THE ECONOMICS PROBLEM SOLVER®

REGISTERED TRADEMARK

A Complete Solution Guide to Any Textbook

Staff of Research and Education Association
Dr. M. Fogiel, Director

special chapter reviews by
Robert S. Rycroft, Ph.D.
Chairperson of Economics Department
Mary Washington College
Fredericksburg, Virginia

Research and Education Association
61 Ethel Road West
Piscataway, New Jersey 08854

THE ECONOMICS
PROBLEM SOLVER®

10th Printing

Printed in the United States of America

Library of Congress Catalog Card Number 97-68333

International Standard Book Number 0-87891-524-0

III-1

WHAT THIS BOOK IS FOR

Students have generally found economics a difficult subject to understand and learn. Despite the publication of hundreds of textbooks in this field, each one intended to provide an improvement over previous textbooks, students continue to remain perplexed as a result of the numerous conditions that must often be remembered and correlated in solving a problem. Various possible interpretations of terms used in economics have also contributed to many of the difficulties experienced by students.

In a study of the problem, REA found the following basic reasons underlying students' difficulties with economics taught in schools:

(a) No systematic rules of analysis have been developed which students may follow in a step-by-step manner to solve the usual problems encountered. This results from the fact that the numerous different conditions and principles which may be involved in a problem, lead to many possible different methods of solution. To prescribe a set of rules to be followed for each of the possible variations, would involve an enormous number of rules and steps to be searched through by students, and this task would perhaps be more burdensome than solving the problem directly with some accompanying trial and error to find the correct solution route.

(b) Textbooks currently available will usually explain a given principle in a few pages written by a professional who has an insight in the subject matter that is not shared by students. The explanations are often written in an abstract manner which leaves the students confused as to the application of the principle. The explanations given are not sufficiently detailed and extensive to make the student aware of the wide range of applications and different aspects of the principle being studied. The numerous possible variations of principles and their applications are usually not discussed, and it is left for the students to discover these for themselves while doing the exercises. Accordingly, the average student is expected to rediscover that which has been long known and practiced, but not published or explained extensively.

(c) The examples usually following the explanation of a topic are too few in number and too simple to enable the student to obtain a thorough grasp of the principles involved. The explanations do not provide sufficient basis to enable a student to solve problems that may be subsequently assigned for homework or given on examinations.

The examples are presented in abbreviated form which leaves out much material between steps, and requires that students derive the omitted material themselves. As a result, students find the examples difficult to understand--contrary to the purpose of the examples.

Examples are, furthermore, often worded in a confusing manner. They do not state the problem and then present the solution. Instead, they pass through a general discussion, never revealing what is to be solved for.

Examples, also, do not always include diagrams/graphs, wherever appropriate, and students do not obtain the training to draw diagrams or graphs to simplify and organize their thinking.

(d) Students can learn the subject only by doing the exercises themselves and reviewing them in class, to obtain experience in applying the principles with their different ramifications.

In doing the exercises by themselves, students find that they are required to devote considerably more time to economics than to other subjects of comparable credits, because they are uncertain with regard to the selection and application of the theorems and principles involved. It is also often necessary for students to discover those "tricks" not revealed in their texts (or review books), that make it possible to solve problems easily. Students must usually resort to methods of trial-and-error to discover these "tricks", and as a result they find that they may sometimes spend several hours in solving a single problem.

(e) When reviewing the exercises in classrooms, instructors usually request students to take turns writing solutions on the board and explaining them to the class. Students often find it difficult to explain the solutions in a manner that holds the interest of the class, and enables the remaining students to follow the material written on the board. The remaining students seated in the class are, furthermore, too occupied with copying the material from the board, to listen to the oral explanations and concentrate on the methods of solution.

This book is intended to aid students in economics in overcoming the difficulties described, by supplying detailed illustrations of the solution methods which are usually not apparent to students. The solution methods are illustrated by problems selected from those that are most often assigned for class work and given on examinations. The problems are arranged in order of complexity to enable students to learn and understand a particular topic by reviewing the problems in sequence. The problems are illustrated with detailed step-by-step explanations, to save students the large amount of time that is often needed to fill in the gaps that are usually found between steps of illustrations in textbooks or review/outline books.

The staff of REA considers economics a subject that is best learned by allowing students to view the methods of analysis and solution techniques themselves. This approach to learning the subject matter is similar to that practiced in various scientific laboratories, particularly in the medical fields.

In using this book, students may review and study the illustrated problems at their own pace; they are not limited to the time allowed for explaining problems on the board in class.

When students want to look up a particular type of problem and solution, they can readily locate it in the book by referring to the index which has been extensively prepared. It is also possible to locate a particular type of problem by glancing at the material within the boxed portions. To facilitate rapid scanning of the problems, each problem has a heavy border around it. Furthermore, each problem is identified with a number immediately above the problem at the right-hand margin.

To obtain maximum benefit from the book, students should familiarize themselves with the section, "How To Use This Book," located in the front pages.

To meet the objectives of this book, staff members of REA have selected problems usually encountered in assignments and examinations, and have solved each problem meticulously to illustrate the steps which are difficult for students to comprehend. Special gratitude is expressed to them for their efforts in this area, as well as to the numerous contributors who devoted brief periods of time to this work.

Gratitude is also expressed to the many persons involved in the difficult task of typing the manuscript with its endless changes, and to the REA art staff who prepared the numerous detailed illustrations together with the layout and physical features of the book.

The difficult task of coordinating the efforts of all persons was carried out by Carl Fuchs. His conscientious work deserves much appreciation. He also trained and supervised art and production personnel in the preparation of the book for printing.

Finally, special thanks are due to Helen Kaufmann for her unique talents in rendering those difficult border-line decisions and in making constructive suggestions related to the design and organization of the book.

Max Fogiel, Ph.D.
Program Director

HOW TO USE THIS BOOK

This book can be an invaluable aid to students in economics as a supplement to their textbooks. The book is subdivided into 33 chapters, each dealing with a separate topic. The subject matter is developed beginning with fundamental economic concepts, business organizations, income and price indices, taxation, business cycles, money, banking, supply and demand, and inflation and unemployment. Included are also sections on competition, monopoly, theory of production, tariffs, and balance of payments.

Each chapter of the book is accompanied by a series of short answer questions to help in reviewing the study and preparation for exams.

TO LEARN AND UNDERSTAND A TOPIC THOROUGHLY

1. Refer to your class text and read the section pertaining to the topic. You should become acquainted with the principles discussed there. These principles, however, may not be clear to you at that time.

2. Then locate the topic you are looking for by referring to the "Table of Contents" in front of this book, "The Economics Problem Solver".

3. Turn to the page where the topic begins and review the problems under each topic, in the order given. For each topic, the problems are arranged in order of complexity, from the simplest to the more difficult. Some problems may appear similar to others, but each problem has been selected to illustrate a different point or solution method.

To learn and understand a topic thoroughly and retain its content, it will generally be necessary for students to review the problems several times. Repeated review is essential in order to gain experience in recognizing the principles that should be applied, and in selecting the best solution technique.

TO FIND A PARTICULAR PROBLEM

To locate one or more problems related to a particular subject matter, refer to the index. In using the index, be certain to note that the numbers given there refer to problem numbers, not to page numbers. This arrangement of the index is intended to facilitate finding a problem more rapidly, since two or more problems may appear on a page.

If a particular type of problem cannot be found readily, it is recommended that the student refer to the "Table of Contents" in the front pages, and then turn to the chapter which is applicable to the problem being sought. By scanning or glancing at the material that is boxed, it will generally be possible to find problems related to the one being sought, without consuming considerable time. After the problems have been located, the solutions can be reviewed and studied in detail. For this purpose of locating problems rapidly, students should acquaint themselves with the organization of the book as found in the "Table of Contents".

In preparing for an exam, locate the topics to be covered on the exam in the "Table of Contents", and then review the problems under those topics several times. This should equip the student with what might be needed for the exam.

CONTENTS

CHAPTER 1

FUNDAMENTAL ECONOMIC CONCEPTS

Basic Attacks and Strategies for Solving Problems in this Chapter. See pages 1 to 39 for step-by-step solutions to problems.

The fundamental problem in economics is scarcity. Our resources (or factors of production such as land, labor, capital, and entrepreneurship that are used to produce goods and services) are inadequate to satisfy our desires for goods and services. Yet the scarcity problem is not simply one of production, of finding the way to "crank out" enough goods and services. It is complicated by the reality that human desires are essentially limitless. Humans refuse to be satisfied with what they have. When they have achieved one standard of living, a higher one becomes the new goal. Consequently, scarcity is a constant and universal problem. It has been a problem in every society in every period of time and is likely to remain a problem in the future.

The term scarcity is not necessarily synonymous with poverty. While scarcity is certainly a problem in poor societies, it is also a problem in the most affluent nations. Consider the following as an illustration. Average family income in the United States is approximately $35,000 per year. Yet, when asked to indicate the level of income the typical family would need to be comfortable, most college students will answer with an amount greatly in excess of $35,000, implying that the average family in the United States is not comfortable, although the United States is arguably the richest nation on earth.

The fundamental business of society then is the production and distribution of the goods and services required to sustain life and to make life worth living. The existence of scarcity creates certain problems that all societies must face. The three basic problems are "What," "How," and "For Whom." The "What" problem is "What goods and services should society produce?" Since there is not enough to go around, society must be concerned with producing the types of goods and services most desired. This goal is known as allocative (or economic) efficiency. The "How" problem is "How should goods and services be produced?" With scarcity, societies clearly want to choose production methods that yield the greatest possible output. This goal is known as technical efficiency. The "For Whom" question is "For whom shall goods and services be produced?" The goods and services produced must be divided among people in some way. The goal of every society is to divide these goods and services equitably.

The discussion above is a bit remote from what people typically hear. The economic problems of our time include such things as stagnant growth, inflation, the power of big business, the efficacy of government action, poverty and the distribution of income, twin deficits, and so on. All these problems are related to, and are manifestations of, the fundamental problem of scarcity.

Economics has been defined by the topics studied by economists or the methods they use. The former definition is not particularly enlightening because there are few topics that modern economists do not study. The latter definition is considerably more enlightening because it emphasizes that economists look at problems in a special way. Distinguishing features of the economic way of thinking include:

1) Methodological Individualism — Societies are composed of individuals. All actions by societies are really the actions of many individuals. Consequently, economists place great emphasis on the study of individuals.

2) Rationality — Individuals are assumed to be self-interested and consider the costs and benefits of all actions before making choices. Being rational simply means that individuals will take actions that promise the greatest benefits relative to costs, given the information they possess.

3) Scarcity — All behavior takes place in an environment characterized by scarcity.

4) The Use of Models — It is only a slight exaggeration to say that economists do not study economies, rather they study models of economies. Models are abstract replicas of reality. They contain the important elements of the thing to be studied, but leave out the extraneous details. The reason models are used is because human beings do not have the capacity to understand the full reality of things.

It is important that students of economics understand the characteristic methodology of the discipline.

An important economic model is the production possibilities curve. Assume an economy is capable of producing just two goods, guns and butter. At a given point in time, its resources (land, labor, capital, and entrepreneurship) and level of technology can be joined to produce various combinations of the goods. The shaded area and line *AD* on the graph indicate the particular combinations feasible. The line *AD* is especially important because it shows the maximum feasible combinations of the two goods obtainable when all resources are used in a technically efficient manner. *AD* is the production possibilities curve. Combinations inside the curve (such as *E*) are feasible, but result from inefficiency. Points such as *F* are

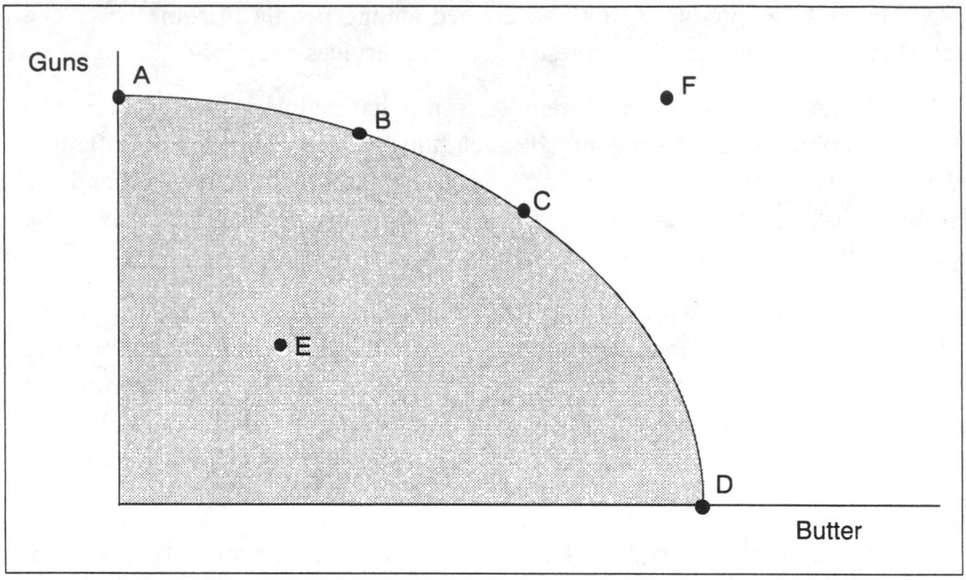

The Production Possibilities Curve

unobtainable given the existing stock of resources and level of technology.

The production possibilities curve represents the limitations of the economy, and, combined with the observation that human wants are essentially limitless, can be used to illustrate several of the concepts and problems associated with scarcity. A goal of all economies is achieving technical efficiency. This means producing the maximum amount possible, which eliminates points inside the curve from consideration. A common definition of technical efficiency is a level of output where more cannot be produced of one good without producing less of the other good. A movement from point *B* to *C*, leading to greater butter production, necessitates a drop in gun production. Consequently, *B* is a point of technical efficiency, as is every other point on the curve.

The goal of allocative efficiency means choosing the point most desired on the curve. Costs are unavoidably associated with any choice. The choice of point *C* over *B* yields more butter, but fewer guns. The guns sacrificed are the **opportunity cost** of the choice. The opportunity cost of any choice is the best alternative foregone by making that choice.

The characteristic "bowed out" or convex shape of the curve shows the law of increasing relative costs. The opportunity cost of either good increases as more of it is produced. The cause of this is the fact that resources tend to be specialized. Some resources tend to be better in the production of one good than the other.

Economic growth means that the economy is capable of producing more of both goods. It is shown by a rightward shift of the curve, and results from increases in the stock of resources or the level of technology.

Step-by-Step Solutions to Problems in this Chapter, "Fundamental Economic Concepts"

THE METHOD OF ECONOMICS

• PROBLEM 1-1

"Economic principles are generalizations." Explain what is meant by this statement and why it is true.

Solution: The data confronting an economist are usually diverse. Since economics deals with the behavior of men, certain factors in an economy act in one way while others act in another. Therefore, since all agents in an economy cannot be expected to react identically to various phenomena, economic principles are generalized and stated either in terms of averages or probabilities. For example, the law of demand states that as the price of a good rises, the quantity of it demanded falls. Suppose, however, that the price of meat becomes so high that people turn more and more to potatoes. Since demand for potatoes increases, the price of potatoes increases also. However, the rising price of meat continues to drive more people to substitute potatoes for meat in spite of their rising price. This increase in potato prices accompanied by an increase in the quantity demanded constitutes an apparent exception to the law of demand, yet does not negate it. The law of demand states that as the price of a good rises, its demand will fall, other things being equal. In this example, other things are not equal--the price of meat changes, affecting the demand for potatoes. The law of demand is a useful tool in explaining economic behavior in spite of any apparent exceptions to it.

The economist is forced to make generalizations due to the nature of his subject--the economy is not readily controllable for experimentation. While a physicist can actually hold other things equal, the economist can only assume them to be equal. In the above example we see the possible danger of this assumption.

• PROBLEM 1-2

Economists construct models for use as tools in interpreting and predicting economic behavior. What are some of the dangers in the use of models?

Solution: The primary danger in constructing an economic model lies in the process of distilling the facts. The economist may eliminate too many facts as irrelevant, severely limiting the validity of the model. For example, if, in studying supply and demand of broccoli during a "good year", the economist may neglect to take the weather into account. Hence the model will work as long as the weather is "good". It will be invalid in a drought year.

The danger in applying models is that it becomes very easy to forget that they are simply generalizations or approximations and people rely too heavily on them. In the above example, twenty years of good weather might lull economists into forgetting that they have left the weather factor out of account so that when drought occurs, they will be unable to account for changes in the broccoli market.

The economist must also keep in mind that economic models have no moral or ethical qualities. They state simply what is, not what ought to be.

• PROBLEM 1-3

"Because economic theories are abstractions from reality they are impractical and unrealistic." True or False? Why?

Solution: When confronted with the massive volume of facts and figures associated with an economy, one of the economist's primary tasks in formulating a useful theory is abstracting from reality--a process in which he must distill the facts and "weed out" all irrelevant data. A theory which involved no such abstraction would prove too unwieldly for practical use. While it would accurately describe the reality of a particular situation, it would be so encumbered by the details of the situation that it would be useless were any of them to change. Therefore, prediction with such a theory would be impossible.

That is not to say that the economist is freed from factuality. The basis of any good theory is its foundation in facts. A theory which does not fit the facts is even less useful than one that tries to incorporate too many of them.

• PROBLEM 1-4

Describe the methodology of economics.

Solution: The first task of the economist is the collection of facts pertinent to a specific aspect of the economy. From these facts, he makes generalizations regarding the problem at hand. He abstracts from specific instances to attempt to formulate a rule which will work in all instances, a rule which will enable him to predict the future behavior of the economy. This formulation of a rule is policy economics, in which the economist attempts to take action based on his prediction to directly influence the performance of the economy.

The question of objectivity clouds economics' status as a science. While physical sciences deal with objective facts, economics deals with men, and, all protestations regarding rationality aside, men's actions are generally not traceable to distinct motives.

On the other hand, the economist has an advantage over the physical scientist. Whereas the physical scientist cannot realistically put himself in the place of the lower life form he is studying, the economist can more or less safely make generalizations since he has approximately the same makeup, motives, and abilities as the subjects of his inquiry.

• PROBLEM 1-5

In what basic respect does the methodology of economics differ from that of the physical and biological sciences? What difficulties is the economist faced with which do not face those in the natural sciences? What advantage does the economist have over the "natural" scientist?

Solution: The methodology of economics differs from that of the physical and biological sciences primarily in that the economist (in most circumstances) cannot conduct controlled experiments, whereas the physical or biological scientist usually can. Because economics is concerned with the activities of people in their everyday affairs, economists must obtain their data from everyday experience, which is subject to innumerable uncontrollable variables, and base their generalizations upon this data while trying to account for the effects of the various uncontrollable variables. Physical and biological scientists, by contrast, can usually isolate the phenomena they are studying under laboratory conditions in which all extraneous variables have been excluded or held to a known, controlled level.

The difficulty facing the economist which does not confront the "natural" scientist (e.g. biologist or chemist) is that while the physical sciences deal only with observable events and natural laws, economics deals with the actions of men whose purposes determine their actions but are not directly observable.

On the other hand, the economist has an advantage over the physical scientist in that the physical scientist cannot "get inside" his subject. That is to say, a chemist cannot learn anything about atomic behavior introspectively, by asking himself the question, "What would I do if I were an atom of uranium?" On the other hand, the economist can make generalizations about human actions from introspection since he has approximately the same nature as the subjects of his study.

• PROBLEM 1-6

What is "economic rationality?"

Solution: Economic rationality refers to a basic assumption made by economists--that human beings are motivated by self interest and will therefore seek, as their primary goal, the maximization of their own economic position, be it in terms of income, quantity of goods, power and prestige, etc. Economists assume that this is the sole motive of all actors in an economy and that such motives,as patriotism, love, etc. will not enter into their economic decision-making processes.

• PROBLEM 1-7

List and give examples of the methods of expressing economic relationships.

Solution: The major methods of expressing economic relationships are equations, tables (in which relationships are enumerated), and graphs (in which relationships are pictorially represented). For example, the concept of total revenue may be viewed in various ways. First, as an equation:

$$TR = f(Q)$$

which is read: "Total revenue is a function of quantity sold." This equation is non-specific, stating only that as sales change, total revenue changes. It does not state by how much. It can be made more specific if it is changed to read TR = PQ or, "Total revenue equals price times quantity." This equation is more specific, telling a producer that his total revenue will equal the quantity he sells times the price he sells each unit for. Once the price is known, the equation is most specific, for example, if the price is $2.00:

$$TR = \$2.00(Q)$$

Now the relationship may be expressed in a table:

Quantity	Total Revenue
10	$20
20	40
50	100
100	200

which gives total revenue values at each of a set of possible outputs. Note that the table is not all-inclusive, leaving out certain possible outputs (say, 57) and their corresponding total revenues.

The third method of expressing the relationship is the graph:

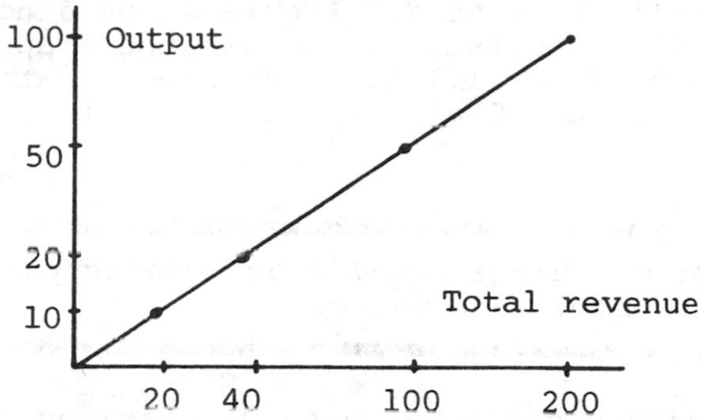

which depicts the value of total revenue for all possible outputs. The graph is useful in that, as a picture, it renders certain information immediately apparent. For instance, since the line is upward sloping, it is clear that the relationship between quantity and total revenue is positive.

• PROBLEM 1-8

Consider the accompanying 4 figures on the relationship of X and Y. 1) In which of these figures is the amount of Y unrelated to the amount of X? 2) In which of these figures is the amount of Y directly related to the amount of X? 3) In which of these figures is Y inversely related to the amount of X?

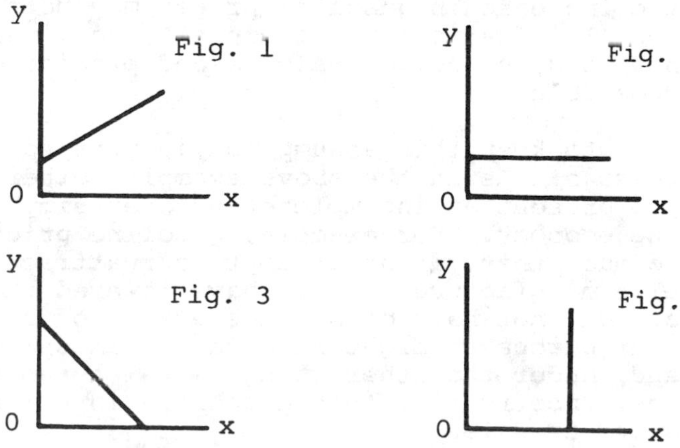

Solution: 1) The amount of Y is unrelated to the amount of X only in Figure 2. Y will always be the same here, no matter what X is.

2) The amount of Y is directly related to the amount of X in Figure 1. If X increases, Y also increases. Alternatively, decreasing X will bring about a corresponding decline in Y.

3) The amount of Y is inversely related to the amount of X in Figure 3 because increasing X will decrease Y and decreasing X will increase Y. Figure 4 would not be the answer to any of the questions because the graph depicts a constant value of X--X will never change no matter what value of Y we choose. That is, X is unrelated to Y.

• PROBLEM 1-9

Explain the "other things equal", or ceteris paribus assumption of economic analysis.

Solution: Economists assume that in analyzing the effect of changes in one of the factors influencing an economic variable, all other factors influencing the variable can be held constant, isolating the effect to that caused by the factor under consideration.

For example, suppose one wished to judge the effect of a change in the price of automobiles in a given year on the amount of automobiles purchased that year. Suppose that in 1976 the average price of a new automobile rose from $3000 to $5000 and the number of new automobiles purchased fell from 10 million to 5 million. Under the other things equal assumption, economists ignore the possible effect of other factors, such as a rise in unemployment or an increase in the cost of gasoline and attribute the decline in sales to the increase in prices.

The advantage of the other things equal assumption is related to the complexity of economics. Since economic variables are so closely related (the rise in automobile prices and the increase in gasoline prices may both be the result of general inflation, for example), that, were this assumption not used, economic analysis and prediction would be nearly impossible.

It is wise to keep this assumption in perspective for these same reasons. As in the above example, other things equal tends to present an incomplete and over simplified picture of the economy. For example, gasoline prices may have risen so much that, in an attempt to reattract customers, automobile manufacturers would have lowered their prices. This price cut may not have offset the effect of rising gas prices (new car purchases might have fallen in spite of the price cut) and, under the other things equal assumption, one might conclude, incorrectly, that a decline in prices had caused a decline in sales.

• PROBLEM 1-10

What is the "Post Hoc" fallacy? Give an example of erroneous economic thinking which may result from this fallacy.

Solution: The "Post Hoc" fallacy takes its name from the Latin phrase "Post Hoc, Ergo Propter Hoc", which means "after this, therefore because of this". The fallacy consists of thinking that, because event A precedes event B in time, event B must have been caused by event A. "Post Hoc" thinking is usually a symptom of ignorance of the relevant facts.

For example, a firm may decide to increase the price of its product, either because of cost pressure or to try to increase its profit margin. Suppose after the price is increased, the firm discovers that the quantity of its product demanded has also increased, i.e., more units are being sold in a given period of time than before the price increase. Without the benefit of further facts, the firm's management might jump to the odd conclusion that the increase in price caused the increase in the quantity demanded. This would be an example of the Post Hoc fallacy. Further investigation might reveal that the true cause of the increase in the quantity demanded is that competitors have increased their prices even more, thus making the firm's product relatively cheaper than before.

• PROBLEM 1-11

What is the fallacy of composition? Give an example of a misconception in economics which results from this fallacy.

Solution: The fallacy of composition is a logical fallacy which may be defined as the belief that what is true for an individual or element of a group is also necessarily true for the group as a whole. An example of an economic misconception which results from this fallacy is the assumption that because one farmer can increase his income by hard work which results in a bumper crop, it necessarily follows that, if all farmers work hard and increase their crop yields, farm income as a whole will increase. The actual result of such an aggregate increase in crop yields may be that the consequent increase in supply of farm products will cause the price of such products to fall so low that total farm income decreases.

• PROBLEM 1-12

One of the reasons Adam Smith supported the Free Market was because he believed that what is good for the individual is good for the country. So, since everyone would like to choose what they want to buy, it must be good for the country to give everyone free choice. Identify the error in Smith's logic and give a counter example.

Solution: Smith commits the error that crops throughout the history of economic theory; he commits the fallacy of composition. This fallacy, stated simply, is claiming what is good for a part, is good for the whole; what is good for part of the country (an individual), is good for the country as a whole. A counter example is relatively easy to present:

"Since it is wise for an individual to save money during a depression (in case of unemployment), it is wise for the entire country to be thrifty also."

If the entire country is thrifty, the depression will get even worse. An increase in savings will reduce demand even further than before. During a depression, demand has to be increased so that businesses will increase production and hire workers. In the case of savings, what is good for the individual is exactly opposite from what is good for the country. From this counter example, it can be concluded that what is good for the individual is not necessarily good for the country.

• PROBLEM 1-13

What is the difference between "caveat emptor" and "ceteris paribus"

Solution: Both phrases come from Latin. "Caveat emptor" is translated to "Let the buyer beware". "Ceteris paribus" is loosely translated to "all other things being equal." "Ceteris paribus" is used when you have several variables and you want to change one but hold all the rest constant. For example, if the price of a product increases, ceteris paribus, the quantity demanded will decrease.

• PROBLEM 1-14

Who was Adam Smith, and what is the principle of the "Invisible Hand"? In what situation will this principle not hold true?

Solution: Adam Smith was an eighteenth century Scottish professor of moral philosophy who is generally credited with founding economics as a science. His book, The Wealth of Nations, published in 1776, was the first notable attempt to explain the workings of a free market. In his book, Smith sets forth the principle of the "Invisible Hand", which asserts that if each individual in society acts in such a way as to maximize his own gain, the functioning of the free market will assure, as a result, the maximum possible benefit to society as a whole.

The Wealth of Nations is undoubtedly the foundation work of modern economic thought. The principles of the book are simple. First, Smith assumes that the prime psychological drive in man as an economic being is the drive of self-interest. Secondly, he contends that in a free market system, one's self-interest is best served by serving that of others. Since it is in the producer's interest to produce something which will be demanded by the public, it follows that the pursuit of one's own self-interest will automatically serve the interest of society. Finally, from these postulates, he concludes that the best program is for government to leave the economic process completely alone--what has come to be known as laissez-faire, economic liberalism or non-interventionism. In formulating the principle of the "Invisible Hand," Smith assumed the existence of perfect competition--a market system with no artificial restrictions or elements of monopoly power. Since government restricts the market in order to compensate for externalities such as pollution, firms are restrained in pursuing their self-interest. Also, some firms have a degree of monopoly power, and therefore are not compelled to accept the wishes of society as guides for their own decision making.

• PROBLEM 1-15

What are three economic roles of government?

Solution: First, minimum standards of life are widespread modern goals. Unfortunately a market system, left unrestrained, does not insure such minimum standards. Therefore through such programs as welfare, government tries to establish such minimum standards.

Secondly the government provides certain indispensable public services which by their nature cannot appropriately be left to private institutions. Some examples of this are the building of highways and the administration of justice. To pay for such public services the government imposes taxes upon its citizens.

Finally the government sets forth laws which establish the framework within which private enterprise operates. Some examples of such government commands are child labor laws and price ceilings.

• PROBLEM 1-16

Define, and distinguish among, descriptive, theoretical and policy economics. How do they relate to each other?

Solution: Descriptive economics is concerned with the collection of economic facts or data. An example of descriptive economics would be the gathering of data necessary to calculate gross national product for a year.

Theoretical economics involves the creation of theories, or generalizations, which are based upon the information supplied by descriptive economics and introspection. For example, a theoretical economist might take GNP data for several years and correlate this data with information on capital formation during the same period. By comparing the two sets of data, he might then develop a theory concerning the relationship between capital formation and growth in GNP.

The task of Policy Economics (also called Applied Economics) is to take this information supplied by descriptive economics, and the theories supplied by theoretical economics, and use them to achieve goals which are desired by a firm or society as a whole. For example, a government economist might use information on GNP and capital formation, along with a theory relating the two, to develop a tax program to encourage capital information and consequent GNP growth. Similarly, a business economist might use information on the production cost of a new product, along with a theory regarding demand for the product, to determine the price which the firm should charge for it.

• PROBLEM 1-17

Define, and distinguish between macroeconomics and microeconomics.

Solution: Macroeconomics is the study of the behavior of the economy as a whole, or of entire sectors of the economy (such as government or business) taken as a whole. The focus of macroeconomics is on the behavior of such variables as average prices, average wages, aggregate supply and aggregate demand. For example, one concept with which macroeconomics deals is gross national product, which is an aggregation, or summing together and treating as a single unit, of the total output of goods and services produced by all industries, businesses, farms, individuals, and government entities in the economy. In focusing on aggregate quantities and the relationships among them, macroeconomics presents a simplified picture of the economy. This simplification is done in order to make intelligible the highly complex and voluminous data with which macroeconomics deals. For example, a typical problem in macroeconomics is how to decrease the aggregate rate of inflation without increasing the aggregate level of unemployment. It would be extremely difficult, if not impossible, to attempt to solve this problem by considering individually all of the variables affecting price and employment policies in all of the individual firms in each industry or sector of the economy. By considering aggregate price and employment data, however, it may be possible to produce a useful, if approximate, model of overall price and employment relationships, in the economy as a whole. This macroeconomic model, or theory, can in turn provide the basis for policy decisions by government regarding how to control inflation without increasing unemployment.

Microeconomics is the study of the behavior of individual components of the economy, such as firms, households or individuals, and the economic relationships among them. Microeconomics focuses upon individual, rather than aggregate, economic data. For example, a typical problem in microeconomics would be to determine the optimum price which a company should charge for a new product. In determining the solution to this problem, it would be necessary to consider such microeconomic data as the company's own production costs, the degree to which price changes affect the quantity demanded of the new product, and the prices which competing firms charge for similar products. Note that all of these data are specific to a particular firm or industry and to a particular product. In the example above, the conclusion which the company reaches regarding the optimum price for its product would not necessarily be the same for another company or another product. Nevertheless, the method of microeconomics can be consistently applied to a variety of problems in order to produce useful answers. For example, the same analysis of supply and demand relationships can be used to determine pricing policy in the automobile and garment industries, even though the specific supply and demand data for these industries may differ greatly.

• PROBLEM 1-18

When we say that macromodels of the economy are mechanistic, does this mean that the economy works like a machine?

Solution: Macromodels of the economy are macroeconomic simplifications of the economy: they work directly on the relationship between aggregates, such as National Income, Consumption, Investment, Money Supply, Government Expenditures, Taxes, Exports and Imports and they take no account of individuals. A macro-economic model represents the economy. The key-word here is 'represents'; a macromodel does not precisely describe or explain the interactions of the millions of individuals living and working together, but it tries to represent the aggregate effect of those millions of interactions. Individuals behave somewhat erratically, but whole cities, regions, or nations show more stable behavior. Whole cities, regions or nations can well be represented by a machine-like model for many purposes.

This may be illustrated by the example of incoming and outgoing highways of New York City. Although the behavior of the millions of individuals, the Smiths, the Jones, the Carters, is unpredictable--we don't know if a particular individual drives his car to or out of New York City at a particular hour--we can with a fair amount of precision predict the total number of cars that will enter or leave New York City over the highways at particular hours of certain days. Traffic statistics are compiled over the course of the year, and on the basis of these we can predict the in-and outgoing traffic flows on certain holidays, and the traffic flows in various hours--for example, before, during, and after the rush hours--of the day. The variety of cars and drivers is enormous, but when the focus is on the number of vehicles alone, an aggregate number for these flows per hour may be found. These traffic flows can also be related to particular events--office hours, holidays, the weather--and the flows can be explained by these 'macro' events that affect millions of individuals simultaneously.

In the same fashion, statistics on economic aggregates can be compiled and related to each other and to outside events that affect the economy as a whole.

Still, the economy does not work as a machine because

all these individuals form their own decisions, sometimes with surprising results. The relationships between the aggregate economic variables are not mechanistic, but probabilistic. The aggregate relationships described by a macroeconomic model are relatively stable, because the eccentricities in the behavior of the individuals comprising the economy are independent of each other. The law of large numbers, applied in physics, is also applied in the social sciences.

SCARCITY

• PROBLEM 1-19

Define "scarcity" in economic terms. From what does economic scarcity result?

Solution: Goods or resources are considered "scarce", in economic terms, if they are not available in sufficient quantity to satisfy all wants for them. Scarcity therefore results from a combination of two factors: Quantities of goods are limited and desire for goods is unlimited. Since wants for virtually all goods are greater than the available supply, most resources are scarce. Only "free goods", such as air (in most situations) are not scarce.

• PROBLEM 1-20

Distinguish economic goods from free goods, and give an example of each.

Solution: Economic goods are distinguished from free goods by their relative scarcity. Free goods are readily available in usable form and in sufficient quantity to satisfy all wants. Examples of free goods include air, ocean water, beachsand etc. Since free goods are plentiful in relation to demand and are not brought about through the use of scarce resources (factors of production), they are precisely that--free,and therefore outside the concern of the economist.

Economic goods and services are brought about through the use of scarce resources. They are found in limited quantity relative to demand; therefore, they command a positive price. Such goods are called economic goods and it is with these that an economist is concerned. For example, oil is an example of an economic good. Not only is there insufficient oil to satisfy all wants for it but it must also be extracted, refined and, in most cases, transported before it can be used. These processes require the use of other scarce, or economic goods, such as land, labor and capital.

• PROBLEM 1-21

What are the three fundamental problems of any society?

Solution: "What, how, and for whom" are the three basic problems of any economic society.

The problem of "what" is: what commodities shall be produced and in what quantities. Do we want e.g., more to eat and less clothing, or vice versa.

The question of "how" asks how shall goods be produced. Who shall do the producing, with what resources, and in what technological manner?

Finally we ask, "For whom shall goods be produced?" How shall we distribute what we produce? Shall all goods be distributed equally among all individuals? Or by what principle shall distribution of goods be distributed among individuals? According to their need, according to their contribution to production, or by some other rule?

• PROBLEM 1-22

What are some widely held economic goals of society?

Solution: Some of the primary goals of an economic system are economic growth, full employment, price stability, economic freedom, an equitable distribution of income, and economic security. (It should be noted however, that these are by no means universal goals.)

An economic system attempts to insure, by the production of certain types of goods and services (e.g. capital goods, education), a growing standard of living i.e., economic growth brought about by the production of more and better goods in the future.

Society attempts to obtain the maximum use e.g., full employment, of all its factors of production.

In order to facilitate economic activity, severe fluctuations in the price level (inflation or deflation) are to be avoided.

To allow for change, innovation, and eventually efficiency, a great degree of freedom in the determination of each individual's employment of his productive resources is sought.

An equitable distribution of income: to some people means that great disparities between society's richest and poorest are unacceptable.

Economic security refers to the attempt to provide for those members of society who are, for one reason or another, unable to produce.

• PROBLEM 1-23

"The free enterprise, capitalist system is a system in which the consumer is sovereign. Consumer preferences determine what shall be produced and how much shall be produced." Evaluate this statement.

Solution: In a free-enterprise, capitalist economy, consumers have, theoretically, no restriction upon their consumption except for a budgetary constraint in that they cannot spend more money than they have. Because of these conditions, they will purchase that set of goods and services which most fully satisfy their desires given their budget constraint. Producers, in an effort to capture limited consumer dollars, must accurately gauge consumer preferences and produce those goods deemed most desirable by consumers. Those producers who fail to do so will eventually be forced out of business by losses.

However, consumers are limited somewhat in their sovereignty by the fact that they are on the opposite side (the supply side) of the resource market. The demand for resources is a derived demand--that is, resources are demanded only if they can produce something profitable. On the aggregate, consumers cannot demand a good the productive resources for which they are unable to supply. Consumers may demand great amounts of coal, but be unwilling to provide the labor to mine it. Under such a situation, the price system will serve to both lower their demand for coal and increase their willingness to mine it, until a point is reached where both urges are to some extent satisfied.

RESOURCES

• PROBLEM 1-24

What is meant by "economic resources" or "factors of production"? Name three categories of resources.

Solution: Economic resources, also called factors of production, include all natural, artificial and human resources which may be used in the production or provision of goods or services. For example, economic resources would include crude oil lying under the surface of the earth, the drilling and pumping equipment used to bring it to the surface, the pipeline which carries it to the dock, the ship (and its crew) which transports it to the refinery, the refinery and its workers and supervisors, the tank farm in which refined gasoline is stored, the truck (and its driver) which transports it to the service station, the service station at which it is sold to consumers (including the land on which it is situated, the building and pumps), and the attendant who pumps it into customers' cars.

Three basic categories into which economic resources, or factors of production, may be classified are land, labor and capital. Some economists (for example, McConnell) consider entrepreneurial ability, or "enterprise", to be a fourth category of economic resource.

• **PROBLEM 1-25**

What is the economic definition of "land"?

Solution: The essential feature of land which differentiates it from other productive resources is that, unlike labor and capital, its supply is virtually fixed and non-augmentable. A change in the rental price of land does not affect the quantity of it available. "Land", as defined in economics, includes not only surface land but all natural resources found on or within the earth, sea or air, which can be used in the productive process. Thus, a coal seam suitable for surface or underground mining would be considered "land", as would a pool of crude oil located beneath the floor of the ocean or edible fish in the ocean. Water suitable for hydroelectric generation would also be considered "land", as would solar energy available for heating water or generating electricity. Land in its traditional sense is also considered "land" in the economic sense, so long as it is suitable for some productive use; for example, fertile land suitable for growing crops or suburban land suitable for housing development.

• **PROBLEM 1-26**

What is the economic definition of "labor"?

Solution: "Labor", in the economic sense, consists of all human abilities or talents which may be used in the production of goods or services. This definition includes both physical and mental abilities or talents. The economic definition of "labor" therefore includes the work of, for example, lawyers and novelists, as well as that of secretaries and steelworkers.

Some economists (for example, McConnell) exclude from the economic definition of "labor" one type of mental ability, entrepreneurial ability, and classify it as a separate economic resource or factor of production.

• **PROBLEM 1-27**

What are the advantages of specialization or the division of labor between individuals? What are some disadvantages?

Solution: The first advantage of specialization is that it allows individuals to take advantage of differences in their abilities. For example, if A has "a way with words" and B has "an ear for music", it would profit them both for A to write lyrics to B's tunes rather than each doing both. Even if A and B are evenly matched in their abilities to write lyrics and music, if each agrees to devote their time to only one of the tasks, the increase in the amount of time and effort expended on the task will presumably cause improvement in their abilities in their respective areas. With increased practice, A might become exceedingly clever and B might further develop his musical talent. Also, limiting themselves to one task eliminates for A and B the time spent switching from job to job. While in the songwriting example this may entail merely turning one's stool from the piano to the desk, in other cases the effort may be enormous.

The decision to specialize may have disadvantages, however. First, specialized tasks are generally more tedious. Whereas A might have looked forward to composing as a break from writing lyrics, the opportunity is no longer present. The two may also lose touch with the requirements of the other end of the job. A might write multi-syllabic lyrics which B finds impossible to set to music, or B might write grandiose symphonies that obscure A's lyrics.

Another disadvantage is that specialization leads to increased interdependence between individuals. After years of writing lyrics, A might lose his touch with the piano, and if B leaves to pursue a career as a cocktail lounge pianist, A's songwriting talent may become less valuable.

• **PROBLEM 1-28**

What is the economic definition of "capital"? Distinguish "real" capital from "money" or "financial" capital.

Solutions: "Capital", as defined for most economic purposes, refers to all man-made goods which are usable in the production of other capital goods or consumer goods. Some examples of "capital", in the economic sense, are machine tools, blast furnaces, oil drilling equipment, farm machinery, railroad tracks and rolling stock, and automobiles used by travelling salesmen.

All of the above are examples of "real capital", which is synonymous with "capital" in the economic sense. Money which is set aside to purchase such real capital goods is sometimes called "money capital" or "financial capital". However, since money itself, until exchanged for real capital, cannot be used as a factor of production "money" or "financial capital" is not included in the economic definition of "capital". The distinction between "money" capital and "real" capital may also be drawn by referring to the latter as "capital goods".

• **PROBLEM 1-29**

Distinguish between consumer goods and capital goods. Is it possible for one good to be both a consumer and a capital good? Give an example.

Solution: Consumer goods directly satisfy the wants or needs of ultimate consumers. Some examples of consumer goods are food, clothing and television sets. Capital goods satisfy consumer wants indirectly by their use in the production of consumer goods. Some examples of capital goods are tractors, textile looms, and machine tools.

It is possible for the same thing to be both a consumer and a capital good. For example, a farmer may own a pickup truck which he uses both to haul produce to market and for personal and family transportation. When the truck is used to haul produce it is a capital good, and when it is put to personal use it is a consumer good.

THE PRODUCTION-POSSIBILITIES CURVE

• PROBLEM 1-30

What is the "production-possibility frontier"? What can be concluded about an economy which is (1) operating on its production-possibility frontier, and (2) operating inside its production-possibility frontier?

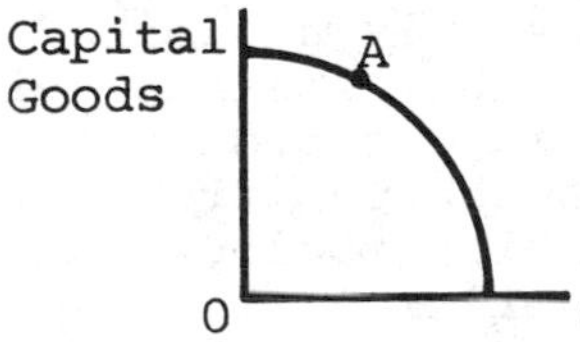

Fig. 1

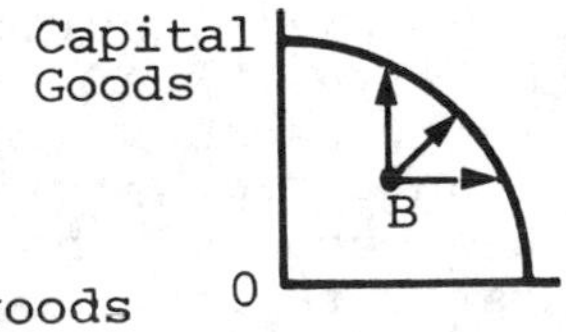

Fig. 2

Solution: The terms "production-possibility curve" and "production possibility frontier" are interchangeable. The production-possibility curve is sometimes called the production-possibility frontier because it defines the limits of what an economy is capable of producing.

Figure 1 shows the production-possibility frontier, or curve, for Country A. The economy of Country A is operating at point "A", which is on its production-possibility frontier. It can be concluded from this that the economy of Country A is operating at peak efficiency, with full employment and the most technically efficient possible use of all factors of production.

A further conclusion can be drawn from the fact that the economy of Country A is operating on its production-possibility frontier. If, for example, the vertical axis in Figure 1 represents capital goods and the horizontal axis represents consumer goods, Country A cannot produce any more capital goods without sacrificing production of some consumer goods, and vice versa.

Figure 2 shows the production-possibility frontier for Country B. The economy of Country B is operating at Point "B", which is inside the production-possibility frontier. This implies that Country B's economy is not operating at peak efficiency. This may reflect unemployment, inefficient use of resources, or both.

It also implies that the economy of Country B could produce more of the goods measured by the horizontal axis without having to forego production of any of the goods measured by the vertical axis, and vice versa. The horizontal arrow from Point "B" to the production-possibility frontier represents the additional amount of the consumer goods, which can be produced without sacrificing production of any capital goods. Likewise, the vertical arrow represents the additional quantity of capital goods which can be produced without sacrificing production of consumer goods. More of both types of goods could be produced, as is indicated by the diagonal arrow.

• PROBLEM 1-31

What is meant by "economic scarcity" and how is the existence of economic scarcity shown in the production possibility frontier?

Solution: The term economic scarcity refers to the basic fact of life that there exists only a finite amount of human and nonhuman resources, which the best technical knowledge is capable of using to produce only a limited maximum amount of each and every good. The existence of economic scarcity can best be depicted in the production possibility frontier, otherwise known as the p-p frontier which shows the menu of choice along which society can choose to substitute one good for another kind of a product, say guns for butter, assuming a given state of technology and a given total of resources. This can be shown graphically as follows:

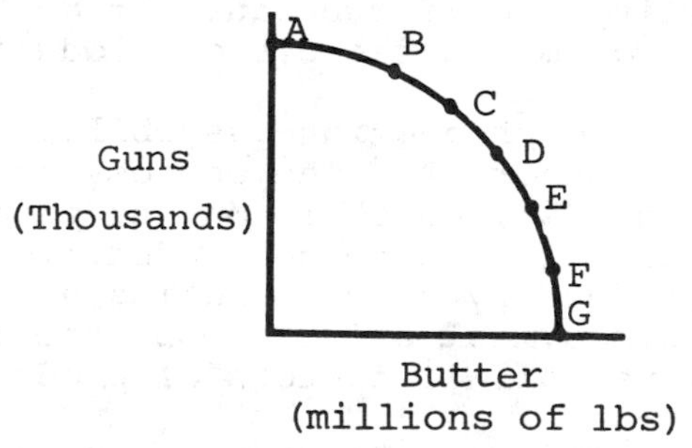

Each point on the production possibilities curve represents some maximum output of any two products. Society must choose which product-mix it desires: more guns means less butter, and vice versa. This will therefore indicate the fact that the total supplies of resources are limited. Thus the total amounts of guns and butter that our economy is capable of producing are limited. Limited resources mean a limited output. A choice must be made as to what quantities of each product society wants produced. This is tantamount to saying that society cannot have the maximum output of both butter and guns to satisfy their wants, and this has been shown in our p-p frontier.

• **PROBLEM 1-32**

What is opportunity cost?

Solution: When resources are scarce, the decision to produce a particular good or service involves an opportunity cost, the sacrifice of a good or service that might have been produced instead. Opportunity cost describes the fact that when we employ resources in a particular way, we are not merely making a decision to produce these goods, but we are also deciding not to produce some other goods or services. That which we implicitly decide not to produce is the opportunity cost of what we do produce. Suppose a farmer has one acre of land, suitable for growing either corn or potatoes. If he plants corn, the opportunity cost of the corn is equal to one acre of potatoes. Because resources are limited, the production of any good necessarily involves an opportunity cost in terms of another.

• **PROBLEM 1-33**

A small country, Ruritania, produces only two goods, shoes and soybeans. Its economic resources are limited, so any factors of production (land, labor or capital) which are added to shoe production must be taken from soybean production, and vice versa. Consequently, to produce more of one good it must be willing to produce less of another. The table below shows various combinations of maximum quantities of shoes and soybeans which Ruritania can produce. Using the data in the table, construct a production-possibility curve for Ruritania.

	Production Possibilities				
Product	A	B	C	D	E
Shoes (Thousands of pairs)	0	10	20	30	40
Soybeans (Thousands of tons)	100	90	70	40	0

Solution: To construct the production-possibility curve, first draw two perpendicular axes. In this illustration, quantity of shoes will be shown on the vertical axis and quantity of soybeans on the horizontal axis. Since the shoe quantity data range from zero to forty in increments of ten, the vertical axis is divided into four equal segments and labelled accordingly. Similarly, the horizontal (soybean) axis is divided into the equal segments and labelled.

Once the axes are constructed, the various production possibilities (A, B, etc.) are plotted by reading from the table the value for shoe production and going up the vertical axis to the point corresponding to that amount, then

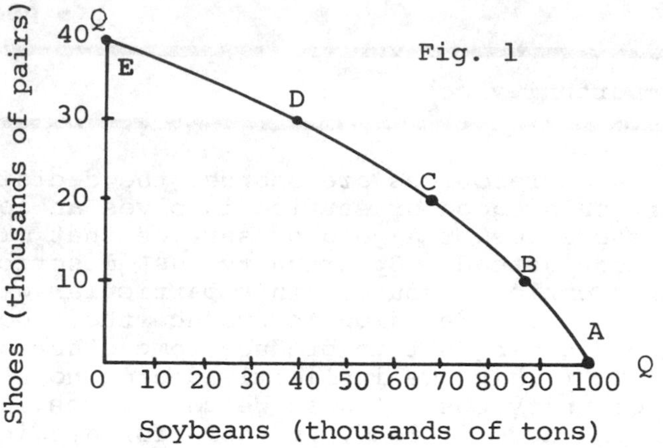

reading the corresponding value for soybean production and going to the right to a point directly above that value on the horizontal axis. When all the production possibilities have been plotted, they are joined by a smooth curve. The correct construction of the production-possibility curve for Ruritania is shown in Figure 1.

• PROBLEM 1-34

Figure 1 below represents the production possibilities curve for an economy which produces only two goods--wheat and tractors. What would be the impact on the economy of a decision to produce 100,000 more tractors? Would your answer be the same if the economy were operating at point "B" or at point "C"? Explain.

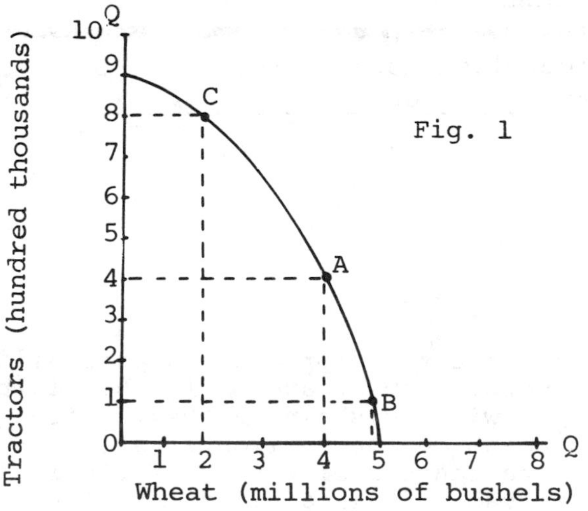

Solution: Suppose the economy is operating at point "A", producing 400,000 tractors and 4,000,000 bushels of wheat, as can be seen from the dashed lines extending from point "A" to the vertical (tractor) and horizontal (wheat) axes. A decision to produce 100,000 more tractors can be implemented only by shifting to a new point "D" on the production

-possibility frontier which corresponds to production of 500,000 tractors. This is illustrated in Figure 2:

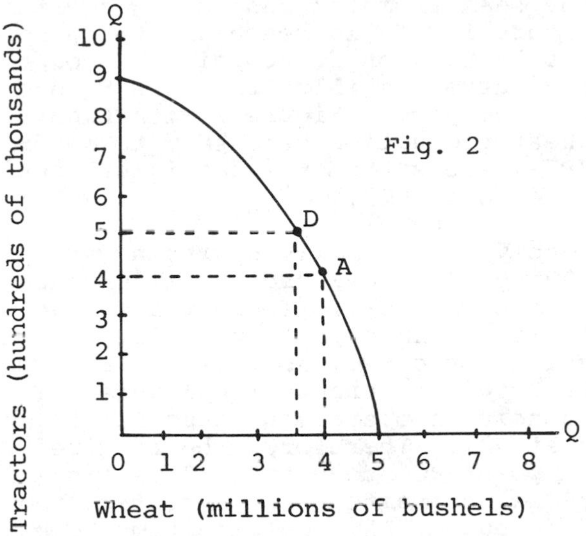

Fig. 2

Note that the dashed line extending downward from point "D" intersects the horizontal (wheat) axis at a quantity of 3,500,000, which is half a million bushels less than the quantity produced at point "A". This means that to produce 500,000 rather than 400,000 tractors and remain on its production-possibility frontier, the economy must give up 500,000 bushels of wheat production. In other words, 500,000 bushels of wheat must be sacrificed for 100,000 extra tractors. This results from the fact that, when the economy is operating on its production-possibility frontier, all available economic resources (such as land, labor and capital) are fully utilized. To produce more tractors requires the use of more economic resources in tractor production. These additional resources can (in this simplified, two-product economy) only be obtained by taking them away from wheat production. The result is a decrease in the quantity of wheat that the economy can produce.

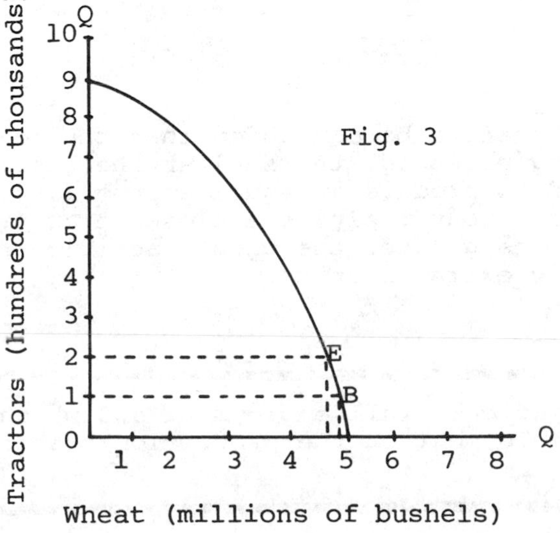

Fig. 3

If the economy is initially operating at point "B", it is producing 100,000 tractors and 5 million bushels of wheat, as can be seen from the dashed lines extending from point "B" on Figure 1. To increase tractor production to 200,000 will result in a shift to point "E" on the production possibility curve, as illustrated in Figure 3. As can be seen by comparing Figure 2 with Figure 3, the sacrifice of wheat production necessary to go from point "B" to point "E" is less than the sacrifice required to go from point "A" to point "D".

If the economy is initially operating at point "C", it is producing 800,000 tractors and 2 million bushels of wheat, as can be seen from Figure 1. To increase tractor production to 900,000 will result in a shift to point "F" on the production-possibility curve, as shown in Figure 4. Note that point "F" is on the vertical axis. This means that, if the economy is operating at point "F", no wheat is being produced at all. Therefore, the required wheat sacrifice to go from point "C" to point "F" is two million bushels. This is four times as great as the sacrifice required to go from point "A" to point "D", and many times greater than the sacrifice required to go from point "B" to point "E".

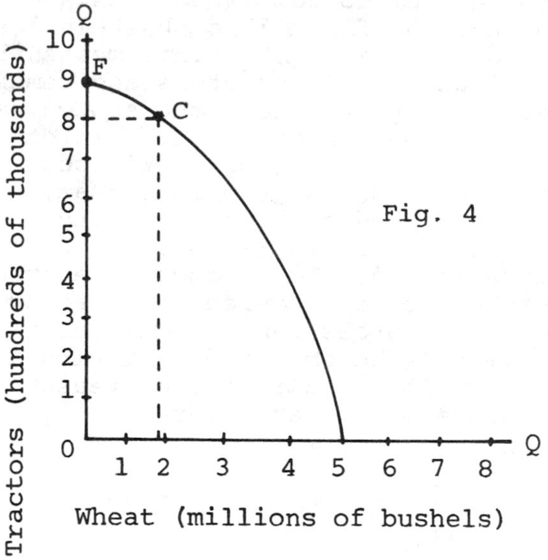

Fig. 4

It can therefore be concluded that the fewer tractors initially being produced, the smaller the sacrifice of wheat required to produce an equal amount (100,000) of extra tractors. Conversely, the closer tractor production is to 900,000 the greater the wheat sacrifice required to produce 100,000 extra tractors.

• PROBLEM 1-35

Which points indicate full employment and which points indicate underemployment on the production-possibilities curve below?

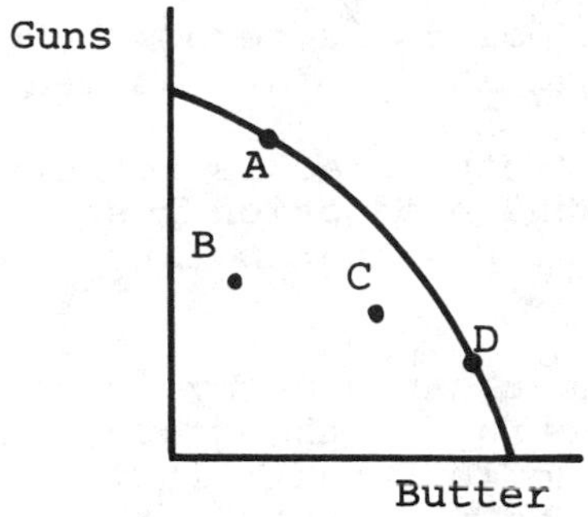

Solution: On a production-possibilities frontier, any point on the curve represents full employment. Therefore A and D represent full employment. Any point inside the curve indicates that resources are not being fully employed in the best-known way, i.e., they are unemployed or underemployed. B and C are such points on the curve above.

• PROBLEM 1-36

Given below is the production possibilities curve for a small country which produces only two goods: nuclear submarines and peanuts.

a) What is the maximum number of submarines produceable by this economy? Of peanuts? When the maxium amount of either peanuts or submarines is produced, how much of the other is produced?

b) Which points represent maximum use of resources?

c) Which points represent unemployment?

d) Which points are impossible to attain?

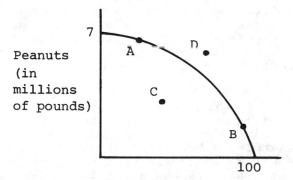

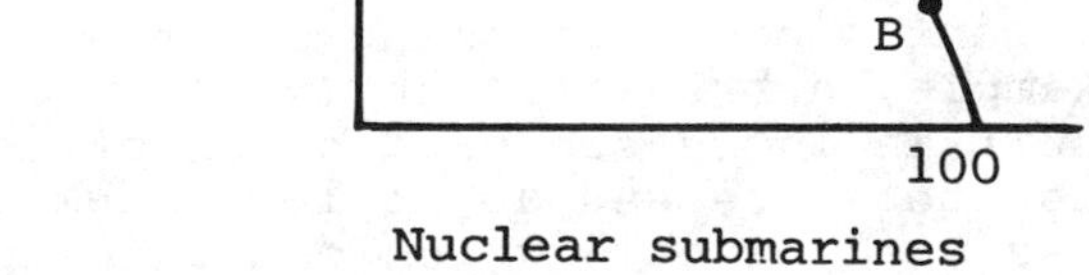

Solution: a) The maximum amounts of the two products will be achieved when all the resources are devoted to one product (submarines or peanuts). When all the resources are devoted to peanuts, we see by looking at the graph that 7,000,000 lbs. of peanuts would be produced. If all resources are devoted to building nuclear submarines, 100 could be built. Since at either of these maximum points, all resources are devoted to one product, the amount of the other product at these points is zero. 7,000,000 peanuts means no submarines, and 100 submarines means no peanuts.

(b) Maximum use of resources is achieved when the point of production lies on the production possibility curve. Looking at the graph, we see that points A and B satisfy this requirement.

c) With unemployment, an economy is not producing at its full capacity. Looking at the graph, we see that point C lies within the production possibilities curve. For the given level of submarines at point C, the economy could be producing about twice as many peanuts as it is. Alternatively, for the given level of peanuts at point C, the economy could be producing nearly twice as many submarines as it is. Clearly, point C represents unemployment (or underemployment).

d) A point that is not possible to attain would be one that lies outside the production possibilities curve. Looking at the curve, we see that D is such a point.

• PROBLEM 1-37

Describe two ways in which an economy's production possibility frontier can be made to expand, or shift outward.

Solution: An expansion, or shifting outward, of the production-possibility frontier indicates economic growth; that is, an increase in the economy's ability to produce goods and services. Two possible causes of economic growth are: (1) an increase in the available supply of factors of production, or economic resources; and (2) technological progress.

Expansion of economic resources can occur in a number of ways. For example, labor can be expanded both quantitatively, through population growth, and qualitatively, through education and training. Capital can be expanded through investment, which allows increased production of capital goods.

Technological progress also causes an expansion of the production-possibility frontier, because improved technology allows more efficient production using existing economic resources. For example, a breakthrough in solar energy technology would result in increased production of usable energy without requiring the increased depletion of existing raw materials, such as coal or oil, which could in turn be used to produce such goods as plastics or synthetic fibers.

• PROBLEM 1-38

Illustrate the effect of capital formation by comparing the production possibility curves, at the present time and ten years in the future, for two economies, one with a high and the other with a low rate of capital formation.

Solution: "Capital formation" means the creation of new or additional capital. "Capital", as defined for economic purposes, means goods (such as machine tools and agricultural implements) which may be used to produce other goods. The effect of capital formation is to increase the resources available for production of goods, and therefore to cause the production-possibility frontier to expand.

If an economy is operating on its production-possibility frontier, it can increase its production of capital goods only by decreasing its production of other goods. In order to increase the share of total output represented by capital goods, output of consumer goods must decrease. In other words, the economy must forego present consumption in order to enjoy greater future production.

Assume that two countries, X and Y, start out with the same production-possibility curve, as shown in Figure 1 below. The vertical axis of Figure 1 represents capital goods, and the horizontal axis consumer goods. The economy of Country X is now operating at point "Ax," producing a relatively large amount of capital goods. In other words, X's economy is experiencing extensive capital formation. The economy of Country Y, on the other hand, is operating at point "Ay" and is engaged almost entirely in the production of consumer goods. It is therefore experiencing very little capital formation.

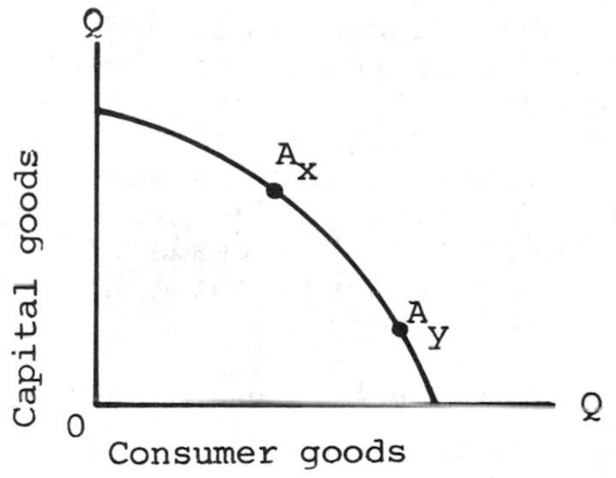

Fig. 1

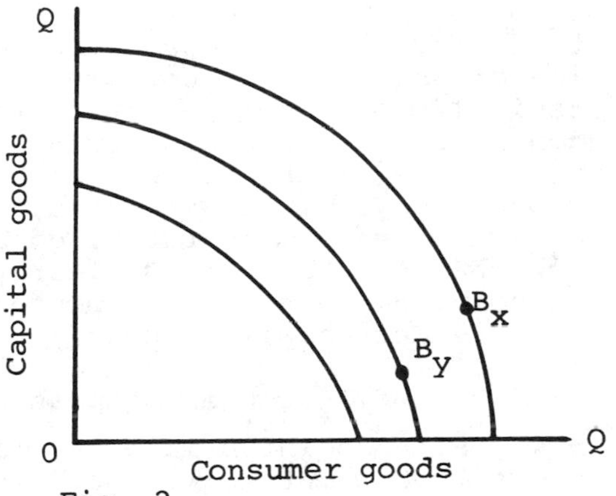

Fig. 2

The situation which is likely to prevail in ten years time is illustrated in Figure 2 below. The innermost curve is the old production-possibility frontier from Figure 1. Country Y's production-possibility frontier has expanded modestly and is represented by the middle curve. Its economy is now operating at the point marked "By". The production-possibility frontier of Country X, because of extensive capital formation, has advanced well beyond that of Country Y, and is now represented by the outermost curve. Country X's economy is now operating at the point marked "Bx". Note that, while it was previously producing fewer consumer goods than Country Y, it is now producing both more capital goods and more consumer goods than is Country Y.

• **PROBLEM 1-39**

Graph P, is a production possibilities curve on which two points, A and B, have been plotted. Graphs P_2 and P_3 represent possible p-p curves ten years in the future. Would P_3 be more likely to be reached in ten years if point A were selected or point B? Explain.

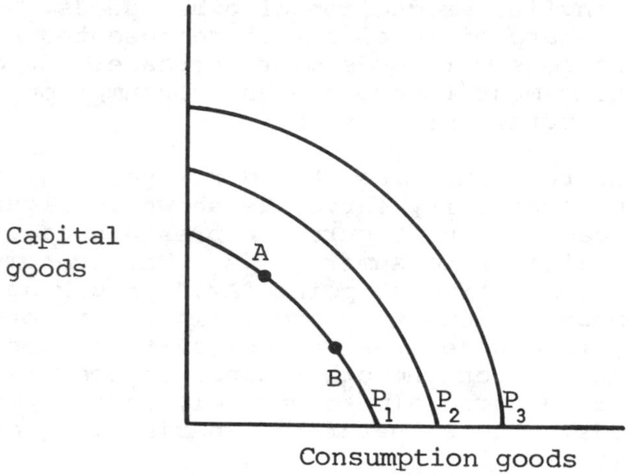

Solution: The production-possibilities curve represents a trade-off between consumption goods such as motorboats and ice cream, which do not produce any further goods, and capital goods, such as tractors and even education, which contribute to producing future goods. If we want to have more goods in the future, we have to sacrifice consumption goods today. In other words, there has to be more saving if we are to have more future goods. Looking at the graph, we see that points A and B clearly represent this trade-off. At point B, we have more present goods than at point A but we have less capital goods.

P_2 and P_3 represent possible p-p curves ten years from now. Since point B involves less production of capital goods than point A, we would expect less growth to take place under B than under A. In other words, there will be less growth during the next decade if we consume more goods today instead of saving and investing in capital goods which provide for more future consumption. Therefore P_2 would be more likely to occur if B were chosen. P_3 would be more likely to occur if A were chosen.

• **PROBLEM 1-40**

The island of Boa-Waku produces only two items: sugar cane and carved utensils. Over the past year, a technological advance has increased the potential production of carved utensils while sugar cane possibilities have remained constant. How would the production possibilities curve change?

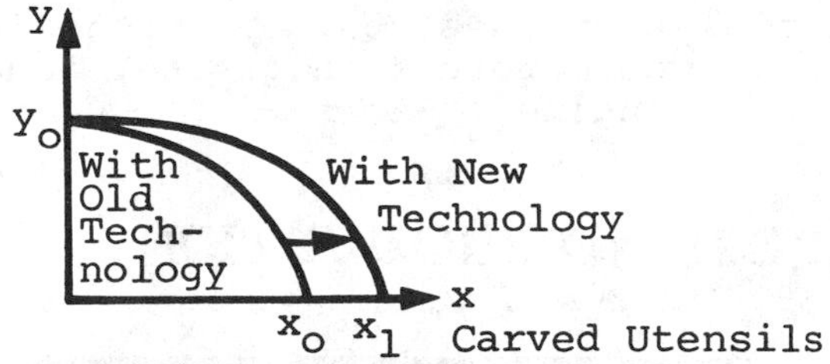

Fig. 1

Solution: This situation clearly represents economic growth. We ordinarily think of economic growth as a shifting outward of the production possibilities curve. However, in this case, there has been no growth in sugar cane's potential output. Therefore the two curves might look something like Figure 1.

Notice that since sugar cane has not increased, the y-intercept of the curve, Y_o, remains the same. But the x-intercept, X_o, moves to the right to X_1 due to the new technology in carved utensil production.

• PROBLEM 1-41

What is meant by "economic efficiency"? Distinguish between economic efficiency and engineering efficiency.

Solution: Economic efficiency occurs when all of society's available economic resources, or factors of production, are fully employed so as to produce the maximum amount of goods and services which the economy is capable of producing. Of course all resources cannot be employed in production all of the time. Workers and managers must have time for eating, sleeping and recreation. Similarly, machines must have periodic "down time" for maintenance. And farm land must occasionally lie fallow to restore its fertility. Within these constraints, however, economic efficiency results when all available factors of production are used to the greatest extent possible and in the most productive possible manner.

The proviso that resources must be used to the fullest possible extent means that underemployment, as well as involuntary unemployment, prevents the attainment of economic efficiency. If a skilled machinist is employed as a dishwasher, or a Wall Street lawyer is forced to type his own legal papers, economic resources are being underemployed, or misallocated and therefore used inefficiently.

Economic efficiency can be distinguished from efficiency in the engineering sense. For example, an automotive engine might be made to produce more horsepower per unit of fuel to increase its "engineering efficiency", if alloys containing rare metals are used in its construction. If, however, such rare alloys could be more productively put to some alternative use, perhaps, e.g., in precision machine tools, their use in automobile engines would be economically inefficient even though it would result in greater "engineering efficiency" in auto engines.

RESOURCES AND PRODUCTION

• PROBLEM 1-42

What is the law of diminishing returns? Give an example of its operation.

Solution: The law of diminishing returns states that, after a point, equal increases in the input of a factor of production, the input of other factors of production remaining fixed, will result in successively less additional output.

For example, a factory may have ten machines, each of which is operated by one worker. Hiring a second worker for each machine will allow the factory to add a second eight-hour shift and double production. A third worker per machine would similarly allow it to triple production by adding a third eight-hour shift. But any additional workers would only serve to relieve other workers during coffee and meal breaks, etc. This would result in a relatively small increase in output. Thus, diminishing returns would set in with the hiring of the thirty-first worker.

• PROBLEM 1-43

Illustrate, using production possibilities curves:

a) the law of diminishing returns

b) a situation in which there are constant returns

c) a situation in which there are increasing returns.

Solution: Diminishing returns describes a situation in which additional units of an input result in decreasing additional output. It is important to keep in mind that this situation exists when at least one other input is held constant. On a production possibility curve, the law of diminishing returns looks like this:

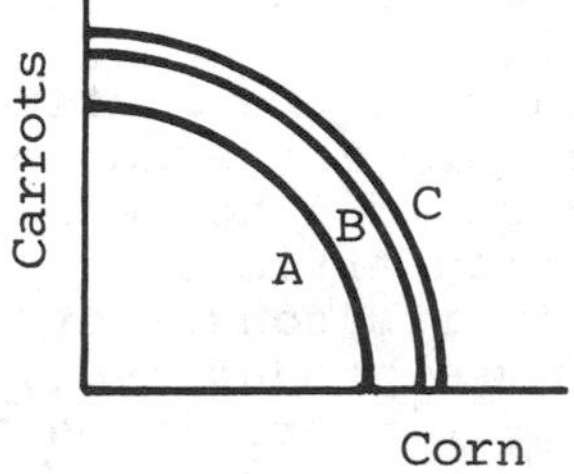

Fig. 1

Where curve A, B, and C each represent an equal increase in one input, say land. Notice the decreasing distance between the curves indicating a decline in additional output.

Constant returns describes a situation where an increase in all inputs brings about a proportionate increase in output. In such a situation, a doubling of inputs would result in a doubling of output, as in Fig. 2:

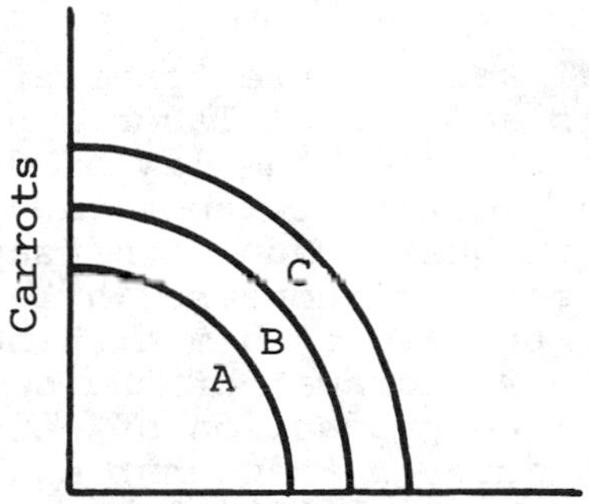

Fig. 2

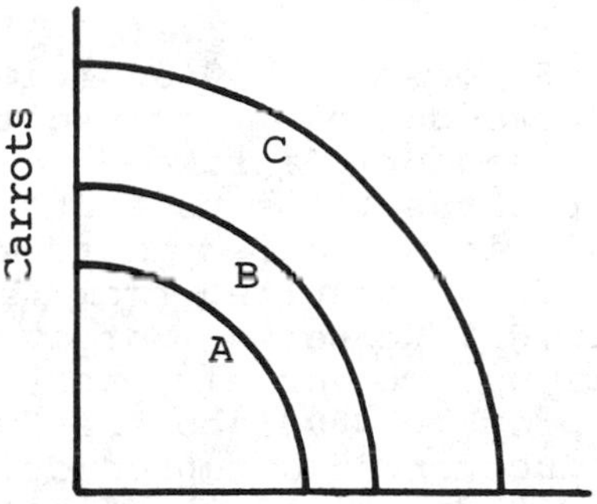

Fig. 3

Where curves A, B, and C represent equal increases in all inputs. Notice the equal distances between the curves, indicating a constant increase in output.

Increasing returns describes a situation in which an increase in all inputs brings about a proportionately greater increase in output, for example, a doubling of inputs causes output to triple. This situation is illustrated in Fig. 3.

Where A, B, and C represent equal increases in inputs. Notice the increasing distance between the curves, indicating an increasing rate of increase of output.

• PROBLEM 1-44

What is the law of increasing relative costs, and how does it relate to the law of diminishing returns? Illustrate the effect of the law of increasing relative costs on the shape of the production-possibility curve.

Solution: The law of increasing relative costs applies when the factors of production required to produce one good are required in different proportions than for the production of another good. In such a case, in order to cause equal increases in production of one good, the economy will have to forego production of increasingly large increments of the other good.

For example, assume that automobile production requires large amounts of labor but very little land. Beef production, on the other hand, requires extensive land but comparatively little labor. Assume further that there is a fixed amount of land available which is suitable for grazing cattle. Finally, assume that, at the outset, the economy's entire labor force of 100,000 is engaged in automobile production, and that 12,000 automobiles per year are being produced.

Now assume that 10,000 workers are withdrawn from the automobile industry and employed in beef production; and, as a result, 2,000 additional head of cattle are produced at the expense of a decline in automobile production of 1000 cars per year.

Suppose 10,000 additional workers are transferred to beef production. Because this additional labor input is being added to a fixed amount of land, the law of diminishing returns tells us that the additional labor input will result in a smaller increase in beef production (say 1,750 head) than resulted from the earlier increase in labor input of 10,000 workers. Moreover, the law of diminishing returns tells us, conversely, that the withdrawal of the second group of 10,000 laborers from the production of cars, causes a reduction in car production greater than that caused by the withdrawal of the first group of 10,000 laborers, say 1250 cars. Thus, the transfer of the first 10,000 laborers from car production to cattle production resulted in an increase of 2000 head of cattle and a decrease of 1000 cars, which means that the cost of each additional head of cattle, in terms of cars foregone, was 1000 cars ÷ 2000 head of cattle = 0.5 car per head of cattle. The cost of the second transfer of 10,000 laborers from car to cattle production was 1250 cars and the gain 1750 head of cattle, so that the cost, in terms of cars foregone, at the higher level of cattle production, is 1250 cars ÷ 1750 head of cattle ≅ 0.72 cars per head of cattle.

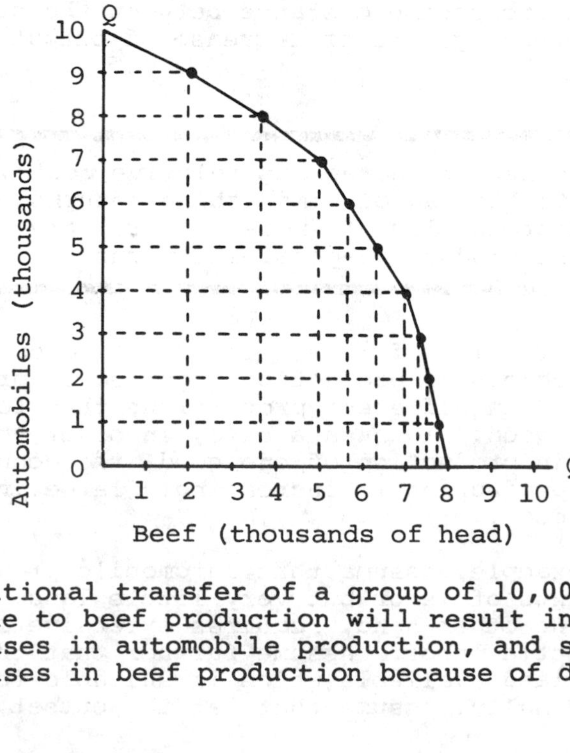

Each additional transfer of a group of 10,000 laborers from automobile to beef production will result in even greater decreases in automobile production, and successively smaller increases in beef production because of diminishing returns.

The law of increasing relative costs may, therefore, be said to be an outgrowth of the law of diminishing returns. It is important to remember that the law of increasing relative costs only applies where the goods in question require factors of production in different proportions or amounts. If, in the hypothetical example above, automobile and beef production required equal proportions of land and labor, each transfer of labor from automobile to beef production could have been accompanied by a proportionate transfer of land. Diminishing returns would not have set in and relative costs may not be increasing.

Where the law of increasing relative costs applies, the shape of the production-possibility curve will be convex, that is, bowed out away from the origin. The figure, which is based on the hypothetical example above, illustrates this.

The successively smaller increases in beef production resulting from equal decreases (note horizontal dashed lines) in automobile production can be seen in the decreasing distances (moving from left to right) between the vertical dashed lines.

• PROBLEM 1-45

What would be the shape of the production-possibility curve if relative costs, rather than increasing, were constant?

Solution: If relative costs are constant, equal decreases in production of one good will always allow equal increases in production of the other. For example, if foregoing production of 1,000 automobiles always frees up enough factors of production to produce 2,000 extra head of beef cattle, this would be a case of constant relative costs. In such a case, the production possibility curve will be a straight line, as shown in the figure.

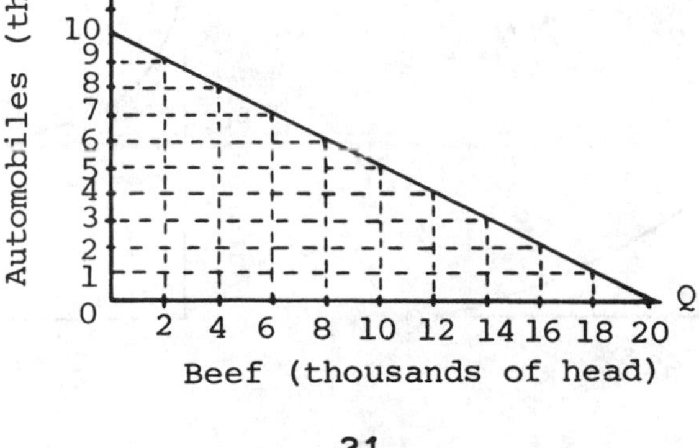

Note that each decrease of 1,000 in automobile production (dashed horizontal lines) corresponds to an increase of exactly 2,000 (dashed vertical lines) in production of beef cattle.

It is unusual to encounter constant relative costs, because constant relative costs imply that the factors of production (such as land, labor and capital) are used in exactly the same proportions to produce both products.

• PROBLEM 1-46

Is it ever possible to have decreasing relative costs? Why or why not? Illustrate the effect which decreasing relative costs would have on the shape of the production-possibility curve.

Solution: It is possible to have decreasing relative costs, at least over part of the production-possibility curve. Such decreasing relative costs result from economies of scale.

For example, suppose that foregoing production of 2,000 head of beef cattle will free up sufficient factors of production to allow the manufacture of 1,000 automobiles. If economies of scale can be realized in the automobile industry, it may be the case that foregoing production of a second 2,000 head of cattle will result in a greater increase (say 1,500) in automobile production. If economies of scale in auto production are realizable, each equal decrease in beef production may allow a successively greater increase in automobile production. If this were true along the entire production-possibility curve, the shape of the curve would be concave, that is, bowed in towards the origin, as in Figure 1.

In reality, economies of scale are likely to prevail only at the extremes of the production-possibility curve. The law of diminishing returns will cause increasing relative costs in the middle region. The shape of the production -possibility curve is therefore more likely to be concave only near the axes and convex in the center, as in Figure 2.

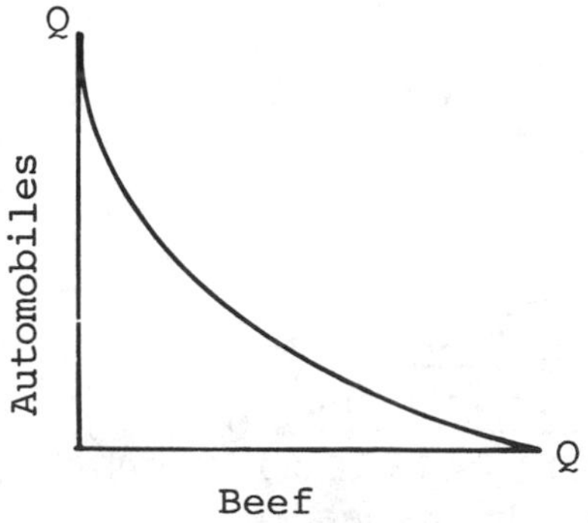

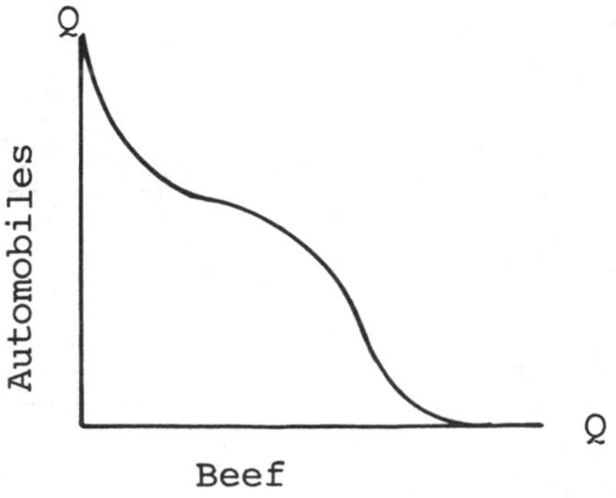

• **PROBLEM 1-47**

What are "economies of scale", and how do they relate to the law of diminishing returns?

Solution: Economies of scale are increases in the engineering efficiency of production which result from increasing the scale of production, that is, increasing the quantity of all required inputs of production (capital, labor, land, etc.) in the same proportion. Doubling the amounts of all inputs may result in more than doubling output because of economies of scale. This results from a number of factors, including, for example, the ability to implement specialization and division of labor, and the possibility of using more technically efficient large-scale energy sources.

The principle of economies of scale does not contradict the law of diminishing returns, because economies of scale result from increasing the inputs of all factors of production in the same proportion. Diminishing returns result when one or more of the factors of production are held constant while others are increased, with the result that the factor proportions become different from what they were.

SHORT ANSWER QUESTIONS FOR REVIEW

Answer
To be covered when testing yourself

Choose the correct answer.

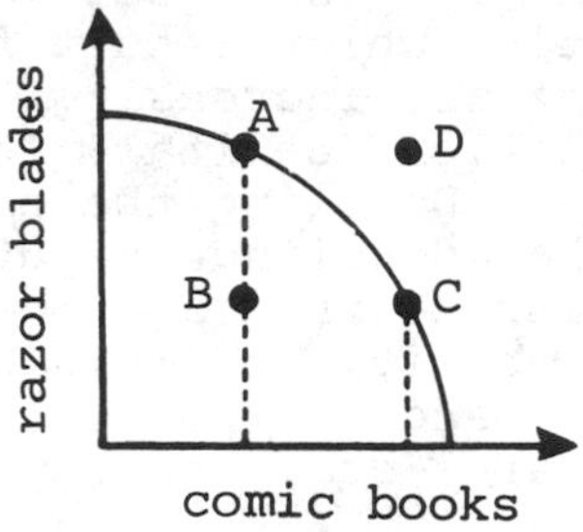

1. The figure is the production possibility curve for nation X. Which of the following is true? (a) Nation X cannot move from point A to point C without an increase in technology or the amount of resources used. (b) Nation X can move from point B to point C with no increase in technology or the amount of resources used. (c) Nation X can move from point D to point A if it ceases to produce razor blades. (d) At point B, nation X can produce either more razor blades or more comic books, but not more of each. (e) If nation X is at point C and decides to produce 10 less comic books, point B must result. — b

2. The economizing problem may be defined as the attempt to allocate resources among various production uses in the most efficient manner. The necessity of dealing with the problem is caused by (a) the law of increasing costs (b) scarcity (c) the "Invisible Hand" doctrine (d) the division of labor (e) the law of diminishing returns — b

3. A coal company owns a mine in Texas. They mine the coal with shovels, load it on a ship and take it to England where it is sold. Which of the following is true? (a) The mine, the shovels and the ship are all examples of capital (b) The mine is land, the coal in it is capital, and the miners are labor (c) The mine and the coal in it are land, and the shovels are capital. (d) The miners and the shovels are both components of labor. (e) The owner of the company (since he draws a salary), is an example of labor. — c

4. According to the law of diminishing returns, as each additional fisherman is added to the crew of a boat, the additional amount of fish caught will (a) increase steadily (b) de-

Answer
To be covered when testing yourself

crease steadily (c) decrease, then increase (d) eventually decrease (e) fluctuate wildly — d

5. Among the various definitions of economics, which of the following is most widely used? (a) The study of exchange (with or without money), between people (b) The study of how production and consumption activities are organized (c) The study of wealth (d) The study of how to improve society (e) The study of how people choose to use scarce or limited productive resources to produce various commodities and distribute them to various members of society for consumption — e

6. Both the unemployed and underemployed workers are (a) out of work (b) involuntarily not working (c) not looking for a job (d) inefficiently used by the economy — d

7. The amount of goods that can be produced in the economy is (a) unlimited when the economy is at full employment (b) limited and finite as described by the production possibility frontier (c) grows indefinitely with the increases in efficiency (d) defined by the amount of resources that are used in production — b

8. Due to the fact that resources are scarce, economics is concerned with the choice between producing one good or substituting the production of another for it. The rate of substitution in production of two goods (a) is more than 1 (b) equals the slope of their production possibility frontier (c) is more than 2 (d) determines how efficiently each good is produced — b

9. The cost of a good in terms of the amount of other goods forgone in order to allow its production is called (a) a fixed cost (b) a variable cost (c) economic rent (d) an opportunity cost — d

10. The production possibility curve of two goods is usually drawn concave, as viewed from the origin, because (a) all resources are scarce (b) of the Law of diminishing returns (c) not all economic resources can be used equally efficiently in the alternative uses (d) of a convention — c

11. Public ownership of economic resources and

Answer
To be covered when testing yourself

central planning are both characteristics of (a) authoritarian socialist economic systems (b) underdeveloped economy (c) laissez-faire capitalism (d) liberal capitalism — a

12. The production possibility (or transformation) curve illustrates the basic principle that (a) an economy will automatically seek that level of output at which all of its resources are employed (b) an economy's capacity to produce increases in proportion to its population size (c) if all the resources of an economy are in use, more of one good can be produced only if less of another good is produced (d) none of the above — c

13. The basic difference between consumer goods and capital goods is that (a) consumer goods are produced in the private sector and investment goods are produced in the public sector (b) an economy that commits a relatively large proportion of its resources to capital goods must accept a lower growth rate (c) consumer goods satisfy wants directly, while capital goods satisfy wants indirectly (d) none of the above — c

Fill in the blanks.

14. The assumption by which an economist isolates the effect of one economic variable in a situation is the ___________ assumption, or _______________. — "other things equal", ceteris paribus

15. A severe drought destroys the corn crop in Nebraska one year. The seeds which Farmer Brown intends to plant the following summer are affected, without his knowledge, by radiation which causes each plant to produce twice as many ears. Upon seeing his bumper crop the following fall, Farmer Brown concludes that a drought one year will cause a bumper crop the next. This is an example of the __________ fallacy. — "post hoc"

16. Mr. Smith produces ashtrays. One year he doubles production and finds that his earnings are doubled. At a meeting of the Association of Ashtray Producers, Mr. Smith advises that each doubles his output in order to double earnings. The Association rejects his advice, — The fallacy of

SHORT ANSWER QUESTIONS FOR REVIEW

	Answer To be covered when testing yourself
though , realizing that his error is ______________________.	composition
17. Mr. Johnson, owner of a coal mine, employs 20 miners who produce 20 tons of coal per week. He hires a new miner and production increases to 22 tons per week. He hires a second and production increases to 25 tons. Hoping to increase productivity to 29 tons per week, Mr. Johnson hires a third miner, but after a week, production only increases to 27 tons. Thus, the law of ______________ has set in.	diminishing returns
18. The pursuit by each individual of his own self interest leads, according to Adam Smith, to the general social good. Smith calls this phenomena the doctrine of the ______________.	Invisible Hand
19. Resources are limited and desires are unlimited. This is ______________, the basic problem of economics.	scarcity
20. A businessman doubles the inputs used in his production process. As a result, his output triples. This is an example of ______________.	increasing returns to scale
21. If an economy is operating inside its production possibility curve, it is either due to ______________ or ______________ of resources.	unemployment or underemployment
22. A good that is used in the production of another good is a ______________________.	capital good
23. The field on which a farmer grows wheat is an example of ______________. The workers who harvest it are ______________. The tractors they use are ______________. The farmer, who rents the field, pays the workers, and buys the tractors, represents ____________________.	land, labor, capital, entrepreneurial ability
24. Al is a "crack shot." Bob is patient and a good sailor. Since both men like both meat and fish, Al agrees to do nothing but hunt and Bob agrees to fish, each trading his surplus to the other. This is known as ______________ ________________.	specialization, or the division of labor
25. A production possibility curve represents the maximum output combinations attainable by an economy with a given level of ________________ and ______________.	resource utilization, technology

Answer

To be covered when testing yourself

SHORT ANSWER QUESTIONS FOR REVIEW

	Answer
26. The fact that two identical situations cannot be created in the real world increases significantly the importance of ______________ in economic theory.	assumptions
27. The method of ______________ is based on the derivation of general principles on the basis of the analysis and systematization of a series of observed facts.	induction
28. The ________________ begins with theoretical hypotheses and then uses observations to check them.	deductive method
29. The hypothesis that what is good for the part is good for the whole leads to a distinction between ______________ and ___________.	macroeconomics, microeconomics
30. Widespread _______________ of certain events in the economy often cause these events to materialize.	expectations
31. When two variables graphically expressed move in the same direction they are said to be _______________ related and the resulting curves ______________ sloping.	directly, upward
32. Inflation directly contradicts the basic economic goal of ______________.	price stability
33. The difference between capital goods,(e.g., machinery), and money capital is that the former is an _______________, while the latter is not.	economic resource
34. People whose skills are not fully utilized in the economy are considered ________________.	under-employed
<u>Determine whether the following statements are true or false.</u>	
35. The wealthier the nation, the more remote its production possibility curve is from the origin.	True
36. The Law of diminishing returns shows that equal additions of all inputs will, at a certain point, begin to result in smaller and smaller increases in output.	False
37. Economics as a science is said to have started with the publication of <u>Wealth of Nations</u> in 1776.	True

SHORT ANSWER QUESTIONS FOR REVIEW

	Answer To be covered when testing yourself
38. The Soviet Union represents a good example of mixed economy since it produces both industrial and agricultural goods.	False
39. The extent to which current income is spent on consumption has no significant effect on the society's future production possibility frontier.	False
40. The Malthusian theory of population predicted the ever decreasing standard of living for human kind in the future.	True
41. The existence of huge powerful enterprises using methods of mass production in their operations is often justified on the basis of increasing returns to scale, which make the large size of a firm economically efficient.	True
42. The fundamental economic problems of what, how and for whom the goods are produced are faced by all societies regardless of their different economic systems.	True
43. All the points on the production possibility frontier are equally desirable to society.	False
44. If goods were not scarce they would be free.	True
45. In a free enterprise economy prices and profit play a decisive role in determining what is produced.	True
46. An economy's movement from one point to another on its production possibility curve represents a change in technology.	False
47. As resources are added to the production of a good or service, the additional amount produced by the addition of an equal amount of resources will usually rise and then fall.	True
48. Economics as a science differs from the "natural" sciences because the economist cannot perform controlled experiments.	True
49. The doctrine of the "invisible hand" means that government, while not taking an active role in the economy, retains the power to control it.	False
50. The principal obstacle to the fulfillment of desires and, hence, the reason for the study of economics, is the scarcity of resources.	True

CHAPTER 2

THE CAPITALIST ECONOMY

Basic Attacks and Strategies for Solving Problems in this Chapter. See pages 40 to 72 for step-by-step solutions to problems.

Societies must design economic institutions to surmount the problems created by the existence of scarcity. One important economic system is capitalism. The distinguishing characteristics of capitalism include: private property, freedom of enterprise, self-interest as the dominant motive, competition, reliance upon the price system, and the limitation of government's role in the economy.

Perhaps the key characteristic is private property. Private property means that individuals can own productive resources and exploit them as they see fit. The locus of decision-making in society is at the individual level. Decisions regarding how and what goods and services to produce are the responsibility of individuals, and individuals reap the rewards or suffer the consequences of their decisions. As a result, capitalism is said to be a system of liberty.

Advocates of capitalism cite several virtues of the system. For one thing, the system is thought to be economically efficient and will promote maximum growth and progress. Individual responsibility and the role of self-interest means that everyone is constantly striving to "build a better mousetrap," and cater to consumer demands. Another feature is that the system maximizes human liberty and is most compatible with democratic political systems.

Critics of capitalism often make the following points. First, capitalism can cause large disparities in living standards and political influence among members of society. Second, capitalistic systems are frequently subject to economic instability. Periods of deep recession, high inflation, or both, are not uncommon. Third, the competitive struggle and production of commodities for profit is at odds with the essential human needs of community and fulfillment.

Modern economies have certain features that distinguish them from primitive economies. These features are not related to the type of economic system used. Rather, they are of a more general nature and include specialization, the use of money, and the use of capital goods.

Specialization means that individuals concentrate on a limited number of productive activities. Instead of individuals who are self-sufficient, society is composed of butchers, bakers, candlestick makers, and others, each of whom devotes him- or herself exclusively to one or a few jobs, and depends on others to produce any additional goods and services desired.

The value of specialization is that by concentrating effort on a limited number of jobs, individuals can become especially proficient. The sum total of all the goods and services produced under specialization will be larger than if each person was self-sufficient, so society's standard of living will be higher. Assume that John can produce four units of food and one unit of clothing from each unit of resources, and that Mary can produce three units of food and two units of clothing from a unit of resources. It clearly makes sense for John to specialize in food production and for Mary to specialize in clothing production.

A harder case is if John can produce four units of food and two units of clothing from each unit of resources, while Mary's production from a unit of resources is three units of food and one unit of clothing. Economists say that John possesses an **absolute advantage** in the production of both food and clothing. Will specialization be beneficial in this case also?

Looking at the matter from the standpoint of opportunity cost, every unit of food that John produces costs ½ unit of clothing. (The unit of resources that produced four units of food could have produced two units of clothing. Therefore, four units of food costs two units of clothing, or one unit of food costs ½ unit of clothing. The cost of good *Y* in terms of *X* = (units of *X* per unit of resources)/(units of *Y* per unit of resources).) The food Mary produces costs ⅓ unit of clothing. Since food is less expensive for Mary to produce, Mary is said to possess a comparative advantage in that activity. John's clothing costs two units of food while Mary's costs three units of food, so John possesses a comparative advantage in clothing production.

The law of comparative advantage states that individuals should specialize in the production of the good or service in which they have a comparative advantage. If John specializes in clothing and Mary in food, they can produce a larger total than if they each produced both goods. By trading they can each get what they want of the good they do not produce. If John can buy food from Mary for anything less than ½ unit of clothing, he will be better off (because that is cheaper than what he could produce it for). Presumably Mary would be willing to sell food for anything more than ⅓ unit of clothing. If Mary can buy clothing for less than three units of food, she will be better off. Presumably John will be willing to sell for anything more than two units of food. While the exact trading ratio cannot be determined, it is certainly possible for the two to bargain for a mutually advantageous arrangement. The point of this example is that the benefits of specialization are quite widespread.

Specialization is also the source of problems. An economy with a high degree of specialization is also characterized by interdependence. Individuals must depend on others to produce a large percentage of what they need. A breakdown in the system, for example a strike in one industry or a natural disaster, can impact everyone else in the system. Another danger is that of alienation. Specialized work may become monotonous and stifling.

Along with specialization comes the necessity of exchange. Specialized producers must bargain with others to trade their surplus product for the other goods and services they desire. From this condition follows the usefulness of money. Money can be defined as anything that is generally acceptable in exchange for goods and services and in payment of debts. An economy without one or more items considered as money is a barter economy. In a barter economy goods and services exchange directly for other goods and services, i.e., John trades clothing to Mary in exchange for food. The problem with a barter economy is that for barter to work, there must be a "double coincidence of wants" – each party must want what the other party has. Since this will not always be the case, resources must be used simply to arrange trades.

With money, this problem disappears. Since money is generally acceptable, everyone always wants money. Consequently, any item can be obtained with money. Reducing the waste of resources associated with exchange will allow society to be more productive.

The third characteristic is the use of capital goods. Capital is defined as man-made means of production. The term includes such items as machinery, factories, and tools. The value of capital is that it multiplies human power. A worker with capital equipment is more productive than a worker without. The drawback of capital goods is that they are part of "roundabout production." In order to use capital goods, resources must first be devoted to their production. This involves a sacrifice of current consumption possibilities and requires waiting for the payoff.

The circular flow model is a diagram showing the process of exchange in a modern economy. Dividing the economy into two sectors, firms (where production takes place) and households (where consumption takes place), the model shows both the real (resources and goods and services) and monetary flows in the economy.

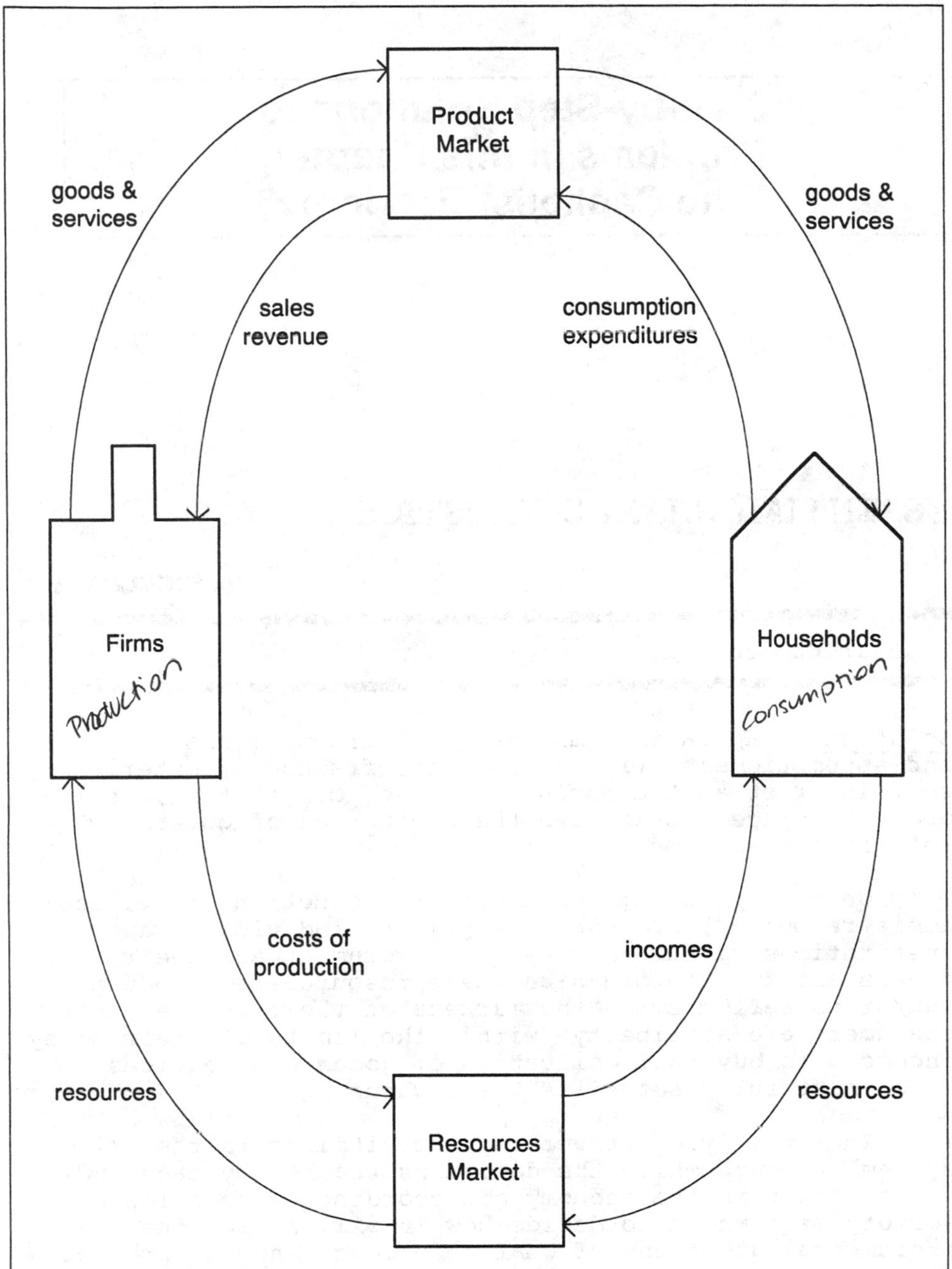

Circular Flow Model

Step-by-Step Solutions to Problems in this Chapter, "The Capitalist Economy"

ESSENTIAL CHARACTERISTICS

• PROBLEM 2-1

What is Capitalism?

Solution: Capitalism embodies the following institutions and assumptions: private property, freedom of enterprise, self-interest as the dominant motive, competition, reliance upon the price system, and the limitation of government's role in the economy.

Under capitalism the means of production (i.e., economic resources) are owned by private individuals and institutions rather than by the government and their owners are free to organize these resources to produce and/or to sell them in the markets of their choice. Also, consumers are at liberty, within the limits of their money incomes, to buy that collection of goods and services which most fully satisfies their wants.

The underlying structure of capitalism is the price system, through which the decisions reached by each individual actor in the economy are coordinated to allow society as a whole to decide how it will answer the fundamental questions of what to produce, how to produce it, and how to distribute it.

• PROBLEM 2-2

What institution is closely identified with capitalism, perhaps more closely than any other?

Solution: The institution of private property, private ownership of the means of production (scarce resources), is perhaps the most famous identifying feature of capitalism. Private property is usually associated with a body of other rights (Freedom of contract, right to bequeath, etc.) that support a person's control over his or her property.

• PROBLEM 2-3

What is meant by the exclusion principle. Give examples of non-exclusive goods.

Solution: If you buy a commodity and are able to prevent others from reaping any benefits from it, that commodity is said to reflect the exclusion principle. The exclusion principle refers to the fact that a good or service can exclude everyone but the buyer from the satisfactions or costs it provides.

Suppose you grow a flower garden. Clearly you derive benefits from your garden. Yet in addition your neighbors and any passersby will also derive aesthetic pleasure from your garden. So the flower garden is non-exclusive in extending benefits.

Alternatively, suppose you ride a motorcycle without a muffler. You derive pleasure from your vehicle, but all your neighbors get is grief from the noise pollution your bike provides. Here is an example of a non-exclusive good which provides costs to others.

Commodities, such as the flower garden and the noisy motorcycle, above are said to possess spillover effects or externalities. Whenever such external costs and benefits exist, the market cannot operate efficiently.

• PROBLEM 2-4

Is pure capitalism adaptable to changes in consumer tastes?

Solution: Pure capitalism adapts to a change in consumer tastes in two ways. Production of consumer goods adjusts to changes in tastes, and the resource markets adjust to changes in the production of consumer goods.

In pure capitalism, if consumer tastes change, (for example if consumers want more sandals and fewer shoes) these changes will be reflected in the demands for the two goods. In the market for sandals, consumers will bid against each other for limited quantity of sandals available. In the shoe market, firms will undercut each other in an effort to sell some of the unwanted shoes. The price of sandals will rise, leading to higher profits in the industry. The price of shoes will fall, leading to lower profits in the shoe industry. The higher profits in the sandal industry will induce firms to expand their output of sandals, leading to an increased supply of sandals. The losses in the shoe industry will drive some firms out of the shoe industry, thus reducing the supply of shoes. The effect of the changes in consumer tastes has been reflected in changes in production; more sandals and fewer shoes are being produced.

The analysis so far assumes that resource markets will adjust to these changes. A sandal-making firm earning high profits will be able to pay more for resources,--higher wages, for example. By paying higher wages, the firm will attract more workers. Similarly, a firm losing money in the shoe business will be forced to cut wages, prompting workers to leave. Resources, in effect, will shift in response to changes in producers' demands, and indirectly, in response to changes in consumer tastes.

• PROBLEM 2-5

What is meant by 'consumer sovereignty'?

Solution: Consumer sovereignty refers to the role of consumers in determining the types and quantities of goods produced. Consumers spend the incomes from the sale of their resources on the goods that they desire most urgently. These consumer expenditures are sometimes called "dollar votes" to emphasize the fact they reflect consumer preferences among products in the market. If there are enough "dollar votes" for a product to provide a profit to its producers, they will produce the good. An increase in "dollar votes" for a good (an increase in demand) will lead to higher prices for the good and higher profits for its producers, and hence, an expansion of the industry as producers attempt to capture the higher profits to be made in the industry. A decrease in demand will result in lower prices and lower profits, and an eventual contraction of the industry as producers seek higher profits in other industries. So changes in consumer demand for various products generate corresponding changes in the supply of those products.

Thus, in the capitalist system, consumers ultimately determine the types and quantities of goods that profit-seeking businesses will produce. This important role of consumer preferences in capitalism is characterized as "consumer sovereignty."

• PROBLEM 2-6

How does pure capitalism determine what goods are to be produced?

Solution: Production under pure capitalism is the result of interactions between consumer preferences and producer profits.

In capitalism, the preferences of consumers, as registered in the demands for specific products, determine what will be produced (the concept of consumer sovereignty). It does not matter how inexpensive or useful a product is:

if consumers are not willing to buy it, it will not be produced. Any firm that continues to produce a good that it cannot sell for a price high enough to cover costs, will lose money and eventually go bankrupt.

If there is a great demand for a good relative to the quantity of it available, the price of the good will be high (consumers will 'bid' against each other for the good). Due to its high price, producers of it will tend to make relatively large profits. These profits will attract resources to the industry. As the industry expands, prices will come down because more of the good is being supplied (as supplies increase, consumers will not have to bid against each other as fiercely as before). As the price comes down, the large profits disappear and no further expansion of the industry occurs.

The analysis is similar for goods experiencing weak demand goods. Here, low prices relative to costs of production imply low profits, which will drive resources out of the industry. The size of the industry will stabilize when firms can earn normal profits.

This description of how the types and quantities of goods to be produced are determined makes several assumptions. The first is that individual firms cannot set their own prices above the competitive market price because of competition. If firms could set their own prices above the competitive market price, they would not produce as much as they possibly could without incurring losses. They would restrict the quantity they produce in order to keep their prices higher than the competitive price. Under competition, any attempt by an individual firm to charge a price higher than the competitive market price results in a loss of its entire sales. With no power to raise the price, the individual producer has no incentive to produce less than the maximum amount he can produce without incurring a loss. A second assumption concerns resource mobility. The analysis assumes firms and the factors of production (labor, capital, etc.) can be easily switched from industry to industry. Without this assumption, industries would not be able to expand and contract so quickly in response to demand. A third assumption is that changes in prices, profits and production are quickly perceived by all economic actors.

In pure capitalism, then, the types and quantities of goods produced are determined by the interaction of consumer sovereignty, producer profits, competition and resource mobility.

• PROBLEM 2-7

How does freedom of choice fit in the capitalist framework?

<u>Solution</u>: Freedom of choice is an essential feature of capitalism. In a capitalist market economy consumer preferences dictate what is to be produced. Restriction of

freedom of choice will lead to production of some goods that are not wanted so urgently as other goods which go unproduced. In short, society will not be as well off as it could have been.

Without freedom of choice, capitalists will not be able to invest where profits indicate that investment is needed to satisfy consumers' demands. Workers will not be able to enter the line of work where they are in greatest demand. As a result of these restrictions of freedom of choice, new industries with huge potential growth would not be able to expand while declining industries would waste large amounts of capital and labor.

There are limits, of course, to this freedom, but within these broad legal limits, however, freedom of choice is an essential feature of capitalism.

• PROBLEM 2-8

What role does competition play in a capitalist economy to regulate self-interest?

Solution: In capitalism, competition channels self-interest to constructive ends. In the marketplace, this means firms will strive to produce goods as efficiently as possible. Because competitive pressure forces these firms to operate efficiently, consumers can buy the products for the lowest price possible and society benefits by getting the most output from a given amount of resources. Competition channels the self-interests of capitalists so that their activities are beneficial to society.

Similarly, competition tends to prevent any person or firm from exploiting other people. When there are a number of competitors in an industry, no firm can charge consumers more than the prevailing market price since consumers would stop buying from the overcharging firm. Each firm also has to pay its workers the prevailing market wage; otherwise, workers will seek employment elsewhere. It would certainly be in the interests of a firm to charge a high price and pay low wages if it could, but competition from other firms in selling products and in hiring labor severely restricts its ability to do so.

In the labor market, each worker would naturally like to get paid a high wage. Competition for jobs, however, forces workers to accept the prevailing wage. No one can charge more than his services are worth to consumers or employers.

In a pure capitalistic society, competition tends to prevent anyone from gaining a large amount of economic power. Because competition diffuses economic power so widely, it is in the self-interest of each producer to produce as efficiently as possible in order to match the competition. Competition tends to channel self-interest into constructive avenues towards achieving greater efficiency. So, in pure capitalism competition regulates how people and firms can achieve their own interests.

• PROBLEM 2-9

Explain how self-interest can lead both capitalists and workers to use their talents to society's advantage.

Solution: Capitalists and workers will both generally want to get as high a payment as possible for their services. Workers will try to learn the skills that are paid the highest, and then they will try to find the positions in their particular fields that pay the highest. Thus, for example, a worker will try to learn the skills of an electrician, and then try to find the electrician's positions that pay the most. Similarly another 'worker' might train to be a lawyer, and then search for the law firm that will pay him the most. Capitalists will try to invest their capital where it can get the highest return. They will search for the most lucrative investment opportunities.

This self-interest on the part of workers and capitalists will be beneficial to society, because it will lead these people to the areas that society values most highly. The price of labor (wages) and the price of capital (interest) both reflect the scarcity of these resources, and the need for these resources. By trying to find the highest-paying occupations and investments, workers and capitalists are actually finding the uses in which society desires labor and capital most. So, by gravitating to these uses, they fill the needs which society has decided (through supply and demand) have the highest priority. Self-interest then can be mutually advantageous to the individual and to society.

• PROBLEM 2-10

"Capitalism is a market economy." Explain.

Solution: Capitalism is a market economy because economic decisions are registered in markets via the price mechanism. The preferences of buyers and sellers are registered in the supply and demand conditions in the various product markets, then reflected in a system of product and resource prices. The pricing mechanism weighs the preferences of everyone, and indicates what should be produced, how it can be produced most efficiently, and how the product is to be distributed. Prices act as incentives directing consumers and producers towards efficient performance. Through markets and the price system, society makes the basic economic decisions, not by resorting to a central authority, but rather by simply weighing individual preferences in the face of scarcity of resources.

• PROBLEM 2-11

Consumer preferences determine what will be produced in pure capitalism. For what types of goods might this system of expressing individual wants be inadequate?

Solution: This system of consumer sovereignty could be inadequate for goods and services which cannot be provided on an individual basis. There are some goods and services over which it is difficult or impossible to exercise exclusive ownership because the benefits generated by them accrue to many people other than the would-be owner. And there are goods and services which can be "consumed" without diminishing the amount of the good available. An example of both types is defense against attack by a foreign nation or terrorist group. It would be extremely difficult for an individual (even if he could afford it) to buy protection services sufficient to repel such an attack without at the same time unintentionally providing a considerable measure of protection to his neighbors, who benefit from it without diminishing its benefits to him.

Because the benefits of such a good could be enjoyed by many people even if only one person were to buy the good, there is an incentive, in the absence of any collective action, for each individual to refrain from buying such a good, hoping instead that someone else will pay for it. The result of such a situation then, might well be that none of the good is purchased by anyone even though each individual would be willing to pay something for such a good. For such goods, the price system is a poor indicator of individual preferences.

"Social goods" such as national defense can be provided and consumed economically only on a social, or collective, basis. Since these preferences cannot be registered by the price system, it cannot allocate the optimal amount of resources to the production of these goods and services.

• PROBLEM 2-12

The major economic argument for pure capitalism is that it provides maximum economic efficiency. What is the major noneconomic argument?

Solution: The major noneconomic argument for capitalism is that capitalism can coordinate the economic activities of large numbers of individuals and businesses without central direction and the use of coercion. The price system is built upon freedom of choice and freedom of enterprise. A worker or consumer cannot be tyrannized by a firm because the worker can switch jobs and the consumer is free to buy a competing product. Competition not only does not use coercion, it prevents coercion. Within the penalties and rewards imposed by the price system itself, each individual is free to pursue his or her own self-interest. This argument states the capitalist competitive price system is conducive to both allocative efficiency, and personal freedom.

• PROBLEM 2-13

Under a pure capitalist system, would the government play a major role in the economy?

Solution: In a pure capitalist economy, all economic decisions would be made, coordinated and carried out through markets and the pricing mechanism. Production would be regulated by competition and self-interest; distribution of output would be based on the inputs to the productive process. In this pure system, there would be no government intervention in the economy.

The government would perform functions such as enforcing contracts, providing a system of justice, and other non-market tasks essential to a smoothly running capitalist economy. Among the functions that the court and criminal system would perform would be to limit the realm of self-interest. Economic efficiency could not justify crimes and tyrannical business practices, even if they were done on the basis of self-interest. Drawing the fine line between criminal self-interest and acceptable self-interest, especially in regard to business practices, would be the closest the government would need to come to interfering with the economy. The ideal capitalist system would provide maximum economic efficiency. The role of government in this system would be limited to maintaining the smoothness of the pure capitalist economy's flow toward this economic efficiency.

• PROBLEM 2-14

Private property, freedom of choice and the pricing mechanism are some features that are peculiar to capitalism. These characteristics alone, however, do not accurately describe modern economies. Identify three essential features of modern economies that are not peculiar to capitalism.

Solution: A heavy reliance on advanced technology and capital goods, extensive specialization, and the use of money are three essential features of modern economies that are not peculiar to capitalism.

All modern economies rely heavily on advanced technology. The use of advanced technology increases productivity and allows a larger potential output from a given amount of inputs.

All societies specialize in production to some extent. At the most basic level, specialization is based on differences in natural abilities among people. At a more sophisticated level, specialization consists of an extensive division of labor, and trade between different regions and countries. With trade, regions produce the goods they are the most efficient at making. Specialization, even at a basic level, can tremendously increase an economy's productive capacity.

Money is used in all but the most primitive economies. Money is simply a convenient means of exchanging goods. With barter, specialization is extremely limited. For any trade to take place at all, a buyer and seller would each have to have exactly what the other wants. With money, this matching-up of wants does not have to take place. In a monetary economy, a person can specialize in an occupation confident that he will be able to trade his products in order to fulfill his consumer needs.

All three of these features are basic to all modern economies, whether they are socialistic, communistic, or capitalistic.

• PROBLEM 2-15

What is meant by the term "mixed economy"? Give an example of a country that has a "mixed economy" and one that doesn't.

Solution: By the term "mixed economy" is meant one in which both public and private institutions exercise economic control. The United States is a good example of a country having a mixed economy. We go to the past to find an example of a non-mixed economy and its operations: Cecil Woodham-Smith's book, The Great Hunger: Ireland 1845-9 (Harper & Row, New York, 1963), relates the unbelievable details of how a non-mixed economy Victorian government let millions of Irish children, women, and men literally starve in the great famine when a fungus destroyed the potato crop. As we can see, a non-mixed economy government is synonymous with a "laissez-faire" government.

SPECIALIZATION

• PROBLEM 2-16

How does specialization, or the "division of labor," increase productivity?

Solution: In a society composed of economically self-sufficient households, each household must produce every variety of good and service which it wishes to consume.

Its consumption is limited to what it can produce with its own land, labor and tools. In a society of specialists, however, each individual or household produces only a very few types of goods or services, which comprise only a small fraction of the types which it may consume. Those types it does not produce directly for itself, it obtains indirectly through exchange with other specialists.

Specialization increases the productivity of a society above that of an otherwise comparable society of self-sufficient households for several reasons. First, it utilizes differences in innate human abilities. Total production of a society is maximized when each task is performed by those whose innate abilities make them the most capable of performing it. Second, where no differences in innate human abilities exist, specialization over a period of time results in a higher acquired level of skill in one's occupation than one could have achieved without specializing. A society of specialists achieves a higher level of proficiency in productive skills than a society of generalists. Third, geographic specialization utilizes differences in climate and soil and natural resources. The English climate and soil is ill-suited for growing wine grapes which grow better in Portugal, but better suited for raising sheep. If England specializes in wool textiles and Portugal in wine, their total production of both goods will be greater than if each country produces as much as it can of both goods. Fourth, specialization saves the time that is lost in production for self-sufficiency in changing tasks. Finally, specialization opens the possibility of discovering and utilizing more technologically advanced techniques, techniques of mass production taking advantage of potential economies of scale.

• PROBLEM 2-17

Given the weekly production possibilities curves for two neighbors, Mr. Davis and Mr. Walker, in Fiqure 1, determine whether they could gain from specialization and trade; what terms of trade would be mutually beneficial; and what their collective gain would be if Davis had previously been producing 3 apples and 30 nuts and Walker had been producing 2 apples and 40 nuts.

Solution: From Figure 1, we can see that Davis can produce a maximum of 6 apples (and no nuts) or 60 nuts (and no apples). And we can see that in order to produce each apple, he must forego the production of 10 nuts. That is, the real cost to Davis of producing 1 apple is (the equivalent of) 10 nuts. Or, the real cost of 1 nut is 1/10 of an apple.

From Figure 1, we can also see that Walker can produce a maximum of 4 apples (and no nuts) or 80 nuts (and no apples). In order to produce each apple, Walker would have to forego producing 20 nuts; or, in order to produce each 20 nuts, he must forego producing 1 apple. That is, the real cost to Walker of producing 1 apple is 20 nuts. Or the real cost of producing 1 nut is 1/20 of an apple.

It is clear from these observations that Davis can produce apples at a lower cost (10 nuts foregone per apple produced) than can Walker (20 nuts foregone per apple produced). But by the same token, it is clear that Walker can produce nuts at a lower cost (1/20 of an apple foregone per nut produced) than Davis can (1/10 of an apple foregone per nut produced). Thus, Davis has a "comparative cost advantage" in producing apples and Walker has a "comparative cost advantage" in producing nuts. If each specializes in the production of the good in the production of which he has a comparative cost advantage, mutually beneficial trade is possible.

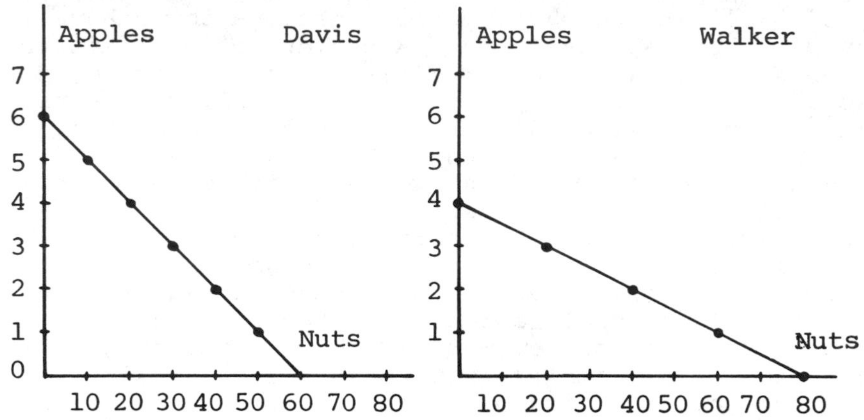

Fig. 1

Let us see why this is so. Davis produces 6 apples and no nuts; Walker produces 80 nuts and no apples. Previously their total production was 3 + 2 = 5 apples and 30 + 40 = 70 nuts. Specialization has yielded a net increase in their total production of 1 apple and 10 nuts. How will this increase be divided? It depends on the terms of trade. Davis will surely not exchange any of his six apples for less than 10 of Walker's nuts, since he could obtain at least 10 nuts by producing them himself at the cost of one apple foregone. Similarly, Walker will not exchange any more than 20 of his nuts for any one of Davis' apples, since he could produce an apple for himself with a sacrifice of no more than 20 nuts not produced. Between these limits set by Davis' and Walker's own production possibilities curves, mutually beneficial exchange can occur. That is, between the exchange ratios of 20 nuts for one apple and 10 nuts for one apple, there are mutually beneficial terms of trade. Let us suppose that Davis and Walker agree on an exchange ratio of 13 nuts for one apple. If they exchange, e.g., 3 apples for 39 nuts, then Davis has 6 - 3 = 3 apples and 39 nuts: the same amount of apples and an additional 9 nuts compared to his situation before specialization and trade. Walker would have 3 apples and 80 - 39 = 41 nuts, 1 more apple and one more nut than before specialization and trade. Clearly both Davis and Walker have benefited through specialization in accordance with their respective comparative cost advantages and subsequent trade.

• PROBLEM 2-18

The following are the production possibility tables for two countries, Saudi Arabia and the United States, for two goods, oil and corn:

U. S. Production Possibility

Product	Production alternatives				
	A	B	C	D	E
Oil (million barrels)	0	5	10	15	20
Corn (million bushels)	80	60	40	20	0

Saudi Arabia Production Possibility

Product	Production alternatives				
	A	B	C	D	E
Oil (million barrels)	0	5	10	15	20
Corn (million bushels)	60	45	30	15	0

Compare the comparative costs to each country of producing each product. Which nation has a comparative advantage in producing oil; In producing corn? Will specialization and trade be profitable?

Solution: By the U. S. Production Possibility table it can be seen that to produce 5 million barrels of oil, 20 bushels of corn must be foregone. The cost equation would be 5 Oil = 20 Corn or, more simply, 1"O" = 4"C". Conversely, 20 million bushels of corn cost 5 million barrels of oil, so 1"C" = .25"O". For Saudi Arabia, 5 million barrels of oil cost 15 million bushels of corn, so 1"O" = 3"C". Conversely, 1"C" = .33"O". It is clear that the U. S. can produce corn more cheaply than Saudi Arabia (each bushel of corn costs the U. S. .25 barrels of oil, while it costs Saudi Arabia .33 barrels). Saudi Arabia, on the other hand, can produce oil more cheaply than the U. S. (each barrel costs Saudi Arabia 3 bushels of corn while costing the U. S. 4). Therefore, the U. S. has a comparative advantage in corn and Saudi Arabia has a comparative advantage in oil. Therefore, specialization (the U. S. producing 80 million bushels of corn and no oil, Saudi Arabia producing 20 million barrels of oil and no corn) will be profitable, each nation trading its surplus to the other.

• PROBLEM 2-19

Suppose that the annual production possibilities of Texas and Louisiana for rice and cotton are those shown in Figure 1. Can specialization and trade benefit both states even though Texas can outproduce Louisiana in both cotton and rice? If so, in which crop would each state specialize, and what would be the limits of mutually beneficial terms of trade?

Solution: There exists scope for specialization and trade whenever the comparative costs of two regions are different: that is, whenever two regions differ in the amount by which the production of good A can be increased by a given decrease in the production of good B. This means, in terms of production possibilities or "transformation" curves, that two regions can specialize in production, and trade to their mutual benefit, when the slopes of their respective production possibilities curves at the points where they are initially producing are different. (For simplicity we assume that production in each region is characterized by constant costs, so that each production possibilities curve has the same slope at each point on the curve.)

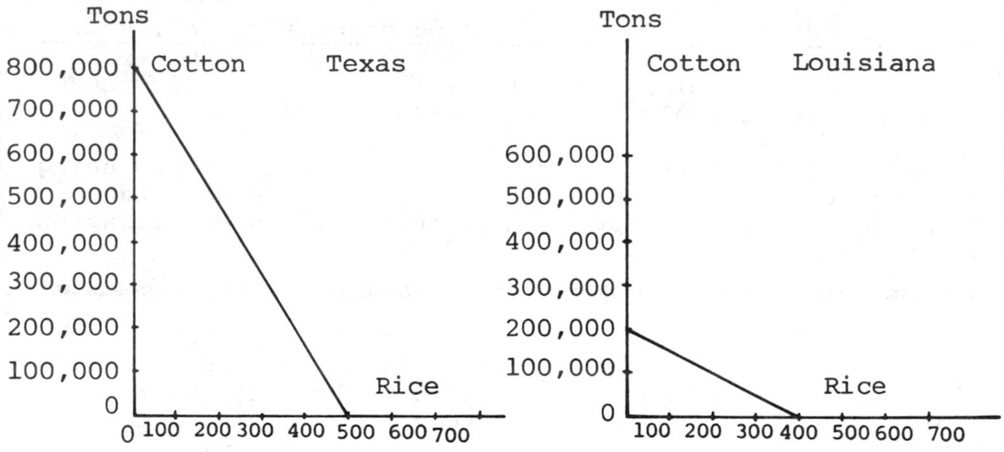

Fig. 1

We can see from Figure 1 that the comparative costs in rice and cotton production are different for Texas and Louisiana. Texas sacrifices the production of 160,000 tons of cotton for each 100,000 tons of rice it chooses to grow instead. The slope of its production-possibilities curve is thus -1.6. Louisiana, on the other hand, sacrifices only 50,000 tons of cotton production for every 100,000 tons of rice it chooses to produce. The slope of its production possibilities curve is -0.5. Clearly, Louisiana can produce rice at a comparatively lower cost (in terms of cotton production foregone) than can Texas. Therefore, Louisiana should be the state to specialize in rice growing, and Texas in cotton growing. We can reach the same conclusion by considering that Texas sacrifices only 62,500 tons of rice production to produce 100,000 tons of cotton, whereas Louisiana must forego production of 200,000 tons of rice production to grow the same 100,000 tons of cotton. Texas clearly has a comparative cost advantage in cotton production, so it should specialize in cotton growing and Louisiana in rice growing.

The limits of the terms of mutually beneficial trade are set by the rates at which the two states can "transform" cotton production into rice production (or vice versa). In Texas, this "rate of transformation," is, as we have seen, 1.6 lb. of cotton per lb. of rice; in Louisiana, it is 0.5 lb. of cotton per pound of rice. Texas would be better off if it could obtain 1 lb. of rice for anything less than 1.6 lb. of cotton. Louisiana would be better off if it could obtain anything more than 0.5 lb. of cotton for 1 lb. of rice. The mutually beneficial terms of trade, therefore, range between 0.5 and 1.6 lb. of cotton per lb. of rice.

These terms of trade can also be stated in terms of lb. of rice per lb. of cotton. The rice/cotton limits to the terms of trade are simply the reciprocals of the above cotton/rice ratios. That is, 0.5 lb. of cotton per lb. of rice = 2.0 lb. of rice per lb. of cotton; and 1.6 lb. of cotton per lb. of rice = 0.625 lb. of rice per lb. of cotton. Mutually beneficial terms of trade, then, lie between 0.625 and 2.0 lb. of rice per pound of cotton. We can see that these are the reciprocals of the slopes of the production possibilities curves of Texas and Louisiana, respectively. Texas would be better off it it could obtain anything more than 0.625 lb. of rice for one lb. of cotton; and Louisiana would be better off if it could obtain one lb. of cotton for anything less than 2.0 lb. of rice.

Mutually beneficial trade can still take place between regions even if one is absolutely more productive in both goods, as long as the cost of producing one good, in terms of the amount of the other good foregone, differs between the two regions.

• PROBLEM 2-20

Let Figure 1 represent the weekly production possibilities tables of Minnesota and North Dakota for wheat and barley.

Figure 1

Minnesota		North Dakota	
Wheat(tons)	Barley(tons)	Wheat(tons)	Barley(tons)
500	0	1000	0
400	200	800	400
300	400	600	800
200	600	400	1200
100	800	200	1600
0	1000	0	2000

Can the two states gain from specialization and trade? If so, which crop does each state specialize in, and what are the limits of the terms of mutually beneficial trade?

Solution: To determine whether specialization and trade yield any gain to Minnesota and North Dakota, we must find out whether each state has a comparative cost advantage in the production of one of the goods. From Figure 1, we can see that for each additional 200 tons of barley which Minnesota grows it foregoes 100 tons of wheat production. Thus, the cost of 200 tons of barley to Minnesotans is 100 tons of wheat; or each ton of barley costs 1/2 ton of wheat.

We see also from Figure 1 that for each additional 400 tons of barley production, North Dakotans must sacrifice (1000-800) = (800-600) = (600-400) = (400-200) = 200 tons of wheat production. That is, the cost of 400 tons of barley to North Dakotans is 200 tons of wheat; or each ton of barley costs 1/2 ton of wheat.

Thus the cost in terms of wheat of a ton of barley is the same in both states. Neither state has a comparative cost advantage in the production of barley. Likewise, neither state has a comparative advantage in wheat production: each additional ton of wheat means the sacrifice of two tons of barley, in either state. (If one state did have a comparative advantage in producing one crop, it would necessarily have a comparative disadvantage in producing the other crop, and the other state would thus necessarily have a comparative advantage in producing the other crop. Similarly, absence of comparative advantage of one state in producing either crop necessarily implies that the other state also has no comparative advantage in producing either crop.)

Since each state has no comparative (dis-)advantage in the production of barley or wheat, there is nothing to be gained by specialization and trade. Neither state would be better off, e.g., exchanging 1/2 ton of their wheat for one ton of the other's barley (or vice versa) than if they simply increased their own production of barley by one ton and reduced their wheat production by 1/2 ton. Yet neither state would be willing to exchange any more than one ton of barley for 1/2 ton of wheat, since it could obtain 1/2 ton of wheat simply by decreasing its own barley production by no more than one ton. And neither state would offer more than 1/2 ton of its wheat for a ton of the other's barley, since it could obtain a ton of barley by reducing its own production of wheat by just 1/2 ton.

When no comparative advantage exists, there is no way in which specialization could increase the total output of the two states. Hence, when no comparative cost differential exists, there can be no gains from trade.

• PROBLEM 2-21

Given the production possibilities curves in Figure 1, show in a similar diagram the consumption possibilities of each country with specialization and trade, assuming that the terms of trade are 1 TV for 2/3 ton of fertilizer.

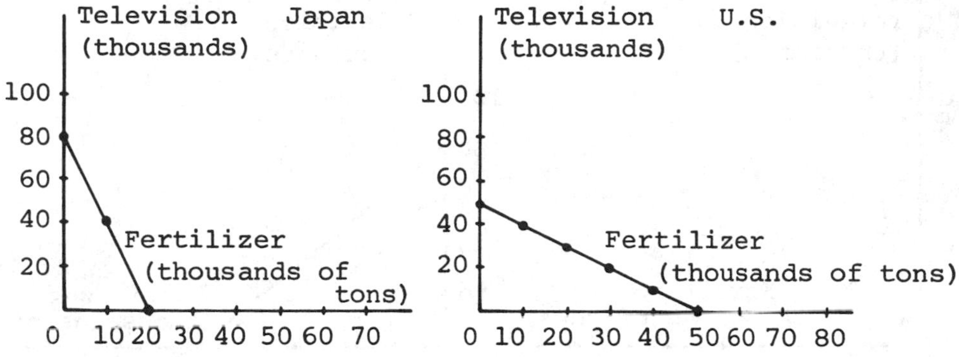

Fig. 1

Solution: From the (constant cost) production possibilities curves in Figure 1, we must first determine whether there are any gains possible from specialization and trade, and, if there are, which country should specialize in which product in order to reap these gains. We must therefore determine whether there exists a comparative cost difference between the two countries in the production of TV's and fertilizer.

From Figure 1, we can see as we move down along Japan's production curve from the Y-intercept to the X-intercept, that Japan must forego 80,000 - 40,000 = 40,000 TV sets in order to produce each 10,000 tons of fertilizer. The cost to Japan in TV sets foregone of each ton of fertilizer produced is 4 sets.

Similarly, we can see that, in the U. S., each additional 10,000 tons of fertilizer requires a sacrifice of TV set production of 10,000 sets. So the cost to the U. S. of each ton of fertilizer is 1 set.

Clearly, fertilizer is produced relatively more cheaply, in terms of TV sets, in the U. S. Therefore TV sets must be produced relatively more cheaply in Japan. (We can see this also by observing that, as we move up the production possibilities curve from the X-intercepts to the Y-intercepts), the sacrifice of 20,000 - 10,000 = 10,000 tons of fertilizer production enables Japan to increase TV production by 40,000 sets, whereas the same reduction of fertilizer production in the U. S. yields a gain of only 10,000 TV sets in the U. S. Therefore, in Japan, each set costs only [10,000 tons fertilizer ÷ 40,000 sets] = 1/4 ton of fertilizer, whereas in the U. S., each set costs [10,000 tons fertilizer ÷ 10,000 sets] = 1 ton of fertilizer. Therefore, TV sets are relatively cheaper to produce, in terms of fertilizer foregone, in Japan than in the U. S.

Clearly, then, it is mutually advantageous for Japan to specialize in producing TV sets, where it has a comparative cost advantage, and for the U. S. to specialize in fertilizer production, where it has a comparative cost advantage. So, with complete specialization, Japan produces 80,000 TV sets and no fertilizer, and the U. S. produces no TV sets and 50,000 tons of fertilizer.

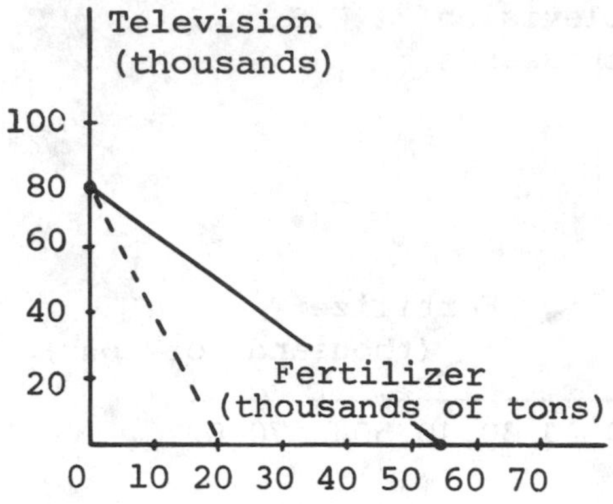

Fig. 2

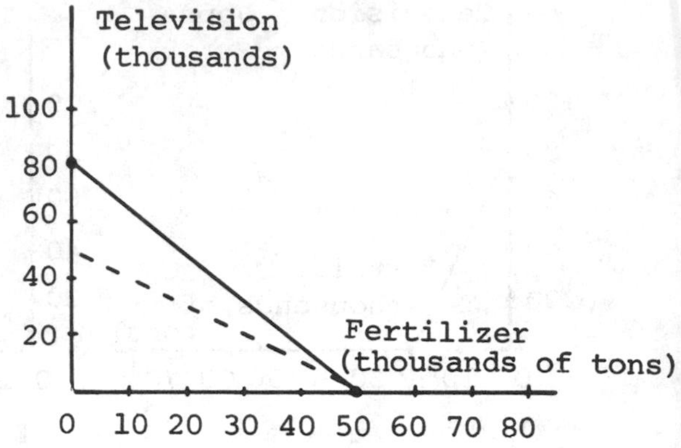

Fig. 3

If the terms of trade are such that 1 TV exchanges for 1/2 ton of fertilizer, what combinations of TV's and fertilizer could Japan consume? If it exchanged its entire production of TV's for fertilizer, it could obtain (80 sets) x $\left(\frac{2/3 \text{ ton fertilizer}}{1 \text{ TV set}}\right) = \frac{160}{3} = 53\text{-}1/3$ tons of fertilizer. If we plot on a graph all the possible combinations of TV's and fertilizer which Japan can attain by trading various amounts (from 0 to 80,000) of its TV's for American fertilizer, we obtain the solid line in Figure 2. The dashed line represents its production possibilities curve. We can see that specialization and trade have enabled Japan to attain larger combinations of the two goods than it could when it produced both for itself.

Likewise, if the U. S. sold all 50,000 tons of its fertilizer to Japan at 2/3 ton per TV, it could obtain (50,000 tons fertilizer) x $\frac{1 \text{ TV}}{3/2 \text{ ton fertilizer}} = \frac{150{,}000}{2}$ = 75,000 TV sets. Plotting on a graph the combinations of TV's and fertilizer the U. S. can obtain by selling to Japan various amounts of its fertilizer (from none to all 50,000 tons) we obtain the solid line in Figure 3. The dashed line represents the U. S.'s production possibilities curve. Just as with Japan, then, specialization and trade enables the U. S. to broaden its menu of choices of combinations of TV's and fertilizer. Specialization and trade, create the same kind of increase in the quantity of goods available than an increase in resources or a technological improvement creates.

• PROBLEM 2-22

What are some of the drawbacks of specialization?

Solution: There are two basic drawbacks of specialization. The first is that work can become so specialized that it becomes monotonous and stifling. Specialization will probably increase the worker's material wealth, but it may do so at the expense of some discontent and frustration. This discontent could be serious enough to undermine the efficiency advantages of specialization.

The second drawback is that specialization tends to create complex networks of interdependent production units. When one of these units ceases to function properly, because of a coal strike or truckers' strike, for example, the whole network can be paralyzed. In a complex factory, one assembly line breakdown can destroy the carefully planned production schedule. Therefore, specialization can create fairly fragile production and trade networks.

These two drawbacks, worker dissatisfaction and intricate interdependencies, are often cited in arguments against further specialization.

USE OF MONEY

• PROBLEM 2-23

What is the advantage of using money in trade as compared to barter trade?

Solution: Barter is the direct exchange of one consumption or production good for another production or consumption good. Monetary trade is the indirect exchange of a consumption or production good for money, which is then exchanged for a different production or consumption good.

The distinguishing characteristic of money is that it is universally acceptable in exchange, while other goods are not. It is that characteristic which makes its use advantageous compared to barter trade.

In order for a (voluntary) trade to occur, each potential trader must have something that the other wants. If A has a good B wants, but B has no goods to exchange that A wants, no trade will occur. Both A and B must look elsewhere for trading partners. They must find someone who (1) wants what they have and (2) has what they want. The number of such potential barter trading partners is relatively small. Therefore, finding trading partners can be a difficult and costly process.

In a monetary economy, on the other hand, it is not necessary to find trading partners who both (1) have exactly the good one wants and (2) want exactly the good one has to exchange. Money makes it possible to trade with individuals who meet only one of these requirements. It is possible instead for B to achieve the exchange he seeks by trading with two different people: C, who is willing to exchange money for the good B has; and A, who is willing to exchange the good B wants for money. Because money is acceptable both to B and to everyone else, there are far more potential partners for a trade involving money than for a barter trade. Hence, the use of money reduces the difficulty of finding a trading partner, and thereby facilitates mutually beneficial exchanges.

• PROBLEM 2-24

What is the relationship between specialization in production (the "division of labor") and the use of money?

Solution: Specialization in production means that households and individuals do not produce all of the various goods which they intend to consume, but rather, that each produces only one or a few of the goods wanted by the community and exchanges its surplus of that good or those goods for those products of other households and individuals which it wants. Specialization, then, unlike production by self-sufficient households or individuals, necessitates the exchange of products among the households and individuals of the community.

Direct exchange, or barter, requires a cumbersome and costly process of searching out trading partners who both have a good that one wants and wants the good one has to sell. But because it is universally accepted in trade, money facilitates finding trading partners.

The greater ease of trading which the use of money achieves enables households and individuals to engage in more highly specialized production, which requires a greater number of exchanges, than could be carried on in a barter economy. The productivity of modern specialized economies would be impossible without the institution of money to facilitate a vast number of exchanges among specializing producers.

USE OF CAPITAL GOODS

• PROBLEM 2-25

What is 'roundabout production'?

Solution: 'Roundabout production' is the method of producing consumption goods by first producing capital goods and then using these as inputs in the production of consumption goods. A primitive farmer, for example, may try to grow food with his bare hands. But if he first makes some simple tools to enable him to grow larger quantities of food, he is engaged in 'roundabout production'. This production of tools is not for immediate consumption, but for enhanced future production of food.

Capital goods (e.g., machines, plants, power stations, etc.) enable producers to make far larger quantities of more sophisticated consumption goods than would be otherwise possible. Capital goods enable producers to produce more with a given amount of resources. In other words, capital goods and roundabout methods of production increase economic productivity. Roundabout production is, at the most basic level, simply an investment of time and effort for increased future consumption.

• PROBLEM 2-26

How does capitalism stimulate and encourage technological advance?

Solution: Pure capitalism stimulates and encourages technological advance by providing opportunities and incentives for technological innovation.

Competition ensures that there are no barriers to the introduction of new techniques and new products. If they can compete successfully in the market place with older techniques, there are no barriers to entry in the marketplace. A firm which introduces a new cost-cutting production technique can realize economic profits. The firm is rewarded for its innovation. By harnessing market incentives, the price system can be very effective in promoting technological advance.

From the social point of view, the innovating firm forces the other firms to adopt the cost-saving technique. If they are slow in adopting the technique, they face the prospect of losses (because the innovating firm can sell the product at a lower price) and eventual bankruptcy. So, the competitive price system forces an entire industry to keep up with the most progressive firms in the industry.

• PROBLEM 2-27

Technological advance usually requires the use of increased amounts of capital goods. Though pure capitalism (the price system) provides incentives for technological innovation, it still must provide for the levels of investment needed to implement the new technologies. Does capitalism provide the means for technological advance? If so, how?

Solution: Capitalism provides the means (investment) for technological advance by way of the price system. Consumer preferences determine the types and quantities of capital goods produced, just as they determine the types and quantities of all other goods produced.

Entrepreneurs register their preferences for the various types and quantities of capital goods, just as ordinary consumers register their preferences for different consumer goods. The entrepreneur, with profits and/or loans (he can borrow money from households by paying interest) registers his demands for various capital goods. If the entrepreneur wants to expand his firm's business, or adopt a new technology, he can simply plow back more of his profits or borrow more money in order to register his preferences for capital goods more strongly.

Capital goods will be supplied if the entrepreneurs are willing to pay a sufficient price. So, pure capitalism can provide the means for technological advance (capital goods), through the workings of the price system.

• PROBLEM 2-28

It would seem that since capital goods increase the quantity of consumer goods that can be produced, economies should drastically increase their production of capital goods. What is the catch in increasing the production of capital goods (investment)?

Solution: If there is full employment and full production, any increase in the production of capital goods must come at the expense of a decrease in the production of consumer goods. Resources must be diverted from elsewhere if there is to be increased investment. So, consumers must sacrifice current consumption in order to increase future consumption. With this in mind, it can be seen why consumers might resist a drastic increase in capital goods production; this increase would come at the cost of a drastic decrease in consumption goods production.

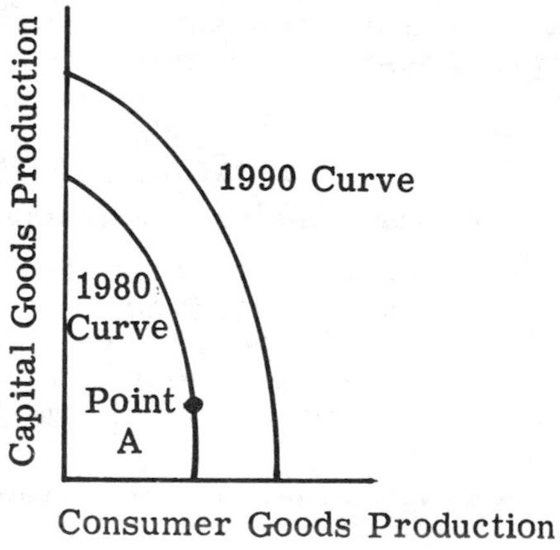

FIG. 1

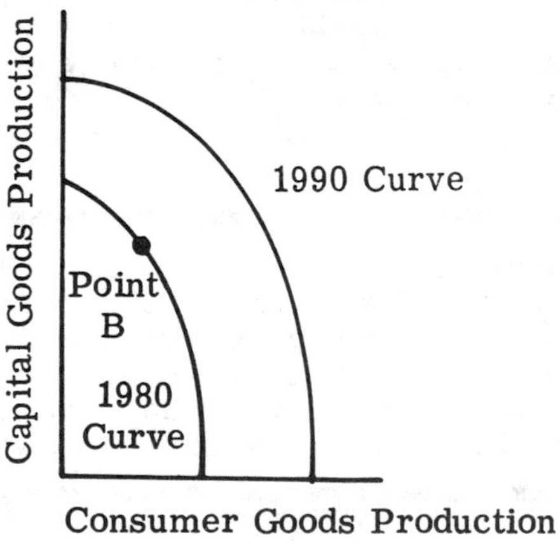

FIG. 2

This tradeoff between present and future consumption can be illustrated by using the production possibilities curve. This curve illustrates the possible combinations of capital goods production and consumer goods production that a society can produce. In Figure 1, country X is producing at point A on the production possibilities curve. At this point, most production is for present consumption. There is enough production of capital goods, however, so that the curve will expand by 1990 to the outside curve in Figure 1. This expansion is the result of the heightened productivity brought about by the increased use of capital goods. Even the low investment level of point A is sufficient to cause an increase in productivity, and hence, potential output.

In Figure 2, country X is producing at point B on the 1980 curve. This point has a much higher level of capital goods production, and a lower level of consumption than point A. The result is that there is a greater shift in the 1990 production possibilities curve. That is, in the second case, the 1990 production possibilities frontier is located farther out. There is more of both consumer and capital goods available than in the 1990 curve of the first case. The higher level of capital goods production leads to a higher level of productivity, which is reflected in the large increase in output potential.

Country X faces a choice between greater present consumption and a greater increase in future consumption. The production possibilities curves illustrate the benefits, and costs, of the alternatives. The sacrifice in current consumption necessary to achieve a large investment (Figure 2) is the catch in increasing the production of capital goods.

THE CIRCULAR FLOW MODEL

• PROBLEM 2-29

What is meant by 'real flows' in a circular flow model? What are 'money flows'?

Solution: Real flows are the flow of resources and the flow of goods and services in an economy. In the circular flow model, resources are transferred from households to businesses; goods and services are transferred from businesses to households. These transfers are the real flows of the model. In a barter economy, real flows would describe the economy completely.

Money flows are the transfers of money that accompany transfers of 'real' goods. Thus the payments of businesses to households for resources, and the payments of households to businesses for goods and services, constitute the money flows of a circular flow model. Money flows are distinguished from real flows because money, as such, cannot be consumed and it is not part of the physical process of production. Its value lies in facilitating exchange; it functions as the medium of exchange.

• PROBLEM 2-30

Describe the two types of markets in the simple circular flow model of pure capitalism.

Solution: In pure capitalism, the two types of markets are the product markets and the resource markets.

The product markets are the markets where finished goods and services are sold by businesses to consumers (households). Here, finished products are transferred from firms to consumers, while money is transferred from consumers to firms.

The resource markets are the markets where productive factors are sold by households (consumers) to businesses. People sell (or rent) the resources in their possession (land, labor, capital) to businesses. Here, there is a transfer of a resource from households to firms and a transfer of money from businesses to households.

These two markets serve essentially different functions. The resource markets are centered around the firms' production of goods and services while product markets focus on households' consumption of goods and services. Distribution of final output among households depends on the relative resource and factor prices.

The relationship between the two markets, and the flow of money and units of production can be illustrated diagrammatically.

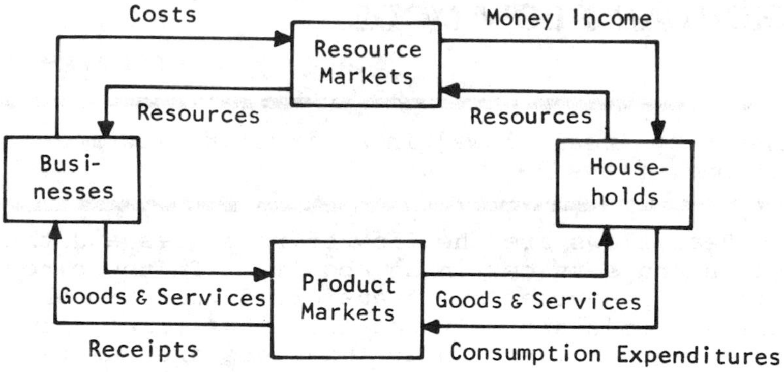

The inside line of this diagram shows the movement of resources and goods through the two markets as each sector (households and businesses) supplies what it can to the markets. In the resource markets, households supply resources, while in the product markets, firms supply goods and services.

The outside line represents the flow of money in the economy. As businesses demand resources, money flows from the business sector to the household sector. Because households demand goods and services, money flows from households to businesses through the product markets.

Through these two markets, supply and demand are equilibrated and economic efficiency is maintained.

• PROBLEM 2-31

How are resource and product prices determined in the circular flow model?

Solution: Resource and product prices are assumed to be determined by the interaction of supply and demand in the market in the circular flow model. Resource prices are determined by the supply schedule of resources of businesses in conjunction with the demand schedule for resources of households. Product prices are determined by the supply schedule of products of businesses in conjunction with the demand schedule for products of households. Though product and resource prices are determined by the interaction of these schedules, the circular flow model assumes these schedules. This model does not offer any explanation of how these schedules are formed. Because of this absence, the circular flow model actually assumes resource and product prices. It does not go into enough detail to explain supply and demand schedules. Because of this, it is overstating the case to say that prices are 'determined' by supply and demand. The circular flow model assumes prices are determined by supply and demand, but it does not really offer any detailed explanation of how they are formed. Until there is an analysis of supply and demand, the circular flow model can only assume the existence of product and resource prices without any concrete proof that they do exist.

• PROBLEM 2-32

Using diagrams, contrast the circular flow model of a barter economy with the model of a monetary economy (omitting markets).

Solution: In both models, the real flows are similar. Households furnish resources for businesses and businesses provide goods and services for households. In Figure 1, the barter economy, this is the extent of the model.

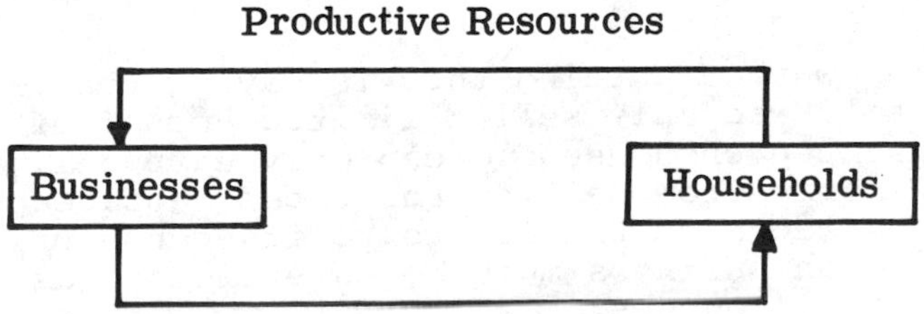

FIG. 1

In Figure 2, the monetary economy, this real flow is complemented by a corresponding money flow in the opposite direction of the "real" flow. This is because whenever there is an exchange, money is used to pay for goods. Money goes into the hands of one sector while goods go into the hands of the other. Money flows and "real" flows must necessarily travel in opposite directions.

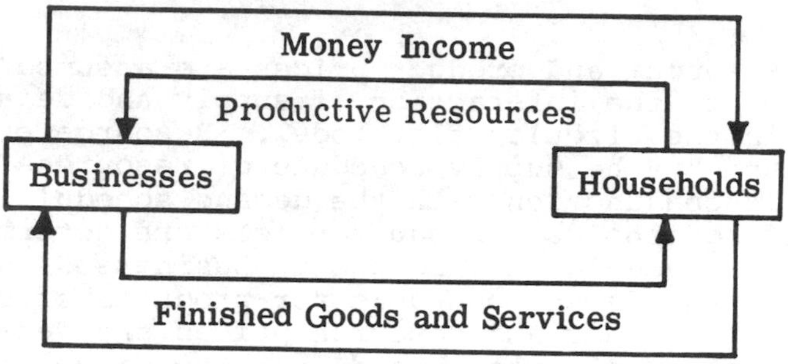

FIG. 2

The difference between the models of the two economies is the addition of the money flow in the monetary economy. The monetary economy is a relatively simple model of a capitalist economy, while the barter economy can only depict the aspects of capitalism which deal with "real" goods. Because the monetary model represents more completely the flows of a capitalist economy, and yet is still simple, the barter model is not used very often.

• PROBLEM 2-33

Economics supposedly deals with the efficient allocation of scarce goods. Where does scarcity fit in the circular flow model?

Solution: Scarcity is implicit in the entire analysis of the circular flow model. Because households have only limited amounts of resources to supply to businesses, businesses can only produce so much output. Because output is limited, consumers can consume only a limited amount.

Another way of putting this is saying that since each household can only sell a limited amount of resources to businesses, each household can only earn a limited amount of income from selling resources. So, each household has to recognize the limits to its consumption. Similarly, each business must be as efficient as possible in its use of resources.

Scarcity and the resultant need for efficiency, then, are not inconsistent with the circular flow model; in fact, these two concepts permeate the entire circular flow analysis.

• PROBLEM 2-34

How does labor fit in the circular flow model?

Solution: Labor is a scarce resource, a factor of production. In the circular flow model, all scarce resources, including labor, are furnished by households. The demand for labor comes from businesses. They want labor because labor is a factor of production; it can be used to produce output.

To determine the position of any economic good in the circular flow model, we must decide whether it is a factor of production, or a finished article ready for consumption. A factor of production will be supplied by households and demanded by businesses; a finished article will be supplied by businesses and demanded by households.

• PROBLEM 2-35

Can there be any economic growth in the simple circular flow model?

Solution: In the simple circular flow model with its two sectors, businesses and households, it is assumed that all output and production is consumed. Households spend all of their income. (Be sure you realize that these two statements mean the same thing. National income equals national output. If all output is consumed, then all income must have been spent on purchasing the output for consumption.)

Since it is assumed in this simple model that all output is consumed, this means there is no economic growth. For economic growth to take place, there has to be investment in expanding productive capacity. In the simple circular flow model, businesses cannot invest. They merely process resources into finished products. Any investment must come from the household sector (remember that this sector even supplies businesses with capital). Since, however, households spend all their income on consumer goods, they do not have any income left over for investment.

The simple circular flow model, then, does not make any allowances for growth because it does not make any allowances for investment.

• PROBLEM 2-36

What important aspects of the workings of a capitalist economy are not captured in circular flow models?

Solution: Simple circular flow models give a general overview of the flow of resources (inputs) and goods and services (outputs) on the one hand and the counterbalancing flow of money payments and receipts on the other which take place in a capitalist economy. The former flows are called 'real' flows to distinguish them from the flows of money payments and receipts which are designated 'money flows'. Because circular flow models attempt to present only a schematic picture of a capitalist economy, they necessarily omit any description of how the principal elements of that picture are constituted.

For example, the flows of "resources" and "goods and services" are aggregated flows of numerous diverse goods from transistors to tractors, from houses to haircuts. The model does not explain how the particular composition of these flows is determined. Nor does it explain how the individual prices of these diverse goods, services and resources are determined by the choices of individual households and businesses so that incomes from the sale of resources by households just match their expenditures on goods and services. The assumption of the model that household incomes and consumption expenditures are equal and constant in volume renders it incapable of illustrating fluctuations in total employment, output, and income or the effects of saving, investment, and capital accumulation. Further, the model's schematic picture omits the public sector, abstracting from the effects of governmental operations and policies on the workings of the private sector. The model assumes that the government remains in the background, merely upholding private property rights and contracts without otherwise influencing the actions of households or businesses. Finally, a circular flow model does nothing to highlight the effects which the use of money to facilitate exchange may have on the real flows in the economy.

• PROBLEM 2-37

The circular flow model of pure capitalism does not include an entire set of transactions which normally occur in a "real-life" economy. What set does it leave out?

Solution: The circular flow model does not include any transactions that occur "within the business and household" sections "of the economy". That is, this model assumes that businesses do not sell goods to each other; they only sell goods to households. These transactions are not included in the circular flow model for the sake of simplicity.

Note that though government is left out of the circular flow model, it would not be included in even more detailed models of pure capitalism. This is because by its very definition, the government has only a very minor role in pure capitalism. It is omitted for an entirely different reason than the omissions of intrabusiness and intrahousehold transactions. These transactions are a major part of the economy but have little analytical value. Government in pure capitalism has not only little analytical value, it also has but a minor role in the economy. So, saying the government is left out of the circular flow model is begging the question; it will be left out of all but the most detailed models of pure capitalism.

SHORT ANSWER QUESTIONS FOR REVIEW

Answer
To be covered when testing yourself

Choose the correct answer.

1. Which of the following is a distinguishing feature of capitalism? (a) Use of capital goods (b) Use of money (c) Private ownership of the means of production (d) Specialization — c

2. Which of the following is not an essential feature of competition as it is usually defined by economists? (a) Large numbers of independent buyers and sellers in a market (b) Freedom of firms to enter and leave the industry (c) Inability of any one firm in the industry to raise product prices by restricting output (d) A high degree of product differentiation between firms — d

3. One function which the price system does not perform is (a) redistribution of incomes among suppliers of resources (b) communication of consumer preferences to producers (c) conservation of the scarcest resources (d) determine the most efficient methods of production — a

4. Under pure capitalism, the government does not (a) enforce property rights (b) fix prices and wages (c) set the ground rules for the operation of private enterprise (d) enforce contracts — b

5. The use of capital goods requires (a) a large number of producers (b) having a comparative cost advantage (c) free entry into or exit from an industry (d) saving — d

6. Which of the following is not a cause of the greater productivity due to the division of labor? (a) It harnesses differences in innate aptitudes and abilities. (b) It permits use of advanced technology and capital goods. (c) It reduces dependence on trade. (d) It allows each person to develop greater proficiency in his occupation — c

7. If Smith can produce 40 shoes or 30 boots per day and Jones can produce 50 shoes or 40 boots per day, Jones has a comparative advantage in producing (a) shoes (b) boots (c) neither shoes nor boots (d) both shoes and boots — b

8. The degree of specialization that a community can attain is greatly increased by (a) use

SHORT ANSWER QUESTIONS FOR REVIEW

Answer
To be covered when testing yourself

of a medium of exchange (b) central direction of production (c) diffusion of economic power (d) competition — a

9. Barter is more cumbersome than monetary trade because (a) it requires a greater number of transactions (b) there are no organized markets (c) it requires different tastes on the part of each trader (d) it requires the wants of the traders to coincide exactly — d

10. The circular flow model of capitalism illustrates (a) how the prices of resources, goods and services are determined (b) how competition achieves economic efficiency under capitalism (c) how resources are allocated (d) how households and firms interact through markets — d

11. Freedom of enterprise means (a) businesses are free to set prices as high as they wish (b) the government imposes no taxes on businesses (c) businesses are responsible for decisions about what to produce and how to produce it (d) business can produce what it wants in defiance of consumer wishes — c

12. Consumer sovereignty means that (a) consumers are protected from fraud by the government (b) the government is the primary consumer of goods and services in the economy (c) the state directs the production of consumer goods (d) consumers ultimately determine what goods are produced — d

13. "Roundabout production" refers to (a) indirect production of consumer goods with the help of capital goods (b) the least efficient production technology (c) production of goods for local markets (d) production of goods and services in the circular flow model — a

14. Without trade there could be no (a) production (b) technological advance (c) specialization (d) freedom of choice — c

15. Capital goods are (a) goods owned by the wealthy (b) goods produced to be used in the production of consumer goods (c) financial assets of businesses (d) goods provided by the government — b

16. Firms will produce at maximum efficiency because

SHORT ANSWER QUESTIONS FOR REVIEW

	Answer To be covered when testing yourself
(a) of government regulation (b) they realize how much society needs scarce resources (c) of the pressure of competition (d) of possible changes in resource prices	c
17. Competitive markets (a) cause malfunctions because of conflicting self-interests (b) insure economic profits for producers in the long run (c) efficiently allocate resources (d) rely heavily on labor-saving devices	c
18. Which of the following is not a feature of American economy? (a) Private property (with a few exceptions) (b) A market system providing freedom of choice (c) The right to a profit, providing the incentive to enter and operate businesses (d) Competition acting as an automatic control on the kinds of goods offered for sale and their price and quantity (e) Central economic planning	e
Fill in the blanks.	
19. ______________ is said to exist in a market in which no seller can unilaterally influence the price of the good.	competition
20. ______________ means that businesses are solely responsible for planning their own production and sales, with no government intervention.	freedom of enterprise
21. Barter trade requires a ______________ between traders.	coincidence of wants
22. Gains from trade are possible only between individuals or countries for which the ________ of producing the traded goods are different.	comparative costs
23. Specialization and trade are greatly accelerated by ______________.	money
24. Under capitalism, directions for coordinating production and consumption and the incentives to coordinate them are communicated by _______ ______________.	the price system
25. The movements of resources, goods and services in the circular flow model are __________ flows of the model.	real
26. In pure capitalism, the institution of _______ _________ plays only a very minor role in allocating resources in the economy.	government

SHORT ANSWER QUESTIONS FOR REVIEW

	Answer (To be covered when testing yourself)
27. Allocative efficiency is achieved in pure capitalism through the mechanism of the ________ ____________.	price system
28. In order to increase the production of capital goods, and thus increase ____________ consumption, consumers must sacrifice some __________ consumption.	future, current
29. The fact that households are the major determinants of what is produced in capitalism has given rise to the statement that capitalism is characterized by ______________________.	consumer sovereignty
30. Without free _______________, there is no assurance that an industry will produce the optimal output with maximum efficiency.	entry/ exit
31. One major problem of specialization is that it creates a fragile, easily disrupted network of _______________.	interdependence
32. The market system probably does not accurately reflect demand for _____________ goods (products that can't be sold on an individual basis).	social or public
33. In the circular flow model, households sell ____________ and businesses sell ___________ and _______________.	resources, goods, services

Determine whether the following statements are true or false.

34. The circular flow model shows how the prices of goods and services are determined.	False
35. Country A has a comparative advantage in the production of good x if it can produce each unit of x with less land, labor, and capital (in money terms) than country B.	False
36. A country must be technologically sophisticated to be counted as a capitalist country.	False
37. The more competition that exists in an economy, the stronger is consumer sovereignty.	True
38. Freedom of businesses to enter or leave product markets as sellers is essential to competition.	True
39. An economy in which productive resources can be sold on markets is a capitalist economy.	True

SHORT ANSWER QUESTIONS FOR REVIEW

	Answer To be covered when testing yourself
40. Roundabout production methods require prior saving out of income.	True
41. Specialization depends on the existence of differences among individuals in their natural abilities.	False
42. Under competition, profit maximization by businesses is inconsistent with consumer sovereignty.	False
43. The price system gives more goods to those with more money votes.	True
44. The transactions in the circular flow model refers to the market where real goods and resources are exchanged for money.	False
45. If the government puts any legal limits at all on the pursuit of self-interest, economic inefficiencies will result.	False
46. There are real flows and monetary flows in the circular flow model of a monetary economy, while there are only real flows in the model of a barter economy.	True
47. While the self-interest of capitalists benefits society, the self-interest of workers always results in a misallocation of resources.	False
48. Only the producer for whom market price is a given quantity is a perfect competitor.	True
49. Perfect competition assures economically optimal and fair income distribution	False
50. The principle of the invisible hand established by Adam Smith, acts in any capitalist market independent of its structure and of its products.	False

CHAPTER 3

BUSINESS ORGANIZATION

Basic Attacks and Strategies for Solving Problems in this Chapter. See pages 73 to 90 for step-by-step solutions to problems.

In a capitalist economy, many of the most important economic decisions are made by privately-owned business firms. In the United States' economy, there are three major types of business firms: the sole proprietorship, the partnership, and the corporation. Each of these types of firms has distinct characteristics, and there are advantages and disadvantages to each type of organization. This chapter provides basic information on each type of business organization.

Step-by-Step Solutions to Problems in this Chapter, "Business Organization"

THE SOLE PROPRIETORSHIP

• PROBLEM 3-1

What are some of the characteristics of a sole proprietorship?

Solution: In a sole proprietorship,

- the owner provides the funds for investment;
- the owner manages the business;
- the owner makes the policy decisions;
- the owner carries responsibility for the acts of the business and is personally without limit liable for all debts of the business; and
- all profit goes to the sole owner.

• PROBLEM 3-2

Why are banks frequently reluctant to lend money to small businesses, especially proprietorships?

Solution: Banks are reluctant to lend money to small businesses because they are frequently bad credit risks. Proprietorships are especially bad risks. Proprietors, or would-be proprietors, have a history of being over-optimistic. They often form a business with unrealistic expectations, and then go out of business after a short while. The result is that the average life of a business is about six years.

A banker, realizing these facts, is extremely skeptical when the owner of a small business asks him for a loan. It is hard for a bank to screen out the potentially successful enterprises from the ones with only a limited potential. Because of the generally poor record of small businesses, banks are not usually very liberal when considering loans for them.

• PROBLEM 3-3

Describe the advantages and disadvantages of a single proprietorship.

Solution: The first advantage of a single proprietorship is that this form of business organization is completely open to new firms. One has merely to "open his doors" to be in business.

Secondly, the individual owner has complete control over the business. He makes all decisions and is entitled to all of the profit. This factor has social benefit as well, as it provides a constant incentive to the proprietor to be efficient.

The single proprietorship, however, carries with it great disadvantages as well. The concentration of decision-making power in the proprietor's hands limits specialization. While his expertise may be in production, he also must make decisions regarding marketing, personnel, etc. Not only will these decisions reflect less-than-expert skill, but, presumably, decisions made in his field of expertise will suffer from a lessening of the amount of attention he can pay to them.

Single proprietorship also presents difficulties in continuity and the raising of funds. If the proprietor is incapacitated, dies, or withdraws from the business, the business will fold. Banks are unwilling to lend to proprietorships because their optimistic origins often lead to unrealizable hopes and short lives, their management is often inefficient, and the existence of a sole owner makes it highly difficult for the bank to totally recoup its losses in the event of default.

The greatest deterrent to a would-be single proprietor is the feature of unlimited liability. Under this provision, the proprietor is solely and completely responsible for all debts of the firm to the full extent of his "personal fortune" and not just to the extent of his investment in the business.

THE PARTNERSHIP

• PROBLEM 3-4

What are some of the characteristics of a partnership?

Solution: In a partnership,

- there is a legal agreement or contract between the partners;
- partners share in policy making and management;

- decisions are made by majority vote of partners;
- partners share profits according to agreement;
- each partner is responsible for any other partner's actions;
- each partner is legally liable, without limit for the total debt of the partnership; and
- the agreement is terminated automatically upon the death, retirement, or withdrawal of a partner In order for the business to continue under these circumstances, a new partnership agreement must be drawn up.

• PROBLEM 3-5

Describe the advantages and disadvantages of a partnership.

Solution: Like a single proprietorship, the partnership form of business allows easy entry into an industry. Also like the proprietorship, partnerships' owners and operators are the same, giving them great flexibility in decision making and assuring the proper incentive for efficiency.

Partnership allows greater specialization in management (and hence, greater efficiency) than a proprietorship, allowing different partners fo concentrate on that area of the business they know best.

Partnership also makes the obtaining of funds somewhat easier. While banks are still reluctant to lend to partnerships, they at least now have two or more "personal fortunes" to draw upon.

Partnership is plagued by many of the same disadvantages of single proprietorship. As noted, it is still difficult to obtain large sums of funds. The division of authority, while leading to greater specialization, can also lead to lack of co-ordination. Partnership also lacks continuity, since the death or withdrawal of an existing partner, or the addition of a new one necessitates the legal formation of a new, distinct partnership.

Like proprietorship, the greatest single drawback to the formation of a partnership is unlimited liability, where each partner is legally responsible, to the full amount of his personal assets (and not just to the extent of his investment in the business) for the debts of the firm.

• PROBLEM 3-6

Define "mutual agency." What are its advantages to a partnership? What are its disadvantages?

Solution: "Mutual agency" is the doctrine by which any of

the partners in a firm has broad powers to act on behalf of the firm and to make commitments in its name.

Its principal advantage lies in streamlining the decision process. This is extremely important particularly in large partnerships, with many partners. Rather than be forced to seek a concensus, any partner can act quickly to take advantage of opportunities on behalf of the firm.

The principal disadvantage is curiously tied in with one of the advantages of partnership. Whereas a partnership allows for greater specialization of management, this leads to less-than-complete knowledge of the workings of the firm on the part of any one partner. The combination of imperfect knowledge and unlimited power to commit the firm can lead to disastrous results.

• PROBLEM 3-7

Define corporation and discuss its advantages and disadvantages.

Solution: Corporations are legal entities, distinct and separate from the individuals who own them. Corporations can acquire resources, own assets, produce and sell products, incur debts, extend credit, sue and be sued, and carry on all those functions which any other type of enterprise performs.

The corporate form of business enterprise has a dominant position in modern American capitalism. The corporations have advantages in raising money capital, by selling stocks and bonds. Through the securities market corporations can pool the financial resources of extremely large numbers of people. Financing by the sale of securities also has decided advantages from the viewpoint of the purchasers of these securities. First, households can now participate in enterprise and share the expected monetary reward therefrom without having to assume an active part in management. Corporations ordinarily have easier access to bank credit than do other types of business organizations. Secondly, corporations have the distinct advantage of limited liability. The owners (stockholders) of a corporation risk only what they paid for the stock purchased. Thirdly, corporations have a certain permanence which is lacking in other forms of business organization. Finally, corporation's have the ability to obtain more specialized, and more efficient management than other forms of business.

The corporation's advantages are of tremendous significance and typically override its disadvantages.

• PROBLEM 3-8

What are some of the characteristics of a corporation?

Solution: The characteristics of a corporation are

- the authority for the chartering of a corporation rests with the states.
- the corporation operates within the provisions of its charter.
- the board of directors is the legal managerial body of a corporation.
- the board of directors appoints further officers of management.
- ownership is represented by shares of stock held by the stockholders.
- stockholders elect the board of directors and vote on policy matters.
- profits can be reinvested in the business in the form of retained earnings, or paid to the stockholders in the form of dividends.
- a stockholder has limited liability for the debts of a corporation, equal to the amount of his investment. That is, if the corporation defaults, a stockholder has no legal recourse to the purchase price of his now-worthless stock, and must absorb the loss.
- the corporation exists as a legal person. That is, when it is involved in legal action, it is addressed in its own person, not in that of any of its owners, directors, or employees.

THE CORPORATION

• **PROBLEM 3-9**

Explain what is meant by a corporation's being called a "legal person." What effect does this have on the firm's actions?

Solution: The corporation's status as a "legal person" means that it is considered distinct from its owners in legal action. That is, a corporation may either take or be subject to legal action. Its owners cannot take or be subject to such action through the corporation. (This is not to say that the owners of a corporation may act illegally on behalf of the firm. They are still personally responsible for their actions.)

The effect of this status is to limit each stockholder's ability to act as the firm's agent. It also guarantees the continuity of the firm, since it exists independently of the particular group of people who own its stock at any one time.

• **PROBLEM 3-10**

Describe the advantages and disadvantages of a corporation.

Solution: Many of the disadvantages of proprietorship and partnership are done away with by the corporation, the greatest being its feature of limited liability. The owners of a corporation (i.e., its stockholders) are liable for the debts of the firm only to the extent of their original investment. Since the corporation exists as a "legal person," its responsibilities do not hinge (as is the case in proprietorships and partnerships) on one person or a small group, but rather, on a large group of small investors. This feature eliminates some of the other difficulties of other forms of business organization. Continuity of the firm is insured since the death or withdrawal of any one owner has little impact. Banks are more willing to lend to corporations owing to their sounder financial position and longer expected life. Size also allows corporations to specialize to a greater extent than any other form of business, increasing efficiency. Another advantage exists in taxation, since the maximum corporate income tax rate is appreciably lower than the maximum personal income tax rate.

However, corporations are not without disadvantages. Corporations must be chartered, and obtaining a charter may involve considerably greater expense and effort than is required to open a proprietorship or partnership. Day to day control of a corporation rests in the hands of a small group of managers, not equally among owners. This division between ownership and control may lead to opposing and/or inconsistent goals and policies, and inefficient policies.

The stockholders of a corporation also suffer a tax disadvantage caused by "double taxation." Corporate receipts are first taxed as corporate income, lowering corporate profits, and therefore dividend payments. Dividend payments are then taxed again, as personal income.

• PROBLEM 3-11

Explain how the reduced personal risk of corporate organization allows for greater efficiency.

Solution: Efficient production often means large-scale production. Since (especially in "heavy industries" such as steel-making) fixed costs are high, a firm often must operate at great scale in order to reach its most efficient point of production, where its average cost is lowest. Large scale production necessitates great financial risk since large amounts of machinery and large pieces of machinery are expensive and must be financed before production begins.

In this context, the limited liability feature of corporate organization is extremely appealing. An investor is much more likely to undertake a great risk on behalf of the firm if his personal liability is limited. This feature induces investors to undertake the large risks necessary for large-scale production and efficiency.

• PROBLEM 3-12

> Four ways a corporation can raise capital are through bonds, common stock, preferred stock, and convertibles. Describe each method.

Solution: Bonds are special kinds of promissary notes that are readily marketable for resale. Ordinarily a bond will insure periodic interest payments and the repayment of its principal when the bond matures. For example a ten year 8% $1000 bond would require annual interest payments of $80 plus the payment of $1000 after 10 years.

The common stockholder provides "equity" capital. He shares in business decisions and profits, but must also share in losses. The common stockholder's income is not limited, as the bondholder's is, but is less regular.

The preferred stockholder lies somewhere between the common stockholder and the bondholder. The preferred stockholder receives at most a stated dividend (as with interest for bonds) but does not get paid his dividend until after the bondholder has been paid his interest. Preferred stock has no "face value" like a bond, hence, holders of preferred stock are not repaid a lump sum of a maturity date, as a bondholder is.

Finally convertibles are bonds which can be converted by the investor for a specified number of shares of common stock.

• PROBLEM 3-13

> What is the difference between callable and convertible preferred stock?

Solution: A callable preferred stock is one which the company has a right to buy back from the stockholder at some previously stated value.

A convertible preferred stock is similar to a convertible bond in that with it, the preferred stockholder has the right to convert each of his shares into shares of common stock at some stipulated ratio.

• PROBLEM 3-14

> What is an investment banking firm? What role does it play in corporate growth and expansion?

Solution: An investment banking firm is a merchandiser of securities. It buys large blocks of stocks from corporations and sells these stocks in smaller blocks, at a profit, to the public. These blocks of stock are new corporate issues; an investment banking firm does not simply facilitate the exchange of already outstanding shares between different stockholders.

A corporation interested in expansion, or a firm that is newly incorporated, might decide to sell shares to finance the expansion. If it does decide to sell shares, the corporation will go to an investment banking firm, which will examine the corporation and decide whether it has a chance to grow or not. If the bank thinks the corporation is sound and growing, it will agree to try to sell the corporation's stock. The bank and corporation will then decide how much the bank will pay the corporation per share. The corporation wants the highest price for its stock, while the bank wants a low price, so it can make a larger profit when it sells the stocks to the public. If the corporation demands too high a price, the bank may not be able to sell all of the shares. In this case, the corporation has to buy back the unsold shares, with the result that it raises less capital than it wanted to. With large, established corporations, the bank might agree to underwrite the stock; that is, the bank will take the loss if all the stocks are not sold.

An investment banking firm, then, is the intermediary that enables a corporation to sell its stocks to the public. As such, it plays an extremely important role in corporate expansion. For small, newly incorporated firms, an investment banking firm can either enable them to obtain needed capital or, by refusing to trade their stock, prevent them from doing so.

• PROBLEM 3-15

From a corporation's point of view, what are the relative advantages and disadvantages of selling bonds, common stock, and preferred stocks?

Solution: For a corporation, the main difference between the three major types of securities is the commitment each makes as regards payments. With bonds, a corporation commits itself to making a fixed payment per year equal to the bond's face value times a specified interest rate, plus a larger sum, the bond's face value, when it reaches maturity. In slow business periods, these inflexible payments can be burdensome. Preferred stock is slightly more flexible. A preferred stock pays, at most, a stated dividend, no matter how profitable the business becomes. If the corporation is doing very badly, however, the full dividend does not have to be paid. These special features of preferred stock ease the problem of fixed payments in bad times and keep the payments low in good times. Common stock offers the most flexibility to a corporation. With common stock, there are no required payments at all, and in bad times, common stock receives no dividends unless preferred stock receives it full dividend.

It must be realized, however, that a firm will usually make some effort to keep both preferred and common stockholders happy. If they are not satisfied with their dividends, the corporation might have trouble raising (money) capital when it tries to sell more stock.

Corporations take other factors into account when deciding which type of security to market. Interest charges can be deducted for tax purposes from corporate earnings, which gives bond debt an advantage, especially when earnings are high. A small corporation might be concerned about new stockholders' taking control, a concern that could lead to the corporation issuing preferred stocks or bonds because bondholders and holders of preferred stock have little power over the running of a corporation.

These relative advantages and disadvantages explain why most corporations use balanced combinations of these types of securities to finance expansion.

• PROBLEM 3-16

Discuss the differences, from their holders' point of view, between stocks and bonds issued by corporations.

Solution: Stockholders are subject to the same fluctuations to which the firm is subject. While the return they may receive is potentially greater than that of bondholders, their potential losses are likewise greater. An important fact to note is the payment schedule - stockholders are paid out of profits, which are calculated after bond payments are made. In the event of financial difficulties, bondholders have less risk at loss than stockholders.

Bondholders' income from the firm is much steadier than that of stockholders, but also more limited. Possible profit from a stock is limitless. That from a bond is fixed.

Unlike stockholders, bondholders have no direct voice whatsoever in corporate decisions. Their relationship with the firm is limited, indirect, while stockholders' is less limited, and more direct.

• PROBLEM 3-17

Describe the "separation of ownership and control" in the corporate structure. In what ways do owners (stockholders) and controllers (e.g., Boards of Directors) conflict? In what ways do they agree?

Solution: Since corporations are owned by such great numbers of stockholders, in order to make smooth operation possible, a certain concentration of decision making power is inevitable. Were a general poll of stockholders necessary each time a decision is made, corporations would be so unwieldy that it is doubtful they would exist. This concentration at power is made possible by the fact that both owners and controllers share at least a fundamental goal - that of profit maximization. Directors of firms are able to maintain their position of power largely through the use of proxy voting. Annual meetings are rarely attended by all, or even a majority of stockholders. Those absent are requested by the directors to relinquish their votes to the directors to use as they see fit. In this way, directors amass large blocs of votes and control the decision making process.

The principle area of disagreement between the two groups is on the question of undistributed corporate profits. Management prefers to reinvest profits in the firm. Such undistributed profits are not taxed as income and they insure the long run growth of the firm. On the other hand, undistributed corporate profits represent a drain on the pool from which dividends are paid to stockholders, who may want dividend payments to be higher.

• PROBLEM 3-18

Explain "double taxation" and the disadvantage it presents to the owners of corporations. What are some ways corporations attempt to avoid it?

Solution: "Double taxation" results from the fact that corporate income is taxed separately from personal income. Corporate income tax lowers corporate profit, out of which dividends are paid to stockholders. After the dividend payment they receive is reduced by taxation, it is lowered once more by direct personal income tax.

Some ways corporations attempt to avoid "double taxation" are through the use of undistributed corporate profits. Since only dividends paid out are subject to personal income taxes, holders of large amounts of stock attempt to keep profits within the firm.

A second way "double taxation" is avoided is through the disguise of profits in the form of high salaries, pension, and expense accounts, which are not taxed as part of corporate income.

• PROBLEM 3-19

Describe both the advantages and disadvantages to society that result from the concentration of economic power in the hands of a relatively small number of firms.

Solution: The greatest argument in favor of the concentration at economic power on the part of a small number of large firms is technical efficiency. Economies at scale in certain industries require large outlays of capital by few firms, for example, public utilities. The fixed costs of building the facilities needed by, say, an electric company, are so high that the facilities must be built to a tremendous scale in order to make production possible. Such a scale also prohibits competition. If an electric company in a city of one million must build a generating plant large enough for 800,000, once it is built, there is no incentive for another firm to build another since the remaining clientele is too small. It is also pointed out by defenders of big business that the majority of major contributions to our standard of living have, over the years, come from "giant corporations."

The arguments against large corporations, on the other hand, are numerous, the foremost being the evils of monopoly. Since the monopolist (or, in the case where a few firms dominate an industry, the oligopolist) faces no (or little) competition, he is able to charge a higher price. This undermines the rationing function of prices. Prices ideally reflect the relative values of different goods, in order that the economy as a whole can correctly allocate resources to the most valuable of them. When an artificially high price is charged for one good, it diverts resources away from more highly valued goods, causing less of them to be produced than ought to be. This situation represents the misallocation of resources and economic inefficiency.

Profits are a normal part of business, so much that the economist counts them as a cost. However, there is a difference between economic profits and monopoly profits. Economic profits reflect a "normal" rate of return, enough to induce an entrepreneur to produce a good deemed valuable by society. Monopoly profits, on the other hand, represent monopoly return, more than that needed to bring about the production of that particular good.

• PROBLEM 3-20

Certain large corporations show slightly lower rates of profit than their next largest competitors. What are some alternative goals that would explain a corporation's opting for greater size over additional profits?

Solution: While profit maximization is undeniably foremost among any corporation's goals, some seem to settle for slightly lower profits in order to increase their size. The principal underlying motives are prestige and power for the managers.

While not necessarily tangible, there is certainly a greater reward for sitting on the Board of Directors of the largest firm in an industry than that of the second. While it may be a rational strategy aimed at opening opportunities both for oneself and the firm, even if it is for a motive as fleeting as impressing one's guests at a cocktail party, the prestige motive for size at the expense of some profits exists.

The power motive is quite similar. A firm's prominence in an industry can often allow them to dictate to others in the industry and even to outsiders dealing with the industry. Size also brings political power, as the largest corporations often receive government contracts and are sometimes in a position to "influence" lawmakers. A giant corporation employing the vast majority of an area's workers may manipulate that area's lawmakers to enact laws favorable to the firm with the threat of widespread unemployment.

• PROBLEM 3-21

What is the predominant form of business organization in the United States in terms of number of firms? What is the predominant form in terms of volume of output?

Solution: In terms of the number of firms, the sole proprietorship is overwhelmingly the predominant type of business organization. In 1973, about 78 per cent of all American businesses were sole proprietorships.

In terms of volume of output, however, corporations easily produce more than any other type of business organization. Generally, corporations, constituting about 14 per cent of all firms, produce about two-thirds of total business output.

SHORT ANSWER QUESTIONS FOR REVIEW

Answer

To be covered when testing yourself

Choose the correct answer.

1. Of the following, which are advantages to a single proprietor? (a) unlimited liability (b) mutual agency (c) ease in obtaining funds (d) control over decisions (e) limited liability — d

2. To establish a single proprietorship, one must: (a) obtain a state charter (b) simply "open his doors" for business (c) sell stock (d) have the ability and knowledge to make the firm successful (e) find a partner — b

3. Under the doctrine of mutual agency: (a) All partners in a firm must agree on all decisions (b) Any one partner can commit the firm financially only to an amount equal to his own investment (c) Any one partner can totally commit the firm financially (d) The partners of a firm must share profits equally (e) A majority of the partners must consent to all decisions — c

4. An advantage of a partnership over a single proprietorship is: (a) limited liability (b) greater specialization of management (c) less "red tape" in forming the business (d) unlimited liability (e) separation of ownership and control — b

5. Fred has $50,000 in personal assets. John has $100,000 in personal assets. They form a partnership, Fred investing $25,000 and John investing $50,000. The firm goes out of business leaving $300,000 in bills owed to their supplier. Their supplier can collect: (a) $25,000 from Fred and $50,000 from John (b) $75,000 from Fred and $75,000 from John (c) $100,000 from Fred and $200,000 from John (d) nothing from either (e) $50,000 from Fred and $100,000 from John — e

6. In order to be an owner of a corporation, one must: (a) purchase any amount of its stock (b) purchase a majority of its stock (c) purchase all of its stock (d) sit on its Board of Directors (e) attend stockholders' meetings — a

7. One million dollars worth of stock, 100% of that issued, in Corporation X is bought by A, B, and C, who purchase $500,000, $300,000, and

Answer

To be covered when testing yourself

$200,000 worth, respectively. A, B, and C each own assets totalling one million dollars. Corporation X goes out of business, leaving two million dollars in outstanding bills. A, B, and C are liable for: (a) $666,666.67 each (b) $500,000, $300,000, and $200,000 respectively (c) $1,000,000, $600,000, and $400,000 respectively (d) $333,333.33 each (e) nothing — b

8. "Double taxation" means: (a) corporate income is taxed at double the personal income tax rate (b) the partners in a firm are taxed at equal personal income tax rates (c) sales tax is imposed on products produced by corporations (d) corporate income is taxed first as corporate income and then as personal income from dividend payments on stock (e) the income tax is twice as high as it should be — d

9. "Separation of ownership and control" means: (a) partners in a firm do not tell each other of the decisions they make (b) a husband and wife cannot be partners in a firm (c) the owners of a corporation do not directly make decisions regarding its operation (d) single proprietors can never be sure if the decisions they make are correct (e) a corporation's Board of Directors makes decisions against the wishes of the stockholders — c

10. As compared to bonds, stocks (a) yield a potentially larger, but much more unpredictable, income (b) yield a "limited but steady" income (c) afford their holders less of a say in the running of the corporation (d) provide the holder with a greater guarantee of recouping his investment (e) are an unattractive asset — a

11. A "convertible bond" is: (a) one whose rate of return changes (b) one that can be returned to its issuer at any time for cash (c) one whose face value changes (d) one that can be redeemed at any time at its issuer's discretion (e) one that can be exchanged for common stock — e

12. Which of the following is not true of a corporation. (a) unlimited liability (b) ease in obtaining funds (c) lower tax rate on corporate income than on personal income (d) greater efficiency brought about by greater size (e)

Answer
To be covered when testing yourself

greater specialization, yielding greater efficiency — a

13. The dominant forms of business organization in the United States, in terms of output and number of firms are: (a) partnerships in output and corporations in number of firms (b) single proprietorships in both (c) single proprietorships in output and corporations in number of firms (d) corporations in output and single proprietorships in number of firms (e) corporations in both — d

14. The corporation's status as a "legal person" means that: (a) its stockholders are immune from prosecution for illegal acts committed in the corporation's name (b) each individual stockholder is limited in his capacity to act as the firm's agent (c) the continuity of the firm is guaranteed since it exists independently of its different owners (d) a and b (e) b and c — e

15. Which of the following relationships is not true? (a) It is easier for a partnership to obtain funds than a single proprietorship and easiest for a corporation (b) A corporation allows the individual owner greater control over the firm than a partnership, and a partnership allows the individual owner greater control than a single proprietorship (c) A partnership allows greater specialization in management than a single proprietorship, and a corporation allows even greater specialization than a partnership (d) In the event of the death or withdrawal of an owner, a partnership has a greater chance of survival than a single proprietorship and a corporation has an even greater chance than a partnership (e) Owners of a single proprietorship and those of a partnership have equal personal liability in the event of the firm's default, and owners of a corporation have even less personal liability — b

<u>Fill in the blanks.</u>

16. Owners of single proprietorships and partnerships are liable for the debts of their firms to the full extent of their "personal fortune." This is known as ____________. — unlimited liability

17. ____________ is the doctrine by which any of the partners of a firm may act as its agent

SHORT ANSWER QUESTIONS FOR REVIEW

	Answer To be covered when testing yourself
and totally commit it financially.	mutual agency
18. The death or withdrawal of an owner does not affect the continuity of a corporation since it exists as a __________.	"legal person"
19. A bond which can be redeemed before maturity at the discretion of its issuer is a __________ bond.	callable
20. Since corporate profits are taxed first as corporate income and then as personal income in the form of divident payments, stockholders' dividends suffer from __________.	double taxation
21. The __________ refers to the fact that the owners of a corporation often do not exercise direct control over management decisions.	separation of ownership and control
22. A bond which can be exchanged for common stock at a previously specified ratio is a __________.	convertible bond
23. High levels of __________ are due to stockholders attempting to avoid double taxation.	undistributed corporate profits
24. Directors of corporations are able to control the votes of stockholders absent from annual meetings, and thus, often, to control the decision-making process, through the use of __________.	proxies
25. The agreement by an investment banker to act as agent in the sale of a corporation's stock and to absorb the loss which might result if all of the stock is not sold, is known as __________ __________.	investment underwriting
26. A firm which invests either directly or indirectly in several countries is a __________.	multinational
27. The __________ is the dominant form of business organization in terms of number of firms, but the __________ is the dominant form in terms of output.	single proprietorship, corporation
28. The statement of a firm's financial position at a given point in time is the firm's __________ __________.	balance sheet

SHORT ANSWER QUESTIONS FOR REVIEW

	Answer To be covered when testing yourself
29. An ______________ is the term given to any item of wealth owned by a firm or individual.	asset
30. A business owned and operated by one person is called a ________________, a business owned and operated by two or more people is called a ______________, and a business owned by a group of persons known as stockholders is called a ______________.	single proprie-torship, partner-ship, corpora-tion
31. The legal responsibility of a stockholder for the debt of a corporation up to the amount of his investment only is called ______________.	limited liability
<u>Determine whether the following statements are true or false.</u>	
32. Owners of single proprietorships are liable for the debts of the firm only to the extent of their investment in the firm.	False
33. One principal reason for the formation of a corporation is the greater ease corporations have in obtaining funds.	True
34. A partnership always involves two people.	False
35. In the event of the death or withdrawal from the firm of one partner, the remaining partners automatically retain control of the firm.	False
36. The separation of ownership and control refers to the fact that the owners of a corporation often do not exercise direct control over its decisions.	True
37. Corporations have a greater chance of succeeding than single proprietorships or partnerships.	True
38. Greater specialization of management is an advantage of a single proprietorship over a corporation.	False
39. There are a great many more corporations than single proprietorships, yet proprietorships produce a greater output than corporations.	False
40. A firm refers to the physical building in which production occurs.	False
41. In order to begin operations, a corporation	

	Answer (To be covered when testing yourself)
must obtain a state charter.	True
42. Because they represent a fixed payment, bonds are a greater burden on a firm than stocks during a period in which receipts are low.	True
43. In comparison with stocks, bonds offer a limited but steady income.	True
44. Banks are generally quite liberal in lending to single proprietorships.	False
45. A callable bond is one which can be exchanged at its issuer's discretion for common stock.	False
46. While the public generally holds the attitude that bigness is bad in business, it is arguable that large firms are necessary for efficiency.	True

CHAPTER 4

NATIONAL INCOME AND PRICE INDICES

Basic Attacks and Strategies for Solving Problems in this Chapter. See pages 91 to 133 for step-by-step solutions to problems.

Gross National Product (GNP) is the most comprehensive and widely-used measure of the economy's "health." It measures the total production of final goods and services over the period of a year. Final goods and services are goods and services which are being purchased for final use and not for resale or further processing or manufacturing.

There are three ways to measure GNP. The output or expenditure approach measures GNP by summing expenditures for final goods and services. Expenditures can be broken down into four components, representing the four sources of spending for final goods and services. They are: personal consumption expenditures, government expenditures, gross private domestic investment, and net exports. The allocations or income approach breaks GNP into seven components: compensation of employees, rents, interest, proprietor's income, corporate profits before taxes, capital consumption allowances, and indirect business taxes. The two approaches must be equivalent because all the money spent from the four sources must be allocated to one of the seven components of income or expense.

The third way to calculate GNP is by adding the value-added of all firms in the economy. Value-added refers to the value a firm creates as the result of processing. For example, a bakery will buy flour and turn it into bread, which is more highly valued. The difference between the value of the flour bought and the bread sold is the firm's value-added. Adding value-added by all firms in the economy will give the value created by the economy as a whole, in short, GNP. Since the source of value-added is the work performed on the intermediate product by factors of production, a firm's value-added will correspond to what it pays its factors of production. Thus, adding value-added will also be equivalent to the income approach.

There are several important alternative measures of income and output that can be derived from GNP. If you subtract Capital Consumption Allowances from GNP, you get a number called Net National Product (NNP). Essentially, NNP measures production less any capital goods which simply replaced worn-out capital. Subtracting Indirect Business Taxes from NNP gives National Income. National Income can be thought of as measuring allocations to factors of production only. In other words, it measures the income earned from production. Personal Income measures income received by households. It starts from National Income and adds all income received but not earned (i.e., social security benefits) and subtracts most income earned but not received (i.e., corporate tax payments). Disposable Income is the money households have free to spend. It is computed by subtracting personal taxes from personal income.

A significant problem in the measurement of GNP has to do with the role of prices. GNP measures production of various types of goods and services, such as apples and oranges and autos and computers. Apples and oranges cannot be directly added, much less autos and computers. The only way they could be added is by putting them into a common unit. The common unit chosen is the nation's currency. In the United States, the market value in dollars of each good and service is added. Market value can be defined as the amount consumers spend or the amount producers receive for the product. If P stands for the price of the product and Q stands for the amount sold, then market value is P^*Q. If there are n goods and services in the economy, then money, or nominal, or current dollar GNP is measured by

$$GNP = P_1Q_1 + P_2Q_2 + \ldots + P_nQ_n.$$

The problem with this approach comes when GNP is compared across two years. For example, assume money GNP in year 0 is compared to money GNP in year 1:

$$GNP^1 = P_1^1Q_1^1 + P_2^1Q_2^1 + \ldots + P_n^1Q_n^1$$

$$GNP^0 = P_1^0Q_1^0 + P_2^0Q_2^0 + \ldots + P_n^0Q_n^0$$

Money GNP in year 1 can be higher than in year 0 for two reasons. First, the Q's could have grown, a desirable state of affairs since it means the economy has actually produced more goods and services. Second, the P's could have increased, a less desirable state of affairs since it simply means there has been inflation. The solution to the problem is to value GNP in both years using the same set of prices. Select a year arbitrarily, say year 0. This will be called the base year. Compute GNP in both years with the year 0 prices:

$$GNP^1 = P_1^0Q_1^1 + P_2^0Q_2^1 + \ldots + P_n^0Q_n^1$$

$$GNP^0 = P_1^0Q_1^0 + P_2^0Q_2^0 + \ldots + P_n^0Q_n^0$$

Using this approach, the only way GNP could increase from year 0 to year 1 is if the Q's increased. GNP calculated this way is known as real or constant dollar GNP.

The data arrived at by the method just described can be used to compute price indices and the rate of inflation. Arbitrarily let the value 100 stand for the price level in the base year. The number 100 is a price index because it is a number that stands for another number. The price index for any year *t* can be computed by using the formula:

$$Price\ Index_t = \left(\frac{Money\ GNP_t}{Price\ Index_t}\right) * 100.$$

The index computed this way is known as the GNP Deflator. It is the most comprehensive measure of prices we have because it includes every final good and service produced. Calculating the percentage change in the price index between any two years will give the rate of inflation between those two years.

Price indices (specifically the GNP Deflator) can be used to "deflate" money GNP data into real terms. The formula is:

$$Real\ GNP_t = \left(\frac{Money\ GNP_t}{Price\ Index_t}\right) * 100.$$

This procedure can be thought of as removing the inflation component from the rise in GNP.

Caution must be used in evaluating GNP statistics. They are often taken to be a measure of national well-being, when they are in fact far from that. For one thing, GNP does not measure all production. Most production that does not enter markets is excluded from GNP. Examples would include produce from backyard vegetable gardens, do-it-yourself activities, criminal activity, and intangibles such as love, friendship, caring, and leisure time. Another consideration is that GNP includes some items that may not really add to human well-being. If there is a crime wave and people begin installing burglar alarms in their homes, GNP may go up as more alarms are manufactured, but are we really better off? Also GNP does not take into account the distribution of the total product. An unequal distribution may reduce well-being in a society that highly prizes equality.

Step-by-Step Solutions to Problems in this Chapter, "National Income and Price Indices"

PURPOSE

• **PROBLEM** 4-1

What is the purpose of the National Accounts?

Solution: The National Accounts try to measure the total value of the output of the economy, and to show where the output originates (by industrial sector; by individual industry; by region; from private as opposed to government production) and how it is allocated (between households and government, between residents and foreigners, and between different regions). Total output may also be represented as the sum of broad categories of goods (consumer durables and non-durables, capital equipment, buildings, etc.). The different presentations are useful for different purposes.

Macroeconomic models use as variables the different (sub)categories of the National Accounts.

• **PROBLEM** 4-2

State the importance of national income accounting.

Solution: The national income accounting is important for the following reasons:

1. It permits us to measure the level of production in the economy over a given period of time, and to explain the immediate causes of that level of performance.
2. By comparing the national income accounts over a period of time, the long-run course which the economy has been following can be plotted.
3. The national income accounts will show growth or stagnation in the economy, alerting economic policymakers to the sort of action which ought to be taken. Since national income accounts break the performance of the economy down into its component parts, they provide policymakers with specific information regarding the formulation and application of economic policy. For example, suppose that,

using the receipts-expenditures approach, it is discovered that GNP has fallen over time and the principle cause of this decline is a decrease in net exports. This alerts policymakers to take action to restrict imports (perhaps by imposing tariffs), which will raise net exports (since X_n = Exports - Imports), and finally, increase GNP.

DEFINING GROSS NATIONAL PRODUCT

• PROBLEM 4-3

Define Gross National Product (GNP).

Solution: Gross National Product, otherwise known as GNP, is defined as the total market value of all final goods and services produced in the economy in one year. An important clarification has to be made here. All goods produced in a particular year may not be sold: some may be added to inventories. Nevertheless, any increase in inventories must be included in determining GNP, since GNP measures all current production regardless of whether or not it is sold.

• PROBLEM 4-4

Compare the output, or expenditures approach with the income, or allocations approach in computing the Gross National Product.

Solution: The Gross National Product via the output, or expenditures approach is arrived at by the following formula:

Consumption expenditures by households	C
plus	+
Government purchases of goods and services	G
plus	+
Investment expenditures by businesses	I
plus	+
Expenditures by foreigners	(Ex - Im)
Equals	=
GNP	Y

while GNP via income, or allocations approach is determined by using the formula:

Wages	W
plus	+
Rents	R
plus	+
Interest	Int
plus	+
Profits	P
plus	+
Non-income charges or allocations	NIC
Equals	=
GNP	Y

• **PROBLEM 4-5**

GNP attempts to measure the annual production of the economy. Non-productive transactions should not be included in its computation. What are 'non-productive transactions'?

Solution: Non-productive transactions are of two major types:

(1) purely financial transactions

(2) second-hand sales

Purely financial transactions include public and private transfer payments and trade in securities.

Transfer payments do not entail production but simply the transfer of funds (as opposed to wage payment) from the government to individuals,

Stock market transactions involve merely the swapping of claims to real assets, these transactions do not involve current production.

Second-hand sales either reflect no current production, or they involve double counting, because the production of the particular good has already taken place, and its value should not be included in (current) GNP.

• **PROBLEM 4-6**

Explain fully why, in the calculation of GNP, the sale of final goods is included while the sale of intermediate goods is excluded.

Solution: First of all, "final goods" means goods and services which are being purchased for final use and not for resale or further processing or manufacturing. Transactions involving intermediate goods, on the other hand, refer to purchases of goods and services for further processing and manufacturing or for resale. Now in the computation of GNP, the sale of final goods is included while the sale of intermediate goods is excluded, because the value of final goods includes all the intermediate transactions involved in their production. The inclusion of intermediate transactions would involve double counting and produce an exaggerated estimate of GNP.

To clarify this point, take the following example. Suppose there are five stages of production in having a suit manufactured and sold to a consumer who is the ultimate or final user. The following table lists the stages of production, sales value of materials or product, as well as the value added:

(1) Stage of production	(2) Sales value of materials or product	(3) Value added
Firm A, sheep ranch	\$ 40	\$ 40
Firm B, wool processor	\$ 65	\$ 25
Firm C, suit manufacturer	\$ 85	\$ 20
Firm D, clothing wholesaler	\$110	\$ 25
Firm E, retail clothier	\$160	\$ 50
Total	\$460	\$160

As the above table indicates, Firm A, a sheep ranch, provides \$40 worth of wool to Firm B, a wool processor. Firm A pays out the \$40 it receives in wages, rents, interest and profits. Firm B processes the wool and sells it to Firm C, a suit manufacturer, for \$65. From this \$65, \$40 goes to Firm A, and the remaining \$25 is used by B to pay wages, rents, interest, and profits for the resources needed in processing the wool. And so on: the manufacturer sells the suit to Firm D, a clothing wholesaler, who in turn sells it to Firm E, a retailer, and then, at last, it is bought for \$160 by a consumer, the final user of the product. At each stage, the difference between what a firm has paid for the product and what it receives for its sale is paid out as wages, rent, interest, and profits for the resources used by that firm in helping to produce and distribute the suit. How much should be included in the GNP in accounting for the production of this suit? The answer is \$160, because this figure includes all the intermediate transactions leading up to the product's final sale. It would be a gross exaggeration to sum all the intermediate sales figures and the final sales value of the product and add the entire amount, \$460, to GNP. This would be a serious case of double counting; that is, counting both the final product and the sale and resale of its various parts in the multistage productive process.

There is an alternative means of determining the \$160 figure which is to be included in the GNP. This is the value-added method; that is, summing the value added to the total worth of the product at each step in the productive process. It is important to note that this measures the total income derived from the production and sale of the suit.

• PROBLEM 4-7

In January 1979, Mr. John sold his 1973 Ford to Mr. Daniel. One month later, Mr. John purchased a brand new Ford which he resold a week later to Mr. Smith. Which of the transactions would be included in the computation of 1979 GNP? Defend your position.

Solution: Neither of the two resale transactions would be included in the computation of GNP. The sale of the 1973 Ford would be excluded because it represents no production in 1979. The inclusion in this year's GNP, of the sales of goods produced some years ago, would be an exaggeration of this year's output. Similarly, the resale by Mr. John of his newly purchased 1979 Ford has to be excluded. When he bought the 1979 Ford, however, its value would have been included in GNP. To include its resale value would be to count it twice.

OTHER ACCOUNTS

• PROBLEM 4-8

Explain the difference between gross investment and net investment. Why is net investment used instead of gross investment in computing net national product? Explain the problem of double counting and how it may be avoided.

Solution: Investment is defined as an addition to the economy's stock of capital (that is, the elements used to produce output, for example, machines and factories.) During the course of a year in which gross national product is computed, the economy as a whole will produce new machines, etc., adding to the stock of capital goods. The total amount of newly produced capital goods is defined as gross investment. However, during that year, a certain amount of capital goods already in use will become obsolete or will be rendered unusable (machines will break down, factories will be destroyed by fire, etc.) Therefore, a certain part of gross investment is used to replace this depreciated capital. That part of gross investment which replaces worn out or obsolete capital goods is defined as depreciation, called capital consumption allowance in the national income accounts. It does not add to the capital stock, but rather replaces capital goods used up producing the year's output. For example, if gross investment equals $100 and depreciation equals $50, the real addition to capital is only $50, not the $100 reported by gross investment. To present a more accurate picture of the investment component of national income accounts, net investment (gross investment minus depreciation, or capital consumption allowance) is used in calculating net national product.

Intermediate goods are goods sold as finished by one business to another, which uses this "finished good" as a raw material in creating another finished good. An example is a producer of wool who sells his wool to a producer of coats. Suppose the wool producer sells $1000 worth of wool to a coat maker who produces $5000 worth of coats. If both the wool and the coats are treated as final goods, a $6000 addition is made to gross national product. However, since the wool is now part of the coats, its value is included in the value of the coats. The real addition to GNP represented by the wool growing and coat-making combined is only $5000.

A solution to the problem of double counting is the use

of the value-added method of calculating GNP. In this method, rather than adding the total amount received by each intermediate producer, only the amount of value which their production adds to the final product is counted. Under this method, the value added by the wool grower, assuming he supplies all the inputs used in producing the wool, is $1000, since the wool is nonexistent and worth $0 before he produces it. The value added by the coat maker is $4000, which equals the value of the final product ($5000) minus the value added to the final product by the wool grower.

• PROBLEM 4-9

What is the relationship between Net National Product and Gross National Product?

Solution: Gross National Product and Net National Product are definable as the sum of three major components: personal consumption expenditure on goods and services, plus government expenditure on goods and services, plus investment expenditure - where it is understood that in GNP, gross investment expenditure on all new machines and construction is included, whereas, in NNP, only the net investment expenditure is included, there having been subtracted from the gross births of capital goods, an appropriate depreciation allowance to take account of deaths, or using up of capital goods.

In equation form, we have the following relationship

GNP = NNP + Depreciation
GNP - Depreciation = NNP

• PROBLEM 4-10

Define, and distinguish between, Gross National Product (GNP) and Net Economic Welfare (NEW). Is it possible (1) to increase NEW by decreasing GNP and (2) to increase both GNP and NEW at the same time?

Solution: Gross National Product, or GNP, is defined as the total value, expressed in money, of the goods and services produced by the economy of a nation during a given period of time (such as a year). New Economic Welfare, or NEW may be defined as GNP expanded to include the values (positive or negative) of factors which do not enter into GNP such as the value of housework performed by (unpaid) housewives, and increased leisure time (both positive), and the discomfort caused by pollution (negative).

It is possible to increase NEW by decreasing GNP. For example, it may be possible to decrease pollution drastically by installing pollution control equipment at power plants which will make these plants somewhat less efficient. If the value to society of the decrease in pollution is greater than the value of the foregone electricity, NEW will increase despite a decrease in GNP.

It is also possible to increase GNP and NEW at the same time. If, for example, a technological breakthrough allows increased efficiency in steel production without increased pollution, both GNP and NEW will increase by an amount equal to the value of the additional steel produced. If this increase in efficiency results in a shortening of the workweek for steelworkers without a decrease in pay, the increase in NEW will actually exceed the increase in GNP because the value of the additional leisure time enjoyed by steelworkers is not included in GNP.

• PROBLEM 4-11

When capital consumption in an economy equals $500,000, and the GNP is $2,050,000, what is the NNP?

Solution: Net National Income equals Gross National Product corrected for the capital consumption

NNP = GNP - Capital consumption

Thus, NNP = $2,050,000 - $500,000 = $1,550,000

This is equal to the sum of total wages, profits, rent and royalties for the use of current resources that are not capital.

• PROBLEM 4-12

If a machine costs initially $1,000,000, lasts for 10 years, and has a scrap value of $100,000 at the end of its lifetime, how much depreciation should be taken into account each year in the current accounts? And how is this shown in the capital account?

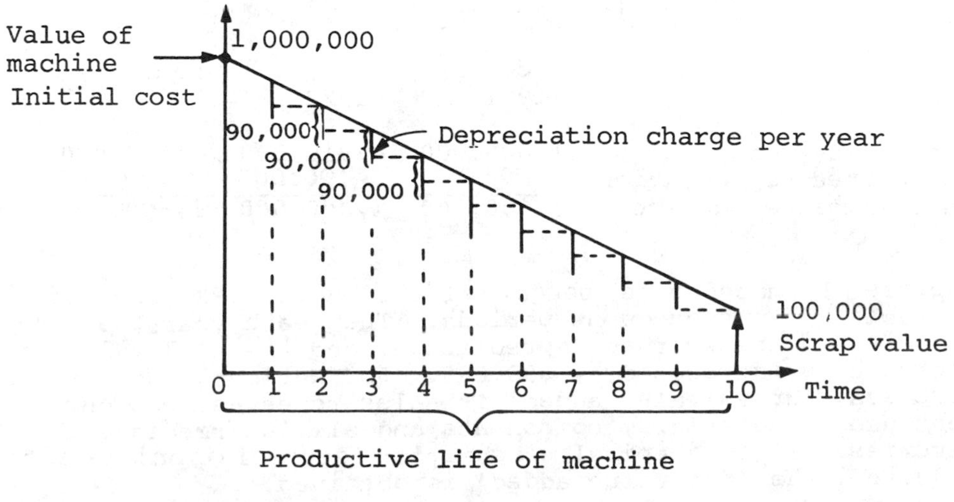

Solution: A machine decreases in value over time because of use, wear and tear, or obsolescence. This decline in value is called capital consumption, or depreciation, and appears as an expense in the current accounts. When the scrap value of the machine at the end of its lifetime of 10 years is $100,000, and its initial cost is $1,000,000, then the difference is the depreciable amount of $1,000,000 - $100,000 = $900,000, to be depreciated over 10 years; thus the depreciation is $\frac{\$900,000}{10}$ = $90,000 per year.

The graph on the preceding page will help to clarify this. The sloping line indicates the declining value of the machine; the 'steps' indicate the depreciation charges. The Current Account compares sales revenues and expensens, and calculates the profit difference.

Current Account

			Sales Revenues -----
less:	expenses:		
	wages	-----	
	materials	-----	
	→ depreciation	$90,000	
	operating profits		------
less:	taxes		------
	profits after taxes		

The Capital Account compares the initial cost of the particular asset (machine or building) with the accrued depreciation, and calculates the book value at any point in time.

Capital Account

	Dec. 31, 19X1	Dec. 31, 19X2	Dec. 31, 19X3
Book value machine	1,000,000	910,000	820,000
Accrued Depreciation	0	90,000	180,000
Initial value machine	1,000,000	1,000,000	1,000,000

Suppose the machine is bought at the end of 19X1, and is depreciated in subsequent periods. Then each year $90,000 is added to the Accrued Depreciation, and the book value of the machine is reduced by $90,000. For National Accounting purposes, 'gross value added' is sales revenues less current use of materials, components and all intermediate deliveries. If the capital consumption (depreciation) is also deducted, the 'net value added' is obtained.

• PROBLEM 4-13

What is the difference between gross national product and national income?

Solution: Gross National Product (GNP) is the dollar value of all goods and services produced in a year in the United States. National Income (NI), which is the total income earned by those who contribute to current production, represents the GNP remaining after deductions are made for indirect taxes, depreciation and thc use of capital.

• PROBLEM 4-14

Why is it that interest payments on government bonds are not included as income currently earned, particularly, when interest on the bonds of private firms is included in national income as earned income?

Solution: The rationale underlying the exclusion is this: much of the government debt has been incurred in connection with

(1) war and defense, and
(2) recession

Unlike public deficits to finance airports or highways, deficits stemming from the military and recessions yield no productive assets (services) to the economy. Hence, interest paid on such debt does not reflect the generation of any current output or income. Similar reasoning underlies the inclusion of interest payments by consumers as a part of transfer payments.

• PROBLEM 4-15

If consumption for a household is \$5000, savings are \$3000, and \$2000 is paid out in taxes, a) What is the personal income? b) What is the disposable income?

Solution: Personal income is equal to the amount consumed + amount saved + amount spent on taxes. In this example, personal income = \$5000 + \$3000 + \$2000 = \$10,000.

Disposable income = amount consumed + amount saved (or Personal Income - taxes). So, DI = \$5000 + \$3000 = \$8000.

• PROBLEM 4-16

What is disposable income?

Solution: Disposable income is the amount of personal income which remains after taxes have been paid. In other words, it is the total amount available for consumption of goods and services and for savings.

CALCULATING NATIONAL PRODUCT AND INCOME

• PROBLEM 4-17

The following are the items of the income statement of the economy for the year 1976 (in billions of dollars):

Rents	$ 24
Personal consumption expendituеs (C)	1,080
Corporate income taxes	65
Undistributed corporate profits	18
Net exports (Ex - Im)	7
Dividends	35
Capital consumption allowance	180
Interest	82
Indirect business taxes	163
Gross private domestic investment (I)	240
Compensation of employees	1,028
Government purchases of goods and services (G)	365
Proprietors' income	97

Determine the Gross National Product using:

a) expenditures approach
b) income approach

Solution: a) The receipts or expenditures approach is determined by using the formula:

$$C + Ig + G + X_n = GNP$$

where

C = personal consumption expenditures;
G = government expenditures on goods and services;
Ig = gross private domestic investment;
X_n = net exports.

For 1976 (referring to the above table), we have:

$1,080 + $240 + $365 + $7 = $1,692.

b) The allocations or income approach is computed as follows:

Capital consumption allowance	$ 180
Indirect business taxes	163
Compensation of employees	1,028
Rents	24
Interest	82
Proprietors' income	97
Corporate income taxes	65
Dividends	35
Undistributed corporate profits	18
Gross National Product	$1,692

Of course, both approaches to the computation of the gross national product must produce the same result (except for minor statistical discrepancies when real world statistics are used.)

• PROBLEM 4-18

There are basically two approaches to GNP: the expenditure approach and the income approach. The following is a list of national income figures for a given year. Arrange them in the form of a consolidated income statement with revenues and allocations ('expenses') for the whole of the economy. The figures are in billions of dollars.

Personal consumption expenditures (C)	660
Transfer payments	127
Rents	40
Capital consumption allowance (depreciation) (D)	95
Social security taxes	46
Interest	20
Proprietor's income	68
Net exports	2
Dividends	6
Compensation of employees	642
Indirect business taxes	101
Undistributed corporate profits	40
Personal taxes	116
Corporate income taxes	35
Corporate profits	81
Government purchases of goods and services	233
Net private domestic investment (I_{net})	57
Personal saving	60

Calculate, in addition, Personal Income (PI) and Disposable Personal Income (DPI).

Solution: An income statement compares total revenues (sales) with total costs (allocations) to determine profits. In the economy, total revenues equal total expenditures by definition: what one person spends as purchaser, is the revenue of the person who sells. Thus, Total Revenues for the economy as a whole are: $GNP = C + G + Ig + X_n$, where Ig is Gross Private Domestic Investment which equals the sum of Net Private Domestic Investment (In) and Depreciation (D); so Ig = In + D = 57 + 95 = 152. And the revenue side of the unconsolidated income statement states:

	Revenues:
Personal consumption expenditures (C)	660
Government purchases of goods and services (G)	233
Gross private domestic investment (Ig)	152
Net exports (X_n)	2
Total GNP	1,047

This figure must first be 'corrected' by subtracting Indirect Business Taxes, since these taxes represent a drain on revenues, so

	Revenues	1,047
less:	Indirect Business Taxes	101
equals	Corrected Revenues	946

This figure is compared with 'Expenses' to determine Profits in the economy.

What are the 'Expenses' of the economy? 'Expenses' are the compensations for the use of labor, machinery, equipment, buildings, land and managerial qualities.

Expenses

Compensation of employees	642
Capital consumption allowance	95
Rents	40
Interest	20
	797

The difference between Corrected Revenues and Expenses equals the sum of Proprietor's Income and Corporate Profits. Thus 'Ownership Income' = Corrected Revenues - Expenses = 946 - 797 = 149.

Then	'Ownership Income'	149
less:	Proprietor's Income	68
equals	Corporate Profits	81

Part of Corporate Profits is paid as Corporate Income Taxes, part is distributed as Dividends, and the rest is kept as Undistributed Corporate Profits, which are retained by the corporations for internal capitalization.

Thus	Corporate Profits	81
less:	Corporate Income Taxes	35
		46
less:	Dividends	6
	Undistributed Corporate Profits	40

The economy can be viewed as one great production enterprise, which has its own income statement.

National Income earned by resource suppliers consists of:

Compensation of Employees	642
Rents	40
Interest	20
Proprietor's Income	68
Corporate Profits	81
	851

Part of this is not received by persons as income but is retained by corporations, thus:

	National Income	851
less:	Undistributed Corporate Profits	40
		811

Also, part has to be paid to the government as Corporate

Income Tax and Social Security Tax. Thus,

		811
less:	Corporate Income Tax	35
		776
Less:	Social Security Tax	46
		730

But this income is enhanced by Transfer payments from persons and from the government before it is received as Personal Income.

Hence,

		730
plus:	Transfer payments	127
equals	Personal Income (PI)	857

Disposable Personal Income is less than this, since they must pay Personal Taxes:

	PI	857
less:	Personal Taxes	116
	Disposable Personal Income (DPI)	741

They save 60 out of it; thus they spend 741 - 60 = 681 on consumption.

• PROBLEM 4-19

Given the following national income accounting data, compute GNP, NNP and NI (all figures are in billions).

- Compensation of employees	195.6
- U.S. exports of goods and services	14.5
- Capital consumption allowance	12.3
- Government purchases of goods and services	60.6
- Indirect business taxes	13.1
- Net private domestic investment	63.4
- Transfer payments	14.2
- U.S. imports of goods and services	17.8
- Personal taxes	43.0
- Personal consumption expenditures	230.9

<u>Solution:</u> Gross National Product (GNP) is the sum of Personal Consumption Expenditures (C), Gross Private Domestic Investment (Ig), Government purchases of goods and services (G) and net exports, equal to the surplus or deficit in the trade balance, or the difference between U.S. exports of goods and services (Ex) and U.S. imports of goods and services (Im). Thus GNP is equal to the total of (net) expenditures: GNP = C + Ig + G + Ex - Im. And Gross Private Domestic Investment equals Net Private Domestic Investment (I) plus the Capital Consumption Allowance (D); so Ig = I + D.

So $\text{GNP} = C + (I + D) + G + (Ex - Im)$

$= 230.9 + (63.4 + 12.3) + 60.6 + (14.5 - 17.8)$

$$= 230.9 + 75.7 + 60.6 - 3.3$$

$$= 363.9$$

Furthermore, Net National Product is Gross National Product less the Capital Consumption allowance:

$$NNP = GNP - D$$

$$= 363.9 - 12.3$$

$$= 351.6$$

National Income equals Net National Product less Indirect Business Taxes (T_{in}).

$$NI = NNP - T_{in}$$

$$= 351.6 - 13.1$$

$$= 338.5$$

• PROBLEM 4-20

The following is a list of national income figures for a given year (amount in billions of dollars):

Gross national product (GNP)	$1,692
Transfer payments	232
Indirect business taxes	163
Personal taxes	193
Capital consumption allowance	180
Undistributed corporate profits	18
Social security contributions	123
Corporate income taxes	65

a) Compute the Net national product (NNP)
b) Determine National income (NI)
c) Determine Personal income (PI)
d) Compute Disposable income

Solution:

	Billions
a) Gross national product (GNP)	$1,692
Capital consumption allowance	-180
Net national product (NNP)	$1,512

Net National product removes the error associated with double counting from gross national product by subtracting the capital consumption allowance or depreciation money spent to replace existing capital rather than to add new capital.

b) Net national product (NNP)	$1,512
Indirect business taxes	-163
National income (NI)	$1,349

National Income translates net national product into income by subtracting the only remaining factor which is not paid out as income, that being indirect business taxes such as sales tax.

c) National income (NI)	$1,349
Social security contributions	-123
Corporate income taxes	- 65
Undistributed corporate profits	- 18
Transfer payments	+232
Personal income (PI)	$1,375

Personal Income subtracts that part of national income which is not paid to the owners of the factors of production, specifically, the income received by corporations, which is distributed among social security contributions, income tax paid by corporations, and undistributed corporate profits or retained earnings.

Personal income also adds transfer payments, which are income received not through a contribution to the product side of national income accounts.

d) Personal income (PI)	$1,375
Personal taxes	-193
Disposable income (DI)	$1,182

Not all of personal income is available to those who receive it, as taxes must be paid. Disposable income, therefore, subtracts personal taxes from personal income to yield the amount of money at individuals' disposal.

• PROBLEM 4-21

Suppose the following data are available for an economy (figures in billions of dollars)

Compensation of Employees	642
Income Taxes	116
Capital Consumption Allowances	95
Income other than Compensation of Employees	209
Indirect Taxes	101
Net Investment	152

Further, it is known that there are no corporations, and all income is paid directly to persons; there are no transfer payments, there is a balanced budget; and government expenditure is exclusively on the provision of services to the economy.

Calculate each of the following:

1. Gross National Product (GNP)
2. Net National Product (NNP)
3. National Income (NI)
4. Personal Income
5. Disposable Personal Income
6. Government Sector Gross Output
7. Private Sector Gross Output
8. Consumption Expenditure
9. Gross Investment

Solution: Start the derivation of the required figures with the calculation of the National Income (NI), which is simply the sum of all the compensations, so

NI = Compensation of Employees + Other Income

= 642 + 209 = 851

In this economy without corporations, the income other than the Compensation of Employees includes proprietor's income, rental income, and interest.

Net National Product (NNP) equals the sum of NI and Indirect Business Taxes, so

NNP = NI + Indirect Taxes

= 851 + 101 = 952

Gross National Product equals the sum of Net National Product and the Capital Consumption Allowances, so

GNP = NNP + Capital Consumption

= 952 + 95 = 1,047

Because there are no corporations (and thus no undistributed corporate profits, or corporate profits taxes); all income is paid directly to persons (no Social Security); there are no transfer payments; and government expenditure is exclusively on the provision of government services. Therefore, Personal Income equals National Income, PI = NI = 851.

Disposable Personal Income equals Personal Income less Personal Income Taxes, so

DPI = PI - Income Taxes

= 851 - 116 = 735

Because there is a balanced budget - i.e. the government expenditures exactly equal taxes - we calculate total taxes first, to determine the Government Sector Gross Output. Total taxes equals the sum of Income Taxes and Indirect Taxes, so

Total Taxes = Income Taxes + Indirect Taxes

= 116 + 101 = 217

Thus, the Government Sector Gross Output = 217.

The Private Sector Gross Output is the difference between the Gross National Product and the Government Sector Gross Output, so

PSGO = GNP - GSGO

= 1,047 - 217 = 830

Gross National Product equals the sum of Consumption Expenditures, Investment, and Government Expenditure (when there are no Exports or Imports, as in this economy)

$$GNP = C + I + G$$

Hence, the Consumption Expenditures are

$$C = GNP - I - G$$

$$= 1,047 - 152 - 217$$

$$= 678$$

The different results are summarized in the following block diagram.

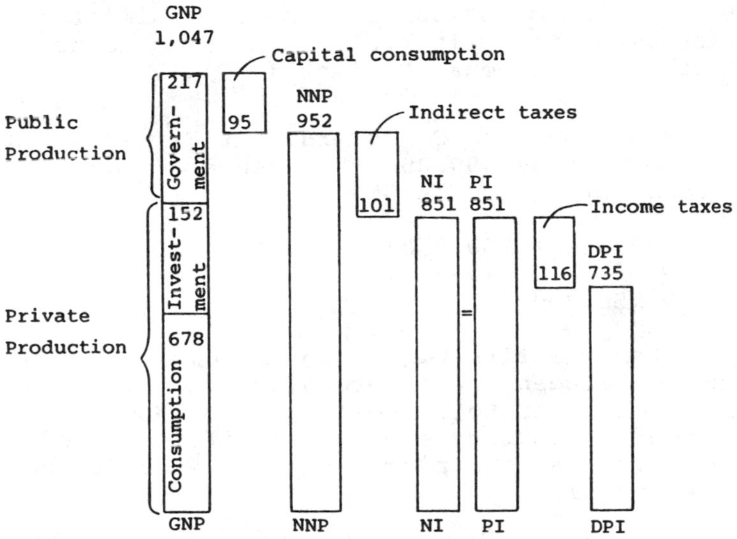

Finally, Gross Investment = Net Investment + Capital Consumption Allowances = 152 + 95 = 247.

• PROBLEM 4-22

There are three firms A, B, and C in the economy, with the following current accounts (figures in millions of dollars):

Firm A

Wages	150,000	Sales to B	200,000
Materials from C	50,000	Sales to C	50,000
Profits paid	?		
Total	?	Total Revenues	250,000

Firm B

Wages	500,000	Sales to C	300,000
Materials from C	200,000	Sales to Consumers	700,000
Materials from A	200,000		
Profits paid	?		
Total	?	Total Revenues	1,000,000

Firm C

Materials from B	300,000	Sales to Consumers	850,000
Materials from A	50,000	Sales to A	50,000
Wages	500,000	Sales to B	200,000
Profits paid	?		
Total	?	Total Revenues	1,100,000

1. What is the total of Final Sales?
2. What is the GNP?
3. Calculate the total of profits paid.

Solution: In this simple economy with no government, no foreign trade and no capital investments, the total of Final Sales equals the total of Sales to consumers; all other sales being intermediate deliveries which do not contribute to the total of Gross National Product (GNP).

Firm A does not sell to Consumers, but Firm B sells 700,000, and Firm C sells 850,000 to Consumers; thus Final Sales equals Consumption equals GNP

$$= 700,000 + 850,000$$

$$= 1,550,000$$

Total profits of a firm (or of an economy) are equal to the difference between total revenues received by the firm (or the economy) and total costs paid out by it. Since profit is regarded as cost by economists, it is included on the cost side of the various firms' current accounts and will equate the two sides.

In firm A's case, total revenues equal total sales (to firms B and C) or 250,000. Total Costs equal Wages plus cost of materials or 200,000. Profit equals total revenue minus total cost or 50,000.

By similar method, Profits of Firms B and C can be calculated at 100,000 and 250,000 respectively. Total Profit for the economy equals the sum of all firms' profits, or 400,000.

• PROBLEM 4-23

Suppose there are three firms in the economy with the following current accounts (figures in millions of dollars):

Firm A

Expenditures		Revenues	
Wages	150,000	Sales to B	200,000
Materials from C	50,000	Sales to C	50,000
Profits	50,000		
Total	$250,000	Total Revenues	$250,000

Firm B

Expenditures		Revenues	
Wages	500,000	Sales to C	300,000
Materials from C	200,000	Sales to consumers	700,000
Materials from A	200,000		
Profits	100,000	Total Revenues	$1,000,000
Total	$1,000,000		

Firm C

Expenditures		Revenues	
Materials from B	300,000	Sales to consumers	850,000
Materials from A	50,000	Sales to A	50,000
Wages	500,000	Sales to B	200,000
Profits	250,000		
Total	$1,100,000	Total Revenues	$1,100,000

What is the total of sales; of consumption; of wages, of profits; of materials used in each of the firms? What is the total GNP?

Solution: This is an economy consisting of three interrelated firms, and consumers.

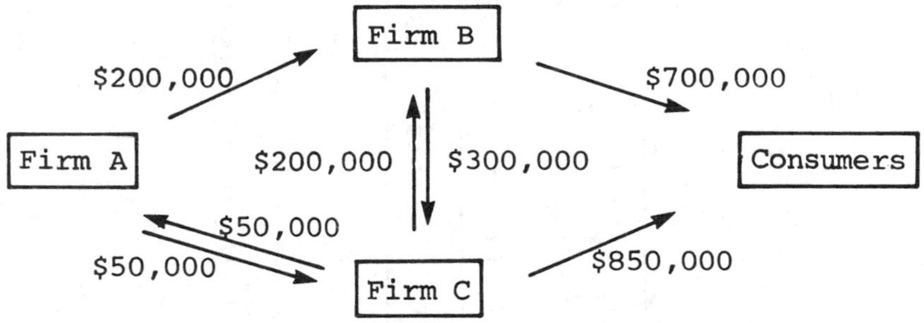

Fig. 1

In the flow diagram in Figure 1 we can easily trace all the deliveries made. This may be tabulated in an input-output table with three sectors: firm A, firm B and firm C, plus the consumers, who deliver the labor and receive wages and profits. This is called an input-output table because the columns of this table tabulate the inputs; for example, in column (2) (firm B) the inputs are $200,000 materials from firm A, and $200,000 materials from firm C, plus $500,000 in wages paid for the labor used, and $100,000 in profits paid for the management and the use of capital. The rows of the input-output table tabulate the outputs; for example, in row (3), firm C produces $50,000 of materials for firm A, $200,000 for firm B, and $850,000 final products for the consumers.

The input-output table, the flow-diagram and the three original business accounts portray the same economy in different ways.

Input-Output Table

		(1) Firm A	(2) Firm B	(3) Firm C	(4) Consumers	(5) Total
(1)	Firm A	0	200,000	50,000	0	250,000
(2)	Firm B	0	0	300,000	700,000	1,000,000
(3)	Firm C	50,000	200,000	0	850,000	1,100,000
(4)	Sub total	50,000	400,000	350,000	0	000,000
(5)	Wages	150,000	500,000	500,000	0	1,150,000
(6)	Profits	50,000	100,000	250,000	0	400,000
(7)	Total	250,000	1,000,000	1,100,000	1,550,000	2,350,000

The total of sales is 250,000 + 1,000,000 + 1,100,000 = $2,350,000 and is found in the bottom right corner cell of the input-output diagram.

The total of consumption may be read also from the input-output table, as the total of column (4): $1,550,000. The total of wages is found as the row total of row (5): $1,150,000; and the total of profits is the row total of row (6): $400,000. Notice that in this economy there are no savings, because all income (= wages + profits) is spent as consumption.

The total of materials used by the different firms is found in row (4); firm A used $50,000 of materials, firm B used $400,000 and firm C used $350,000 of materials.

But what is the total of GNP? Avoid the 'trap of double counting': delete all the intermediate deliveries.

GNP will be equal to the sum of the values added by all firms in the economy. The value added by firm A is its total sale output, minus the materials from firm C, or 250,000 - 50,000. Hence, for the whole economy, it equals total sales minus the total of materials used, or [$2,350,000 - (50,000 + 200,000 + 200,000 + 300,000 + 50,000) = $1,550,000. This equals the sum of the total wages and profits: [$150,000 + $500,000 + $500,000) + ($50,000 + $100,000 + $250,000)] = ($1,150,000 + $400,000) = $1,550,000.

The value added approach measures the difference in value between the firms' inputs and their outputs. Note also that in this simple economy the sum of value added (GNP) is also equal to the value of Final Sales to consumers (there is no government), or $1,550,000, which equals Consumption. Thus GNP = sum of gross value added = total Final Sales.

That National Product = GNP = National Income of this simple economy without government, or foreign economic transactions, may be calculated in 3 different ways.

National Product = GNP =

1. Sales to Final buyers (consumers) =

   $700,000 + $850,000 = $1,550,000

2. Total Sales minus intermediate sales =

   $2,350,000 - $800,000 = $1,550,000

3. Total wages plus profits =

   $1,150,000 + $400,000 = $1,550,000

which is equal to the sum of all values added.

• PROBLEM 4-24

Suppose in an economy the income from the private sector is $1,550 million. The government in this country may choose either to levy a 5% sales tax or to levy an income tax to finance its expenditures. It balances its budget. What is the National Product of this economy, its National Income, and its Disposable Income under both proposed tax systems?

Solution: If there were no government, the total of incomes from the private sector would have represented National Income = National Product = $1,550 million. When the newly-introduced government uses a sales tax to finance its expenditures, the 'real' output will remain the same $1,550 million; but this output, assuming that it will be unchanged, will be sold at higher market prices, which incorporate the sales tax. The private output at market prices will be $1,550 + (0.05 x 1,550) = $1,627.50 million. The total of the taxes, (0.05 x 1,550) = 77.50 million, will be used for government expenditures, adding value to the total output at market prices, so that the National Product will be the sum of the private cutput at market prices and the output provided by the government = 1,627.50 + 77.50 = $1,705 million.

National Income is the sum of income from the private sector and income from the government = 1,550 + 77.50 = $1,627.50 million. Under the sales tax plan there is no income tax; thus, Disposable Income equals National Income = $1,627.50 million.

Under the second proposal, that of financing government expenditures by an income tax, private output at market prices equals the income generated in the private sector = $1,550 million, since there is no sales tax. The 'product' provided by the government is still worth $77.50 million, so the National Product is the sum of the private output and the public output = $1,550,000 + 77.50 = $1,627.50 million. National Income is the sum of the income generated in the private and the public sectors, and remains unchanged under both proposals: = $1,627.50 million. But Disposable Income is now equal to National Income less the income tax of $77.50 million, = $1,627.50 - 77.50 = $1,550 million.

In summary (figures in millions of dollars):

		Plan 1 Sales Tax	Plan 2 Income Tax
1.	Private output at market prices	1,627.50	1,550.00
2.	Less sales tax	77.50	--
3.	Income from private sector	1,550.00	1,550.00
4.	Product = Income from public sector	77.50	77.50
5.	NATIONAL PRODUCT (1 + 4)	1,705.00	1,627.50
6.	NATIONAL INCOME (3 + 4)	1,627.50	1,627.50
7.	Less income tax	--	77.50
8.	DISPOSABLE INCOME	1,627.50	1,550.00

Conclusion: the type of tax used to finance the public sector (government) affects the figures of the National Product, and of Disposable Income, but not the National Income figures (= National Product at Factor Cost).

In both cases the consumers receive $1,550 million in private goods and $77.50 million in public goods; thus the 'real' goods and services are unaffected by the method of finance.

The point of this discussion is that the government gives its output 'free' to the economy, but buys resources on the market. The main totals of the national accounts, when the government finances its operations by a sales tax, are different from what they are when the government uses an income tax.

• PROBLEM 4-25

The Z Government is contemplating a flood-control project in one of its localities. Its economists are studying the various alternatives open to them corresponding to the project's total annual cost as well as its total annual benefit (reduction of damage). The following table enumerates such options.

(1) Plan	(2) Total annual cost of project	(3) Total annual benefit (reduction of damage)
Without protection	$ 0	$ 0
A: Levees	$ 3,000	$ 6,000
B: Small reservoir	$10,000	$16,000
C: Medium reservoir	$18,000	$25,000
D: Large reservoir	$30,000	$32,000

a) Is the flood control project economically justifiable on the basis of given data?
b) What is the optimum size or scope for this project?

Solution: This is an illustration of the benefit-cost analysis which not only indicates whether a public program is worth undertaking but also provides guidance concerning the extent to which a given project should be pursued.

a) An examination of the plans indicates that in each instance total benefits exceed total costs indicating that a flood-control project for this locality is economically justifiable.

b) To answer part b, it is necessary to compute and compare marginal costs and marginal benefits associated with each plan.

The guidelines are as follows

Pursue an activity or a project so long as the marginal benefits exceed the marginal costs. Stop the activity or project as close as possible to the point at which marginal benefits equal marginal costs. In our problem, option C - the medium-sized reservoir - is the best because the marginal benefits it offers are the closest to the marginal cost of a project. Plans A and B are too modest; in both cases marginal benefits exceed marginal costs. Plan D cannot be justified because it entails marginal cost of $12,000 in excess of marginal benefits of $7,000. Plan D therefore involves an overallocation of resources to this flood-control project. Plan C is closest to the optimum; it "pushes" flood control so long as marginal benefits exceed marginal cost.

Benefit-Cost Analysis For a Flood-Control Project

(1) Plan	(2) Total Annual Cost of project	(3) Extra or Marginal cost	(4) Total Annual Benefit	(5) Extra or marginal benefit
Without protection	$ 0		$ 0	
		$ 3,000		$ 6,000
A: Levees	$ 3,000		$ 6,000	
		$ 7,000		$10,000
B: Small reservoir	$10,000		$16,000	
		$ 8,000		$ 9,000
C: Medium reservoir	$18,000		$25,000	
		$12,000		$ 7,000
D: Large reservoir	$30,000		$32,000	

Therefore, the optimum size or scope for this project would be Plan C, the medium reservoir.

• PROBLEM 4-26

In a closed economy, there are four firms. The following diagram shows their sales.

Firm	Sells	To	For
Iron Mine Inc.	Iron Ore	United Steel Co.	$ 100
United Steel Co.	Steel	Acme Automobiles	$ 300
Acme Automobiles	Cars	Honest John's Car Dealership	$ 500
Honest John's Car Dealership	Cars	Consumers	$1000

1. Calculate value added by each firm.
2. Calculate GNP using both the value-added approach and the final goods approach.
3. A value-added tax of 10% is imposed. Calculate each firm's tax payment and tax receipts for the economy.

4. Compare the results of a 10% value-added tax with a 10% sales tax imposed on final goods. Is there a difference in total tax collected?

Solution:

1.) Value added by each firm is the difference between the value of the product they received and the value of the product they sold, as follows:

Firm	Sells	To	For	Value Added
Iron Mine Inc.	Iron Ore	United Steel Co.	$ 100	$ 100
				$ 200
United Steel Co.	Steel	Acme Automobiles	$ 300	
				$ 200
Acme Automobiles	Cars	Honest John's Car Dealership	$ 500	
				$ 500
Honest John's Car Dealership	Cars	Consumers	$1000	
		Total	$1900	$1000

2.) Summing Values added, GNP is calculated at $1000. The only goods sold as final goods are the cars sold by Honest John to consumers, this total also equalling $1000. (The problem of double-counting can be seen in the difference between the total of all sales, $1900, and the total of value added. If care is not taken to eliminate intermediate goods from the computation, GNP is overstated by $900, or 90%)

3.) A value-added tax is simply a tax levied on each firm's value-added:

	Value Added	Tax (@ 10%)
Iron Mine Inc.	$100	$ 10
United Steel Co.	200	20
Acme Automobiles	200	20
Honest John's Car Dealership	$500	50
	Total:	$100

4.) If a 10% sales tax were imposed on final goods, consumers would be taxed on the $1000 worth of cars they bought, for a total of $100. This is the same amount of total tax paid under a value-added tax. It should be noted that the reason for this is that the value-added approach to GNP and the final goods approach are necessarily equal.

REAL VS. MONETARY MEASUREMENT

• **PROBLEM 4-27**

What is the difference between money income and real income?

Solution: Money income is the amount of dollars a person receives. Real income, on the other hand, is the amount of goods and services a person can buy with his money income. Real income represents the "purchasing power" of money wages. It is equal to money income adjusted by the price index.

• PROBLEM 4-28

What are 'withdrawals' from, and 'injections' into the income-expenditure flow?

Solution: A withdrawal is any use of income other than as consumption expenditure on the current output of the domestic economy. For example:

1) expenditures on imports, Im;
2) increase in money balances, } "savings"
3) purchase of government bonds or corporate stocks; and } = S
4) taxes, T.

An injection is any expenditure on domestic output that does not arise directly from consumer income-expenditure decisions.

For example:

1) expenditures in exports, Ex;
2) investments in capital items, I; and
3) government expenditures, G.

• PROBLEM 4-29

Explain the concept of a price index. Why is it important?

Solution: A price index is a device which attempts to measure output in "real terms," as opposed to money terms by taking inflation or deflation into account.

For example, suppose that GNP doubles from year one to year two, the money value of all final goods rising from, say, $1 million to $2 million. However, suppose that the prices of final goods also doubled on average. The "real output" of the economy in year two is given by dividing year two's GNP by an index of year two's prices. The price index is the ratio of year two's prices to year one's prices, i.e., 2 in our example. Thus, real GNP in year two has remained constant at $2,000,000 ÷ 2 = $1,000,000.

The Price Index is important in order to allow for accurate monitoring of economic performance which will lead to the making of correct decisions by economic policymakers.

Suppose, for example, in the year described above, that prices had risen from $1 to $3. Now money GNP has doubled, but real GNP has fallen from $1 million to $666,667,

$(\frac{\$2 \text{ million}}{\$3})$. If GNP were not deflated by the price index, policymakers would be unable to detect the economy's falling performance and would thus be unable to correct it.

• PROBLEM 4-30

What are the two different ways of looking at the index of the general price level?

Solution: 1. The index number of the prices is the weighted average of the individual prices, all taken relative to 100 in the base year, with weights which are proportional to the expenditures on the various goods in the base year;

2. This index number is the cost, in the current year, of the actual basket of goods purchased in the base year, relative to a base-year expenditure of 100. A price index may not cover all prices. The retail price index (CPI = consumer price index) is an index number of prices of consumer goods, with weights corresponding to total household expenditures on these items; the wholesale price index (WPI), covers raw materials, farm products and some manufactures, weighted according to their importance to the whole economy, not simply households; and several stock market price indices (Dow Jones, for example), try to summarize the general level of prices of thousands of corporate stocks.

• PROBLEM 4-31

Explain how inflation and deflation complicate the computation of the gross national product.

Solution: Inflation and deflation complicate the computation of gross national product because GNP is a price-times-quantity figure. The raw data from which the national income accountants estimate GNP are the total sales figures of business firms; these figures embody changes in both the quantity of output and the level of prices. This means that a change in either the quantity of total physical output or the price level will affect the size of GNP. However, it is the quantity of goods produced and distributed to households which affects their standard of living, not the size of the price tags which these goods bear. The hamburger of 1965 which sold for 30 cents would have yielded the same satisfaction as a similar hamburger selling for $1.50 in 1980 will yield. The problem, then, is one of adjusting a price-times-quantity figure so that it will accurately reflect changes in physical output, not changes in prices.

• PROBLEM 4-32

In 1933, the Consumer Price Index was 38.3 (1967 = 100) and Babe Ruth received a salary of $80,000, his highest ever. Near the end of the 1978 baseball season, the Consumer Price

Index hit 200. Using this information, what would Ruth's salary be in 1978?

Solution: To compute a salary for Babe Ruth in 1978, we multiply his 1933 salary by the ratio of the indexes, i.e.

$$\text{Salary}_{1978} = \text{Salary}_{1933} \times \frac{\text{Consumer Price Index(1978)}}{\text{Consumer Price Index(1933)}}$$

$$= 80{,}000 \times \frac{200}{38.8}$$

$$= \$412{,}371.13$$

• PROBLEM 4-33

Given the following figures:

	Year 1	Year 6
Total income	\$400 billion	\$550 billion
Price index	1.00	1.10

find the increase in real income from Year 1 to Year 6.

Solution: First, convert the two income figures to real income by the formula

$$\text{Real Income} = \frac{\text{Total Income}}{\text{Price Index}}$$

For Year 1, Real Income = \$400 billion/1.00 = \$400 billion.
For Year 6, Real Income = \$550 billion/1.10 = \$500 billion.

Increase in real income = \$500 billion - \$400 billion = \$100 billion.

• PROBLEM 4-34

Consider the following hypothetical data:

Year	Annual output	Market Value
1	3 oranges and 2 apples	3 at 10 cents + 2 at 15 cents = 60 cents
2	2 oranges and 3 apples	2 at 10 cents + 3 at 15 cents = 65 cents

In which year is society better off? Why?

Solution: Society is better off in Year 2 than in Year 1 because society values Year 2's output more highly than it does that of Year 1. In other words society is willing to pay more for the collection of goods produced in Year 2, the value of which amounts to 65 cents, than that of goods produced in Year 1, the value of which totals only 60 cents.

• PROBLEM 4-35

Suppose that in the base year, GNP = $1000 billion. Since the base year, money GNP has increased $500 billion while real GNP has increased $250 billion. What is the current price index?

Solution: The price index is used to adjust money GNP for changes in the price level. Specifically, this formula is used:

$$\text{Real GNP} = \frac{\text{Money GNP}}{\text{Price Index}} \times 100$$

or $$\text{Price Index} = \frac{\text{Money GNP}}{\text{Real GNP}} \times 100$$

In the problem, money GNP increases by $500 billion from $1000 billion to $1500 billion, while real GNP increases by $250 billion from $1000 billion to $1250 billion. Substituting these figures into the price index formula yields:

$$\text{Price Index} = \frac{1500 \text{ billion}}{1250 \text{ billion}} \times 100$$

$$= 120.$$

An interpretation of price index = 120 (where base year price index = 100) is that in the period since the base year, the prices of products under consideration have, on the average, risen by 20%.

• PROBLEM 4-36

The following data provides a "real-world" illustration of adjusting GNP for changes in the price level (selected years, in billions of dollars).

(1) Year	(2) Money, or unadjusted GNP	(3) Price level index, percent	(4) Adjusted GNP
1946	$ 209.6	44.06	?
1951	330.2	57.27	?
1958	448.9	66.06	?
1964	635.7	72.71	?
1968	868.5	82.57	?
1972	1,171.5	100.00	?
1974	1,406.9	116.20	?
1975	1,498.9	126.37	?

Determine the adjusted GNP for each year.

Solution: Since the long-run trend has been for the price level to rise, the problem is one of increasing, or inflating, the pre-1972 figures, since the base year is 1972. The upward revision of money GNP to be made acknowledges that prices were lower in years prior to 1972 and, as a result, money GNP figures understated the real output of those years. Also, the rising price level has caused the money GNP figures for the post-1972 years to overstate real output; hence these figures must be reduced, or deflated. Accordingly, the following computations may be arrived at:

(1) Year	Real or adjusted GNP (1972) dollars
1946	\$ 475.7 (= 209.6 ÷ 0.4406)
1951	\$ 576.6 (= 330.2 ÷ 0.5727)
1958	\$ 679.5 (= 448.9 ÷ 0.6606)
1964	\$ 874.3 (= 635.7 ÷ 0.7271)
1968	\$1,051.8 (= 868.5 ÷ 0.8257)
1972	\$1,171.1 (= 1,171.1 ÷ 1.0000)
1974	\$1,210.8 (= 1,406.9 ÷ 1.1620)
1975	\$1,186.1 (= 1,498.9 ÷ 1.2637)

• PROBLEM 4-37

Given below are the money NNP and Price Index (1929 base) for 1929 and 1933:

	Money NNP (billions of current dollars)	Price Index
1929	\$96	100
1933	\$48	75

a) What is the real NNP in 1933 using 1929 as a base?
b) What is the real NNP in 1929 using 1933 as a base?

Solution: a) To find real NNP, divide money NNP by the price index for the year in question, and then multiply the result by 100. For 1933, the price index in terms of 1929 dollars is given as 75.

$$\text{Therefore real NNP} = \frac{\$48}{75} \times 100$$

$$= \$64.$$

b) To find real NNP for 1929 in terms of 1933 dollars, it is necessary to first make 1933 the base; i.e., Price Index (1933) = 100.

To find the price index for 1929, use the following relationship obtained from the Price Indices that held 1929 as a base.

$$\frac{\text{Index (1929)}_{\text{base=1929}}}{\text{Index (1933)}_{\text{base=1929}}} = \frac{\text{Index (1929)}_{\text{base=1933}}}{\text{Index (1933)}_{\text{base=1933}}}$$

DATE:

TOPIC:

230.9
63.4
60.6
354.9
− 3.3
351.6
+ 12.3
363.9
363.3
− 12.3
351.6
+ 13.1
338.5
− 13.1
362.7
− 13
349.7

14.5
− 17.8
−3.3

17.8
14.5
3.3

+ 95
889
209
1098
1041

1692
− 182
1510 = NNP
− 163
1347 = NI
− 123
936
− 65
1191
− 8
1193
+ 232
1375
− 193
1183

DATE: November 17, 1995

TOPIC: Homework number Eight

Elizabeth Elson

GDP Expenditure method

(8) (A) ~~[illegible]~~ 245 + 33 + 72 + (11 − 0)

33
72

350 + 11 = $361

C = 245
I = 33
27
G = 72
X − M = 11

388

37
~~38~~ 360
339
49

~~13 + 14 + 56 + 223 =~~ ✓

223 = wages
13 = interest
14 = rent
33 = Prop. income
~~[illegible]~~
56 = Corp. profit

223
13
14
33
339

339 + 18 + 4 = 361
27
388

W + I + R + P +

+ corp. dividends
+ corp. income tax
+ undistributed corp. profits

National Income

223
13
14
33
283
16
19
21
56

339 = NI

339
339 NI

durable − more

Leading indicator — happens 6/7 mnths. b4 all economy. there are 11 leading indicators.

(1) 642

$$\frac{100}{75} = \frac{x}{100}$$

$$x = 133\ 1/3$$

Price Index (1929) = 133 1/3; now compute the real NNP by using the same formula as in part a).

$$\text{Real NNP} = \frac{\$96}{133\ 1/3} \times 100$$

$$= \$72.$$

• PROBLEM 4-38

Assume our economy produces only one good, product X, and that its quantities and prices over time are given in the following table:

Year	(1) Units of Output	(2) Price of X
1	5	$ 10
2	7	20
3	8	25
4	10	30
5	11	28

a) Compute the price index in percent using Year 1 as the base year; i.e., (Year 1 = 100).
b) Compute the unadjusted, or money GNP.
c) Compute the adjusted, or real GNP.

Solution: a) The formula for computing the price index is given by:

$$\text{Price index} = \frac{\text{Price in any given year}}{\text{Price in base year}} \times 100$$

Multiply the price comparison by 100 in order to express it as a percentage. Using Year 2 as the given year yields

$$\text{Price index} = \frac{\$20}{\$10} \times 100 = 200 \text{ percent}$$

For Year 3,

$$\text{Price index} = \frac{\$25}{\$10} \times 100 = 250 \text{ percent}$$

For Year 4,

$$\text{Price index} = \frac{\$30}{\$10} \times 100 = 300 \text{ percent}$$

And for Year 5,

$$\text{Price index} = \frac{\$28}{\$10} \times 100 = 280 \text{ percent.}$$

These index numbers indicate that the price of product X in Year 2 was 200 percent of what it was in Year 1; in Year 3, it was 250 percent of Year 1's price and in Years 4 and 5, the prices were 300 and 280 percent respectively.
b) To arrive at the unadjusted, or money GNP, multiply the units of output by the corresponding prices. Thus:

Year 1	5 × $10	=	$ 50
2	7 × $20	=	$140
3	8 × $25	=	$200
4	10 × $30	=	$300
5	11 × $28	=	$308

c) Then money GNP greatly overstates the increases in real output occuring in those four years. That is, the monetary measure of production (money GNP) does not accurately reflect the actual changes which have occurred in physical output (real GNP). Considerable portions of the sharp increases in money GNP in Years 2, 3, 4 and 5 are due to drastic inflation as shown in the price column -- except in Year 5, where the unit price declines but where its money GNP still increases due to an increase in physical output.

It is therefore necessary to use the computed index numbers to deflate the inflated money GNP figures in order to arrive at the real GNP figures. This can be computed as follows:

$$\text{Adjusted, or real GNP} = \frac{\text{Unadjusted, or money, GNP}}{\text{Price index in decimals}}$$

Thus,

Year 1 $\frac{\$50}{1.00} = \$50$ = Real GNP

Year 2 $\frac{\$140}{2.00} = \$70$ = Real GNP

Year 3 $\frac{\$200}{2.50} = \$80$ = Real GNP

Year 4 $\frac{\$300}{3.00} = \$100$ = Real GNP

Year 5 $\frac{\$308}{2.80} = \$110$ = Real GNP

These real GNP figures measure the value of total output in Years 1, 2, 3, 4, and 5 as if the price of product X had been constant at $10 throughout the five-year period. Real GNP thus shows the market value of each year's output measured in terms of constant dollars; that is, dollars which have the same value, or purchasing power, as in the base year.

Real GNP is clearly superior to money GNP as an indicator of the economy's productive performance over a given period of time since it measures the real value of production and not its artificially inflated value.

Suppose an economy produces 5 different goods, A, B, C, D, and E, which have different prices Given data for two different years:

Goods	Year 1 quantity	Year 1 price	Year 2 quantity	Year 2 price
A	85	$1.25	86	$1.50
B	84	0.96	50	1.30
C	225	5.60	227	5.50
D	113	3.58	150	3.15
E	34	2.28	66	2.35

it is necessary to calculate:

1) The value of output in Year 1, in current dollars.
2) The value of output in Year 2, in current dollars.
3) The percentage change in current dollars from Year 1 to Year 2.
4) The price index for Year 2 to base Year 1.
5) The real output in Year 2, expressed in Year 1 dollars.
6) The price index for Year 1 to base Year 2.
7) The real output in Year 1, expressed in Year 2 dollars.
8) The percentage change in real output, in terms of Year 1 dollars, from Year 1 to Year 2.
9) The percentage change in real output, in terms of Year 2 dollars, from Year 1 to Year 2.

And, give a general evaluation of the economy's performance.

Solution: 1,2) The value of output is the sum of the products of the prices times the quantities of the different products, so $Y = \sum_{i=A,B,C,D,E} p_i q_i$ ($\sum$ is the sum sign); thus we calculate

Goods	Year 1 quantity (1)	Year 1 price (2)	(3)=(1)×(2)	Year 2 quantity (4)	Year 2 price (5)	(6)=(4)×(5)
A	85	$1.25	$ 106.25	86	$1.50	$ 129.00
B	84	0.96	80.64	50	1.30	65.00
C	225	5.60	1,260.00	227	5.50	1,248.50
D	113	3.58	404.54	150	3.15	472.50
E	34	2.28	77.52	66	2.35	155.10
Y(sum)			$1,742.06			$2,070.10

3) GNP in current dollars has grown from \$1,742.06 to \$2,070.10, an increase of \$328.04, or

$$\frac{328.04}{1,742.06} \times 100 = 18.83\%$$

4) The price index for Year 2 to base Year 1 is the value of output in Year 2, calculated by using the quantities of Year (1) as 'weights', divided by the value of output of Year 1, as previously calculated. Thus the price index is $\frac{\sum p_i^2 q_i^1}{\sum p_i^1 q_i^1} \times 100$, where p_i^2 denotes the prices of Year 2, and p_i^1, q_i^1 the prices and quantities of Year 1.

Calculate:

Goods	(7) = (5) × (1) = $p_i^2 q_i^1$
A	\$1.50 × 85 = \$ 127.50
B	109.20
C	1,237.50
D	355.95
E	79.90
$\sum p_i^2 q_i^1$ =	\$1,910.05

Thus the price index for Year 2 to base Year 1 is

$$\frac{\sum p_i^2 q_i^1}{\sum p_i^1 q_i^1} \times 100 = \frac{1,910.05}{1,742.06} \times 100 = 109.64$$

Notice inflation of 9.64% from Year 1 to Year 2.

5) The real output in Year 2, expressed in Year 1 dollars, is the value of output in **Year 2** in current dollars divided by the price index for Year 2 just calculated:

$$Y_2 = \frac{\sum p_i^2 q_i^2}{\frac{\sum p_i^2 q_i^1}{\sum p_i^1 q_i^1}} = \frac{2,070.10}{1.0964} = \$1,888.09$$

6) Now calculate the price index for Year 1 to base Year 2. The quantities of Year (2) serve here as 'weights'. The price index is

$$\frac{\sum p_i^1 q_i^2}{\sum p_i^2 q_i^2}$$

Calculate:

Goods	$(8) = (2) \times (4) = p_i^1 q_i^2$
A	$1.25 × 86 = $ 107.50
B	48.00
C	1,271.20
D	537.00
E	150.48
$\sum p_i^1 q_i^2 =$	$2,114.18

Thus the price index for Year 1, expressed in Year 2 dollars is

$$\frac{\sum p_i^1 q_i^2}{\sum p_i^2 q_i^2} \times 100 = \frac{2,114.18}{2,070.10} \times 100 = 102.13$$

and we notice a deflation (sic.) of 2.13% from Year 1 to Year 2 (Year 2 = 100).

7) The real output in Year 1, expressed in Year 2 dollars, is the value of output in Year 1 in current dollars, divided by the price index for Year 1, just calculated:

$$Y_1 = \frac{\sum p_i^1 q_i^1}{\frac{\sum p_i^1 q_i^2}{\sum p_i^2 q_i^2}} = \frac{1,742.06}{1.0213} = \$1,705.72$$

8) Real output in Year 1 in Year 1 dollars = $1,742.06
Real output in Year 2 in Year 1 dollars = $1,888.09

output has increased by $1,888.09 - 1,742.06 = $146.03. Output has grown by $\frac{146.03}{1742.06} \times 100 = 8.38\%$ from Year 1 to Year 2, expressed in year one dollars.

9) Thus real output has grown by $2,070.10 - 1,705.72 = $364.38, or $\frac{364.38}{2070.10} \times 100 = 17.60\%$, when measured in Year 2 dollars.

Although there is some doubt about the occurrence of inflation, from these results it may be safely concluded that the real output of this economy has been increased, and by 8.38% when measured in Year 1 dollars (a rather conservative estimate); by 17.60% when measured in Year 2 dollars. The discrepancies in the results when using differently calculated price indices should serve as a warning against using the aggregates, in particular those of real output, unthinkingly.

LIMITATIONS

• PROBLEM 4-40

What are some reasons why the correlation between real GNP and social welfare is weak?

Solution: GNP might understate or overstate real output, and more GNP will not necessarily make society better off.

1. Certain productive transactions do not appear in the market; and GNP, as a measure of the market value of output, does not include such transactions as the productive services of the housewife or do-it-yourself production. Thus GNP will be understated. However, the portion of the farmer's output which he consumes himself, will be estimated and included in GNP.

2. GNP does not value leisure, although it may add considerably to our well-being, nor does it value the satisfaction derived from one's work, or dissatisfaction caused by alienation felt in factories and offices; it may overstate our welfare.

3. GNP does not measure quality improvements, although they contribute to our well-being; it therefore understates our welfare.

4. GNP reflects only the size of output, and does not tell us anything about the composition of the output, or its distribution, although these two aspects influence the state of social well-being tremendously.

5. GNP does not measure the cost of dirty air and water, automobile junkyards, congestion, noise, and other forms of environmental pollution. Thus current GNP will overstate social welfare, at a cost to future generations.

6. GNP measures the size of total output; it may therefore conceal the changes in the standard of living of individual households in the economy. Even GNP divided by total population (i.e. the per capita output), although a better measure, does not say anything about the income distribution.

• PROBLEM 4-41

Why is the change in the quantity index from Year 1 to Year 2, using as weights the prices of Year 1, not always equal to the change in the quantity index, using as weights the prices of Year 2? Explain this with the help of the conventional price line - indifference curve diagram.

Solution: We use the following diagram for our explanation, in which good X_1 is measured on the abscissa and good X_2 on the ordinate.

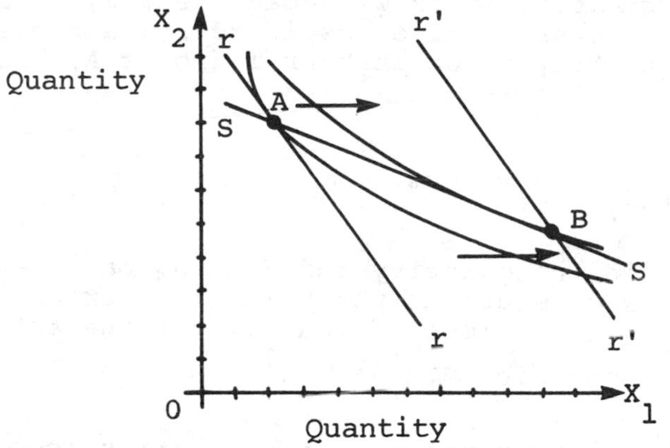

In Year 1 the consumers buy the combination of quantities of X_1 and X_2 represented by point A, and in Year 2 the combination represented by point B. In Year 2 they buy more of good X_1 and less of good X_2, than in Year 1. The slope of the price lines rr and r'r' gives the relative prices of goods X_1 and X_2 in Year 1: X_1 is then more expensive than good X_2, because 1 unit of good X_1 can buy more units of good X_2. The slope of price line s gives the relative prices of goods X_1 and X_2 in Year 2: then X_2 is more expensive than good X_1, because 1 unit of good X_2 can buy more units of good X_1. When the prices of Year 2 are used as weights in the calculation of the quantity index, it can be seen that there is no change in the total value of the quantity index; because the total value of the basket of goods bought at point A equals the total value of the basket of goods bought at point B, since both points lie on the same price - (income-) line. To clarify this further, suppose that the absolute price of good X_1 is P_1, and that of good X_2 is P_2; then the total amount spent in point B is $P_1X_1 + P_2X_2 = R$. After rearranging we get

$$X_2 = \frac{R}{P_2} - \frac{P_1X_1^2}{P_2}$$

as representation of the priceline ss, where $-\frac{P_1}{P_2}$ is the slope of this line. When the quantity of X_1 is lower, the quantity of X_2 is higher and vice versa, since R and P_1 and P_2 are fixed. Point A lies on the same line, thus also in point A, $P_1X_1^1 + P_2X_2^1 = R$, where accents have been added to the quantities in order to indicate that they are different from those in point B.

$$\frac{P_1X_1 + P_2X_2}{P_1X_1 + P_2X_2} = \frac{R}{R} = 100\%$$

represents the quantity index with base Year 2, thus for point B; but if the same prices as in Year 2 are used to calculate the quantity index in Year 1 (point A) they yield again

$$\frac{P_1X_1^1 + P_2X_2^1}{P_1X_1 + P_2X_2} = \frac{R}{R} = 100\%.$$

Thus the change in the quantity index using base Year 2 prices is nil. Now return to the pricelines rr and r'r'. In point A, using the prices of Year 1, for the total amount spent in Year 1 there is $P_1^1X_1^1 + P_2^1X_2^1 = Q$. And

$$\frac{P_1^1X_1^1 + P_2^1X_2^1}{P_1^1X_1^1 + P_2^1X_2^1} = \frac{Q}{Q} \equiv 100\%$$ represents the quantity index with

base Year 1. However, proceeding to point B in Year 2, and using the prices of Year 1, one jumps to a different priceline, although it has the same slope $P_1^1X_1 + P_2^1X_2 = Q^1$. The income spent on goods X_1 and X_2 in point B is larger than in point A, $Q^1 > Q$. The quantity index, using the prices of Year 1, measures now

$$\frac{P_1^1X_1 + P_2^1X_2}{P_1^1X_1^1 + P_2^1X_2^1} = \frac{Q^1}{Q} > 1,$$

thus larger than 100%.

It may be concluded that the change in the value of the quantity index measured with the prices of Year 1 as weights, is unequal to the change in the value of the quantity index measured with the prices of Year 2 as weights.

SHORT ANSWER QUESTIONS FOR REVIEW

Answer
To be covered when testing yourself

Choose the correct answer.

1. National income or product means: (a) the amount of money received by the people over an interval of time (b) the money measure of the overall flow of final goods and services over an interval of time (c) the total amount of money (d) the income of the government over an interval of time (e) the net value of tangible goods in existence at a point in time — b

2. Net investment is (a) the difference between capital consumption allowance and indirect business taxes (b) positive when net private domestic investment is zero (c) the difference between depreciation and gross private domestic investment (d) negative when the economy is static — c

3. Personal income equals disposable income plus: (a) personal income taxes (b) personal savings (c) dividend payments (d) payroll taxes (e) transfer payments — a

4. Transfer payments do not include (a) social security payments (b) payments to farmers, under certain agricultural programs (c) aid to the handicapped (d) government expenditures on education and manpower — d

5. Not included in "investment" for an economy is: (a) the purchase of a new motor truck by a firm (b) the installment of new machinery in a factory (c) the addition of a new wing to a factory (d) an increase in inventories (e) the purchase of a factory previously used for another purpose — c

6. GNP is not a very good measure of economic welfare because: (a) it is a monetary measure (b) it takes into account pollution and abatement services (c) the expenditures and income approaches to GNP yield different results because the units of measurement are not the same (d) it does not include nonmonetized activities — d

7. An important difference between personal income and personal disposable income consists of: (a) dividends (b) consumption expenditures (c) personal savings (d) investment income (e) personal income taxes — e

8. When a country's level of income rises it is most likely that: (a) the import of goods

Answer

To be covered when testing yourself

and services will remain constant (b) there is an increased propensity to import (c) export earning is falling (d) the economy's stock of capital goods is declining — b

9. The general test for including any item in national income is whether it is: (a) a return to labor (b) representative of productive income rather than profit (c) spent for economic goods but not for intangible services (d) a current return for one of the productive factors (e) none of the above — d

10. NNP is (a) GNP adjusted for depreciation charges (b) national income plus corporate income taxes (c) NI minus indirect business taxes (d) NI plus personal income and disposable income (e) NI minus transfer payments — a

11. When the domestic economy is experiencing inflation one of the following is true: (a) investors are making wise decisions about investment opportunities (b) relative prices are moving strictly downwards (c) exports to foreign nations have risen more rapidly than imports (d) the purchasing power of the dollar has risen (e) people on fixed income are seriously affected — e

12. An economy's capital stock must decline if: (a) consumption exceeds investment (b) net investment is zero (c) government expenditures for goods and services are greater than tax collections (d) depreciation is greater than net investment (e) depreciation is greater than gross investment — e

13. Real GNP and Nominal GNP are similar in the sense that: (a) Real GNP and Nominal GNP are both adjusted for changes in the price level (b) they refer to all economic activities, monetized and nonmonetized (c) they determine the market value of all monetized goods and services produced in an economy, usually for a year (d) they are good measures of the distribution of resources in the world economy — c

14. The sum of all stages value-added in the production of some good: (a) is not a meaningful concept at all (b) bears no relationship to final selling price of that good (c) is greater than final selling price of that good (d) is less than final selling price of that good (e)

SHORT ANSWER QUESTIONS FOR REVIEW

	Answer (To be covered when testing yourself)
is equal to final selling price of that good	e
15. The economy is: (a) a growing economy because net private domestic investment is positive (b) experiencing inflation because disposable income exceeds personal income (c) in a depression because personal income exceeds disposable income (d) a declining economy because net private domestic investment is negative	d

Fill in the blanks.

16. ______________ measures the market value or cost of the resources used in the production of the GNP.	National Income
17. The calculation of NNP does not include ______ ______________.	depreciation allowances
18. If money GNP rises, ________________ GNP may either rise or fall.	real
19. That part of corporate profits included in ______________ is equal to total corporate profits minus both corporate taxes and undistributed profits.	Disposable Income
20. Personal income is most likely to exceed national income during a period of ____________ or depression.	recession
21. GNP per capita in __________ dollars can be used as a true measure of the standard of living because it ignores inflation and deflation.	constant
22. _______________ refers to net investment plus replacement investment.	gross investment
23. Gross national product (GNP) is an inferior measure of a nation's product because it counts _________________.	depreciation
24. The ______________ of national product would result from adding together total output of iron ore and total output of iron.	double counting
25. The concept of _______________ refers to total investment less the amount of investment goods used up in accomplishing the year's production.	net domestic investment
26. "Capital formation" of an economy means ______.	investment

	Answer
# SHORT ANSWER QUESTIONS FOR REVIEW	To be covered when testing yourself
27. In a declining economy, __________ exceeds gross investment.	depreciation
28. Interest on the federal debt is an example of a __________ that does not enter into the computation of net national product.	transfer payment
29. The total income earned in any given year by resource suppliers is measured by __________.	National Income
30. If corporations paid all their profits in the form of dividends, the immediate impact on the national-income accounts would be an increase in __________.	personal income
Determine whether the following statements are true or false.	
31. Interest paid by business firms represents a cost of producing the national output and is therefore included in NNP.	True
32. GNP is the sum total of all wages, plus rents, plus interest, minus profits.	False
33. If over some period of time prices have doubled and money income has doubled, then real income is unchanged.	True
34. If indirect business taxes are subtracted from net national product the result is national income.	True
35. Because personal income usually shows much the same percentage moves as disposable income, it is a satisfactory indicator of disposable income.	True
36. For an economy that consumed more than it produced in a given year, the drop in inventories should be added to GNP in measuring current production.	False
37. Except for government service and international transactions, GNP is equal to the sum of the sales revenues of all business enterprises.	False
38. A good indicator of economic growth is the relationship between gross investment and depreciation.	True
39. In order to calculate DI, given NNP, one of the things we must do is subtract transfer payments from NNP.	False

SHORT ANSWER QUESTIONS FOR REVIEW

		Answer To be covered when testing yourself
40.	Personal income is a measure of income earned.	False
41.	It is possible for net private investment to be negative.	True
42.	If government and corporations could be ignored, then DI and NNP would be identical.	True
43.	Social Security payments and Veterans' payments are productive financial transactions that should be included in GNP calculations.	False
44.	Goods and services which are completely processed are called intermediate goods.	False
45.	The total sales of Chrysler cars depend on the level of disposable income to a greater extent than on net national product.	True

CHAPTER 5

CONSUMPTION, SAVINGS, AND INVESTMENT

Basic Attacks and Strategies for Solving Problems in this Chapter. See pages 134 to 174 for step-by-step solutions to problems.

A key variable in Keynesian macroeconomic theory is aggregate demand—total planned spending by all sectors of the economy. Aggregate demand determines firms' production plans and, consequently, the level of prices and employment. In Keynesian theory, aggregate demand is composed of four components: consumption, investment, government spending, and net exports. Each category of spending has unique determinants and is analyzed separately. This chapter looks at consumption and investment spending.

The determinants of consumption at both the household and national levels are similar. Key factors influencing the level of consumption are disposable income (Y_d), tastes, wealth, taxes, and expectations. The consumption function (or "propensity-to-consume" schedule) is a schedule showing the relationship between disposable income and consumption.

Although in principle the consumption function could have any functional form, in elementary theory it is common to represent it using a linear equation: $C = mY_d + B$. The parameter B represents autonomous consumption, the amount of consumption spending if income were zero. Obviously, consumers cannot continue to spend over long periods of time without income. A positive value for B should be interpreted to represent temporary spending financed by previous savings, perhaps during an emergency caused by illness or being on strike. The parameter m represents the increase in consumption resulting from a one dollar increase in income. This parameter is known as the marginal propensity to consume ($m = \Delta C / \Delta Y_d$), and is assumed to be between 0 and 1 in value.

The figure shows the graph of a linear consumption function. The parameter B is the vertical axis intercept of the function. The parameter m measures the slope of the function. A useful device is the 45° line which bisects the quadrant. Any point on the 45° line represents equal values for the variables measured along the horizontal and vertical axes. The intersection of the consumption function and the 45° line is called the break-even point. Here $C = Y_d$. The vertical distance from the consumption function to the 45° line measures the amount of saving. To the right of the break-even point saving is positive. To the left, saving is negative. Negative saving can be called dissaving.

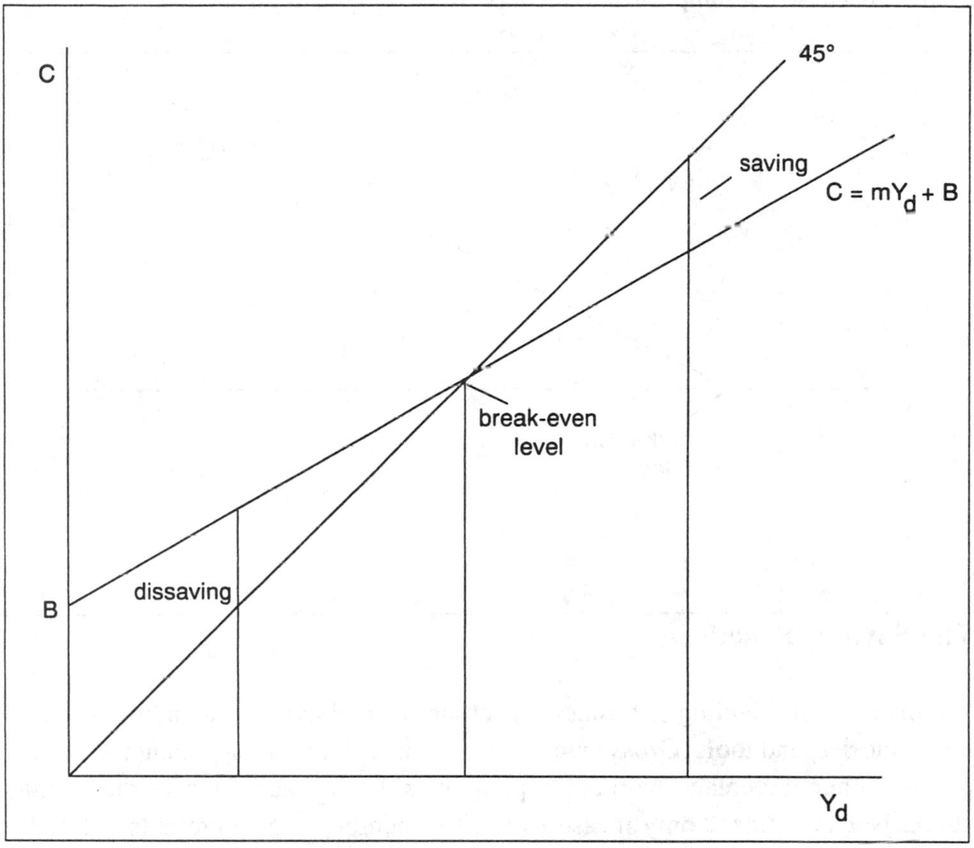

The Consumption Function

A related concept is the savings function (or "propensity-to-save" schedule). By definition, any money not consumed is saved. Therefore, $S = Y_d - C$. Substituting in the consumption function, $S = Y_d - mY_d - B$. Factoring, $S = (1 - m)Y_d - B$. The parameter $(1 - m)$ is called the marginal propensity to save $((1 - m) = \Delta S/\Delta Y_d)$. Similarly to the case of consumption, the marginal propensity-to-save represents the increase in savings resulting from a one dollar increase in income. Note that the sum of the marginal propensity to consume and marginal propensity to save must equal 1, because an additional dollar of income can only lead to either more consumption or savings. The determinants of savings must be the same as the determinants of consumption.

The graph of the savings function is shown on the accompanying figure. The parameter $-B$ is the vertical axis intercept. The parameter $1 - m$ is the slope of the function. The intersection of the function and the horizontal axis corresponds to the break-even point.

The average propensity to consume is the proportion of income consumed (C/Y_d). The average propensity to save is the proportion of income saved (S/Y_d). The sum of the average propensity to consume and the average propensity to save must equal 1, because consumption and savings are the only uses for income.

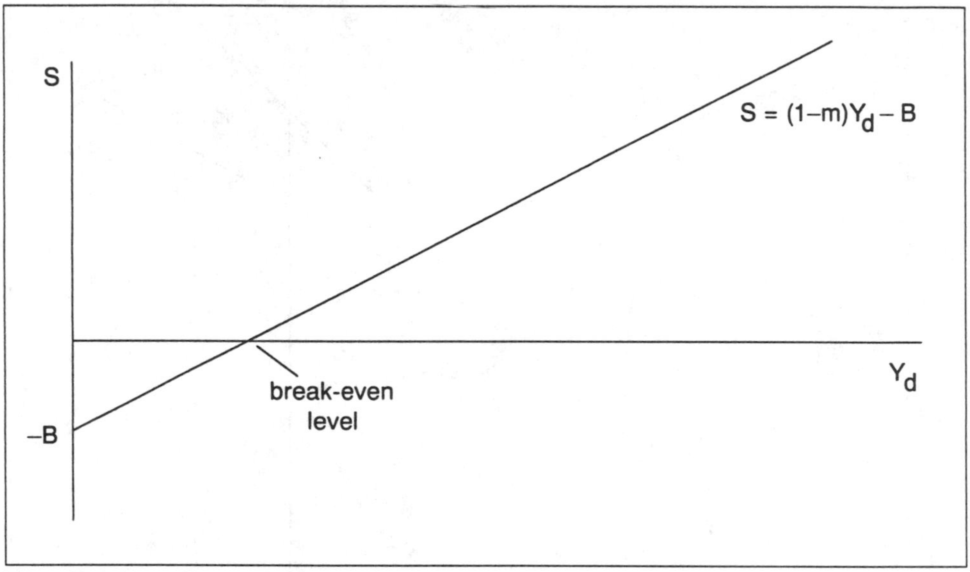

The Savings Function

Investment spending is business spending for real capital, including machinery, factories, and tools. Gross investment is a measure of all spending for capital goods, either to replace wornout capital or make net additions to the capital stock. Net investment only measures capital spending that represents net additions to the capital stock. The category of Gross Private Domestic Investment in the National Income Accounts also includes consumer spending on new housing and unplanned changes in business inventories.

The chief determinants of investment include the rate of interest, expectations about future profitability and sales, technological change, the cost of capital, and taxes.

It is common practice to graph the level of investment (I) against the rate of interest (i). The interest rate measures the opportunity cost of investment funds. The lower the interest rate, the more investment projects will become viable. Changes in the other factors mentioned cause shifts in the curve. Events causing investment to appear more profitable (more optimistic expectations regarding the economy, reduced taxes and capital costs, technological breakthroughs) shift the curve to the right. Events causing investment to appear less profitable (the opposite of those mentioned earlier) shift the curve to the left.

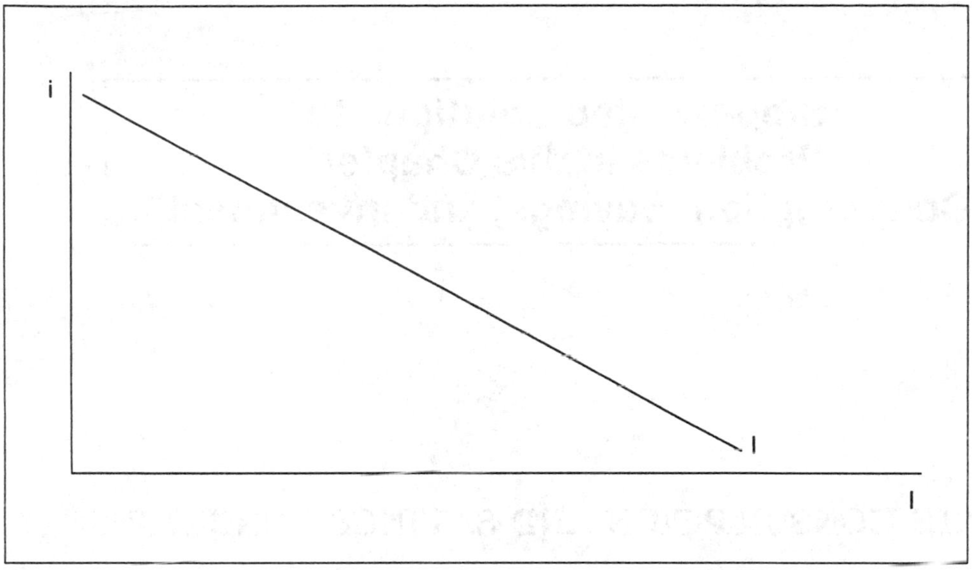

The Investment Function

Investment spending is one of the flashpoints in the debate between Keynesian and classical economists. To Keynesians, investment is a highly volatile form of spending. This is because future expectations regarding profitability and sales is particularly influential in determining the level of investment, and expectations are easily subject to change. Since this major type of spending is volatile, aggregate demand and the economy will be subject to considerable instability.

Classical economists see the interest rate as exerting a stronger influence on investment. This is important because it helps preserve the equality between savings and investment. Macroeconomic equilibrium requires that the amount saved (a leakage from the circular flow) be offset by the amount invested (an injection to the circular flow). If savings rises, this will put downward pressure on interest rates and stimulate additional investment. If savings falls, this will put upward pressure on interest rates and reduce investment. Assuming this process always works smoothly, the economy is likely to be relatively stable (The attainment of full employment requires more explanation, and will be discussed in a later chapter.).

Step-by-Step Solutions to Problems in this Chapter, "Consumption, Savings, and Investment"

THE CONSUMPTION AND SAVINGS FUNCTIONS

• PROBLEM 5-1

What is the consumption function?

Solution: The consumption function, also known as the "propensity-to-consume schedule", traces out the relationship between different income levels and the amount of money that will be spent on consumption at each of these income levels for some specific point in time. Consumption functions may be graphed for individuals, where consumption expenditures are generally plotted against possible levels of the individual's disposable income (gross income minus taxes). Consumption functions may also be aggregated to the community or even the national level. In determining the national consumption function, the National Income Accounting categories of consumption and disposable income are generally used.

Mathematically, the simple linear consumption function takes the form:

$$C = mY_d + B$$

where C is consumption, m is the marginal propensity to consume, Y_d is disposable income and B is the level of consumption when no income is earned. This mathematical formula is a shorthand way of describing people's consumption habits. That is, when no income is earned ($Y_d = 0$) people will borrow, or dissave, to consume some minimal amount (C = B).

As income increases from this point, people will consume only part of their increased earnings and devote the rest to saving more (or dissaving less).

Graphically, the simple linear consumption function appears as shown in Figure 1.

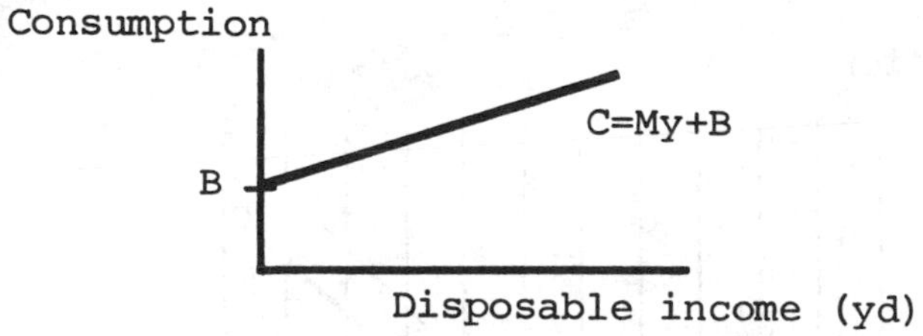

Fig. 1

Its slope is "m", the marginal propensity to consume (MPC), and its vertical axis intercept is B, "autonomous consumption".

• **PROBLEM 5-2**

What is the significance of the 45° line that is often included in the consumption function diagram?

Fig.

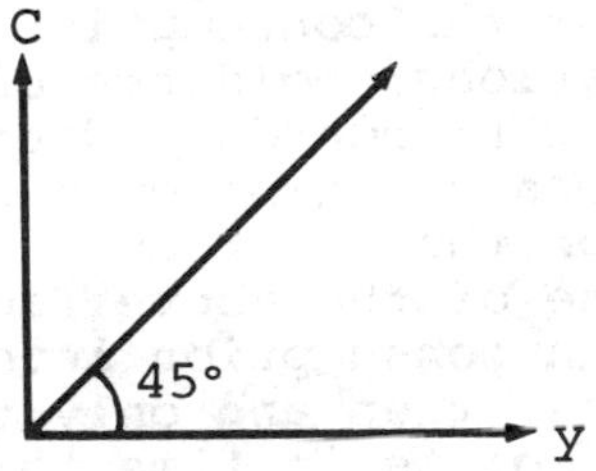

Solution: The 45° line, as shown in the figure, traces out the only points in the entire diagram where the quantity being measured on the vertical axis is exactly equal to the quantity being measured on the horizontal axis. In the consumption function diagram, consumption is measured on the vertical axis and income is measured on the horizontal axis. Here, the significance of the 45° line is that it indicates the points where consumption is exactly equal to income. Wherever a given consumption function crosses this line, income is equal to consumption at this income level, and so saving is equal to zero.

• **PROBLEM 5-3**

A. A. Wingit, a noted macroeconomist, has derived the community consumption function C, shown in the figure, estimated by using National Income Accounts data for 1955 through 1975. What assumptions did Prof. Wingit make in formulating his function about the effects on consumption of factors other than income?

Solution: A consumption function traces out the relationship between potential levels of income and the corresponding amounts that will be allotted to consumption from these income levels for some specific moment in time. There are

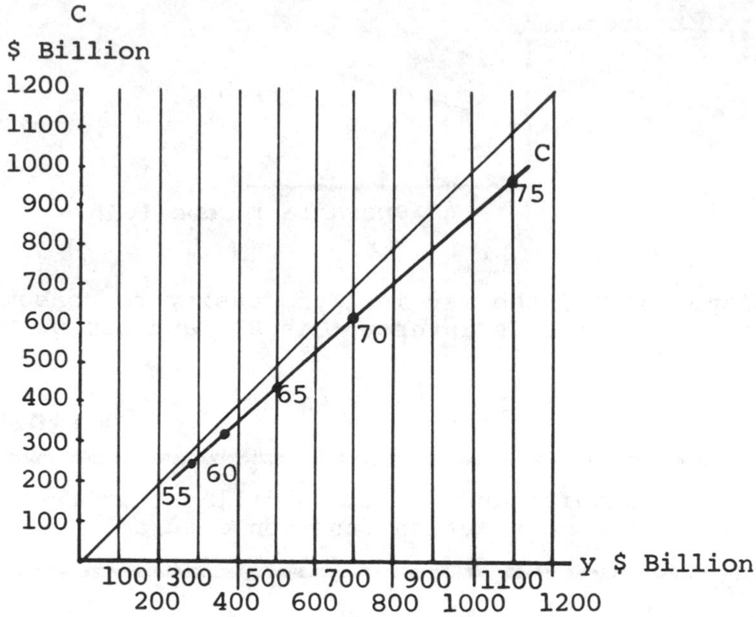

several determinants of the consumption function, including such things as expectations, holdings of assets, credit availability and living standards. When the economist is attempting to estimate a consumption function, he can observe only one point on the function at any given moment. If he assumes that none of the above factors have changed and that any changes in consumption levels are due strictly to income level changes, then and only then can he use data points from different points in time to estimate his function. For example, in 1975, consumption in the U.S. was \$973.2 billion while disposable income was \$1,080.9 billion. If the economist assumes that nothing else has changed between 1975 and 1976, then the data points C = \$1079.7 and Y_C = 1181.7 can be used to help him draw the function. This is precisely what has been done in the function given in the question. Prof. Wingit has assumed that time has not affected any of the non-income factors underlying the consumption function from 1955 to 1975.

• PROBLEM 5-4

What is the primary factor affecting the level of consumption? How can the simple consumption function be represented algebraically? Show what role the marginal propensity to consume plays in a simple linear consumption function.

Solution: The most important determinant of consumer spending, C, is disposable income = personal income - personal taxes $\equiv$ Y - T. Therefore the consumption schedule may be represented as follows:

$$C = f(Y - T) + \overline{C}$$

where the first term on the right-hand side is dependent

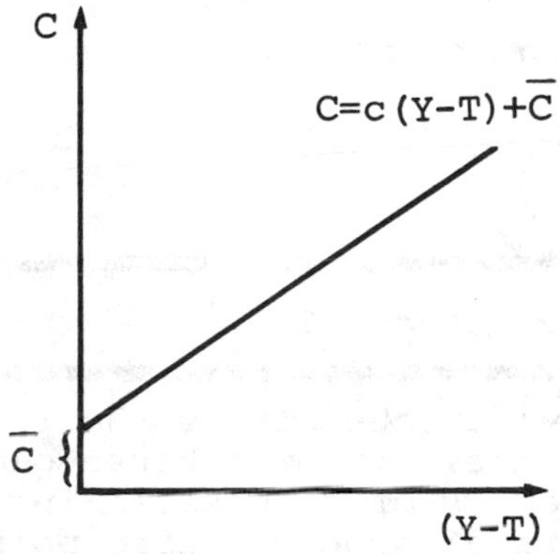

on disposable income, and $\overline{C}$ - autonomous consumption - is independent of disposable income.

It is convenient to approximate this consumption schedule linearly:

$$C = c(Y - T) + \overline{C} .$$

The coefficient C is the marginal propensity to consume out of disposable income, (Y - T). The linear relationship can be presented by a straight line in a graph, as shown.

Suppose taxes are fixed (lump sum taxes). Then a change in consumption caused by a change in personal income, Y, can be presented as

$$\Delta C = c\Delta Y, \text{ because}$$

$\Delta\overline{T} = o$, and $\Delta\overline{C} = 0$.

But then $c = \frac{\Delta C}{\Delta Y}$, the marginal propensity to consume out of additional personal income, Y.

• PROBLEM 5-5

What are some of the non-income factors that cause shifts in consumption?

Solution: Some of the influences which can cause changes in the consumption schedule are:

1) expectations about the future (what consumers think will be happening to prices, income, and availability of goods)

2) changes in holdings of financial assets

3) amount of durable goods on hand

4) credit facilities

5) changes in living standards

6) taxation.

• PROBLEM 5-6

What is the saving schedule?

Solution: The saving schedule is the relationship which shows how much of their incomes households plan to save for the various levels of disposable income which they might possibly earn at some specific point in time. Economists assume that people will allocate all of their disposable income to either consumption C or saving S. Algebraically, this can be written:

$$Y_d = C + S$$

Subtracting C from both sides gives: $S = Y_d - C$.

That is, savings is that part of disposable income which is not used in consumption.

• PROBLEM 5-7

What is the relationship between the consumption function, the saving function, and the "income function" or 45°-line?

Solution: For any potential level of income, consumption expenditures are charted by the consumption function, while saving is shown by the saving function. In the very simple model, income can be divided only between consumption and saving. That is, consumption plus saving always equals income at any given income level.

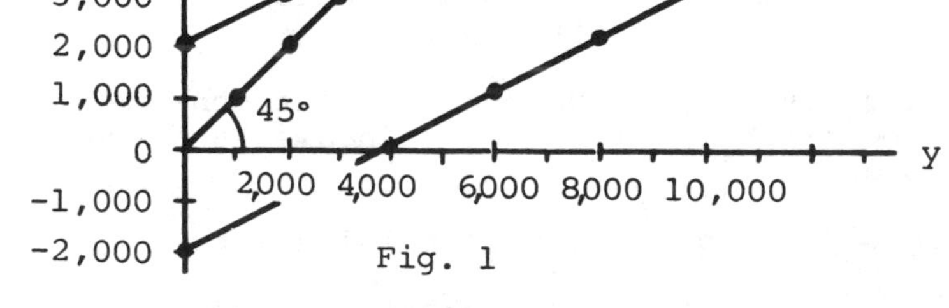

Fig. 1

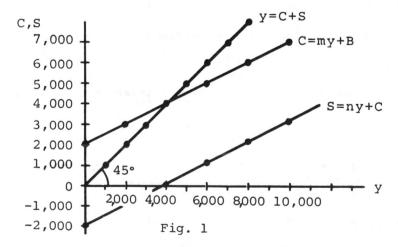

Graphically, a summation of the two functions (a vertical summation, since this addition is valid at any given level of income) would yield an "income function", or more specifically, the 45° line where the quantity being measured by the horizontal axis is equal to the quantity measured by the vertical axis.

Table 1 and Figure 1 illustrate this relationship between the consumption and saving functions.

TABLE 1

Consumption	(C)	2000	3000	4000	5000	6000	7000
Saving	(S)	-2000	-1000	0	1000	2000	3000
Income	(Y)	0	2000	4000	6000	8000	10,000

• PROBLEM 5-8

If the saving function in Figure 1 was derived from the consumption function in the figure, was it derived correctly? If not, derive the correct saving function.

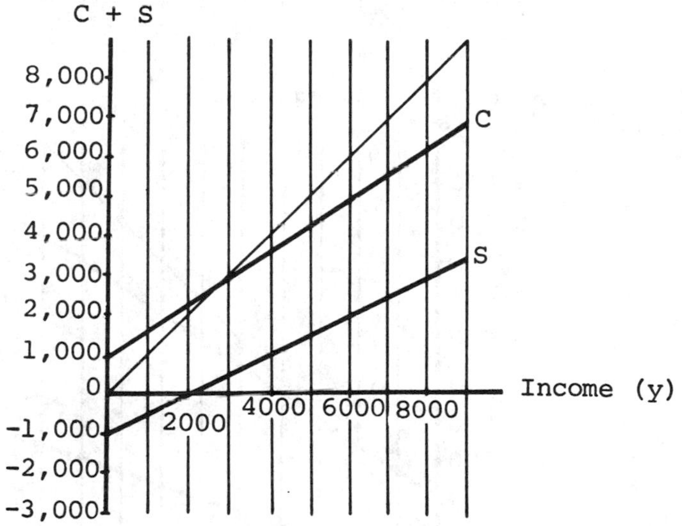

Fig. 1

Solution: To solve this problem, recall that in this simple model, all income is used for either consumption or spending, that is, Y ≡ C + S. Under this assumption, a vertical summation of C and S should add up to the 45° line (where Y ≡ C + S for all income levels). Therefore, to see if the savings curve was derived correctly, add the two curves and see if they equal the 45° line. This vertical summation is shown in Figure 2 by the line C + S.

Since the C + S summation lies above the 45° line, the saving function in Figures 1 and 2 was not correctly derived. To derive the saving function correctly, find the difference between the consumption function (which shows the level of consumption for every income level) and the 45° line (which shows all points where the verti-

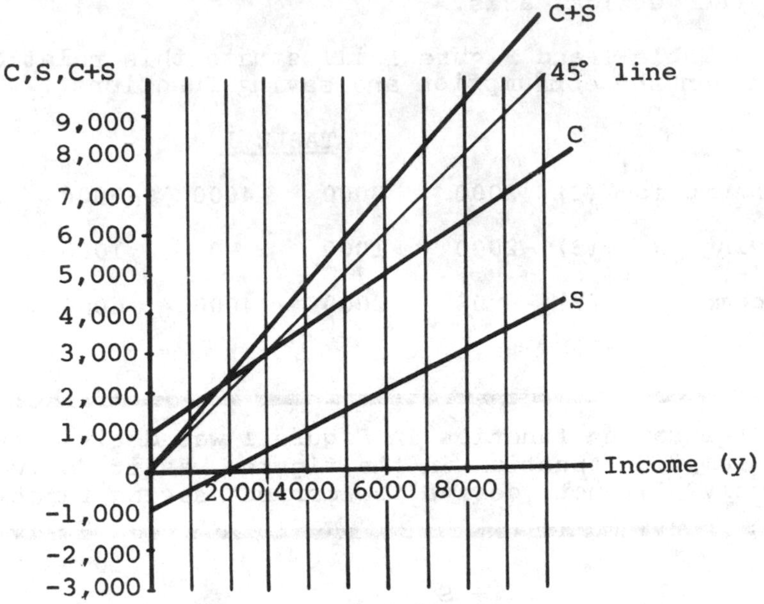

Fig. 2

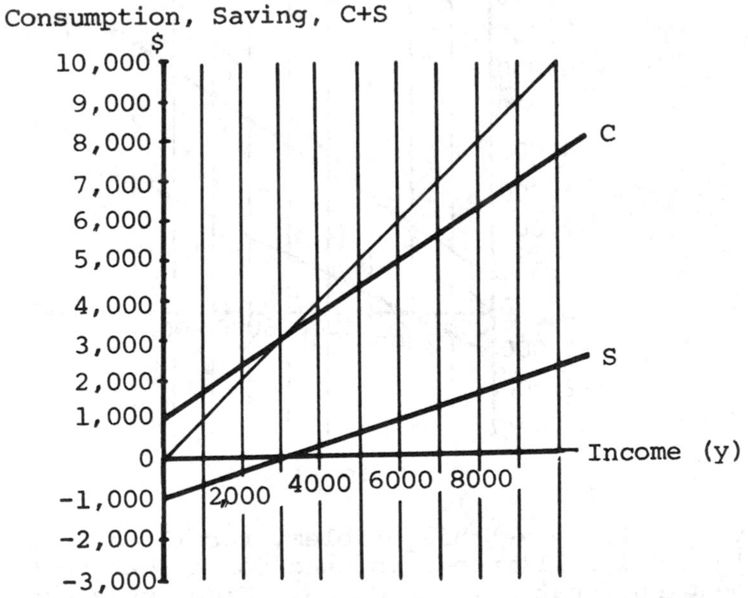

Fig. 3

cal axis is exactly equal to the horizontal axis). The correctly derived saving function is shown in Figure 3.

• PROBLEM 5-9

Complete the table given in Figure 1 (in billions of dollars).

Figure 1

Level of output and income (NNP = DI)	Consumption	Saving
$370	$_____	$ -4
390	_____	0
410	_____	4
430	_____	8
450	_____	12
470	_____	16
490	_____	20
510	_____	24
530	_____	28

From the above data, determine the break-even point, and state its significance.

Solution: Disposable Income = Consumption + Saving. Therefore, Consumption = Disposable Income - Saving.

Using this formula for consumption, we can fill in the table as in Figure 2.

Figure 2

Level of output and income (NNP = DI)	Consumption	Saving
$370	$374	$ -4
390	390	0
410	406	4
430	422	8
450	438	12
470	454	16
490	470	20
510	486	24
530	502	28

The break-even point occurs at the income level of $390 billion, where the households consume their entire income. The significance of this point is that, at it, disposable income equals consumption expenditure and consequently, savings are zero.

• PROBLEM 5-10

Letting C be consumption, S be savings, and Y be disposable income, suppose the consumption schedule is as follows: $C = 200 + \frac{2}{3} Y$.

a) What would be the formula for the savings schedule?

b) When would savings be zero?

Solution: a) When Y = C + S, total income Y will be used only for consumption, C, and savings, S. Substituting for C in the above equation, yields

$$S + (200 + \frac{2}{3} Y) = Y ,$$

from which is obtained

$$S = -200 + \frac{1}{3} Y ,$$

the required savings schedule.

b) To find the point where savings would be zero, set S = 0 and solve for Y.

Starting with the savings schedule

$$S = -200 + \frac{1}{3} Y ,$$

substitute S = 0 , yielding $0 = -200 + \frac{1}{3} Y$,

or $\frac{1}{3} Y = 200$. Dividing by 1/3 results in Y = 600.

Therefore, savings = 0 when disposable income = 600. If Y < 600, dissaving occurs. If Y > 600, saving occurs.

• PROBLEM 5-11

The figure shows Bill's consumption function.

a) If Bill earns $8,000 this year, how much will he spend on consumption?

b) If he earns $2,000, how much will he spend on consumption? At this income level, how much will he have to borrow?

c) At what income level will he spend exactly as much as he earns on consumption?

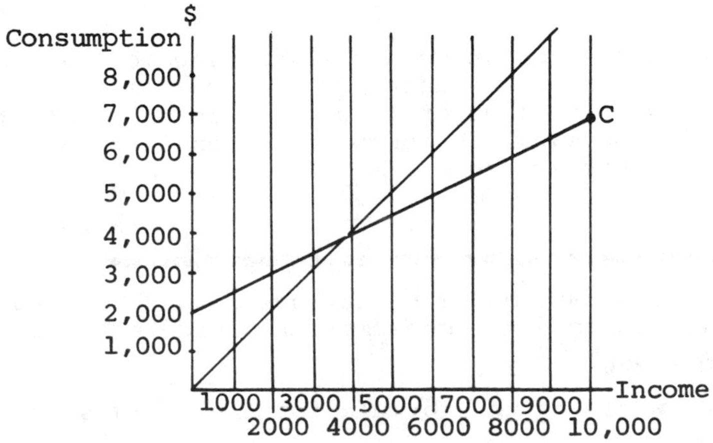

Solution: An individual's consumption function shows how much money will be spent on consumption by the individual out of any level of income.

a) If Bill earns $8,000 this year (8,000 on the horizontal, or income axis), the given consumption function says that he will consume $6,000 (the 6,000 on the vertical, or consumption, axis).

b) If Bill's income = $2,000, then the consumption function indicates that his consumption = $3,000. At this income level, since he is earning $2,000 and spending $3,000, Bill will have to borrow (or dissave) the difference of $1,000.

c) The point where Bill spends exactly all that he earns occurs at income = 4,000, since here consumption = 4,000 also. Note that it is at this income level that the consumption function crosses the 45° line.

• PROBLEM 5-12

Figure 1 shows the Smith family's consumption function for 1980.

a) If the Smiths earn no income at all in 1980, how much dissaving will they have to do?

b) If the Smiths earn $8,000 in 1980, how much will they save?

c) Draw the Smiths' savings function for the potential income range of $0 to $18,000.

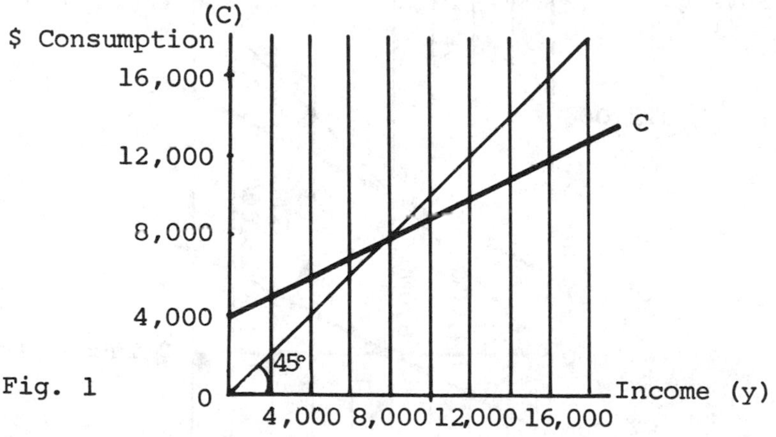

Fig. 1

Solution: A family's consumption function indicates how much money that family will spend on consumption at different levels of income. Keep in mind that for this analysis, it is assumed that all income is spent, for either consuming or saving.

a) If the Smiths earn no income at all, i.e., Y = 0, that is, they are at the zero point on the horizontal axis. To find out how much they will consume at this income level, find the point on the consumption function at which Y = 0. Using the graph, this is the point C = 4,000. If the Smiths are earning no income at all, and yet they are consuming $4,000 worth of goods, then they must be dissaving the entire amount, $4,000. Mathematically, this can be derived using the identity $Y \equiv C + S$. Substituting the values Y = 0 and C = 4,000 gives:

$$0 = \$4000 + S, \text{ which gives:}$$

$$S = -\$4,000, \text{ or } \$4,000 \text{ of dissaving.}$$

<u>Figure 2</u>

Y	C	S
0	4,000	-4,000
2,000	5,000	-3,000
4,000	6,000	-2,000
6,000	7,000	-1,000
8,000	8,000	0
10,000	9,000	1,000
12,000	10,000	2,000
14,000	11,000	3,000
16,000	12,000	4,000
18,000	13,000	5,000

These points are plotted to form the savings function as shown in Figure 3.

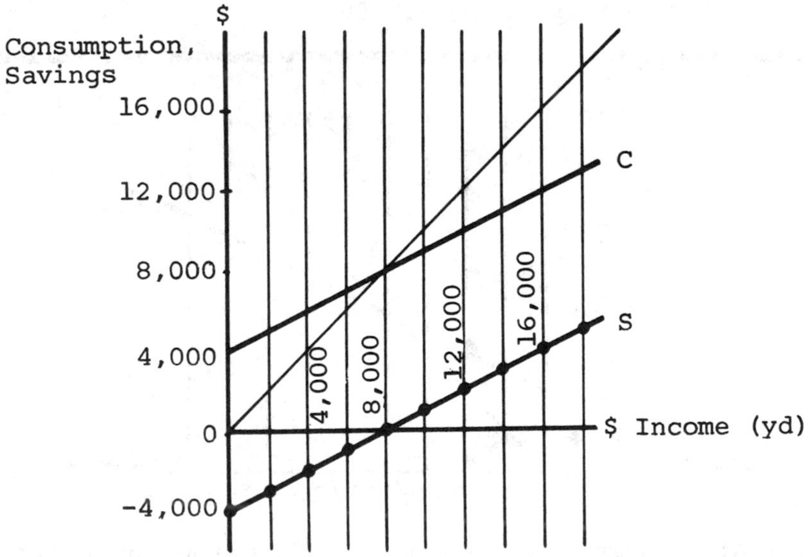

Fig. 3

b) If the Smiths earn $8,000 in 1980, then, using the given consumption function, they will consume $8,000 worth of goods and services. Since they earn $8,000 and spend $8,000, they will save nothing. Mathematically,

$$Y \equiv C + S \text{ or } \$8,000 = \$8,000 + S,$$

which gives $S = 0$.

c) Using the procedure outlined in parts a) and b), determine the savings level for the various levels of income, as shown in Figure 2.

• PROBLEM 5-13

Mr. D consumes all his income. Draw his consumption and saving schedules.

Solution: To solve this problem, first recall that

Income (Y) = Consumption (C) + Savings (S).

The problem states that Mr. D. consumes all his income. Therefore, consumption = income at every point on his consumption schedule, while savings is zero throughout. Now, recall that the 45° line shows the set of all points where the quantity being measured by the vertical axis is exactly equal to the quantity being measured by the horizontal axis. Since Mr. D's consumption (the vertical axis quantity) is equal to his income (the horizontal axis quantity) throughout, Mr. D's consumption schedule would be this 45° line.

Algebraically this is the line $c = Y$, shown in Figure 1.

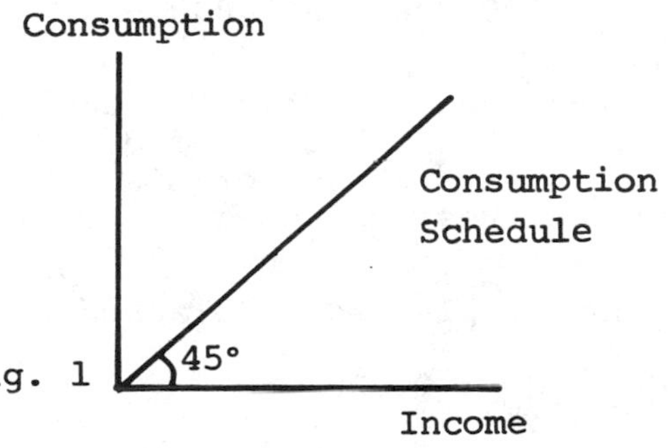

Fig. 1

Since Mr. D consumes all his income, his savings must at all points be zero. Therefore the savings schedule will be the line $S = 0$ for all $Y \geq 0$, and will appear as in Figure 2.

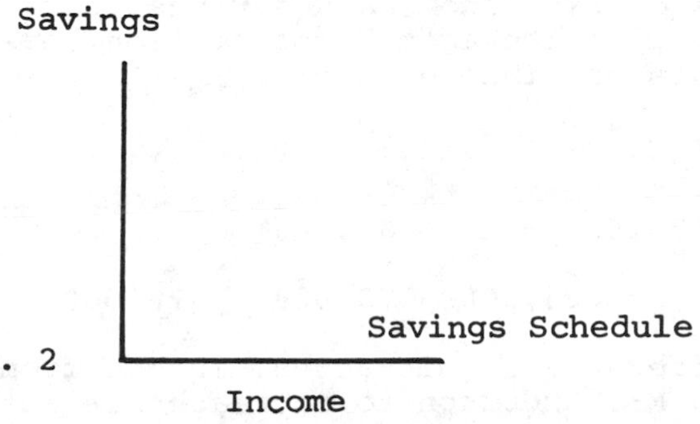

Fig. 2

THE MARGINAL PROPENSITY TO CONSUME

• PROBLEM 5-14

During 1979, Mr. Anderson expected to earn \$20,000. From this income he had planned to save \$2,000. However, during 1979, Mr. Anderson got a raise which boosted his income to \$23,000. If Mr. Anderson ended up saving a total of \$3,000 out of his \$23,000 income, what was his marginal propensity to consume (MPC)? (It may be assumed that if he had not received his raise, Mr. Anderson would have actually saved the \$2,000 that he had planned to save.)

Solution: The marginal propensity to consume is defined as the change in consumption that results from a one dollar change in income, or $\frac{\Delta C}{\Delta Y}$, where Δ means "the change in". To solve this problem, first determine the change in Mr. Anderson's income and the resulting change in his consumption, and then apply the definition to obtain his MPC.

The problem states that originally Mr. Anderson expected to earn \$20,000. Instead he earned \$23,000. This means that his income increased by \$3,000, or

$$Y_{actual} - Y_{planned} = \$23,000 - \$20,000 - \Delta Y = + 3,000$$

To calculate the change in his consumption, the income identity, $Y \equiv C + S$, will be needed. Originally, Mr. Anderson was going to save \$2,000 of his expected \$20,000 income. Substituting these values into the equation gives:

$$Y_{planned} = C_{planned} + S_{planned}$$

$$20,000 = C_p + 2,000$$

which gives:

$$C_p = 20,000 - 2,000 = 18,000$$

Thus, his originally planned consumption was \$18,000. The increase in his income to \$23,000 caused Mr. Anderson actually to save \$3,000 instead of \$2,000. Substituting the actual values of his income and savings into the income identity will give the actual consumption level that corresponds to his new income level:

$$Y_{actual} = C_{actual} + S_{actual}$$

$$\$23,000 = C_a + \$3,000$$

$$C_a = \$23,000 - \$3,000 = \$20,000$$

Thus, the difference in his actual income from planned income caused Mr. Anderson to increase his actual consumption from the \$18,000 he had planned to \$20,000 for 1979, or, $C_a - C_p = \Delta C = + 2{,}000$.

Using the definition of marginal propensity to consume,

$$MPC = \frac{\Delta C}{\Delta Y} = \frac{2{,}000}{3{,}000} = \frac{2}{3} \text{ or } .666....$$

That is, Mr. Anderson's marginal propensity to consume is 2/3. Note that the MPC could also have been arrived at by first calculating the change in Mr. Anderson's savings due to the change in income to get the MPS (marginal propensity to save). From this, MPC could then have been derived by using the formula: MPS + MPC = 1, or 1 - MPS = MPC.

• PROBLEM 5-15

Disposable income after taxes	Net Savings
\$8,000	100
\$9,000	250

What is the marginal propensity to consume in the range \$8,000-\$9,000 for the family given in the figure?

Solution: Two definitions are needed to solve this problem. First, the marginal propensity to consume = the change in consumption/the change in income. Second, recall that

Consumption + Savings = Disposable Income

or,

Consumption = Disposable Income - Savings.

In the example above, income increased by \$9,000 - \$8,000 = \$1,000. Savings increased by \$250 - \$100 = \$150. Therefore, consumption increased by \$1,000 - \$150 = \$850.

Then MPC = 850/1000

= 0.85.

• PROBLEM 5-16

Suppose that the marginal propensity to consume is constant at 1/2 and the break-even point is \$8,000. If income is \$10,000, then how much will be consumed and how much will be saved?

Solution: This question is asking for a linear consumption function, given the slope of the line and a point on the line, from which the levels of consumption and saving at some given income level can be determined. Since the MPC is constant at 1/2, the consumption function is a straight line with a slope of 1/2. This means that every time income is increased by 2 units, half of it, or 1 unit, goes towards more consumption. One point on the line is given, the break-even point, where Y = C = \$8,000. The equation for a simple linear consumption function is $C = mY + B$, where m is the slope of the line, or the MPC, and B is the level of consumption when Y = 0. It is given that m = MPC = 1/2, but B is not given. To find B, note that the point Y = 8,000, and C = 8,000 is given as one point on the line. Since the formula for the line must hold true for all points on the line, the following substitutions into the original equation must be true:

$$8000 = 1/2(8000) + B = 4000 + B.$$

Subtracting 4,000 from both sides gives:

$$B = 8{,}000 - 4{,}000 = 4{,}000.$$

Substituting this value for B back into the consumption function gives:

$C = 1/2\, Y + 4{,}000$, the consumption function for this problem.

To find what C, consumption, is when income is \$10,000, substitute Y = 10,000 into the consumption function equation:

$$C = 1/2(10{,}000) + 4{,}000 = 5{,}000 + 4{,}000 = 9{,}000.$$

That is, when income is \$10,000, consumption is \$9,000 and the remainder, \$1,000, is saved.

• PROBLEM 5-17

Suppose that John's MPC is constant at 4/5. If he had no income at all, he would have to borrow \$2,000 to meet all his expenses. Graph John's consumption function and write it out algebraically. Using the formula for John's consumption function, find his break-even point.

Solution: It is given that the MPC, or slope of the function, is constant throughout at 4/5. This means that the consumption function is a straight line with a slope of 4/5. It is also given that at the point Y = 0, C = 2,000. To draw a graph of the consumption function, plot the initial point, Y = 0 and C = 2,000. To construct a line with slope of 4/5 through this point, count up 4,000 and over 5,000 to reach a second point at Y = 5,000 and C = 6,000 = (4,000 + 2,000), and draw a line through these two points (points (0,2) and (5,6) on the graph given in the figure). This line is John's consumption function, as shown in the figure.

To write this consumption function algebraically, recall that the form taken by a simple linear consumption function is $C = mY + B$, which is the formula for a line

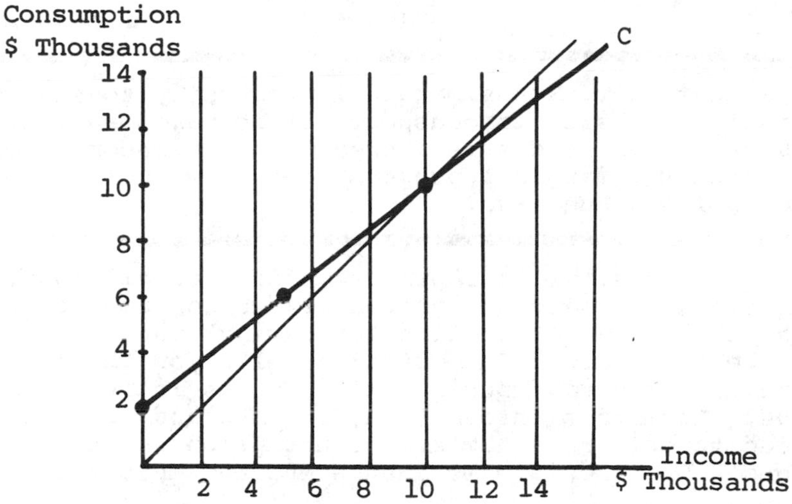

with a slope of m and a vertical axis intercept of B. Since the slope of the consumption function is the MPC, which is 4/5 in this case, then m = 4/5. The vertical axis intercept (or the point where the consumption function crosses the consumption axis and where Income is at Y = 0) is C = 2,000. Therefore, B in the formula above is equal to $2,000. Substituting these two values into the formula gives:

$$C = (4/5)Y + 2{,}000,$$

which is the algebraic formula for John's consumption function.

To find the break-even point algebraically, recall that at this point, all income is used for consumption, or Y = C. To find this point substitute Y for C in the equation above:

$$Y = (4/5)Y + 2{,}000 \quad (=C).$$

Subtract (4/5)Y from both sides to get:

$$Y - (4/5)Y = 2000.$$

Simplify to get

$$(1 - 4/5)Y = (1/5)Y = 2000.$$

Multiply both sides of the equation by 5 to get:

$$Y = 10{,}000.$$

This income level satisfies both the original consumption function (that is, it is on the consumption line) and the condition for a break-even point (that is, it is a point where consumption is equal to income). Therefore, it is the break-even point. To confirm this, note that on the graph, the consumption function crosses (is equal to) the 45° line (where Y = C) at the point Y = 10,000 = C.

• PROBLEM 5-18

Assume that A. T. Hun's marginal propensity to save = marginal propensity to consume. If he makes an extra $1000 this year, and this increase in his income does not change his marginal propensities, how much of this $1000 will Mr. Hun save?

Solution: To solve this problem, first recall that, by definition, the marginal propensity to consume (or save) is the change in consumption (or saving) that comes from a change in income. The question tells you that Mr. Hun's income has changed, specifically, it has increased by $1,000. With this information, the MPC and the MPS can be used to determine how much consumption and savings have changed. To calculate Mr. Hun's MPC and MPS, recall that:

$$MPC = MPS = 1.$$

In this problem, it is given that MPC = MPS. Therefore,

$$MPC + MPS = 2MPS = 1$$

$$MPS = 1/2, \; MPC = 1/2$$

Since Mr. Hun's MPS is 1/2, he will save half of this new income, or $500. That is, the amount saved = (1/2)(1000)= $500.

• PROBLEM 5-19

Mr. Krinsky is a wealthy lawyer who knows how to live well. No matter what his disposable income is, he will always devote at least $30,000 to consumption each year. In addition, once his disposable income rises above $40,000, he saves half of the portion above $40,000 and spends the rest on various luxuries.

a) Draw Mr. Krinsky's consumption function.

b) Over what range does dissaving occur, and over what range does saving occur?

c) Describe the marginal propensity to consume over the course of the graph.

Solution: a) The problem states that Mr. Krinsky will always spend at least $30,000, and once his income rises above $40,000, he spends half of the part above $40,000. Therefore his consumption schedule would be represented by graph K in the figure.

The line $C = Y_d$ is called the 45° helper line and lies exactly halfway between the vertical and horizontal axes. Along this line, Consumption (C) = Disposable income (Y_d) at all points. In other words, along this line no saving or dissaving takes place.

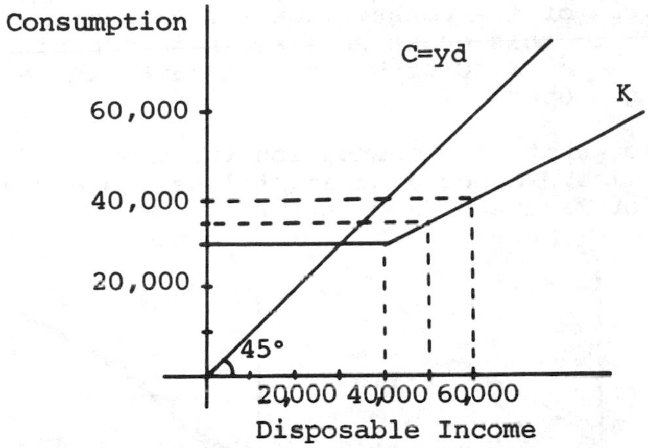

b) To find out where saving and dissaving occur, we must compare Mr. Krinsky's consumption schedule with the 45° helper line in the graph from part (a). Whenever the consumption function lies above the 45° helper line, dissaving occurs because consumption is greater than disposable income. Whenever the consumption function lies below the 45° helper line, saving occurs because consumption is less than disposable income. The graph shows that in the range, $0 \leq$ Income $<$ \$30,000, dissaving occurs. If Income $>$ \$30,000, saving occurs. If Income = \$30,000, the two graphs intersect and Mr. Krinsky consumes exactly all of his disposable income. Therefore at Income = \$30,000, no saving or dissaving occurs.

c) To study the marginal propensity to consume (MPC), once again make use of the graph. From Income = 0 to Income = \$40,000, consumption is constant at \$30,000. MPC is given by the formula, $MPC = \Delta C/\Delta Y_d$. Over this range, $\Delta C = 0$. Therefore from Income = 0 to Income = \$40,000, $MPC = 0/\Delta Y_d = 0$.

If Mr. Krinsky earns over \$40,000, he spends 1/2 of the portion over \$40,000. Therefore, if the increase in disposable income = ΔY_d, the increase in consumption = $\Delta C, = \frac{1}{2} \Delta Y_d$. Therefore, $MPC = (1/2)\Delta Y_d/\Delta Y_d$, and MPC = 1/2.

Thus,

$$MPC = \begin{cases} 0 & \text{if income} \leq \$40,000 \\ 0.5 & \text{if income} > \$40,000 \end{cases}$$

• PROBLEM 5-20

Which of the given consumption functions exhibits a) constant MPC, b) increasing MPC and c) decreasing MPC?

Solution: MPC, or the marginal propensity to consume, is the change in consumption that is caused by a \$1 change in income. Graphically, it is the slope of the consumption function at any given point. Since the MPC is the value of the slope of the consumption function at any given point, the answer to this question lies in determining whether the functions in A, B, C or D have constant, increasing or decreasing slopes.

Notice that the consumption function in Figure D is a straight line. Since a straight line has a constant slope, the MPC for Figure D is constant.

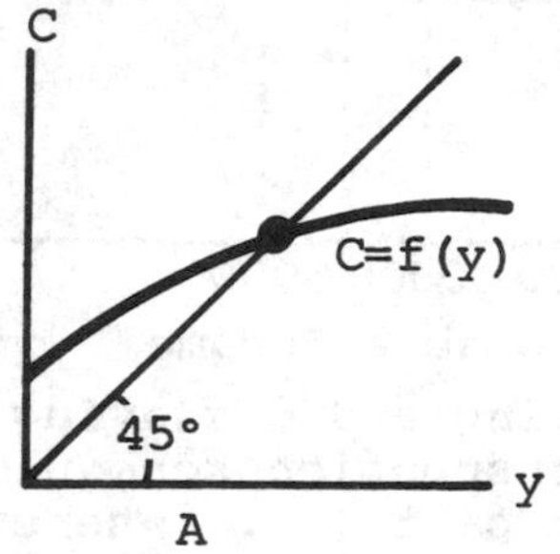

A

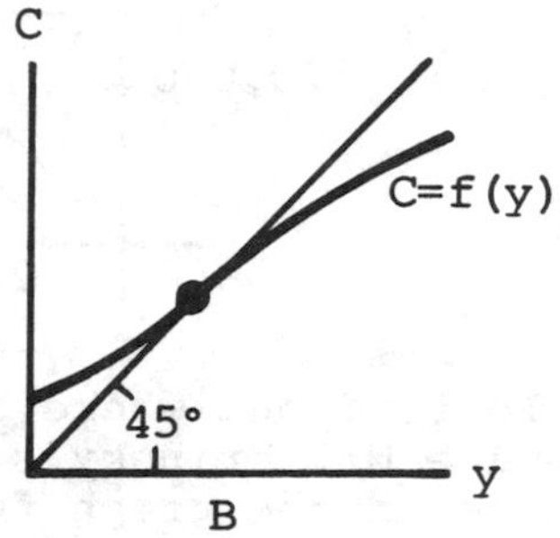

B

In Figure A, slope of the consumption function decreases as income increases. Therefore, Figure A shows a decreasing MPC.

The slope of the consumption function in Figure B at first gets steeper (increases) but then flatter (decreases). Thus, this function shows first increasing MPC and then, after the break-even point, decreasing MPC, a case not asked for in the question.

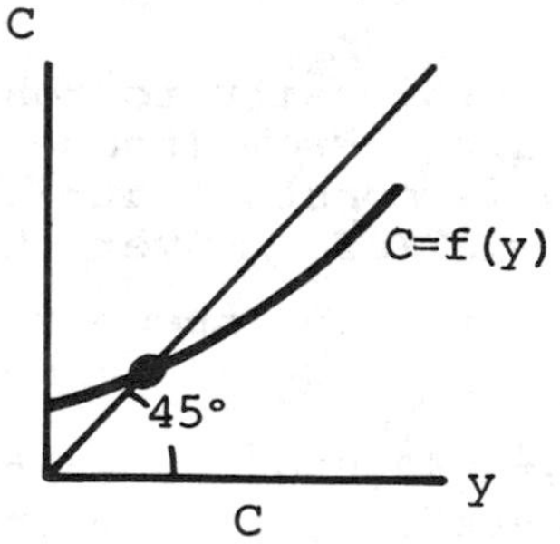

C

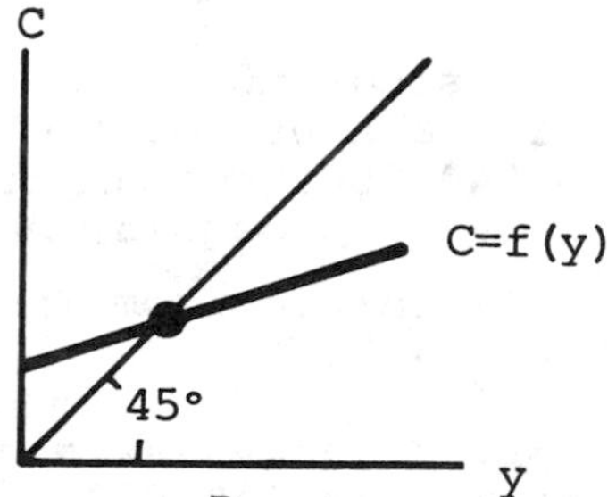

D

Figure C shows a curve whose slope gets steadily steeper (increases); therefore it exhibits an increasing MPC.

Thus, the answer to the question is that constant MPC is shown by Figure D, increasing MPC by Figure C and decreasing MPC by Figure A.

• PROBLEM 5-21

Explain why the sum of the MPC and the MPS for any given change in disposable income must always be equal to 1.

Solution: By definition, the MPC, or marginal propensity to consume, is that proportion of any change in income which is consumed. It is defined by

$$MPC = \frac{\Delta C}{\Delta Y},$$

where ΔC = change in consumption, and ΔY = change in total disposable income.

Similarly, the MPS, or marginal propensity to save, is that proportion of any change in income which is saved, and is defined by

$$MPC = \frac{\Delta S}{\Delta Y},$$

where ΔS = change in saving, and ΔY = change in disposable income.

If total disposable income Y is allocated either to consumption (C) or saving (S), any increase in income Y must be accounted for completely by the sum of the change in consumption C and the change in saving S.

Algebraically, total income Y is used for consumption C and saving S:

$$Y = C + S.$$

Any change in income is reflected in a change in consumption and in savings:

$$\Delta Y = \Delta C + \Delta S.$$

When both sides of this equation are divided by the change in income ΔY, the result is:

$$\frac{\Delta Y}{\Delta Y} = \frac{\Delta C}{\Delta Y} + \frac{\Delta S}{\Delta Y},$$

or

$$1 = \frac{\Delta C}{\Delta Y} + \frac{\Delta S}{\Delta Y}.$$

By definition, $MPC = \frac{\Delta C}{\Delta Y}$

and $MPS = \frac{\Delta S}{\Delta Y}$.

Therefore, by substitution:

$$1 = MPC + MPS.$$

• PROBLEM 5-22

What is the geometric meaning of the marginal propensity to consume?

Solution: The marginal propensity to consume is the change in consumption that results from a change in income. Since the consumption curve graphs the relationship between consumption and income, it can be used to geometrically interpret the MPC. Figure 1 illustrates a hypothetical consumption curve.

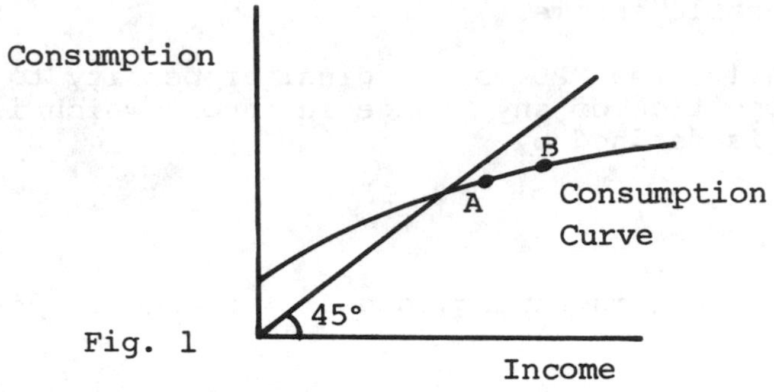

Fig. 1

Now pick two points on the curve, A and B, close enough together so that the shape of the curve between A and B can be approximated with the straight line, AB. By definition, MPC from A to B is

$$\frac{\text{Consumption}_B - \text{Consumption}_A}{\text{Income}_B - \text{Income}_A} = \frac{\text{change in C}}{\text{change in Y}} = \frac{\Delta C}{\Delta Y}$$

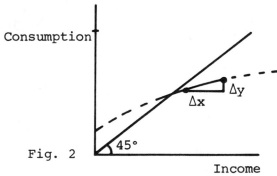

On the graph of the consumption schedule given in Figure 2 it can be seen that the geometrical interpretation of the MPC is the slope of the consumption curve, $\Delta y/\Delta x$, where $\Delta y = \text{consumption}_B - \text{consumption}_A$ and $\Delta x = \text{Income}_B - \text{Income}_A$.

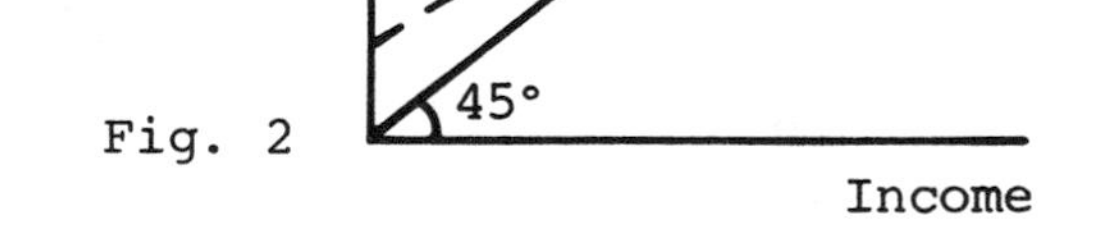

Fig. 2

For those with a background in differential calculus, it is clear that as point A is allowed to approach point B, the marginal propensity to consume is the derivative of the consumption function.

• PROBLEM 5-23

Suppose that John's MPC is constant at 3/4. If his breakeven point occurs at $7,000, how much will John have to borrow when his income is $3,000?

Solution: This question is asking for the level of dissaving at a specific income level. It is given that MPC is constant at 3/4. Therefore John's consumption function is a straight line with slope of 3/4. You are also given one point on his consumption function, the break-even point, where Y = C = 7,000.

To solve this problem algebraically, first obtain the formula for John's consumption function. Recall that the basic formula for a simple linear consumption function is C = mY + B, where m is the slope of the line and B is the point where the consumption function crosses the consumption axis (that is, where Y = 0). It is given that m - MPC = 3/4, but you must solve for B. This is done by noting that the given break-even point, Y = C = 7000, is one point on the consumption function line. Therefore the following substitutions into the consumption function formula are valid:

$$C = 7,000 = (3/4)(7,000) + B.$$

Subtracting (3/4)(7000) from both sides gives:

$$7,000 - (3/4)(7000) = B.$$

Simplifying gives:

$$B = 7000 - 5250 = 1750.$$

Using this, John's consumption function is:

$$C = (3/4)Y + 1750.$$

To find his consumption level when he earns \$3,000, substitute Y = \$3,000 into the consumption function as follows:

$$C = (3/4)(3000) + 1750.$$

$$C = 2250 + 1750 = 4000.$$

Since John consumes \$4,000 when he earns \$3,000, the amount that he dissaves at this income level is the difference between the two, or \$1,000.

• PROBLEM 5-24

A family is above its break-even point: out of \$10,000 of income, it saves \$2,000. Assuming that its consumption function is linear, with normal shape and a positive consumption axis intercept, then its marginal propensity to consume, MPC, should be:

a) 1; b) less than 1 but greater than 4/5;

c) 4/5; d) less than 4/5 but greater than 0;

e) anywhere from 1 to zero, no more than this can be determined from the given data.

Solution: This question is asking if anything can be said about a family's MPC, given one point on the family's linear consumption function. That is, without specifically determining the consumption line, can something be said about its slope?

To solve this problem, begin by constructing a graph with the given point, Y = 10,000 and C = 8,000 (= Y - S = 10,000 - 2,000), plotted as shown in the figure.

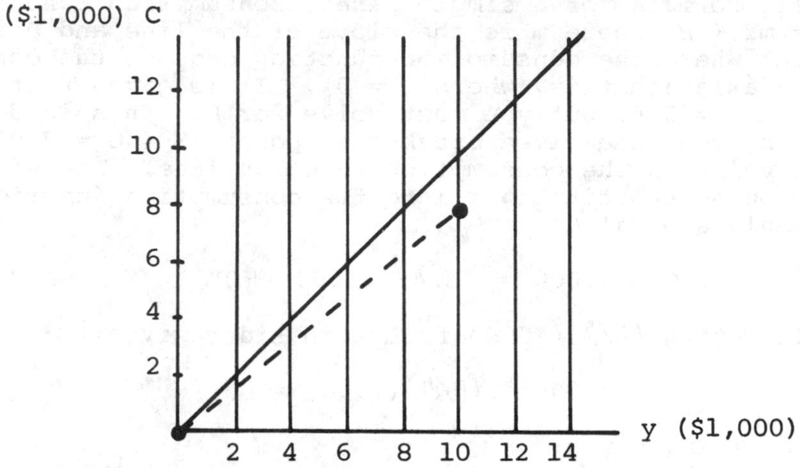

The question states that the assumption may be made that the consumption function has normal shape, that is, that its slope will be positive, less than one but greater than zero and that its consumption-axis intercept (where Y = 0) will be positive. Since it is given that this family's consumption function contains a point C > 0 at Y = 0, then the consumption function would have to be somewhat flatter than the dashed line in the diagram, because this line connects the known point with the point C = 0 at Y = 0.

The slope of the dashed line is the change in the vertical distance, from 0 to 8, divided by the change in the horizontal distance, from 0 to 10, or:

$$\frac{\Delta C}{\Delta Y} = \frac{0 - 8}{0 - 10} = \frac{-8}{-10} = \frac{4(-2)}{5(-2)} = \frac{4}{5} .$$

Since the real consumption function must have a slope that is flatter, or less than, the slope of the dashed line, the correct answer is d, the slope of the consumption function, or its MPC, is less than 4/5 but greater than zero.

• PROBLEM 5-25

A. A. Wingit, a noted professor of economics, claims to have derived a consumption function for the U.S. for 1980. Prof. Wingit claims that the U.S. marginal propensity to consume will be constant for all ranges of income at .9. The professor also claims that if no income were earned by anyone in the entire nation, $100 billion would need to be "dissaved". Graph Prof. Wingit's consumption function. What is his break-even point?

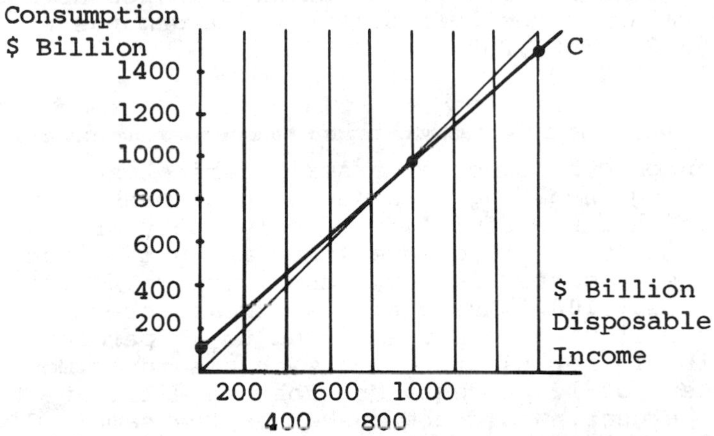

Solution: This question is asking for the construction of a consumption function, given a constant MPC and given the value of consumption when income is equal to zero. Since the MPC is given as constant at .9, this consumption function is a straight line with a slope of 9/10. To construct the graph, begin with the given point, Y = 0 and C = $100 billion. From this point, construct a line with a slope of 9/10, by counting upward 900, and over 1000, from the given point, and drawing a line through these two points (Y = 0 and C = 100, and Y = 1000 and C = 900 + 100 = 1000). This line, as shown in the figure, is Wingit's consumption function, with its constant MPC at .9.

The break-even point occurs where all Disposable Income goes to consumption, or, graphically, where the consumption function crosses the 45° line. In Prof. Wingit's consumption function, this point occurs at Disposable Income = $1,000 billion (or $1.0 trillion) = consumption.

• PROBLEM 5-26

If a household chose to save 10 percent of its income and to add three quarters of its saving to cash balances, what would be the value of the loan contracts it demanded when its income totaled $30,000 per year?

Solution: A loan contract, which is traded in the loan contract market, is defined as an interest-bearing promissory note or IOU. It is a piece of paper stating that somebody has undertaken the obligation of repaying the dollars that he has borrowed from someone else. It represents an exchange of today's dollars for future dollars.

In this case, the household has chosen to save 10 percent of its income of $30,000 per year, i.e., it saves $3,000 per year. It defers $3,000 worth of consumption to the future. Part of these dollars saved will go into its cash balances, earning no interest, and part will be invested in loan contracts, so earning interest. This second decision is based on two considerations: the convenience of having cash on hand for transactions, and the opportunity cost of not earning interest. The household decides to invest 3/4 of its savings in loanable contracts, so the value of the loan contracts it demands will be 3/4 x $3,000 = $2,250.

• PROBLEM 5-27

Mr. Johnson, the owner of a small cabinetmaking shop, is considering investing in a new sanding machine which costs $1000 and has a useful life of only one year. It is expected that the net revenue (that is, net of such operating costs as power, lumber, labor, and so forth) from the machine is $1100. Assuming that the interest rate Mr. Johnson will have to pay amounted to 12 percent, would it be advisable for him to go on with his investment plan? If instead of 12 percent, Mr. Johnson will have to pay only 7 percent, would the answer be the same? Given that he will not loan the $1000, is cost still associated with it?

Solution: This problem illustrates the two basic determinants of investment, i.e., (1) the expected rate of net profits which businesses hope to realize from investment spending, and (2) the rate of interest. One generalization can be made here. If the expected rate of net profits exceeds the interest rate, it will be profitable to invest. But if the interest rate exceeds the expected rate of net profits, it will not be advisable to invest.

Our expected rate of net profit on the machine is computed as follows:

$$\text{Expected Rate of Net Profit} = \frac{\text{Net Profit}}{\text{Cost of the Equipment}}$$

$$= \frac{\$1100 - 1000}{\$1,000} = \frac{\$100}{\$1,000}$$

$$= 10 \text{ percent.}$$

Since for the first alternative, the expected rate of net profit, 10 percent, is less than the interest rate, 12 percent, it would not be advisable for Mr. Johnson to go on with the investment plan. Given that Mr. Johnson will have to pay only 7 percent, he would be better off to go along with the plan.

To answer the last question, the following point has to be considered:

The role of the interest rate as a cost in investing in real capital is valid even if the firm does not borrow, but rather finances the investment internally out of funds saved from past profits. By using this money to invest in the sander, the firm incurs a cost in the sense that it forgoes the interest income which it could have realized by lending the funds to someone else. The interest rate, therefore, represents the opportunity cost of capital for the investor, because he could have invested the $1,000 in bonds instead of in the sanding machine, and earned the 7 percent.

THE AVERAGE PROPENSITY TO CONSUME

• PROBLEM 5-28

a) What is meant by average propensity to consume?

b) Suppose that $1000 out of $10,000 disposable income is saved. What is the average propensity to consume?

Solution: A propensity is a tendency to do something. Most people will save some part of their disposable income (saving) and spend part of it on goods and services (consumption). Dividing the amount spent for consumption (C) by the total amount of disposable income (Y) will yield the average propensity to consume (APC).

In the formula, APC= C/Y; correspondingly, the average propensity to save (APS) = S/Y.

b) Consumption = Disposable Income - Savings. Since savings is $1000 and disposable income is $10,000, consumption = $10,000 - $1,000 = $9,000. Then

$$\begin{aligned} APC &= C/Y \\ &= 9{,}000/10{,}000 \\ &= 0.9. \end{aligned}$$

• PROBLEM 5-29

Consider the given aggregate consumption schedule.

Income (in billions)	Consumption (in billions)	Savings (in billions)
$600	$600	0
700	660	40
800	720	80
900	780	120

Comment on the MPC, MPS, APC, and APS in this situation.

Solution: A study of the table shows that each time income goes up $100, consumption goes up $60 and savings increase by $40. Therefore, both MPC and MPS are constant, where

$$MPC = \Delta C/\Delta Y$$
$$= 60/100$$
$$= 0.6$$

and

$$MPS = \Delta S/\Delta Y$$
$$= 40/100$$
$$= 0.4$$

On the other hand, APS and APC are different at each point on the schedule.

At income = 600, APC = 600/600 = 1, and APS = $\frac{0}{600}$ = 0.

At income = 700, APC = 660/700 = 0.9428, and APS = (1 - .9428) = 0.0572.

At income = 800, APC = 720/800 = 0.9, and APS = (1 - 0.9) = 0.1.

At income = 900, APC = 780/900 = $0.86\overline{6}$ and APS = (1 - $.86\overline{6}$) = $0.13\overline{3}$.

Thus, it is shown that, although MPS and MPC remain constant, APS becomes larger as income increases and APC becomes smaller.

• PROBLEM 5-30

Assume that in a given year, consumption and saving schedules are as given (columns 1 through 3 in billions of dollars).

(1) Level of output and income (NNP = Dl)	(2) Consumption	(3) Saving
$510	480	30
530	495	35

a) Determine the average propensity to consume (APC) and the average propensity to save (APS).

b) Compute the marginal propensity to consume (MPC) and the marginal propensity to save (MPS).

Solution: To solve this problem, first recall that:

a) $APC_1 = \frac{\text{consumption}}{\text{income}}$

Substituting the values given in the problem gives:

$$\frac{\$480}{\$510} = .94$$

$$APC_2 = \frac{\$495}{\$530} = .93$$

$$APS_1 = \frac{\text{Saving}}{\text{Income}} = \frac{\$\ 30}{\$510} = .07$$

$$APS_2 = \frac{\$\ 35}{\$495} = .08$$

b) $$MPC = \frac{\text{change in consumption}}{\text{change in income}} = \frac{\$495 - 480}{\$20} = \frac{15}{20} = 0.75$$

$$MPS = \frac{\text{change in saving}}{\text{change in income}} = \frac{\$35 - 30}{\$20} = \frac{5}{20} = 0.25$$

• PROBLEM 5-31

Prove that the sum of the average propensity to save and the average propensity to consume is always equal to one.

Solution: Given that APC = C/Y and APS = $\frac{S}{Y}$,

where C = consumption

S = saving

Y = income,

$$APC + APS = \frac{C}{Y} + \frac{S}{Y}$$

$$APC + APS = (C + S)/Y$$

Then, since Y = C + S, i.e., the income is allocated over consumption and saving,

$$APC + APS = Y/Y\ ,$$

or $APC + APS = 1.$

Intuitively, what the result is stating is that if all income must be spent, and it can only be spent in two ways, on either savings, or consumption, then the percentage spent on consuming plus the percentage spent in saving will add up to 100% or all of the original income to be allocated.

• PROBLEM 5-32

Differentiate between investment in layman's terminology and investment as it applies to economics.

Solution: "Investment" in layman's terminology does not always have the same meaning as in economics. "Net investment," or capital formation, in economics has been defined to be the net increase in the community's real capital (equipment, buildings, inventories). But the plain man speaks of "investing" when he buys a piece of land, an old security, or any title to property. For economists, these are clearly transfer items. What one man is buying, someone else is selling. There is net investment only when additional real capital is created.

In short, even if there are no real investment opportunities that seem profitable, an individual may still wish to nonconsume--to save. He can always buy an existing security asset; he can accumulate, or try to accumulate, cash.

THE INVESTMENT FUNCTION

• PROBLEM 5-33

What is gross private domestic investment?

Solution: Gross private domestic investment refers to all investment spending by domestic (= non-foreign) business firms. It includes:

1) all final purchases of machinery, equipment and tools by business enterprises;

2) all construction; and

3) changes in inventories.

The buying of stocks and bonds is excluded from the economist's definition of investment, because such purchases merely transfer the ownership of existing assets. Investment in the economist's definition is the construction or manufacture of new capital assets. It is the creation of such earning assets that give rise to jobs and income, not the exchange of claims to existing capital goods.

Gross private domestic investment includes those investment goods which are to replace the machinery, equipment, and buildings used up in the current year's production plus any net additions to the economy's stock of capital. Gross investment includes both replacement and added investment. For example, if the gross investment is $260 billion, and if the depreciation (capital consumption) is $200 billion, then net investment (= addition to capital stock) would be $60 billion.

• PROBLEM 5-34

There are many factors which affect the amount of investment undertaken at any given time. List six important factors.

Solution: The six main "non-interest" determinants of investment are:

1) acquisition, maintenance and operating costs to the producer;

2) business taxes;

3) technological change;

4) the stock of capital goods on hand;

5) expectations about future sales and future profitability; and

6) the rate of interest.

• PROBLEM 5-35

Keynesian economists claim that investment is the most volatile component of private spending. If this is so, why is the investment function, as shown, drawn as a straight line, rather than as an erratic curve?

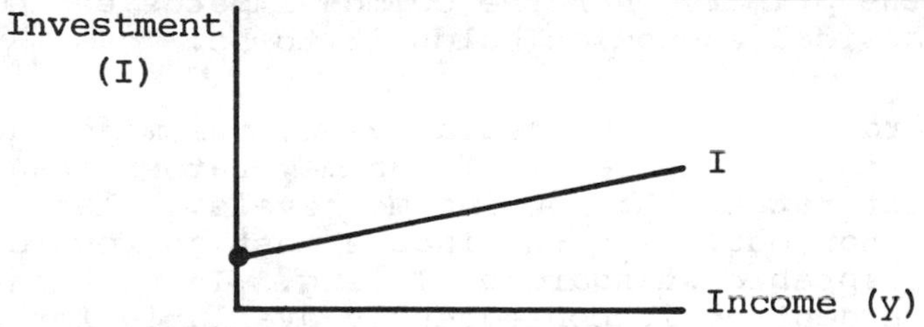

Solution: The instability of investment is generally attributed to the following four factors:

1) the durability of capital goods;

2) the irregularity of innovation;

3) the variability of profits; and

4) the variability of expectations.

Note that the investment function is plotted as the relationship between the money value of investment and money income. Since none of the causes of investment's volatility is strongly related to income, the effects due to the four factors cited above cannot be shown by the shape of the investment function as graphed. That is, these factors, which cause the investment function to be so variable, are not represented on the axes. Therefore, a single investment line represents the relationship between investment and income, given that the other 4 factors affecting the money value of investment besides income remain the same. Thus it cannot show great fluctuations caused by these factors. Rather, these underlying factors shift the entire curve, often dramatically, upward or downward. Thus the instability of investment is represented by shifts in the investment function rather than by the shape of this function.

Contrast the Keynesian, or modern, economic theory of saving and investment with the classical economic view.

Solution: The keystone to the classical economic view is the claim that there is a direct relationship between saving and capital investment. Specifically, the claim is that dollars invested will exactly equal dollars saved at, and only at, an equilibrium interest rate. Thus, the interest rate is the only factor which determines the amount of both saving and investment.

In Keynesian economics, this relationship between saving and investment is rejected. Rather, savers and investors are looked on as two distinct groups, generally with entirely distinct and unrelated motives for saving and investing, respectively. While the interest rate may have some effect on both saving and investment, it is neither the primary, nor the common impetus behind the two which classical economics holds it to be.

According to the Keynesian view, the major determinant of saving is the level of income, rather than the level of interest rates. At low income levels, a larger percentage of a household's total income must go towards achieving an acceptable standard of living. In such cases, a smaller percentage is consequently available for saving, and in fact dissaving, or borrowing, may occur at lower income levels. As the income level increases, however, both a higher percentage of a household's total income and a greater amount of income will become available for saving. (A higher income level will also tend to result in an increase in a household's consumption.) This direct relationship between income level and saving is held to be valid for households both individually and as a group (national income).

On the investment side, while the interest rate, or the cost of obtaining dollars with which to invest, will probably at least be taken into consideration during investment planning, under the Keynesian system it is far from being the only, or even primary, determinant. Rather, investments are made according to the expected rate of profit--that is, how much profit can be accrued by the business at various levels of investment. In fact, some economists hold that the interest rate hardly figures at all in corporate investment planning (although if the interest rates are higher than the expected rate of net profits, that is, than the amount above and beyond the original loan which will be accrued as profits, then of course it would be inadvisable to borrow at that rate for investment). In any case, under the Keynesian view, if profit expectations, determined by levels of consumption, are low, then the level of investment will be low and perhaps even decline, no matter what the interest rates are.

In summary, it is seen that classical economics maintains a direct relationship between interest rate and the amount of both saving and investment, with the amounts of saving and investment being equal. Modern Keynesian economics, on the other hand, holds that the motives behind saving and investment are distinct; and that if there is a relationship between the two, it is directly between the level of consumption and level of production, it being reasoned that, generally, more saving results in less consumption, which produces a decline in profit expectations of businesses, which in turn results in less investment. (As indicated in the parenthetical remark above, interest rates play a role in determining profit expectations, a point which is covered in detail in another question. However, this is not the same as the direct relationship between interest rates and amount of investment which is maintained by classical economic theory.)

● PROBLEM 5-37

What is meant by an autonomous increase in spending?

Solution: An autonomous increase in spending is an increase in total spending that is not the result of an increase in income. Examples of this are increases in spending financed from savings, increases in government spending, and increases in investment resulting from lower interest rates.

● PROBLEM 5-38

How does classical economic theory answer the claim that the existence of saving undermines Say's Law, that is, that saving results in underspending, or a deficiency of total demand?

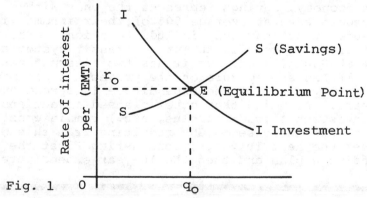

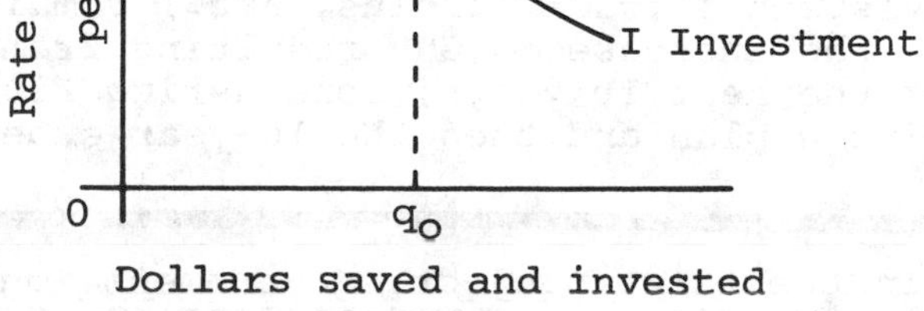

Fig. 1

Solution: Classical economic theory claims to extricate itself from the charge that the existence of saving breaks the perfect relationship between supply and demand given in Say's Law, by the introduction of a special market contained in capitalism called the money market. The money market, supposedly ensures equilibrium between saving and investment, thus allowing for the return of the "leakage" caused by saving back into the income-expenditure flow.

Classical economic theory claims that the money market operates basically as follows:

The only incentive to save rather than to spend income in immediate consumption is interest, i.e., a reward of further income given for thriftiness. The greater this reward (the higher the interest rate), the more consumers are induced to save. This results in an upward-sloping supply of savings curve, as shown by the curve SS in Figure 1.

The cost of borrowing these savings is incurred by the businesses to which the savings are lent. Business demands money capital in order to invest it in replacing and enlarging their plants and their stocks of capital equipment. Business firms prefer to borrow at low rates rather than at high ones. This results in a downward-sloping investment (demand-for-dollars) curve for businesses, as shown by the curve II in the figure.

According to the classical theory, this interplay between the supply of and demand for savings results in an equilibrium interest rate being established where the two curves, saving and investment, intersect (point E on the graph). At this point, where the interest rate $= r_o$, the quantity of dollars saved, or supplied, equals the quantity of dollars demanded for investment (both equal to q_o in Figure 1). The gap in spending caused by the withdrawal of saved dollars is thus filled in by the exactly equal amount of investment spending by businesses.

• PROBLEM 5-39

In a given economy, savings represent the only withdrawals; people save at average 50% of their income (it may be assumed that 'savings' include taxation). The government plans to rebuild the urban transit system at a total cost of $30 billion, but it has two alternatives for spending: 1) The expenditure on the project is all made in the first 2 years. 2) The expenditure is spread evenly over 10 years. Assuming that other planned injections (private investment, trade surplus, etc.) remain constant, what will be the increase in GNP resulting from this mass-project over the next 10 years, considering first the 2-year expenditure plan and then the 10-year expenditure plan?

Solution: In the first project, government would step up investment in the first year by $15 billion, keep investments at that level during the second year, and let investments drop to zero during the remaining 8 years. A multiplied increase effect on GNP can be expected in the first year, and a decrease effect at the end of the second year.

In the second project, government spends \$3 billion each year over a period of 10 years. The step-up effect on GNP would be less than that of the first project in the first year, but there will be no drop in GNP in any of the following 9 years.

Given that people save at average 50% of their income, the propensity to save is thus MPS = 0.5, and the Keynesian multiplier is

$$\frac{1}{MPS} = \frac{1}{0.5} = 2.$$

Consider first the project with the major investments concentrated in the first two years. In the first year the injection is ΔI = \$15 billion, thus the increase in GNP ΔY = 2 x \$15 = \$30 billion. This level of investment of \$15 billion is sustained in the second year, so there is no increase or decrease in GNP, and GNP remains at the higher level reached in the first year. In the third year, investment drops back to zero, so there is a 'withdrawal' of ΔI = -15, and GNP decreases by ΔY = 2 x (-15) = \$30 billion. During the rest of the 10 year period, GNP remains at the lower level. See Table 1 and Figure 1.

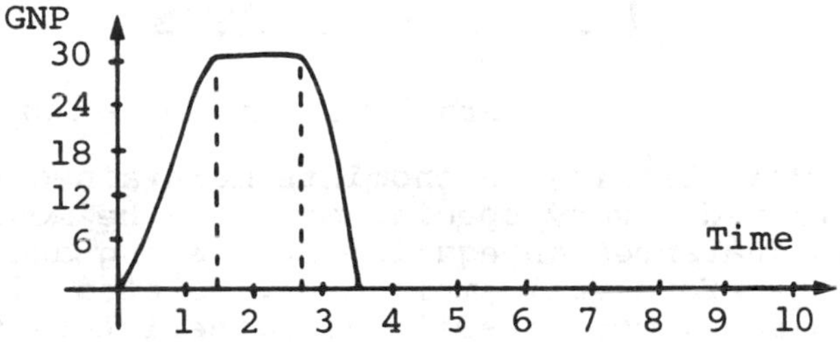

Fig. 1 Project 1

Table 1

Period	1	2	3	4	5	6	7	8	9	10
Change in GNP, ΔY	+30	0	-30	0	0	0	0	0	0	0

In the second project plan the total expenditure of \$30 billion is spread evenly over 10 years. In the first year the injection is ΔI = \$3 billion, thus the increase in GNP is ΔY = 2 x 3 = \$6 billion. In the following 9 years GNP will remain at the higher level reached in the first period. Only after the 10 year period, when no other investment projects will be initiated, will a drop of \$6 billion in GNP occur. See Table 2 and Figure 2.

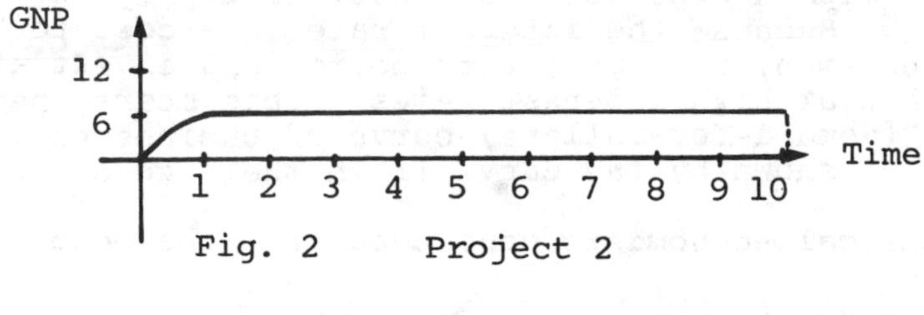

Fig. 2 Project 2

Table 2

Period	1	2	3	4	5	6	7	8	9	10
Change in GNP, ΔY	+6	0	0	0	0	0	0	0	0	0

• PROBLEM 5-40

How did the classical economists use the money market mechanism as their defense in giving guarantee to the equality of saving and investment plans and therefore full employment?

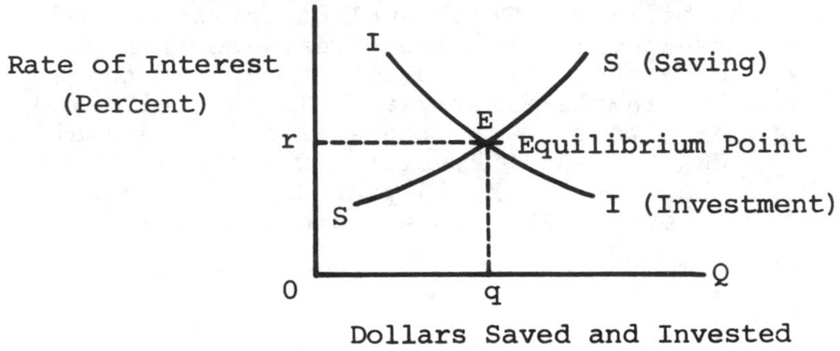

Solution: The classical economists maintained that capitalism contained a very special market--the money market--which would guarantee an equilibrium saving and investment plans and therefore full employment. Stated differently, the money market, more specifically the interest rate (the price paid for the use of money)--has been given the role of seeing to it that dollars stocked as saving would automatically reappear as dollars spent on investment goods. The rationale underlying the saving and investment equating adjustments of the interest rate was given by the classical economists who contended that, other things being equal, households normally prefer to consume rather than to save. The consumption of goods and services satisfies human wants; idle dollars do not. Hence, it was reasoned that consumers would save only if someone would pay them a rate of interest as a reward for their thriftiness. The greater the interest rate, the more dollars would be saved; that is, the saving (supply-of-dollars) curve of households would be upsloping. This could be verified by the figure.

Furthermore, the classical economists maintained that it is the business owners who seek (demand) money capital to replace and enlarge their plants and their stocks of capital equipment who would be inclined to pay for the use of saving. Because the interest rate is a cost to borrowing businessmen, they prefer to borrow and invest at low rather than at high interest rates. This means that the investment (demand-for-dollars) curve of businesses is downward sloping, as shown by the curve II in the figure.

Classical economists concluded that the money market,

wherein savers supply dollars and investors demand dollars, would establish an equilibrium price for the use of money--an equilibrium interest rate--at which the quantity of dollars saved (supplied) would equal the number of dollars invested (demanded).

Answer

SHORT ANSWER QUESTIONS FOR REVIEW

To be covered when testing yourself

Choose the correct answer.

1. A straight line consumption function, which cuts the 45° line from above: (a) has an MPC which is constant and less than one for all income levels (b) has an MPC which is constant and greater than one for all income levels (c) has an MPC which is greater than one above the break even point and less than one below it (d) has an MPC which is greater than one below the break even point and less than one above it (e) exhibits none of the traits listed above — a

2. The community consumption function will be shifted by all of the following except: (a) the discovery of vast amounts of a valuable natural resource (b) changes in the population level (c) changes in the overall price level (d) changes in family incomes (e) changes in the value of the community's liquid assets — d

3. If consumption is $9,000 when disposable income is $10,000, then the marginal propensity to consume is (a) .10 (b) .9 (c) 9/1 (d) 10/9 (e) indeterminate — e

4. At the break even point: (a) saving is equal to zero (b) consumption is equal to disposable income (c) the consumption function intersects the 45° line (d) MPS + MPC = 1 (e) all of the above — e

5. The marginal propensity to consume is the ratio of: (a) total consumption to total income (b) the increase in saving to an increase in income (c) the increase in consumption to an increase in income (d) the increase in consumption to an increase in saving (e) break even consumption to break even income — c

6. If the community as a whole decides to become less thrifty, that is, to consume more out of every paycheck, then: (a) the consumption function would shift upward while the saving function would shift downward (b) the consumption function would shift downward while the saving function would shift upward (c) the consumption function and the saving function would both shift upward (d) the consumption function and the saving function would both shift downward (e) none of the above would happen since this is an example of a shift along

SHORT ANSWER QUESTIONS FOR REVIEW

Answer (To be covered when testing yourself)

the consumption function, not a shift of it — a

7. The level of consumer income determines: (a) the stock of liquid assets (b) the level of consumer indebtedness (c) the purchasing power (d) the distribution of wealth (e) none of the above — c

8. If MPS is .25, then MPC is: (a) .25 (b) .25 x .75 (c) .25 - 1.0 (d) 1.0 - .25 (e) .75 - .25 — d

9. On a chart which shows consumption and income, a 45° line shows: (a) the set of all points where consumption equals saving (b) the set of all points where saving equals income (c) the set of all points where consumption equals income (d) all by itself, the level of saving for all income levels (e) none of the above — c

10. Which of the following would not shift the consumption function downward? (a) An increase in taxes (b) An increase in income (c) An increase in thriftiness (d) A very high level of consumer indebtedness (e) None of these — b

11. Say's law maintains that: (a) demand creates its own supply (b) consumption creates its own demand (c) savings creates its own consumption (d) saving creates its own investment (e) none of the above. — d

12. Which of the following would tend to shift the investment schedule downward? (a) An increase in the interest rate (b) A technological advance which causes costs to decrease sharply (c) Vigorous stock market activity on Wall Street (d) Declining wages (e) Overall optimism in the business community — a

Use the diagram for questions 13 through 15.

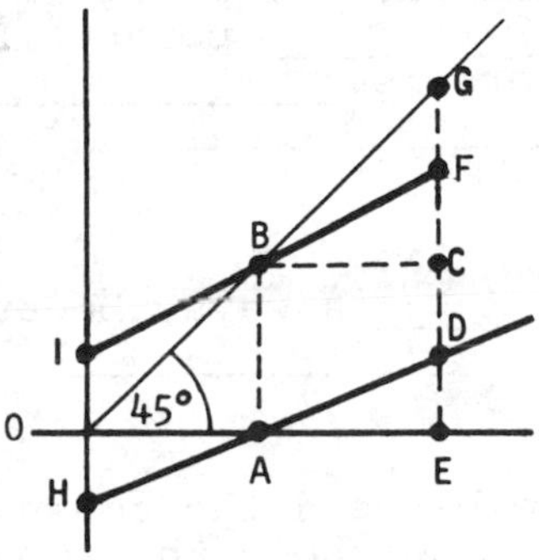

SHORT ANSWER QUESTIONS FOR REVIEW

	Answer (To be covered when testing yourself)
13. The average propensity to consume (APC) is one at point: (a) F (b) B (c) I (d) D (e) E	b
14. Which two line segments are equal in length? (a) GF = DE (b) AB = BC (c) OB = BC (d) IB = BF (e) OA = AE	a
15. The marginal propensity to save (MPS) is equal to: (a) BG/BC (b) BF/BC (c) IB/OA (d) 1 - BG/BC (e) DE/AE	e
<u>Fill in the blanks.</u>	
16. _____________ is defined by the economist as the act of refraining from present consumption.	saving
17. The undertaking of the maintenance and improvement of productive capacity is known as ______.	investment
18. (Consumption/Investment) tends to be much more variable than (consumption/investment).	investment, consumption
19. The percentage of any income increment that is consumed is called the ______________.	marginal propensity to consume, or MPC
20. The percentage of any income increment that is saved is called the ______________.	marginal propensity to save, or MPS
21. Savings is equal to zero when consumption is equal to ______________.	disposable income
22. In a very simple model, the economist claims that disposable income = ______________ + ______________.	saving, consumption
23. The income level where savings is equal to zero is known as the ______________ point. Below this income level there is ______________, and above it, there is ______________.	break even, dissaving or negative saving, positive saving
24. MPS + MPC = ______________ always, because Saving + Consumption = ______________.	1, Total Disposable Income
25. The vertical distance between the consumption function and the 45° line shows the amount	

Answer To be covered when testing yourself

(positive or negative) of ____________. — saving

Determine whether the following statements are true or false.

26. If during a period of very low income, money is borrowed (dissaved) to live on, then the MPC must be greater than 1 for this point in time since consumption is greater than disposable income. — False

27. The act of buying a share of common stock in IBM would be called investment by the economist. — False

28. As income rises, a family's MPS tends to fall. — False

29. The value of the slope of the consumption function at any point is its MPC at that point. — True

30. If the marginal propensity to save schedule is known, then the marginal propensity to consume schedule can be derived. — True

31. Investment fluctuates so much because people's savings habits fluctuate so much. — False

32. If the consumption function for every family is known, then these schedules may be aggregated to find the exact community consumption function. — False

33. If saving is zero and consumption is positive, then the break even point has been reached. — True

34. Assumptions about the inter-family distribution of national income are essential in the construction of the community consumption function. — True

35. The savers in our economy are also the investors, which is why the government sector is needed to assure a smoothly functioning economy. — False

36. MPS - 1 = MPC. — False

37. For a normal individual consumption function, the APC may be greater than one below the break even income level, and less than one above it. — True

38. An increase in the interest rate will tend to shift the investment schedule upward. — False

39. According to classical theory, an increase in the desire to save will lower the interest rate

Answer
To be covered when testing yourself

and, in so doing, will increase investment by a corresponding amount. | True

CHAPTER 6

INCOME DETERMINATION: THE SIMPLE MULTIPLIER THEORY

Basic Attacks and Strategies for Solving Problems in this Chapter. **See pages 175 to 198 for step-by-step solutions to problems.**

An important element of Keynesian theory (frequently called the multiplier theory) is the determination of the equilibrium level of income and output. The equilibrium level is defined as the sustainable level—the level of income and output that can continue to be produced assuming no unexpected changes in the economy.

Assume a closed, pure market economy (an economy without a government sector or any international economic relationships). In such an economy, aggregate demand (Y_d) is equal to the sum of (planned) consumption and (planned) investment, where consumption is induced spending (dependent on the level of income) and investment is autonomous spending (not dependent on the level of income)

$$Y_d = C + I.$$

Using the GNP identity of output and income, aggregate supply (Y_s), a measure of output, is equal to income, which can be broken down into two components, (planned) consumption and (planned) savings

$$Y_s = C + S.$$

In such an economy, there are three ways to locate the equilibrium level of income:

1) Since equilibrium can be defined as the level of income where total spending is just sufficient to purchase all the goods produced, it follows that in equilibrium $Y_d = Y_s$.

2) The equality of Y_d and Y_s means $C + I = C + S$. Therefore in equilibrium $I = S$. The economic rationale for this is as follows. The income generated from production is just sufficient to buy all the goods and

services produced (from the fundamental equality between output and income). Equilibrium is obtained if all that income is spent. Money that is saved represents a leakage from this circular flow of income and expenditure. Only if all the money saved is borrowed and invested (injected back into the circular flow), can there be equilibrium, which implies that I must equal S.

3) If aggregate demand is less than the amount produced, the surplus goods will be placed in inventory. This increase in inventory is unintended and undesired, and will cause firms to reduce production, meaning the economy could not have been in equilibrium. If aggregate demand exceeds the amount produced, the excess demand can only be satisfied by firms making unintended and undesired reductions in their inventories, which will spur them to increase production in the future, a situation which likewise could not have been equilibrium. Consequently, a third way to locate equilibrium is the level of income where there is no unintended inventory changes.

In a closed economy with a simple government sector, the equilibrium conditions are similar, only they must be modified to take into account government spending and taxes. In such an economy, $Y_d = C + I + G$ and $Y_s = C + S + T$, where both G and T are autonomous.

The three equilibrium conditions are:

1) $Y_d = Y_s$ or $C + I + G = C + S + T$.

2) $I + G = S + T$.

3) Unintended inventory investment is 0.

The multiplier effect refers to the fact that changes in autonomous factors (for example ΔI, ΔG, ΔT) cause changes in the equilibrium level of income (ΔY) that are a multiple of the change in spending. This multiple ($\Delta Y/\Delta I$, $\Delta Y/\Delta G$, $\Delta Y/\Delta T$) is known as the multiplier.

The reason for the multiplier effect can be simply stated. Assume the economy is in equilibrium and a form of autonomous spending increases. This increase in spending will be associated with an increase in demand for output in some sectors of the economy, leading to an increase in the incomes of people who work in those sectors. The higher incomes thus generated will stimulate greater spending on the part of those individuals. This added spending will be associated with higher demand in some other sectors of the economy leading to higher incomes there. These higher incomes will in turn stimulate more spending which will lead to higher incomes elsewhere, and so on. In short, spending increases income, which will lead to more spending, which will increase incomes still more, leading to more spending and more income, and so on.

In the simplest model, with induced and autonomous consumption, a MPC =

m, and autonomous I, G, and T, the important multipliers are:

Consumption spending multiplier = $1/(1-m)$ so that

$$\Delta Y = \left(\frac{1}{1-m}\right)\Delta C$$

Investment spending multiplier = $1/(1-m)$ so that

$$\Delta Y = \left(\frac{1}{1-m}\right)\Delta I$$

Government spending multiplier = $1/(1-m)$ so that

$$\Delta Y = \left(\frac{1}{1-m}\right)\Delta G$$

Tax multiplier = $-m/(1-m)$ so that

$$\Delta Y = \left(\frac{-m}{1-m}\right)\Delta T$$

Step-by-Step Solutions to Problems in this Chapter, "Income Determination: The Simple Multiplier Theory"

EQUILIBRIUM INCOME DETERMINATION

• PROBLEM 6-1

Give the significance of the equilibrium level of output.

Solution: The equilibrium level of output is that level of output which the economy is capable and willing to sustain. Stated differently, the equilibrium level of output whose production will actually create total spending just sufficient to purchase that output; in other words, the total quantity of goods supplied (NNP) is precisely equal to the total quantity of goods demanded (C + In). This is the only level of output at which the economy is willing to spend precisely the amount necessary to take that output off the market. Here, the annual rates of production and spending are in balance. There is no over production, which results in a piling up of unsold goods and therefore cutbacks in the rate of production, nor is there an excess of total spending, which draws down inventories and prompts increases in the rate of production.

• PROBLEM 6-2

Assuming that equilibrium GNP can be found at the intersection of the savings and investment schedules, show that equilibrium GNP can be found at the intersection of the consumption plus investment schedule and the 45° line.

Solution: Look at the graph below to help visualize the problem. Aggregate demand equals consumption plus investment

$$Y_d = C + I \qquad (1)$$

Aggregate supply = aggregate income which equals the sum of consumption and savings

$$Y_s = C + S \qquad (2)$$

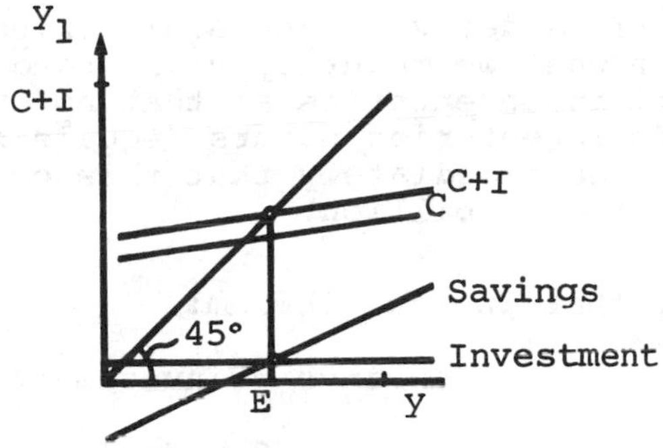

In equilibrium aggregate demand equals aggregate supply

$$Y_d = Y_s \qquad (3)$$

i.e., the intersection of the consumption-investment schedules and the 45° line. Substituting (1) and (2) into (3) results in

$$C + I = C + S$$

Suppressing consumption at both sides of the equation gives

$$I = S$$

i.e., the intersection of the investment and savings schedules.

• PROBLEM 6-3

Based on the following hypothetical data, determine the equilibrium level of output:

Savings billions	Investment billions	Aggregate demand (C + In), billions	Unintended investment (+) or disinvestment (-) in inventories
$ - 5	$ 20	$ 395	$ - 25
0	20	410	- 20
5	20	425	- 15
10	20	440	- 10
15	20	455	- 5
20	20	470	0
25	20	485	+ 5
30	20	500	+ 10
35	20	515	+ 15

Solution: Before deriving the equilibrium level of output, let's explain what we meant by unintended investment and disinvestment in inventories so that no unintended (dis-) investment in inventories occurs (equals zero). From the schedules we see immediately that this occurs at an aggregate demand of $470 billion.

We know also that in equilibrium:

savings = investment

$$S = I$$

and also this occurs at an aggregate demand of $470 billion.

In equilibrium:

aggregate supply = aggregate demand

Thus the equilibrium level of output is $470 billion.

• PROBLEM 6-4

The existing level of output of the economy is $ 1,700 billion. Planned savings are $ 255 billion, the government plans to levy taxes of $ 470 billion, and businesses are intending to spend $ 240 billion. What level of government expenditure will balance the economy at its existing output level, if there are no international transactions?

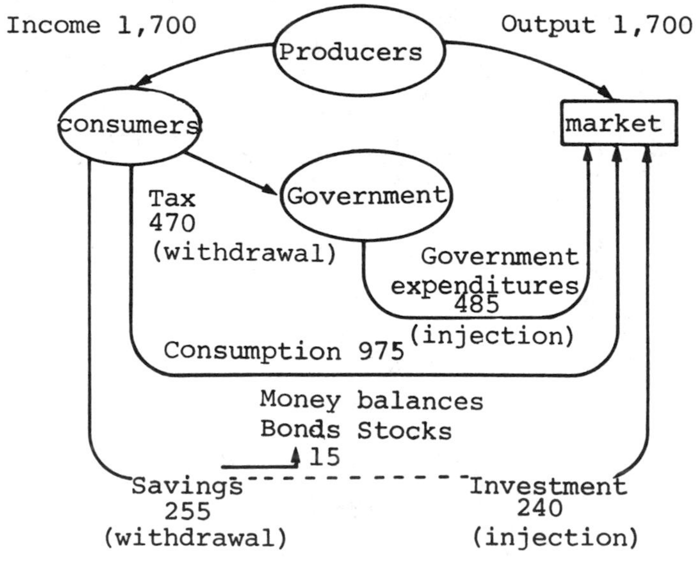

Fig. 3

Solution: The output of the economy must be matched by the demand for it, if the level of output is to remain at its existing level. The output of this economy is $ 1,700 billion. The total value of income is, per definition, equal to the total value of output; thus total income is also $Y = \$ 1,700$ billion. The government will levy a tax of $T = \$ 470$ billion, which is a withdrawal. Disposable income, therefore, is $Y_d = Y - T = 1,700 - 470 = \$ 1,230$ billion. The disposable income will be used for consumption and savings, $Y_d = C + S$. Planned savings are \$ 255 billion, thus consumption plans amount to $C = Y_d - S = 1,230 - 255 = \$ 975$ billion. The total aggregate demand consists of consumption, C, investment, I, and government expenditures, G, when there are no international transactions, that is, when there are no exports or imports. So

$$\begin{aligned} Y &= C + I + G \\ &= 975 + 240 + G \\ &= 1,215 + G. \end{aligned}$$

For income to remain in equilibrium, output must be demanded in total. Thus

$$1,700 = 1,215 + G$$

and the government expenditures must be

$$G = 1,700 - 1,215 = \$ 485 \text{ billion}$$

in order to balance the economy.

This situation is pictured in the flow diagram shown.

The planned savings and taxes are planned withdrawals from the income-expenditure flows, while the planned investments and government expenditures are planned injections.

Note: government has a budget deficit. Its expenditures exceed the tax revenues by $G - T = 485 - 470 = \$ 15$ billion. And savings exceed investments by $S - I = 255 - 240 = \$ 15$ billion. These \$ 15 billion are diverted into money balances; or into U.S. securities in order to finance the public debt.

• PROBLEM 6-5

Economic theory tells us that the intersection of the savings and investment schedules, as shown below, is the equilibrium toward which national income will gravitate. Explain why national income will move toward E if national income is above or below E.

Solution: Suppose that national income is above point E. At any point above E, savings surpass investment. At such a point, families intend to save more than firms will be willing to go on investing. Firms will then find a lack of customers and inventories pile up. Not wanting to be forced into undesired inventory investment, firms will cut

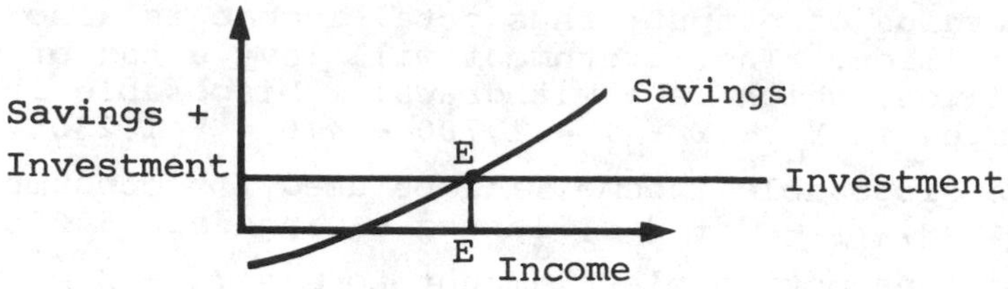

production and lay off workers, moving national income gradually downward toward E.

If national income were below E, families' intended saving falls short of business firms' intended investment. The result is consumption being greater than current production. Businesses will find inventories depleting and will then expand production and hire more men, causing national income to increase toward E.

• PROBLEM 6-6

> Suppose that investment is always zero and the savings and consumption schedules are linear so that MPS = S and equilibrium GNP = $\overline{Y}$. Show that if GNP = 0, scheduled consumption = $S\overline{Y}$.

Solution: Since investment = 0, the Consumption plus Investment Schedule is simply the Consumption Schedule. Therefore equilibrium occurs at the point where the consumption schedule intersects the 45° line. Also, since investment = 0 and equilibrium occurs when savings = investment, equilibrium is at the point where the savings schedule crosses the horizontal axis. (See the accompanying figure).

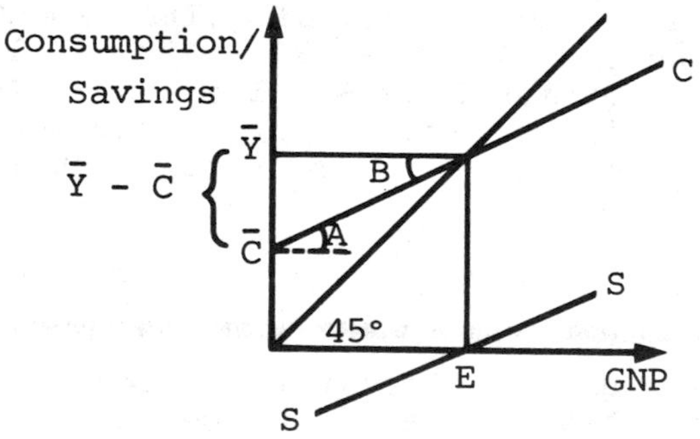

At the equilibrium point, E, GNP = $\overline{Y}$ as stated in the assumption. Since at E, CC intersects the 45° line, consumption is also equal to $\overline{Y}$ at E. Therefore $(\overline{Y},\overline{Y})$ is a point on our consumption schedule, CC. Our job now is to find the Y-coordinate of the point (0,Y) which shows what consumption would be if GNP = 0. To find this we must know the slope of the Consumption schedule. Given is MPS = s. Using the definition 1 - c = S, which implies that c + s = 1, we have $c = 1 - s$ (1)

The Consumption schedule is

$$C = c \cdot Y + \overline{C} \qquad (2)$$

where $\overline{C}$ is the autonomous consumption. Substituting (1) into equation (2) results in

$$C = (1 - s) Y + \overline{C}$$

When GNP = Y = 0 there is no induced, only autonomous consumption

$$C = \overline{C}$$

From the figure we notice that the slope of the linear Consumption schedule,

$$\text{slope A} = \text{slope B} = \frac{\overline{Y} - \overline{C}}{\overline{Y}}$$

Thus

$$1 - s = \frac{\overline{Y} - \overline{C}}{\overline{Y}}$$

Multiplying both sides by $\overline{Y}$ results in

$$\overline{Y} - s\,\overline{Y} = \overline{Y} - \overline{C}$$

Subtracting $\overline{Y}$, and deleting the negative signs at both sides of the equation gives

$$s\overline{Y} = C$$

Conclusion: the autonomous consumption, i.e., the consumption when GNP = 0, equals the product of the Marginal Propensity to Save and equilibrium GNP.

• PROBLEM 6-7

A simple economy, in which both the desired savings and the intended investment depend only on the value of the disposable income (the interest rate is assumed to be fixed, r = c, MPS > 0, MPI > 0), reaches its equilibrium at a point where I = S. Will the assumption MPI > MPS significantly alter the ability of this economy to settle at the equilibrium point? How?

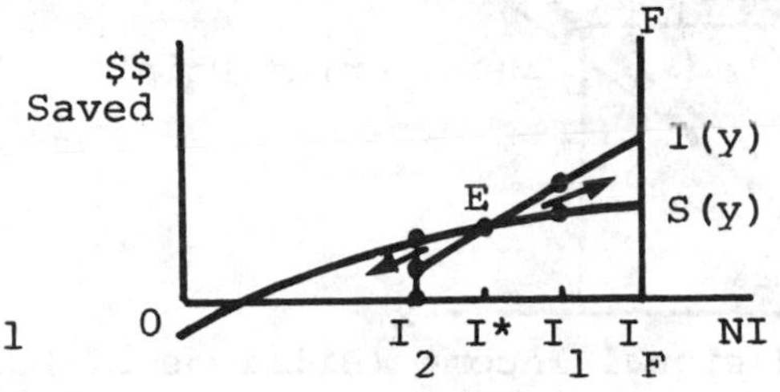

Fig. 1

Solution: The assumptions of the problem tell us in effect that an increase in the aggregate level of national income in our economy will induce higher levels of desired savings and desired investment. The statement MPI > MPS means simply that a given change in NI will cause a larger change in the value of I than it will in the value of S in our economy. Graphically the model can be described in the following way: Consider a point to the right of E where the value of NI is I, (NI is bigger than I* but smaller than I_F which is a full employment output). As Fig. 1 shows, at this level of aggregate income the desired investment by business firms exceeds the desired savings by the households. It means that the aggregate value of withdrawals from our economy represented by planned savings is insufficient to match the total value of injections into the economy represented by the intended investment. Consequently the demand for goods produced in the economy will start exceeding the available supply, the firms' inventories will be depleting, and the businessmen will be pushed into further investment and expanded production as a result of excess demand. Therefore at a point I, our economy will tend to move rightward toward higher investment and employment, and away from E.

Similar analysis will show that at I_2 the economy will tend to contract rather than expand and will again move in the direction away from E. The described above tendencies are represented by black arrows in Fig. 1. Clearly, the assumption MPI > MPS alters the nature of the economy significantly in that it makes it unstable. At any level of NI higher (lower) than I* the natural forces of our economy will make it expand (contract) even further away from the point E where I = S (see Fig. 1). In this situation point E in Fig. 1 becomes meaningless as an equilibrium point and the economy has no self-stabilizing qualities.

• PROBLEM 6-8

Prove that the aggregate supply schedule is the 45-degree line in the aggregate demand - aggregate supply approach to the equilibrium NNP.

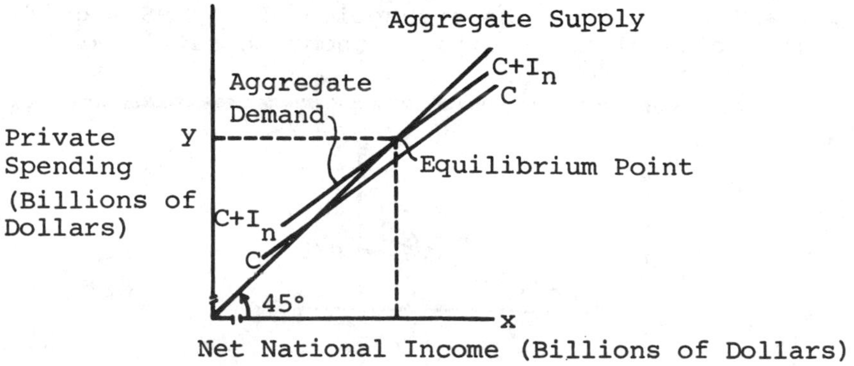

Solution: The aggregate demand- aggregate supply approach determines the equilibrium levels of employment, output, and income at the point where the aggregate supply consisting of output = income (NNP), is equal to the aggregate demand (Consumption + Net Investment).

By definition, each point on the aggregate supply schedule indicates (on the vertical axis) the amount which the business community must receive as total spending, = total revenue from business' point of view, in order to be induced to produce the corresponding level of national output = national income (on the horizontal axis). Business in the aggregate is willing to undertake the production of, χ (billions of dollars) of national output only if anticipated expenditures are Y (billions of dollars), where $\chi = Y$. If business expects total spending to be greater or less than Y it will find it profitable to offer an equally larger or smaller national output. Thus, a series of points--a line-- equidistant from the total output (NNP) axis and the total spending (C + In) axis will summarize the aggregate supply plans of business. Being equidistant from the two axes, this line is necessarily the 45-degree line. The 45° line being the aggregate supply schedule, the intersection of the 45° line with the aggregate demand schedule (C + In) will determine the equilibrium level of NNP.

• PROBLEM 6-9

How can the IS-schedule be derived from the savings and the investment schedules?

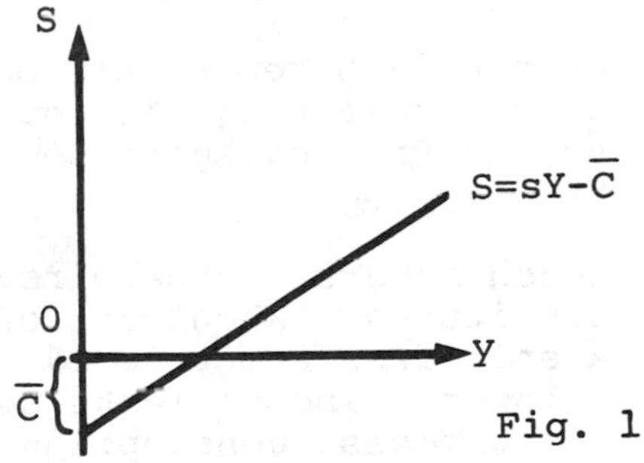

Fig. 1

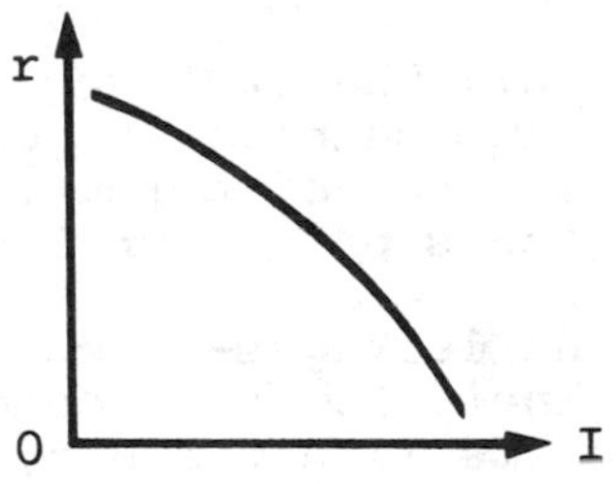

Fig. 2

Solution: The IS-scheldule is the collection of points in the interest rate - income plane that represent equilibria in the commodity market, i.e., savings = investment: S = I, which is equivalent to the income-expenditure equilibria C + S = C + I. The savings schedule can be described as

$S = sY - \overline{C}$ (see Fig. 1).

The investment schedule is $I = I(r)$. (see Fig. 2).

And equilibrium requires that the amount of savings equals the amount of investment, S = I (see Fig. 3).

These three schedules can be combined so that

$$sY - \overline{C} = 1(r)$$

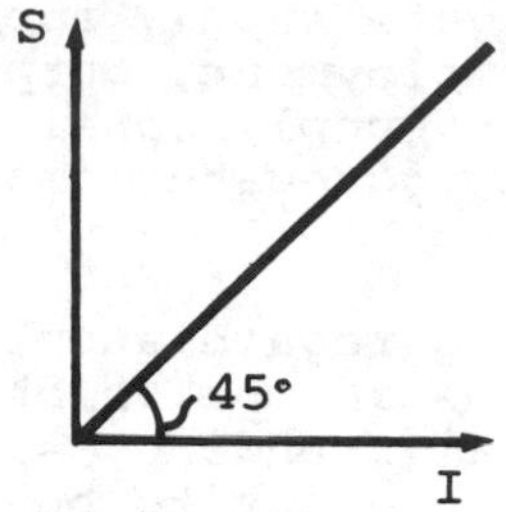

Fig. 3

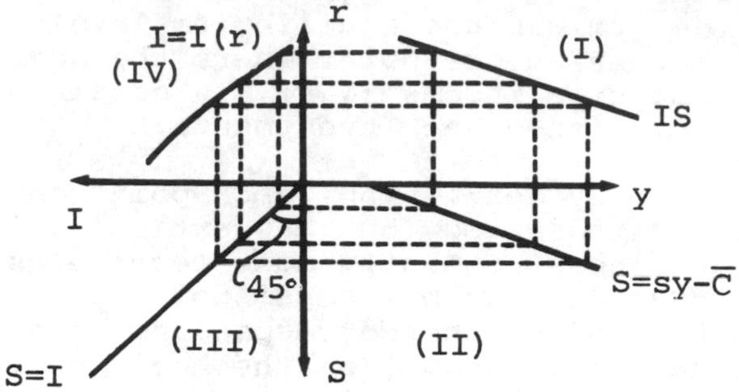

Fig. 4

or sY - $\overline{C}$ - I(r) = 0 i.e., the relationship between Y and r that describes the IS-schedule, (see Fig. 4).

Placing the savings schedule in quadrant (II), the equilibrium conditions in quadrant (III) and the investment schedule in quadrant (IV) results in the IS schedule in quadrant (I).

LEAKAGES-INJECTIONS APPROACH TO EQUILIBRIUM

• PROBLEM 6-10

Explain the essence of the leakages-injections approach in the determination of the equilibrium levels of output.

Solution: The leakages-injections approach represents one of the two methods in determining and explaining the equilibrium level of output. The other is the aggregate demand-aggregate supply (or C + In = NNP) approach.

The leakages-injections approach refers to the circular 'pipeline' flow of income and expenditures. When part of the income is not spent, total expenditures are reduced and income in the next period will be lower: income leaks away. Recall that income is used for two purposes, consumption and saving

$$Y_{in} = C + S \qquad (i)$$

or, saving is that part of income that is not spent

$$S = Y - C \qquad (ii)$$

Recall also the Consumption Function

$$C = c \cdot Y + \overline{C} \qquad (iii)$$

Substituting (iii) into (ii) gives us

$$S = Y - (c \cdot Y + \overline{C})$$

$$= (1 - c) Y - \overline{C}$$

$$= s \cdot Y - \bar{C}$$

where c = Marginal Propensity to Consume

s = 1 - c = Marginal Propensity to Save.

Savings therefore represent a leakage in the potential spending or demand from the income-expenditures flow. The consequence of saving is that consumption falls short of aggregate output or NNP; hence, by itself consumption is insufficient to take aggregate supply off the market, and this fact would seem to set the stage for a decline in total output. However, the business sector does not intend to sell its entire output to consumers; some of the national output will take the form of capital or investment goods which will be sold within the business sector. Investment can therefore be thought of as an injection into the income-expenditure flow, supplementing consumption; Total Expenditures consist of consumption and investments.

$$Y_{ex} = C + In \qquad \text{(iv)}$$

In equilibrium

$$Y_{in} = Y_{ex}$$

Substituting (i) and (iv) in

$$C + S = C + In$$

Subtracting C from both sides

$$S = In$$

Only at the point of equilibrium households plan to save the amount business wants to invest.

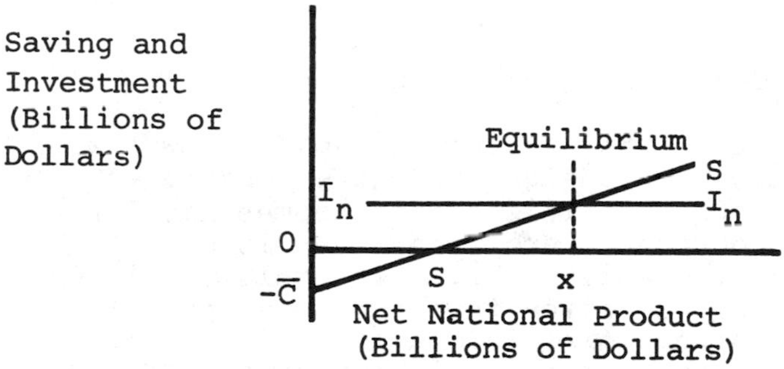

The accompanying graph illustrates this point.

• PROBLEM 6-11

Calculate the total of withdrawals from the economic income-expenditure circuit, when it is given that the marginal propensity to consume is 0.90 and the income tax rate is 0.26; for the following levels of total output: $ 1,100 billion.
1,050
1,000
950
900

Why is this calculation important?

Solution: Withdrawals from the income-expenditure circuit consist of savings and taxes. But taxes affect disposable income, and because savings are based on disposable income, taxes also affect savings.

National income of the economy equals its total output.

To determine the aggregate savings, we have to determine what percentage of disposable income is saved, i.e., the marginal propensity to save. The marginal propensity to save is equal to one minus the marginal propensity to consume:

$$s = 1 - c = 1 - 0.90 = 0.10$$

Total Output = Total National Income Y (1)	Taxes T = 0.26Y (2)	Disposable Income Y - 0.26Y (3)=(1)-(2)	Savings S = 0.10(1-0.26)Y (4)=0.10x(3)	Total With-drawals T + S (2)+(4)
1,100	286	814	81.4	367.4
1,050	273	777	77.7	350.7
1,000	260	740	74.0	334.0
950	247	703	70.3	317.3
900	234	666	66.6	300.6

The solution is developed in the table above.

Notice that both taxes and savings go up (or down) with total national income. When the government expenditures G remain constant, the budget deficit G - T becomes smaller when national income increases, and wider when it decreases. Suppose that the full employment level is \$ 1,000 billion. From the table we notice that the total of withdrawals at that level of national income is \$ 334.0 billion. Suppose that it is estimated that total private planned investments will be \$ 50 billion. This is an injection in the income-expenditure circuit. The total of injections consists of investments and government expenditures I + G. For equilibrium the total of withdrawals should equal the total of injections:

$$T + S = I + G$$

Thus, $334 = 50 + G,$

and we infer that the government expenditures should be fixed at G = 334 - 50 = \$ 284 billion. There will be a budget deficit of G - T = 284 - 260 = \$ 24 billion to sustain a full-employment level of income.

MULTIPLIER ANALYSIS

• PROBLEM 6-12

Prove that the multiplier is equal to 1/(1 - MPC).

Solution: Suppose you purchase an item for \$ 100. This first \$100 will result in an increase in income throughout the economy. The \$100 will find its way into the hands of other households in the form of wages, rent, interest, and profits. There it will be subject to MPC. Suppose MPC = 0.8. Then (100)(0.8) = \$80 will be spent. This \$80 will contribute to income and will once again pass on to other households. There it will once again be subject to MPC. So $(80)(0.8)[=(100)(0.8)^2] = \$64$ will be spent. The process will keep going.

Generalizing, we see that if x is the original expenditure and c is MPC, the amount of eventual income, I, can be determined by this formula:

$$I = x + xc + xc^2 + xc^3 + \ldots$$
$$= x(1 + c + c^2 + c^3 + \ldots)$$

This is an infinite series with c smaller than one; therefore, $\left(1 + c + c^2 + c^3 + \ldots = \frac{1}{1-c}\right)$. Substituting back into the original equation, we get $I = x\left(\frac{1}{1-c}\right)$ or $I = x\left(\frac{1}{1 - MPC}\right)$. So we see that the Income generated, I, is equal to the original investment multiplied by $\left(\frac{1}{1 - MPC}\right)$, which is therefore the multiplier.

• PROBLEM 6-13

In 1978, Government increased its investment spending by \$ 5 billion. Given that the MPC (Marginal Propensity to Consume) is 0.75, and assuming further that the economy is initially in equilibrium at \$ 470 billion,

a) Determine its effect on equilibrium NNP;

b) Assuming that instead of an increase by \$ 5 billion, there was a drop in investment by \$ 5 billion, what will happen to equilibrium NNP?

c) Give the significance of your results.

Solution: This is an application of the Keynesian Multiplier Principle, which is based upon two facts:

1. That the economy is characterized by repetitive continuous flows of expenditures and income wherein the dollars

spent by Mr. Clarke are received as income by Mr. Grove. (See Fig. 1)

Fig. 1

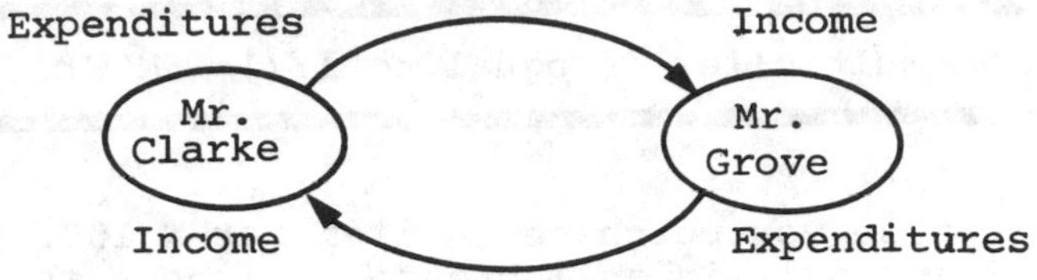

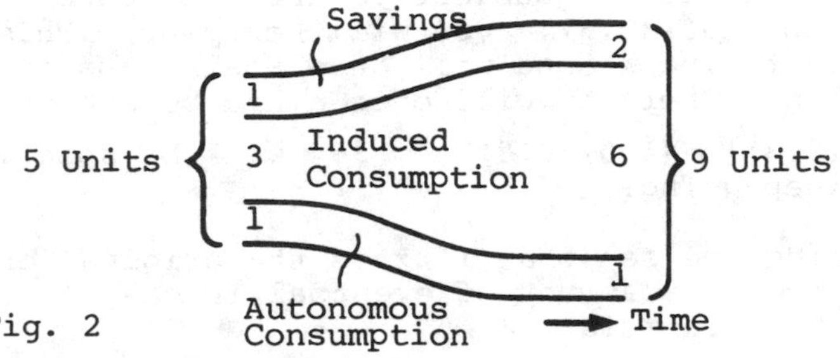

Fig. 2

2. That any change in income will cause consumption to vary in the same direction, as, and by a fraction of, the change in income. (See Fig. 2)

The Multiplier Principle states that an initial change in the rate of spending will cause a chain reaction which, although of diminishing importance at each successive step, will cumulate to a multiple change in NNP.

In any economy total aggregate income is equal to total aggregate spending.

With a constant MPC, here $c = 0.75$, an increase in income carries a proportional increase in both, savings and consumption. How this Multiplier Principle is based upon these two facts becomes clear from the following derivation.

Fact 1, the Income Identity, states that total aggregate income = total aggregate spending

= investment + consumption

$$Y = In + C \qquad \text{(i)}$$

Fact 2, the Consumption Function, states that consumption is proportional to income.

$$C = c \cdot Y + \overline{C} \qquad \text{(ii)}$$

Where c = Marginal Propensity to Consume

$\overline{C}$ = autonomous consumption

Substituting (ii) into (i) we derive the following equation

$$Y = In + (c \cdot Y + \overline{C})$$

Bringing all the terms including Y to the left-hand side,

$$Y - c \cdot Y = (1 - c)Y = In + \overline{C}$$

Dividing both sides by (1 - c) gives

$$Y = \frac{1}{1-c} \cdot (In + \overline{C}).$$

The coefficient $\frac{1}{1-c}$ is called: the multiplier because any change in investment, ΔIn, and in autonomous consumption, $\Delta \overline{C}$, is multiplied by this factor to produce a magnified change in income, ΔY. Thus

$$\Delta Y = \frac{1}{1-c} (\Delta In + \Delta \overline{C}) \qquad \text{(iii)}$$

To see that this represents a chain reaction with diminishing effect over time, we increase investment. Income will in first instance be affected directly by this increase in spending. (Refer to equation (i)).

$$\Delta Y_0 = \Delta In$$

In the next round, part of the increase in income will be consumed, (no change in autonomous consumption).

$$\Delta C_1 = c \cdot \Delta Y_0$$

thereby increasing income further. This next increase in income is also partly spent on consumption.

$$\Delta C_2 = c . \Delta C_1 = c^2 \Delta Y_0 = c^2 \Delta In$$

Etcetera, (the indices indicate time periods).

The ultimate change in income is the accumulated sum of all these changes.

$$\Delta Y_f = \Delta C_1 + \Delta C_2 + \Delta C_3 + \ldots + \Delta In$$

$$= c\Delta I + c^2 \Delta I + c^3 \Delta I + \ldots + \Delta In$$

$$= (1 + c + c^2 + c^3 + \ldots) \Delta In$$

$$= \frac{1}{1-c} \cdot \Delta In,$$

It is also seen that the effect over time diminishes because c is a fraction smaller than 1, so that the higher powers of c become smaller and smaller, and the effect of the initial increase in investment lessens.

a) Government increased investments by $ 5 billion, $\Delta In = 5$

The Marginal Propensity to Consume is 0.75. Using formula (iii) we can calculate the effect on NNP. $(\Delta\bar{C} = 0)$.

$$\Delta Y = \frac{1}{1-c} \cdot \Delta In$$

Substituting the given values in

$$\Delta Y = \frac{1}{1 - 0.75} \cdot 5 = \frac{5}{0.25} = 20$$

NNP is increased by $ 20 billion, so the new equilibrium NNP is

$$NNP_{new} = 470 + 20 = 490 \text{ billion dollars.}$$

b) Following the same procedure, $\Delta In = -5$

$$\Delta Y = \frac{1}{0.25} \cdot -5 = -20$$

Thus NNP will decrease by $ 20 billion and the new equilibrium NNP will be

$$NNP_{new} = 470 - 20 = 450 \text{ billion dollars.}$$

c) From the above results, we can see that a relatively small change in the investment plans of businesses and government or the consumption - saving plans of households can trigger a much larger change in the equilibrium level of NNP. Furthermore, it is also of no coincidence that the multiplier effect ends at the point where exactly enough saving has been generated to offset the initial $ 5 billion increase in investment spending. It is only then that the disequilibrium created by the investment increase will be corrected. In this case, NNP and total incomes must rise by $ 20 billion to create $ 5 billion in additional saving to match the $ 5 billion increase in investment spending. Income must increase by 4 times the initial excess of investment over saving, because households save one-fourth of any increase in their incomes.

• PROBLEM 6-14

Show that if the multiplier is one, the slope of the savings schedule is one.

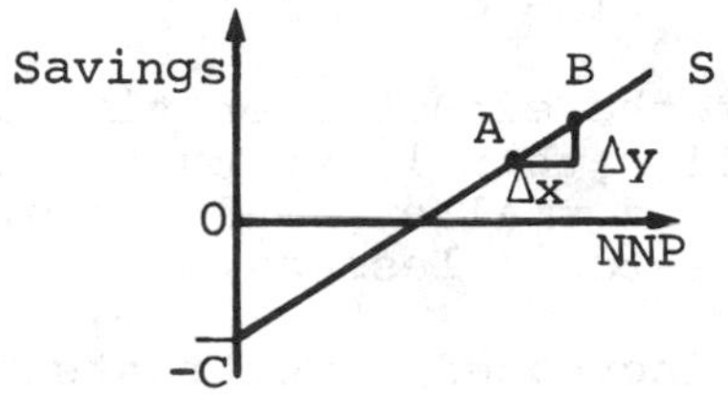

Solution: Since Multiplier = $\frac{1}{1 - MPC} = \frac{1}{MPS}$ we get MPS = 1 from the above information. Looking at the savings schedule, Δx represents change in GNP and Δ_y represents change in savings, we know from the fact that MPS = 1 that $\Delta y/\Delta x = 1$. Recall that the savings schedule can be derived from the Consumption function; it is virtually its complement.

The Consumption function is, in linear form,

$$C = c \cdot Y + \bar{C} \qquad (1)$$

where c is the Marginal Propensity to Consume and $\bar{C}$ the autonomous consumption, i.e., consumption not induced by income Y.

Income is used for consumption and savings

$$Y = C + S \qquad (2)$$

Substituting (1) into equation (2) results in

$$Y = c \cdot Y + \bar{C} + S$$

Bringing the first two terms at the right hand side to the left gives

$$S = Y - cY - \bar{C} = (1 - c)(Y - \bar{C})$$

But 1 - c = s, the Marginal Propensity to Save, thus

$$S = s \cdot Y - \bar{C},$$

i.e., the savings schedule. And we see that a marginal change in the savings caused by a marginal change in income can be represented by $\frac{\Delta S}{\Delta Y} = s$, i.e., the 'slope' of the savings schedule.

• PROBLEM 6-15

By how much must investment rise to bring about a $ 300 M change in income if MPC = 0.75.

Solution: The multiplier formula tells us that

$$\Delta \text{ income} = \frac{1}{MPS} \times \Delta \text{ investment}$$

$$\Delta \text{ income} \times MPS = \Delta \text{ investment}$$

$$\Delta \text{ income} \times (1 - MPC) = \Delta \text{ investment.}$$

Substituting the numbers above, we get

$$\$\ 300M \times (1 - 0.75) = \Delta \text{ investment.}$$

Therefore the required rise in investment is
$\$ 300M \times 0.25 = \$ 75M.$

• **PROBLEM 6-16**

Suppose the government decides to increase its expenditures by 50 billion dollars. What effect will this have on NNP if the marginal propensity to consume is 0.75?

Solution: This is a simple Keynesian multiplier problem. Aggregate demand equals the sum of consumption, investment and government expenditures.

$$Y = C + In + G \qquad (1)$$

Households consume out of their income

$$C = c \cdot Y + \overline{C} \qquad (2)$$

where c is the Marginal Propensity to Consume, and $\overline{C}$ is the autonomous consumption.

Substituting (2) into equation (1) results in

$$Y = c\,Y + \overline{C} + In + G$$

or

$$Y - cY = (1 - c)Y = \overline{C} + In + G$$

Dividing both sides by 1 - c

$$Y = \frac{1}{1 - c}\,(\overline{C} + In + G)$$

Taking changes and ignoring investment and autonomous consumption, $\Delta In = \Delta\overline{C} = 0$

$$\Delta Y = \frac{1}{1 - c} \cdot \Delta G$$

$\frac{1}{1 - c}$ is called the multiplier.

Substituting the given values c = 0.75 and $\Delta G = 50$

$$Y = \frac{1}{1 - 0.75} \cdot 50 = \frac{1}{0.25} \cdot 50 = 200$$

Thus the National Income will increase by $200 billion.

DISEQUILIBRIUM NNP ANALYSIS

• **PROBLEM 6-17**

Why is it that when aggregate demand (C + I) exceeds aggregate supply, the effect is to increase employment?

Solution: When the aggregate demand (C + In) exceeds aggregate supply, this produces a signal to increase production and, assuming a direct relationship between production and employment, the increased production results in more employment. This is due to the fact that businessmen are producing at a lower rate than buyers are taking goods off the shelves; the consequence is an unintended decline in business inventories, signaling that production has to be stepped up. More employment means more income available to spend.

The reverse holds true when aggregate demand is less than aggregate supply. That is, businesses will find that the production of these total outputs fails to generate the levels of spending needed to take them off the market, and an unintended accumulation of inventories will occur, absorbing capital. Being unable to recover the costs involved in producing these outputs, businesses will cut back on their production. This would mean fewer jobs and a decline in total income.

• PROBLEM 6-18

Suppose the production process is lengthy and 75% of the capital input at present is dependent on the output in the next period, and 25% is dependent on the output in the period thereafter. The technical capital/output ratio is 3. Furthermore, business reacts cautiously to capital shortages; it will only provide capital for 80% of the present gap and 10% of the preceding gap. Can you describe this distributed lag accelerator process?

Solution: The technical capital/output ratio is $a = \frac{K_t}{Y_t} = 3$.

However only 75% of the present capital input is reflected in the output in the next period, the rest being reflected in the following period. Thus the K capital required at present is

$$K_t = 0.75\ a\ Y_{t+1} + 0.25\ a\ Y_{t+2}$$

$$= 0.75 \times 3 \times Y_{t+1} + 0.25 \times 3 \times Y_{t+2}$$

$$= 2.25\ Y_{t+1} + 0.75\ Y_{t+2}.$$

The capital required at present is $K_t = 2.25\ Y_{t+1} + 0.75\ Y_{t+2}$, and the capital available at present is the capital of the preceding period

$$K_{t-1} = 2.25\ Y_t + 0.75\ Y_{t+1}.$$

The time-indices are simply shifted one period backward.

The present capital gap is the difference between the

capital required and the capital available. Thus

$$K_t - K_{t-1} = (2.25\ Y_{t+1} + 0.75\ Y_{t+2})$$

$$- (2.25\ Y_t + 0.75\ Y_{t+1})$$

$$= 0.75\ Y_{t+2} + 1.50\ Y_{t+1} - 2.25\ Y_t.$$

Taking 0.75 before brackets shows the weights given to the outputs between the brackets:

$$K_t - K_{t-1} = 0.75\ (Y_{t+2} + 2\ Y_{t+1} - 3\ Y_t).$$

This is the present gap.

To find the preceding gap, shift the time indices again one period backward. The preceding capital gap is then $K_{t-1} - K_{t-2} = 0.75\ (Y_{t+1} + 2Y_t - 3Y_{t-1})$. Investments provide additional capital for 80% of the present gap and 10% of the preceding capital gap, as given. Thus the present investments are $I_t = 0.80\ (K_t - K_{t-1}) + 0.10\ (K_{t-1} - K_{t-2})$. Substituting the expressions above for both gaps results in the desired distributed-lag-accelerator expression:

$$I_t = 0.80\ [0.75\ (Y_{t+2} + 2\ Y_{t+1} - 3\ Y_t)]$$

$$+ 0.10\ [0.75\ (Y_{t+1} + 2\ Y_t - 3\ Y_{t-1})]$$

After substituting for the terms Y_{t+2}, Y_{t+1}, Y_t, Y_{t-1}, the distributed-lag-accelerator is obtained:

$$I_t = 0.6\ Y_{t+2} + 1.275\ Y_{t+1} - 1.65\ Y_t - 1.80\ Y_{t-1}$$

From this expression note that investments are based partly on expectation of GNP in the future, whereby the nearest future - Y_{t+1} - is more influential than Y_{t+2}, two periods ahead; partly on present GNP, Y_t; and partly on past GNP, Y_{t-1}. In this economy GNP must progressively grow, otherwise the investments required become negative. For example, assume that GNP remains constant, i.e.,

$$Y_{t-1} = Y_t = Y_{t+1} = Y_{t+2} = Y.$$

Thus

$$I_t = 0.6\ Y + 1.275\ Y - 1.65\ Y - 1.80\ Y$$

$$= - 1.575\ Y.$$

In other words, in this unrealistically pessimistic economy there is a strong tendency for investments to fall, and head for a deep depression. Only if the behavior of the business changes, towards becoming less conservative, can this economy be "saved." (The 'conservative' investment behavior can also be explained by capacity limitations of the capital goods producing industries; even if business wants to add quickly new capital, it is constrained to do so. There may be a serious backlog in the investment projects.)

Answer
To be covered when testing yourself

SHORT ANSWER QUESTIONS FOR REVIEW

Choose the correct answer.

1. The values of MPC and MPS always add up to 1 because (a) any two marginal quantities add up to 1 (b) both MPC and MPS schedules are straight lines (c) every $1 of the national income is either saved or used for consumption (d) the level of investment in the economy is assumed to be constant — c

2. The equilibrium point at which I = S makes an economy stable due to the fact that (a) anywhere away from this point the economy is naturally driven towards the equilibrium (b) people want to use their resources productively and therefore reinvest all that they save (c) government stops intervening at this point (d) all of the above — a

3. The multiplier can not (a) be equal to 2 (b) be equal to 1000 (c) act to decrease the equilibrium NI (d) be equal to 0 — d

4. If a multiplier is 1 then (a) consumers save all of their income (b) there is no multiplier effect (c) the aggregate demand is practically nonexistent (d) all of the above — d

5. The fact that intended investment exceeds the desired saving suggests that (a) for the simple closed economy aggregate supply is not matched by aggregate demand, i.e., more is supplied than demanded (b) there will be a tendency to increase employment unless the economy is already at a full employment level (c) there is an inflationary gap (d) the economy is in an undesirable condition — b

6. When the government expenditure is accounted for in the calculation of national income (a) the new schedule of spending in the economy will be parallel to the one including only consumption and investment (b) the new spending schedule will lie everywhere above the one including only consumption and investment (c) the equilibrium value of national product will rise (d) all of the above — d

7. Suppose total withdrawals from the economy exceed total injections. The disequilibrium can be corrected by (a) inducing additional investment (b) lowering taxes (c) (a) and (b) (d) inducing savings in order to produce a

SHORT ANSWER QUESTIONS FOR REVIEW

Answer
To be covered when testing yourself

paradox of thrift — c

8. Actual investment is always equal to actual saving. MPI is (a) always equal to MPS (b) probably less than MPC (c) usually positive but less than 1 (d) negative — c

9. The intended investment and desired savings schedules intersect at a point where the equilibrium NP is even larger than the full employment output. As a result (a) there is an inflationary gap (b) the prices are likely to rise (c) nothing definite can be said (d) (a) and (b) — d

10. The recessionary gap is likely to have a stronger impact on the economy when (a) MPS is small (b) MPC is small (c) MPS is large (d) (b) and (c) — a

11. Given a certain interest rate (r_o) the point of equilibrium in both the product market and the money market is: (a) where the IS curve crosses the LM curve at r_o (b) where the IS curve just crosses the LM curve (c) where the LM curve is decreasing (d) where the LM curve and IS curve come close to r_o — a

12. If aggregate supply exceeds aggregate demand in a private (non-government) economy, then: (a) consumption plus investment equals savings (b) savings equals investment (c) savings is greater than intended investment (d) national output will remain at break-even level (e) none of these — c

13. An alternative to the aggregate demand-aggregate supply approach in determining NNP is the: (a) income and wealth approach (b) leakages-injections approach (c) employment-wage approach (d) import-export approach — b

14. An inflationary gap exists if: (a) the aggregate demand schedule crosses the 45-degree line above the full employment NNP (b) the aggregate demand schedule crosses the 45-degree line below equilibrium at the full employment NNP (c) intended investment is greater than savings at the full employment NNP (d) none of the above — a

SHORT ANSWER QUESTIONS FOR REVIEW

Answer
To be covered when testing yourself

Fill in the blanks.

15. The (de)inflationary gap is measured at the _____________. — full employment level of national income

16. Investment and government expenditure are examples of _____________. — injections into an economy

17. The intersection of a consumption schedule with the _____________ occurs at a point where aggregate saving is equal to 0. — 45° line

18. When the planned investment is consistently below actual investment _____________ are building up. — inventories

19. The _____________ of goods and money is a good practical explanation of the multiplier effect. — circular flow

20. _____________ takes place when an increased desire to save causes the reduction of actual saving. — The paradox of thrift

21. Thriftiness is more appropriate and should be encouraged in the _____________ economy, not in the _____________ economy. — inflated, depressed

22. Only _____________ increases in the NI can occur when the economy is producing at full employment. — nominal

23. _____________ is a major factor determining the value of the multiplier in a closed economy characterized by a constant investment function. — MPS or MPC

24. When the economy is at a break even point (nothing is saved) the value of the multiplier approaches _____________. — infinity

Determine whether the following statements are true or false.

25. When the economy is at equilibrium MPC = MPS necessarily holds. — False

26. The simple closed economy contains self-equilibrating forces which push the national income towards a level where aggregate desired

SHORT ANSWER QUESTIONS FOR REVIEW

	Answer (To be covered when testing yourself)
savings and aggregate intended investment are equivalent.	True
27. The terms gross national product and disposable income are interchangeable by definition.	False
28. Since actual savings always equal actual investments the real economy is always at equilibrium, at least theoretically.	False
29. A rising investment function ensures that the equilibrium level of national income will be reached at a point where the savings schedule intersects the investment schedule from below.	True
30. For a simple closed economy with a constant level of income MPS = MPC is another way of saying that $1 invested into the economy will become a $2 addition to its disposable income.	True
31. If a rising investment function is included in the calculation of the multiplier effect, its value, as a result, has to increase.	True
32. The equilibrium level of gross national product ensures that the economy is stable; therefore, it is optimal and desirable for any economy to produce at equilibrium.	False
33. Everything else unchanged, a bigger value of MPI makes the paradox of thrift more visible.	True
34. Unless the national income is at equilibrium, some inflationary or deflationary gap will exist.	False
35. With a constant level of investment the economy is always in equilibrium.	False

CHAPTER 7

FISCAL POLICY AND THRIFTINESS

Basic Attacks and Strategies for Solving Problems in this Chapter. See pages 199 to 250 for step-by-step solutions to problems.

Fiscal policy is the use of government spending and tax policy (the budget or the fisc) to achieve social goals. These social goals fall into three categories: allocational, distributional, and stabilization. Allocational goals refer to the impact of government budget policy on society's allocation of resources. Government provides public goods, regulates externalities, and can influence private spending through incentives built into the tax code. Distributional goals refer to the impact of budget policies on the distribution of income in society. All government policies have differential impacts on different groups of people. Stabilization goals refer to government's impact on inflation, unemployment, and economic growth.

A major debate in the discipline is between the classical economists (and their contemporary descendants such as the monetarists and rational expectations school) and the Keynesians. The classicals believe that market economies tend to be efficient, equitable, stable, and capable of achieving a rapid rate of growth. Consequently, there is little need for government to involve itself too deeply in the workings of the economy. Keynesians believe market economies are prone to inefficiency, inequity, instability, and stagnation. Consequently, active government is called for to deal with these problems.

More specifically with respect to the stabilization goal of government, the classical view is that while the economy may be subject to some economic fluctuations – periods of mild recession and inflation – fiscal policy is unlikely to have much success in smoothing things out, and may, in fact, make the fluctuations more severe. Keynesians believe that more severe fluctuations – periods of boom and bust – are a natural part of the working of the economy. Society should make a commitment to the use of fiscal policy to combat recession and inflation.

In the Keynesian view, the main channel by which fiscal policy affects the economy is through its influence on aggregate demand. Government spending is a component of aggregate demand, as the equation $Y_d = C + I + G$ makes clear. Tax policy has its impact on aggregate demand through its influence on consumer disposable income, and hence on consumption and firm profits, and hence on investment.

In simple models, the multipliers for fiscal actions can easily be derived. Assuming an economy where *I* is autonomous and the only tax is on consumption and is of the lump-sum variety (every household pays the same absolute amount), the equations for the effect of government spending, tax policy, and balanced budget policy are (let *c* be the MPC)

Government Spending

$\Delta Y = \left(\frac{1}{1-c}\right) * \Delta G$, where $1/(1-c)$ is the government spending multiplier.

Taxation

$\Delta Y = \left(\frac{c}{1-c}\right) * \Delta T$, where $-c/(1-c)$ is the tax multiplier.

Note that the government spending policy contemplates an increase (decrease) in spending with no change in taxes. This will result in an increase (decrease) in the government's budget deficit. Deficit spending is expansionary in Keynesian economics. Running a surplus is contractionary. The tax policy contemplates tax changes without spending changes, with similar impacts on the budget deficit.

Balanced Budget

$\Delta Y = 1 * \Delta B$, where 1 is the balanced budget multiplier and

ΔB stands for the change in the budget. The balanced budget case contemplates that both *G* and *T* are changed by the same amount in the same direction so the balance of the budget is not affected. Note that balanced budget increases are expansionary and decreases are contractionary.

The type of fiscal policy analyzed above is known as discretionary policy. Discretionary policy occurs when government consciously sets spending and taxes to achieve particular goals. In reality, setting fiscal policy is no simple task for a number of reasons. For one thing, fiscal actions have their affect in the future, so wise policy requires the ability to forecast accurately, something we do not do very well. Second, the actual budget process is slow and cumbersome. Our political process is incapable of making the quick decisions sometimes required. Third, we do not know the actual value of the parameters needed for the various multipliers. We only have imprecise estimates. Fourth, fiscal policy is ultimately an exercise in political decision-making, with all the pitfalls that phrase implies. Frequently allocational, distributional, and, sometimes, purely political goals can interfere with wise stabilization policy.

Fortunately, we do not have to rely on discretionary fiscal policy. Some parts of our fiscal system work automatically to stabilize the economy. They are called automatic stabilizers. An example would be our system of unemployment compensation. Assume the economy falls into a recession. Automatically the system begins paying out benefits to unemployed workers, allowing them to maintain a level of spending higher than they could achieve in the absence of benefits. This prevents the recession from being as severe as it might otherwise be. During expansion, the level of benefits falls and government collects tax revenues to fund the system during the next recession. This decline in benefits and increase in tax collections restrains the growth of spending. Other examples include income taxes and welfare spending. Automatic stabilizers cannot completely offset an economic fluctuation, but they can make it less severe than it might otherwise be, and they have the added advantage of working without requiring immediate human judgment.

An important point is that the level of government spending and taxation cannot be set exactly by the government. The state of the economy, to the extent that it influences required expenditures and the government's ability to collect taxes, also influences the budget. This means that one cannot simply look at the actual level of government spending and taxation and come away with much of an idea of what the government was trying to accomplish. A deficit may have been the result of deliberate policy, or simply a weak economy which reduced tax collections and raised benefit payouts. A way to avoid this problem is to use the Full Employment Budget concept. The Full Employment Budget estimates what government spending and taxes would be if the economy were at full employment. This allows observers to compare government budgets over any two years and determine the direction of policy. Regardless of the state of the economy, a more expansionary policy will lead to an increase in the full employment deficit between the two years.

A consequence of an activist Keynesian fiscal policy during a time of recession will be a budget deficit. It is clear that in the Keynesian view, deficits are not to be feared. The bigger problem is unemployed resources. To Keynesians, since budget deficits are mainly internal debts, there is no danger of national bankruptcy. A valid concern with budget deficits is that they may "crowd out" capital formation. If government borrowing drains away savings that could have gone for investment, there will be less capital formation, and the economy will grow more slowly in the future. In effect, we will bequeath our grandchildren a less productive economy. Keynesians do not fear this scenario because deficit spending should only occur during periods of recession, periods when there is too much saving and too little spending. Deficit spending puts saving into circulation, reviving the economy, and creating an environment that will be more conducive to investment.

During periods of inflation, the government can run a surplus and pay back the debt. In reality, our debt has grown over time, suggesting that restraining deficit spending is not an easy task.

Step-by-Step Solutions to Problems in this Chapter, "Fiscal Policy and Thriftiness"

BUDGETARY EXPENDITURE PATTERNS

• PROBLEM 7-1

What is fiscal policy?

Solution: Fiscal policy is the policy of the government with regard to the level of government spending and the tax structure.

The national income identity states

$$C + I + G \equiv Y \equiv S + (T - R) + C$$

where C = consumption, I = investments, G = government expenditures, S = saving, T = taxes and R = transfers. Fiscal policy determines quantities G, R, and T directly and, through the income determination process, determines Y, C, and S indirectly.

• PROBLEM 7-2

What are the three types of budget used by the U.S. government? Indicate the reason for their existence. Which is the most indicative of macroeconomic policy problems?

Solution: The three types of budget used by the U.S. government are the Unified Budget, the National Income Accounts Budget and the Full Employment Budget.

The Unified Budget shows the cash flows of the U.S. Treasury. The trust accounts, such as those of the Social Security Administration, are included. Also shown is the amount lent by the various federal credit agencies for housing, agriculture, and international assistance. The net lending, equal to the excess of loan disbursements over loan repayments, has become more important because of the expansion in the activities of the federal credit agencies.

The National Income Accounts Budget is based on the conception of output used in the national income accounts. All types of income-generating purchases of goods and services, compensations for the government employees, and transfer payments that enhance the purchasing power of the private sector are included. Net lending, however, is not included in the expenditures, as it is in the unified budget. In addition, the purchase and sale of existing real and financial assets are excluded because they do not represent current income or production.

The Full-Employment Budget shows the estimated tax revenues and expenditures of the national income account budget adjusted to what they would be were the economy operating at a steady and high level of employment.

If the Full-Employment Budget shows a growing deficit, it can be supposed that the federal government has altered its tax and expenditure programs to make fiscal policy stimulating; if it shows a growing surplus, the government has adopted a more restraining fiscal policy. The Unified and National Income Accounts are affected by changes in the level of economic activity (see, for example, the explanation of the 'fiscal drag'). The High-Employment Budget provides a measure of fiscal policy that does not reflect these changes; it is a better measure of the direction of fiscal policy. But what is considered to be 'full employment': 4, 5 or 7% unemployment?

• PROBLEM 7-3

Discuss the classical economists' contention that the level of output which business producers can sell depends not only upon the level of total spending but also upon the level of product prices.

Given the above argument, what would be the repercussions upon the resource market, particularly labor?

Solution: The classical economists argued that the level of output is dependent also upon the product price level and not only upon the level of total spending. This is tantamount to saying that even if the interest rate should somehow temporarily fail to equate the amounts which households wanted to save with the investment intentions of businesses, any resulting decrement in total spending would be offset by proportionate declines in the price level. This can be illustrated clearly by the following example. Suppose $20 will buy four shirts at $5, $10 will buy the same quantity of shirts only if their price should fall to $2.50. Therefore, if it happens that households somehow managed to succeed in saving more than businesses were willing to invest, the consequent diminution in total spending would not result in a decline in real output, real income, and the level of employment if product prices would decline in proportion to the decline in expenditures. The classical economists furthermore used competition among the sellers as the factor which would guarantee its occurrence. As declines in product became general, competing producers would lower their prices to dispose of accumulating surpluses. Stated differently, the result of saving would be to lower prices; and lower prices, by increasing the value of the dollar, would allow nonsavers to obtain more goods and services with their current money incomes. Saving would therefore lower prices, but not output and employment.

This would boil down to the question whether the above argument doesn't ignore the resource market. Wouldn't businesses find it unprofitable to accept lower product prices in the face of declining demand? As product prices decline, won't resource prices--particularly wage rates--have to decline significantly to permit businesses to produce profitability at the now lower prices?

All of these questions were answered by the classical economists by saying that wage rates must and would decline. General declines in product demand would be reflected in the decrease of the demand for labor and other resources. The immediate consequence for this would be a surplus of labor, that is, unemployment, at the wage rate prevailing prior to these declines in the demand for labor. Producers, though not willing to employ all workers at the original wage rates, would find it profitable to employ additional workers at lower wage rates. Those workers unable to locate employment at the old higher wage rates could find jobs at the new lower wage rates.

A question might be raised here of whether workers are willing to accept lower wage rates. This was answered by saying that competition among unemployed workers would guarantee it. In competing for scarce jobs, idle workers would bid down wage rates until these rates (wage costs to employers) were so low that employers would once again find it profitable to hire all available workers. And this would happen at the new lower equilibrium wage rate. The classical economists therefore concluded that involuntary unemployment was impossible. Anyone who was willing to work at the market-determined wage rate could readily find employment.

• PROBLEM 7-4

What is the position of the New Left on Keynesian fiscal policy?

Solution: Although the radicals acknowledge that increased government spending does reduce unemployment, they contend that in the United States such spending has been channelled into unproductive activities.

The New Left asserts that Keynesian fiscal policies have contributed to the consolidation of a quasi-military state, imperialist expansion, wasteful private consumption, and continuing inequality of income distribution.

Government is severely restricted in its expenditure alternatives. Disbursement of funds to poor people would sustain an increase in consumption spending, and thus in aggregate demand, but capitalist ideology sees this as weakening work incentives and social discipline. Entrenched interests oppose many possible public work projects, such as the upgrading of housing conditions in urban slums, or improving the urban transit system. Also, government investment in and ownership of factories and other productive facilities is strongly opposed by capitalist interests. The only way out seems to be an increase in spending on the ultimate waste products: military equipment and operations. In every year since World War II, the United States has spent more on national defense than any other nation.

It is also charged that these extensive defense expenditures have resulted in a powerful alliance between the Defense Department, the armed services, and the major corporations that supply them with arms. There appears to be a close connection between this military-industrial complex and American foreign policy, particularly in developing nations. Big business--the international corporations--seeks to maintain the conditions of low-cost labor and raw materials in these countries by thwarting indigenous movements toward industrialization. Frequently the local governments, comprised largely of the land-owning elite, are supported by the American corporations and their ally, the U.S. government, in order to maintain the status quo.

The critics also argue that the increase in consumption induced by an expansive fiscal policy has not always led to an increase in the quality of life. The possibilities created by an increase in productivity, such as a shorter work week, more leisure, and an improved environment, are forgotten in the rush for an ever-increasing quantity of goods and services.

Finally, the emphasis on aggregate economic performance obscures many of the important structural features of the American society. An overall 4 percent unemployment rate, considered to be the 'acceptable' natural rate, hides an unemployment rate of 8 percent for the blacks, 15 percent for all teenagers, and 40 percent for black teenagers. Aggregate policies appear to fail to solve the problems of discrimination and poverty.

The Radicals also point to the inequities of the tax system: the sales and property taxes of the state and local governments are highly regressive. Many of the aggregate fiscal spending and taxing programs do not assist in the redistribution of income but aggravate the existing inequality in income distribution.

Competition in the labor market ruled out involuntary idleness. However, the classical economist's forgot, so to speak, that wages are not only costs of production for the employer who decides how much he will produce, but income for the workers, to be used for their expenditures, i.e., for the aggregate demand.

What is the effect of an increase in government spending, where no change in taxes takes place and the deficit is financed by borrowing?

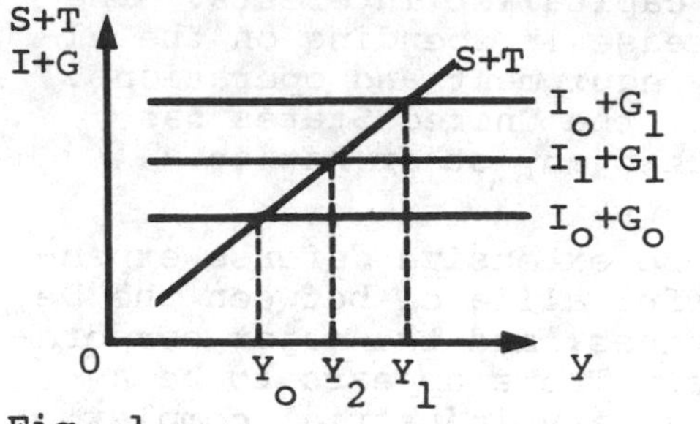

Fig. 1

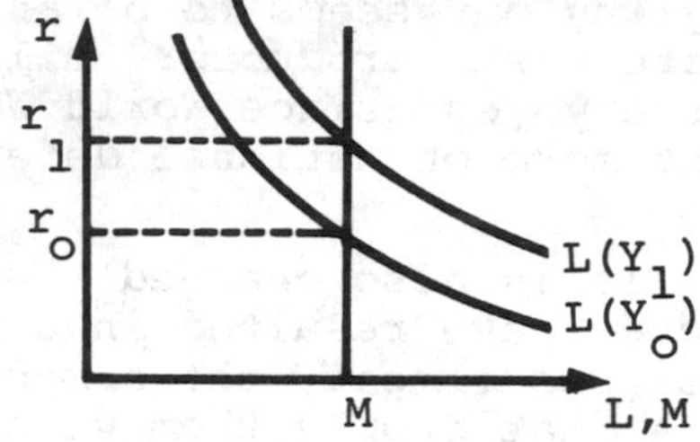

Fig. 2

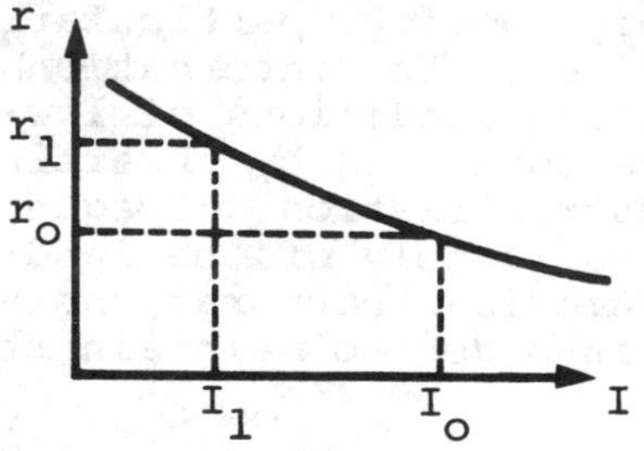

Fig. 3

Solution: The initial effect of an autonomous increase in government spending is an increase in aggregate demand, triggering a multiplier process. (See Fig. 1.)

In this graph Y denotes GNP; (I + G) is the total of investment I and government spending G; and S + T is the total of savings S and taxes T. Where the two graphs (I + G) and (S + T) intersect exists an equilibrium; C + I + G = C + T + S between total expenditures and total 'revenues.' When government spending is increased from G_o to G_1, equilibrium income rises from initial Y_o to Y_1. The deficit is financed by borrowing in the financial markets, and therefore the money supply is unchanged. (See Fig. 2.) L is the liquidity preference, which is dependent on income, L = L(Y); M is the autonomous money supply as determined by the monetary authorities; and r is the rate of interest.

The increase in income, induced by the increased government expenditures, results in an upward shift of the liquidity preference schedule, because people want to hold larger cash balances due to the increased number of their transactions. The rise in the rate of interest, from r_o to r_1, resulting from this increased demand for money, causes a reduction in planned investments. (See Fig. 3.) This graph depicts the marginal efficiency of investment.

The reduction in investments means a reduction in aggregate demand and, in terms of Fig. 1, a downward shift in the I + G schedule. The final outcome is the equilibrium income level Y_2, which is higher than the original level of Y_o, but lower than the expanded income level without the interest effect. This problem may also be analyzed in the IS - LM framework. (See Fig. 4.)

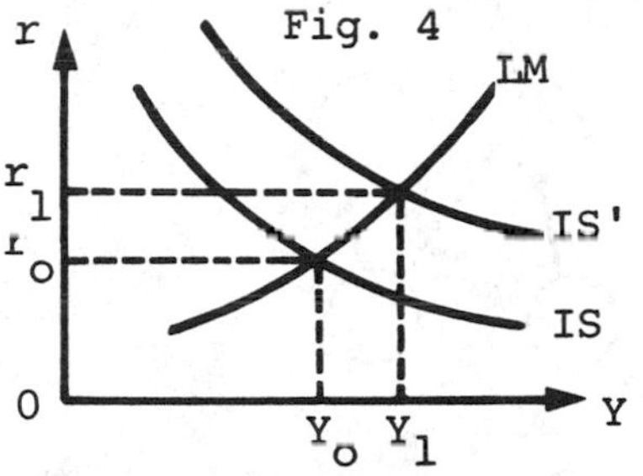

Fig. 4

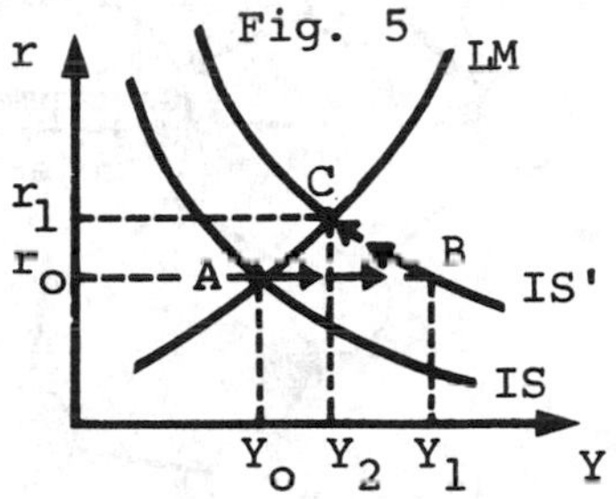

Fig. 5

The IS-schedule represents the points of equilibrium in the commodities markets (so I + G = S + T), while the LM-schedule represents the points of equilibrium in the financial markets (so L(Y) = M). The increase in government spending and its consequences shift the IS-schedule to the North-East, thereby simultaneously increasing the national income and the rate of interest. For clarity, the steps involved are analyzed. The increase in government spending shifts the IS-schedule to the right when the interest rate is fixed. (See Fig. 5.)

The equilibrium shifts from A to B, and income from Y_o to Y_1. Then the interest rate is allowed to rise from r_o to r_1; equilibrium shifts back from B to C, and equilibrium income from Y_1 to Y_2.

The precise effect of the fiscal policy depends on the shapes of the IS and LM schedules.

• PROBLEM 7-8

Does the type of government expenditure matter (in terms of income generation)?

Solution: From the point of view of income generation, it does not matter whether or not the immediate result of the expenditure is to create something 'useful.' John Maynard Keynes provided in his General Theory of Employment, Interest and Money the contrived example that the government would bury bottles filled with newly printed money in old mines, and let private enterprise dig the bottles up. This useless activity would have the effect of infusing income into the economic circuit.

But the effect of government expenditure does depend on who the initial (first-round) income recipients are and whether the expenditure affects injections in other sectors.

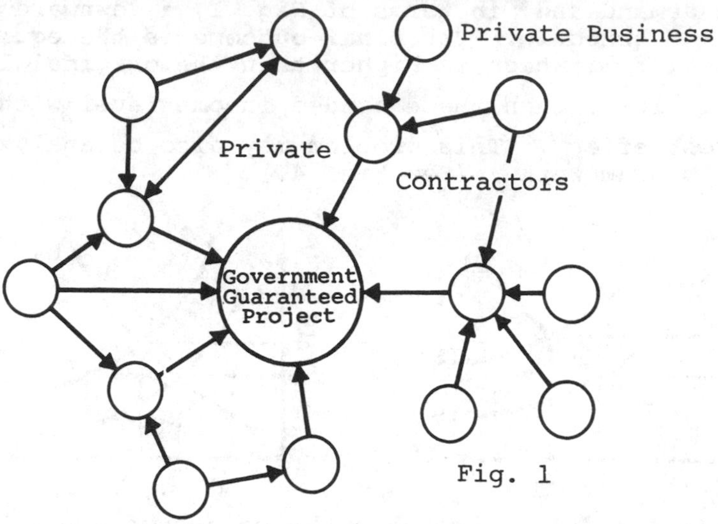

Fig. 1

The marginal propensity to consume is not uniform throughout the society. It is expected to be lower among the rich than among the poor. Thus, expenditures which initially increase incomes of the rich have a lower multiplier effect than expenditures which initially increase incomes of the poor. For example, assume that the marginal propensity to consume of the rich is $c_1 = 0.5$, and of the poor $c_2 = 0.9$ (there is no autonomous consumption and no taxes). Thus the multiplier of the rich is $\frac{1}{1 - 0.5} = 2$ and of the poor $\frac{1}{1 - 0.9} = 10$, respectively.

But even when the marginal propensities to consume are identical $c_1 = c_2 = 0.8$, the progressive income tax system produces the same type of effect. The tax rate (t_1) of the higher income brackets is higher than the tax rate of the lower income brackets (t_2).

Supposing $t_1 = 0.4$ and $t_2 = 0.1$, the consumption of the rich can be described by $C_1 = c(1 - t_1)Y = 0.8 \times 0.6 \times y = 0.48Y$ and the consumption of the poor can be described by $C_2 = c(1 - t_2)Y = 0.8 \times 0.9Y = 0.72Y$. It follows that, the multiplier of the rich is $\frac{1}{1 - 0.48} = 1.923$ and the multiplier of the poor is $\frac{1}{1 - 0.72} = 3.57$. Therefore, when a government expenditure of, for instance, \$4 billion is received by the rich, national income increases by \$7.692 billion. When these \$4 billion are received by the poor, however, national income increases by \$14.28 billion. Thus a simple redistribution of income--from the rich to the poor--may increase the propensity of the economy enough so that equilibrium income increases with no increase in government expenditure. For example, when the government transfers $2 billion from the rich to the poor the effects are as follows:

There is a decrease in initial income of the rich by $2 billion. This reduces national income by 2 x 1.923 = $3.846 billion. These $2 billion are transferred to the poor, so that their initial income is raised by $2 billion. The effect on national income will be an increase of 2 x 3.57 = $7.14 billion. Thus, the resulting total effect on national income of this income redistribution project would be an increase in national income by 7.14 - 3.846 = $3.294. The problem of boosting the economy has been considered in this example. But when the government tries to dampen the economy, the situation is reversed. In this case the income transfer will be from the poor to the rich.

A second effect to be considered when discussing which type of government expenditure is to be applied is the effect on the expenditures in the other sectors: the so-called 'spin-off' effect. When government spends on projects that could equally well be undertaken by private business it is likely to replace private activities by government activities, and the beneficial effect on national income could be small. But government expenditures on space programs or massive urban passenger transport, which would never be undertaken in the private sector, may even encourage additional private investment in electronics, light metal, and other related industries. The government undertakes the most risky part of these large scale projects--contracting private enterprises--and private industry supplements with the less risky and costly products (see accompanying figure).

• PROBLEM 7-7

The economy has an overall tax rate of 27% of national income.

The full employment income level is $980 billion. In order to sustain this level, the government must keep its expenditures at $296 billion in addition to private investment and other injections.

1. Calculate the full employment balance (surplus or deficit for a budget which will just sustain full employment).

2. Calculate also the surplus or deficit, at an income level of $970 billion, for a budget which has the full employment balance calculated under 1.

Solution: The full employment income level is Y = $980 billion; thus the full employment taxes are

$$T_f = t \cdot Y_f = 0.27 \times 980 = \$264.6 \text{ billion.}$$

Full employment government expenditures are G_f = $296 billion. Hence when the economy operates at full capacity the government would experience a budget deficit of

$$G_f - T_f = 296 - 264.6 = \$31.4 \text{ billion.}$$

Or, full employment government expenditures are $G_f = tY_f + 31.4$ billion dollars. It appears that the actual income level of $970 billion is below the full employment level: the economy is in a recession. Lower income means less tax revenues for the government which now receives only $T = tY = 0.27 \times 970 = \$261.9$ billion.

The government expenditures are autonomous and do not change by a change in income; the expenditures in the recession are the same as they are when the economy operates at full capacity. Thus the actual deficit is $G_f - T = 296 - 261.9 = 34.1$. Because the actual deficit is larger than the full-employment deficit, the government assists in pulling the economy out of the recession by enlarging the aggregate demand.

• PROBLEM 7-8

Why does an accurate economic policy require accurate predictions?

Fig. 1

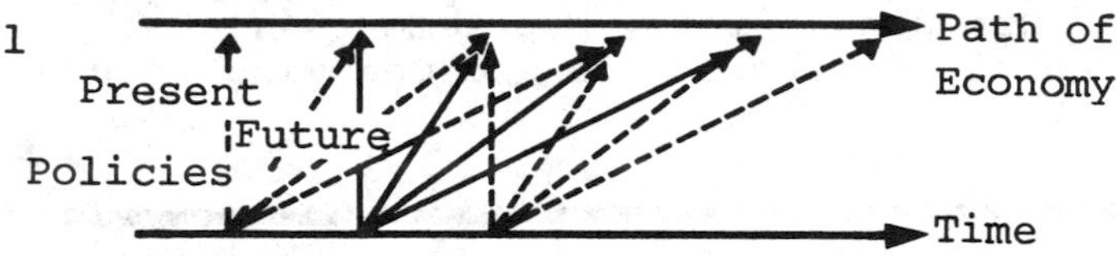

Solution: Economic policy is aiming at a moving target, not a stationary one. Not only must a decision be made as to which policy instrument is to be used for which purpose, but also how much of the policy instrument should be applied and when. The 'how much' and 'when' problems are interrelated, as can be seen from the dynamic Keynesian multiplier, or the money multiplier of the banking system. Current actions will have effects on the economy next year and possibly the year thereafter. It follows that last year's actions influence the present economy and will influence it next year. (See Figure 1.) Therefore the economy never starts from scratch; there is a history of policies influencing the present and the future, together with the policies that are currently enacted. And before the results of present policies can be predicted, the continuing consequences of former policies must be predicted, i.e., the path of the economy at present and in the future when no further action is taken. This prediction is done presently by large econometric models which simulate the operation of the economy; like the Wharton model, IBM model, Michigan model, the models of the Federal Reserve Bank of St. Louis, and the First National City Bank.

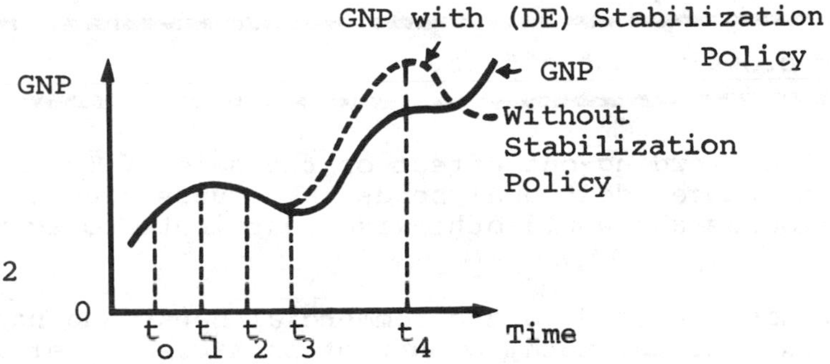

Fig. 2

We give an example of what happens if the path of the economy is not accurately foreseen. (See Figure 2.) At t_1 a recession starts, which is detected only some time (say a quarter) later, at t_2. To make a decision to take expansionary action costs some time, and before the policy is starting to get hold, we are already at time t_3. The effect of the expansionary policy builds up momentum and, unfortunately, it reaches its peak at t_4, when the economy without stabilization policy happens to be in its booming phase. The consequence is strong inflationary pressure. Conclusion: the expansionary policy came too late; it had almost no beneficial effect upon the recession, and even contributed to the inflation.

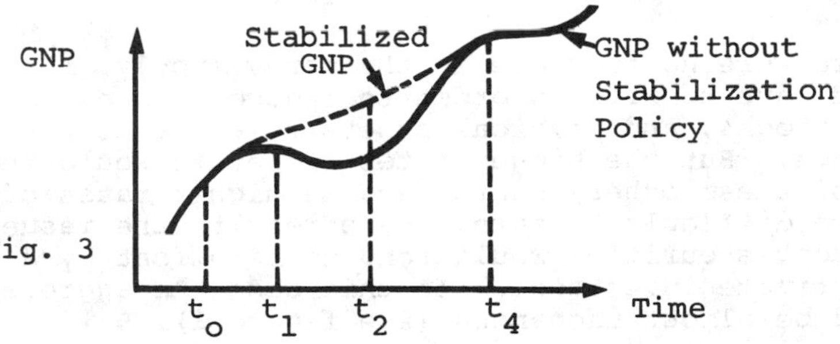

Fig. 3

Suppose now we apply an accurate 'reliable' econometric forecasting model at time t_0. (See Figure 3.) We foresee at time t_0 that a recession will start at t_1, the period from t_0 to t_1 is called the prediction lag; we can then take the decision and enact the policy in the period from t_0 to t_1 preceding the actual recession. The policy starts at or even before the recession begins at time t_1, builds up momentum in the first phase of the predicted recession and gains its peak at time t_2 when the economy reaches its trough. Thereafter the expansionary stabilization policy is gradually phased out, so that there is no inflationary pressure when the economy reaches a peak by its own forces. The resulting path of the stabilized GNP is a smooth growth path, with the business cycle almost eliminated.

Explain the crowding-out effect.

Solution: The crowding-out effect of the sale of Treasury bonds is that these additional bonds take funds away from private borrowers who would otherwise contribute to aggregate demand.

When bonds are sold to the commercial banks and bank reserves, and thus the total amount of bank credit remains unchanged, commercial banks must cut down on the volume of loans made to the private sector of the economy. This reduces the private capital expenditures that might have been financed by these loans.

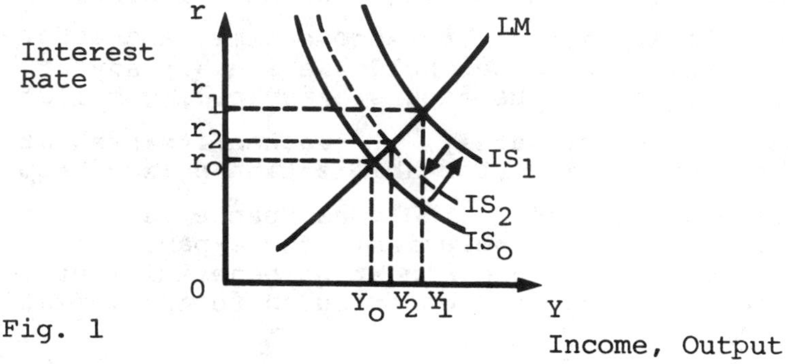

Fig. 1

If there were no increase in the money supply, rates of return would have to rise in order to induce persons to hold more bonds, stocks, and physical assets relative to their money holdings. But the higher rates of return would reduce the supply of these other assets because higher rates of return are more difficult to earn. As a result, the issue of U.S. government securities would tend to be offset by a reduction in private investment. In this case the aggregate demand would be almost unchanged (see figure 1).

The initial stimulus of the government deficit shifts the IS schedule from IS_0 to IS_1, and income and interest rate have the tendency to rise to Y_1 and r_1 respectively. But the crowding-out effect reduces private investment, the IS curve shifts back to position IS_2, and income and interest rate reach only the levels Y_2 and r_2 respectively.

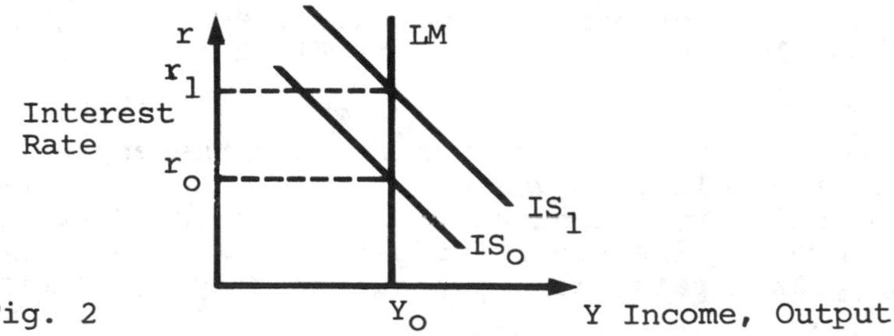

Fig. 2

Monetarist economists, such as Milton Friedman, hold the view that government spending merely crowds out private spending. The crowding-out effect is also implied when it is assumed that the LM curve is vertical. This implies that the demand for money is not related to the interest rate: there is only a unique level of income at which the money market is in equilibrium (see figure 2).

When government spending increases and the IS schedule shifts to the North-East, only the interest rate is increased, but the income remains unchanged. Investment spending is reduced by an amount exactly equal to the increase in government spending.

BALANCING THE BUDGET

• PROBLEM 7-10

Show that the net effect of a balanced budget (where government expenditures = taxes) is an increase in NNP by the amount of the budget.

Solution: We know that the net effect on NNP = ΔNNP_1 (due to G) - ΔNNP_2 (due to tax)

$$\Delta NNP_1 = G \times \text{Multiplier}$$

$$= G \times \frac{1}{1 - MPC}$$

$$\Delta NNP_2 = \Delta \text{ Consumption} \times \text{Multiplier}$$

$$= \text{Tax} \times (MPC) \times \frac{1}{1 - MPC}$$

If we combine the two, we get

$$\Delta NNP = \left(G \times \frac{1}{1 - MPC}\right) - \left(T \times \frac{MPC}{1 - MPC}\right)$$

Since in a balanced budget, G = T, we can substitute G for T in our equation.

$$\Delta NNP = \left(G \times \frac{1}{(1 - MPC)}\right) - \left(G \times \frac{MPC}{(1 - MPC)}\right)$$

$$\Delta NNP = \frac{G}{(1 - MPC)} - \frac{(G)(MPC)}{(1 - MPC)}$$

$$\Delta NNP = \frac{G}{(1 - MPC)}(1 - MPC)$$

$$\Delta NNP = G \cdot \frac{1 - MPC}{1 - MPC}$$

$$\Delta NNP = G$$

How can an expansionary budget deficit cause a worsening of the balance of payments?

Solution: An expansionary budget deficit leads to an increase in output and income. More income will be spent on imports. Assuming that exports remain unchanged and that imports are being increased, the balance of payments worsens.

The national income identity of an open economy states that total expenditures equal the total of the income allocations

$$C + I + G + Ex \equiv Y \equiv C + S + T + Im$$

where C = Consumption, I = Investment,
G = government expenditure, Ex = exports, Y = income,
S = saving, T = taxes, and Im = imports

After rearrangement of the components and deleting consumption C there remains

$$(G - T) = (S - I) + (Im - Ex) \tag{1}$$

The excess of government expenditures over taxes--i.e., the budget deficit (G - T)--equals the sum of the surplus of available private loanable funds S over private, planned investments I (S - I), and the deficit on the balance of payments (Im - Ex)--i.e., the excess of imports over exports. Or, the extra injection into the economy of the government deficit equals the sum of the extra leakages in the economy, the excess of savings over investments, and the excess of imports over exports.

Suppose that imports Im are proportional to disposable income $Im = m(Y - T)$. A fixed percentage of disposable income is therefore spent on imported commodities; and exports, being autonomous, are thus uninfluenced by domestic economic activity; $Ex = \overline{Ex}$. Further savings are also proportional to disposable income, $S = s(Y - T)$; and investments are autonomous, $I = \overline{I}$. Finally, government expenditures are autonomous, $G = \overline{G}$, and taxes are proportional to income $T = t \cdot Y$.

When these relationships are substituted into equation (1), the result is

$$(\overline{G} - T) = [s(Y - T) - \overline{I}] + [m(Y - T) - \overline{Ex}] \tag{2}$$

$$= (s + m)(Y - T) - \overline{I} - \overline{Ex}$$

Bringing the investments $\overline{I}$ and exports $\overline{Ex}$ to the left and taxes T to the right yields

$$\overline{G} + \overline{I} + \overline{Ex} = (s + m)(Y - T) + T$$

Substituting the final relationship $T = tY$ results in

$$\bar{G} + \bar{I} + \bar{E}x = (s+m)(Y - tY) + tY$$

$$= (s + m)(1 - t)Y + tY$$

Collecting all the terms involving Y:

$$(s + m + t)(1 - t)Y = \bar{G} + \bar{I} + \bar{E}x$$

Dividing by $(s + m + t)$,

the multiplier relationship

--disposable income $(1 - t)Y = \dfrac{1}{s + m + t}(\bar{G} + \bar{I} - \bar{E}x)$--

is finally obtained. It can be seen that it does not matter if the government increases its government expenditures, creating a larger deficit, or business plans bigger investments, or the consumers abroad buy more of our exports: the end result is an increase in disposable income. The disposable income multiplier is

$$\frac{1}{(s + m + t)} ,$$

and the income multiplier is

$$\frac{1}{(s + m + t)(1 - t)}$$

Returning to equation (2),

$$(\bar{G} - T) = [s(Y - T) - \bar{I}] + [m(Y - T) + \bar{E}x] ,$$

it may be observed that an increase in the budget deficit by enlarging government expenditures $\bar{G}$ (or by lowering the tax rate), reflected in a higher disposable income, will induce a larger surplus of available loanable funds (savings) over planned investments and a larger deficit on the trade balance, because imports $Im = m\ (Y - T)$ have been increased with unchanging exports. Thus an expansionary budget deficit applied, for example, to reduce unemployment, may have negative repercussions on the balance of payments.

• PROBLEM 7-12

From an economic point of view, what is the danger of a balanced government budget?

Solution: The danger of a Balanced Budget is that it intensifies cyclical swings in the economy: inflations and depressions will hit harder.

During a recession, a declining national income Y reduces the government revenues in the form of taxes, thus:

$T = t \cdot Y$; and a budget deficit may result $(T - G < 0)$. If the budget is to be balanced, government expenditures must be sharply curtailed and tax rates may have to be increased. Both actions result in a decline in aggregate demand: G and C will fall.

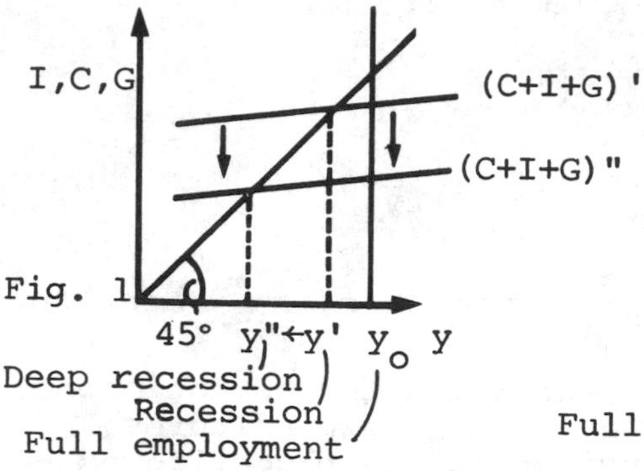

Fig. 1

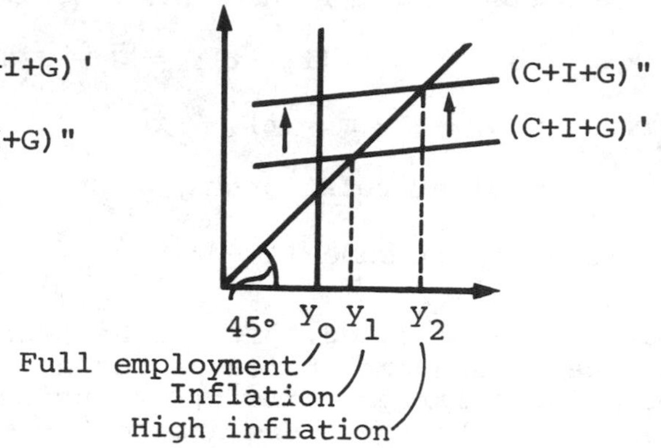

Recall that consumption $C = c(1 - t)Y + \overline{C}$ where

c is marginal propensity to consume

t is income tax rate

and $\overline{C}$ is autonomous consumption.

The fall in aggregate demand hastens the decline in economic activity. (See figure 1)

The recession will be intensified. However, if the government maintains the unbalanced budget with the budget deficit $G - T > 0$, this may give a counteracting input and the recession may be reversed. An inflationary boom would result in increased revenue in the form of taxes, because of the rising income. This may create a budget surplus; $T - G > 0$. The government may also decide on a tax cut. Both these actions will intensify the inflation, (see Figure 2).

But if the government maintained the unbalanced budget with the budget surplus, this would have a counteracting, dampening effect and the inflation would be reversed. Conclusion: a balanced budget intensifies the fluctuations in the business cycle.

• PROBLEM 7-13

Suppose the government seeks to achieve a balanced budget by levying taxes of $100 billion and making expenditures of $100 billion. How will this affect NNP if MPC = 0.8?

Solution: The levying of a tax will reduce NNP, while expenditures by the government increase NNP. Here it is necessary to find the joint effect of the two.

First, find the multiplier by the formula

$$\text{Multiplier} = \frac{1}{1 - \text{MPC}}$$

$$= \frac{1}{1 - 0.8} = \frac{1}{0.2} =$$

$$= 5$$

Then, to evaluate the effect of the increase in expenditures, use the definition of the multiplier:

$$\text{Multiplier} = \frac{\Delta \text{NNP}}{\Delta G}$$

$$\Delta \text{NNP} = \Delta G \times \text{multiplier}$$

$$\Delta \text{NNP} = \$100 \text{ billion} \times 5$$

$$\Delta \text{NNP} = \$500 \text{ billion}$$

To evaluate the effect of the increase in taxes, it is essential to realize that consumption will not fall by the full amount of the tax. Instead, savings will drop somewhat. To find out the effect of the tax on consumption, multiply the drop in disposable income by the MPC.

$$\text{Drop in private consumption} = (\text{Drop in Disposable Income})(\text{MPC})$$

$$= (\$100 \text{ billion})(0.8)$$

$$= \$80 \text{ billion}$$

Then, applying the multiplier to the drop in consumption yields:

$$\Delta \text{NNP (decrease)} = \Delta \text{Consumption} \times \text{Multiplier}$$

$$\Delta \text{NNP} = \$80 \text{ billion} \times 5$$

$$\Delta \text{NNP} = \$400 \text{ billion}$$

Therefore the increase in government expenditures of $100 billion raises NNP by $500 billion, and the levying of a tax decreases NNP by $400 billion. The net effect will be an increase of $100 billion in NNP.

• PROBLEM 7-14

In the economy, households save 10% of their disposable income; business plans to invest an amount of $50 billion, and the government initially has a balanced budget. It appears that the income level is under the capacity level of the economy, and the Republicans want to lower expenditures by 1% and the tax rate by 6%, in an effort to boost the economy. Does this initiative create a budget deficit, or a budget surplus? The Democrats think this policy is too conservative and propose to increase expenditures by 4% and the tax rate by 1%. What effect will this second policy have on the budget?

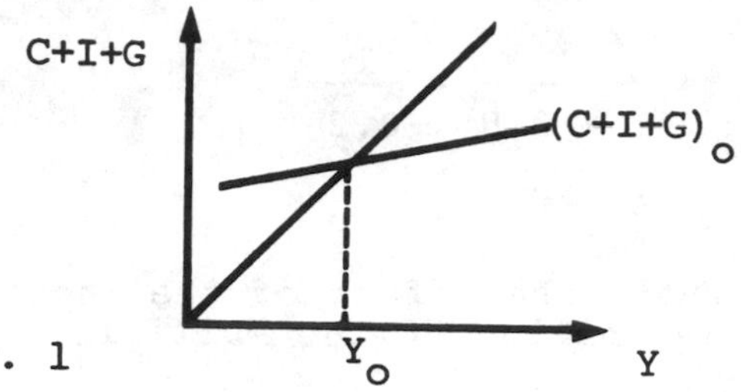

Fig. 1

Solution: The economy is initially in equilibrium (see figure 1).

At this level of income Y_o, the budget is in balance $G_o = T_o$.

First calculate the initial equilibrium level of income, and then trace the repercussions of the two policy proposals.

In the initial equilibrium there prevails, by definition, the condition that total injections = total withdrawals:

$$I_o + G_o = T_o + S_o$$

and a balanced budget:

$$G_o = T_o$$

Thus, in initial equilibrium, planned investments equal savings $I_o = S_o$

The marginal propensity to save s = 0.10, the tax rate t = 0.25 and planned investments $I_o = 50$. When equilibrium prevails and the budget is balanced, equilibrium income Y_o can be calculated as follows

$$I_o = S_o$$

and savings are $S_o = s(Y_o - T_o) = s(Y_o - t_oY_o)$, where $Y_o - t$ is disposable income, so that

$$S_o = s(1 - t_o)Y_o \; .$$

Thus $\quad I_o = s(1 - t_o)Y_o \; .$

Substituting the given values into the equation,

$$50 = 0.10(1 - 0.25)Y_o =$$

$$= 0.075Y_o$$

Dividing both sides by 0.075 yields equilibrium income

$$Y_o = \frac{50}{0.075} = 666.666$$

In this situation there is a balanced budget

$$G_o = T_o$$

and taxes $T_o = t_oY_o$

thus $G_o = t_oY_o$.

Substituting the newly found value of initial equilibrium income $Y_o = 666.666$ results in the government expenditures

$$G_o = 0.25 \times 666.666 = 166.666$$

Suppose we create a surplus of ε on the budget so that

$T_1 - G_1 = \varepsilon$, where

ε is positive, and T_1 and G_1 are the new taxes and government expenditures. It follows that in the new equilibrium

$$I_o + G_1 = T_1 + S_1$$

or $I_o = T_1 - G_1 + S_1 = \varepsilon + S_1$

Thus the new level of savings is definitely lower than the old level of savings

$$S_1 < I_o = S_o$$

But this does not necessarily mean that income has contracted, because what is of interest here is the total of injections $I_o + G_1$ versus the total of withdrawals, $T_1 + S_1$. Government expenditures are lowered by 1% and the tax rate is lowered by 6% in an effort to boost the economy; so the new level of government expenditures is $G_1 = 0.99 \times 166.666 = 164.999$, and the new tax rate $t_1 = 0.94 \times 0.25 = 0.235$.

In equilibrium total injections = total withdrawals:

$$I_o + G_1 = T_1 + S_1$$

or

$$I_o + G_1 = t_1Y_1 + s(1 - t_1)Y_1 \qquad (1)$$

Substituting the new values into this equation results in

$$50 + 164.999 = 0.235Y_1 + 0.1(0.765)Y_1$$

or

$$214.999 = 0.3115Y_1$$

Thus the new equilibrium income is

$$Y_1 = \frac{214.999}{0.3115} = 690.205 \quad \text{and}$$

taxes $T_1 = 0.235 \times 690.205 = 162.198.$

Conclusion: this policy proposal will boost income and result in a budget deficit of

$$G_1 - T_1 = 164.999 - 162.198 = 2.801.$$

In the second policy proposal, government expenditures are $G_1 = 1.04 \times 166.666 = 173.333$ and the new tax rate $t_1 = 1.01 \times 0.25 = 0.2525$, so that when these values are substituted in equation (1), the result is

$$50 + 173.333 = 0.2525Y_1 + 0.1(0.7475)Y_1$$

$$223.333 = 0.32725Y_1$$

The new equilibrium income is

$$Y_1 = \frac{223.333}{0.32725} = 682.45$$

The tax revenues will be

$$T = 0.2525 \times 682.45 = 172.318.$$

Thus this policy will also boost the economy, although less than will the 'conservative' policy, and in this case there will be a budget deficit of

$$G_1 - T_1 = 173.333 - 172.318 = 1.015.$$

This is less than half of the budget deficit under the 'conservative' proposal of the Republicans.

In summary:

	GNP (in billions	deficit of dollars)
Republicans: lower government expenditures by 1% and taxes by 6%	690.205	2.801
Democrats: increase government expenditures by 4% and taxes by 1%	682.45	1.015

• PROBLEM 7-15

The government decides to levy a lump-sum tax which will reduce disposable income by \$50 billion. If the MPS = 0.25, what effect will this have on NNP?

Solution: When government increases its expenditures, apply the multiplier to the increase to find the change in NNP. When government levies on additional tax, two calculations must be performed in order to compute the effect the tax has on NNP. First it is necessary to find out how the tax affects consumption. Then the effect which the change in consumption has on NNP can be determined.

Given that MPS = 0.25, it follows that MPC = 0.75. Therefore, if disposable income falls by \$50 billion as a result of the tax, consumption will fall by (\$50 billion)(0.75) =

\$37.5 billion.

To determine the drop in NNP due to the tax, apply the multiplier to the drop in consumption

$$\text{Drop in NNP} = (\text{drop in consumption})\left(\frac{1}{1 - \text{MPC}}\right)$$
$$= (\text{drop in consumption})\left(\frac{1}{\text{MPS}}\right)$$
$$= (37.5 \text{ billion})\left(\frac{1}{0.25}\right)$$
$$= \$150 \text{ billion.}$$

• PROBLEM 7-16

If planned output is expected to have a money value of \$1,700, but aggregate demand turns out to be only \$1,500, how can aggregate output, in theory, adjust to aggregate demand?

Solution: The money value of output Y is equal to the (general) price level, P, times real output, y:

$Y \equiv P \cdot y$. Producers expect that aggregate demand $Y_0 = P_0 \cdot y_0 = \$1,700$, but in fact aggregate consumer demand is $Y_1 = P_1 \cdot y_1 = \$1,500$.

The adjustment in the money value of the output may come from a drop in the aggregate price-level, caused by a price cut of $\frac{\$1700 - \$1500}{\$1700} = \frac{\$200}{\$1700} \cong 12\%$; this implies that all prices, including factor prices and thus wages, will fall by ~ 12% on average. The drop otherwise might come from a decline in real output y of 12%. Or, finally, it may come from a combination of a fall in the general price level, P, and a fall in real output y.

In a diagram we can draw the money value of total output as a "rectangular hyperbola" with the price level and real output on the vertical and horizontal axes, respectively, as shown.

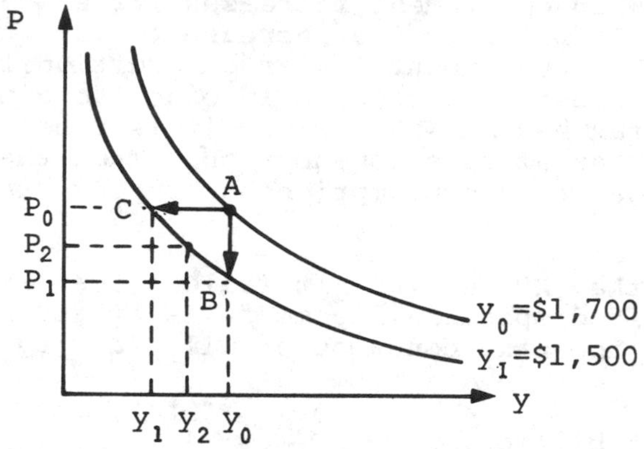

If producers expected aggregate demand to be somewhere on Y_0, e.g., at point A, the fall of aggregate demand can be followed by a drop in output as follows:

1) From A to B is a pure price level reduction. $Y_1 = P_1 \cdot Y_o$
2) From A to C is a pure recession in real output. $Y_1 = P_0 \cdot y_1$.
3) From A to a point on curve Y_1 = \$1500 between B and C, combines a recession in real output with a price level reduction. $Y_1 = P_2 \cdot Y_2$.

• PROBLEM 7-17

What does the expression 'fiscal drag,' popular in the 1960's, mean?

Solution: The expression 'fiscal drag' refers to the fact that as national income increases under the expansionary influence of a budget deficit, the increase will become smaller and smaller because the budget deficit will be closed; the higher incomes generate more taxes and, assuming that government expenditures remain constant, the budget deficit $G - T = G - t \cdot Y$ will disappear. Where G = autonomous government expenditures, T = proportional income taxes, t = income tax rate, and Y = income.

To see how this mechanism works, use the diagram on the following page.

Where I + G is the sum of autonomous investment I and government expenditures G. This remains constant when income Y changes; therefore, it is represented by a horizontal line.

S + T is the sum of the savings S(= s · Y) and the taxes T (= t · Y)

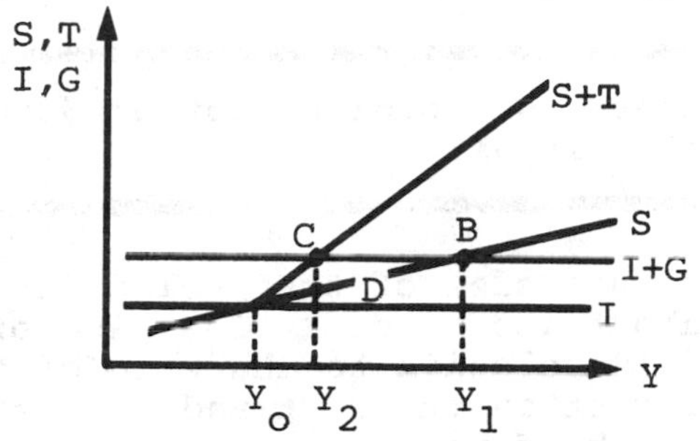

Begin, for example, in equilibrium A, where there are no government expenditures and no taxes, and where savings S equal investments I; so S = I.

First, introduce the government expenditures G and add them to the investments I, so that the result is the uplifted horizontal line I + G. At point A, where the income is Y_o, there occurs a budget deficit equal to G - 0 = G (no taxes). Through the multiplier effect the income starts to rise up to Y_1, and a new equilibrium, S = I + G, is reached at point B.

Now return to the initial equilibrium point A, and suppose this time that at the moment government expenditures are introduced, a proportional tax system will be introduced also. The taxes T are added to the savings S and the result is the rotated line S + T. The initial budget deficit of G will now be reduced because, when income Y starts to rise, taxes T = t · Y are generated; and this time it is not point B, where income is Y_1, that is reached but only point C, where income is Y_2 . The reason for this is that more income has leaked out of the income circuit in the form of taxes.

Again, at point C equilibrium is reached and S + T = I + G. Keep in mind that the budget deficit is not completely closed, however, because at income level Y_2, savings equal the distance from D to the horizontal axis; and taxes equal the distance CD which is smaller than G. The conclusion that a deficit does not necessarily indicate that fiscal policy is expansionary. At point C, the fiscal policy is not expansionary although there is a deficit. The 'fiscal drag' effect is clear: it is not income level Y_1 but only Y_2 that is reached.

Note: a big part of the government expenditures is tied and can hardly be reduced (it can only be increased). Government expenditures are for military equipment, social security benefits, services for teachers and subsidies to farmers, for example.

THE PUBLIC DEBT

• PROBLEM 7-18

Is the fact that there is a public debt of $350 billion a reason for concern? Discuss.

Solution: The absolute size of the public debt does not tell us anything about its burden. The size of any debt must be considered in relation to the size of the income from which the interest on the debt and the repayment of the principal has to be financed.

In 1935 the gross federal debt was only about $35 billion,--one-tenth of the current debt. Gross national product was $72 billion. Thus in 1935 the income/debt ratio, or debt turnover ratio, was 72/35 = 2.06. Nowadays national income is about $980 billion. Thus the income/debt ratio has increased to 2.8. The present economy can better afford to carry this debt than in the 1930s. The interest paid by the Federal government is about $18 billion. The whole of the American debt is held internally: the American people owe the money to themselves. Paying off the internally held debt does not therefore mean a change in the total wealth of the nation, but it will probably result in a redistribution of this wealth.

Wars have been chiefly responsible for the large size of the debt, and they imposed most of their burdens on those who were living at the time: productive factors were used for the production of military goods instead of civilian goods and services. No additional capital goods were supplied to increase the production for the succeeding generation. Not the public debt, but the real economic sacrifice, forms the real burden.

• PROBLEM 7-19

Suppose the government runs a budget deficit of $30 billion, and the FED does not want to increase the money supply by more than $40 billion. By how much must the national debt increase?

Assume that the legal reserve requirement of the banking system is 20%.

Solution: Budget deficits of the government, i.e., the surplus of expenditures over taxes, can be financed in two ways: by newly created money, and by borrowing. Symbolically,

$$\text{Budget deficit} = G - T = B + M,$$

where G = government expenditures,

T = taxes,

B = borrowing, and

M = newly created money.

The borrowing (B) by the government adds to the national debt. The Treasury sells government securities to the public to raise the needed funds. An increase in national debt adds to the burden of interest to be paid by the government; and the Treasury will try to keep this burden small.

The second way to finance the government deficit is by creating money, either in the form of demand deposits or in the form of papernotes ('banknotes'). In this case the Treasury sells the securities, but these are immediately purchased by the Federal Reserve banks in the open market. Thus no additional borrowing from the public takes place, but the money supply increases. The Treasury and the FED work in tandem to finance the budget deficit by money creation.

The consolidated balance sheet of the twelve Federal Reserve banks shows the following changes when, for instance, $1 billion in government securities is sold by the Treasury and bought by the Federal Reserve banks:

Consolidated Balance

Assets	Liabilities
U.S. government securities + $1 billion	Federal Reserve notes $0.5 billion U.S. Treasury deposits $0.5 billion

It has been assumed that half of the $1 billion is used to add to the Federal Reserve notes and half to add to the U.S. Treasury deposits; other allocations are possible. But the effect is that it contributes to high-powered money, i.e., to the reserves that the commercial bank may hold with the FED.

The legal reserve requirement is 20%: each $5 deposit must be supported by at least $1 reserves. When the total of the deposits, which form part of the money supply are allowed to increase by $40 billion, then the reserves (i.e., the high-powered money) must rise at least by M = 0.20 x 40 = $8 billion.

The budget deficit = 30 = B + M

= B + 8

Thus the national debt must increase by

B = 30 - 8 = $22 billion.

This is an example of a rather forceful expansionary policy. Not only does the government deficit boost the economy through the multiplier process; in addition there is an increase of $40 billion in the money supply. One of the reasons why the Treasury-FED would opt for this policy is that the increased money supply would keep the interest rates low. Otherwise the increased economic activity resulting from the stimulus of the budget deficit would increase the demand for money and drive the interest rates upward; in which case the stimulus of the budget deficit would be partly offset by a reduction in planned investments.

• PROBLEM 7-20

How can the debt management of the U.S. Treasury contribute to economic stabilization?

Solution: Debt management consists of the decisions as to what kind of securities to issue--short-term, intermediate-term, or long-term--i.e., the composition of the U.S. debt.

To have a stabilization effect, the Treasury must issue short-term debt when there is a recession and long-term debt when there is too much inflation.

The sale of short-term securities in order to finance a deficit increases the supply of liquid assets, which tends to lower long-term interest rates. This is because the financial institutions will buy more long-term bonds when they have more liquid assets. This drives the prices of these bonds upward and their interest yields will fall. If the economic effect of this decline in long-term interest rates offsets the effect in short-term rates, the net effect is expansionary.

The sale of the long-term bonds tends to lower the prices of these bonds and increase interest rates, not only for the long-term bonds but also for the other long-term investments that compete with bonds. The higher interest rates discourage private borrowing and investment. This has a restraining effect on the economy. Historically, however, the U.S. Treasury has not managed its debt in this way. It is hesitant to create long-term debt in times of prosperity when interest rates are high, because this would contribute to its interest service costs.

• PROBLEM 7-21

How can the public debt exert an inflationary pressure on the economy?

Solution: The Treasury finances the public debt by selling U.S. securities. These government securities are very liquid assets; they can easily be converted into money. Consequently the buyers of these securities tend to allot more of their current income to consumption spending than they would if their savings were tied up in relatively non-liquid real estate or private business investments--in stocks, obligations, consumer durables, etc. And such an increase in consumption spending, adding to the aggregate demand, can have an inflationary pull.

A second reason for the inflationary influence of the public debt is also connected with the liquidity of the securities. The huge amount of securities in the hands of households, securities that can easily be converted into cash, represents a backlog in buying power that may be converted at inconvenient times. Inflation will normally induce this conversion if it appears more rational to households to buy at the present time since they expect inflation to continue.

These two tendencies explain why every addition to the public debt may create extra fuel for inflation.

FISCAL POLICY AND TAXATION

• PROBLEM 7-22

A country which previously had no tax system must decide if it will introduce a proportional, progressive, or regressive tax system. It is considered important that the stability of the economy is maintained. Discuss and illustrate which system should be introduced, ignoring only political implications. Assume that the proposed regressive system is a lump-sum tax system, collecting $20 billion in taxes at all levels of NNP; the proportional system has a rate of 20%; and the progressive system has a tax rate of zero at the level of NNP = $100 billion, with a 10 percent increase for every additional $100 billion.

The consumption schedule is as follows:

NNP (billions)	Consumption (billions)
$100	120
200	200
300	280
400	360
500	440
600	520
700	600

Solution: The stability of the economic system is dependent on the size of the (Keynesian) multiplier, and the rate at which the tax revenues vary directly with NNP (= Net National Product). Government budget deficits will stimulate the economy, but an increasing NNP will gradually eliminate that budget deficit. Similarly, a budget surplus will exert a deflationary influence, but the decreasing NNP will, by diminishing tax revenues, gradually eliminate the budget surplus.

When the economy has no tax system, the marginal propensity to consume can be determined from the given consumption schedule. It is to be noted from this schedule that every \$100 billion increase in NNP (ΔY) is accompanied by an \$80 billion increase in consumption (ΔC); thus the marginal propensity to consume

$$c = \frac{\Delta C}{\Delta Y} = \frac{80}{100} = 0.8$$

We may plot the schedule in a graph (See Fig. 1.)

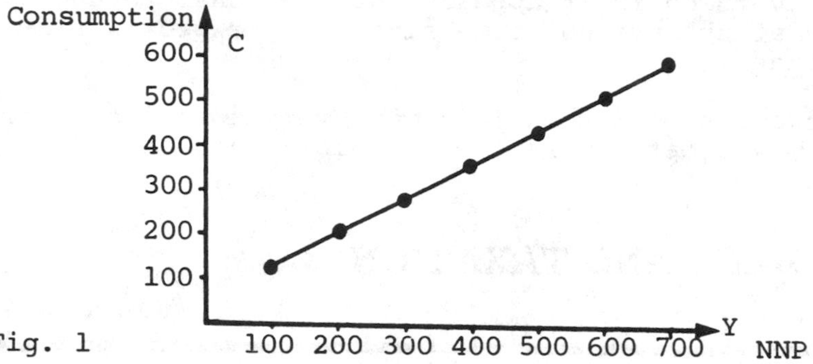

Fig. 1

The Keynesian multiplier is $\frac{1}{1 - c} = \frac{1}{1 - 0.8} = 5$

for this country without a tax system. It will first be determined why a lump-sum tax system is called regressive. Suppose a \$20 billion tax is imposed at all levels of NNP and calculate the tax rate at all levels of NNP.

NNP (billion), Y	Lump Sum Tax, T	Tax Rate t	Disposable Income (Y - T)	Consumption $C=c(Y-T)+\overline{C}$
\$100	20	0.20	80	104
200	20	0.10	180	184
300	20	0.06	280	264
400	20	0.05	380	344
500	20	0.04	480	424
600	20	0.03	580	504
700	20	0.03	680	584

Notice that the tax rates for the higher levels of NNP are lower than for the lower levels, and therefore a lump-sum tax qualifies as a regressive tax.

Disposable income (Y - T) is also calculated. Assuming that the marginal propensity to consume remains unaffected by the imposition of the lump-sum tax system, consumption may be calculated. First, autonomous consumption, which is unrelated to income, is determined from the original consumption schedule. A reduction in income by the imposition of the tax system does not affect this. The MPC = 0.8; thus out of an income of \$100 billion, 0.8 x \$100 billion = \$80 billion is induced consumption. The actual level of consumption is \$120 billion, however; thus the difference, \$120 billion - \$80 billion = \$40 billion is the autonomous consumption $\overline{C}$. (This result can be calculated from the other levels of NNP, and $\overline{C}$ remains the same.) Thus, total consumption, the sum of autonomous and induced consumption, can be calculated using the formula $C = c(Y - T) + \overline{C}$

This equals $C = c(Y - tY) + \overline{C}$

$$= c(1 - t)Y + \overline{C}$$

where t is the tax rate.

The Keynesian multiplier in this case is $K = \frac{1}{1 - c(1 - t)}$, using c = 0.8 and the tax rates already calculated, it can be seen that with a lump-sum tax the multiplier is no longer constant for all levels of NNP, but increases with NNP. The calculation of the multiplier is as follows:

NNP	1-t	c(1-t) = 0.8(1-t)	1-c(1-t)	$k = \frac{1}{1-c(1-t)}$
100	0.80	0.64	0.36	2.8
200	0.90	0.72	0.28	3.6
300	0.94	0.75	0.25	4.0
400	0.95	0.76	0.24	4.2
500	0.96	0.77	0.23	4.3
600	0.97	0.78	0.22	4.5
700	0.97	0.78	0.22	4.5

Notice that the multiplier is more powerful at the higher levels of NNP than at the lower levels of NNP. The budget deficit (surplus) remains constant at all levels of NNP under this lump-sum tax system: $\overline{G} - \overline{T} = \overline{G} - 20$, where $\overline{G}$ = government expenditures. So there is no built-in stabilizer in this system. And as NNP increases it can be seen that small distortions, such as a fall in investments because of pessimistic expectations, have wider repercussions because of the larger multiplier.

In summary, the lump sum tax system is destabilizing over time when NNP gradually increases. Under the proportional tax system with a tax rate of 20% at all levels of NNP, the consumption schedule is calculated as follows:

NNP (billions)	Tax Rate t=0.20	Proportional Tax T	Disposable Income Y - T	Consumption $C=c(Y-T)+\overline{C}$
100	0.20	20	20	104
200	0.20	40	160	168
300	0.20	60	240	232
400	0.20	80	320	296
500	0.20	100	400	360
600	0.20	120	480	424
700	0.20	140	560	488

In this case, the tax rate remains constant but the taxes collected increase with an increase in NNP.

The Keynesian multiplier remains constant in this case because both the marginal propensity to consume and the tax rate are constant; thus

$$k = \frac{1}{1-c(1-t)} = \frac{1}{1-0.8(1-0.20)} = \frac{1}{1-0.8x0.8} = \frac{1}{1-0.64} =$$

$$= \frac{1}{0.36} \cong 2.8$$

A proportional tax system tends to be stabilizing because a budget deficit, (surplus) decreases in size when income increases, (decreases). (See figure 2.)

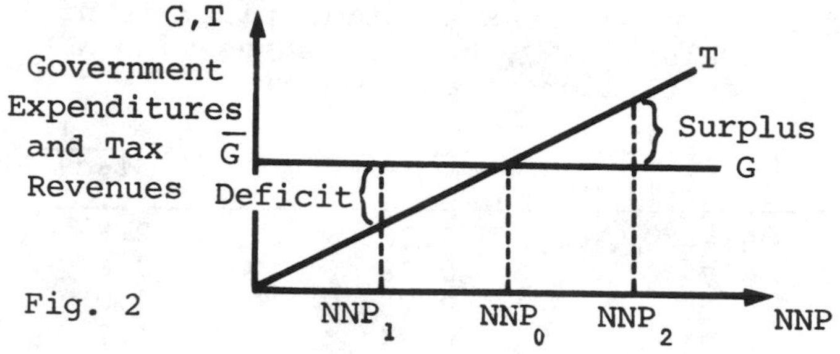

Fig. 2

At income level NNP_1 the economy experiences a deficit which will be eliminated when NNP increases, and at income level NNP_2 there is a surplus which will be eliminated when NNP decreases.

The Keynesian multiplier remains constant; thus distortions have the same effects on high as well as low levels of NNP. In summary, a proportional tax system is stabilizing.

Finally, a "progressive" tax system will be discussed. Again calculate the consumption schedule:

NNP	Tax Rate t	Progressive Tax T	Disposable Income Y - T	Consumption $C=c(Y-T)+\overline{C}$
\$100	0.00	0	100	120
200	0.10	20	180	184
300	0.20	60	240	232
400	0.30	120	280	264
500	0.40	200	300	280
600	0.50	300	300	280
700	0.60	420	280	264

Under the progressive tax system, when income increases, the tax rate as well as the taxes collected increase. The Keynesian multiplier is no longer constant but decreases with increasing NNP as can be seen from the following calculations

NNP	1 - t	c(1 - t)	1 - c(1 - t)	$k = \frac{1}{1 - c(1 - t)}$
100	1	0.8	0.20	5
200	0.90	0.72	0.28	3.6
300	0.80	0.64	0.36	2.8
400	0.70	0.56	0.44	2.3

500	0.60	0.48	0.52	1.9
600	0.50	0.40	0.60	1.7
700	0.40	0.32	0.68	1.5

Taxes increase when the level of income increases: thus a budget deficit, (surplus) will be eliminated when income increases (decreases). The influence of the Keynesian multiplier becomes weaker when NNP grows, so that possible distortions have less powerful repercussions throughout the economy.

Conclusion: a progressive tax system is a powerful instrument for stabilization, because budget discrepancies will be eliminated rather quickly while the stability of the economic system improves owing to a decrease in the size of the multiplier.

• PROBLEM 7-23

Government can apply various measures to fight inflation; one of the available measures is a structural change in the tax system. Explain how a progressive tax structure, a proportional tax structure, and a regressive tax structure respectively affect inflation. Assume that incomes are gradually increasing.

Solution: First, what is meant by progressive, proportional and regressive tax structures will be explained, and then the effects on inflation will be analyzed.

A progressive tax structure is one in which the percentage of income collected in taxes is greater for higher incomes than for lower ones.

A proportional tax structure is one in which the percentage of income collected in taxes is the same for all levels of income.

A regressive income tax structure is one in which the percentage of income collected in taxes is lower for higher incomes than for lower incomes.

The effect of a progressive tax structure when incomes are rising is to reduce inflationary pressure, because an increasing percentage of income is collected and therefore is not available to add to demand. In terms of fiscal policy, this means that government tax revenues automatically increase more rapidly, closing the budget deficit and thereby lessening the inflationary pressure also.

The effect of a proportional tax structure on inflation is much less than that of a progressive tax structure, because the percentage taken from rising income remains the same. Still, because the total tax revenue increases, the budget deficit slowly closes when incomes rise--assuming that the government expenditures remain unaltered. This automatic stabilizer effect helps to reduce the inflationary pressure too, but less than the progressive tax structure.

The regressive tax structure adds to inflationary pressure because a greater percentage of income will be left available to consumers when incomes rise, and hence more can be consumed. When incomes rise it depends on the degree of regressiveness of the tax whether more or less tax revenue will be received by the government, and thus whether an existing budget deficit will be closed or widened. A widening deficit will add more inflationary pressure. But even if the deficit will gradually be closed under a regressive tax structure with rising incomes, it can still be said that the effect will be much less than it would be under a progressive or proportional tax structure.

• PROBLEM 7-24

How can taxes be used to achieve the economic goals of full employment, price stability, and economic growth?

Solution: When the government levies personal income taxes T_P the disposable personal income $Y - T_P$ is decreased and thereby personal consumption expenditures are decreased also. When the government levies corporation income taxes T_C, it influences investment out of retained earnings of business, I. When retail sales taxes are also levied, the spending power of the consumers, the sales revenues, and thus the retained earnings and investments, are affected. Property taxes affect the wealth owned by individuals and businesses and will thereby again affect consumption and investment. By changing the tax rates and/or the structure of the tax system (e.g., proportional versus lump-sum taxes) the government--i.e., federal, state and local authorities--can influence the aggregate demand, particularly the consumption expenditures C and the planned investments I.

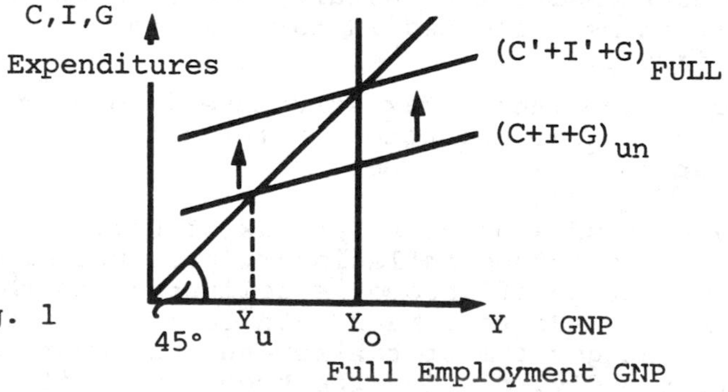

Fig. 1

In figure 1 it can be seen that if the aggregate demand --consumption plus investment plus government spending (C + I + G)--is lower than the potential output capacity of the economy, unemployment results. To reach the goal of full employment, expenditures should be increased. One method is lowering the taxes to increase C and I.

$Y_o - Y_u$ is the deflationary unemployment gap in GNP.

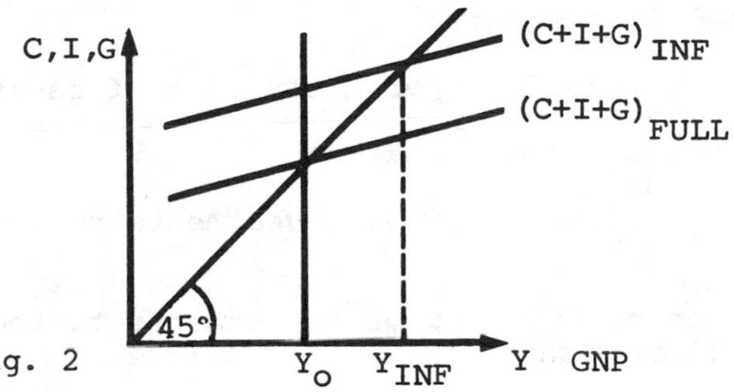

Fig. 2

The opposite situation exists if the aggregate demand is higher than the potential output capacity: the excess purchasing power results in inflation because real output is fixed at Y_o, and only nominal income $Y = P \cdot \bar{y}$ can be increased by raising general price level P. (See figure 2.)

$Y_{inf} - Y_o$ is the inflationary gap in GNP. An increase in the taxes would reduce the purchasing power available to the public, and so also reduce the primary inflationary pressure. To see some of the contentions above in detail, the impact of the taxes on consumption expenditures and planned investments will be discussed. Consumption can be thought of as being dependent on income Y, taxes T, and wealth owned.

A: $C = C(Y, T, A)$

For simplicity, assume the following linear functional form

$$C = c_1(1 - t_1)Y + c_2(1 - t_2)A \qquad (1)$$

where

C = consumption expenditures

c_1 = marginal propensity to consume out of income, say $c_1 = 0.8$

c_2 = marginal propensity to consume out of wealth owned, say $c_2 = 0.1$

t_1 = personal income tax rate

t_2 = personal property tax rate

Investment can be thought of as being dependent on the interest rate r, taxes T, and earnings before income taxes R

$$I = I(r, T, R)$$

For simplicity, assume the following linear functional form

$$I = \alpha r + \beta(1 - t_3)R \qquad (2)$$

where

I = planned investments

r = interest rate (= Opportunity cost of capital)

t_3 = corporation income tax rate

α = reaction coefficient of investments to the interest rate

β = reaction coefficient of investments to the earnings after taxes

Total aggregate demand consists of consumption, planned investments and government expenditures

$$Y = C + I + \overline{G} \tag{3}$$

Substituting equations (1) and (2) into equation (3) yields

$$Y = c_1(1 - t_1)Y + c_2(1 - t_2)A$$

$$+ \alpha r + \beta(1 - t_3)R + \overline{G}$$

Bringing all the terms with Y to the left hand side gives

$$[1 - c_1(1 - t_1)]Y = c_2(1 - t_2)A + \alpha r + \beta(1 - t_3)R + \overline{G}$$

Dividing both sides by the coefficient between square brackets $[1 - c_1(1 - t_1)]$

gives

$$Y = \frac{1}{1 - c_1(1 - t_1)} \left\{c_2(1 - t_2)A + \alpha r + \beta(1 - t_3)R + \overline{G}\right\}$$

At this point something remarkable may be observed. The personal income tax rate t_1 affects the Keynesian multiplier $\frac{1}{1 - c_1(1 - t_1)}$: when t_1 is increased, $1 - t_1$ becomes smaller, therefore the denominator $1 - c_1(1 - t_1)$ becomes larger, and thus the Keynesian multiplier $\frac{1}{1 - c_1(1 - t_1)}$ smaller. Supposing $t_1 = 0.25$, an increase of one percentage point up to $t_1 = 0.26$ changes the value of the multiplier from

$$\frac{1}{1 - 0.8(1 - 0.25)} = 2.5 \quad \text{to} \quad \frac{1}{1 - 0.8(1 - 0.26)} = 2.45$$

so if the autonomous expenditures were \$400 billion, GNP would be reduced from 2.5 x 400 = \$1,000 to 2.45 x 400 = \$980 billion.

Suppose now that there is a multiplier $\frac{1}{1 - c_1(1 - t_1)} = 2.5$, and $t_2 = 0.40$.

The income wealth multiplier relationship is

$$\Delta Y = \frac{c_2(1 - t_2)}{1 - c_1(1 - t_1)} \Delta A;$$

a marginal change in wealth is multiplied to a larger income change. The income/wealth multiplier has the value of

$$\frac{c_2(1 - t_2)}{1 - c_1(1 - t_1)} = \frac{0.1(1 - 0.4)}{0.4} = 0.15$$

If it is supposed that wealth amounts to $10,000 billion, a property tax rise of 1 percentage point from $t_2 = 0.40$ to $t_2 = 0.41$ changes the income wealth multiplier from 0.15 to

$$\frac{0.1(1 - 0.41)}{0.4} = 0.1475, \text{ and GNP drops by}$$

$$(0.15 \times 10{,}000) - (0.1475 \times 10{,}000) = \$25 \text{ billion.}$$

The analysis of the corporation income tax rate is analogous to the property tax rate. Of course t_1, t_2 and t_3 do not include only the personal income tax, the property tax, and the corporation income tax respectively, but also the effects of the excise taxes on the consumption and investment goods that are sold.

• PROBLEM 7-25

What is the effect on savings of a tax cut of $10 billion? Is this inflationary or deflationary?

Assume that the marginal propensity to consume is 0.85.

Solution: Because taxes affect disposable income, they affect savings. A cut in taxes increases disposable income Y - T, where Y is income before taxes and T is taxes. The marginal propensity to save out of income is 1 minus the marginal propensity to consume: $s = 1 - c = 1 - 0.85 = 0.15$. When taxes are cut by $10 billion, the effect on savings will be an increase of

$$\Delta S = s\,[-\Delta T] =$$

$$= 0.15\,[-(\$10 \text{ billion})] = 0.15 \times \$10 \text{ billion} = \$1.5 \text{ billion.}$$

The remainder of the addition to disposable income, $\Delta T - \Delta S$ = $10 billion - $1.5 billion = 8.5 billion will go to increased consumption demand. This increased consumption demand will be amplified by the multiplier process. The multiplier is $\frac{1}{1 - c} = \frac{1}{0.15} = 6.67$; thus the effect on the economy will be an increase in income of $\Delta Y = \frac{-c\Delta T}{1 - c} = \frac{8.5}{0.15} = \$56.67$ billion.

• PROBLEM 7-26

In a given economy, households save 10% of their incomes; the current income tax burden is 25%; planned investments are expected to be \$60 billion; and the trade deficit is about \$2.5 billion. Current government expenditures are \$270 billion per year. The full capacity GNP level is \$1,060 billion.

What is the current deficit? What is the full employment deficit?

Compare the two. Is the current budget expansionary or contractionary? Explain.

Solution: First, it is necessary to calculate the current level of GNP and infer the taxes in order to see the current budget deficit. Then the full employment deficit must be calculated and compared with the current budget deficit. National income equals the total of expenditures, consumption, planned investments, government expenditures, and the trade surplus. (The trade surplus equals exports-imports.) Thus:

$$Y = C + I + G + (Ex - Im)$$

Consumption can be described by the relationship wherein households consume 90% of their disposable income; the rest--10%--is saved. Thus

$$C = 0.90\ (Y - T),$$

where Y - T is disposable income. Taxes are proportional to income:

$$T = 0.25Y.$$

Substituting this in the income relationship results in

$$C = 0.90(Y - 0.25Y) = 0.90 \times 0.75Y$$

$$= 0.675Y$$

Substituting this new figure into the income identity yields

$$Y = 0.675Y + I + G + (Ex - Im)$$

Next, bring the elements with the common term Y to the left side of the equation:

$$0.325Y = I + G + (Ex - Im)$$

Dividing by 0.325 yields

$$y = \frac{1}{0.325} \times [I + G + (Ex - Im)]$$

The multiplier is thus equal to $\frac{1}{0.325} = 3.077$. Current GNP can now be determined by substituting the values of planned investment, government expenditures and the trade balance into the relationship above:

$$Y = 3.077 \times [60 + 270 + (-2.5)]$$

$$= 3.077 \times 327.5 = \$1007.72 \text{ billion}$$

Notice that the trade deficit is a negative trade surplus. Unemployment exists because GNP is below its full capacity level. Current taxes are

$$T = 0.25 \times 1007.72$$

$$= \$251.93 \text{ billion.}$$

The government expenditures are larger than the tax revenues; thus the current budget deficit is

$$G - T = 270 - 251.93 = \$18.07 \text{ billion.}$$

The full capacity GNP is \$1,060 billion. Total tax revenues in the full employment situation would be $T = 0.25 \times 1{,}060 = \$265$ billion, so that the full employment deficit would be $G - T_f = 270 - 265 = \$5$ billion. The actual, or current budget deficit depends on the initial position of the economy and the tax revenues at that level of income. The current budget has an ultimate inflationary effect because the full employment budget--based on the current savings behavior, tax rates, investment plans, and trade-balance--shows a deficit. The full employment balance, therefore gives a clearer picture of what the ultimate effect of the introduced budget policy will be than does the actual budget.

• PROBLEM 7-27

Suppose households consume 85% of their disposable income. What is the effect on national income if income taxes are increased by 4%? If sales taxes are increased by 4%? Assume the initial tax rate is 20% in both cases.

Solution: Sales taxes and excise taxes are related to expenditure rather than income. Their totals move up and down with income because consumption expenditures do so. In other words, income taxes fall on both consumption and saving, while sales taxes fall only on consumption.

Consumption expenditure is given by the equation

$$C = c(Y - T)$$

where $(Y - T)$ is income minus taxes, or disposable income.

Taxes are proportional to income:

$$T = tY.$$

Thus $C = c(Y - tY) = c(1 - t)Y$

$$= 0.85\ (1 - 0.20)Y = 0.68Y$$

When the income tax rate is increased by 4% consumption expenditures decrease.

The multiplier is initially $\frac{1}{1 - 0.68} \cong 3.1$

However, when the tax rate is raised by 4%, the multiplier decreases in value to

$$\frac{1}{[1 - 0.85(1 - 0.24)]} = \frac{1}{[1 - 0.646]} = \frac{1}{0.354} \cong 2.9$$

Taking into consideration that only 85% of disposable income is consumed, the amount of income affected by the tax is .85 x 4% = 3.4%.

Thus income falls by 2.9 x 3.4% = 9.9%

The sales tax falls on expenditures only. Thus the multiplier of 3.1 remains unaffected:

Expenditures are lowered by 4%; income will then fall by

$$3.1 \times 4\% = 12.4\%$$

THE PARADOX OF THRIFT

• PROBLEM 7-28

Discuss the paradox of thrift.

Solution: According to the paradox of thrift, an attempt to save more can result in a decrease in actual savings and investment.

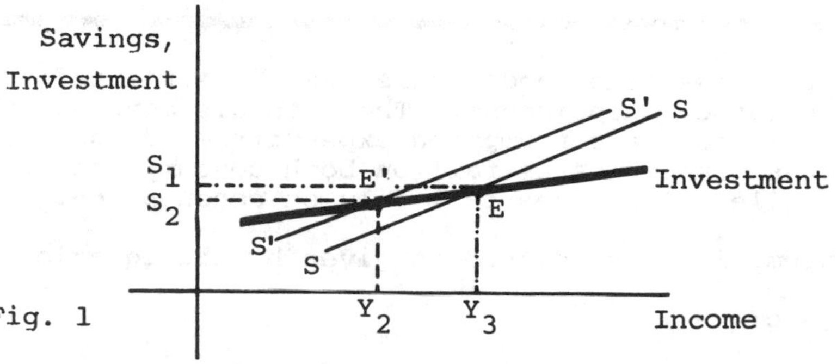

Fig. 1

We can see in Figure 1 that if the planned savings schedule shifts from SS to S'S' due to peoples' attempt to save more, the actual amount of savings and investment will decline, from I_1 to I_2, as long as the slope of the investment line > 0. Here, the investment schedule slopes slightly upward, and as the savings schedule shifts, the equilibrium point moves from E to E'. This illustrates the paradox: instead of increased savings, a slight drop in savings from S_1 to S_2 occurred. Note also how income dropped from Y_1 to Y_2 as the equilibrium point shifted.

• PROBLEM 7-29

Evaluate the following statement: "If society attempts to save more, it may end up actually saving the same amount, or even less" (The Paradox of Thrift).

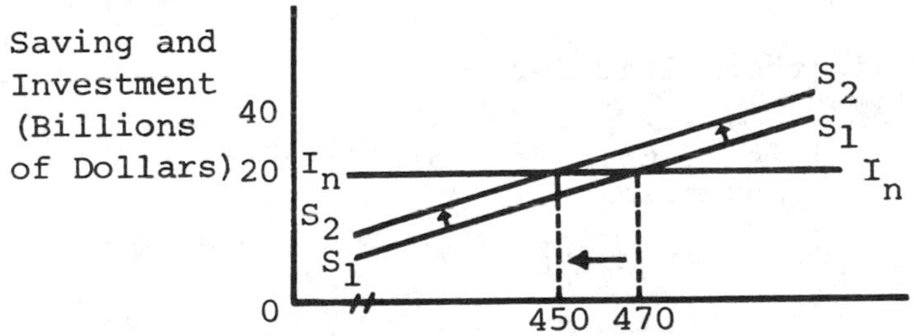

Solution: The above statement is the curious paradox suggested by the leakages-injections approach to NNP determination and by the analysis of the multiplier. And as was stated above, the paradox is that if society attempts to save more, there is the probability that it may end up actually saving the same amount, or even less. To make this point clearer, the accompanying graph is presented.

Suppose In and S_1 are the current investment and saving schedules which determine a \$470 billion equilibrium NNP. Now, assume that households, perhaps anticipating a recession, attempt to save \$5 billion more at each income level in order to put aside a nest egg against the expected bad times. This attempt to save more is reflected in an upward shift of the saving schedule from S_1 to S_2. But this shift creates an excess of planned saving over planned investment at the current \$470 billion equilibrium output. The multiplier effect of this will cause this small increase in saving (decline in consumption) to be reflected in a much larger decline in equilibrium NNP--namely 5 x 4 = \$20 billion, if we assume a MPC of 0.75, because then the simple multiplier is

$$\frac{1}{1 - c} = \frac{1}{1 - 0.75} = \frac{1}{0.25} = 4 .$$

In terms of formal analysis: when the society suddenly decides to save more, the autonomous consumption is decreased in size.

The savings schedule is

$$S = sY - \overline{C} \tag{1}$$

Equilibrium is defined by

$$S = I \tag{2}$$

Substituting (1) into equation (2) results in

$$sY - \overline{C} = I$$

or $$sY = I + \overline{C}$$

Dividing both sides by s yields

$$Y = \frac{1}{S}(I + \overline{C})$$

where $\frac{1}{s} = \frac{1}{1-c}$ is the multiplier.

When $\overline{C}$ decreases in size this decrease is amplified by the multiplier. In the example

$$\Delta Y = \frac{1}{0.25}(-5) = -20$$

A sudden increase in saving by \$5 billion reduces income by \$20 billion. Still, total actual saving = total investment in equilibrium (S = I)

This results in the following paradoxes:

First, note that at the new \$450 billion equilibrium NNP, households are saving the same amount they did at the original \$470 billion NNP. Society's attempt to save more has been frustrated by the multiple decline in the equilibrium NNP causing the decline in actual savings. Second, this analysis suggests that thrift, which has always been held in high esteem in our economy, can be something of a social vice. From the individual point of view, a penny saved may be a penny earned. But from the social point of view, a penny saved is a penny not spent, and therefore causes a decline in someone else's income. The act of thrift may be virtuous from the individual's viewpoint but undesirable from the social standpoint, because of its negative effects upon total output and employment.

Third, households may be most strongly induced to save more (consume less) at the very time when increased saving is most inappropriate and most economically undesirable; that is, when the economy seems to be backsliding into a recession.

THE DEFLATIONARY GAP

• PROBLEM 7-30

What is a deflationary gap?

Solution: This describes a situation in which total demand is too small to absorb the total supply that an economy can produce at the full employment level of national income. The difference between total supply and total demand is then called the deflationary gap.

• PROBLEM 7-31

A government is encountering a deflationary gap of $250 billion in the economy. It would like to reach a full employment level of income and can do this by either increasing expenditures only, or by increasing expenditures and taxes.

a) Supposing that MPC = 0.8, discuss the two alternative policies.

b) How do these policies change if government is required to balance its budget?

c) Is there another alternative policy besides the two mentioned?

Solution: By increasing expenditures alone the government avoids raising taxes, but will not be able to keep a balanced budget. To see by how much government expenditures must increase to eliminate the deflationary gap and reach full employment use the multiplier formula

$$\Delta Y = \frac{1}{1 - c} \Delta G$$

where ΔY = deflationary gap = $250

ΔG = change in government expenditures

and the factor $\frac{1}{1 - c}$ = the Keynesian multiplier; $c = 0.8$

The amount of the deflationary gap to be counteracted is

$$\Delta Y = 250$$

Thus $\Delta Y = 250 = \frac{1}{1 - 0.8} \cdot \Delta G$

$$= \frac{1}{0.2} \Delta G$$

$$250 = 5 \cdot \Delta G$$

Government expenditures must increase by $\Delta G = \frac{250}{5} = 50$ billion dollars, to reach full employment of income. There are two types of income tax systems: the proportional tax, and the lump-sum tax. The proportional tax takes a certain percentage t from income Y, so that the disposable income left is

$$Y_{disp} = Y - tY = (1 - t)Y \qquad (1)$$

Households consume out of disposable income

$$C = c \cdot Y_{disp} + \overline{C} \qquad (2)$$

Substituting (1) into (2) yields

$$C = c(1 - t)Y + \overline{C} \qquad (3)$$

Total aggregate demand is equal to the sum of consumption, investment and government expenditures

$$Y = C + In + G \qquad (4)$$

Substituting (1) into equation (4) results in

$$Y = c(1 - t)Y + \overline{C} + In + G \qquad (5)$$

Bringing all terms, including Y, to the left side:

$$[1 - c(1 - t)]Y = \overline{C} + In + G \qquad (6)$$

Divide both sides by the term [1 - c(1 - t)]:

$$Y = \frac{1}{1 - c(1 - t)} \cdot (\overline{C} + In + G) \qquad (7)$$

Notice that the multiplier has become more complicated; it is in effect reduced in value. This can be explained by recalling that taxes form a leakage in the income-expenditure flow.

Changes in autonomous consumption or investment are not the focus of interest here, so $\Delta\overline{C} = \Delta In = 0$ and there remains:

$$\Delta Y = \frac{1}{1 - c(1 - t)} \Delta G \qquad (8)$$

What tax rate should be set, and how much should the government spend to beat the deflationary gap? There are two variables, ΔG and t, and only one equation, so the only thing that can be determined is a relationship between ΔG and t that has to be fulfilled if the deflationary gap is to be completely defeated.

From equation (8) there was obtained:

$$[1 - c(1 - t)]\Delta Y = \Delta G \qquad (9)$$

$$[1 - 0.8\ (1 - t)]\ 250 = \Delta G$$

$$[0.2 + 0.8t]\ 250 = \Delta G$$

$$50 + 200\ t = \Delta G$$

This is the relationship sought after. For example, if $t = 0.30$, then

$$\Delta G = 50 + 200\ (0.30) = 110,$$

and if the tax rate is 20% then

$$\Delta G = 50 + 200\ (0.20) = 90.$$

The lower the tax rate, the less leakage in the income-expenditure flow that occurs, the more effective government expenditures are, and the less government has to spend to beat the deflationary gap. An interesting question arises when the government is required to balance its budget.

Assuming that the budget is balanced in the beginning, this means that the total increase in government expenditures must equal the total increase in taxes.

$$\Delta G = t\Delta Y$$

Substituting this in equation (9) gives

$$[1 - c + ct]\Delta Y = t\Delta Y$$

or $$(1 - c)\Delta Y + ct\Delta Y = t\Delta Y$$

Bring the second term to the right hand side:

$$(1 - c)\Delta Y = (t - ct)\Delta Y$$

$$= t(1 - c)\Delta Y$$

This can only be true if $t = 1.00$. In other words, in the case of a balanced budget, total government expenditure equals the deflationary gap

$$\Delta G = \Delta Y = 250$$

and the increase in the households' disposable income equals zero.

From equation (1) taking changes at both sides,

$$\Delta Y_{disp} = (1 - t)\Delta Y$$

$$= (1 - 1)\Delta Y = 0$$

The lump-sum tax is a deduction 'over the board' T from income Y, so that the disposable income left is

$$Y_{disp} = Y - T \qquad (10)$$

Households consume out of disposable income.

Substituting (10) into equation (2) yields

$$C = c(Y - T) + \overline{C}$$

Substituting this into equation (4) results in

$$Y = c(Y - T) + \overline{C} + In + G$$

Bring all terms including Y to the left side:

$$Y - cY = (1 - c)Y = \overline{C} + In + G - cT$$

Divide both sides by the term 1 - c:

$$Y = \frac{1}{1 - c} (\overline{C} + In + G - cT)$$

Notice that in this case the simple multiplier has not changed. But total expenditures are decreased by cT, i.e., that part of income that would have gone into consumption had it not been taxed_away. Again there is a leakage, but it is final. Again $\Delta\overline{C} = \Delta In = 0$,

so $$\Delta Y = \frac{1}{1 - c} \cdot (\Delta G - c\Delta T) \qquad (11)$$

The increase in the lump-sum tax only reduces the total expenditures, reducing the effect of the increase in government expenditures ΔG.

Substituting the values for ΔY and c into equation (11) yields

$$250 = \frac{1}{1 - 0.8} (\Delta G - 0.8T)$$

or $$50 = \Delta G - 0.8T$$

i.e., the required relationship between the increase in government expenditures ΔG and the increase in the lump-sum tax.

For example, if T = 50, then

$$\Delta G = 50 + 0.8(50) = 90$$

and if T = 100, then

$$\Delta G = 50 + 0.8(100) = 130$$

in order to beat the deflationary gap.

What happens if the government is again required to balance its budget? In the case of a lump-sum tax this means

$$\Delta G = \Delta T$$

Substituting this in equation (11) results in

$$\Delta Y = \frac{1}{1 - c} (\Delta G - c\Delta G)$$

$$= \frac{1 - c}{1 - c} \cdot \Delta G$$

so $$\Delta Y = \Delta G .$$

Again it is concluded that the balanced budget requirement implies that the increase in the government expenditures equals the deflationary gap $\Delta G = \Delta Y = 250$ billion dollars. The increase in the lump-sum tax would equal this, and disposable income would be reduced once and for all by the same $250 billion.

The other alternative would be not to change government expenditures, $\Delta G = 0$, but to decrease taxes.

In the case of the proportional tax rate use equation (9), substituting $\Delta G = 0$.

Then $[1 - c(1 - t)]\Delta Y = 0$

or $[1 - 0.8\ (1 - t)]\ 250 = 0$

or $[0.2 + 0.8t]\ 250 = 0$

or, $50 + 200t = 0$.

$$200t = -50$$

$$t = -\frac{50}{200} = -0.25$$

Thus the tax rate should be reduced by 25% to beat the deflationary gap. In case of the lump-sum tax use equation (11), substituting $\Delta G = 0$

$$\Delta Y = \frac{-c}{1 - c}\ \Delta T,$$

$$250 = \frac{-0.8}{0.2}\ \Delta T$$

$$= -4\Delta T\ .$$

$$\Delta T = -62.5$$

Thus there should be a final reduction of $62.5 billion in the lump-sum tax in order to beat the deflationary gap.

STABILIZING AND DESTABILIZING FACTORS

• PROBLEM 7-32

List some automatic stabilizers in the economy and explain their workings.

Solution: There are some structural, behavioral, and institutional relationships in the economy that have a stabilizing effect on it, besides the concrete stabilizing policy measures.

For example, if planned investments fall (because of

worsening prospects) and planned savings remain on the previous level, that is $I < S$, the economy glides into a recession. However, much of the saving is business saving from the depreciation reserves and retained earnings (= undistributed profits) of corporations. To some extent investment and business saving are linked. Business saving will also fall if investment falls, though not to the same extent. Thus the investment-saving gap is smaller. Secondly, the permanent income effect works as a stabilizer. As incomes start to fall, households tend to adhere to the previous, higher consumption levels, because they expect the fall in income to be only transitory. Declining income and high consumption means rapidly falling savings. This also helps to keep the investment-saving gap small.

For a while, too, the downward pressure of accelerator effects is comparatively small. Investment plans are made in advance, and will probably be carried out if businesses believe that the recession is only temporary. This keeps the investment level high.

But the concrete policy measures act as stronger stabilizers. The rate of tax of the progressive income tax is lower on low incomes than on high incomes. Therefore, a fall of 7% in pre-tax incomes, for example, will result in a decline in disposable income that is smaller than 7%.

Since consumption plans are based on disposable income, the downward influence from falling consumption will be lessened by the progressiveness of the income tax. For example, suppose Person One is in a low income-tax bracket with a tax rate of $t_1 = 10\%$, and Person Two is in a high-income tax bracket with a tax rate of $t_2 = 40\%$. Assume further that both persons have the same marginal propensity to consume of 0.8, and there is no autonomous consumption. Then the respective consumption can be described by

$$C_1 = C(1 - t_1)Y_1 = 0.8 \times 0.9 \times Y = 0.72\ Y_1$$

$$C_2 = c(1 - t_2)Y_2 = 0.8 \times 0.6 \times Y = 0.48Y_2$$

If the economy consisted only of Person One, the multiplier would be

$$k_1 = \frac{1}{1 - 0.72} = 3.57\ ;$$

if the economy consisted of Person Two, the multiplier would be

$$k_2 = \frac{1}{1 - 0.48} = 1.92\ .$$

It is clear that the higher the tax rate, the lower the multiplier, and the less destabilizing the multiplier will be. When a fall in total consumption is distributed fifty-fifty over the income brackets, the multiplier is the weighted average of the two above

$$k_3 = 0.5 \times 3.57 + 0.5 \times 1.92 = 1.785 + 0.96 = 2.745$$

A second policy stabilizer built into the system is the automatic growth of government transfer payments as the economy declines. As incomes move downward and unemployment increases, both unemployment benefits and welfare payments will increase. This slows the fall in personal incomes and thus the decline in planned consumption expenditure.

The basic weakness of all these stabilizers is their lack of predictive ability. These stabilizers rely on restorative influences which appear only when an actual deviation occurs, and they often react too late.

• PROBLEM 7-33

List 4 destabilizing processes in the economy and explain why they are destabilizing.

Solution: It appears that the multiplier process, the accelerator process, the effects of expectations, and the inflationary process exert destabilizing influences on the economy.

The multiplier exerts such influences because an initial, relatively small decline or increase in expenditure somewhere in the economy will decrease or increase other incomes and thus other expenditures. The consequence is a multiplied effect of a relatively small initial impulse or disturbance; i.e., the 'noise,' or disturbance, in the economy is amplified.

The accelerator effect works along the same lines: a fall in output will cause a decline in investment, lowering expenditure. Thus, via the multiplier, output falls further. There is an equivalent upward push on output if output increases.

The expectation of recessions or booms in the near future will tend to lower or raise investment plans, and thus help to cause the expectations to come true. This is an example of 'self-fulfilling prophecies.'

The 'built-in' inflationary process will sustain inflation even though its initiating causes have been removed. The inflation is built into the expectations, the inflation-clauses of contracts, the financial transactions, etc.

SHORT ANSWER QUESTIONS FOR REVIEW

Answer
To be covered when testing yourself

Choose the correct answer.

1. Built-in stabilizers: (a) are sufficient to maintain full stability (b) reduce the size of the multiplier resulting from, say, an increase in investment spending (c) are found primarily in the fiscal policy of grass-roots government (d) tend to lessen fluctuations in GNP through their effect on disposable income, but do not in themselves change the size of the multiplier (e) were endorsed by Adam Smith — b

2. Our large public debt is undesirable because: (a) there is a definite danger that the Federal government may go bankrupt (b) when the entire debt falls due, it must be paid out of higher taxes (c) it has increased at a faster rate than has the GNP (d) the Treasury as a creditor, may strongly endorse policies which conflict with a tight money policy (e) none of the above — d

3. A countercyclical fiscal policy would include (a) raising government expenditures and cutting taxes in times of depression (b) raising government expenditures and cutting taxes in times of boom (c) raising government expenditures and raising taxes in times of boom (d) cutting government expenditures and cutting taxes in times of depression (e) none of the above — a

4. In determining the government's fiscal posture, one should look at: (a) the actual surplus or deficit (b) the full-employment budget surplus or deficit (c) the personal income tax (d) the inflationary impact which the automatic stabilizers have in full employment economy — b

5. "Automatic stabilizers" tend to: (a) adjust tax rates to keep the full employment budget in balance (b) adjust pay to cost-of-living changes (c) adjust tax rates to keep the actual budget in balance (d) reduce national income fluctuations (e) keep the money supply at a steady 4 to 6 per cent increase per annum — d

6. Economists are in general agreement that discretionary fiscal policy will stabilize the economy most when: (a) the budget is balanced

Answer
To be covered when testing yourself

each year (b) budget deficits are continuously incurred (c) deficits are incurred during recessions and surpluses during inflations (d) deficits are incurred during inflations and surpluses during recessions (e) budget surpluses are continuously incurred — c

7. The government can worsen an inflationary situation when it: (a) increases taxes (b) increases debt-financed spending (c) exercises money and credit policies to reduce private spending (d) makes its public activities more efficient (e) does any of the above — b

8. An expansionary fiscal policy requires: (a) increased government spending, higher taxes or both (b) lowered government spending, lower taxes (c) increased money supply and increased interest rates (d) increased government spending, lower taxes, or both — d

9. In an inflationary period, an appropriate policy for the Federal Reserve would be to: (a) encourage member banks to increase their loans (b) sell government securities on the open market (c) lower legal Reserve requirements (d) decrease the discount rate (e) reduce margin requirements — b

10. A large public debt may: (a) impair incentives to innovate and invest (b) decrease inflationary pressures in a full-employment economy (c) shift the consumption schedule down (d) create a larger stock of private capital for future generations — a

11. The ultimate rule of fiscal discipline in modern mixed economies is to: (a) permit the automatic stabilizers to balance the budget (b) balance the budget every four years (c) balance the budget over the cycle (d) balance the budget every year (e) do none of the above, since there are no rules — e

12. The effect of a government surplus upon the equilibrium level of NNP is substantially the same as: (a) a decrease in saving (b) an

increase in investment (c) an increase in consumption (d) an increase in saving d

13. "Old-fashioned public finance" refers best to which of the following views? (a) The "full-employment budget" should, in peacetime, be balanced (b) An example of a good tax for revenue purposes is a head tax, since its tax revenue is stable over the business cycle. (c) The public debt is less of a burden in peace than in war because only under wartime conditions is it necessary to write a blank check to finance national survival (d) The government budget should be balanced over the cycle rather than every year b

14. Imagine an economy at full employment. If receipts fall short of expenditures, it can be concluded that: (a) investments exceed savings (b) savings exceed investments (c) the tax structure has been adjusted upwards (d) an equality of tax receipts and expenditures b

15. Which of the following is not a public good? (a) city hall (b) fire station (c) TV set (d) national defense program c

16. A major purpose of the Federal Trade Commission is to: (a) increase trade between businesses (b) curb inflation (c) take action against fraudulent and misleading advertising (d) increase employment c

17. The very nature of social goods and services makes it: (a) easier to measure precisely the manner in which benefits are apportioned among individuals or institutions (b) easier to understand how the tax burden is allocated among taxpayers (c) difficult to measure precisely the manner in which benefits are apportioned among individuals or institutions (d) useful in redistributing income c

18. Sales and excise taxes are considered "hidden taxes" in that they are shifted by sellers to consumers via (a) increased sales (b) higher substitute-product prices (c) lower product prices (d) higher product prices d

19. The rationale behind the ability-to-pay taxation is that (a) households and businesses

	Answer To be covered when testing yourself
should purchase goods and services of government in the same manner in which other commodities are bought (b) larger income receivers should pay more than proportionate amount (c) consumers act rationally, therefore need tax breaks (d) smaller income receivers should pay less than proportionate amount (e) the first dollars of income received in any period of time will be spent upon basic high-urgency goods	e
20. A disadvantage of public works as a medium of positive fiscal policy is that: (a) the taxes needed to pay for the projects might result in lowered spending (b) most public works programs yield little or no benefit to the public (c) the increase in spending is particularly likely to lead to inflationary price rises (d) it necessarily means diverting resources into public works when they are more needed elsewhere (e) once under way, it is difficult or expensive to stop many public works programs	e
Fill in the blanks.	
21. ____________ means the budget surplus that would develop, given the existing tax rates and spending structure, if the economy were to be at its full-employment level.	Full employment surplus
22. ____________ refers to the fact that with given tax rates and expenditure policies, a rise in national income will tend to produce a surplus while a decline will tend to result in a deficit.	Built-in stability
23. The federal debt may best be viewed by an economist as a burden primarily to the degree that it reduces the growth and level of the __________.	real capital stock
24. A ____________ tax is generally desirable from the standpoint of fiscal policy because the changes in total collections will vary proportionately more than the changes in GNP.	progressive income
25. The effectiveness of the built-in or automatic stabilizers is limited by the fact that the offset which the stabilizers provide to a change in private spending is less than the change in ____________.	private spending
26. Fiscal policy is a course of government action to stabilize the level of national output	

Answer
To be covered when testing yourself

chiefly through the use of the government's taxing and spending powers toward controlling the total volume of ____________ in the economy. — purchasing power

27. The basic consideration which underlies the balanced budget multiplier is that individuals and businesses reduce their expenditures by some amount less than any increase in their ______. — taxes

28. A ____________ stabilizer reduces the size of the multiplier resulting from, say, an increase in investment spending. — built-in

29. The notion that the basic purpose of the Federal budget is to stabilize the economy regardless of resulting increases in the size of the public debt describes ____________ finance. — functional

30. By the idea of ____________, we mean the idea that the government should always collect current taxes sufficient to cover its current peacetime expenditures. — old fashioned public finance

31. The partial freezing on federal construction expenditures during the 1969 Vietnam inflation is an example of ____________ fiscal policy. — discretionary

32. Generally speaking, public works expenditures tend to be more ____________ than transfer payments. — expansionary

33. An argument against a large public debt is that the transfer payments which are involved in meeting interest charges may impair _________. — production

34. ____________ principle suggests that increases in government spending will increase the interest rate and thereby reduce investment. — "Crowding out effect"

35. If government adhered strictly to a(n) ________ budget, then the government's budget would tend to destabilize the economy. — annually balanced

Determine whether the following statements are true or false.

36. Automatic stabilizers can never fully offset the instabilities of an economy. — True

37. A system of unemployment insurance is automatically stabilizing in its effects upon GNP. — True

SHORT ANSWER QUESTIONS FOR REVIEW

	Answer (To be covered when testing yourself)
38. An "inflationary gap" can be eliminated by increasing government purchases and reducing taxes.	False
39. Consumers fulfill a built-in stabilizing function if they quickly adjust their standards to changes in their incomes	False
40. There is strong evidence to support the theory that increased government spending reduces private investment on balance.	False
41. The lower the levels of government spending and taxation at which a deficit of a given size occurs, the greater will be its contractionary impact upon the economy.	True
42. The equilibrium level of NNP will not change in response to changes in the investment schedule.	False
43. It is possible for the full-employment budget to be in surplus while the actual budget is in deficit.	True
44. During a period of prolonged inflation, compensatory fiscal policy might contribute to the overproduction of private goods relative to social goods.	True
45. Positive fiscal policy means nothing more than increasing government expenditures in depressions and reducing it in prosperity.	False
46. To achieve an annually balanced budget during a recession, the government must decrease the tax rates.	False
47. Corporations fulfill a built-in stabilizing function if they pay the same annual dividend no matter what their earnings.	True
48. A disadvantage of using public works as a weapon of fiscal policy is that tax collections would have to be raised in depressions in order to finance the expenditure.	False
49. The MPS indicates what fraction of a drop in DI will result at the expense of consumption.	False
50. Automatic stabilizers can never fully offset the instabilities of an economy.	True

CHAPTER 8

TAXATION

Basic Attacks and Strategies for Solving Problems in this Chapter. See pages 251 to 298 for step-by-step solutions to problems.

Taxes are the main way that modern governments, whether at the federal, state, or local level, raise money. Other methods include user fees (direct charges for the use of government services, such as highway tolls), tariffs (essentially taxes on imported goods), and borrowing.

An important issue in the economics of taxation is what constitutes a "good tax." Most economists agree that a good tax has four fundamental characteristics: it raises enough revenue, it is equitable, it is not damaging to economic efficiency, and it is simple.

The first characteristic of a good tax is unexceptional and does not merit extended comment. Equity in taxation is a principle everyone agrees on, but what it actually means for the design of tax systems is ambiguous. We want tax systems to be both horizontally and vertically equitable. Horizontal equity means that equals are treated equally. Vertical equity means that unequals are treated unequally. However, there are at least two general approaches to taxation that would meet both tests of equity.

The benefit principle states that people should be taxed in proportion to the benefits they receive from government. This system is horizontally equitable because those receiving the same benefits pay the same taxes. It is vertically equitable because those receiving more benefits pay more taxes. Unfortunately, there are at least three major problems with this approach. First, it is difficult to quantify the value of benefits people receive from government. What is the monetary value of national defense to particular individuals? Second, how do we deal with different tastes of people? While a "hawk" may value a unit of national defense quite highly, a "dove" is likely to have a decidedly different opinion. Third, what should we do about people who cannot afford to pay for the benefits they receive? The poor may receive proportionately more benefits from the government, but be unable to pay for them.

The second competing principle is that of ability-to-pay. This says that the tax burden should be proportional to the ability to pay taxes. This is horizontally equitable because people with the same level of income end up paying the same taxes. This is vertically equitable because people with higher incomes should pay more taxes. There are at least two problems with the practical application of this principle. First, people with high ability-to-pay but limited need for benefits may end up paying for more than they receive. Second, measuring ability-to-pay is no easy task. Allowances presumably should be made for geographical variations in the cost-of-living, different family sizes, different ages of family members, unexpected events, and so on.

The tax system should not create disincentives to work, save, and invest. The average tax rate (ATR) can be defined as the proportion of income taxed $\left(ATR = \frac{Tax}{Income}\right)$. The marginal tax rate (MTR) can be defined as the proportion of **additional** income taxed $\left(MTR = \frac{\Delta Tax}{\Delta Income}\right)$. The MTR is the more relevant concept from the standpoint of incentives because it measures the proportion of additional income earned that must be transferred to the government. For example, assume the wage rate is \$20.00 per hour, but the MTR is .50. If an additional hour is worked, the individual will earn \$20.00, but only receive \$10.00 (= \$20.00 * .50). The larger the MTR, the smaller the reward to the individual for the effort required to earn the additional income. If the MTR is "too high," individuals may begin substituting leisure for productive activity.

Individuals need to take the MTR into consideration to make rational economic decisions. For example, assume an investor is choosing between a \$1,000.00 investment in corporate bonds paying 8% and government bonds paying 7% tax-free. The investor's MTR is .25. The investor will receive annual interest payments of \$80.00 (.08 * \$1,000.00) from the corporate bonds, but be required to pay \$20.00 (.25 * \$80.00) in taxes. His after-tax return is 6% (\$60.00/\$1,000.00), which equals the before-tax interest rate times 1 – MTR (.08 * (1 – .25) = .06). The tax-free government bonds are the better investment.

There are three main types of tax structures. A progressive system is one where households with higher incomes have a higher ATR. Under such a system, the MTR also rises with higher income. A proportional system is one where the ATR is constant at all levels of income. Households with higher incomes do pay more money, however. The MTR is constant and equal to the ATR in this type of system. A regressive system is one where the ATR falls as income rises. Higher income households may or may not pay more money, depending on how the tax rate is set. The MTR also falls for higher levels of income.

The goals of equity and efficiency can collide. For example, advocates of ability-to-pay systems frequently support progressive tax structures, yet such systems have the highest MTR. Regressive tax systems have the least built-in disincentive to effort, but may be the most unfair.

A simple tax system is one with the lowest resource cost of compliance. The goal of simplicity can conflict with both equity and efficiency. Frequently provisions in the tax code are used to stimulate or discourage various activities in the public interest or for the sake of equity (the two are not always the same thing). For example, the deductibility of mortgage interest in the United States system acts as a distinct stimulus to home buying and building. These provisions tend to make the tax code more complex. In addition, they may direct resource allocation in ways other than what the market would dictate and influence the distribution of income.

An important issue in the evaluation of taxes is tax incidence. The legal incidence of a tax is on whoever is legally required to pay the tax bill. The economic incidence of a tax is on whoever suffers reduced purchasing power because of the tax. For example, the legal incidence of the state gasoline tax is on the individual service station owners. If the owner responds to the tax by raising the price of gasoline, the economic incidence of the tax may have been shifted forward to the consumer. If the owner responds to the tax by reducing his demand for resources, the economic incidence of the tax may have been shifted backward to the factors of production.

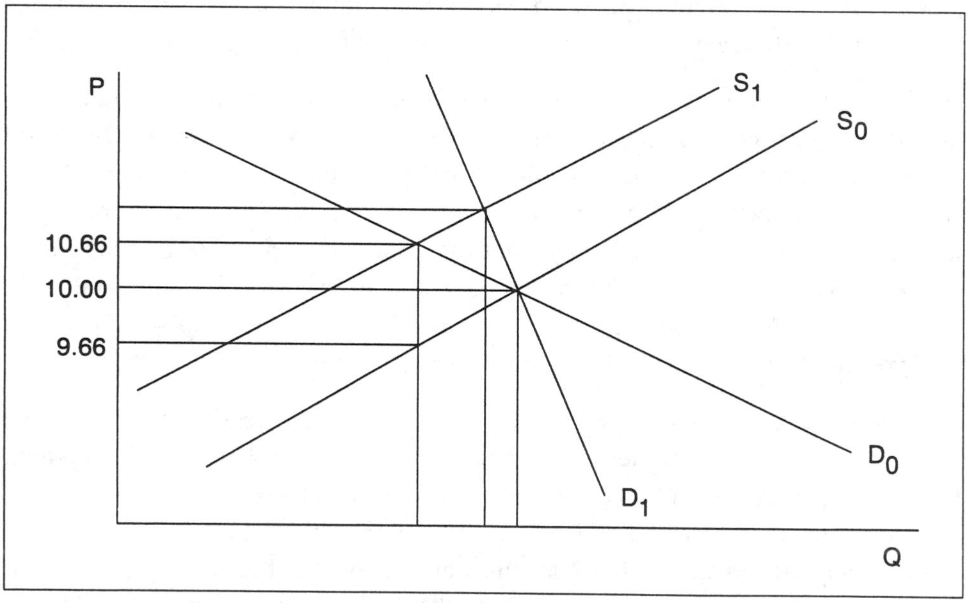

Incidence of a Tax

The theory of demand and supply can be used to analyze the issue of tax incidence. Consider the case of an excise tax placed on good A. Refer to the figure for what follows. Prior to the imposition of the tax, market demand is D_0

and market supply S_0. In equilibrium, consumers pay $10.00 and producers receive $10.00 for each unit. Now assume a $1.00 per unit tax is legislated with the producer bearing the legal incidence. The tax will cause the supply curve to shift vertically upward by $1.00 to S_1. The market demand curve will remain stationary, but there will be a new equilibrium price and quantity in the market. At the new equilibrium, consumers will pay $10.66 per unit. Out of that money, the producer will send $1.00 to the government, retaining $9.66. Compared to the initial equilibrium, consumers are paying $.66 more and producers are receiving $.34 less. The economic incidence of the tax is then shared between the consumer and the producer, with the consumer bearing 66% and the producer bearing 34%.

The sharing of the economic incidence depends on the slopes of the demand and supply curves. Using the same figure, note that if market demand were D_1, the consumer would bear relatively more of the tax. In general, the steeper (less elastic) the demand curve, the greater the economic incidence borne by the consumer. In the case of supply, the flatter (more elastic) the supply curve, the greater the incidence borne by the consumer.

An important source of tax revenue in the United States is the taxation of corporate profits. Under the Tax Reform Act of 1986, corporations pay a marginal tax rate of 15% on the first $50,000 in taxable income, 25% on income between $50,000 and $75,000, and 34% on all income earned over $75,000. Among the most important issues associated with corporate income taxation are the following.

First is the incidence of the corporate tax. Many people fail to recognize that the burden of all taxes are ultimately on people. Economists have yet to agree fully on how the corporate tax burden is shared among consumers, workers, and owners.

Second is the issue of double taxation. A corporation's profits are taxed. Dividend payments are then made out of what is left, but these dividends are taxed as normal income once they reach individuals. In essence, the money has been taxed twice. The fairness and efficiency of doing this remains an open question.

Third is depreciation. It is standard accounting procedure to charge against costs of production an estimate of the value of a firms' capital stock that has "worn-out" during the year. The problem arises because there is no generally accepted method to accurately measure the "true" amount of depreciation. Consequently, accountants have devised various formulas to allocate depreciation charges. The particular formula used could have significant tax consequences depending on the time pattern of depreciation charges. Inflation creates interesting problems regarding depreciation. It is common to base depreciation formulas on the cost of the capital when it was purchased, but if inflation raises capital costs, the formula will not allow enough expense to permit replacement when the time comes.

Fourth is inventory valuation. When unsold products are placed in inventory, should they be valued at the price they would have sold for when produced, or the price they would sell for currently? Depending on the rate of inflation, the choice of valuation technique could have significant tax consequences.

Tax subsidies refer to payments that the government makes to particular industries or groups to achieve specified social goals. An example would be subsidies given to American shipbuilding firms to allow them to stay in business. The reason is the belief that America needs a shipbuilding industry for national defense purposes. From the standpoint of analysis, a tax subsidy can be considered a negative tax which shifts the supply curve outward, lowering price and raising quantity. The impact of a subsidy on an industry is its effect on industry revenue which ultimately depends on the elasticity of demand and supply in the market.

Externalities occur when the costs and benefits of production or consumption are shared by people who are neither the buyer nor the seller of the product. For example, assume a by-product of the production of some good or service is sludge, which is dumped into a river and carried downstream to damage a beach. This pollution is one of the costs of production, but the cost is avoided by both the producer and the consumer of the product. For another example, one of the benefits of receiving a vaccination is that other people are made safer because they cannot catch the disease from the recipient of the shot. Under current laws, they do not have to pay for that benefit.

The problem with externalities is that they send the wrong signal to the market. In the first example, the producer thinks the cost of production is lower than it actually is and is likely to produce too much. In the second example, the recipient of the shot is likely to consider the benefit of the shot to be lower than it actually is and may end up getting too few shots.

Many economists believe the most efficient solution to the problem is to "internalize the externality," to somehow incorporate the added costs or benefits of the activity in the decision-making process of producers or consumers. One way to do this is by using taxes. Judicious taxation could be used to charge producers for the pollution damage they cause, and reward consumers for the consumption benefits they create. The practical application of taxes for this purpose is a complicated issue.

Step-by-Step Solutions to Problems in this Chapter, "Taxation"

BASIC CONCEPTS

• **PROBLEM 8-1**

Distinguish between the two main principles of taxation.

Solution: The first main principle of taxation is the benefits principle. It holds that, as nearly as possible, the persons who benefit from a particular government service should pay the taxes to support that service. We can see the benefits principle roughly applied when we examine gasoline taxes. Here the costs of constructing and maintaining roads are met by a tax on each gallon of gasoline. However, in other cases, it is not possible to apply the benefits principle. For example, it is difficult to quantify the benefit received by each individual from national defense. Would people living in an area more likely to be attacked benefit more than others? Would owners of large investments such as factories, which might be destroyed in a war, benefit more from defense than those who do not have such investments? If either were the case, according to the benefits principle, these persons ought to pay higher taxes. However, the difficulty in applying the benefits principle in this case is that it would be impossible to determine exact "quantities" of benefit and corresponding tax rates. Also, some citizens might actually suffer from national defense (those who live near Air Force bases and are annoyed by the noise of airplanes, for example). According to the benefits principle, the government should actually pay them.

The second main principle of taxation is the ability-to-pay principle. It holds that one's tax burden should be geared directly to one's financial position, i.e. tax would depend upon income, family size, situation in life, etc. The ability-to-pay principle is most readily realized through a tax on income itself, with some allowance for family size and such special circumstances as medical expenses.

• **PROBLEM 8-2**

What is meant by direct and indirect taxes? Give examples of each.

Solution: Direct taxes are taxes that are levied directly on people. Examples of this would be income tax, inheritance taxes, and poll taxes.

Indirect taxes are levied against goods and services and thus only indirectly on people. Examples of this would be gasoline taxes, cigarette taxes and sales tax.

• PROBLEM 8-3

What is a value-added tax?

Solution: A value-added tax, or VAT, collects tax on a product at each stage of production. Suppose a flour mill buys $75 worth of wheat from a farmer, grinds it into flour, and then sells the flour for $100. A value-added tax imposed upon the flour mill would be based solely on the $25 that the mill added to the value of the wheat by converting it to flour, i.e. the raw-materials costs used from earlier stages of production are subtracted from the flour mill's selling price in calculating his "value added" and the VAT tax is levied on this value added.

• PROBLEM 8-4

What is the difference between a specific and an ad valorem tax?

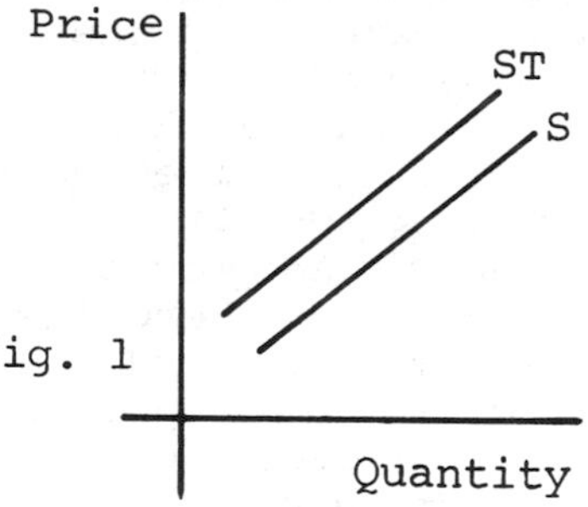

Fig. 1

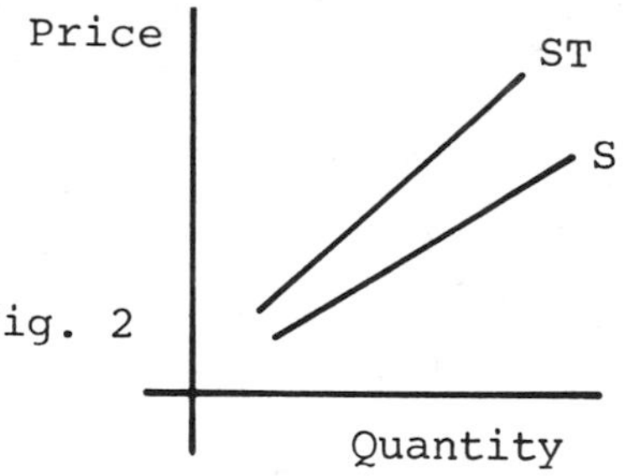

Fig. 2

Solution: Specific, or per unit, taxes add a flat amount to the price of every unit of a product sold. The amount of the tax never varies, even though the price of the product may.

A specific tax, by adding a constant amount to each unit, creates a new supply curve, S_T, which is parallel to the original supply curve, S, as shown in Fig. 1.

An ad valorem tax is a sales tax where the government takes a percentage of the sale price of a product as tax. In the United States, sales taxes characteristically imposed by states and some city governments, are ad valorem taxes.

As you move up the supply curve to the right, price increases. The absolute dollar amount of an ad valorem tax will also increase, therefore, since the tax maintains a constant percentage of a growing price, the supply curve after tax, S_T, will then diverge from the original supply curve, S, as shown in Fig. 2.

• PROBLEM 8-5

Discuss the following taxes that state and local governments impose: property tax, sales tax, inheritance and estate taxes.

Solution: Almost half of the total revenues of state and local government come from property tax. The property tax is levied primarily on real estate - land and buildings. Each locality sets an annual tax rate, e.g. $50 on each $1000 of assessed valuation. (Note, however, that in many localities, assessed valuations tend to be much smaller than market value.)

Most consider the property tax to be regressive relative to income. For one thing small properties tend to be assessed relatively higher (in relation to their market values) than large properties. Also, in today's society, so much of wealth and income has become divorced from real estate, that is we no longer expect a rich man to necessarily have tremendous amounts of property, whereas two hundred years ago, we might have.

While local governments draw most of their tax revenue from property taxes, state governments rely a great deal upon sales tax for revenue. Some local governments also impose sales taxes. What a sales tax does is impose a constant percentage tax on items bought at the retail level. Items such as food and medicine are sometimes exempt from a sales tax.

Sales taxes are regarded as regressive since the poor must spend a larger fraction of their total dollars than the rich on items which are affected by a sales tax.

Inheritance and estate taxes come into play only upon the death of an individual. The inheritance and estate tax is regarded as a progressive tax. A poor person's inheritance usually involves no tax because of liberal exemptions, while a rich man's estate pays at a progressive rate. With such a policy, the government is trying to prevent the development of a permanent moneyed caste, living off property passed on from one generation to the next. In recent years, such maneuvers as complex "trusts" and the right to make certain gifts have helped the rich reduce death-tax collections to a lower level.

• PROBLEM 8-6

What is the overall difference between Federal taxes and State and Local taxes? Explain.

Solution: Federal taxes consist mainly of personal income taxes and corporate income taxes. The personal income tax is progressive and the corporation tax is only slightly progressive because there are only two rates, 22% on earnings up to $25,000 a year and 48% on all other earnings. Thus Federal taxes in total are mildly progressive.

State taxes consist mainly of retail sales taxes. Retail sales taxes are regressive because the spending of lower income groups consumes a larger part of their income than the spending of higher income groups. This regressive feature can be lessened by exempting food, fuel, medicine and utilities from retail sales taxation. Local tax systems rely mainly, (for 86%), on property taxes. Because cheaper property tends to be overassessed in comparison with high-priced property; wealthier people are more likely to have influence with assessors or to threaten court action because of overassessment; and tenants usually have property taxes shifted to them as part of their rent; property taxes are considerably regressive. Thus State and Local taxes, due to general retail and property taxes are slightly regressive.

• PROBLEM 8-7

Arrange the following in their proper sequence for the determination of the income tax base of an individual.

(a) Adjusted gross income
(b) Personal exemptions
(c) Expenses (nonbusiness and personal)
(d) Taxable income
(e) Gross income
(f) Expenses (related to business or specific revenue.)

Solution: Notice that we have three measures of income here: gross income, adjusted gross income, and taxable income. As we go down that line, we arrive at smaller and smaller measures of income. Specifically, various expenses and exemptions are deducted from gross income to arrive at adjusted gross income and from adjusted gross income to arrive at taxable income.

The actual steps are as follows:

Gross Income
Less: Deductions:
Expenses (related to business or specific revenue)

Adjusted Gross Income
Less: Deductions:
Expenses (nonbusiness and personal)
Personal Exemptions

Taxable Income

• PROBLEM 8-8

Miss Lane had the following income tax information in 1978 while she worked as a reporter on a large metropolitan newspaper:

Taxable income	$15,000
Exemptions	1,500
Business Expenses	6,000
Nonbusiness Expenses	3,000

Find Miss Lane's adjusted gross income and gross income for 1978.

Solution: Under ordinary circumstances, we start with gross income, make deductions, arrive at adjusted gross income, make further deductions, and then arrive at taxable income. In this problem, we must work this procedure backwards.

First let us calculate deductions from gross income and adjusted gross income. Of the items listed for Miss Lane, only Business Expenses constitute a deduction from Gross Income. Exemptions and Non-business Expenses constitute deductions from Adjusted Gross Income. Thus we have the following two findings:

Deductions from Gross Income:	
Business Expenses	$6,000
Deductions from Adjusted Gross Income:	
Non-business Expenses	$3,000
Exemptions	$1,500
	$4,500

Now we can add back the deductions in the following manner to arrive at figures for Adjusted Gross Income and Gross Income.

Taxable Income	$15,000
Deductions from Adjusted Gross Income	$ 4,500
Adjusted Gross Income	$19,500
Deductions from Gross Income	$ 6,000
Gross Income	$25,500

RATE STRUCTURE

• **PROBLEM 8-9**

Mr. Gribbon earns $10,000 annually as an accountant and pays $1500 of this amount to the government in taxes. Mr. Doyle earns $50,000 as a frankfurter vendor, of which he takes home $45,000 after taxes. Is the tax structure here progressive, proportional, or regressive?

Solution: We must first find the individual tax rates for the two men. Mr. Gribbon's tax rate = $1,500/$10,000 = 15%. Mr. Doyle takes home $45,000 of his $50,000 earnings. Therefore his taxes paid are:

$$\$50,000 - \$45,000 = \$5,000.$$

Mr. Doyle's tax rate is:

$$\$5{,}000/\$50{,}000 = 10\%.$$

We see now that as income increases from $10,000 to $50,000, the tax rate decreases from 15% to 10%. Therefore the tax structure is regressive.

• PROBLEM 8-10

Given are the tax tables for 3 systems of income taxation. Which one is progressive? Proportional? Regressive? Calculate the tax rates levied in each case.

Income Tax Tables (in 1000 dollars)

Tax base	A	B	C
10	3	3	3
20	6	6	5
30	9	8	6
40	12	10	8
50	15	12	15
60	18	15	18
70	21	18	28
80	24	19	32
90	27	20	45
100	30	20	50

Solution: From a short look at the table is becomes clear that income tax system A is proportional, B is regressive, and C progressive, but it becomes even more graphic when we plot the values in a diagram with the tax base on the horizontal axis and the taxes on the vertical axis (see figure 1) In order to evaluate the income taxes according to the ability-to-pay principle, we divide these taxes by the tax base to find the tax rate connected with a particular tax base.

Tax rates (in %)

Tax base in $1000 dollars	Systems A	B	C
10	30%	30%	30%
20	30	30	25
30	30	27	20
40	30	25	20
50	30	24	30
60	30	25	30
70	30	26	40
80	30	24	40
90	30	22	50
100	30	20	50

Now our analysis can be more detailed. Income tax system A is undoubtedly proportional: the tax rate is constant at 30%. Tax system B is proportional in its first two income brackets, becomes regressive in the next three brackets,

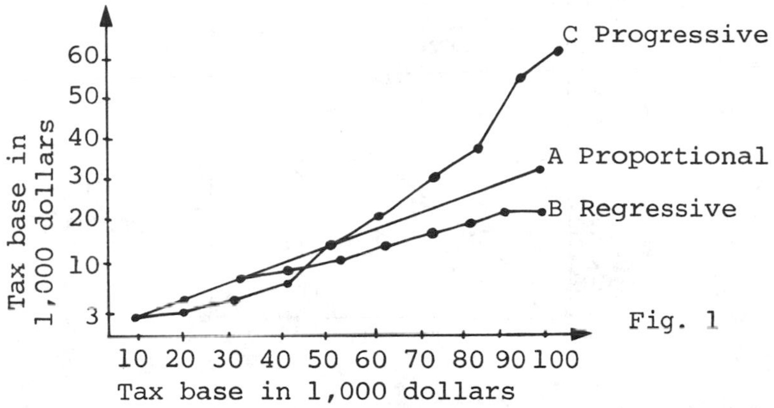

Fig. 1

progressive in the next two, and again regressive in the last three brackets. But the system as a whole is regressive, since the tax rate falls as income rises. Tax system C is regressive in its first three brackets, and then becomes progressive, the tax rate increases by 10% for every two brackets. A picture also clarifies these relationships (see figure 2), where the tax base is on the horizontal axis and the tax rate on the vertical axis.

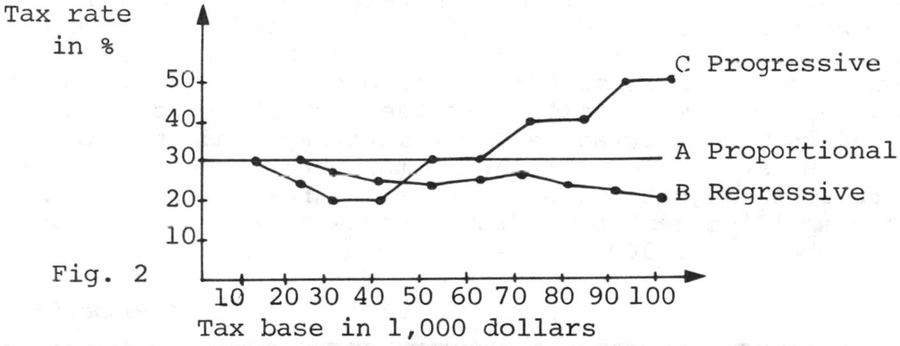

Fig. 2

The regressive tax system B places the greatest burden on lower income groups; while the progressive tax C falls most heavily on people with higher incomes. Notice that in our example both systems C and B favor the middle class groups with lower tax rates: system C the brackets of $30,000 and $40,000, and system B the bracket of $50,000.

• PROBLEM 8-11

Why does the fact that there are high tax rates on high incomes not mean that people in higher income groups pay most of the taxes?

Solution: A far higher percentage of the population is in the lowest tax bracket than in the higher ones, as may be inferred from the Lorenz curve which describes graphically the distribution of family income in the U.S. (See figure 1). The top 5% of the population receives 14% of total income in the U.S. The top 20% of the population receives 40% of total income, but the lowest 20% of the population receives only 6% of total income. The cake is not equally divided.

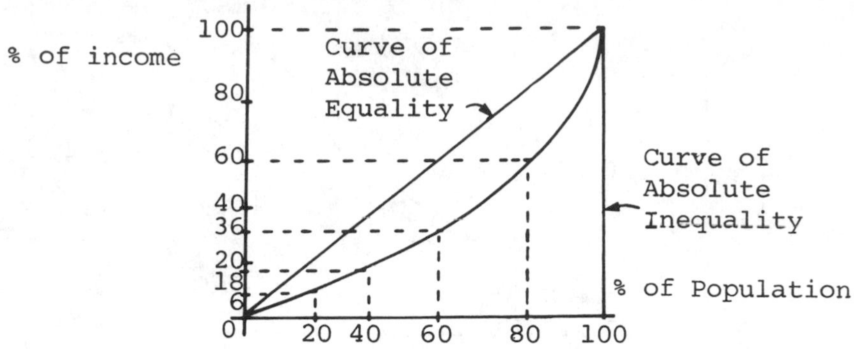

Fig. 1

And we see that the highest 50% of the population receives about 75% of total income and the lowest 50% only 25% of total income. The U.S. total tax system is perhaps regressive. Suppose, for example, that the higher income group spends 60% of its income and the lower income group 95% and there is a retail sales tax of 5%, then the effective tax the highest group pays is only 0.05 × 0.60 = 0.03, or 3%, but the lowest income group pays 0.05 × 0.95 = 0.0475 or 4.75% of its income on taxes. If, in actuality, the lowest 50% of the population pays an effective tax rate that is only a bit higher than 3 times the effective total tax rate of the highest 50% of the population - the lowest group would pay more taxes than the highest group.
The United States Treasury Department reported that in 1968, 52 percent of all federal income tax money came from taxpayers whose adjusted gross income was below $15,000, and less than 10 percent came from those with adjusted gross income above $100,000.

• PROBLEM 8-12

Suppose the following table represents the tax system in the fictional land of Kannana

Total taxable income	Total tax
$ 1,000	$ 0
3,000	150
6,000	600
10,000	1,500
20,000	5,000

Find the average and marginal tax rates in Kannana.

Solution: To find the average tax rate at any level of income, we divide total tax by total taxable income. Therefore, at an income of $1000, where total tax = $0, average tax rate = 0/1000 = 0%. Similarly, at an income of $3000, average tax rate = 150/3000 = 5%. At $6,000, tax rate = 600/6000 = 10%. At $10,000, tax rate = 1500/10,000 = 15%. Finally, at an income of $20,000, average tax rate = 5000/20,000 = 25%.

To find average tax rate, we used the two figures, total tax and total taxable income. Since marginal tax rate is a concept which involves change, we will use here the change in total tax and the change in total taxable income. To ease computations, let us reconstruct our original tax chart, adding in the average tax rates and two new columns, Δtotal tax and Δtotal taxable income. To compute these two columns, we just subtract each two consecutive entries in the total tax and total taxable income columns.

Total Taxable Income	Total Tax	Average Tax Rate	ΔTotal Taxable Income	ΔTotal Tax
$ 1,000	0	0%		
			$ 2,000	$ 150
3,000	150	5		
			$ 3,000	$ 450
6,000	600	10		
			$ 4,000	$ 900
10,000	1500	15		
			$10,000	$3,500
20,000	5000	25		

Now, we saw above that the formula for average tax rate is:

$$\text{Average tax rate} = \frac{\text{Total Tax}}{\text{Total Taxable Income}}$$

Similarly, we now will use the following formula for marginal tax rate:

$$\text{Marginal tax rate} = \frac{\Delta\text{Total Tax}}{\Delta\text{Total Taxable Income}}$$

Therefore, as income rises from $1,000 to $3,000, marginal tax rate = $150/$2,000 = 7.5%. From $3,000 to $6,000, marginal tax rate = 450/3000 = 15%. From $6,000 to $10,000, it is 900/4000 = 22.5%. Finally, from $10,000 to $20,000, marginal tax rate = 3500/10,000 = 35%.

Finally, let us present our figures for average and marginal tax rates together. Using the same table form as above, we have:

Total Taxable Income	Total Tax	Average Tax Rate	Marginal Tax Rate
$ 1,000	$ 0	0%	
			7.5%
3,000	150	5	
			15.0%
6,000	600	10	
			22.5%
10,000	1,500	15	
			35.0%
20,000	5,000	25	

Looking over the new chart, we discover the progressive tax structure used in Kannana. As income increases, average tax rate increases. Also, marginal tax rate rises as income increases and remains higher than average tax rate.

• PROBLEM 8-13

Precisely what is meant by a progressive tax? A regressive tax? A proportional tax? Give an example for each.

Solution: a) A tax is progressive if its rate increases as income increases. Such a tax claims not only a larger absolute amount, but also a larger fraction or percentage of income as income increases.

As an example, suppose the rate structure is such that a household with an annual taxable income of less than $1000 pays 5 percent in income taxes, a household realizing an income of $1000 to $2000 pays 10 percent, while those earning from $2000 to $3000 pay 15 percent. This would be an illustration of a progressive income tax.

b) A regressive tax is one whose rate declines as income increases. Such a tax takes a smaller and smaller proportion of income as income increases. A regressive tax may or may not take a larger absolute amount of income as income expands.

An example of this would be the following structure. One pays 15 percent if he earns less than $1000, 10 percent if he earns $1000 to $2000, 5 percent if he earns $2000 to $3000, and so forth.

c) A tax is proportional when its rate remains the same, regardless of the size of income. Suppose the tax rates are such that everyone pays 10 percent of his income in taxes, regardless of the size of his income. This would be a proportional income tax.

• PROBLEM 8-14

Describe the behavior of the marginal tax rate under a proportional, progressive, and regressive tax system.

Solution: In a proportional tax system, all incomes are taxed at the same rate. If the tax rate at an income of $2000 is 20%, it will be 20% at all other incomes. Therefore the marginal tax rate, or the tax rate paid on an additional dollar of income, will be constant since the tax rate itself is constant. In this example, marginal tax rate = 20% (= actual tax rate).

In a progressive tax system, as income increases, a higher proportion of this income goes to taxes. Suppose $2000 income is taxed at 20% and $3000 income is taxed at 30%. This is a progressive tax system where as income rises by $1000 from $2000 to $3000, tax increases from $400 to $900.

Therefore

$$\text{Marginal tax rate} = \frac{\Delta \text{tax}}{\Delta \text{income}}$$

$$= \frac{900 - 400}{1000}$$

$$= 50\%$$

As this example shows, the marginal tax rate in a progressive tax system will be greater than the actual tax rate. And since the actual tax rate rises in a progressive system, the marginal tax rate will also rise.

Finally, under a regressive tax system, the proportion of income going to taxes decreases as income increases. Suppose at income of \$2000, tax rate = 25%, while at \$3000, tax rate = 20%. This represents a regressive system, where a \$1000 increase in income from \$2000 to \$3000 brings about a \$100 change in tax from \$500 to \$600. Therefore

$$\text{Marginal tax rate} = \frac{\Delta \text{tax}}{\Delta \text{income}}$$

$$= \frac{\$\ 100}{\$1000}$$

$$= 10\%$$

In this example, marginal tax rate = 10%, while actual tax rate = 20%. So, in general, under a regressive tax system, marginal tax rate is less than actual tax rate. And since actual tax rate falls in a regressive system, marginal tax rate will also fall.

There are some odd cases where the marginal tax rate takes on special meaning.

If marginal tax rate > 100%, an increase in before-tax income, will actually mean a decrease in after-tax income. If marginal tax rate = 100%, any increase in pay will be totally devoured by taxes. Both of these situations represent highly progressive tax systems.

If marginal tax rate < 0%, an increase in income actually results in one paying less total income taxes. If marginal tax rate = 0, an increase in income will have no effect upon taxes, i.e. whatever before-tax income increases by, after-tax income will also increase by the same amount. These two situations represent highly regressive tax systems.

• PROBLEM 8-15

Mr. Balfour has \$1,000 which he wishes to invest. He is having trouble choosing between tax-free municipal bonds which pay 6% interest and a savings account which pays 8%

interest. If Mr. Balfour has a marginal tax rate of 30%, where should he invest his money?

Solution: The tax-free municipal bonds pay 6% and Mr. Balfour has $1,000 to invest. Therefore, in one year, the municipal bonds would pay $1,000 × 6% = $60 interest. Since these bonds are tax-free, Mr. Balfour will receive, after taxes, $60.

The savings account offers Mr. Balfour 8% interest on his $1,000, or $80. This is greater than the $60 interest offered by municipal bonds, but we must still subtract taxes in order to get the real income from the savings account. Since Mr. Balfour's marginal tax rate = 30%, extra income over his present income will be taxed at a rate of 30%. Interest from a savings account represents just such income. Therefore, of the $80 interest, $80 × 0.30 = $24 will be taken out for taxes. That leaves Mr. Balfour with $80 - $24 = $56 interest after taxes.

Since $60 > $56, we would advise Mr. Balfour to select the municipal bonds.

• PROBLEM 8-16

Suppose there is a poll tax of $2 per head. How is this a regressive tax?

Solution: According to this poll tax, each person pays the same amount ($2) as tax. But $2 would be a higher percentage of a poor man's income than a rich man's income. Therefore the tax is regressive.

• PROBLEM 8-17

How is the federal payroll tax that supports the Social Security program a regressive tax?

Solution: As it currently stands, the Social Security tax has each employee contribute 6.05% of his first $ of income. The reason this tax is regressive is because there is a dollar limit on the amount of income, $, subject to the tax.

To see the regressive nature of this kind of structure, let us examine a simpler case. Suppose the Social Security tax were instead 6% of the first $10,000 of income. Then a man earning $10,000 would pay $600, or 6% of his income, to the Social Security system. Now, a worker earning $20,000 would pay $600 also (since only his first $10,000 is taxed) but this would represent only 3% of his $20,000 income. Thus as income rises above $10,000, the actual tax rate drops. Thus above incomes of $10,000, this tax is regressive.

Notice also the behavior of the marginal tax rate. From income of \$0 to \$10,000, the actual tax rate is constant at 6%. Therefore the marginal tax rate is also constant at 6%. But after you earn \$10,000, your Social Security tax bill remains constant. Therefore, for all incomes above 10,000, marginal tax rate = 0%.

• PROBLEM 8-18

Why is a retail sales tax of 4% not proportional but regressive?

Solution: A retail sales tax of 4% appears to be proportional because it holds on all sales, those of a person with a high income as well as those of a person with a low income. However in reality the 4% retail tax works as a regressive income tax because lower income groups spend a greater proportior of their income (frequently all of it) than upper income groups on consumption (the rest being saved), the spending of those in the high income brackets is relatively less affected by the sales tax.

For example, assume that the lower income groups spend 95% of their income and the higher income groups only 60%. The retail sales tax is 4% on sales, thus on what the consumers spend. Then the lower income group pays in effect $0.04 \times 0.95 = 0.038$, or 3.8% of its income on retail taxes and the higher income group only $0.04 \times 0.60 = 0.024$, or 2.4%; thus a higher effective rate of taxation in the lower brackets than in the higher brackets. It appears that any "proportional" tax, in which all taxpayers pay an equal amount, is actually regressive, since that amount will be a relatively larger portion of a low income than of a high income. In that sense Federal taxes, other than income taxes, and estate and gift taxes, are regressive.

• PROBLEM 8-19

Suppose that the sales tax rate is 3%. The rate is the same on all purchases, yet it is not considered a proportional tax. What type of tax is it considered and why?

Solution: Sales tax is generally considered a regressive tax. This is due to the fact that people with small incomes spend a larger percentage of their incomes on taxed commodities. To illustrate, assume a man earning \$3,000 annually spends 2/3 of his earnings on products which require sales tax, while a man earning \$30,000 annually spends 1/5 of his earnings on such products. For the first man,

$$\text{Sales tax} = \$3,000 \times 2/3 \times 3\%$$

$$= \$60$$

Computing the percentage of earnings given to sales tax, we have:

$$\$60/\$3000 = 2\%$$

For the second man,

$$\text{Sales tax} = \$30{,}000 \times 1/5 \times 3\%$$
$$= \$180$$

Computing the percentage of earnings given to sales tax, we have:

$$\$180/\$30{,}000 = 0.6\%$$

Since the percentage of income paid as taxes decreases as income rises, the tax is regressive.

• PROBLEM 8-20

How does a progressive income tax help to stabilize the economy?

Solution: A progressive tax system can help to stabilize an economy. Suppose a country is going through prosperous times, with money income and total demand rising so as to outrun productive capacity. In this situation, inflation occurs. But with a progressive income tax, tax collections will rise at a more rapid rate than incomes. These rising tax collections have the effect of diverting income from the expenditures stream, thereby lessening inflationary pressures.

On the other hand, suppose an economy backslides into a recession and total demand is inadequate to maintain full employment. In this situation, tax collections will decline at a more rapid rate than income, so as to bolster the income-expenditures stream and cushion the recession.

In short, the automatic changes in tax collections which are inherent in a progressive income tax system add an element of built-in stability to an economy.

INCIDENCE

• PROBLEM 8-21

a) What is meant by the incidence of a tax?
b) Suppose a tax is placed on land. Describe its incidence.

Solution: a) The incidence of a tax refers to the identification of the person who ultimately pays the tax. Economic theory shows us that a tax which might intuitively seem to fall upon producers can often be passed on so that its incidence is upon consumers.

b) Land is an example of a market situation where the supplier cannot pass on the incidence of a tax to consumers. This is due to the nature of the supply curve of land. Looking at the graph, we see that land has a perfectly inelastic supply curve, that is, quantity supplied is constant.

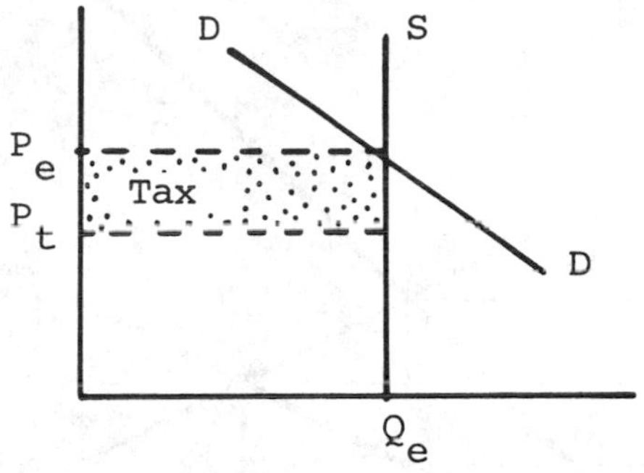

Since quantity supplied is fixed, no tax can change the supply curve. And since the tax is imposed upon the supplier, it will have no effect upon the demand curve, DD. So market equilibrium price will remain at P_e. Landlords will be unable to charge a price higher than P_e, since above Pe some land will remain unrented. Even with tenants paying P_e, however, landlords will only receive P_t, $P_e - P_t$ representing that part of rental income claimed by the government as tax. Since the price of land to the tenant has not increased as a result of this tax, it is clear that the incidence of a tax on land is on the supplier.

• PROBLEM 8-22

What is meant by forward and backward shifting?

Solution: We speak of forward and backward shifting when discussing tax incidence. The incidence of a tax refers to who actually bears the ultimate burden of paying that tax.

Suppose a tax is imposed on a businessman. Forward shifting occurs when this businessman is able to pass the burden of that tax onto its customers in the form of higher prices. Backward shifting occurs when this businessman is able to pass the burden of that tax onto its workers, in the form of lower wages, or onto its suppliers, in the form of lower resource payments. The full analysis of a particular business tax may find some of the burden shifted forward, some of the burden shifted backward, and some of the burden borne by the owners of the business.

• PROBLEM 8-23

The accompanying graph illustrates two market situations, one before the imposition of 100% tax on walnuts and one after the tax was imposed.

Evaluate the tax incidence by discussing the change in equilibrium when the tax is imposed.

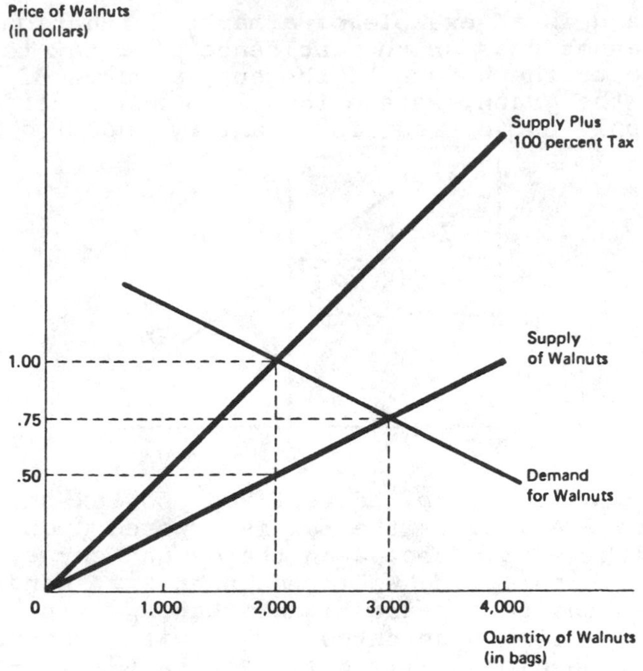

Solution: Before the imposition of the tax, market equilibrium occurs where the demand curve intersects the supply curve, indicating a quantity bought and sold of 3,000 bags and a price of 75¢ per bag.

Now a 100% tax is imposed. The inexperienced economics student might simply expect the price of walnuts to rise from 75¢ to $1.50 to take care of the tax. This is not the case. Instead we must draw a new supply curve, shown as the Supply Plus 100 percent Tax curve. To draw this curve, we simply take the original supply curve and double the price at every quantity sold, since now, with the 100% tax, our suppliers can keep only 1/2 of what the customer pays. Therefore, after the imposition of the tax, market equilibrium occurs where the demand curve intersects the Supply Plus 100 percent Tax curve. At this point, quantity bought and sold is 2,000 bags and the price paid by the consumer is $1.00 per bag.

Now, for each bag that is sold for $1.00, the government takes 50¢. To evaluate the incidence of this 50¢ tax, we notice that price to the consumer at market equilibrium has risen from 75¢ to $1.00, while the price that the supplier receives has fallen from 75¢ to 50¢ ($1.00 - 50¢ tax taken by government). To pay the government 50¢, the consumer is paying an extra 25¢ while the suppliers are getting 25¢ less for their product. Thus, the incidence of this particular tax is shared equally by customers and sellers.

• PROBLEM 8-24

Suppose a 100% sales tax is placed on a good. Explain with the use of graphs what will determine the incidence of that sales tax.

Solution: The incidence of a sales tax on a good will be determined by the nature of the supply and demand curves for that particular good, i.e. the elasticities of supply and demand. To show this, let us deal with the extreme cases of perfect elasticity and perfect inelasticity.

First, suppose supply is perfectly elastic as in Fig. 1.

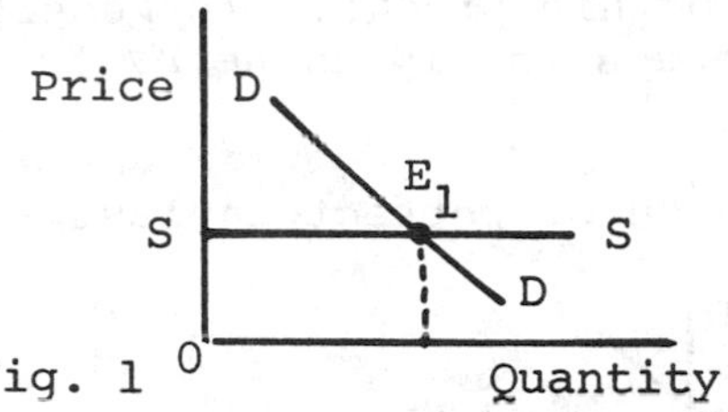

Fig. 1

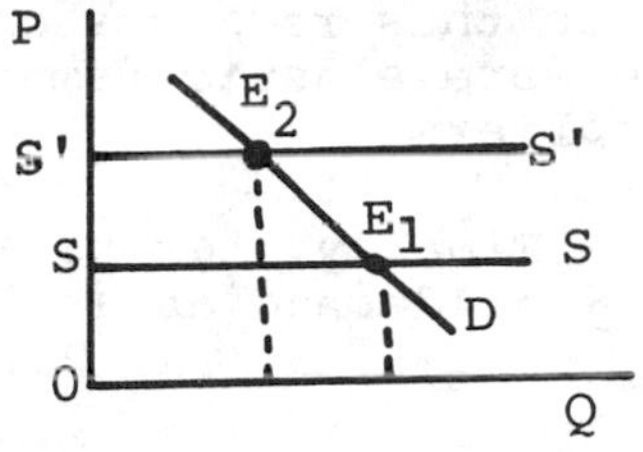

Fig. 2

In a perfectly elastic supply situation, price will double and supply will now be S'S', as in Fig. 2.

Before the tax, the suppliers received OS for their product. After the tax, they are still receiving OS. So the supplier has not felt the tax at all. Instead it is the buyer who feels the incidence of the tax. The price has doubled from OS at E to OS' at E_2. Thus, the consumer has full incidence of the sales tax when supply is perfectly elastic. In general, the more elastic the supply, the more the buyer pays for the sales tax. Now suppose that supply is perfectly inelastic. Since quantity is fixed in this supply situation, the supply curve will not be changed by the 100% sales tax, as illustrated in Fig. 3.

The graph shows that equilibrium will remain at E, so that buyers will still pay OP for the product, thus paying none of the tax. Now since the government takes half of the revenue from the product now (100% sales tax), the suppliers will not be realizing a price of OP for their product, but rather only 1/2(OP). Therefore, in this situation, the supplier assumes full burden of the sales tax. In general, the more inelastic supply, the more the supplier bears the sales tax's incidence.

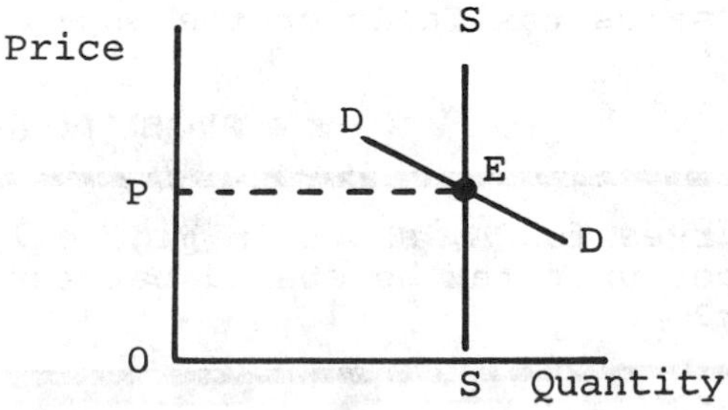

Fig. 3

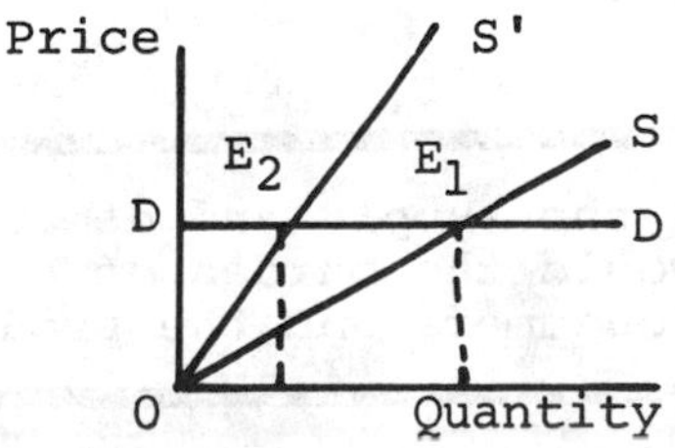

Fig. 4

Now, we shall hold supply fixed and vary the elasticity of demand. If demand is perfectly elastic, a 100% sales tax will oause a shift in equilibrium as in Fig. 4.

In such a situation, buyers will only pay one price,

no matter what the quantity. Therefore a tax will not affect price. Before the tax, at E_1, and after the tax, at E_2, price is OD. Therefore, as in the situation of inelastic demand, it is the supplier upon whom the incidence of the tax will fall. Whereas before the tax, the supplier received OD for each unit of output, he must now pay 50% of his price to the government in the form of tax. The supplier thus receives only 1/2(OD) for his product. In general, the more elastic demand is, the more a tax is borne by the suppliers.

Finally, let us examine the case of perfect inelasticity of demand as in Fig. 5.

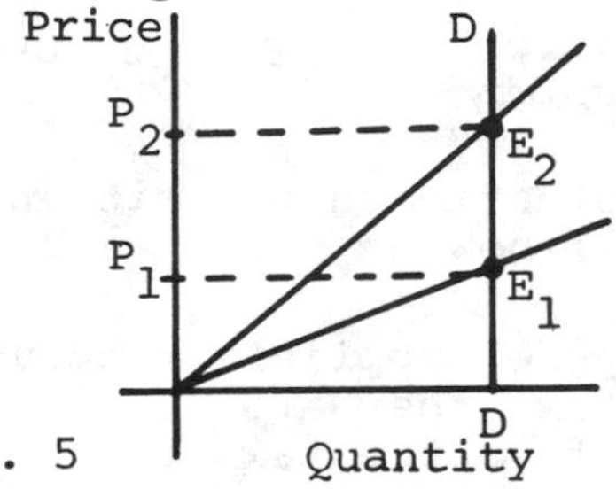

Fig. 5

Here, quantity demanded is fixed, no matter what the price. Therefore, as the tax is imposed, price to the consumer will rise from OP_1 to OP_2 (the full amount of the tax). The supplier, on the other hand, will receive OP_1 before the tax and OP_1 after the tax (once P_1P_2 is paid to the government for the tax). Thus, in a perfectly inelastic demand situation, the consumer will pay completely for a sales tax. In general, the more inelastic demand is, the more the buyer pays for a tax.

To sum up, we have shown here that the incidence of a sales tax is determined by the elasticities of supply and demand. As a general rule, the incidence of a sales tax falls on the buyer as inelasticity of demand increases or elasticity of supply increases. On the other hand, as elasticity of demand increases or inelasticity of supply increases, the incidence of a sales tax falls on the suppliers.

• PROBLEM 8-25

Given the supply and demand curves for $\overline{A}$, shown in Figure 1, how would the burden of a $2 per unit tax be shared between the consumers and the producer?

Solution: By asking for a discussion of the burden of a tax, the question is essentially asking, "Who will lose the most if a $2 per unit tax is implemented?" To construct the new market situation, the new supply curve, S'S', in Figure 2, is drawn $2 above the old curve, SS, in Figure 2, to represent the implementation of the tax. The old equilibrium occurred at P = \$3, Q = 300. The new equilibrium occurs at P = \$4, Q = 200. At this new equilibrium, note that the consumer pays \$4 per unit, but the producer only receives \$2 per unit, the remaining \$2 going to the government. Thus for each unit sold, the consumers are paying \$1 to the government {\$4 (the new price) - \$3 (the old price)}, while the producers also pay \$1 to the government {\$3 (the old price) - \$2 (the price received with the tax)}. In this example, the burden of the tax is shared equally.

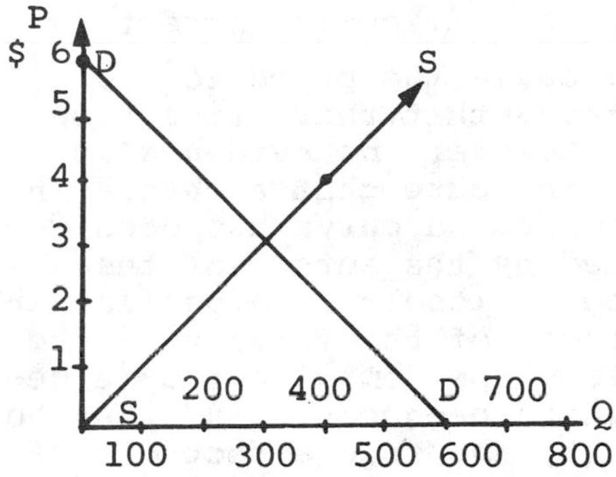

Fig. 1

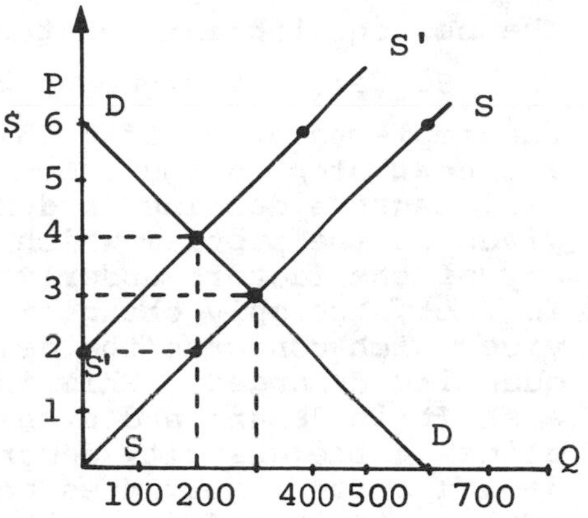

Fig. 2

• PROBLEM 8-26

> "If a tax is levied on gasoline, the initial effect will be a rise in price. This price rise will lead to a decline in demand which will cause the price to fall. In the end the equilibrium price may even be lower than it was to begin with." If the goal of government policy is to lower gasoline prices, should this advice be followed? Why or why not?

<u>Solution:</u> The solution to the problem lies in the determination of whether or not a fallacy is inherent in the argument. Begin by constructing the initial market situation, as shown in Figure 1.

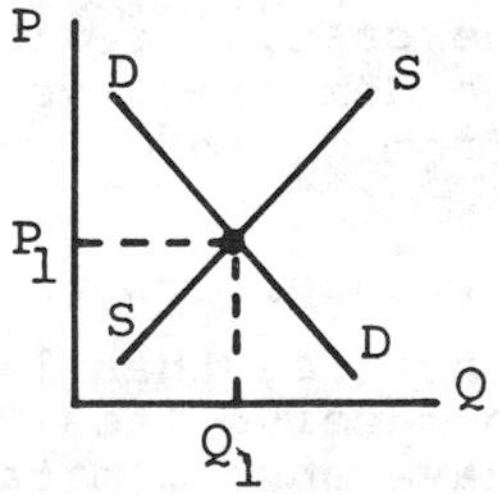

Fig. 1

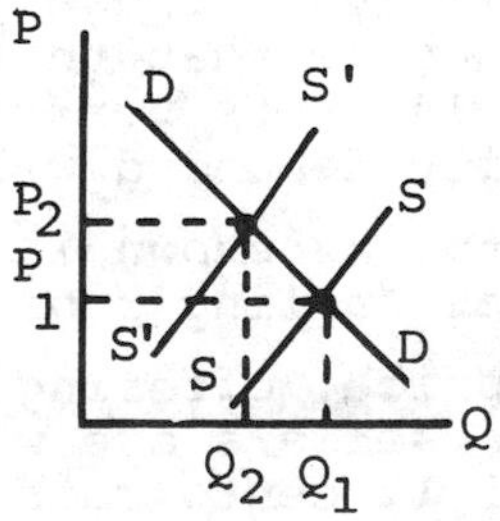

Fig. 2

The initial equilibrium point occurs at price P_1 and quantity Q_1. The first step listed in the advice is to levy a tax. A tax would effectively raise the cost of the commodity to the market at all levels of production (for any Q). The after-tax supply of gasoline is shown in Figure 2 by S'S'.

The new equilibrium point occurs at price P_2 and quantity Q_2. So far, the argument behind the advice is correct, as the implementation of a tax does cause the price to rise. The next step in the argument states that this price rise will cause a decline in demand. However, no evidence is given in the problem which would indicate that a change in any of the factors underlying the demand curve has occurred. In fact, the only change mentioned by the author of the advice which concerns the demand curve itself is a decline in quantity demanded. This is the root of the fallacy. Here, a shift in demand and a shift along the demand curve (a decline in the quantity demanded) have been confused. As the demand curve itself does not shift, the true effect of the implementation of a tax would be higher prices to the consumer and lower prices received by the producer, with the difference going to the government.

• PROBLEM 8-27

Suppose potatoes are selling for 12 cents per pound under a free market situation, as shown in figure 1, The government now imposes a tax of 2 cents per pound of potatoes. What will happen to the price of potatoes and the quantity sold?

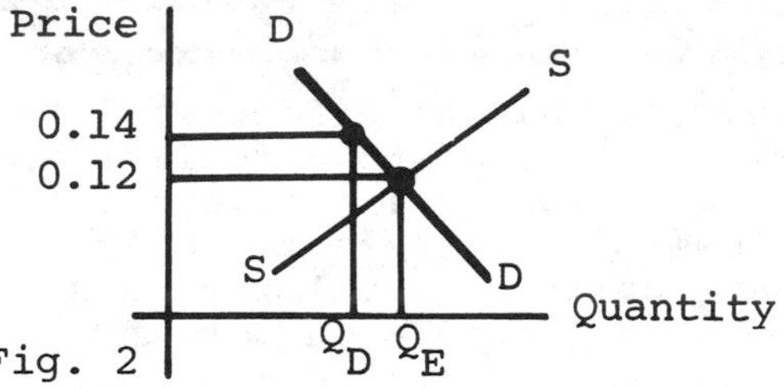

Fig. 2

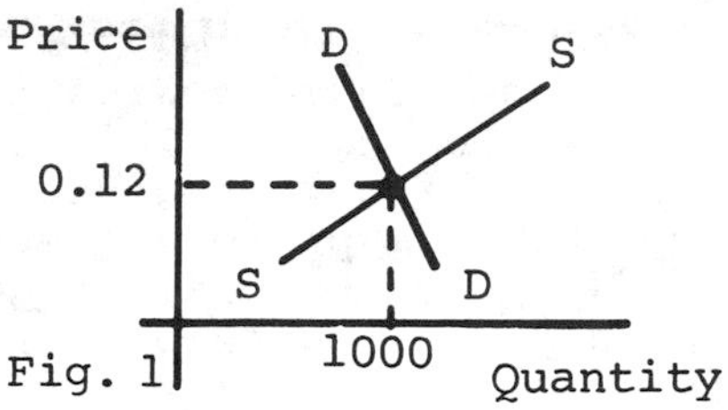

Fig. 1

Solution: First,note that, at whatever equilibrium the market settles after the tax is imposed, the buyer will be paying 2 cents per pound more for potatoes than the seller will be receiving, the difference going to the government as tax. Thus it might seem at first glance that the effect of the tax will be simply to cause the buyer to pay 2 cents more per pound. Suppose that this were the case, i.e. the price would rise to 14 cents per pound. The demand curve tells us that quantity demanded will fall from Q_E to Q_D if price goes up 2 cents, as shown in Fig. 2.

With sales falling from Q_E to Q_D, suppliers will start lowering the price, offering to sell at less than 14 cents: in effect, the sellers are willing to receive less than their original 12 cents rather than have unsold potatoes. Thus we see that the outcome will generally be that the price paid by consumers will end up somewhere between 12 cents and 14 cents per pound, and the price received by sellers (net of tax) will be less than the original 12 cents per pound.

Let us also attack this problem by asking what will happen to supply and demand curves when the tax is imposed. Demand is unchanged by a tax imposed on a product. (Demand is altered by a change in price which occurs as producers attempt to shift the burden of the tax to consumers.) Supply, however, is shifted. Consider each quantity supplied. With a per-unit tax of 2 cents, the suppliers must add in 2 cents at each quantity supplied as another cost. Thus, the supply curve will shift upward by 2 cents at each quantity supplied, as shown in Fig. 3.

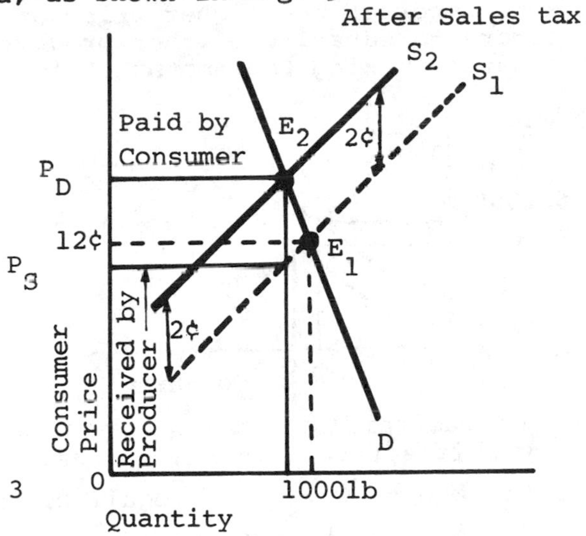

Fig. 3

At the original pre-tax equilibrium, E_1, price is 12 cents per pound and quantity is 1000 lb. After the tax, supply is represented by S_2 and equilibrium has changed to E_2. Here we see that the price paid by buyers, P_D, has risen, but not by the full 2 cents per pound because of the slope of the demand curve. Also, the price received by producers, P_S, must be less than 12 cents, since $P_D < 14$ cents and $P_S = P_D - 2$ cents. Once again, notice also that quantity demanded and supplied at E_2 is less than at E_1.

• PROBLEM 8-28

The city of Rutland wished to place a tax on ice cream so as to increase revenue for the city. Currently approximately 40,000 pints of ice cream are sold annually at a price of $1/pint. The city hoped to collect $2000 through the ice cream tax. The treasurer of the city therefore recommended a 5 cent tax on every pint of ice cream. At the end of the year, much less than $2000 had been collected. What went wrong?

<u>Solution:</u> Before we can say what went wrong, let us try to see why the treasurer picked a 5 cent per pint tax in the first place. We are told that annual sales amount to 40,000 pints and that the city wishes to collect $2000 in revenue. Therefore it appears that the treasurer calculated that in order to collect $2,000 from the sales of 40,000 pints, the city should collect 5 cents on every pint. This arithmetic is perfectly legitimate since

$$\frac{5 \text{ cents}}{\text{pint}} \times 40{,}000 \text{ pints} = \$2{,}000$$

However, what is not valid is the assumption by the treasurer that 40,000 pints will be sold after the tax is imposed. The 0,000 pint figure represents the before-tax sales. After the tax is imposed, the higher price of ice cream will convince consumers to substitute other products or shop in other towns, thereby making the amount of ice cream sold fall.

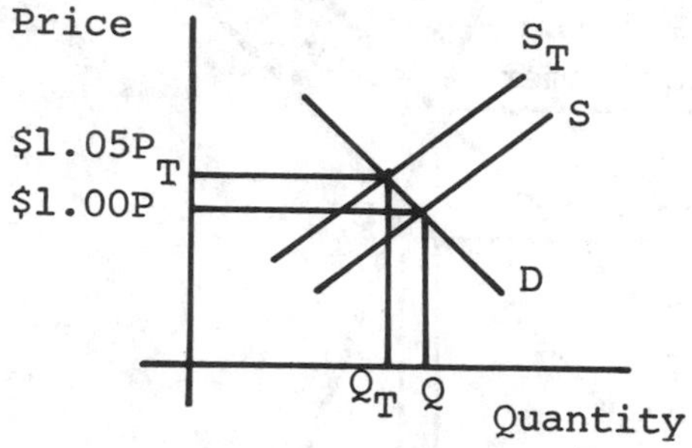

In the graph, we see this situation. When the tax is imposed, supply shifts from S to S_T, so that equilibrium quantity falls from Q to Q_T. Since equilibrium quantity is bound to fall (except in the extreme cases of completely inelastic demand or supply), the treasurer's estimate of tax revenue was bound to fail. Rather than relying on the known before-tax quantity, Q, some estimate of the after-tax quantity, Q_T, should have been employed.

• PROBLEM 8-29

The Yankee Soda Co. currently produces two carbonated beverages with identical cost curves. Reggie Cola which has highly elastic demand and Yankee Root Beer which has highly inelastic demand. Both products currently sell for 40 cents per can and sell approximately 20 million cans per year. If the government wishes to impose a 4 cent per can tax on one of these two products, which would it choose to maximize revenue?

Solution: To answer this problem, we must construct supply and demand curves for the two products. We are told that Reggie Cola and Yankee Root Beer have identical cost curves. Therefore S_R (the supply curve for Reggie Cola) = S_Y (the supply curve for Yankee Root Beer). Also, we are told that the demand for Reggie Cola (D_R) is highly elastic while the demand for Yankee Root Beer (D_Y) is highly inelastic. We are told that at equilibrium prior to the tax $Q_D = Q_Y$ = 20 million and $P_D = P_Y$ = 40 cents. So, the supply and demand curves before the tax would be as shown in Fig. 1.

Now, the government's revenue on any tax collection is equal to the amount of the tax times the after-tax equilibrium quantity. In this case the amount of the tax is the same for Reggie Cola and Yankee Root Beer. Therefore government revenue is strictly a function of the after-tax equilibrium quantity. Whichever soda has the greater equilibrium quantity will be chosen so as to maximize revenue.

Let us now return to our supply and demand curves and observe what happens when a tax is imposed.

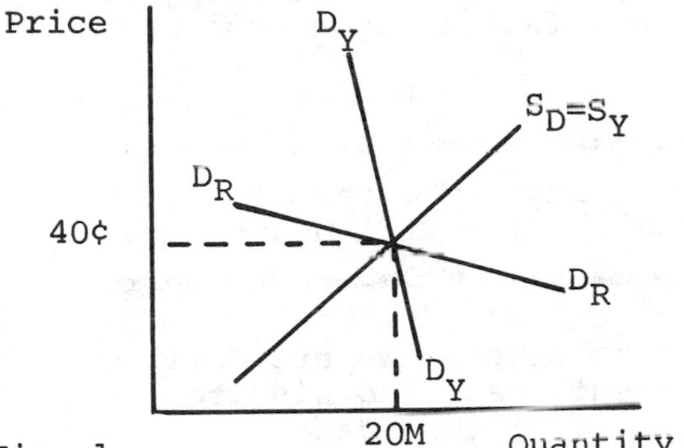

Fig. 1

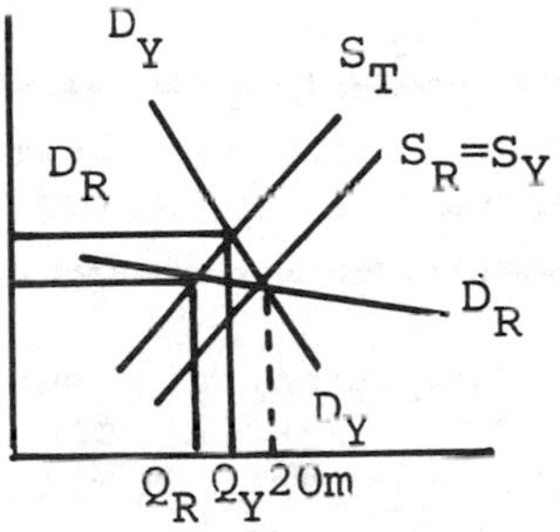

Fig. 2

On the graph shown in Fig. 2, S_T represents the supply curve after the tax has been imposed. We notice that with a tax, the new equilibrium quantities for Reggie Cola and Yankee Root Beer are no longer the same. In fact, Q_R, the equilibrium quantity for Reggie Cola, is less than Q_Y, the equilibrium quantity for Yankee Root Beer. Therefore putting a tax on Yankee Root Beer would maximize revenue.

In general, the more inelastic demand is, the less equilibrium quantity will fall when a tax is imposed, thereby making government revenue greater. Similarly, government revenue will be greater the more inelastic supply is.

• PROBLEM 8-30

Suppose a corporation is able to set prices where it chooses, i.e. demand is not perfectly elastic. If a per-unit tax is imposed on this corporation's product, how will demand elasticity affect pricing decisions and the incidence of the tax?

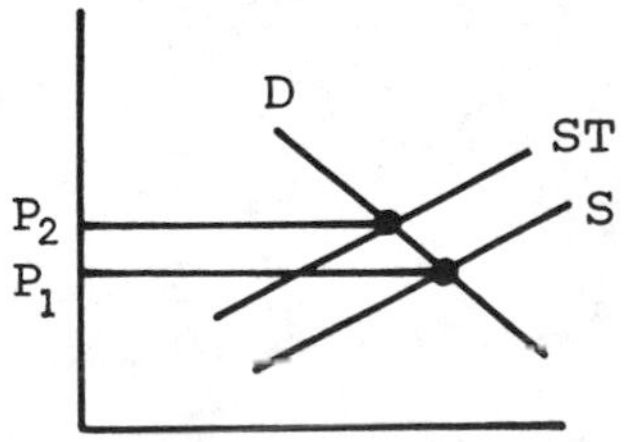

Solution: Ordinarily, we speak of a firm accepting a new market equilibrium price, when a tax is imposed. As shown we would expect price to change from P_1 to P_2 if a tax were imposed.

However, demand elasticity affects a company's reaction to a tax imposition, specifically, an elastic demand schedule means that an increase in price will bring about a decrease in total revenue. Therefore, in general, we would say that the probability of a price hike when a tax is imposed decreases as elasticity of demand increases.

When demand is inelastic, a price hike will increase total revenue. So, in a tax imposition, we would expect prices to rise with the incidence falling upon consumers.

• PROBLEM 8-31

How is it that if the government imposes a tax of a flat amount on a product, market equilibrium will not change?

Solution: To answer this, let us suppose we are dealing with a perfect competitor, currently selling his product for \$6, with the following total cost (TC) data:

Q	TC
0	10
1	13
2	15
3	17
4	20
5	25
6	32

Now, to find market equilibrium, we must know the marginal revenue (MR) and the marginal cost (MC). Since we are dealing with a perfect competitor, MR = constant = \$6. To figure out MC, we use the TC data as follows. $MC = \Delta TC/\Delta Q$. So, we now have

Q	TC	MC
0	10	
		3
1	13	
		2
2	15	
		2
3	17	
		3
4	20	
		5
5	25	
		7
6	32	

Now, as long as MC < MR, we can make more profit by adding another unit to production. Looking at the table, we see that up to the fifth unit of production, MC < MR. Therefore, at profit maximization, Q = 5. Since P = \$6, Profit = TR - TC = 30 - 25 = \$5.

Suppose now that the government imposes a flat tax of \$2. MR will remain the same since demand is unaffected by the tax. Total costs will increase by \$2 at all levels of production, but MC will remain the same, as shown below:

Q	TC	MC
0	12	
		3
1	15	
		2
2	17	
		2
3	19	
		3
4	22	
		5
5	27	
		7
6	34	

Since both MC and MR remain unchanged, market equilibrium will remain at the same point, i.e. Q = 5, P = 6. Profit now is TR - TC = \$30 - \$27 = \$3. With a \$2 tax, profit has fallen from \$5 to \$3. The producer therefore, is burdened with the entire tax.

• PROBLEM 8-32

Suppose you purchase a transistor radio and pay 6% sales tax on it. Is this the only tax which you are paying? Explain.

Solution: No, the sales tax is not the only tax for which the consumer must pay. There are many other hidden taxes which most people are unaware of, but which are included in the selling prices of goods.

In our transistor radio example, taxes have been paid by the manufacturer on the labor and raw materials that were required to produce that radio. Clearly, some of that tax burden is passed onto the consumer in the form of higher prices. Also, transportation costs, which affect product cost, include a certain amount of taxes in their charges, thereby giving another kick forward to the price of the transistor radio.

Many of these taxes cannot be traced definitely to their original sources, but it has been estimated that hidden taxes represent almost 20% of every dollar of retail sales.

• PROBLEM 8-33

Discuss the single-tax movement.

Solution: The fact that land is a free gift of nature which would be available even in the absence of rental payments has led many to question exactly what a landowner is entitled to. After all, why should rent be paid to those who by historical accident or inheritance happen to be landowners?

The socialists argue that all land rents represent unearned income. Therefore all land should be nationalized so that payments for its use can be used to improve the well-being of the entire population, rather than improve the well-being of just a landowning majority.

In the United States, criticism of the land rental situation has taken the form of a single-tax movement. Spearheaded by Henry George's book Progress and Poverty, this movement maintained that a tax on land rent could serve as the only tax levied by a government, thus giving it the name single-tax.

To understand how George and his followers could claim that a single tax on land rent would suffice in a country, we must return to our original consideration of taxes and elasticity of supply. In a normal situation, taxes are shared by producer and consumer. However, the supply of land does not represent a normal situation. Instead land is a fixed resource which has a perfectly inelastic supply. Now consider the situation in the late 1800's when Henry George wrote his book. As population grew and the geographic frontier closed, landowners came to enjoy larger and larger rents from their landholdings as demand increased. On the graph shown in Fig. 1, we see that as demand increases from DD to D_1D_1, the price of land jumps drastically while quantity supplied and demanded remains constant due to the inelasticity of supply.

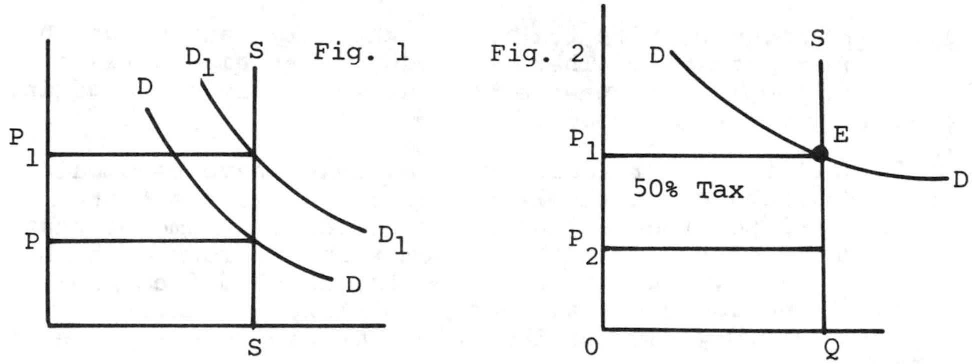

Henry George took the position that these increases in land rent belonged to the economy as a whole and that land rents should be taxed away and spent for public uses. Now if a tax was imposed the fact that supply is perfectly inelastic means that the tax will be totally borne by the landowner. This is due to the fact that the tax causes no shift in the perfectly inelastic supply curve, keeping market equilibrium constant, while forcing producers to pay a tax.

Suppose the situation is as shown in Fig. 2.

Before the tax is imposed, each landowner receives OP_1 in rent for each unit in land. After the tax, equilibrium is still at E, but each landowner must pay 50% of his revenue in tax, so that now landowners only receive OP_2 in rent for each unit.

With such a situation in mind, George held that there was no reason to tax away only 50% of the landowner's unearned rental income. Indeed, the government could squeeze even 99% tax out of the landowners since the landowner would not withdraw his land from production when no land means no rental income at all.

Of course, George's single-tax movements did not escape criticism. For one thing, it is clear that a land tax alone could not bring in enough revenue to support current levels of government spending. Also, one cannot say that a rent payment is completely unearned income since land typically contains some improvements made by the landowner. Just how much of the rental income is actually economic rent is often difficult to determine. Finally, the question of unearned income goes beyond land and land ownership. One can argue that many individuals and groups benefit from "unearned" income. For instance, suppose by chance, you invested in IBM stock 50 years ago and are now quite wealthy because of it. How is this income different from the landowner's rental income?

CORPORATE TAXATION

• PROBLEM 8-34

What are the current tax rates for American corporations? What are some of the arguments raised against and for heavy taxation of corporations?

Solution: On its first $25,000 of net income, a corporation must pay 22% to the federal government as tax. Beyond this point, a corporation must pay 48% of each dollar above $25,000 as tax.

Some experts argue that corporations should not be taxed because the corporate tax simply becomes a cost that is passed on to consumers. The prices of goods are higher than they would be without taxation and in many cases, the resultant higher prices represent a regressive tax structure for consumers. Also, it is argued that "double taxation" exists since the corporation pays taxes on net income and stockholders also pay taxes on dividends received from the corporation.

On the other hand, some argue that corporations should be taxed heavily, with the bigger corporations taxed at progressively heavier rates. Such a group holds that if government needs large sums of money and further increases in personal income tax are not feasible, then a corporate tax is better than a sales tax. It is also pointed out that there are loopholes present in the structure of capital-gains taxation which should be remedied.

• PROBLEM 8-35

What is meant by the "double taxation" problem in the corporate income tax system?

Solution: The "double taxation" problem deals with the fact that some corporate income is taxed twice. Specifically, the corporation must pay tax on its income. Then after it passes on after-tax dividends to its stockholders, the stockholders must pay personal income taxes on the dividends.

Suppose a firm makes $50,000 and pays $20,000 in taxes, leaving $30,000 to pay out as dividends or reinvest in the firm. The company then decides to pay out $15,000 in dividends. Now this $15,000 has already been drained by taxes, but when each stockholder gets his check from the corporation for a piece of that $15,000, he will have to pay further taxes. This double taxation of dividends is felt by many economists to be a glaring inequity in the present structure of income taxes.

• PROBLEM 8-36

What are tax loopholes? Can a loophole be considered an instance of tax evasion?

Solution: Loopholes are instances of legal tax avoidance made possible by Congressional legislation that permits income to go untaxed or be taxed at low levels. An example of this would be the fact that profit made on the sale of an asset above its original cost, capital gain, is taxed at a lower rate than ordinary income.

A loophole does not constitute tax evasion. Evasion involves illegal means to reduce one's tax burden. An example of such means would be the claiming of a false expense account.

• PROBLEM 8-37

What are long-term capital gains and how do they represent a loophole in our current tax system?

Solution: A capital gain is income from the sale of a piece of property (including shares of stock) for more money than it originally cost. The capital gain is classified as long-term if the property is held for six months or longer before reselling.

Long-term capital gains have come to be associated with loopholes because of the way in which they are taxed. Specifically, U.S. federal income tax law says that income from long-term capital gains will be taxed at no more than one-half the rate that applies to ordinary income. Thus $20,000 of income realized through speculation on the stock market may be taxed only one-half as much as $20,000 of income earned as an economics researcher. Typically, low-income taxpayers receive very little of their income in the form of capital gains. Instead, it is the upper-income taxpayers who make use of this loophole. Thus, the high-income earners are paying a good deal less in federal income tax than a glance at the schedule of tax rates might suggest.

• PROBLEM 8-38

What is depreciation? How does a method such as straight-line depreciation affect taxes differently than an accelerated method?

Solution: Suppose a piece of capital equipment is bought by a firm for $10,000. At the end of one year, that firm might be able to sell this same piece of equipment for only $8,000 on the open market. What has happened is that this equipment has worn out with usage of the year and its utility has decreased with the passage of time. Thus the market value of the asset has gone down by $2,000. We call this decrease in value depreciation.

When a firm makes an investment in a capital good (such as our example above), tax laws typically permit the firm to deduct the cost of the asset over a period of time. The rationale for this is as follows: Like the costs of other inputs (labor, raw materials), outlays for capital goods represent costs incurred by the firm in the productive process.

Yet, a firm must still determine how much of the cost of using the capital good is borne during each year of its useful life. In theory, the firm would find the market price for the capital good at the beginning and end of each year and use the difference as a measure of depreciation. In practice, this is often impractical or impossible. The result is that the tax authorities turn to somewhat arbitrary rules in instructing firms on evaluating depreciation. We shall see evidence of the arbitrary nature of depreciation by examining two very different methods currently used.

Before we examine these methods of depreciation, an understanding of how depreciation affects profits and taxes is needed. Suppose a firm has $20,000 income in its first year of operation before depreciation is accounted for and has capital assets worth $50,000. If this firm can somehow say that depreciation for the year is $20,000, its income after depreciation will be $0 and its taxes will be $0. If it can only claim $5,000 as depreciation, its taxable income will be $15,000. Of course, in the end, the amount of depreciation deducted will be $50,000 (the value of the capital goods). However it is important to realize that it is to the firm's advantage to postpone taxes as much as possible, thereby giving it money to work with now. Therefore it is often to the firm's advantage to make large depreciation deductions as quickly as possible, thereby reducing its tax burden.

Suppose now we return to our asset which cost $10,000 and let us say that this asset has a useful life of 4 years with no value at the end of this 4-year period. In the straight-line method of depreciation, equal amounts of depreciation expense are deducted during each year of the asset's useful life. To find this, we take the cost of the asset above, $10,000, and divide it by the useful life of 4 years to get an annual depreciation expense of $2,500.

Under accelerated depreciation method, depreciation expenses are made larger during the early years of the asset's life. One such method is called the "sum-of-the-year's-digits" method. With this approach, the useful life is first determined. Then the digits, starting with 1 and continuing to the useful life, are summed. In our example, the sum = 1 + 2 + 3 + 4 = 10. Then, to figure out the depreciation expense for each year, we multiply the cost of the capital good by a fraction determined as follows: the denominator is the sum obtained above, 10. The numerator is a progressively smaller integer, starting with the largest digit (i.e. the useful life) in year 1, the second largest digit (useful life - 1) in year 2, and so on until the numerator is 1 in the last year. In our example, we would have the following:

Year	Depreciation Expense
1	$\frac{4}{10} \times \$10,000 = \$4,000$
2	$\frac{3}{10} \times \$10,000 = \$3,000$
3	$\frac{2}{10} \times \$10,000 = \$2,000$
4	$\frac{1}{10} \times \$10,000 = \$1,000$

Looking at the different results for straight-line and sum-of-the-year's digits (SYD) depreciation, we see that in years 1 and 2, straight-line depreciation is less than SYD, while in years 3 and 4, straight-line is greater than SYD. Therefore, in years 1 and 2, taxable income will be greater under straight-line while in years 3 and 4, taxable income will be smaller. The effect of this is that under straight-line depreciation, taxes will be paid on profits sooner than under an accelerated method such as SYD. As shown earlier, it is often to the firm's advantage to postpone taxes to a later date. Therefore it is clear why many business firms approve of accelerated depreciation methods such as sum-of-the-year's-digits.

• **PROBLEM 8-39**

What are the FIFO and LIFO methods of inventory evaluation? How do they affect taxation differently?

Solution: Suppose a company sells a beverage which it stores in a 2000-gallon vat. Every day it purchases a few hundred gallons, from large producers, which it pours directly into the vat. This vat represents our beverage company's inventory. Now when it makes a sale, it does not know on which day it bought the goods it is selling since all the inventory is blended together. Therefore some method must be devised to identify for the purpose of tax accounting on what day each amount of the beverage sold was purchased.

In this case, it is impossible to discriminate between different purchases. In most cases, it is not impossible but highly impractical. Therefore methods such as LIFO and FIFO have been devised.

FIFO, the first-in, first-out method of costing inventory is based on the assumption that when a sale is made, the unit of inventory which has been on hand the longest should be used to evaluate cost. Suppose you sold canned vegetables and loaded your shelves from behind. Then you would be constantly pushing your oldest merchandise forward to sell, and the FIFO principle would be justified.

LIFO, the last-in, first-out method of costing inventory is based on the assumption that the most recent units of inventory purchased should be used to evaluate cost. Suppose you are once again selling canned vegetables, but this time you stock the shelves from the front. Now you will constantly be pushing back old cans and putting brand new cans up front. In this case LIFO is justified.

The ways in which LIFO and FIFO affect taxes depend upon the way prices are moving. In the United States, rising prices have become the norm, so we will assume that costs are rising over time. If costs are rising, FIFO will evaluate costs at a lower level than LIFO. Therefore profit under FIFO will be higher than profit under LIFO. And finally, tax under FIFO will be higher than profit under LIFO. And finally, tax under FIFO will be higher than tax under LIFO.

With such a situation, the wise businessman would choose LIFO so as to minimize taxes. However, it is a different story when reporting to the stockholders. Here the businessman wishes to show a nice profit to the shareholders. Since LIFO shows a smaller profit than FIFO, the businessman would prefer using FIFO for the financial statements which shareholders (and possible future investors) read.

• PROBLEM 8-40

In corporation XY sales in year 197X amount to $3,000,000; the cost of goods sold is $1,500,000; administrative expenses are $300,000; depreciation $800,000; all other expenses are $100,000; retained earnings are $100,000; when the corporation income tax rate is 48%, how much dividend is declared? How much could be declared if the tax rate fell to 45%?

Solution: The data indicate that we have to write up the income statement of corporation XY for the year 197X, and calculate the Earnings Before Income Taxes (EBIT), the Earnings After Taxes (EAT) and, finally, the Dividends Declared.

Income Statement of XY for 197X

	Sales revenues		$3,000,000
less:	Cost of Goods Sold		$1,500,000
	Operating income		$1,500,000
less other expenses:			
	depreciation	$800,000	
	administration	$300,000	
	other	$100,000	
			$1,200,000
	EBIT		$ 300,000
less:	Income Taxes 48%		$ 144,000
	EAT		$ 156,000
less:	Retained Earnings		$ 100,000
	Dividends Declared		$ 56,000

When the income tax rate is lowered to 45%, the Earnings Before Income Taxes remain unchanged. So,

	EBIT	$ 300,000
less:	Income Taxes 45%	$ 135,000
	EAT	$ 165,000

When there will be no earnings retained to be added to the Owner's Equity, these $165,000 could be declared as dividends for shareholders.

But if it is decided to reinvest $100,000 of the EAT (= 'profits') as Retained Earnings to increase the net wealth of the company, only 165,000 - 100,000 = $65,000 is declared as dividend. If it is however decided to declare the same amount of dividend, $56,000, $109,000 instead of $100,000 can be reinvested.

TAX SUBSIDIES

• PROBLEM 8-41

How are transfer payments different from government purchases?

Solution: When the government makes a purchase, it receives a good or service in return. Government purchases are often called exhaustive in that they directly absorb or employ resources, with the resultant production contributing to national output.

Transfer payments, on the other hand, are disbursements for which government currently receives no goods or services in return. Some examples of transfer payments are unemployment insurance and social security payments to the aged. Since transfer payments rechannel tax revenues back to households and businesses, they are in effect "negative taxes." Transfer payments are often called nonexhasutive because, as such, they do not directly absorb resources or account for production.

We can also distinguish between government purchases and transfer payments in the way they affect consumption of private and social goods. Being financed with tax money, government purchases tend to reallocate resources from private to social goods consumption. In the case of transfer payments, however, the tax money collected is rechanneled to other citizens. Therefore, there is no increase in social goods consumption here, but rather a change in the composition of private goods output. In this sense, transfer payments involve a lesser degree of government intervention in the economy than do government purchases.

• PROBLEM 8-42

Explain and give examples of income replacement and income support programs in the United States.

Solution: Programs giving transfer incomes to the retired or disabled are sometimes referred to as income replacement programs, since they are concerned with replacing incomes from other sources that have been stopped for one reason or another. The most important income replacement program in the United States is Social Security, a program which covers about 90% of employed persons in the country. It includes payments to retired and disabled persons and also to their survivors.

Considered as a policy with the aim of providing a minimum base income for its recipients, the Social Security program presents some problems. In 1970, the average monthly payment for a retired husband-wife family from social security was below the officially defined poverty level for that type of family. The benefits, however, are raised from time to time, especially during election years.

Income support programs are designed to supplement other income sources (which may be zero) for persons neither retired nor physically disabled. Such programs, which make payments to "able-bodied" members of the community, can be divided into unemployment benefits and "need" programs.

Unemployment payments are not generally related to income, i.e. the president of a corporation could draw payments in July, even if he received $150,000 working January to June, provided he lost his job and cannot find another.

"Need" programs are the only transfer payments made to persons simply because they are poor. "Welfare" falls into this category.

• PROBLEM 8-43

Suppose a certain industry is subsidized by the federal government. How will this affect market equilibrium? How will the elasticity of supply and demand affect the impact of the subsidy?

Solution: If we think of a subsidy as a negative tax, it is quite simple to discuss the above problem. Indeed we must only know how a tax affects the market, and from this we can deduce how a subsidy will affect the market.

Suppose the market for product X is currently operating freely as shown in graph 1.

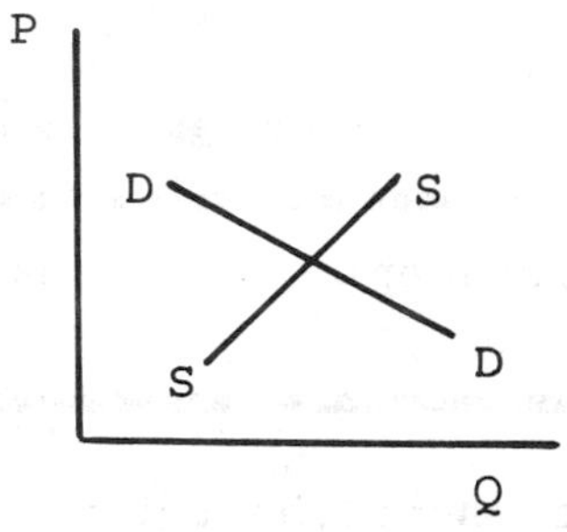

Graph 1

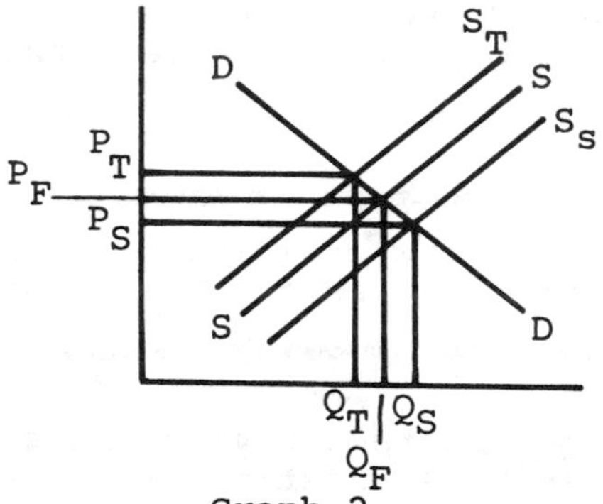

Graph 2

Graph 2 shows the effects of a tax and a subsidy upon the market situation:

Whereas a tax will cause supply SS to shift to the left to S_TS_T, a subsidy (negative tax) will shift supply to the right to S_SS_S, while a tax causes quantity to fall and price to rise, a subsidy will cause price to fall and quantity to rise.

The elasticity of supply and demand will be related to subsidies in much the same way the elasticity is related to tax.

In graph 3, demand is perfectly inelastic. Hence, quantity demanded will not change no matter what the subsidy or tax. Therefore in this situation, the price of the good will fall by the full amount of the subsidy, i.e. the con-

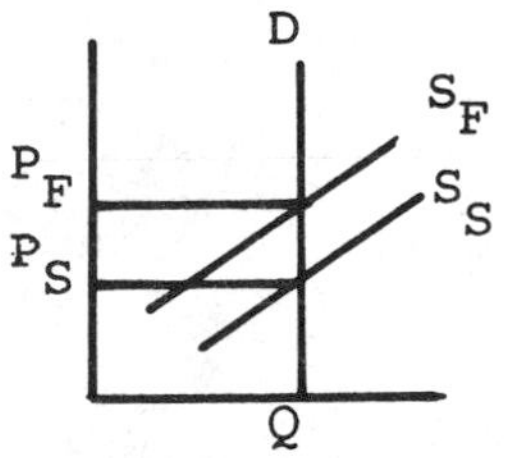

Graph 3

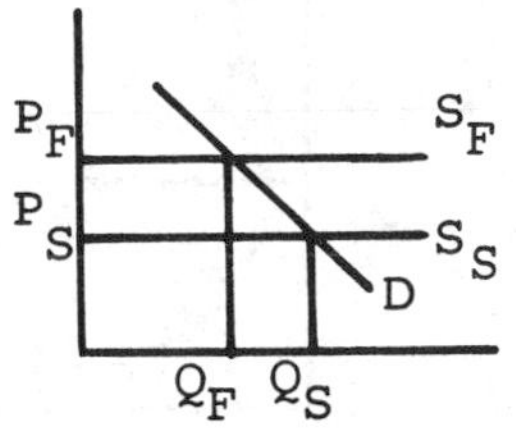

Graph 4

sumer will benefit completely from the subsidy. Similarly, in graph 4, when supply is perfectly elastic, the subsidy will be totally reaped by the consumer as equilibrium price falls from P_F to P_S.

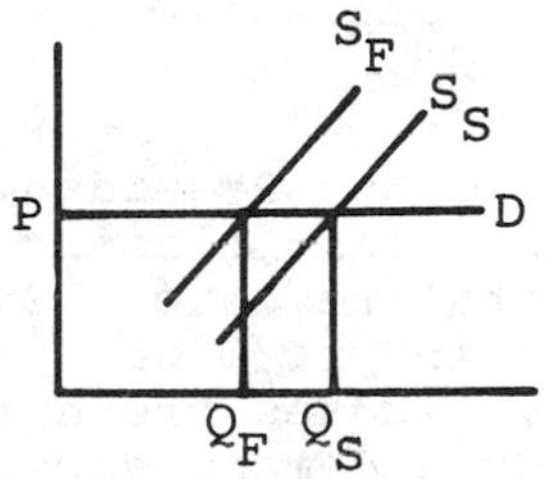

Graph 5

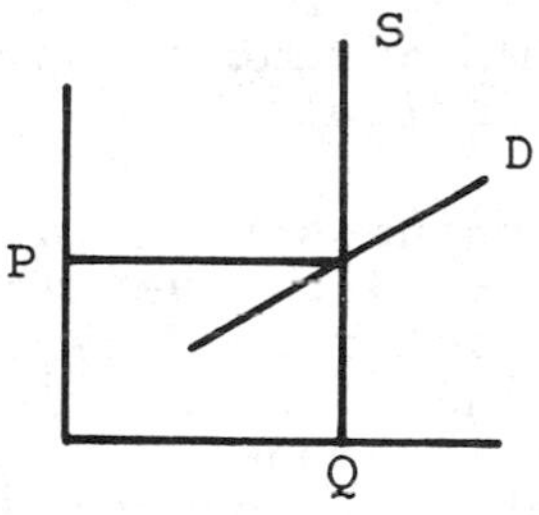

Graph 6

On the other hand, if demand is perfectly elastic or supply perfectly inelastic, the supplier reaps all the benefits of the subsidy. In graph 5, demand is perfectly elastic. Therefore, no change in supply will change the price without demand changing first. Finally, in graph 6, supply is not affected by the subsidy. A perfectly inelastic supply means that quantity is fixed, and no amount of subsidy will change that quantity. Therefore since a subsidy does not affect the demand curve, equilibrium will remain at P and Q. But since the producer is also receiving a subsidy from the government which is not affecting the market situation, the producers benefit totally from a subsidy when supply is perfectly inelastic.

To sum up, the more inelastic supply or elastic demand is, the more a producer benefits from a subsidy. The more elastic supply or inelastic demand is, the more a consumer benefits from a subsidy.

• PROBLEM 8-44

The leaders of an industry went to see the President to complain about falling revenues in recent years. Among the data supporting their case, industry A's leaders presented the President with demand elasticity figures, indicating an industry average of 0.3. Not wanting to waste his time on what he thought was a trivial problem, the President recommended subsidization of the industry. Why would the President's plan backfire?

Solution: The key to solving this problem is an understanding of the nature of elasticity of demand and the effect of a government subsidy upon a supply curve.

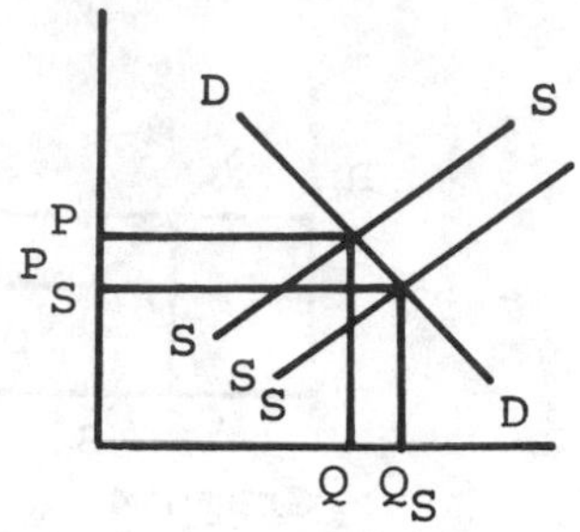

Since a subsidy is nothing more than a "negative tax," a subsidy would affect supply by shifting it down and to the right (as shown).

In such a situation, price will fall while quantity demanded will increase.

Now, the industry leaders came to the President complaining of falling revenues. We know that elasticity of demand is a factor in determining total revenue. Specifically, if demand is inelastic, a drop in price will cause a drop in total revenue. The industry figures presented to the President in this problem include a demand elasticity of 0.3. This is a very highly inelastic demand curve, inelastic meaning an elasticity less than one. Therefore any drop in price would bring about even further drops in total revenue.

But, as the subsidy graph shows , the establishment of a subsidy will cause a drop in price, and therefore a drop in total revenue since demand is inelastic. Such a move would result in the exact opposite of what the President had originally intended.

• PROBLEM 8-45

Mr. Errol makes deliveries by bicycle for a living and earns \$200 a week. He is currently taxed at a rate of 20%. Because of his superior work record, his boss gave Mr. Errol a \$10 raise in pay. Mr. Errol is excited, but does not realize that this raise in pay puts him in a 25% tax bracket.

a) How much of an increase in take-home salary does this raise amount to?

b) Discuss Mr. Errol's marginal tax rate.

Solution: a) When Mr. Errol was earning \$200 a week, his tax rate was 20%. Therefore his total tax paid = 20% × \$200 = \$40, and his take-home salary was \$200 - \$40 = \$160.

Now Mr. Errol has received a raise to \$210. But his tax rate becomes 25%, due to a progressive tax system. Therefore his new tax charge = 25% × \$210 = \$52.50, with a resulting take-home salary of \$210 - \$52.50 = \$157.50.

So we see that what looked originally like a \$10 increase in pay is in reality a drop in pay of \$2.50, due to the tax structure.

b) To find Mr. Errol's marginal tax rate, we must look at the change in taxes and the change in salary. Since Mr. Errol's salary was raised from $200 to $210, the change in salary, ΔS, = $210 - $200 = $10. Part a) of this problem tells us that the amount of tax paid by Mr. Errol goes from $40 to $52.50. Therefore, the change in tax, Δt, = $52.50 - $40.00 = $12.50.

Using the formula for marginal tax rate, we get

$$\text{Marginal tax rate} = \frac{\Delta t}{\Delta S}$$

$$= \frac{12.50}{10}$$

$$= 125\%$$

This extremely high marginal tax rate offers us another way of looking at a situation where a raise in salary actually means a drop in take-home pay. In general, if marginal tax rate > 100%, the increase in tax is greater than the increase in salary. Therefore take-home pay will always drop if marginal tax rate is greater than 100%.

• PROBLEM 8-46

Suppose Country X has the following tax structure:

Net Income	Tax
$10,000	$1,000
20,000	3,000
30,000	6,000

At each of the three income levels, what is the average tax rate and the marginal tax rate?

Solution: To find the average tax rate, we divide the amount of tax paid by net income.

Therefore, at a net income of $10,000,

$$\text{average tax rate} = \frac{\text{tax}}{\text{Net Income}}$$

$$= \frac{\$\ 1{,}000}{\$10{,}000}$$

$$= 10\%$$

At a net income of $20,000

$$\text{average tax rate} = \frac{\$\ 3{,}000}{\$20{,}000} = 15\%$$

At a net income of $30,000,

$$\text{average tax rate} = \frac{\$\ 6,000}{\$30,000} = 20\%$$

So we see that this is a progressive tax structure, i.e. as income increases, one pays a higher fraction of income to taxes.

The marginal tax rate is the tax rate paid on the additional, or marginal, dollar of income. In our example, we will assume that for a net income of $0, tax = 0. Then, using the formula,

$$\text{Marginal Tax Rate} = \frac{\Delta\ \text{Tax}}{\Delta\ \text{Income}}$$

We can compute the marginal tax rate for each income level.

For the first step, income increases from $0 to $10,000 while tax increases from $0 to $1,000. Therefore

$$\text{Marginal Tax Rate} = \frac{\$\ 1,000 - \$0}{\$10,000 - \$0} = 10\%$$

which is the same as the average tax rate at $10,000 income.

When income rises to $20,000, tax rises to $3,000. Therefore, at an income of $20,000,

$$\text{Marginal Tax Rate} = \frac{\$\ 3,000 - \$1,000}{\$20,000 - \$10,000}$$

$$= \frac{2,000}{10,000} = 20\%$$

When income rises to $30,000, tax increases to $6,000. Therefore, at an income of $30,000,

$$\text{Marginal Tax Rate} = \frac{\$\ 6,000 - \$\ 3,000}{\$30,000 - \$20,000}$$

$$= \frac{\$\ 3,000}{\$10,000} = 30\%$$

So, with the progressive tax system shown above, we see rising marginal tax rates.

EXTERNALITIES

• PROBLEM 8-47

What are externalities?

Solution: Externalities are costs and benefits associated

with the production and consumption of certain goods and services which the price system fails to account for. Externalities are often referred to as spillover costs and benefits.

Two distinctions are made in discussing externalities. They can accompany acts of either production or consumption, and they can be either positive (benefits) or negative (costs). From these two distinctions, we describe four basic types of externalities.

First, we have positive production externalities. Anyone who has walked past a bakery and smelled the fresh bread has experienced positive production externalities. Here, the consumer (or society) has received a benefit without paying for it. Similarly, one would experience negative production externalities by walking past a polluting factory and smelling the air. Here society is incurring costs which the producing firm has failed to recognize.

On the consumption side, positive consumption externalities exist when one family grows beautiful flowers in its garden and the whole neighborhood benefits. On the other hand, negative consumption externalities exist when a camper throws his beer cans in the forest or a moviegoer chews his popcorn so loudly that no one else can watch the movie.

• PROBLEM 8-48

Suppose Figure 1 shows typical supply and demand curves describing the notebook paper market.

However, in producing notebook paper, the market fails to take into account an external cost of $75 per ton arising from water pollution caused by the paper production process.

How might the government tax the producers of this industry?

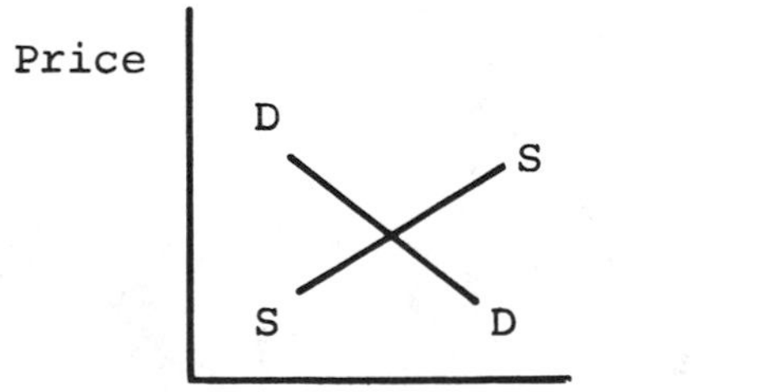

Fig. 1

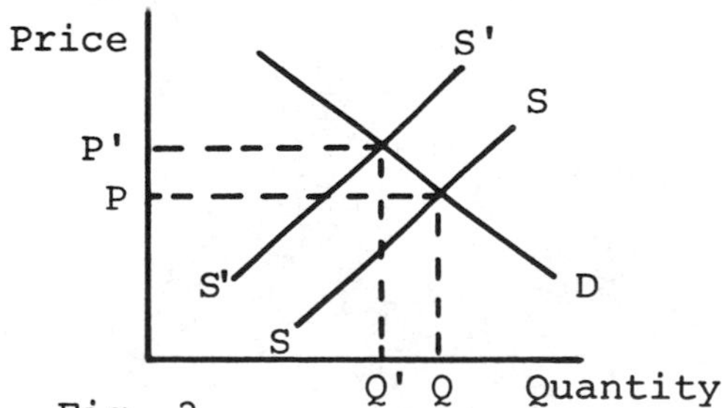

Fig. 2

<u>Solution:</u> The above situation represents a case of externalities. Specifically a negative production externality exists whereby the paper producers are not realizing the full costs of their production. As it stands now the producers' supply curves are based only upon the private marginal cost. The social marginal cost must include the $75 extra cost due to pollution associated with each unit of output. Figure 2 illustrates this.

SS represents Supply Based on Private Marginal Cost while S'S' represents Social Marginal Cost. With only private costs assessed, equilibrium occurs at a quantity of Q and price of P. When social costs are accounted for, quantity falls to Q' while price rises to P'.

The role of government here is to force the paper producers to internalize - meaning to bear themselves - the costs of any externalities they generate. To do this the government should simply impose a tax of $75 per ton of paper since each ton produces $75 of pollution that goes unpaid. The effect would be to raise the private marginal cost of producing paper to equal the social marginal costs. Thus, the external cost would be internalized, and the manufacturer would be forced to cut back his production in recognition of the full social costs. The new price would be P' and quantity sold would be Q'. With the tax revenue of $75 per ton, the government could grant subsidies to clean up the pollution or to compensate the residents of the area for the costs of the pollution.

Notice the incidence of the tax here. One might at first guess that the producers would pay the full amount of the tax. However, unless demand is perfectly elastic or supply is perfectly inelastic, the customer will have to pay for a portion of the tax.

Answer
To be covered when testing yourself

SHORT ANSWER QUESTIONS FOR REVIEW

Choose the correct answer.

1. An income tax is regressive if: (a) the amount paid as taxes decreases as income increases (b) the percentage of income paid as taxes decreases as income increases (c) the absolute amount paid as taxes varies directly with income (d) the tax rate is constant — b

2. Federal: state: local as (a) property: income: excise (b) corporate income: sales: transportation (c) personal income: sales: property (d) personal income: excise: transportation (e) corporate income: sales: property — c

3. Of the following, which is not a regressive tax, considering income as the tax base? (a) payroll tax (b) a 10 percent general sales tax (c) the Federal personal income tax (d) property tax — c

4. The personal distribution of income in an economy is actually unequal because: (a) the economy is not very competitive and discrimination exists (b) the economy is very competitive (c) the tax structure is progressive (d) the economy is in a recession — a

5. Which of the following taxes is least likely to be shifted? (a) a Federal excise tax on Scotch whiskey (b) a general sales tax on all foodstuffs and clothing (c) a personal income tax (d) a state excise tax on baseball tickets — c

6. The ability-to-pay philosophy is most evident in: (a) an excise tax on coffee (b) an excise tax on gasoline (c) a tax on residential property (d) a progressive income tax — d

7. Which of the following relate directly to the benefits-received principle of taxation? (a) progressive tax rates (b) proportional tax rates (c) Federal excise tax on alcoholic beverages (d) personal income tax — c

8. A tax structure is said to be progressive if: (a) the tax rate remains the same, regardless of the size of income (b) the tax increases the total volume of consumer expenditures (c) the tax rate increases as income increases (d) the tax rate declines as income increases — c

9. Property taxes like taxes on land are borne by

the property owner because: (a) the tax payments are his obligation (b) they tend to be regressive for a certain period of time (c) even when land is sold, the property tax is not likely to be shifted (d) the same rate applies to all income levels — c

10. The maximum marginal tax rate on personal income currently is (a) 35 percent (b) 70 percent (c) 45 percent (d) 27 percent (e) 90 percent — b

11. The Federal corporate income tax is (a) proportional if corporation owners bear the tax (b) regressive when corporation owners (shareholders) pass the tax to consumers in the form of higher product prices (c) progressive when corporation owners pass the tax to employees (d) regressive when corporation owners bear the tax — b

12. **Personal income tax: (a) generally falls as individual income rises (b) cannot be shifted from one individual to another during inflation and deflation except at full employment NNP (c) does not generally fall on the individual upon whom the tax is levied, since there is chance for shifting (d) may be regarded by unions as part of the cost of living and, as a result, they may bargain for higher wages** — d

13. The significant difference between the transactions of the private and public sectors of the economy is: (a) the former are voluntary, and the latter compulsory (b) the latter are voluntary, and the former compulsory (c) the former allocate resources and the latter do not (d) the latter allocate resources and the former do not — a

14. The marginal tax rate is (a) the decrease in taxes paid as additional income is obtained (b) the ratio of total taxes paid to total income (c) the increase in taxes paid as additional income is obtained, divided by that increase in income (d) the total tax rate less the average tax rate — c

15. Transfer payments are frequently labeled: (a) exhaustive, in that they directly absorb resources and contribute to the national out-

Answer
To be covered when testing yourself

put (b) allocative, in that they tend to reallocate resources from private to social goods consumption (c) non-exhaustive because, as such, they do not directly absorb resources or account for production (d) non-exhaustive, in that they directly absorb resources but do not contribute to the national output — c

16. Avoidance: evasion as: (a) increase: reduce (b) legal: illegal (c) inflationary: deflationary (d) progressive: regressive — b

17. Which of the following is not an important source of revenue for the Federal government? (a) personal income taxes (b) payroll taxes (c) property taxes (d) corporate income taxes — c

18. Sales and excise taxes are levied upon retailers, but retailers add these taxes to the prices of their products. This illustrates: (a) the benefits-received principle of taxation (b) the ability-to-pay principle of taxation (c) the equal-sacrifice theory of taxation (d) the shifting of taxes to consumers — d

19. About what percentage of its income does the average family pay in taxes? (a) 66 percent (b) 33 percent (c) 10 percent (d) 20 percent (e) 25 percent — b

20. The two largest items in the combined budgets of state and local governments are for: (a) police and fire protection (b) welfare and Medicaid (c) highways and education (d) legislators' and judges' salaries (e) none of the above — c

21. To eliminate double taxation of income originating in corporations, we could: (a) halve the corporate tax rate only (b) halve both the corporate and personal income tax rates (c) divorce the artificial personality of the corporation from the personalities of its owner (d) give the dividend receiver a tax credit for the taxes his corporation has paid on his share of the earnings — d

22. The value-added tax differs from a turnover tax in that the former: (a) taxes each transaction (b) collects at each stage of production (c) includes a percentage of earlier taxes (d) taxes at the final source — b

23. The single largest U.S. tax loophole is the fact that: (a) capital gains are taxed less heavily

SHORT ANSWER QUESTIONS FOR REVIEW

than ordinary income (b) each person is allowed an exemption of $750 (c) over 150 persons with income of more than $200,000 per year pay no tax (d) dividends often escape untaxed — a

24. For which of the following purposes would a sales tax on consumer expenditures be most useful? (a) Raising government revenue (b) Stimulating total demand for goods and services (c) Reducing deflationary pressures (d) Achieving a more equal distribution of income — a

25. Of the following, the most "progressive" system for income redistribution is: (a) a graduated income tax applied to all incomes (b) a graduated income tax applied to all incomes above the minimum exemption level (c) a graduated income tax applied to all incomes above the minimum exemption level together with subsidies to those whose incomes are very low (d) a graduated income tax applied to all incomes above the minimum exemption level and below a certain maximum level (e) none of the above are progressive — c

26. In a full-employment economy, aggregate demand is inflationary if: (a) it exceeds full-employment output (b) the aggregate demand curve just equals full-employment output at the equilibrium point (c) it is lower than full employment output (d) none of the above — a

27. The negative income tax proposal holds that: (a) individuals and families whose incomes fall below specified "poverty levels" should receive payments from government up to the poverty level (b) individuals and families whose incomes rise above the poverty line should give back to the poor in the form of transfer payments (c) income taxes should at all times be subtracted from income (d) the negative portion of income be given to individuals and families at the end of the year — a

28. In an economy, if spillover costs of a particular product are substantial, the market is: (a) over-allocating resources to the production of that good or service (b) under-allocating resources to that commodity (c) neutralizing the effect for all goods (d) optimally allocating resources — a

29. The Pure Food and Drug Act of 1906 is an

Answer
To be covered when testing yourself

illustration of: (a) the allocative function of government (b) the redistributional function of government (c) government provision of a suitable legal framework for the price system (d) how competition is maintained in the price system — c

30-32. Answer Questions 30 through 32 on the basis of the following data:

Taxable Income	Total Tax
$ 1500	$ 5
2500	110
3000	200
4500	400
5000	600
6000	900

30. The tax illustrated here is: (a) structural (b) perverse (c) proportional (d) progressive — d

31. If your taxable income is $5000, your average tax rate will be: (a) 15% (b) 13% (c) 12% (d) 18% (e) 10% — c

32. If your taxable income increases from $5000 to $6000, your marginal tax rate will be: (a) 40% (b) 11% (c) 6% (d) 20% (e) 30% — e

Fill in the blanks.

33. A federal tax levied on a domestically produced commodity is called ______________. — an excise tax

34. The largest single source of the federal government's tax revenue is ______________. — personal income tax

35. The major source of government revenue in Russia is the ______________ tax. — turnover

36. Mr. A earns $3000 a year and pays $350 in taxes. Mr. B earns $10,000 a year and pays $1000 in taxes. The tax system here is ______________. — regressive

37. When a per-unit tax was placed on the producers of product X, the price rose by the full amount of the tax, due to the demand for the product. X's demand is therefore ______________. — perfectly inelastic

38. If we only examine incomes less than $10,000,

SHORT ANSWER QUESTIONS FOR REVIEW

	Answer (To be covered when testing yourself)
then we could consider the Social Security tax _______________.	propor-tional
39. The idea that tax burden should be linked directly to one's financial position is called the _______________ principle of taxation.	ability-to-pay
40. The idea that households and businesses should purchase the goods and services of government in basically the same manner in which other commodities are bought is called the _______________ principle of taxation.	benefits-received
41. Taxes do not always stick where the government puts them. When a tax can be shifted among various parties in the economy, we examine the final resting place or _______________ of that tax.	incidence
42. Legal tax avoidance that lets income go untaxed or be taxed at a low level is called ___________.	tax loopholes
43. Miss W earns $20 each time she works but does not pay any taxes. Miss X pays $1 in taxes and earns more than Miss W. The tax structure here is _______________.	progressive
44. Negative taxes is another name for _____________.	transfer payments
45. If Mr. R works 41 hours instead of 40 hours the additional dollars earned place him in a higher tax bracket. In such a situation, take-home pay is the same for 41 hours as it is for 40 hours. Mr. R's marginal tax rate is therefore _________.	100%
46. An income tax with _______________ rates causes after-tax income to be more equally distributed than before-tax income.	progressive
47. In a regressive tax structure, marginal tax rate falls _______________ than average tax rate as income rises.	more rapidly
48. Aside from the highest and lowest income classes, the total tax system in the United States is roughly _______________.	propor-tional
49. The fact that dividends are taxed as both corporate income and personal income is referred to as _______________.	double taxation
50. The tax which collects on a product at each	

SHORT ANSWER QUESTIONS FOR REVIEW

	Answer To be covered when testing yourself
stage of production is called the ____________ tax.	value-added
51. If demand is elastic, a per-unit tax on a product will cause total revenue for a firm to _______.	decrease
52. Spillover costs cause a market equilibrium where quantity supplied and demand is too __________ and price is too ____________.	high, low
<u>Determine whether the following statements are true or false.</u>	
53. The federal income tax is the only major tax on individuals in the United States that is progressive.	True
54. If demand is inelastic, a government subsidy to a business firm will cause total revenue to fall.	True
55. In a regressive tax structure, tax revenue decreases as income increases.	False
56. In a progressive tax structure, marginal tax rate is always greater than or equal to average tax rate.	True
57. In general, state and local governments have more progressive tax structures than the federal government.	False
58. The benefits-received principle of taxation supports the case for highly progressive taxation.	False
59. Historically, total government spending and tax collections have risen both absolutely and as a percentage of total output.	True
60. The property tax is progressive since tax rates are constant and wealthy people own much more taxable property than do poor people.	False
61. The major problem with the corporate income tax is that the consumer must pay for the entire tax through higher product prices.	False
62. Sales taxes are proportional since the same tax rate applies regardless of the size of a purchase.	False
63. Because of deductions and loopholes, less than one-half of all true income is included in the	

SHORT ANSWER QUESTIONS FOR REVIEW	Answer To be covered when testing yourself
tax base.	True
64. The value-added tax is termed an indirect tax, even though it specifically taxes the new costs at each stage of production.	True
65. If a progressive tax structure causes after-tax income to fall, as before tax income rises, then marginal tax rate is negative.	False
66. Progressive income taxes tend, through redistribution of income, to expand purchasing power.	True
67. The exclusion of food from a general sales tax would make it considerably less regressive.	True

CHAPTER 9

BUSINESS CYCLES

Basic Attacks and Strategies for Solving Problems in this Chapter. See pages 299 to 323 for step-by-step solutions to problems.

Business cycles are the alternating periods of boom and bust which characterize market-based economies. A diagrammatic representation of a typical business cycle is shown below. On the vertical axis is some measure of business conditions, quite possibly GNP. A business cycle consists of four phases: peak, recession, trough, and recovery. Both the peak and trough occur at a point in time, typically a specific month. The recession and recovery phases occur during the time that elapses between peak and trough and trough and peak, respectively.

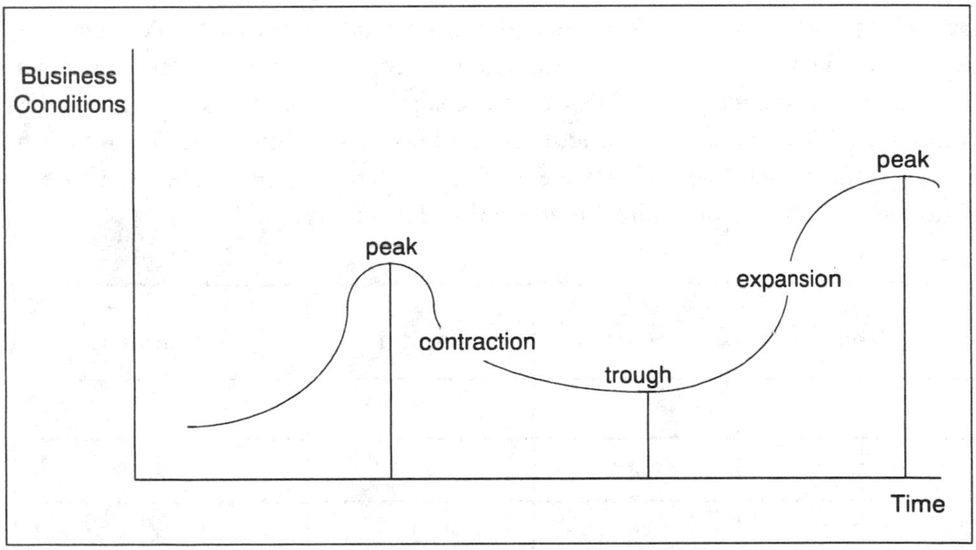

The word cycle is potentially misleading as a description of the phenomenon. "Cycle" implies regular and periodic movements, but actual business cycles are anything but regular. Every business cycle in history has been unique. Cycles have differed in their duration and magnitude. Some have been long and severe, others have been short and mild. There have been long and mild and short and severe cycles also.

Cycles are only one of the "movements" that business activity is subject to. Other movements include trends, seasonal fluctuations, and stochastic movements. Trends refer to the long run direction of movement of business activity. In the United States, the trend in business activity has been upward as our nation's standard of living has grown. Seasonal fluctuations reflect movements in the economy that are influenced by the season of the year or national customs. For example, toy sales dramatically rise every December, but decline in January. Electricity consumption is high every summer as people use air conditioners, but declines during spring and fall. Stochastic movements are the result of random and unpredictable factors.

Specific economic variables also display cyclical movements. Some variables have the characteristic that they consistently hit their peak before the business cycle peak and hit their trough before the business cycle trough. These variables are known as leading indicators. The "best" (most reliable) leading indicators are grouped together into the Index of Leading Indicators, a well-known forecasting tool.

The Acceleration Principle is a simple theory of investment with dramatic implications. It predicts that investment spending depends on the rate of growth of a firm's sales, and that small changes in sales growth can cause large fluctuations in investment. Assume firms use $2 of capital for every $1 of sales; new investment can be put in place instantaneously, and there is no depreciation. The table shows that in year 1, $2 of sales requires a capital stock of $4. As sales rise by 2 units in years 2 and 3, the capital requirement increases, leading to an investment of 4 each year. Sales increase again in year 4, but by a smaller amount, and investment falls to **half** its previous value. Constant sales in year 5 causes a further decline in investment. The accelerator principle is used to explain the volatility of investment in the national economy.

Year	Sales	Capital	Investment
1	2	4	0
2	4	8	4
3	6	12	4
4	7	14	2
5	7	14	0

There are many theories explaining business cycles. The major categories of theories include external versus internal theories and real versus monetary theories. External theories attribute business cycles to events that take place external to the economy. Schumpeter's innovation theory is an example. In this theory, technological innovations that occur at random intervals set off investment booms leading to cycles. Internal theories attribute cycles to the inner workings of the economy. Sammuelson's multiplier-accelerator model is an example. While external shocks are required to start a cycle, the cycle is kept moving by the interaction of the multiplier and accelerator principles. The latter principle is a theory that shows how small changes in spending can lead to dramatic changes in investment.

Real theories locate the source of business cycles in the movements in "real" variables, such as investment or government spending. The Keynesian theory, which emphasizes the volatility of investment, is an example. Monetary theories look at fluctuations in financial variables. Monetarist theory serves as an example here.

Step-by-Step Solutions to Problems in this Chapter, "Business Cycles"

DEFINITION

• **PROBLEM 9-1**

What are "business cycles" or "business fluctuations"?

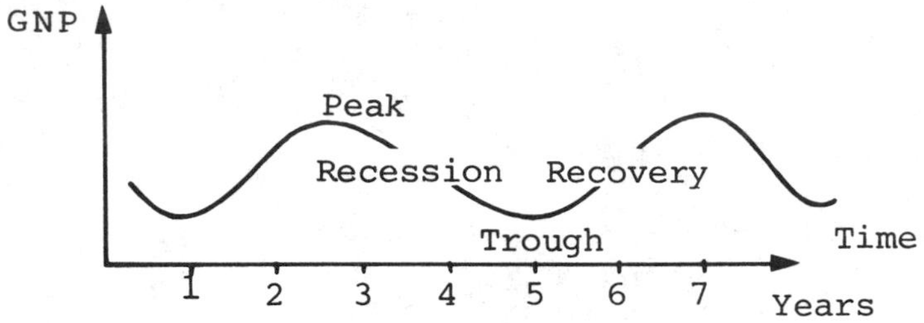

Solution: The term "business cycles" refers to variations in the level of economic activity over a period of years. Some economists prefer the term "business fluctuations," rather than business cycles, because it implies no regularity, as the former does. Business "cycles" vary greatly in duration and intensity, but the general form is presented in the accompanying figure, with GNP as the main indicator.

The four phases of the business cycle, indicated on the graph, are prosperity (peak, upper turning point), recession (contraction, downswing), depression (trough, lower turning point), and recovery (expansion, upswing).

• **PROBLEM 9-2**

Give a short analysis of the anatomy of the business cycles.

Solution: The business cycle represents a certain process in the economy that can be described by the wavelike fluctuations in GNP shown in the accompanying figure.

Suppose, for example, gross investment falls. The lower

investment level generates, via the multiplier process, a lower income level (in the absence of a counterbalancing policy). The downswing in GNP causes a decline in savings, and also in total taxes, because income taxes and sales taxes are directly related to income. But the fall in savings or in taxes will be less than the fall in income.

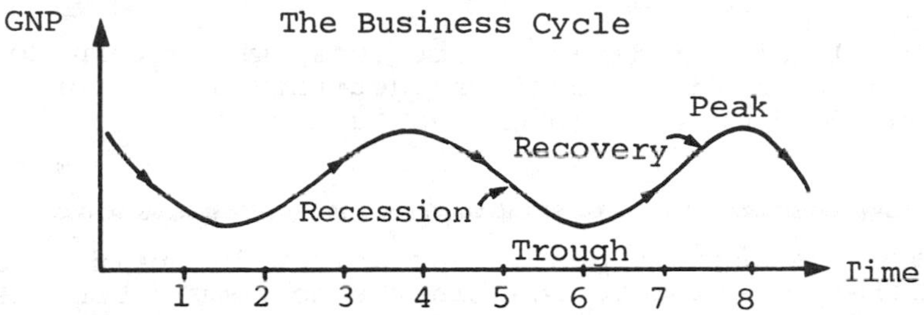

The initial capital stock will be deemed too high relative to expected sales, so the accelerator process will induce a further reduction in investment. Since tax receipts are falling, the government will face a budget deficit. If the government is committed to a balanced budget, it will cut government expenditures, thereby contributing to a further fall of GNP. If, on the other hand, the government is committed to a "full employment policy," it will try to increase expenditures to counteract the fall in GNP.

Because government expenditures cannot be reduced below a certain level, and because the actual capital stock will eventually reach the desired lower level, the downswing will come to a halt as business resumes replacement of its depreciated capital stock. This means an increase in investment.

Once investment starts to rise, it will have a multiplied effect on income. Income will start to rise and the economy enters the phase of the upswing.

Savings will rise with income; taxes will also rise; and investments will rise as described by the accelerator theory. Government spending is still a matter of policy. Since tax receipts are rising there will be strong political pressures to increase government expenditures, giving an extra upward impulse to total expenditure.

MEASUREMENT

• PROBLEM 9-3

What are leading, coincidental, and lagging indicators of economic activity?

Solution: When a statistical series has a pattern that conforms to the business cycle, but turns downward prior to the peak in business activity and upward prior to the trough, it is called a leading indicator. Examples of leading indicators are the rate of change in the (broadly defined) money supply (including time deposits) and the National Bureau of Economic Research's index of stock prices and the industrial material prices.

Coincidental indicators completely coincide in time to the business cycle. Their turning points, peaks and troughs coincide with the turning points in the business activity.

Finally, lagging indicators are those which turn downward after the peak in the business activity has occurred, and upward after the trough has been passed.

• PROBLEM 9-4

What are the basic types of variations in business activity, comprising the fluctuations in the economy? Use GNP as main indicator.

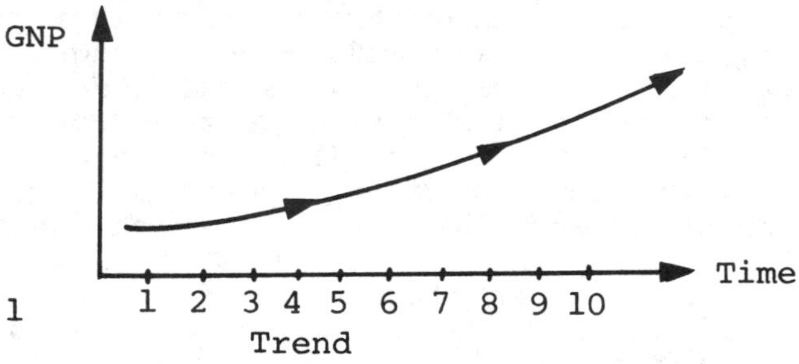

Fig. 1

Solution: There are four types of movements in business activity: trend, cyclical, seasonal and stochastic (or erratic) movements.

The trend movement refers to an extended period of time and indicates the long-range direction of the economy. Trends are analyzed in growth and development economics. (See Fig. 1.) For example, the trend growth may average 2% per year. The trend is related to population and productivity growth.

Business cycles are the most important movements from a macroeconomic viewpoint; they are the movements about which the government and the monetary authorities are concerned. Four phases may be discerned in the business cycle: the upswing, or expansion phase; the peak, or prosperity phase; the downswing, or contraction phase; and the trough, or recession phase. The expansion phase is also called the "boom," and the contraction phase--recession. (See Fig. 2.)

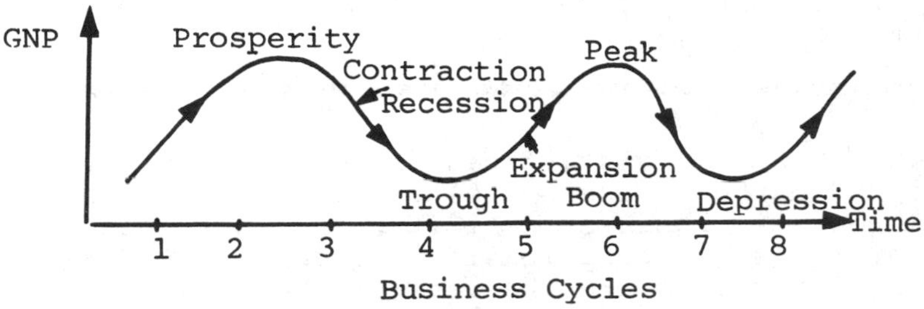

Recovery is associated with increases in demand, production, employment, prices, and income. Recession is associated with a decline in demand, and decreases in production, employment, prices, and income.

Seasonal movements are caused partly by nature; for example, agriculture and construction are affected by weather conditions. But they are also partly determined by man: for example, the sales-spree before Christmas. (See Fig. 3.) Economists try to make allowances for the

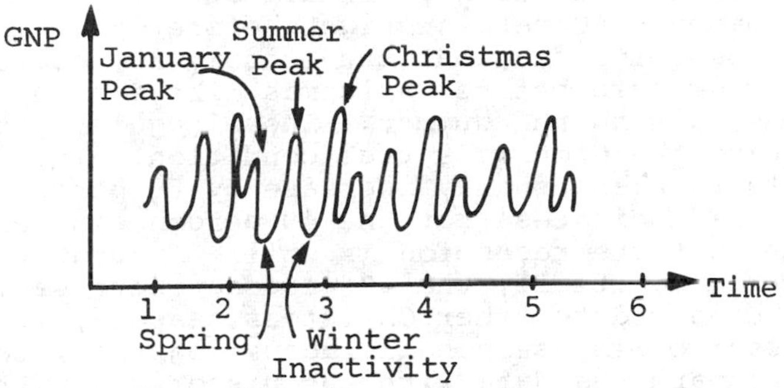

Fig. 3 SEASONAL MOVEMENTS

seasonal fluctuations in their macroeconomic data. Seasonal fluctuations are important for day-to-day, monthly and quarterly decision making. For example, the Federal Reserve has to decide when to create more money to accommodate the seasonal upsurge in buying activities. Government will allow for seasonal fluctuations when it evaluates the effects of its policy on, say, unemployment.

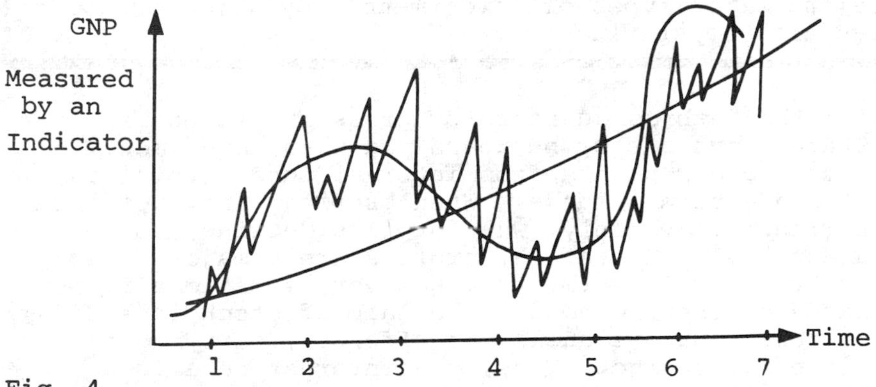

Fig. 4

When we add the trend, the business cycles and the seasonal fluctuations we get an impression of how GNP fluctuates over time in reality. (See Fig. 4.) In reality GNP fluctuates even more because of the erratic "shocks."

Stochastic movements, or "shocks," are unpredictable, like the oil-price-shock in 1973. The causes can be any unexpected event: an earthquake, a "black-out," a revolution, the outbreak of a war, the discovery of a spectacular improvement in the transport system, or a geological discovery (oil, gas).

• PROBLEM 9-5

Why do economists make seasonal adjustments in economic data before trying to isolate long-term trends?

Solution: Economists make seasonal adjustments in economic data because regular seasonal patterns can give a distorted picture of the actual economic situation. If the economy is in a recession, but sales at retail outlets (or consumer demand) increase by 40 percent right before Christmas, it still cannot be concluded that the economy is recovering. Retail sales increase before Christmas like suntan lotion sales increase during the summer. These regular patterns do not indicate the economy's true condition. If, for example, retail sales usually increase by 60 percent before Christmas, this indicates that the 40 percent increase is another sign that the recession is still plaguing the economy. Taken by itself, the 40 percent increase looks impressive; compared to other Christmas seasons, it is not so impressive. By seasonally adjusting the data, economists compare the data with the historical pattern, and not just with last month's figures, and so gain a more accurate picture of the actual trend.

ROLE OF INVESTMENT

• PROBLEM 9-6

What are the major types of investment? By which economic variables are they influenced?

Solution: About three-quarters of gross investment in the United States consists of business plant and equipment. Firms finance their plants from internal funds (retained earnings) and external funds. When profits rise, retained earnings rise. Conversely, when profits decline, so do retained earnings. Therefore, profits are a major determinant of business investments. However, sometimes firms borrow funds by issuing bonds (the sale of stock is a different process, but has analogous effects), carrying a certain interest charge. Thus, the interest rate is a major factor influencing investment.

There are also investments in inventories of goods in process, i.e. inventories of unfinished goods somewhere in the production "pipeline," and of finished goods. When these inventories increase there is a positive investment; when they decrease there is a negative investment (disinvestment). In a recession, inventories pile up, so inventory investment increases. However, this is considered to be involuntary investment. In a boom, inventories are run down.

The last type of investment is in residential construction. It is influenced by the average income levels. Because mortgage interest is a major cost, interest rates also play a substantial role in residential construction investment decisions.

• PROBLEM 9-7

Why is it that the fluctuations in private investment, I, are regarded as being the main cause (or potential cause) of fluctuations in economic activity?

Solution: When discussing the fluctuations in "economic activity" in measurable terms, the fluctuations in GNP, and so fluctuations in Y, National Income, are the main objects of examination. The level of income Y is determined by the equality of aggregate demand and aggregate supply:

$$C + I + G + (Ex - Im) = Y = C + S + T.$$

Or, subtracting consumption from both sides:

$$I + G + (Ex - Im) = S + T.$$

From this equality it follows that changes in the level of income Y are caused by changes in investments I, in government expenditures G, in exports Ex and imports Im, in savings S, or in taxes T. If the propensity to consume is constant, i.e. the consumption intentions of the society do not change over time, and the tax rates also remain constant, there will be no fluctuations in savings and taxes if income is stable.

For independent impulses we have to look at investments I, government expenditures, G, and exports, Ex, the so-called injections. Although government expenditures have been high since World War II, the factors of present interest are those that influence the level of economic activity independently of deliberate government policy, which often has a counterbalancing character. Changes in the amount of private investment then are likely to be the major cause of potential changes in economic activity.

Investment, more than any other type of expenditure, is subject to the uncertainties of the future. This is due to the fact that capital goods invested in today yield their output only sometime in the future. Thus capital owners must make guesses as to what the future pattern of demand for goods will be, and what line of production will be the most profitable. If they are wrong, they risk the loss of their capital. Hence, investment demand is closely related to the expectations and state of confidence of capital owners, and these forces may vary considerably from time to time.

• PROBLEM 9-8

Why are the industries producing capital goods and consumer durables typically hit hardest by a recession, insofar as production and employment are concerned?

Solution: The vulnerability of the industries producing housing and commercial buildings, heavy capital goods, farm implements, automobiles, refrigerators, gas ranges and similar products can be explained by the facts of postponability and of monopoly power. "Postponability" simply means that, within limits, the purchase of such durable goods is postponable. Hence, as the economy slips into a recession, producers delay the acquisition of modern productive facilities and the construction of new plants. As a result, investment in capital goods declines sharply. Also, consumers will defer the purchase of, for example, a new car, or a new color TV, until better times arrive.

But the purchase of the basic necessities, such as food, clothing, and fuel for heating, can not be postponed.

The effect of monopoly power on these industries is the second reason for their vulnerability. Most industries producing capital goods and consumer durables are industries of high concentration. This means that only a small number of firms dominate the market. These big firms "have sufficient monopoly power to resist lowering prices by restricting supply in the face of a declining demand." Thus a fall in the demand for capital goods and consumer durables will not have much impact on the prices, but will have on output, and thus on employment.

Nondurable goods industries, for example agriculture, food, and textile, are for the most part highly competitive, i.e. characterized by many firms. Price declines therefore can not be resisted. The impact of a declining demand falls to a greater extent upon prices than upon the levels of production and employment.

• PROBLEM 9-9

Which would you expect to fluctuate more over time, washing machine production or electric-power production? Why?

Solution: Electric-power production has shown a relatively stable rate of growth; recessions do not particularly affect this good (electric power). Washing machine sales, however, can be affected by recessions, sometimes severely, and this affects washing machine production.

This result is consistent with the general observation that durable and capital goods experience greater fluctuations in sales and production than do perishable and consumer goods. (Electricity is a perishable good; it cannot be stored on a wide scale. It is also consumed by households, though quite a bit of electricity consumption is by firms.) The reason why durable goods experience greater fluctuations is because in bad times, their purchase can be put off indefinitely. During prosperous times, everyone might decide to buy a washing machine at once, thus destroying the washing machine market for the next few years. The purchase of perishable goods, however, cannot be postponed. A consumer cannot put off the purchase of food, clothing or energy until the economy has recovered; he is forced to purchase these perishable goods near his usual levels of consumption.

This observation that the production of durable goods fluctuates because their purchase can be postponed, is good reason to believe that movements of durable goods represent fundamental causes of economic fluctuations.

• PROBLEM 9-10

How can business expectations affect the economy?

Solution: Business expectations can affect the economy by affecting the level of investment. If business leaders feel optimistic about the future, they will be more likely to invest. If they feel that an increase in demand is permanent, they will be more likely to increase output. Their decisions, based on their expectations, will then increase output, leading to a higher level of national income. Similarly, if business leaders are pessimistic about the future of the economy, they could stop investment and trigger a downswing.

Two aspects of business expectations are worth noting. The first aspect is that, to a certain extent, business expectations are self-fulfilling. If business leaders feel the economy is heading for a recession, whether it actually is or not, their actions (cutting investment) will tend to reduce output and push the economy into a recession. Subject to limits (such as government policy and consumer expectations), business expectations dictate the economic future.

The second aspect is that these expectations are not formed in a vacuum. In forming their opinions, business leaders do pay attention to consumer expectations, government policy, past economic performance, and many other factors. Because so many factors go into these opinions, they lose some of their independence and influence. A proposed change in government policy, for example, might dramatically change business expectations, and so change investment plans. It would be hard to conclude that business expectations were the determining factor in the consequent change in the economy; it would seem that business expectations were dependent on government policy. The expectations could even have been consciously manipulated by the government.

Because of these factors, some economists do not think that "business expectations" offers a basis for economic analysis. Until the formation of these expectations can be adequately explained, any explanation of the business cycle based on them will necessarily be vague and imprecise. Economists, however, do use surveys of business intentions to invest in formulating their forecasts of future economic activity.

THE ACCELERATOR

• PROBLEM 9-11

Explain briefly the "acceleration principle."

Solution: The acceleration principle asserts a direct relationship between changes in sales and net business investment. If sales are steady, business will see no need for additions to their productive capacity, i.e., net investment. So, the only business investment will be replacement investment to offset depreciation. This investment can be assumed to be fairly steady. If sales rise rapidly, however, say by 50 percent, net business investment will increase even more rapidly. Instead of replacing machines at, say, 10 percent a year, business now not only replaces 10 percent, but also increases capacity by 50 percent. This means gross business investment has increased over its old level by a multiple of 6 (10 percent of machines, at the old level, as compared to 10 percent + 50 percent = 60 percent of machines, at the new level). If for some reason sales stop rising, investment will return to its former level of 10 percent per year. (Note that for the first few years, at least, this 10 percent is 10 percent of the old capital stock because it will be a while before the newly acquired machines will have to be replaced.)

As an example, suppose a firm must have \$2 of capital equipment to produce \$1 of output per year. This means that for yearly sales of \$30 million, the firm needs to have a capital stock of \$60 million. If the \$30 million sales figure has been steady for a few years, the firm will have built up its capital stock to the \$60 million level and will need only to offset depreciation. If the firm's capital stock consists of 20 machines of different ages, with one wearing out each year, depreciation costs will be \$3 million per year, a figure arrived at by dividing the \$60 million of capital stock by the number of machines which comprise that capital stock, 20 in this case. \$60 million ÷ 20 = \$3 million, or the cost of one machine which is replaced each year. This means that the firm's gross investment is \$3 million per year while its net investment is zero. Table 1 shows the stable investment over the years as sales remain stable.

Year	Sales	Capital Stock	Net Investment	Gross Investment
1972	\$30	\$60	\$0	1 machine at \$3 = \$3
1973	30	60	0	1 machine at \$3 = \$3
1974	30	60	0	1 machine at \$3 = \$3

Table 1 (all figures in millions)

However, if sales increase by 50 percent (to $45 million) in 1975, investment will increase at a higher rate. With sales of $45 million, the firm must increase its capital stock to $90 million. This requires a net investment of $30 million ($90 million - $60 million = $30 million). This will increase the number of machines by 10, increasing the firm's output capacity by 50 percent (the same increase as sales).

Year	Sales	Capital Stock	Net Investment	Gross Investment
1975	$45	$90	$30	(10+1)machines at $3 = $33
1976	60	120	30	(10+1)machines at $3 = $33
1977	75	150	30	(10+1)machines at $3 = $33

Table 2 (all figures in millions)

In calculating gross investment, it must be remembered that the firm will still have to replace one aging machine a year. This gives us a gross investment of 11 machines, or $33 million. An increase in sales of 50 percent in this case increases gross investment by a multiple of 11. Notice in Table 2 that if sales continue to increase by $15 million dollars per year, gross investment will hold steady at $33 million per year.

If sales stop increasing, and hold steady, a different picture emerges. Instead of investment remaining steady, net investment will drop to zero. Without any increase in sales, there is no need to expand capacity. See Table 3.

Year	Sales	Capital Stock	Net Investment	Gross Investment
1972	$30	$60	$0	1 machine at $3 = $3
1973	30	60	0	1 machine at $3 = $3
1974	30	60	0	1 machine at $3 = $3
1975	45	90	30	(10+1)machines at $3 = $33
1976	60	120	30	(10+1)machines at $3 = $33
1977	75	150	30	(10+1)machines at $3 = $33
1978	75	150	0	1 machine at $3 = $3
1979	75	150	0	1 machine at $3 = $3

Table 3 (all figures in millions)

The importance of the acceleration principle is that it shows that investment fluctuates much more than sales fluctuate. Minor changes in sales can trigger larger changes in investment. This is because the level of gross investment depends on the level of sales, but the level of net investment depends on changes in the level of sales.

• PROBLEM 9-12

What is meant when it is said that "the accelerator is asymmetric"?

Solution: When the stock of capital that is required to

produce a certain level of output is greater than the stock of capital available, the additional capital is provided by investment. If Y_t is the level of output in period t, then the level of capital required is $K_t = aY_t$, where a is the fixed capital/output ratio. K_{t-1} is the level of capital available at the beginning of period t, which corresponds to the level of output in the preceding period t-1. Then $K_{t-1} = aY_{t-1}$, and the additional capital, which is to be provided by investment, is $K_t - K_{t-1} = I_t = aY_t - aY_{t-1} = a(Y_t - Y_{t-1})$; or, $I_t = a\Delta Y$. This is the simple accelerator statement: investment per period is proportional to the change in output per period.

However, when the required capital K_t is less than the capital available K_{t-1}, i.e., $K_t - K_{t-1}$ is negative, then no quick disinvestment process exists. There is no reverse process by which the excess capital $K_{t-1} - K_t$ can be converted back into resources except for the running down of inventories of consumer goods or intermediate goods. Thus, "the accelerator is asymmetric"; that is, the acceleration principle applies only when the required capital for a certain level of output is greater than the available capital. The acceleration principle does not apply in the reverse situation, where required capital is less than available capital.

In the real economy, though, eventually the capital stock can decline gradually in the case of available capital exceeding required capital, because capital goods wear out or become obsolete, and so need replacement. By not replacing depreciated capital stock, or part of it, the capital stock can be reduced, but only at the rate of depreciation.

• PROBLEM 9-13

How does the acceleration principle affect the business cycle?

Solution: The acceleration principle can be a powerful factor in the instabilities of the business cycle. The increase in investment stimulated by an increase in demand can, through the effects of the multiplier, dramatically increase economic growth. So, minor increases in demand can stimulate the economy powerfully through the interactions of the multiplier and the "accelerator" (new investment).

The economy, however, can not expand forever. Eventually the full-employment level of income and output will be reached. Once this level is reached, the accelerator will then force the economy away from full-employment; the economy will not be able to maintain a steady full-employment output. This is because once demand stops increasing, net investment will fall to zero. This drop in investment will reduce output, and will lead to further decreases in income and output due to multiplier effects. When the demand for goods drops, the acceleration principle works in reverse; firms will try to get rid of the machinery that they no longer need. They will not only refuse to replace obsolete, worn-out equipment, they will even try to get rid of machinery faster than depreciation would allow for. This is because part of the stock of machinery will be superfluous, and place an extra burden in depreciation and maintenance expenses on the earning capacity of the firms, which are confronted with a reduction in sales revenues. The overall effect is that once the economy reaches full employment and demand stops growing, the accelerator and the multiplier will combine to immediately propel the economy into a recession. The negative gross investment of firms will, through the multiplier, feed upon itself and further reduce demand, which in turn will cause firms to try to "disinvest" even more (as happened during the Depression).

The economy will eventually bottom out because firms cannot disinvest all their capital. Though they can run down inventories (a form of negative investment), they cannot reconvert machines back into resources. The depreciation rate places a limit on the rate of disinvestment. As disinvestment slows down, the drops in demand will become smaller and smaller. At some point, firms will have the level of capital stock needed for the low level of income. So, disinvestment will stop. Another increase in demand will occur, and the next business cycle will start.

The acceleration principle, then, is one explanation of the instability in the capitalist economy. It can exaggerate and intensify any fluctuations in the economy caused by other factors.

• PROBLEM 9-14

Explain the business cycle with the help of the accelerator and multiplier principles. Assume that the labor force and labor productivity experience trend growth at a constant rate.

Solution: Assume that the requested analysis begins with a depression. The government will inject extra government expenditures into the economy, and via the multiplier this injection will have an amplified effect on national income. The rising income, and the consequent expansion of purchasing power will induce increases in consumption and business sales. Firms, confronted with this increase in sales, and hence higher profits, will be motivated to expand their producing facilities. The increase in the demand for capital, whether inventory or equipment, will trigger an increase in investment, due to the accelerator effect. The increase in investment will increase incomes in the capital goods industries, and will contribute to the rise in total income even further via the multiplier.

If the labor force grows at a constant rate, and the productivity per worker does also, then the trend growth of potential output also will be limited to a constant rate of growth, the so-called "natural rate of growth," given by the sum of the rates of growth of the labor force and of its productivity.

Say that the labor force grows by 2% per year and the labor productivity by 2%. Then the potential output can only increase by 2 + 2 = 4%. The interaction of the accelerator and multiplier described above produces a cyclical upswing in aggregate income from its depression level towards its potential full employment level. The actual rate of expansion of national income exceeds the trend potential rate of growth of output, 4%, since it includes the trend rate of growth of potential income and output (4%) cyclical expansion due to the multiplier-accelerator process. As unemployment is eliminated, the economic system will reach its full-employment output capacity. Output from then on will be able to grow only as fast as the potential rate of growth of output, 4%, which is lower than the rate of growth during the upswing of the depression. The reduction in the growth rate which must occur as full employment is reached in the upswing has further consequences. According to the acceleration principle, consumption must continue to increase at the same rate as it did during the upswing, in order for investment to continue at the rate at which it proceeded during the upswing. But when the rate of growth in income and hence consumption decreases, investment will drop because business will not want so much additional equipment. The drop in investment will have amplified reduction effects, via the multiplier, on total national income. The economic system will move into a recession, as the interaction of the accelerator and multiplier send the system on a downward course. When the output decreases rapidly, the acceleration principle posits a disinvestment in capital stock. The rate of disinvestment determines a floor below which national income can not fall. When eventually the capital stock is reduced to the level corresponding to the lower income and consumption levels, the acceleration principle posits a termination of disinvestment. The economy will have reached its trough and will move into an upswing again, from a depression into a recovery. And the cycle may start anew.

• PROBLEM 9-15

Suppose that the amount that people consume is equal to 80% of their disposable income of the preceding year, and autonomous consumption is $200 billion. Net investment equals the addition to the capital stock of the preceding period. The capital stock in any year is always equal to 2.5 times the level of the same year's consumption. What is the equilibrium income in the economy? How would the economy behave if it is confronted by a sudden drop in aggregate income of $50 billion?

<u>Solution</u>: First construct the multiplier model; second,

the accelerator model; and finally the combined accelerator-multiplier model which will be used to calculate equilibrium income, and the consequences of the exogenous "shock" of the drop in national income.

Autonomous consumption $\bar{C}$ = 200 (leaving out the dollar signs, and the billions), and people consume in addition 80% of their preceding year's income. Thus the consumption function can be represented by

$$C_t = 0.80\ Y_{t-1} + 200 \tag{1}$$

where subscripts t and t-1 indicate year t and year t-1 (the preceding year). The income identity states that income equals the sum of consumption and investment:

$$Y_t = C_t + I_t \tag{2}$$

Substituting equation (1) into equation (2) yields

$$Y_t = 0.80\ Y_{t-1} + 200 + I_t \tag{3}$$

This represents the multiplier model of income determination.

As regards the accelerator-model, first, net investment equals the addition to the capital stock of the preceding period, so

$$I_t = K_t - K_{t-1}\ . \tag{4}$$

Second, the capital stock is 2.5 times the consumption sales:

$$K_t = 2.5\ C_t \tag{5}$$

Substituting equation (5) into equation (4) gives the accelerator relationship between investments and the increase in consumption sales:

$$I_t = 2.5\ C_t - 2.5\ C_{t-1} = 2.5\ (C_t - C_{t-1}) \tag{6}$$

Substituting the consumption function (equation 1) into equation (6) gives

$$\begin{aligned} I_t &= 2.5\ [(0.80\ Y_{t-1} + 200) - (0.80\ Y_{t-2} + 200)] \\ &= 2.5\ (0.80)\ [Y_{t-1} - Y_{t-2}] \\ &= 2\ (Y_{t-1} - Y_{t-2}) \end{aligned} \tag{7}$$

This is the accelerator model.

Now combine both models. Substitute the accelerator model, equation (7) into the multiplier equation, equation (3). This gives

$$Y_t = 0.80\ Y_{t-1} + 200 + [2(Y_{t-1} - Y_{t-2})]$$
$$= 2.8\ Y_{t-1} - 2.0\ Y_{t-2} + 200 \qquad (8)$$

This is the combined accelerator-multiplier model of the economy. Equilibrium prevails when the income in the present period is equal to the income of the preceding period; thus when $Y_t = Y_{t-1} = Y_{t-2} = \overline{Y}$, a constant. When this unknown equilibrium condition is imposed onto equation (7), equilibrium $\overline{Y}$ can be determined:

$$\overline{Y} = 2.80\ \overline{Y} - 2.00\ \overline{Y} + 200 = .80\ \overline{Y} + 200$$

Collecting all terms gives

$$0.20\ \overline{Y} = 200.$$

Thus, the equilibrium income level is

$$\overline{Y} = \frac{200}{0.20} = 1000.$$

Now use the combined accelerator-multiplier model to calculate its behavior when the economy is confronted by a sudden drop in income of \$50 billion. Suppose the economy is initially in equilibrium, so $Y_0 = 1000$. When the shock occurs, $Y_1 = 1000 - 50 = 950$. With the help of equation (8) we calculate the income level for period 2:

$$Y_2 = 2.80\ Y_1 - 2.00\ Y_0 + 200$$
$$= 2.80 \times 950 - 2.00 \times 1000 + 200$$
$$= 2660 - 2000 + 200 = 860$$

a very drastic drop in national income. In the third period,

$$Y_3 = 2.80\ Y_2 - 2.00\ Y_1 + 200$$
$$= 2.80 \times 860 - 2.00 \times 950 + 200$$
$$= 2408 - 1900 + 200 = 708.$$

Using this procedure, the values of national income over several years have been calculated, as shown in the table, to show the force of the combined effect of the accelerator and consumption interaction.

year	0	1	2	3	4	5
Y_t	1000	950	860	708	462	78

The drop of \$50 billion in the first period plunges the economy into an ever worsening recession.

ALTERNATIVE THEORIES

• PROBLEM 9-16

What is the major difference between external and internal theories of the business cycle? What is the modern view of the two types of theories?

Solution: An external theory of the business cycle looks for a basis of economic fluctuations outside of the economic system. These theories point to wars, revolutions, rates of population growth and migrations, scientific discoveries and technological innovations as possible reasons for economic instability.

Internal theories of the business cycle look for mechanisms within the economic system which give rise to regular, self-generating fluctuations. In these theories, something inherent in the system will give rise to expansion, which will cause recession, which will lead to another expansion. Here, cyclical instability is built into the system.

The major difference between these types of theories, then, is implicit in their names. One theory looks for causes of the business cycle within the organization of the economy, while the other looks for causes in outside jolts to the system.

The mainstream view today combines the two different types of theories. Most economists believe that any purely external theory ignores the internal reactions of the economy to external stimuli. Even an outside factor, technological innovation for example, will be dependent to a large extent on the internal workings of the system. If an innovation is introduced which leads to the birth of an industry, the multiplier effect will increase total output beyond the level indicated by a simple addition of a new industry's output. In addition to this, the growth stimulated by the new industry could lead firms to take a more optimistic view of the economy. As a result, investment increases, which further stimulates output. A purely external theory ignores how the economic mechanism reacts internally to exogenous changes.

Purely internal theories have a different defect. Most economists place a crucial emphasis on the role of investment in explaining fluctuations. A cursory examination of the interaction between wars, political instability or technological innovation, and investment will show that external factors are probably the main cause of investment fluctuations. Ignoring these external factors will cripple any explanation of the business cycles.

So, economists today rely on theories which combine two types of theories. In short, they see business cycles as the result of the interplay between external stimuli, and the internal reactions to those stimuli.

• PROBLEM 9-17

Explain the monetary theory of the business cycle.

Solution: The monetary theory holds that the supply of money is the prime determinant of business activity. In a very simplified form, the mechanism of the monetary theory is based on the relations between interest rate, money supply, and investment. When the economy is in a recession, banks have plenty of money available and interest rates are low. The low interest rates and the ease in getting loans encourage businessmen to borrow and to expand operations. This leads to a general expansion. As more and more businessmen react to the expansion and invest, the availability of money declines and the interest rate rises. As a result, investment drops. In this view, the economy's expansion inevitably leads to a contraction. As investment decreases, and as output decreases even further because of multiplier effects, the interest rate will fall and the availability of money will increase. So, with each contraction, the stage is set for a further expansion. This theory, an internal theory of the business cycle, concerns itself completely with the self-regulated fluctuations of the economy.

• PROBLEM 9-18

Discuss Schumpeter's innovation theory of the business cycle.

Solution: Schumpeter theorized that innovations (new ideas and processes, like assembly-line production, computers and supermarket shopping) are introduced in clusters. A few daring innovators will put money into developing them and introduce them into the economy. If accepted, these innovations will induce a wave of investments, stimulating output and income. Other entrepreneurs, less willing to take risks, will imitate the innovators and rush into the marketplace with variations of the original idea. Eventually, however, this wave of innovation and imitation will run its course. Investment will dry up and the economy will head for contraction and recession, until the next cluster of innovations is introduced. This is primarily an external theory of the business cycle, because the driving impetus of the business cycle in this particular model, namely, the introduction of innovations into the production process, is thought to operate independently from the economic activity.

• PROBLEM 9-19

What is Kalecki's theory of political business cycles in economics?

Solution: Michael Kalecki, a Polish econometrician,

formulated a political theory of the business cycle that comes close to the view of the "accelerationists," who state that the long-run effect of a Keynesian "full employment" policy of the government is an acceleration in the rise of the general price level.

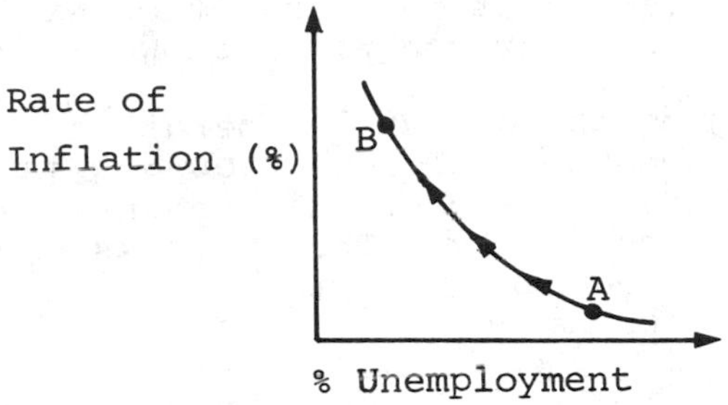

Fig. 1
Short-Run Phillips Curve

Kalecki stated that if government succeeds with its aggregate demand management in approaching full employment, it will also induce a "cost-push inflation"--in which wage rates rise and push up prices. A possible explanation for this effect may be that in order to reduce unemployment, inflation will necessarily be induced, when the government moves along the short-term Phillips-curve. (See Figure 1.)

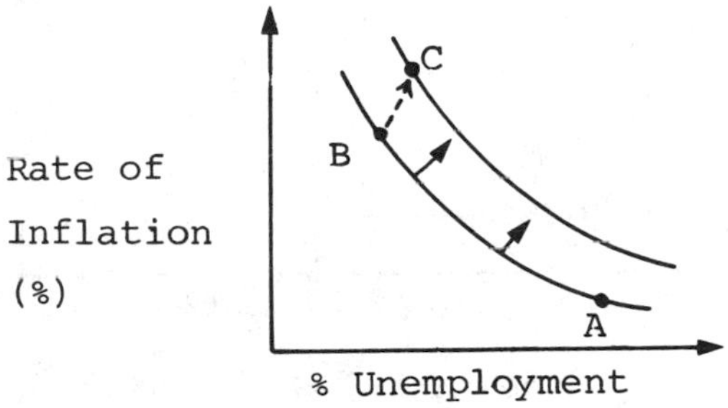

Fig. 2
Cost Push Inflation

Workers find their real wages to be reduced and bargain for higher money wages; the wage rates rise and employers, confronted with squeezed profits, push prices upward. (See Figure 2.) The Phillips curve is pushed upward, and the trade-off between inflation and unemployment worsens.

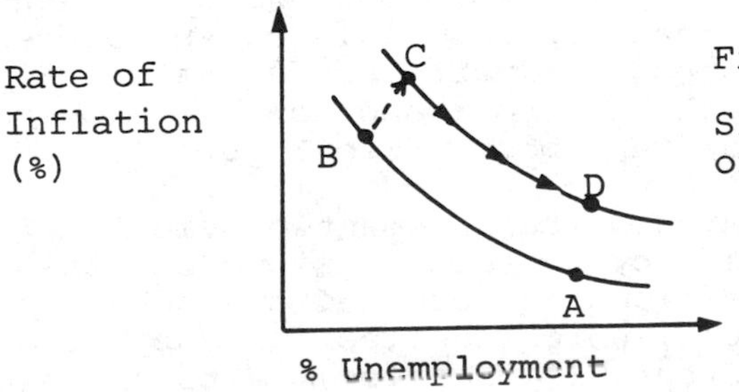

Fig. 3
Slowdown of Economy

The government, wanting to check this extra amount of cost-push inflation, will deliberately engineer a stagnation and slowdown of the economy, creating more unemployment. (See Figure 3.) The ultimate effect is that inflation is increased for all levels of unemployment, including the original level.

But a democracy, such as the USA, will find the higher rates of unemployment unacceptable, and government will be politically forced to try to reach full employment again. However; the resulting cost-push inflation will lead government inevitably to another contrived slowdown.

The mixed economy of the USA will generate a political, activistic, governmental cycle of "stop-go" in the economy, because of the fundamental contradiction between full employment and price stability. The business cycle is therefore an unavoidable companion of the mixed capitalist economy, according to Kalecki.

• PROBLEM 9-20

Explain the "echo waves of replacement" theory of the business cycle. Is it an internal ("endogenous") or external ("exogenous") theory? What weakness(es) does it have?

Fig. 1

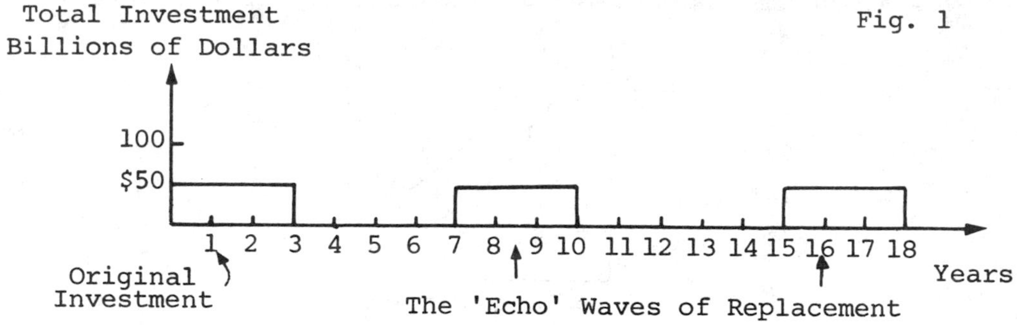

Solution: Suppose that machinery, and other durable goods wear out (or become obsolete) and have to be replaced every 8 years. Suppose further that during an initial 3 year period there is a build-up of the stock of capital at an annual rate of $50 million, as shown in Table 1. These machines will be used in the following 5 years without becoming completely worn out and hence none needs to be replaced in that period. This causes depressed demand in the capital goods industries. But after 8 years the capital equipment wears out and needs replacement, giving rise to an investment boom. See Figure 1.

These "echo" waves of replacement provide the basis of an internal business cycle theory, since it attempts to explain economic fluctuations in terms of the behavior of a factor, namely investment, which is itself a subject of economic theorizing. "External" theories try to explain economic fluctuations as consequences of phenomena that are outside the scope of economic theory, e.g., sunspots.

The weakness of the theory is its assumptions that (a) the initial investments are made simultaneously and (b) all different types of capital goods have the same life-span, and therefore will all need to be replaced at the same time. In actuality there are numerous types of capital goods with widely varying economic life-spans, so that capital goods are continually being replaced.

Table 1

year	net investment	replacement investment	total investment
1	+50	0	+50
2	+50	0	+50
3	+50	0	+50
4	0	0	0
5	0	0	0
6	0	0	0
7	0	0	0
8	0	+50	+50
9	0	+50	+50
10	0	+50	+50
11	0	0	0
12	0	0	0
13	0	0	0
14	0	0	0
15	0	0	0
16	0	+50	+50
17	0	+50	+50
18	0	+50	+50
19	0	0	0

SHORT ANSWER QUESTIONS FOR REVIEW

Answer
To be covered when testing yourself

Choose the correct answer.

1. Which of the following is not a phase of the business cycle? (a) recession (b) expansion (c) inflection (d) peak (e) trough — c

2. The secular trend refers to: (a) fluctuations in business activity which average 40 months in duration (b) fluctuations in business activity which occur around Christmas, Easter, and so forth (c) fluctuations in business activity which average 8 or 9 years in duration (d) the long-run increase in the relative importance of durable goods in the American economy (e) the long-term expansion or contraction of business activity which occurs over 50 or 100 years — e

3. What component of total spending changes by the greatest percentage during the typical business cycle? (a) local government spending (b) consumer spending on goods and services (c) business spending on wages and salaries (d) business spending on capital goods (e) state government spending — d

4. What was the basic cause of prosperity in the early forties? (a) rapid expansion and growth in the automobile industry (b) a high level of government spending on war goods (c) the rapid expansion of foreign trade as trade barriers were lowered (d) none of the above — b

5. In forecasting the economic future, models: (a) build up consistent estimates of spending based upon past patterns (b) redefine the cycle so that stagnant growth is called recession (c) derive as output from "black boxes" estimates of the money supply (d) continue to be more artistic than scientific (e) even when carefully constructed, perform much less satisfactorily than the forecasts of the most experienced economists — a

6. A good example of an "internal" theory of the business cycle is: (a) random-walk shocks (b) multiplier-accelerator process (c) multiplier reactions of income to innovational waves (d) none of the above — b

7. Which of the following is least likely to be hurt by moderate inflation? (a) a disabled laborer who is living off accumulated savings (b) a pensioned steelworker (c) a stenographer (d) a small businessman (e) none of the above — d

SHORT ANSWER QUESTIONS FOR REVIEW

Answer

To be covered when testing yourself

8. The replacement-wave theory of business cycles rests on the assumption that (a) invention of new machinery will result in a surge of new orders from buyers interested in reducing their costs (b) a rise in consumption spending will prompt many firms to replace their equipment at about the same time (c) a large amount of newly installed machinery will require replacement at about the same time (d) when retail-store inventories fall below a critical level in depressions, orders to replace those inventories will result in a revival of business (e) none of the above — c

9. Most of the causes of cyclical instability are: (a) exogenous (b) endogenous (c) political (d) due to changes in the rate of growth of the money supply (e) clearly attributable to none of the above — e

10. The factor most responsible for fluctuations in the level of national income is: (a) fluctuations in the volume of transfer payments (b) consumer demand (c) the demand for imports (d) investment demand (e) the procyclical character of the tax structure — d

11. If we study the statistics of production over past business cycles, the greatest relative fluctuations will be found in: (a) consumption goods, because of the multiplier effects of consumption respending (b) government-purchased goods, because of the efforts of government to stem the business cycle (c) durable or capital goods, because of the variability of investment spending and postponability (d) any of the above, fluctuations being typically about the same in all kinds of production (e) none of the above, cyclical movements being typically movements of prices rather than production — c

12. The major factor underlying the prosperity of the twenties was: (a) the market decline in the relative importance of consumer durables which occurred after 1922 (b) the strong inflationary pressures which stimulated speculative spending on inventories (c) the remarkably constant level of productivity which labor achieved (d) the high level of investment spending stimulated by the rise of a number of new industries — d

13. In the past half-century, it is unlikely that an

SHORT ANSWER QUESTIONS FOR REVIEW

Answer
To be covered when testing yourself

important source of the business cycle can be attributed to: (a) variations in government defense expenditures (b) an uptrend in the per cent of income saved by individuals (c) fluctuations in inventory investment (d) pervading swings in residential construction — b

14. The immediate determinant of the volume of output and employment is: (a) the level of wholesale prices (b) the composition of consumer spending (c) the size of the labor force (d) the level of total spending (e) the ratio of social goods to private goods production — d

15. According to Kalecki's views of business cycles: (a) governments deliberately expand and contract activity because of the dilemma between unemployment and inflation (b) business cycles occur at about the same time in all countries (c) business activity grows less than the growth rate of a fully employed economy (d) cost-push inflation is corrected by appropriate monetary policies (e) any or all of the above are true — a

16. Which of the following is not a characteristic of an economic boom? (a) wage increases. (b) high level of employment. (c) decrease in the interest rates. (d) high profits. — c

Fill in the blanks.

17. During the course of typical business fluctuations, there is more variation in ______________ production than in nondurable-goods production. — durable-goods

18. The United States' economy is generally considered to be at ______________ when 4 percent of the labor force is unemployed. — full employment

19. The ______________ principle says that in order for the demand for investment goods to keep increasing, the demand for consumer goods must increase more and more. — accelera-tion

20. The basic factor underlying the 1955-1957 boom was business and consumer spending on __________ goods. — durable

21. ______________ expenditures have been the least subject to fluctuations over the 1929-1973 period. — consumer services

22. In the late 1950's, the U.S. economy rather per-

SHORT ANSWER QUESTIONS FOR REVIEW

Answer
To be covered when testing yourself

sistently faced a problem of above-normal ______ ________. — unemployment

23. In forecasting the economic future, models build up consistent estimates of spending based upon ______________ patterns. — past

24. As contrasted with the 1949 and 1954 recessions, the 1958 recession was accompanied by some ______________. — inflation

25. An interacting accelerator and multiplier are a ______________ that generates business cycles. — model

26. By far, the majority of all commodities produced through specialization of labor are produced by ______________. — businesses

27. By a ______________ cycle, we mean one in which the government itself is the source of cyclical instability. — political

28. The ______________ theory of the business cycle is called an external theory because the inner mechanisms of the economy do not affect sunspots. — sunspots

29. It is not necessarily a violation of the acceleration principle if investment decreases while ______________ increases. — consumption

30. During the Great Depression, prices fell by relatively more in the agricultural commodities industry than in the agricultural ______________ industry. — implements

31. Inflation benefits ______________ at the expense of creditors. — debtors

<u>Determine whether the following statements are true or false.</u>

32. The peak of a business cycle is readily recognizable because, by definition, a period of full employment has been reached. — False

33. Generally speaking, output and employment are more variable over the business cycle in "low concentration" industries than they are in "high concentration" industries. — False

34. The major pre-World War II cycle, on the existence of which economists are generally agreed,

SHORT ANSWER QUESTIONS FOR REVIEW

	Answer To be covered when testing yourself
is approximately 8 to 10 years in length.	True
35. Recent recessions have not been severe because economists and statisticians have been able to predict their occurrence and intensity with great accuracy.	False
36. Two main corrections necessary if one is to use statistics to measure business cycles are the (a) seasonal and (b) long-term or secular trend.	True
37. The production of durable goods is more stable than the production of nondurables over the business cycle.	False
38. We speak of recession as soon as activity grows less than the growth rate of the economy at full employment.	True
39. A good example of a leading indicator would be new orders.	True
40. The "trough" of the business cycle comes when economic magnitudes are falling fastest.	False
41. If the government uses its fiscal and monetary policies wisely, it can nonetheless be an originating source of cyclical instability.	False
42. Business cycles in European countries have tended to be less extreme than they have in the United States.	True
43. Replacement waves refer to a bunching up of new orders for capital goods.	True
44. The 17-to-18 year business cycle is sometimes referred to as the "long-wave."	False
45. A recession has started only when business activity has declined absolutely.	False
46. If consumer spending rises and then levels off and becomes constant, then according to the acceleration principle, net investment spending will fall to zero.	True

CHAPTER 10

INFLATION AND UNEMPLOYMENT

Basic Attacks and Strategies for Solving Problems in this Chapter. See pages 324 to 376 for step-by-step solutions to problems.

Inflation can be defined as an increase in the general price level. Inflation should not be confused with increases in the prices of individual goods. In an economy where tastes and technology are constantly changing, we should expect prices of some goods to rise while others fall. Inflation can only be said to exist if the average level of all prices rises.

An alternative but equivalent definition of inflation is a fall in the purchasing power of the dollar. The purchasing power of the dollar is a measure of the quantity of goods and services a dollar could buy. If prices rise, the dollar cannot buy as much, leading to the definition.

Deflation is a fall in the general price level or an increase in the value of the dollar.

Stagflation is defined as a period when both inflation and unemployment are high.

The three most widely-used measures of inflation are:

1) the GNP Deflator (discussed in Chapter 4)
2) the Consumer Price Index (or Cost of Living Index)
3) the Producer Price Index (or Wholesale Price Index)

The theory behind the construction of both the CPI and PPI is similar and fairly straightforward. In both cases, a "market basket" of goods is constructed. In the case of the CPI, the market basket consists of the goods and services the typical consumer buys each month. In the case of the PPI, the market basket consists of intermediate goods at the wholesale level. Then period after period, the cost of both market baskets is computed, using the prices prevailing during each period.

For example, in year 0 the price of the CPI market basket is found by multiplying each item in the basket by its year 0 price.

$$\sum P_i^0 Q_i^0$$

Year 1 prices are used to compute the cost of the market basket in year 1.

$$\sum P_i^1 Q_i^1$$

The percentage change in the cost of the market basket between the two years is the change in the cost of living.

Typically, index numbers are used to express the cost of the market baskets. A base year is arbitrarily chosen and given an index value of 100. The index for the other year is simply scaled up or down by the change in the cost of living. If the cost of living was 5% higher in the other year, its index value would be 105. Assume year 0 is chosen as the base year, the index value for year 1 (X) is determined by solving the following ratio problem:

$$\frac{X}{100} = \frac{\sum P_i^1 Q_i^1}{\sum P_i^0 Q_i^0} \text{ where } X = \frac{\sum P_i^1 Q_i^1}{\sum P_i^0 Q_i^0} * 100$$

Index numbers are used to deflate nominal into real values, or, in other words, to compute the purchasing power of a nominal value. If Y_i is the nominal value of something in year i, and CPI_i is the price index that year, then the real value of Y (R_i) is given by:

$$R_i = \frac{Y_i}{CPI_i} * 100$$

For example, median family income in the United States in nominal terms was $3,031.00 in 1947 and $30,853.00 in 1987. Did family living standards rise 10 times over the 40-year period? Using 1982-84 as the base year, the consumer price index was 22.3 in 1947 and 113.6 in 1987. Prices, therefore, rose 5 times. To compare incomes we need to compute their real equivalent, or, in other words, compute the purchasing power of the income in both years. The formulas are as follows:

$$1947\text{:} \quad \frac{\$3{,}031.00}{22.3} * 100 = \$13{,}591.00$$

$$1987\text{:} \quad \frac{\$30{,}853.00}{113.6} * 100 = \$27{,}1591.00$$

Real median family income has actually doubled over the 40-year period.

Is inflation a good or bad thing? An unambiguous answer cannot be given. On the basis of business cycle history, it is the case that inflation problems have been more common during periods of prosperity than periods of recession. Nonetheless, there are some very real problems associated with inflation even in the best of times. For one thing, some people's incomes are relatively fixed in the sense that they do not keep pace with prices. These people lose purchasing power and end up worse off through no real fault of their own. Of course, a rise in prices increases the value of goods and services produced and incomes equally. So if some people fall behind it means others must enjoy incomes rising at a rate faster than prices.

Inflation will exact a toll on wealth whose value is relatively fixed in nominal terms. Money balances decrease in purchasing power during a time of inflation. It is well-known that interest rates tend to rise during periods of inflation. This is likely related to the effect that inflation can have on wealth. Lenders will attempt to protect the real value of the wealth they lend by adding the expected rate of inflation to the rate of interest they charge. Unfortunately, the prediction of inflation rates is hazardous.

An important distinction is between the nominal and real interest rates. The nominal rate is the rate actually charged. For example, assume a nominal rate of 10% is charged on a one-year loan of $1,000.00. On the due date, $1,100.00 would be repaid ($1,000 principal plus $100.00 interest). This amount has a purchasing power $1,100.00/$1,000.00 = 10% more than the amount originally lent. The real rate of interest is the rate charged in terms of purchasing power. Assume there was 5% inflation during the year. On the due date, $1,100.00 would be repaid, but the money has a purchasing power of approximately $1,050.00. (If the CPI is 100 at the beginning of the year, it will be 105 at the end. Deflating the amount repaid as explained above will give the purchasing power of the money repaid, which is $1,050.00/$1,000.00 = 5% more than the amount originally lent.) The real rate of interest is approximately 5%. If we subtract the rate of inflation from the nominal interest rate, we get an approximation of the real rate. A 10% nominal rate is only a 5% real rate if there has been 5% inflation. During periods of inflation, lenders determine the nominal rate of interest they charge by adding the expected rate of inflation to the real rate they wish to receive.

Inflation exacts a cost in terms of economic efficiency. There are numerous ways this can take place. Probably the most general statement of the problem is that during a period of inflation, the future is made to appear more uncertain. Consequently, people will devote more resources to current consumption and less to investment, reducing the economy's ability to grow.

Inflation can be categorized by type. This categorization is useful because it provides a guide to the proper anti-inflation policy. One type of inflation is demand-pull. In demand-pull inflation, aggregate demand exceeds the economy's ability to produce goods and services, causing prices to be "pulled up." Excessive demand can be the result of overly-stimulative fiscal or monetary policies, investment or export booms, or consumption binges. The description of the problem suggests the solution. If the problem is too much demand, the solution is to reduce demand. Restrictive monetary or fiscal policy will usually be called for.

Another type is cost-push inflation. Cost-push occurs when factors on the supply-side of the economy increase costs of production, forcing firms to pass the increased costs on to consumers in the form of higher prices. There are several variants of the cost-push model, each suggesting a different sector of the economy as the "culprit." Wage-push models suggest that irresponsible wage demands, particularly on the part of unions, cause the cost increases that are passed on to consumers. Profit-push models spotlight greedy big business's grab for higher profits. Supply-shock models start with resource scarcity that pushes up costs, necessitating price increases.

As in the case of demand-pull inflation, the description of the problem suggests the solution, although the solution is not always painless. Wage- or profit-push situations suggest either labor or business is too powerful and consequently government may have to step in to curb their power. Wage and Price controls is a commonly advocated policy to reduce cost-push inflation. Wage and Price controls are government laws which limit how much wages and prices are permitted to rise. The solution to supply-shock inflation is to eliminate the bottleneck or natural condition that made the resources scarce in the first place.

Many economists think that much inflation results from so-called "self-inflicted wounds," frequently government policies that restrict economic growth and cause other inefficiencies. For example, excessive taxes may stifle the incentive to work, save, and invest. An overly-generous welfare system may reduce the incentive to become self-supporting. Tariffs and other restrictions against foreign competition may protect "lazy" firms. A revision of government policies is called for in all these cases.

The labor force is defined as those individuals who are either working or are actively seeking work. Only about 65% of the population is in the labor force at any one time. The unemployment rate is the proportion of the labor force that is without work but actively seeking a job.

A non-controversial national goal is full employment. Achieving full employment does not mean a 0% unemployment rate. There is some unemployment at full employment—the full employment unemployment rate—also known as the natural unemployment rate. The reason for this is related to the different types of unemployment.

There are three main types of unemployment. Frictional unemployment is people "between jobs," individuals who have just been laid off or fired or just entered the labor force to begin looking. They are likely to find a job but have not done so immediately because information about job opportunities is not readily available, but must be discovered by a time-consuming process of search. Structural unemployment is people unemployed when job vacancies exist, but who cannot apply for the vacancies because they lack the appropriate skills. Technological change may be an important cause of this problem.

Both types of unemployment are inevitable in an economy such as ours. Consequently, when only frictional and structural unemployment are present, we may consider ourselves at full employment. Economists cannot say exactly what number constitutes full employment. Most economists today say anything between 4% and 5.5% represents full employment. This is not to imply that full employment is an immutable level. Labor market policies to provide better job market information or job retraining may reduce the amount of both types of unemployment we have to put up with.

Cyclical unemployment is unemployment resulting from too few jobs. Its seriousness is not doubted by anyone.

An important economic relationship is Okun's law. The law says that real GNP drops 3 percentage points for every 1 percentage point increase in the level of unemployment. If full employment is considered to be 5%, and actual unemployment is 7%, then GNP is approximately 6 percentage points below potential.

A simple way to calculate the employment consequences for occupations or industries of the changes in output in a particular industry i (ΔY_i) is to use the labor-input ratio $\left(\frac{L_i}{Y_i} \right)$ for that industry. The change in employment, ΔL_i, is equal to $\frac{L_i}{Y_i} * \Delta Y_i$. Aggregating across all industries gives employment consequences for the economy as a whole. This method is frequently used to make forecasts of future skill needs for the economy, but suffers from the strong assumption that labor-input ratios are fixed for occupations and industries.

The Phillips curve refers to an empirically-observed relationship between inflation and unemployment. Periods of high unemployment have usually been associated with low inflation. Periods of high inflation have usually been associated with low unemployment. Reductions in unemployment have usually been associated with rising rates of inflation, even before the economy has achieved full employment. The Phillips curve then represents the trade-off that is thought to exist between the two problems. The diagram gives an example of a simple Phillips curve.

It is now recognized that the Phillips curve is not a stable relationship. The Phillips curve may shift in or out, representing an improving or worsening trade-off. Shifts in the Phillips curve may result from economic inefficiency, cost-push or supply-shock factors, or changing inflationary expectations.

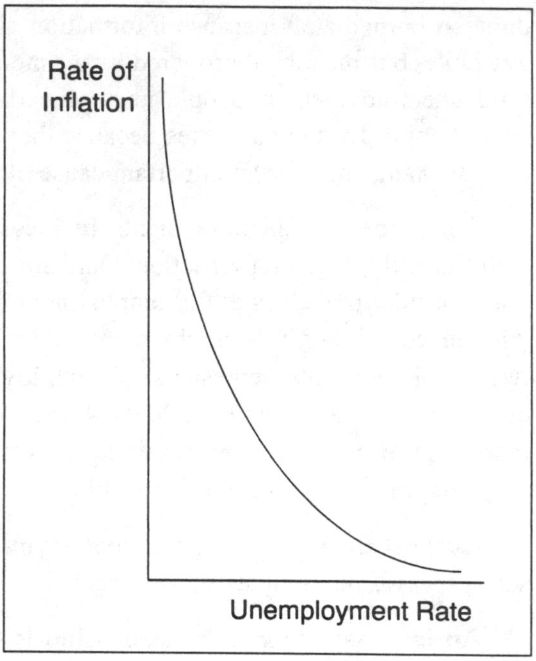

The Phillips Curve

The Federal Reserve System (Fed) has tools at its command which permit it to influence the level of spending in the economy. Through open-market operations, changes in the required reserve ratio, and changes in the discount rate, the Fed can influence the ability of banks to extend credit. The ability of banks to lend will influence interest rates, stimulating or reducing the investment spending which is a component of aggregate demand.

Monetarism is a school of thought within the economics profession. There are two basic tenets to remember. First, Monetarists believe that changes in the money supply are the most important factor influencing the health of the economy. They do not believe that money is the only factor influencing the economy. Second, they do not believe that the Fed should pursue an activist monetary policy, attempting to combat every slowing of the economy or hint of higher inflation. Since Fed actions do not affect the economy immediately, but only after a potentially long period of time, perhaps a year or two, and since our ability to forecast that far ahead is pitiful, Fed attempts to pursue an activist policy are likely to lead to the wrong policy as often as the right one. The better decision is for the Fed to cause the money supply to grow at a constant rate no matter what. By reducing fluctuations in the money supply, the Fed will have reduced the major source of economic instability and will not be attempting to do what it truly cannot do.

Step-by-Step Solutions to Problems in this Chapter, "Inflation and Unemployment"

INFLATION, DEFLATION AND STAGFLATION

• **PROBLEM** 10-1

A rise in the general price level is called ___________? How is this change measured?

Solution: A rise in the general price level is called inflation and it is usually measured with the help of 3 indices:

1. the consumer price index (CPI);
2. the wholesale price index (WPI), which are both published by the Bureau of Labor Statistics; and
3. the GNP deflator, published by the Department of Commerce.

The CPI or WPI, is the ratio of today's cost of a basket of goods of fixed composition. If we denote the base year quantities of the various goods by q_0^i and their base year prices by p_0^i, the cost of the basket in the base year is

$$\Sigma p_0^i q_0^i$$

where the summation (Σ) is over all goods in the basket. The cost of a basket of the same quantities but at today's prices is

$$\Sigma p_1^i q_0^i$$

where p_1^i is today's price. Then the price index $= \dfrac{\Sigma p_1^i q_0^i}{\Sigma p_0^i q_0^i} \times 100$.

The GNP deflator is the ratio of the nominal GNP to the real GNP

$$P = \frac{\text{nominal GNP}}{\text{real GNP}}$$

so that real GNP is nominal GNP deflated

$$\text{real GNP} = \frac{\text{nominal GNP}}{P}$$

• **PROBLEM** 10-2

Elaborate on the following statement: "Inflation also casts its evil eye upon savers". Give an example to make your point clear.

Solution: "Inflation also casts its evil eye upon savers". This means that as prices rise, the real value, or purchasing power, of a liquid saving will deteriorate. Savings accounts, insurance policies, annuities, and other fixed-value paper assets which were once adequate to meet rainy-day contingencies or to provide for a comfortable retirement, decline in real value during inflation. Mortgage holders and bondholders will be similarly affected. A household's accumulated claims upon the economy's output become less in value as prices rise.

However, two important clarifications have to be noted. First, stock values are flexible and determined by current market conditions; hence, savings in this form will tend to increase in value with, or in some cases ahead of, the general level of prices. Secondly, so long as the interest rate on savings exceeds the rate of inflation, the purchasing power of savings will increase rather than diminish. For example, the purchasing power of a $1000 savings account will increase if the annual interest rate is, say 5 percent and the annual increase in the price level is only 3 percent.

• PROBLEM 10-3

What are some of the undesirable effects of inflation?

Solution: Inflation results in the following effects:

1) Unjustified wealth transfers occur from net money creditors to net money debtors.

2) When union wage contracts do not have inflation escalator clauses, and workers notice an actual decline in their real wages, they may more frequently resort to strikes creating social instability.

3) Assume the country has fixed rates of exchange and its domestic inflation rate is higher than the inflation rate in the countries with which it is trading. Then it becomes less competitive in the world markets, i.e., exports less, and imports more. This situation may result in a serious balance of payments deficit. Inflation is therefore, a major cause for international monetary crises.

4) The tax revenues of the government are automatically increased because inflation pushes income earners into higher tax brackets: the rates of the federal income tax are progressive. This may defeat the economic policy of reaching full employment because total spending decreases, automatically.

5) The usefulness of money as a store of value may be reduced and people will start to use money substitutes, preferably those that are interest-earning, like credit accounts (credit cards); and they will reduce their money balances and invest more in real assets, like houses, education, automobiles.

6) All sorts of distortive effects on the allocation of resources will occur; the operation of the credit markets will be less effective by increasing risk of borrowing and lending; the built-in price rigidities of wage and installment contracts also create distortions.

• PROBLEM 10-4

What is the difference between open and repressed inflation?

Solution: When the planned expenditures are unattainable because the economy is already operating at full capacity the adjustment process results in inflation.

Open inflation results when the price stability breaks down and prices start rising to match the value of the planned expenditures with the value of the full capacity output. Repressed inflation results when the prices are not allowed to rise by explicit price controls, i.e., the prices are legally fixed, and waiting lines and backlog-lists are formed in consequence. The expenditure plans of investors and consumers are curtailed to match the existing capacity. Open inflation exists in most of the non-communist industrial economies; repressed inflation exists in most of the communist industrial economies. Note that if equilibrium income exceeds the output capacity and inflation results, the events cannot be analyzed any more in terms of the simple income determination model.

Also, inflation usually commences with the creation of an inflationary gap; thereafter, however, it acquires its own momentum and mechanism; inflationary expectations develop and the inflation becomes self-generating.

• PROBLEM 10-5

What is meant when it is stated that "suppressed inflation" existed in the United States from 1942 to 1947?

Solution: In the period 1942 to 1947 prices were stable; therefore, the unaware reader might conclude that inflation was not a factor of the American economy at that time. However closer examination reveals that during this period wartime price controls were in effect. In 1947, when the price controls were removed, we notice that prices shot upward. Therefore we speak of the years 1942-1947 as a period of suppressed inflation. During this time, inflation-causing factors were in operation but price controls suppressed, or rather postponed the inflationary impact until the prices were freed in 1947. The main inflationary factor during this period was the enormous aggregate demand for military goods and services when the economy operated at a full-employment level. Thus there was a repressed demand-pull inflation, that could be detected from long waiting lists and delivery times of the various products.

• PROBLEM 10-6

a) The theory which attributes inflation to excessive wage demands by unions or price demands by large producers is called the ___________ .

b) The theory which attributes inflation to excessive aggregate demand is called the ____________________.

c) Give an explanation of both theories.

Solution: a) cost-push theory of inflation.

b) demand-pull theory of inflation.

The cost-push theory, or cost-price spiral theory of inflation requires the existence of the 'ratchet-effect', or stickiness of prices: this means that prices move flexibly upward but are rather 'sticky' downward. The union demands for higher wages, backed by the oligopolistic character of the trade-unions in the labor market, or the demands for higher prices for oil supplied (a raw material input) by the Oil Producing and Exporting Countries (OPEC is a cartel in the raw material markets), or the autonomous price increases by large industrial producers of intermediate products (for example, of steel) increase the costs of producing. These raised costs are passed on to the consumers in the increased prices of the final products, inducing the general price level to increase. The consumers feel the brunt of inflation by noticing a decline in their purchasing power, (thus in their real income), and will require an increase in their nominal income, i.e., their wages and salaries, etc. This process is circular and leads to the cost-price-spiral) (See Fig. 1).

If prices were generally flexible and moved easily downward then a reallocation of resources would take place from the unionized and oligopolistic sectors to the non-unionized and more competitive sectors, thus from the 'controlled' sector of the economy to the 'uncontrolled' sector of the economy.

The demand-pull theory of inflation states that aggregate demand is bigger than the potential output of the economy, pulling the general price level upward:

$$Y_{\text{potential}} = \frac{Y_{\text{demand}}\uparrow}{P\uparrow} = \text{constant}$$

There is an inflationary gap: $Y_{\text{demand}} - Y_{\text{potential}}$. Such an inflationary gap may be caused by an increase in autonomous consumption $\bar{C}$ and investment In, caused by optimistic expectations, new technological developments or lower taxes on business profits.

It may also be caused by fiscal policy: increasing government expenditures, decreasing income taxes, or both, or by monetary policy: increasing the money supply and lowering the interest rates, thereby inducing more investment. (See Fig. 2).

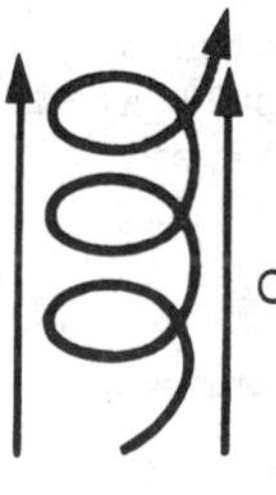

Fig. 1

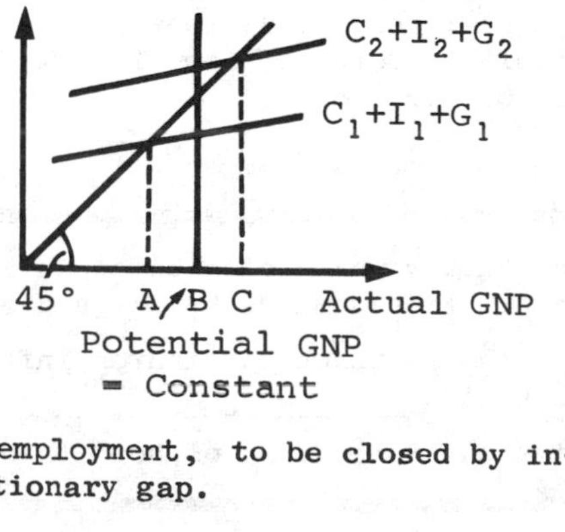

Fig. 2

AB is the deflationary gap with unemployment, to be closed by increased spending. BC is the inflationary gap.

• PROBLEM 10-7

Suppose the government decides that in order to fight inflation, labor unions will not be allowed any wage increases until further notice. What type of inflation would this be aimed at?

Solution: This program would be aimed at cost-push inflation. By freezing wages, the government is hoping to stop the wage-price-spiral which is causing the inflation.

• PROBLEM 10-8

Suppose the government has decided to combat inflation by raising taxes on disposable income. What specific type of inflation would this be used against?

Solution: This approach would be used to fight demand-pull inflation. By increasing taxes on disposable income, consumers will have less money available to spend, and aggregate demand would be reduced, taking into account the multiplier effect. (See Chapter 6 Income Determination: The Simple Multiplier Theory).

• PROBLEM 10-9

Describe the circumstances leading to the existence of a demand-pull inflation. How does this differ from the so-called "wage-push" or "cost-push" inflation, and the alternative "profit-push" inflation.

Solution: Generally speaking, the levels of output and employment, on the one hand, and the level of prices, on the other, have a common determinant: the level of total spending or demand. In an economy which is market directed such as the American economy, businesses produce only those goods which can be sold profitably. Stated differently, if total demand is at a low level, many businesses will not find it profitable to produce a large volume of goods and services. The consequence of this would be that output, employment, and the level of incomes will be low. If the level of total demand will be at a high level, then it will be profitable to produce more. The consequence of this would be that output, employment, and incomes will also increase correspondingly. Finally, the economy may strive to spend beyond its capacity to produce. However, the business sector cannot respond to this excess demand by expanding real output for the reason that all available resources are fully employed. Therefore, this excess demand will bid up the prices of the fixed real output, causing the so-called demand-pull inflation.

The cost-push inflation is based upon the assumption that labor unions and big businesses both possess significant amounts of monopoly or market power with which to raise wages and prices and that this power becomes easier to exert as the economy approaches full employment. Hence, the "wage-push" or "cost-push" inflationary condition may be outlined as follows: As the economy moves toward full employment, labor markets tighten and unions become more aggressive in their wage demands. Futhermore, increasing prosperity will tend to enhance the willingness of businesses to grant union wage demands. It will become harder for firms to resist union demands and risk a costly strike at the very time when business activity is becoming increasingly profitable. The overall effect of a more profitable business environment is that the economic expansion provides gradually a more favorable environment for the use of monopoly power to pass wage increases on to consumers in the form of higher product prices.

Alternatively, market-power inflation may be "profit-push"; that is, inflation may be initiated by businesses as they seek higher profit margins. Large corporations which have the ability to manipulate or administer their prices may decide to increase prices to expand their profits.

• PROBLEM 10-10

What is the importance of the so-called "rule of 70"?

Solution: Given the annual rate of inflation, the "rule of 70" allows one to quickly calculate the number of years required for a doubling of the price level. Specifically, the number of years necessary for the price level to double is found by dividing 70 by the annual rate of inflation. For example, a 3 percent annual rate of inflation will double the price level in about 23 (= 70 ÷ 3) years. An 8 percent annual rate of inflation will double the price level in about 9(= 70 ÷ 8) years.

• PROBLEM 10-11

When your cash balances are at present $1,000 and inflation is expected to be 12% per year, what will be your real balances after 4 years in terms of current prices?

Solution: Real balances are money holdings expressed in the terms of goods and services they can buy; they are held in relation to the customary expenditures on goods and services.

The cash balances buy $1,000 worth of goods and services in current prices; so your real balances are at present in current prices equal to $1,000.

After one year inflation the purchasing power of one dollar is decreased by 12%, so your real balances after one year in current prices are only $(1 - 0.12) \times 1{,}000 = 0.88 \times 1{,}000 = \$880$. One other year of inflation reduces the purchasing power to

$$(1 - 0.12) \times 880 = \$744.40.$$

In the third year your real balances are $(1 - 0.12) \times 744.40 = \$681.47$, in current prices; and in the fourth year $(1 - 0.12) \times 681.47 = \$599.69$. This is a dramatic decrease in real value.

Looking at the process we see that we could also calculate the real value in the fourth year more directly by

$$(1 - 0.12)(1 - 0.12)(1 - 0.12)(1 - 0.12) \times 1{,}000 =$$

$$(1 - 0.12)^4 \times 1{,}000 = 0.59969 \times 1{,}000 = \$599.69.$$

In general, the real balances in current prices after n years are $(1 - \pi)^n \times A$ where π = inflation rate, n = number of years, A = present cash balances.

The drop in the purchasing power of your money can be counteracted when you invest part of your cash balances in some form of wealth, like corporate stock, bonds, consumer durables, the prices of which will rise along with the general price level.

• PROBLEM 10-12

What happens to the purchasing power of money when there is inflation? What does it mean?

Solution: The purchasing power of money is the real value of money, i.e., what you can buy for each dollar. Nominal GNP is the sum of the products of the quantities of goods purchased times their prices:

$$\text{nominal GNP} = P_1Q_1 + P_2Q_2 + P_3Q_3 + \dots + P_nQ_n .$$

It is also equal to real GNP times the GNP-deflator: nominal GNP = real GNP $\times$ deflator = Q $\times$ P. The deflator is the general price level. From the exchange equation we know that nominal GNP = P $\times$ Q = M $\times$ v where M is the quantity of money supplied and v is the velocity of the money turnover, i.e., the frequency with which money changes hands. Suppose the quantity of money supplied and the velocity do not change over time, so that nominal GNP is constant. Then when there is inflation and the general price level P creeps up, real income = real GNP decreases, $\overline{MV}$ = constant = $P\uparrow \times Q\downarrow$, and less goods can be purchased with the same amount of money.

• PROBLEM 10-13

What is the inflation tax?

Solution: The value of the inflation tax is the amount that individuals have to add to their cash balances every year to keep the real value of their cash balances constant. ΔM is the amount of nominal balances added to the cash balances, P the general price level and T_{infl} the real value of the inflation tax, so that

$$T_{infl} = \frac{\Delta M}{P}.$$

When we multiply and divide by M we obtain

$$T_{infl} = \frac{\Delta M}{M} \cdot \frac{M}{P}$$

M/P is the holding of the real balances, and $\Delta M/M$ is the growth rate of the money supply. In the long run the growth of the money supply M is equal to the rate of inflation π, because the real output Q is determined by the autonomous forces of increase in the population and in the labor productivity. So

$$T_{infl} = \pi \cdot \frac{M}{P}$$

For example, when the real money holdings are 2000 and the rate of inflation is 9%, the inflation tax is

$$0.09 \times 2000 = 180.$$

• PROBLEM 10-14

What is the portfolio adjustment theory of inflation? Explain.

Solution: The portfolio adjustment theory of inflation is the theory of inflation that is based on the increase in spending caused by the decrease in the money balances held by the public. According to the theory, people adjust money balances to the lower desired levels of money holdings. Inflation occurs if at the full employment level of income, the supply of money is greater than the demand for money.

FIG. 1

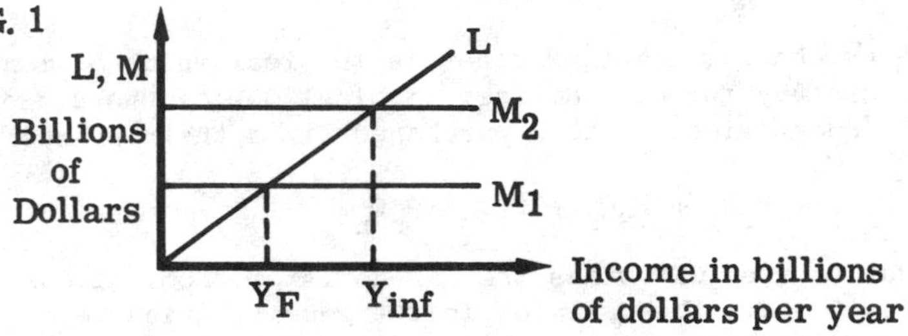

The money demand L in Figure 1 is related to the level of income (transactions demand for money). The money supply M is autonomously determined by the Federal Reserve (FED)(see Fig. 1).

If the money supply is increased from M_1 to M_2, the quantity of money supplied at the full employment level Y_F exceeds the demand. The portfolio adjustment theory explains then that total spending, or transactions, increase because the money balances people hold are too high; prices are bid up, thereby causing nominal income Y to rise to Y_{infl}, the level of inflationary nominal income.

As prices rise, the demand for money increases because people notice that the real value of their money balances, i.e., the balance difference between their money debts and money assets, diminishes. Here inflation is induced by monetary policy. But the L-schedule may also shift upward autonomously because of expectations of inflation, thereby causing the existing money supply to become inflationary. (See Fig. 2).

FIG. 2

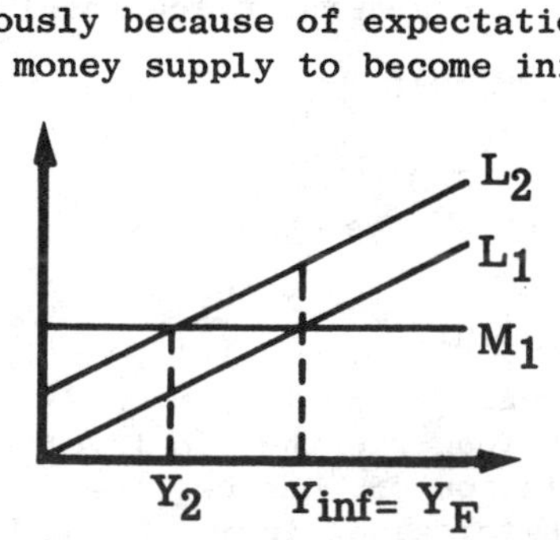

This accelerates the already existent inflation, and may create unemployment because the new income level is below the full employment level. The money balances of the people are too high and they will spend their money, bidding up the prices further and thus reducing the real value of their balances.

• PROBLEM 10-15

What is the Structuralist theory of inflation, used mainly to explain the inflations, and hyper inflations, in Latin America? Explain.

Solution: The structuralist theory contends that inflation is a necessary accompaniment of economic development. Rapidly rising per capita income Y_D/N and fast growth of the population N tend to increase the aggregate demand, $Y_D = (Y_D/N) \times N$, so much that it surpasses the available aggregate supply. Supply consists of domestically produced goods and imported goods, (generally of inelastic supply). Excess aggregate demand thus creates an almost permanent inflationary gap, pushing the general price level quickly upward. Otherwise stated: the supply of imported goods and domestically produced goods is inelastic. The inelastic output of domestic production is caused by an inadequate increase in the productivity per worker, and by the high unemployment rate. Assuming an inflexible technology we have

$$\text{Total output } Y_s = qh(1 - u)\bar{N},$$

where q is the productivity per worker, h the average number of hours worked, u is the unemployment rate and $\bar{N}$ the labor force, which is only a part of the total population N, but directly related to it in less developed countries with their traditional work distributive roles. If the unemployment rate u is high, and thus that part of the labor force that is actively employed $(1 - u)\bar{N}$ is low, and q the labor productivity is low (the average number of hours h is fixed) then the total output Y_s is low, and will fall short of the aggregate demand.

• PROBLEM 10-16

Which of the following is not a part of deflation?

a) depressed business
b) reduced production
c) higher prices
d) unemployment

Solution: c) higher prices. In deflation, there is a fall in the general price level.

• PROBLEM 10-17

What are the characteristics of stagflation?

Solution: Stagflation is a combination of stagnation in the growth of real output, resulting in high unemployment rates, coupled with inflation, a rapidly rising price level. Stagflation was characteristic of the macroeconomic scene of the early 1970's; it is best represented by the Phillips curve which shows that there is always a trade-off between unemployment and inflation. A lower rate of inflation is accompanied by a higher unemployment rate and vice versa. When stagflation occurs, the inflation is not caused by an excessive level of demand, because then we would expect to have a high level of output, and a low level of unemployment, but by forces on the supply or cost side of the market. The rising costs of the input materials push the prices of the products upward causing the increase in the general price level, i.e., inflation, without a concomitant growth in output and reduction in unemployment. Furthermore, the rapid inflation erodes the real income, or purchasing power of consumers, and reduces the aggregate demand.

• PROBLEM 10-18

What were some causes of the stagflation in the early 1970's?

Solution: Stagflation is the simultaneous occurrence of stagnation in the growth of real output, high or even rising unemployment levels, and rapid inflation.

It appears that part of the unemployment in the early 1970's occurred because of the rapid acceleration of the price level. The oil price increases in 1973/74 were tantamount to a gigantic excise tax paid by the customers and businesses of the western industrialized countries to the OPEC nations. The effect of this 'excise tax' was, of course, contractionary with respect to output and employment.

Secondly, the built-in stability feature of the proportional and progressive tax systems of the western industrial countries worked perversely during this period. The money incomes of households and businesses inflated rapidly; and so, in consequence, did their personal and corporate income tax payments. The OPEC 'tax' and higher domestic tax bills left consumers and businesses with less to spend on domestic consumer and investment goods. The result was falling real output and unemployment.

In addition some macroeconomic policy mistakes were made. The government and the monetary authorities used contractionary fiscal and monetary policies in an attempt to restrain the inflation. Since the causes of the inflation were largely on the cost side because of the higher prices of the imported raw materials, the restriction of the aggregate demand did not control the rate of inflation, but intensified the declines in output and employment.

• PROBLEM 10-19

What are possible explanations for the recent failure of fiscal and monetary policy to solve the stagflation problem?

Solution: Stagflation is the situation of a simultaneous occurrence of inflation and unemployment. This is often illustrated by the Phillips curve which shows the trade-off between the level of unemployment and the level of inflation for a given economy.

Monopolistic power concentration, international trade problems, and a changing composition of the labor force help to explain the stagflation phenomenon. Monopolistic concentration in a number of key industries can raise prices without excess demand. Strong unions can win wage increases, even in the face of substantial national unemployment. 'Monopolies', meanwhile, can set their prices irrespective of a general situation of competition.

Consequently, periodic declines in the level of aggregate demand no longer function as an effective restraint on price increases. An expansionary monetary policy which lowers the interest rate increases the U.S. payments deficit, because businesses (either foreign or domestic) borrow dollars here and send them abroad to build plants or make investments. An accelerating balance of payments deficit may force a series of official and de facto dollar devaluations. This fuels inflation because the now cheaper American products will be in higher demand on the world markets. In other words, the stabilizing domestic monetary (but also fiscal) policies are restricted by their effects on the balance of payments.

An industrial society experiences an increasing demand for more highly skilled and well-educated workers. But new entries into the labor force consist of a growing percentage of unskilled, poorly educated teen-agers and women, and a large number of those whose job skills have become obsolescent through technological advances.

The highly skilled and well-educated maintain high employment levels even in times of recession. The unskilled and poorly educated, on the other hand, often find it difficult to obtain employment even in prosperous times because of a declining demand for their labor. An increase in aggregate demand does not necessarily create the kinds of jobs for which the unskilled are suited.

UNEMPLOYMENT

• PROBLEM 10-20

What are frictional, structural and cyclical unemployment?

Solution: Frictional unemployment occurs as workers change jobs. Structural unemployment occurs when workers become unemployed because the industry is replacing workers by machines or reducing the number of employees because of an increase in the efficiency of use of labor. Economists consider frictional and structural unemployment to be more or less unavoidable since workers are free to choose employment and to search for a job, and the modern industrial economy fosters and encourages technological advancement.

Cyclical unemployment occurs when the economy is for some reason producing at a lower level than that desired by society. The economy in general does not have jobs for all those who are able and willing to work because aggregate demand is deficient; cyclical unemployment occurs in the recession phase of the business cycle.

• PROBLEM 10-21

Differentiate between apparent unemployment and disguised unemployment or underemployment.

Solution: Apparent unemployment (or, simply, unemployment) is the situation wherein a worker is involuntarily out of work.

On the other hand, disguised unemployment or underemployment is the case wherein the worker may have a job but in a sense still not be employed to the limits of his capability. For example, a lawyer who is employed as a court reporter is considered to be "partially unemployed". The lawyer here has a job, but he is not being employed efficiently.

• PROBLEM 10-22

Classify unemployment based on its cause. Describe and give examples for each. Which of the three do you think is the most desirable?

Solution: The three classifications of unemployment based on its cause are as follows:

1. Frictional unemployment
2. Structural unemployment
3. Cyclical unemployment

Frictional unemployment results when given the freedom of occupational choice, at any point in time, some workers will be "between jobs". That is, some workers will be in the process of voluntarily switching jobs. Others will have job connections, but will be temporarily laid off because of seasonality or adversive environmental conditions (for example, bad weather in the construction industry) or model changeovers (as in the automobile industry). This will include also young people who will be looking for their first jobs, and enter the labor force for the first time.

Structural unemployment is brought about when important changes occur over time in the structure of consumer demand and in technology, which in turn alter the structure or the composition of the total demand for labor. Unemployment results because the composition of the labor force does not respond quickly or completely to the new structure of the labor demand. As a consequence, some workers find that they have no readily marketable talents; their skills and experience have been rendered obsolete and unwanted by changes in technology and consumer demand. Examples: Years ago, highly skilled glassblowers were thrown out of work by the invention of bottlemaking machines. More recently, unskilled and inadequately educated blacks have been dislodged from agriculture in the South as a result of the mechanization of agriculture. Because of this, many of the workers have migrated to the ghettos of northern cities and have suffered prolonged unemployment because of insufficient skills.

By cyclical unemployment we mean unemployment caused by the business cycle, that is, by a deficiency of aggregate or total demand. Unemployment increases when the overall level of business activity decreases. Conversely, as business activity increases, unemployment declines. An example for this cyclical unemployment would be the Great Depression in 1933 which reached about 25 percent of the labor force.

Of the three, frictional unemployment is regarded to be as inevitable and, at least in part, desirable. It is considered to be desirable because workers typically move from low-paying, low-productivity jobs to higher-paying, higher-productivity positions. This means more income for the workers and a better allocation of labor resources - and therefore, a larger real output- for the economy as a whole.

• PROBLEM 10-23

What are the differences between frictional, seasonal, and technological unemployment?

Solution: All three types contribute for the situation with less than full employment. Frictional unemployment results from the constant labor turnover. Since people are free to switch jobs, there is always a small percentage of the work force that are searching for jobs and thus not employed. Seasonal unemployment means a reduction of jobs due to diminished activities in some industries at certain times of the year like in the building industry or agriculture. Technological unemployment is caused by innovation and advancement in machinery which replaces human workers. This causes the labor-capital ratio to decrease, i.e., the labor intensity of the production process is reduced.

• PROBLEM 10-24

What is natural unemployment and what are its determinants?

Solution: The natural rate of unemployment is that rate of unemployment at which flows in and out of unemployment just balance, and at which expectations of firms and workers as to the behavior of prices and wages are correct, (see Figure.)

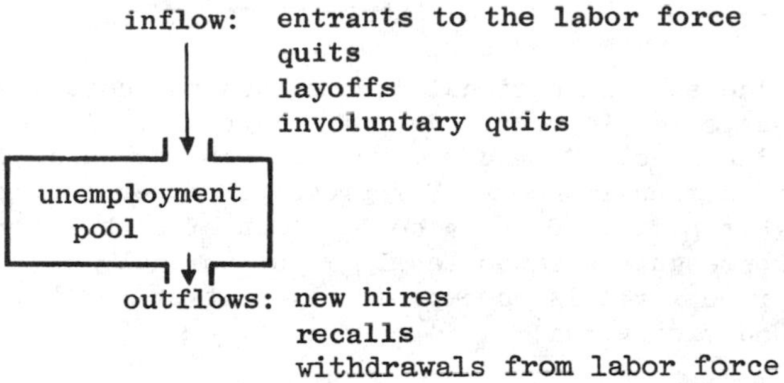

The determinants of the natural rate of unemployment are grouped under the duration and frequency of unemployment.

The duration of unemployment is the average period of time to find and accept a job, after entry into the pool of unemployed. It depends on:

1. The organization of the labor market, its informational structure, in regard to the presence or absence of employment agencies, youth employment services, etc.;

2. The demographic make-up of the labor force (males vs. females; whites vs. non-whites; various age groups);

3. The ability and desire of the unemployed to keep looking for a better job; and

4. The availability and type of jobs.

The two basic determinants of the frequency of unemployment are:

1. The variability of demand for labor across different firms in the economy: some firms are growing and some are contracting. The higher this variability, the higher the natural unemployment rate will be.

2. The rate at which new workers enter the labor force: the faster the growth of the labor force, the higher the natural unemployment rate will be.

All of these determinants may change; therefore,the natural rate of unemployment is not a constant over time. Because the natural rate of unemployment is primarily determined by institutional arrangements and not by aggregate demand, it is considered to be the rate corresponding to 'full' employment.

The natural rate of unemployment is presently considered to be 5.5%.

• PROBLEM 10-25

Is an increase in national income equivalent to an increase in employment?

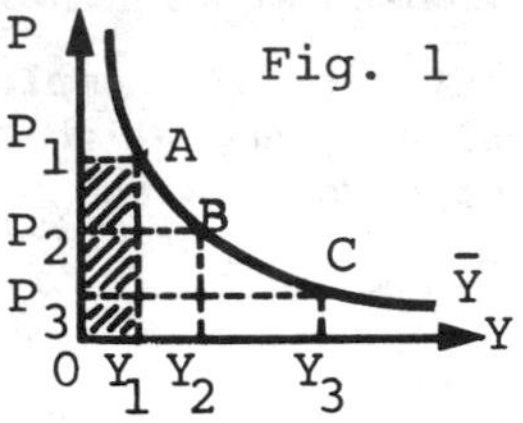

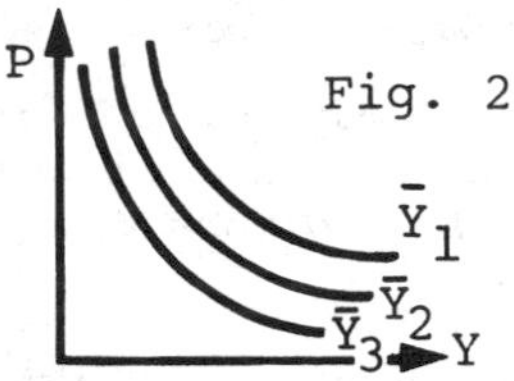

Solution: Every increase in national income does not necessarily result in an increase of employment. National income Y is the product of the general price level P and the real income y, thus $Y = P \times y$. Therefore a higher national income Y represents either a larger real income y or higher prices P, or a combination of both. The hyperbola in Fig. (1) represents a fixed level $\bar{Y}$ of nominal national income; a higher price level is accompanied by a lower level of real income y and vice versa.

The area of quadrangle $OP_1Ay_1 = OP_2By_2 = OP_3Cy_3 = \bar{Y}$ does not change. And $\bar{Y}_1 > \bar{Y}_2 > \bar{Y}_3$ (see Fig. 2).

Why does the increase of national income sometimes represent a pure price increase (inflation)? For example, when real output y is at the full employment level, and employment cannot be further increased due to an inadequate supply of labor, a stimulus to increase the national income will result in inflation: when Y goes up, and y = constant, P goes up.

• PROBLEM 10-26

On average every person in the U.S.A. is unemployed once per 2 years, and the average duration of unemployment is 7 weeks. Given these data, what do you expect the unemployment rate to be? And what does it indicate?

Solution: The unemployment rate = duration $\times$ frequency. The average duration of unemployment, or the average length of the period that a person is unemployed is 7/52 = 0.135 year. The average frequency with which a person is unemployed is 1/2 = 0.5 times per year. Thus the unemployment rate u is expected to be u = 0.135 x 0.5 = 6.75%. The unemployment rate is defined as the ratio of the total number of unemployed to the total labor force

$$u = \frac{\text{total number of unemployed}}{\text{total labor force}} .$$

• PROBLEM 10-27

When the natural (= 'full') unemployment rate, $\bar{u}$ = 6%, and the actual unemployment rate, u = 9%, how much loss of output does the economy suffer? And what is necessary to create 'full' employment?

Assume that the potential output of the economy is $1600 billion, and the marginal propensity to save s = 10%.

Solution: This question relates to Okun's Law which states, GNP gap = $3(u - \bar{u})$. Okun's Law is an empirical relationship found by Arthur Okun, former chairman of the Council of Economic Advisors, that was used by the Kennedy and Johnson administrations as a basis for economic policy. It states that for every 1% actual unemployment above the natural rate of natural unemployment there is a 3 percent GNP gap.

The GNP gap is the percentage shortfall of actual output Y from the full-employment = potential output Y_F, so

$$\text{GNP gap} = \frac{Y_F - Y}{Y_F}$$

Given the data the GNP gap 3(9 - 6) = 9% of the potential output, which is Y_F = $1600 billion. Thus the loss of output $Y_F - Y = 0.09Y_F = 0.09 \times 1600$ = 144 billion dollars. In order to create 'full' employment, $u = \bar{u}$, we must reduce the GNP gap to zero, and bring the actual output up to potential output, so $\Delta Y = Y_F - Y$. The Kennedy and Johnson administrations applied the New Economics as founded on the teachings of John Maynard Keynes. (see the chapter on the simple multiplier theory).

When we want to increase actual GNP by $144 billion, spending by households, business and government should be increased by much less thanks to the multiplier effect. The multiplier has the value of

$$\frac{1}{s} = \frac{1}{0.1} = 10$$

Thus households and business should be induced to spend more on consumption and investment, by i) lowering the taxes, ii) through an increase in the money supply, lowering the interest rates, and iii) an increase in the budget deficit.

$$\Delta Y = 144 = \frac{1}{s}(\Delta C + \Delta I + \Delta G)$$

$$= 10(\Delta C + \Delta I + \Delta G)$$

The total spending should therefore increase by $\Delta C + \Delta I + \Delta G = \frac{144}{10}$ = $14.4 billion.

• PROBLEM 10-28

When GNP grows by 3.5%, the labor productivity by 1.6% and the labor force by 2.2% per year, is unemployment increasing or decreasing?

Solution: The short term output is given by $Y = qh(1 - \bar{u})\bar{N}$, where Y is GNP, q the labor productivity, h the average number of hours worked, u the actual unemployment rate, and $\bar{N}$ is the labor force.

When we turn this relationship among levels into a relationship among growth rates we get the sum

$$g_Y = g_q + g_h + g_{1-u} + g_N ,$$

where g means growth rate. The average number of hours worked per week is relatively constant (say 40 hours per week), so $g_h = 0$. The other growth rates are given

$$3.5 = 1.6 + g_{1-u} + 2.2$$

$$= 3.8 + g_{1-u}$$

We find that g_{1-u}, the growth rate of employment is negative, $g_{1-u} = -0.3\%$.

Employment decreases, and thus unemployment, if it already exists, is increasing.

• PROBLEM 10-29

Assume there are only 5 kinds of labor in the economy, engineers, secretaries, truckers, steel workers and farm workers. It is impossible to move from one category to another without several years of training. Suppose that in each category there are 1,000,000 people unemployed (thus in total there are 5,000,000 people unemployed), and each increase of $1 billion in GNP causes an increase of 20,000 in the demand for engineers, 30,000 for secretaries, 25,000 for truckers, 15,000 for steel workers, and 5,000 in the demand for farm workers.

1) By how much must GNP be increased to remove all unemployment?

2) If GNP is increased to remove all unemployment, from which source would you anticipate inflationary pressure?

Solution: The category with the slowest reduction in unemployment when GNP is increased, is the category which determines by now much GNP must be increased to remove all unemployment.

The category with the fastest reduction in unemployment indicates from which source inflationary pressure may be anticipated. We will first show this for the secretaries and engineers only, and then develop the total solution. This is a problem of structural unemployment and inflation, and is based on the assumption of fixed labor input ratios in the production process. For example, the labor input ratio of engineers in the total economy is

$$\left(\frac{\Delta L}{\Delta Y}\right)_E = \frac{20,000}{1 \text{ billion}} ,$$

i.e., every increase in GNP of 1 billion is accompanied by an increase in the demand for engineers of 20,000.

To eliminate the total number of unemployed engineers of 1,000,000, we must increase GNP by

$$\Delta Y = L_E \times \left(\frac{\Delta Y}{\Delta L}\right)_E ,$$

so by the product of the engineering labor available and the reciprocal of the labor input ratio, called the (marginal) output/labor ratio. Thus in this case we must increase GNP by

$$\Delta Y = 1,000,000 \times \frac{1}{20,000}$$

$$= \$50 \text{ billion}$$

to eliminate completely the unemployment of engineers.

To eliminate the unemployment of secretaries, however, we have to increase GNP by only

$$\Delta Y = L_S \times \left(\frac{\Delta Y}{\Delta L}\right)_S = 1,000,000 \times \frac{1}{30,000}$$

$$= \$33.33 \text{ billion}$$

so by \$16.66 less. The reason is, of course, that the labor input ratio of the secretaries is higher, i.e., each increase of GNP of \$1 billion employs 10,000 (= 30,000 - 20,000) more secretaries than engineers. The unemployment of engineers is more slowly reduced by an increase in GNP than the unemployment of secretaries. We can make the above calculations for all five categories, to see by how much GNP must be increased to wipe out unemployment in each category. The results are displayed in the following table.

Table 1	Engineers	Secretaries	Truckers	Steel workers	Farm workers
ΔY increase in GNP to eliminate structural unemployment (in \$billion)	50	33.33	40	66.66	200

From this table it is clear that the unemployment of the farm workers forms the real stumbling block: to eliminate this unemployment GNP is required to be increased by \$200 billion. So, when GNP is increased by \$200 billion, not only are all the farm workers employed, but also all the steel workers, engineers, truckers and secretaries. However, because these other employment categories required less increase in GNP to close the GNP gap, in all these categories inflationary pressure results. The fiercest inflationary pressure will result from the secretaries. Why?

When GNP is increased by \$200 billion and assuming fixed labor input ratios, the demand for secretaries will increase by

$$\Delta L_S = \Delta Y \times \left(\frac{\Delta L}{\Delta Y}\right)_S$$

$$= 200 \times 30,000 = 6,000,000 \text{ persons.}$$

In the labor market there will be an excess demand of 6,000,000 - 1,000,000 = 5,000,000 secretaries. And employers will start to offer higher salaries to attract the scarcely available secretaries, thereby increasing the costs of production. This cost-push will be reflected in higher prices for goods and services, reducing the purchasing power of the dollar, i.e., reducing the real value of salaries and wages. This will also trigger off demands for higher wages and salaries in the neighboring sectors, and the inflationary pressure spreads as quickly as a drop of oil on a water surface.

The inflationary pressure will also be felt in the other labor categories where excess demand appears. See the following table which is constructed using the expression

Table 2 -- i	Engineers	Secretaries	Truckers	Steel workers	Farm workers
$\Delta L_i - U_i$ Excess demand in category i resulting from ΔY = $200 billion	3,000,000	5,000,000	4,000,000	2,000,000	0

$$\Delta L_i - U_i = \Delta Y \times \left(\frac{\Delta L}{\Delta Y}\right) - U_i$$

$$= 200 \times \left(\frac{\Delta L}{\Delta Y}\right)_i - 1,000,000$$

where ΔL_i is the increase in the demand for labor in category i, (i= engineers, secretaries, truckers, steel and farm workers); $(\Delta L/\Delta Y)_i$ is the (marginal) labor-input ratio for labor category i; U_i is the unemployment experienced in labor category i; and ΔY is the particular increase in GNP that is investigated; in this case ΔY is the increase of $200 billion that eliminates the unemployment of the farm workers. This calculatory example is rather extreme, but it shows that if the labor-input ratios are rather fixed, for example, in-consequence of sticky salaries and wages, there is always a trade-off situation between unemployment and inflation on the aggregate macro-level. If we employ all the secretaries, requiring an increase in GNP of $33.33 billion, there will still be 1,000,000 - (33.33 x 20,000) = 333,333 engineers, 1,000,000 - (33.33 x 25,000) = 166,750 truckers, 500,050 steelworkers and 833,350 farm workers unemployed. Conversely, if we employ all the farm workers, requiring, as we have seen, an increase in GNP by $200 billion, a tremendous inflationary pressure is induced in all the other labor categories. The 'normal' situation, under the influence of the parties lobbying Congress, will be that GNP will be increased somewhere inbetween $33,33 and $200 billion, say $50 billion. The resulting situation is indicated in the next table, which can be

Table 3 -- i	Engineers	Secretaries	Truckers	Steel workers	Farm workers
Inflationary labor gap	0	500,000	250,000		
Unemployment				250,000	750,000

derived now easily using the preceding discussion. There is some inflationary pressure (secretaries, truckers), some unemployment (steel workers, farm workers) and in one category the labor market is in equilibrium.

The decision, how much inflation and unemployment, and where the brunt of each of them is allocated, is a political decision.

• PROBLEM 10-30

For every $5 billion output, manufacturing requires $2 billion inputs from primary production and 300,000 workers in manufacturing. Primary production requires no other inputs, but needs 200,000 workers for every $1 billion of primary output. Suppose the regional economy consists of only these two sectors, manufacturing and primary production. What will the total increase in unemployment be if a recession causes manufacturing output to fall by $50 billion?

Solution: The labor input ratio in the manufacturing industry is

$$\frac{L_m}{Y_m} = \frac{300{,}000}{5 \text{ billion}} = 0.06$$

and the primary product input ratio in the manufacturing industry is

$$\frac{Y_p}{Y_m} = \frac{2 \text{ billion}}{5 \text{ billion}}$$

while the labor input ratio in the primary production sector is much higher

$$\frac{L_p}{Y_p} = \frac{200{,}000}{1 \text{ billion}} .$$

There are no additional inputs in the primary production industry. The reduction of manufacturing output of ΔY_m = \$50 billion causes a reduction in employment in the manufacturing industry by

$$\Delta Y_m \times \frac{L_m}{Y_m} = 50 \text{ billion} \times \frac{300{,}000}{5 \text{ billion}} =$$

$$= 3 \text{ million workers.}$$

But it also causes a demand for primary output products of

$$\Delta Y_m \times \frac{Y_p}{Y_m} = 50 \times \frac{2}{5} = 20 \text{ billion.}$$

This reduction in the output of the primary production industry also causes a reduction in the employment in this industry. The reduction in employment of the primary production workers is

$$\Delta Y_p \times \frac{L_p}{Y_p} = 20 \text{ billion} \times \frac{200{,}000}{1 \text{ billion}}$$

$$= 4 \text{ million workers.}$$

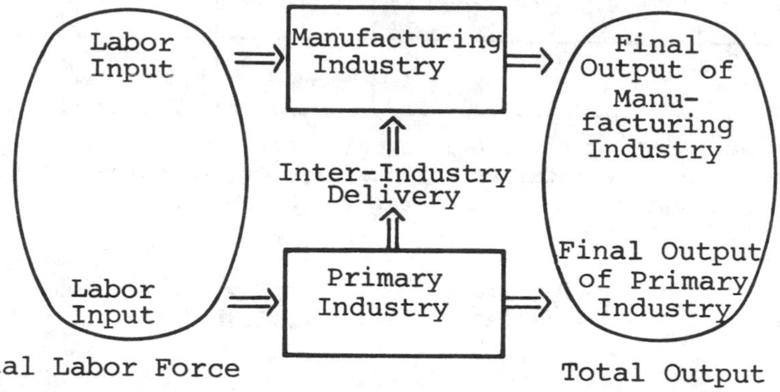

Thus the recession causes unemployment to increase by the unemployment increase in the manufacturing industry plus the unemployment increase in the primary production industry, that is by 3 + 4 = 7 million workers. The interconnections become clear in the diagram.

• PROBLEM 10-31

Suppose there are three industrial sectors in the economy, defense production, home construction and transportation, and only two categories of workers, machinists and electricians. Assume that it takes a long time and much investment in retraining programs before one category of workers can do the work of the other category.

Defense production needs 30,000 machinists and 50,000 electricians for every $1 billion output, home construction needs 20,000 machinists and 70,000 electricians per $1 billion of output, and transport needs 60,000 machinists and 30,000 electricians per $1 billion of output.

If the defense production is cut by $40 billion, because of a reduced involvement in war, by how much should home construction and transport be increased to insure as low as possible unemployment of either type of worker.

Solution: We trace first the logistic interconnections between the output and the employment with the help of a diagram:

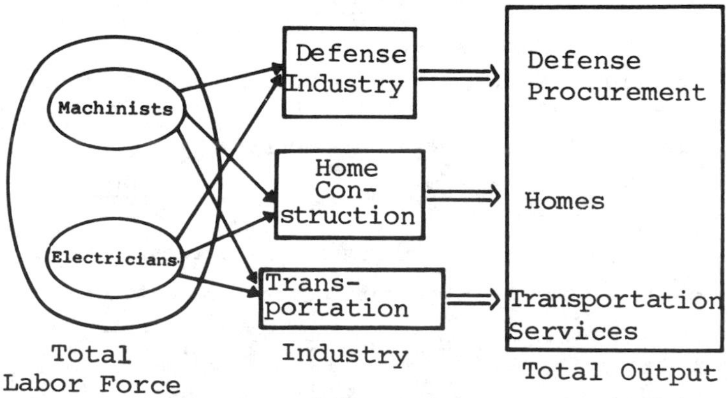

We calculate first the labor input ratios to see how reductions and increases in output affect employment.

The labor-input ratio in the defense industry is

$$\frac{L_m^D}{Y^D} = \frac{30,000}{1 \text{ billion}}$$

for machinists, and

$$\frac{L_E^D}{Y^D} = \frac{50,000}{1 \text{ billion}}$$

for electricians, respectively. The labor-input ratios in the home construction industry are

$$\frac{L_m^H}{Y^H} = \frac{20,000}{1 \text{ billion}}$$

for machinists and

$$\frac{L_E^H}{Y^H} = \frac{70,000}{1 \text{ billion}}$$

for electricians, respectively. And, finally, the labor ratios for transport are

$$\frac{L_m^T}{Y^T} = \frac{60,000}{1 \text{ billion}}$$

for machinists, and

$$\frac{L_E^T}{Y^T} = \frac{30,000}{1 \text{ billion}}$$

for electricians, respectively.

If the defense construction is cut by $\Delta Y = \$40$ billion, then

$$\Delta Y^D \times \frac{L_m^D}{Y^D} = 40 \times 30,000 = 1,200,000 \text{ machinists, and}$$

$$\Delta Y^D \times \frac{L_E^D}{Y^D} = 40 \times 50,000 = 2,000,000$$

electricians loose their jobs in the defense industry. The government tries to place them in the home construction industry by increasing the demand for homes through providing cheap loans, and by investing in public transportation. The question is by how much must the output of homes and of transport be increased to absorb the 1,200,000 unemployed machinists and the 2,000,000 unemployed electricians?

Of course we look at the labor intensities of each of the two industries, home construction and transport, for the respective labor categories. The more labor intensive an industry, i.e., the higher its labor-input ratio, the more workers will become employed by every dollar of increased output. Let us compare the labor input ratio of both industries:

(per $1 billion)	Machinists	Electricians
Home construction	20,000	70,000
Transport	60,000	30,000

It appears from this tabulation that transport is more labor intensive for machinists, and home construction for electricians.

We can now set up the following inequalities. The total labor absorption of machinists is the labor absorption in home construction plus the labor absorption in transport:

$$\Delta Y^H \cdot \frac{L_m^H}{Y^H} + \Delta Y^T \cdot \frac{L_m^T}{Y^T} = \Delta Y^H \cdot 20{,}000 + \Delta Y^T \cdot 60{,}000 \leq 1{,}200{,}000 \; .$$

The labor sbsorption of machinists must be smaller or equal (preferably equal) to the unemployed machinists. The same type of inequality holds for the electricians

$$\Delta Y^H \cdot \frac{L_E^H}{Y^H} + \Delta Y^T \cdot \frac{L_E^T}{Y^T} = \Delta Y^H \cdot 70{,}000 + \Delta Y^T \cdot 30{,}000 \leq 2{,}000{,}000 \; .$$

We have now to determine the mix of home-construction/transportation output necessary to absorb all unemployed workers. This means that we have to solve the system of two simultaneous equations:

$$2 \;\; \Delta Y^H + 6 \;\; \Delta Y^T = 120$$

$$7 \;\; \Delta Y^H + 3 \;\; \Delta Y^T = 200$$

for the two unknowns: ΔY^H and ΔY^T, the increases in output of the home construction and transport industry, respectively. We divided by a factor of 10,000 to simplify the notation.

Divide the first equation by 2

$$\Delta Y^H + 3 \; \Delta Y^T = 60$$

and subtract this from the second equation to obtain

$$6 \; \Delta Y^H + 0 = 140.$$

Thus the increase in the home construction must be

$$\Delta Y^H = \frac{140}{6} = 23.33$$

billion dollars. From the preceding relationship

$$\Delta Y^H + 3 \; \Delta Y^T = 60.$$

We can then easily derive, by substitution

$$23{,}33 + 3 \; \Delta Y^T = 60$$

or

$$3 \; \Delta Y^T = 60 - 23.33 = 36.67 \; .$$

Dividing by 3,

$$\Delta Y^T = 12.22 \text{ billion dollars.}$$

Thus the output of the home construction industry must increase by \$23,33 billion dollars, and the output of the transport industry by \$12.22 billion dollars to absorb all the machinists and electricians who lost their job because of the cut in defense expenditures by \$40 billion.

INFLATION VS. UNEMPLOYMENT: THE PHILLIPS CURVE

• PROBLEM 10-32

It is observed that attempts by the Federal Reserve to combat inflation have caused output to decline and the rate of unemployment to increase. Can you give a possible explanation of this trade-off between inflation and unemployment within the Classical framework of aggregate supply and demand schedules?

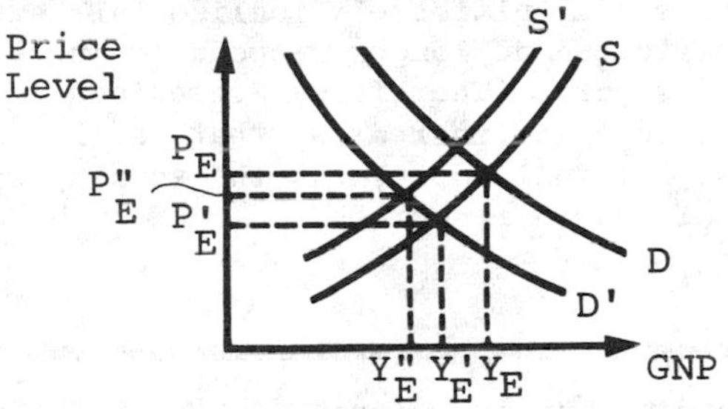

Solution: The basic cause of the trade-off between inflation and cyclical unemployment seems to be the wage and price inflexibilities, caused by the wage policies of the trade unions and the price policies of the business firms. The existence of the system of wage and price contracts provides lags in the reaction patterns of wages and prices. During the expansionary phase of the business cycle, wage increases typically lag behind the increase in aggregate demand, and when the Federal Reserve tightens the money supply to restrict the increase in inflation and aggregate demand falls, wage increases are still trying to catch up with the loss of real income caused by the inflation in the expansionary phase. These wage increases mean increases in production-costs of business which is confronted at the same time with a drop in the sales = fall in aggregate demand.

A fall in aggregate demand moves the aggregate demand schedule D (see accompanying figure) to the left to D' , causing a slight fall in equilibrium income Y_E to Y'_E , and a drop in equilibrium price p_E to p'_E . An increase in production costs shifts the supply schedule S up to S' because the producers are only willing to supply the same output at a higher price. This upward movement of the supply schedule depresses the equilibrium income even further to Y'_E and pushes the price level up again. The total result is a sharp fall in total output, and thus in employment, and almost no change in the price level.

• PROBLEM 10-33

Evaluate the following statements: "The price level generally begins to rise before full employment is reached. At full employment, additional spending tends to be purely inflationary".

Solution: As the production activities continue to expand, the supplies of unemployed resources will not vanish simultaneously in the various industries and sectors of the economy. To illustrate, the full employment of labor and capital may be realized in industry A , while industry B has excess capacity and unemployed workers. Industry A is therefore being characterized by a fixed supply, and increases in demand will have substantial price-increasing effects. In industry B, increases in demand will result in offsetting supply responses and prices are constant. Briefly stated, because the full employment of resources is not achieved simultaneously in all industries, prices in some industries will rise as the economy approaches overall full employment. Therefore the resulting inflation is called "premature" simply because it occurs before the economy in the aggregate reaches full employment.

Now, if we assume still further increments in total demand, then all sectors and industries will ultimately realize full employment. Industries in the aggregate can no longer respond to increases in demand with increases in supply. Therefore, accretions in demand for products will result in price increases, that is, in general inflation. In other words, at full employment the economy encounters the production barrier of scarce resources.

• PROBLEM 10-34

Assume the following information is relevant for an industrially advanced economy in the 1980-1982 period:

Year	Price level index	Rate of increase in labor productivity	Index of industrial production	Unemployment rate	Average hourly wage rates
1980	181	2.5 %	205	5.8 %	$3.55
1981	188	2.0	202	6.4	3.80
1982	199	1.8	200	7.1	4.10

Describe in detail the macroeconomic situation faced by this society. Is cost-push inflation in evidence?

Solution: This society is confronted with growing unemployment, and inflation. The inflation rate in 1981 is 188-181 = 7% and in 1982, 199-188 = 11%, while the rate of unemployment in 1981 is 6.4%, and in 1982, 7.1%, respectively. The industrial production fell from 205 in 1980 to 202 in 1981, to 200 in 1982, so a reduction in output took place in 1981 of 205-202 = 3%, and in 1982 of 202-200 = 2%.

Nominal income Y = general price level P x real output y ;

$$Y = P.y$$

So the growth in nominal income (GNP) equals the increase in the general price level (= inflation) plus the growth in real output. So, this society experiences a growth in National Income of 7-3 = 4% in 1981, and of 11-2 = 9% in 1982. National income increases, although real output declines, because of the excessive inflation.

The average hourly wage rate increases by

$$\frac{3.80 - 3.55}{3.55} = 7\% \text{ in 1981, and by}$$

$$\frac{4.10 - 3.80}{3.80} = 8\% \text{ in } 1982$$

Labor productivity increases by 2.0% in 1981 and by only 1.8% in 1982.

Nominal wage W = general price level P $\times$ real wage w ,

$$W = P \times w$$

or

$$w = W/P \ .$$

So the increase in real wage is the difference between the rise in nominal wage and inflation. The real wage in 1981 increased, therefore 7-7 = 0%, but fell in 1982 by -(8-11) = 3%, while labor productivity increased by 2% and 1.8%, in the respective years.

Finally, industrial output y = employment L $\times$ labor productivity, q . Thus the growth in industrial output g_y equals the growth of employment g_L plus the growth in labor productivity, g_q

$$g_y = g_L + g_q$$

In 1981, $-3 = g_L + 2$, and we expect employment to fall by $g_L = -3-2 = -5\%$ but unemployment increases at an even worse rate of

$$\frac{6.4 - 5.8}{5.8} = 10\%$$

In 1982, $-2 = g_L + 1.8$, we expected employment to fall by $g_L = -2 - 1.8 = -3.8\%$ but, unemployment increased by 11%.

Conclusion: This industrially advanced society experiences the worst of two macroeconomic worlds, unemployment and a severe cost-push-inflation. Nominal income increases, but real output falls. The cost-push comes from outside the economy, because the labor productivity rose, while the real wage remained constant in 1981, and fell by 3% in 1982. And secondly, the fall in real output and the insufficient growth in labor productivity implied already an increase in unemployment, but the actual increase in unemployment has been even more dramatic than was expected.

On the basis of the increase in nominal wage rates and increases in labor productivity we could expect an inflation rate of 7 - 3 = 4% in 1981, and 8 - 1.8 = 6.2% in 1982 but the actual inflation rates were 7% and 11%, respectively. Inflation therefore must be caused by increases in the prices of raw materials, and/or increases in profit margins, while the profits are not spent but retained. Real purchasing power has leaked away, either abroad, or into reserves.

• PROBLEM 10-35

What is the Phillips curve? And what is the expectations-augmented Phillips curve?

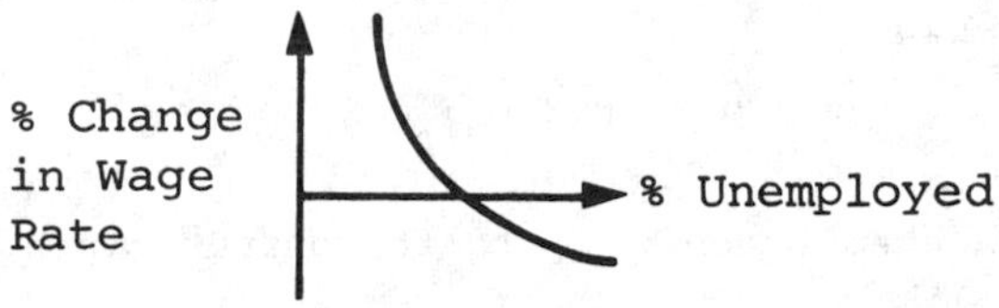

Fig. 1

Solution: The Phillips curve, as conceived by Professor A.W. Phillips of the London School of Economics in the 1950's, was an empirical relationship between the percentage of wage increase and the percentage of unemployment. (See Fig. 1). Because of the direct relationship between the percentages of price and wage increase, respectively, it became fashionable in the 1960's to relate the percentage of price increase = inflation rate π to the unemployment rate u (see Fig. 2).

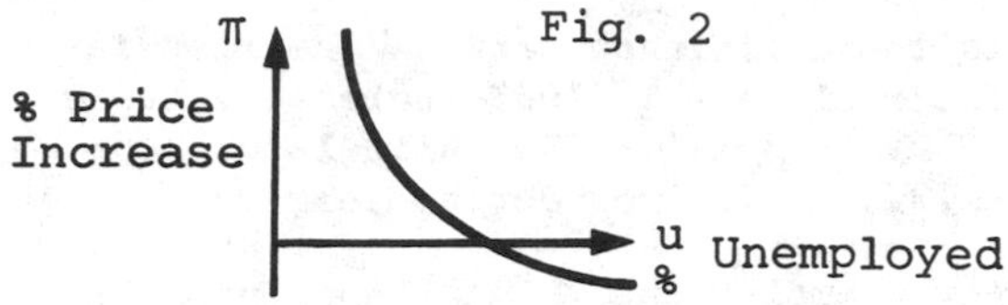

Fig. 2

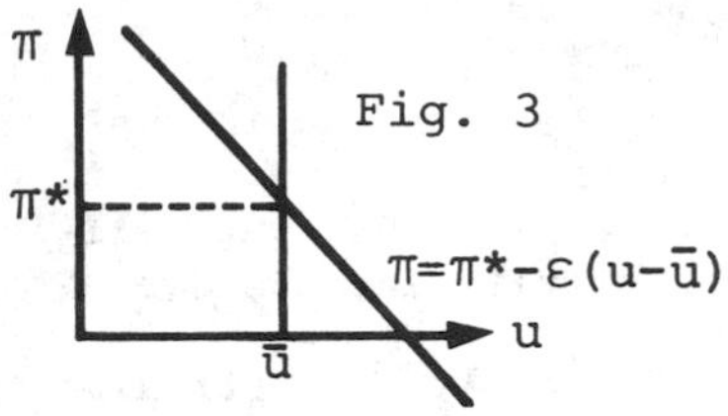

Fig. 3

In the 1970's the expectations-augmented Phillips curve was introduced: this is a relationship between actual inflation π, expected (or anticipated) inflation π^*, and the difference between the actual unemployment rate u, and the natural rate of unemployment $\bar{u}$. A linear form of the expectations-augmented Phillips curve can be presented as $\pi = \pi^* - \epsilon(u - \bar{u})$. (See Fig. 3).

From Figure 3 we notice that when the actual rate of inflation u is equal to the natural rate of inflation $\bar{u}$, $u = \bar{u}$, the actual rate of inflation π equals the expected rate of inflation π^*.

The Phillips curve is also called the price-job trade-off curve, because a higher rate of inflation is accompanied by a lower rate of unemployment, and a lower rate of inflation with more unemployment.

• PROBLEM 10-36

How do modern economists, using the anticipated inflation theory, project the long-run Phillips curve, and why?

Solution: The long-run Phillips curve is projected to be vertical at a level of employment where the economy is working at full capacity, when expectations adjust to the actual rate of inflation.

The modern aggregate supply equation, or, price-equation, relates output not to the price level but to the relative change in the price level, i.e., to inflation. Such a relationship can be written as $\pi = \pi^* + \alpha(Y - Y_p)$, $\alpha > 0$, where π is the actual rate of inflation, π^*-the expected rate of inflation, Y-output, Y_p-potential output (so that $Y - Y_p$ is the capacity gap), and α a positive coefficient. This relationship can be derived from the expectations-augmented Phillips curve

$$\pi = \pi^* - \epsilon(u - \bar{u}) \qquad (1)$$

where u = rate of unemployment, and $\bar{u}$ = the natural rate of unemployment, and Okun's Law

$$u - \bar{u} = -\beta(Y - Y_p) \qquad (2)$$

which relates the unemployment gap to the output gap.

Substituting equation (2) into equation (1) gives

$$\pi = \pi^* + \epsilon\beta(Y - Y_p) = \pi^* + \alpha(Y - Y_p) ,$$

where $\alpha = \epsilon\beta$ (ϵ and β are positive coefficients).

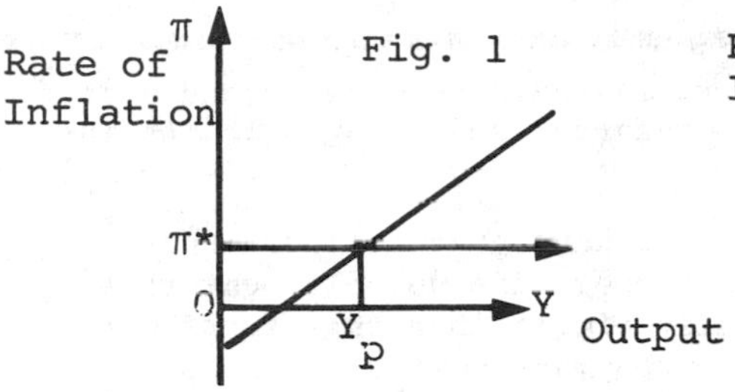

Fig. 1

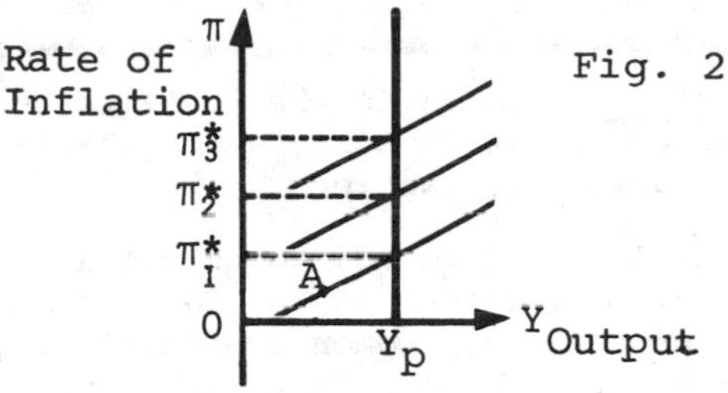

Fig. 2

The aggregate supply schedule can be pictured as in Figure 1.

The current rate of inflation equals the expected rate of inflation when current output equals potential output. It is also clear that inflation is higher when actual output Y relative to potential output Y_p is higher and when expected inflation π^* is higher. An increase in the expected rate of inflation shifts the aggregate supply schedule upwards (see Fig. 2).

So inflation depends on the state of the labor market, here measured by the GNP gap, and on inflationary expectations. In the short run we may have both inflation and unemployment (point A). That possibility arises because the expectations of inflation cause wages and prices to rise, and unemployment may not exert sufficient dampening pressure on wage settlements to restore full employment. This combination of inflation and unemployment was observed in the seventies.

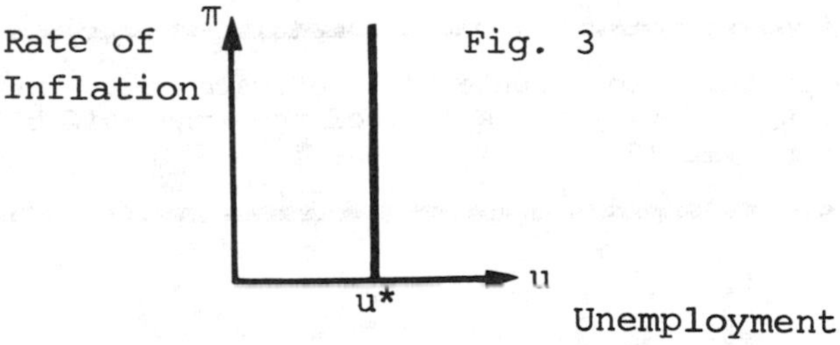

Fig. 3

But in the long-run the aggregate supply schedule is vertical, because in the long-run $Y = Y_p$. The reason is that expectations will ultimately adjust to the actual rate of inflation so $\pi^* = \pi$, and

$$\pi^* = \pi^* + \alpha(Y - Y_p)$$

from which it follows that $Y = Y_p$. Deviations of output from the full-employment level require expectational errors or deviations of the inflation rate from its habitual level. In the long-run, by definition, there are no errors in expectations, and therefore output is at the full-employment level. The aggregate supply schedule is vertical (see figure 2). But when $Y = Y_p$, then it follows that unemployment is at its 'natural' level (see equation 2), $u = \bar{u}$. Thus the Phillips-curve is also vertical (see figure 3).

• PROBLEM 10-37

Keynesians, in defense of the Phillips curve, have contended that in the late 1960's and in the 1970's the Phillips curve has shifted to the right. What could have caused such a shift?

Solution: Shifts in the Phillips curve may have occurred because of changes in the composition of the labor force, and changes in the inflationary expectations.

In the past decade teenagers and women have come to constitute larger proportions of the total labor force. The unemployment rates of teenagers and women are substantially higher than that for the whole labor force. This influx of unemployment dominated groups in the labor force pushes the general rate of unemployment upward, at the same levels of existing inflation.

The Phillips curve shifts, consequently, to the right. Secondly, if the public, workers and businesses expect substantial inflation in the future, these expectations will be included in their wage demands and price policies, pushing inflation upward at the same level of existing unemployment. Again the Phillips curve shifts to the right in consequence.

Keynesian policy becomes, therefore, more complicated. In a recession, Keynesian demand policies are effective in moving the economy toward full employment. But, as full employment is approached, an acceleration in the rise of the general price level will occur, and, worse yet, inflationary expectations may evolve. Therefore greater emphasis will be put upon manpower or wage-price policies in addition to the Keynesian demand management.

• PROBLEM 10-38

How can income policies contribute to a leftward shift in the Phillips curve thereby reducing the effect of the trade-off between inflation and unemployment?

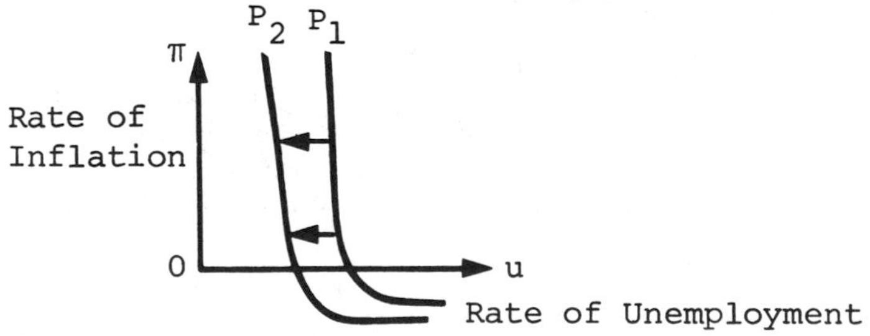

Solution: The term income policy refers to any method, voluntary or compulsory, that attempts to restrain inflation by direct limitations on increases in wages or prices. Also called wage and price controls, these government measures affect the prices firms charge and the wages labor earns directly, rather than through the indirect way of affecting aggregate demand and expectations.

When prices and wages are temporarily not allowed to change in a so-called 'price freeze', the inflationary expectations, which account for much of the difficulty in reducing actual inflation, are directly affected. However this works only when the price-freeze is announced and imposed without prior warning, because when a long debate precedes the imposition of the controls, many firms would find the time to hike their prices prior to the controls and frustrate the entire program by accelerating inflation rather than containing it.

But when the income policy is effective it reduces the levels of inflation connected with the various rates of unemployment. Thus the Phillips curve is shifted leftward, from P_1 to P_2, (see Fig.). It appears that price-wage controls are most affective in handling cost-push inflation in a period of high unemployment. Instead of a temporary price freeze, as used by the Nixon administration, price-wage guidelines can be used, as was done by the Kennedy administration. In this case, wage increases are limited to the rate at which the productivity is increasing. Employers can meet such wage increases out of productivity gains, and therefore prices are expected to remain stable.

THE GOVERNMENT, FIRM AND INDIVIDUAL: FIGHTING INFLATION

• PROBLEM 10-39

What are some of the ways for government, business, and the consumer to halt or control inflation?

Solution: Government can control the supply of money and credit, thereby avoiding over-expansion of business.

This relates to Monetary Theory and Policy which assumes a direct relationship between the supply of money and aggregate income:

$$Y = f(M)$$

where f( ) denotes a functional relationship, which may be linear

$$Y = k.M$$

thus

$$\Delta Y = k.\Delta M ,$$

a reduction in the money supply causes a preferably multiplied reduction in the aggregate demand (k is assumed to be greater than one). Taxes can be increased, thus reducing personal consumption. Increases in the national debt should be avoided and nonessential government expenditures should be reduced.

This relates to the simple Keynesian Multiplier Theory and Fiscal Policy, which states a direct relationship between aggregate autonomous spending and aggregate income

$$Y = \frac{1}{1-c}(I + \bar{C} + G - cT)$$

Fiscal policy controls government expenditures G and taxes T; (T - G) is the budget deficit financed by issuing government paper (obligations, Treasury Bills, money), thereby contributing to the national debt.

Business can help fight inflation by trying to increase the productivity of workers. This would decrease costs. Construction should be postponed insofar as feasible because this reduces investment in buildings, machinery and inventory and thereby reduces aggregate demand. Also production should be geared toward reasonable demand and unnecessary stockpiling of raw materials and semi-finished products should be avoided.

Labor can help fight inflation by also trying to increase productivity and cooperating with management in controlling the wage-price spiral, i.e., not setting excessive wage-bids.

Consumers can help by increasing personal savings, and thus decreasing personal spending, again reducing aggregate demand. Of course, these suggestions look rather flimsy when held up in the light of the real world. For government, before any economic issue can be decided, the political half of the issue must be solved. This often causes government to ignore the economic issue or try to solve it in a roundabout, often unsuccessful manner.

The business world understands that if we were to all work together, inflation could be controlled. But self-interest is the motivating force in the American industrial (capitalist) system, which is highly competitive. In this situation it seems risky to postpone expansion of the production facilities, to keep prices steady and profits low.

Finally, the consumer is confronted by the savings paradox. He knows that more savings and less consumption would help fight inflation, but it is inflation itself that is preventing the consumer from saving more, by inducing him to spend now.

• PROBLEM 10-40

When are wage-price controls appropriate and why?

Solution: We can best answer this question by stating when wage-price controls are not appropriate. That is when the initial cause of inflation, i.e., excess demand, is not removed. Price-wage controls will ultimately break down into wide spread avoidance, public disobedience and soaring black markets if the excess demand continues. The inflationary gap may be removed by fiscal and monetary policies.

But when the initial cause for inflation is removed and inflation perpetuates in an inflationary spiral, because it is built-in in the economy (inflationary expectations, inflation clauses in contracts), then it is appropriate to apply wage and price controls to change the dynamics of the inflationary process (change the expectations, the clauses). Thus wage-price controls are supplementary to fiscal and monetary policy.

Price and wage controls are difficult and costly to apply: literally tens of thousands of pay scales and hundreds of thousands of commodity prices have to be controlled.

• PROBLEM 10-41

If productivity is increasing by a uniform 2 percent in all industries, what should the wage guideline be if the inflation is to be held at 6 percent?

Solution: If productivity is increasing by a uniform 2 percent in the whole economy functioning at full-employment, real-output increases by 2 percent. Thus the real purchasing power is allowed also to increase by 2 percent, i.e., real wages can rise by 2 percent. Inflation should be controlled to be 6 percent, so nominal wages are allowed to increase 2 + 6 = 8%. In general:

Nominal wages = general price level x real wages

or

$$W = P \times w$$

The growth rate of nominal wages = rate of inflation + growth rate of real wages

$$g_W = \pi + g_w$$

$$= 0.06 + 0.02 = 0.08$$

• PROBLEM 10-42

When can a government budget deficit be considered to be neutral with respect to monetary factors? Explain.

Solution: A budget deficit can be considered neutral with respect to monetary factors if,

1) the amount of financing by new money is just sufficient to maintain the desired ratio of money balances to income at the new level. Some proportion of the budget ought always to be financed by monetary expansion since, if output is rising because of the stimulating fiscal policy, an increased quantity of money is required to keep the ratio M/y constant, where M is the money stock and y is national income. If this is not done then this ratio declines; the actual money balances become lower than the desired ones and people begin to spend less in order to hoard money; and the original stimulus of the budget deficit will be neutralized.

When the money stock is too rapidly increased and becomes larger than the public wishes to hold, people will try to reduce their money balances by increasing expenditures, exerting an inflationary pressure on the economy. Only when the ratio M/y remains constant and M increases as rapidly as y - assuming there was monetary equilibrium in the beginning, is the fiscal policy in this respect neutral.

A second condition for neutrality of the fiscal policy is that the amount of borrowing is exactly the amount that absorbs the gap which would otherwise exist between savings available for lending and the borrowing for private investment.

Total withdrawals must equal total injections in equilibrium; thus,

$$S + T = I + G$$

where S = private savings; I = private investments; T = taxes; G = government expenditures.

When there is a deficit, (government expenditures are larger than the tax revenues), $G - T > 0$; then, in equilibrium we see

$$G - T = S - I > 0$$

so that the funds being borrowed for investments I are as much less as new funds available for lending S (savings).

The budget deficit can be financed by selling bonds and by creating new money. Hence,

$$G - T = B + H,$$

where B is bond sales and H is high-powered money. Thus, if the government finances its deficit only by borrowing B, for example, and it sells bonds, it can absorb precisely the excess savings that private investors are not using.

Under these two conditions fiscal policy is neutral: the quantity of money-income ratio is unchanged, and the interest rates remain unchanged because the total supply of loanable funds is demanded by private investors and government together.

• PROBLEM 10-43

Which institutions and/or persons gain from anticipated inflation and why?

Solution: Inflation becomes anticipated if it is permanent and stable: the inflation rate does not change erratically over time but follows a smooth path.

Bankowners and the United States Treasury gain from anticipated inflation. Bankowners gain because the total of their monetary assets that earn no interest for the banks (cash in vault, deposits at the Federal Reserve Banks and the 'float', i.e., the checks in process of collection), is less than the total of their monetary liabilities on which they pay no interest, (or a very low one) like demand deposits. Thus banks are net money debtors. The United States Treasury gains through its connection with the Federal Reserve (FED). The Federal Reserve banks gain for the same reason that bankowners in general gain: the total of their monetary debts on which they do not pay interest (Federal reserve notes and their deposits) exceeds the total of their monetary assets on which they earn no interest (gold certificates). The equity (= 'net wealth') of the Federal Reserve banks is limited by law, so their inflationary gains are passed on to the United States Treasury. This way the Treasury earns the so-called inflation-tax. This reduces the needs for other tax revenues, so the people as tax payers should ultimately benefit by a tax reduction.

• PROBLEM 10-44

How does the anticipation, or expectation, of inflation affect aggregate supply? In your solution you may use Okun's Law and the modern expectations-augmented version of the Phillips curve.

Solution: The expectation of inflation will influence the behavior of wages, therefore costs, and therefore the prices for which output is supplied.

In face of anticipated inflation, labor wants to protect its real wages by having nominal wages rise, for example by including escalator clauses in the wage contracts; and firms can afford to pay the higher wages because they expect to be able to pass on rising costs in the form of higher prices.

Expectations can be included in the Phillips curve, when we conceive it as a relationship among actual inflation π, anticipated inflation π^*, and the difference between the actual unemployment rate u, and the natural rate of unemployment $\bar{u}$:

$$\pi = \pi^* - \varepsilon(u - \bar{u}) \tag{1}$$

(see Fig. 1). Okun's Law relates the

$$\text{GNP gap} = \frac{Y_F - Y}{Y_F},$$

where Y_F is full employment GNP, and Y is actual GNP, to the difference between the actual and the natural rate of unemployment:

$$\frac{Y_F - Y}{Y_F} = 3(u - \bar{u})$$

Call $3Y_F = \frac{1}{\alpha}$, then we can rewrite Okun's Law as $u - \bar{u} = -\alpha(Y - Y_F)$. (2)

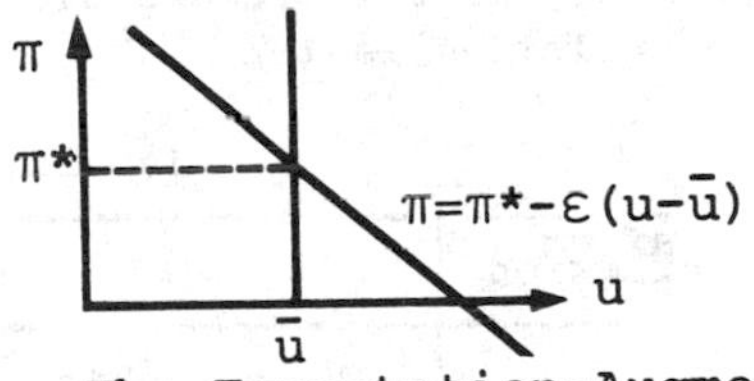

Fig. 1 The Expectation-Augmented Phillips Curve

When we substitute this expression (2) for $u - \bar{u}$ into equation (1), we find the modern version of the aggregate supply schedule:

$$\pi = \pi^* + \varepsilon\alpha(Y - Y_F) = \pi^* + \gamma(Y - Y_F),\ \gamma > 0. \tag{3}$$

This modern version of the aggregate supply schedule relates the actual and anticipated rates of inflation to the absolute value of the GNP gap.

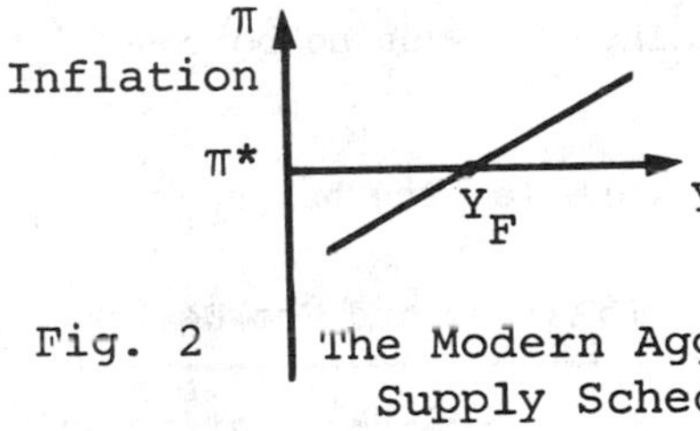

Fig. 2 The Modern Aggregate Supply Schedule

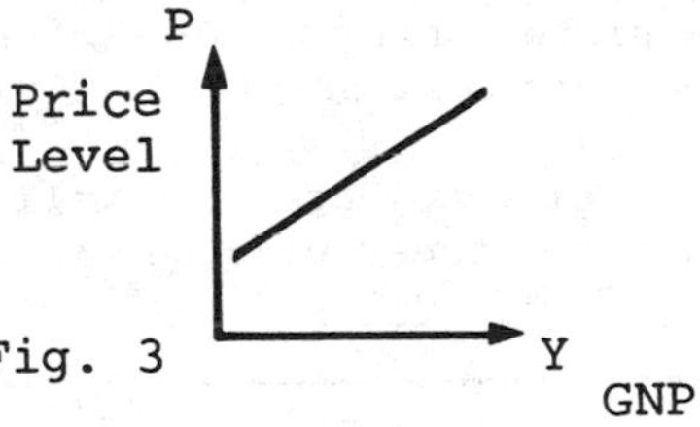

Fig. 3

(See Fig. 2). The classical aggregate supply schedule related not the price change to the actual GNP, but the price level P to the actual GNP. (See Fig. 3).

The modern aggregate supply schedule (Eq. 3 and Fig. 2) has two important properties:

1. Current inflation π is related to anticipated inflation π^*. When the anticipated inflation π^* is higher, the actual rate of inflation π will be higher.

2. A high GNP gap, $Y - Y_P < 0$, which means a high actual employment rate in the labor market, reduces the actual inflation rate below the expected inflation rate.

A more than full employment situation, so $u - \bar{u} > 0$, and thus $Y - Y_P > 0$, pushes the actual inflation π above the anticipated inflation rate π^*.

• PROBLEM 10-45

What is the consequence of unanticipated inflation? Explain and give an example.

Solution: When part of the inflation rate is intermittant and cannot be fully anticipated the interest rates do not fully discount inflation and wealth will be transferred from net money creditors to net money debtors.

For example: the balance sheet of a net money debtor may look like the following; he is a net money debtor because his money debts surpass his money assets; the inflation is 10%.

Assets			Liabilities and Net Wealth		
	original	after inflation		original	after inflation
Money assets	500	500	Money debts	3000	3000
Real assets	4000	4400	Net wealth	1500	1900
Total	$4500	$4900	Total	$4500	$4900

Money assets and liabilities do not change under inflation. The net money debtor has benefitted from inflation because his net wealth increased by

$$\frac{1900 - 1500}{1500} = 26.7\%$$

which is higher than the 10% inflation. He gained because he borrowed to finance his real assets.

But a net money creditor will lose. For example: the balance sheet of a net money creditor may look like:

Assets			Liabilities and Net Wealth		
	original	after inflation		original	after inflation
Money assets	500	500	Money debts	-	-
Real assets	1000	1100	Net wealth	1500	1600
Total	$1500	$1600	Total	$1500	$1600

The net money creditor incurs a loss by inflation because his net wealth increased by

$$\frac{1600 - 1500}{1500} = 6.7\% ,$$

lower than the 10% inflation. He has a loss because he used his equity to finance his real assets. Households on the average are net money creditors, while government and businesses are net money debtors. Inflation in the United States has caused a transfer of wealth from households to the federal government, and increasingly, in recent years, to business.

INFLATION AND INTEREST RATES

• PROBLEM 10-46

What would the money rate of interest have to be at an inflation rate of 6% to induce people to hold the same proportion of their assets in the form of money as they would with stable prices, if the real rate of interest was 5% and was not affected by the inflation?

Solution: The money rate of interest i equals the sum of the real rate of interest r and the inflation rate π

$$i = r + \pi$$
$$= 0.05 + 0.06 = 0.11$$

The money rate of interest has to be 11% to allow for no portfolio adjustments.

• PROBLEM 10-47

What is the consequence of permanent inflation for the interest rates?

Solution: When inflation is permanent and relatively steady it becomes anticipated and interest rates become discounted by the anticipated rate of inflation; nominal interest rate = real interest rate + inflation

$$i = r + \pi .$$

For example: inflation is 9% and the nominal rate is 11% then the real rate of interest is

$$r = i - \pi = 11 - 9 = 2\% .$$

• PROBLEM 10-48

Suppose that the trade-unions are strong enough to bargain a 5% increase in nominal wages. How much do you expect the prices will rise? In the U.S.A. productivity increases on average of 2% per year. How much are the workers better off?

Solution: Inflation is induced here by an increase in the labor costs; it will be a form of cost-push inflation.

We assume that the employers will leave their profit share unchanged at the conventional level. Thus the cost increase will be directly reflected in the product prices. The productivity is supposed to increase by 2%; this means a relative cost reduction of 2%. Thus the prices are expected to rise by

$$\pi = 5 - 2 = 3\% .$$

The nominal wage increase consists of the real wage increase and the increase in the general price level = inflation rate. What counts for the worker is how much he can purchase for his money, i.e., his real wage. His real wage increase is

$$5 - 3 = 2\%$$

The real wage increase equals the productivity increase.

What is the Gibson Paradox, and why is it called a paradox?

Fig. 1 Price and Interest Movements Overtime: The Gibson Paradox

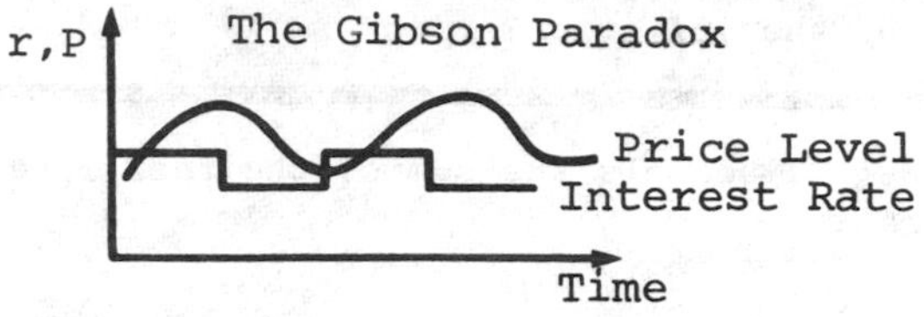

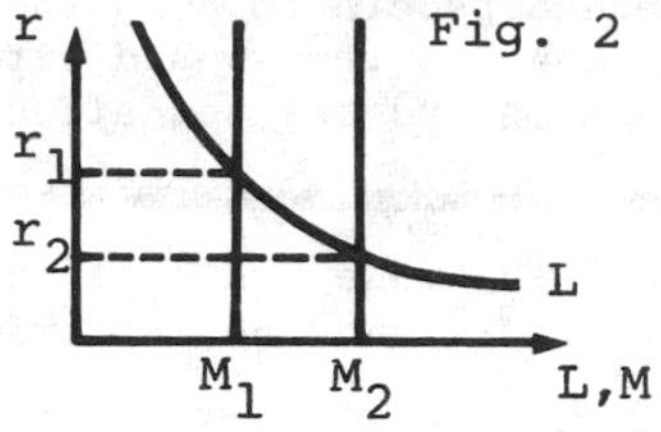

Fig. 2

Solution: The Gibson Paradox observes that when prices rise, interest rates rise and vice versa. (See Fig. 1). It is called a paradox because it contradicts the Classical Theory which states that an increase in the money supply would cause prices to rise and interest rates to fall. Looking at the money exchange equation $MV = PQ$ this becomes more transparant. We notice that, if the velocity V of the money turnover, i.e., the number of times that money changes hands in transactions, remains constant, and also real output is constant, and the money supply M increases, the price level P must increase. This can be explained by the portfolio adjustment theory: people spend their money when their money balances are too high, bidding up the prices.

But an increased money supply lowers the interest rate in the financial market (see Fig. 2). When the money supply M_1 increases to M_2, the interest rate r drops from r_1 to r_2 along the money-demand, i.e., Liquidity Preference, schedule.

The Gibson Paradox can be reconciled with classical theory by introducing time lags: the drop in the interest rate takes place immediately but the price increase is delayed so that the interest rate is already increased again when prices actually start to rise. And it can also be reconciled by acknowledging the difference between nominal and real interest rates.

The nominal interest rate i is the sum of the real interest rate r and inflation π : $i = r + \pi$. When the nominal rate i drops it may be caused by a drop in the real interest rate r, or by a drop in the rate of inflation π.

• PROBLEM 10-50

Which interest rate-nominal or real-represents the opportunity cost of holding cash? Explain.

Solution: The real rate represents the opportunity cost of holding cash; cash does not earn interest. The real cost of holding cash is equal to the rate of inflation times the cash hold, if there is no alternative. But this cash may be invested in bonds and earn a nominal interest. The opportunity cost of not investing the cash in bonds is the nominal interest minus the cost of inflation, which gives us the real interest.

• PROBLEM 10-51

Suppose we have a bond that sells for $1,000. The annual interest paid is $80. However, the monetary authorities have predicted that the general price level will increase next year by 5 percent. Given these facts, compute the;

a) nominal interest rate.

b) real interest rate.

Solution: a) The nominal interest rate is the rate that is actually paid and is computed as follows:

Amount of the interest paid ÷ Amount of the bonds = $\frac{\$80}{\$1,000}$ = 8 percent per year.

b) The real interest rate is one that expresses the real return on lending money, taking into account expectations about the future rate of inflation. Since it is predicted that the general price level will increase next year by 5 percent, that means the real value of the $1,000 is expected to decline over the year by

$$\$1,000 \times 5\% = \$50.$$

To calculate the real interest rate that will be earned, the $50 will be deducted from the $80 interest payment. This indicates a real gain of only $30 on the $1,000 bond - or a real interest rate of only

$$\$30 \div \$1,000 = 3 \text{ percent}.$$

We notice from these calculations that the nominal interest rate i is the sum of the real interest rate r and the rate of inflation π, thus

$$i = r + \pi .$$

• PROBLEM 10-52

Suppose that the interest rate has risen from 8% to 10% over a three year period while inflation has risen from 3% to 5%. What has happened to the real interest rate.

Solution: Whenever examining interest rates, we must realize that the "real interest rate" is equal to the "money interest rate" minus "the percentage price rise." Using the inflation rate above as an indicator of the percentage price rise, we see that at the beginning of the three year period, the real interest rate = 8% - 3% = 5%. At the end of the three year period, real interest = 10% - 5% = 5%. Therefore when prices are rising, money interest rate must rise in order to keep real interest rate constant.

• PROBLEM 10-53

Mr. Riley loaned his friend, Mr. Gillis, $400 to purchase a second-hand car. One year later Mr. Gillis returned $420 to Mr. Riley. During that period, the consumer price index rose by 5%.

a) What is the nominal rate of interest in this example?

b) What is the real rate of interest?

Solution: a) The nominal, or market, rate of interest, is the actual percentage represented by the interest paid by a borrower. Therefore, in this example Mr. Gillis paid \$20 in interest (\$420 - 400). This represents \$20/400 = 5% nominal rate of interest.

b) The real rate of interest takes inflation into account. It is defined as the nominal rate minus the rate of inflation (as represented by the consumer price index). In this example, prices rose by 5%. Therefore real rate of interest =

$$5\% - 5\% = 0 .$$

THE FEDERAL RESERVE AND THE MONEY SUPPLY

• PROBLEM 10-54

How will an increase in the money supply, effectuated by the FED through an open market operation, have the result of increasing the national income?

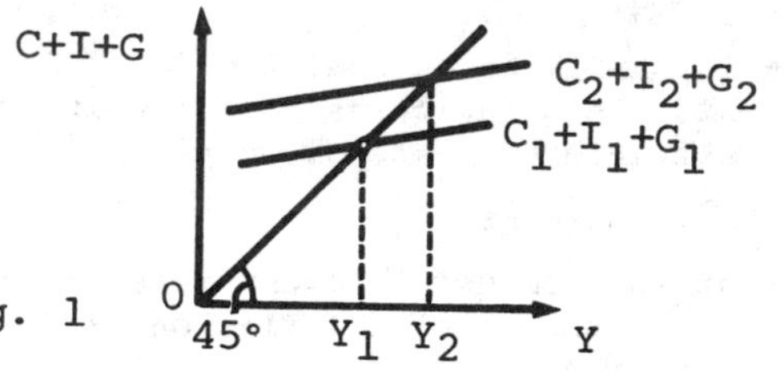

Fig. 1

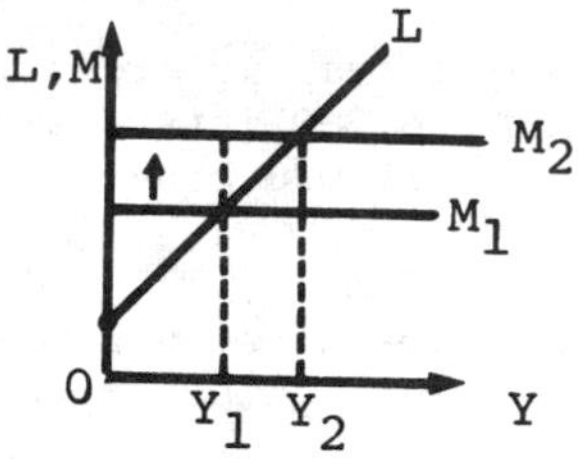

Fig. 2

Solution: There are two coexistent explanations of this process. The Monetary Theorists rely on the portfolio adjustments, while the Keynesian Theorists use the effects on interest rates and investment.

In both theories an increase in the national income results from an increase in aggregate demand $Y = C + I + G$. In Fig. 1 the new equilibrium income Y_1 is higher than the old equilibrium income Y_2, because of an upward shift in aggregate demand from $C_1 + I_1 + G_1$ to $C_2 + I_2 + G_2$ (see the chapter on income determination). Most of this autonomous shift comes from an increase in investment I, and monetary policy concentrates on this component of the aggregate demand. The national income will expand by more than the autonomous increase in spending because of the multiplier effect (see chapter on the multiplier).

1) The monetary theorists use the following explanation for the connection between the increase in the money supply and the shift in autonomous spending. Suppose that the demand for money is related proportionally to income (see Fig. 2). L is the demand for money and M the supply of money, determined by the FED, independently of income Y. Let there be an increase in the money supply from M_1 to M_2. At income level Y_1 the supply of money is larger than the demand; people have excess money balances. They will increase their spending to reduce their money balances to the desired level; but this autonomous increase in the aggregate demand raises the level of the national in-

come from Y_1 to Y_2. The desired levels of the money balances increase simultaneously along L, and the gap between actual and desired levels of the money balances becomes closed by this portfolio adjustment process. The people adjust their money holdings relative to the other assets they own. In case of an open market operation when the FED buys securities in exchange for money, the money holdings of banks and public are increased relative to their holdings of bonds and other assets. The increase in the bank reserves will result in a multiple expansion of their deposits (the money-multiplier effect), affecting further the portfolios of the public. When commercial banks receive additional reserves, say through an open market operation, they usually react by expanding their investments and loans, stimulating the investment component in the aggregate demand. The open market purchases by the FED raise the security prices and lower the interest rates. This causes a rise in bond prices inducing the public to adjust their portfolios by selling their securities. The high bond prices tend to increase the demand for money and reduce the demand for bonds. The increased supply of money and the lower interest yields on bonds makes other assets, like corporation stock, physical capital and consumer goods relatively more attractive, and autonomous spending I + C increases. Thus the portfolio adjustment explanation of the monetarist theorists relies on the changes in the relative prices of the different assets as the principal way in which the stimulus is transmitted from the financial markets to the real sector of the economy.

2) The Keynesian theorists used the interest rate-investment theory. The liquidity preference schedule and the money supply are exhibited in Fig. 3.

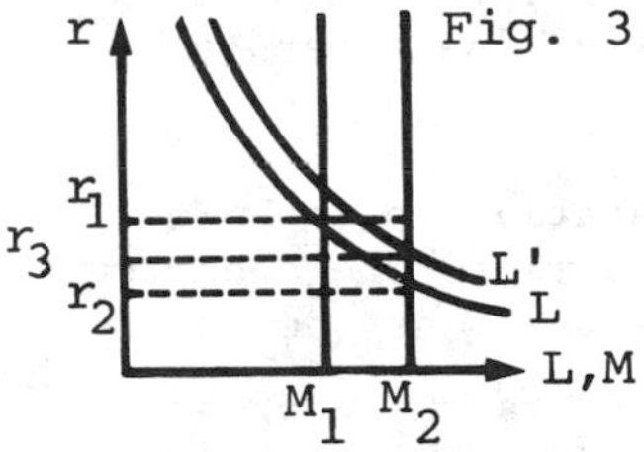

Fig. 3

Fig. 4
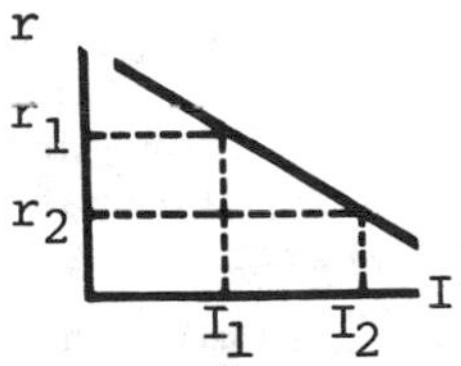

Fig. 5
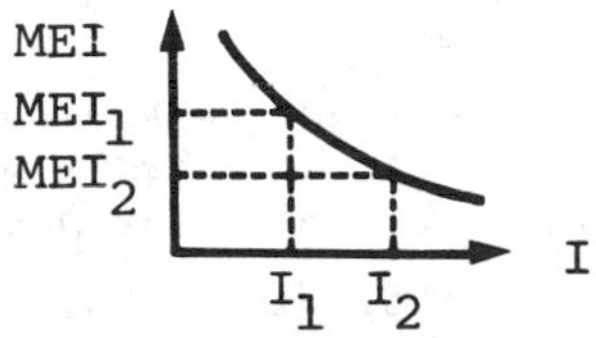

An increase in the money supply from M_1 to M_2 causes the interest rate to fall from r_1 to r_2: the people will have excess money balances at interest rate r_1 and therefore start buying bonds. The bond prices are bid up, and thus the yield goes down to r_2. At the lower interest rate people are willing to hold more money relative to their holdings of other assets. This decline in the interest rate is the liquidity effect of an increase in the money supply.

The fall in the interest rates makes borrowing for business cheaper and investments will expand (see Fig. 4), because the cost of borrowing funds will be lower than the expected rate of return on new investments. The expected rate of return on a new investment, is also called the marginal efficiency of investment (MEI) and is defined as the ratio

$$MEI = \frac{\text{expected annual net return}}{\text{cost of investment (machine, building, etc.)}}$$

When the expected rate of return is higher than the interest rate, more funds will be borrowed and invested. The marginal efficiency of investment is decreasing (see Fig. 5) and at a certain level of investment the expected rate of return = interest rate = cost of capital and no more funds will be invested. This expansion of investment means an increase in aggregate demand moving national income upward.

This simple explanation becomes more sophisticated when we add the following: the increase in income induces an increase in the transactions demand for money. This income effect shifts the liquidity preference schedule L (see Fig. 3) to the right and restricts the fall in the interest rate to r_3, and therefore the increase in investment.

• PROBLEM 10-55

Does the total wealth possessed by the public change when the FED increases the money supply by an open market purchase of securities?

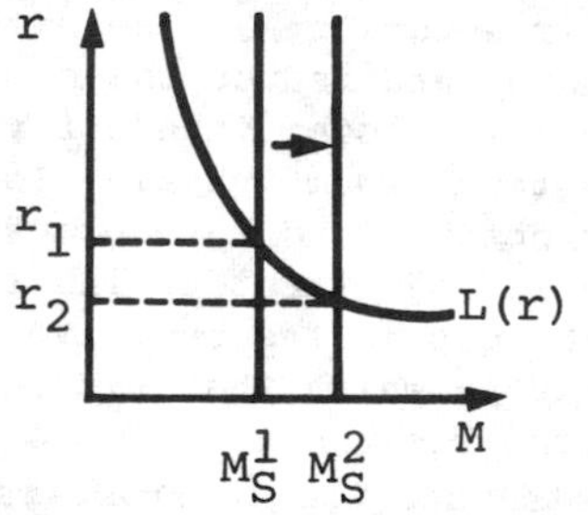

Solution: No. If additional money is supplied by an open market operation, the FED buys securities from the public in exchange for cash. The public thus substitutes their holdings of bonds for holdings of cash balances, and there is no change in total wealth. As a result there is also no wealth effect on total spending.

The important effect of such an open market operation is to lower the interest rates (see accompanying figure), and to raise the security prices. The money supply M_s^1 shifts to M_s^2 while the money demand schedule remains unchanged. As a result the interest rate r drops from r_1 to r_2.

• PROBLEM 10-56

Which of the following should the Federal Reserve not do during a recession:

a) lower required reserve ratios
b) sell securities in the open market
c) reduce down payment requirements for installment buying
d) lower the discount rate

Solution: b) sell securities in the open market.

Clearly this should not be done because such a policy move would reduce the money supply and hence reduce the aggregate demand for goods and services at the prevailing price level, further exacerbating the negative impact of the current recession on output and employment.

• PROBLEM 10-57

Suppose that real GNP doubles while the quantity of money increases by

80%. If the velocity of money is constant, what happens to the price level?

Solution: From the Equation of Exchange, we have

$$MV = PQ$$

where

$$M = \text{money supply}$$
$$V = \text{velocity of money}$$
$$P = \text{price level}$$
$$Q = \text{real GNP} .$$

We hold V fixed while M and Q change and we then must determine P. Therefore

$$V' = V$$
$$M' = M + 80\% M = 1.8M$$
$$Q' = 2Q$$
$$P' = P + \Delta P ,$$

where the primed symbols represent the values of the variables after the increase in the quantity of money.

By the equation of exchange

$$M'V' = P'Q'$$

Substituting, we get

$$(1.8M)(V) = (P')(2Q)$$
$$1.8MV = 2P'Q$$
$$P' = 0.9 \frac{MV}{Q} , \text{ but } \frac{MV}{Q} \equiv P$$

thus

$$P' = 0.9P$$
$$\Delta P = P' - P = 0.9P - P$$
$$= -0.10P$$

Therefore the price level drops by 10%.

• PROBLEM 10-58

What are the effects of an increase in the money supply on output and on prices in the short run and in the long run?

Solution: The effect in the short run is an increase in output, and in the long run an increase in the general price level.

Use the equation of exchange as frame of reference:

$$MV = PQ$$

where M denotes the money supply, V the velocity of circulation, P the general price level and Q the real aggregate output, or total of business transactions in the economy. When the money supply M increases there is usually a small drop in the velocity V, but on average we are allowed to assume that V is constant (V is about 3.5). The increase in the money supply M, increases the money balances above their desired levels and people start to buy. The aggregate demand increases and the producers react by increasing their output, as long as it has not yet reached its full-employment output.

In the long run, however, the growth of real output Q is limited by the available labor and capital supply. When Q cannot increase rapidly enough, the increase in the money supply will be reflected in a more rapid increase in the general price level P, that is, in a demand-pull inflation.

MILTON FRIEDMAN AND MONETARISM

• PROBLEM 10-59

Can you explain the two basic tenets of Monetarism?

Solution: Monetarism emphasizes the importance of the behavior of the money stock, M, in determining:

1. The rate of inflation,

$$\pi \equiv \frac{\Delta P}{P},$$

in the long run, and

2. The behavior of real GNP, Y, in the short run.
   In an economy with a constant growth rate of money,

$$M \equiv \frac{\Delta M}{M},$$

a constant level of output, and with full anticipation of inflation, the prices will rise exactly at the rate at which the nominal money stock is increasing: $\pi = m$. Thus in a stationary economy the rate of inflation equals the growth rate of the nominal quantity of money.

How to derive this equality?

Recall the equilibrium condition in the money market: the real money supply M/P equals the real money demand L(i,Y) which is dependent on the interest rate and income, so

$$M/P = L(i,Y), \qquad (1)$$

(Note: this relation describes the LM-schedule in the IS-LM analysis), or

$$M = PL(i,Y), \qquad (2)$$

the nominal money supply equals the nominal money demand. In a stationary economy output and interest rates are constant $i = \bar{i}$ and $Y = \bar{Y}$; but then there is also the real money demand constant,

$$L(\bar{i},\bar{Y}) = \bar{L}.$$

Also, in order to maintain the equality between the supply and demand for money, changes in the nominal money supply, $\Delta M/M$, must equal changes in the price level $\Delta P/P$; so $m = \pi$. Even if we allow for constant growth of real income, the relationship between m and π is fixed.

The income elasticity of the demand for money is the relative marginal change in the real money demand caused by the relative marginal change in real income:

$$\frac{\Delta L}{L} \Big/ \frac{\Delta Y}{Y}.$$

For example: when the elasticity of the money demand is 0.75 we mean that a 1% increase in real income, $\Delta Y/Y = 1\%$, causes an increase in real money demand of $\Delta L/Y = 0.75\%$

$$\left(\frac{\Delta L}{L} \Big/ \frac{\Delta Y}{Y} = \frac{0.75\%}{1\%} = 0.75\right).$$

Suppose that real income grows at an average rate of 3% per year, $\Delta Y/Y$, then we know that the real money demand increases by

$$\frac{\Delta L}{L} = 0.75 \times 3\% = 2.25\%.$$

Returning to relation (2), $M = PL(i,Y)$ we notice that the growth rate of the nominal money supply equals the sum of the inflation rate and the rate of increase in the real demand for money:

$$\frac{\Delta M}{M} = \frac{\Delta P}{P} + \frac{\Delta L}{L}$$

or

$$m = \pi + \frac{\Delta L}{L}$$

Thus the inflation rate equals the rate of increase in the money supply minus the rate of increase in the real money demand: $\pi = m - \Delta L/L$. With an elasticity of the money demand of

$$\frac{\Delta L}{L} \Big/ \frac{\Delta Y}{Y} = 0.75 ,$$

this can be expressed as

$$\pi = m - 0.75 \frac{\Delta Y}{Y}$$

and we have a constant relationship between the inflation rate, the rate of money supply and the growth rate of real income, which is relatively constant in the long run, say 3%, so that $\pi = m - 2.25$. Inflation in the long run appears to be a monetary phenomenon: it arises from growth in the nominal money supply in excess of growth in real money demand. Secondly, how is the behavior of real GNP, Y, in the short run, determined by the behavior of the money stock M? We know from the income determination theory that changes in the aggregate demand in the short run are due to changes in real balances (adjustments in portfolios to changes in the money stock) or changes in the fiscal policy of taxes and expenditures; and that the aggregate supply relationship is affected by the expected rate of inflation π^*, because it influences labor and material costs.

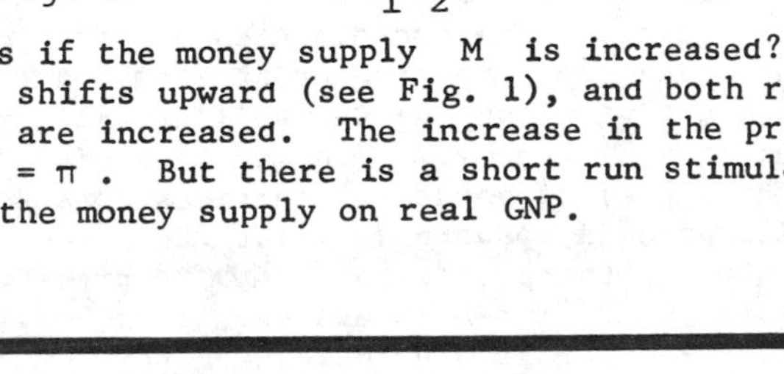

Fig. 1

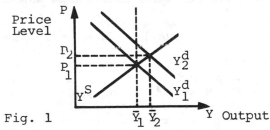

What happens if the money supply M is increased? The aggregate demand schedule shifts upward (see Fig. 1), and both real output and the price level are increased. The increase in the price level means inflation, $\Delta P/P = \pi$. But there is a short run stimulative effect of an increase in the money supply on real GNP.

• PROBLEM 10-60

What is the monetary rule of Milton Friedman and why did he propose it?

Solution: According to Professor Milton Friedman of Chicago University the monetary authorities should follow the rule that the money supply be increased at a fixed rate.

He argues that, because the behavior of the money stock is of critical importance for the behavior of real GNP (in the short run) and nominal GNP (in the long run), and because money operates with long, often variable lags, monetary policy should not attempt to 'fine tune' the economy. Because of insufficient knowledge and understanding of the processes involved errors are made in forecasting and judging the time lags. Thus an active discretionary monetary policy might actually accentuate the instability of the economy. Therefore the money supply should be kept growing at a constant rate, $\Delta M/M$ = constant. Friedman's money rule is essentially a non-activist rule: the money supply is kept growing at, say, $\Delta M/M = 4\%$

An example of an activist rule would be that the growth rate of the money supply would be increased by 2.5% per year, for every 1% unemployment in excess of the natural unemployment rate of, say, 6%. Algebraically such a rule would be expressed as

$$\frac{\Delta M}{M} = 4.0 + 2.5(u - 6.0)$$

where $\Delta M/M$ = growth rate per year and u = unemployment rate. By linking the monetary growth to the unemployment rate an activist, anticyclical monetary policy is achieved, but without any discretion.

However, given that the economy and our knowledge of it are both changing overtime, there is no case for permanent rules that would tie the controls of fiscal and monetary authorities permanently, and some discretion appears to be desirable.

• PROBLEM 10-61

How can the Automatic Monetary Policy of a fixed growth rate in the Money Supply as proposed by Milton Friedman, have a stabilizing effect on the economy?

Solution: As automatic policy deals, without discretionary interference, with the random disturbances to which any real economy is subjected.

Suppose the economy is below its capacity level; there is unemployment. The supply of money growing at a constant rate is then relatively high to the lowered level of activity. The public will consider their money balances excessive. Their desired money balances are lower, so the public will decrease their money balances by increasing their expenditures. In the aggregate the consolidated balances cannot be decreased because the money stock is growing at a constant rate, but the increase in economic activity, buying and selling, will provide an expansionary stimulus on the economy. This may cause initially price increases, because the supply of goods and services does not react immediately to the increase in spending: first the inventories will be run down. But eventually there will be an upward pressure on real output too. The existing unemployment keeps wage increases moderate. The rapidly rising prices and the slowly increasing wages makes the expansion of (real) output profitable for business. Initially, as an additional effect, the excess money supply depresses the interest rates, and these encourage investments. All these effects are directed towards an expansion of real output.

Suppose now, in a different case, that an external disturbance, for example, a raw-materials-cost-price-shock (oil!) has caused prices to rise at 'full employment'. Nominal incomes will increase with the price level, because of wage and salary demands, but the money balances will only grow as fast as real output does. Thus the money balances will become low relative to the income levels and expenditures, and people will cut down their expenditures to build up their balances. The lower than desired money supply causes the interest rates to increase, discouraging investments. In this way the effects are all directed towards a contraction, because the money stock is growing at a constant rate.

• PROBLEM 10-62

How would Monetarists stabilize the fluctuations of the economy?

Solution: Monetarists believe that changes in the growth rate of the quantity of money are responsible for changes in the level of economic activity. The supply of money effects interest rates, which in turn affects investment. So, the key to stabilizing economic fluctuations is stabilizing the growth rate of the quantity of money.

Monetarists generally do not recommend trying to counter fluctuations in the level of business activity by varying the growth rate of the money supply. They feel that the effects of monetary policy are too unpredictable to use against specific disturbances in the economy. So, Monetarists would stabilize the fluctuations of the economy by stabilizing the growth rate of the money supply.

• PROBLEM 10-63

Some monetarists, like Milton Friedman contend that the Phillips curve does not exist as a stable, 'long-run' phenomenon. These 'accelerationists' conclude that Keynesian full-employment policies, based on the incorrect assumption that the Phillips curve does exist, will result in an accelerating rate of inflation. Can you explain this accelerationist theory?

Solution: We use the accompanying figure in our explanation.

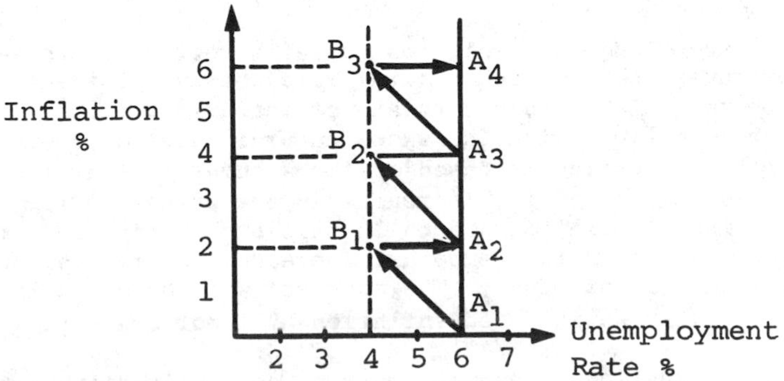

Suppose that the natural, or 'full-employment' rate of unemployment is higher than believed. Suppose, it is 6% (point A, in the figure) rather than 4%. The government, obliged to steer the economy towards full employment by the Employment Act of 1946, believes that the 'full-employment' rate of unemployment is 4%, and regards 6% unemployment as economically and politically intolerable. It invokes therefore expansionary fiscal and monetary policies. The resulting increase in aggregate demand pulls up the price level, and, given the level of money wages, business profits increase. The money expenses remain constant, but the sales revenues increase because of the price increase. Firms respond to expanded profits by increasing output, and hire additional workers. The economy moves from point A_1 to point B_1. This move is consistent with the Keynesian conception of the Phillips curve. Some higher inflation is traded for a reduction in unemployment.

The accelerationists contend, however, that point B_1 is not a stable equilibrium position. The workers will recognize that their real wages and incomes have fallen, because their money incomes didn't rise when the level of product prices has increased. The workers will demand, and receive, a money wage increase to restore the purchasing power they have lost. But when the money wages are raised, with constant sales revenues, business profits will be reduced to their earlier level. And the motivation of businesses to increase output and employment will be eroded. Unemployment will return to its true 'natural' rate of unemployment of 6%. The economy moves from point B_1 to point A_2. But the economy experiences as a result of these two processes a higher rate of inflation, here 2%. The effectual shift is from point A_1 to point A_2. The shift from A_1 to B_1 was only a 'short-run', transient phenomenon. In the 'long-run' unemployment returns to its 'natural rate'.

The process may now be repeated. A frustrated government will try again to expand the economy. Aggregate demand increases, prices rise, money wages remain temporarily constant, profits increase, output increases, and employment rises, the economy moves to B_2. But the workers will catch up; raise their money wages; the profits increase will be eroded, employment falls; and the economy moves to A_3; etc. So, say the accelerationists, the expansionary policies of the government move the 'short-term' Phillips curve upward, from $A_1 B_1$, to $A_2 B_2$, to $A_3 B_3$, to more unfavorable positions.

Secondly, the 'long-run' Phillips curve is vertical: the economy always gravitates back to the 'natural rate' of unemployment. And in the long-run there is no constant rate of inflation. Each rate of inflation is compatible with the same 'natural rate' of unemployment. However, this explanation is based on the assumption that increases in money wages lag behind the increases in the price level. If the workers anticipate inflation and build this expectation into their wage demands, then even the temporary increases in profits, output and employment will not occur. The movement will be directly from A_1 to A_2. Fully anticipated inflation by labor means there will be no short-run decline in unemployment. The implication is that Keynesian measures to achieve a (misspecified) full-employment rate of unemployment will generate an accelerating rate of inflation, not a lower rate of unemployment.

• PROBLEM 10-64

How did the Monetarists, using the anticipated-inflation-theory, project the Phillips-curve, and why?

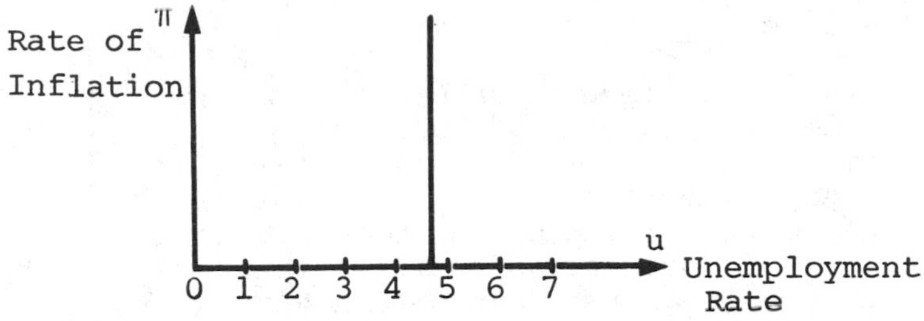

Solution: The Monetarists claim that the current Phillips-curve is essentially vertical (see accompanying figure).

When an economy experiences a steady rate of inflation for a longer period, inflation becomes anticipated. And workers, expecting that their wage increases will be eroded, will bargain for nominal wage increases with the expected inflation in mind. Workers will not only ask for wage increases that will compensate them for current productivity gains and past inflations, but also for the price increases they expect. As a result inflation will be accelerated. The accelerating rate of inflation is not due to an increasingly tight employment situation, but rather to expectations of future inflation. A trade-off between inflation and employment no longer exists and the Phillips curve will be a vertical line. The line can be thought of as the natural rate of unemployment, i.e., 'full employment' given the structure of the economy.

Answer
To be covered when testing yourself

SHORT ANSWER QUESTIONS FOR REVIEW

Choose the correct answer.

1. By "cost-push (or sellers') inflation," economists are referring to: (a) attempts by labor and industry to set prices and wages that will give them together more than 100 per cent of the available product (b) rising prices due to excessive levels of government spending financed by open-market operations through the Fed (c) rising prices due to excessive levels of aggregate demand (d) the rise in total sales revenue attributable to price-tag changes rather than to real volume changes (e) none of the above — a

2. "Stagflation" refers to: (a) a simultaneous increase in output and the price level (b) a simultaneous reduction in output and the price level (c) an increase in the price level accompanied by decreases in real output and employment (d) a decline in the price level accompanied by increases in real output and employment — c

3. To improve the "natural rate of unemployment": (a) pursue contractionary macroeconomic policies (b) try to improve on structural imperfections in the labor market (c) raise the minimum wage (d) pursue expansionary macroeconomic policies (e) don't bother with any of the above — b

4. The Humphrey-Hawkins bill: (a) denounces the use of monetary and fiscal policy as means of combating cost-push inflation (b) proposes that the United States control its exports of food to offset the higher prices on OPEC petroleum (c) advocates the manipulation of the international value of the dollar for the purpose of stabilizing the domestic economy (d) endorses economic planning as a means of achieving full employment and designates government as an employer of last resort — d

5. The structural bind which characterizes many modern economies is that of: (a) stagflation, where there has been excessive expansion of both monetary and fiscal policies (b) not having adequate statistics for determining what are the proper doses of monetary and fiscal policies (c) braking inflation without engineering a slowdown in output and employment (d) not knowing how to limit the rate of demand pull in-

SHORT ANSWER QUESTIONS FOR REVIEW

flation (e) being overly expansionist in the short run and ignoring long-run consequences — c

6. The basic problem portrayed by the Phillips Curve is: (a) that unemployment tends to increase at the same time the general price level is rising (b) that changes in the composition of total labor demand tend to be deflationary (c) the possibility that automation will increase the level of noncyclical unemployment (d) that a level of aggregate demand sufficiently high to result in full employment may also cause inflation — d

7. If everybody learns to anticipate the rate of inflation correctly, the long-run Phillips tradeoff between price change and unemployment becomes: (a) a "kinked curve" as in oligopoly (b) an L-shape formed by the two axes (c) a vertical line (d) a horizontal line (e) none of the above — c

8. If people come to fear and expect price inflation, they: (a) are not likely to shift any Phillips curve, for any such curve depicts only a short-run relationship (b) bring on stagflation by shifting their Phillips curves to a horizontal line (c) bring on stagflation by shifting their Phillips curves to a vertical line (d) shift their effective Phillips curves, but it is not known in which direction (e) shift upward their effective Phillips curves — e

9. The proposal for an "excess wage settlements tax" holds that: (a) workers who receive inflationary wage increases, will be forced to pay higher income taxes (b) firms which grant inflationary wage increases must pay a special surtax on their profits (c) unions which negotiate wage increases in excess of productivity increases will be fined by the Federal government (d) corporations which are successful in limiting wage increases will qualify for rebates on their corporate income tax payments — b

10. We speak of demand-pull inflation when: (a) MV is no longer exactly equal or proportional to PQ (b) M changes and prices go up (c) aggregate demand, prices, and employment are all rising at equivalent rates (d) aggregate demand is greater than the value of what the economy can produce at full employment (e) the Germans greatly contracted their money supply in the 1920s — d

SHORT ANSWER QUESTIONS FOR REVIEW

Answer
To be covered when testing yourself

11. During periods of unemployment: (a) the unemployment rate for women is lower than that for men (b) the unemployment rate for blacks is roughly twice the rate for whites (c) the unemployment rate for teen-agers is below the rate for the labor force as a whole (d) the burden of unemployment is quite evenly distributed among males and females, blacks and whites, and young and old workers — b

12. If the modern mixed economy wishes to enjoy both full employment and price stability, then it should: (a) control all prices permanently (b) control all prices (c) institute mandatory wage-price guidelines (d) institute voluntary wage-price guidelines (e) consider all of these, but not necessarily choose any one — e

13. Inflation is undesirable because: (a) it arbitrarily redistributes real income and wealth (b) it tends to be cumulative; that is, creeping inflation invariably causes hyperinflation (c) it always tends to make the distribution of income less equal (d) it is typically accompanied by a declining real output — a

14. In order to secure a better Phillips curve, it might be necessary to: (a) make minimum wages more flexible, which may mean reducing rather than increasing the wage rate (b) make the government the employer of last resort (c) increase the size and scope of manpower training programs (d) reduce structural unemployment (e) do any or all of the above — e

15. The equation of exchange suggests that, if aggregate demand is constant, an increase in the price level due to cost increases or shortages will: (a) shift the Phillips Curve to the left (b) reduce the velocity of money by a compensating amount (c) be compatible with a growing real GNP (d) reduce real output and employment — d

<u>Fill in the blanks.</u>

16. By ______________, we mean, a course of action aimed at securing long-run price stability with simultaneous full employment. — incomes policy

17. A ______________ shift of the Phillips curve suggests that a lower rate of inflation is now associated with each rate of unemployment than previously. — leftward

SHORT ANSWER QUESTIONS FOR REVIEW

Answer
To be covered when testing yourself

18. ______________ are kinds of government expenditure which have the largest ultimate impact upon the level of GNP. — Roads and schools

19. The ______________ suggests a conflict or trade-off between a high level of employment and price level stability. — Phillips curve

20. To go from a short-run Phillips curve to a long-run Phillips curve, we shift the former ______________. — clockwise

21. The wage-price guideposts suggest that wage increases should not exceed the rate of increase in the nation's ______________. — productivity

22. Eisenhower's running a slack economy with high unemployment in the late 1950s probably gave Kennedy a ______________ Phillips curve to the left. — short-run

23. Congress' Joint Economic Committee claimed that unions and management in the steel industry priced steel out of the international market in the 1950s. This process is best described by the ______________ inflation. — cost-push

24. The wage-price guideposts were designed to limit wage rate increases to the annual increase in ______________ productivity. — labor

25. If we wish to improve the position of the Phillips curve, we would pursue policies such as making minimum wage rates more ______________. — flexible

26. Keynesians feel that in the 1970s, the Phillips curve may have shifted to the right because of changes in the composition of the ______________. — labor force

27. If the price of a product or resource is frozen at some level below the equilibrium price, a ______________ of that product or resource will occur. — shortage

28. According to ______________ and Luxemburg, capitalist economies' markets could not operate to support consumption and purchasing power at high enough levels. — Lenin

29. By ______________, we mean the existence of both inflation and unemployment. — stagflation

30. We usually expect that, when demand is inadequate

SHORT ANSWER QUESTIONS FOR REVIEW

Answer
To be covered when testing yourself

prices fall--or at least do not rise; ________ phenomena contradict this expectation. | cost-push

Determine whether the following statements are true or false.

31. Milton Friedman believes unions and monopolies are the main reasons for inflation. | False

32. The wage-price guideposts of the Kennedy and Johnson administrations made it illegal to raise wage rates by more than the increase in national productivity. | False

33. Every mixed economy has the knowledge to create whatever domestic purchasing power it needs for full employment. | True

34. If national productivity rises by 4 percent and money wages increase by 2 percent, then unit costs of production will decline. | True

35. There can be no inflation without an increase in the money supply. | False

36. A shift in the Phillips Curve to the left will improve the "rate of inflation-rate of unemployment" choices available to society through the application of monetary and fiscal policy. | True

37. Society has really only one choice: that of less unemployment now at the cost of more unemployment later. | False

38. Demand-pull inflation and cost-push inflation are essentially identical concepts because both entail rising money wages and rising prices. | False

39. The wage guideposts constitute a good example of what is meant by an "incomes policy." | True

40. The Phillips curve relationship suggests an inverse relationship between increases in the price level and the level of employment. | False

41. The wage-price guidelines state that the average money-wage increase is to be no higher than the average increase in physical productivity. | True

42. A long-term or permanent wage-price freeze is consistent with the goal of efficiency in the allocation of resources. | False

SHORT ANSWER QUESTIONS FOR REVIEW

Answer

To be covered when testing yourself

43. Under the wage guideposts, wages in each industry are held down to the productivity increase in that industry. — False

44. If the Phillips curve shifts to the right and the economy has been applying wage-price guidelines or controls, we can conclude that this wage-price has been successful. — False

45. Cost-push phenomena are observed in both unionized and nonunionized industries. — True

CHAPTER 11

MONEY

Basic Attacks and Strategies for Solving Problems in this Chapter. See pages 377 to 408 for step-by-step solutions to problems.

Sweeping all the alleged mystical features of money aside, at its heart money is a commodity (a thing that can be bought or sold) with a characteristic that sets it apart from all the other commodities in our economy. Namely, money is the only commodity that is generally acceptable in exchange for goods and services and in payment of debts.

Assume you wish to acquire an item that you cannot produce yourself. To get that item, you must trade something you have for it. Potentially any good or service could be traded—a loaf of bread, a towel, a chicken, and so on—but most of these items will not be accepted by everyone. In other words, they are not generally acceptable. Items that everybody will always accept become known as money, because they are generally acceptable.

Money serves three major functions. First, it is a medium of exchange. It is the commodity people use to buy goods and services. By allowing us to forego the problems associated with barter, namely, the double coincidence of wants difficulty discussed in Chapter 2, money makes exchange more efficient. Second, money is a measure of value. The worth of commodities is measured in money terms, not in terms of any other commodities, like chickens. Third, money is a store of value. It is a convenient way to store wealth.

Money is valuable for three reasons. First, it has general acceptability. People are willing to accept money in exchange for goods and services because they know they can use it anywhere else in the country to buy things. Second, it has relative scarcity. The supply of money is limited relative to the demand for it. Third, money has legal tender status. Governments have decreed that people are legally obligated to accept the national currency in exchange for goods and services and in payment of debts.

Throughout history many commodities have been used as money at one time or another. American Indians used wampum (shells), the Virginia colonists used tobacco, and the Yap Islanders used huge boulders, to name three unusual cases. More commonly, gold, silver, paper, cheap metal, and bits stored in a computer's memory have and are being used. In the United States today, there are two competing definitions of money. The definition called Ml includes currency and coins, demand deposits (checking accounts at commercial banks), other checkable accounts (other types of deposits at commercial banks or other institutions on which a check can be drawn), and traveler's checks. Every item under this definition can be used as a medium of exchange. The definition M2 includes all of Ml plus savings deposits, small time deposits (under $100,000), Money Market Mutual Funds and Deposit Accounts (special investment funds managed by professionals), and several smaller items that households typically do not use. Some of these items cannot be directly used as a medium of exchange, but all are highly liquid.

An examination of the portfolios of households and businesses indicates that everyone holds some money. An important problem in economics is explaining why people hold (demand) money and what factors influence how much. According to Marshall and Fisher, people demand money for two reasons: transactions and as an asset. The transactions demand says that people demand money to have some available to finance normal expenditures. The amount demanded will depend on the amount normally spent and the difficulty people have in liquidating non-money assets. The asset demand is money available to take advantage of unexpected investment opportunities or emergencies of all types. The amount demanded will depend on the foregone interest costs of holding it.

The Quantity Equation of Exchange is the identity $MV = PQ$, where M is the money supply, V is the velocity of money (the number of times money changes hands during a period of time), P is the average price level, and Q is real output. The quantity PQ can be thought of as nominal GNP. If a dollar bill changes hands 5 times, it must have created $5 in income. Consequently, the national money supply times the number of times it changes hands must give us nominal GNP, so the Quantity Equation of Exchange must be true by definition. Rearranging terms, we can see that V can easily be computed from readily available data: $V = PQ/M$. If GNP = $5,000 and M = $750, then V = $5,000/$750 = 6.67. If the money supply rises to $850 and V remains constant, then GNP should rise to $850*6.67 = $5,669.50.

Certain assumptions allow us to transform the Quantity Equation of Exchange into a theory. If we assume the velocity of money is constant, and the economy is at full employment equilibrium, making Q constant also, it follows that changes in M will lead to proportional changes in P. This is known as the Quantity Theory of Money. By multiplying both sides of the equation by $1/V$, and letting $k = 1/V$, we also have a theory of money demand: $M = kPQ$, the demand for money is proportional to the level of income.

The IS/LM model is a simple general equilibrium model of the economy. A general equilibrium model is one that attempts to analyze all markets in the economy simultaneously. In the IS/LM model, there are two markets, the goods market and the money market. The IS curve shows all combinations of the interest rate and real GNP at which the goods market is in equilibrium. The LM curve shows all combinations of the interest rate and real GNP at which the money market is in equilibrium. The intersection of the two curves shows the interest rate and level of real GNP at which both markets are simultaneously at equilibrium.

The value of the model is that it can be used to analyze the impact of various events—increased government spending, increased taxes, decreased money supply, investment boom, increased money demand, and so on—on all the markets of the economy.

Step-by-Step Solutions to Problems in this Chapter, "Money"

NATURE AND FUNCTION

• PROBLEM 11-1

What are the functions of money?

Solution: First, money serves us as a medium of exchange. Suppose Mr. Kastner would like to have some tobacco but can only offer philosophy books in return. Now Mr. Voelkle, the owner of a cigar shop, can offer Mr. Kastner some tobacco, but has no desire to read philosophy. Therefore no exchange will take place unless each man has something that the other man will trade for. When money is introduced as a medium of exchange, it provides a solution. Mr. Kastner can sell his books for money on the outside and then spend the proceeds from the sale to buy tobacco at Mr. Voelkle's store. No longer is there any need for the two men to be restricted to making only exchanges of goods and services. Instead Mr. Kastner will pay an amount of money for a good (tobacco).

Money also serves us as a measure of value. Just as scales measure weights in pounds and ounces, money measures value in dollars and cents. Suppose in the preceding example, Mr. Voelkle agreed to accept philosophy books for his tobacco. Just how much tobacco is equivalent in exchange for the complete works of Nietzsche? The use of money alleviates this problem of measurement.

Money is also a store of value. If Mr. Kastner sells his books, he need not go right out and buy a tremendous amount of tobacco. Rather he can save a portion of it to purchase tobacco in the future. The money saved represents purchasing power deferred to the future.

TYPES OF MONEY

• PROBLEM 11-2

What are the major forms of money in use?

Solution: Fractional currency which accounts for about 2% of total currency is composed of pennies, nickels, dimes, quarters and half-dollars. These are all fractions of the unit of account, the dollar, and are useful for the very large number of small purchases.

Paper money, also referred to as currency, accounts for about 20% of the quantity of money. The bulk of it is issued by the Federal Reserve Banks as Federal Reserve Notes.

Checkbook money, or demand deposits, account for nearly 75% of the money supply.

• PROBLEM 11-3

Why are United States coins called "token money"?

Solution: These coins are called "token money" because the value of the metal in each coin is far less than the coin's monetary value. Suppose that coins were minted with metallic value equal or nearly equal to their face value. If the market price of the metal contained in the coin were to rise above the face value of the coin, people would melt down the coins for the use of the metal.

• PROBLEM 11-4

What is the danger inherent in the issuance of fiat money?

Solution: Fiat money is money that circulates by order of the government. It is often resorted to in order to meet emergencies, for example, for buying military supplies during a war. The danger inherent in the issuance of fiat money is that its quantity is controlled by the government rather than by market forces within the economy. If money is issued faster than the output of goods and services grows, prices will tend to rise and the real value of the money unit (dollar, pound, etc.), i.e., the reciprocal of the price level, $1/P$, will tend to fall.

• PROBLEM 11-5

What is meant by near-money? Give an example.

Solution: Near-monies are any assets that can be quickly converted (liquidated) into currency or demand deposits. According to the M_1 definition of money, a savings account is considered to be near-money, rather than money proper, because giving a bank book to a person for payment of a debt is not an accepted practice. The funds in a savings account may, however, be quickly liquidated by withdrawing funds from the account and converting them to cash or check before paying the debt. Hence, savings accounts are an example of a "near-money." Other examples are government bonds, savings and loan accounts, high-grade corporate bonds, etc.

THE SUPPLY OF MONEY

• PROBLEM 11-6

What are the three sources of money creation?

Solution: The United States Treasury in collaboration with the Federal Reserve issues coins and currency. The Federal Reserve Banks and the commercial banks create demand deposits, or "checkbook money," and time or savings deposits.

• PROBLEM 11-7

Two definitions of money supply are M_1 and M_2. Differentiate between the two.

Solution: M_1 is comprised of coin and currency held by the (non-bank) public, and demand deposits in commercial banks. This is the money supply narrowly defined. M_2, on the other hand, includes all of M_1 plus time and saving deposits. M_2 represents the broader definition of money supply.

THE DEMAND FOR MONEY

• PROBLEM 11-8

According to Marshall and Fisher, what are the components of the demand for money?

Solution: This analysis divides the demand for money into two components.

1) Transactions Demand

2) Asset Demand

In both cases it must be remembered that money in its most liquid form, cash on hand, earns no interest. It can, however, be "invested," with varying degrees of liquidity and riskiness to earn interest. This implies that people will retain from their paychecks only as much money in cash as they will need until the next paycheck. It is this cash on hand that is determined by the two demands. The transactions demand is directly proportional to income. That is, the greater the level of income is, the higher the transactions demand will be.

The Asset Demand for money deals with money as an asset. It describes the relationship between money retained and the interest rate. It is assumed that money may be retained for either precautionary or speculative reasons and that any increases in the general interest rate will cause people to invest their extra cash. This is because as the general interest rate rises, increasing opportunity costs will result, that is, the money holder will forfeit increasing returns on any cash which is not invested.

• PROBLEM 11-9

What causes the fluctuations in the money supply (M_{II})? Can you analyze the determinants? Give an example.

Solution: The fluctuations in the money supply M_{II} are the result of fluctuations in the monetary base H (= high powered money = reserves), the public's ratio of currency to deposits $c = \frac{C}{D}$, and the banks' ratio of reserves to deposits $r = \frac{R}{D}$ (= reserve requirement).

The money supply M_{II} consists of currency C, demand deposits and time deposits--together called 'the deposits', D.

Thus $$M_{II} = C + D \qquad (1)$$

The monetary base H consists of the currency outside of banks C and the bank reserves R; thus

$$H = C + R \qquad (2)$$

Dividing (1) by equation (2) gives us the ratio of the money supply M_{II} to the high powered money H;

thus $$\frac{M_{II}}{H} = \frac{D + C}{C + R}$$

Dividing both the numerator and denominator by D, deposits, results in

$$\frac{M_{II}}{H} = \frac{1 + \frac{C}{D}}{\frac{C}{D} + \frac{R}{D}}$$

Multiplying both sides by high powered money H gives the money supply M_{II} analyzed in its determinants

$$M_{II} = \frac{1 + \frac{C}{D}}{\frac{C}{D} + \frac{R}{D}} \cdot H$$

and we notice that fluctuations in M_{II} are caused by fluctuations in the monetary base H, the currency deposit ratio $\frac{C}{D}$ and the reserve deposit ratio $\frac{R}{D}$.

Example 1: Suppose that the currency deposit ratio is $\frac{C}{D}$ = 0.30 and the reserve deposit ratio is $\frac{R}{D}$ = 0.20 and both are known to have been constant, then a change of $1 billion in the money supply M_{II} is caused by a change of

$$\frac{1}{\frac{1 + 0.25}{0.30 + 0.20}} = \frac{1}{2.5} = \$0.4 \text{ billion in the reserves H.}$$

Example 2: Suppose the reserves are $1 billion, the currency deposit ratio is 0.30, by how much must the reserve requirement be lowered to cause an expansion of $5 billion in the M_{II}?

$$\Delta M_{II} = 5 = \frac{1 + 0.30}{0.30 + \Delta\left(\frac{R}{D}\right)} = \frac{1.3}{0.30 + \Delta\left(\frac{R}{D}\right)}$$

Taking reciprocals results in

$$\frac{0.30 + \Delta\left(\frac{R}{D}\right)}{1.3} = \frac{1}{5}$$

Multiplying both sides by 1.3 gives

$$0.30 + \Delta\left(\frac{R}{D}\right) = \frac{1.3}{5} = 0.26$$

$$\Delta\left(\frac{R}{D}\right) = -0.04$$

Thus the reserve requirement must be lowered by 4 percent to effectuate the desired expansion of M_{II}.

Professor Phillip Cagen has noted that variations in the currency deposit ratio C/D accounted on average for 50% of the cyclical variability in the rate of increase in the money supply. Changes in the monetary base H and in the reserve deposit ratio R/D each accounted for about 25% of the variations. The Federal Reserve has hardly any control over C/D and R/D but controls H. The changes in C/D and R/D are caused by banks and consumers.

• PROBLEM 11-10

What is the transactions demand for money? How would you relate the transactions demand concept to one's lifestyle?

Solution: People will hold a certain amount of money in anticipation of normal expenditures or "transactions" which they conduct. For example, if you were paid \$50 a week for your part-time job, you may want to carry \$10 with you for "transactions" you wish to conduct. A business will have a similar "transactions" demand in conducting its purchases and paying its workers.

• PROBLEM 11-11

Assume you are paid \$140 every two weeks, and at the end of the two weeks you have entirely spent your salary. Also, assume that you spend your salary at a constant rate.

a. Construct a graph showing your pattern of expenditure for four weeks.

b. What would be your average transactions balance during each two week period? Remember, you are spending all your salary at a constant rate every two weeks.

c. How much money would you have on hand 2 days after payday, 7 days, 10 days, and 14 days?

Solution: a. Let us use the Y axis of the graph to represent cash on hand, and the X axis to represent time. We know we will have \$140 the first day, and \$0 at the end of two weeks.

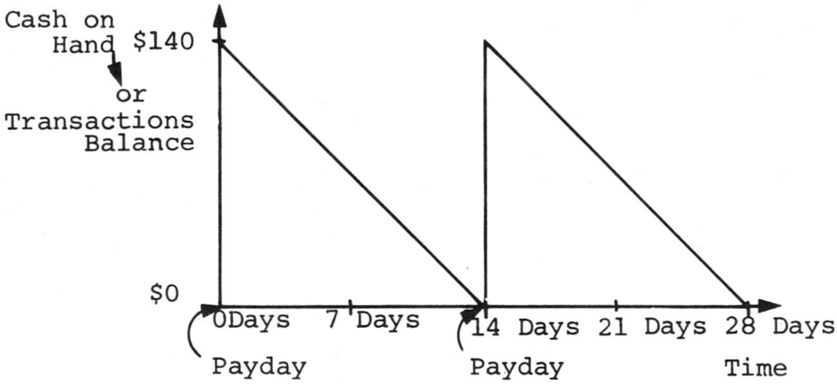

Note that, since the salary is spent at a constant rate, the graph slopes downward in a straight line or constant rate.

b. By dividing the salary by the time between paydays we can find the average transactions balance:

$$\frac{140 \text{ Dollars}}{2 \text{ Weeks}} = 70 \text{ Dollars}$$

c. To answer this question we must find the amount we spend each day. Knowing that we spend \$140 in 14 days, divide the salary by the number of days:

$$\frac{140 \text{ Dollars}}{14 \text{ Days}} = \$10/\text{Day}$$

Thus, after 2 days, 2 x $10/day or $20 has been spent, and $140 - $20 or $120 remains.

In 7 days: 7 X $10 = $70 is spent, $140 - $70 = $70 remains.

In 10 days: 10 x $10 = $100 is spent, $140 - $100 = $40 remains.

In 14 days: 14 X $10 = $140 is spent, $140 - $140 = 0 remains.

• PROBLEM 11-12

> If you owned interest bearing bonds, and periodically converted a portion of them to cash for transactions purposes, what factors would influence your decision as to how often you converted the bonds to cash?

Solution: Besides considering your need for transactions balances, you would consider the loss of interest on the bonds as well as the cost of selling them. For example, if the interest on the bonds was high, and the cost of selling them low, it would be to your advantage to hold as many of the bonds as possible, converting them to cash frequently. You would maintain a small transactions balance in this case.

If the interest rate on bonds was low, and the cost of selling them was high, you would not lose much interest income by cashing in large amounts of bonds at once. It would also be to your advantage to make few sales of the bonds if the cost of selling them is high. In this case, you would have a large transactions balance.

• PROBLEM 11-13

> Using the formula for maximizing the net income or holding bonds and selling them for transactions purposes
>
> $$\left(n = \sqrt{\frac{Zi}{2b}}\right)$$
>
> where n = number of transactions, Z = amount of bonds, i = the interest rate on the bonds, and b = the transactions cost:
>
> a. What would happen if i increased? Why?
>
> b. What would happen if b increased? Why?

Solution: a. If the rate of interest increased, the number

of transactions would increase (holding all things constant) as can be seen in the formula. Intuitively, we know that since the rate of interest is high, the net income from the bonds is higher. It would be desirable to hold as much in bonds as possible, selling them for cash in small amounts frequently and when needed. You would hold little money for transactions purposes.

If the cost of transactions increased, it can be seen in the equations that the number of transactions would decrease to maximize income. The extra cost of transactions would exceed to some extent the amount of interest lost from frequent withdrawals of a small amount of bonds.

• PROBLEM 11-14

a. If you are holding interest bearing bonds (Z), the interest rate is (i), and the cost of transactions is (b), what is the optimal number of transactions to make (n) so as to maximize the amount of interest received from the bonds?

b. If you have $10,000 in bonds, the interest rate is 10%, the cost of transactions is $5, what would be the optimal amount of transactions?

Solution: a. The optimal amount of transactions to make can be found from the formula.

$$n = \sqrt{\frac{Zi}{2b}} .$$

b. In the example, we substitute into the above formula:

$$n = \sqrt{\frac{10000 \times .1}{2 \times 5}}$$

$$n = \sqrt{\frac{1000}{10}}$$

$$n = \sqrt{100} \quad , \qquad n = 10$$

So, 10 transactions will maximize the interest income on $10,000, at 10% interest, with a $5 transactions fee.

• PROBLEM 11-15

a. What would be the average holding of money (M) in relation to transactions cost (b), amount of bonds (Z), and the interest rate (i)?

b. How is the average money holding related to transactions cost and the interest rate?

Solution: The average amount of money (M) you are holding in cash for transactions is found by the formula:

$$M = \sqrt{\frac{bZ}{2i}} \ .$$

As can be seen by the formula, average money holdings are an increasing function of transactions costs (b), and a decreasing function of the rate of interest (i).

Intuitively, we know that if the interest rate is high, we will want to hold most of our assets in interest bearing bonds, and little in cash.

If the transactions costs are high, we will desire less transactions, and convert large amounts of bonds to cash at once, and give us a high average money balance.

• PROBLEM 11-16

Wealth may be held in several types of financial assets. List some of these financial assets.

Solution: Financial wealth may be held as:

a. currency (or paper money) and coins, which are the most "liquid" or easily convertible assets;

b. demand deposits, which banks are obligated to pay currency "on demand" to a deposit holder or a holder of his check;

c. time deposits, or deposits that earn interest for their holders in savings bank accounts, mutual savings banks and deposits at savings and loan associations;

d. liabilities of governments, of which U.S. savings bonds are an example, or obligations of the Treasury Department and other government agencies;

e. corporate bonds, that are obligations of private firms and may often be sold on a stock exchange;

f. ownership shares of business, through common stock or other means;

g. other financial assets include the value of life insurance policies, and pension funds for retirement.

• PROBLEM 11-17

The three basic reasons for holding money are for a) transactions purposes, b) precautionary purposes and c) possible profit or speculation purposes.

Given these three motives, indicate which might be most important for the following people:

a) a student on a small allowance from his parents
b) a financially conservative professor with young children to support
c) a "wheeler-dealer"

Solution: a) It is unlikely that a student would keep large precautionary or speculative balances. Rather it is more likely that a student would hold a balance for transactions purposes, that is to meet daily demands for cash that accompany scholastic life.

b) Since our professor here is financially conservative, we would expect him to hold money for precautionary reasons. Just in case an unforeseen event occurs, having money on hand gives you some added power to cope with it.

c) Finally, the wheeler-dealer would hold onto money for speculative purposes. In case an investment opportunity came along which could not be resisted, the wheeler-dealer would want to have a store of funds on hand.

THE VALUE OF MONEY

• PROBLEM 11-18

Why does our paper money have value, that is, why is it worth more than just the paper it is printed on?

Solution: There are three main points to the answer of this question.

1) Acceptability - money has value because we all accept it in exchange. Workers accept salaries in terms of dollars (rather than in terms of some product) because they know that their dollars will buy them the goods they desire.

2) Relative Scarcity - money, like any other economic good, must be scarce in relation to the desire for it in order to have exchange value.

3) Legal Tender - money derives part of its value from the fact that the government has decreed that a creditor must accept the legal currency in payment of debt.

• PROBLEM 11-19

What is the Quantity Equation of Exchange?

Solution: The Quantity Equation of Exchange is the identity

$$PQ \equiv MV,$$

where P is an index of the average price level; Q stands for the real GNP, that is, it measures the total volume of goods and services produced, in money terms, but with the effects of inflation removed; M is the money supply; and V is the velocity of money, that is, it measures the speed with which the money supply circulates through the economy. Income velocity measures the average number of times the same dollar turns up as income for someone.

In other words, the Quantity Equation is just another way of looking at GNP. The average price of all goods and services times the real quantity of all goods and services is the same thing as GNP. Also, the total Money Supply times the average number of times each dollar became income for someone equals the total income or GNP. Thus,

$$PQ \equiv MV.$$

• PROBLEM 11-20

What is the Quantity Equation of Exchange and how can it be derived?

Solution: The Quantity Equation of Exchange is the formal identity

$$MV \equiv PQ.$$

P is the average price level, and Q stands for real GNP, which is computed statistically by "deflating" money GNP by the price index. M is the total money supply and V the velocity of circulation of money.

The velocity of money, or income turnover is defined as the ratio of GNP to the money supply

$$V \equiv \frac{GNP}{M} \equiv \frac{p_1q_1 + p_2q_2 + \cdots}{M} \equiv \frac{PQ}{M}$$

When we multiply both sides of this identity by M, we get a new identity, the Quantity Equation of Exchange $MV \equiv PQ$.

Example: the money supply M is about \$290 billion, GNP about \$1,500 billion. So $\frac{GNP}{M} = \frac{1,500}{290} = 5.2$ per year is the income velocity. This means that each unit of money was used for GNP transactions about 5.2 times per year.

Or, differently stated, people hold at average a money balance equivalent to 70 days income.

The principal causes of changes in the velocity appear to be changes in interest, the rate of inflation, and real income; all three affecting the money balances people prefer to hold.

• PROBLEM 11-21

If GNP = $2,000 billion and the velocity of money is 4, what is the money supply?

Solution: To solve this problem, we use the equation of exchange MV = PQ. We know that GNP ≡ PQ.

Substituting this into the equation of exchange we get

$$GNP = MV.$$

Multiplying both sides of the equation by $\left(\frac{1}{V}\right)$ we get

$$\frac{GNP}{V} = \frac{MV}{V} = M.$$

Substituting the numerical values gives us:

$$M = \frac{2000}{4} = 500.$$

The money supply is $500 billion.

• PROBLEM 11-22

Suppose that the total value of all transactions in the United States is $100,000 and the money supply is $10,000. Calculate the velocity of money.

Solution: The velocity of money is the number of times each dollar is spent during a certain period. At any point in time, there is a given supply of money in the economy. In this case money supply = $10,000. This money finances the daily transactions of the economy, with each dollar being used more than once since when one person receives a dollar, he then spends it. Therefore the money supply, $10,000, is less than the total dollar value of transactions, $100,000.

To compute the velocity of money then, we simply divide the total value of transactions by the money supply, i.e. velocity, V, = $100,000/$10,000 = 10. Thus during the period in question, each dollar was spent 10 times.

• PROBLEM 11-23

If 1964 GNP = $622 billion and the average money supply was $155 billion, what was the income velocity of money?

Solution: To solve this problem we first need to know the Equation of Exchange, MV = PQ. We know that GNP = PQ, where P is the price level and Q is the physical volume of all goods produced. Therefore,

$$PQ = GNP$$

$$PQ = \$622 \text{ billion}$$

From the equation of exchange, we know that PQ = MV, where M is the money supply and V is the income velocity of money. Substituting we get

$$GNP = MV.$$

Multiplying both sides of the equation by $\left(\frac{1}{M}\right)$ we get

$$\frac{GNP}{M} = \frac{MV}{M} = V$$

Substituting in the appropriate values of GNP and M we get

$$V = \frac{\$622 \text{ billion}}{\$155 \text{ billion}}$$

or

$$V = 4.0129$$

So we see that the money circulated 4.0129 times in 1964.

• PROBLEM 11-24

If GNP = $600 billion and the money supply is $200 billion, what is the velocity of money?

Solution: The definition for the velocity of money for the economy as a whole is

$$V = \frac{GNP}{\text{money supply}} = \frac{PQ}{M}$$, where P is the general price level, and Q the real quantity of output. Substituting our given numerical values into the equation, we get the velocity of money

$$V = \frac{\$600 \text{ billion}}{\$200 \text{ billion}} = 3$$

This means that each dollar changes hands an average of 3 times per year.

• PROBLEM 11-25

If output of goods and services in real terms was $1600

billion last year, the money supply was \$500 billion and the velocity of money was 4, then what was the price level? Was last year an inflationary period or a deflationary period?

Solution: This problem can be solved using the quantity equation of exchange,

$$MV = PQ$$

The question asks us to determine the price level, so we multiply both sides of the equation by $\left(\frac{1}{Q}\right)$ to get:

$$\frac{M \cdot V}{Q} = P$$

The question gives the values for M, V, and Q. Substituting them into our equation we get:

$$P = \frac{500 \times 4}{1600} = \frac{2000}{1600} = 1.25$$

Thus the price level was 1.25.

The second part of the question asks whether these numbers indicate inflation or deflation, that is, did P change? In order to determine this we would need to know what P was at the beginning of the year and at the end of the year. Since we are only given one set of numbers to cover the entire period, we cannot determine whether P changed. The answer to the second part of the question would be that not enough information was supplied.

• PROBLEM 11-26

If real GNP is expanding at a steady annual rate of 2 percent and the nominal money stock at a steady annual rate of 5 percent, what is the effect on the average price level if the income velocity of circulation of money is unchanged?

Solution: The equation of exchange says that $MV \equiv PQ$, where M is the quantity of money, V is the velocity of circulation of money, P is the average price level and Q is real GNP. If we divide both sides of the equation by $Q \cdot V$, we have $\frac{M}{Q} \equiv \frac{P}{V}$. When real GNP, Q, is expanding at an annual rate of 2 percent and the nominal money stock M is increasing at a rate of 5 percent per year, the ratio of peoples' total money balances to their total real income (GNP), $\frac{M}{Q}$, is increasing. This means that $\frac{P}{V}$, the ratio of the average price level to the velocity of circulation of money, must be increasing. Since we assumed that V remains constant, P must be increasing. The rate of change of this ratio, assuming a constant income velocity of circulation, is the rate of change of the price level, g_P.

Thus $g_P = g_M - g_Q = 5 - 2 = 3$ percent,

where g_M is the rate of change of the stock of money, and g_Q is the rate of change of real GNP.

Because the money supply is increasing faster than real output (= real income) peoples' money balances will be in excess of their desired balances, and they will step up their expenditures to reduce these money balances. This increased spending will expand nominal aggregate demand and have an inflationary impact.

• PROBLEM 11-27

What is the "Crude Quantity Theory of Money and Prices"? How might it be used?

Solution: The Crude Quantity Theory states that the price level moves in direct proportion to the money supply. Arithmetically it is:

$$P = kM$$

It is derived from the Quantity Equation of Exchange, $PQ = MV$, with $k = \frac{V}{Q}$. The Crude Quantity Theory implies that both V and Q are constant.

One way this equation might be used is to predict changes in the price level from changes in the money supply. That is, if the money supply increases, an adherent of this theory would say that prices would be expected to increase also.

• PROBLEM 11-28

Define the Quantity Theory of Money.

Solution: The theory can be stated as follows: Assuming no change in the volume of goods and services exchanged or the velocity of money circulating, price level variations are directly dependent upon changes in the quantity of money. Symbolically,

$$M\bar{V} = P\bar{Q}, \text{ where } \bar{V} \text{ and } \bar{Q} \text{ are both constant.}$$

Dividing both sides of the equation by $\bar{Q}$ results in

$$P = \frac{\bar{V}}{\bar{Q}} M = kM.$$

Since both $\bar{V}$ and $\bar{Q}$ are constant, and will not change, we can define $k = \frac{\overline{V}}{\overline{Q}}$. This crude form of the Quantity Theory of money is useful for the understanding of hyperinflations and long term price increments.

A modern form of the Quantity Theory does not use the levels of the prices and the money supply but the relative rates of change:

$$\frac{\Delta P}{P} = k \cdot \frac{\Delta M}{M}$$

Because k is only a proportionality constant that depends on the units used it can be omitted for all practical purposes; and the modern version reads

$$\pi = m$$

where π is the rate of change in the general price level (if upward it is called inflation; if downward--deflation), and m is the rate of the money supply.

A more sophisticated form of the Quantity Theory of Money recognizes the fact that the ratio $\frac{V}{\overline{Q}}$ is not constant. It is then assumed, however, that the changes in this ratio are gradual and predictable (Milton Friedman).

IS-LM ANALYSIS

• PROBLEM 11-29

How can the Pigou effect be explained?

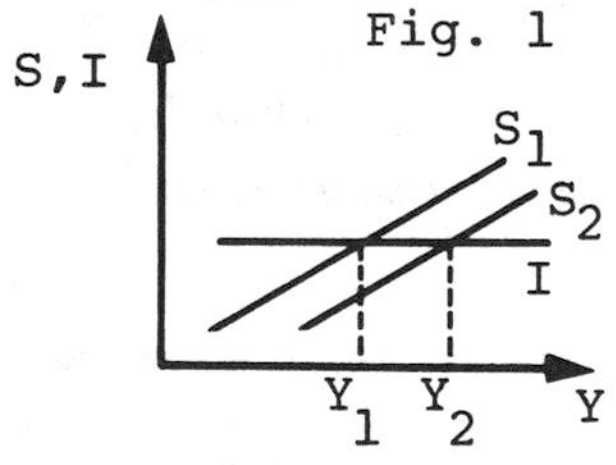

Fig. 1

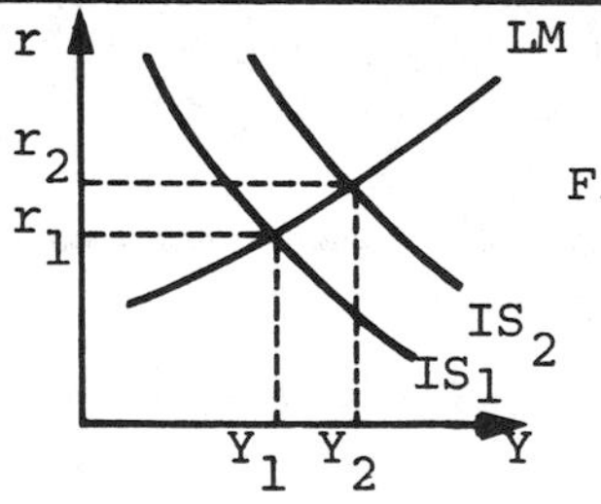

Fig. 2

Solution: The Pigou effect is the shift in the IS schedule, i.e. the equilibrium points of savings = investments in the interest rate - income plane, as a result of a change in the real balances $\frac{M}{P}$; where M is the money supply and P the general price level.

An increase in real cash balances is an increase in net wealth and may stimulate spending because there is less need to save. The savings schedule is lowered causing investment to be equal to saving at a higher income level (see Fig. 1).

Because interest rates are initially unchanged the IS schedule shifts to the right. (See Fig. 2.)

This causes both income Y and interest rate r to rise from Y_1 to Y_2, and from r_1 to r_2 respectively. The reason is that when income starts to rise, the demand for money increases too and the equilibrium in the financial market, L = M, becomes established at a higher level of the interest rate (see Fig. 3).

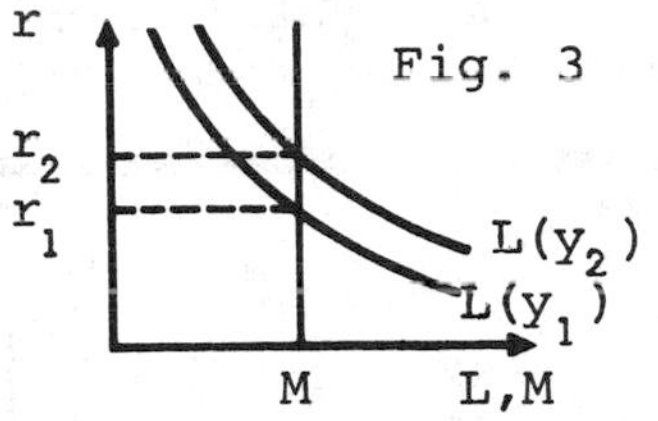

Fig. 3

Recall that the IS schedule is based on the points of equilibrium in the commodities market, S = I, and the LM schedule on the points of equilibrium in the financial market, M = L.

• PROBLEM 11-30

> With the use of supply and demand curves, explain how interest rates are determined (Loanable Funds Theory).

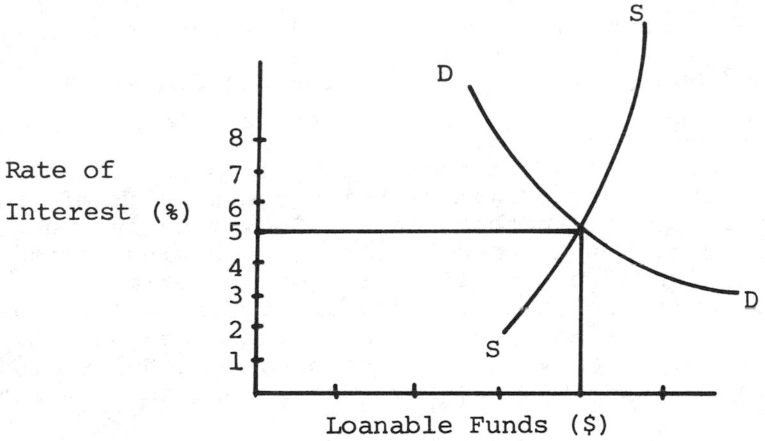

Solution: Using the interest rate as the price of borrowing money we can draw the supply and demand schedule shown.

The demand for loanable funds tends to vary inversely with the rate of interest, i.e. the demand curve slopes down and to the right, meaning that as the interest rate rises the amount of money people want to borrow will decrease.

The supply of loanable funds varies directly with the rate of interest, i.e. the supply curve slopes upward and to the right, meaning that the amount of money which people are willing to lend will increase as interest rates rise.

The equilibrium interest rate is determined by the intersection of the supply and demand curves. At this point, quantity of funds demanded by those seeking loans equals quantity of funds supplied by those seeking to loan out their cash balances and an equilibrium rate is achieved. In our example, the rate is 5%.

• PROBLEM 11-31

Analyze graphically the Keynesian criticisms in terms of the classical conception of the money market.

Fig. 1

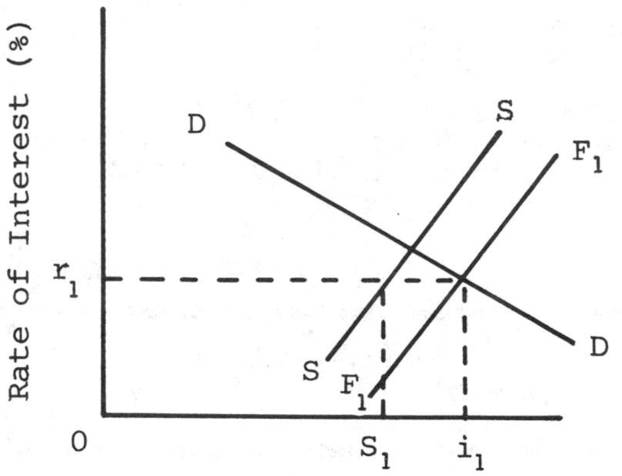

Dollars Saved and Invested

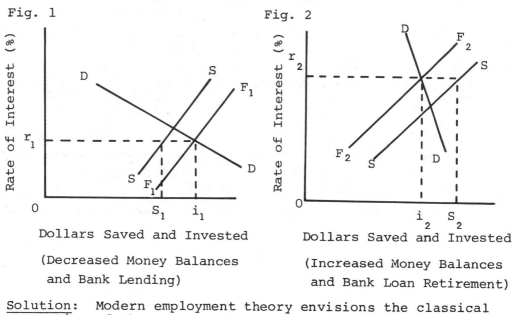

(Decreased Money Balances and Bank Lending)

Fig. 2

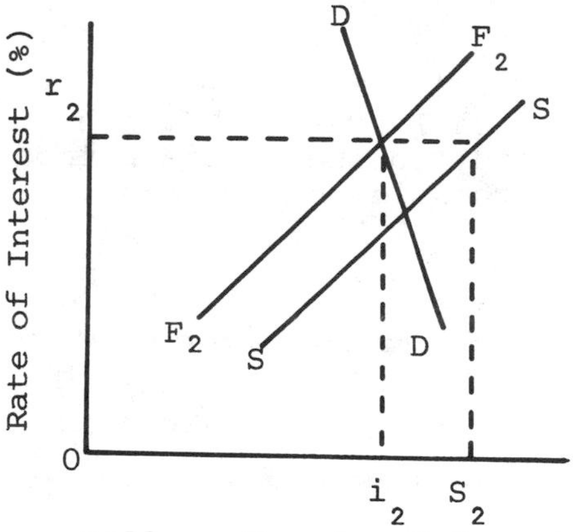

Dollars Saved and Invested

(Increased Money Balances and Bank Loan Retirement)

Solution: Modern employment theory envisions the classical conception of the money market as being oversimplified and therefore incorrect in another sense. Specifically, the classical money market assumes that current saving is the only source of funds for the financing of investment. Keynesian economics holds that there are two other sources of funds which can be made available in the money market: (1) the accumulated money balances held by households, and (2) commercial banks. Graphically, these work as shown in Figures 1 and 2.

In Figure 1, funds are shifted by households from their money balances to the money market and banks create funds (money) by lending. Adding these amounts horizontally to current saving S_1 , the supply of funds curve F_1F_1 is obtained. At the resulting equilibrium interest rate r_1 , investment is i_1 and obviously in excess of current saving s_1. In the second case (Figure 2), the supply-of-funds curve, F_2F_2 , is less than current saving s, because portions of current saving have been subtracted horizontally from the SS curve to derive the F_2F_2 curve. At the relevant equilibrium interest rate r_2, investment is only i_2, while current saving is more at s_2. The conclusion is that the money market does not ensure the equality of the saving and investment. Say's Law is therefore invalid, and the economy is prone to macroeconomic instability.

• PROBLEM 11-32

How can the LM (Money market equilibrium) schedule be derived from the transactions demand for money and the liquidity preference curve?

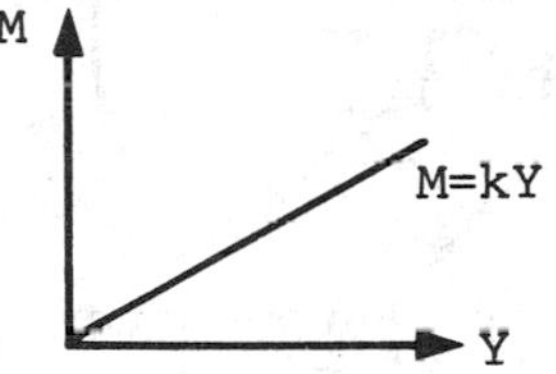

Fig. 1

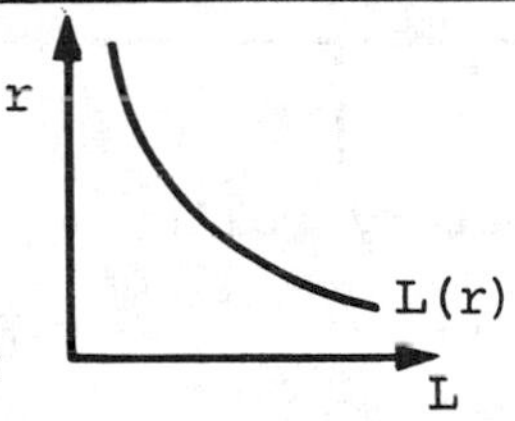

Fig. 2

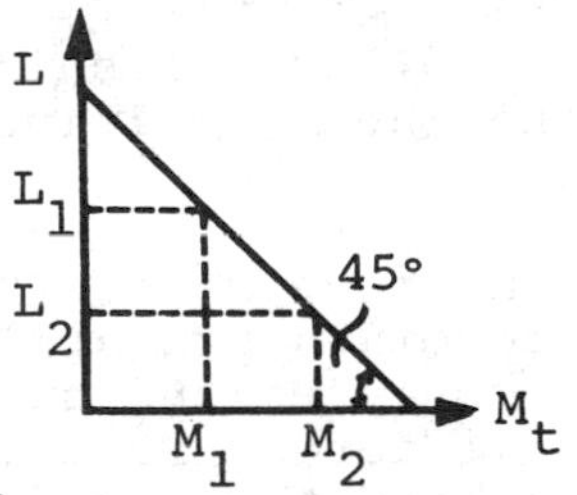

Fig. 3

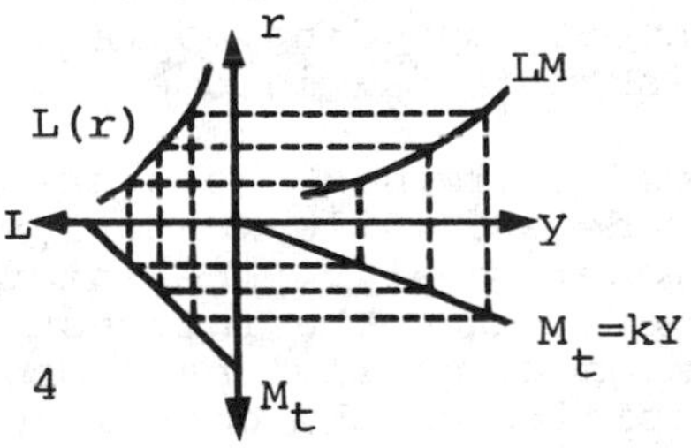

Fig. 4

Solution: The LM-schedule is the collection of points in the interest rate-income plane that indicate the equilibriums in the money market.

The transactions demand for money is proportional to income, $M_t = kY$ (see Fig. 1).

The liquidity preference schedule is dependent on the interest rate $L = L(r)$ (see Fig. 2).

We assume that the money supply is autonomous $M_s = \overline{M}$; determined by the monetary authorities and the banking system.

The total money demand is the sum of the transactions demand for money and the liquidity preference $M_d = M_t + L = kY + L(r)$ (see Fig. 3).

$$\overline{M} = L_1 + M_1 = L_2 + M_2$$

Equilibrium in the money market requires that the money supply equals money demand $M_s = M_d$, and thus

$$\overline{M} = kY + L(r).$$

Thus, $kY + L(r) - \overline{M} = 0$ is the relationship describing the

LM-schedule (see Fig. 4).

The logical structure of the IS-LM model may be clarified by a flow chart as shown.

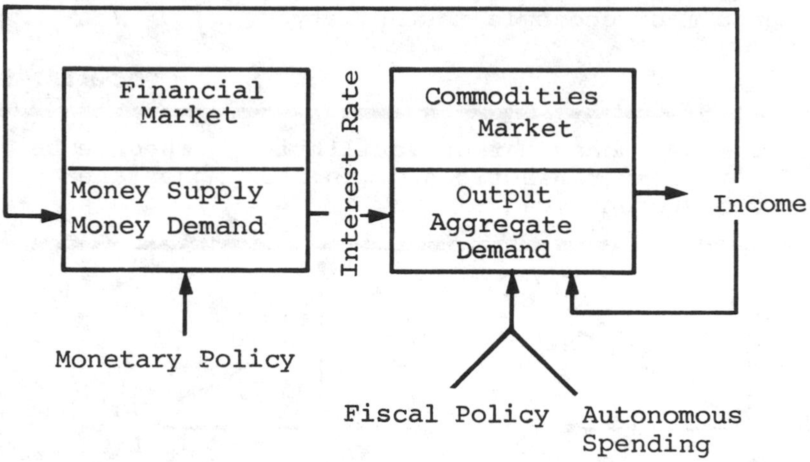

Aggregate demand, influenced by fiscal policy and shifts in autonomous spending, determines via the income multiplier process, national income.

Income determines, together with the interest rate, the money demand while monetary policy determines primarily the money supply. The interaction of money demand and supply determines the interest rate. The interest rate influences primarily investment spending, and the portfolio composition of the consumers. Aggregate demand is a composite of consumption, investment and government spending.

• PROBLEM 11-33

An economy is described by the following equations:

$$C = 0.85\,(1 - t)\,Y \qquad (1)$$

$$t = 0.30 \qquad (2)$$

$$I = 300 - 15i \qquad (3)$$

$$\overline{G} = 400 \qquad (4)$$

$$L = 0.25Y - 12i \qquad (5)$$

$$\frac{\overline{M}}{\overline{P}} = 295 \qquad (6)$$

where
C - consumption (in \$ billion)
Y - income (in \$ billion)
t - tax rate
I - investment (in \$ billion)
i - interest rate (in %)
$\overline{G}$ - government + autonomous spending (in \$ billion)

L - demand for money (in \$ billion)
$\overline{M}$ - money supply (in \$ billion)
$\overline{P}$ - general price level

What are the equations describing the IS and LM schedules, respectively, and what are the equilibrium levels of income and the interest rate? Also calculate the Keynesian and the monetary multipliers of this economy. The monetary multiplier indicates the change in the equilibrium income caused by a one dollar change in the real money stock.

Solution: First we will solve the equations describing the IS and LM schedules.

The IS schedule indicates the points in the interest rate-income plane where equilibrium in the commodities markets prevails, i.e. where savings equal investment plus government spending $S = I + \overline{G}$. Savings is disposable income (= income less taxes) minus consumption,

thus $S = (1 - t)Y - C$

Substituting for consumption in equation (1) gives $S = (1 - t)Y - 0.85(1 - t)Y$. Combining terms in Y,

$$S = 0.15(1 - t)Y. \qquad (7)$$

The tax rate is 30%, so savings is

$$S = 0.15(1 - 0.30)Y = 0.105Y \qquad (8)$$

This is set equal to investment plus government spending:

$$S = I + \overline{G}$$

Substituting for I and $\overline{G}$ equations (3) and (4) respectively yields

$$0.105Y = 300 - 15i + 400$$

Rewriting this expression results in the equation of the IS schedule

$$i = \frac{700 - 0.105Y}{15}$$

or $$i = 46.67 - 0.007Y \qquad (9)$$

The LM schedule indicates the points in the interest rate-income plane where equilibrium in the financial market prevails, i.e. where the real supply equals the money demand

$$\frac{\overline{M}}{\overline{P}} = L$$

Substitution of equations (5) and (6) gives

$$295 = 0.25Y - 12i.$$

Rewriting this expression results in the equation of the LM schedule

$$i = \frac{0.25Y - 295}{12}$$

or $$i = 0.021Y - 24.58 \qquad (10)$$

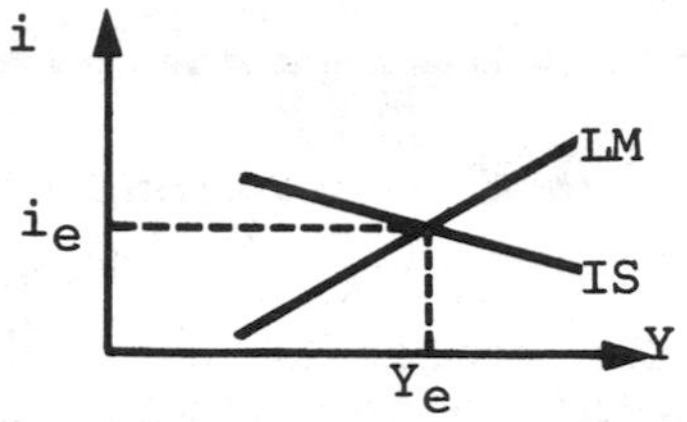

The equilibrium levels of income and interest are determined from the intersection of the IS and LM schedules (see the figure). At the equilibrium point, i.e. the point of intersection, the interest rate of the IS-schedule equals the interest rate of the LM-schedule; thus we set equations (9) and (10) equal

$$0.021Y - 24.58 = i_e = 46.67 - 0.007Y$$

Bring all Y_e to the left hand side (LHS) and the constants to the right hand side (RHS)

$$0.028Y_e = 71.25 \qquad (11)$$

Dividing both sides by 0.028 gives us the equilibrium income Y_e

$$Y_e = \$2,544.64 \text{ billion}$$

The equilibrium interest rate follows from substituting Y_e into equation (10) (or into equation (9))

so $$i_e = 0.021 \times 2,544.64 - 24.58 = 28.86\%$$

This is the equilibrium interest rate.

Our third task is to calculate the Keynesian multiplier. The simple Keynesian multiplier abstracts from the asset markets and is defined as

$$k = \frac{1}{s(1-t)}$$

Here $$k = \frac{1}{0.15(1-0.30)} = \frac{1}{0.105} = 9.5$$

But when we include the financial markets in this IS-LM model we will see that the value of the Keynesian multiplier will be lower due to the rising interest rate. To understand this it is useful to return to equation (9) and see how it is derived

$$0.105Y = 700 - 15i$$

where the 700 consists of autonomous investment and government expenditures; let it equal A.

$$0.105Y = A - 15i \qquad (12)$$

Set (12) equal to (10)

$$0.021Y - 24.58 = i_e = \frac{A}{15} - 0.007Y$$

Bringing the Y to the LHS and the constants to the RHS results in

$$0.028Y = 24.58 + \frac{A}{15}$$

Dividing both sides by 0.028 gives

$$Y = 877.86 + \frac{A}{15 \text{ X } 0.028} = 877.86 + 2.38A.$$

A change in Y caused by a change in autonomous spending A is then described by

$$\Delta Y = 2.38\Delta A.$$

Thus the Keynesian multiplier including the financial markets k = 2.38, is considerably less than the simple Keynesian multiplier.

Finally we will solve for the monetary multiplier: $m = \Delta Y / \Delta(\overline{M}/\overline{P})$.

In this case we return to equation (10) and how it is derived

$$i = 0.021Y - \frac{\overline{M}/\overline{P}}{12}$$

Again setting this equal to equation (9)

$$0.021Y - \frac{\overline{M}/\overline{P}}{12} = i_e = 46.67 - 0.007Y$$

or

$$0.028Y = 46.67 + \frac{\overline{M}/\overline{P}}{12} .$$

Dividing both sides by 0.028 gives

$$Y = 1666.79 + \frac{\overline{M}/\overline{P}}{12 \text{ X } 0.028} = 1666.79 + 2.98\ \overline{M}/\overline{P}.$$

And thus the monetary multiplier

$$m = \Delta Y / \Delta(\overline{M}/\overline{P}) = 2.98$$

This means that if the real money supply $\overline{M}/\overline{P}$ is increased by \$1 billion, income increases by \$2.98 billion. In this economy the monetary multiplier is stronger than the Keynesian (fiscal) multiplier.

(Note: Don't confuse the monetary multiplier with the money (- expansion) multiplier.)

• PROBLEM 11-34

When my expected annual income is \$20,000 and the rate of interest is 9.8% what is my total wealth?

Solution: Considering the fact that total wealth W is the source of all income Y, we have the relationship that income is a certain annual percentage of return on total wealth (supposing an infinite time-horizon): Y = rW.

Dividing both sides by r gives the capitalization formula

$$W = \frac{Y}{r} .$$

Thus my total wealth is $W = \frac{20,000}{0.098} = \$204,082$.

• PROBLEM 11-35

What is the optimal amount of cash to be held for transactions, when the return on bonds is i = 5%, real income Q = \$20,000 per year, and the unit real transactions cost b = \$5?

Solution: This problem can be solved by the Tobin-Baumol inventory approach to the management of cash inventories. Real income per year is \$20,000 which is paid out at a regular rate. Thus the stock of assets diminishes over time. The question is will these assets be held in bonds or money?

If all income is held in the form of money, interest income that could be earned on bonds--in total 5% of \$20,000 = \$1,000--is foregone. But if all income is invested in bonds, every time that money is needed for transactions some bonds have to be converted into money accompanied by some transaction costs. The rate is \$5 per transaction, thus the total transaction costs depends on the frequency that bonds are converted into money. In other words, there is a trade-off between holding wealth in the form of bonds and in the form of money. What is the optimal average cash balance C*/2?

When C is the amount of money taken out at the moment of a

transaction the number of transactions is the total of income \$20,000 divided by C, (\$20,000/C), and the cost of transactions is this number multiplied by the transactions rate b = 5.

Total transactions costs are $5 \times \frac{20,000}{C}$.

The opportunity cost of holding the average cash balance C/2 is $0.05 \frac{C}{2}$.

Total cost of holding the cash inventory

$$T = 0.05 \frac{C}{2} + 5 \times \frac{20,000}{C} \qquad (1)$$

We want to minimize the total cost T by an appropriate selection of C. There are two approaches to the solution in this case: the algebraic approach and the calculus approach.

The algebraic approach is the simplest. It can be seen from expression (1) that the total cost is the sum of two elements 0.025 X C, a linear element, and 100,000/C, a hyperbolic element (see Fig. 1).

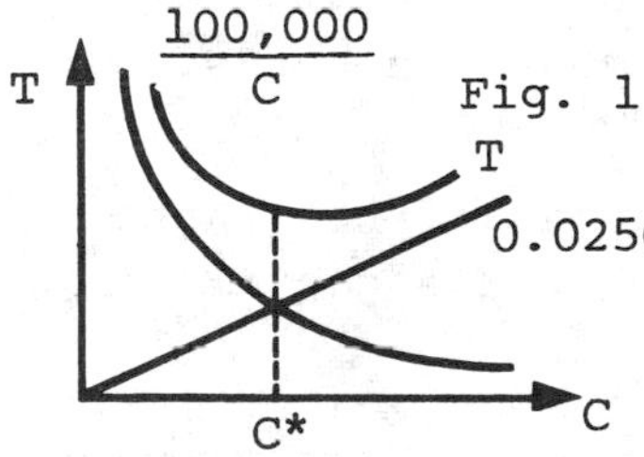

Fig. 1

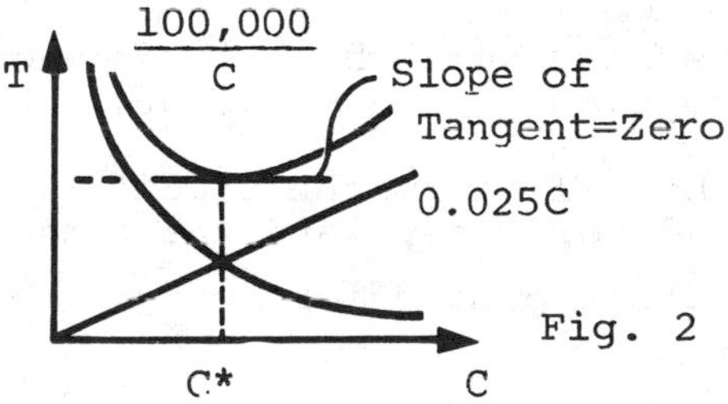

Fig. 2

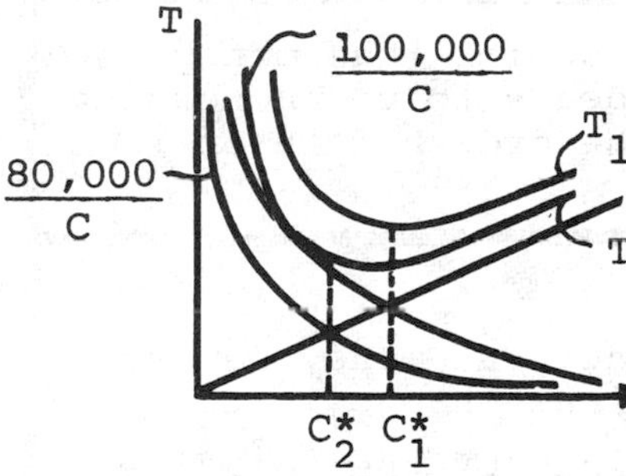

Fig. 3

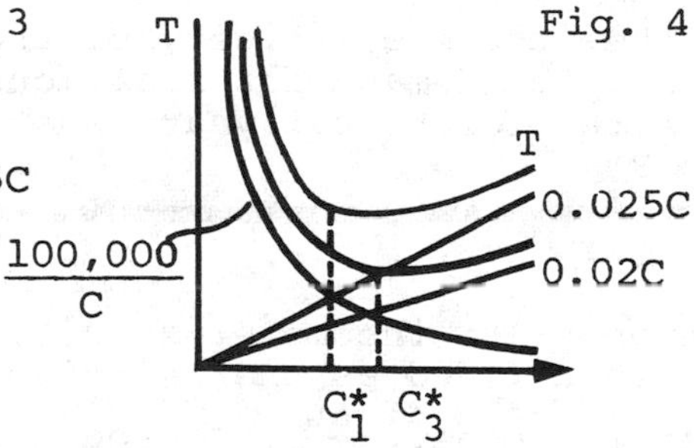

Fig. 4

The minimum of T occurs exactly above the crossing of the straight line and the hyperbola, thus where they are equal:

$$0.025C = \frac{100,000}{C}$$

Multiplying both sides by C results in $0.025\ C^2 = 100,000$. Thus $C^2 = 4,000,000$ and the optimal cash amount to be taken out is C* = \$2,000 and the optimal average cash balance is $\frac{C^*}{2} = \frac{2,000}{2} = \$1,000$.

The calculus approach requires that the slope of the tangent to the minimum equals zero (see Fig. 2).

Thus $\frac{dT}{dC} = 0.025 - \frac{100,000}{C^2} = 0$

And again we find $0.025 = \frac{100,000}{C^2}$

Thus $C^2 = 4,000,000$ and $C^* = 2,000$.

Thus the optimal average cash balance to be held is $\frac{C^*}{2} =$ \$1,000.

From the expression (1) for the total cost of holding cash balances it is to be noticed that when the transactions cost, b, become lower, because of the development of credit institutions, the optimal cash balance is lower too (see Fig. 3).

The hyperbola shifts to the origin. Say the new b = \$4, then the new hyperbola is $\frac{4 \times 20,000}{C} = \frac{80,000}{C}$. The new optimum is $C_2^* = \$1789$.

When the return on bonds decreases say to 4%, the optimal cash balances are bigger (see Fig. 4), because the straight line turns downward.

It is less worthwhile to invest the money in bonds. The new optimum is $C_3^* = \$2,236$. The component $\frac{iC}{2} = \frac{0.05}{2} \times C$ may be called in the tradition of Keynes: the transactions demand for money; and the component $b \cdot \frac{Q}{C} = 5 \times \frac{20,000}{C}$: the asset demand for money.

• PROBLEM 11-36

When the income elasticity of the demand for real money is 0.8, and the demand for real money appears to be increasing at a rate of 2.6% per year, what is the growth rate of real income?

Solution: The income elasticity of the real money demand, E_{in}, is defined as the relative marginal change in the real demand for money, $\frac{\Delta L}{L}$, caused and divided by the relative marginal change in real income, $\frac{\Delta Y}{Y}$.

Thus
$$E_{in} \equiv \frac{\Delta L}{L} \Big/ \frac{\Delta Y}{Y} \qquad (1)$$

Recall that the real demand for money depends on the interest rate r, and income Y, so L = L(r,Y). It is given that the real demand for money increases by $\frac{\Delta L}{L} = 2.6\%$ and the income elasticity of the demand for money $E_{in} = 0.8$, so that we may substitute these values in the relationship $\frac{\Delta L}{L} = E_{in} \cdot \frac{\Delta Y}{Y}$, which is derived by multiplying both sides of equation (1) by $\frac{\Delta Y}{Y}$.

Thus $\quad 2.6\% = 0.75 \frac{\Delta Y}{Y}$.

The growth rate of real income equals then

$$\frac{\Delta Y}{Y} = \frac{2.6}{0.75}\% = 3.47\% \text{ per year.}$$

• PROBLEM 11-37

If members of the economy wish to hold money balances equal to 5 weeks of expenditure, and all income is spent, what will be the desired level of money balances when aggregate income is $1,600 billion per annum?

Solution: The velocity of money equals the reciprocal of the number of years of transactions that the money balances will finance; 5 weeks are 5/52 = 0.096 year, so the velocity of money $V = \frac{1}{0.096} = 10.4$.

On average, each dollar changes hands 10.4 times per year. The velocity of money is defined as the ratio of transactions to balances

$$V = \frac{PT}{M}$$

Because all income is said to be spent, total transactions = total income and

$$V = \frac{PY}{M},$$

where $\quad$ P = general price level and
$\quad\quad\quad$ Y = real income,
so that $\quad$ PY = nominal income.

Multiplying both sides by M results in the money-income equation of exchange MV = PY.

Nominal income is $1,600 billion per year, thus MV = $1,600 billion.

The velocity of money V was found equal to 10.4, so

$$10.4M = \$1,600 \text{ billion}$$

Dividing both sides by 10.4 gives the desired level of money balances

$$M = \$153.846 \text{ billion.}$$

• PROBLEM 11-38

Which factors affect a person's demand for real cash

balances, and how? (Friedman)

Solution: A person's demand for real cash balances $\left(\frac{M}{P}\right)^d$, where M indicates the nominal value of the cash balances, and P the general price level, depends on

1) his income, y; if his income increases he will hold more cash, needed for transactions, contingencies and/or speculation, and vice versa;

2) nonhuman wealth, w, i.e. bonds, equity, physical capital; here also we notice a proportional relationship;

3) human capital;

4) the expected rates of return on money r_m, on bonds, r_b, and on equities, r_e, respectively; when r_m increases, the demand for real cash balances $\left(\frac{M}{P}\right)^d$ increases, but when r_b and/or r_e increase, part of the money holdings will be substituted by bonds and/or equities, because of the higher expected return on the wealth invested;

5) the expected rate of change in prices of goods and services $\frac{1}{P}\frac{dP}{dt} = \pi$ the inflation rate; when inflation increases, the real value of cash diminishes, but physical assets, for example, retain their value so physical assets will be substituted for money.

In summary: the demand for money can be analyzed like the demand for consumer goods and services, with "income" and "substitution" effects. The difference is that money, as a form of wealth, provides services in the future. It is convenient to summarize the factors affecting the demand for real cash balances in the following function:

$$\left(\frac{M}{P}\right)^d = f\left(y, w;\ r_m, r_b, r_e, \frac{1}{P}\frac{dP}{dt};\ u\right)$$

where f denotes the function relationship. The aggregate demand for real cash balances for the economy as a whole is the sum of the demands of the individuals and business firms in the economy. This aggregate demand varies with the size of the population, and changes with the income distribution.

Answer

To be covered when testing yourself

SHORT ANSWER QUESTIONS FOR REVIEW

Choose the correct answer.

1. The value of money depends on: (a) the cost of producing it (b) the amount of gold the government backs each dollar with (c) how much each dollar will buy (d) what the government says each dollar is worth — c

2. The money supply in the U.S. is backed by: (a) government bonds (b) gold in the Fed's vaults (c) gold and silver in a one to one ratio (d) the government's ability to keep the dollar's value stable by controlling the money supply — d

3. The largest portion of M_2 is: (a) cash (b) government bonds (c) demand deposits (d) time deposits (e) none of the above — c

4. Inflation is beneficial to: (a) a retired person on a fixed income (b) a home owner with a mortgage (c) a common stock holder (d) nobody — b

5. Unforeseen inflation is likely to result in: (a) more banks seeking to lend to marginally secure customers (b) relative hardship to those on fixed incomes (c) an increase in the value of government bonds (d) all of the above (e) none of the above — b

6. Savings deposits are not a part of M_1 because: (a) they are insignificant compared to demand deposits (b) they are not recognized as legal tender by the Fed (c) they are not a medium of exchange (d) they are more "liquid" than regular demand deposits (e) none of the above — c

7. The price level and the purchasing power of money: (a) are not related in any immediate way (b) are always equal (c) vary directly (d) vary inversely (e) vary directly during inflations and inversely during deflations — d

8. Near-money does not include: (a) savings accounts (b) government bonds (c) demand deposits (d) all of the above (e) none of the above — c

9. The precautionary demand for money will increase when: (a) people are more confident about future bond prices (b) the interest rate fluctuates within a range which is considered nor-

Answer
To be covered when testing yourself

mal (c) a larger "velocity of circulation" prevails (d) uncertainty is increasing — d

10. Using the crude Quantity Theory of Money and Prices, in the form of P = KM, a doubling of the money supply will: (a) result in a change in Q which we cannot estimate (b) double P (c) cut V in half (d) cut K in half (e) none of the above — b

11. A proponent of the more sophisticated Quantity Theory of Money would say: (a) "prices always double when the money supply doubles" (b) "velocity never changes" (c) "real GNP always increases whenever the money supply increases" (d) nothing; there is no "sophisticated" version of the Quantity Theory (e) none of the above — e

Fill in the blanks.

12. In the early history of the United States colored beads woven into long patterned belts were widely used to purchase goods and services. In this example (a barter system was being used./the beads served as money.) — the beads served as money

13. Money that circulates by decree of the government is ______________. — fiat money

14. A coin or currency whose physical value in terms of metal or paper and ink is below its nominal value, in terms of what it will purchase is known as ______________. — token money

15. A system where gold does not circulate, and paper currency cannot be converted into gold is known as ______________. — an inconvertible paper standard

16. If a family decides that it must retain $500 from each monthly paycheck in order to pay its bills on time, this $500 represents the family's ______________ demand for money. — transaction

17. If this same family retains an extra $100, "just in case . . .," this amount would be its _______ ________ demand for money. — precautionary

18. Mr. Jones' stock broker recently told Mr. Jones that United Widgets stock would probably bottom out next week at $50 per share and then take off after that. In fact, he said that he wouldn't

SHORT ANSWER QUESTIONS FOR REVIEW

	Answer
be surprised if the stock had hit $100 per share by the end of the quarter. As a result, Mr. Jones decided to set aside some cash from this month's pay check, just in case United Widgets really did hit $50 per share. This is an example of a change in Mr. Jones' ____________ demand for money.	speculative
19. A decline in the value of money with an upward movement of the price level is called ________.	inflation
20. A rise in the value of money with a downward movement of the price level is called ________.	deflation
21. During times of unforeseen inflation (debtors/creditors) tend to gain at the expense of (debtors/creditors).	debtors, creditors
22. The Crude Quantity Theory is often considered to be most useful in analyzing ____________.	long term trends in pricing or hyperinflation
23. One asset is considered to be more ____________ than another when it can be exchanged for currency faster and with less expense.	liquid
24. $\frac{PQ}{M}$ is equal to ____________.	velocity
25. The ____________ can be thought of as the price for borrowing money.	interest rate

<u>Determine whether the following statements are true or false.</u>

26. U.S. dollars are called Federal Reserve Notes because the Fed has reserved one dollar's worth of gold or silver for every dollar in circulation.	False
27. The dollar, twenty years ago, would buy roughly twice what it buys now.	True
28. M_1 is a part of M_3.	True
29. Unused credit limits on credit cards are currently considered part of M_3.	False
30. The value of money may be calculated as the inverse of the price level, that is, $\frac{1}{\text{(price index)}}$.	True
31. Land is an example of a near-money.	False

SHORT ANSWER QUESTIONS FOR REVIEW

	Answer To be covered when testing yourself
32. A creditor who thinks that a deflationary period is coming would be wise to collect all his outstanding debts as soon as possible.	False
33. Velocity changes dramatically over the business cycle.	False
34. The Transaction Demand for Money generally increases as income increases.	True
35. The Speculative Demand for Money depends only on income.	False
36. Income velocity has recently been estimated at 3.	False
37. Money must be kept relatively scarce in order to maintain its value.	True
38. Coins and currency make up only about 10% of the actual money supply.	False
39. More than 3/4 of all payments in the U.S. are made by check.	True
40. Money is anything that is widely accepted as a medium of exchange.	True

CHAPTER 12

THE BANKING SYSTEM

Basic Attacks and Strategies for Solving Problems in this Chapter. See pages 409 to 455 for step-by-step solutions to problems.

The largest proportion of our money supply is the deposits of banks and similar institutions. Consequently, their actions have an enormous influence on our nation's money supply, and, through that, inflation, unemployment, and the rate of growth. Understanding how the financial system works is vital in the study of macroeconomics.

Commercial banks and other financial institutions, such as savings and loans, credit unions, investment banks, and insurance companies, all play a similarly important role in our economy. They are a channel by which savings get changed into investment funds. The various deposit instruments they offer are safe, may pay interest, and are easy to use (i.e., you can write checks against many of them). Many savers, especially households and small businesses, may prefer to place their excess funds with these institutions rather than find credit-worthy borrowers themselves. The financial institutions' ability to accumulate large amounts of funds and lend money at attractive terms make them a preferred source of borrowing for firms intent on investment. By making it easier for society to save and invest, these institutions contribute to the economy's ability to grow.

All financial institutions are profit-seeking businesses. Their revenue comes from the interest paid on loans and fees for various and sundry financial services provided. Their costs of production include the interest paid on deposits, salaries of employees, capital charges, and so on. If revenues exceed costs, a profit is earned. What makes these institutions unique is that some of their liabilities circulate as money.

A balance sheet can be used to represent a businesses' financial condition at a particular point in time. All balance sheets contain a listing of the assets of the business. Assets are all productive items that the bank owns. Major assets for banks are the "IOU's" of borrowers, government bond holdings, property, and reserves. Reserves are money that the bank holds, either in the form of cash in the vault or as checking accounts with the Federal Reserve System. Liabilities are what the business owes. Major liabilities of banks include the various types of deposits they offer. These deposits are a liability because they represent an obligation the institution has to its depositors, either to pay interest, provide services, or both. The difference between assets and liabilities is called net worth (Assets – Liabilities = Net Worth). This is a measure of the economic value of the business. It is a common accounting tool to represent a balance sheet by a "T-account" with assets listed on the left and liabilities and net worth on the right. Because of the way net worth is defined, the total of both sides must always be equal. Balance sheets always balance.

A glance at the balance sheet of any financial institution would show that its reserves are always a small fraction of its deposits. In other words, if all depositors were to show up at the institution at the same time and request withdrawal of all their money from their accounts, the institution would be unable to honor their requests. Fortunately, the danger of this occurring is extremely small. Depositors like to hold deposits. They make life easier. Of course, everyday some depositors make withdrawals, but these withdrawals are typically offset by new deposits. In fact, the only cash a financial institution needs is a small amount to offset daily imbalances between new deposits and withdrawals. In short, a financial institution does not need a lot of reserves and can operate quite safely with reserves equal to only a tiny fraction of its deposits. This is known as **fractional reserve banking,** and it is the key to an institution's ability to "create" money.

An important aspect of the study of banking is understanding the process by which banks create money. In the United States, the minimum amount of reserves a bank must hold, called required reserves (R), is determined by the Federal Reserve System through the required reserve ratio (r). The required reserve ratio is a number between 0 and 1 indicating what reserves must be as a percentage of deposits (D). To get the amount of required reserves, simply multiply r times the amount of deposits the bank holds ($R = r * D$). For example, if $r = .10$ and $D =$ \$1,000,000, required reserves are .10 * \$1,000,000 = \$100,000. If a bank holds more reserves than R, the additional amount is called excess reserves (E), where E = total reserves – R.

Excess reserves are the key to money creation. Instead of holding excess reserves (which do not earn interest), a bank can "lend them out," creating demand deposits along the way (A bank lends money by, in essence, creating a demand deposit for the borrower to use.). As the money lent is spent and deposited in other banks, these other banks can do the same thing. Potentially, the money supply can increase by a multiple of the initial amount of excess reserves. The equation is $\Delta D = (1/r) * E$. If $r = .10$ and the banking system holds $E =$ \$200,000, then the money supply can be increased (1/.10) * \$200,000 = \$2,000,000.

The actual process requires the cooperation of all banks in the banking system, with each individual bank lending no more than its excess reserves. The simple formula shown here only shows the maximum expansion. Other factors can intervene to reduce the system's ability to create new money.

The implication of this is that if the amount of reserves or the required reserve ratio can be controlled, then the lending activities of financial institutions can be controlled, and through that, total spending and eventually inflation, unemployment, and economic growth.

Step-by-Step Solutions to Problems in this Chapter, "The Banking System"

INSTITUTIONS

• **PROBLEM 12-1**

What main functions are performed in the economy by commercial banks?

Solution: Commercial banks perform two main functions. First, they accept and store money (cash or checks) deposited with them, and provide in exchange demand accounts ("checkbook money") subject to withdrawal on demand by the depositor. Second, they make loans (grant credit).

Because depositors as a whole do not generally withdraw all their funds at once, banks keep only a fraction of the money deposited with them in reserve to cover withdrawals. The remainder is available to be lent at interest to households, firms, and governments.

• **PROBLEM 12-2**

What is the basic principle of the commercial loan theory of banking?

Solution: The basic principle of the commercial loan theory of banking is that when bank loans are restricted to short-term commercial loans the stability of the entire banking system in times of financial crisis is assured. Only short-term self-liquidating loans to business firms are thought to be appropriate, because the bank can stagger the due dates of its loans; and the merchant or manufacturer acquires the funds to repay the loan with interest when he sells his inventory or output.

This theory today is not generally accepted. It is thought that financial panics can only be avoided if the deposits are insured, for example, by the Federal Deposit Insurance Company (FDIC), or if a central bank exists regulating the reserve requirements.

• **PROBLEM 12-3**

What are the functions of a commercial bank? How do its functions differ from those of a savings bank?

Solution: The primary economic function of commercial banks is to hold demand deposits and to honor checks drawn upon them--in short, to provide us, the economy, with the most important component of the money supply.

A second important function of commercial banks is to lend money to merchants, homeowners, farmers, and industrialists, and to hold government and municipal bonds.

Other miscellaneous functions include accepting savings or time deposits; selling money orders or traveler's checks; handling "trusts" and estates; buying bonds, mortgages and securities and even counseling for firms.

The functions of the commercial banks are much broader in scope as compared to the mutual savings banks which accept only time deposits and other related banking activities in much smaller scale as compared to the commercial banks' activities.

• **PROBLEM 12-4**

What are the major financial institutions in the American economy; what are their functions and which of them are able to create money?

Solution:

1. Commercial banks: create demand deposits (checking accounts) and provide commercial loans.

2. Savings institutions:

   a. mutual savings banks

   b. savings and loan (building and loan) associations

   c. savings departments in commercial banks

These institutions create savings accounts (time deposits) where people can place the money they don't immediately need.

3. Personal trusts: invest the funds of people with financial security who want to provide income for their families.

4. Insurance companies: pool the resources of the public in order to minimize the risk associated with

accident, sickness, death and other unpredictable circumstances.

5. Consumer credit institutions: provide quick, cheap consumer credit.

6. Investment banks, brokerage houses, the federal government provide long-term loans.

Only a commercial bank is able to create money by using its demand deposits as the basis for loans which become additional deposits in other banks.

• PROBLEM 12-5

What is credit?

Solution: Credit is the transfer from one economic agent (person, firm, or bank) to another of immediate purchasing power in exchange for a promise to repay the principal amount borrowed plus the interest accrued on the principal at a certain date in the future.

• PROBLEM 12-6

What is the FDIC? How does it contribute to financial stability when the general public fears that a bank might fail?

Solution: FDIC stands for the Federal Deposit Insurance Corporation, and was established in 1933 following the failure of a large number of banks during the Great Depression. Banks that are members of the Federal Reserve System are required to belong to the FDIC. Today the FDIC insures deposits up to $40,000. The premium for coverage is one-twelfth of one percent, paid by the bank.

When the general public fears that a bank might fail, the psychological effect of insuring deposits diminishes the prospect of having runs on banks. Before the FDIC was established, people would withdraw their deposits if they feared bank failure. Because banks typically have very small cash reserves, such runs would cause extreme difficulty. In the century before the FDIC was established, runs on banks contributed to the financial panics that accompanied most recessions. By eliminating this incentive to withdraw deposits, FDIC has made an important contribution to financial stability.

THE BALANCE SHEET

• PROBLEM 12-7

Describe a commercial bank's balance sheet.

Solution: The balance sheet of a bank, like that of any firm, is a statement which lists, on the one side, all the categories of "assets," claims owned by the bank, with their monetary values; and, on the other side, all categories of claims against the bank, "liabilities," with their monetary values; and the net worth of the bank, which is simply defined as the difference (positive, negative, or zero) between the total value of assets and the total value of liabilities. Thus total assets are always "balanced" by total liabilities plus net worth, i.e., Assets = Liabilities + Net Worth, since Net Worth = Assets - Liabilities by definition.

A bank's assets are principally the cash it receives from depositors, the loans it has made and expects to be repaid, and the securities (bonds, etc.) it has bought with a part of the cash received from depositors. Its liabilities (ignoring the possibility of time deposits) consist of the demand accounts which it created for depositors upon receipt of their cash and which it is liable to redeem in cash on demand.

A major difference between the balance sheet of a commercial bank and that of a solvent non-bank firm is that the bank's "current liabilities," i.e., those which are due to be met immediately, as the bank's demand deposits are, exceed the value of their "current assets," i.e., those assets which can be immediately converted to cash. Conversely, a solvent non-bank firm has on hand enough assets which are immediately convertible to cash to meet present obligations. If all depositors at once demanded that a bank redeem their accounts in cash, the bank would be unable (without a loan from the Fed) to do so. Part of the depositors' cash is out on loan and thus not available to the bank until the loan is due to be paid back. However, because the current liabilities of banks (checkbook money) are a generally accepted means of payment whereas the IOU's of non-bank firms are not, banks, unlike non-bank firms, are not generally called upon to meet all their current liabilities at once in cash. Thus they do not face insolvency as long as the public is confident enough in the bank's ability to redeem its deposit accounts in cash on demand to leave its cash in the bank.

• PROBLEM 12-8

Suppose Mr. X has a checking account in Bank A, and Mr. Y has a checking account in Bank B. Banks A and B each have $100,000 in deposit liabilities and $30,000 in reserves, and the required reserve ratio is 20%. Show what happens to each bank's deposit liabilities, reserves, and excess reserves if Mr. X writes a check for $10,000 to Mr. Y, Mr. Y deposits the check into his account at Bank B, and Bank B collects from Bank A.

Solution: Let us first construct the initial balance sheets of Bank A and Bank B from the given data.

Bank A

Assets		Liabilities	
Reserves	$30,000	Deposits	$100,000
Loans	$70,000		
Total	$100,000	Total	$100,000

Bank B

Assets		Liabilities	
Reserves	$30,000	Deposits	$100,000
Loans	$70,000		
Total	$100,000	Total	$100,000

The effect of Mr. X's check on the balance sheet entries of Bank A is, first, to reduce the balance in Mr. X's deposit account by $10,000, which also reduces its total deposit liabilities by $10,000. Second, collection by Bank B of the check from Bank A means an outflow of $10,000 in reserves from Bank A. These changes can be represented as follows:

Bank A

Assets		Liabilities	
Reserves	- $10,000	Deposits	- $10,000

After these changes then, Bank A's balance sheet will be:

Bank A

Assets		Liabilities	
Reserves	$20,000	Deposits	$90,000
Loans	$70,000		
Total	$90,000	Total	$90,000

To determine the effect of the checking transaction on Bank A's excess reserves, recall that excess reserves are (actual reserves - required reserves). Required reserves in turn are equal to (Deposit liabilities x required reserve ratio). Initially, Bank A's required reserves were $100,000 x 20% = $20,000. Thus its excess reserves were $30,000 - $20,000 = $10,000. After the checking transaction, actual reserves have fallen to $20,000. Required reserves are equal to $90,000 x 20% = $18,000. Thus Bank A's excess reserves are now equal to $20,000 - $18,000 = $2,000, down by $ 8,000.

Turning now to Bank B, the deposit of Mr. X's $10,000 check by Mr. Y increases the balance in Mr. Y's deposit account, and thus the total deposit liabilities of Bank B, by $10,000. In addition, collection of the check from Bank A increases the reserves of Bank B by $10,000. These changes can be represented as:

Bank B

Assets		Liabilities	
Reserves	+ $10,000	Deposits	+ $10,000

After these changes, then, Bank B's balance sheet will be:

Bank B

Assets		Liabilities	
Reserves	$40,000	Deposits	$110,000
Loans	$70,000		
Total	$110,000	Total	$110,000

To calculate the change in Bank B's excess reserves, we must find the amount of their required reserves before and after the transaction. Before, they were ($100,000 x 20%) = $20,000. After, they are ($110,000 x 20%) = $22,000. Thus, before, excess reserves were (actual reserves - required reserves) = ($30,000 - $20,000) = $10,000. After, they are ($40,000 - $22,000) = $18,000, up by $8,000.

• PROBLEM 12-9

Suppose Chemical Bank makes a loan of $100,000 to Mr. Gerard. Mr. Gerard uses the loan to buy a house from Ms. Furey, and Ms. Furey deposits Mr. Gerard's check into her account at Citibank. Show what happens at each stage of this process to the deposit liabilities and the reserves of each of the two banks.

Solution: The initial loan of $100,000 is made by creating a demand deposit account with a balance of $100,000 in

Mr. Gerard's name at Chemical Bank. The bank's deposit liabilities are increased at the same time and by the same amount as the loan (an asset). In terms of Chemical Bank's balance sheet, the making of the loan is represented by the following changes:

Chemical Bank

Assets		Liabilities	
Loans	+ $100,000	Deposits	+ $100,000

When Mr. Gerard writes a check to Ms. Furey, and she deposits it in her account at Citibank, her balance with Citibank increases by $100,000, and thus Citibank's deposit liabilities increase by $100,000. Similarly the deposit increases Citibank's reserves by $100,000. These changes are represented on its balance sheet in the following way:

Citibank

Assets		Liabilities	
Reserves	+ $100,000	Deposits	+ $100,000

Presentation of the check to Chemical Bank by Citibank for payment will reduce Chemical Bank's reserves by $100,000. And it will also reduce the balance in Mr. Gerard's account, and thus Chemical Bank's total deposit liabilities, by $100,000. These changes are represented on the balance sheet of Chemical Bank as follows:

Chemical Bank

Assets		Liabilities	
Reserves	- $100,000	Deposits	- $100,000

The final changes in the position of Chemical Bank's balance sheet, then, after the loan has been made, used to make a payment, and collected by the payee's bank (Citibank) is as follows:

Chemical Bank

Assets		Liabilities	
Loans	+ $100,000	Deposits	+ $100,000
Reserves	- $100,000	Deposits	- $100,000
Total	0	Total	0

The position of Citibank's balance sheet will have undergone the following changes:

Citibank

Assets		Liabilities	
Reserves	+ $100,000	Deposits	+ $100,000
Total	+ $100,000	Total	+ $100,000

• PROBLEM 12-10

Suppose you decide to open a bank and issue $100,000 of capital stock to set it up. $80,000 of this is used to buy the building. The other $20,000 is kept as cash.

What will the original balance sheet be and how will it change with each of the following transactions:

a. Customers deposit $30,000 in demand deposit accounts in your bank;

b. The bank decides to buy $20,000 of government bonds.

Solution: The original balance sheet is as follows:

Assets		Liabilities and Net Worth	
Cash	$ 20,000	Capital Stock	$100,000
Property	$ 80,000		
Total	$100,000	Total	$100,000

Notice that Assets ≡ Liabilities + Net Worth. Liabilities are the claims of the non-owners against the assets; net worth represents the claims of the owners against the assets.

a. If customers deposit $30,000 in demand deposit accounts, cash will rise to $50,000. But a corresponding liability will be created, since the bank is obligated to pay out on demand any or all of the $30,000. We'll call this account Demand deposits.

Therefore the balance sheet would now be:

Assets		Liabilities and Net Worth	
Cash	$ 50,000	Demand deposits	$ 30,000
Property	$ 80,000	Capital stock	$100,000
Total	$130,000	Total	$130,000

b. If the bank buys $20,000 of government bonds, its cash will decrease to $30,000. But the possession of the bonds represents a new asset which we will call Government Securities.

Therefore the new balance sheet is:

Assets		Liabilities and Net Worth	
Cash	$ 30,000	Demand deposits	$ 30,000
Govt. securities	$ 20,000	Capital stock	$100,000
Property	$ 80,000		
	$130,000		$130,000

FRACTIONAL RESERVE BANKING

• PROBLEM 12-11

What is meant by "fractional reserve" banking?

Solution: Fractional reserve banking means that banks keep less than 100% of their deposits in cash, placing the rest in income-earning investments. Such a policy is built on laws of probability, which protect the bank from having all its depositors come in at the same time and demand cash. In the United States the Federal Reserve Board controls the percentage of total deposits which must be kept as reserves by member banks. In the end the government now stands behind the fractional cash reserve policy, ready even to print up new money in the case of a run on the banks, in order to avoid a wave of bankruptcies, a collapse of the banking system, and massive deflation of the money supply.

• PROBLEM 12-12

What are "required reserves"? What are "actual reserves" and "excess reserves"?

Solution: "Required reserves" are those funds which a commercial bank must keep, either in cash or on account with the Federal Reserve Bank, and which it may not lend out. The amount of a bank's required reserves is a certain percentage, called the required reserve ratio, of its demand (and time) deposits specified by the Federal Reserve.

"Actual reserves" are the funds which a commercial bank possesses at any given time in the form either of cash or balances in its account with the Federal Reserve Bank.

"Excess reserves" is the difference (positive, negative, or zero) between a commercial bank's "actual reserves" and its "required reserves." A commercial bank with positive excess reserves is in a position to increase its loans; a bank with negative excess reserves must decrease the amount it is lending; a bank with zero excess reserves is "loaned up," and may not increase its lending any further, although it may reduce the amount of its loans if it wishes.

• PROBLEM 12-13

How did the government stand behind the banks through the formation of the Federal Deposit Insurance Corporation?

Solution: Through the formation of the Federal Deposit Insurance Corporation all bank deposits are now being protected by government insurance. Thus all banks are safe today because everyone realizes that it is a vital function of government to stand behind them should a depression and panicky "run" on the banking system ever recur.

• PROBLEM 12-14

Define reserve ratios. What are the latest reserve requirements of member banks?

Solution: In banking, the reserve ratio is the "specified percentage" of their deposit liabilities which the commercial bank must have on deposit in the central bank or in vault cash. This ratio is expressed as follows:

$$\text{Reserve ratio} = \frac{\text{commercial bank's required deposit in Federal Reserve Bank}}{\text{commercial bank's demand-deposit liabilities}}$$

To take an example, if the reserve ratio were 10 percent, our bank, having accepted \$100,000 in deposits from the public, would be obligated to keep \$10,000 as a deposit, or reserve, in the Federal Reserve Bank in New York City. If the ratio were 20 percent, \$20,000 would have to be deposited in the Federal Reserve Bank. If 50 percent, \$50,000 and so forth.

The reserve requirements of member banks as of January 1977 are as follows:

Demand deposits	Reserve requirement
\$ 0 - 2 million	7%
\$ 2 - 10 million	9 1/2%
\$ 10 - 100 million	11 3/4%
\$ 100 - 400 million	12 3/4%
Over \$ 400 million	16 1/4%

• PROBLEM 12-15

Suppose a bank has $250,000 in deposits, and $10,000 in excess reserves. If the required reserve ratio is 20%, what are the bank's actual reserves?

Solution: A bank's actual reserves are the sum of its required reserves and its excess reserves. We are given the information that its excess reserves are $10,000. We need to calculate its required reserves. We do this by multiplying its deposits by the required reserve ratio. Thus, required reserves = (deposits) x (required reserve ratio) = ($250.000) x (20%) = $50,000. Actual reserves, then are (required reserves + excess reserves) = ($50,000 + $10,000) = $ 60,000.

• PROBLEM 12-16

Suppose a commercial bank has deposits of $400,000 and has made loans and investments of $315,000. Assume also that deposits are its only source of reserves. If the required reserve ratio is 20%, how much are its excess reserves?

Solution: In order to calculate the bank's Excess reserves, we need to find out what its Total reserves are and what its Required reserves are, for Total reserves = Required reserves + Excess reserves, or Excess reserves = Total reserves - required reserves. The bank's Total reserves, after making its loans, are $400,000 (Deposits) - $315,000 (Loans) = $85,000. The amount of its required reserves is given by multiplying the amount of its deposits by the required reserve ratio. That is, Required reserves = required reserve ratio x total demand deposits = (0.20) x ($400,000) = $ 80,000. Excess reserves, then are Total reserves - Required reserves = $85,000 - $80,000 = $5,000.

• PROBLEM 12-17

Suppose a commercial bank's required reserves are $100,000, and the required reserve ratio is 16 2/3%. What must its deposits be?

Solution: The amount of reserves which a bank is required to have on account with the Federal Reserve Bank or in vault cash is in direct proportion to its deposit liabilities. The ratio of reserves to deposits is the required reserve ratio.

In our example, the bank's required reserves of $100,000 must be equal to 16 2/3% of its deposits. That is:

Required reserve = Required reserve ratio x Deposits

$100,000 = 16 2/3% x Deposits

$$\text{Deposits} = (\$100{,}000) \div 16\ 2/3\%$$

$$= \$600{,}000.$$

• PROBLEM 12-18

Mr. Jones is president of the First National Bank of St. Louis and wishes to determine if his bank is holding too much of its demand deposits as reserves. The bank's total deposits = $1,700,000 and the reserve ratio is 20%. If Mr. Jones finds that reserves = $850,000 what might he conclude about excess reserves?

Solution: For this bank, the required amount of reserves

$$= (\text{deposits}) \times (\text{reserve ratio})$$

$$= (\$1{,}700{,}000) \times (20\%)$$

$$= \$\ 340{,}000$$

But in fact the bank has reserves of $850,000 (or $\frac{\$850{,}000}{\$1{,}700{,}000}$ = 50% of its total deposits). The excess reserves = $850,000 - $340,000 = $510,000, or as a percentage, 50% - 20% = 30%. Mr. Jones may conclude that too much is being held as reserves. Some of the excess reserves should be invested where they can give the bank a positive return.

• PROBLEM 12-19

Suppose a bank has made a total of $100,000 in loans and still has excess reserves of $25,000. If the required reserve ratio is 10%, how much must the bank's demand deposit liabilities be? Assume that other liabilities and net worth are just matched by assets other than loans and reserves.

Solution: The balance sheet identity tells us that Assets = Liabilities + Net Worth. If the bank's net worth and liabilities other than demand deposits are just offset by its assets other than loans and reserves, then its loans plus its actual reserves (assets) must equal its demand deposit liabilities. We know the amount of its loans, $100,000. We know its excess reserves are $25,000. Actual reserves consist of excess reserves plus required reserves, the latter we do not know. We do know, however, that required reserves are 10% of demand deposits, since the required reserve ratio is 10%. Therefore, if we let X be the (unknown) amount of the bank's demand deposits, then 0.10X will be the amount of required reserves. We can now write the balance sheet equation for this bank as:

Loans + Actual Reserves = Loans +

Excess reserves + Required reserves =

$$\$100,000 + \$25,000 + 0.10X = \text{Demand Deposits} = X. \quad \text{Or,}$$

$$\$100,000 + \$25,000 + 0.10X = X$$

Subtracting 0.10X from both sides of the equation, we have

$$\$125,000 = 0.9X.$$

Dividing both sides of the equation by 0.9, we have

$$X \cong \$138,889 = \text{Demand Deposits}$$

We can check this result by calculating from it the amount of Required reserves, and, with that, total Loans plus Actual reserves and see if they are equal to total demand deposit liabilities. Thus, Required reserves are 10% of demand deposits, i.e., 0.10 x \$138,889 ≅ \$13,889. Total assets are thus \$100,000 (Loans) + \$25,000 (Excess reserves) + \$13,889 (Required reserves) = \$138,889. Thus, total Loans plus Actual reserves do equal total demand deposits, so the solution value of \$138,889 for the bank's total demand deposits must be correct.

• PROBLEM 12-20

Suppose a commercial bank has \$600,000 in demand deposits, has made \$375,000 worth of loans and investments, and has \$25,000 in excess reserves. Assuming that the bank's initial reserves were provided exclusively by deposits, what must be the required reserve ratio of the banking system?

Solution: The required reserve ratio is the ratio of reserves that must be kept in cash or on account with the Federal Reserve Bank to demand deposit liabilities. Required reserves are equal to Actual reserves minus Excess reserves. The amount of Actual reserves is what remains after part of the bank's initial reserves, which were acquired through deposits, have been used to make loans and investments. The Actual reserves of the bank, then, are \$600,000 (Deposits) - \$375,000 (loans and investments) = \$225,000. Since Required reserves are Actual reserves less Excess reserves, and we are given the information that Excess reserves are \$25,000, Required reserves must be equal to \$225,000 - \$25,000 = \$200,000.

The Required reserve ratio, Required reserves ÷ demand deposit liabilities, then is \$200,000 ÷ \$600,000 = 1/3 = 33 1/3%.

• PROBLEM 12-21

Suppose a bank has the following balance sheet:

Assets		Liabilities	
Reserves	$ 30,000	Deposits	$ 90,000
Loans & Securities	$ 70,000	Capital Stock	$ 10,000
Total	$100,000	Total	$100,000

Assume a required reserve ratio of 20%. How much additional money can the bank lend? Show how the balance sheet changes when that amount is lent, and when the borrower's checks drawing on the loans are cleared against the bank.

Solution: The bank can lend an additional amount equal to its excess reserves. Its excess reserves are its actual reserves less required reserves. Actual reserves are $30,000. Required reserves are given by the product of the required reserve ratio and demand deposits, i.e., (20%) x ($90,000) = $18,000. Thus excess reserves are equal to $30,000 - $18,000 = $12,000. The bank can increase its total loans by $12,000.

If the bank does lend an additional $12,000, it does so by creating demand account balances for its borrowers. Thus, loans of $12,000 are reflected in changes in the balance sheet as follows:

Assets		Liabilities	
Loans	+ $12,000	Demand Deposits	+ $12,000

The bank's balance sheet will look like this

Assets		Liabilities	
Reserves	$ 30,000	Deposits	$102,000
Loans & Securities	$ 82,000	Capital Stock	$ 10,000
Total	$112,000	Total	$112,000

When the borrowers use their loans to make payments, they will write checks drawn on the bank. When these checks are presented to the bank for payment, the bank will lose reserves in the amount of the checks; and the same amount will be deducted from the deposit balances of the borrowers who wrote the checks. The bank's balance sheet will undergo these changes:

Assets		Liabilities	
Reserves	- $12,000	Deposits	- $12,000

After collection of the borrowers' checks, then, the bank's balance sheet looks as follows:

Assets		Liabilities	
Reserves	$ 18,000	Deposits	$ 90,000
Loans & Securities	$ 82,000	Capital Stock	$ 10,000
Total	$100,000	Total	$100,000

• PROBLEM 12-22

Suppose a bank has $500,000 in deposit liabilities, loans and securities of $380,000, and $120,000 in reserves. If the required reserve ratio is 20% and the bank decides to lend an additional $50,000, what happens to the bank's reserves and what must the bank do to adjust to the change in its reserves?

Solution: In lending an additional $50,000, the bank creates a deposit account of $50,000 in the name of the borrower, thus adding to its deposit liabilities (claims against the bank) by $50,000. The loan, being a future claim against the borrower, represents an asset to the bank. Thus the bank's balance sheet will show the following:

Assets		Liabilities	
Reserves	$120,000	Deposits	$500,000
Loans & Securities	$380,000		
Loans	+ $ 50,000	Deposits	+ $ 50,000
Total	$550,000	Total	$550,000

When the new borrower uses his loan by writing checks against his account, and the checks are presented to the bank for payment, the bank's balance sheet will again change. If the borrower has written checks for the entire $50,000 of the loan, then $50,000 will be deducted from his deposit account. Also, the bank will have to surrender $50,000 of its reserves to the payees or their banks. Thus, the balance sheet will change as follows:

Assets		Liabilities	
Reserves	$120,000	Deposits	$500,000
Loans & Securities	$380,000		
Loans	+ $ 50,000	Deposits	+ $ 50,000
Reserves	- $ 50,000	Deposits	- $ 50,000
Total	$500,000	Total	$500,000

Netting out all changes, then, the bank's balance sheet will come to look as follows:

Assets		Liabilities	
Reserves	$ 70,000	Deposits	$500,000
Loans & Securities	$430,000		
Total	$500,000	Total	$500,000

Note, however, that the amount of reserves required for $500,000 in deposit liabilities is $500,000 x required reserve ratio = $500,000 x 20% = $100,000. The bank's actual reserves are only $70,000, $30,000 below reserves required. In other words excess reserves are - $30,000. In order to restore its reserves to the required level ($100,000), the bank must call $30,000 of its loans in for payment (e.g., it can sell government bonds, which are loans to governments). This reduction of loans in order to build up its reserves can be represented on the bank's balance sheet as follows:

Assets		Liabilities	
Reserves	$ 70,000	Deposits	$500,000
Loans & Securities	$430,000		
Loans	- $ 30,000		
Reserves	+ $ 30,000		
Total	$500,000	Total	$500,000

Thus the final position of the bank's balance sheet is:

Assets		Liabilities	
Reserves	\$100,000	Deposits	\$500,000
Loans	\$400,000		
Total	\$500,000	Total	\$500,000

MULTIPLE DEPOSIT CREATION

• PROBLEM 12-23

What features of commercial banking make banks unique among financial institutions in their ability to expand the money supply?

Solution: The money supply (M_1) is defined as demand deposits and currency held by the public. Commercial banks alone provide demand deposit accounts subject to withdrawal by check in exchange for deposits of cash or checks. If they simply provided the public with the convenience of accounts subject to withdrawal by check and storage of its cash, however, commercial banks' operations could neither add to nor subtract from the total quantity of money. Deposits into or withdrawals from checking accounts would change the composition but not the quantity of the stock of money.

It is the practice of banks of keeping only a fraction of their deposits on reserve and lending the remainder that enables commercial banks to create money. Loans made by one bank are withdrawn from it and generally deposited, in whole or in part, in other banks, adding to total bank deposits. Thus, due to banks' practice of keeping only a fraction of deposits on reserve to cover withdrawals from their demand accounts, and lending out the remainder, a \$1 deposit of cash into a checking account reduces total currency holdings by \$1 but increases total checking account balances by more than \$1, and thus increases the total quantity of money in the economy (currency plus checking account balances).

• PROBLEM 12-24

True or false: Because of "multiple expansion of bank deposits," individual commercial banks are able to lend several dollars for each dollar deposited with them.

Solution: False. As a whole, the banking system is able to create money, but individual banks have no such power as suggested by the statement above. Money expansion by the system as a whole is possible when the assets (loans) of one bank form the liabilities (deposits) of another. Because the banks are required to keep only a fraction of their total demand deposits in reserve, a 'blow-up' of the original amount of money is possible. A single bank could not lend more than it has on deposit because people who borrow money withdraw all or part of it from their accounts. When the checks of the borrowers were presented to the bank for payment, the single bank would not have the reserves or cash to make the payments if it had created more loans than it had received in deposits.

But when there are several banks, then money borrowed from one bank is usually deposited in another bank in the system. That bank in turn expands its loans by a fraction of the new deposits, by creating new demand accounts. These borrowers in turn draw on these accounts to make payments which the payees deposit in their banks, enabling those banks to expand their loans. And so on.

• PROBLEM 12-25

Why is it that the banking system as a whole can produce a multiple expansion of deposits while a single bank within that system cannot?

Solution: An individual commercial bank, let us recall, is required to keep as reserves a certain percentage (the required reserve ratio), say 20%, of its deposits. It can, therefore, lend out only a fraction (100% - 20% = 80%) of new reserves it acquires from deposits made into the bank. Hence, an individual bank alone could increase its deposit liabilities by only a fraction (80% in this case) of an increase in its reserves.

In conjunction with the lending operations of other banks in the banking system, however, the effects on total bank deposit liabilities of an increase in an individual bank's reserves go much further. Borrowers from a commercial bank A will use their loans to make various payments, usually by writing checks. Recipients of these checks drawn on bank A will generally deposit them in their banks, call them B, thus increasing the deposits of the B banks. When the B banks present the checks to bank A for payment, bank A will lose reserves, up to the entire 80% of its reserves which it lent out; and these reserves will be transferred to the B banks. The B banks are able to lend out 80% of these reserves newly acquired from Bank A, an amount equal to 80% x 80% = 64% of the initial increase in Bank A's reserves. As loans made by the B banks are used by borrowers to make payments, recipients of these payments generally deposit them in their banks, the C banks, adding to C bank deposits.

The chain of loans, payments, and deposits initiated by a new deposit in one bank can continue to increase deposits in the banks as a group by several times the amount of initial new deposit. This is the result when the reserves lent out by the A bank are deposited in the B banks, and they in turn lend part of these reserves, which are in turn deposited in the C banks, etc. The outflow of reserves from an individual bank that occurs when the bank makes a loan is not an outflow of reserves from the banks as a whole if the loan funds are deposited in another bank in the system. When the loans of any individual bank become deposits in other banks, and these deposits are (partly) used to make new loans, total deposits in banks taken together can be increased by a multiple of the increase in the deposits of any one of them.

• PROBLEM 12-26

If $1,000 in currency is deposited in a commercial bank, what is the potential change in the total money supply resulting from this transaction if the required reserve ratio, r, is 15% ?

Solution: The initial effect of the deposit of currency is to reduce the public's holdings of currency by $ 1000 and increase its demand deposits by $ 1000. The money supply, which is the sum of currency held by the public and demand deposits, is thus unaffected up to this point.

However, the deposit of $1000 in currency adds $1000 to the reserves of the commercial bank. If the bank was previously "loaned up," i.e., its excess reserves were 0, the bank must keep in reserve, against the additional $ 1000 in deposit liabilities, 15% x $ 1000 = $ 150 in required reserves. That leaves $ 1000 - $ 150 = $ 850 in excess reserves E, available to be lent out. The banking system as a whole can potentially create loans in the form of demand deposits equal to $\frac{E}{r}$ =

$\frac{\$850}{.15} \cong \$\ 5667.$

The total potential increase in the money supply (currency held by the public and demand deposits) is (currency + demand deposits) = (- $ 1000 + $ 1000 + $ 5667) = $ 5667.

• PROBLEM 12-27

What is the immediate effect on the money supply if Bank A receives a deposit of $ 1000 in currency from Mr. X and grants a loan of $ 500 to Mr. Y?

Solution: The money supply consists of demand deposits and currency held by the public. When Mr. X deposits $ 1000 in currency into Bank A, the bank adds $ 1000 to his deposit balance. The money supply remains unchanged, since the $ 1000 reduction in currency held by the public is offset by an increase in demand deposits. The transaction changes the composition, but not the amount, of the money supply.

When the bank makes a loan to Mr. Y, it adds $ 500 to the balance in his deposit account, or opens an account in his name with a $ 500 balance. There is no change in his holdings of currency. So there is an immediate addition to the money supply of $ 500 as a result of the loan.

The net immediate impact of the two transactions, then, is to add $ 500 to the money supply.

• PROBLEM 12-28

Suppose a commercial bank has \$ 100,000 in deposits and has made loans of \$ 65,000. If the required reserve ratio is 20%, (a) how much additional money can the bank lend, and (b) how much can the banking system as a whole add to the money supply as a result of the loan?

Solution: In order to calculate how much additional lending the bank can engage in, we must calculate its Excess reserves. Its Excess reserves are the difference between its Actual reserves and its Required reserves. Actual reserves are that portion of its deposits which it has not lent out but has kept either in its account with the Federal Reserve Bank or in the form of cash in its own vaults. In our bank's case, Actual reserves (Deposits - Loans) are \$ 100,000 - \$ 65,000 = \$ 35,000 of Actual reserves. Required reserves are that portion of deposits which the Fed requires that banks keep on reserve, either in their Fed accounts or in vault cash. A bank's Required reserves are given by multiplying its deposits by the required reserve ratio. In our bank's case, this is \$ 100,000 x 20% = \$ 20,000 of Required reserves. Its Excess reserves (Actual reserves - Required reserves) are thus \$ 35,000 - \$ 20,000 = \$ 15,000.

Excess reserves may be lent out by the bank. If the whole \$ 15,000 is lent out, withdrawn, spent, and eventually deposited in other banks, those banks' reserves are increased by \$ 15,000. Assuming that all of them were heretofore "loaned up," i.e., that their Excess reserves were zero, they now have Excess reserves available to lend, equal to Additional Deposits - Required reserves = \$ 15,000 - (20% x \$ 15,000) = (100% - 20%) \$ 15,000 = \$ 15,000 - \$ 3,000 = \$ 12,000. If this \$ 12,000 in loans is spent and deposited in still other banks, the deposit and loan expansion continues, but by decreasing amounts. The total expansion of deposits by the banking system is given by $E + (1 - r)E + (1 - r)^2 E + (1 - r)^3 E + \dots$

$$= \$15,000 + (1.0 - 0.20)(\$15,000) + (1.0 - 0.20)^2(\$15,000) + (1.0 - 0.20)^3(\$15,000) \dots$$

$$= \$15,000 + (0.8)(\$15,000) + (0.8)^2(\$15,000) + (0.8)^3(\$15,000) + \dots$$

$$= \$15,000 + \$12,000 + (0.8)(\$12,000) + (0.8)(\$9,600) + \dots$$

where "E" is the amount of its excess reserves which our bank decides to lend, and "r" is the banking system's required reserve ratio. The sum of the terms of the mathematical series is given by the expression $\frac{E}{r}$. In our example, then, total potential expansion of deposits is equal to $\frac{E}{r} = \frac{\$15,000}{0.20} =$

$ 75,000. Since currency held by the public has not changed in amount through this process, the total money supply (currency held by the public plus demand deposits) has risen by $ 75,000 also.

• PROBLEM 12-29

Suppose a bank has $250,000 in deposit liabilities, $ 175,000 in loans and $ 75,000 in reserves. What is the direct effect on the money supply if the bank lends an additional $ 25,000? What is the direct effect on the money supply when the loan is repaid (ignoring interest)?

Solution: The initial balance sheet of the bank looks like this:

Assets		Liabilities	
Reserves	$ 75,000	Deposits	$250,000
Loans	$175,000		
Total	$250,000	Total	$250,000

The additional $25,000 loan is made by adding $25,000 to the demand account of the borrower, in exchange for his promise to pay (IOU). Deposit liabilities are increased by $25,000 as are loans in the asset column. The addition of these assets and liabilities is represented in balance sheet form by:

Assets		Liabilities	
Loans	+ $25,000	Deposits	+ $25,000

The bank's revised balance sheet looks as follows:

Assets		Liabilities	
Reserves	$ 75,000	Deposits	$275,000
Loans	$200,000		
Total	$275,000	Total	$275,000

The bank's deposits have increased by $25,000. The money supply is defined as the sum of demand deposits and currency held by the public. Since no change has occurred in people's cash holdings, the change in the money supply coincides with the change in demand deposits. That is, the money supply has increased by $ 25,000.

When the loan is repaid, the reverse process will take place. The borrower repays the $ 25,000, either by writing a check against his deposit account, thus reducing the bank's deposit liabilities, or by payment of cash. In either case, the money supply, being the sum of demand deposits plus currency held by the public, decreases by $ 25,000 when the loan is repaid.

• PROBLEM 12-30

Show that an initial deposit of $ 1000 in a bank can cause an increase in total deposits of the banking system of up to $ 5000/r dollars, if the required reserve ratio is 20%.

Solution: Suppose the required reserve ratio = 20% and someone deposits $ 1000 in a bank. The bank must keep 20% of that $ 1000, or $ 200, but can lend out the remaining $ 800. The recipient of the $ 800 deposits the money in a second bank, where 20% of it, or $ 160, is kept in reserve, and $ 640 is lent out. The process will continue in this manner as illustrated in the accompanying table.

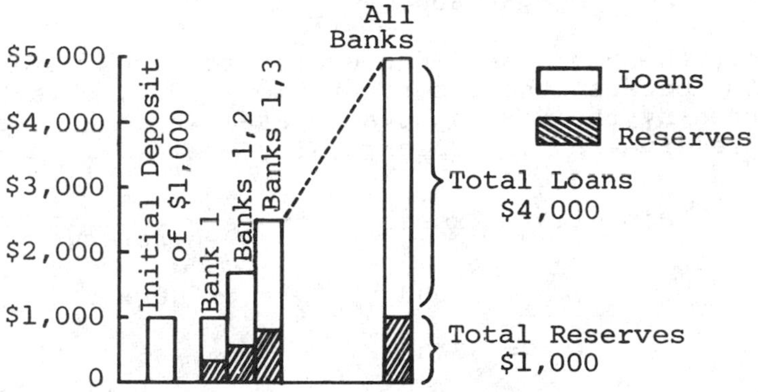

The money creation process of the entire banking system (with 20% reserve requirement)

An illustration:

Bank	deposits	reserves	loans
1	1,000	200	800
2	800	160	640
3	640	128	512
4	512	102	410
5	410	82	328
6	328	66	262
etc.	... +	... +	... +
All Banks in total	$5000	$1000	$4000

• PROBLEM 12-31

If a bank has total reserves of \$ 1000 and demand deposits of \$ 2000, what is the amount by which demand deposits can expand in the banking system, assuming a 20% required reserve ratio.

Solution: Our first step is to figure out how much the required reserves are, using the formula:

$$\text{Required reserves} = \text{deposits} \times \text{reserve ratio}$$

$$= \$\ 2000 \times 20\%$$

$$= \$\ 400$$

Then we must find excess reserves, using the formula

$$\text{Excess reserves} = \text{Actual reserves} - \text{required reserves}$$

$$= \$\ 1000 - \$\ 400$$

$$= \$\ 600$$

Therefore the bank has \$ 600 excess reserves which it can lend out. But because the reserve ratio < 100%, this \$ 600 can be expanded by the banking system as a whole as a function of the reserve ratio. Specifically

$$\text{Additional Deposits} = \text{Excess reserves} \times \frac{1}{\text{reserve ratio}}$$

$$= \$\ 600 \times \frac{1}{0.2} = \$\ 600 \times 5$$

$$= \$3000$$

So the money supply, i.e., total demand deposits of the banking system as a whole, can increase by \$ 3000.

• PROBLEM 12-32

Suppose that in the banking system as a whole demand deposits are equal to \$ 80,000,000 and reserves are equal to \$ 17,000,000 with a legal reserve ratio of 10%. If the Federal Reserve doubles the required ratio, by how much will the money-creating potential of the banking system as a whole drop?

Solution: The money-creating potential of the banking system as a whole depends upon two factors: the legal reserve ratio and the amount of excess reserves. Of course, the amount of excess reserves is a function of the legal reserve ratio. In this case, with \$ 80,000,000 of demand deposits, and a 10% reserve requirement the required reserves are \$ 8,000,000. Since actual reserves are \$ 17,000,000, there are excess reserves of \$ 17,000,000 - \$ 8,000,000 = \$ 9,000,000. Therefore in the old situation, the money-creating potential of the banking system as a whole is equal to the amount of excess reserves divided by the required reserve ratio, or \$ 9,000,000/ 0.10 = \$ 90,000,000.

In the new situation, the required reserve ratio = 20%. With \$ 80,000,000 of demand deposits, required reserves are \$ 16,000,000. If actual reserves are \$ 17,000,000, excess reserves are \$ 1,000,000. Therefore, the money-creating potential of the banking system as a whole here = \$ 1,000,000/ 0.20 = \$ 5,000,000.

Thus by doubling the required reserve ratio, money-creating potential of the banking system as a whole drops from \$ 90,000,000 to \$ 5,000,000.

• PROBLEM 12-33

Suppose the banking system as a whole has \$ 100,000,000 in deposits, with no excess reserves. What is the potential change in the money supply if the Fed a) lowers the reserve requirement from 25% to 20%; b) raises the reserve requirement from 25% to 33 1/3%?

Solution: To compute the potential change in the money supply arising from a change in the required reserve ratio, we need first to calculate the amount of required reserves presently held by the banking system. With deposits of \$ 100,000,000 and a required reserve ratio of 25%, required reserves are (0.25) x (\$ 100,000,000) = \$ 25,000,000. Since excess reserves are 0 (zero), actual reserves of the banking system are \$ 25,000,000.

If the Fed lowers the required ratio to 20%, then required reserves are (0.20) x (\$ 100,000,000) = \$ 20,000,000. Since actual reserves are \$ 25,000,000, the banking system now has Excess reserves = (Actual reserves - Required reserves) = \$ 25,000,000 - \$ 20,000,000 = \$ 5,000,000. If each bank in the system lends out its entire excess reserves, and none of the loans is withdrawn from the banking system as a whole (although they are withdrawn from the individual lending banks, they are redeposited in other banks in the system), the \$ 5,000,000 total excess reserves can fulfill the reserve requirements for an increase in deposits given by: Reserve requirement = reserve ratio x Deposits.

$$\$ 5,000,000 = r \times (\text{Additional Deposits})$$

$$\text{Additional deposits} = \$ 5,000,000 \div (0.20)$$

$$= \$25,000,000.$$

Since the amount of currency held by the public has not been affected by the change in reserve requirements, this \$ 25,000,000 is a net addition to the money supply.

We can check this result by comparing the reserve requirements for the new amount of deposits with the actual reserves of the system. The additional \$ 25,000,000 of deposits brings total deposits to \$ 125,000,000. With a required reserve ratio of 20%, the required reserves of the system are (\$ 125,000,000) x (20%) = \$ 25,000,000. This is exactly the amount of reserves which the banking system does in fact have, so our computation of the potential change in deposits must be correct.

If the Fed raises the required reserve ratio to 33 1/3%, then Required reserves for \$ 100,000,000 in deposits are \$ 33,333,333. Excess reserves = Actual reserves - Required reserves = \$ 25,000,000 - \$ 33,333,333 = - \$ 8,333,333. The banks must reduce their loans until their actual reserves (\$ 25,000,000) are sufficient to fulfill the new reserve requirement (33 1/3% of deposits). Using the same identity as above to compute the reduction in deposits required by the change in the reserve ratio:

$$- \$ 8,333,333 = r \times (\text{Deposit reduction})$$

$$\text{Deposit reduction} = (-\$ 8,333,333) \div (0.333)$$

$$= - \$ 25,000,000.$$

Again, currency held by the public is unaffected, hence the total change in the money supply is - \$ 25,000,000.

We can check this result by seeing that the new amount of demand deposits of \$ 100,000,000 - \$ 25,000,000 = \$ 75,000,000 is the maximum that can be supported by \$ 25,000,000 in reserves with a required reserve ratio of 33 1/3%:

$$\text{Reserves} = \text{required reserve ratio} \times \text{Deposits}$$

$$\$ 25,000,000 = (33\ 1/3\%) \times (\$ 75,000,000)$$

$$= \$ 25,000,000$$

• PROBLEM 12-34

> Suppose a bank acquires an additional \$ 1 of deposits and no required reserve ratio exists. By how much could this one dollar deposit theoretically expand the money supply?

<u>Solution</u>: To find the amount by which the money supply could expand with fractional reserve banking, when one additional dollar is lent, we would normally divide \$ 1 by the reserve ratio. But in this case, reserve ratio = 0%, and since we cannot divide any number by 0, we can not calculate the change in the money supply by this method. But if we think about what having no reserve ratio implies, the solution becomes apparent.

With a reserve ratio of 0, each additional \$ 1 deposited in one bank adds \$ 1 to its reserves and permits that bank to lend \$ 1 additional. If the additional \$ 1 loan is deposited in another bank, it too can expand its loans by \$ 1. And so on, ad infinitum. There is no constraint upon this process so that theoretically, the money supply could expand infinitely if no part of additional deposits is kept in reserve by any bank in the system.

• PROBLEM 12-35

What is meant by the term "monetary (or demand deposit) multiplier," and how is it calculated?

Solution: The monetary multiplier is the ratio of total demand deposits in the banking system to the total reserves of the system. It is also the multiple of an increase (decrease) in the system's reserves by which the amount of demand deposits in the system expands (contracts) as a result of the increase (decrease) in reserves.

The money multiplier, barring "leakages" of reserves into excess reserve holdings of banks or into the cash holdings of the public, is always the reciprocal of the required reserve ratio, r, i.e., $\frac{1}{r}$. If banks decide to hold excess reserves equal to a certain proportion, e, of their demand deposits, the effect on the money multiplier is the same as that of required reserves held by the bank, so that the money multiplier is $\frac{1}{r+e}$ $\left(< \frac{1}{r} \right)$ the reciprocal of the sum of the required reserve ratio and the excess reserve ratio. Both categories of reserves reduce in the same manner the lending capacity, and thereby the deposit creating capacity of the banking system, from what it would be if banks kept no reserves, but lent them all out.

• PROBLEM 12-36

If the required reserve ratio, "r," is 20%, and banks retain excess reserves equal to 10%, "e," of deposits, calculate the demand deposit multiplier and the total increase in the demand deposits of the banking system as a whole that would result from an initial deposit of $ 10,000.

Solution: The demand deposit multiplier is the reciprocal of the sum of the required reserve ratio and the excess reserve ratio. Thus, in this example, the demand deposit multiplier is equal to $\frac{1}{r+e} = \left(\frac{1}{.20 + .10}\right) = \frac{1}{.30} = 3\ 1/3$.

The demand deposit multiplier tells us the multiple of an addition to the reserves by which total demand deposits of the banking system can be expanded. The initial deposit of $ 10,000 added $ 10,000 to bank reserves. Hence total demand deposits of the banking system increase as a result of the initial deposit by 3 1/3 x $ 10,000 ≅ $ 33,333, including the initial $ 10,000 deposit.

Alternatively, we could calculate the total increase in

deposits of the banking system as the sum of the initial deposit and the amount of loan money created by the banking system. The latter can be calculated by first determining the amount of reserves lent out by the bank receiving the initial deposit and multiplying this amount by the demand deposit multiplier. The reserves lent out by the bank are equal to (\$ 10,000 - required reserves - retained excess reserves)=

$$(\$ 10{,}000 - [r \times \$ 10{,}000] - [e \times \$ 10{,}000]) = (\$ 10{,}000 - [(r + e) \times \$ 10{,}000]) = (\$ 10{,}000 - [(20\% + 10\%) \times \$ 10{,}000]) = (\$ 10{,}000 - [30\% \times \$ 10{,}000]) = \$ 10{,}000 (1 - 30\%) = 70\% \times \$ 10{,}000$$

= \$ 7,000. Multiplying this amount, which is lent out by the initial bank, and received as deposits and additions to the reserves by other banks in the system, by the demand deposit multiplier, 3 1/3, we have \$ 7,000 x 3 1/3 = \$ 23,333 as the amount of loan money created by the banking system. Adding to this the initial \$ 10,000 deposit, we again achieve the result that total demand deposits in the banking system increase by \$ 33,333.

• PROBLEM 12-37

Suppose \$ 100 is deposited into a bank. If the required reserve ratio is 100%, what is the demand deposit multiplier and what is the total addition to demand deposits of the banking system resulting from the initial deposit?

Solution: In the absence of "leakages" of reserves into excess reserves or the cash holdings of the public, the demand-deposit multiplier is equal to the reciprocal of the required reserve ratio. In this case, the required reserve ratio is 100%, or 1.0. The demand deposit multiplier, its reciprocal, is $\frac{1}{1.0} = 1$. That is, each increase in the banking system's reserves permits an increase in its deposit liabilities of 1 x the increase in its reserves. Thus, the \$ 100 deposit, which increases bank reserves by \$ 100, permits a total increase of deposits of 1 x \$ 100 = \$ 100. The initial deposit (\$ 100), then, constitutes the entire increase in demand deposits of the banking system that is possible with a 100% reserve requirement. No additional deposits over and above the initial deposit can be created by the banking system. With a 100% reserve requirement, and thus a "multiplier" of 1, no multiple deposit expansion is possible. The banks can lend out no part of their reserves. Thus, in contrast to a fractional reserve banking system, there can be no deposit expansion process, in which the reserves lent out by one bank can be deposited in another, thus adding to the second bank's deposits, and to its reserves, part of which addition it can lend out, etc.

• PROBLEM 12-38

Suppose a bank has \$ 250,000 in deposits and reserves of \$ 62,500. If the required reserve ratio, r, is 25%, what happens to the potential money supply if a depositor withdraws and keeps \$ 10,000 in currency, assuming all other banks in the system are "loaned up"?

Solution: With a required reserve ratio of 25%, the required reserves of the bank (r x Deposits) are (0.25) x (\$ 250,000) = \$ 62,500. This is also the amount of its actual reserves. Thus, this bank is fully "loaned up," i.e., it has no excess reserves. Actual reserves - Required reserves ≡ Excess reserves = 0.

When a depositor withdraws \$ 10,000 from the bank, its actual reserves are reduced by \$ 10,000, to \$ 52,500, and its deposit liabilities are also reduced by \$ 10,000, to \$ 240,000. The required reserves for \$ 240,000 in deposit liabilities are (r x Deposits) (0.25) x (\$240,000) = \$ 60,000. Excess reserves (= Actual Reserves - Required reserves) have gone from zero to (\$52,500 - \$ 60,000) = - \$ 7,500. Alternatively, we could compute the change in excess reserves as the difference between the change in actual reserves and the change in required reserves. The change in actual reserves is the same as the amount of the change in deposits, i.e., - \$ 10,000. The bank has \$ 10,000 less in vault cash as a result of the withdrawal. Required reserves, however, do not change by the full \$ 10,000. For, since the amount of reserves the bank is required to keep is only a certain fraction of its deposits (25% in our example), a change in its deposit liabilities via a deposit or withdrawal will change the amount of its required reserve by only that same fraction of the change in deposits. In our example, the change in required reserves ≡ (required reserve ratio) x (change in deposits) = (0.25) x (- \$ 10,000) = - \$ 2,500. Thus, the change in Excess reserves due to the \$ 10,000 withdrawal is equal to the change in Actual reserves less the change in Required reserves = (Change in Deposits) - (required reserve ratio) x (Change in Deposits) = (1 - r) (Change in Deposits) = (1 - 0.25) (- \$ 10,000) = (0.75) (- \$ 10,000) = - \$ 7,500. Since Actual reserves and required reserves were equal before the withdrawal, and thus excess reserves were 0 (zero), the amount of the change in excess reserves is equal to the amount of excess reserves in the new situation.

The bank's actual reserves are now below the amount required by \$ 7,500. In order to restore them to the required level, the bank must sell \$ 7,500 worth of securities or call in \$ 7,500 of its loans. If the bank's debtors withdraw this \$ 7,500 from their banks, in order to repay their loans, their banks, too, if they had been fully "loaned up" (no excess reserves), will be short of required reserves, by (1 - r) (Change in Deposits)=(1 - 0.25) (- \$ 7,500) = - \$ 5,625, and have to call in that amount of their loans to restore their reserves to the required level. If this process of withdrawals requiring contractions of bank loans necessitating further deposit withdrawals, etc., runs its full course, total demand deposits in the banking system will be reduced by the sum of the reductions at each successive stage. If we let ΔH_1 represent the initial change in deposits (- $ 10,000, in our example), then as we saw the second stage reduction caused by the initial change, $\Delta H_2 = (1-r)(\Delta H_1)$.

The third stage reduction, $\Delta H_3 = (1 - r)(\Delta H_2) = (1 - r)(1 - r)(\Delta H_1) = (1 - r)^2 (\Delta H_1)$; the fourth stage reduction, $\Delta H_4 = (1 - r)(\Delta H_3) = (1 - r)(1 - r)(1 - r)(\Delta H_1) = (1 - r)^3 (\Delta H_1)$; and so on. The sum of the changes in deposits at each stage is thus given by: $\Delta H_{total} =$

$$\Delta H_1 + (1 - r)\,\Delta H_1 + (1 - r)^2(\Delta H_1) + (1 - r)^3\,\Delta H_1 \; . \; . \; .$$

In our example, $\Delta H_{total} = -\$10,000 + (-\$7,500) + (-\$5625) + (-\$4219) \; . \; . \; . \; .$ The sum of this infinite mathematical series is given by the expression $\frac{\Delta H_o}{r}$.

Thus, the initial $10,000 withdrawal can result in a cumulative contraction of $-\frac{\$10,000}{0.25} = \$40,000$ in the amount of demand deposits in the economy if all banks are "loaned up" and all loans are repaid by withdrawals from demand deposits. The effect on the total money supply is the sum of this effect plus the effect on currency holdings of the public, which have risen by the $10,000 of the withdrawal. Thus the net effect of the $10,000 withdrawal on the money supply (demand deposits plus currency held by the public) is (-$40,000) + ($10,000) = - $30,000, i.e., a reduction of the money supply by $30,000.

• PROBLEM 12-39

Suppose that the public wishes to hold 15 percent of its total money balances as cash, the remainder in the form of bank deposits, and banks hold cash reserves equal to 12 percent of the deposits. What total amount of cash will be required, for use both by the banks and the public, for a total money supply of $ 200 billion?

Solution: The total money supply consists of bank deposits (checking account balances) and cash in the hands of the public. The total money supply, or total money balances held by the public is M = $ 200 billion; 15 percent of it is in the form of cash; the remainder, 85 percent in the form of checking accounts: M = 0.15 M + 0.85 M where M = $ 200 billion. Thus the cash balances of the public are 0.15 x 200 = $ 30 billion, and the total deposits of the public 0.85 x 200 = $ 170 billion. The banks hold cash reserves equal to 12 percent of the deposits. We have calculated the deposits to be \$ 170 billion thus the cash reserves of the banks are 0.12 x 170 = \$ 20.4 billion. The total amount of cash in the economy consists of the cash held by the public and the cash held by the banks on reserve against demands by depositors. The cash balances of the public are calculated to amount to \$ 30 billion and the cash reserves of the banks to \$ 20.4 billion. Thus the total amount of cash required in the economy is the sum \$ 30 billion) +\$ 20.4 billion = \$ 50.4 billion.

• PROBLEM 12-40

Suppose city banks have a reserve requirement of 20 percent, and country banks have a reserve requirement of 25 percent. What would happen to (a) total country bank deposits, (b) total city bank deposits, (c) the total deposits of the banking system, if a large group migrated from the country to the city and brought with them \$ 200 million dollars in deposits?

Solution: The migrants withdraw \$ 200 million from their deposit accounts in the country banks, and reduce the cash reserves of these banks by \$ 200 million. This would reduce the total country bank deposits by

$$\frac{\$200 \text{ million in reserves}}{0.25 \text{ required reserve-deposit ratio}} = \$800 \text{ million}$$

in demand deposits. There occurs a multiplied effect of deposit reduction in consequence of the reduction of the cash reserves. The migrants deposit their money in the city banks where the legal reserve requirement is 20%. When the money is deposited, the city banks' reserves are increased by \$ 200 million. Not all of it has to be kept in the vaults; part of it can be used for creating loans. The total amount of new loans that can be created by city banks as a whole is equal to the amount of their new deposits, which are also additions to their reserves, divided by the required reserve-deposit ratio, i.e.,

$$\frac{\$ 200 \text{ billion in new reserves}}{0.20 \text{ required reserve-deposit ratio}} =$$

\$ 1,000 million in new loans, which take the form of demand deposit balances. So the demand deposits may be increased by \$ 1,000 million. Thus, the total banking system experiences an increase of \$ 1000 million - \$ 800 million = \$ 200 million in deposits because of this initial transfer of demand deposits from country banks with higher required reserve-deposit ratios to city banks with lower required reserve ratios.

• PROBLEM 12-41

In the extreme case, \$ 1,000 of new reserves put into a bank will ultimately result in an increase of \$ 5,000 of bank deposits, assuming that the reserve ratio is 20%. But in reality this is rarely the case. What stops the extreme case from being realized?

Solution: First, it is likely that somewhere along the chain of deposit expansion, some individual who receives a check will withdraw the proceeds into cash holdings outside the banking system. If \$ 200 of the original \$ 1000 were immediately withdrawn, new demand deposits created would be

$\$ 4,000\ [\$ 1,000 - \$ 200 = \$ 800;\ \$ 800 \times (1.0 + 0.8 + [0.8]^2 + [0.8]^3 \ldots) = \$ 800 \times \frac{1}{0.2} = \$ 800 \times 5]$ instead of \$ 5,000.

It is also possible that a bank might not strictly adhere to the reserve ratio, keeping instead an excess over the legally required amount. If the banks in this system hold 25% instead of 20%, \$ 1,000 of new reserves would result in

$\$ 1,000 \times (1 + .75 + (.75)^2 + \ldots) = \$ 1,000 \times \frac{1}{.25} = \$ 1,000 \times 4 = \$ 4,000$ of bank deposits, instead of \$ 5,000. Such withdrawals of reserves from the banking system, or "leakages," reduce the multiple deposit creating capacity of the banking system below the limit theoretically possible if all reserves remain in the banking system, and used to the maximum extent allowed by law to make loans.

• PROBLEM 12-42

Suppose all banks in the banking system were merely branches of one monopoly bank. How would the process of multiple-deposit creation (or destruction) differ from the process that takes place in a banking system composed of independent banks?

Solution: In order to compare the processes in their simplest form, let us assume that there are no "leakages" of bank reserves into the public's currency holdings or into banks' excess reserves in either case.

In the case of a banking system in which there are a number of independent banks, an increase (or decrease) in the reserves of an individual bank resulting from a deposit (or withdrawal) does not enable (or require) it to expand (or contract) its deposits by the full amount by which the banking system as a whole is able (or required) to expand (or contract) total deposits, i.e., by the change in reserves divided by the required reserve ratio. That is, if ΔR_1 represents the change in reserves resulting from a deposit (or withdrawal) of an individual bank, all other banks' reserves remaining initially the same, and the required reserve ratio, r, is 20%, the banking system as a whole can potentially expand total demand deposits in all banks taken together by $\frac{\Delta R_1}{r} = \frac{\Delta R_1}{0.20} = 5\Delta R_1$. The individual bank whose reserves increase, however, cannot expand its own deposits by $5\Delta R_1$ by lending an additional amount $4\Delta R_1$. For, since loans are not generally left in the lending bank but withdrawn to spend, the bank must be prepared to lose a quantity of its reserves equal to the amount of the loan. In our example, the bank which had experienced an increase of reserves by ΔR_1, would, by making an additional $4\ \Delta R_1$ of loans be adding $4\ \Delta R_1$ to its deposit liabilities and hence be subject to the loss of $4\ \Delta R_1$ of reserves when the loan is withdrawn from the bank (reducing deposit liabilities again by $4\ \Delta R_1$). Reserves initially increase by ΔR_1, then would decrease by the $4\Delta R_1$ of the loan, for a net decrease of $3\Delta R_1$. Deposit liabilities increase by ΔR_1 with the initial deposit, increase again by $4\Delta R$ when the loan is made, and decrease by $4\Delta R_1$ when the loan is withdrawn for a net increase of ΔR_1. If the bank was initially "loaned up" (i.e., its reserves were just equal to r x Deposits), then the bank's reduced reserves are insufficient to fulfill the reserve requirements for its increased deposit liabilities. Thus an individual independent bank cannot lend a multiple of an increase in its reserves, since such an amount of loans withdrawn from the bank would leave it with a shortage of required reserves. Loans granted would be withdrawn to pay for whatever the recipient of the loan bought and wind up in the accounts at other banks of the paymant recipients. The additional deposits at other banks add to their reserves, and enable them to lend a fraction (1 - required reserve ratio) of the increase. These loans are withdrawn and soon deposited, assuming no leakages, in other banks, which can now expand their loans. This multi-stage deposit and loan expansion process continues until deposits in banks as a whole have increased by (the increase in reserves) ÷ (required reserve ratio).

In the case of a monopoly bank, however, the bank need not be concerned that loans it makes will deplete its reserves. For, assuming no leakages, loans made by the bank will be redeposited in other accounts at the same bank by recipients of the loanee's payments, since it is the only bank in the system. The monopoly bank is the "banking system as a whole," and can (or must) thus expand (or contract) its loans immediately by $[(1 - r) \div r] \times [\Delta R_1] = [(1 - .20) \div .20] \times [\Delta R_1] = [(.80) \div (.20)] \times [R_1] = 4\ \Delta R_1$ and hence its total deposits by $\Delta R_1 / r = \Delta R_1 / 0.20 = 5\ \Delta R_1$ without going through the multi-stage process by which a non-monopoly banking system expands deposits.

• PROBLEM 12-43

Describe the role of a financial intermediary. Give an example.

Solution: A financial intermediary acts as an agent in negotiating loan contracts between the ultimate demanders (households) and the ultimate suppliers (investors). It intermediates between the suppliers of short term funds (the households) and the demanders of long term funds. A Savings and Loan Association is an example of a non-bank financial intermediary.

Suppose a potential borrower, say, a construction company, wants a loan of $100,000 from a Savings and Loan association (S&L); and the S&L is convinced that it will be a profitable transaction. The S&L must attract the money in order to grant the borrower a loan.

If households find the interest rate the S&L pays on its savings accounts worthwhile, they deposit their savings totaling $100,000 in the accounts of the S&L. The S&L credits the households' savings accounts by $100,000 and at the same time adds the $100,000 to an asset category called Cash.

Assets	S&L	Liabilities
Cash + $100,000	Savings Accounts +	$100,000

In the second step the S&L grants the $100,000 loan and gives the borrower $100,000 in cash:

Assets	S&L	Liabilities
Cash - $100,000		
Loans + $100,000		

When all these steps have taken place, the S&L has a $100,000 loan asset that precisely matches its liability total of $100,000 consisting of the savings accounts of the households.

Assets		S&L	Liabilities
Loan Contracts	$100,000	Savings Accounts	$100,000

The construction company pays the S&L a certain interest for the use of the funds; the S&L, after subtracting the remuneration for its services of intermediation, passes these interest payments to the households who were willing to deposit their savings in the savings accounts of the S&L. Because the interest the borrower pays to the S&L is higher than the interest paid by the S&L to the households, the S&L can be a profitable operation.

• PROBLEM 12-44

What is the economic effect of the increase in the number of financial intermediaries?

Solution: The expansion of financial intermediaries affects:

1. the velocity of money

2. the supply of credit, and

3. the stability of the savings.

The money velocity is the ratio of income received to the money supply held; it represents the number of times money circulates. An increase in the number of financial intermediaries, in particular mutual savings banks and loan associations, increases the savings deposits, and there is less need to hold money relative to income. Thus the ratio

$\frac{\text{income}}{\text{money}} = \frac{Y}{M} = V$, the velocity of money increases. This loosens the effect of the FED's control over the economic output, because spending $Y = P \times Q$ depends both on the velocity V and the quantity of money M : $Y = P \times Q = M \times V$. The Fed controls M, but V is largely autonomous; so when V fluctuates erratically, the direct link between the money supply M and total spending Y is broken. Also wide variations in the annual growth of total credit provided by the financial intermediaries causes wide variations in consumer and investment spending, thereby destabilizing the level of economic activity. When the amount of credit provided is not only influenced by the interest rates, but also by the amount of financial intermediation provided, this is again a cause of concern for the FED which loosens its control over total spending in the economy. And the sometimes lack of stability of the thrift institutions is a third reason for concern for the FED. Accelerated inflation is the fundamental cause for this lack of stability. The assets of financial intermediaries are long-term, while their deposits are very short-term. A sharp increase in the interest rates caused by accelerated inflation causes troubles, because the rates earned on the long-term assets cannot be changed so quickly. The income on the long-term assets, for example mortgages, is fixed. Therefore the intermediaries are unable to raise the rates they pay on their deposits, and they can't compete with the other, higher paying, forms of saving. So they risk customers withdrawing their deposits to place them in the more conventional savings institution. This would cause a liquidity crisis for the financial intermediaries.

• PROBLEM 12-45

What is meant by a bank loan that is called a 7 percent discount?

Solution: Some loans are called discounts due to the way interest is charged. On a regular 7%, one year loan, the borrower receives \$ 100 today and pays back \$ 107 in a year. On a 7 percent discount, the borrower would receive \$ 93 today and pay back \$ 100 in a year. It can be seen that in the latter case, the borrower is paying an interest rate that is slightly higher than the stated discount rate of 7%. In fact the rate = 7/93 = 7.52688%.

• PROBLEM 12-46

What might happen to the housing construction industry if commercial banks are allowed to compete freely with mutual savings banks?

Solution: If free competition were allowed, commercial banks would raise the interest rates offered to savers in an attempt to lure customers away from the mutual savings banks. As savers moved their money to commercial banks, deposits in mutual savings banks would drop. Consequently the amount of money available for mortgages would drop. With less mortgage money available, fewer houses could be bought, and the housing industry would slump.

• PROBLEM 12-47

A building company plans to construct a series of houses with a total value of \$ 2,000,000. A commercial bank is interested in this housing project and is willing to provide the funds. How does this transaction take place?

Solution: The building company needs to borrow the money for this investment project because it must pay the current wages and costs of materials used in the building process, while it only starts to receive money when the project is finished in the future and it sells or rents the houses built. It is willing to pay a certain interest on the money borrowed (= the principal) from the commercial bank, and promises to repay the principal in the future when the project is finished. This promise has the form of a loan contract provided by the building company and accepted by the bank. From the viewpoint of the bank, the bank buys this loan contract and gives immediately the money to the building company in the form of a new checking account with the commercial bank whose value is equal to the purchase price of the loan contract. A loan contract is an asset of the commercial bank, and the checking account a liability. In other words, increase in the real value of the checking accounts held by the public at commercial banks

$$D_L^B = \Delta \left(\frac{M}{P}\right)$$

where M - the nominal value of the checking accounts (= money) and P - the general price level. The commercial bank is interested in buying the loan contract because the building company pays interest on the money borrowed. In general a higher interest rate will induce the commercial banking system to expand the quantity of new loans supplied. It does so, because the purchases of the loan contracts are accompanied by the creation of new money in the form of checking accounts with the commercial banking system.

Thus this loan operation is presented as

Commercial Bank

Assets	Liabilities
Loan Contract + \$ 2,000,000	Checking Account + \$ 2,000,000

This process shows us that if D_L^B represents the real value of the demand for loan contracts by the commercial banking system (the real value is expressed in terms of the prices of goods and services that prevailed in the base period), this D_L^B is directly connected with the opportunity cost borne by the commercial banks whenever it holds reserves in excess of the amount of reserves required by the Fed.

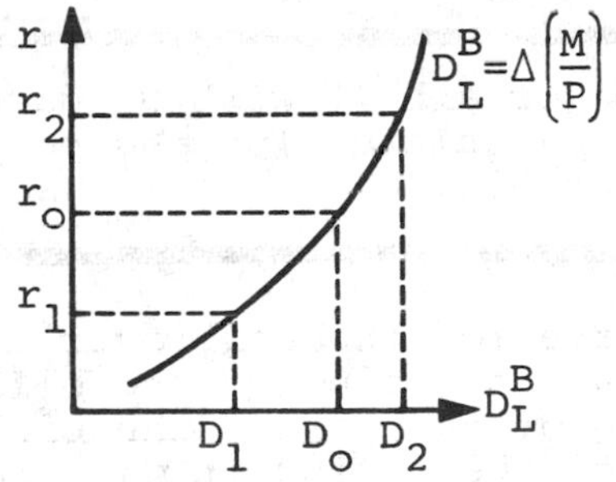

The opportunity costs of excess reserves is the interest income that banks could have earned had they instead decided to purchase loan contracts to the full extent permitted by their reserves. Thus the commercial banking system's demand for loan contracts is positively sloped with respect to the interest rate. (See the accompanying figure.)

• PROBLEM 12-48

What is the rate of interest you pay when you agree with your bank to 1) borrow a loan of \$ 5,000 at 10% interest, and 2) conclude a life-insurance with a premium of \$ 30? This enables you to buy a new car; the loan has to be repaid in monthly installments over 24 months.

Solution: This is an example of a consumer loan to buy a consumer durable, the new car. The loan amounts in total to the sum of the actual amount borrowed and of the life-insurance you have to conclude with your bank:

$$P = 5{,}000 + 30 = \$\ 5{,}030$$

You pay an interest of A = 0.10 x 5,030 = \$ 503 over 24 months. The relevant interest rate is the interest rate on the unpaid balance

$$r = \frac{m}{n+1} \times \frac{A}{P/2} \qquad (1)$$

where P/2 is the average amount borrowed, so that $\frac{A}{P/2}$ is the interest you agreed upon for the loan, i.e., 10%; m is the number of payments to the bank per year, while n is the number of payments needed to discharge the debt (n + 1 includes the final repayment of the principal). Reordering formula (1) gives

$$r = \frac{m}{n + 1} \times \frac{2A}{P}$$

Substituting in the data, m = 12, n = 24, A = 503 and P = 5,030 gives the actual interest rate that you as borrower pay:

$$r = \frac{12}{25} \times \frac{1006}{5030}$$

$$= 9.6\%$$

• PROBLEM 12-49

What is the bill rate for a bill with 91 days to maturity and a price of $ 97,987? Calculate also the coupon-issue yield equivalent for the same bill.

Solution: The bill rate for the bill over a 91 day period is the relative increase in value of the bill over the period. At the beginning of the period the bill is worth $ 97,987; at the end of the period it will be worth its face value of $ 100,000. So the relative increase in value is $\frac{100 - 97.987}{100} = 0.02013$. The 'year' for bill rates has 360 days. There are $\frac{360}{91} = 3.956$ periods of 91 days in this 'year.' So the bill rate on an annual basis is

$$r = 0.02013 \times 3.956$$

$$= 0.0796 = 7.96\%$$

The coupon issue yield does not use the face value as basis, but the price paid; and secondly the 'year' for the coupon issue yield has 365 days.

Thus the coupon issue yield is calculated as:

$$i = \frac{100 - 97.987}{97.987} \times \frac{365}{91}$$

$$= 0.0205435 \times 4.010989$$

$$= 0.0824 = 8.24\%$$

• PROBLEM 12-50

A security has a maturity value of $ 100,000; its coupon rate is 4% and its yield is required to be 8%. What would a buyer pay for this security if the security is due 5 years from now?

Solution: We will calculate the bid price, or present value, of this security. The bid price P consists of the sum of the present values of the annual interest payments A and the present value of the maturity value M.

$$P = \frac{A}{1 + r} + \frac{A}{(1 + r)^2} + \frac{A}{(1 + r)^3} + \frac{A}{(1 + r)^4} + \frac{A}{(1 + r)^5} + \frac{M}{(1 + r)^5}$$

The annual interest payment

$$A = \text{maturity value} \times \text{coupon rate}$$

$$= 100{,}000 \times 0.04$$

$$= 4{,}000$$

The yield $r = 0.08$, so that the bid price P =

$$\frac{4000}{1.08} + \frac{4000}{(1.08)^2} + \frac{4000}{(1.08)^3} + \frac{4000}{(1.08)^4} + \frac{4000}{(1.08)^5}$$

$$+ \frac{100{,}000}{(1.08)^5} = \qquad (1)$$

$$= 3{,}703.70 + 3{,}429.35 + 3{,}175.32$$

$$+ 2{,}940.12 + 2{,}722.33 + 68{,}058.00$$

$$= \$\ 84{,}028.82$$

(note: it is more convenient to use actuarial tables to calculate present values, but the explicit calculation is shown here for purposes of exposition). From formula (1) it is clear that:

1. the higher the coupon rate--the higher the bid price.

2. the higher the yield--the lower the bid price.

This last relationship is important from an economic point of view. With high yields, smaller investments are needed to achieve a given flow of income in the form of interest payments than with low yields.

• PROBLEM 12-51

When a security has a maturity value of $ 100,000 and the coupon rate is 5%, what are you willing to pay for it when it is due next year and the yield is 9%?

Solution: We calculate the bid price P, or present value of the interest payment A over the year and the maturity value M.

$$P = \frac{A}{(1 + r)} + \frac{M}{(1 + r)}; \text{ combining gives}$$

$$P = \frac{A + M}{(1 + r)}$$

Substituting the given values gives the bid price

$$P = \frac{(0.05 \times 100{,}000) + 100{,}000}{1 + 0.09}$$

$$= \frac{105{,}000}{1.09} = \$\ 96{,}330.28$$

When you invest \$ 96,330.28 now and you receive 5% interest over the year plus the principal sum of \$ 100,000 at the end of the year you make a yield of 9% on your investment:

investment + return

= interest + principal

$$96{,}330.28 + 0.09 \times 96{,}330.28$$

$$= (0.05 \times 100{,}000) + 100{,}000$$

$$\text{Or } (1.09) \times 96{,}330.28 = 105{,}000$$

When you invest more at present the yield will be lower than 9% because the maturity value + interest payment = \$ 105,000 does not change.

• PROBLEM 12-52

How can you explain the interest-term-structure, i.e., the relationship between short-term and long-term interest rates?

<u>Solution</u>: There are two principal theories explaining the interest-term-structure:

1. the expectations theory, and
2. the theory of market segmentation.

The expectations theory states that long-term interest rates are an average of consecutive expected short-term interest rates over the long period.

Thus

$$(1 + R_n)^n = (1 + r_1)(1 + r_2)(1 + r_3) \ldots (1 + r_n)$$

where R_n is the interest rate on a long-term security; n, the number of years to maturity of the long-term security; and $r_1, r_2, r_3, \ldots r_n$, the expected interest rates on one-year securities from the first to the final year of the long period security, i.e., r_1, is the interest rate expected to prevail in the first year, r_2 in the second year, etc., until r_n which is expected to prevail in the final year.

When we take the nth-root of both sides of the equation

$$1 + R_n = \sqrt[n]{(1 + r_1)\ (1 + r_2)\ .\ .\ .\ (1 + r_n)}$$

we see that one plus the long-term interest rate on the n-year security is equal to the geometric average of one plus the individual single-period interest rates. From this formula we note that if long-term rates are lower than present short-term rates, the short term rates are expected to fall somewhere in the next few years. This situation is typical of periods of prosperity. When investment is high, borrowing becomes difficult, and thus interest rates are high: it is expected that they will fall later. The situation that long-term rates are higher than present short-term rates is typical for a recession. Also one may expect on the basis of this relationship that short-term interest rates fluctuate more widely than long-term rates, because any change in a short-term rate, as one of the elements of the geometric average, has only a small effect on the average, i.e., the long-term interest rate.

The theory of market segmentation states that differences in interest rates are due to the imperfections in the information flows between segmented markets: in the segmented markets different conditions of supply and demand for securities with different maturities prevail.

• PROBLEM 12-53

Explain why yield curves may slope downward in periods of prosperity and high interest rates; and why they may slope upward in periods of recession.

Fig. 1

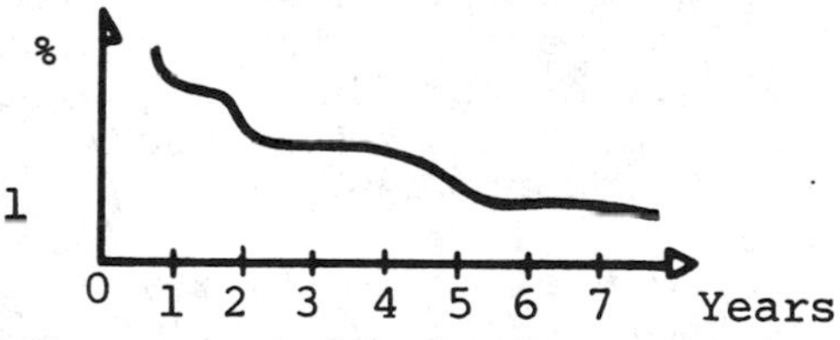

Yield Curve in Period of Prosperity

Fig. 2

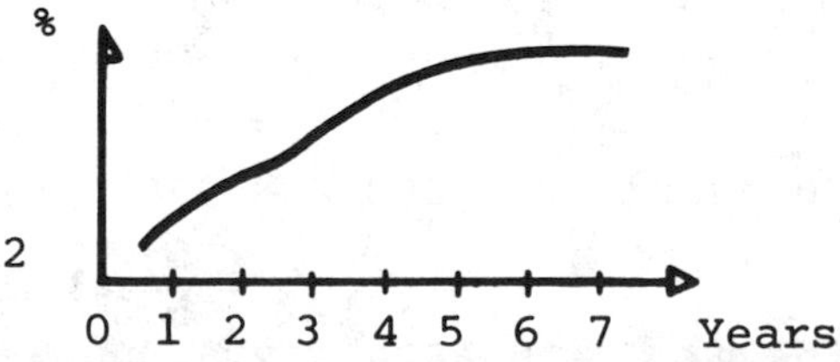

Yield Curve in Period of Recession

Solution: A yield curve is a schedule of the interest yields of bonds with differences in maturity (see accompanying graphs).

The downward-sloping yield curve of figure 1 is typical of periods of prosperity when interest rates are high. The relatively high interest rates lead to expectations that they will fall later. Borrowers, for whom the interest rate is a cost rate on the funds borrowed, will tend to borrow for short terms, so that later on, after repayment of the principal, they can borrow on more profitable terms. The increased demand for short term securities drives the short term yield rates up. Lenders on the other hand, will try to lend their funds for long terms. The increased supply of long term funds tends to decrease the long-term rates.

In a period of recession, the reverse holds true. In a recession the interest rates are generally low and the usual expectation is that in the future interest rates will rise. Borrowers will tend to borrow on the prevailing easy terms for the long term. The increased demand for long-term securities drives their rates upward. In this situation the lenders are only willing to lend their funds for the short term, expecting better yield rates in the future. The increased supply of short-term funds presses their rates down.

So yield curves, obtained by charting the closing yields on a certain date, indicate the prevailing expectations in the financial markets.

• PROBLEM 12-54

Suppose you are considering buying some United States Treasury Bonds, say a \$ 1,000,000, 6 year bond, which has a coupon rate of 3.5%, and is offered after half a year for \$775,000; your opportunity cost of capital is 7%. Would you invest in such a bond?

Solution: To answer this question we have to calculate the yield on the bond and compare it with the opportunity cost of capital; if the yield is higher than the opportunity cost of capital, we invest in the bond, otherwise we invest in the alternative investment opportunity.

The "yield" is the yield to maturity on the bond if purchased at the price shown and held until it matures. On a bond we earn the interest payments per year: A = 1,000,000 x 3.5% = \$35,000, plus a capital gain per year. The total capital gain equals the difference between the face value and the asked price:

$$1,000,000 - 775,000 = \$\ 225,000.$$

The capital gain per year is $\frac{1}{6 - 1/2} = \frac{1}{5.5} = 18.18\%$ of the total capital gain, or C = 0.1818 x 225,000 = \$ 40,909 per year. Thus the total return each year on the investment in this bond is the sum of the interest payment received each year and the capital gain per year.

A + C = 35,000 + 40,909 = \$ 75,909. What does the investment amount to? The average investment over the 5 1/2 year period is the average of the asked price P and the maturity value M,

$$\frac{P + M}{2} = \frac{775,000 + 1,000,000}{2} = \$\ 887,500$$

The yield is the return on investment per year

$$i = \frac{75,909}{887,500} = 8.55\%,$$

which is higher than the cost of capital of 7%. Conclusion: you should invest in this bond.

In abstracto, the estimate of the yield we used is $i = \frac{A + C}{(P + M)/2}$.

• PROBLEM 12-55

Suppose you buy a 91-day \$ 500,000 Treasury bill at the price of \$ 485,000 and you hold the bill until it matures. What is the interest rate you earn?

Solution: The formula for the bill rate is $r = \frac{F - P}{F} \cdot \frac{360}{d}$ so we calculate the difference between the face value F = 500 and the price paid for the bill P = 485 and divide it by the face value F, $(\frac{F - P}{F} = \frac{15}{500} = 0.03)$, to get the interest return over the 91 day period. On year basis, this has to be multiplied by the number of periods involved,

$$\frac{360}{d} = \frac{360}{91} = 3.956$$

Thus the bill discount rate

$$r = 0.03 \times 3.956 = 0.11868;$$

$$\text{or } 11.8\%$$

The year is conventionally taken to be consisting of 360 days.

SHORT ANSWER QUESTIONS FOR REVIEW

Answer
To be covered when testing yourself

Choose the correct answer.

1. A bank's assets include its (a) loans and deposits (b) net worth and reserves (c) reserves and loans (d) deposits only — c

2. A bank's deposits are (a) liabilities (b) assets (c) net worth (d) reserves — a

3. Which of the following is not true of a bank's required reserves: (a) they are equal to its deposits multiplied by the required reserve ratio (b) they consist of vault cash plus balances on account with the Federal reserve (c) they are equal to actual reserves minus required reserves (d) they are kept to protect the solvency of the bank — d

4. When a check written on Bank A for $100 is collected, Bank A's loss of reserves is (a) a fraction of $100 (b) $100 (c) a multiple of $100 (d) zero — b

5. A bank's excess reserves are (a) deposits minus required reserves (b) actual reserves minus loans (c) actual reserves minus required reserves (d) deposits minus loans — c

6. If a bank has deposits of $10,000, loans of $6000 and the required reserve ratio is 15%, the bank's excess reserves are (a) $1500 (b) $900 (c) $2500 (d) $600 — c

7. If a bank has actual reserves of $3000, excess reserves of $2000, and the required reserve ratio is 25%, its deposits must be (a) $8000 (b) $4000 (c) $12,000 (d) $20,000 — b

8. If the required reserve ratio is 20%, a bank which has $150,000 in deposits and $50,000 in actual reserves can lend an additional (a) $50,000 (b) $100,000 (c) $10,000 (d) $20,000 — d

9. If the required reserve ratio decreases, the lending capacity of banks (a) increases (b) decreases (c) remains unchanged (d) first decreases then increases — a

10. If a bank's actual reserves fall below its required reserves, it must (a) increase its loans to earn more interest (b) buy government bonds (c) sell bonds or call in loans

SHORT ANSWER QUESTIONS FOR REVIEW

Answer

To be covered when testing yourself

(d) use its excess reserves to make up the difference — c

11. If the banking system has $650,000,000 in deposits, $175,000,000 in actual reserves, and the required reserve ratio is 20%, by how much can the money supply be expanded? (a) $225,000,000 (b) $175,000,000 (c) $130,000,000 (d) $45,000,000 — a

12. Suppose a bank has excess reserves of $1000. How is the money supply affected if one depositor withdraws $200 from his account and a borrower repays a $500 loan? (a) It increases by $300 (b) It decreases by $500 (c) It decreases by $200 (d) It increases by $700 — b

13. If the required reserve ratio is 10%, a bank with $800,000 in deposits and $75,000 in excess reserves has actual reserves of (a) $7500 (b) $80,000 (c) $5000 (d) $155,000 — d

14. If the banking system has $5000 in excess reserves and the required reserve ratio is 25%, what effect on the money supply does a withdrawal of $15,000 in currency have? (a) Increases it by $10,000. (b) Decreases it by $40,000. (c) Decreases it by $60,000. (d) Increases it by $15,000. — b

15. The money multiplier is equal to (a) 1 ÷ the required reserve ratio (b) 1 ÷ the marginal propensity to spend (c) 1 - the required reserve ratio (d) 1 ÷ the marginal propensity to save — a

16. When a bank makes a loan (a) its assets decrease, its liabilities remain unchanged and its net worth decreases (b) its assets increase, its liabilities increase, and its net worth decreases (c) its assets remain unchanged, its liabilities decrease, and its net worth increases, (d) its assets increase, its liabilities increase, and its net worth remains unchanged — d

<u>Fill in the blanks.</u>

17. The banking practice of keeping only part of the bank's demand deposits in the forms of vault cash and balances on account with the Federal Reserve and lending the remaining part is called ______________. — fractional reserve banking

SHORT ANSWER QUESTIONS FOR REVIEW

	Question	Answer (To be covered when testing yourself)
18.	The fraction of deposits which the Federal Reserve requires that commercial banks keep in vault cash or balances at the Fed is called ____________.	the required reserve ratio
19.	The difference between a bank's actual reserves and its required reserves is its ____________.	excess reserves
20.	The ____________ is the American central bank, which controls the quantity of reserves in the commercial banking system.	Federal Reserve Bank
21.	A bank's balance sheet shows the bank's ______, ____________ and ____________.	assets, liabilities, net worth
22.	In balance sheet terms, a bank's deposits are ____________.	liabilities
23.	____________ are the only financial institutions with the ability to create money.	commercial banks
24.	The ____________ is the governmental agency responsible for safe-guarding all bank deposits.	Federal Deposit Insurance Corporation
25.	The reciprocal of the required reserve ratio gives the ____________ or ____________.	monetary, demand deposit multiplier
26.	If we multiply a bank's deposits by the required reserve ratio, we get the ____________ of that bank.	required reserves
27.	At any given time, a bank can make new loans of the same amount as its ____________.	excess reserves
28.	The principle assets of banks are their ______.	loans
29.	The largest component of the money supply is ____________.	demand deposits
30.	Commercial banks expand the money supply by increasing their ____________.	loans
31.	When a bank loan is made, the bank's ____________ are increased.	demand deposits
32.	When a check written by one of Bank A's depositors is collected by the payee's bank, Bank A's ____________ and ____________ are reduced.	reserves, deposits

SHORT ANSWER QUESTIONS FOR REVIEW

Answer
To be covered when testing yourself

Determine whether the following statements are true or false.

Statement	Answer
33. One of the assets of a commercial bank is its demand deposits.	False
34. The Federal Reserve requires commercial banks to maintain its reserve requirement to ensure that they can withstand sudden massive withdrawals by depositors.	False
35. The reserve requirement imposed on commercial banks by the Federal Reserve limits their lending capacity.	True
36. A commercial bank may lend out all of its excess reserves.	True
37. Commercial banks have the power to print money.	False
38. Commercial bank loans are made by crediting the deposit accounts of borrowers with additional balances.	True
39. New loans made by commercial banks increase the money supply.	True
40. With a required reserve ratio of 20%, a commercial bank can lend out an amount equal to 5 times its reserves.	False
41. Commercial banks and the Federal Reserve are not the only money-creating institutions in the economy.	False
42. The banking system as a whole can create a quantity of money equal to several times its reserves.	True
43. It is fractional reserve banking that enables commercial banks to create money.	True
44. Excess reserves are reserves of currency in excess of those needed to cover withdrawals by depositors.	False
45. The amount of reserves a commercial bank is required to keep depends on the volume of its loans.	False
46. A deposit of currency into a commercial bank may result in an increase in the money supply since the bank can expand its loans.	True

SHORT ANSWER QUESTIONS FOR REVIEW

Answer
To be covered when testing yourself

47. The reason that the process of multiple deposit creation can take place in the banking system as a whole is that reserves lost by any individual bank are acquired by others. — True

CHAPTER 13

FEDERAL RESERVE BANKS AND MONETARY POLICY

Basic Attacks and Strategies for Solving Problems in this Chapter. See pages 456 to 477 for step-by-step solutions to problems.

The Federal Reserve System (Fed) is a unique institution. Its main purpose is to oversee the operation of the banking system. It was chartered by an act of Congress so it can be considered an agency of the government, but it is nominally owned by the banks that choose to be members of it. The top officials of the Fed (the Board of Governors) are appointed by the President and confirmed by the Senate, but their terms are for 14 years, which gives them and the institution considerable independence from the politicians. In addition, the Fed is so profitable that it gives money back to the Treasury each year, although Congress exercises oversight on its expenditures, including salaries of officials and other employees. The Fed can set some rules and regulations that must be adhered to by both member and non-member institutions. In short, the Fed can be considered an independent agency of the government charged with promoting the public interest.

The System consists of 12 banks located around the country, each with special responsibilities to oversee banking in its region. There are many smaller banks in each region also. The Fed is directed by a seven-member Board of Governors from Washington D.C. The most influential member of the board is the Chairperson, who is appointed by the President and confirmed by the Senate for a four-year term. Reappointment is possible.

The major functions of the Fed include 1) the issuance of legal tender currency, 2) setting the legal reserve requirement, 3) acting as the banker's bank by maintaining accounts for individual bank reserves and clearing checks between banks, 4) acting as the "lender of last resort," providing emergency loans to banks with inadequate reserves, 5) performing banking services for the Federal Government, 6) acting as one of several regulators of the banks, and 7) conducting monetary policy.

Monetary policy refers to using changes in the nation's money supply to influence credit conditions, total spending, and the rates of inflation, unemployment, and economic growth. The Fed is able to change the nation's money supply by using tools which allow it to influence the amount of excess reserves in the banking system. By increasing excess reserves, the Fed makes banks more willing and able to lend. As banks reduce interest rates and ease up on credit requirements, more money will be borrowed which will be used to finance additional consumption and investment spending. Through the multiplier process this additional spending will cause an increase in national income. By decreasing excess reserves, the Fed will make banks less willing and able to lend. Banks will raise interest rates and credit requirements, leading to a reduction in borrowing and credit-sensitive spending.

The three major tools which the Fed can use are 1) changes in the reserve requirement, 2) open market operations, and 3) changes in the discount rate. By changing the reserve requirement, the Fed can make the existing level of reserves support more or less deposits. It is a powerful, but blunt tool, and is not used that often.

Open market operations refers to the Fed buying or selling U.S. government bonds in the open market. Decisions about open market operations are made by the Federal Open Market Committee (FOMC), a 12-person group composed of the seven members of the Board of Governors and five Federal Reserve System bank presidents who serve on an alternating basis. If the Fed buys bonds in the open market, this has the effect of adding reserves to the banking system. Banks can then extend credit, leading to an increase in spending. If the Fed sells bonds, this has the effect of decreasing reserves in the banking system. This will lead to "tighter" credit and less spending.

The discount rate is a special interest rate. It is the rate the Fed charges to member banks that borrow from it to restore their reserve position. The higher the discount rate, the more "painful" borrowing becomes and thus banks will follow more cautious lending policies. This will make credit conditions "tighter" and reduce borrowing and spending. The lower the rate, the less cautious banks will have to be.

There are other tools that the Fed can use which have a more selective impact.

An important problem in the implementation of monetary policy is time lags. The inside lag is the period of time elapsing between when a policy action becomes necessary and when it takes place. It is made up of three shorter lags: the recognition lag, the length of time between when a problem takes place and it is recognized; the decision lag, how long it takes to decide what to do; and the action lag, how long it takes to implement the decision. The outside lag is the length of time between taking action and its effect on the economy. The existence of lags means that good policy-making requires the ability to forecast accurately, something economists do not do very well. Our inability to forecast weakens the case for discretionary policy and strengthens the case for the use of rules.

The issue of time lags is also relevant to a comparison between fiscal and monetary policy. A widespread opinion is that monetary policy has a shorter inside lag, but longer outside lag than fiscal policy.

Step-by-Step Solutions to Problems in this Chapter, "Federal Reserve Banks and Monetary Policy"

EXPLANATION

• **PROBLEM 13-1**

What is the main objective of modern central banking? Explain.

Solution: The main objective of modern central banking is the formulation of policies that affect the factors in the bank reserve equation, and thus influence the monetary base. The bank reserve equation reads:

Factors supplying reserve funds, F_1 - Factors absorbing reserve funds, F_2 at the Federal Reserve banks = Member bank reserves with Federal Reserve banks, R. Thus written in concise form:

$$F_1 - F_2 = R \qquad (1)$$

F_1 is the sum of Federal Reserve credit (= U.S. government securities + loans and acceptances + float + other Federal Reserve assets), the gold stock, special drawing rights certificate account and Treasury currency outstanding.

F_2 is the sum of currency in circulation C, and the sum C' of 5 other elements: Treasury cash holdings; Treasury, Foreign and other deposits in Federal Reserve banks; and other Federal Reserve liabilities and capital accounts. Thus,

$$F_2 = C + C' \qquad (2)$$

Combining equations (1) and (2) results in $F_1 - (C + C') = R$. Adding C to both sides

$$F_1 - C' = R + C = H.$$

The monetary base ,H, is the sum of the member bank reserves with the Federal Reserve banks R and the currency in circulation C. To give some meaning to these symbols we supply the values of them on December 31, 1973:

$$F_1 = \$106,755 \text{ million}$$

$$F_2 = \$79,695 \text{ million}$$

and the $R = F_1 - F_2 = \$27,060$ million

$$C = \$72,497;$$

thus $$C' = F_2 - C = 79,695 - 72,497 = \$7,198 \text{ million}$$

and the monetary base

$$H = \begin{cases} F_1 - C' = 106,755 - 7,198 = \$99,557 \text{ million} \\ C + R = 27,060 + 72,497 = \$99,557 \text{ million.} \end{cases}$$

Modern central banking tries to influence the factors underlying F_1 and C'. The bulk of F_1 consists of U.S. government securities, \$80,495 million out of the total of \$106,755, or 75%. The purchase and sale of U.S. government securities, i.e., the open market operations is controlled by the Federal Open Market Committee. It is the most important policy to influence the monetary base H.

Recall that the monetary base is the most important variable determining the expansion of the money supply.

Another item belonging to F_1, the loans and acceptances, comprising only 2% of F_1 is influenced by the changes in the discount rate. The member banks react to changes in the discount rate by increasing or decreasing their borrowing from the Federal Reserve banks.

• PROBLEM 13-2

Which are the three possible monetary systems in the world? Explain their working.

Solution: 1) automatic systems; 2) discretionary systems; 3) systems with monetary rules.

If monetary policy is used to balance a country's imports and exports it is basically an automatic system: the money supply increases when the exports surpass the imports and there is a surplus in the balance of payments and decreases when there is a deficit. When exports surpass the imports, the economy 'earns money'. This surplus on the balance of payments increases the bank reserves and so the money supply. The increase in the money supply increases real income and thereby stimulates the demand for imports, and increases the price level so that the exports become less competitive on the world markets and will be reduced by lack of demand for exports. The monetary ease will reduce the short term interest rates and stimulate investment in foreign enterprises and the purchase of foreign securities, which are both types of imports. The consequence is a reduction in the surplus on the balance of payments = exports - imports.

A deficit on the balance of payments would produce a reverse process. This automatic monetary system uses income and price movements to balance the international payments and keep the exchange rate fixed. Examples of countries which have used this automatic system in the past World War II period are Japan, France and West Germany.

A second type of monetary system is the dicretionary system as it is used, for example, in the United States. Monetary policy is used for goals other than controlling the balance of payments only, like full employment, price stabilization and economic growth. This is made possible primarily by the execution of the open-market operations of purchasing

and selling securities. A discretionary policy requires the use of targets because of the time lags of the impact of monetary policy on income, prices or the rate of growth. At present, targets related to the money stock, like 'reserves available for private deposits' are favored by the FED. In a discretionary system the targets may be changed. Under a discretionary system, fixed, flexible or 'pegged' exchange rate remains virtually fixed for long periods.
long periods.

A monetary system using rules is not yet existent. In such a system the discretion of the monetary authorities is replaced by a relatively precise rule that governs the monetary actions taken. Professor Milton Friedman suggests to increase the money supply at a fixed rate $\Delta M/M$ = constant, say 4% annually.

Another rule was advocated by Irving Fisher: to stabilize the price index, or $\Delta P/P$ = constant. And Henry Simons suggested in the 1930's to fix the quantity of money, so $\Delta M/M = 0$, or $M = \bar{M}$. (i.e., Simons' rule was a historic variant of the modern Friedman-rule). All these proposals imply non-activist rules. A possible activist rule could link the monetary growth to the unemployment rate, like

$$\frac{\Delta M}{M} = 4.0 + 2.5\ (u - 6.0)\ .$$

The growth rate of the money stock would be increased by 2.5% for every 1% unemployment in excess of the natural unemployment rate of 6%.

Suggestions for monetary systems based on rules usually include a proposal for flexible exchange rates to provide an adjustment mechanism for balancing imports and exports, so that income and prices can be controlled separately from the balance of payments.

• PROBLEM 13-3

What are the primary functions of the Federal Reserve Banks?

Solution: First, the Federal Reserve System has the exclusive legal right to issue legal tender currency. No commercial bank may issue currency.

Second, the "FED" sets the legal reserve requirements for commercial banks. That is, it determines the proportion of deposits that each commercial bank must keep "in reserve" to cover withdrawals by depositors, and thus also the proportion which each bank may lend out. The authority to set reserve requirements gives the FED power to control the maximum quantity of money and credit in the economy.

Third, the FED acts as the commercial banks' bank, providing accounts in which commercial banks may keep their reserves. It also clears interbank checks like the way in which a commercial bank clears checks between its depositors.

Fourth, it can provide loans to commercial banks, whose reserves fall to inadequate levels, e.g., due to large expected withdrawals.

Fifth, the FED performs most of the Federal government's banking services, holding part of the Treasury's revenues, and assisting in tax collection and bond sale and redemption.

Sixth, the FED plays a role along with state and national governments in regulating the operation of its member commercial banks.

FUNCTION OF THE FED

• PROBLEM 13-4

What are the three major controls which the Federal Reserve System uses to manage money?

Solution: (a) raise or lower the required reserve ratio; (b) buy or sell bonds in the open market; (c) raise or lower the discount rate.

• PROBLEM 13-5

The Federal Reserve's most important control instrument is open-market operations. How is it that selling government bonds can reduce bank reserves?

Solution: Suppose the Federal Open Market Committee (FOMC) decides to sell $2 billion of government bonds. To accomplish this, the bonds are sold on the open market. The buyer will most likely pay for the bonds by a check drawn on his bank account. When the FED presents this check for payment to the bank, the bank will lose an equivalent amount of reserve balances with the Federal Reserve.

So reserves go down by $2 billion. But the process doesn't stop here. Due to the multiple contraction of money, a drop of $2 billion in reserves tends to set off a $10 billion contraction of demand deposits (assuming a reserve requirement of 20% and no leakages).

• PROBLEM 13-6

What are the principal and selective instruments of control of which the Federal Reserve System makes use?

Solution: The Federal Reserve has three principal instruments of control: open-market operations, changes in the discount rate, and changes in the reserve requirements of the member banks. There are also several selective instruments of control : margin requirements on stock purchases, ceilings on bank deposit interest rates, and eligibility requirements for discounting at the Federal Reserve banks.

• PROBLEM 13-7

What are the five minor tools which the Federal Reserve Board possesses?

Solution: The Federal Reserve Board's five minor weapons are:

1) moral suasion
2) selective control over "margin requirements"
3) control over maximum interest rate allowed on time deposits
4) selective credit controls over installment contracts and consumer credit
5) selective controls over the terms of housing mortgage contracts.

Moral suasion refers to "jawbone control". Here the FED expresses its displeasure to the banks or to the public if the banks are not doing what it wants of them.

Control over "margin requirements" means that the FED decides what percentage of a stock price people can borrow in order to buy and carry common and preferred stock. When the stock market crashed in 1929, there was no control over margin requirements.

Since the Great Depression, the FED has placed various controls on bank interest rates, including an interest ceiling for time deposits, and a ban on interest for checking accounts until the 1970's.

Control over installment terms, the so-called Regulation W, was used during the Korean crisis in 1950-52 but was allowed to lapse afterward. It required a minimum down-payment when buying goods on credit and required consumers to pay up charge accounts before buying more goods on credit.

Control over mortgage terms was established by Regulation X, but allowed by Congress to lapse in 1953. Through it the FED had the power to set terms for mortgage down payments and the number of years for amortization of principal.

• PROBLEM 13-8

What is a margin requirement?

Solution: A margin requirement refers to the percentage of the value of a stock purchase which is required by the Federal Reserve Board to be paid immediately upon purchase, and not deferred.

• PROBLEM 13-9

Which unit of the Federal Reserve System controls each of the 5 control instruments of the FED?

Solution: Responsibility for the 3 most important control instruments, open market operations, changes in the discount rate, and changes in the reserve requirements, is assigned as follows:

1) The Federal Open Market Committee (FOMC) determines the open-market policy, i.e., the purchase and sale of U.S. government securities, and thereby influences the monetary base. The FOMC consists of 12 members: the seven governors of the Federal Reserve Board and presidents of five of the twelve Federal Reserve banks. It meets every 4 weeks in Washington, D.C.

2) Changes in the discount rate are initiated by the individual Federal Reserve banks but must be approved by the Federal Reserve Board. Thus the responsibility for the discount rate is shared. Changes in the discount rate influence the borrowings of the member banks from the Federal Reserve banks, and so also the monetary base.

3) Changes in the reserve requirements of member banks are the sole responsibility of the Board of Governors. Changes in the legal reserve requirements determine changes in the ratio of the demand deposits to the monetary base, i.e., the money multiplier. Two less important in-

struments are also to the full responsibility of the Board:

4) The controls over interest rates on savings deposits in member banks, and

5) Controls over margin requirements on loans to purchase securities. In summary the following figure illustrates the division of functions:

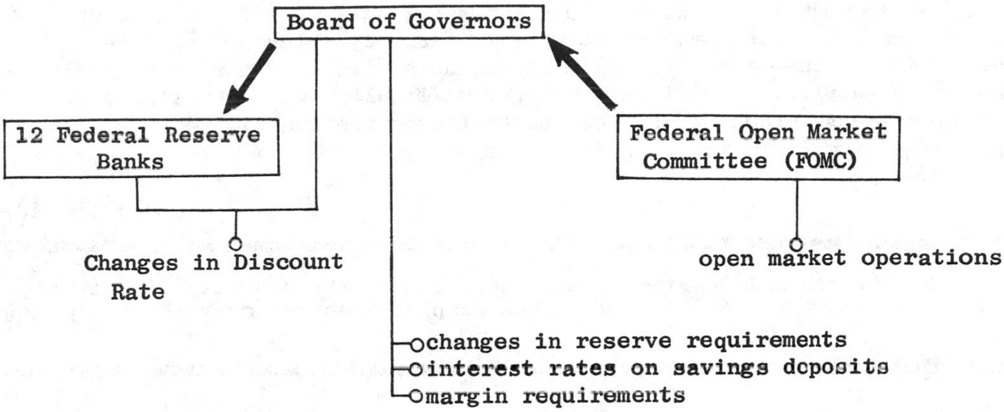

THE RESERVE REQUIREMENT

• PROBLEM 13-10

What is the primary purpose of the legal reserve requirement imposed by the FED on all commercial banks?

Solution: The FED requires that each bank retain on account with the FED or in cash an amount of money equal to a certain proportion of its demand deposit liabilities. This requirement is the legal reserve requirement. It limits the proportion of a bank's reserves which the bank can lend out and hence the amount of deposits which the banking system as a whole can create.

It might be thought that the principal function of such a requirement is to prevent banks from lending out more of their reserves than is prudent, thereby jeopardizing their solvency and the safety of their customer's deposits. This is not, however, its principal function. Protecting bank customers' deposits is the responsibility of the Federal Deposit Insurance Corporation. And it is examinations by federal and state authorities that are supposed to ensure that banks remain solvent. Moreover, if, in a panic, depositors attempt to withdraw their funds from commercial banks, there is no reserve requirement short of 100% which absolutely ensures that banks will remain solvent. In the absence of a 100% reserve requirement only readiness on the part of the Central Bank (FED) to provide banks with all the reserves they need to redeem their deposits can prevent bank insolvency in a panic.

The primary purpose of the FED'S reserve requirements is to give the FED greater control over the money supply. The existence of legal reserve requirements enables the FED to predict with greater accuracy how great an impact on bank deposits and the money supply it can have by increasing or decreasing commercial bank reserves. The FED knows, for example, that, with a 20% required ratio, if it increases (decreases) commercial bank reserves by a given amount, the maximum increase (decrease) in the money supply this action can produce is 5 times the increase (decrease). If the FED can estimate the extent of "leakages" into (from) currency held by the public and commercial bank excess reserves, it can estimate the actual impact on the money supply of an increase (decrease) in commercial bank reserves that it effects.

If, on the other hand, there is no uniform legal reserve requirement, and commercial banks may lend out any fraction of their reserves, the FED will be unable to predict the multiple by which an increase (decrease) in bank reserves which it produces will increase (decrease) the money supply. It will have greater difficulty achieving its money supply targets, since it has less control over the reaction of the banking system to an increase (decrease) in reserves.

• PROBLEM 13-11

Although the Federal Reserve authorities control the quantity of commercial bank reserves why is it that they lack complete control over the money supply?

Solution: A change in the quantity of commercial bank reserves will result in a predictable change in the money supply M_1, only if the money multiplier, the ratio of the change in demand deposits to the change in reserves which caused it, is known.

Although the monetary authorities have considerable control over the legal reserve requirements for demand deposits and time deposits, they have almost no control over leakages of reserves into or from the currency holdings of the public and the excess reserves of commercial banks, and the ratio of excess reserves to demand deposits. The ratio of currency to demand deposits is determined by the desires of the public and appears to vary with fluctuations in economic activity; while the amount of excess reserves kept by banks is affected by transfers of deposits to banks with different reserve requirements and also depends largely on the actions of the individual banks. Thus to control the money stock, M_1, by increasing or decreasing the reserves of commercial banks, the monetary authorities would have to know the money multiplier m, which it cannot do with exactness since it cannot predict exactly the extent of the two main leakages from the banking system, i.e., the public's desire for currency (as opposed to demand deposits) or the bank's decisions as to how much to hold in excess reserves.

• PROBLEM 13-12

When does the lowering of the reserve requirements have the same effect as open market purchases on the money supply?

Solution: Open market purchases increase the monetary base H, consisting of currency held by the public C and the total reserve deposits of member banks at the Federal Reserve banks R, and the bank's vault cash, or V. (H = C + R + V.) The lowering of the legal reserve requirement increases the amount of demand deposits, D, that can be supported by the given reserve, R.

The formula for the expansion of the Money Supply M_I is

$$\Delta M_I = \Delta V \Delta D + c\Delta D = (1 + c)\Delta D = (1 + c)\frac{\Delta H}{r + c}$$

where c is the currency-demand deposit-ratio and r the reserve requirement. We abstract from the excess reserves and the time-deposits (see the chapter on the banking system). We compare now the situation in which an increase in the monetary base H has the same effect on the money supply M_I, as a lowering of the reserve requirements.

$$\frac{(1 + c)\Delta H}{(r + c)} = \Delta M_I = \left[\frac{(1 + c)H}{(r + \Delta r + c)} - \frac{(1 + c)H}{(r + c)}\right]$$

Dividing both sides by 1 + c results in

$$\frac{\Delta H}{r + c} = \left[\frac{H}{r + \Delta r + c} - \frac{H}{r + c}\right]$$

Bringing the second term at the right-hand side to the left-hand side gives

$$\frac{H + \Delta H}{r + c} = \frac{H}{r + \Delta r + c}$$

When this equation holds the effects of the two policies on Money Supply M_I are equivalent. For example: suppose the monetary base H = 100 and is increased by $\Delta H = 5$: the reserve requirement r = 20% and the currency-demand deposit ratio c = 1.75. Then

$$\frac{H + \Delta H}{r + c} = \frac{105}{1.95} = \frac{H}{r + c + \Delta r} = \frac{100}{1.95 + \Delta r}$$

or

$$53.85 = \frac{100}{1.95 + \Delta r}$$

Multiplying both sides by $1.95 + \Delta r$ results in $105 + 53.85\Delta r = 100$. Subtracting 105 from both sides, $53.85\ \Delta r = -5$, and dividing both sides by 53.85 gives the change in the legal reserve requirement that is necessary:

$$\Delta r = -0.093 = -9.3\% .$$

• PROBLEM 13-13

Why do the Treasury and the FED usually attempt to lower the long-term rates of interest, and simultaneously to raise the short-term rates?

Solution: Lowering the long-term interest rates stimulates the domestic economy, while raising the short-term rates encourages foreign speculators to keep their dollar balances invested in short-term securities in the United States.

Long-term interest rates form the cost of capital for long-term investment projects, i.e., investments in buildings, machinery, equipment, and therefore influence the total investment expenditures which form part of the aggregate demand; and the aggregate demand determines the level of employment.

Short-term interest rates are important in the international money markets. High short-term interest rates in the U.S. make portfolio investments in short-term securities in the U.S. attractive for foreign speculators; thereby providing short-term capital that can be pooled through banks and financial intermediaries for more long-term lending purposes. In this way the increased desires for long-term borrowing can be complemented.

OPERATIONS BY THE FED

• PROBLEM 13-14

Suppose the Federal Reserve System has initiated an expansionary monetary policy by using $25 billion in newly printed money to buy government bonds from bond holders. What will be the repercussions of such an action by the Federal Reserve System with regard to the following:

a) the interest rate
b) bond holders
c) Borrowers

Solution: The increase in the money supply may be depicted graphically by means of the following figure:

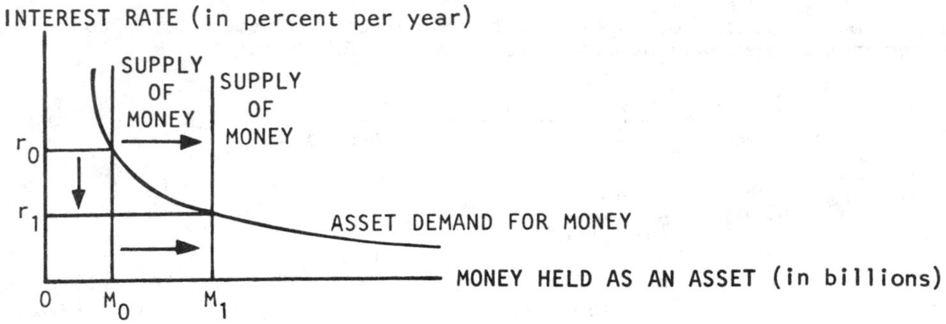

As a result of the increase in the money supply by $25 billion, interest rate falls from r_0 to r_1.

Bond holders are willing to hold more in money assets only if the interest rate falls. The equilibrium interest rate would indeed fall - as the above figure indicates - since bond holders would sell their bonds and hold more money only if the bonds earned a lower return.

With lower interest rates, more individuals and firms would be interested in borrowing money to finance new factories, homes, automobiles etc.

• PROBLEM 13-15

Suppose the FED enlarges the monetary base through open market operations by $150 million:

1) What is the theoretically possible maximum expansion in demand deposits of the total banking system, when the reserve requirement is 18%?

2) What is the expansion in demand deposits and the money supply if we, let ΔH = the amount of the change in the monetary base (reserves), let r = the required reserve ratio, and let ΔD = the change in demand deposits taking into consideration all the leakages which the public maintains? The ratio of currency to demand deposits is 0.30, the ratio of excess reserves to demand deposits is 0.125, the reserve requirement for the time deposits is 0.04, and the ratio of savings and time deposits to demand deposits which the public wishes to maintain is 1.75.

Solution: 1) Eighteen percent of demand deposits have to be held in the form of reserves. Thus 18% of the increase, in the demand deposits ΔD made possible by the enlargement of the monetary base must be equal to this increase in the reserves, where m is the so-called money multiplier for Money Supply M_1. $\Delta H = r\Delta D$ or

$$\Delta D = \frac{\Delta H}{r} = \frac{\$150 \text{ million}}{0.18} = \$833 \text{ million.}$$

2) Leakages occur if there are increases in (a) currency held outside banks, (b) in excess reserves of commercial banks, or (c) in savings and time deposits.

a) The withdrawal from commercial banks of part of the increase in monetary reserves in the form of currency directly lessens the initial increase in reserves of the banking system and consequently lessens potential expansion of deposits. The increase in the monetary base (potencial demand deposit reserves) ΔH, is divided, as a first approximation, between an increase in commercial bank reserves and an increase in the amount that the public wishes to hold in the form of currency (= currency drain). So, $\Delta H = \Delta R + \Delta C = r\Delta D + c\Delta D = (r + c)\Delta D$, where ΔR is the change in commercial bank reserves held against demand deposits, ΔC is the change in currency held by the public, and c is the ratio of the public's currency holdings to its demand deposits $(\Delta C = c\Delta D)$.

b) Banks also hold small balances of excess reserves to cover possible shartages of required reserves. So a certain part of the enlargement of the monetary base will be set apart as excess reserves (= excess reserves drain). Where ΔI is the increase in excess reserves and $i(= 0.125\%)$ is the percentage of demand deposits that banks hold as excess reserves $(\Delta I = i\Delta D)$, we may write as a second approximation

$$\Delta H = \Delta R + \Delta C + \Delta I = r\Delta D + c\Delta D + i\Delta D$$
$$= (r + c + i)\Delta D .$$

c) Commercial banks create time deposits as well as demand deposits. Because banks must hold reserves against time deposits too, they will have less in reserves to support demand deposits. Where ΔT is the change in commercial bank reserves held against time deposits (time deposit drain) and t is the ratio of time deposits to demand deposits, and r' is the reserve requirement for time deposits, then $r' \times t = (0.08 \times 1.75)$ is the ratio of time deposit reserves to demand deposits. And we may write

$$\Delta H = \Delta R + \Delta C + \Delta I + \Delta T \equiv r\Delta D + c\Delta D + i\Delta D + (r')t\Delta D$$
$$= [r + c + i + (r')t]\Delta D .$$

Dividing both sides of the equation by the sum between the square brackets results in

$$\Delta D = \frac{\Delta H}{[r + c + i + (r')t]} . \qquad (1)$$

The possible increase in the demand deposits, taking into account the various leakages, is considerably less than the theoretically possible maximum increase in demand deposits. Substituting the given data into the equation results in

$$\Delta D = \frac{\$150 \text{ million}}{[0.18 + 0.30 + 0.125 + (0.04 \times 1.75)]}$$
$$= \frac{150}{0.675}$$
$$\cong \$222 \text{ million} .$$

We see also that when the public shifts from demand deposits to time deposits, implying an increase in t, the possible increase in demand deposits will be smaller, and vice versa.

Money Supply 1, M_1, consists of currency in circulation C and demand deposits D: $M_1 = C + D$. The total amount of currency equals a certain percentage, c, of the demand deposits: C = cD; thus

$$M_1 = D + cD = (1 + c)D .$$

A change in M1, ΔM_1, caused by a change in the monetary base, ΔH, can then be presented as (recall equation (1))

$$\Delta M_1 = (1 + c)\Delta D = \frac{(1 + c)\Delta H}{[r + c + i + (r')t]} = m\Delta H ,$$

where m is the so-called money multiplier for Money Supply M_1. Using the result we found already, the increase in M_1 resulting from an increase in the monetary base by $150 million is

$$\Delta M_1 = (1 + 0.30)\$222 \text{ million}$$

$$= 1.30 \times \$222 \text{ million} = \$288.6 \text{ million.}$$

• PROBLEM 13-16

Suppose the FED buys $100,000 of government bonds from a commercial bank. What will be the effect of this purchase on the money supply, if the required reserve ratio is 10%, if banks maintain no excess reserves, and if there is no change in the public's currency holdings?

Solution: The sale of bonds expands the bank's reserves by $100,000 and enables it to make new loans of (1 - 0.10)($100,000) = $90,000. Withdrawal and expenditure of the $90,000 by the bank's loanees increase by $90,000 the receipts of the payees, who deposit this amount into their banks. These banks now have $90,000 additional reserves, of which they can lend (1 - 0.10)($90,000) = $81,000. The chain of deposit and loan creation continues until New Deposits = Increase in Reserves ÷ Required Reserve Ratio - $100,000 ÷ 10% = $1,000,000.

• PROBLEM 13-17

Suppose the FED adds $500,000 to the reserves of the banking system. If the required reserve ratio is 30%, if banks maintain no excess reserves and if the public increases its holdings of currency by $200,000, what is the effect on the money supply?

Solution: The $500,000 increase in reserves of the banking system would allow the creation of additional loans which, if all those individuals paid with the borrowed funds deposited them into their bank accounts, would ultimately increase total deposits by

(Increase in Reserves) ÷ (Required Reserve Ratio)

= ($500,000) ÷ (30%) = $1,666,667 .

But, the public withdraws $200,000 to increase its holdings of currency, and thus reduces reserves by that amount. The contraction of deposits caused by this withdrawal is (Decrease in Reserves) ÷ (Required Reserve

Ratio)

$= (\$200,000) \div (30\%) = \$666,667.$

Thus the net change in total deposits is $1,666,667 - $666,667 = $1,000,000, i.e., an addition of $1 million.

Alternatively we could calculate the net change in deposits by dividing the net change in the reserves of the banking system by the required reserve ratio. That is, ($500,000 - $200,000) ÷ (30%) = ($300,000) ÷ (30%) = $1,000,000.

The Money Supply (M_1) is defined as the sum of demand deposits and currency held by the public. The former has risen, as we calculated, by $1,000,000; and the latter rose by $200,000 due to withdrawals from banks. Hence the total change in the Money Supply (M_1) is

$$\$1,000,000 + \$200,000 = \$1,200,000.$$

• PROBLEM 13-18

Suppose the FED buys $125,000,000 of government bonds from commercial banks. If currency held by the public remains unchanged, but banks decide to increase their excess reserves by $50,000,000, and the required reserve ratio is 20%, what happens to the total money supply?

Solution: The purchase by the FED from commercial banks of government bonds adds $125,000,000 to commercial banks' reserves. They could make loans and generate a multiple-deposit expansion of

(Increase in Reserves) ÷ (Required Reserve Ratio)

$= (\$125,000,000) \div (20\%) = \$625,000,000$.

However, they choose to accumulate an additional $50,000,000 of excess reserves. Hence, reserves which are used to support deposits increase by (Actual Reserves) - (Excess Reserves) ≡ (Required Reserves);

$$(\$125,000,000) - (\$50,000,000) = (75,000,000).$$

If additional required reserves are $75,000,000, then the increase in deposits in the entire banking system is given by:

(Required Reserves) = (Required Reserve Ratio) x (Deposits).

Substituting the values from our problem:

($75,000,000) = (20%)(Deposits)   Deposits = (75,000,000) ÷ (20%)

$= \$375,000,000$.

Since currency held by the public has been unaffected by the FED purchase of bonds, the change in total money supply ≡ change in deposits + change in currency held by the public = change in deposits = $375,000,000.

• PROBLEM 13-19

What is the potential impact on the money supply of an open market sale by the FED of $3,000,000 in government bonds, assuming all commercial banks are fully "loaned up" (i.e., their excess reserves are zero), and the required reserve ratio is 25%?

Solution: When the FED sells government bonds on the open market, they are purchased either by commercial banks or by the non-bank public. When a commercial bank buys government bonds from the FED, payment is made by means of a deduction from the bank's reserve balance with the FED. The commercial bank has smaller reserves.

If, as we have assumed, commercial banks are "loaned up", i.e., have no excess reserves, then actual reserves, which were equal to required reserves, will fall below required reserves, which remain unaffected, since the bond purchase has no direct effect on commercial bank demand deposits. In our example, total commercial bank reserves will fall by $3,000,000. In order to comply with the FED's required reserve ratio, banks must reduce their demand deposit liabilities to the level at which their reserves are equal to at least 25% (the required reserve ratio) of their demand deposit liabilities. The commercial banks achieve this reduction in demand deposits when they call in loans, each individual bank attempting to add to its reserves. In the aggregate, however, the commercial banks cannot increase their reserves, but only reduce their outstanding loans and demand deposit liabilities.

Let us illustrate this point. Those banks which bought the $3,000,000 in government bonds will have lost $3,000,000 in reserves. Their demand deposit liabilities remain unchanged, however, and hence the level of their required reserves remains unchanged. In order for each of these banks to re-achieve the required reserve against its demand deposit liabilities, it must call for payment of some of its loans. All together, banks which have purchased the $3,000,000 in government bonds will need to call in $3,000,000 in loans to replace their $3,000,000 loss of reserves. We will assume that these loans are repaid entirely by checks drawn on the borrowers' demand deposit accounts. Thus, at this first stage, total demand deposit accounts are reduced by $3,000,000. And when the checks clear, $3,000,000 in reserves is transferred from banks against which the checks are drawn to those banks whose loans are being repaid. But the process cannot stop here since the demand deposit liabilities of the former banks are now lower by $3,000,000 which means that required reserves are (25% x $3,000,000) = $750,000 less, while actual reserves are $3,000,000 less. These banks' actual reserves are thus ($3,000,000 - $750,000) = $2,250,000 below their required reserves. They in turn will have to call in loans for payment, in the amount of $2,250,000, in order to build up their reserves to the required level. Their debtors in turn will write checks on a third group of banks for a total of $2,250,000, which will result in destruction of an additional $2,250,000 in demand deposit liabilities, and the transfer from the third group to the second group of banks of $2,250,000 in reserves. Now the third group of banks will be short of required reserves by (1 - 25%)($2,250,000) $\cong$ $1,687,500, and will have to call in loans, and so on. Altogether, the demand deposits of the banking system will be reduced by

$$\$3{,}000{,}000(1 + (1 - 25\%) + (1 - 25\%)^2 + \dots) =$$

$$\$3{,}000{,}000(1/25\%) = \$3{,}000{,}000 \times 4 = \$12{,}000{,}000$$

as a result of a sale by the FED of $3,000,000 of government bonds to commercial banks. Since currency holdings of the public are unaffected by the transaction (by assumption), the total effect on the money supply is a $12,000,000 reduction.

When the FED sells $3,000,000 in government bonds to the non-bank public, bond buyers make payment by writing $3,000,000 in checks in favor of the FED against their demand deposit accounts in their commercial banks. The FED collects from these commercial banks by reducing their reserve balances with the FED by $3,000,000; and the commercial banks deduct $3,000,000 from the checking accounts of the bond buyers. But, just as in the previous case when the FED sold bonds to the commercial banks, the process does not end here. The banks of the bond buyers have $3,000,000 less in demand deposit liabilities, and thus their required reserves are lower by ($3,000,000 x 25%) = $750,000.

But their actual reserves are $3,000,000 lower than before, so that required reserves exceed actual reserves by $3,000,000 - $750,000 = $2,250,000. Thus these banks will be required to call in $2,250,000 of loans. If we assume these are repaid by checks drawn on the borrower's demand deposit accounts (rather than by currency), then these second banks have their demand deposits and reserves reduced by $2,250,000. The process continues as in the previous case, and the resulting effect on the money supply is the same: a reduction of $12,000,000.

• PROBLEM 13-20

Suppose commercial banks have a total of $500,000,000 in demand deposits, $100,000,000 in reserves, and the required reserve ratio is 20%. What would be the potential effect on the money supply if the FED (a) raised the required reserve ratio to 25%, (b) lowered the reserve ratio to 10%?

Solution: The money supply (M_1) consists of demand deposits and currency held by the public. Bank loans constitute a major source of bank deposits, since banks usually make loans by adding the amount of the loan to the account balance of the borrower.

Thus, factors affecting the lending capacity of the bank will have an impact on bank deposits and hence on the money supply. The required reserve ratio is such a factor, since it determines each bank's required reserves and thereby also the amount of excess reserves it has available to lend.

In our example, the banks' required reserves are initially ($500,000,000) x (20%) = $100,000,000, as are their actual reserves. Therefore, the banking system has no excess reserves (actual reserves - required reserves) and no capacity to make additional loans.

If the FED raises the required reserve ratio to 25%, required reserves are ($500,000,000) x (25%) = $125,000,000. Actual reserves are still only $100,000,000, however. The banks must therefore act to reduce their demand deposit liabilities and thereby also the amount of their required reserves, to the level at which required reserves are no more than actual reserves. They achieve the reduction in demand deposits by calling in loans. The banks must continue to call in loans until their $100,000,000 in reserves are equal to at least 25% of their demand deposits, that is, until their total demand deposits are no more than 1/25% = 4 times their reserves. Total demand deposits of the banking system must be reduced to 4 x $100,000,000 = $400,000,000 from $500,000,000, as a result of the increase in the required reserve ratio from 20% to 25%. It thus reduces the money supply by $100,000,000. An increase in the required reserve ratio represents "contractionary" monetary policy by the FED.

If the FED lowered the required reserve ratio from 20% to 10%, the required reserves for the initial $500,000,000 of demand deposits in the banking system would be ($500,000,000 x 10%) = $50,000,000. Since actual reserves of the system are $100,000,000, the banking system has $100,000,000 - $50,000,000 = $50,000,000 in excess reserves (actual reserves - required reserves), with which it can create new loans (demand deposits). The amount of new deposits (loans) which the banking system as a whole can create from $50,000,000 in excess reserves is that amount of which $50,000,000 is 10%, i.e., it can create an additional ($50,000,000 ÷ 10%) = $500,000,000 in deposits. Total deposits will be $1,000,000,000 as a result of the reduction of the required reserve ratio. Required reserves are (\$1,000,000,000 $\times$ 10%) = \$100,000,000, just equal to the system's actual reserves. Thus, reduction by the FED of the required reserve ratio, since it increases demand deposits, and hence the money supply, is a form of "expansionary" monetary policy.

• PROBLEM 13-21

The basic goals of monetary policy, or of macro-economic policy in general, are reduction of the rate of unemployment, stabilization of prices, economic growth and control of the balance of payments. What are the targets of monetary policy and how is the realization of this policy monitored?

Solution: The implementation of Monetary Policy requires that the policy instruments (open market operations, reserve requirements, discount rate, Regulation Q) will be applied in such a way that certain operational targets will be reached. (See Fig. 1).

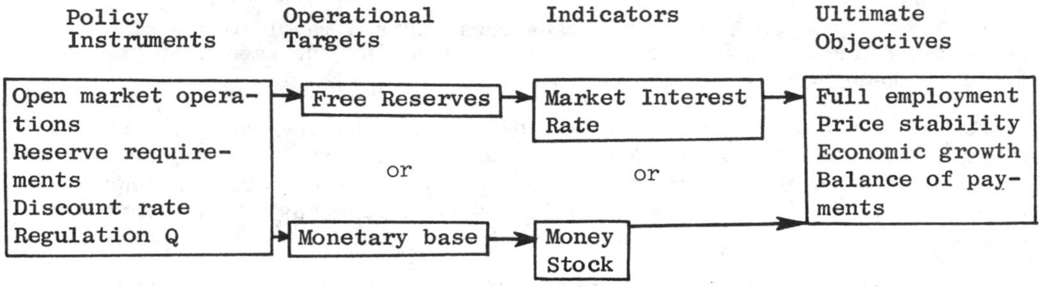

These targets function as beacons to guide the policy implementation. The next step is to monitor certain monetary indicators in order to be able to judge if the results are contributing to the ultimate objectives of macro-economic policy (full employment, price stability, economic growth and control over the balance of payments). These ultimate objectives cannot serve as targets for monetary policy, because of the long-time-lags between a change in monetary policy and its effects on real national income (6 months) and on prices (2 years); and because real output and prices are also affected by fiscal policy, price controls and other more structural economic policies.

At present the FED uses two targets, the level of free reserves, and the more important monetary base. The two accompanying indicators used are the market interest rates and the money stock.

Free reserves = excess reserves of member banks - their borrowing from the Federal Reserve banks = E - B. Using free reserves as target, the FED would purchase securities to raise the level of the free reserves and sell them to reduce it. The level of free reserves is usually only temporarily increased by increasing the excess reserves E, so that the new free reserves = $(E + \Delta E) - B = E' - B$.

The next step is then to use part ΔE of the new excess reserves E' to pay off borrowings at the Federal Reserve banks, so that

$$\text{free reserves} = E - (B - \Delta E) = E - B + \Delta E .$$

We notice that this keeps the free reserves at the higher level. When free reserves are used as a target, short-term interest rates are used as an indicator. When the level of free reserves is high, interest rates are expected to be low, and vice versa. These changes in the interest rates are then expected to affect the economy.

A possible chain reaction is also the following:

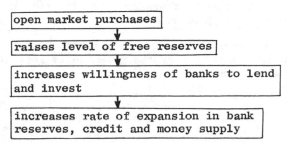

open market purchases

↓

raises level of free reserves

↓

increases willingness of banks to lend and invest

↓

increases rate of expansion in bank reserves, credit and money supply

However, the links between changes in the level of free reserves and the credit and money supply expansion is extremely weak, and confusion may arise easily. Secondly, if interest rates are used as an indicator, they ought to be discounted for the expectations of inflation: real interest rates should be used.

A better target of monetary policy is the monetary base H, in combination with the rate of change in the money supply as an indicator. It appears that the changes in the money supply have significant effects on aggregate demand. (See the portfolio adjustment theory). The monetary authorities control the most important part of the monetary base by their purchase and sale of U.S. Government securities. When the money-multiplier is relatively stable - and so far it has been, the control of the money supply through the control of the monetary base, appears to be rather strict.

• PROBLEM 13-22

Economic stabilization policy usually works with time-lags. Which lags in the effects of economic policy may you discern?

Solution: 1) The inside time-lag (the period between which a policy action becomes necessary and when it is taken).
2) The outside lag (the period between which a policy action is taken and when it affects the economy). The outside lag is generally a distributed lag: the effects of a policy action build up over the course of time. The inside lag is divided into recognition, decision and action lags. The recognition lag is the period between the time a disturbance occurs and the time it is organized by the policy makers that action is required. When the disturbance is predicted, this lag is negative: the event will be known in advance of the actual disturbance. Because of this, accurate fore-casting and prediction assists in shortening the inside lag considerably so that the policy action can be taken in time. Because the Federal Reserve Board, the Treasury and the Council of Economic Advisors share their predictions, the recognition lag is equal for them.

But there exists a difference in the decision lags (the delays between the recognition of the need for action and the policy decisions) and in the action lags (the lags between the policy decisions and their implementation) between monetary and fiscal policy. The decision and action lags of monetary policy are relatively short in comparison with those of fiscal policy. While the inside lag is discrete, the outside lag is distributed: the effects of economic policy are spread over time. Think for example about the Keynesian multiplier process, or the money-multiplier process. Government spending acts immediately on aggregate demand and the national income, while an increase in the money supply works only via the adjustments of the portfolios on aggregate demand. It appears therefore that the outside lag of fiscal policy is shorter than that of monetary policy.

Fiscal policy seems attractive because of this short outside lag but that advantage is offset by the potentially long inside lag of a lengthy legislative process.

SHORT ANSWER QUESTIONS FOR REVIEW

Answer
To be covered when testing yourself

Choose the correct answer.

1. Which of the following is not a contractionary policy? (a) Raising the discount rate (b) increasing the legal reserve ratio (c) selling bonds (d) persuading commercial banks to approve less loans — c

2. The legal reserve ratio is changed (a) quite often. (b) once in a few years. (c) every month. (d) when Congress decides they should be changed. — b

3. A tighter money supply (a) increases the value of bonds. (b) activates private investment. (c) causes the interest rate to rise. (d) raises the price of bonds. — c

4. Chicago monetarists propose (a) to use fiscal and monetary policies equally often. (b) to fix the annual rate of growth of the money supply. (c) to accept long-term unemployment in exchange for less inflation. (d) all of the above. — b

5. When a country exports more than it imports its domestic money supply (a) becomes tighter. (b) increases. (c) does not change. (d) none of the above. — b

6. Commercial banks tend to (a) just fulfill the reserve ratio requirement. (b) often fall below the legal ratio. (c) create reserves in excess of legal requirements for safety purposes. (d) accept new deposits reluctantly in times of inflation. — c

7. Lower discount rates (a) increase the banks willingness to lend, as they usually accompany the policy of easing the money supply. (b) tend to reduce economic activity. (c) act in the same way as a higher legal reserve ratio. (d) always result in a reduction in the price of bonds. — a

8. A Federal Reserve action (a) has a direct impact on GNP. (b) affects the National Income through a complicated multi-stage process. (c) has generally no impact on GNP. (d) always makes real GNP rise in the end. — b

9. The Fed's open market operations in the 1970's considered stability of the market interest

Answer
To be covered when testing yourself

rates as (a) their secondary target. (b) their primary target. (c) the requirement for the effectiveness of any monetary policy. (d) something to be entirely disregarded. a

10. The higher the legal reserve ratio (a) the more prone to lending the banks are. (b) the larger is the money supply in the economy. (c) the harder it is for commercial banks to create new money. (d) the more likely inflation is. c

11. An increase in the demand deposits of a commercial bank (a) will result in the reduction of excess reserves or in the creation of new reserves by a bank. (b) is represented on the bank's balance sheet by an increase in its assets. (c) has to be matched by an increase in time deposits in order to maintain an accounting balance. (d) is equivalent to an increase in its net worth. a

12. The existence of positive expectations regarding the future performance of the economy (a) will have no effect on the banks' policies. (b) will make banks particularly concerned with their safety and consequently with the holding of sufficient amount of excess reserves. (c) will probably cause banks to step up their lending activities and to reduce the amount of 'safety' reserves. (d) is always inflationary. c

13. The money supply in the economy (a) is actually determined by the amount of currency printed by the Treasury. (b) includes both demand deposits and time deposits when broadly defined. (c) is usually growing during depressions. (d) should, in view of Milton Friedman, be increased by 10% every year if the economy is to be stable. b

14. As the market interest rate rises (a) government bonds fall in value. (b) government bonds grow in value. (c) the price of government bonds is not affected. (d) people want to hold as much money as possible. a

15. During open-market operations (a) bonds inevitably fall in price. (b) the goals of Federal Reserve often change. (c) bonds are sold to or bought from anonymous customers. (d) many banks fail. c

SHORT ANSWER QUESTIONS FOR REVIEW

	Answer To be covered when testing yourself
Fill in the blanks:	
16. The banks which are part of the __________ attract over 80% of total demand deposits.	Federal Reserve System
17. The assets of commercial banks consist mainly of __________, __________ and __________.	reserves, loans, investments
18. The __________ determines the ability of the banking system to create new money.	legal reserve ratio
19. Changes in the legal reserve requirements are used by the Fed __________ as a tool of monetary policy.	once every few years
20. The __________ makes a decision on the prospective target of the open market operations.	FOMC
21. The discount rate is always __________ __________ the market interest rate.	less than
22. The Fed often uses __________ instead of explicit monetary actions to achieve its economic goals.	moral suasion
23. The result of the balance of trade deficit will be the __________ of reserves in the economy.	reduction
24. The real money supply is __________ related to price level.	inversely
25. Professor Friedman believes that economic instability results exclusively from the irresponsible __________.	changes in the money supply
26. The reduction in the discount rate ultimately has as its purpose __________.	economic expansion
27. When the reserves of the banking system are increased by $1 the total money supply eventually increases by the amount equal to __________.	the inverse of the legal reserve ratio
28. The profits made by the Fed accrue to the __________.	government

SHORT ANSWER QUESTIONS FOR REVIEW

	Answer To be covered when testing yourself
29. The __________ banks are required to be members of the Federal Reserve System.	national
30. The basic policy of the Federal Reserve System is to __________ undesirable economic tendencies using monetary tools.	counteract
<u>Determine whether the following statements are true, or false.</u>	
31. The U.S. Federal Reserve System consists of a central Federal Reserve Board and twelve Federal Reserve Banks.	True
32. The Fed extensively uses fiscal policy tools to control inflation.	False
33. The Federal Reserve System's major function is to control the national money supply.	True
34. The Fed's policies are counter cyclical as a rule.	True
35. The Federal Reserve Banks can control the size of their member banks' reserves not the size of demand-deposits.	False
36. A $5 bill is part of the Fed's liabilities.	True
37. Changes in the discount rate represent one of the major monetary policy tools which the Fed uses in order to stabilize the national economy.	True
38. Changes in the legal requirement on the proportion of the total demand-deposits which each member bank has to maintain as a reserve is the monetary policy tool most extensively used by the Federal Reserve Board.	False
39. Open market operations are performed by the Fed approximately once a month.	False
40. When the legal reserve ratio is 20% the rise in the banks' reserves of $1 million will lead to a $5 million increase in total demand-deposits.	True
41. Selling government bonds and securities is an effective way to expand economic activity because it results in money and credit being more readily available.	True

SHORT ANSWER QUESTIONS FOR REVIEW

<u>**Answer**</u>
To be covered when testing yourself

Question	Answer
42. The right of member banks to borrow from the Federal Reserve is automatic.	False
43. The Federal Reserve is in complete control of the inflow of money into the U.S. from abroad.	False
44. Banks do not rely exclusively on the Federal Reserve for borrowed funds.	True

CHAPTER 14

SUPPLY AND DEMAND

Basic Attacks and Strategies for Solving Problems in this Chapter. See pages 478 to 542 for step-by-step solutions to problems.

Markets are institutions that facilitate the process of exchange by providing regularized channels of communication between potential buyers and sellers of commodities. The operation of markets is enormously complicated, and probably beyond the ability of any individual to comprehend completely. Consequently, economists analyze markets using models. The leading model of markets is the supply and demand model.

The purpose of the supply and demand model is to explain how prices and quantities are determined and change in the market. The behavior of buyers is represented by the demand curve. The demand curve is a schedule or equation that shows the quantity buyers are willing and able to buy at each price (or the highest price buyers are willing to pay for any quantity of the product). By the law of demand, the relationship between price and quantity demanded is negative.

Referring to the figure on the following page, measure quantity of the product along the horizontal axis and price along the vertical axis. A demand curve is a negatively sloped line, such as D_0, D_1, or D_2. The demand curve can be interpreted two ways. One, it shows the quantity consumers are willing and able to buy at each price. If price was P_1, consumers would demand Q_1 units. Two, it shows the maximum price consumers will pay for units of the good. Consumers will pay up to P_1 for Q_1 units of the good.

There are, of course, other factors that affect the quantity buyers are willing and able to buy. These factors include buyer income and tastes, the prices of substitute and complement goods and services, price expectations, population trends, and many others. Graphically, any change in these factors that would increase the willingness and ability of buyers to buy can be represented by an outward (or upward or rightward) shift in the demand curve (from D_0 to D_1). This is called an increase in demand, and needs to be distinguished from an increase in quantity demanded, which results from a drop in the price of the product. Opposite changes will shift the demand curve inward (or downward or leftward) (from D_0 to D_2). This is called a decrease in demand, and needs to be distinguished from a decrease in quantity demanded which results from an increase in the price of the product.

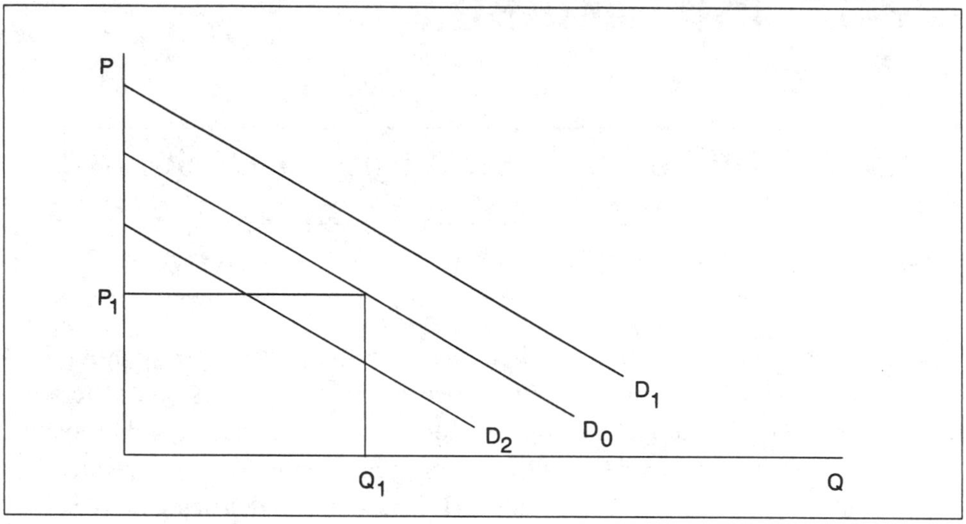

Demand Curves

The supply curve is a schedule or equation that shows the quantity sellers are willing and able to sell at different prices (or the lowest price sellers are willing to accept for any quantity of the product). By the law of supply, the relationship between price and quantity supplied is positive.

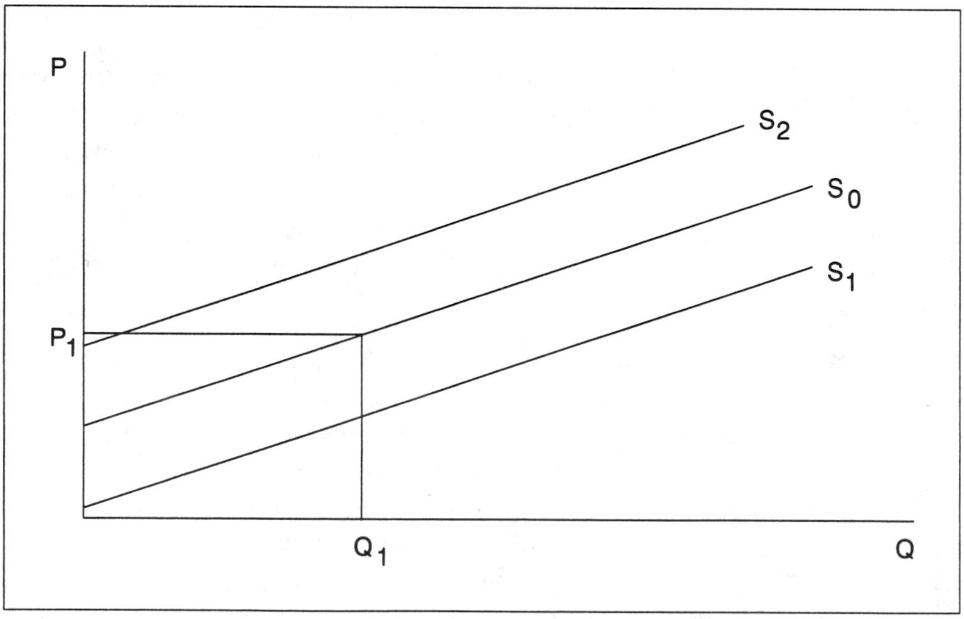

Supply Curves

Graphically, the supply curve is a positively sloped schedule, such as S_0, S_1, or S_2. The supply curve can be interpreted two ways. First, it shows the quantity firms are willing and able to supply at different prices. If the price was P_1, firms would be willing and able to supply Q_1. Second, it shows the minimum price firms would require to supply a given quantity of the good. Q_1 units would not be supplied unless firms could receive a price of at least P_1.

As in the case of demand, there are other factors influencing the willingness and ability of sellers to sell. Some of these factors include technology, resource prices, prices of other goods, price expectations, the number of sellers in the market, and taxes and subsidies. Any change in these factors that increases the willingness and ability of sellers to sell will be represented by an outward (or downward or rightward) shift in the supply curve (from S_0 to S_1). This is called an increase in supply, and needs to be distinguished from an increase in the quantity supplied which occurs when the price of the product rises. An opposite change will cause the supply curve to shift inward (or upward or leftward) (from S_0 to S_2). This is called a decrease in supply, and needs to be distinguished from a decrease in quantity supplied, resulting from a decrease in the price of the product.

The intersection of the demand and supply curves determines the equilibrium price and quantity in the market. In the figure, the equilibrium price is P^* and the equilibrium quantity is Q^*. The word equilibrium is virtually synonymous with stable. The key to understanding the concept is to realize that the intersection of the curves does not necessarily indicate the price the product sells for (market price) and the amount bought and sold (market quantity). The market price and quantity could either be greater or less than the equilibrium levels, but disequilibrium situations are unstable.

Compared to equilibrium, if the price is above equilibrium (for example, at P_1 in the figure), the quantity demanded will be less and the quantity supplied will be greater, causing a surplus of the good. The existence of a surplus will send a signal to sellers that price is "too high," causing them to reduce price and quantity supplied while stimulating a greater quantity demanded. Compared to equilibrium, if the price of the good is below equilibrium (for example, at P_2 in the figure), the quantity demanded will be greater and the quantity supplied less, causing a shortage of the good. The existence of a shortage will send a signal to sellers that the price is "too low," causing them to raise price and quantity supplied while reducing the quantity buyers want to buy. If the price is at equilibrium, the quantity supplied equals the quantity demanded. Since sellers can sell all they want and buyers can buy all they want, there is no reason for the price to change. Therefore, the market is in equilibrium.

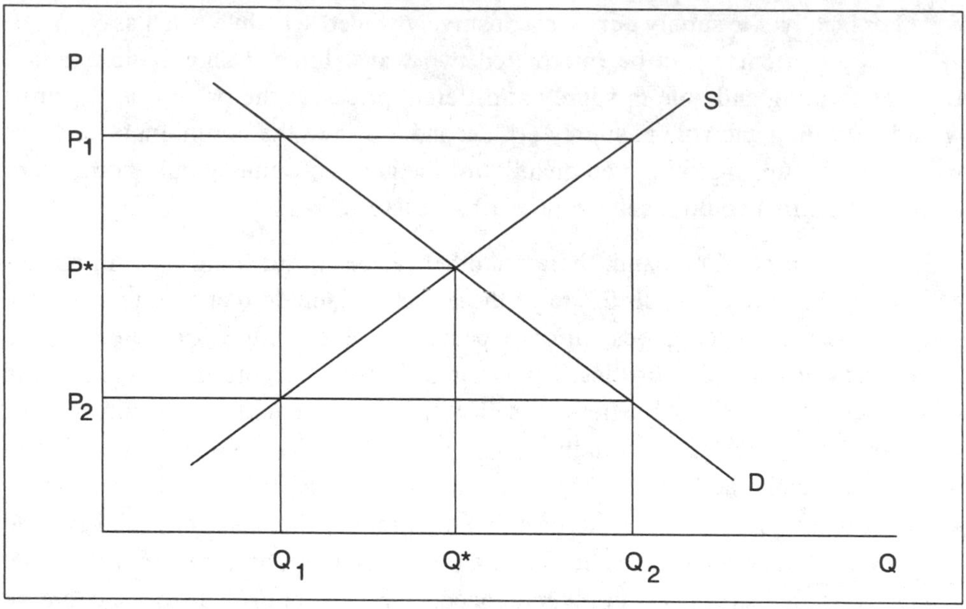

Market Equilibrium

Markets are seldom in equilibrium. The value of the model is that it gives a logical explanation of why prices change. If prices are falling, it must be because there was a surplus in the market. If prices are rising, it must be because there was a shortage in the market.

A common problem is to solve for the equilibrium price and quantity in a market. Let the demand equation be $Q_d = a - b^*P$, where Q_d is quantity demanded, P is price, a is the vertical axis intercept, and $-b$ is the slope of the function. Let the supply equation be $Q_s = c + d^*P$, where Q_s is quantity supplied, c is the vertical axis intercept, and d is the slope of the function. Since quantity supplied equals quantity demanded in equilibrium, it follows that $a - b^*P = c + d^*P$, and you can solve for the equilibrium value of P. In equilibrium, $P = \dfrac{a-c}{b-d}$. Substituting the value for P in either the demand or supply equation will give the equilibrium quantity.

Increases in demand for a product will raise both the equilibrium price and quantity. An increase in demand means buyers are willing and able to buy more and pay a higher price. Sellers will respond by producing and selling more. Decreases in demand do the opposite. Increases in supply will lower equilibrium price and raise equilibrium quantity. An increase in supply means sellers are willing to sell more and accept a lower price. Buyers will buy more at the lower price. Decreases in supply raise equilibrium price and lower equilibrium quantity. A decrease in supply means sellers want to reduce the amount they sell and charge a higher price. Buyers will react to the higher price by buying less.

The equilibrium price in a market is not necessarily the "best" price in the sense of being "fair." In some markets, prices may be higher than society considers desirable. In other markets, prices may be lower than society considers desirable. Throughout history, societies have reacted to "problem prices" by enacting price controls. A price floor is a rule that specifies that the price of a product cannot fall below some level. A price ceiling is a rule that specifies that a price cannot rise above a certain level. The supply and demand model can be used to analyze the impact of these rules.

If a price floor is set above the equilibrium level, one consequence will be a surplus of the good as quantity supplied exceeds, and quantity demanded is less than, the equilibrium level. If a price ceiling is set below the equilibrium level, a consequence will be a shortage of the good, as quantity supplied is reduced below, and quantity demanded increased above, the equilibrium level. Price controls may keep prices from their equilibrium levels, but there can be undesirable side-effects. The worth of price controls cannot be determined scientifically, but an evaluation of them cannot ignore the side-effects and whether the ultimate goals of the price controls can be achieved by other means.

Step-by-Step Solutions to Problems in this Chapter, "Supply and Demand"

DEFINITION

• PROBLEM 14-1

Define "Market", "Supply", and "Demand", and explain their connections.

Solution: Markets are institutions that facilitate the process of exchange by providing regularized channels of communication between potential buyers and potential sellers of commodities. Despite their diversity, certain basic economic principles apply to all of them. The law of supply and demand is a proposition predicting how individuals tend to behave in response to changes in their economic environment. If individual suppliers tend to be willing to sell more of a commodity as its price increases, and if individual buyers tend to be willing to purchase more of a commodity as its price falls, then all transactions taking place in a market will tend to be carried out at a particular, determinate price, which is a price such that the quantity of the commodity buyers wish to purchase exactly equals the quantity which suppliers are willing to sell. Consider the following illustration on the next page.

Suppose that the good we are interested in is beef. The table gives hypothetical data on the quantity of beef per week which suppliers would tend to bring to market and consumers would tend to purchase at various possible prices. The data are in the form of what we call supply and demand schedules (column 2 is the supply schedule and column 3 the demand schedule.) From column 3, we see that consumers tend to buy more beef when its current market price is low. Column 2 indicates that suppliers tend to be willing to sell more when the current market price rises, and this also seems to agree with our everyday experience that the greater the incentive offered, the greater the response.

An Illustration of Supply and Demand

Supply and Demand Schedules for Beef.

(1) Price of Beef	(2) Quantity Supplied (Millions of lbs/week)	(3) Quantity Demanded (millions of lbs/week)	(4) Excess Supply	Excess Demand
1. $1.50	650	200	450	--
2. 1.40	600	240	360	--
3. 1.30	550	280	270	--
4. 1.20	500	320	180	--
5. 1.10	450	360	90	--
6. 1.00	400	400	--	--
7. .90	350	440	--	90
8. .80	300	480	--	150
9. .70	250	520	--	270
10. .60	200	560	--	360
11. .50	150	600	--	450

THE DEMAND CURVE

• PROBLEM 14-2

What is meant by "demand" and what is a "demand curve"?

Solution: "Demand" refers to the relationship between the quantity of a good that an individual or group desires and is able to buy at a particular time, and the price per unit of the good, factors other than price being equal. The desire to buy is not by itself sufficient to constitute demand: it must be accompanied by sufficient purchasing power.

The demand relationship can be viewed in either of two ways. It can be viewed as specifying the maximum quantity of a good that an individual or group desires and is able to purchase at a given price. Or, alternatively, it can be viewed as specifying the maximum price per unit that an individual or group of individuals is willing and able to pay for a given quantity of a good.

A "demand curve" is a graphic representation of this relationship between the quantity of a good demanded and the price of the good (other factors remaining constant). For example, let the following schedule represent Smith's demand for shirts on October 1, 1979:

Price	$25	$22	$20	$18	$15	$12	$11	$9	$6
Quantity Demanded	0	1	2	3	4	5	6	7	8

This information can be represented in graphic form as a demand curve or schedule as follows (it is customary to designate the vertical axis to measure price and the horizontal axis to measure quantity):

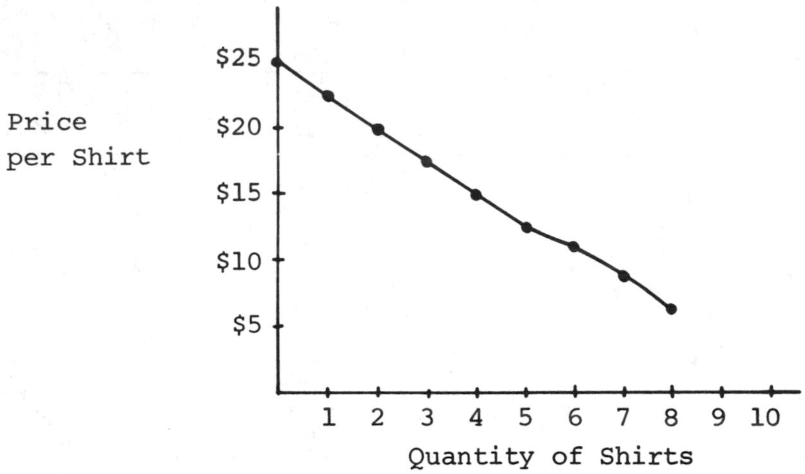

Here we have Smith's demand curve for shirts on October 1, 1979.

• PROBLEM 14-3

Define the term "demand" in economics. Give an example to illustrate demand.

Solution: Demand is defined as a schedule which shows the various amounts of a product which consumers are willing and able to purchase at each specific price in a set of possible prices during some specified period of time. Note the phrase, "willing and able", because willingness alone is not effective in the market. One may be willing to buy a Mercedes-Benz, but if this willingness is not backed by the ability to buy, that is, by the necessary dollars, it will not be effective and, therefore will not be reflected in the market.

Figure 1 represents hypothetical data for an individual buyer's demand for corn.

Figure 1

Price per bushel	Quantity demanded per week
$5	10
4	20
3	35
2	55
1	80

The demand schedule in and of itself does not indicate which of the five possible prices will actually exist in the corn market. This depends on both demand and supply. Demand is simply a tabular statement of a buyer's plans, or intentions, with respect to the purchase of a product.

It is important to note that to be meaningful, the quantities demanded at each price must relate to some specific time period--a day, a week, a month, and so forth. The phrase "a consumer will buy 10 bushels of corn at $5 per bushel" is vague and meaningless. The phrase " a consumer will buy 10 bushels of corn per week at $5 per bushel," however, is clear and very meaningful.

• PROBLEM 14-4

In constructing demand and marginal revenue curves, it is often convenient to start off with a downward-sloping straight line to represent demand. We then draw a straight line for marginal revenue (MR) such as drawn in figure 1.

a) Show that if demand is linear, marginal revenue is linear

b) Show that if demand is linear with slope-b and y-intercept a, marginal revenue has slope -2b and y-intercept a.

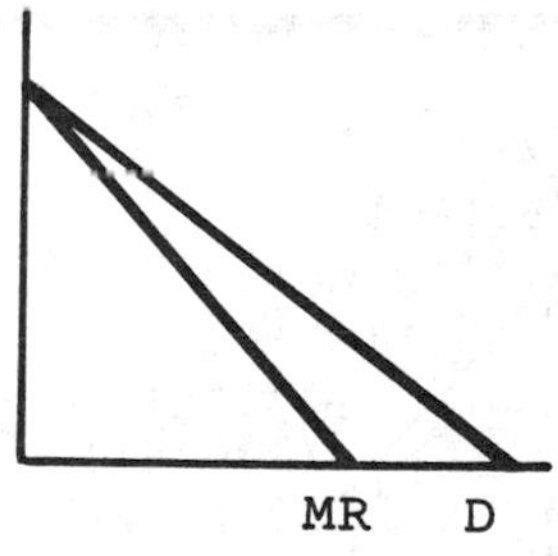

Fig. 1

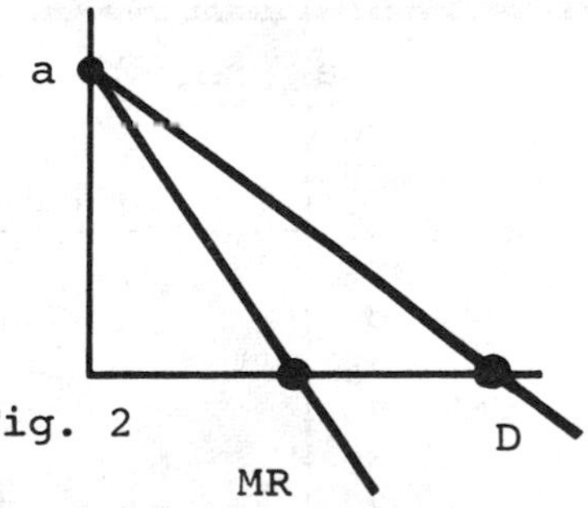

Fig. 2

Solution: (a) To solve this problem, begin by using the function $P = a - bQ$ to represent a linear demand function. Since total revenue (TR) $= P \cdot Q$, we get $TR = (a - bQ)(Q)$ or multiplying through, $TR = aQ - bQ^2$. The next step is to find MR in terms of TR. Since $TR = f(Q)$ and $MR = \Delta TR/\Delta Q$, then $MR = d(TR)/dQ$, that is, the marginal revenue function is the derivative of the total revenue function with respect to the quantity produced mathematically, this is

$d(aQ - bQ^2)/dQ = a - 2bQ$. Thus when the demand curve is assumed linear, $MR = a - 2bQ$, and a and b are constants (because in the original definition of a linear demand, $P = a - bQ$, where a and b were both constants), then MR is linear.

(b) Part (a) above shows that if demand is defined by $P = a - bQ$, then MR has the function $MR = a - 2bQ$. To determine the vertical axis value for both MR and Demand, find their value when $Q = 0$. In both cases, the vertical-axis intercept occurs at a. The slope of either D or MR can be determined by its derivative. The slope of demand $= \frac{d(\text{Demand})}{dQ} = -b$ and the slope of $MR = \frac{dMR}{dQ} = -2b$, i.e., slope of MR = two times slope of demand. When constructing these curves, both should originate at the same point on the vertical axis, with MR falling twice as fast as demand, that is, MR should intersect the quantity-axis at a point halfway between the origin and the intersection of demand with the quantity axis, as shown in figure 2.

• PROBLEM 14-5

Given the demand schedule in Figure 1 for cream soda in Sioux City, construct the demand curve.

Figure 1

Price per quart	Quarts purchased per day
$0.70	80,000
0.65	90,000
0.60	100,000
0.55	110,000
0.50	120,000
0.45	130,000
0.40	140,000

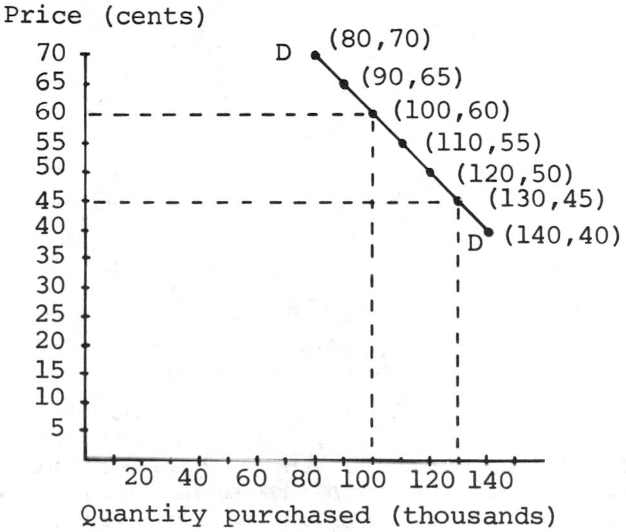

Solution: To construct the graph, first define the axes. The x-axis (the horizontal axis) will represent quarts purchased per day. The y-axis (the vertical axis) will represent price per quart. Second, plot points as shown in figure 2.

• PROBLEM 14-6

The demand schedules of Smith, Jones and Green for wool suits during the week of September 4, 1979 are shown in Figure 1.

Figure 1

Smith	Price	$201	$200	$150	$100	$75	$50	$40		
	Quantity	0	1	2	3	4	5	6		
Jones	Price	$351	$350	$300	$250	$200	$175	$150	$125	$75	$40
	Quantity	0	1	2	3	4	5	6	7	8	8
Green	Price	$151	$150	$100	$75	$50	$40			
	Quantity	0	1	1	2	3	4			

Construct the total demand schedule for Smith, Jones and Green and draw their individual demand curves, and their total demand curve for wool suits.

Solution: The total demand schedule for a group of individuals is found by summing the quantities demanded by each of the individuals at each price. Thus, for example, at a price of $150 per suit, Smith demands 2 suits, Jones demands 6 suits, and Green demands 1 suit. So the total quantity demanded by the three of them at a price of $150 is 9. The table in Figure 2 shows their individual and total demand schedules.

Let us consider how some of the entries in the table above were arrived at, for example, the zeros in Smith's column at prices above the price of $200 and in Green's column above the price of $150. Although these zeros do not appear explicitly in the individual demand schedules of Smith and Green, they are implied by the entries Price = $201, Quantity = 0, and Price = $151, Quantity = 0 in Smith and Green's respective demand schedules. This is true because we know that a demand schedule shows the maximum price that an individual will pay for a given quantity of a good. Hence, we know that at a price of $201 or more, Smith will demand no suits, and at a price of $151 or more, Green will demand no suits.

Similarly, no explicit entry is made in Smith's demand schedule at a price of $175. But we know from the information given in his demand schedule that, while he will buy one suit at a price of up to (and including) $200, he will not buy two suits unless the price is as low as $150. Thus, at any price between $150 and $200, Smith demands only one suit.

Jones' demand schedule shows no entry at a price of $50. But from the fact that Jones demands 8 suits at a price of $75, and still demands only 8 suits at a price of $40, it can be inferred that at $50 he would also demand just eight suits.

Figure 2

Price	Quantity Demanded by Smith	by Jones	by Green	Total
$351	0	0	0	0
$350	0	1	0	1
$300	0	2	0	2
$250	0	3	0	3
$200	1	4	0	5
$175	1	5	0	6
$150	2	6	1	9
$125	2	7	1	10
$100	3	7	1	11
75	4	8	2	14
50	5	8	3	16
40	6	8	4	18

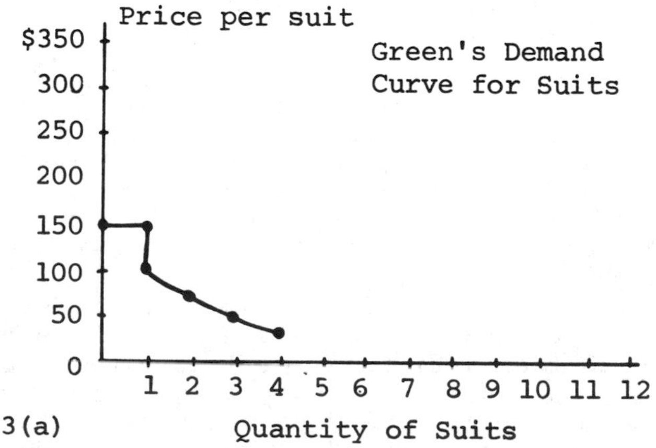

Fig. 3(a)

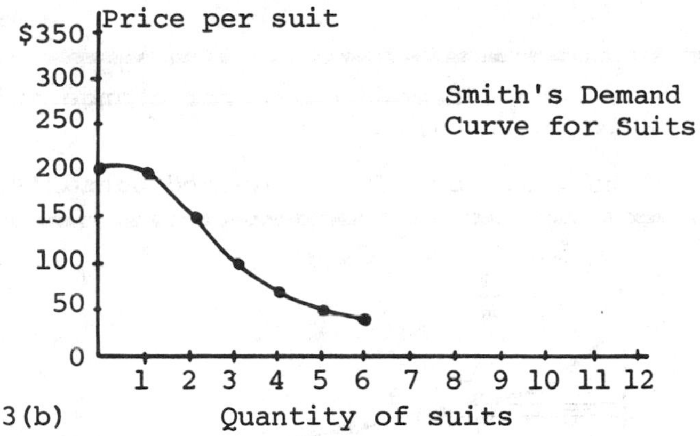

Fig. 3(b)

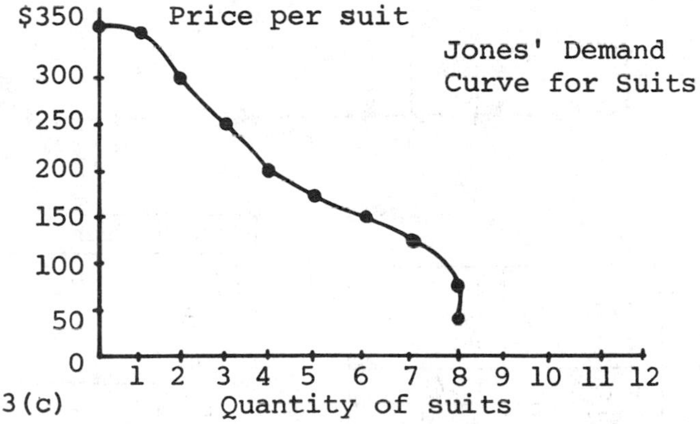

Fig. 3(c)

We can draw the individual demand curves of Smith, Jones and Green by plotting the price-quantity combinations given by their respective demand schedules on a graph, with the vertical axis representing price and the horizontal axis representing quantity, as shown in Figure 3.

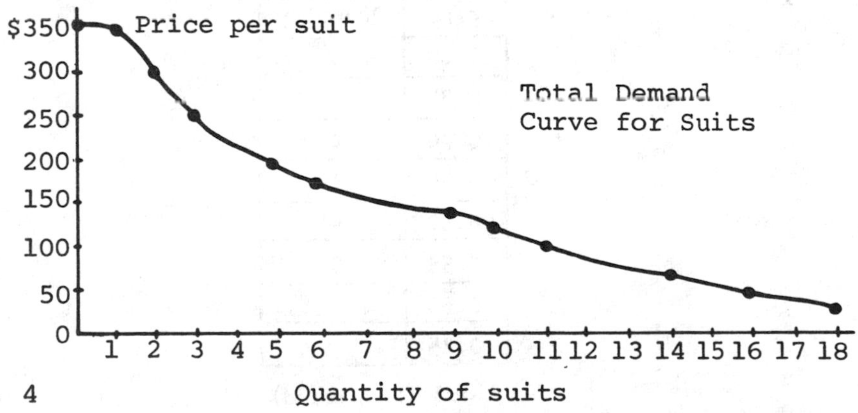

Fig. 4

The total demand curve of Smith, Jones and Green for wool suits is the "horizontal sum" of their individual demand curves. It is also a graph of the total demand schedule (Figure 2). Figure 4 shows the total demand curve for wool suits of Smith, Jones and Green.

• **PROBLEM 14-7**

Figure 1 shows John's demand curve for orange juice (measured in quarts per week).

Use Figure 2 to write out John's demand schedule.

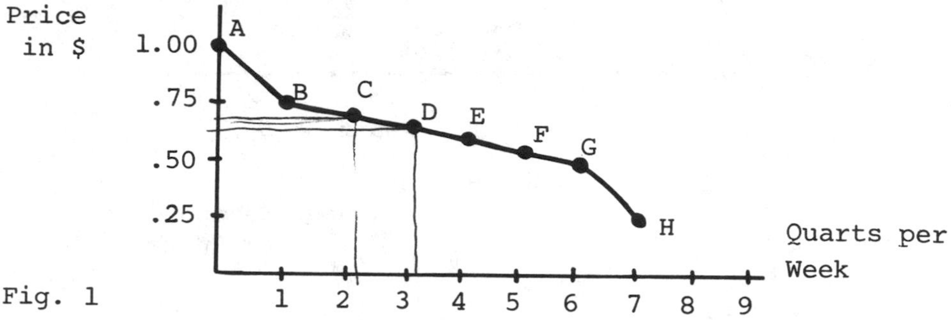

Fig. 1

	Price($)	Quantity quarts per week
A	1.00	0
B	.75	1
C	.70	2+
D	.65	3+

Price	Quantity
1.00	0
.75	1
.70	2
.65	3
.60	4
.55	5
.50	6
.25	7

FIG. 2

Price	Quantity
1.00	0
0.75	1
0.70	2
0.65	3
0.60	4
0.55	5
0.50	6
0.25	7

Fig.2 (completed)

Solution: John's demand curve for orange juice shows the quantity of orange juice that he will buy over the given range of prices. Since the demand curve is a graphical representation of the demand schedule, Figure 2 may be filled in by reading points A through H off the graph. That is, the coordinates of point A are P = 1.00 and Q = 0: of point B, P = .75 and Q = 1; of point C, P = 0.70, Q = 2; of point D, P = 0.65, Q = 3; of point E, P = 0.60, Q = 4; of point F, P = 0.55, Q = 5; of point G, P = .50, Q =6; and of point H, P = .25 and Q = 7. Figure 2 shows the demand schedule with these values written in,

Price	Quantity
1.00	0
0.75	1
0.70	2
0.65	3
0.60	4
0.55	5
0.50	6
0.25	7

• PROBLEM 14-8

The accompanying figure represents the demand for widgets.

(1) If the price of widgets was $4, how many widgets would people buy?

(2) Why wouldn't they buy 60?

(3) Given that 50 widgets were sold last week, what was the price?

(4) Why wouldn't the price have been $6?

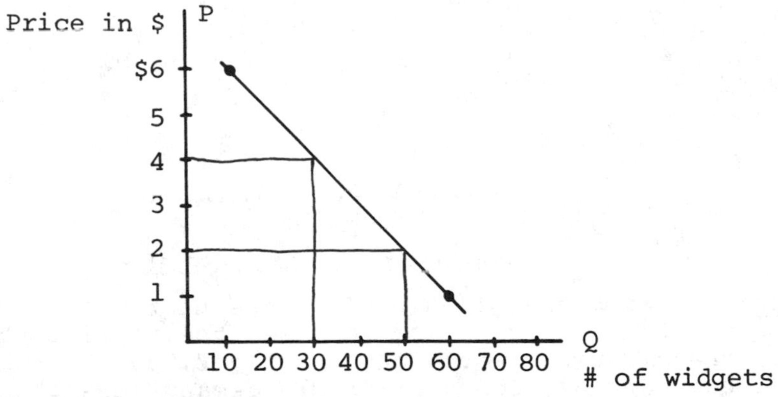

Solution: A demand curve is defined as the relationship between price and quantity demanded. In this case, the graph shows how many widgets people will buy at any given price.

(1) According to the graph, the value of Q that is associated with P = 4 is 30. Thus, people will buy 30 widgets when the price is $4.

(2) The point Q = 60 and P = 4 is located off the demand curve. The graph indicates that there is a demand for only 30 widgets when the price of each widget is $4. In order for people to demand 60 widgets, the price would have to

be $1. That is, 30 more widgets could be sold if the price was lowered by $3 (per widget).

(3) Since the graph shows the relationship between price and quantity demanded, specifying the quantity demanded will indicate the price offered for that quantity. The graph shows that the price associated with a quantity demanded of 50 is $2.

(4) The point Q = 60 and P = 6 is not located on the demand curve. If the price were $6, only 10 widgets would be sold.

• PROBLEM 14-9

The accompanying graph represents the consumers' demand for freshly caught fish.

(1) On Monday, the fishermen caught 2,000 lbs. of fish. If they want to sell their entire catch, at which price must they sell their fish?

(2) If on Tuesday they caught 4,000 lbs. of fish, what price should they charge to sell the entire catch?

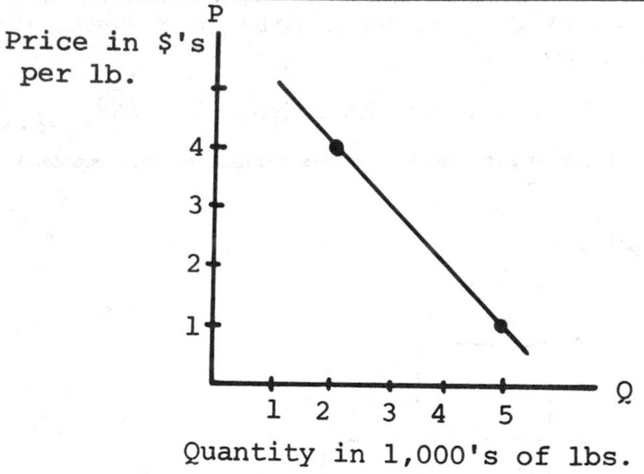

Solution: 1) From the graph one can see that when Q = 2,000, P = 4. Therefore, if the fishermen set their price at $4 per lb., the consumers would buy exactly 2,000 lbs. At any price higher than $4, consumers would demand less than 2,000 lbs. At any lower price, they would demand more than 2,000 lbs.

In order to sell all 2,000 lbs. the fishermen should charge at most $4 per pound.

2) From the graph, when Q = 4,000, P = $2. On Tuesday, they should charge at most $2 in order to sell all their fish.

• PROBLEM 14-10

Mrs. White is buying trees to landscape her family's new

residence. The accompanying demand schedule characterizes her behavior as a buyer.

Price of Trees	Quantity Demanded
$10	1
9	2
8	3
7	4
6	5
5	6
4	7
3	8
2	9
1	10

The price is quoted at $6. Accordingly, she buys five trees. Then, after she buys the five trees, the seller offers her one more for $5.

a) Does she take it?

b) Suppose the seller offers her an opportunity to buy more trees (after she has already agreed to purchase five at $6 each and one more for $5) at the price of $3. How many more does she buy?

c) If the price had been $3 initially, would she have bought more than eight trees?

d) Suppose she has to pay a membership fee of $5 to buy at this nursery, after which she could buy all the trees she wanted for her garden at $3 each. How many would she buy? (Assume price at other nurseries is $4, with no membership fee.)

e) If she could buy trees at $3 each from some other store without a membership fee, would she still buy only eight trees, saving the $5 for use on all her other consumption activities?

f) Explain why, according to the demand schedule, her purchase of eight trees at $3 each, at a total cost of $24, is a consistent alternative to her purchase of eight trees under the former sequential offers, in which she pays a total of $41 (five at $6, one at $5, and two at $3).

<u>Solution</u>: a) Mrs. White has bought 5 trees at $6 each, in accordance with her demand schedule. When the sixth tree is offered at $5, she takes it also.

b) Since she has already agreed to purchase five at $6 each and one more for $5, she will buy two more, for a total of eight trees.

c) If the price had been $3 initially, she wouldn't have bought more than eight trees. Remember, the eighth tree is worth at most $3. What she paid for "earlier" trees is irrelevant except insofar as it affects her remaining income and thus her demand for everything else. But this effect is spread over all purchases, and we assume it is a trivial amount compared to her total income.

d) As per her demand schedule, Mrs. White will buy 8 trees because her total cost here would be $5 membership fee plus $24 (cost of trees) = $29. The other alternative has a total cost amounting to $32 (cost of 8 trees at $4 each), despite the fact that it has no membership fee cost.

e) Yes, she would still buy only eight trees.

f) According to the demand schedule, her purchase of eight trees at $3 each, at a total cost of $24, is a consistent alternative to her purchase of eight trees in which she pays a total of $41 (five at $6, one at $5, and two at $3). Marginal price is the same under each circumstance, and the price of extra units is adjusted to.

• PROBLEM 14-11

What are some of the major determinants of the demand for a good?

Solution: Some of the major determinants of the demand for a good are:

(1) tastes of consumers,

(2) the number of potential buyers and their incomes,

(3) the prices of substitute and complementary goods, and,

(4) consumer expectations of future prices and their future incomes.

Demand has been defined as desire plus ability to buy. Consumer tastes determine their desires to buy various goods. The greater their taste for a good, the more they will buy at a given price, or the higher the price they are willing to pay for a given quantity.

Similarly, with given tastes for a good, the quantity that consumers demand at a given price is generally greater, the greater their incomes.

The prices of other goods in the market also affect the demand for any good. Relatively low prices for goods which are regarded as close substitutes for the goods under consideration (e.g., margarine for butter) mean less demand for that good, whereas relatively high prices for substitutes mean more demand for it. Prices of complementary goods, i.e., goods that are often consumed in conjunction with the good in question (e.g., bread and butter) have a different effect. A relatively high price for complementary goods means less demand for the good in question, while relatively low prices mean a greater demand for it.

Finally, consumers' expectations of their future incomes and of future prices affect their current demands for goods. If consumers expect to have greater incomes in the future than they have presently, they will tend to demand greater quantities of at least some goods than if they expected their incomes to remain the same. And, of course, they will demand less if they expect their incomes to fall. Also, expectations of a higher price in the future will stimulate a greater present demand for a good than there would be if its price were expected to remain at its current height. And, naturally, expectations of a lower price in the future will cause buyers to delay some of their purchases and thus reduce current demand.

THE LAW OF DEMAND

• PROBLEM 14-12

What is the Law of Demand?

Solution: The Law of Demand states that the quantity of a good demanded by an individual or group is greater (less) the lower (higher) the per unit price of the good, other things being equal. Alternatively expressed, it states that the maximum per unit price at which an individual or group member is willing and able to buy a given quantity of a good is greater (less) the smaller (larger) the quantity of that good, other factors remaining the same.

The Law of Demand, then, asserts that there is an "inverse" or "negative" relationship between the price of a good and the quantity of it demanded by an individual or group. That is, as one variable increases, the other decreases.

• PROBLEM 14-13

Graphically, why does the demand curve, which represents all price and quantity demanded possibilities, slope downward and to the right?

Solution: The demand curve slopes downward and to the right because there is an inverse relationship between price and the quantity demanded. The law of demand, which states that people buy more of any good at a lower price than they do at a higher price, is reflected in the downward slope of the demand curve.

Graphically, the downward sloping demand curve can

be shown as in the figure.

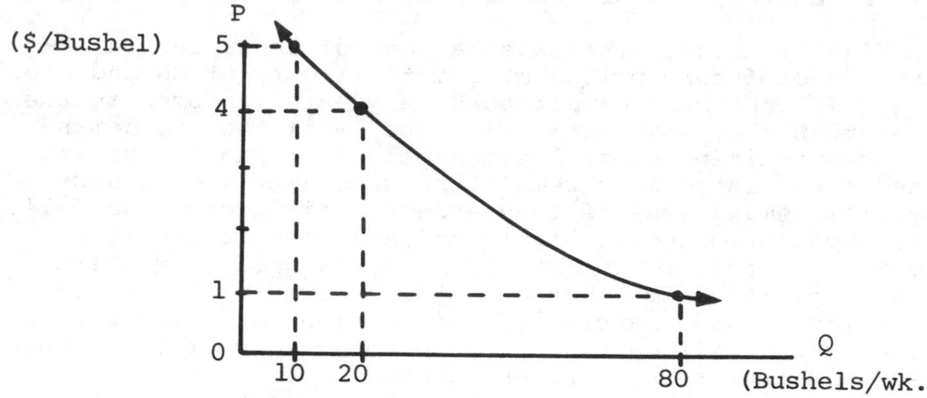

As can be seen in the figure, the quantity demanded at a price of $5 would be 10 bushels per week. If the price is reduced to $4, the quantity demanded will increase to 20 bushels. At a price of $1, people are able and willing to buy 80 bushels per week.

• PROBLEM 14-14

What would be implied about the relationship between prices and quantity demanded, if a demand curve sloped upward and to the right? Might this situation normally be expected to occur?

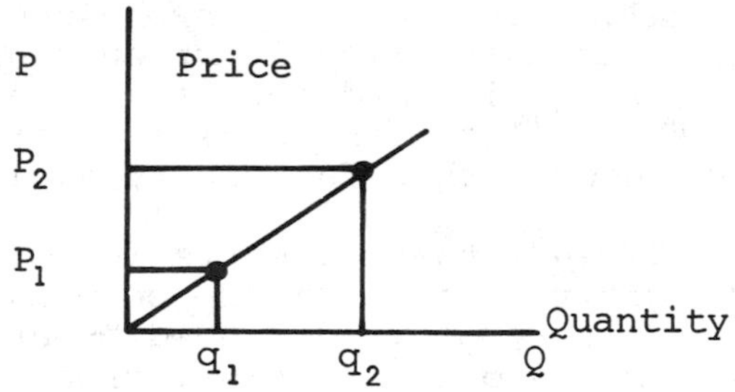

Solution: Graphically, a demand curve that slopes upward and to the right can be drawn as in the figure. This would imply that increases in price would always cause increases in the quantity demanded. That is, this implies a direct relationship between price and quantity demanded.

In general, economists assume that people do not act in this manner. For example, suppose that the price of one brand of dishwashing detergent doubled. Generally, consumers would not buy more of this product at the higher price. In fact, it would be expected that they would substitute other brands for the more expensive brand, and that the quantity demanded of the more expensive brand, and hence its sales, would decrease. Even if this particular brand were the only dishwashing detergent available, we would still expect consumers to use less of the product as it became more expensive. In either case, consumers would not be expected to increase the quantity of a product they demand if it becomes more expensive. Therefore, it would not normally be expected that a demand curve sloping upward would occur.

There are, however, a few examples of this sort of curve. Suppose a certain good has "snob appeal", that is, people buy it precisely because it is expensive. If this good's price were to fall, it would lose its "snob-appeal" and sales might decline. For example, suppose Mr. Jones wants to buy a Cadillac for the sole purpose of impressing people with the fact that he can afford its $20,000 price tag. Now, suppose that the price of Cadillacs was to fall to some point below the price of Pintos, and that this drop in price was widely advertised. It is very likely that Mr. Jones would no longer want to buy a Cadillac since the "snob-appeal" of the $20,000 price tag has been removed. Examples such as this however, are fairly rare, making it safe to assume that, in general, demand curves slope down and to the right.

DEMAND VS. QUANTITY DEMANDED

• PROBLEM 14-15

What is the difference between an increase in demand and an increase in the quantity demanded?

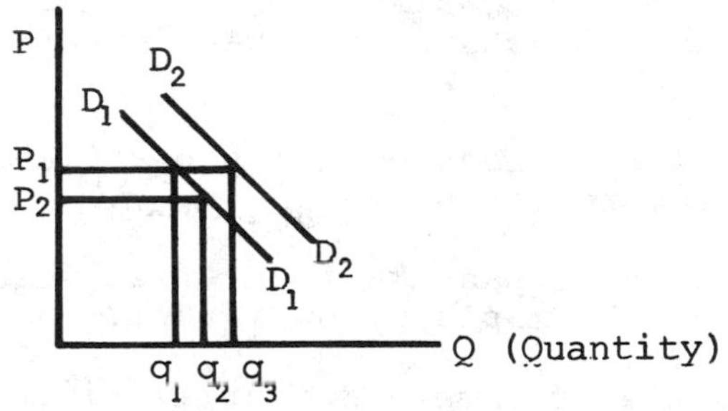

Fig. 1

Solution: An increase in quantity demanded is caused by a reduction in price. It involves movement along the demand curve. In the figure, using D_1D_1 as the demand curve, as price decreases from p_1 to p_2, quantity demanded increases from q_1 to q_2. The demand curve itself is unchanged, but a change in price has caused a change in the quantity demanded.

An increase in demand involves an actual shift of the entire demand curve to the right. At each price, a greater quantity is demanded than was previously demanded. It can be seen in the figure that along D_1D_1, at p_1, the quantity demanded is q_1. But if demand increases to D_2D_2, at p_1, the quantity demanded increases to q_3.

• PROBLEM 14-16

What is the difference between a change in demand and a change in quantity demanded?

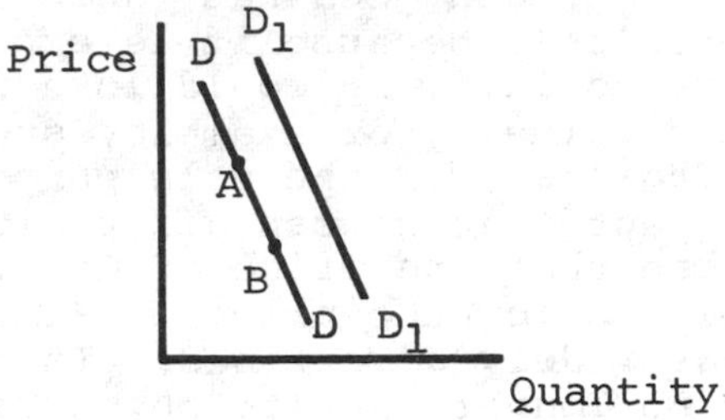

Solution: A change in demand means that one or more of the determinants of demand has changed, resulting in an entirely new demand curve. A change in quantity demanded means that none of the determinants of demand has changed. Change occurs only within the original demand curve.

On the accompanying graph a shift from DD to D_1D_1 represents a change in demand, while movement from point A to point B represents a change in quantity demanded.

• PROBLEM 14-17

In each of the following situations, indicate whether a change in demand or a change in quantity demanded is taking place:

a) The price of lettuce falls by 5¢ a head and consumers purchase more lettuce. quant. demand

b) The price of pancake flour rises drastically. How does this affect the maple syrup market?

c) The price of home heating oil rises. Consequently, thermostats are kept at a lower temperature than previously.

d) A consumer gets a raise and goes shopping at a Mercedes-Benz showroom. demand

Solution: A change in demand occurs when one of the factors underlying demand changes, shifting the entire demand curve. On the other hand, a change in quantity demanded occurs if there is a change only in price, the change being represented by movement along the demand curve.

a) In this case, the price of lettuce falls so quantity demanded increases. Thus this situation represents a change in quantity demanded.

b) Here, a change in the price of flour is affecting

the demand for a complementary good, maple syrup. At a higher price for flour, consumers will purchase less flour for making pancakes. Consequently, with fewer pancakes, consumers are less eager to buy maple syrup; i.e., at each possible price, they are not willing to buy as much as previously. Thus, the demand for syrup decreases, i.e., the entire demand curve for maple syrup is shifted to the left. Thus, the effect of a change in the quantity demanded of flour (due to the higher price), is a change in demand for maple syrup. Graphically, movement along the flour demand curve from P_0Q_0 to P_1Q_1 causes a shift of the maple syrup demand curve from D_0D_0 to D_1D_1:

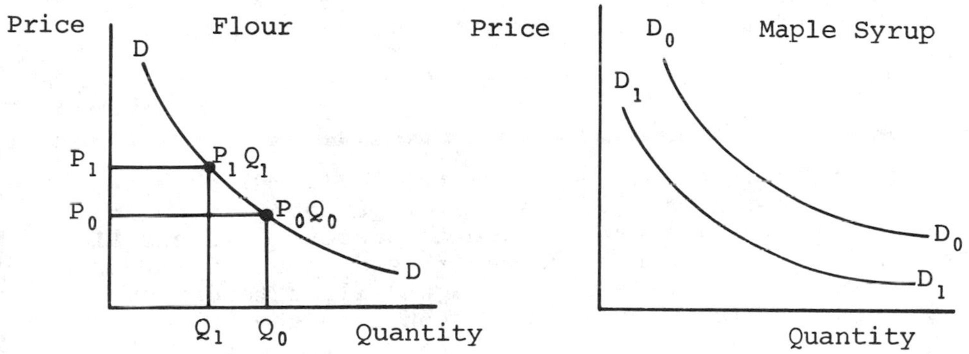

(c) Here again, price changes and quantity demanded changes as a consequence, without the demand curve itself shifting. So, as in a), a change in quantity demanded, is what is taking place.

d) Finally, getting a raise represents a change in income. The rise in income will cause one's demand for certain products to increase, i.e., for one's demand curve to shift to the right. The now wealthier consumer is willing to buy a greater quantity than previously (probably one compared to none in this case), at the same price. Therefore, there is a change in demand for Mercedes-Benz'.

• PROBLEM 14-18

Sandy went to a sporting goods store to buy a can of tennis balls. When she got there, she discovered that tennis balls were 50¢ per can less than she had thought they would be. She bought two cans instead of one. Had Sandy's demand for tennis balls changed?

Solution: When economists speak about demand, they are generally referring to a demand schedule or a demand curve. Quantity normally refers to quantity demanded (or quantity supplied, when dealing with supply curves).

In this case, the question asks, "Has Sandy's demand curve shifted?" The demand curve is defined as the relationship between price and quantity demanded. It is determined by such things as the consumer's tastes, income, the price of goods which could be substituted for the good being analyzed, and the consumer's expectations about the future price and availability of the good.

In this question, Sandy's tastes have not changed. Her income hasn't been increased or decreased. Nothing was said about the price of any substitute for tennis balls. Nothing has been mentioned which should cause Sandy to suspect a decrease in the availability of tennis balls in the future. Therefore, since none of the factors involved in the determination of Sandy's demand for tennis balls have changed, Sandy's demand has not changed. In this case, the quantity demanded has changed due to a change in (the expected) price. This is an example of movement along the demand curve, not of a shift in the demand curve.

• PROBLEM 14-19

The Lincoln Theatre had been showing old films for two months. Admission was $2.00 and average daily attendance was 200. Then, the owner decided to present a recent blockbuster film. Admission price was raised to $4.00 to cover the cost of the new film and average daily attendance rose to 600. Does this example cast doubt upon the law of demand?

Solution: The law of demand states that as price increases, quantity demanded decreases. At the Lincoln Theatre, quantity demanded increased as the price of admission rose. At first glance, it might be thought that this would imply an upward-sloping demand curve. But in actuality, two separate demand curves are necessary in order to accurately represent the situation, as a single commodity is not being offered throughout the example. At first, old films are shown; then new blockbuster films are shown. Hence, as it is clear that two distinct demand curves are needed, the law of demand remains intact.

• PROBLEM 14-20

Sam owns a fresh vegetable stand. Last week he decided to raise his carrot prices from 59¢ per bunch to 69¢ per bunch. Subsequently, Sam noticed that several of his regular customers were buying 2 bunches instead of their usual one. In fact, his carrot sales had gone up appreciably. When he finally asked one of his customers why she was buying so many carrots, she replied, "My neighbor told me that you had recently raised your price because carrots were in short supply, and that I ought to stock up before you ran out." Does this contradict the law of demand? Why or why not?

Solution: The question states that by raising his price from 59¢ to 69¢, Sam increased the quantity demanded by his customers. The law of demand states that when the price of a good is raised (and at the same time all other factors are kept constant), the quantity demanded will decrease.

At first glance, the described situation would seem to contradict the law of demand. However, the important thing to notice is that all other factors have not remained constant. Sam's customers' demand for carrots has changed, shifting their demand curve. The original demand was for carrots for current consumption, as the customers operated under the belief that they would be able to purchase carrots for future consumption. The demand increased when it became their demand for both current and future carrot consumption. That is, their demand had changed from "carrots for dinner tonight" to "carrots for dinner tonight" plus "carrots to save for future dinners." This problem is an example of a shift in a demand curve, rather than an illustration of movement along that curve, and hence does not violate the law of demand.

• PROBLEM 14-21

The community demand for a particular product (e.g., wheat) in the vicinity of the market price of $2.00 per bushel is shown in the accompanying table. (Conventionally, wheat prices are expressed to the nearest eighth of a cent per bushel.)

Demand Function

Price	Quantity
$2.01	9,986,000
2.00 7/8	9,987,000
2.00 6/8	9,988,000
2.00 5/8	9,990,000
2.00 4/8	9,992,000
2.00 3/8	9,994,000
2.00 2/8	9,996,000
2.00 1/8	9,998,000
2.00	10,000,000
1.99 7/8	10,002,000

With 1,000 bushels, could an individual seller affect the market price by withholding all of his supply from the market?

Solution: This question is designed to illustrate the demand situation facing an individual seller in a price-takers' market, in which each seller in the market provides such a small portion of the total market supply that he could not affect the price by offering to sell either more or less of his product. Neither would his actions significantly affect any other seller's situation. Applying this principle to the problem, 1,000 bushels is very small compared to the total market supply. Therefore, the price cannot be affected by withholding 1,000 stocks of wheat. The best price that one could get is the market price of

$2.00, whether 1 or 1,000 bushels are sold. It is important to note also that this price-takers' market is the so-called perfectly competitive market.

• PROBLEM 14-22

What is a derived demand?

Solution: This is a demand which is derived from the demand for a final product which is being produced. Labor is a case in point. The demand for labor could not exist outside of the demand for the products which this labor is helping to produce. Therefore the demand for labor is a derived demand.

• PROBLEM 14-23

What is a demand schedule, a supply schedule, and market price?

Solution: A demand schedule is a listing of the quantities of a good a consumer is willing to buy and the corresponding prices he will pay for each quantity. A supply schedule is a listing of the quantities of a good a producer is willing to offer and the corresponding prices he will charge for each quantity. Market price is the price at which the quantity demanded (from the demand schedule) is equal to the quantity supplied (from the supply schedule).

• PROBLEM 14-24

In the table below, column 1 gives the price per ton of coal. Column 2 shows the amount of coal, in tons, which coal companies are willing to supply per year at each price ("Supply"). Column 3 shows the amount which consumers will buy per year in tons, at each price. ("Demand"). Illustrate graphically the relationships between price and supply and between price and demand. Are the relationships direct or inverse?

Price (per ton)	Tons Supplied	Tons Demanded
$ 10	1,000	10,000
20	2,000	8,000
30	3,000	6,000
40	4,000	4,000
50	5,000	2,000

Solution: To draw the graph, first construct two perpendicular lines, or "axes", one labelled "P" for price and the other labelled "Q" for quantity. By convention, the vertical axis is the "P" axis and the horizontal axis is the "Q" axis. The point at which the two axes intersect is called the "origin". It represents both zero price and zero quantity, and is therefore labelled "0".

Since the price data from column 1 of the table range from $10 to $50, five equal divisions are marked off on the "P" axis. The points of division are labelled with each price, increasing from bottom to top.

Columns 2 and 3 contain quantity data ranging from 1,000 to 10,000 tons. The "Q" axis is therefore divided into ten equal segments, and the points of division are labelled accordingly.

The correct construction and labelling of the axes is illustrated in figure 1:

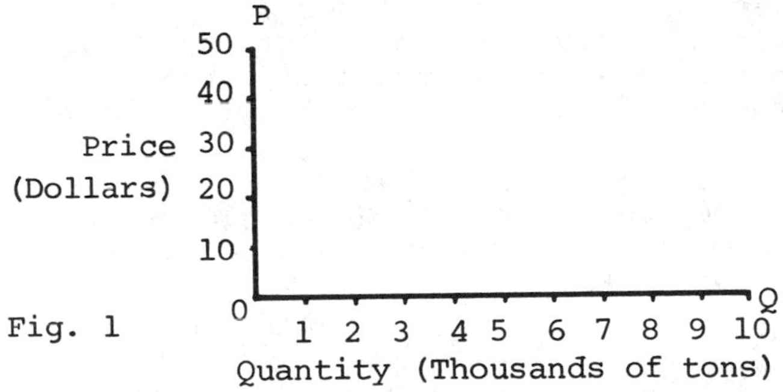

Fig. 1

To graph the relationship between price and supply, read across from column 1 of the table to column 2, and plot in the space to the right of the "P" axis and above the "Q" axis points which correspond to each price (from column 1) and its associated quantity supplied (from column 2). For example, the first price listed in column 1 is $10. Going across to column 2, the associated quantity supplied is 1,000 tons. This is plotted by going up the "P" axis to the $10 mark, and then going to the right to a point directly above the 1,000 ton mark on the "Q" axis. The same procedure is followed for the remaining prices and their associated quantities supplied ($20, 2,000 tons; $30, 3,000 tons, etc.). when all the points have been plotted, they are joined by a line running through all of them. This line, which is labelled "S", is the supply curve. The correct construction of the supply curve is illustrated in figure 2.

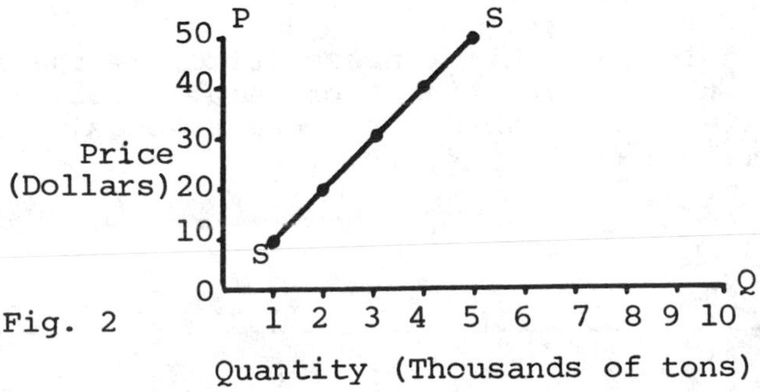

Fig. 2

The demand curve (labelled "D") is drawn by plotting points for each price (from column 1 of the table) and its associated quantity demanded (from column 3), and connecting these points with a line. Figure 3 shows both the demand and supply curves.

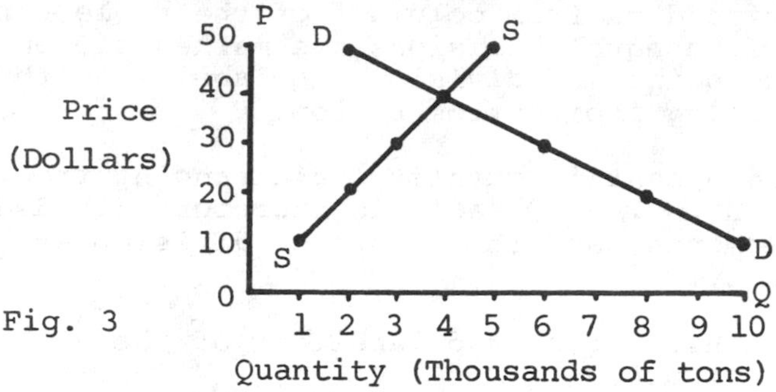

Fig. 3

Note that the supply curve "S" rises as it goes to the right from the origin. This means that for each increase in price there is an increase in the quantity supplied. Price and supply are, therefore, said to be directly related.

Price and demand, on the other hand, are inversely related. This can be seen from the downward slope of the demand curve as it goes to the right from the origin, indicating that as price rises, quantity demanded falls.

THE SUPPLY CURVE

• PROBLEM 14-25

What is meant by the term "supply", and what is a "supply curve"?

Solution: The "supply" of a good refers to the relationship, at a particular time, between the price offered for the good and the quantity of it that sellers are willing to sell. The quantity of a good that an individual or group is willing to sell depends, other factors being equal, on the per unit price of the good. Or, to describe the same relationship in a different way, the minimum per unit price which will induce an individual or some members of the group to sell units of the good depends on the number of units, other factors again being equal.

A supply curve is a graphic representation of the relationship between the (hypothetical) price of a good and the quantity supplied. Let Table 1 represent Jones' supply schedule of watermelons on July 4, 1976:

Table 1

Price	$1	$2	$3	$3.50	$4	$4.50	$5	$5.50	$6	$7	$8	$9
Quantity	0	0	1	2	3	4	5	6	7	8	9	10

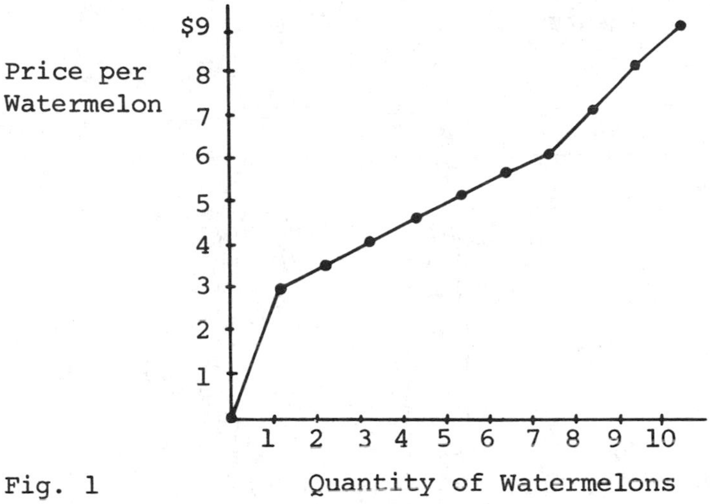

Fig. 1

The information in the table can be presented in graphic form as Jones' supply curve, as shown in Figure 1.

• PROBLEM 14-26

State the law of supply.

Solution: The law of supply states that there is "a direct relationship between price and quantity supplied. As price rises, the corresponding quantity supplied rises, and as price falls, the quantity supplied also falls." In other words, "it simply states that producers are willing to produce and offer for sale more of their product at a high price than they are at a low price."

• PROBLEM 14-27

Given the accompanying supply schedule for milk chocolate bars (Figure 1), construct its supply curve.

Price per bar	Quantity supplied
$0.10	5,000
0.15	15,000
0.20	25,000
0.25	35,000
0.30	45,000

Figure 1

Solution: To construct the graph, first define the axes. Quantity supplied will be on the x-axis, (the horizontal axis), and price per bar will be on the y-axis (the vertical axis). Then plot the points given above, as shown in Figure 2.

The supply function is linear and there is a direct

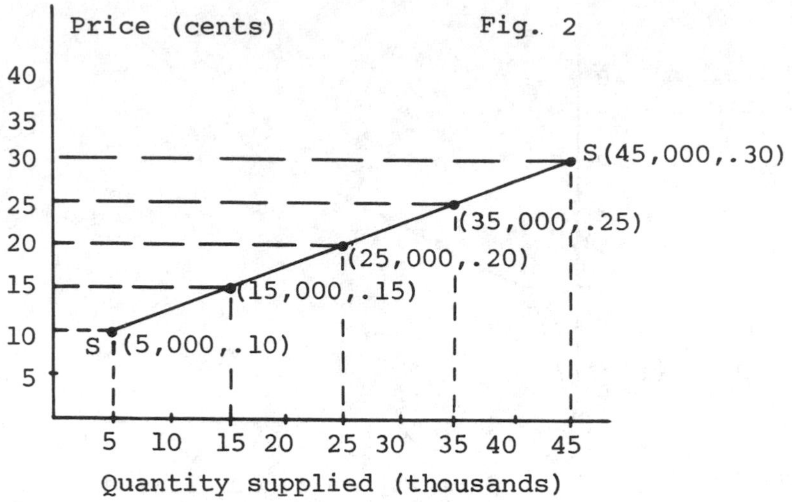

relationship between quantity supplied and price; that is, a change in one co-ordinate will produce a corresponding change in the same direction in the other co-ordinate.

• PROBLEM 14-28

Figure 1 shows a supply curve for corn (in millions of bushels per month).

Use Figure 2 to write out the supply schedule.

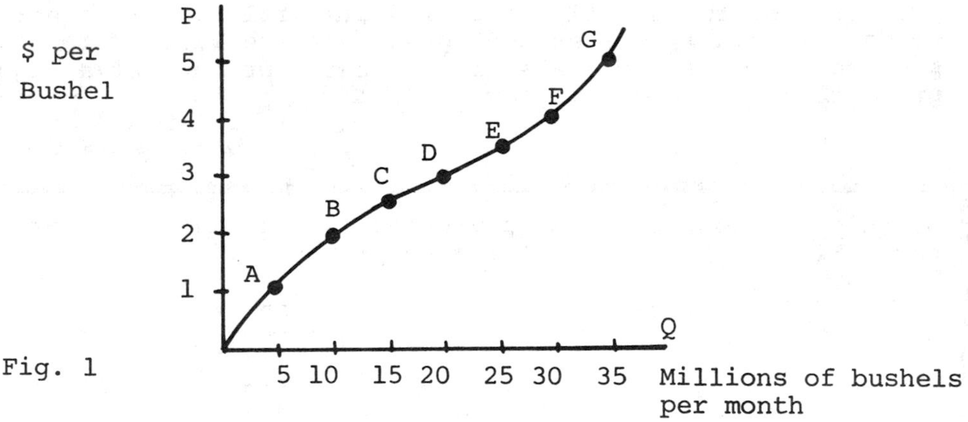

Fig. 1

Figure 2

	A	B	C	D	E	F	G
Price	1	2	2.5	3	3.5	4	5
Quantity (millions)	5	10	15	20	25	30	35

Solution: The supply curve shows the quantity of corn that

the farmers will supply over the given range of prices. Since the supply curve is a graphical representation of the supply schedule, Figure 2 may be filled in by reading the coordinates of the points A,B,C,D,E,F, and G from the graph. For example, at Point A, P = $1 and Q = 5 million bushels. Figure 2, when completed, should read as given in Figure 3.

Figure 3

Price	1.00	2.00	2.50	3.00	3.50	4.00	5.00
Quantity	5	10	15	20	25	30	35

• PROBLEM 14-29

Suppose that the supply schedules of the three largest automobile producers in 1978 were as shown in figure 1.

Figure 1

Price	Quantity Supplied (in millions) by General Motors	by Ford	by Chrysler
$8,000	2.5	1.5	1.2
7,000	2.2	1.3	1.0
6,000	2.0	1.1	0.8
5,000	1.9	1.0	0.6
4,000	1.8	0.9	0
3,000	.7	0	0
2,000	0	0	0

Construct the total supply schedule of "Big Three" automobiles in 1978, and draw their individual and total supply curves.

Solution: The total supply schedule is found by summing the quantities supplied by each producer at each price to give the total quantity supplied at each price. This is done in Figure 2.

Figure 2

Price	Quantity Supplied (in millions) General Motors		Ford		Chrysler		Total
$8,000	2.5	+	1.5	+	1.2	=	5.2
7,000	2.2	+	1.3	+	1.0	=	4.5
6,000	2.0	+	1.1	+	0.8	=	3.9
5,000	1.9	+	1.0	+	0.7	=	3.6
4,000	1.8	+	0.9	+	0.6	=	3.3
3,000	0.7	+	0	+	0	=	0.7
2,000	0	+	0	+	0	=	0

The individual supply curve of each supplier can be constructed by plotting on a graph the price-quantity combinations given in its supply schedule and connecting the points, as shown in Figure 3.

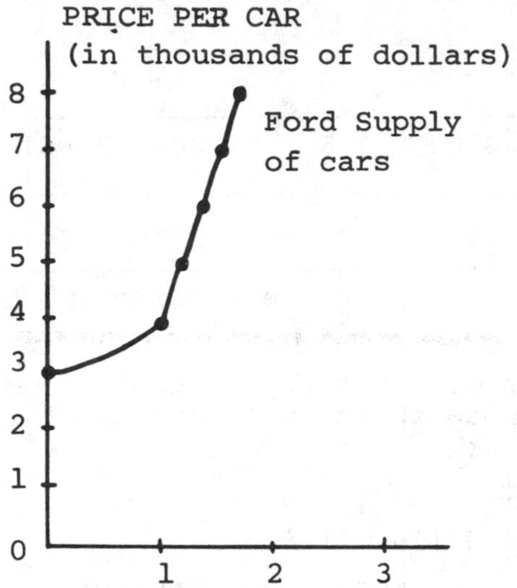

Fig. 3(a) Quantity in millions

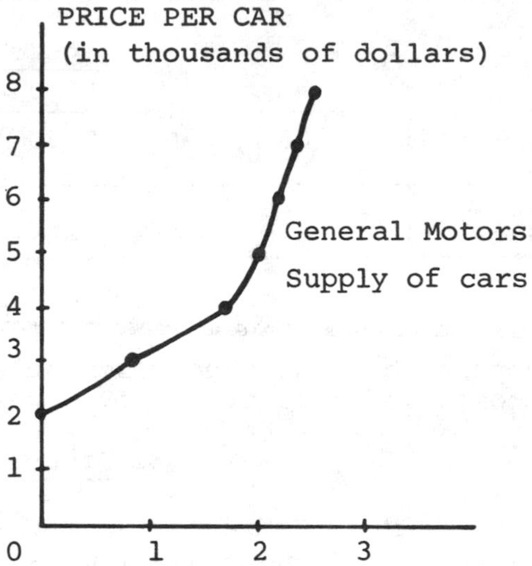

Fig. 3(b) Quantity in millions

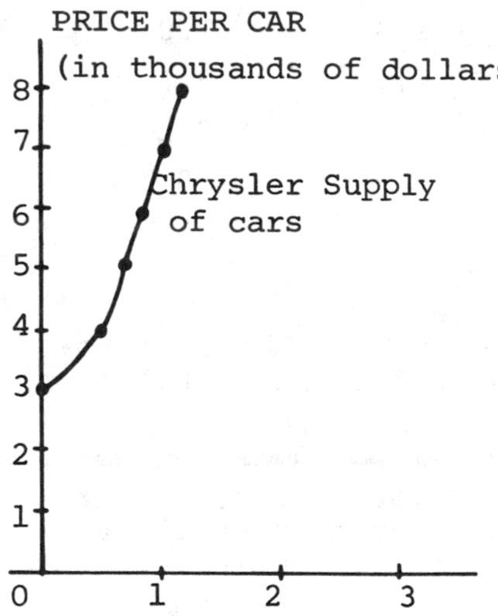

Fig. 3(c) Quantity in Millions

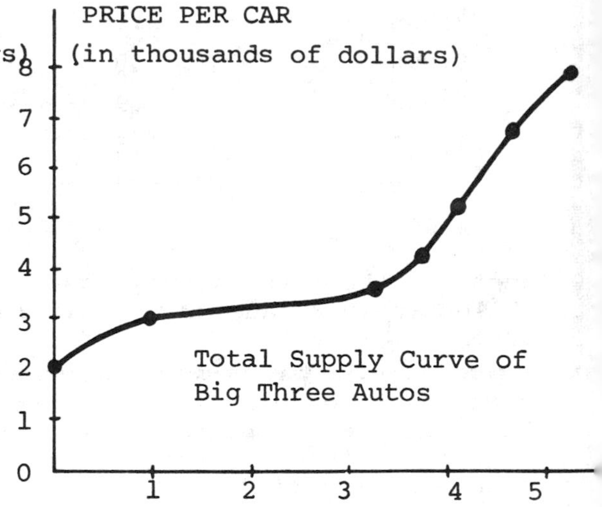

Fig. 4 Quantity in Millions

The total supply curve of the three car producers is the "horizontal sum" of their individual supply curves, where "quantity" is shown on the horizontal axis. It is the graph of the total supply schedule, as well, and is shown in Figure 4.

• **PROBLEM 14-30**

The accompanying figure represents the supply curve for widgets:

1) If the going price for widgets is $2, how many widgets will producers supply? 30

2) Why wouldn't they be willing to supply 50?

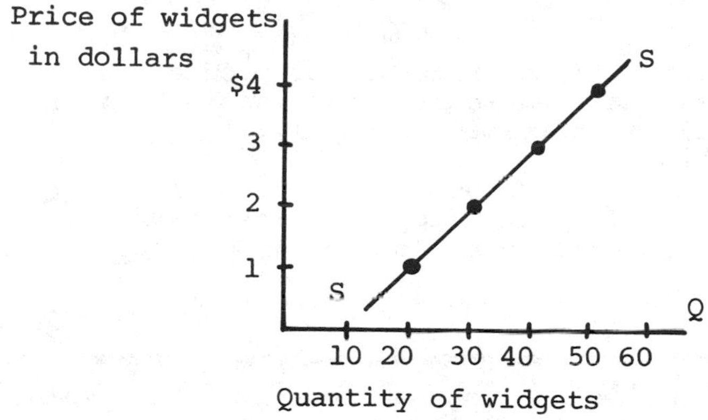

Solution: The supply curve maps the relationship between price and quantity supplied. That is, at any given price, it tells you how much producers will supply; or, in order for producers to supply any given quantity, it tells you what price they must receive.

1) According to the supply curve, if Price = $2, then Quantity = 30. That is, the producer will supply 30 widgets.

2) The point P = $2, Q = 50 is located off the supply curve. In order for the producer to supply 50 widgets, the price would have to be $4. That is, in order for the producer to increase the supply by 20 widgets, an inducement, in the form of a $2 increase in price, must be offered.

• PROBLEM 14-31

What are the major determinants of supply, i.e., the position of the supply curve?

Solution: The first major determinant of supply is the cost of the resources used to produce a good. An increase in resource costs will reduce supply, i.e., push the supply curve upward and to the left; and a decrease in resource costs will move the supply curve down and to the right. The second major determinant of supply is the technology by which a good is produced, that is the technique according to which resources are combined to produce it. A new technique that, e.g., allows use of a smaller physical quantity of resources increases supply (resource prices being assumed unchanged), since resource costs are less with the new technique.

The prices of other goods (substitutes and complements) also affect a particular goods'supply. A rise in the price of a substitute may encourage suppliers to offer more of their particular good at each possible price in anticipation of a shift of demand from the substitute to their product. A rise in the price of a complementary good, however, results in less demand for their own, and suppliers may react by supplying less at each possible price, reducing supply.

Expectations regarding the price of the product, its complements and substitutes, and customers' incomes can play a significant role in determining supply.

Total market supply depends on the number of suppliers, given the size of each. The more suppliers in a market, the further to the right will be the market supply curve.

• PROBLEM 14-32

Suppose an artist paints a landscape and offers it for sale. What does his supply curve look like?

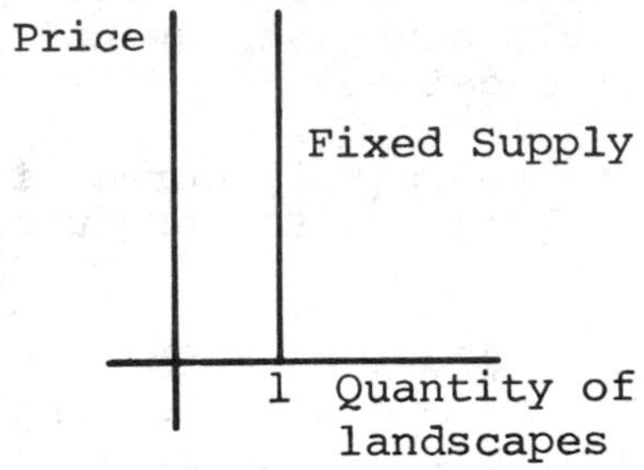

Solution: The artist faces a situation of completely fixed or inelastic supply. As such, no matter what the price offered by his customers, his quantity supplied is constant (= 1). His supply curve would look as shown in the figure.

THE LAW OF SUPPLY

• PROBLEM 14-33

A statistician in the Department of Agriculture observed that every year the temperature in Florida dropped below 20° F, the price of oranges was above normal while the quantity sold was below normal. He concluded that Florida oranges did not obey the law of supply. Is he correct?

Solution: What our statistician observed is that after cold winters, the size of the orange crop was less than normal while the price of oranges was greater than normal. Plotting his observations on a graph he would see something like Figure 1. P_1Q_1, P_2Q_2, P_3Q_3, and P_4Q_4 represent "normal" prices and quantities, while P_5Q_5 and P_6Q_6 represent the higher prices and lower quantities of years with cold weather and poor crops.

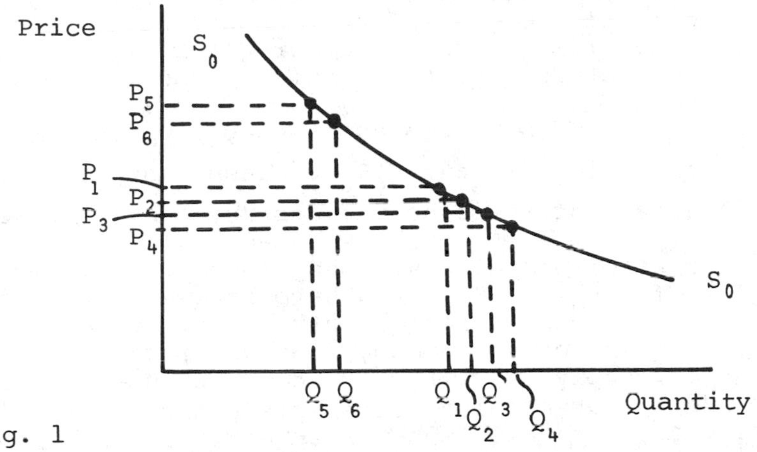

Fig. 1

There is evidently a negative relationship between the size of the orange crop and the price of oranges. He concludes that the supply curve of Florida oranges is S_0S_0, and unlike normal supply curves which slope upward, is downward sloping in contradiction to the law of supply.

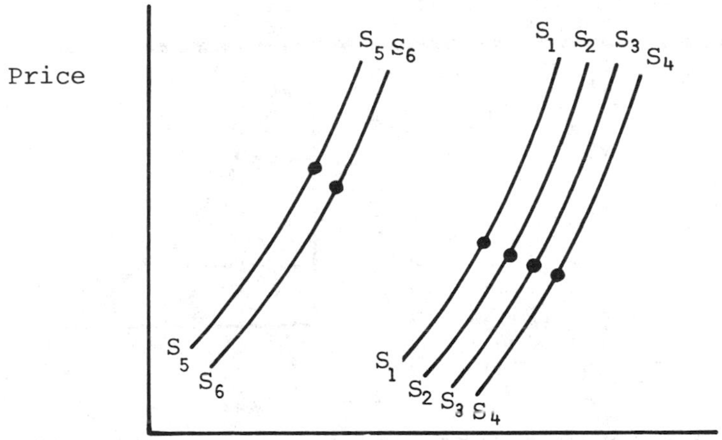

Fig. 2

Our statistician has made the mistake of confusing "changes in quantity supplied" corresponding to price changes with "changes in supply", which are due to factors other than price changes, confusing movements, along a supply curve with shifts in the position of the supply curve. He has assumed that all of the price-quantity points he has observed lie on the same supply curve, and that the variations in weather cause movements from point to point along a given curve. We know, however, that a given supply curve represents the relationship between the price of a good and the quantity of it that will be supplied, as long as other factors which affect the quantity supplied remain the same. But not all of these other factors have remained the same. Poor growing weather has an effect on the supply of oranges.

It reduces the number of oranges that suppliers are willing to sell at any given price. That is, it shifts the supply curve to the left. Thus, each of the points observed by our statistician lies on a different supply curve, each of which corresponds to different weather conditions. Figure 2 shows the correct interpretation of his observations.

S_1S_1, S_2S_2, S_3S_3, and S_4S_4 represent supply curves in "normal" years while S_5S_5 and S_6S_6 represent supply curves in years when part of the crop was destroyed by cold weather.

Our statistician's observations, then, do not contradict the law of supply. He would have realized this if he had known that changes in factors other than price which affect the quantity of a good supplied are represented by a shift in the supply curve rather than a change in position along the supply curve which represents a change in price and quantity supplied with non-price factors held constant.

• PROBLEM 14-34

What does the supply curve shown in Figure 1 imply about the relationship between prices and quantity supplied?

Might such a situation actually occur?

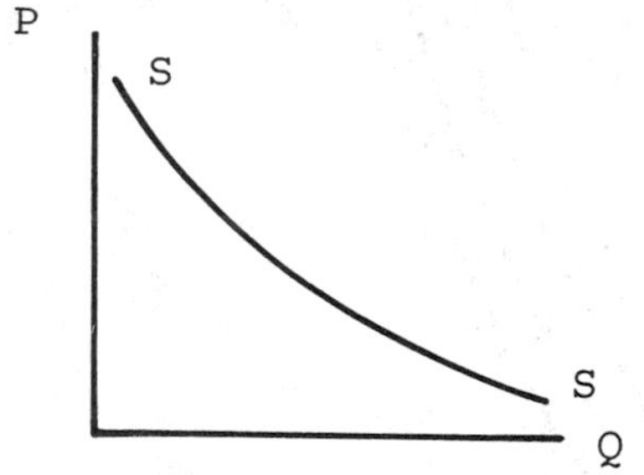

Fig. 1

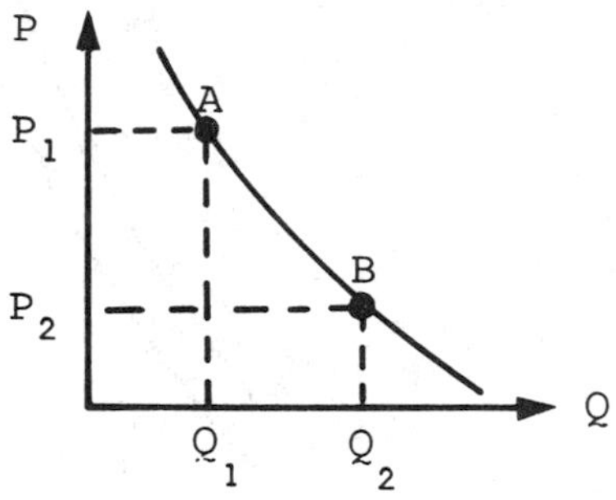

Fig. 2

Solution: One way of determining the relationship between prices and the quantity supplied described by this supply curve would be to pick two points A and B, as shown in Figure 2.

Notice that in moving from Point A to Point B, the price decreases from P_1 to P_2 and the quantity supplied increases from Q_1 to Q_2. This means that there is an inverse relationship between price and quantity supplied in this supply curve. Normally we do not expect supply to increase as the price decreases. If the element of time is added to the supply curve, a downward sloping supply curve becomes more realistic. Consider the example of the very early automobile manufacturers. At any specific and isolated moment in time, the doubling of their output in some short period of time, for example in one month, would have resulted in sharply rising costs. One reason for these rising costs could have been the working overtime of both men and machines, since it takes time to train workers or to expand production capacity. However, over longer periods of time, there are fewer restrictions on how the product must be produced. New factories can be built, new workers can be trained, and entirely different methods of production may even be discovered. For the early automobile manufacturers, the implementation of a mass production, assembly line technique resulted in decreasing per unit costs to the manufacturer. Thus, over a fairly long period of time, the early automobile manufacturers increased the quantity supplied while lowering price.

SUPPLY VS. QUANTITY SUPPLIED

• PROBLEM 14-35

What is the distinction between a "change in supply" and a "change in quantity supplied"? Illustrate using supply curve diagrams.

Solution: A supply curve represents the relationship between the quantity of a good that potential sellers will supply and the per unit price offered for the good, other factors remaining the same. A "change in supply" refers to a change in the relationship between the quantity of a good that suppliers are willing to sell and the per unit price of the good due to a change in one of the factors which affect this relationship. That is, a change in supply means that at any given price sellers are willing to sell more or less than they were previously. A "change in supply" is represented graphically, therefore, by a change in the position of the supply curve, as illustrated in Figure 1.

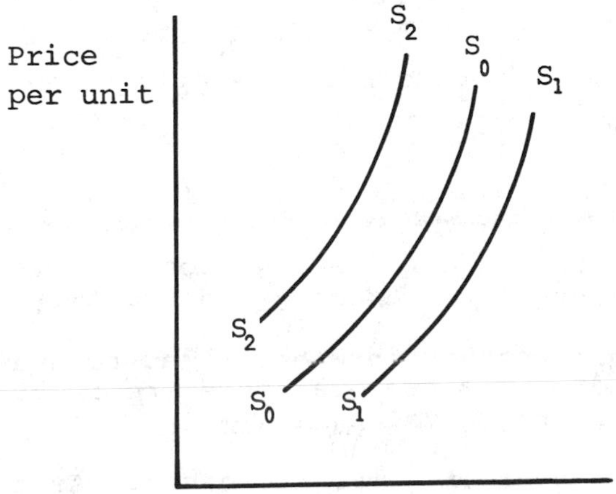

Fig. 1

If S_0S_0 represents the initial state of supply, an increase in supply is indicated by a rightward and downward shift in the supply curve, e.g., to S_1S_1. At any given price, a larger quantity will be supplied than initially at S_0S_0 Similarly, a leftward and upward shift in the supply curve e.g., to S_2S_2, indicates a decrease in supply, for, at any given price, a smaller quantity will be supplied than initially at S_0S_0.

If, on the other hand, the quantity of the good that will be supplied at each possible price remains unchanged, but price changes, the response to the price change is a "change in the quantity supplied." The set of different quantities that will be supplied at different prices, other factors remaining the same, is just what a supply curve represents. A change in quantity supplied in response to a price change is represented, then, by movement to a different point on the same supply curve. For example, if, other factors remaining the same, price rises from P_0 to P_1

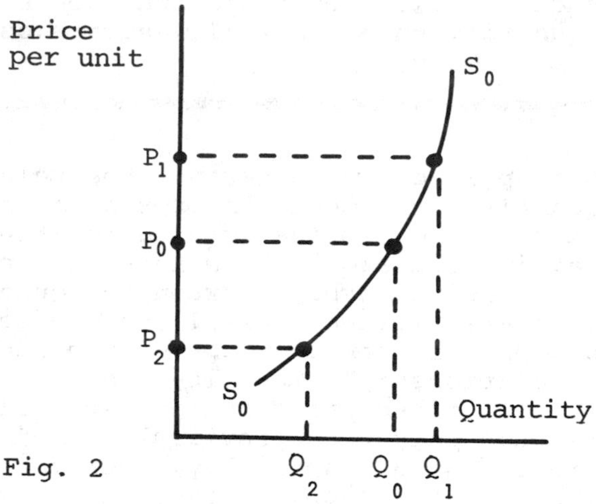

Fig. 2

in Figure 2, suppliers will supply a larger quantity, Q_1, as compared to Q_0 at P_0. Similarly, if the price falls from P_0 to P_2, suppliers will supply a smaller quantity, Q_2 as compared to Q_0 at P_0.

• PROBLEM 14-36

Indicate whether the following economic events represent a change in supply or a change in quantity supplied.

a) Cold weather in Florida destroys a great deal of the orange crop. Therefore there are fewer oranges in the country's supermarkets.

b) The cost of limes increases. As a result, bar owners raise the price of gin and tonics.

c) The price of leather shoes goes up. This induces manufacturers of leather shoes to increase production.

Solution: A change in quantity supplied is caused by a change in price, and is represented by movement from one point to another along a fixed supply curve. A change in supply occurs when a factor underlying supply changes, thus causing a shift of the entire curve.

a) The first example represents a change in supply. The weather, one of the factors underlying supply in this instance, has changed for the worse and caused supply to shift to the left.

b) To the bar owner, limes represent a raw material basic to his finished product, the gin and tonic. As such, the cost of limes is one of the factors underlying supply. Therefore, an increase in the price of limes causes a change in supply.

c) Finally, in this case, price alone has changed for leather shoes, and quantity supplied has increased. This represents a change in quantity supplied only.

• PROBLEM 14-37

Consider the supply curve for product A given in Figure 1. Suppose the producer's costs suddenly rise. Now, it costs the producer $1.00 more to produce each unit of A. Draw the new supply curve.

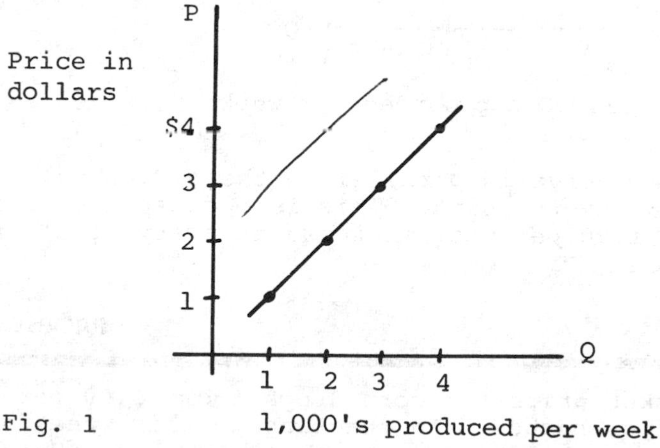

Fig. 1

Solution: The supply curve is drawn from the points specified in the supply schedule. One approach to this problem is to write out the supply schedule corresponding to this supply curve. This is shown in Figure 2.

Price in $	Quantity (1,000's per/week)
1	1
2	2
3	3
4	4

Figure 2

The producer must add $1.00 to the price of each unit of A at every level of production (quantity supplied). Recognizing that price means per unit price, the new supply schedule appears as in Figure 3, where each price has been increased by $1.00.

Price in $	Quantity (1,000's per/week)
2	1
3	2
4	3
5	4

Figure 3

Replotting this gives the new supply curve as shown in Figure 4.

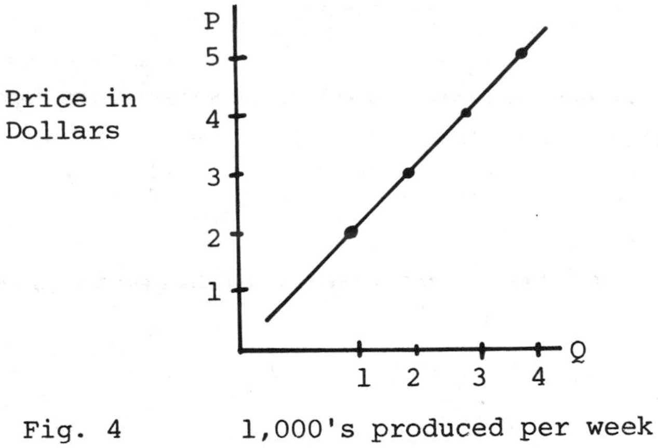

Fig. 4

Note that the new curve is parallel to the old curve, lying $1.00 above it at every point. This is because the cost increase was a $1.00 per unit increase at every level of quantity supplied.

• PROBLEM 14-38

Suppose the market price for corn drops from $1,00 per bushel to $.75 per bushel. In reaction to this, the farmers decide to sell one third less corn to the market. Has the supply of corn to the market decreased?

Solution: Restated, this question asks, "Has the supply curve shifted?" The answer to this lies in the analysis of the two changes given in the problem.

First, the market price drops and second, the farmers decrease the quantity of corn supplied to the market. No other changes are specified in the problem. Therefore, the farmers have decreased the "quantity supplied" due to a decrease in the market price of corn, not the "supply" of corn. This is an example of a shift along the supply curve and not of a shift in the supply curve, i.e., a change in supply, as the position of the curve itself has not changed.

• PROBLEM 14-39

Suppose a farmer has just 2 acres of land. He finds from experience that these 2 acres are equally prolific in the production of corn and wheat. Specifically, he has found that each acre is capable of producing either 20 bushels of wheat or 20 bushels of corn. Suppose, too, that no matter how our farmer decides to apportion his 2 acres between wheat and corn, his total costs of production remain at $25. If the price of corn is $1 per bushel and that of wheat is $2 per bushel, what will the farmer do to maximize his profits?

Solution: This problem is an illustration of the principle of product substitution, which is based on the direct relationship between the price of a product and the quantity supplied. As the market price of a product rises, a producer will shift his resources from other commodities to that product whose price has been increased. In order to gain maximum profits, the farmer in the example will plant all his land in wheat, producing 40 bushels. Total revenue will be 40 bushels x $2 = $80, and profits will be $80 - $25 = $55 (where $25 are the total costs of production).

The output of corn in that case, will be zero. To plant any corn at a price of $1 per bushel will necessarily result in profits of less than $55, which is verified by the following computations.

Total revenue = 40 bushels x $1 = $40

Total costs of production = $25

Net profit = $40 - $25 = $15

Suppose the market price of corn rises to $3, while the price of wheat remains at $2. It would then be profitable for the farmer to shift all his resources to corn, that is, to substitute corn for wheat production. By doing so, his total revenue will be increased to $120 (= 40 bushels x $3) and his profits to $95 (= $120 - $25).

From the above illustration, it is demonstrated that it is profitable to substitute the production of relatively high-priced goods for the production of relatively low-priced ones by shifting resources accordingly.

• PROBLEM 14-40

The supply and demand curves, shown in Figure 1 represent the market for commodity A. What would be the effect of the implementation of a $1 per unit tax legally imposed on the seller?

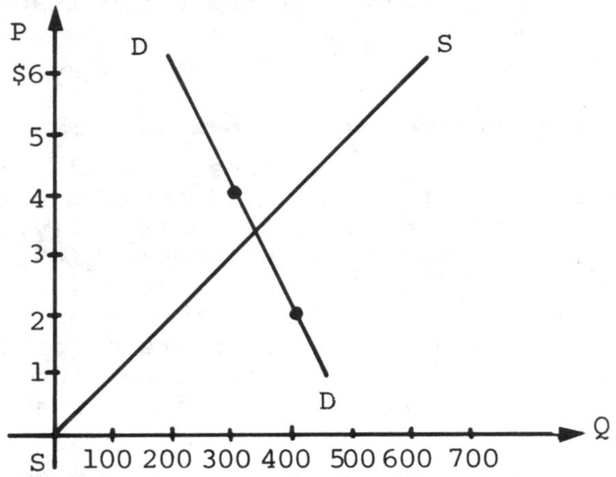

Fig. 1

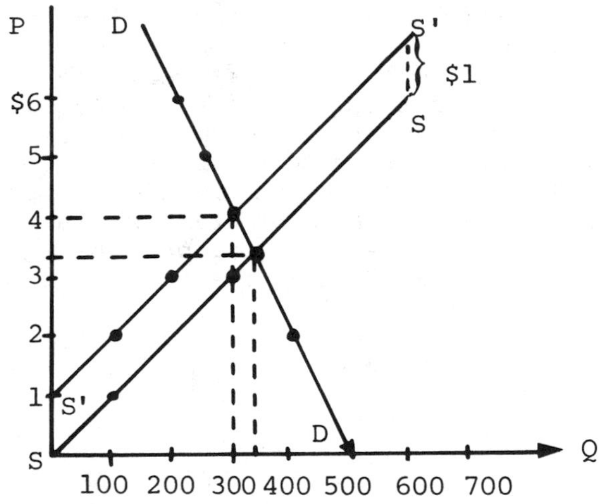

Fig. 2

Solution: This question can be rephrased as, "What happens to the equilibrium point if the government imposes a $1 per unit tax on the seller?" The first step in its solution is the construction of the new market situation. The implementation of a tax will not change any of the factors which determine the demand curve, therefore DD does not shift. A $1 per unit tax legally imposed on the seller would cause the producer's costs to change. Since this tax is a one dollar per unit tax, at any given quantity, price must be $1 higher to induce the producer to supply the given quantity. That is, the new supply curve S^1S^1 in

Figure 2, will be parallel to the old SS in Figure 2, with a distance of $1 between them. Using the diagram, note that the new equilibrium occurs at a higher price with a smaller quantity purchased than the before-tax equilibrium.

• PROBLEM 14-41

List the basic nonprice determinants of supply. Explain how each affects the supply curve.

Solution: The basic nonprice determinants of supply are:

(1) the technique of production (technology)

(2) resource prices

(3) prices of other goods

(4) price expectations

(5) the number of sellers in the market

(6) taxes and subsidies

The first two determinants of supply, technology and resource prices, are the two components of production costs. Anything which serves to lower production costs, that is, any technological improvement or any decline in resource prices, will increase supply. With lower costs, businessmen will find it profitable to offer a larger amount of the product at each possible price. An increase in the price of resources (a deterioration of technology being unlikely) will cause a decrease in supply.

Changes in the prices of other goods can also shift the supply curve for a product. A decline in the price of wheat may cause a farmer to produce and offer more corn at each possible price. Conversely, a rise in the price of wheat may make farmers less willing to produce and offer corn in the market.

Expectations concerning the future price of a product can also affect a producer's current willingness to supply that product. Farmers might withhold some of their current corn harvest from the market, anticipating a higher corn price in the future. This will cause a decrease in the current supply of corn. On the other hand, in many types of manufacturing, expected price increases may induce firms to expand production immediately, causing supply to increase.

Given the scale of operations of each firm, the larger the number of suppliers, the greater will be market supply. The smaller the number of firms in an industry, the less the market supply will be.

Finally, certain taxes, such as sales taxes, add to production costs and therefore reduce supply. Conversely, subsidies lower costs and increase supply.

The above explanations can be shown in a figure which illustrates changes in the supply of corn.

A change in one or more of the determinants of supply will cause a change in supply. An increase in supply shifts the supply curve to the right, as from S_1S_1 to S_2S_2. A decrease in supply is shown graphically as a movement of the curve to the left, as from S_1S_1 to S_3S_3. A change in the quantity supplied involves a movement, caused by a change in the price of the product under consideration, from one point to another -- as from a to b -- on a fixed supply curve.

• **PROBLEM 14-42**

"Allowing the prices of goods to rise in periods when none of the good is being produced is immoral, because the higher prices do not induce a larger output. They merely give unwarranted profits to those who are lucky enough to own the goods. Either prices should be prevented from rising or the government should take over ownership in order to prevent unjust enrichment quotas." Do you agree with this analysis? If so, why? If not, why not?

Solution: We should disagree. A higher price permits a re-allocation of existing goods--a re-allocation that would not occur in the absence of higher prices. Immorality is a gratuitous judgment. That the profits to those who own the goods when prices rise are "unwarranted" is also a gratuitous judgment. The point is to note that higher prices do have a consequence--re-allocation--and that personal judgments should not blind one to that fact.

MARKET EQUILIBRIUM

• **PROBLEM 14-43**

Given in Figure 1 are supply and demand data for Farmer Dean's apricots.

Price per bushel	Quantity supplied	Quantity demanded
$3	100	500
4	200	400
5	300	300
6	400	200
7	500	100

Figure 1

a) What is the equilibrium price and quantity? Illustrate using supply and demand curves.

b) How many bushels of apricots will be produced if the government sets a price support at $6? How many bushels will the government have to purchase at $6?

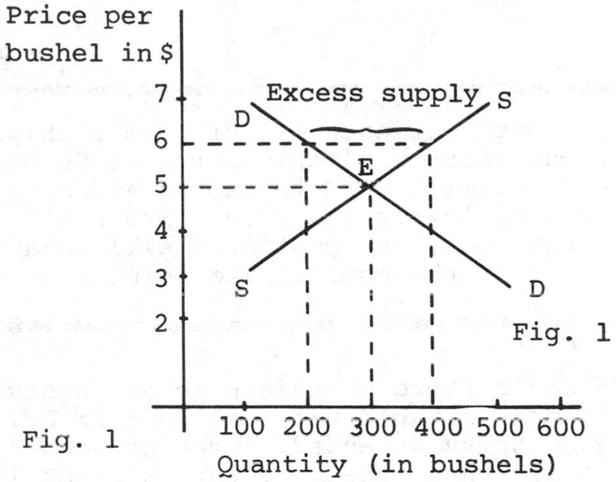

Fig. 1

Solution: If we graph the data given above, we obtain Figure 2.

a) To find the equilibrium price and output, examine the intersection of the supply curve SS and the demand curve DD. At this equilibrium point, E, the price per bushel is $5 and the quantity demanded (supplied) is 300 bushels.

b) Under a price support program, the government sets a price below which the price of a product is not allowed to fall. With Farmer Dean's apricots, a price support has been set at $6 per bushel. At $6 per bushel, Farmer Dean is willing to supply 400 bushels of apricots. Since the quantity demanded at a price of $6 is only 200 bushels, there will be an excess supply of 200 bushels. It is these 200 bushels that the government will have to purchase at $6 from Farmer Dean.

• PROBLEM 14-44

Show graphically the effect of an increase in demand on equilibrium price and output.

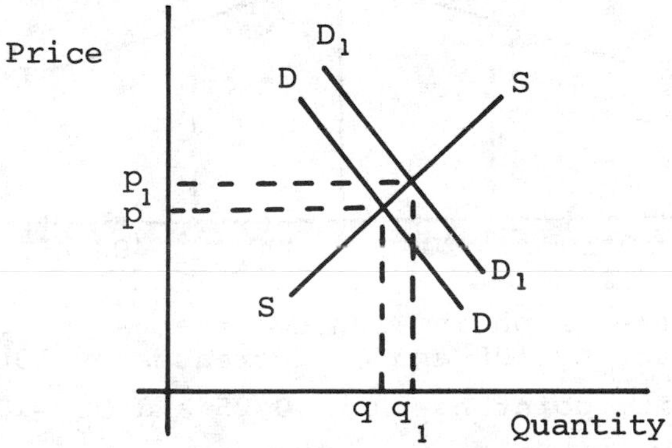

Solution: Consult the figure. As demand increases from DD to D_1D_1, quantity demanded increases from q to q_1, and price increases from p to p_1. Correspondingly, a decrease in demand will cause equilibrium price and output to decrease.

• PROBLEM 14-45

If price is 35 cents for each bag of potato chips at Frank's Deli, customers will only purchase 50 bags per week, whereas Frank will want to supply 450 bags. But for every five cents he lowers the price, Frank will supply 100 less bags per week, and customers will demand 100 more bags per week. Find the equilibrium point.

Solution: We could approach this problem in several ways. First we could draw a table with columns for Price, Quantity Supplied, and Quantity Demanded. Then go down the table, lowering the price until the equilibrium point is reached.

Price	Q_D	Q_S
0.35	50	450
0.30	150	350
0.25	250	250

We see that at Price = 25 cents, $Q_D = Q_S = 250$ bags, equilibrium prevails; the amount demanded equals the amount supplied.

Alternatively, we could draw the graphs (Figure 1) for supply and demand since we know the behavior of Q_S and Q_D as price falls:

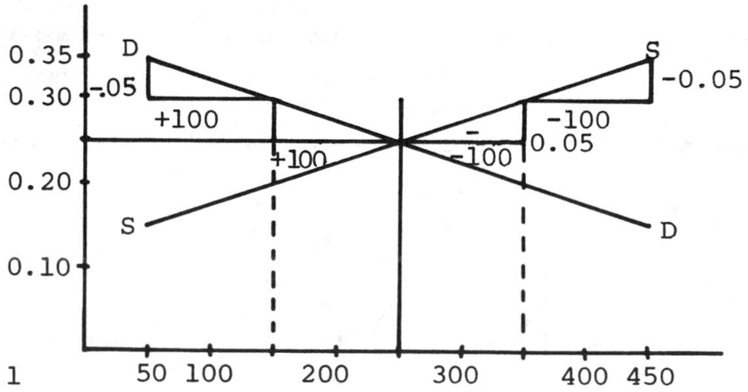

Fig. 1

We see on the graph in Figure 1 that as price falls by \$0.05, Q_D increases by 100 and Q_S decreases by 100. Once again, equilibrium point has P = 0.25 and $Q_D = Q_S = 250$.

Finally, we could evaluate the equilibrium point algebraically. For the demand schedule, we are given the point $(Q_1, P_1) = (50, \$0.35)$. Then we are told that as price falls by $\Delta P = 0.05$, Q_D increases by $\Delta Q = 100$. Therefore

$$\text{slope} \equiv \frac{\Delta P}{\Delta Q} \equiv \frac{P_d - P_1}{Q_d - Q_1} = \frac{P_d - 0.35}{Q_d - 50} = \frac{-0.05}{100}$$

Cross-multiplying, we get

$$100\ P_d - 35 = -0.05\ Q_d + 2.5$$

or $\quad 100\ P_d = -0.05\ Q_d + 37.5$;

dividing both sides by 100 results in

$$P_d = -0.0005\ Q_d + .375$$

For the supply schedule, we are given the point $(Q_2, P_1) = (450, 0.35)$ and the fact that Q_S decreases by $\Delta Q = 100$ as price decreases by $\Delta P = 0.05$. Therefore

$$\text{slope} = \frac{\Delta P}{\Delta Q} = \frac{P - P_1}{Q - Q_2} = \frac{P_S - 0.35}{Q_S - 450} = \frac{0.05}{100}$$

Cross-multiplying, we get

$$100\ P_S - 35 = 0.05\ Q_S - 22.5$$

or $100\ P_S = 0.05\ Q_S + 12.5$; dividing both sides by 100 gives $P_S = 0.0005\ Q_S + .125$

Finally, at the equilibrium point, we know that the demand and supply prices and quantities are equal, so:

$$P_D = P_S$$

or $-0.0005\ Q_D + .375 = 0.0005\ Q_S + .125$

Since $Q_d = Q_S$, we can combine the Q_S and Q_d terms to get

$$0.25 = 0.001\ Q$$

$Q = 250$, the equilibrium quantity. Substituting the equilibrium value for Q back into the equation for supply,

we get $\quad P = (0.0005)(250) + .125$

$P = 0.25$, the equilibrium price, which is the same as the two other methods shown. We could just as well substitute the equilibrium value of Q into the demand equation to get the equilibrium value of P.

• PROBLEM 14-46

Given that the demand schedule is represented by P = 100 - 5Q, and the supply schedule is represented by P = 40 + 10Q (where P is price and Q is quantity), find the equilibrium price and quantity.

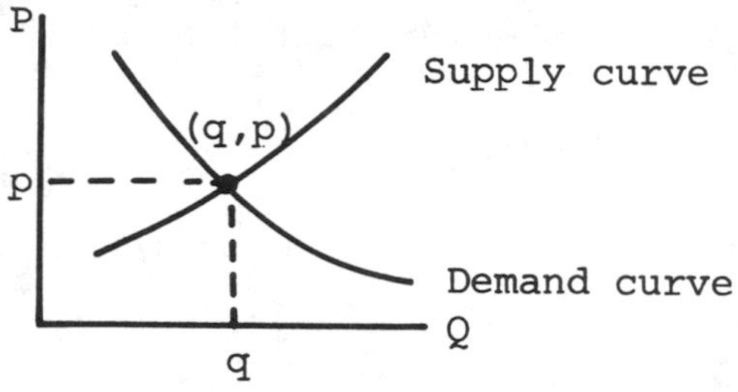

Fig. 1

Solution: Equilibrium occurs when supply and demand are equal. Graphically, this is represented as the point where the supply and demand curves intersect; that is, the point at which the co-ordinates (Q,P) are the same on both the supply and demand curves. In Figure 1, this point is represented as (q,p).

To determine this point, values must be found for both p and q. As, at the equilibrium point, the price for supply and the price for demand are equal (P = P) q can be found by setting the equations for the supply and demand schedules equal to each other, and solving for Q.

$$\text{(demand) } 100 - 5Q = 40 + 10Q \text{ (supply)}$$

Adding 5Q to both sides of the equation and subtracting 40 from both sides we obtain the equation:

$$60 = 15Q.$$

Dividing both sides of the equation by 15 yields:

$$Q = \frac{60}{15} = 4 .$$

Thus the equilibrium quantity (q) is 4.

To find the equilibrium price p, substitute the value of q into either the supply or demand schedule equations, and solve for P.

$$P = 100 - 5(4) = 100 - 20 = 80 \text{ (demand)}$$

$$P = 40 + 10(4) = 40 + 40 = 80 \text{ (supply)}$$

Thus, the equilibrium price p = 80, and the equilibrium point would be:

$P = 80$ and $Q = 4$.

• PROBLEM 14-47

Show graphically the effect of an increase in supply on equilibrium price and output.

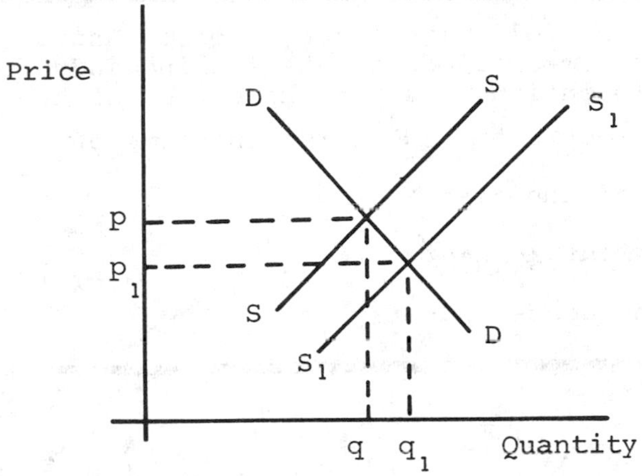

Solution: Consult the figure. As supply increases from SS to S_1S_1, quantity supplied increases from q to q_1 while price decreases from p to p_1. Correspondingly, a decrease in supply will cause output to decrease and equilibrium price to increase.

• PROBLEM 14-48

Show graphically the effect of a decrease in demand on equilibrium price and quantity.

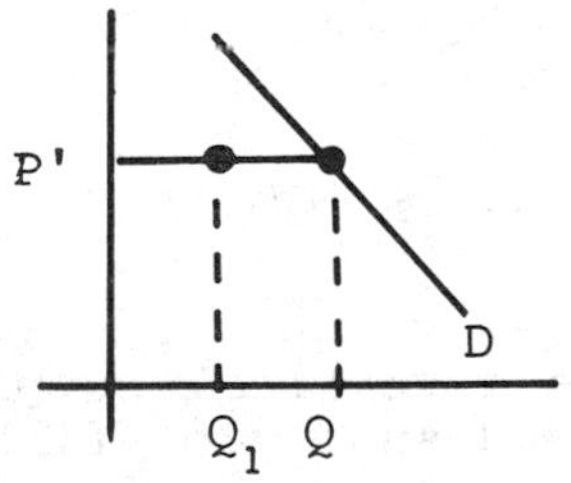

Fig. 1

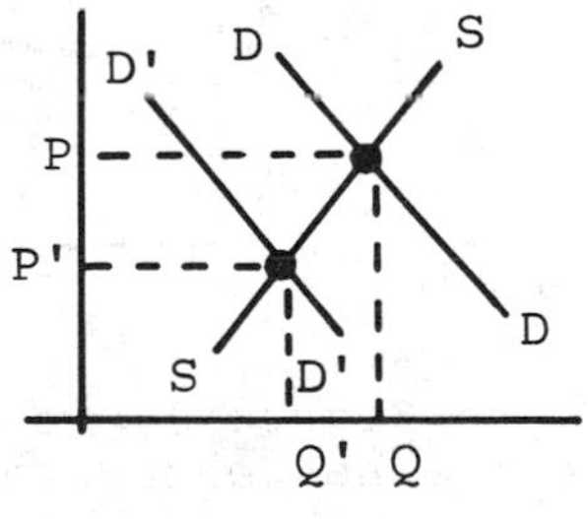

Fig. 2

Solution: The question is asking for the effects on equilibrium of a shift downward in the demand curve. Figure 1 shows the initial demand curve. A decrease in demand causes the demand curve to shift to the left. The reason for a leftward shift is that a decrease in demand implies that at any given price P', people will demand less of the commodity (Q') than before (Q). Plotting this decrease in quantity demanded at each price would give you a new demand curve, D'D' in Figure 2, lying to the left of DD.

The initial equilibrium point is (Q,P). The new equilibrium point is (Q'P'). Thus, a decrease in demand causes the equilibrium price to fall from P to P', and the equilibrium quantity to fall from Q to Q'.

• PROBLEM 14-49

Consider the following three graphs. Assume that these are the three time periods of the fishing industry. Given the above information, analyze the effect of the shift of the dd demand curve to d^1d^1 curve in terms of

a) Price of the fish

b) employment

c) fishing boats industry

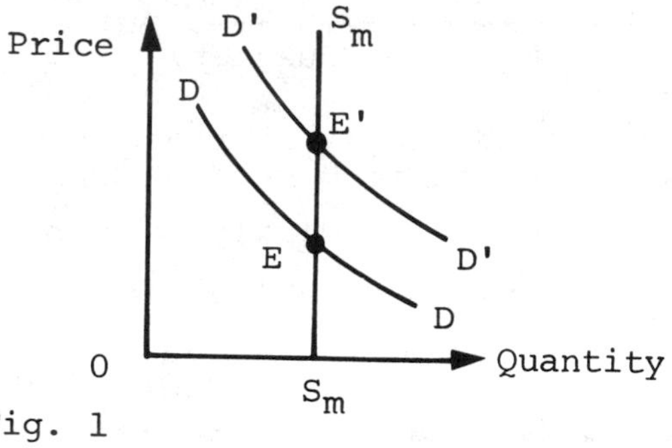

Fig. 1

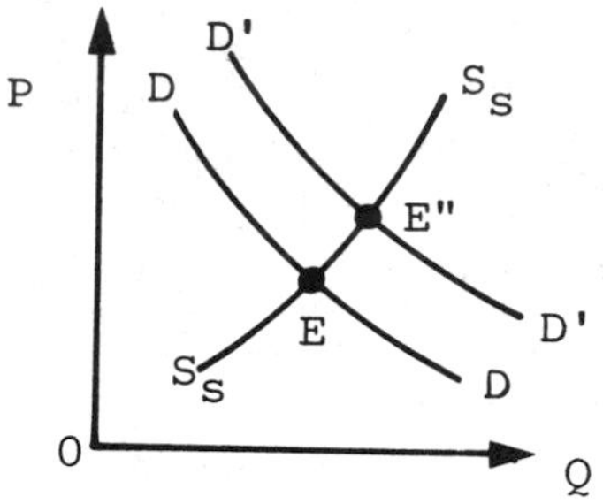

Fig. 2

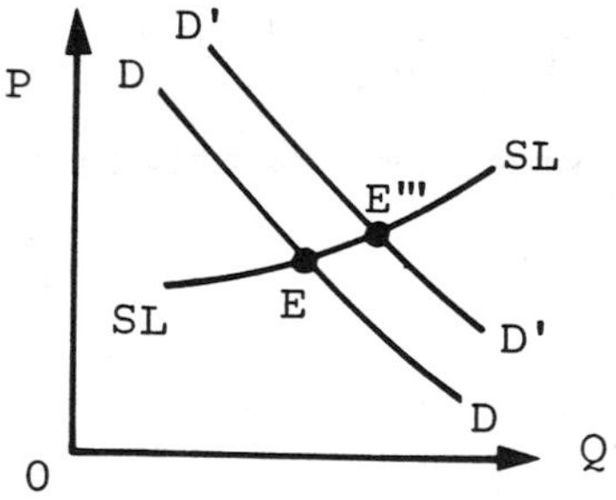

Fig. 3

Solution: In Figure 1, we have a vertical supply curve S_mS_m, which means we have a fixed supply of fish. If demand increased in such a level that it exceeds the constant supply of fish, then such stronger demand will sharply raise the momentary price of fish. This is shown in Figure 1, where the constant supply curve S_mS_m intersects the new demand curve d^1d^1 at the new, momentary equilibrium price at E^1. The rationale for such price accretions is to ration the limited supply of fish among the excess demanders.

With such prevalent high prices in the market, skippers

of the fishing boats will be induced to hire more men (i.e., increased employment in the area) and to use more nets. They will in the short run begin to bring to the market a greater supply of fish than they did at the old momentary equilibrium, even if they do not have the time to get new boats built. Figure 2 shows the new S_sS_s short-run supply schedule, and indicates that it intersects the new demand curve at E", the point of short run equilibrium. It is important to note that the equilibrium price is a little lower than the momentary E' price because of the extra supply of fish induced in the short run by more intensive use of the same number of boats.

The final long-run equilibrium, otherwise known as the "normal" price, is illustrated in Fig. 3. The prevailing higher prices have resulted in more shipbuilding and attracted more sailors into the industry. The final equilibrium E"' is found at the intersection of the long-run supply curve S_LS_L and the long run demand curve d'd'. The final equilibrium is reached after all economic factors (including number of ships and shipyards) have adjusted to the new demand level.

We can see that the long run equilibrium price is lower as compared to that of the momentary and short-run equilibrium prices. Yet when we consider the price that prevailed previously when demand was lower, it is a little bit higher. This case was termed by Marshall as the case of "increasing cost" which he considered to be normal in most sizable competitive industries. He rationalized such normality by saying that when large industry operating under large scale production expands, it can only "pirate" men, ships, nets and other productive factors away from other industries by increasing only their prices and thus its own cost. So this is why our long run supply curve S_LS_L will usually be sloping upward gently.

The case of the constant cost, wherein our long-run supply curve S_LS_L in Fig. 3 is horizontal, would be applicable only if the industry is small as compared with the total of all other users of its factors.

• PROBLEM 14-50

Sam owns a fresh vegetable stand. If a new apartment building opens across the street from him, what will probably happen to the prices he can charge for his vegetables? Illustrate using supply and demand curve diagrams.

Solution: Using supply and demand curves (SS and DD, respectively, in Figure 1), we can illustrate the situation before the new building opens.

The equilibrium point determined by these two curves is E with price P and quantity Q. The opening of a new apartment building would give Sam new potential customers, causing the demand curve for his vegetables to shift out to D'D', as shown in Fig. 2.

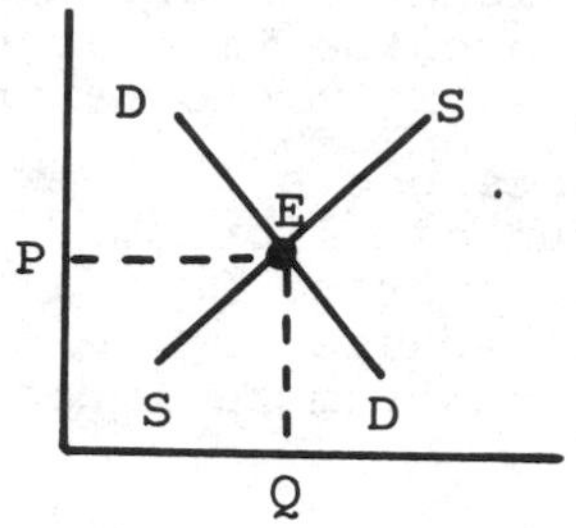

Fig. 1

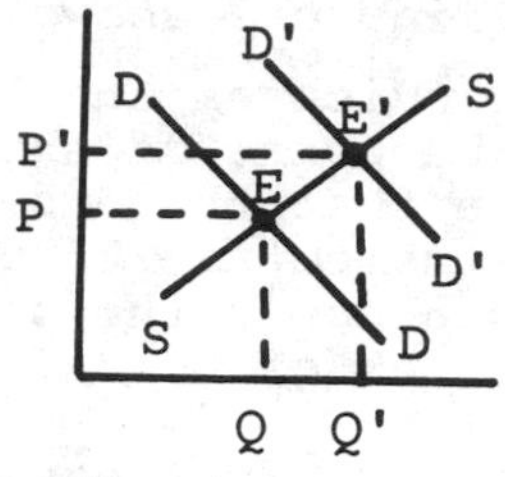

Fig. 2

This new demand leads to a new equilibrium point at E', with a new price of P' and a new quantity (supplied and demanded) of Q'. Thus, an increase in demand results in an increase in both the equilibrium price and the equilibrium quantity.

• PROBLEM 14-51

Due to a new breakthrough in electronic circuitry, the cost of producing hand calculators drops dramatically. What would be the effects of this on the equilibrium price and quantity in the calculator market (assuming all other things remain unchanged)?

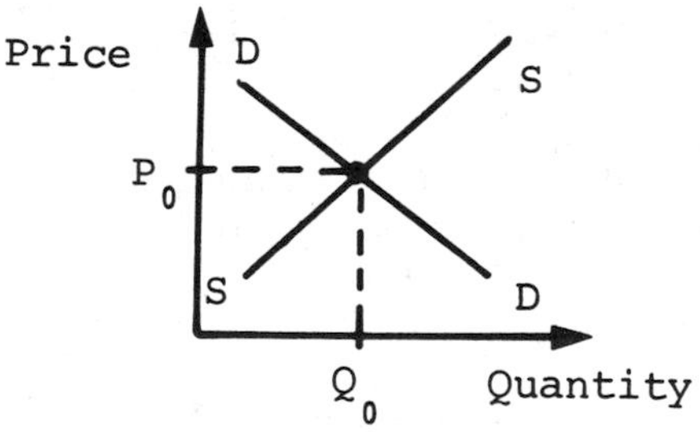

Fig. 1

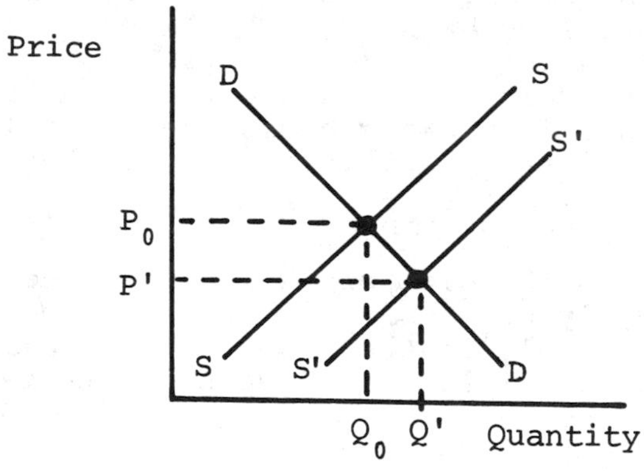

Fig. 2

Solution: The problem is asking for an analysis of the effects on the market situation of a decrease in costs to the producer. Figure 1 shows the market before the change occurs, with the equilibrium point at (P_0Q_0).

The problem states that the costs of producing the calculators has dropped. This change is likely to result in a decrease in the price that the producer is willing to accept for his product at any quantity supplied. That is, a downward shift occurs in the supply curve, from SS to S^1S^1 in Figure 2.

Therefore, the new equilibrium point (P^1, Q^1) shows that price will decrease from P_0 to P^1 and the quantity sold will increase from Q_0 to Q^1.

• PROBLEM 14-52

Using supply and demand curves, explain (a) why roses are expensive in the winter and (b) Christmas trees are inexpensive on December 26.

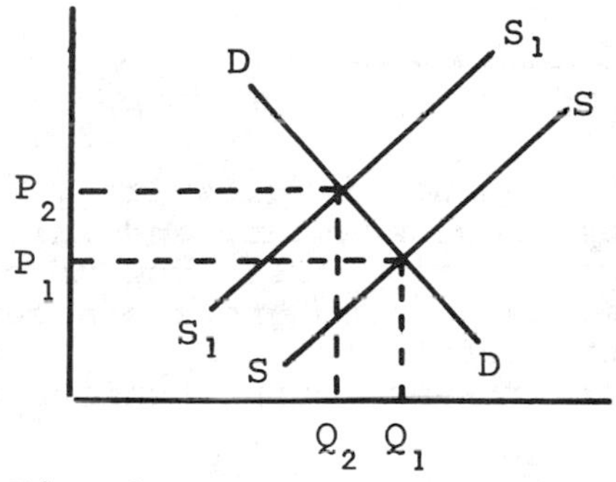

Fig. 1

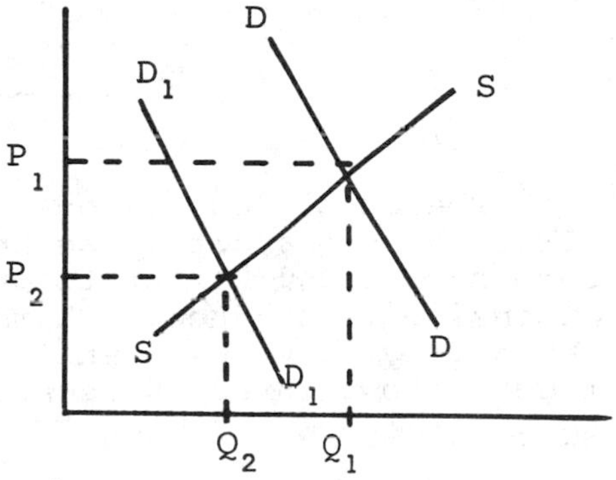

Fig. 2

Solution: During the winter, roses do not grow in most climates. Hence, the supply of roses decreases drastically.

Graphically, Figure 1 shows that as supply decreases from SS to S_1S_1, quantity demanded falls from Q_1 to Q_2, but price rises considerably, from P_1 to P_2. Christmas trees, on the other hand, can be obtained from the woods as easily a week before Christmas as a week after. The reason these trees are so inexpensive on the 26th is because demand has dropped drastically overnight. See Figure 2.

Here, both quantity demanded and price fall as demand decreases from DD to D_1D_1. Price decreases from P_1 to P_2, and quantity sold decreases from Q_1 to Q_2.

• PROBLEM 14-53

How are the supply and demand curves of a product affected as that product grows scarcer?

Solution: As a product or resource becomes scarce, we would not expect any change to take place in its demand curve. Scarcity, per se, would not cause the demand curve to shift. Of course there is the possibility that the news of the scarcity might affect the demand for the product, but this can be considered an outside factor in this instance, and is more properly the concern of marketers and psychologists.

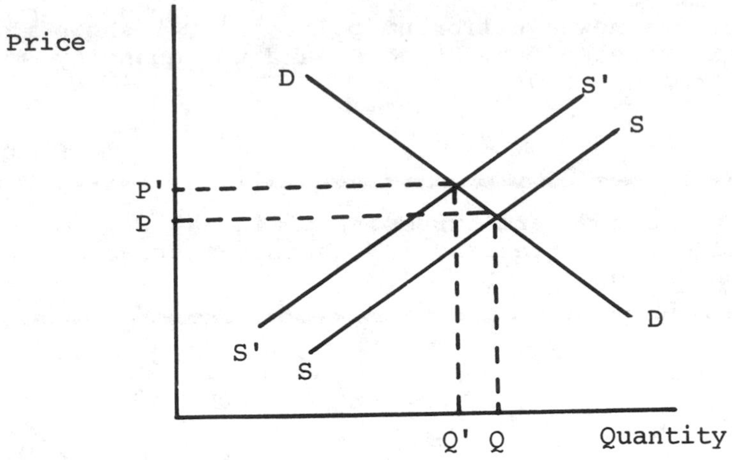

The supply curve, on the other hand, is definitely affected by scarcity. As an item grows scarcer, and therefore harder and harder to produce, it also will grow more expensive to produce. Therefore, as an item grows scarcer, the supply curve will shift to the left. The graph in the figure shows this. As scarcity increases, supply shifts from SS to S^1S^1.

On the graph, it is shown that scarcity will cause price to rise from P to P_1 and quantity demanded and supplied to fall from Q to Q_1.

• PROBLEM 14-54

Explain rationing in terms of supply and demand curves. What difference will it make if the maximum quantity that each consumer can buy is to the left or to the right of the equilibrium point?

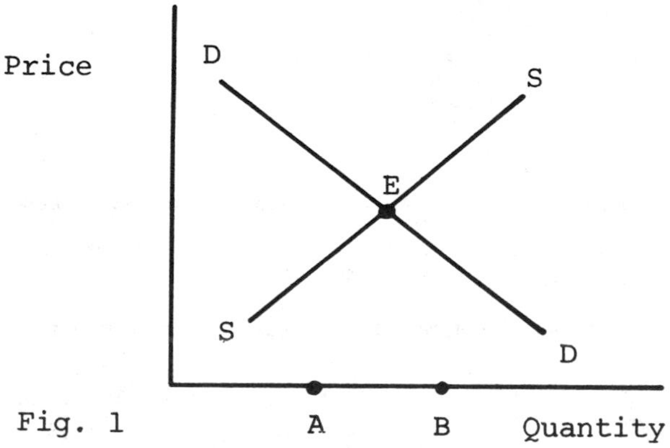

Fig. 1

Solution: Rationing is a system of distributing goods and services in which there is a maximum limit to the quantity of a good or service that each consuming unit can purchase or obtain.

Consumer Z's demand curve for product X is plotted in Figure 1 along with the supply curve for product X. Suppose two possible rations are being considered. One would set the maximum quantity that each consumer could purchase at point A (on the graph), and the other would set its ration at point B.

To show how these rations would affect market operations, draw the line perpendicular to the x-axis and passing through the ration points. Any part of the graph to the right of the perpendicular line will no longer be a part of market operations.

On the graph in Figure 2, by drawing the perpendicular for point A, it is shown that a ration of A is to the left of the equilibrium point, E. Thus, if rationing were to be put into effect at point A, consumer Z would be willing to pay P_2 for quantity A, while supply of A existed for a price of P_1. This market would hence be out of equilibrium. If price were kept below P_2, Consumer Z would look elsewhere to get more of product X.

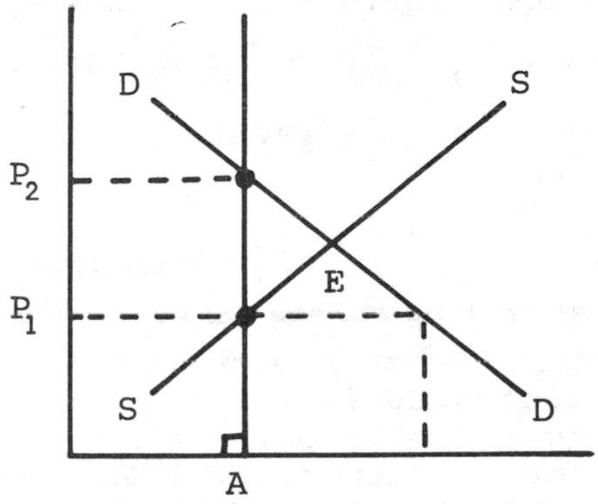

Fig. 2

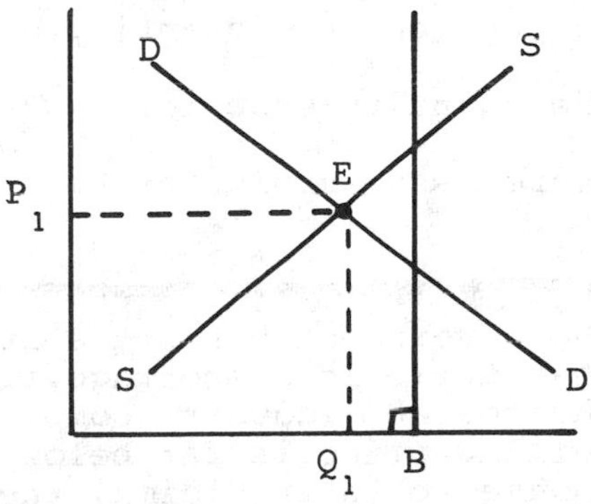

Fig.3

If the ration were to be set at point B, the graph would appear as shown in Figure 3.

Here, the ration of B is to the right of the equilibrium point, E. Because of this, the ration would have no direct effect upon market operations. Consumer Z would continue to buy and producers would continue to supply a quantity Q_1 at a price of P_1. The producers would not supply the maximum that Consumer Z is allowed to purchase by the ration of B, as Figure 3 shows that the consumer's willingness to purchase that quantity occurs at a price far less than that at which the producer's willingness to supply that quantity occurs; that is, a surplus would exist.

• PROBLEM 14-55

Given the supply and demand schedules for product A as shown in Figure 1, suppose that the price is currently P. Assuming that there are no price floors or ceilings, to what equilibrium price will this market tend?

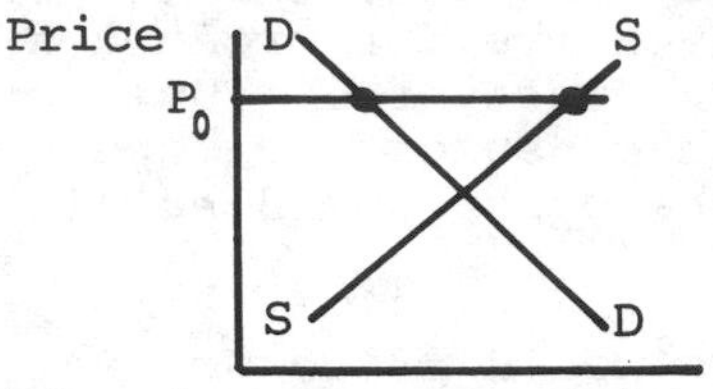

Fig. 1

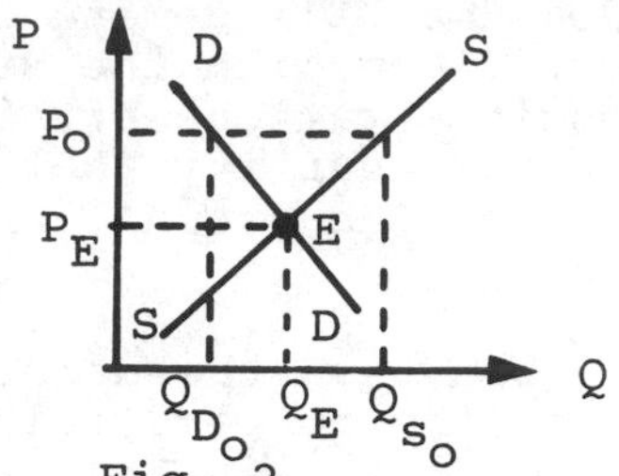

Fig. 2

Solution: By definition, an equilibrium point is a point from which there is no tendency to move, that is, things are at rest. In supply and demand analysis, this occurs at the price when the amount supplied and the amount demanded are equal. In a competitive market, this occurs where the supply and demand curves intersect. The equilibrium point for product A occurs at E with price equal to P_E and the quantity equal to Q_E, as shown in Figure 2.

P_O does not represent the equilibrium price, since, at that price, the quantity demanded, Q_{D_O}, is not the same as the quantity supplied. Q_{S_O}. $Q_{S_O} > Q_{D_O}$, so that, at P_O there is a surplus of A.

• PROBLEM 14-56

The government has set a price ceiling on cigarettes so that there is a shortage, as illustrated in the figure. The tobacco industry complains to the government that the ceiling price is far below the equilibrium price. In response to their claims, the government, which does not have access to the above graph, sends an economics student into the market place to investigate the situation. After a week of study, he concludes that since the quantity sold by the stores equals the quantity bought by consumers, the market is in equilibrium, and there is no need to reconsider the ceiling price. What is the fallacy in his argument?

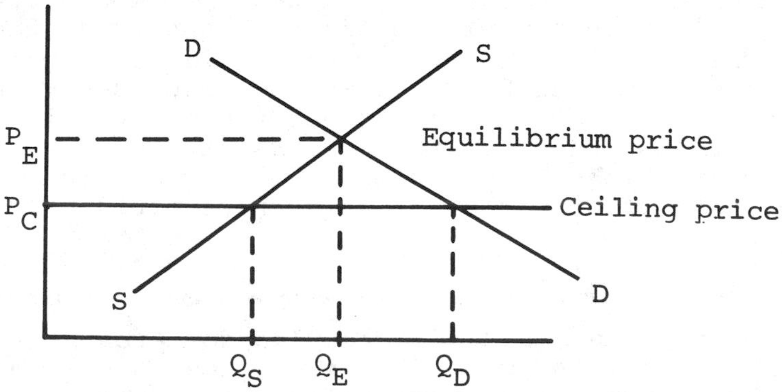

Solution: The student is correct in saying that quantity sold = quantity bought. But this equality is true in any situation, no matter what the price. What the student fails to realize is that equilibrium occurs at that price at which the amount consumers are willing to buy is just matched by the amount producers are willing to sell. If the student had taken the correct approach to studying the market, he would have discovered the amount consumers are willing to buy at the ceiling price, Q_D, is considerably higher than the amount producers are willing to sell Q_S. The difference, $Q_D - Q_S$, represents the amount of the shortage. Although consumers demand the amount Q_D at price P_c, they can find only amount Q_S for sale at that price. So Q_S is the amount actually bought and sold, and the demand for the additional quantity $Q_D - Q_S$ goes unsatisfied. Thus the equality of the quantity bought and the quantity sold, which always exists, at any price, does not imply equality of the quantity demanded and the quantity supplied, which occurs only at the equilibrium price, P_E.

• PROBLEM 14-57

Explain with the use of graphs when and why black markets exist.

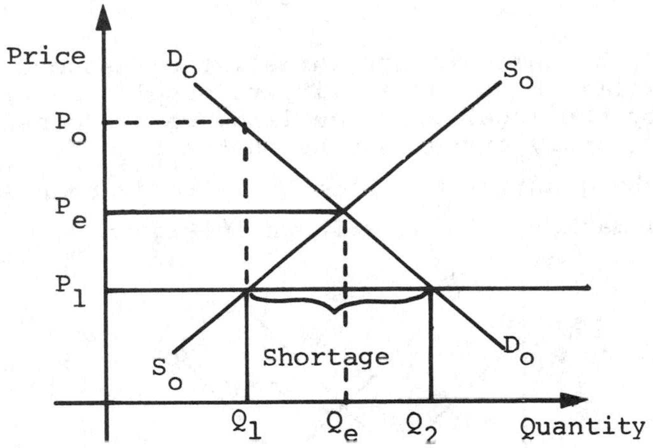

Fig. 1

Solution: A black market arises when the government sets a maximum legal price for a product below the equilibrium price. By graphing supply and demand curves for such a situation, it can be shown that if the maximum legal price is set at P_1, quantity demanded will exceed quantity supplied (see figure 1). Therefore a shortage of $(Q_2 - Q_1)$ will exist.

With a shortage of $(Q_2 - Q_1)$ at P_1, black markets may develop to alleviate the shortage. The quantity actually bought and sold in the legal market is the lesser of the quantity demanded at P_1 and quantity supplied, in this case, the quantity supplied, Q_1. Thus the demand for Q_1

units is satisfied. The remaining demand unsatisfied in the legal market can be determined by subtracting distance Q_1 from the original demand curve D_oD_o at each price, as shown in Figure 2.

D_1D_1 represents the demand for the product on the black market (assuming no potential demander refuses to patronize the black market for moral reasons or for fear of legal penalties, etc.).

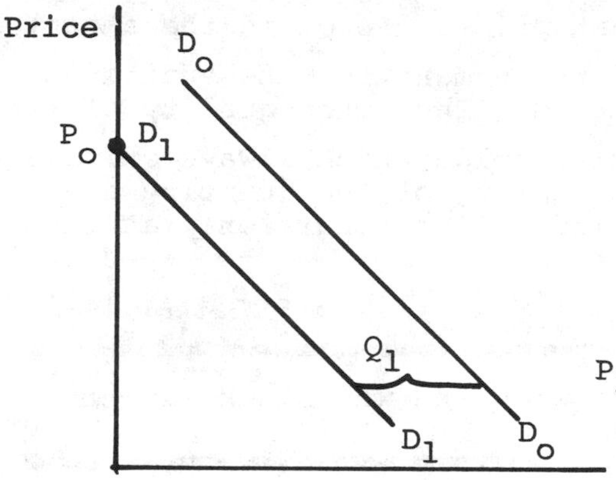

Fig. 2

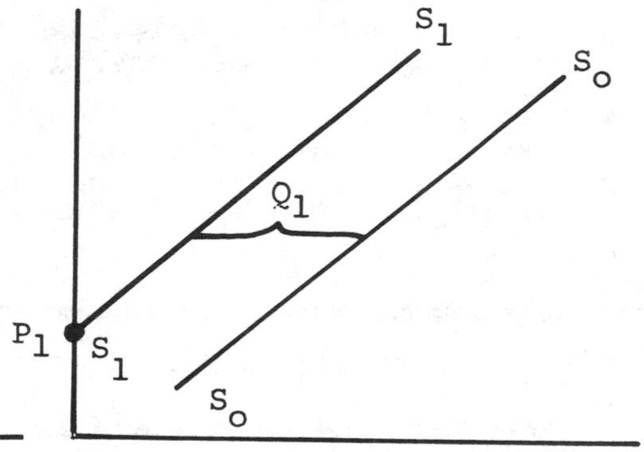

Fig. 3

Under, the same--rather unrealistic--assumption, that suppliers' willingness and ability to supply the product is unaffected by the legal price ceiling, we can construct the black market supply curve also by subtracting from S_oS_o at each price the quantity Q_1 which has already been supplied in the legal market. This is shown in Figure 3.

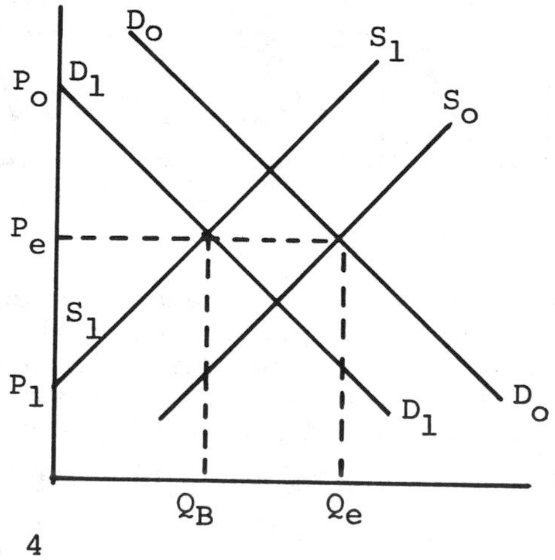

Fig. 4

Under the above assumptions, then, both the black market demand and black market supply curves lie to the left of the original demand and supply curves by Q_1. Their intersection, then, takes place at a price equal to the pre-ceiling equilibrium price, P_e; and at a quantity, Q_B equal to the pre-ceiling equilibrium quantity minus Q_1, $Q_e - Q_1 = Q_B$, as shown in Figure 4.

Hence, under our assumptions, Q_B units of the product will be sold on the black market at price P_e, the original equilibrium price.

• PROBLEM 14-58

Given the supply and demand schedules for product B as shown in Figure 1, why wouldn't price P_o be an equilibrium price?

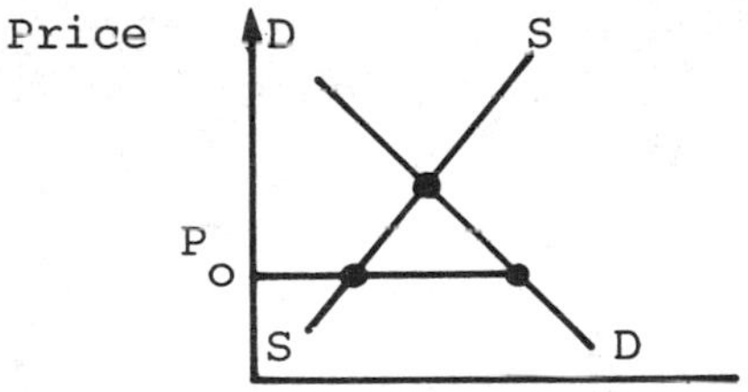

Fig. 1

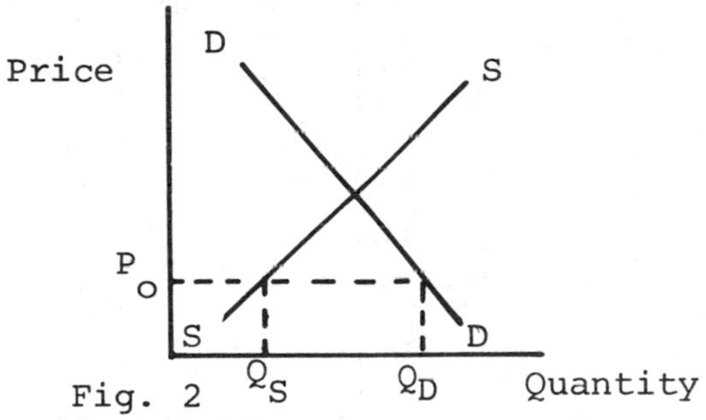

Fig. 2

Solution: An equilibrium point is a point from which there is no tendency to change. That is, if P is an equilibrium price, neither the suppliers of product B nor demanders of product B would have any incentive to change the price of B or the quantity of B which is actually exchanged in the market.

Using Figure 2, note that the quantity supplied by the producers of B is Q_S. Excluding the possibility of any interference in the market (such as a government decree), the only way to change the quantity of B supplied is to change the price. However, note also that the quantity of B which the consumers would willingly demand at price P_o is Q_D. Q_D is greater than Q_S, that is, the quantity demanded is greater than the quantity supplied at this price. At price P_o consumers are willing to buy more but producers are not willing to sell more. Therefore, Q_S represents the quantity of B which actually is exchanged in the market at price P_o. Producers would be willing to increase the quantity supplied only at a higher price than P_o and this higher price will discourage some buyers, reducing the quantity demanded. Thus the excess of the quantity demanded over the quantity supplied will decrease as the price becomes higher and higher. Ultimately, at the point where the two curves intersect, the quantity willingly supplied by the producers will be equal to the quantity demanded by the consumers, and equilibrium will be reached.

Suppose the demand schedule in the motorcycle market is given by the equation $P_D = 100 - 5Q_D$, where P represents price, and Q represents quantity. If the supply schedule is given by the equation $P_s = 40 + 10Q_s$, what is the equilibrium price and quantity in the motorcycle market?

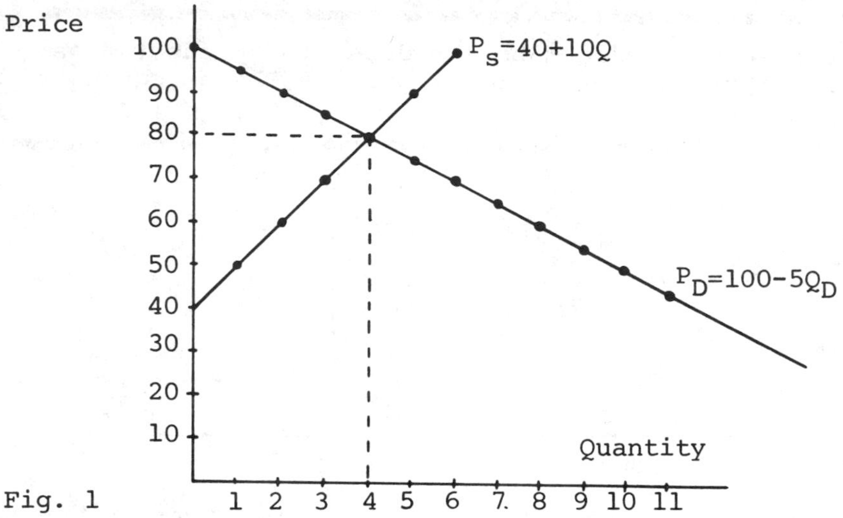

Fig. 1

Solution: The equilibrium price is that price at which the quantity demanded, Q_D, is equal to the quantity supplied, Q_s.

Likewise, the equilibrium quantity is that quantity for which buyers are willing and able to pay the same per unit price, P_D, that sellers will sell for, P_s. Thus, equilibrium exists when $Q_D = Q_s$ and $P_D = P_s$.

Let us first use the latter equality to solve our problem, since the demand and supply equations are written with P_D and P_s alone on the left hand side of the equations. Equilibrium means that $P_D = P_s$. Since $P_D = 100 - 5Q_D$ and $P_s = 40 + 10Q_s$, $100 - 5Q_D = 40 + 10Q_s$. Since, in equilibrium, $Q_D = Q_s$, we can treat Q_D and Q_s as the same variable. Therefore,

$$60 = 15Q_{D,s}$$

$$Q^* = 4 = Q_D = Q_s$$

The equilibrium quantity, Q*, is 4 motorcycles.

Using this piece of information we can determine the equilibrium price. The equilibrium quantity, Q* = 4, can be substituted into either the demand equation or the supply equation to give the equilibrium price. The demand equation $P_D = 100 - 5Q_D$ gives us $P_D = 100 - 5(4) = 100 - 20 = 80$. The supply equation will give the same value for price ($P_s = P_D = 80$) if the equilibrium quantity, Q*, is indeed 4. Let us substitute $Q^* = Q_s = 4$ into the supply equation

$$P_s = 40 + 10Q :$$

$$P_s = 40 + 10(4) = 40 + 40$$

$$P_s = 80 = P_D$$

Hence, P*, the equilibrium price, is indeed 80.

Graphically, this motorcycle market is depicted by Figure 1.

• PROBLEM 14-60

As the price of gasoline rises, what should we expect to happen to the demand for big "gas-guzzling" cars? Illustrate with supply and demand curves.

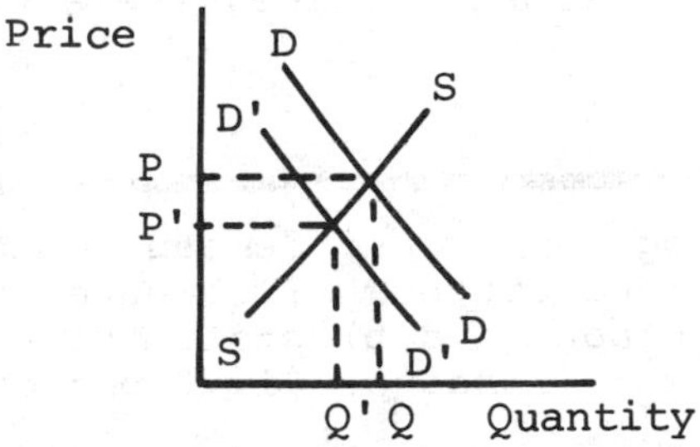

Solution: This question asks what happens to the equilibrium price of a good when the price of a complementary good changes, here, cars and gasoline, respectively. As gasoline prices rise, the demand for big cars will decrease, as shown in the diagram, from DD to D'D'. This causes a decrease in the equilibrium price, from P to P', and a decrease in the quantity supplied, from Q to Q'.

SURPLUS AND SHORTAGE

• PROBLEM 14-61

Given the accompanying supply and demand schedules,

Quantity demanded	Price	Quantity supplied
3000	$4.00	1200
2800	$4.05	1600
2500	$4.10	1900

Quantity Demanded	Price	Quantity Supplied
2100	$4.15	2100
2000	$4.20	2450
1700	$4.25	2900

(contd.)

a) find the equilibrium price, and

b) determine whether there would be a surplus or a shortage if price were set at $4.00.

Solution: a) Equilibrium price is that price at which quantity demanded equals quantity supplied. In this schedule, we see that at Price = $4.15, quantity demanded is 2100 and quantity supplied is 2100. Therefore, equilibrium price is $4.15.

b) If price were to be set at $4.00, quantity demanded would be 3000, but quantity supplied would be only 1200. Therefore a shortage would exist of (3000 - 1200 =) 1800 units. Note that whenever the price is below the equilibrium price, there will be a shortage, while whenever the price is above the equilibrium price, there will be a surplus.

• **PROBLEM 14-62**

Given the accompanying supply and demand schedules (Fig. 1) for yogurt in the United States, a) compute the equilibrium price and output by graph, and b) state the effect on the market if the price were fixed at $1.70 per quart.

Figure 1

Price per quart	No. of Quarts Demanded (in millions) (Q_D)	No. of Quarts Supplied (in millions) (Q_s)
$0.50	49	40
0.80	48	42
1.10	47	44
1.40	46	46
1.70	45	48
2.00	44	50

Solution: a) By graphing supply and demand together (Fig. 2), it is shown that at Price = $1.40, quantity demanded equals quantity supplied equals 46 million. Therefore, the equilibrium price is $1.40 and the equilibrium quantity is

46 million quarts.

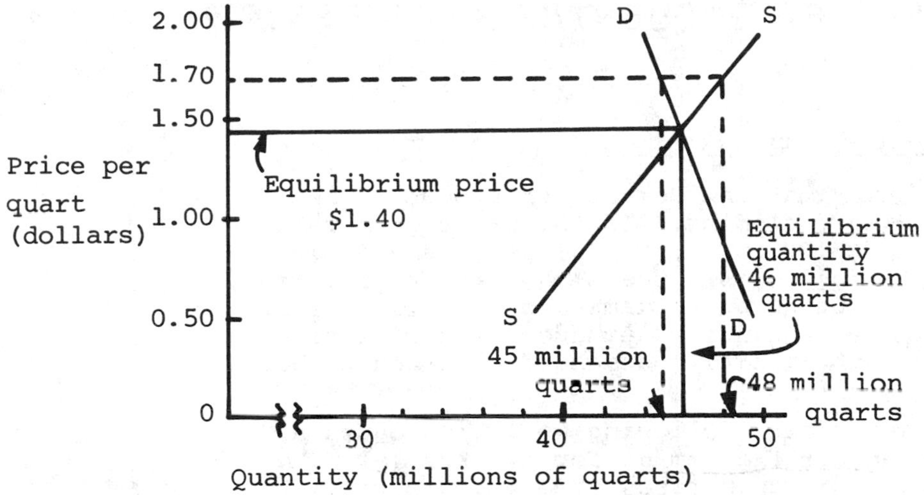

Fig. 2

b) Looking at the graph, it can be seen that, at a price of $1.70, there is a difference between the quantity supplied, Q_s, and quantity demanded, Q_D. Specifically, $Q_s = 48$, $Q_D = 45$. Thus at $1.70, there will be a surplus of $Q_s - Q_D = 48m. - 45\ m. = 3$ million quarts.

• PROBLEM 14-63

At each of the three prices given in the figure ($2, $3 and $4), determine whether a market surplus, shortage, or equilibrium exists.

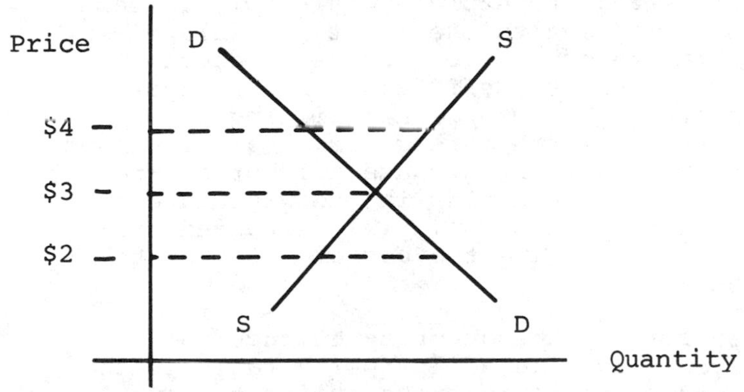

<u>Solution</u>: At price = $2, quantity demanded is greater than quantity supplied. Therefore a shortage exists.

At price = $3, quantity demanded = quantity supplied. Therefore a market equilibrium exists.

At price = $4, quantity demanded is less than quantity supplied. Therefore a surplus exists.

Answer

To be covered when testing yourself

SHORT ANSWER QUESTIONS FOR REVIEW

Choose the correct answer.

1. Assume that the demand for product A is downward sloping. If the price of A falls from $3.00 to $2.75 (a) the demand for A will fall. (b) the demand for A will rise. (c) the quantity demanded of A will fall. (d) the quantity demanded of A will rise. (e) the quantity demanded of A won't change. d

2. Which of the following would not cause a change in the demand for steak? (a) The price of steak rises from $3.00 per lb. to $3.50 per lb. (b) Cattle producers launch an advertising campaign on the vitamin content of beef. (c) The Surgeon General determines that beef consumption is hazardous to your health. (d) The price of hamburger falls from $2.00 per lb. to $1.50 per lb. a

3. If the demand curve for product B shifts to the right as the price of product A declines, it can be concluded that (a) A and B are substitutes. (b) A and B are complementary goods. (c) A is an inferior good and B is a superior good. (d) A is a superior good and B is an inferior good. (e) both A and B are inferior goods. b

4. A false reason to explain why supply curves slope upward and to the right is (a) diminishing returns. (b) extra production brings in the less efficient, higher-cost producers. (c) people are willing to pay a higher price for more goods. (d) expanded industry output might cause a labor shortage and subsequently a rise in the wage rate and the cost of production. (e) expanded production may require the use of inferior resources. c

5. One reason why the quantity demanded of a good tends to rise as its price falls is that (a) the decrease in price shifts the supply downward. (b) the decrease in price shifts the demand curve upward. (c) people's real incomes are greater so they increase their consumption of the good. (d) demand has to rise to restore equilibrium after a price fall. (e) none of the above. c

6. Income and tastes are (a) factors underlying

supply. (b) factors underlying demand. (c) ignored in economic analysis. (d) complements of demand. (e) substitutes for demand. — b

7. As the equilibrium price of butter decreases (a) the demand curve for margarine shifts to the left and downward. (b) the demand curve for margarine shifts to the right and upward. (c) the demand curve for margarine remains the same. (d) the supply curve for margarine shifts left and downward. (e) the supply curve for margarine shifts right and upward. — a

8. All of the following will cause the supply curve for soybeans to shift except (a) a new union contract which increases wages by 20%. (b) a drop in the price of a complement. (c) an increase in the market price of soybeans. (d) the weather being good and there being a bumper crop of soybeans. — c

9. Which of the following is most likely to be an inferior good? (a) Steak (b) Imported foreign sports cars (c) Butter (d) Potatoes (e) Summer lake-houses — d

10. If the economy is fully employed, an upward shift in the demand for wheat alone (a) will lead to a gradual fall in the price of wheat. (b) will lead to unemployment of wheat farmers. (c) cannot alter the output of wheat. (d) will lead to an increase in the amount of wheat supplied with a consequent decrease in the supply of some other commodities. (e) will lead to an increase in the quantity supplied of corn. — d

11. Price ceilings and price floors (a) shift supply and demand curves and, therefore, have no effect on the rationing of prices. (b) clear the market. (c) always result in shortages. (d) interfere with the rationing function of prices. — d

12. Cameras and film are (a) complementary goods (b) inferior goods (c) substitute goods (d) superior goods (e) independent goods. — a

13. An equilibrium price occurs when (a) P is set equal to Q. (b) there is a shortage and no surplus. (c) quantity supplied is equal to quantity demanded. (d) all of the above.

Answer
To be covered when testing yourself

(e) none of the above. c

14. A price at which the amount consumers wish to buy exceeds the amount that producers will supply, (a) lies above the equilibrium price. (b) lies below the equilibrium price. (c) will induce a shift in the demand schedule. (d) is impossible. (e) none of the above. b

15. Which of the following statements is incorrect? (Hint: use diagrams.) (a) If supply declines and demand remains constant, equilibrium price will rise (b) If supply increases and demand decreases, equilibrium price will fall (c) If demand increases and supply decreases, equilibrium price will rise (d) If demand decreases and supply increases, equilibrium price will rise (e) If supply increases and demand remains constant, equilibrium price will fall d

16. Given the supply of lamb chops, a reduction in the supply of pork chops (a substitute) will tend to (a) shift the demand curve for lamb chops to the right (b) shift the demand curve for pork chops to the right (c) shift the demand curve for pork chops to the left (d) lower the price of pork chops (e) lower the price of lamb chops a

17. If the demand schedule may be written P = 100 - 4Q, and the supply schedule may be written P = 40 + 2Q, then the equilibrium price and quantity are (a) P = 60, Q = 10 (b) P = 10, Q = 6 (c) P = 40, Q = 6 (d) P = 20, Q = 20 (e) none of the above. a

18. A "disequilibrium price" (a) is no different from an "equilibrium price" because the amount bought must equal the amount sold. (b) is a price at which the quantities demanded and supplied are not equal. (c) has no significance at all in real life, because such supply and demand analysis takes no account of incomes, tastes or other factors that influence demand. (d) has no application except where some monopoly is present, so that the supplier can influence and stabilize the price. (e) none of the above. b

19. Which of the following would not cause a shift in the demand curve for corn? (a) An increase in consumers' incomes (b) An increase in the

Answer

To be covered when testing yourself

SHORT ANSWER QUESTIONS FOR REVIEW

price of corn (c) A large decrease in the supply of peas (d) An increase in the price of peas (e) A decrease in the price of peas — b

20. A market demand curve (a) can be obtained by adding the demand curves of all the largest purchasers in the market. (b) is always horizontal. (c) is the sum of the demand curves of all the individuals in the market. (d) can only be derived if all buyers belong to a purchasing cooperative. (e) represents the government's demand for the good in question. — c

21. Good growing conditions would probably (a) lower the prices of substitutes for wheat. (b) induce greater demand for wheat, yielding a higher price. (c) cause wheat suppliers to move up their supply curves to a higher point. (d) cause people to reduce their demand for wheat. (e) induce a downward and rightward shift in wheat's supply curve. — e

22. A price that is said to be "too high for equilibrium," means that (a) no producer can cover his costs of production at that price. (b) quantity supplied exceeds quantity demanded at that price. (c) producers are leaving the industry. (d) consumers are willing to buy all the units produced at that price. (e) quantity demanded exceeds quantity supplied at that price. — b

23. If Congress reinstituted the draft as a necessary measure in order to maintain the armed forces at a size which they deem adequate, an economist might comment that (a) the price of military labor services was an equilibrium one. (b) the quantity of military services was an equilibrium one regardless of price. (c) the price of military labor services was a disequilibrium one and is set too high. (d) the price of military military services is a disequilibrium one and is set too low. (e) this particular issue has absolutely no economic content. — d

Fill in the blank.

24. A ___market___ is the interaction of supply and demand; the buying and selling of goods. — market

25. The sum of all individual demands is called the ___market demand___. — market demand

SHORT ANSWER QUESTIONS FOR REVIEW

Answer

To be covered when testing yourself

26. The relationship between the price of a commodity and the quantity of it offered for sale is called ____________.

supply

27. The relationship between the price of a commodity and the quantity buyers are willing and able to purchase is called ____________.

demand

28. When quantity demanded at a particular price is more than quantity supplied at that price, a ____________ exists.

shortage

29. The ____________ can be put as follows: There is an inverse relationship between the price of a commodity and the quantity of that good demanded at that price.

law of demand

30. The cost of producing A goes up. This results in decrease in the ____________.

supply

31. A ____________ is a legal price, imposed by the government, which is above the equilibrium price.

price floor

32. When tastes shift away from commodity A, (A goes out of fashion), the demand curve would normally (shift to the right/shift to the left/remain the same) while the supply curve would (shift to the right/shift to the left/remain the same).

shift to the left, remain the same

33. A substantial increase in the cost of producing A is likely to result in (an upward shift/downward shift/no change) in the demand curve and (an upward shift/downward shift/no change) in the supply curve.

no change, an upward shift

Consider the accompanying diagram in answering questions 34 through 37.

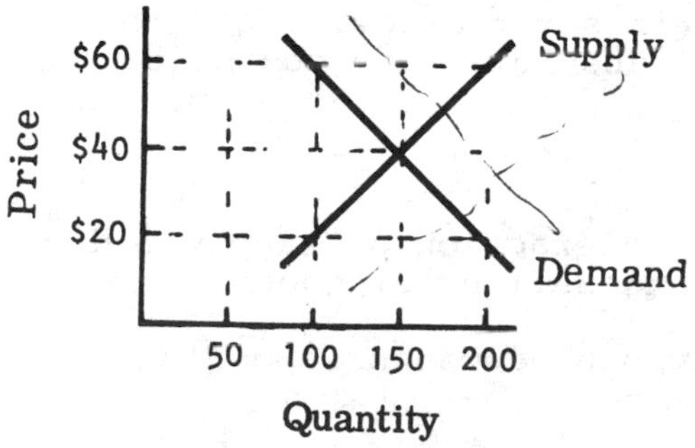

HORT ANSWER QUESTIONS FOR REVIEW

	Answer To be covered when testing yourself
4. A price of $60 in this market will result in a surplus of ________ units.	100
5. A price of $20 in this market will result in a ________ of 100 units.	shortage
6. The highest price that buyers will be willing and able to pay for 100 units of this product is ________.	$60
7. If this is a competitive market, price and quantity will gravitate toward ________ dollars and ________ units respectively.	$40, 150 units
8. Cameras and film are ________ goods.	comple-mentary
9. To increase the amount of capital goods in a full employment-full production economy, someone must necessarily decrease ________.	con-sumption

<u>etermine whether the following statements are rue or false.</u>

0. The higher the legal minimum wage is set, the more jobs will be available for the unskilled.	False
41. A supply curve shifting to the right means that producers will supply more at each price.	True
42. A change in tastes will cause people to shift along their demand curves. This differs from a change in income, which causes a shift in demand curves.	False
43. Advertising a product is an attempt by the advertiser to cause people to shift upward along their demand curves.	False
44. What occurs in the rye market will have some effect on the markets for wheat and corn.	True
45. At some given price, if sellers do not wish to continue selling and buyers do not wish to continue buying, then a shortage exists.	False
46. An increase in demand accompanied by an increase in supply will increase the equil-	

Answer
To be covered when testing yourself

	ibrium quantity, but the effect on equilibrium price will be indeterminate.	True
47.	An "increase in the quantity supplied" may be due to a decrease in production costs. T	False
48.	The market demand curve is simply a horizontal summation of all individual demand curves. T	True
49.	Given normally sloped curves, a shift in the demand curve will cause a shift along the supply curve. T	True

CHAPTER 15

DEMAND AND UTILITY THEORY

Basic Attacks and Strategies for Solving Problems in this Chapter. **See pages 543 to 574 for step-by-step solutions to problems.**

Economists have developed an analysis that purports to explain the wide range of household decisions, including such choices as spending versus saving, types and quantities of specific goods and services purchased, quantity of labor supplied, and so on. The basis for the theory is the belief that households act "as if" they weigh the benefits and costs of alternative courses of action before they make decisions. Given the household's goal of maximizing its well-being, the courses of action chosen will always be those that promise to provide the greatest benefits relative to their costs.

The benefit received from consuming goods and services is called utility. The term utility refers to the satisfaction obtained from goods and services. Utility cannot be measured directly. It could be measured indirectly by determining how much of other goods and services people are willing to give up for the good and service in question. For example, the utility of an item may be measured by how much money you are willing to give up to get it. This approach suffers from the practical problem that most people cannot say precisely how much they would be willing to give up, and everyone has an incentive to conceal that amount if they did know.

The amount of utility a specific individual receives from a particular good or service depends on 1) individual tastes, 2) the amount of complementary goods and services available, and 3) the amount of the particular good or service already consumed. The latter point is relevant to the law of diminishing marginal utility. Marginal utility is the increase in total utility from consuming one more unit of the product. The law says that as you consume more of a product, the additions to total utility eventually begin to diminish. Essentially it means that as you consume a product additional units provide less and less satisfaction.

The graph shows the marginal utility schedule for good *X* of a particular individual. The negative slope is indicative of the law of diminishing marginal utility. Assuming good *X* is the only good available, the utility maximizing rule can be easily derived. Assume good *X* sells for price *P*. The individual should increase consumption of the good whenever the benefit received from a unit exceeds what it costs. In symbols, consumption should increase when $MU > P$. Individuals should not consume a good when the benefit received is less than what it costs. In symbols, consumption should not take place when $MU < P$. The individual should consume no more than the quantity where $MU = P$, the utility maximizing point.

Note that each unit of good *X* except the last one provides more utility than it costs ($MU > P$ for each unit except the last one, where $MU = P$). If we add up all this "surplus" utility over all units of good *X*, we get a quantity known as consumer surplus. On the graph this corresponds to the area under the *MU* and above the *P* schedule. In other words, consumer surplus is the consumer's total utility from consuming good *X* less the total cost of the good. Maximizing utility is equivalent to maximizing consumer surplus.

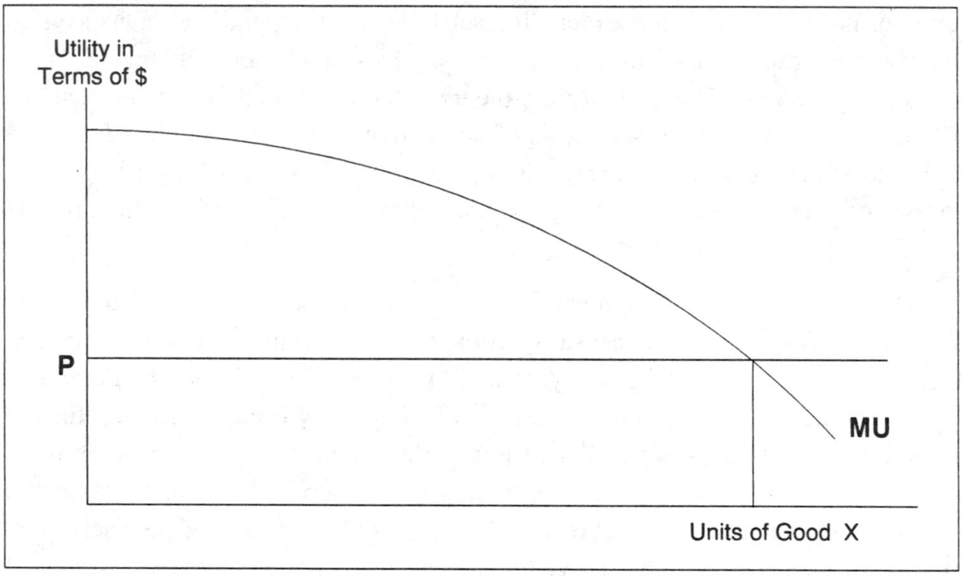

Consumer Equilibrium for Good X

When there is more than one good, the condition for utility maximization follows from that above and will be illustrated using the case of two goods, a and b. Utility maximization occurs when the following condition holds:

$$\frac{MU_a}{P_a} = \frac{MU_b}{P_b}$$

This says that utility is maximized when the marginal utility of the last dollar spent on each good is equal. To understand why, assume the condition does not hold, $MU_a/P_a > MU_b/P_b$. This says that the last dollar spent on good *a* brings more utility than a dollar spent on good *b*. It follows that if you spent one less dollar on good b (surrendering MU_b/P_b in utility) and used that dollar for good a (receiving MU_a/P_a utility), you would be better off. This reallocation of your consumption dollars should continue until the condition of equality is obtained.

Using the diagram again, if you know the price of a product, you can determine the amount purchased by finding where the price line intersects the *MU* schedule. In other words, the *MU* schedule tells us how much consumers are willing to purchase at different prices. This means that the *MU* schedule is simply the consumer's demand schedule for the good.

To get the market demand schedule for a product, simply add horizontally the demand schedules of every consumer in the market.

When the price of a good drops, the consumer is affected in two ways. The substitution effect means that the good is now relatively cheaper than its substitutes, which will lead the consumer to buy more of the item. The income effect means that the purchasing power of the consumer's income has been increased since at least one of the prices she faces is now lower. The consumer will proceed to purchase more of all normal goods and less of all inferior goods. The law of demand comes about as a result of both these effects. If the good is normal, a lower price will lead to greater quantity demanded because both the substitution and income effect work in the same direction. If the good is inferior, the substitution and income effects of a price decrease work in opposite directions. As long as the good is not "too inferior," the net result will be greater quantity demanded. If the good is "too inferior," we will have the Giffen good case of an item whose quantity demanded falls as its price falls. We may be assured that the Giffen good case is rare, if indeed it has ever occurred.

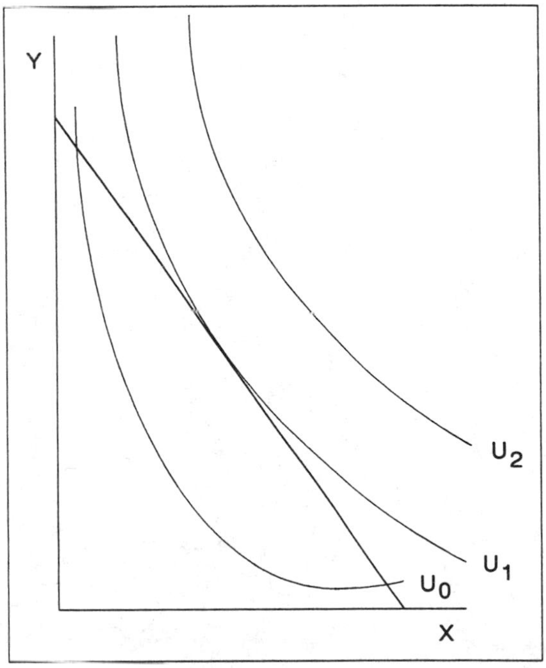

Consumer Equilibrium Using Indifference Curves

The modern analysis of consumer behavior does not rely on the concept of utility. Rather, it uses the concept of indifference. In comparing bundles of goods containing different amounts of X and Y, consumers can easily decide if they prefer one bundle to another or are indifferent between the two. An indifference curve (for example U_1 on the graph) displays all combinations of goods X and Y that provide equal amounts of utility (all combinations the consumer is indifferent toward). Indifference curves to the right provide higher levels of utility.

The negative of the slope of an indifference curve is called the marginal rate of substitution (MRS). It indicates how many units of *Y* the consumer is willing to give up to get one more unit of *X*. As you move down to the right along an indifference curve, the MRS decreases, indicating that additional units of *X* have become less valuable.

The negatively-sloped straight line is called the budget constraint. It shows all combinations of the two goods that the consumer could purchase, given her income and the prices of the two goods. The negative of the slope of the budget constraint is the ratio of the price of *Y* to the price of *X* (P_x/P_y). It measures how many units of *Y* the consumer must give up to get an additional unit of *X*.

Utility maximization occurs at the point of tangency between the budget constraint and an indifference. The point of tangency is a feasible point, an amount the consumer can purchase, and provides the highest level of utility of all the possible combinations of the goods.

Step-by-Step Solutions to Problems in this Chapter, "Demand and Utility Theory"

UTILITY

• PROBLEM 15-1

What is utility? What is marginal utility?

Solution: Utility is the power to satisfy a want. When one is thirsty, water has utility, i.e., it is able to quench one's thirst. If a person prefers a strawberry sundae to hot fudge, it is said that the utility or want-satisfying power, to that person of a strawberry sundae is greater than that of hot fudge.

"Utility" and "usefulness" need not be synonomous. Pet rocks may be "useless" yet be of tremendous utility to Christmas shoppers who can't think of what to buy their friend "who has everything".

Also, utility is a subjective notion. The utility of a specific product will vary widely from person to person. That first cigarette upon waking up in the morning will yield a great deal of utility to the chain smoker, but would have little or negative utility for someone who doesn't smoke.

Marginal utility is the extra utility, or satisfaction, which a consumer derives from an additional unit of a specific good.

• PROBLEM 15-2

What is the law of diminishing marginal utility?

Solution: Marginal utility refers to the additional utility derived from successive units of a good or service. The Law of Diminishing Marginal Utility refers to the fact that as successive units are consumed during some short period of time in which the consumer's tastes do not change, the utility derived from each additional unit decreases beyond some point. For example, the first strawberry sundae on a hot day might yield the average consumer ten "units of utility". The second sundae is still good, but the first has already gone some way in satisfying him, so the second yields only nine units of utility, etc. (Note however that total utility increases from ten to nineteen.)

The law of diminishing marginal utility is used to explain the downward slope of demand curves. If successive units of a product yield smaller and smaller amounts of marginal, or extra, utility, the amount that a consumer will pay for additional units will decline as well.

• PROBLEM 15-3

Suppose marginal (MU) and total utility (TU) look as graphed in the accompanying figure.

a) Explain the shape of the total utility (TU) curve up to point M.

b) What is happening at point A ?

c) Explain the TU curve after point M.

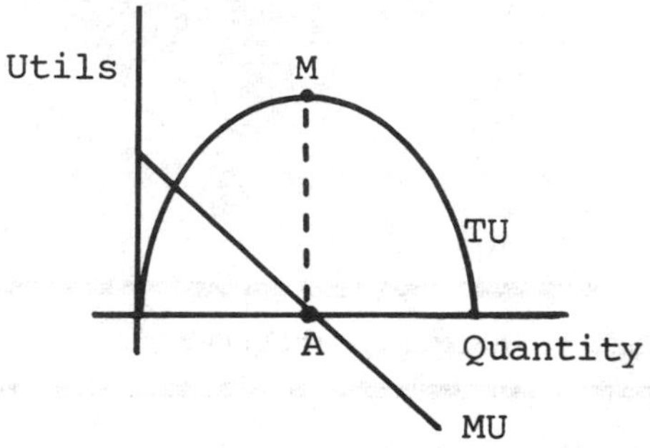

Solution: a) Total utility curves typically, as above are shaped like upside-down U's. The reason for this is the law of diminishing marginal utility. We start at $Q = 0$. The first unit of the product brings about a certain level of satisfaction (utils) but all units after the first bring less and less satisfaction. This is also illustrated by the shape of the MU curve. As more and more units of the product are consumed, MU grows smaller and smaller, hence the negative slope.

To explain the U-shape of the total utility curve, we say that, at first, it is increasing at a decreasing rate. MU is the rate of change of TU. As long as $MU > 0$, TU is increasing. But since MU is getting smaller, TU is increasing, but at a slower and slower rate. Hence, the levelling off of the TU curve appears.

b) At point A, $MU = 0$. Also when Quantity = A, TU is at a maximum. These two concepts go hand-in-hand. To the left of A, $MU > 0$. Therefore to the left of M, TU is increasing. To the right of A, $MU < 0$. Therefore, to the right of M, TU is decreasing. If TU is increasing as it approaches M and decreasing as it goes away from M, it must reach a maximum at M.

c) After point M, TU is decreasing. Here the consumer has reached maximum satisfaction. More consumption of the product can only bring about dissatisfaction. (It's like eating too much of a good thing. After a while, your stomach starts to hurt). This is represented by the shape of the MU curve. Since $MU < 0$ after point A, this means that the change in TU is negative, i.e., TU is decreasing. Since MU itself is becoming more and more negative, TU will fall at a quicker and quicker pace. Thus the upside-down U-shape is explained.

• PROBLEM 15-4

Differentiate between the cardinal approach and the ordinal approach to the study of consumer demand theory.

Solution: Cardinal numbers are those that assign a concrete quantity such as 1, 2, 3, and 4. These numbers say that 2 is twice as great as 1 and that the absolute difference between them is 1. On the other hand, ordinal numbers are those that establish a rank or order among the things to which they have been assigned, such as first, second, and third. These numbers do not say anything about the absolute difference or any other relationship between them, other than "first" is greater than "second" if we are viewing the numbers in descending order.

The classical approach to the study of consumer demand theory is generally called the cardinal utility approach. It involves the use of marginal utility and as such requires the measurement of satisfaction in absolute terms. The ordinal approach to the study of consumer demand theory, on the other hand, uses indifference analysis, relying only on a ranking of preferences for various goods.

• PROBLEM 15-5

What is meant by the law of diminishing marginal utility? Illustrate by giving an example.

Solution: The law of diminishing marginal utility states, that as you consume more of the same good, your total (psychological) utility increases. However, let's use the term marginal utility to refer to the extra utility added by one extra last unit of a good. Then, with successive new units of the good, your total utility will grow at a slower and slower rate because of a fundamental tendency for your psychological ability to appreciate more of the good to become less keen. This fact, that the increments in total utility fall off, economists describe as follows:

As the amount consumed of a good increases, the marginal utility of the good (or the extra utility added by its last unit) tends to decrease. To illustrate the law of diminishing marginal utility, let's consider the following table:

(1) Quantity of a Good Consumed	(2) Total Utility	(3) Marginal Utility
0	0	
		4
1	4	
		3
2	7	
		2
3	9	
		1
4	10	
		0
5	10	

Column (2) of the table shows that total utility enjoyed increases as Q grows, but at a decreasing rate. Column (3) measures marginal utility as the increment of total utility resulting when one last unit of the good is added; the fact that marginal utilities in the table are declining exemplifies the law of diminishing marginal utility.

• **PROBLEM 15-6**

How is the theory of diminishing marginal utility used to justify the "progressive" income tax? What is the weakness of the argument?

Solution: The theory of diminishing marginal utility states that each additional unit of a good or service results in less-and-less added satisfaction for an individual. It is the theory of diminishing marginal utility which helps account for the downward slope of a demand curve.

Under a progressive tax system, a higher proportion of income goes to taxes as income increases. For example, an income of $20,000 might be taxed at 25% while an income of $30,000 might be taxed at 30%.

The whole idea of progressive taxes can be seen as an extension of the theory of diminishing marginal utility, where we examine the marginal utility of an individual's income. When applied to a progressive tax system, the theory says that those people with high incomes are sacrificing less when they are asked to pay x dollars in the tax than poor people would sacrifice to pay that same amount, since the utility derived by the relatively rich from an additional x dollars is lower than that derived by the relatively poor due to their respective utility positions. For example, a poor family might have to go without some of the necessities of life to meet a $100 tax bill, but a rich family would simply have to give up some luxuries for a few days.

The weakness of the argument stems from the fact that it overlooks the subjective nature of utility. That is, while a given individual can compare the utilities to him or her of different goods, the utility that a given good has for two different individuals cannot be compared. There is no basis in economics for the claim that the marginal utility of a dollar is less to a wealthy person than to a poor person, since utility is subjective. Interpersonal comparisons of utility would require that utility be something objective.

UTILITY MAXIMIZATION

• **PROBLEM 15-7**

What is the utility-maximizing rule?

Solution: In dealing with the behavior of the so-called "rational" consumer, economists assume that he attempts to dispose of his money income in such a way as to derive the greatest amount of satisfaction, or total utility, from it. The consumer's goal is assumed to be utility maximization. In making his choices of goods and services, the typical consumer has a limited number of dollars in his pocket and the products he wants have price tags on them. Therefore he will be able to purchase only a limited amount of goods.

Since his purchases are limited by his budget, the consumer must decide which specific collection of goods and services will yield the greatest amount of satisfaction. To do this, the rational consumer uses the utility-maximizing rule which prescribes the allocation of money income in such a way that the last dollar spent on each product purchased yields the same amount of extra (marginal) utility.

To help explain this rule, let us examine an illustration. Suppose

Mr. X is trying to decide which combination of goods A and B he should buy with his limited budget of $10. Assume product A costs $1 and product B costs $2. The table provides utility data necessary for solving. Notice how diminishing marginal utility sets in.

(1) Unit of product	(2) Product A: price = $1 (a) Marginal utility, utils	(b) Marginal utility per dollar (MU/price)	(3) Product B: price = $2 (a) Marginal utility, utils	(b) Marginal utility per dollar (MU/price)
First	10	10	24	12
Second	8	8	20	10
Third	7	7	18	9
Fourth	6	6	16	8
Fifth	5	5	12	6
Sixth	4	4	6	3
Seventh	3	3	4	2

In columns 2a and 3a, we see the marginal utility of products A and B "measured" in utils. We must also construct columns 2b and 3b where we have marginal utility (MU) per dollar = MU/price. The point is this: To make the amounts of extra utility derived from differently priced goods comparable, marginal utility must be put on a per-dollar-spent basis, as is done in columns 2b and 3b.

Now that we have Mr. X's marginal utility data, it must be decided in what order he should allocate his dollars on units of A and B to achieve the highest degree of utility. Concentrating on columns 2b and 3b, we see that Mr. X should first purchase one unit of B since it yields the greatest utility. This costs $2 and leaves $8 to spend. Next Mr. X is indifferent about buying A or B since they both yield ten utils. Suppose he buys both of them: Mr. X now has 1 unit of A and 2 units of B and $5 left. Note that with this combination of goods, the last dollar spent on each yields the same amount of extra utility. But Mr. X keeps going since he has $5 more.

Since the third unit of B yields 9 utils, Mr. X will choose that, leaving him with $3. Then finally, Mr. X will purchase one more unit of A and B each since the second unit of A and the fourth unit of B each yield 8 utils. This leaves Mr. X without any money. So, to maximize utility, Mr. X will purchase four units of B and two units of A with total utility equalling 10 + 8 + 24 + 20 + 18 + 16 = 96 utils. If the reader examines some of the other possible combinations of A and B, it will become apparent that A = 2 and B = 4 is the optimal combination. Looking at columns 2a and 3a, we see that trading off the fourth unit of B for the third and fourth unit of A would be giving up 16 utils for 7 + 6 = 13 utils in return.

Alternatively, giving up the original two units of A for a fifth unit of B would give up 18 utils for 12 utils in return. Once again, a loss in total utility would take place. So A = 2 and B = 4 represent the point of utility maximization.

• PROBLEM 15-8

Restate the utility-maximizing rule in algebraic terms.

Solution: The utility-maximizing rule states that a "rational" consumer allocates his money income so that the last dollar spent on each product purchased yields the same amount of extra (marginal) utility. It is important to remember that since different products may have different prices, we cannot always directly compare only the marginal utility of these different products. We must find the marginal utility per dollar for the various products we are considering where marginal utility (MU) per dollar = MU/Price. Once we have the ratio of MU/Price for all the relevant products, we simply equate these ratios to maximize utility. If there are four products, A,B,C,D, we have

$$\frac{MU_A}{Price_A} = \frac{MU_B}{Price_B} = \frac{MU_C}{Price_C} = \frac{MU_D}{Price_D}$$

where prices are constant and the consumer exhausts all of his available income, as the condition for utility to be maximized.

• PROBLEM 15-9

Mrs. McCoy is trying to decide how much beer, wine, and soda to buy. Soda costs $1 for a large bottle. Beer is $2 for a six-pack. Wine cost $4 per liter. Her marginal utility figures for the beverages are as presented below:

Unit of product	MU of soda(utils)	MU of Beer(utils)	MU of wine(utils)
First	10	50	60
Second	9	40	40
Third	8	30	32
Fourth	7	20	24
Fifth	6	16	20
Sixth	5	12	16

If Mrs. McCoy wishes to spend $17 what combination of beverages should she select in order to maximize her total utility.

Solution: To solve this problem, use the utility-maximizing rule which says that a consumer will purchase amounts of products so that the last dollar spent on each product yields equal marginal utility.

In this problem, the products are priced differently so that the marginal utilities alone are not the sole criterion for her choice. Instead, the given marginal utilities must be converted to MU per dollar. For soda, MU per dollar = MU/price = MU/$1 = MU, that is, division by $1 yields the original MU. For beer, divide MU by 2. For wine divide MU by 4. The table below shows these calculations.

Unit of product	Soda		Beer		Wine	
	MU	MU/dollar	MU	MU/dollar	MU	MU/dollar
First	10	10	50	25	60	15
Second	9	9	40	20	40	10
Third	8	8	30	15	32	8
Fourth	7	7	20	10	24	6
Fifth	6	6	16	8	20	5
Sixth	5	5	12	6	16	4

Now going down the columns marked MU/dollar for each product, pick out the highest possible values. Keep in mind that Mrs. McCoy has only $17 to spend.

Going across the first unit row, note that the greatest satisfaction per dollar will come from the first six-pack of beer, 25 utils/dollar. The second six-pack of beer still yields more utility per dollar than either the first bottle of soda or the first liter of wine, so the second six-pack would also be bought. This leaves Mrs. McCoy with $17 - 2 ($2) = $17 - $4 = $13. Now we have 15 utils/dollar from the third six-pack and the first liter of wine. So Mrs. McCoy buys them both, leaving her with $13 - $2 - $4 = $7. Then finally, Mrs. McCoy buys one unit each of beer ($2), wine ($4) and soda ($1) since the next unit of each beverage yields 10 utils/dollar. This exhausts her budget.

So, if Mrs. McCoy wished to maximize utility, she would buy a total of 1 bottle of soda, 4 six-packs of beer, and 2 liters of wine. Total utility (TU) can be found by adding up the marginal utilities given originally in the problem for each of the purchases. $TU_{soda} = 10$; $TU_{beer} = 50 + 40 + 30 + 20 = 140$; $TU_{wine} = 60 + 40 = 100$; so $TU = 10 + 140 + 100 = 250$. To show that this is a maximum, find MU/price for the last unit purchased of each beverage:

$$\frac{MU_{soda}}{price_{soda}} = \frac{10}{1} = 10$$

$$\frac{MU_{beer}}{price_{beer}} = \frac{20}{2} = 10$$

$$\frac{MU_{wine}}{price_{wine}} = \frac{40}{4} = 10$$

Since they are equal and all of the $17 has been spent, this combination is the utility maximizing one.

• PROBLEM 15-10

Given in Figure 1 is Mr. Brody's marginal utility curve for beer consumption. Explain the shape of this curve and show how much beer Mr. Brody would drink in order to maximize his total utility.

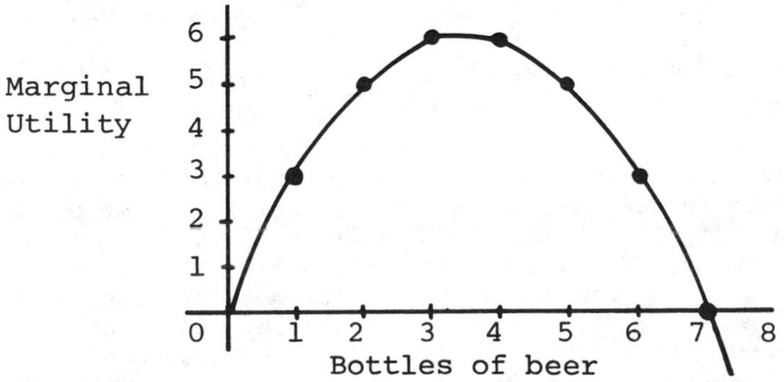

Fig. 1

Solution: Since marginal utility indicates the satisfaction derived from each additional beer, the shape of the curve can be explained as follows: at first each additional bottle of beer gives Mr. Brody more and more satisfaction. That is, the second beer is more satisfying to him than the first and the third is more satisfying than the second. After three beers, the MU curve stops rising. This is because the fourth beer is only as satisfying as the third. After four beers, the curve slopes downward as each additional beer is less and less satisfying. Finally at the point of consumption of the seventh beer, marginal utility = 0. This means that the seventh beer yields no addition to Mr. Brody's total satisfaction. Finally, after seven beers, the marginal utility of beer is negative. This means that all beers after the seventh one detract from Mr. Brody's total satisfaction.

Now we must explain how Mr. Brody would maximize total utility. Clearly, as long as marginal utility is greater than zero, drinking additional beer will increase his total utility. Therefore Mr. Brody will drink seven beers. By the time he has finished his seventh beer, the marginal utility of beer to him is zero as indicated in Figure 1 by the intersection of his marginal utility curve with the x-axis. After seven beers, the marginal utility of beer is negative, so drinking any more beer after the seventh bottle would decrease his total utility.

• PROBLEM 15-11

The Blarney Beer Co. advertises its ale as "the only ale to drink when one bottle is just not enough". Since the introduction of this slogan, sales have risen dramatically at the expense of Blarney Beer's major competitor, Rock of Ages Ale, Inc. Recently research workers at Rock of Ages have developed a machine called a utilometer which measures utility achieved as beer is consumed.

In a study of beer drinkers, Rock of Ages obtained the graphs in Figure 1 for Blarney ale, Rock of Ages ale, and Derry Lite Beer, a quickly growing competitor.

Explain what is meant by the graphs and show why Rock of Ages should be concerned over Blarney Beer's advertising claim.

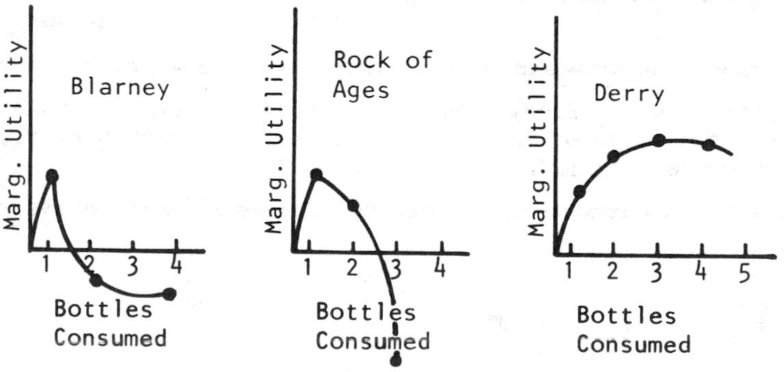

FIG. I

Solution: Looking at the three graphs, we see that the marginal utility of the first bottle is the same for all three beers. But after the first beer, marginal utility diminishes for Blarney and Rock of Ages while it increases for Derry. For Blarney in fact, marginal utility becomes negative before finishing the second beer. For Rock of Ages, marginal utility is still positive for the second beer (i.e., total utility increases) but becomes negative before finishing the third beer. Derry Lite has a curve which does not show diminishing marginal utility until after three beers.

Blarney Beer claims that its ale is "the only ale to drink when one bottle is just not enough". Looking at the graph for Blarney, we see that this claim is not true. While drinking the second beer, the marginal utility becomes negative; after this point total utility decreases. It would hardly be sensible for someone to finish two bottles when one and part of a second would leave his total utility highest.

If anyone has a right to use that advertising claim, it is Derry Lite. We see from its marginal utility curve that marginal utility increases through the third bottle and total utility continues to grow even beyond this point.

• PROBLEM 15-12

Could the curve in Figure 1 represent a consumer's total utility curve? Why or why not?

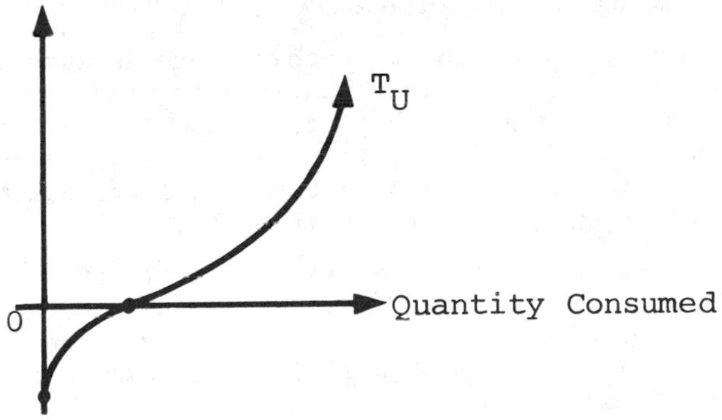

Solution: The method for solving this problem is

1) to examine exactly what kind of relationship is being described by this line, and

2) to decide if this relationship is one permissible under the standard economic assumptions. That is, what is Figure 1 saying and is it realistic?

The two axes measure utils and the quantity of the good consumed. The curve states that when none of the commodity is consumed, the individual is experiencing disutility, a negative level of utility. This premise is acceptable under standard economic assumptions. The curve shows that as the level of the good consumed is increased, the disutility is diminished. This too is a permissible statement. However, the curve further shows that as the quantity consumed is increased beyond the 0 util level, satisfaction increases at an increasing rate. That is, the individual's total utility is ever increasing from the consumption of this good; he has an insatiable appetite for it. While this kind of behavior is not typical, it can, to some extent, occur. For example, a miser with his hoard of gold, who feels that as much as he owns is never enough, and the more he has the more he wants. He will never reach a point where his utility from accumulating the gold is less than the disutility of having its bulk crowding his house.

Unlike the miser, most people will finally reach a saturation point with any good, after which its total utility to each of them will begin to diminish. Therefore, the economist generally assumes that the curve pictured does not trace a typical total utility curve.

• PROBLEM 15-13

Using a marginal utility approach, explain why air, so vitally important to the maintenance of life, is free.

Solution: First of all, let us realize that air is not a free good in many parts of the world. Indeed, although we might not pay cash for it, our bodies pay dearly every time we breathe polluted air.

When we question the price of petroleum rising above \$1/gallon, we are told that we have become so dependent upon oil, it has become such a necessity of life, that there is nothing we can do but pay whatever price it costs. If there were ever a necessity of life, it is oxygen which we get from the air we breathe. Yet, even with the cost of pollution involved in breathing it, air still seems incredibly cheap for something we can't live without.

The reason it is so cheap is that there is much more breathable air on the earth at any one time than is ever needed so its marginal utility is zero. It is not a scarce good. Since the last breath of available air has no marginal utility, it is apparent why a necessity could have no price. Price depends not on total utility, which in the case of air is extremely high, but on marginal utility.

Pricing depends upon the marginal utility of the last little bit of air available to breathe. The price of this last little bit will depend on the usefulness of it. And since every unit of air is like any other unit, every unit must sell for the same price, i.e., what the last unit sells for.

• PROBLEM 15-14

Suppose the marginal utility to David Jones of product A is defined by the function, $MU_A = 10 - x$, where x is the number of units of A produced. For B, $MU_B = 21 - 2y$, where y is the number of units of B produced. Assume that the price of A = price of B = \$1.

How much of A and B would David buy if he had \$7 to spend?

Solution: There are two conditions that must be met here: (1) all \$7 must be spent; (2) at maximum utility, $MU_A/Price_A = MU_B/Price_B$.

(1) Since all \$7 must be spent and both A and B cost \$1, we know that the number of units of A(x) times the price of A(\$1) plus the number of units of B(y) times the price of B(\$1) must equal \$7. Stated algebraically, we have $(x)(\$1) + (y)(\$1) = \$7$ or $x + y = 7$.

(2) Here, we must equate $MU_A/Price_A$ and $MU_B/Price_B$. But since $Price_A = Price_B = \$1$, the equation reduces to $MU_A = MU_B$, or $10 - x = 21 - 2y$.

Now we have a system of two equations in two unknowns:

$$x + y = 7$$

$$10 - x = 21 - 2y$$

Since $x + y = 7$, we can add $(-y)$ to both sides, getting

$$x = 7 - y .$$

Substituting this in the second equation above, we get

$$10 - x = 21 - 2y$$

$$10 - (7 - y) = 21 - 2y$$

Eliminating the parenthesis,

$$10 - 7 + y = 21 - 2y$$

$$3 + y = 21 - 2y$$

Adding 2y to both sides

$$3 + 3y = 21$$

Subtracting 3 from both sides

$$3y = 18$$

$$y = 6$$

Since $x = 7 - y$, $x = 7 - 6 = 1$.

So, according to the formulae above, utility maximization occurs when one unit of product A and six units of product B are produced.

• PROBLEM 15-15

Economist Gary Becker, points out that the traditional marginal-utility theory of consumer behavior is inadequate because it lacks a time dimension. Explain.

Solution: Becker contends that the "prices" of consumer goods (as when evaluating MU/Price) should include, not merely the market price, but also the value of the time required in the consumption of the good. In other words, the denominators of the MU/Price ratios are inadequate because they do not reflect the "full price".

Suppose you are debating whether to eat out or go to a baseball game. The baseball ticket costs \$6 while dinner will cost \$12. If you feel both give you equal utility, theory tells us that you would select going to the ball game. However, Becker tells us we must take account of the fact that baseball games are more time consuming than dinners at restaurants. Suppose a ballgame will take 3 hours of your time, while dining out will only take 2 hours. If your time is worth, say \$9 per hour, then the full price of the ballgame is \$6 + (3)(\$9) = \$33 while the full price of dining out = \$12 + (2)(\$9) = \$30. Now the dinner out becomes the rational choice when the value of time is taken into account.

INDIFFERENCE

• PROBLEM 15-16

What is indifference analysis? What is an indifference curve?

Solution: Indifference analysis is a consumer behavior theory which expresses the consumer's tastes by using curves (indifference curves) that show his preferences among various combinations of goods. It is a different approach to consumer behavior from cardinal utility analysis, which relies on the measurability of tastes and preferences. Indifference analysis relies only on the ability to rank goods in order of preference. For example, cardinal marginal utility analysis assumes that a consumer is able to express his tastes for products A and B by assigning a specific number of "utils" to each. Thus, he may indicate that he likes A twice as much as he likes B. Indifference analysis, on the other hand, only asks the consumer to rank his preferences - to say whether he likes A more than B, B more than A, or is indifferent between them.

An indifference curve is a smooth graph which represents the various combinations of two goods that an individual would wish to consume in order to attain a constant given level of satisfaction. That is to say, a person is "indifferent" as to whether he consumes one or another combination of goods on the same indifference curve.

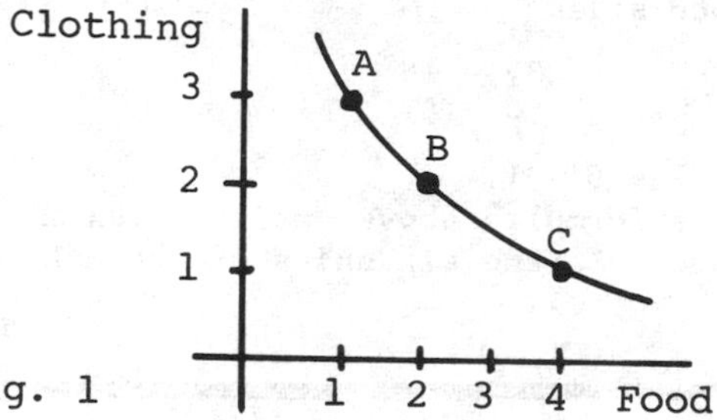

Fig. 1

Figure 1 represents a typical indifference curve. At point A, our consumer has 3 units of clothing and 1 unit of food. At B, he has 2 units of clothing and 2 units of food. At C, he has 1 unit of clothing and 4 units of food. Given the choice among A, B, and C, our consumer would be indifferent, since each of these three points yields exactly the same level of satisfaction.

• PROBLEM 15-17

Consumer x is indifferent as to which of the following combinations of items he will receive.

	Food	Clothing
A	1	6
B	2	3
C	3	2
D	4	1½

Draw and explain consumer x's indifference curve.

Solution: We are told that consumer x is indifferent to combinations A,B,C, or D, i.e., he derives the same amount of utility from each of the four combinations. One unit of food and six units of clothing is just as satisfying as three units of food and two units of clothing.

To graph consumer x's indifference curve, we measure units of food on one axis and units of clothing on the other. Each of the four combinations, A,B,C, and D, is represented by a point. But these four points are not the only points on the graph. Instead the indifference curve is plotted as a continuous function along which utility is constant. Figure 1 is an indifference curve for consumer x.

It should be noted that this indifference curve is of convex curvature when viewed from below. As we move down the curve, the slope be-

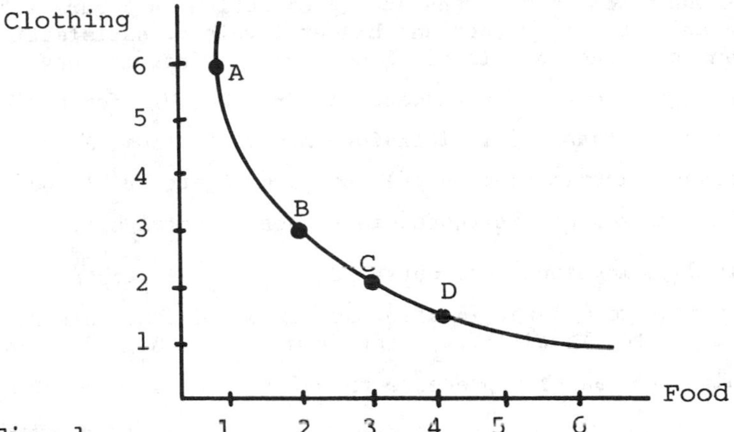

Fig. 1

comes more and more horizontal due to the law of substitution.

• PROBLEM 15-18

The curves labeled U_1, U_2, and U_3 in Figure 1 represent indifference curves.
Describe the effects on total utility as a consumer moves from point A to points B_1, B_2, B_3, or B_4.

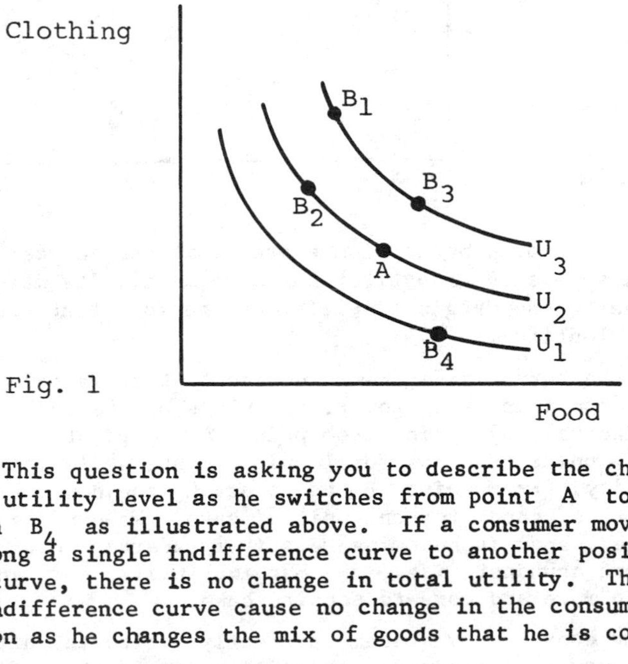

Fig. 1

Solution: This question is asking you to describe the change in the consumer's utility level as he switches from point A to the points B_1 through B_4 as illustrated above. If a consumer moves from one postion along a single indifference curve to another position along that same curve, there is no change in total utility. That is, shifts along an indifference curve cause no change in the consumer's total satisfaction as he changes the mix of goods that he is consuming.

This kind of movement is illustrated when the consumer moves from point A to point B_2. Here the amount of clothing consumed increases and the amount of food consumed decreases in such a way that the consumer is still on his original indifference curve, the mapping of constant utility. That is, in moving from A to B_2 the consumer's total utility has remained unchanged.

As one moves in a northeasterly direction in Figure 1 to higher indifference curves, higher and higher levels of satisfaction are represented by each new indifference curve. That is curve U_2 stands for a higher level of satisfaction than U_1; U_3 for a higher level of satisfaction than U_2. Therefore movements from A to B_3 (food increases, clothing increases) and from A to B_1 (food decreases, clothing increases) represent increases in total utility.

Finally, movement from curve U_2 to U_1 is southwesterly representing a move to a lower indifference curve so that this represents a decline in total utility. Going from A to B_4 (food increases, clothing decreases) represents therefore a drop in total utility.

• PROBLEM 15-19

Explain the law of substitution by using the convex curvature of the indifference curve in Figure 1.

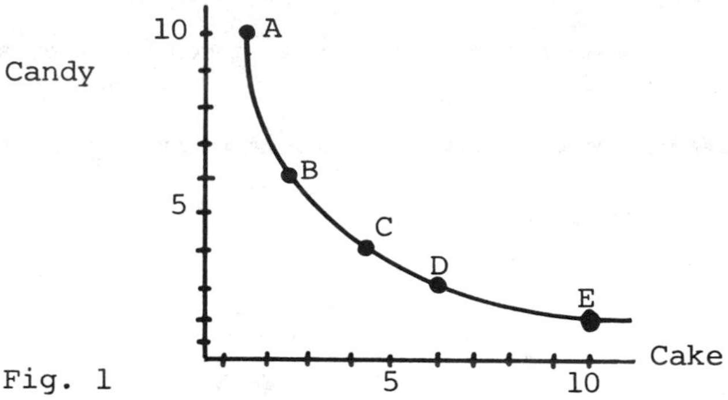

Fig. 1

Solution: The law of substitution states that the scarcer a good is, the greater its relative substitution value, i.e., its marginal utility rises relative to the marginal utility of the good that has become relatively more plentiful.

Examining the curve in Figure 1, notice that as we move along the convex curve from points A to E, the slope of the curve grows more and more horizontal. In going from point A to point B, our consumer is giving up 4 units of candy for 1 unit of cake while maintaining constant utility. From point B to point C, the consumer will give up only 2 units of candy for one unit of cake. We can see that farther down the curve, candy is becoming relatively scarcer to him and cake relatively more abundant, i.e., the marginal utility of candy is rising as he gives up more and more to acquire cake.

Suppose our convex curve became perfectly horizontal after the point E. Then the amount of candy necessary to maintain this utility level would never fall below one unit. In other words, no amount of cake could induce our consumer to give up any more of his candy.

In general, the law of substitution and the convex indifference curve are saying the same thing: the fewer units of product A you have, the more units of B you must be given in return in order to maintain a constant level of utility.

• PROBLEM 15-20

In indifference curve analysis, what is meant by the marginal rate of substitution?

Solution: Suppose we are dealing with two products, A and B. Then the marginal rate of substitution of B for A, abbreviated as MRS_{BA}, is defined as the amount of B the consumer is just willing to give up in order to get one additional unit of A and still maintain the same level of satisfaction.

Table 1

A	B
3	7.0
4	6.4
5	5.9
6	5.5

Table 1 above represents various combinations of A and B where the level of satisfaction is assumed to be constant. Suppose the consumer has 3 units of A and 7.0 units of B. To get the 4th unit of A, he would give up no more than 0.6 units (7.0 - 6.4) of B. Therefore $MRS_{BA} = 0.6$. Then as he acquires more A and holds less B, each unit of A becomes less important to him. Thus, he will give up a relatively small amount of B to get A as we move down the table and the MRS_{BA} falls from 0.6 to 0.5 to 0.4.

• PROBLEM 15-21

Suppose that at a given level of satisfaction the marginal rate of substitution of product B for product A is constant. What does this imply about the relevant indifference curve?

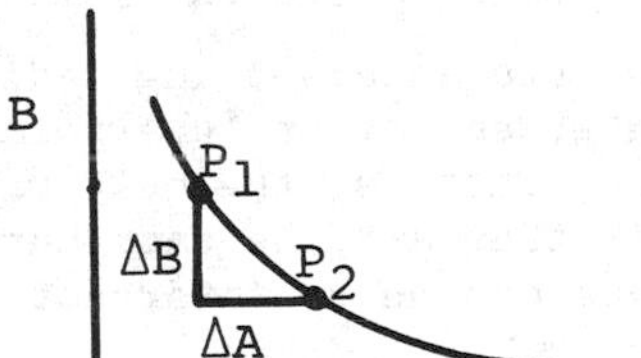

Fig. 1

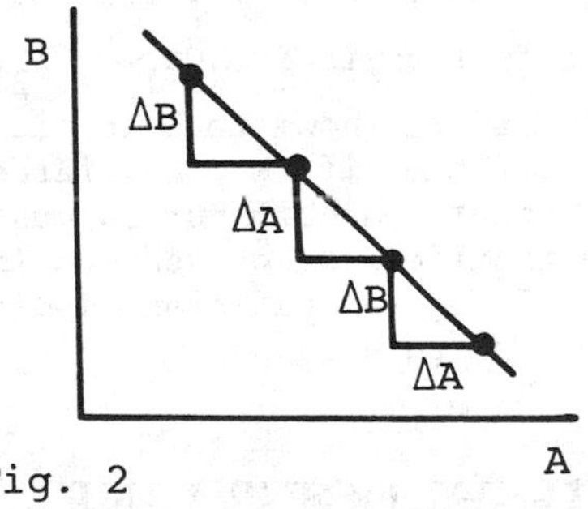

Fig. 2

Solution: The marginal rate of substitution of B for A, MRS_{BA}, is defined as the amount of B the consumer is just willing to give up in order to get one additional unit of A and maintain the same level of satisfaction.

On the indifference curve in Figure 1, $MRS_{BA} = \Delta B/\Delta A$, which is a slope concept. Therefore if $\Delta B/\Delta A$ is constant, the indifference curve is a downward-sloping straight line, as shown in Figure 2.

When two products present a straight line indifference curve, they are perfect substitutes.

• PROBLEM 15-22

Explain why indifference curves cannot intersect.

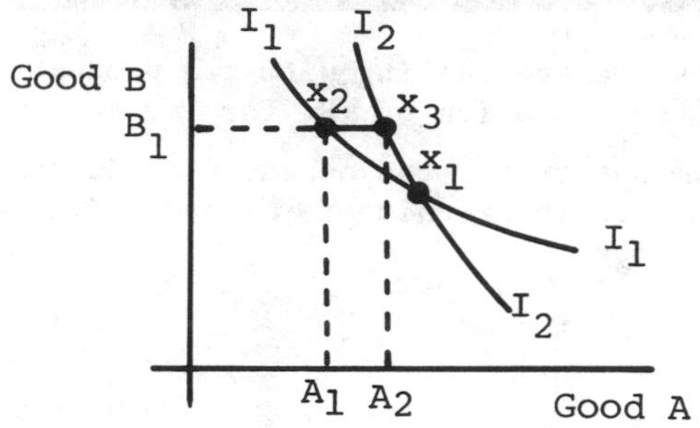

Solution: Suppose two indifference curves intersected as shown below:

If the two curves intersected at point x_1, then it would follow that the levels of satisfaction corresponding to I_1 and I_2 would be the same since each indifference curve traces out the combination of goods which yields equal satisfaction. This implies that the levels of satisfaction at x_2 and x_3 would be equal. At both x_2 and x_3, the quantity of good B is OB_1. For x_2, quantity of good A is OA and for x_3, quantity of A is OA_2.

Since, the satisfaction derived at x_2 must be the same as at x_3, we have: satisfaction from OB_1 + satisfaction from OA_1 = satisfaction from OB_1 + satisfaction from OA_2. Subtracting OB_1 from both sides, we get

satisfaction from OA_1 = satisfaction from OA_2.

Looking at the graph, we see that this cannot possibly be true since $OA_2 > OA_1$. That is, the only way that x_2 and x_3 could yield equal satisfaction is if: $OA_1 = OA_2$, or if x_2 and x_3 were the same point. This can be shown to hold for all points on two intersecting indifference curves, thus if two indifference curves intersect at any one point, then all points on both curves must be the same. That is, the only way that two indifference curves can intersect is if they are the same curve. Therefore, two different indifference curves can never intersect at only one point.

THE BUDGET LINE

• PROBLEM 15-23

Suppose Consumer X has $6 to spend on food and clothing, where food costs $1.50 a unit and clothing costs $1.00 a unit. Draw his consumption-possibility line.

Solution: The consumption-possibility line, or, as it is often called, the budget line, shows the possible combinations of food and clothing which Consumer X can buy for a given amount of expenditure, in our example, \$6. Let's first look at the extreme cases. X could buy all food and get \$6/1.50 = 4 units. Or he could buy all clothing and get \$6/1.00 = 6 units. These two possibilities represent the endpoints of the consumption-possibility line. To draw the rest of the function, draw the straight line connecting the endpoints as shown in Figure 1. This line is straight, because clothing can be exchanged for food at a constant ratio (3 units of clothing = \$6 = 2 units of food); i.e., slope = constant = -3/2 .

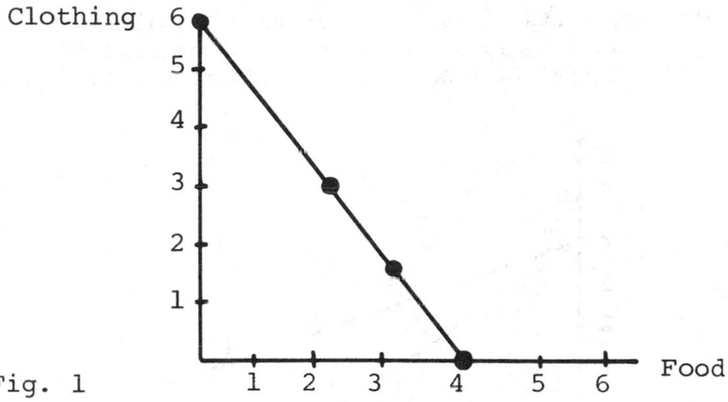

Fig. 1

To prove to yourself that this line is really straight, note several other points on the line, including 2 units of food and 3 units of clothing or 3 units of food and $1\frac{1}{2}$ units of clothing. When plotted, these two points, as well as any other of the many possible combinations of the two goods that are affordable to the consumer, fall on a straight line.

This problem can also be approached algebraically. We have \$6 to spend where each unit of food costs \$1.50 and each unit of clothing costs \$1. Letting x = # of units of food and y = # of units of clothing, \$1.50x and \$1.00y represents the total amounts spent on food and clothing respectively. Therefore, since we have \$6 to spend, the equation of the budget line is

$$\$1.50x + \$1.00y = \$6$$

or

$$\$1.50x + \$y = 6$$

$$= -\$3/2x + \$6$$

Once again, we see the budget line is a straight line with slope = - 3/2.

• PROBLEM 15-24

Line AB in Figure 1 represents a consumer's budget line.

a) If he has a \$12 budget, what are the per-unit prices of food and clothing.

b) If the price of food falls by \$1 per unit, how will AB shift.

c) Suppose these prices remain constant, if his budget rises to \$18, how will AB shift.

Solution: a) To find the per-unit prices of food and clothing, it is easiest to work with the endpoints of the line AB. At point A, no food is purchased while 4 units of clothing are purchased for \$12.

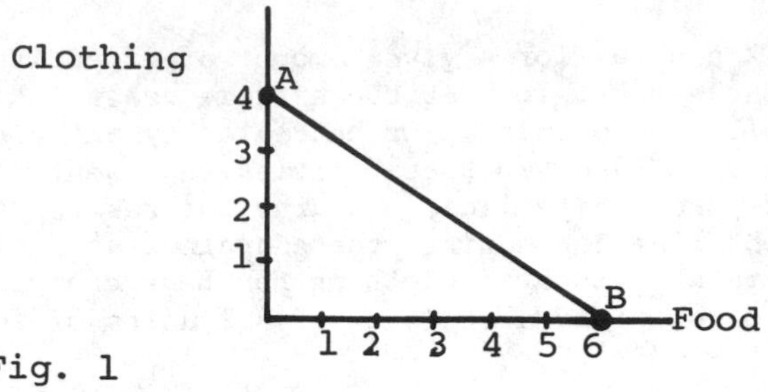

Fig. 1

Therefore clothing costs 12 dollars/4 units = 3 dollars per unit. At point B, no clothing is purchased while 6 units of food are purchased for $12. Therefore food costs 12 dollars/6 units = 2 dollars per unit .

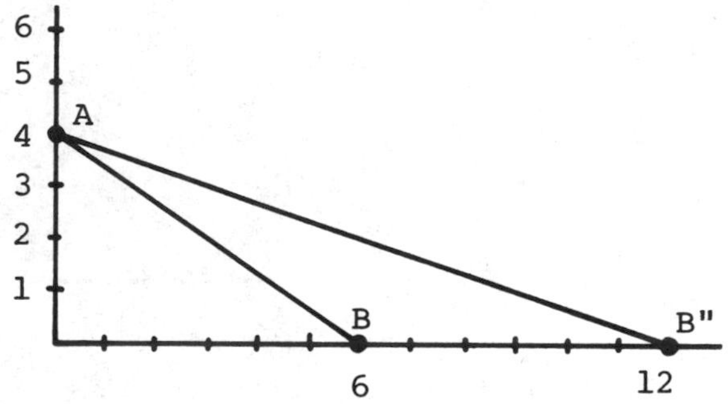

Fig. 2

b) Now a shift in price has taken place. Specifically, the price of food has fallen from $3 to $2. This will not affect point A since the price of clothing has not changed at all. Point B however will shift. Whereas before a $2 price bought 6 units for $12, a $1 price will now enable a consumer to buy 12 units for $12. Therefore B will shift to B", where food bought = 12 units as shown in Figure 2.

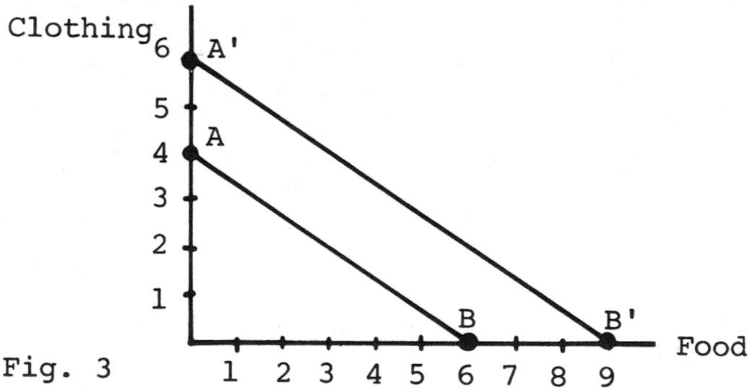

Fig. 3

c) If this consumer's budget rises to $18, he will be able to buy more of both food and clothing than before. Therefore his budget line will shift up and to the right, as shown in Figure 3.

Whereas the consumer could purchase 4 units of clothing previously at $3 per unit for $12, he can now purchase 6 units of clothing for $18. This is shown as point A' on the graph. Also, he previously could purchase 6 units of food at $2 per unit. Now $18 buys the consumer 9 units, as shown by point B'. Then the straight line connecting A' and B' represents the new budget line. Notice that A'B' is parallel to AB. As long as the prices of A and B do not change, a shift in the budget will not affect the slope of the budget line.

Show with the use of an example that a doubling of all money prices and a halving of income will affect a consumer's budget line identically.

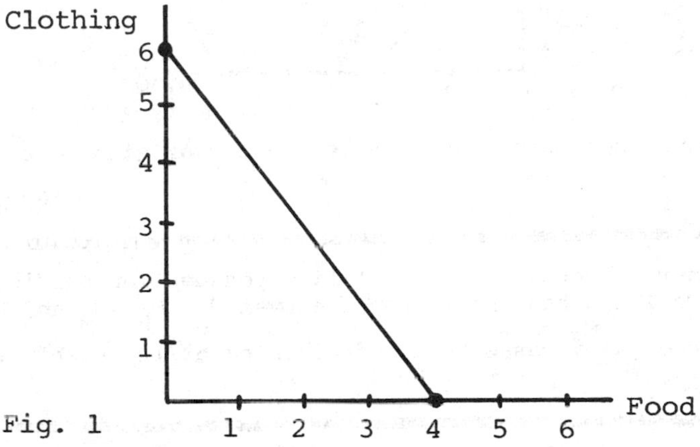

Fig. 1

Solution: Suppose that food is currently $6 per unit and clothing costs $4 per unit. With a budget of $24, one's budget line would appear as in Figure 1.

If prices double, food is $12 per unit and clothing is $8 per unit. Whereas previously one could buy 6 units of clothing at point A or 4 units of food at point B, the new prices allow $24 ÷ $8 per unit = 3 units of clothing at point A_1 or $24 ÷ $12 per unit = 2 units of food at point B_1, as shown in Figure 2.

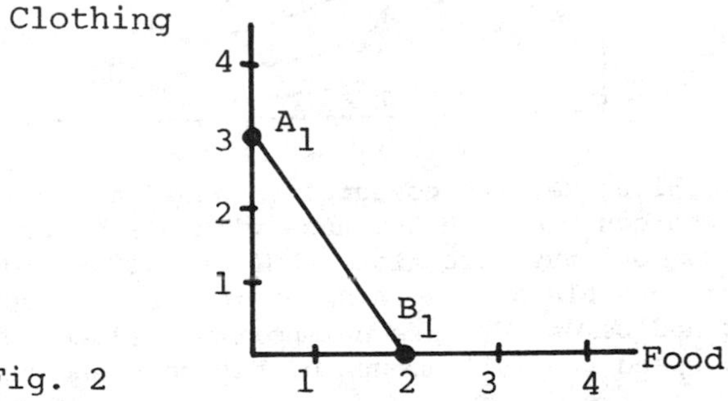

Fig. 2

Now suppose, prices are once again $6 for food and $4 for clothing, but the budget is now $12, i.e., the budget is cut in half. This means that at most 3 units of clothing, at point A_2, or 2 units of food, at point B_2, can be bought, as shown in Figure 3.

Examination of Figures 2 and 3 will show that they are identical, i.e., a halving of one's budget has the same effect upon a budget line as a doubling of prices. Both represent a parallel shift of the budget line down and to the left from the original budget line in Figure 1. The shift in prices kept the budget lines parallel because both prices (of food and of clothing) changed in the same proportion, so that the slope (ratio of the price of clothing to the price of food) remained the same. Had the prices shifted by different percentages, the new

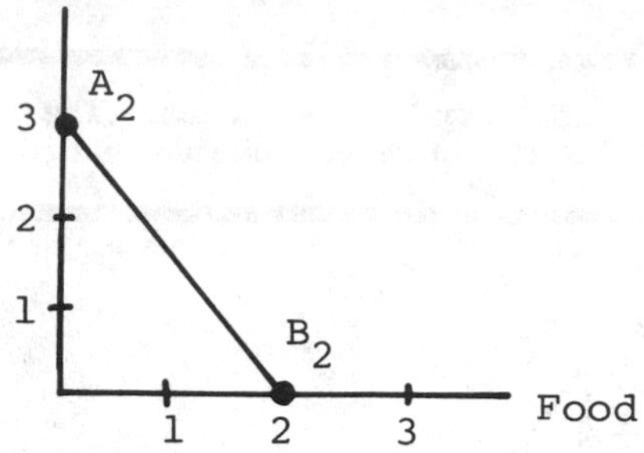

Fig. 3

budget line would not have been parallel to the original one.

• PROBLEM 15-26

Suppose Consumer X faces the straight-line consumption-possibility line shown in Figure 1 and has indifference curves U_1, U_2, U_3 and U_4.

Why will Consumer X purchase food and clothing at the combination given by point B?

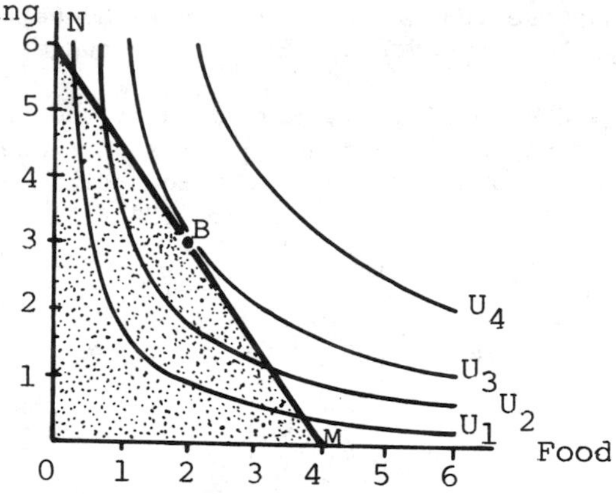

Fig. 1

Solution: Since the line NM, the consumption-possibility line, shows the limits of what the consumer can purchase with his given amount of income, he is free to move anywhere along NM. Positions to the right and above NM are impossible unless he had more money to spend. Positions to the left and below NM are unimportant, since we assume Consumer X wants to spend the full amount of his food and clothing budget.

We assume that Consumer X is out to maximize total satisfaction. Therefore he should choose a combination of goods located on line NM where NM is tangent to the highest possible indifference curve.

Let us examine the way NM intersects the various indifference curves. NM intersects both U_1 and U_2 in two places. This is due to the curved shape of indifference curves. Note that by moving from U_1 to U_2 the consumer has increased his utility level. To gain the maximum utility level, the consumer will want to continue to jump to higher indifference curves. NM touches U_3 in only one point while it does not intersect U_4 at all. Therefore, Consumer X would plan his budget at point B since the intersection of his budget line with U_3 represents the highest possible indifference curve that the consumer can reach given the budget level which has put him on the consumption possibility line NM. When a budget line intersects an indifference curve in two points (as with U_1 and U_2) it means that there are higher attainable indifference curves. When a budget line is tangent to an indifference curve, the highest attainable satisfaction has been reached.

THE DEMAND CURVE

• PROBLEM 15-27

A market demand curve is defined as a horizontal summation of all the individual demand curves. Why is this summation taken horizontally rather than vertically?

Solution: The market demand curve is also defined as a schedule which, for any given price, shows the total quantity demanded by the market, or the summation of all individual quantities demanded at this given price. Price is measured on the vertical axis while quantity is measured by the horizontal axis. Therefore, at any given level on the vertical axis, the proper horizontal point is a summation of all the individual quantities demanded.

Alternatively, consider what is actually being scheduled by a vertical summation. If all individual demand curves were summed vertically, then for any given quantity demanded, this new summed curve would show the sum of all the prices that would be offered for this quantity by all individuals. Since this schedule does not fit the definition of a market demand curve, a vertical summation would not be correct.

• PROBLEM 15-28

The following four diagrams in Figure 1 represent the demand for widgets in the North, South, Mid-West and West respectively. Using these curves, draw the U.S. market demand for widgets.

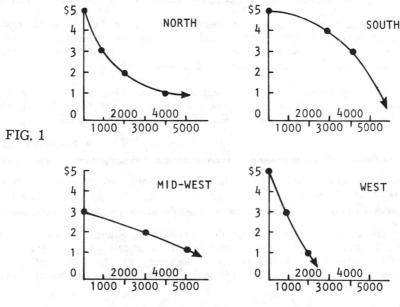

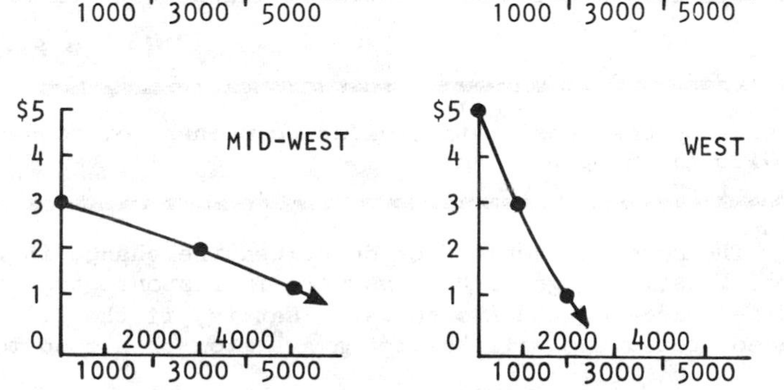

FIG. 1

Solution: Given four "individual" demand curves, this question is asking you to derive a market demand curve. A market demand curve for a good is defined as a horizontal summation of all the individual demand curves for that good. That is, at any given price, the market demand curve shows how much of the commodity will be purchased by the entire market. To form the market demand for widgets, begin by noting that at $5 per widget, the entire market will demand 0 widgets. At $4 per widget, market demand will be 500 + 3,000 + 0 + 500 = 4,000. $3 per widget caused 1,000 + 4,000 + 0 + 1,000 = 6,000 to be demanded. When all points are computed and plotted, the resulting market demand is as shown in Figure 2.

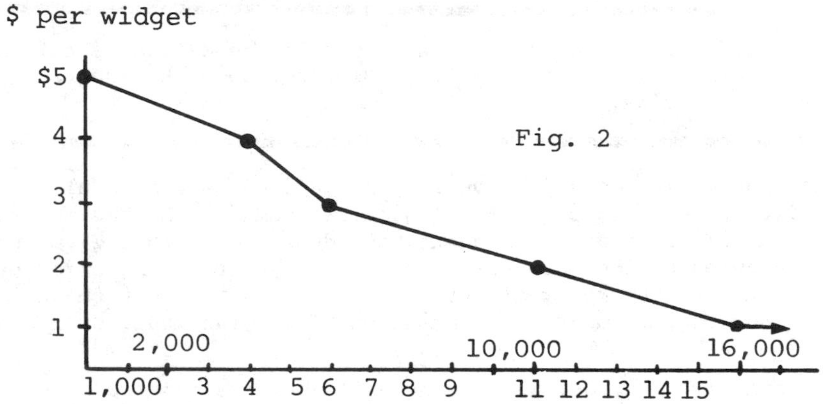

Fig. 2

• **PROBLEM 15-29**

> When speaking about the cross relations of demand, an economist may describe two products as being substitutes, complements, or independent commodities. Explain each case and give an example.

Solution: Substitutes are rival, or competing, products. That is, A may be used instead of B or vice versa. Thus, if products A and B are substitutes, a rise in the price of A will cause an increase in demand for B. An example of substitute goods would be coffee and tea.

Complements are co-operating commodities. That is, A will most often be used with B. Thus, if A and B are complements, a rise in the price of A will lower the demand for B. An example of complementary goods would be frankfurters and sauerkraut.

Finally, two products are independent commodities if a change in the price of A has no noticeable effect upon the demand for B. Wallpaper and frozen orange juice are an example of independent commodities.

• **PROBLEM 15-30**

> What is meant by the substitution effect component of downward-sloping demand? Give an example.

Solution: The substitution effect describes the change in the amounts consumed of substitute goods by consumers in response to a change in the relative prices of the two goods. That is, if the price of a good is increased, consumers will "switch away" from this good to its substitutes. Conversely, if the price of a good is decreased, consumers will "switch toward" this good, consuming more of it than before while decreasing the amounts consumed of its substitutes.

For example, suppose veal cutlets cost $3/pound and shrimp cost $4/pound. If the price of shrimp falls to $2/pound while the price of veal cutlets remains unchanged, shrimp will become more attractive to the consumer. At $2/pound it is a "better buy" than at $4/pound. Consequently, the lower price will induce the consumer to substitute some shrimp for some veal and other items. A lower price increases the relative attractiveness of a product and makes the consumer willing to buy more of it. This is known as the substitution effect and helps explain the downward slope of demand curves.

• PROBLEM 15-31

What is meant by the income-effect? Give an example of an exception to the law.

Solution: Suppose the price of steak rises. When your money income is fixed, being forced to pay a higher price for steak is equivalent to having your real income or purchasing power decreased. With a lower real income, you will now want to buy less steak.

The 1845 Irish famine gives us an odd exception to this rule. When the famine raised the price of potatoes, poor families actually ended up consuming more potatoes! This is due to the fact that the rise in potato prices lowered their real income and hence made it quite impossible to afford any meat at all. With nowhere else to turn to for sustenance, they were forced to become even more dependent on potatoes.

• PROBLEM 15-32

What is meant by the terms "normal good" and "inferior good"?

Solution: Normal goods are those whose demand curve varies directly with income. They are also called superior goods.

Inferior or "poor man's" goods are those whose demand curve shifts downward with an increase in income. An example is margarine. As people earn more, they are able to afford butter and will cut down their demand for margarine.

• PROBLEM 15-33

The following figure shows the market demand for coffee. Match each of the following events, a) through d) with a shift in the diagram from the original equilibrium point, ϵ, to the new equilibrium positions, (1) through (4).

a) the price of tea increases
b) the price of coffee increases
c) the price of cream increases
d) the price of shoes decreases

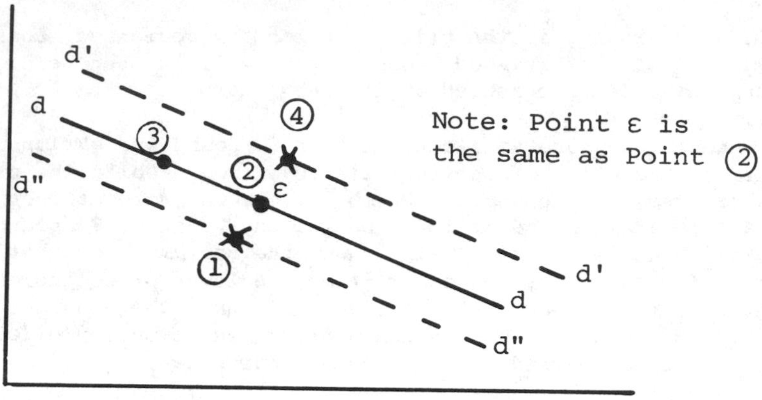

Solution: This question is asking you to determine what the effect on an equilibrium, market-determined price will be, given changes in the prices of a complement, a substitute and an independent commodity.

a) Tea is a substitute for coffee. An increase in the price of tea will cause some tea drinkers to become coffee drinkers. Therefore an increase in the price of tea will be likely to lead to a shift to point (4), representing an increase in demand for coffee to d'd'.

b) The demand curve in question is for coffee. This event illustrates a shift along a curve rather than a shift in a curve. Therefore, an increase in the price of coffee is shown by point (3).

c) Cream is a complement to coffee, that is, they are generally used together. Therefore an increase in the price of cream will lead to an increase in the total price of a cup of coffee with cream and will lead to a decline in demand for coffee. This is shown by position (1), which represents a downward shift in the demand curve to d"d".

d) The demand for shoes would be considered independent from the demand for coffee. Therefore a change in the price of shoes should have no noticeable effect on the price of coffee. So equilibrium remains at point (2).

CONSUMER'S SURPLUS

• PROBLEM 15-34

What is meant by consumers' surplus?

Solution: The notion of consumers' surplus is the result of two phenomena First is the idea that people will buy more and more of a particular good or service only at lower and lower cost to them. This is due to the law of diminishing marginal utility. The second phenomenon is that if a single price prevails in a market, the price consumers pay for each unit of a good or service represents the value they place on the last unit (the marginal unit) bought. Therefore, except for the very last unit purchased, consumers gain more utility from each unit bought than they sacrifice when they purchase it. Since consumers pay only according to the marginal value of the last unit bought, they receive "surplus" of value, from all prior units, which have higher (marginal) utilities than the last unit bought.

• PROBLEM 15-35

Figure 1 shows a typical consumer's demand for ties. If this person buys 4 ties, what will his consumer surplus be?

Price of Ties

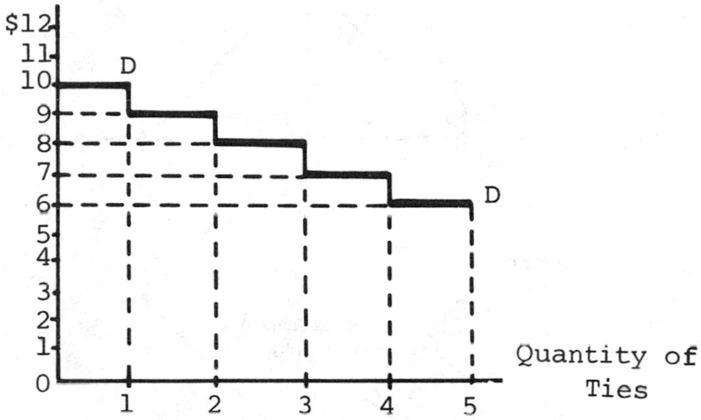

Fig. 1

Solution: Looking at the graph above, we see that at a price of $10, this consumer would be willing to buy one tie. He would not pay $10 for a second tie, but if the price were lowered by $1 to $9, he would buy a second tie. Similarly, he would pay $8 for a third tie and $7 for a fourth tie. Therefore, in all, he would be willing to pay $10 + $9 + $8 + $7 = $34 for four ties. However, according to his demand curve, this consumer will only pay $7 for each of the four ties he buys so that his total expenditure is $28, rather than $34. His consumer surplus is therefore $34 - $28 = $6.

In Figure 2, it is the shaded region.

Price of Ties

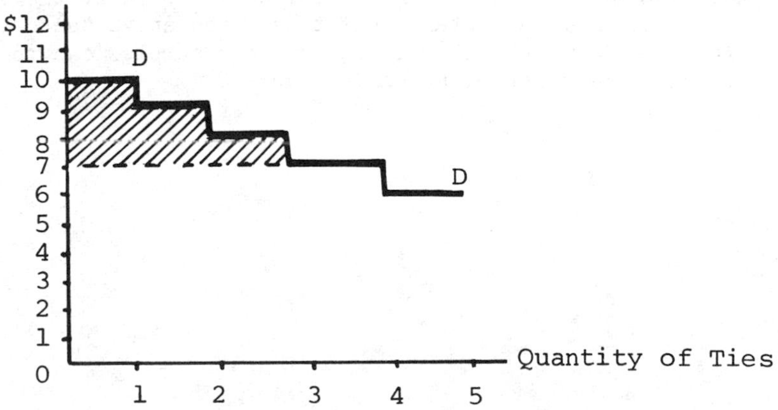

Fig. 2

• PROBLEM 15-36

The diagram, (Fig. 1), shows a market equilibrium for a commodity. Show graphically the total consumer surplus derived by the buyers of this commodity.

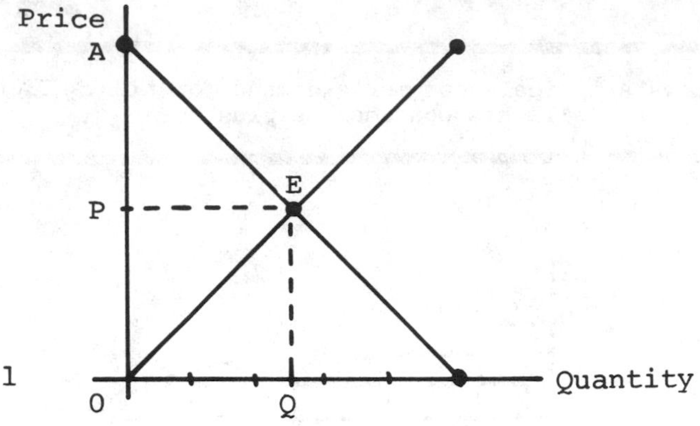

Fig. 1

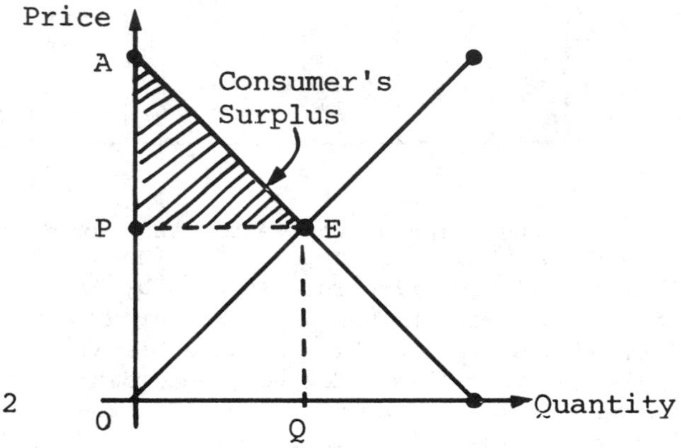

Fig. 2

Solution: **In any transaction, the consumer's surplus is the measure of the benefit to the consumer over and above his cost. Graphically the total benefit to the consumer of quantity OQ of the commodity can be measured by the area of** OAεQ. The amount paid by the consumer is OPεQ. The portion of the total benefit over and above the cost is the area OAεQ - OPεQ = PAε. Therefore, consumer surplus can be shown graphically as the area PAε as shown in Figure 2.

Answer

To be covered when testing yourself

SHORT ANSWER QUESTIONS FOR REVIEW

Choose the correct answer.

1. A consumer prefers having less of a given good in his consumption basket to having more of it. This means (a) that a given good is inferior (b) that a given good has no substitutes (c) that a consumer is irrational (d) none of the above — c

2. Any two points on a given indifference curve represent (a) two ways of consuming the same amount of each good contained in the consumption basket (b) combinations of goods a consumer can purchase which give him the same total amount of utility (c) the optimal points of consumption (d) the consumer's lack of preference among the goods he purchases — b

3. The substitution effect alone would imply that the indifference curves (a) have a convex shape (b) are straight lines (c) have a concave shape (d) have irregular shape — a

4. If a consumer is to maximize utility it is necessary and sufficient (a) that the bundle of goods he purchases is somewhere on the budget constraint (b) that he purchases as many goods as possible (c) that no inferior goods are purchased (d) that marginal utilities of all the consumed goods per $1 of income are equal to each other — d

5. The difference between the total utility derived from the consumption of a certain amount of a given good and the amount of money actually paid for it is called (a) marginal utility (b) average utility (c) consumer surplus (d) producer surplus — c

6. Unless discriminated against, the price a consumer pays for every unit of a commodity purchased is equal to the (a) marginal utility derived from the consumption of the last unit of a commodity (b) utility derived from the consumption of the first unit of a commodity (c) utility derived from the consumption of an average unit of a commodity (d) total utility derived from the consumption of a commodity — a

7. Which of the following pairs of goods are com-

SHORT ANSWER QUESTIONS FOR REVIEW

Answer
To be covered when testing yourself

plements? (a) watches and paintings (b) pencils and pens (c) TV sets and radios (d) ski boots and skis — d

8. Which of the following pairs of goods can be considered substitutes? (a) salami and ham (b) salt and pepper (c) milk and honey (d) cars and calculators — a

9. Cigarettes and ladies' hats are an example of (a) two complementary goods (b) independent goods (c) substitutes (d) inferior goods — b

10. Two indifference curves intersect (a) at a point where a consumer maximizes utility given a certain income constraint (b) at a point where marginal utilities of purchased goods are equal to each other (c) only if a consumer displays illogical or irrational behavior (d) in at least two points — c

11. The consumer's maximal attainable utility is given (a) by an indifference curve which lies everywhere above the budget line (b) by an indifference curve which is tangent to the consumer's budget line (c) by an indifference curve which lies everywhere below the budget line (d) by a middle point of the budget line — b

12. Consider a world where only two goods are available for consumption. Neither one of the goods is assumed to be inferior. The price of one of them falls and consequently a second good becomes relatively more expensive. (a) A consumer will necessarily reduce his purchases of a second good (b) A consumer will purchase more or less of a second good depending on the relative strengths of the income and substitution effects (c) A consumer will be likely to increase his purchases of a second good (d) The consumer will not change the amount purchased of both goods — b

13. Suppose two goods are substitutes. Other things being equal, when the price of one of them rises (a) the demand for a second good will rise (b) the demand for a second good will fall (c) the price of a second good will also rise (d) the price of a second good will fall — a

14. When the consumer's real income rises he (a)

SHORT ANSWER QUESTIONS FOR REVIEW

Answer
To be covered when testing yourself

buys less of an inferior good (b) increases consumption (c) moves to a higher indifference curve (d) all of the above — d

15. A budget line of a given consumer shifted outward. This means (a) the indifference curve tangent to a new budget line lies everywhere above the previous indifference curve (b) the consumer's real income has increased (c) a consumer is better off (d) all of the above — d

16. When it is said that for any particular individual the Marginal Disutility of hours spent picking berries is equal to the Marginal Utility of the berries picked, it is implied that: (a) the individual has a larger consumer surplus at this point than he would have anywhere else (b) the price of the berries should equal the cost of leisure (c) the cost of the berries cannot be stated in terms of forgone opportunity cost (d) this individual has no consumer surplus to speak of (e) none of the above — a

17. The area of consumer surplus is correctly shaded in which area? (a) A. (b) B. (c) C. (d) D. (e) E. — b

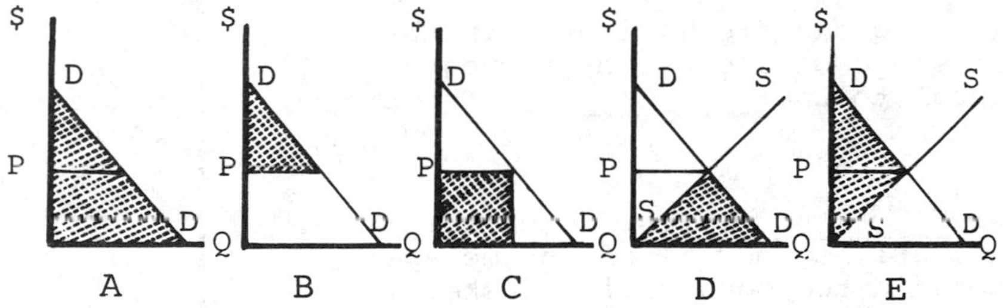

Fill in the blanks.

18. The fact that discount prices are often offered contingent on the purchase of extra units of a given good is a direct consequence of the law of __________. — diminishing marginal utility

19. All possible combinations of goods which give a consumer equal satisfaction describe the __________. — indifference curve

20. __________ is essentially the difference between the total value of a certain amount of a

SHORT ANSWER QUESTIONS FOR REVIEW

Answer
To be covered when testing yourself

Question	Answer
good to a consumer and its exchange value in the market.	Consumer surplus
21. If two goods are __________ the higher price of one of them is likely to have an adverse effect on the demand for both goods.	complements
22. The more substitutes for a given good are readily available the more __________ its demand curve is likely to be.	elastic
23. Coffee and tea are __________ while coffee and sugar are __________.	substitutes, complements
24. __________ utility of the last unit of a good purchased determines the price a consumer is willing to pay for it.	Marginal
25. __________ is the sum of marginal utilities of all units of a good purchased.	Total utility
26. A fall in the price of a good not only makes it relatively more attractive but also __________ the consumer's real income.	increases
27. The level of utility derived from the consumption of a given bundle of goods is __________ for every consumer.	different
28. When only two goods are available in the market the slope of a consumer's budget line is equal to the __________ of the two goods.	price ratio
31. A consumer __________ satisfaction only if marginal utility per $1 of income spent on each good in the consumption basket is equivalent.	maximizes
32. A consumer can only be on an indifference curve which has __________ common points with his budget line.	one or more
29. Both __________ and __________ changes cause shifts in the market demand curve.	income price
30. If marginal utility per $1 of income spent on good A exceeds marginal utility per $1 of income spent on good B, a consumer will want to __________ the consumption of B.	reduce

SHORT ANSWER QUESTIONS FOR REVIEW

Answer

To be covered when testing yourself

33. The shaded area in the figure represents __________. — consumer surplus

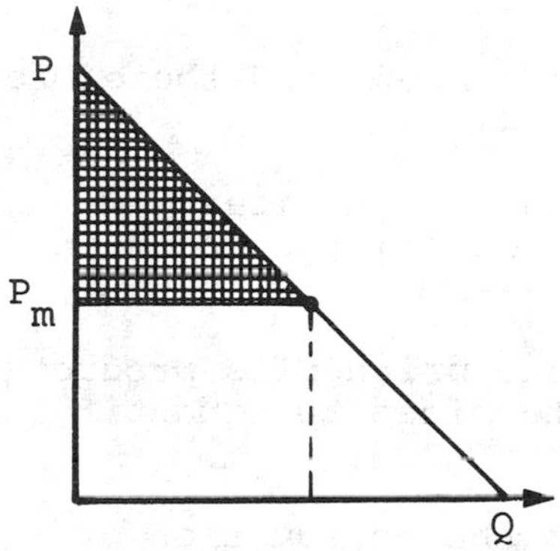

34. An outward shift in the market supply curve would cause an (increase/decrease) in consumer surplus. — increase

Determine whether the following statements are true or false.

35. The market demand curve is nothing but a horizontal summation of the consumer demand curves for a product. — True

36. The direction of the slope of a demand curve usually varies from consumer to consumer and depends largely on individual taste. — False

37. The economic definition of inferior goods describes them as goods produced below certain accepted standard of quality. — False

38. The position of the individual demand curve is affected by changes in income. — True

39. When the price of a product rises the demand for its complement rises too. — False

40. Butter and margarine can be called substitutes since most consumers can easily switch from one to another. — True

41. A statistical study showed the consumption of margarine eventually falling with the growth of income. The result entitles the author to claim that margarine is an inferior good. — True

42. The amount of satisfaction derived from the

	Answer To be covered when testing yourself
consumption of each successive unit of a given good is greater than the amount of satisfaction derived from the consumption of a previous one.	False
43. Utility is a psychological concept and therefore cannot be precisely measured.	True
44. A consumer is best off when he equalizes marginal utilities per dollar of all the goods in his consumption basket.	True
45. Total utility determines the price of a product while marginal utility determines the quantity consumed.	False
46. Total utility derived from the consumption of water exceeds the total utility gained from the acquisition of diamonds.	True
47. Consumers tend to buy more of a good when its price is lowered because their real incomes become higher and they can afford to buy more.	True
48. The impact of the income effect on consumption patterns is always greater than the impact of the substitution effect.	False
49. A consumer can choose to consume at any point on a given indifference curve with the exception of those indifference curves which are located outside the area bounded by the budget constraint, the axes, and the origin.	True
50. The consumer surplus of a good is not the same thing as its total economic value.	True

CHAPTER 16

ELASTICITY OF SUPPLY AND DEMAND

Basic Attacks and Strategies for Solving Problems in this Chapter. See pages 575 to 620 for step-by-step solutions to problems.

The coefficient of elasticity is a measure of the responsiveness of a dependent variable to a change in an independent variable. The formula is:

$$\textit{coefficient of elasticity} = \frac{\%\Delta \textit{dependent variable}}{\%\Delta \textit{independent variable}}$$

Some of the most widely-used elasticities include:

1) Price-elasticity of Demand (E_p). E_p is a measure of the responsiveness of quantity demanded to changes in price. The formula is

$$E_p = -\left(\frac{\%\Delta \textit{quantity demanded}}{\%\Delta \textit{price}}\right).$$

Numerical values for E_p fall into five categories:

(a) $E_p = 0$, demand is perfectly inelastic

(b) $0 < E_p < 1$, demand is inelastic

(c) $E_p = 1$, demand is unit elastic

(d) $1 < E_p <$ infinity, demand is elastic

(e) $E_p =$ infinity, demand is perfectly elastic

2) Price-elasticity of Supply (E_s). E_s is a measure of the responsiveness of quantity supplied to changes in price. The formula is

$$E_s = \frac{\%\Delta \textit{quantity supplied}}{\%\Delta \textit{price}}$$

Numerical values for E_s fall into five categories:

(a) $E_s = 0$, perfectly inelastic

(b) $0 < E_s < 1$, inelastic

(c) $E_s = 1$, unit elastic

(d) $1 < E_s <$ infinity, elastic

(e) $E_s =$ infinity, perfectly elastic

3) Cross-elasticity of Demand ($E_{A,B}$) . $E_{A,B}$ is a measure of the responsiveness of the quantity demanded of good A to a change in the price of good B. The formula is

$$E_{A,B} = \frac{\%\Delta quantity\ demanded\ of\ good\ A}{\%\Delta price\ of\ good\ B}$$

Numerical values for $E_{A,B}$ fall into two categories:

(a) $E_{A,B} > 0$, goods are substitutes

(b) $E_{A,B} < 0$, goods are complements

4) Income-elasticity of Demand (E_y). E_y is a measure of the responsiveness of quantity demanded to a change in income. The formula is

$$E_y = \frac{\%\Delta quantity\ demanded}{\%\Delta income}$$

Numerical values for E_y fall into two categories:

(a) $E_y > 0$, normal good

(b) $E_y < 0$, inferior good

Using price-elasticity of demand as the example and the diagram on the following page there are two ways to compute elasticity: point elasticity and arc elasticity. Point elasticity measures elasticity at a particular point on the demand curve. At point a

the formula for elasticity is $E_p = -\left(\frac{\delta q}{\delta p} * \frac{P_a}{Q_a}\right)$, where $\frac{\delta q}{\delta p}$ is the inverse of the slope of the demand curve at the point.

Arc elasticity measures E_p between two points on the demand curve, such as a and b. Measurement of arc elasticities presents some interesting problems. For example, what is the percentage change in Q between a and b? The change in Q is $Q_a - Q_b$, but to calculate the percentage change you need to divide the change by a base. Using Q_a as a base is perfectly valid so that the percentage change would be $(Q_a - Q_b)/Q_a$. However using Q_b as a base is equally valid. This would make the percentage change $(Q_a - Q_b)/Q_b$, which would be a different value from the first case. Economists arbitrarily solve this problem by using the midpoint formula. The base for calculating percentage changes is taken to be the average of the two endpoints. Therefore, the percentage change in Q is given by:

$$\%\Delta Q = \frac{Q_a - Q_b}{\left(\frac{Q_a + Q_b}{2}\right)}$$

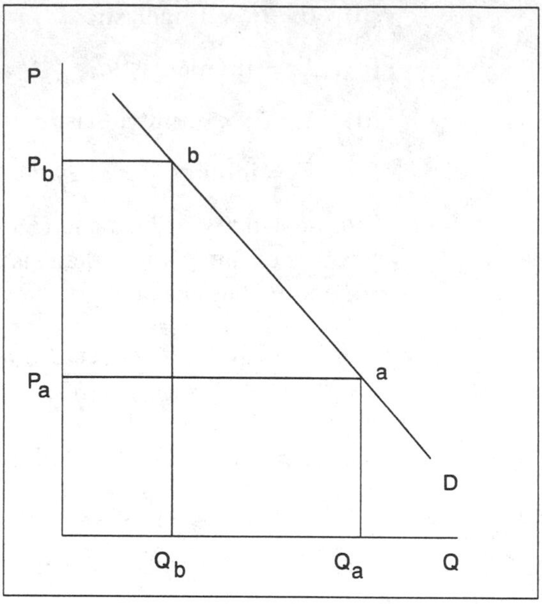

A similar formula is used for $\%\Delta P$. The arc elasticity formula then is

$$E_p = -\left(\frac{\left(\frac{Q_a - Q_b}{Q_a + Q_b}\right)}{\frac{P_a - P_b}{P_a + P_b}}\right)$$

Note that the 2 drops out in the formula.

The formulas for the other elasticities are constructed using similar principles and are shown in the text which follows.

There are four determinants of price-elasticity of demand.

1) Necessity or luxury — The more necessary a good is the more inelastic the demand.

2) Availability of close substitutes — The fewer substitutes a good has the more inelastic the demand.

3) Share of budget absorbed — The smaller the share of a consumer's budget allocated to the good, the more inelastic the demand.

4) Length of time considered — The shorter the length of time considered, the more inelastic the demand for the good.

Step-by-Step Solutions to Problems in this Chapter, "Elasticity of Supply and Demand"

THE ELASTICITY CONCEPT

• PROBLEM 16-1

What is the elasticity of demand?

Solution: The elasticity of demand is a measure of the extent to which quantity of a good demanded, Q, responds to changes in the price, P, of the good. Specifically,

$$\text{Elasticity, E,} = -\frac{\text{Percentage change in quantity demanded}}{\text{Percentage change in price}}$$

$$= -\frac{\Delta Q/Q}{\Delta P/P} = -\frac{\Delta Q}{\Delta P}\cdot\frac{P}{Q},$$

where ΔP represents the change in the price of the good, and ΔQ represents the resulting change in the quantity of the good demanded.

• PROBLEM 16-2

Why do we always insert a negative sign in front of demand elasticity?

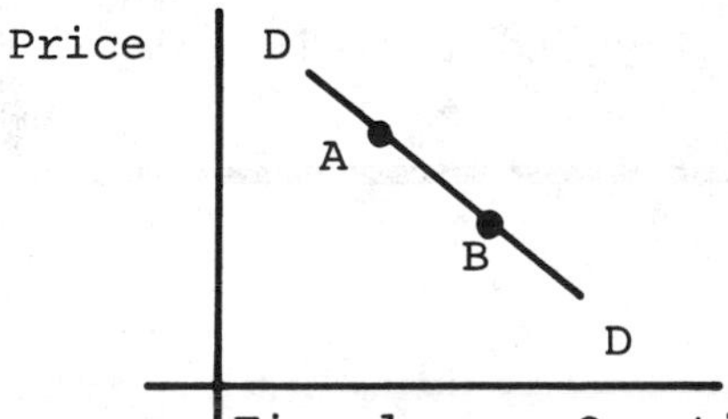

Fig. 1

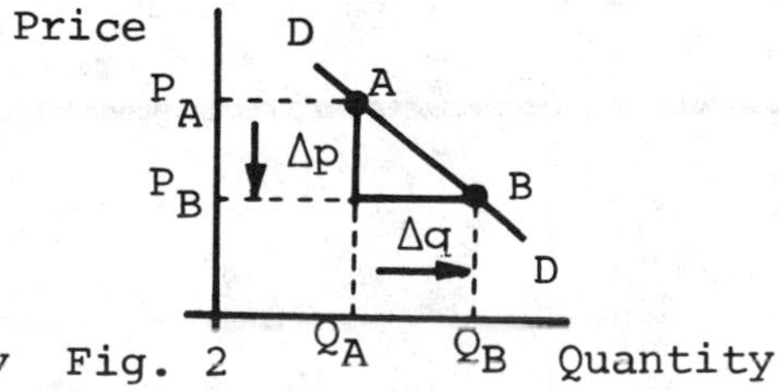

Fig. 2

Solution: The graph in Figure 1, representing a typical demand curve, is downward-sloping. This means that price and quantity demanded move in opposite directions. As price increases, quantity demanded decreases while as price decreases, quantity demanded increases.

Let us examine the demand curve in Figure 1 to see why the negative sign is employed. Suppose we move from point A to point B as shown in Figure 2.

As the graph indicates, $\Delta P = P_B - P_A$ is negative while $\Delta_q = Q_B - Q_A$ is positive. Since, in determining elasticity, we would be dividing a positive number $(\Delta q/q)$ by a negative number $(\Delta p/p)$, our elasticity coefficient would be negative. By convention we add the minus sign to make the elasticity coefficient positive.

Let's also show why we need the minus sign when we go from point B to point A, by examining Figure 3.

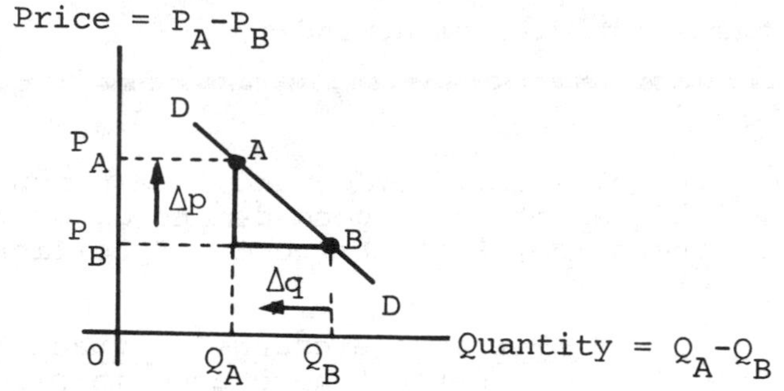

Fig. 3

Here $\Delta p = P_A - P_B$ is positive while $\Delta q = Q_A - Q_B$ is negative. Then, in determining elasticity, we will have a negative number $(\Delta q/q)$ divided by a positive number $(\Delta p/p)$, yielding a negative elasticity coefficient. Here, once again, we add the minus sign to make the negative elasticity coefficient positive.

In the case of supply, we do not need a minus sign since quantity demanded and price change in the same direction.

• PROBLEM 16-3

What is meant by perfect inelasticity and infinite elasticity?

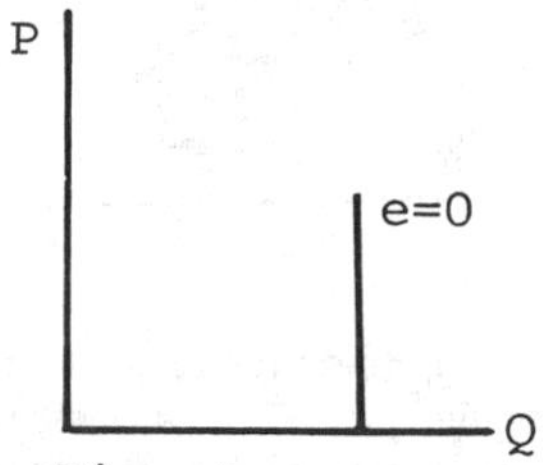

Fig. 1

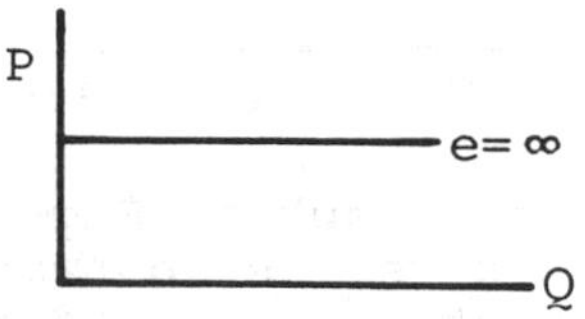

Fig. 2

Solution: We we speak of elasticity, e, we follow the rule that $\infty > e > 0$ at all times. Most of the time, we do not expect to meet a situation where $e = 0$ or $e = \infty$. Perfect inelasticity and infinite elasticity are just such extreme cases.

Perfect inelasticity is the case where $e = 0$. It is graphed as a vertical line, as shown in Figure 1.

Suppose that this graph in Figure 1 represents a supply function. The interpretation of the vertical line is that there is a fixed quantity being supplied regardless of price and the suppliers will not change the quantity supplied in response to any price. Therefore no matter how much you raise or lower price, Q is constant. The same graph could be a demand curve. Here the consumer would demand a certain amount of a good, no more, no less, regardless of its price per unit. And according to this graph, he would be willing to pay any price for it. Thus the change in Q,

$$\frac{\Delta Q}{Q}$$

remains zero when there is a change in price, $\frac{\Delta P}{P} > 0$. Thus

$$e = \frac{\Delta Q/Q}{\Delta P/P} = 0$$

Infinite elasticity represents the other end of the spectrum. Here we graph a perfectly horizontal line, as shown in Figure 2.

Suppose this were a market demand curve. The horizontal line tells us that the consumers will buy as much of the good as exists at the same price. If producers raise the price, consumers will buy none of the product at all. If the producer lowers the price, it will result in an indefinitely large demand. This curve is used to portray perfect competition. If it were a supply curve, a horizontal line would represent the "constant-cost case." The slightest cut in price will cause quantity supplied to fall to zero, while a rise in price will draw out an indefinitely large supply. Thus the change in the quantity demanded is infinite, $\Delta Q/Q = \infty$, when there is any change in the price, $\Delta P/P > 0$.

So $e = \frac{\Delta Q/Q}{\Delta P/P} = \infty$.

• PROBLEM 16-4

Describe and illustrate the five categories of supply elasticity.

Solution: Economists have grouped supply elasticity into these five categories: infinitely elastic, elastic, unitarily elastic, inelastic, and perfectly inelastic.

Infinitely elastic supply, as seen in Figure 1, is the extreme case in which any rise in price would cause quantity

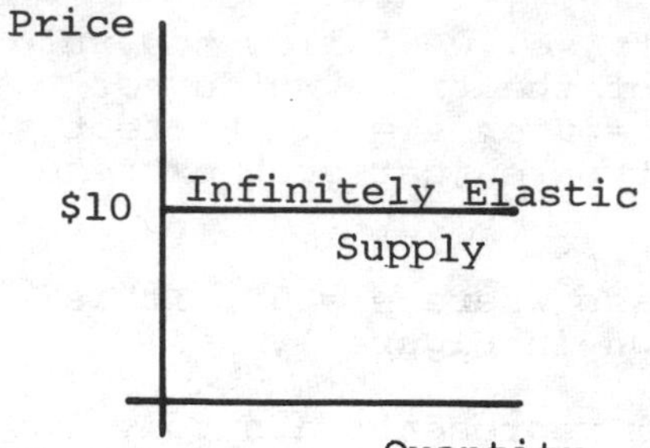

Fig. 1

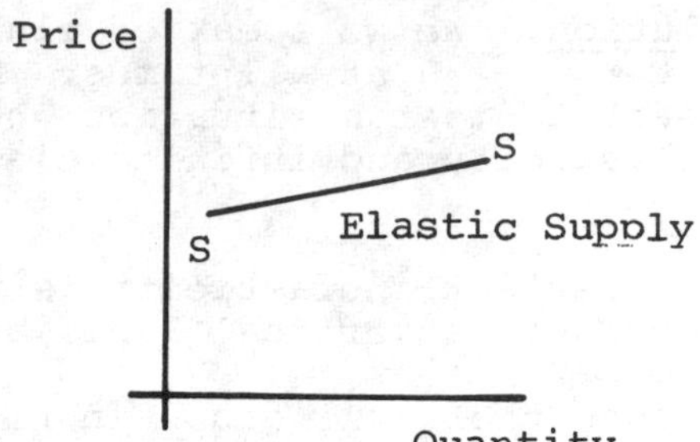

Fig. 2

supplied to increase by an infinite amount and any drop in price would cause quantity supplied to fall to zero. In Figure 1 supply is infinitely elastic at a price of $10. There are no actual cases of infinite elasticity of supply in reality, but it is still a useful concept to study.

Supply is elastic when a given percentage change in price brings about an even greater percentage change in quantity supplied. Since elasticity of supply =

$\frac{\Delta Q}{Q} \Big/ \frac{\Delta P}{P}$ and $\frac{\Delta Q}{Q} > \frac{\Delta P}{P}$, an elastic supply curve will have an elasticity coefficient >1. In Figure 2, we see a typical straight-line elastic supply curve--upward sloping, but not at all steep and it crosses the vertical axis above the origin. Along the curve, particular values of elasticity will vary.

Unitary elasticity occurs when a given percentage change in price causes an equivalent percentage change in quantity supplied. Since $\frac{\Delta P}{P} = \frac{\Delta Q}{Q}$, elasticity $= \frac{\Delta Q}{Q} \Big/ \frac{\Delta P}{P} = 1$. Any straight line supply curve that passes through the origin, such as in Figure 3, has unitary elasticity.

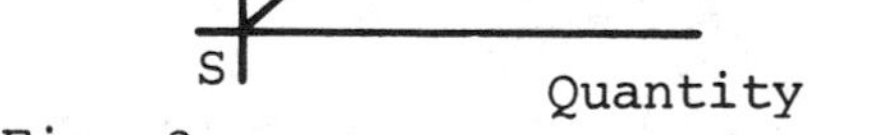

Fig. 3

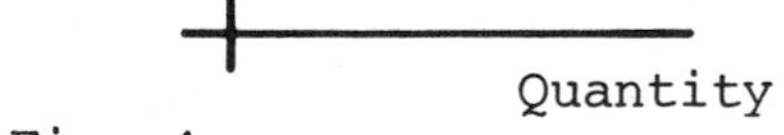

Fig. 4

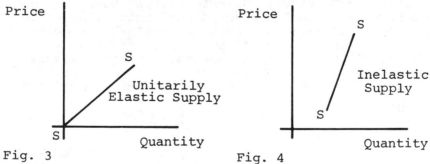

Because the elasticity $e = \frac{\Delta Q}{Q} \Big/ \frac{\Delta P}{P} = \frac{\Delta Q}{P} \cdot \frac{P}{Q}$,

and for a straight line through the origin, $\frac{P}{Q} = \frac{\Delta P}{\Delta Q}$, or

$\frac{P}{Q} = 1 \Big/ \frac{\Delta Q}{\Delta P}$, so $e = \frac{\Delta Q}{\Delta P} \times \frac{1}{\frac{\Delta Q}{\Delta P}} = 1.$

Supply is said to be inelastic when the percentage change in quantity supplied is less than the percentage change in price. Since $\frac{\Delta Q}{q} < \frac{\Delta P}{P}$, elasticity = $\frac{\Delta Q}{q} \Big/ \frac{\Delta P}{P} < 1$. Figure 4 shows a straight-line inelastic supply curve. It is much steeper than an elastic supply curve and somewhat steeper than a unitarily elastic supply curve and it crosses the horizontal axis to the right of the origin. As in the case of the elastic supply curve, elasticity is not constant along the curve.

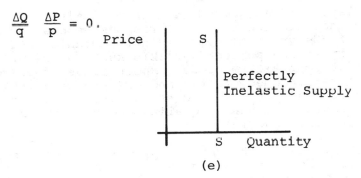

Lastly, there is the other extreme case of perfectly inelastic supply. Here quantity supplied is fixed, so that no matter what the change in price, quantity supplied can not possibly change. Since $\frac{\Delta Q}{Q} = 0$ elasticity =

$$\frac{\Delta Q}{q} \Big/ \frac{\Delta P}{p} = 0.$$

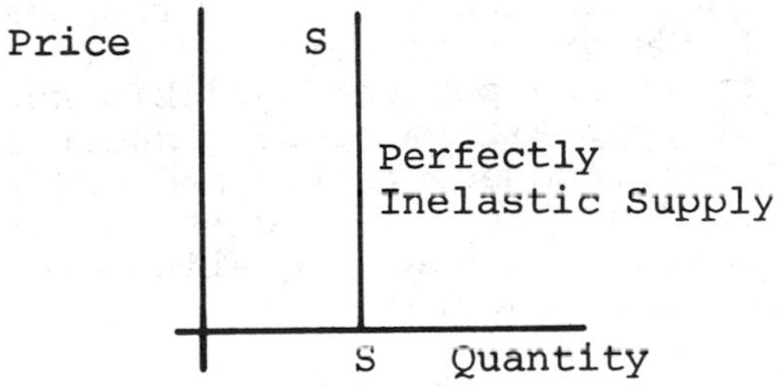

(e)

Graph (e) above represents the case of perfect inelasticity. Examples of perfect inelasticity include paintings by Goya and land.

• PROBLEM 16-5

The figure represents Joe's demand curve for wine per week. What does this demand curve imply about Joe's demand for wine?

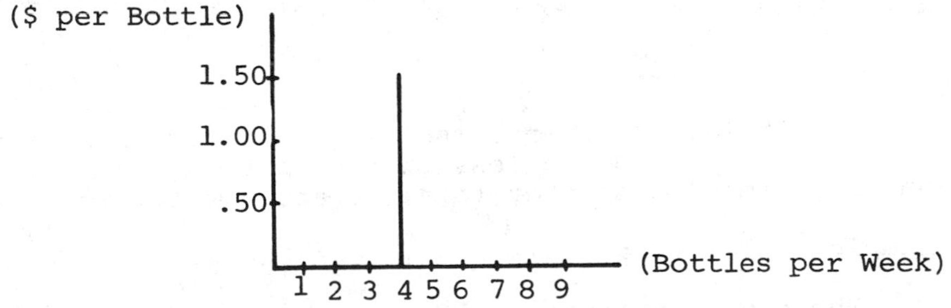

Solution: An individual's demand curve shows how much of a product he will purchase at any given price. Here, the demand curve shows how much wine Joe will buy given the set of prices being charged by the local liquor stores.

In this case, the demand curve implies that Joe will buy 4 bottles of wine per week, regardless of price. That is, even at very high prices, Joe would buy 4 bottles of wine doing without other goods in order to purchase the wine. Also, Joe's demand is very rigid. If the price falls to zero, that is, wine becomes free, Joe will still demand only 4 bottles.

This is called a perfectly inelastic demand curve as the quantity demanded remains constant at all prices.

• PROBLEM 16-6

Define elasticity of demand.

Solution: Elasticity of demand is a term widely used in economics to indicate the degree of responsiveness, or sensitiveness, of the quantity demanded attributable to a given change in an independent variable such as the price of X, prices of competitive goods, expectations of price changes, consumer incomes, tastes and preferences, or advertising expenditures. Let us discuss the price-elasticity of demand. Elasticity ends up qualitatively in one of three alternative categories.

1. Unitary elasticity where $|\varepsilon p| = 1.0$. This is the situation where the percentage change in quantity demanded divided by the percentage change in price equals 1. Since price and quantity are inversely related, this means that the effect on revenues of a price change is exactly offset by a change in quantity demanded, with the result that total revenue, the product of $P \cdot Q$ or (Price x Quantity), remains constant.

2. Elastic demand (that is, $|\varepsilon p| > 1$), results when the relative change in quantity demanded is larger than that in price. So a given percentage increment in price causes demand to decrease by a larger percentage, resulting in a decrease in total revenue. Thus, if demand is elastic, a price increase will lower total revenue, and a decrease will raise total revenue

Example: $\varepsilon p = +3.0$

3. Inelastic demand, $|\varepsilon p| < 1.0$, occurs when a price increase will produce a less than proportionate decrease in quantity demanded so that total revenues will rise.

Example: $\varepsilon p = +0.5$

The equation for calculating any elasticity is

$$\text{Elasticity} = \frac{\text{Percentage Change in Q}}{\text{Percentage Change in X}}$$

$$= \frac{\Delta Q}{(Q_1 + Q_2)/2} \div \frac{\Delta P}{(P_1 + P_2)/2} \, .$$

Dividing by a ratio is equal to multiplying by its inverse,

thus

$$\varepsilon_p = \frac{\Delta Q}{\Delta P} \cdot \frac{(P_1 + P_2)/2}{(Q_1 + Q_2)/2}$$

and $$\varepsilon_p = \frac{\Delta Q}{\Delta P} \cdot \frac{(P_1 + P_2)}{2} \cdot \frac{2}{(Q_1 + Q_2)} ,$$

so $$\varepsilon_p = \frac{\Delta Q}{\Delta P} \cdot \frac{(P_1 + P_2)}{(Q_1 + Q_2)}$$

Where Q is quantity demanded, P is the independent variable, i.e., in the discussion, the price, and Δ designates the amount of change in a variable.

• PROBLEM 16-7

Mr. Caponi is a butcher who recently raised the price of steak at his market from \$1.50 to \$2.00 a pound. Correspondingly, his sales dropped from 200 pounds per day to 100 pounds per day. Is the demand for steak at Caponi's market elastic or inelastic?

Solution: To evaluate the elasticity of demand, we use the total revenue test. If demand is elastic, total revenue (TR) $\equiv$ Price (P) x Quantity (Q) will decrease as price increases. If demand is inelastic, total revenue will increase as price increases. So, when price = \$1.50,

$$TR = P \times Q$$

$$= (\$1.50) \times (200)$$

$$= \$300$$

Now, when price rises to \$2.00,

$$TR = P \times Q = (\$2.00) \times (100)$$

$$TR = \$200$$

So, as price increases, total revenue decreases. Therefore, the demand for steak is elastic.

• PROBLEM 16-8

At 25 cents apiece, Mr. Krinsky sells 100 chocolate bars per week. If he drops his price to 20 cents, his weekly sales will increase to 110 bars. Is the demand for chocolate bars elastic or inelastic?

Solution: To evaluate the elasticity of demand, we use the total revenue (TR) test.

When price = 25 cents,

TR = Price x Quantity

TR = (0.25) x (100)

TR = $25

When price is reduced to 20 cents,

TR = (0.20) x (110)

TR = $22

So, as price decreases, total revenue decreases. Therefore demand is inelastic.

• PROBLEM 16-9

Suppose that the price of bubble gum fell by a penny and the quantity demanded doubled while a one cent drop in the price of automobiles caused one additional car to be demanded. Does this mean that demand for bubble gum is more elastic than the demand for automobiles? Explain.

Solution: The information given above does not tell us whether demand for bubble gum is more elastic than demand for automobiles. The reason is that the change in price given above is an absolute change (one cent) rather than a relative change. In order to determine elasticities, we must study the percentage changes in prices.

• PROBLEM 16-10

Alan's father gave him $3 to spend at the county fair. On his way there Alan decided he would spend the entire $3 on pizza, no matter what the price. Describe and draw Alan's demand curve.

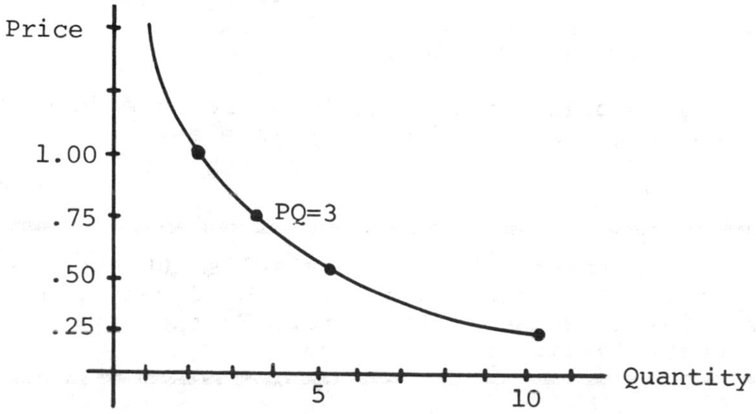

Solution: If pizza cost 50¢ a slice, Alan will buy 6 slices.

If it costs 75¢ a slice, he will buy 4 slices. We arrive at these figures by the fact that Alan plans to spend his entire \$3 on pizza. In other words, (Slices bought) x (Price per slice) = \$3, or in demand terms,

$$TR = PQ = \$3$$

To graph this function, PQ = 3, we graph the inverse function (P = 3/Q as shown in Figure 1 using only quadrant 1 since P > 0, Q > 0

Since Total Revenue (TR) = PQ, we have

TR = constant = \$3 which is a case of unitary elasticity.

• PROBLEM 16-11

Graphically, show the results of a successful advertising campaign begun by the producers of a product A on the equilibrium price and quantity of product A.

Solution: The problem asks what will happen to both the quantity of A sold in the market and the price at which it is sold if A's producer begins a successful advertising campaign. To solve this problem, begin by drawing a supply and demand diagram to represent the market situation before any changes take place (Figure 1).

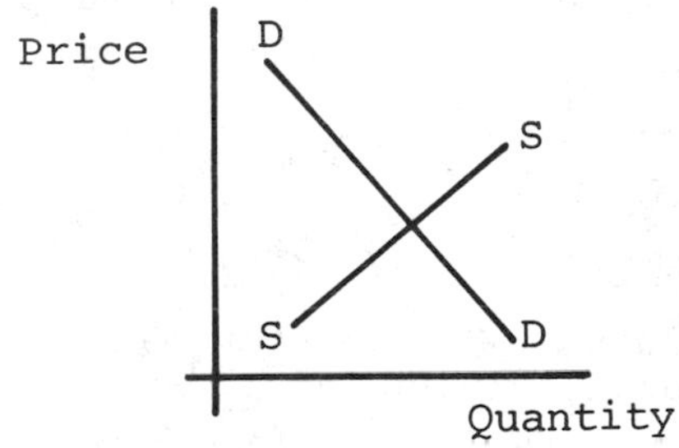

Fig. 1

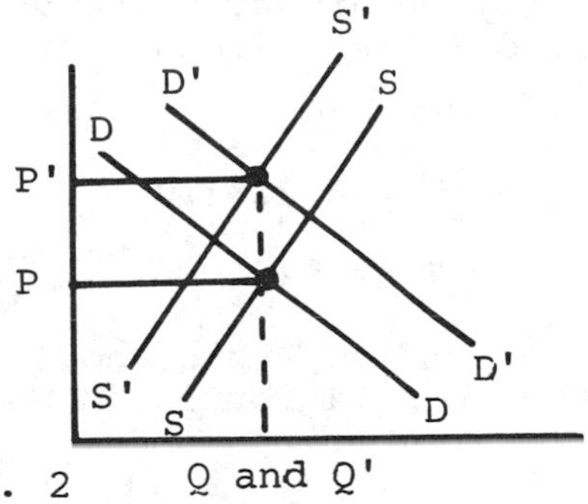

Fig. 2

The only cause for change given in the problem is a successful advertising campaign. The aim of any advertising campaign is to increase demand. A successful advertising campaign would cause demand to shift outward, from DD to D'D' in Figure 2. Advertising might also increase costs to the producer, causing the supply curve to shift up, from SS to S'S' in Figure 2. The resulting equilibrium would occur at co-ordinates (P', Q').

In Figure 2, it is shown that price rises from P to P'. Notice that the change in Q is indeterminate. That is, as the curves are drawn in Fig. 2, both Q and Q' occur at the same point, indicating no change in Q as a result of the advertising campaign. However, as shown in Figures 3 and 4, the change in Q depends on the shapes of the curves and the estimate made on how much each changes.

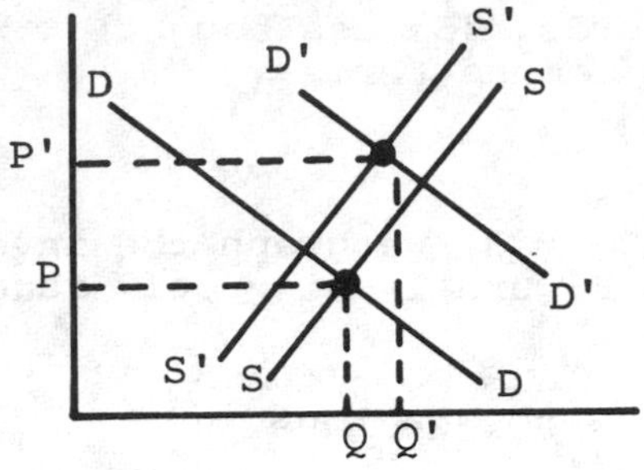

Fig. 3

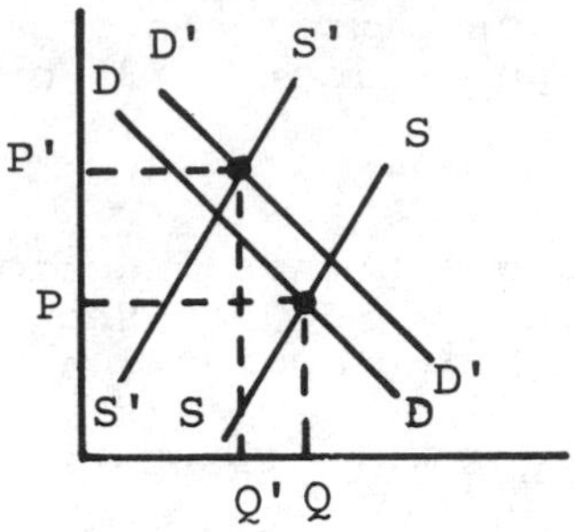

Fig. 4

Therefore, the change in the equilibrium price resulting from a successful advertising campaign is produced by an increase in the price combined with an indeterminate change in the quantity.

• PROBLEM 16-12

> Suppose the demand for a certain product is unitarily elastic throughout its entire schedule. If quantity demanded is 100 units when price is $1, sketch the curve.

Solution: Since the curve is unitarily elastic throughout, we know that total revenue is constant for all Price-Quantity combinations. Computing total revenue for the given Price-Quantity combination, $Q_D = 100$ when the related price $P = \$1$, we have

$$TR = (\$1)(100)$$

$$TR = \$100$$

Therefore, throughout the curve, $PQ = \$100$. This will be the formula for our demand curve. Graphing this, we get Figure 1:

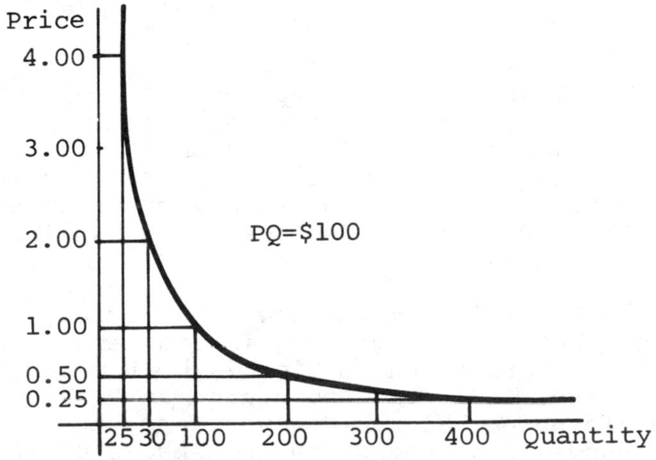

Fig. 1

The rectangles formed underneath the curve will all have areas of 100 since that area = P x Q = TR = \$100.

• PROBLEM 16-13

Examine the demand curve shown. Is it possible for demand to be elastic at the point where the demand curve intersects the Q-axis?

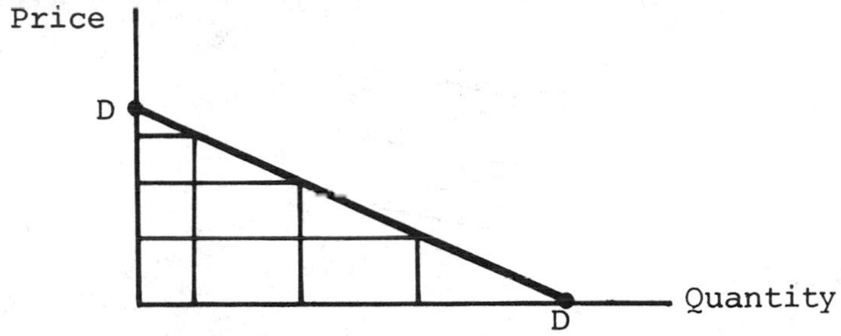

Solution: Such a situation is impossible. We can see this by remembering our definition of elastic demand. Under elastic demand, total revenue increases as price decreases. This can easily be shown over much of the graph above with the use of rectangles to indicate TR = P x Q. But at the intersection of the curve with the x-axis, P = 0. ∴ Total Revenue = 0.

Since TR decreased when we lowered price to P = 0, the curve cannot be elastic at this point.

• PROBLEM 16-14

Suppose you are given the linear demand function in Table 1.

Q	P
3	7
4	6
5	5
6	4
7	3

Table 1

a) Find the point of unitary elasticity.

b) Suppose you were given the general linear equation for demand: P = a + bQ. Use calculus to find the point of unitary elasticity.

c) Solve part a) using the information obtained in part b).

Solution: a) The first step in finding the point of unitary elasticity on a linear demand function is to compute the total revenue (TR) and the change in total revenue, ΔTR, at each of the points given, using the formula TR = P x Q, i.e., total revenue is the product of price times the quantity sold.

Q	P	TR = P · Q	ΔTR
3	7	21	
			3
4	6	24	
			1
5	5	25	
			-1
6	4	24	
			-3
7	3	21	

Table 2

If you examine the ΔTR column above, you will see that as Q increases from 3 to 5, ΔTR > 0. Therefore, in the range $3 \leq Q < 5$, demand is elastic. Similarly in the range $5 < Q \leq 7$, ΔTR < 0 so that here demand is inelastic.

What we have left now is the one point where Q is exactly equal to 5. At this point, demand is unitarily elastic.

b) We must find the point of unitary elasticity when only the general equation, P = a - bQ, is given. In this situation, since TR = P x Q, TR = (a + bQ)(Q) = $aQ + bQ^2$. At the point of unitary elasticity, not only is TR constant, but

$MR = \frac{d(TR)}{dQ} = 0$. Since MR = d(TR)/dQ, substituting TR = $aQ + bQ^2$ in gives $MR = d(aQ + bQ^2)/dQ$,

so $MR = a + 2bQ$

Now we must find the point where MR = 0.

$$MR = 0 = a + 2bQ$$

thus $-2bQ = a$

Dividing both sides by -2b, results in Q = -a/2b

Therefore, when demand is defined by P = a + bQ, unitary elasticity occurs at the point where Q = -a/2b. Also, at this point, we can find the price by using

P = a + bQ and substituting for Q the

value found, so $P = a + b \; - \frac{a}{2b}$; after cancellation of of the b, $P = a - \frac{a}{2}$; which equals

$$P = a/2$$

c) We are asked to take the information from part b) and apply it to part a). The demand function given in part a) only extends from Q = 3 to Q = 7. To use part b), we must find out what "a" is, and in order to do this, we must find out what "P" is when Q = 0 in order to find the intercept of the vertical axis.

Let us first examine two sets of points, (Q, P): (3, 7) and (4, 6). The slope between these points is

$$\frac{7 - 6}{3 - 4} = -1 = b .$$ Therefore our general equation

P = a + bQ becomes P = a - Q. Substituting the point (5, 5) in the equation, results in 5 = a - 5, so a = 10. Therefore our derived equation is P = 10 - Q.

To find the point of unitary elasticity, we simply use the fact that a = 10, b = -1 and the rule that when e = 1, $Q = -\frac{a}{2b}$ and $P = \frac{a}{2}$. So Q = - a/2b ; substituting in b = -1 and a = 10, gives Q = -10/-2

= 5

and P = a/2

= 10/2

= 5

The result, (5, 5), is the same as in part a).

CROSS ELASTICITIES

• PROBLEM 16-15

What is meant by cross elasticity of demand?

Solution: Cross elasticity is the ratio between the percentage change in the quantity demanded of a good and the percentage change in the price of another good. Like all elasticity formulas, it takes the general form of the expression for elasticity of demand. Specifically,

$$e_{A,B} = \frac{\frac{\Delta Q_A}{Q_A}}{\frac{\Delta P_B}{P_B}}$$

where $e_{A,B}$ = cross elasticity of demand for product A with respect to the price of product B

Q_A = quantity of product A

ΔQ_A = change in quantity of product A

P_B = price of product B

ΔP_B = change in price of product B

If the cross elasticity of demand is positive, then an increase in the price of product B will increase the quantity demanded of product A; products A and B are substitutes. If the cross elasticity of demand is negative, then an increase in the price of product B will cause the quantity demanded of product A to fall; products A and B are complements.

• PROBLEM 16-16

How will the cross elasticity of demand differ, depending upon whether product A is a complement of or substitute for product B?

Solution: We will be using the following formula to evaluate cross elasticity:

$$e_{A,B} = \frac{\Delta Q_A/Q_A}{\Delta P_B/P_B}$$

Suppose the price of frankfurters $\Delta P_F > 0$ rises. As a result, fewer frankfurters are being bought and so, fewer frankfurter rolls Q_R are being bought $\Delta Q_R < 0$. The two products, frankfurters and frankfurter rolls, are complements of each other.

Since $\Delta P_F > 0$ and $\Delta Q_R < 0$, $\dfrac{\Delta Q_R/Q_R}{\Delta P_F/P_F} < 0$.

Therefore, if good A is a complement of good B, the cross elasticity of demand for A with respect to the price of B will be negative.

Now let us consider what will happen to the sales of hamburgers as the price of frankfurters rises. Since frankfurters have become more expensive, hamburgers will now become relatively more attractive to the consumers, and some people will start buying more hamburgers, $\Delta Q_H > 0$ and fewer frankfurters. These two products are thus substitutes for one another. So, with $\Delta P_F > 0$ and $\Delta Q_H > 0$, $\Delta Q_H/Q_H/\Delta P_F/P_F > 0$. Therefore, when good A is a substitute for good B, the cross elasticity of demand for A with respect to the price of B will be positive.

DETERMINANTS OF ELASTICITY

• **PROBLEM 16-17**

What are some of the determinants of elasticity of demand?

Solution: 1) Availability of substitutes is an important factor in determining elasticity of demand. The more substitutes a product has, the more elastic the demand will be for that product. As the price of that product rises, people will switch to the substitutes. As the price of that product falls, people will search for ways to substitute it for a higher priced product.

2) The number of uses a product has, will also have an effect on its elasticity. The more uses a product has, the more elastic its demand is.

3) The necessity of a product will also affect elasticity of demand. The more necessary a product is, the more price-inelastic it tends to be. For example, the demand for food is, usually, inelastic.

• **PROBLEM 16-18**

Describe each of the following situations in terms of demand elasticity.

a) You have a cold and the only medicine that can help you used to cost $1.50 per bottle but now costs $20.00 a bottle. You buy it anyway.

b) At $80 per ticket you would buy 2 tickets, but scalpers want $100 a seat for the Stanley Cup finals, so you stay at home and watch the games on television.

c) Chocolate bars double in price overnight from 10¢ to 20¢, yet you buy the same number as before.

Solution: a) Here we see a highly inelastic demand situation since the cure is necessary (you want to get rid of your cold) and there are no substitutes (there is only one medicine that can help you).

b) Here the fact that you refuse to pay the $100 price for seats indicates your demand is elastic. The price differential is $100 - $80 = $20 = ΔP, a $\Delta P/P$ = $20/$80 = 25% increase in price. But the price increase results in a decrease in the number of tickets you buy of 0 - 2 = -2 = ΔQ, a $\Delta Q/Q = -2/2 = -100\%$ decrease in the number of tickets bought. Elasticity,

$$e, = \frac{-\Delta Q/Q}{\Delta P/P} = -\left(\frac{-100\%}{25\%}\right) = 4.$$

Several reasons could be cited for this elasticity.

First, you feel that watching the game on TV is a partial substitute for watching it in person. Second, there is no necessity to being there in person.

c) Here prices double yet you buy the same quantity as before thus indicating inelastic demand.

• **PROBLEM 16-19**

What is the coefficient of elasticity?

Solution: The coefficient of elasticity is defined as the percentage change in the dependent variable divided by the percentage change in the independent variable. Suppose we were studying the effect of automobile pollution on lung cancer. If automobile pollution increased by 10% and incidence of lung cancer increased by 5%, we would evaluate elasticity as follows:

$$\text{coefficient of elasticity} = \frac{\%\ \Delta\ \text{dependent variable}}{\%\ \Delta\ \text{independent variable}}$$

$$= \frac{5\%}{10\%}$$

$$= 0.5$$

In the above example, the dependent variable increased as the independent variable increased. This is called a direct relationship. If this had been an indirect relationship, i.e., if one variable increased as the other decreased, the coefficient of elasticity would have been less than zero. In such a case, we ordinarily drop the minus sign so that all elasticities can be expressed as positive numbers greater than or equal to zero.

MEASURES OF ELASTICITY

• **PROBLEM 16-20**

Using average values find the coefficient of elasticity for the following:

Price	Quantity
\$45	65,000
\$55	35,000

Solution: Here $\Delta Q = Q_1 - Q_2 = 65,000 - 35,000 = 30,000$. $-\Delta P - (P_1 - P_2) = P_2 - P_1 = \$55 - \$45 = \$10$. $Q_{avg.} =$

$(Q_1 + Q_2)/2 = (65,000 + 35,000)/2 = 50,000$. $P_{avg.} = (\$45 + \$55)/2 = \$50$. Substituting into the formula, coefficient of Elasticity =

$$\frac{\Delta Q}{Q_{avg.}} \div \frac{-\Delta P}{P_{avg.}} = \frac{30,000}{50,000} \div \frac{\$10}{\$50} = 0.6 \div 0.2 = 3$$

• PROBLEM 16-21

How would you define the following two elasticities: income elasticity of imports and interest elasticity of investments?

Solution: Income elasticity of imports measures the responsiveness of imports, M, to a change in income, Y. In formula terms, we have income elasticity of imports

$$\varepsilon_y^m = \frac{\text{percentage change in imports M}}{\text{percentage change in income Y}}$$

or $\varepsilon_y^m = \dfrac{\Delta M/M}{\Delta Y/Y}$, which can also be written as

$$\varepsilon_y^m = \frac{\Delta M}{\Delta Y} \cdot \frac{Y}{M}$$

Interest elasticity of investments measures the responsiveness of investment, I, to a change in the interest rate, i. So we have interest elasticity investments =

$$\frac{\text{percentage change in investment I}}{\text{percentage change in interest i}}$$

$$\varepsilon_i^I = \frac{\Delta I/I}{\Delta i/i}$$

or $\varepsilon_i^I = \dfrac{\Delta I}{\Delta i} \cdot \dfrac{i}{I}$

• PROBLEM 16-22

What is meant by income elasticity of demand?

Solution: Income elasticity of demand is defined as the percentage change in quantity of a good demanded divided by the percentage change in a consumer's income. The difference between this elasticity and price elasticity of demand is that income has taken the place of price in the role of independent variable. Mathematically, the concept can be expressed as follows:

$$e_Y = \frac{\Delta q/q}{\Delta Y/Y}$$

where e_Y = Income elasticity of demand

q = quantity demanded

and Y = income

Suppose that $e_Y > 0$ for product A. Then as income increases, you spend more of your income on product A than you did before the increase. Such products are called superior, or normal, goods. Examples of normal goods would be shoes and steaks. If $e_I < 0$ for product B, then you spend less on product B after an increase in income than you spent before the increase. Such products are called inferior, or "poor man's", goods. An example of this would be the potato. If you are very poor, you might have to eat a lot of potatoes because they are relatively inexpensive. However, as income rises, you would find yourself able to purchase meats and vegetables that are more expensive than potatoes, but at least bring some variety to your menu. Consequently, as income increases, your potato consumption will most likely fall.

A further break-up of income elasticities is also used. Specifically, if $e_Y > 1$, income elasticity of demand is said to be high and goods of such elasticity are considered luxuries. Remember that if $e_Y > 1$ for product c, this means that as income increases, not only does your absolute consumption of product c increase, but also the percentage of income spent on product c is increasing. Suppose you are making $2,000 per year and can afford steak once a year. If your income increases to $20,000, you can now afford steak every week. Here is an example of elasticity greater than 1. However, the reader should be careful not to assume that $e_Y > 1$ over all income ranges. Suppose income now rose from $20,000 to $200,000. Surely, you could now afford steak every night and if e_Y were greater than 1, you would eat steak every night. Yet you won't because you would get sick of steak eventually. Therefore we must remember that income elasticities often vary and must be defined over a range of income.

Those goods that have $e_Y < 1$ are considered necessities.

making $2,000 per year and can afford steak once a year. If

• PROBLEM 16-23

What is the difference between arc elasticity and point elasticity? Use an example.

Solution: To make easier the explanation of elasticities,

let us make use of the following demand function: Q = 7 - P. The following points are contained in that function

P	Q
4	3
3	4
2	5

Suppose we were asked to find the elasticity of the demand function on the interval P = 2 to P = 4. This elasticity between two points (2, 5) and (4, 3), is called arc elasticity. Let us use the midpoint formula for price elasticity of demand, as follows:

$$e = -\frac{q_1 - q_2}{q_1 + q_2} \Big/ \frac{p_1 - p_2}{p_1 + p_2}$$

$$e = -\frac{q_1 - q_2}{q_1 + q_2} \cdot \frac{P_1 + P_2}{P_1 - P_2}$$

where (2, 5) = (P_1, q_1) and (4, 3) = (P_2, q_2) so that

$$e = -\left(\frac{5 - 3}{5 + 3} \cdot \frac{2 + 4}{2 - 4}\right)$$

or $$e = -\left(\frac{2}{8} \cdot \frac{6}{-2}\right)$$

$$= -\left(\frac{-3}{4}\right) = 3/4$$

Notice that by using the midpoint formula, we have computed the elasticity at a point halfway between (2, 5) and (4, 3). This point is (3, 4), because the demand curve is a straight line.

Let us now evaluate the elasticity at (3, 4) by finding the point elasticity. To do this, we must return to our original definition of elasticity, where it was said that $e = \frac{\Delta q}{\Delta P} \cdot \frac{P}{q}$. Now, if we are only dealing with one point, we can't very well evaluate Δ_q and Δ_p. Therefore we must imagine starting out with an arc elasticity and letting Δ_p become very small. As $\Delta_p \to 0$, calculus tells us that $\frac{\Delta q}{\Delta p} \to \frac{dq}{dp}$, so that for point elasticity, $e = \frac{dq}{dp} \frac{p}{q}$. Notice that this is simply the reciprocal of the slope multiplied by a factor of P/q. At the point (3, 4), p/q = 3/4 and since demand is given by the formula Q = 7 - P, dQ/dP = -1. Then

$$e = \frac{dQ}{dp} \; \frac{P}{q} = (-1)\left(\frac{3}{4}\right) = -3/4.$$

Dropping the minus sign, we once again have e = 3/4 at point (P, Q) = (3, 4)

A simple diagram clarifies the issue. First we draw a non-linear demand curve DD,

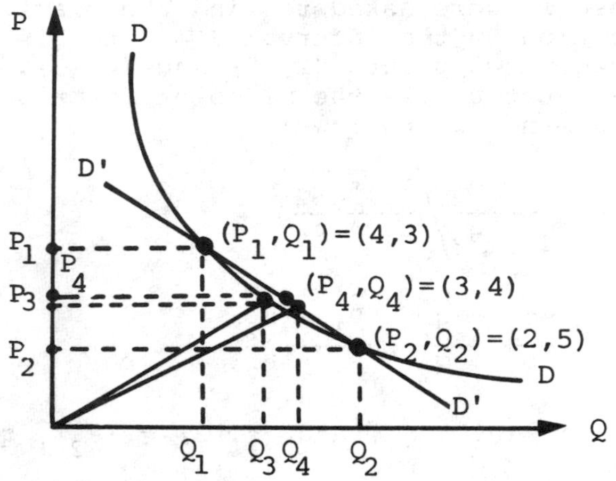

and then the linear demand curve D'D'. Suppose the slope of the non-linear demand curve at point (P_3, Q_3) equals the slope of the linear demand curve, i.e., the line tangent at DD in point (P_3, Q_3) is parallel to D'D', say

$\frac{\Delta Q_3}{\Delta P_3}$. Then the point-elasticity in point (P_3, Q_3) is

$$e_3 = \frac{\Delta Q_3}{Q_3} \Big/ \frac{\Delta P_3}{P_3} = \frac{\Delta Q_3}{\Delta P_3} \cdot \frac{P_3}{Q_3},$$ and in point (P_4, Q_4)

is $$e_4 = \frac{\Delta Q_4}{Q_4} \Big/ \frac{\Delta P_4}{P_4} = \frac{\Delta Q_4}{\Delta P_4} \cdot \frac{P_4}{Q_4}$$

But we stated that $\frac{\Delta Q_3}{\Delta P_3} = \frac{\Delta Q_4}{\Delta P_4}$;

substituting in gives us $e_3 = \frac{\Delta Q_4}{\Delta P_4} \cdot \frac{P_3}{Q_3}$

and we see that the point elasticities in (P_3, Q_3) and (P_4, Q_3) are in general not equal. The arc elasticity measured over the arc from (P_1, Q_1) to (P_2, Q_2), equals the point elasticity of (P_3, Q_4), but not of point (P_4, Q_3).

• PROBLEM 16-24

> Show that any straight-line supply curve passing through the origin has $e_s = 1$.

Solution: Let us first draw a straight-line supply curve through the origin and examine it.

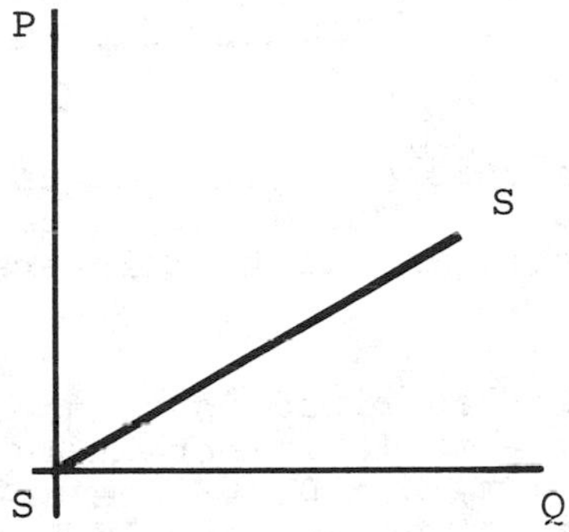

Now let us define the function, Q = f(p). Since it is linear, we have the equation Q = mP + b. Since it passes through the origin, b = 0. Therefore our equation of interest is Q = mP, where M can be any number ≥ 0, since the problem asked to be solved for "any straight-line supply curve."

Now, we must choose a definition of price elasticity of supply to use. Since we have a function defined, Q = mP, it will probably be best to use the definition of point elasticity, i.e,

$$e_s = \frac{P}{Q}\ \frac{dQ}{dP}\ .$$

Since Q = mP, the slope $\frac{dQ}{dP} = m$, substituting this into

$$e_s = \frac{P}{Q}\ \frac{dQ}{dP}\ ,\text{ we have}$$

$$e_s = \frac{P}{Q} \cdot m\ ,\text{ substituting } Q = mP \text{ in}$$

gives $e_s = \frac{P}{mp} \cdot m$

or $\quad e_s = \frac{m}{m} = 1$

So, any straight line supply curve through the origin has unitary elasticity throughout.

• PROBLEM 16-25

> Show that a straight line supply curve that cuts the price

axis has elasticity greater than 1.

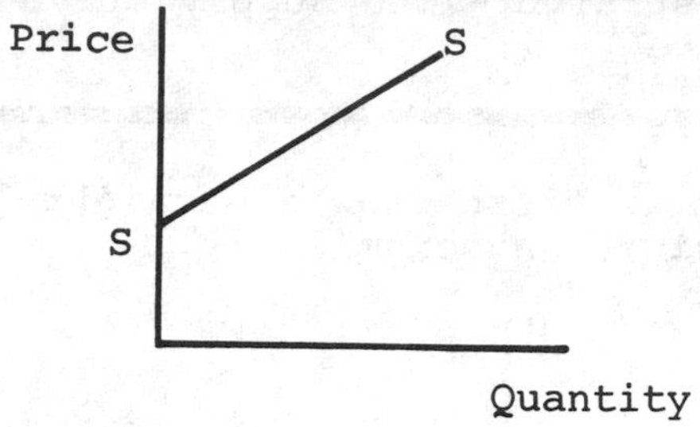

Fig. 1

Solution: To solve this problem, let us first draw an appropriate supply curve. The question tells us that the supply curve is linear and that it intersects the price axis, as shown in Figure 1.

The graph, when described in terms of x and y takes the general form, $y = mx + b$, where m is the slope, b is the y-intercept, and $m, b > 0$. Since are are using price (p) and quantity (q) above, we should change $y = mx + b$ to $p = mq + b$. Also, we must remember that Q is a function of p, so that we should rearrange $p = mq + b$ to show $Q = f(p)$. Specifically, $p = mq + b$

Now, let us evaluate elasticity, using the formula

$$e_s = \frac{P}{Q}\,\frac{dQ}{dP}\ . \quad \text{Since } Q = \frac{P}{m} - \frac{b}{m}\ ,\ \frac{dQ}{dP} = \frac{1}{m}\ .$$

Therefore

$$e_s = \frac{P}{Q}\,\frac{dQ}{dP}\ , \text{ and substituting for Q and } \frac{dQ}{dP}$$

results in
$$e_s = \frac{p}{\frac{p}{m} - \frac{b}{m}} \cdot \frac{1}{m}$$

$$e_s = \frac{P}{p - b}$$

since $b > 0$, $P - b < P$. Therefore $\frac{P}{P - b} > 1$ and

$e_s > 1$

• PROBLEM 16-26

Show that a straight line supply curve that cuts the quantity axis has elasticity less than 1.

Solution: We draw an appropriate supply curve. Since it is linear and cuts the quantity axis, the supply curve will look like this:

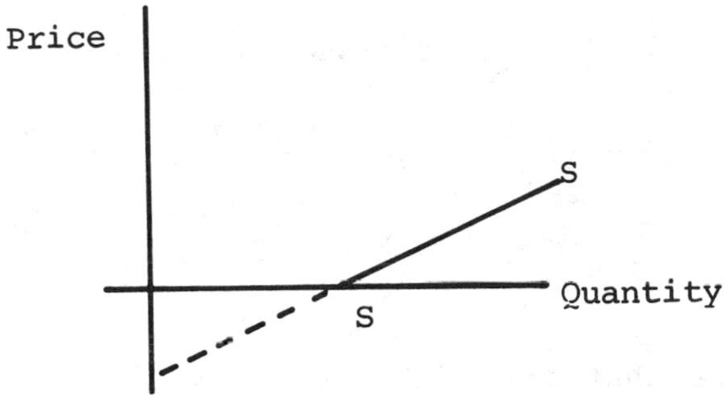

Notice the dotted portion of the curve above. This is not part of the actual supply curve (since price is negative here) but is drawn to show where the equation for the supply curve comes from. We will use the constants m and b, where m, b > 0, to describe the supply curve. Since the dotted line intersects the p-axis when p < 0, our equation is $p = mq - b$. Rearranging so that $q = f(p)$, we get $p + b = mq$

$$q = \frac{p}{m} + \frac{b}{m} .$$

Now let us evaluate elasticity using the formula

$e_s = \frac{P}{Q} \frac{dQ}{dP}$. Since $Q = \frac{P}{m} + \frac{b}{m}$, $\frac{dQ}{dP} = \frac{1}{m}$. Substituting for Q and $\frac{dQ}{dP}$ gives

$$e_s = \frac{P}{\frac{P}{m} + \frac{b}{m}} \cdot \frac{1}{m}$$

$$= \frac{P}{P + b}$$

Since $b > 0$, $P < P + b$. Therefore $\frac{P}{P + b} < 1$,

Thus $e_s < 1$, the elasticity of supply is less than 1.

• PROBLEM 16-27

At Price = \$q, quantity demanded, $Q_D = 11$. At Price = \$11, $Q_D = 9$. Find the elasticity of demand using

a) $P = 9$, $Q_D = 11$ as a base

b) $P = 11$, $Q_D = 9$ as a base

c) average values as a base

Solution: a) The general formula for elasticity of demand,

E_D , is $\quad E_d = -\frac{\Delta Q}{Q} \Big/ \frac{\Delta P}{P} = -\frac{\Delta Q}{Q} \cdot \frac{P}{\Delta P}$

Using P = 9, Q = 11 as a base we have

$$E_d = -\left[\frac{(9 - 11)}{11} \cdot \frac{9}{(11 - 9)}\right] = -\left[\frac{-2}{11} \cdot \frac{9}{2}\right] =$$

$$\frac{2}{11} \times \frac{9}{2} = 9/11$$

So we see here that demand is inelastic, because

$E_d < 1$.

b) Using P = 11, Q = 9 as a base we get

$$E_d = -\left[\frac{(11 - 9)}{9} \cdot \frac{11}{(9 - 11)}\right] = -\left[\frac{2}{9} \cdot \frac{11}{-2}\right] =$$

$$\frac{2}{9} \times \frac{11}{2} = 11/9$$

This time relative to our second base, demand is elastic, because $E_d > 1$

c) Finally if we use average values we have

$$E_d = -\left[\frac{\Delta Q}{\frac{(Q_1 + Q_2)}{2}} \Big/ \frac{\Delta P}{\frac{(P_1 + P_2)}{2}}\right]$$

or $\quad E_d = -\left[\frac{\Delta Q}{(Q_1 + Q_2)} \cdot \frac{(P_1 + P_2)}{\Delta P}\right]$

Substituting the values in, gives

$$E_d = -\left[\frac{2}{(11 + 9)} \cdot \frac{(9 + 11)}{-2}\right]$$

$$= -\left[\frac{2}{20} \cdot \frac{20}{-2}\right]$$

$$= 1.$$

So our final method tells us that demand is unitarily elastic.

• **PROBLEM 16-28**

Below are given the prices in two different months for a product and the corresponding quantities demanded. But we do not know whether the price rose from \$.80 to \$1.00 or fell from \$1.00 to \$.80. Show how each assumption will give a different answer for elasticity of demand and how using average values will alleviate this problem.

Price	Quantity demanded
\$1.00	4000
\$ .80	5000

Solution: The formula for elasticity of demand is

$$e = \frac{\Delta Q/Q}{\Delta P/P}$$

. The problem here is to determine just what Q and P are.

No matter what Q and P are, ΔQ and ΔP are constant.

$\Delta P = \$1.00 - \$.80 = \$0.20$. $\Delta Q = 5000 - 4000 = 1000$.

If we assume that the price was originally \$1.00 and use \$1.00 and 4000 units for P and Q respectively, we will get

$$\text{Elasticity} = \frac{\Delta Q}{Q}\Big/\frac{\Delta P}{P} = \frac{1000}{4000}\Big/\frac{0.20}{0.80}$$

$$\text{or } e = 0.25/0.2$$

$$= 1.25$$

If we assume that the price was originally \$0.80 and Q_D was originally 5000 units,

$$\text{Elasticity} = \frac{\frac{1000}{5000}}{\frac{\$0.20}{\$0.80}}$$

$$\text{or } e = 0.2/0.25$$

$$= 0.8$$

So we see that by using two different assumptions, we come up with two very different elasticities. In the first case, demand is elastic. In the second, demand is inelastic. In order to alleviate this problem, we use "average values" as our denominators when finding percentage changes. Rather than just using Q and P, we use the average values of Q and P.

So, we get $Q_{avg.} = \dfrac{Q_1 + Q_2}{2} = \left(\dfrac{4{,}000 + 5{,}000}{2}\right)$

$= 4500$; and $P_{avg.} = \dfrac{P_1 + P_2}{2} = \left(\dfrac{\$1.00 + \$.80}{2}\right)$

$= \$0.90$. Then Elasticity $= \dfrac{\Delta Q}{Q_{avg.}} \div \dfrac{\Delta P}{P_{avg.}} =$

$$\left[\frac{1000}{4500}\Big/\frac{\$0.20}{\$0.90}\right] = \frac{1000}{4500} \cdot \frac{\$0.90}{\$0.20} = \frac{900}{900} = 1.0$$

• PROBLEM 16-29

> The ABC Pencil Co. was considering a price increase and wished to determine the elasticity of demand. An economist and a market researcher, Key and Worce, were hired to study demand. In a controlled experiment, it was determined that at 8¢, 100 pencils were sold while at 10¢, 60 pencils were sold, yielding an elasticity of 2.25. However, Key and Worce were industrial spies, employed by the EF Pencil Co. and sent to ABC to cause as much trouble as possible. So Key and Worce decided to change the base for their elasticity figure, measuring price in terms of dollars instead of pennies (i.e., \$.08 for 8¢ and \$.10 for 10¢). How will this sabotage affect the results?

Solution: First, let us see how Key and Worce arrived at their original elasticity figure of 2.25. We will use the formula,

$$e_d = \frac{\dfrac{Q_2 - Q_1}{Q_1 + Q_2}}{\dfrac{P_2 - P_1}{P_1 + P_2}}$$

Where e_d = price elasticity of demand, Q_1 and P_1 are the original quantity and price, and Q_2 and P_2 are the new quantity and price. In this problem, we are told that $Q_1 = 100$, $P_1 = 8¢$, $Q_2 = 60$, $P_2 = 10¢$. Therefore

$$e_d = \frac{\dfrac{60 - 100}{100 + 60}}{\dfrac{10¢ - 8¢}{8¢ + 10¢}}$$

$$= \frac{\dfrac{-40}{160}}{\dfrac{2}{18}}$$

$$= \frac{-40}{160} \times \frac{18}{2}$$

$$= -2.25$$

Dropping the minus sign, we have 2.25, as we should. Clearly, Key and Worce were misled in believing that changing the method of measuring price from pennies to dollars would change the elasticity figure. The reason the figure for elasticity was unaffected is that elasticity measures the percentage changes in price and quantity. The percentage change from 8¢ to 10¢ is the same as from \$0.08 to \$0.10. So elasticity is independent of the unit of measurement employed.

Now let us see how changing the price base will affect elasticity. Specifically, we will now have $P_1 = 0.08$ and $P_2 = 0.10$.

so
$$e_d = \frac{\frac{60 - 100}{100 + 60}}{\frac{0.10 - 0.08}{0.08 + 0.10}}$$

$$= \frac{\frac{-40}{160}}{\frac{0.02}{0.18}}$$

$$= \frac{-40}{160} \times \frac{0.18}{0.02}$$

$$= -2.25$$

DEMAND ELASTICITY AND REVENUE

• PROBLEM 16-30

Suppose a producer determines that above his current price of \$1.00, demand for his product is highly elastic, while below the \$1.00 price, demand is highly inelastic.

a) What might his demand curve look like?

b) Why would you not expect this producer to alter his price, given only the information above?

Solution: All we are told is that demand is highly elastic above a point, K, and highly inelastic below that point. Let us draw , in Figure 1, a highly inelastic and a highly elastic demand curve which intersect at K.

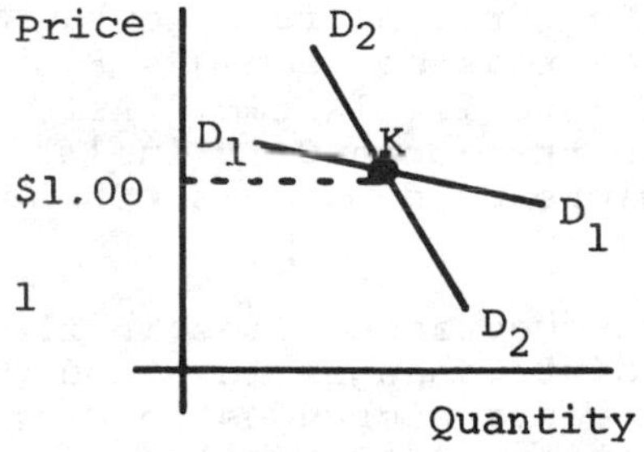

Fig. 1

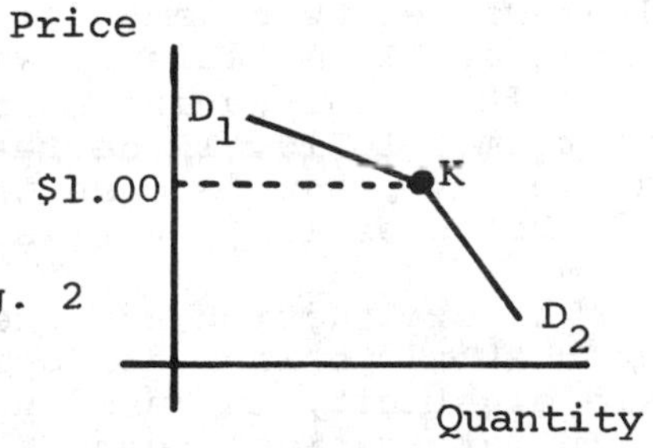

Fig. 2

D_1D_1 is highly elastic. D_2D_2 is highly inelastic.

Now let us imagine the case of the producer originally given. Above point K, we are told that demand is highly elastic. Therefore, above point K, D_1D_1 represents the producer's demand curve. Similarly, below K, we are told that demand is highly inelastic. Therefore, below K, demand is represented by D_2D_2. Combining the appropriate portions of the two curves, we get the demand curve in Figure 2 for the product.

b) With the information we have been given, we can only assume that this producer wishes to maximize profits. However, we do not have enough information to discuss profit maximization. Instead we must talk about maximization of total revenue. The producer is currently selling Q units for $1.00 each so that TR = $Q. He now has three choices. He can remain at point Q, increase price, or lower price. If he increases price, he will be facing a highly elastic demand curve. Since an increase in price brings about a drop in total revenue when demand is elastic, this move would not be taken. If he lowers the price, the producer will be facing a highly inelastic demand curve. Here, since a decrease in price brings about a drop in total revenue when demand is inelastic, we would not expect our producer to lower price either. Therefore only one choice is left. The producer, in his attempt to maximize revenue, will remain at point Q, since a movement of price in either direction, would decrease total revenue.

• PROBLEM 16-31

How is it that if the slope of the demand curve is constant, elasticity can change along the demand curve?

Solution: Suppose we have the following demand situation:

P	Q	TR = P x Q
10	8	80
9	9	81
8	10	80

Table 1

If we examine the sets of possible combinations for P and Q, we see that demand is a straight line function. But looking at TR in Table 1, we notice that between Q = 8 and Q = 9, TR is increasing so that demand is elastic. As Q goes from 9 to 10, TR decreases so that demand is inelastic. Thus we have shown a case where slope of demand is constant, = -1, but elasticity varies.

The explanation for the above occurrence lies in the fact that slope is based upon absolute changes in P and Q, while elasticity is based upon percentage changes in P and Q. In mathematical terms, the slope = $\Delta P/\Delta Q$, while elasticity $e = \frac{\Delta Q/Q}{\Delta P/P}$. For slope, $\Delta Q = 1$ and $\Delta P = -1$ throughout the demand curve so that slope = -1. But for elasticity, the percentage change by going from 8 to 9 is different from that obtained when going from 9 to 10. Thus demand elasticity is not constant.

• PROBLEM 16-32

Given in Figure 1 is a linear demand curve which has been divided into 3 sections. Point M represents the one point on the curve where demand is unitarily elastic, or $E_d = 1$. The section to the left of M has elastic demand throughout, or $E_d > 1$ while the section to the right of M has inelastic demand throughout, $E_d < 1$.

Given the linear demand function and its corresponding total revenue (TR) function in Figure 1, explain why the point of unitary elasticity will necessarily occur at the quantity, Q*, where TR is maximized.

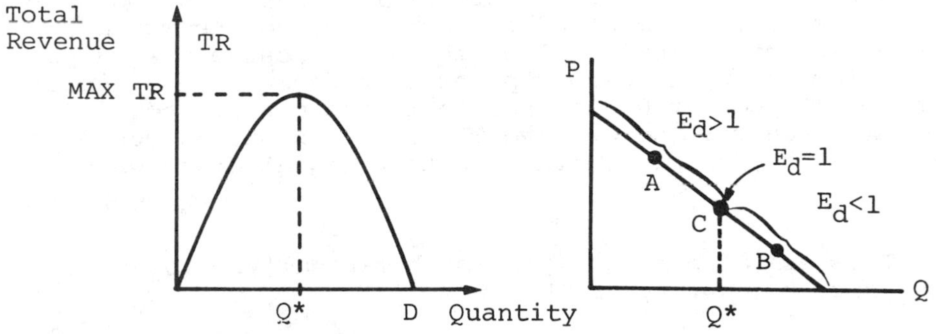

Fig. 1

Solution: All linear demand curves can be divided into three sections: an elastic portion, a point of unitary elasticity, and an inelastic portion, as shown in Figure 1.

Suppose we start initially at point A in the elastic portion of the demand curve, i.e., where the elasticity of demand, E_d, is greater than unity (1). The elastic portion of the demand curve is, by definition, that portion in which any given percentage change in price will result in a larger percentage change in the opposite direction of the quantity demanded, that is, where

$$\frac{\text{(Change of price)}}{\text{price}} < \frac{\text{change in quantity demanded}}{\text{quantity demanded}},$$

Therefore, on the elastic portion of the demand curve, a given percentage increase in price,

$$\frac{\Delta P}{P},$$

results in a larger percentage decrease in the quantity demanded

$$\frac{\Delta Q}{Q}.$$

Hence, total revenue, TR $\equiv$ P x Q, decreases; that is, the change in total revenue, ΔTR, is negative. Conversely, when the price is lowered, on the elastic portion of the demand curve, total revenue increases; that is, the resulting change in total revenue, ΔTR, is positive. Hence, to increase his total revenue, a seller who starts initially at point A would lower his price, moving toward C. Similarly, if we start at point B, on the inelastic portion of the demand curve, we could increase TR by increasing price. This is so because, on the inelastic portion of the demand curve, a given percentage change in price produces a smaller percentage change in the opposite direction of the quantity demanded. Thus, a price increase will not be completely offset by a reduction in the quantity demanded. Hence, a higher price produces a greater total revenue along the inelastic portion of the demand curve. So, if our seller started at point B on the inelastic segment of the demand curve, he would increase his price, moving along the demand curve toward point C. Increasing price beyond point C, however, would decrease TR since the seller would then be in the elastic portion of the demand curve. So we have TR being maximized when Q = Q* which also happens to be the quantity (point C) at which $E_d = 1$.

This can also be analyzed mathematically. Total revenue = price x quantity or TR = P x Q

At the point of maximum total revenue, Max TR, the marginal revenue equals zero

$$MR \equiv \frac{\Delta TR}{\Delta Q} = 0$$

But the marginal revenue is

$$MR \equiv \frac{\Delta TR}{\Delta Q} = P + Q\frac{\Delta P}{\Delta Q}$$

Taking P outside brackets gives

$$MR = P\left(1 + \frac{Q}{P} \cdot \frac{\Delta P}{\Delta Q}\right)$$

We recognize $\frac{Q}{P} \cdot \frac{\Delta P}{\Delta Q}$ as the reciprocal of the demand elasticity

$$e = \frac{\Delta Q}{\Delta P} \cdot \frac{P}{Q},$$

thus, substituting this into the formula for the marginal revenue, gives us the inverse relationship between marginal revenue MR and the elasticity e.

$$MR = P(1 + \frac{1}{e})$$

When at the Maximum total revenue the marginal revenue equals zero

$$MR = 0 = P(1 + 1/e) \quad ,$$

we see that the elasticity of demand must equal e = -1, because

$$MR = P(1 + \frac{1}{-1}) = 0$$

Thus the point of unitary elasticity will necessarily occur at the quantity Q* where total revenue TR is maximized.

At point C, elasticity of demand, E_d is unity (1). A given percentage change in price will cause an equal percentage change in the quantity demanded in the opposite direction of the quantity demanded. Hence, total revenue remains the same where the demand curve is unit-elastic.

• PROBLEM 16-33

In Figure 1, how can you decide where the point of unitary elasticity is on the demand curve?

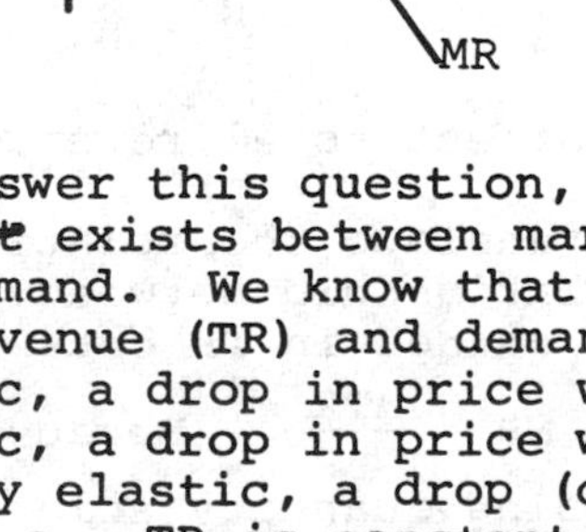

Fig. 1

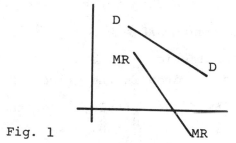

Solution: To answer this question, one must understand the relationship that exists between marginal revenue (MR) and elasticity of demand. We know that a relationship exists between total revenue (TR) and demand. Specifically, if demand is elastic, a drop in price will increase TR; if demand is inelastic, a drop in price will decrease TR; if demand is unitarily elastic, a drop (or rise) in price will not affect TR, i.e., TR is constant.

For the algebraically inclined this relationship is easy to derive. The total revenue TR is the product of price P and quantity Q: TR = P · Q A marginal change in the TR caused by a marginal change in P can then be presented as

$$\frac{\Delta TR}{\Delta P} = Q + P \cdot \frac{\Delta Q}{\Delta P}$$

Bringing Q outside brackets gives

$$\frac{\Delta TR}{\Delta P} = Q(1 + \frac{P}{Q} \cdot \frac{\Delta Q}{\Delta P})$$

and we recognize

$$\frac{P}{Q} \cdot \frac{\Delta Q}{\Delta P} = \frac{\Delta Q/Q}{\Delta P/P} = e$$

as the elasticity which is always negative because the slope of the demand curve,

i.e., $\frac{\Delta Q}{\Delta P}$, is negative.

We call the demand elastic when $e < -1$, inelastic when $-1 < e < 0$, and unitary elastic when $e = -1$.

Let us return to the expression for the marginal change in the total revenue TR caused by a marginal change in the price P:

$$\frac{\Delta TR}{\Delta P} = Q(1 + \frac{P}{Q} \cdot \frac{\Delta Q}{\Delta P})$$

$$= Q(1 + e)$$

When the demand is elastic, $e < -1$, for example $e = -2$, then

$\frac{\Delta TR}{\Delta P} < 0$ (because $Q > 0$); thus a drop in the price, $\Delta P < 0$, will increase the total revenue, $\Delta TR > 0$.

When the demand is inelastic, $-1 < e < 0$, for example, $e = -1/2$, then $\frac{\Delta TR}{\Delta P} > 0$, and a drop in the price, $\Delta P < 0$, will cause a fall in TR, $\Delta TR < 0$. Finally, when the demand is unitary elastic, $e = -1$, then $\frac{\Delta TR}{\Delta P} = 0$, and a drop in price, $\Delta P < 0$, does not affect total revenue, $\Delta TR = 0$.

Now our job is to translate the relationship between TR and elasticity into a relationship between MR and elasticity. By definition, MR is the change in TR obtained by selling one more unit of product, or $MR = \frac{\Delta TR}{\Delta Q}$. Because demand is downward-sloping, increasing quantity sold by one will lower price by a certain amount, ΔP. Suppose now that demand is elastic. If we lower the price (by increasing production by one unit) TR will increase. The change in TR (ΔTR) is therefore positive and since $MR = TR/\Delta Q$, MR will also be positive. Similarly, if demand is inelastic, a drop in price will decrease TR. ΔTR is therefore negative, and $MR < 0$. Finally, if demand is unitarily elastic, TR is constant and $\Delta TR = 0$. Therefore $MR = 0$.

With such information in mind, we can tackle the problem above. We are asked to determine where the point of unitary elasticity is. Our above analysis pointed out that if MR = 0, demand is unitarily elastic. This point occurs when the MR curve intersects the x-axis, as shown in Figure 2.

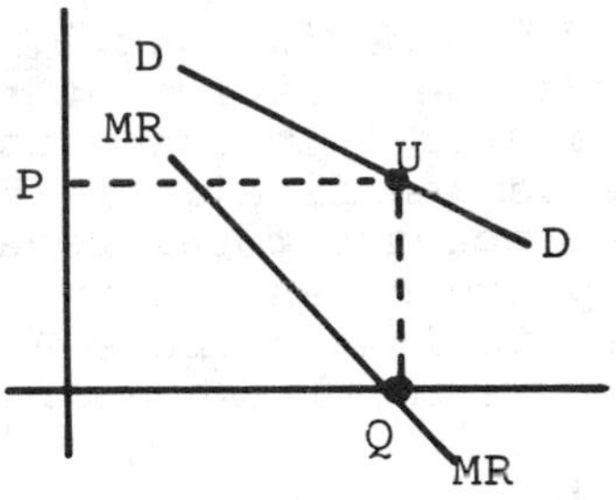

Fig. 2

Point V is therefore the point of unitary elasticity.

Again we can tackle this problem also mathematically. Instead of relating a marginal change in total revenue, ΔTR, to a marginal change in price, ΔP, we relate it to a marginal change in quantity so the marginal revenue is

$$MR = \frac{\Delta TR}{\Delta Q} = P + Q \cdot \frac{\Delta P}{\Delta Q}$$

Bringing P outside brackets, gives

$$\frac{\Delta TR}{\Delta Q} = P(1 + \frac{Q}{P} \cdot \frac{\Delta P}{\Delta Q})$$

and we recognize $\frac{Q}{P} \cdot \frac{\Delta P}{\Delta Q}$ as the reciprocal of the elasticity of demand; $\frac{Q}{p} \cdot \frac{\Delta P}{\Delta Q} = \frac{1}{\frac{P}{Q} \cdot \frac{\Delta Q}{\Delta P}} = \frac{1}{e}$

Substituting this in the above relationship results in

$$MR = \frac{\Delta TR}{\Delta Q} = P(1 + \frac{1}{e})$$

When the demand is unitary elastic; so e = -1, then

$$MR = P(1 + \frac{1}{-1}) = P(1 - 1) = 0,$$

i.e., the marginal revenue is zero; the marginal revenue line cuts the horizontal axis.

• PROBLEM 16-34

Mr. Mavis runs a beer distributorship and currently sells a case of beer for $4.00. In an informal study of 61 customers in his store one day, Mr. Mavis determined that above the price of $4.00, demand is slightly inelastic, while below the price of $4.00, demand is slightly elastic.

If Mr. Mavis wishes to maximize total revenue, should he raise or lower price?

Solution: To see whether Mr. Mavis should lower or raise his price, we must observe the behavior of total revenue. When demand is elastic, a drop in price causes an increase in total revenue. Since demand is elastic below P = $4.00, lowering the price would increase total revenue. When demand is inelastic, a rise in price causes an increase in total revenue. Since demand is inelastic above P = $4.00, raising the price would increase total revenue.

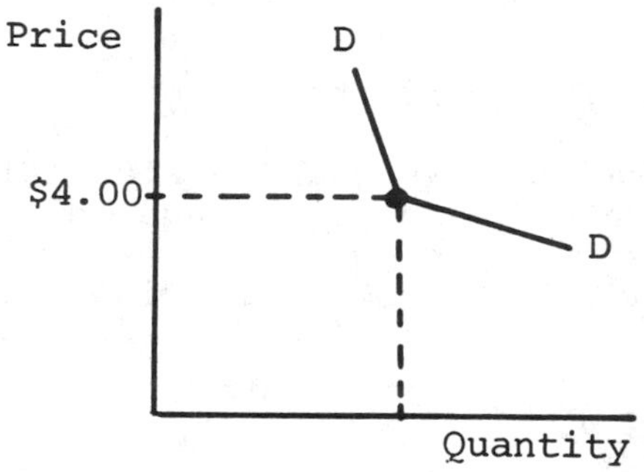

Now Mr. Mavis has found out that both lowering and raising the price will increase total revenue, but since we do not know by how much total revenue will increase in each direction, we cannot say which way Mr. Mavis should go.

• PROBLEM 16-35

Mr. Ellis sells "Buzzbee Frisbees" door-to-door. In an average month, he sells 500 frisbees at a price of $5 each. Next month, his company is planning an employee contest whereby if any employee sells 1,000 frisbees, he will receive an extra two weeks vacation with pay. Never one to work too hard, Mr. Ellis decides that instead of trying to push $5 frisbees on unwilling customers for 12-hours a day, he will maintain his normal work schedule of 8 hours each day. His strategy is to lower the price which he charges his customers. If demand elasticity, e = -3, what price should Mr. Ellis charge in order to sell 1000 "Buzzbee Frisbees." Use average values for P and Q.

Solution: When dealing with elasticity of demand, we utilize the following four pieces of data:

Q_0 = quantity demanded before price change

Q_1 = quantity demanded after price change

P_0 = price before the change

P_1 = price after the change

In this case, $Q_0 = 500$, $Q_1 = 1000$, $P_0 = \$5$, P_1 is unknown, and $e = -3$.

The basic formula for elasticity is:

$$e = \frac{Q_1 - Q_0}{P_1 - P_0} \cdot \frac{P_1}{Q_1} \quad \text{or} \quad e = \frac{Q_1 - Q_0}{P_1 - P_0} \cdot \frac{P_0}{Q_0}$$

However, it is often a good idea to use the average value $\frac{P_1 + P_0}{2}$ instead of P_1 or P_0 to compute the percentage price change. Similarly, we will use the average value $\frac{Q_1 + Q_0}{2}$ instead of Q_1 or Q_0. So our equation for elasticity becomes

$$e = \frac{Q_1 - Q_0}{P_1 - P_0} \cdot \frac{(P_1 + P_0)/2}{(Q_1 + Q_0)/2}$$

$$= \frac{Q_1 - Q_0}{P_1 - P_0} \cdot \frac{P_1 + P_0}{Q_1 + Q_0}$$

$$e = \frac{Q_1 - Q_0}{Q_1 + Q_0} \cdot \frac{P_1 + P_0}{P_1 - P_0}$$

Now all we have left to do is to substitute the values given for e, Q_0, Q_1 and P_0 into the equation above and solve for P_1:

$$-3 = \frac{1000 - 500}{1000 + 500} \cdot \frac{P_1 + 5}{P_1 - 5}$$

or $$-3 = \frac{1}{3} \cdot \frac{P_1 + 5}{P_1 - 5}$$

$$-9(P_1 - 5) = P_1 + 5$$

$-9P_1 + 45 = P_1 + 5$; collecting the terms including P_1

$10P_1 = 40$; dividing both sides by 10

results in $P_1 = \$4$

So, if Mr. Ellis lowers his price to \$4 for each "Buzz-bee Frisbee", he will sell 1000 of them in the next month without increasing his daily work schedule at all.

In the old situation the total revenue of Mr. Ellis was \$5 x 500 = \$2500. In the new situation his total revenue is \$4 x 1,000 = \$4,000.

• PROBLEM 16-36

Why is it that a profit-maximizing businessman would always raise prices when facing an inelastic demand curve but might or might not raise prices when facing an elastic demand curve?

Solution: When talking about profit maximization, one must realize that not only total revenue must be taken into account. In addition total costs must be considered. Specifically, profit π = Total Revenue - Total Costs = TR - TC.

Let's first consider the case of the businessman facing the inelastic demand curve. By raising the price, TR will increase. Also, since a raise in price causes a decrease in quantity demanded, TC, which is an increasing function of quantity, must decrease. Therefore, since TR is increasing and TC is decreasing, profit will increase as price rises. So the profit-maximizing businessman would always raise prices with an inelastic demand curve.

Now examine the case of a price rise when demand is elastic. Since a price rise implies a drop in quantity demanded, total output and total costs will fall. However, total revenue will also decrease because demand is elastic. Therefore, since TR and TC are both falling, we can not say in general what will happen to profit. If TR falls by more than TC falls, profit will fall. If TR falls by less than TC falls, profit will increase. Therefore the profit-maximizing businessman might or might not increase price when faced with an elastic demand curve, depending on the behavior of TR and TC.

• PROBLEM 16-37

Why is it that a profit-maximizing businessman would never lower prices when facing an inelastic demand curve and might not lower price when facing an elastic demand curve?

Solution: The price elasticity of demand reveals much about the behavior of total revenue (TR). Specifically, when demand is elastic, a reduction in price will cause an increase in total revenue. On the other hand, when demand is inelastic, a reduction in price will cause a decrease in total revenue.

In talking about profit-maximization, we also must discuss total costs. Here elasticity of demand is unimportant since costs and demand elasticity are unrelated. The only point about costs that we must remember is that as output increases, so do total costs (TC). And since a price drop results in an increase in quantity demanded (output), total costs will be increasing in this case.

Now examine each of the cases individually. The businessman facing the inelastic demand curve would have decreasing TR and increasing TC if he were to lower his price. Therefore profit would fall, since profit = TR- TC. It would make no sense then for the profit-maximizing businessman facing an inelastic demand curve to lower prices.

In the case of elastic demand, we once again face increasing TC as output increases. However, TR will also be increasing as output increases. Therefore, since profit = TR - TC, we can not decide at this point whether a profit-maximizing businessman would or would not lower price and increase output along the elastic portion of the demand curve. For if the increase in TC is greater than the increase in TR, then profits will be less than before. However, if the increase in TC is less than the increase in TR, then profits would be greater than before. Therefore, we can not say in general whether the profit-maximizing businessman would or would not lower prices when facing an elastic demand curve.

• PROBLEM 16-38

If demand is inelastic, total revenue increases as price increases. If demand is elastic, total revenue decreases as price increases. In the case of supply, total revenue does not depend upon elasticity. Why?

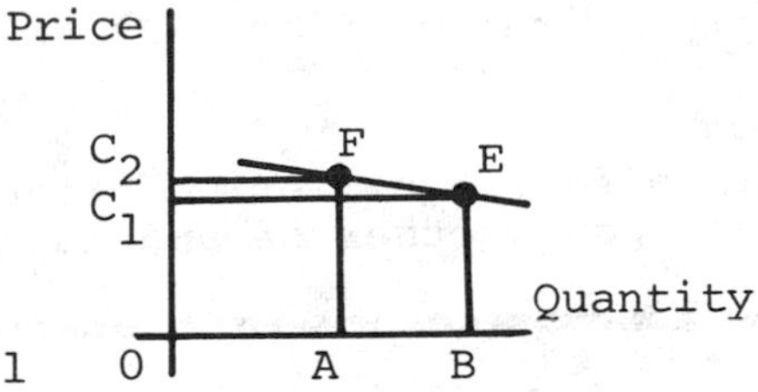

Fig. 1

Solution: Let us first illustrate the change in total revenue as price increases for an inelastic and elastic demand curve.

Since total revenue (TR) = (Price x Quantity), we represent it with rectangles under the demand curves in Figure 1. For both curves, before the price increase, TR = area of rectangle OC_1EB. As price increases, the TR along the elastic curve decreases to area of OC_2FA while the TR along the inelastic curve increases to area of OC_2GA.

The reason TR is a function of demand elasticity is because demand is downward sloping. Remember TR = P x Q and as we move along a demand curve, Q increases as P decreases and Q decreases as P increases. With one going up and one going down, we can not tell ahead of time how TR will be affected by a change in price, unless we know the elasticity.

In dealing with supply curves, however, elasticity does not affect the sign (positive or negative) of the change in total revenue that results from moving along the supply curve, since P and Q are directly related, i.e., Q increases as P increases. Let us use the curve below to illustrate:

Fig. 2

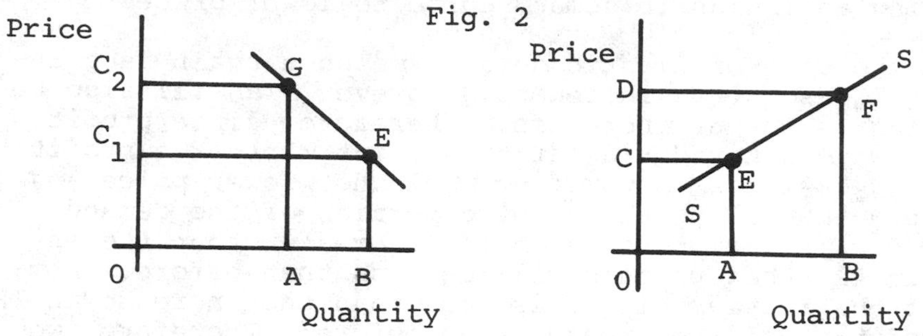

As price goes from C to D, P increases and Q increases. Therefore, since TR = P x Q, TR must increase as P increases, no matter what elasticity is. Similarly, TR must decrease as P decreases. In the figure above, TR goes from area of OCEA to area of ODFB as price goes from C to D.

ELASTICITY AND MARKET EQUILIBRIUM

• PROBLEM 16-39

Suppose that supply increases from SS to S'S' as shown in Figure 1.

How will this affect equilibrium price and output differently depending upon whether demand is elastic or inelastic?

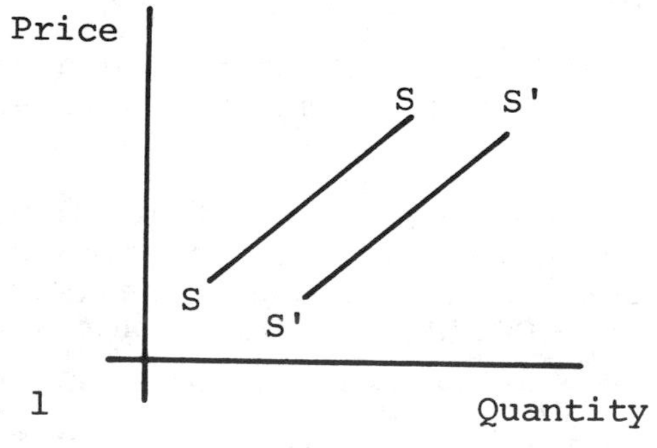

Fig. 1

Solution: Below are drawn a relatively elastic demand curve, D_1D_1 and a relatively inelastic demand curve, D_2D_2 , along with the two given supply curves, SS and S'S'.

Before supply increases, equilibrium occurs at E for

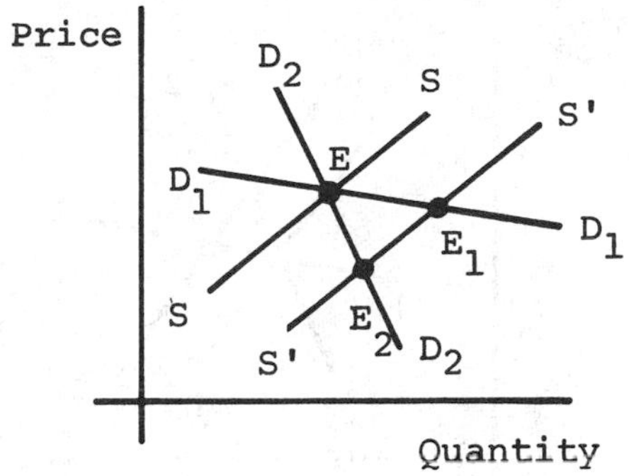

Fig. 2

both D_1D_1 and D_2D_2 . Once supply increases to S'S', the equilibrium point for D_1D_1 is E_1 and the equilibrium point for D_2D_2 is E_2 . In the elastic demand case, an increase in supply has triggered a relatively small decrease in price, along with a relatively large increase in quantity demanded. Since we are moving down an elastic demand curve by increasing supply, total revenue will increase. In the case of inelastic demand, however, the increase in supply brings about a relatively small rise in quantity demanded along with a relatively large drop in price. Since there is a decrease in price on an inelastic demand curve, total revenue will fall.

• PROBLEM 16-40

How does an increase in demand affect equilibrium differently, depending upon whether supply is elastic or inelastic?

Solution: Let DD represent demand before the increase and D'D' represent demand after the increase. S_1S_1 is an elastic supply curve while S_2S_2 is an inelastic supply curve. Both S_1S_1 and S_2S_2 originally have equilibrium at E. After the increase in demand, S_1S_1 has equilibrium at E_1 and S_2S_2 has equilibrium at E_2.

As the graph above shows, the increase in demand from DD to D'D' has quite different effects, depending on the elasticity of supply. If the supply is elastic, as in S_1S_1, an increase in demand represents a movement up the supply curve from point E to E_1 . Since supply is elastic, the percentage increase in equilibrium quantity will be greater than the percentage increase in equilibrium price. For S_2S_2 , an increase in demand represents a percentage increase in price which is greater than the percentage increase in quantity since supply is inelastic.

In general one should remember that the more inelastic supply is, the more an increase in demand will be re-

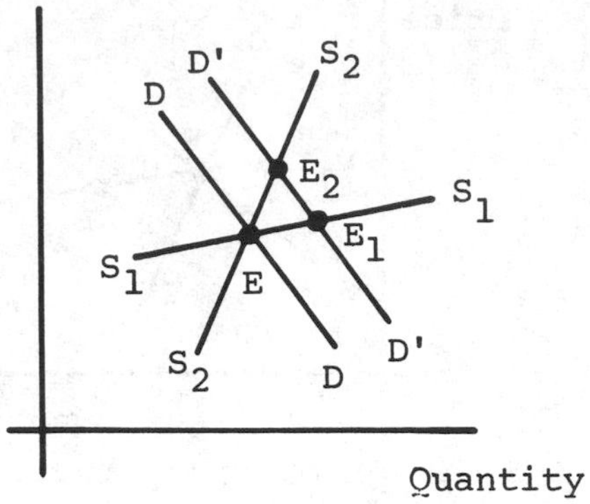

flected in an increase in the price of the product. The extreme case is perfect inelasticity, as in land, where quantity is fixed so that an increase in demand must be completely translated into a price (rent) increase. On the other extreme, the more elastic supply is, the more an increase in demand will be reflected in an increase in equilibrium quantity.

• PROBLEM 16-41

Alfred Marshall spoke of three different time periods (1) momentary equilibrium (2) short-run equilibrium and (3) long-run equilibrium. Compare the elasticities of supply in the three periods.

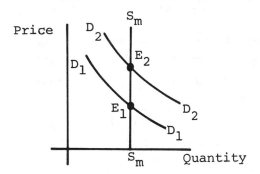

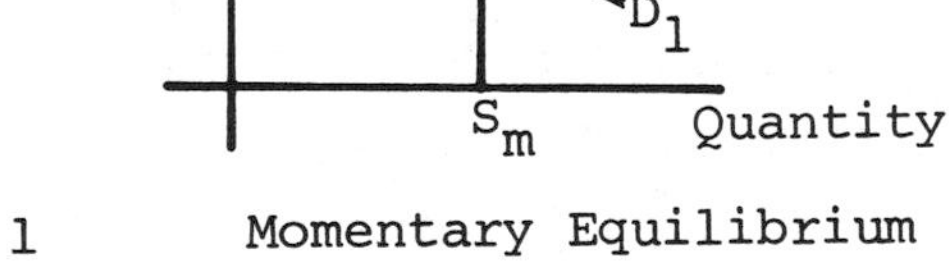

Fig. 1 Momentary Equilibrium

Solution: Momentary equilibrium is the situation in which suppliers have no time to make adjustments in output therefore making supply perfectly inelastic. As the graph in Figure 1 shows, with a perfectly inelastic supply curve, SmSm, a change in demand represented in Figure 1 by the shift from D_1D_1 to D_2D_2 will not affect the momentary equilibrium quantity, but rather will alter the momentary equilibrium price as we go from E_1 to E_2.

During the short-run some adjustments of labor and other variable factors are possible, thereby altering the supply curve from the perfectly inelastic supply curve of momentary equilibrium. The supply curve in Figure 2, SsSs, illustrates the less inelastic supply curve of the short run.

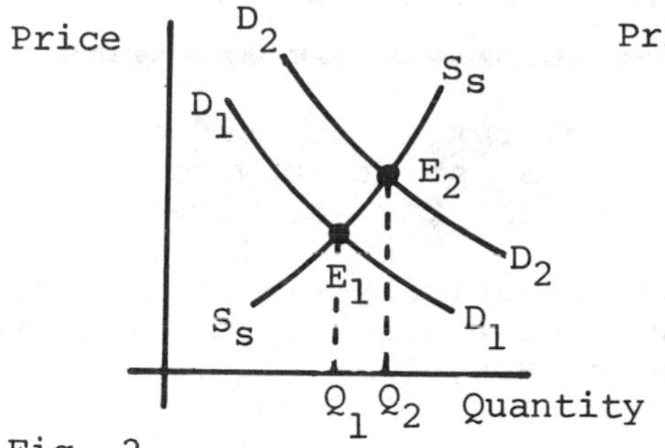

Fig. 2

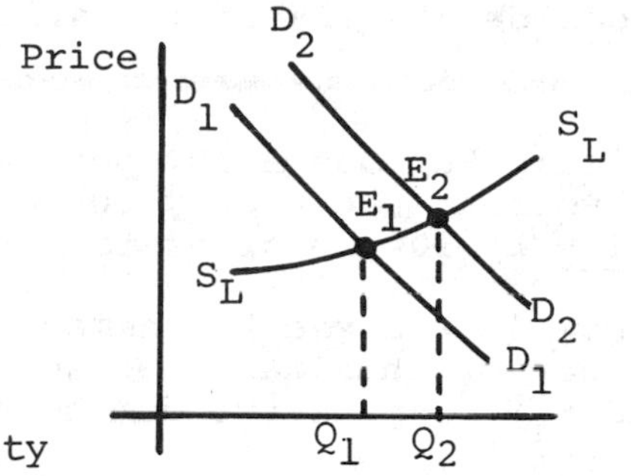

Fig. 3

Finally, the long-run represents the time period during which full adjustments of all factors to changes in demand can take place. Firms can abandon old plants or build new ones. They can leave old industries or enter new industries. The supply curve, S_LS_L, has even greater elasticity than the previous two time periods, as illustrated in Figure 3.

• PROBLEM 16-42

The farm sector is typically characterized by low demand price elasticity. How does this affect the farmer's situation when supply varies from year to year?

Solution: Suppose demand for farm products is inelastic as shown below. Also imagine that good weather causes supply to increase from S_1S_1 to S_2S_2 with equilibrium going from E_1 to E_2 .

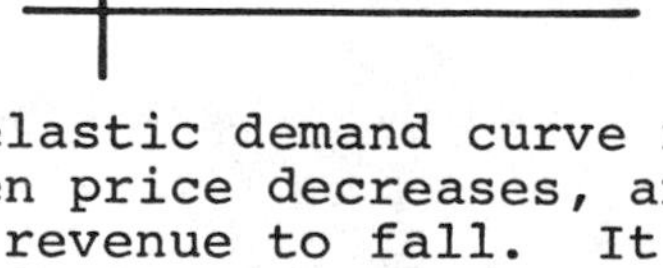

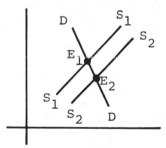

Since an inelastic demand curve represents decreasing total revenue when price decreases, an increase in supply will cause total revenue to fall. It seems quite strange but it is theoretically accurate to say that if a farmer has a good year and goes to the market with larger crops than usual, he will have lower sales revenue than usual.

On the other hand, if the farmer had a bad year, supply would decrease, causing a decrease in quantity sold but a greater percentage increase in price, which would cause total revenue to rise.

• **PROBLEM 16-43**

How does demand elasticity affect tax incidence?

Solution: Suppose a 10¢-per pack tax is imposed on cigarettes so that the supply curve, SS, shifts upward at each quantity by 10¢ in order to meet the tax (as shown below).

Now let us see how demand elasticity will affect the incidence of this tax. We see below our two supply curves, SS and S_1S_1 , plus two demand curves, D_1D_1 and D_2D_2 .

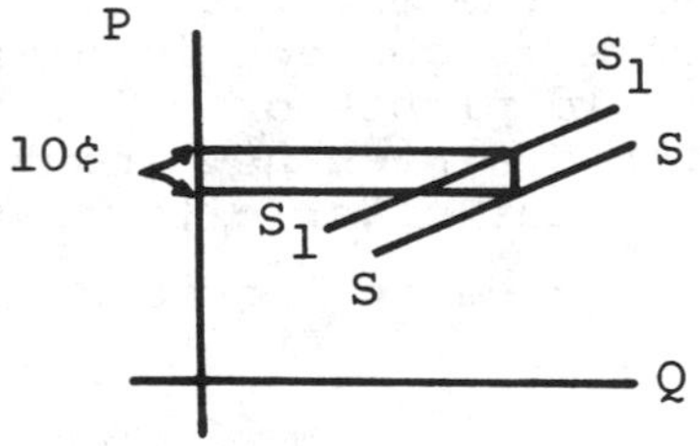

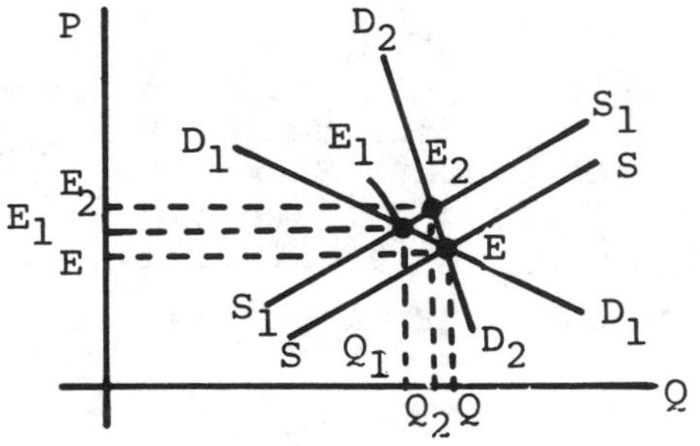

D_1D_1 is highly elastic while D_2D_2 is highly inelastic. With demand as D_1D_1 , the 10¢ tax shifts equilibrium from E to E_1 . With demand as D_2D_2 , the 10¢ tax shifts equilibrium from E to E_2 . Notice now that the price rises more when demand is inelastic, i.e., the consumer pays more of the tax burden as demand grows more inelastic. On the other hand, in the highly elastic demand situation, D_1D_1 , price has risen considerably less. Here, the tax incidence is primarily upon the producer. The demand for cigarettes will be sharply decreased.

SHORT ANSWER QUESTIONS FOR REVIEW

Answer
To be covered when testing yourself

Choose the correct answer.

1. The elasticity coefficient of demand indicates: (a) the slope of the demand function (b) the degree of concentration in the market (c) the extent to which a demand curve shifts as income changes (d) consumer responsiveness to price changes — d

2. Suppose Product A is reduced in price from \$9 to \$8 and, as a result, the quantity demand increases from 50 to 60 units. Demand is: (a) inelastic (b) elastic (c) unitarily elastic (d) cannot be determined from the information given — b

3. Suppose the elasticity coefficients of demand are 2.3, 0.40, 1.27, and 0.77 for demand schedules D_1, D_2, D_3 and D_4 respectively. A 1 percent increase in price will result in an increase in total revenue for: (a) D_1 only (b) D_1 and D_3 (c) D_2 and D_4 (d) D_3 and D_4 — c

4. Product B is reduced in price from \$10 to \$9 and, as a result, quantity demanded increases from 70 to 75 units. Demand is: (a) inelastic (b) elastic (c) unitarily elastic (d) cannot be determined from the information given — a

5. If the quantity demanded remains almost unaffected by a per unit price change, demand is said to be: (a) inelastic (b) elastic (c) kinked (d) fixed — a

6. Product C is reduced in price from \$5 to \$4 and, as a result, quantity demanded increases by 100 units. Demand is: (a) inelastic (b) elastic (c) unitarily elastic (d) cannot be determined from the information given — d

7. In which of the following cases will total revenue fall? (a) price rises and demand is inelastic (b) price rises and demand is elastic (c) price falls and demand is elastic (d) price rises and supply is elastic — b

8. The demand schedule faced by the individual purely competitive firm is: (a) perfectly inelastic (b) relatively inelastic (c) relatively elastic (d) perfectly elastic — d

SHORT ANSWER QUESTIONS FOR REVIEW

Answer
To be covered when testing yourself

9. Consumer X's money income decreased and his demand for product Y increased. Product Y is therefore: (a) an inferior good (b) a substitute good (c) a complementary good (d) a normal good — a

10. Suppose the supply of product A is perfectly elastic. If there is an increase in demand for this product: (a) equilibrium price and quantity will both increase (b) equilibrium price and quantity will both decrease (c) equilibrium quantity will increase but price will not change (d) equilibrium price will increase but quantity will not change — c

11. If the marginal revenue associated with a given decline in price is negative, it can be said that: (a) the product is an inferior good (b) demand is inelastic in this price range (c) a price hike would decrease profits (d) the elasticity coefficient is greater than one — b

12. If demand is perfectly inelastic, the incidence of an excise tax will be: (a) entirely on the seller (b) mostly on the seller (c) mostly on the buyer (d) entirely on the buyer — d

13. For a given increase in demand, the quantity effect is largest and the price effect is smallest: (a) in the long run (b) in the short run (c) in the immediate market period (d) when supply is least elastic — a

14. A vertical supply curve indicates that: (a) an unlimited amount of the product will be supplied at a constant price (b) a change in price will have no effect upon quantity supplied (c) price and quantity supplied are inversely related (d) the industry is organized monopolistically — b

15. The elasticity of a straight-line demand curve is: (a) constant throughout (b) inelastic in high price ranges and elastic in low price ranges (c) elastic in high price ranges and inelastic in low price ranges (d) unitary at several points — c

Fill in the blanks.

16. If total revenue falls as price rises, demand is _______________. — elastic

SHORT ANSWER QUESTIONS FOR REVIEW

	Answer To be covered when testing yourself
17. You decide to raise ticket prices in order to provide more funds to finance your concerts. You are assuming that demand is ______________.	inelastic
18. Supply curves tend to be more elastic in the ______________ run.	long
19. The elasticity between two points on a curve is called ______________ elasticity.	arc
20. A horizontal line is used to draw ____________ demand.	perfectly elastic
21. The ratio between the percentage change in the quantity demanded of one good and the percentage change in the price of another good is called the ______________.	cross elasticity of demand
22. If the cross elasticity of demand for product A with respect to the price of product B is negative, A and B are ______________.	complements
23. If your consumption of product A increases as income increases, product A is a ______________ good.	normal, or superior
24. On a straight-line demand curve, the point of unitary elasticity occurs where ______________ is zero.	marginal revenue
25. Any straight-line supply curve passing through the origin has ______________ elasticity.	unitary
26. In a highly elastic demand situation, the incidence of a per-unit sales tax will fall primarily upon the ______________.	producer
27. As the availability of ______________ for product A increases, the elasticity of product A increases.	substitutes
28. ______________ refers to the ratio of the percentage change in quantity supplied to the percentage change in price.	Price elasticity of supply
29. An increase in supply will raise equilibrium quantity unless demand is ______________.	perfectly inelastic
30. If price rises and total revenue increases, the coefficient of elasticity of supply ______ ______________.	cannot be determined

Determine whether the following statements are true or false.

SHORT ANSWER QUESTIONS FOR REVIEW

	Answer To be covered when testing yourself
31. If the demand for wheat is highly inelastic, a bumper crop may reduce farm incomes.	True
32. In general, the demand for necessities is less elastic than the demand for luxury goods.	True
33. If price and total revenue are directly related, demand is elastic.	False
34. If price and quantity demanded both increase from one time period to another, we can conclude that the law of downward-sloping demand has encountered an exception.	False
35. A drop in the price of soda failed to increase sales. Demand must be perfectly inelastic over this price range.	True
36. For a given shift in demand, one would expect the equilibrium price to change more in the long run than in the short run.	False
37. The more inelastic the demand for a good which is taxed, the greater the total tax receipts of the government tend to be.	True
38. Infinite elasticity is where a change in price has no effect on total revenue.	False
39. A producer can always increase profit by lowering price when demand is elastic.	True
40. Inelastic demand, when drawn on a graph, will always show a steep slope.	False
41. Income elasticity of demand measures the effect of a change in income on the demand for certain products.	True
42. Following a shift in demand, equilibrium price rose by 10% and equilibrium quantity rose by 10%. Therefore demand is unitarily elastic.	False
43. By measuring price in cents instead of dollars, elasticity measurements can be distorted.	False
44. On a straight-line demand curve, total revenue is maximized at the point of unitary elasticity.	True
45. Even if the slope of a demand curve varies from point to point, elasticity may be constant along the curve.	True

CHAPTER 17

ANALYSIS OF COSTS

Basic Attacks and Strategies for Solving Problems in this Chapter. See pages 621 to 645 for step-by-step solutions to problems.

Economists look at costs differently than accountants do. Explicit costs are defined as those costs that entail an actual outlay of money. Implicit costs are the opportunity costs of production, those sacrifices a firm must make that do not entail actual outlays of money. As a general rule, the accounting analysis of cost concentrates on explicit costs, while economists also consider implicit costs.

Assume an individual is earning $40,000 per year at a job and receiving interest payments of $10,000 per year from financial investments. Now assume the same individual quits her job, liquidates her financial holdings, and starts her own business, using her own money for the initial investment and working full time in the business. At the end of the first year of operation, an accountant is called in to prepare a profit and loss statement. The accountant would total all revenues from sales and explicit costs. Assume the statement looks like this:

Total Revenues		$100,000
Explicit Costs		
Employee's Wages	$20,000	
Materials	$40,000	
Utilities	$10,000	
Other	$10.000	
Total Explicit Costs		–$80,000
(Accounting) Profit		$20,000

According to the accountant, a profit of $20,000 was earned.

An economist would similarly total revenues and explicit costs, but also include implicit costs. In this case, if the individual had continued at her job, she would have received $40,000 in compensation. Leaving the job forced her to sacrifice this income, an implicit cost of doing business. Likewise with her financial investments. The $10,000 in interest foregone is another implicit cost of doing business. Adding these costs to explicit costs gives total costs of production of $130,000 and an (economic) loss of $30,000. How do economists turn profits into losses? If she had not gone into business for herself, she would have received $40,000 + $10,000 = $50,000 in income for the year. By going into business, her monetary profit was only $20,000, or $30,000 less than she could have earned.

In this instance, the accountant's approach is misleading. The economist's approach provides a sounder basis for making decisions. In real life, accounting rules and regulations and practical problems with computing implicit costs limit our ability to apply the economist's approach generally.

An important element in the consideration of costs is an analysis of the various cost curves. In the short run, total costs (TC) can be divided into fixed (FC) and variable (VC) components, where fixed costs include items that do not vary with the level of output (such as depreciation and certain contractual commitments), and variable costs include items varying with the level of output (such as labor and raw material costs).

The graph shows the relationship of *TC*, *FC*, and *VC* to the level of output (Q). Note that *FC* must be paid even if the plant shuts down and produces nothing, and does not change as output rises. The *VC* curve has a distinctive shape. *VC* initially rises at a decreasing rate (to output *a*), after which it rises at an increasing rate. Expansion to point ***a*** is associated with greater efficiency, likely resulting from specialization and division of labor. After point *a*, diminishing returns set

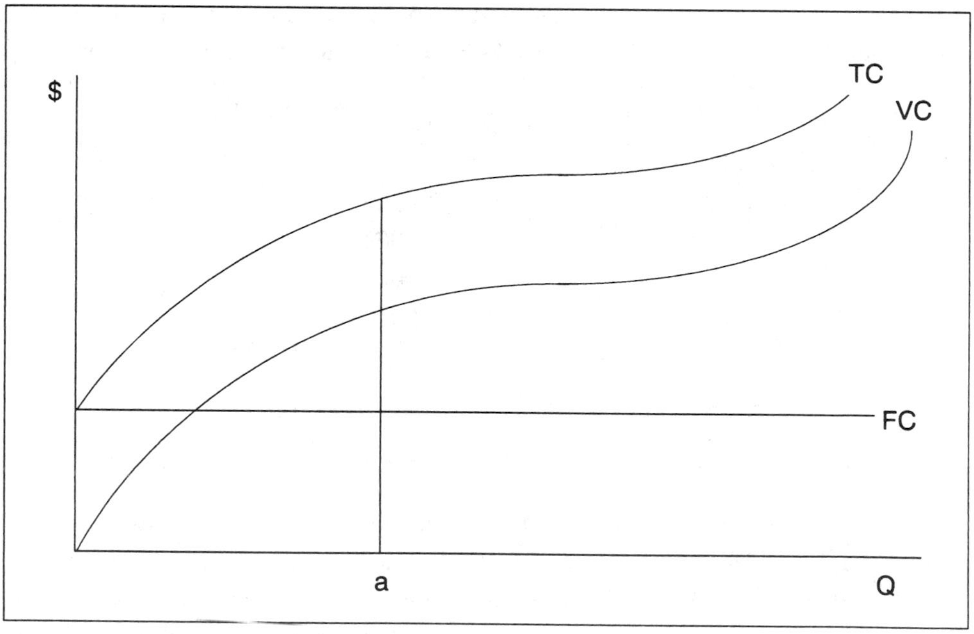

Costs of Production

in, leading to decreased efficiency. The *TC* curve has the same shape as *VC*, differing from it only by the level of *FC*.

Using the cost categories just discussed, a family of average cost curves can be determined. Average fixed cost (AFC) equals *FC/Q*; average variable cost (AVC) equals *VC/Q*; average total cost (ATC) equals *TC/Q*. Another important concept is marginal cost (MC), which measures the increase in total cost from producing one more unit $\left(MC = \frac{\Delta TC}{\Delta Q} \right)$. Since *TC* increases only if *VC* does, *MC* also equals the increase in variable cost from producing one more unit $\left(MC = \frac{\Delta VC}{\Delta Q} \right)$.

The graph shows the relationship of the curves to each other. *AFC* approaches the horizontal axis asymptotically. Both *AVC* and *ATC* have a distinctive U-shape. The *MC* schedule lies below both *AVC* and *ATC* when they are falling, above them when they are rising, and must intersect each at its low point. The relationship of costs to output is an important determinant of business decisions, and students of economics need to understand these relationships.

In the long run, there are no fixed costs. The important concepts are long run average cost (LAC) and long run marginal cost (LMC). *LAC* measures the minimum average cost of producing any level of output, assuming the firm can build

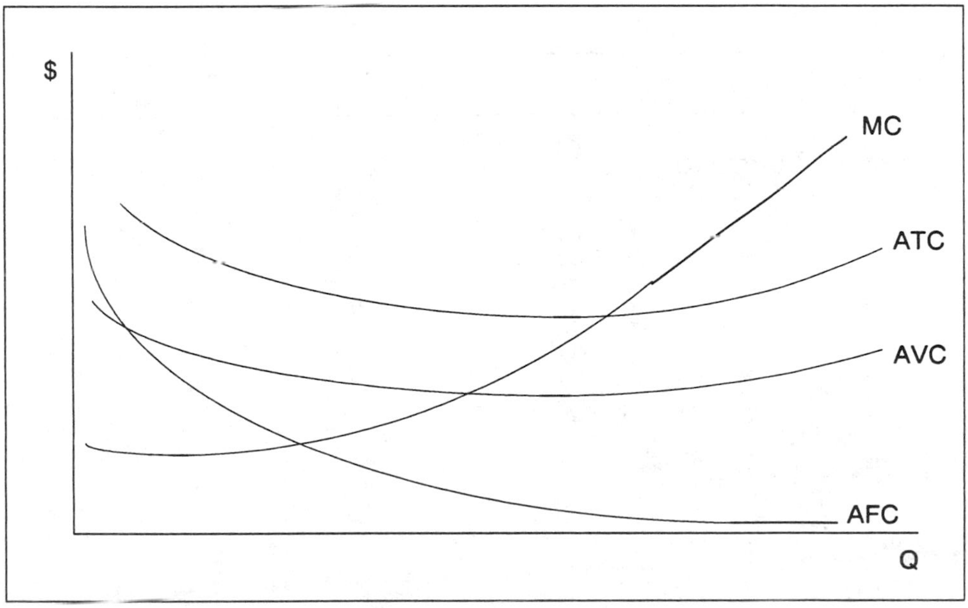

Average and Marginal Costs

any size factory it wants for that output. *LMC* measures the increase in total cost of producing one more unit, again assuming the firm can make any adjustment desired in its factory. Refer to the figure. Each short run average cost curve (SAC) represents a particular size factory, one that is most efficient in producing a particular level of output. *LAC* is the "envelope" of the *SAC* curves. For example, the minimum *LAC* of producing output *a* is *b*. This can be achieved by building and operating the plant giving SAC_2. Consequently, if it were to increase output to c, its average costs would be higher (*d*) than if it were able to build a more efficient plant. Average costs of *e* could be achieved in the long run with a different plant (not shown). *LAC* can be considered a planning curve. After choosing an expected long run level of output, the firm will then choose the plant that will allow it to produce that output at minimum cost.

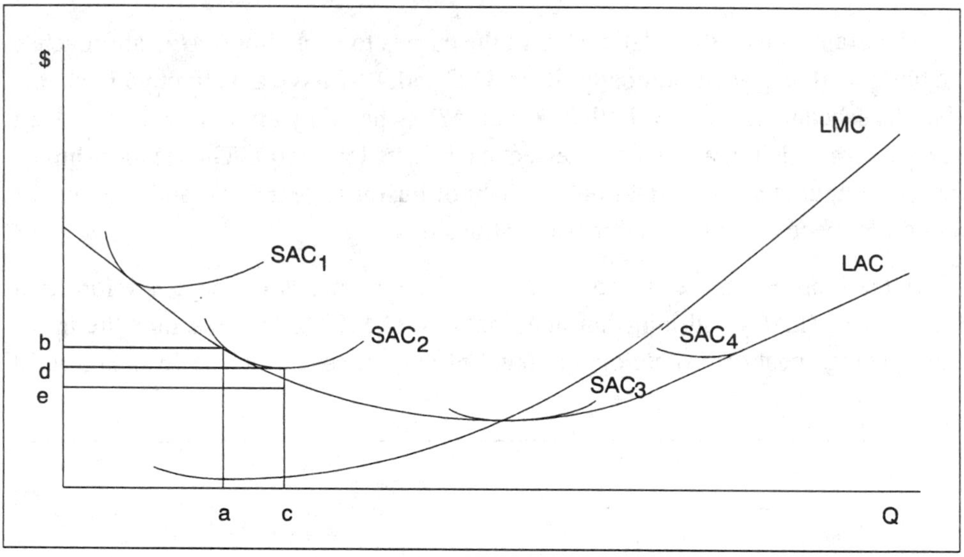

Costs in the Long Run

Step-by-Step Solutions to Problems in this Chapter, "Analysis of Costs"

IMPLICIT, EXPLICIT, AND OPPORTUNITY COSTS

• PROBLEM 17-1

What is meant by opportunity cost? Illustrate by giving an example.

Solution: In economic analysis, cost does not necessarily refer to simple dollar outlay but refers to what must be given up in order to attain a stated objective. Therefore, the concept of opportunity cost covers not merely direct payments but the value of opportunities foregone by an owner as a result of devoting his time and other resources to the business in question.

To understand what we mean by opportunity cost, consider the following examples:

a) The steel that is used for armaments is not available for the manufacture of automobiles or apartment buildings. The opportunity cost of the armaments is the automobiles, apartments, and other goods which the steel could and would have been used to produce if it were not used to produce armaments instead.

b) If an assembly-line worker is capable of producing either automobiles or washing machines, then the cost to society in employing this worker in an automobile plant is the contribution he would otherwise have made in producing washing machines.

c) The cost to you in studying this question is the alternative uses of your time which you must forego.

• PROBLEM 17-2

Mr. Brennan owns an open field adjacent to his house. The coach of the local high school football team offered Mr. Brennan $250 to rent the field from him for his team's summer football drills. Mr. Brennan could also grow vegetables on the field. The cost of seed, fertilizer, and hiring neighborhood teenagers to plant and harvest the field he estimates would be $200 and Mr. Brennan expects to receive $500 if he sold the vegetables. What are the explicit and implicit costs to Mr. Brennan of growing vegetables, and will he choose to grow vegetables or rent the field?

Solution: The explicit costs are the payments to outsiders that are necessary to hire their productive factors, in this case, the payments necessary to buy seed and fertilizer and to hire labor. Thus the explicit costs are $200.

The implicit costs of using a resource for one purpose, e.g., to grow vegetables, are the payments which the resource could have earned if used for the best available alternative purpose, in this case as a football field. The implicit cost of growing vegetables is $250.

The total of the explicit and implicit costs to Mr. Brennan of growing vegetables on his empty plot of land is ($200 + $250) = $450. Since his revenue from selling the vegetables, $500, exceeds his total explicit and implicit costs, $450, it is worthwhile for him to use the land to grow vegetables, and not rent to the football team. We can also see that it is not worthwhile for Mr. Brennan to rent the field by considering the costs of that choice. While Mr. Brennan need not incur any explicit costs to rent the field, the implicit cost is the net revenue he could receive from the sale of vegetables grown on it, that is, $500 less $200 of explicit costs to grow the vegetables, or $300. Since the costs of renting the field, namely $300 in implicit costs, are greater than the revenue that could be made from renting it, $250, it is not worthwhile for Mr. Brennan to rent the field to the football team.

• PROBLEM 17-3

What are pure profits?

Solution: Pure profits are the difference between the total receipts of the firm and all explicit and implicit costs, including "normal" profit, an implicit cost which compensates the entrepreneur for his labor. Some sources of pure profit are (a) the inherent uncertainty of future business conditions and (b) gains from monopoly power.

TOTAL, AVERAGE, AND MARGINAL COSTS

• PROBLEM 17-4

What is meant by the term marginal cost?

Solution: Marginal cost may be defined as the additional

cost of one more unit of production. That is,

$$\text{Marginal Cost} = \frac{\text{Change in Total Cost}}{\text{Change in Quantity Produced}} .$$

For instance, suppose that a firm has been producing two units of output at a total cost of $3000. It then decides to produce an additional unit of output, raising total cost to $4000, $1000 more than the total cost at an output level of two units. The $1,000, then, is the marginal cost--the extra cost of producing the additional unit of output.

• PROBLEM 17-5

From the data supplied in Table 1, determine the marginal cost of each unit produced.

Table 1

Output	Average Fixed Cost	Average Variable Cost
0	$10.00	0
1	10.00	$20.00
2	5.00	19.50
3	3.33	19.00
4	2.50	18.50
5	2.00	18.00
6	1.67	17.50
7	1.42	17.29
8	1.25	17.25
9	1.11	17.33
10	1.00	17.50

Solution: Marginal cost means the addition to the total cost attributable to each additional unit of output. To determine marginal cost at each level of output we must subtract the total cost of that output from the total cost of that output less one unit.

Total cost is the sum of total fixed cost and total variable cost. Total fixed cost is the product of Average Fixed Cost and Output. From Table 1 we can compute Total Fixed Cost as shown in Table 2.

Table 2

Output	x	Average Fixed Cost	=	Total Fixed Cost
1	x	$10.00	=	$10
2	x	5.00	=	10
3	x	3.33	=	10
4	x	2.50	=	10
5	x	2.00	=	10
6	x	1.67	=	10
7	x	1.42	=	10
8	x	1.25	=	10
9	x	1.11	=	10
10	x	1.00	=	10

As must be the case by definition, Total Fixed Cost must be the same for all levels of output.

Total Variable Cost can similarly be found by multiplying Average Variable Cost by the corresponding output, as is done in Table 3.

Table 3

Output	x	Average Variable Cost	=	Total Variable Cost
0	x	0	=	0
1	x	$20.00	=	$20.00
2	x	19.50	=	39.00
3	x	19.00	=	57.00
4	x	18.50	=	74.00
5	x	18.00	=	90.00
6	x	17.50	=	105.00
7	x	17.29	=	121.00
8	x	17.25	=	138.00
9	x	17.33	=	156.00
10	x	17.50	=	175.00

The Total Cost of each level of output is given by the sum of Total Fixed Cost and Total Variable Cost, as given in Table 4.

Table 4

Output	Total Fixed Cost	+	Total Variable Cost	Total Cost
0	$10	+	0	$10.00
1	10	+	$19.00	30.00
2	10	+	39.00	49.00
3	10	+	57.00	67.00
4	10	+	74.00	84.00
5	10	+	90.00	100.00
6	10	+	105.00	115.00
7	10	+	121.00	131.00
8	10	+	138.00	148.00
9	10	+	156.00	166.00
10	10	+	175.00	185.00

To determine the marginal cost at each level of output, we subtract the total cost at that level of output from the cost of producing one less unit. The marginal costs are shown in Table 5.

Table 5

Output	Total Cost	Marginal Cost		
0	$10.00			
1	30.00	(30.00-10.00)	=	$20.00
2	49.00	(49.00-30.00)	=	19.00
3	67.00	(67.00-49.00)	=	18.00
4	84.00	(84.00-67.00)	=	17.00
5	100.00	(100.00-84.00)	=	16.00
6	115.00	(115.00-100.00)	=	15.00
7	131.00	(131.00-115.00)	=	16.00
8	148.00	(148.00-131.00)	=	17.00
9	166.00	(166.00-148.00)	=	18.00
10	185.00	(185.00-166.00)	=	19.00

Given the information in Table 1, construct a table showing the average and marginal costs (per thousand units) at each level of output.

Table 1

Autos produced (thousands)	Total Cost
10	$50,000,000
11	56,000,000
12	62,500,000
13	69,500,000
14	79,000,000
15	90,000,000

Solution: The marginal cost of 1000 automobiles at each level of output is found by subtracting the total cost of that output from the total cost of that output plus 1000. Thus, for example, at an output of 10,000 automobiles, the marginal cost of 1000 automobiles is found by subtracting the total cost of 10,000 automobiles from the total cost of 10,000 + 1000 = 11,000 automobiles. Subtracting $50,000,000 from $56,000,000 gives a marginal cost of $6,000,000 per 1000 automobiles when output is 10,000. Following the same procedure at each successive output level, we obtain the following table of marginal costs:

Table 2

Autos produced (thousands)	Marginal Cost (per 1000)
10	$6,000,000
11	6,500,000
12	7,000,000
13	9,500,000
14	11,000,000

The average cost at each output level is found simply by dividing total cost by the corresponding output. For example, 15,000 cars cost $90,000,000, so the average cost is $90,000,000 ÷ 15,000 = $6,000,000 per 1000 cars. Following the same procedure at each successive level of output, we obtain the following table of average costs:

Table 3

Autos produced (thousands)	Average Cost (per 1000)
10	$5,000,000
11	5,090,909
12	5,208,333
13	5,346,154
14	5,642,857
15	6,000,000

• PROBLEM 17-7

Suppose that the average cost of mining a ton of coal varies with the total weight of coal mined each day in the way shown in Table 1.

Table 1

Tons mined	100	101	102	103	104	105
Average Cost per Ton	\$300	\$299	\$298	\$297	\$296	\$295

Compute the marginal cost at each level of production of mining a ton of coal.

Solution: Marginal cost is defined as the change in total cost due to a change in quantity produced divided by the amount of the change in the quantity produced. In order to find the changes in total cost resulting from the mining of each additional ton of coal, we must calculate the total cost at each level of production. This is done simply by multiplying the average cost of production by the number of units (tons of coal) produced. Doing that gives the total cost schedule in Table 2.

Table 2

Tons mined	100	101	102	103	104	105
Total Cost	\$30,000	\$30,199	\$30,396	\$30,591	\$30,784	\$30,975

Since marginal cost is the difference in total cost due to each change in production level, we find the marginal cost of each additional ton by subtracting the total cost at each level of production from the total cost at the next higher level. E.g., the marginal cost of the 101st ton is \$30,190 - \$30,000 = \$190. Table 3 shows the marginal cost of mining each additional ton of coal.

Table 3

Ton	101st	102nd	103rd	104th	105th
Marginal Cost	\$199	\$197	\$195	\$193	\$191

• PROBLEM 17-8

The following table shows National Widget Corporation's total costs.

Output	Total Cost
0	90
1	95
2	100
3	105
4	110
5	115

6	126
7	146
8	186
9	270
10	490

Compute the firm's
a) Marginal Cost
b) Variable Cost
c) Average Total Cost
d) Average Variable Cost

Solution: a) Marginal Cost is defined as the extra cost incurred by increasing output by one unit. For example the Marginal Cost associated with increasing output from 4 to 5 units is 115 - 110 = 5. Figure 1 shows NWC's Marginal Cost.

Output	Total Cost	Marginal Cost
0	90	
		5
1	95	
		5
2	100	
		5
3	105	
		5
4	110	
		5
5	115	
		11
6	126	
		20
7	146	
		40
8	186	
		84
9	270	
		220
10	490	

Figure 1

b) Variable Cost is defined as those costs which increase with the level of output. That is, they are Total Costs minus Fixed Costs (TC - FC = VC). NWC's Fixed Costs are 90, so Variable Costs can be calculated by subtracting $90 from Total Costs at all levels of production, as shown in Figure 2.

Output	Total Cost	Variable Cost
0	90	0
1	95	5
2	100	10
3	105	15
4	110	20
5	115	25
6	126	36

7	146	56
8	186	96
9	270	180
10	490	400

Figure 2

c) Average Total Cost is defined as Total Cost at any given output divided by that output (ATC = TC/Q). Similarly, Average Variable Cost is the Variable Cost at any given output divided by that output (AVC = VC/Q). For Q = 5, from Figure 2, TC = 115 and VC = 25. Using the formulas gives, ATC = 115/5 = 23 and AVC = 25/5 = 5. NWC's completed cost schedule is shown by Figure 3.

Output	Total Cost	Variable Cost	Average Total Cost	Average Variable Cost	Marginal Cost
0	90	0	00	00	
					5
1	95	5	95	5	
					5
2	100	10	50	5	
					5
3	105	15	35	5	
					5
4	110	20	27-1/2	5	
					5
5	115	25	23	5	
					11
6	126	36	21	6	
					20
7	146	56	20-6/7	8	
					40
8	186	96	23-1/4	12	
					84
9	270	180	30	20	
					220
10	490	400	49	40	

Figure 3

• PROBLEM 17-9

The value of the slope of a line is defined as "rise over run." That is, given any two points on a line (in Figure 1, points A and B) the value of the slope is defined as the rise, or the vertical distance between A and C (in Figure 1) divided by the run, or the horizontal distance (CB in Figure 1).

With this in mind, what is the economic significance of the slope of line OD in Figure 2?

Solution: Given the definition of the slope of a line, the question is asking for the economic meaning behind the slope of a line drawn from the origin to a point on a Total

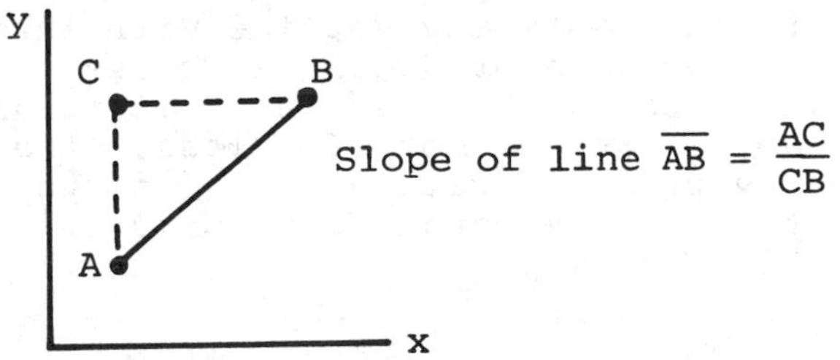

Fig. 1

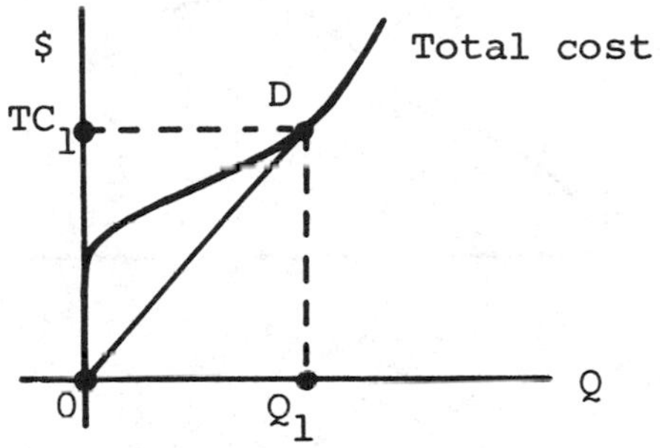

Fig. 2

Cost curve. To find the solution to this problem, begin by writing out the value of the slope of line OD. With slope defined as rise over run, the value of the slope of OD would be the rise, or OTC_1 divided by the run, or OQ_1, that is, $\frac{OTC_1}{OQ_1}$. Remember that the Total Cost of producing a given quantity of output divided by the quantity produced is equal to the average cost for that quantity. Therefore, the slope of line OD can be defined as the average cost for quantity produced, Q_1.

This result may be generalized. Given any Total Curve (that is, Total Cost, Total Revenue, or Total Profit) the Average Curve may be constructed by finding for each quantity the value of the slope of the line from the origin to the point on the Total Curve corresponding to that Quantity.

• PROBLEM 17-10

Could the Total Cost curve ever look like the curve in Figure 1? Why or why not?

Solution: The Total Cost curve maps out the Total Costs incurred by a producer over any level of production. That is, if you know how much output the producer is producing, then the Total Cost curve will give a dollar figure for the total costs of producing that quantity of output. The Total Cost curve in the figure shows that, as this producer increases the quantity of his output, his total costs increase, rapidly at first, then at a slower rate until finally his Total Costs begin to decline. While average or marginal costs may decline with larger output, it is unlikely that as a producer increases the amount produced, his Total Costs will decline. It is always assumed that you can "never get more for less," that is, increasing the quantity produced will always cost the producer more. For this reason, the Total Cost curve will never appear as drawn in Figure 1.

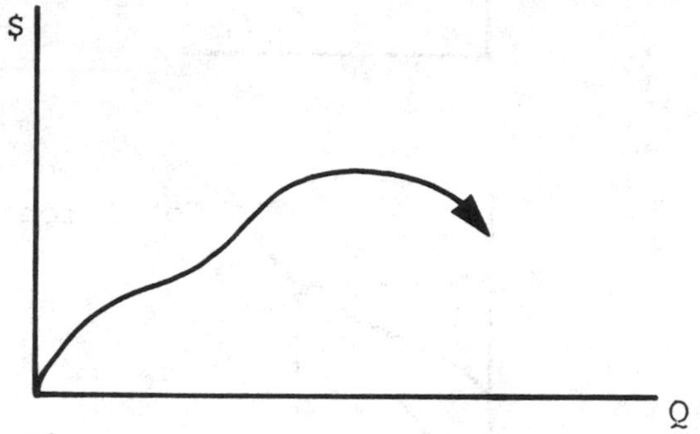

Fig. 2

• PROBLEM 17-11

Does the diagram in Figure 1 accurately depict a set of cost curves? Why or why not?

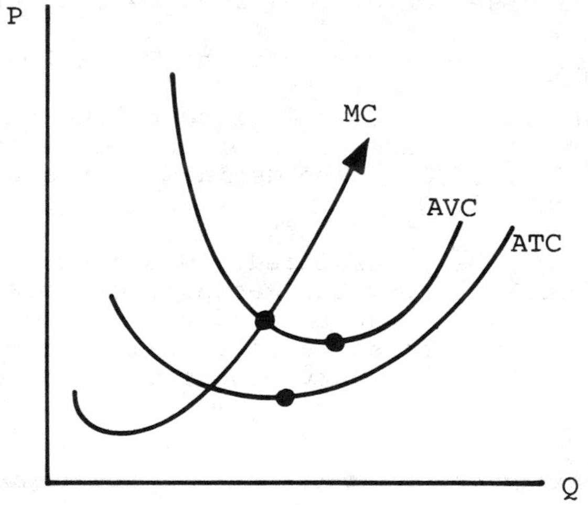

Fig. 1

Solution: The question is asking if these curves, as drawn in the figure, represent cost-quantity relationships that might occur. The solution to this problem lies in noticing that the Marginal Cost Curve cuts both the Average Variable Cost Curve and the Average Total Cost Curve at points other than their respective minima. The Marginal Cost Curve always pierces the Average Cost Curve (both Average Variable Cost and Average Total Cost) at the Average Cost Curve's minimum point.

Intuitively, the reasoning behind this is that if Marginal

Cost is less than Average Cost, then the Marginal Cost will pull the Average Cost down. That is, if the cost of producing the 100th unit of output is lower than the average cost of producing the first 99 units, then the average cost of producing 100 units will be less than that of producing 99 units. Similarly, if the Marginal Cost Curve is above the Average Cost Curve, then the Marginal Cost Curve will pull the Average Cost Curve up. Thus, where the Marginal Cost Curve crosses the Average Cost Curve, it causes the Average Cost Curve to change direction, that is where the MC Curve crosses the AC Curve, the AC Curve is at its minimum point. The MC Curve will never cross the AC Curve at any point other than its minimum.

FIXED AND VARIABLE COSTS

• PROBLEM 17-12

How are fixed and variable costs different?

Solution: Fixed costs are the portion of the total costs of a firm which do not vary with the level of output. That is, fixed costs are always the same whether the firm is producing at full capacity or producing nothing, or somewhere in between. Therefore even if production is stopped completely, fixed costs will have to be paid. Often called "overhead cost," fixed costs include depreciation and contractual commitments (including rent).

Variable costs represent the remainder of total costs, that is the costs which vary with the level of output. At output = 0, variable costs = 0. Some examples of variable costs are fuel and raw materials.

• PROBLEM 17-13

Given the total cost and total fixed cost data of Table 1, calculate the total variable cost incurred at each level of output.

Table 1

Quantity Produced	Total Fixed Cost	Total Cost
1	$1000	$1500
2	1000	1950
3	1000	2350
4	1000	2700
5	1000	3000
6	1000	3300
7	1000	3650
8	1000	4000
9	1000	4400
10	1000	4900

Solution: Costs of production can be subdivided into fixed

costs, which are unaffected by the level of production, and variable costs, which are called that because they vary with the level of output produced. Total costs are the sum of total fixed and total variable costs of production.

Since Table 1 gives us Total Cost and Total Fixed Cost data at each output level, we can find Total Variable Costs of production by subtracting Total Fixed Costs from Total Costs at each level of output. For example, at 5 units of output, Total Variable Cost ≡ (Total Cost - Total Fixed Cost) = \$3000 - \$1000 = \$2000. Table 2 shows similar calculations of Total Variable Cost for other output levels.

Table 2

Quantity Produced	Total Cost		Total Fixed Cost	Total Variable Cost
1	\$1500	-	\$1000	\$ 500
2	1950	-	1000	950
3	2350	-	1000	1350
4	2700	-	1000	1700
5	3000	-	1000	2000
6	3300	-	1000	2300
7	3650	-	1000	2650
8	4000	-	1000	3000
9	4400	-	1000	3400
10	4900	-	1000	3900

• PROBLEM 17-14

Suppose a shoe manufacturer has an average fixed cost of \$0.50 per shoe at an output of 10,000 shoes. If he expanded production to 12,500 shoes, what would his average fixed costs be?

Solution: Average Fixed Cost is defined as Total Fixed Cost divided by the Quantity produced. Hence, multiplying Average Fixed Cost by the corresponding output gives us Total Fixed Cost. If we know Total Fixed Cost, we can find the Average Fixed Cost corresponding to any level of output by dividing Total Fixed Cost by that output.

Let us, then, calculate the shoe manufacturer's Total Fixed Cost: (Average Fixed Cost x Output) = (\$0.50 x 10,000) = \$5000 = Total Fixed Cost. To find his Average Fixed Cost at an output of 12,500 shoes, we divide Total Fixed Cost by Output:

(\$5000 ÷ 12,500) = \$0.40.

• PROBLEM 17-15

Explain why the average fixed cost curve (AFC) slopes downward throughout, while the average variable cost curve (AVC) slopes down at first, but then turns upward.

Solution: By definition, fixed cost (FC) is constant, no matter what the level of output (Q) is. Also by definition, AFC ≡ FC/Q. Since FC is constant, the only variable upon which AFC depends will be Q. Therefore, as Q increases, AFC will become smaller and smaller. For example, suppose FC = \$10,000. Then AFC = \$10,000/Q. If Q = 10, AFC = \$1000. If Q = 100, AFC = \$100. If Q = 1000, AFC = \$10. That is, as the quantity produced is increased, the Average Fixed Cost per unit decreases.

Average variable cost (AVC) tends to drop at first, as the marginal product, and the average, product per unit of variable input, increases due perhaps to fuller utilization of the fixed inputs and/or to the extension of specialization. But eventually, AVC rises as a result of the law of diminishing returns. This law states that as more and more units of a variable factor of production are added to a fixed factor of production, a point will be reached after which the output accounted for by each additional unit of the variable factor will decline. The decrease of the marginal product of the variable input means that the average product of the variable input will also eventually decrease as additional units of it continue to be applied. At the point where the average product per unit of variable input begins to decrease, the average variable cost (input) per unit of output begins to increase.

• PROBLEM 17-16

Could the Average Fixed Costs curve ever look like the curve in Figure 1? Why or why not?

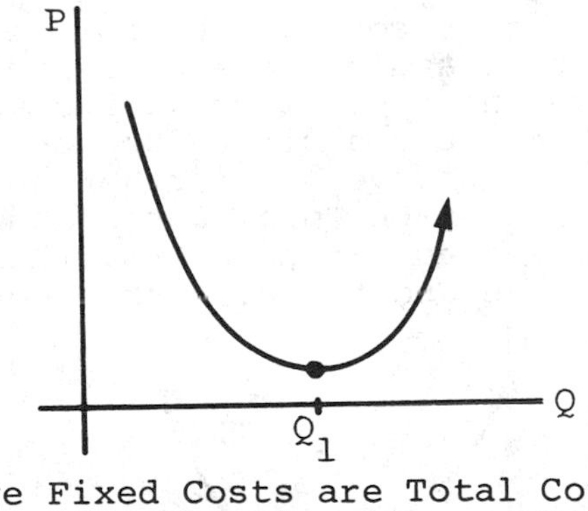

Fig. 1

Solution: Average Fixed Costs are Total Costs divided by the quantity produced. That is, Average Fixed Cost is that portion of the firm's fixed cost that is attributable to each unit. For example, if rent were the only Fixed Cost, then Average Fixed Cost would be the amount that each unit of output would be "charged" as its "share" of the rent bill. With this in mind, the question is asking whether, as the quantity produced is increased, Average Fixed Costs can first decline, reach a minimum and then rise again. Using the example of rent as the only fixed cost, dividing the portion of the rent bill among an increasing group of units of output could never result in an increasing amount being attributed to each of them. Mathematically,

$$AFC = \frac{FC}{Q}$$

Since Fixed Costs are constant, as Q increases (as in $\frac{FC}{2}, \frac{FC}{3}, \frac{FC}{4}, \frac{FC}{5}, \ldots$) the value of AFC will always get smaller. For this reason, the AFC curve will never look like the one pictured in Figure 1.

• PROBLEM 17-17

Does figure 1 accurately depict a possible set of Average Variable Cost, Average Total Cost and Marginal Cost Curves? Why or why not?

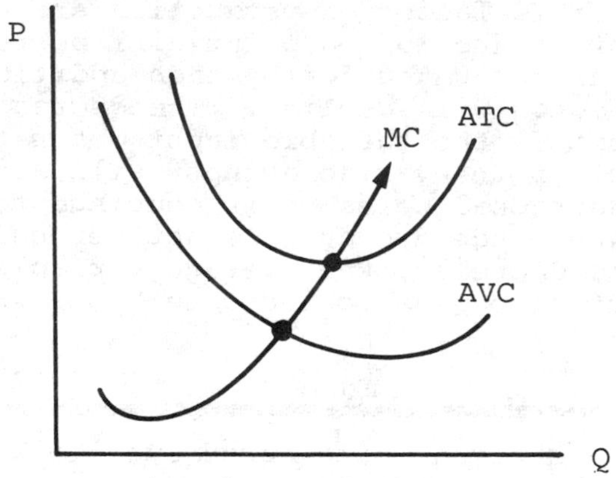

Fig. 1

Solution: This question is asking you to examine the cost-quantity relationships depicted by these graphs and determine whether or not they follow the assumptions normally made about a producer's costs. The solution to this problem lies in noticing that at low levels of production (small Q's) the ATC curve and the AVC curve are very close to each other, while at high levels of production (larger Q's) the ATC curve and the AVC curve get farther apart. Since the difference between Average Total Costs and Average Variable Costs is equal to Average Fixed Costs, then the distance between the ATC curve and the AVC curve would be the AFC

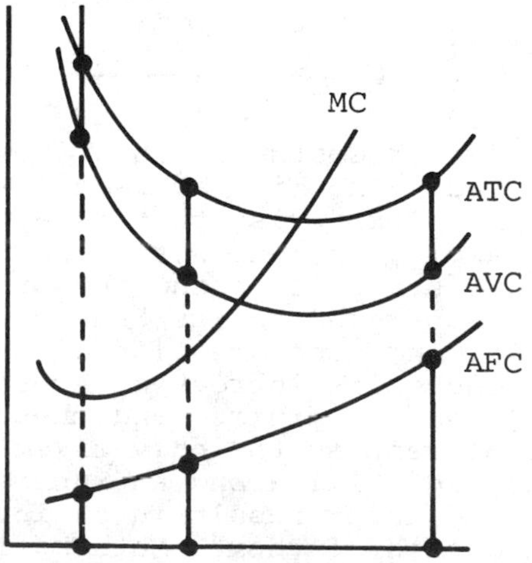

Fig. 2

curve. By figuring out the distance between the two curves at every point, the AFC curve can be drawn as in Figure 2.

This diagram shows that the curves as drawn in the diagram imply an increasing AFC. But as Total Fixed Costs, a constant, is divided between increasing quantities of output, the Average Fixed Costs should decline. For example if rent was the only Fixed Cost, then as output was increased, the portion of the rent bill attributed to each unit of output would decrease not increase. Mathematically,

$$AFC = \frac{TFC}{Q}$$

Since TFC is a constant, as Q is increased. AFC will decrease. Therefore, when properly constructed, the AVC curve will approach the ATC curve as Q is increased, not when it is decreased as shown in the diagram.

• PROBLEM 17-18

Given:

$$TC = FC + VC,$$

prove that:

$$ATC = AFC + AVC.$$

Solution: To solve this proof it must first be recalled that:

$$ATC = \frac{TC}{Q}, \quad AFC = \frac{FC}{Q} \text{ and } AVC = \frac{VC}{Q}.$$

With this in mind, the given equation is multiplied by $\frac{1}{Q}$ to get:

$$\frac{TC}{Q} = \frac{FC}{Q} + \frac{VC}{Q}$$

which, by the definitions is equivalent to

$$ATC = AFC + AVC.$$

Intuitively, this equation means that cost per unit may be divided up into two parts, AFC, or the portion of Fixed Cost attributed to any one unit of output, and AVC, or the portion of Variable Cost attributed to any one unit of output.

• PROBLEM 17-19

Does Figure 1 accurately depict a set of cost curves? Why or why not?

Solution: The question is asking if these curves describe

cost-quantity relationships that might normally be expected to occur. The solution to this question lies in noticing that while all three curves have the proper shape, the Average Variable Cost curve is greater than the Average Total Cost curve at every quantity level. That is, at any level of output, the Average Variable Costs are higher than the Average Total Costs. This would imply that Average Fixed Costs are negative. Mathematically, this can be shown by remembering that:

$$ATC \equiv AVC + AFC$$

Subtracting AVC from both sides of the equation gives:

$$ATC - AVC \equiv AFC.$$

Since the curves imply that:

$$AVC > ATC \text{ for all points,}$$

this implies that AFC is negative for all points. Since the quantity produced can never be negative and since Total Fixed Costs are defined as:

$$AFC \times Q = TFC,$$

then these curves imply that Total Fixed Costs are negative. For example, if rent was the producer's only Fixed Cost, this would imply that the landlord paid the company to produce on his property. Since this sort of situation is generally assumed not to occur, that is, since Fixed Costs are assumed to be positive, the Average Total Cost Curve will always lie above the Average Variable Cost Curve, not below it as depicted in Figure 1.

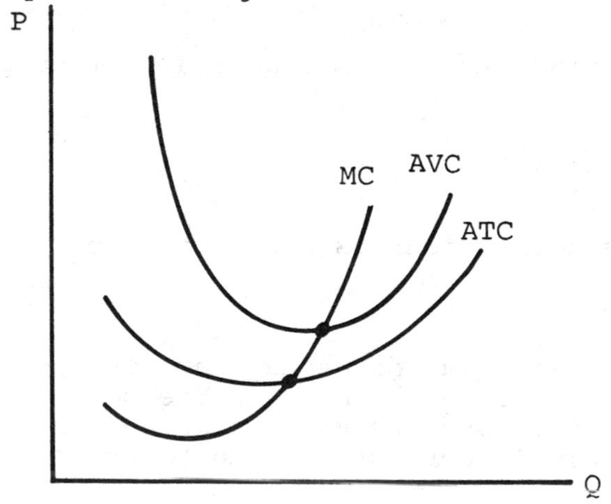

Fig. 1

• PROBLEM 17-20

Determine Fixed Costs for firm A and firm B from the Total Cost curves in Figure 1.

Solution: Fixed Costs are defined as those costs which do

Fig. 1

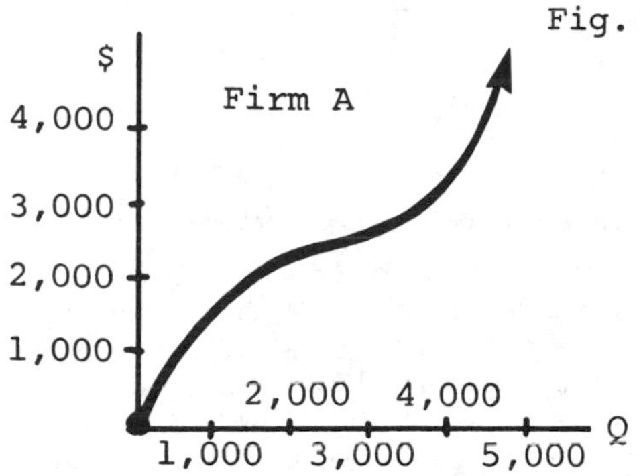

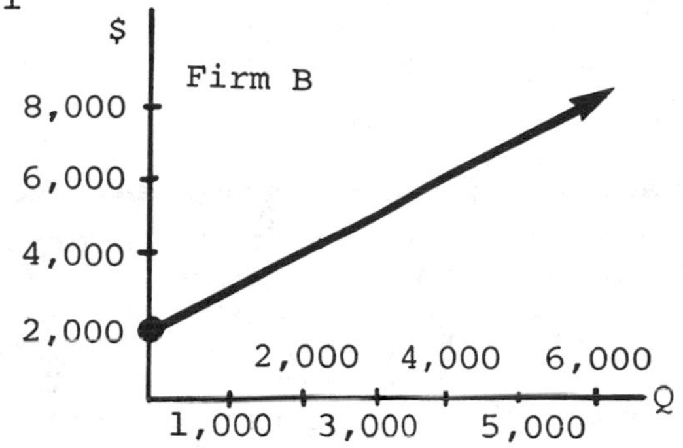

not vary with changes in output. They are the costs which a firm incurs just by existing, whether it produces any output or not. That is, Fixed Costs are constant, they are the same at Q = 0 as they are at any other level of production. Variable Costs, on the other hand, are incurred only if it produces some output. Total Cost is the sum of Fixed Costs and Variable Costs.

With these definitions in mind, note that the way to determine Fixed Costs, given a Total Cost curve, is to find the Total Cost incurred by the firm at zero output, Q = 0. Producing no output, the firm incurs no variable costs, only fixed costs. Hence, Total Cost ≡ Variable Costs plus Fixed Costs = 0 + Fixed Costs = Fixed Costs at zero output (Q = 0).

Using this, note that Firm A has Total Costs = 0 at Q = 0. Therefore its Fixed Cost = 0. For Firm B, at Q = 0, Total Costs = $2,000. Therefore Fixed Costs for Firm B are $2,000.

• **PROBLEM 17-21**

What are the differences between Marginal Fixed Cost (MFC), Marginal Variable Cost (MVC) and Marginal Total Cost (MC)?

Solution: To solve this problem, recall that "marginal," whether it's marginal cost, marginal utility or anything else, always means "extra" to the economist. Therefore Marginal Fixed Cost would be defined as the extra amount of Fixed Cost that would result from an extra unit of output. Since Fixed Costs are constant by definition, a change in the quantity produced will result in no change in Fixed Costs. That is, Marginal Fixed Cost will always be equal to zero.

Remember that the difference between Variable Cost and Total Cost is a constant, Fixed Cost. Therefore any change in Variable Cost must cause a change of equal value in Total Cost. That is, Total Cost grows by exactly the same amounts as Variable Cost does. For this reason, any change in the quantity produced will add exactly the same amount to Total Cost as it does to Variable Cost. Therefore Marginal Total Cost is the same as Marginal Variable Cost. In summary:

MFC = 0

MVC = MC.

• PROBLEM 17-22

> The National Widget Corporation currently holds a five-year lease on their factory, on which they have four more years left before the lease runs out. Beginning this month, the landlord has been allowed to pass along a $100 per month "fuel adjustment surcharge." If, every month, NWC's economists (by some miracle) are able to chart their cost curves for the upcoming month, how would the cost curves have changed to reflect this fuel surcharge, assuming that no other factors have changed?

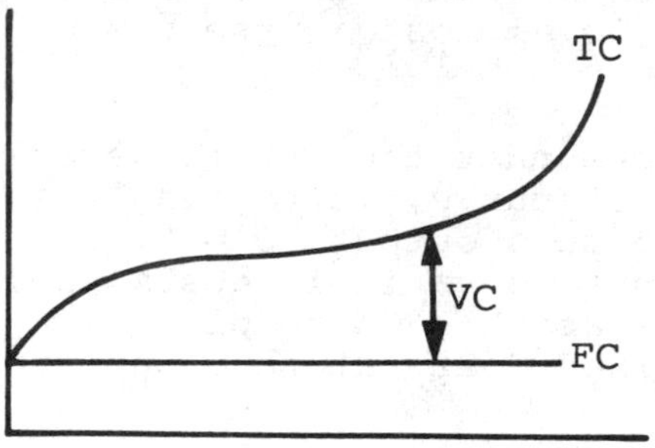

Fig. 1

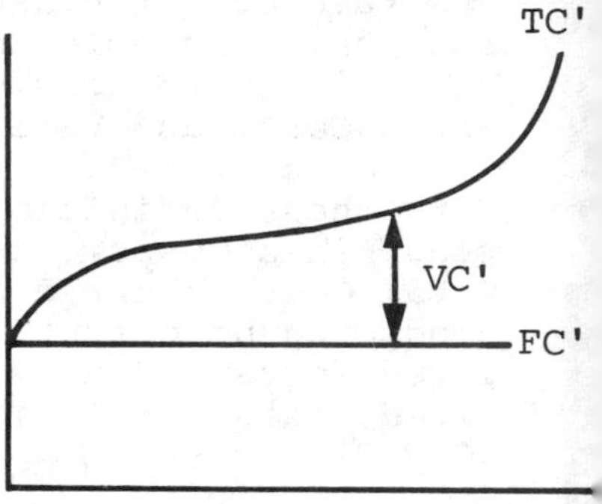

Fig. 2

Solution: Since, for any given month, the problem allows rent to be considered a fixed cost, this question is asking how an increase in Fixed Costs will affect NWC's cost curves. Figure 1 shows a normal TC = VC + FC curve. Figure 2 shows these same curves with the new Fixed Costs: TC' = FC' + VC'. Note that since only Fixed Costs have changed, VC = VC'. This implies that AVC do not change. It also implies that MC do not change since "extra" costs can only be incurred from costs that change with output.

Fig. 3

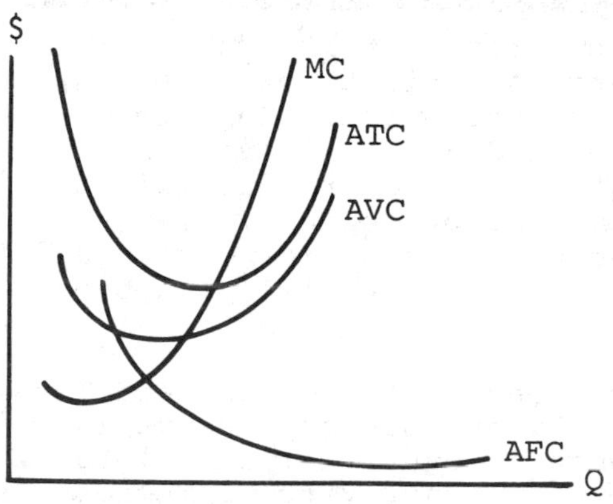

Fig. 4

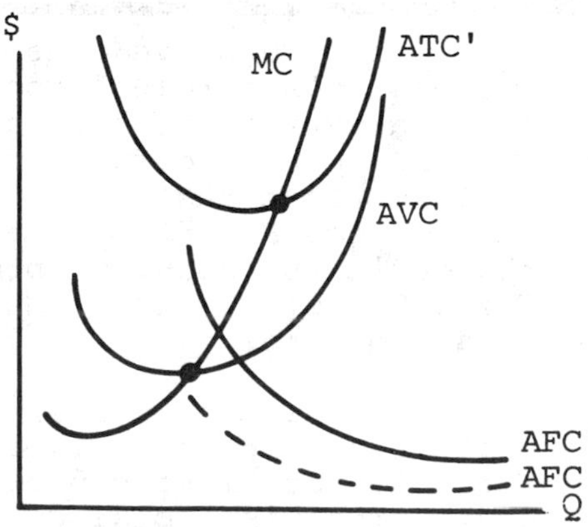

AFC would be expected to rise with the new AFC' approaching the old AFC in a manner similar to the way the old AFC approaches the Q axis. Since ATC = AFC + AVC, the new ATC'

would also be shifted up. Thus an increase in Fixed Costs would result in no change in: Variable Costs, Marginal Costs and Average Variable Costs. It would result in upward shifts in: Total Costs, Average Fixed Costs and Average Total Costs.

LAW OF DIMINISHING RETURNS

• PROBLEM 17-23

What is the principle of diminishing marginal returns?

Solution: The principle states that, as the quantity of one factor input in a production process (e.g. capital) is increased, while the quantity of other factor inputs is held constant, there is a point beyond which the (increase in total) output attributable to each additional unit of factor input will become less and less.

• PROBLEM 17-24

Use Table 1 to determine what range of factor input levels exhibits increasing marginal returns and what range exhibits decreasing marginal returns.

Table 1

Acres of Land	Man-Hours/ Week	Tons Fertilizer	Tons Wheat
100	50	0	50
100	50	10	100
100	50	20	160
100	50	30	200
100	50	40	225
100	50	50	245

Solution: We must recall that the concepts of increasing and decreasing returns refer to a factor of production the amount of which that is used in a production process is varied while the amounts of other factors used are held constant. In this case the variable factor is fertilizer. Hence, the question asks for a determination regarding the productivity of successive increments of fertilizer.

The data given in Table 1 shows the changes in the amount of wheat that is grown on a given area of land with a given amount of labor due to 1-ton increments of fertilizer. To determine the marginal return to each 1 ton increment, we must subtract from each output level, the output resulting from the application of 1 ton less of fertilizer. Thus, for example, the marginal return due to the 3rd 1-ton increment is (200 tons of wheat - 160 tons of wheat) = 40 tons of wheat. Table 2 shows the marginal return to each 1-ton increment of fertilizer.

Table 2

Increment of Fertilizer (1 ton)	Marginal Product (Tons of Wheat)
1st	(100-50) = 50
2nd	(160-100) = 60
3rd	(200-160) = 40
4th	(225-200) = 25
5th	(245-225) = 20

From Table 2, we can see that the marginal product of each ton of fertilizer (given the levels of the two fixed inputs, land and labor) increases from the first to the second ton, and decreases from the second ton onward.

SHORT RUN VS. LONG RUN

• PROBLEM 17-25

What is meant by the term "long run"?

Solution: The long run is that time period over which every input in the production process may be considered variable. That is, it refers to a period of time extensive enough to allow a firm to change the quantities of all factors of production. The length of the long run can vary widely depending upon what industry or production process is being described.

• PROBLEM 17-26

Could a Short Run Average Cost curve ever contain a point below the Long Run Average Cost curve? Why or why not?

Solution: The Long Run Average Cost curve (LAC) traces out the lowest possible Average Cost for any given quantity produced, under the assumption that every input into the production process is variable, including, among other things, plant size and machinery. Any given Short Run Average Cost curve (SAC) shows the lowest possible Average Cost for each quantity produced, assuming that at least one input is held constant. The example most commonly used to illustrate this point is plant size. For example, if a producer is currently producing in a factory designed to produce 100,000 units most efficiently, then this factory will produce 80,000 units less efficiently, that is, at a higher cost per unit, than would a factory designed to produce exactly 80,000 units.

Using these definitions, it is impossible for a SAC to ever contain a point below its LAC. If some point on a SAC could produce at lower per unit costs then this point would be included in the LAC. Therefore since only the lowest possible average costs for any given quantity produced are included on the LAC, the SAC will never contain a point below the LAC.

Given the Long Run Average Cost curve, LAC, could the Short Run Average Cost curves SAC_1, SAC_2, SAC_3 and SAC_4 all correspond to the given LAC in Figure 1?

Solution: The LAC is, by definition, the curve containing all the lowest points on the SAC's. That is, no point on any SAC may fall below the LAC. Therefore, SAC_1 and SAC_4 cannot be Short Run Average Cost curves associated with the LAC in Figure 1.

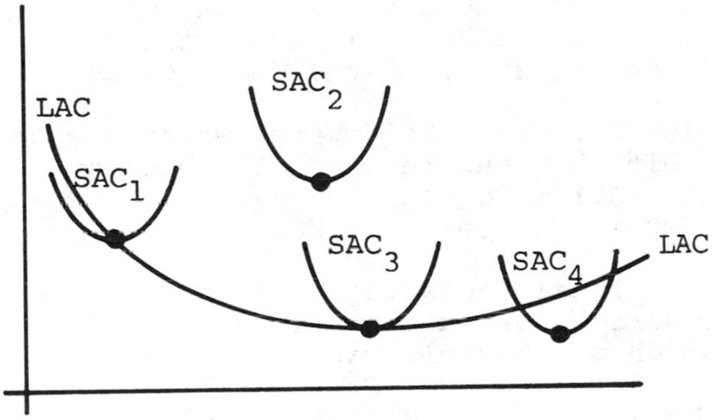

Fig. 1

SAC_2 does not touch LAC at any point. This means that for any given quantity produced there exists some SAC, some combination of inputs, which will produce the product at a lower cost per unit (AC) than any point on SAC_2. While it is possible that a manufacturer would construct a factory that is less efficient at all levels of output than some other factory might be, this is generally not assumed to be the case. Therefore, SAC_2 would not really be a Short Run Average Cost curve associated with LAC. SAC_3 touches LAC at one point, and it does not contain any points which lie below LAC. That is, it represents an efficient combination of inputs but not more efficient than is possible in the Long Run. Therefore, SAC_3 is the only one of the four Short Run curves drawn that corresponds to LAC.

Answer

To be covered when testing yourself

SHORT ANSWER QUESTIONS FOR REVIEW

Choose the correct answer.

1. Marginal cost is (a) Total Cost divided by the number of units produced (b) Fixed Cost divided by the number of units produced (c) Average Cost divided by the number of periods over which the product is produced (d) the extra Total Average Cost of producing an additional unit of output (e) the extra Total Cost of producing an additional unit of output. e

2. Which of the following holds true where Average Cost per unit, AC, has reached it's minimum level? (a) AVC = FC (b) MC = AC (c) P = AVC (d) MC = AVC (e) P = MC. b

3. Knowledge of Total Variable Costs and Fixed Costs for various outputs enables one to determine which of the following? (a) Average Costs (b) Average Fixed Costs (c) Average Total Costs (d) Marginal Costs (e) All of the above. e

4. With a given plant size, an increase in output cannot produce an increase in (a) Total Cost (b) Average Fixed Cost (c) Average Total Cost (d) Average Variable Cost (e) Total Variable Cost. b

5. A driver wishes to buy gasoline and have his car washed. The car wash costs $1.00 when he buys up to 19 gallons of gas at $1.10 each. However, if he buys 20 gallons, the car wash is free. The Marginal Cost of the twentieth gallon to him is (a) $1.00 (b) $1.10 (c) 10¢ (d) cannot be determined from this information (e) none of the above. c

6. If the Total Cost of producing 10 units is $100 and the Marginal Cost of the eleventh unit is $21, then (a) Total Variable Costs of 11 units are $21 (b) Total Fixed Costs are $79 (c) the Marginal Cost of the tenth unit is more than $21 (d) the Average Total Cost of eleven units is $11 (e) the Average Total Cost of twelve units is $12. d

7. If Marginal Cost is above Average Total Cost, then: (a) Average Variable Costs are falling (b) Average Fixed Costs are rising (c) Average Total Costs are falling (d) Average Total Costs are constant (e) Average Total Costs are rising. e

SHORT ANSWER QUESTIONS FOR REVIEW

Answer

To be covered when testing yourself

8. Which of the following does not involve an externality? (a) Flood control (b) Oil drilling on boundaries (c) Neighbor's bees (d) Pollution (e) An outside sales force. — e

9. Which of the following economically justifies an interference with Laissez-faire? (a) Higher rent of factory space as industry A grows (b) An external economy or diseconomy (c) lower price of B due to a decrease in B's popularity (d) an increase in the availability of C due to a cheaper production technique (e) Nothing; economists have proven that a laissez-faire economy should never be tampered with. — b

10. The alternative cost doctrine can best be defined as: (a) the marginal product revenue needed to keep MC=MR (b) the opportunity cost (c) costs that do not vary with changes in output (d) costs that increase with the level of output (e) none of the above — b

11. Which of the following is most likely to be a fixed cost? (a) expenditures for raw materials (b) wages for unskilled labor (c) shipping charges (d) property insurance premiums (e) none of these are fixed costs, even in the very short run. — d

12. Which of the following is likely to be a variable cost? (a) real estate taxes (b) rental payments on IBM equipment (c) interest on bonded indebtedness (d) fuel and power payments (e) none of these are variable costs even if the time frame is a very long one. — d

13. Average Fixed Cost: (a) always declines with increases in output (b) is U-shaped only if there are increasing returns to scale (c) is U-shaped only if there are decreasing returns to scale (d) may be constructed by adding ATC and AVC for any output level (e) is intersected by MC at its minimum point. — a

14. The concept of explicit costs differs from that of implicit costs in that the former:

SHORT ANSWER QUESTIONS FOR REVIEW

Answer
To be covered when testing yourself

(a) are opportunity costs and the latter are rent and interest payments (b) are out of pocket payments to factors of production and the latter are solely opportunity costs (c) are out of pocket payments to factors of production and the latter are externalities (d) can only be represented by short run cost curves and the latter can only be represented by long run cost curves (e) are never actually paid while the latter always are.

b

15. Externalities (a) shift the firm's cost curves upward and to the right (b) cause the firm to move along all of its cost curves (c) are always a "bad thing" (d) are hardest on the individual entrepreneur (e) do none of the above.

e

Fill in the blanks.

16. __________ is the loss in value of a capital good due to wear or absolescence.

Depreciation

17. Wages, fuel and raw materials are examples of __________ costs.

variable

18. Interest, property taxes and insurance are examples of __________ costs.

fixed

19. The labor provided by the owner of a store is an example of an __________.

implicit cost

20. Costs that are incurred regardless of the level of production are called __________.

fixed costs

21. Costs that depend on the production level are called __________ .

variable costs

22. A favorable effect on one or more persons which emanates from the actions of a different person or firm is known as an __________.

external economy

23. At its minimum, the Average Cost curve is crossed by __________.

the Marginal Cost Curve

24. If the owner of a store has his entire life savings tied up in his stock, then the return on this money had it been invested elsewhere represents ______________.

an opportunity cost

25. The __________ is that time span for which no input in the production process need be considered a cost.

long-run

SHORT ANSWER QUESTIONS FOR REVIEW

Answer
To be covered when testing yourself

Determine whether the following statements are true or false.

	Statement	Answer
26.	If external economies prevail in an industry, expansion of industry output could shift the cost curves of single firms downwards.	True
27.	Marginal cost is equal to the change in total cost.	True
28.	The Marginal Cost curve can only intersect the Average Variable Cost curve at its minimum.	True
29.	With the Total Cost schedule being given, it is possible to draw a Marginal Cost curve.	True
30.	If all factors of production could be bought at existing prices in unlimited quantity and output were to show constant returns to scale, then the long-run Marginal Cost curve could horizontal out to an infinite quantity.	True
31.	From the long-run Average Cost curve, one can derive the long-run Marginal Cost curve.	True
32.	Average Fixed Cost intersects Average Variable Cost at Average Variable Cost's minimum.	False
33.	Whenever Marginal Cost is rising, Average Cost is also rising.	False
34.	MC often declines at first because there are increasing returns in production.	True
35.	Marginal Cost is not generally the same as Average Cost.	True
36.	A high tax on an external diseconomy, like smog creation in Los Angeles, might fail to raise any revenue at all and therefore be pointless.	False

CHAPTER 18

PERFECT COMPETITION

Basic Attacks and Strategies for Solving Problems in this Chapter. See pages 646 to 696 for step-by-step solutions to problems.

Economists are interested in studying the behavior and performance of business firms. One of the most important factors influencing behavior and performance is the structure of the industry in which the firm operates. Economists have developed models of the four basic industry types: perfect competition, monopoly, monopolistic competition, and oligopoly. Each of these models should be understood to be abstract replicas of a very complicated reality.

The chief characteristics of perfect competition are:

1) There Are Many Buyers and Sellers in the Market—This means that each buyer and seller is small relative to the size of the market, preventing anyone from exerting significant influence on market events. This also means that firms are price-takers, unable to influence the price they charge.

2) Homogenous Product—Each firm sells an identical product. This implies that the only factor consumers will consider when making purchase decisions is price, so no firm can successfully charge a price higher than the market level.

3) Freedom of Exit and Entry—There are no substantial barriers limiting the ability of firms to enter and leave the industry. This implies that there is nothing preventing new competitors from trying to share in the prosperity of an industry. Likewise, there is nothing preventing firms from "bailing out" of an industry undergoing hard times.

4) Perfect Information—Each buyer and seller has enough information to make fully informed purchase and sale decisions. This implies that inferior products will quickly get driven out of the market while superior products will always find buyers.

These assumptions, particularly 1 and 2, imply that the demand curve facing the individual firm will be horizontal at the market price. The standard interpretation of this demand curve is that the firm can sell all it wants at the market price.

Another important assumption is that firms are considered to be profit-maximizers.

The major issues in the analysis of perfect competition are the determination of the firm's short run and long run equilibrium positions, and an evaluation of the long run equilibrium. In the short run, firms will produce the quantity of output where the price they charge (P) will equal the marginal cost (MC) of production. Whenever $P > MC$, the firm can add to its profits by selling units that add more to its revenues (P) than to its costs (MC). When $P < MC$, additional sales add more to costs than to revenues.

Refer to the figure for a graphical depiction of short run equilibrium. The graph on the left represents industry demand and supply. The intersection of the curves gives equilibrium price, which is treated as a given by the firm. The graph on the right represents the typical firm. The horizontal line is the firm's demand curve. Other curves depicted are marginal cost (*MC*), average variable cost (*AVC*), and average cost (*AC*). Short run equilibrium is at the level of output where *P* equals *MC*. The firm's total revenue is area *0PcQ**. Its total cost is area *0bdQ*. It earns an economic profit of area *bPcd*.

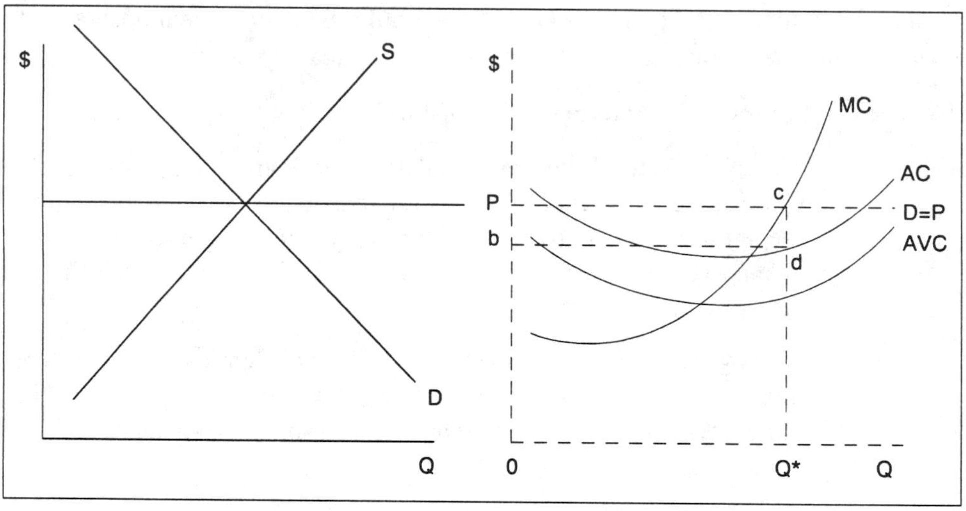

Short Run Equilibrium

Short run losses are also possible. If the firm is charging *P* greater than minimum *AVC*, but less than *AC*, the firm will continue to produce in the short run, despite the losses. The reason has to do with the distinction between fixed and variable costs. The firm must pay its fixed costs in the short run, regardless of whether it produces or not. A *P* in excess of *AVC* provides a surplus which can be used to partially offset the fixed costs.

If $P <$ minimum *AVC*, the firm will shut down in the short run. If it shuts down, it must pay its fixed costs. If it produces, it must pay its fixed costs, and its failure to cover its variable costs will only add to the loss.

Where do the market demand and supply curves come from? Market demand is the horizontal summation of the individual consumer demand curves for the product. Market supply is the horizontal summation of the individual firm supply curves. Where do the individual firm supply curves come from? From the earlier discussion, if you know the price of the product (assuming $P >$ minimum AVC), you can find the quantity the firm will supply from its MC curve. If $P <$ minimum AVC, then nothing will be supplied. Consequently, the firm's supply curve is simply the segment of its MC curve above minimum AVC.

Freedom of exit and entry is the dominant factor determining long run equilibrium. If the industry is earning economic profits, entry will take place. The new firms will help increase the supply of the product, leading to a lowering of the market price. The added demand of the new firms for factors of production may raise production costs, also. The result is that economic profits will disappear. Another result is that firms will be forced to build and produce in the most efficient factories possible, because to do otherwise would result in losses. Consequently, in long run equilibrium, firms will be producing at the low point of their long run average cost curve.

If there are losses in the industry, exit will take place, leading to an increase in the market price as the supply of the product is reduced and costs of production fall as a result of a decreased demand for factors of production. Production at the low point of the long run average cost curve will also occur.

Perfect competition is viewed by many economists as an "ideal." Firms in perfect competition are in a constant struggle for survival. They must produce products to the specifications of consumers, a condition known as consumer sovereignty. They must produce output as efficiently as possible. For their troubles, firms can only hope to earn normal profits in the long run, preventing any undue concentration of political or economic power in a few hands. Evaluations of industry performance typically use the perfectly competitive model as the point of comparison. Policy recommendations to improve industry performance frequently call for industries to be made more competitive.

Step-by-Step Solutions to Problems in this Chapter, "Perfect Competition"

CHARACTERISTICS OF PERFECT COMPETITION

• PROBLEM 18-1

Define pure competition.

Solution: Pure competition occurs in a market with numerous buyers and sellers exchanging a homogenous product, and with free entry into the market for this product. Because there are so many buyers and sellers, no one person or firm has any influence over the price; they are all "price-takers". There is only a single homogenous product in the market, and consumers of the product possess complete information regarding the price charged by all the producing firms, so no firm can charge a higher price than any other firm without losing all its customers. So the demand conditions for each firm are the same. No firm has an advantage from brand-name recognition.

Free entry in (and exit from) the market make it impossible for firms to earn economic profits in the long run. If there are economic profits being made, additional firms will enter the industry. They will continue to enter until there are so many firms that no one firm can earn any more than 'normal' profits on its operations. Any industry that has these three characteristics (numerous buyers and sellers, a homogenous product, and free entry) is called purely competitive.

• PROBLEM 18-2

What are the conditions necessary for perfect competition?

Solution: The conditions are

a) that there are many buyers and sellers in the market;

b) that no single buyer or seller is able to influence the price of the good;

c) that the product is standardized and uniform;

d) that new firms are free to enter and existing firms are free to leave the industry; and

e) that there is virtually no room for nonprice competition.

• PROBLEM 18-3

What is meant by atomistic competition?

Solution: Atomistic competition is another name for perfect, or pure, competition. The term "atomistic" is used to convey the notion of numerous small firms which combine like a multitude of tiny atoms to make up the industry.

• PROBLEM 18-4

What are the two essential features of competition?

Solution: The essential aspects of competition are numerous buyers and sellers, and free entry into and exit from markets. The condition that there be numerous buyers and sellers prevents any one person or firm from dominating the market. That is, there is a widespread diffusion of economic power. This prevents manipulation of prices and so, allows the price system to reflect accurately supply and demand conditions.

Free entry and exit helps to keep competition operative. If an industry experiences an increase in demand, the absence of barriers to the entry of new firms into the industry allows the industry to expand rapidly to meet the wishes of consumers. In an industry experiencing a decline in demand, firms must be able to leave the industry, if the manpower and resources used by these firms are to be used more efficiently somewhere else.

These two features, competition and free entry and exit are the defining characteristics of economic competition.

• PROBLEM 18-5

Which of the curves represents the demand faced by a producer under perfect competition?

Solution: A perfectly competitive firm is one that is so small compared to the size of the entire market that it can-

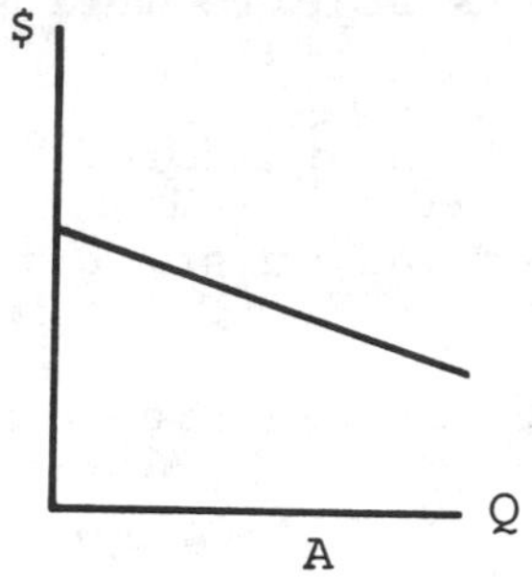

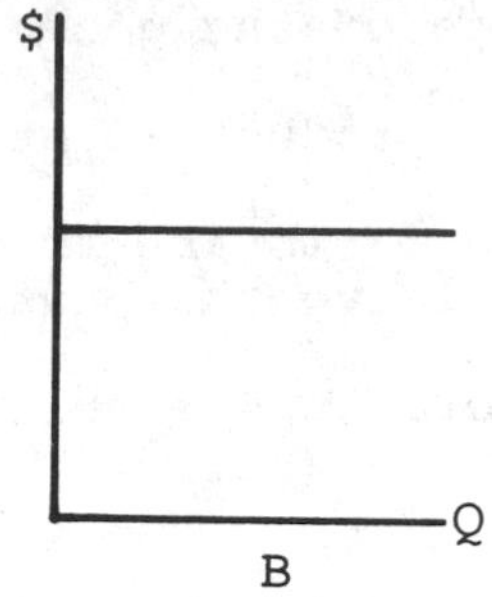

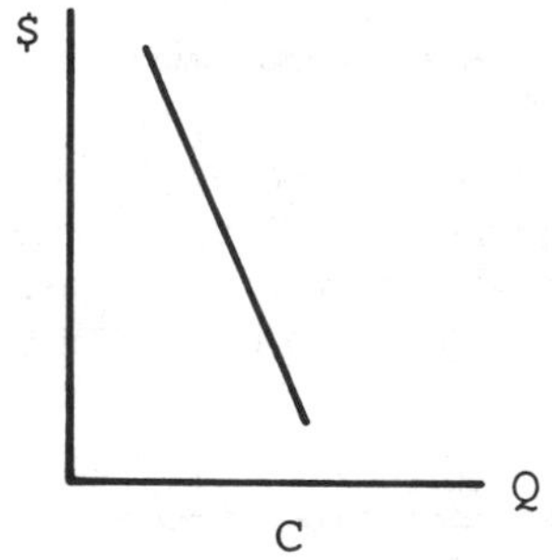

not affect market price regardless of how much it decides to supply. That is, whether the perfect competitor supplies nothing (Q = 0) or the maximum that he can produce, market price will always be the same to him. Note that the demand curves A and C both show that as the producer increases his output, i.e., moves to the right along the Q-axis, the price offered to him declines. Therefore A and C do not represent demand to a perfectly competitive firm. Demand curve B shows a constant price, regardless of the quantity of output level chosen. Therefore, B, a horizontal line, does show demand to a perfectly competitive firm.

• PROBLEM 18-6

Given the cost and demand curves for three producers, can you determine which, if any, represent a perfect competitor?

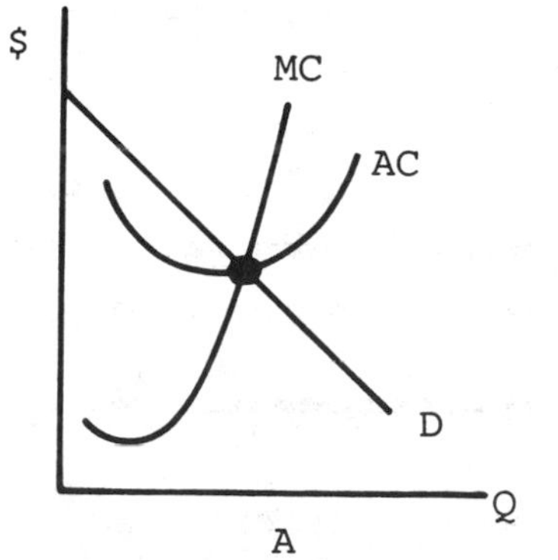

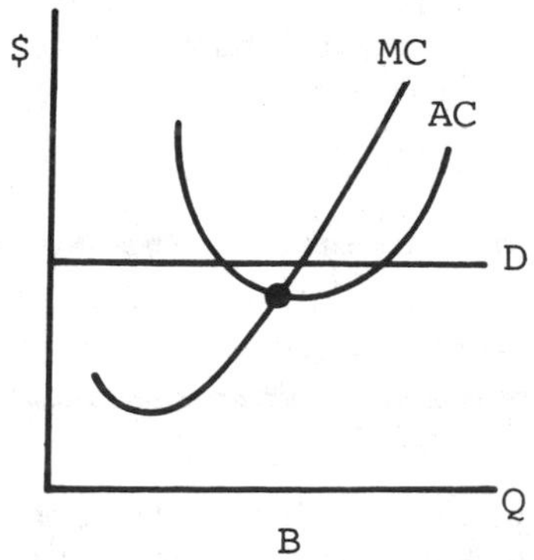

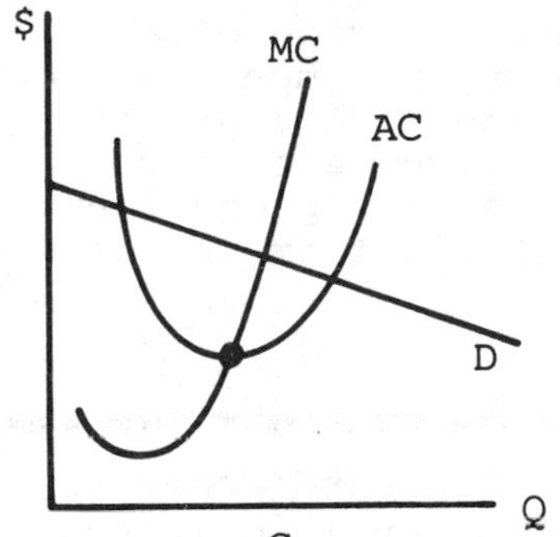

C

Solution: By definition, a perfect competitor is so small compared to the size of the total market, that increasing or decreasing the amount which he produces will not affect the market price. Consider cases A and C. Note that in both cases the demand curve facing the firms is downward sloping. This means that, at any production level, for the firms to increase their output and sell all of this additional output, the market price must decline. Similarly, if the firms decreased their output, in order to maintain market equilibrium, the market equilibrium price would rise. Therefore, these two producers, regardless of the shapes of their cost curves, cannot be perfect competitors.

In case B, note that the demand curve is a horizontal line. This means that no matter what quantity firm B decides to produce, the equilibrium market price will not change. Therefore, firm B is a perfect competitor.

• PROBLEM 18-7

In a price-takers' market, does the marginal revenue of each seller equal the average revenue (price)? Why?

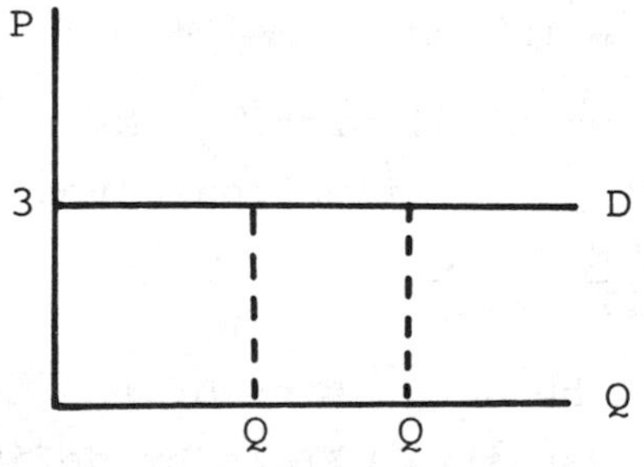

Fig. 1

Solution: Yes, under the conditions of perfect competition, which imply that all the producers are price-takers, the marginal revenue of each seller equals the average revenue or the price of a product.

A producer can sell any amount of output at the market price (see fig. 1). This is precisely the meaning of the horizontal demand schedule a producer is facing (fig. 1). Marginal revenue is simply the revenue obtained from the sale of the last unit of output. In case of a price-taker; no matter what quantity he chooses to produce, the last unit will still be sold at the prevailing market price of \$3 (see fig. 1). Therefore, marginal revenue of our producer will always be \$5 which is the price of a product and also, of course, average revenue received from the sale of any amount of output.

• PROBLEM 18-8

Adam Smith's 'invisible hand' operates in the free market system, with active competition, that aligns the self-interests of individuals with the "public interest". What exactly is the "public interest"?

Solution: The "public interest" is to use the scarce resources as efficiently as possible. So, if land is scarce, it is in the public interest to use the land (for food, for housing, etc.) in the most efficient manner. This is the same as saying the public interest is to get the highest possible quantity of goods at the lowest price. Any system which can do this is in the public interest. This is exactly why economics concerns itself with efficiency, with the allocation of scarce goods.

• PROBLEM 18-9

Prove, through the use of derivatives, that if a firm is trying to maximize its profits it should produce where marginal revenue equals marginal cost.

Solution: Recall that Total Profit may be written as follows:

$$T\pi = TR - TC$$

Also recall that marginal profit = $M\pi = \frac{d\pi}{dQ}$. Taking the derivative of the profit function gives:

$$M\pi = \frac{d\pi}{dQ} = \frac{dTR}{dQ} - \frac{dTC}{dQ}$$

Recall that $\frac{dTR}{dQ}$ (the derivative of the total revenue (TR) with respect to quantity (Q)) is by definition the expression for marginal revenue, MR, and that $\frac{dTC}{dQ}$ (the derivative of the total cost (TC)with respect to quantity (a) represents marginal cost, MC. Substituting MR and MC into the derivative yields:

$$M\pi = MR - MC$$

Now, since the maximization of any function requires that the first derivative be set equal to zero, profit maximization will occur where

$M\pi = MR - MC = 0$

Therefore, at the point of profit maximization,

$MR = MC.$

• PROBLEM 18-10

Given the demand curve in Figure 1, construct its associated Marginal Revenue (MR) and Average Revenue (AR) Curves.

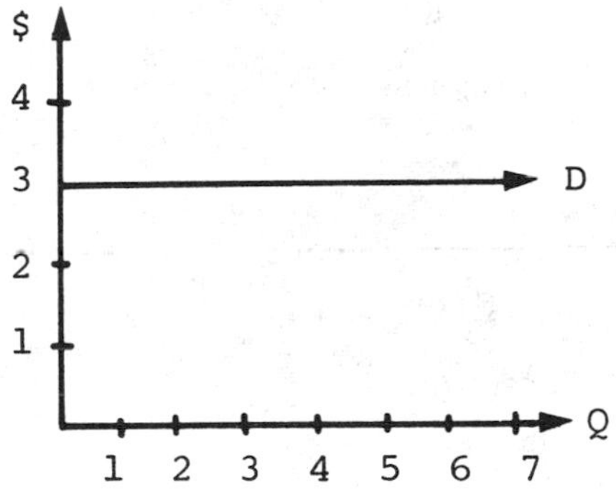

Fig. 1

Solution: Given the demand curve in Figure 1, there are several ways to approach the problem of constructing its MR and AR curves. The most straightforward approach is to note that since this demand curve is a horizontal line at \$3, every unit that the producer sells will sell for \$3; so producer's Average Revenue per unit at any level of production, is \$3. Also any additional unit of output, at all production levels, will also bring the producer an additional \$3 of revenue, that is, his Marginal Revenue is also \$3 at all quantity levels. Therefore, Demand, Market Price, Average Revenue and Marginal Revenue are all co-incident straight lines at P = \$3 as shown in Figure 1(a).

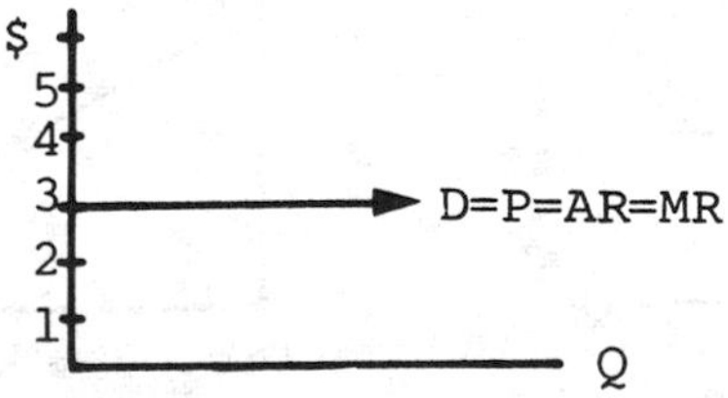

Fig. 1(a)

A second approach to this problem would be to set up a Total Revenue schedule, as shown in Figure 2 which would correspond to the given demand curve. That is, list the market price and the corresponding quantity demanded for several values of Q. Remember that TR = P X Q to get the values for Total Revenue. Then determine the extra amount of Total Revenue gained by increasing output by one unit to determine

Price	Quantity Demanded	Total Revenue	Marginal Revenue	Average Revenue
$3	1	3		3
3	2	6	3	3
3	3	9	3	3
3	4	12	3	3
3	5	15	3	3
3	6	18	3	3
3	7	21	3	3
3	8	24	3	3

Figure 2

Marginal Revenue. Then use

$$AR' = \frac{TR}{Q}$$

to calculate Average Revenue. Note that, when graphed, the results of this table are identical with Figure 1.

• PROBLEM 18-11

Economists claim that to derive the market demand curve, one should take the horizontal sum of the individual demand curves. If this is so, how can the horizontal demand curves to the many small perfect competitors, figure 1, sum to the downward-slope demand curve, figure 2, which represents the entire market demand?

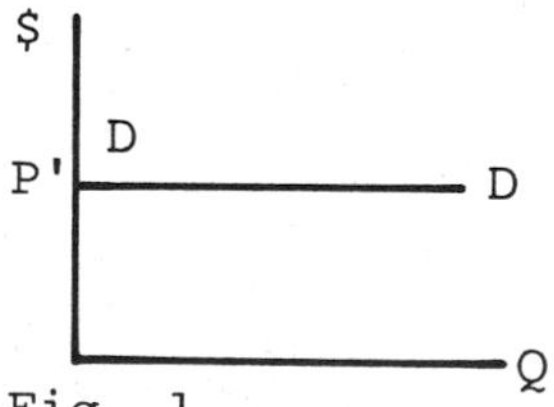

Fig. 1

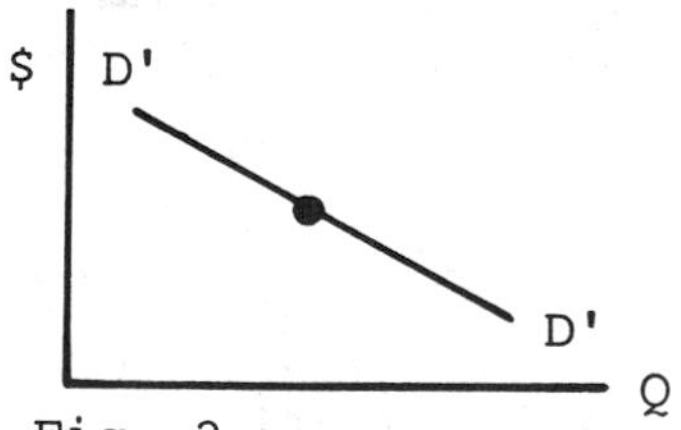

Fig. 2

Solution: The solution to this problem lies in realizing that demand to each individual perfectly competitive firm is not the same as the demand of each consumer, or individual demand. The economist sums each individual's demand to obtain the market demand, that is, the quantities which all consumers together will purchase at any given price, represented in Figure 2.

Market demand may be broken down into components which

represent the market demand for each individual firm's product, that is, as the relationship between price and the quantity which the market will demand of any single producer. By the definition of a perfectly competitive market, each firm in such a market produces such a small quantity in relation to the entire market that no matter what quantity it decides to produce, that quantity is not large enough to affect the price that consumers as a whole are willing to offer for each unit of the product. Hence, what the individual producer "sees" as the demand curve facing him appears perfectly horizontal, because he "sees" such a small segment of it.

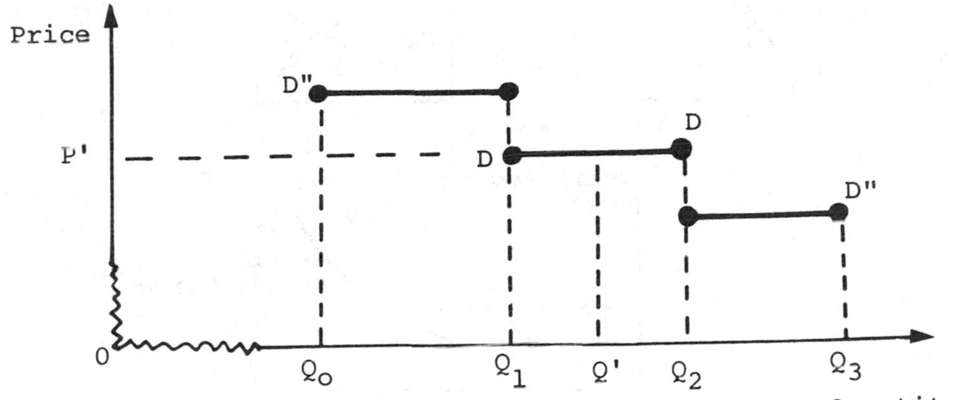

Fig. 3

A much magnified view of the market demand curve in Figure 2 would appear as in Figure 3.

Suppose the prevailing market price is P', and the quantity supplied by all producers except one is Q' (which lies halfway between Q_1 and Q_2). If the one producer's maximum production is less than $\frac{(Q_2 - Q_1)}{2}$, any amount he chooses to bring to market will leave the market equilibrium at some point along DD (between Q' and Q_2). Hence, only the segment DD of the entire demand curve D^1D^{21} is relevant to our single producer Thus, the demand curves facing individual perfectly competitive producers are horizontal. These demand curves, unlike individual consumers' demands, may not be summed to obtain the market demand.

• PROBLEM 18-12

How does one arrive at the aggregate supply curve (for an entire industry)?

Solution: To get the aggregate SS supply curve for a good, we must add horizontally the SS supply curves of the independent producers of that good. For example, suppose we are dealing with a competitive market for fish. How much of this commodity will be brought to market at each different level of market price? Firm A will bring so much to market at a particular price; Firm B will bring so much at this same price; Firm C will bring the amount shown on its supply curve; and so it goes. The total Q that will be brought to market at a given market P will be the sum of all the qs which firms will want to supply at that price, and similarly at any other price.

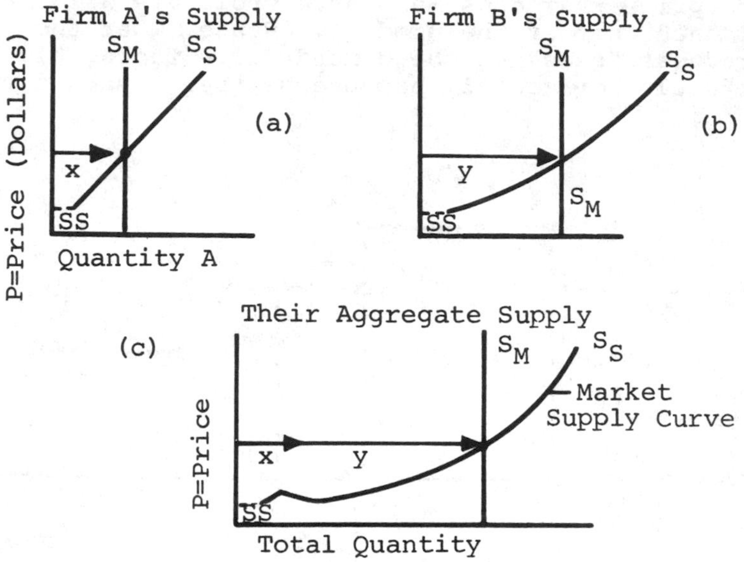

This can be shown graphically in the accompanying diagrams.

where Sm represents the fact that supply is fixed

Ss represents the situation when firms can produce more within given plants.

To get the industry's vertical momentary supply curve SmSm, add horizontally, at the same P, all firms' vertical momentary supply curves.

Again, to get the industry's short-run supply curve SsSs, add horizontally, at the same P, the short-run supply curves of the fixed number of firms existing in that short run.

INDIVIDUAL AND MARKET SUPPLY

• PROBLEM 18-13

When summing individual supply curves to get the market supply curve, why does the economist add the curves "horizontally" rather than "vertically."

Solution: A market demand curve shows the relationship between each possible market price measured along the vertical axis and the quantity that the entire market will supply at that price, measured along the horizontal axis. The quantity that the market will supply at any given price is a sum of the quantities that each individual seller will supply at that price. Since at any given price, the total quantity supplied in the market is composed of the quantities supplied by many individual firms, the total quantity supplied in the market is the sum of these quantities. These quantities are determined by reading off the supply curve the horizontal co-ordinate corresponding to the given price (represented by the vertical co-ordinate of the supply curve). Therefore, the sum of the horizontal co-ordinates of the individual supply curves gives us the horizontal co-ordinate of the total market supply curve which corresponds to the given price (vertical co-ordinate). Repeating the summation of the horizontal co-ordinates of the individual demand curves at each possible price (vertical co-ordinate) and plotting the results gives us the total market supply curve.

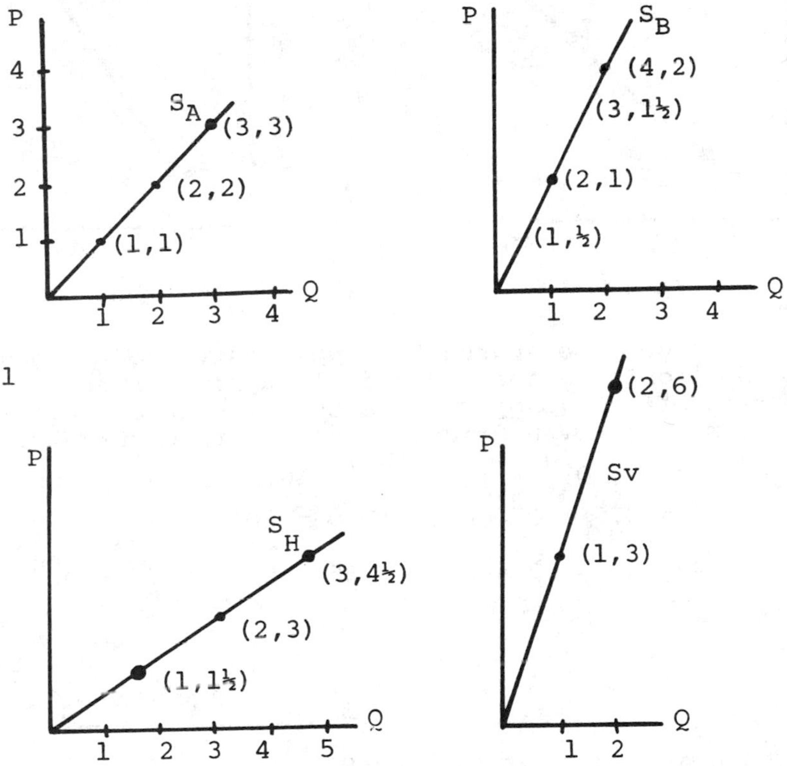

Fig. 1

For example, consider the two individual supply curves, A and B in Figure 1. S_H shows a horizontal summation of S_A and S_B. It shows the relationship between any given market price and the total quantity supplied by individual producers A and B, that is, a market supply curve.

Sv, on the other hand, shows a vertical summation of S_A and S_B. That is, for any given quantity supplied, it shows the market price that A would require to produce that quantity, plus the market price that B would require to produce that quantity. Since the economic interpretation of a vertical summation of S_A and S_B is not the same as the definition of a market supply curve, a vertical summation of individual supply curves will not form a market supply curve. S_V has no economic significance.

• PROBLEM 18-14

Given below are the short-run supply curves for Firms A and B. Construct their aggregate supply curve.

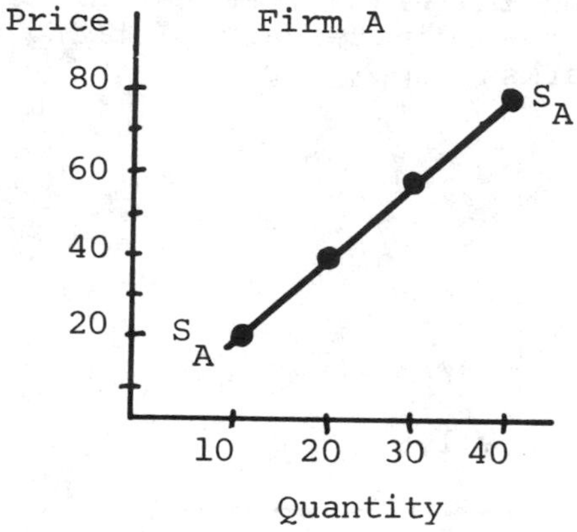

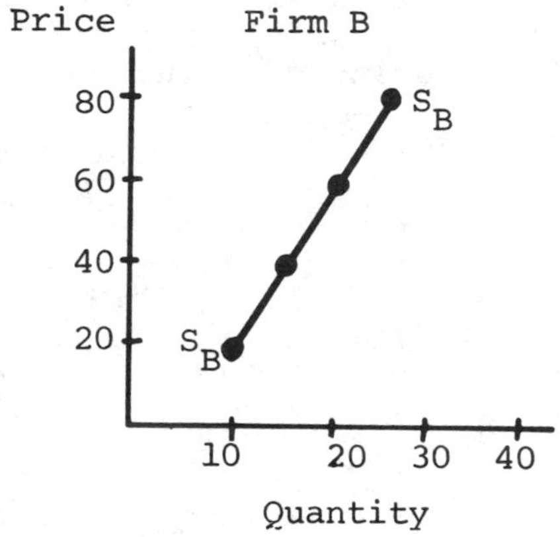

Solution: To get the aggregate supply curve for a good we must add horizontally the individual supply curves. To do this we read off the supply curve the quantities supplied by each firm at a given price, Q_A and Q_B respectively. For example at P = 20, $Q_A^{20} = 10$, $Q_B^{20} = 10$. Therefore at P = 20, aggregate $Q_T^{20} = Q_A^{20} + Q_B^{20} = 10 + 10 = 20$

At P = 40, $Q_A = 20$ and $Q_B = 15$. $Q_T^{40} = Q_A^{40} + Q_B^{40} = 20 + 15 = 35$.

(Figure 1)

P	Q_A		Q_B		Aggregate Q_T
20	10	+	10	=	20
40	20	+	15	=	35
60	30	+	20	=	50
80	40	+	25	=	65

Figure 1 shows the results of such calculations of Q_T at prices of 20, 40, 60, and 80. That is the supply schedule. Figure 2 shows the corresponding aggregate supply curve.

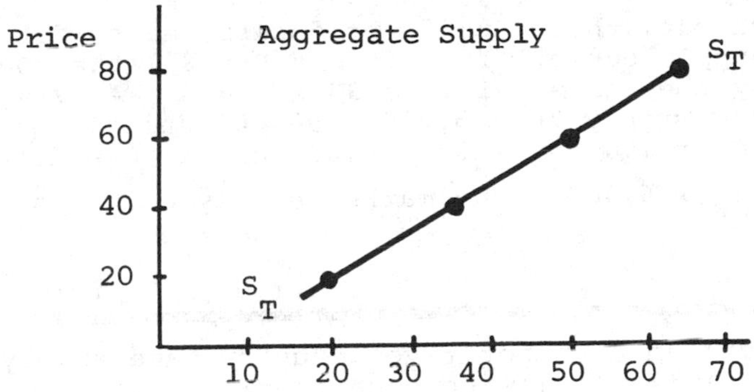

Fig. 2

• **PROBLEM 18-15**

> Suppose there are 30 independent producers in a given market, each with supply curves SS_i like the one shown in figure 1. Construct the market supply curve.

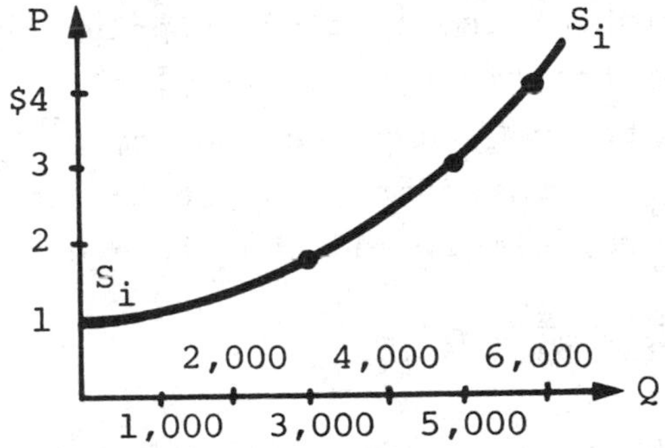

Fig. 1

Solution: The market supply curve is the horizontal summation of the supply curves for all the independent producers in the market. To construct this market supply curve, note that at any given price, P, the quantity supplied in the market will be exactly 30 times the quantity that any individual producer would supply at that price. This is because

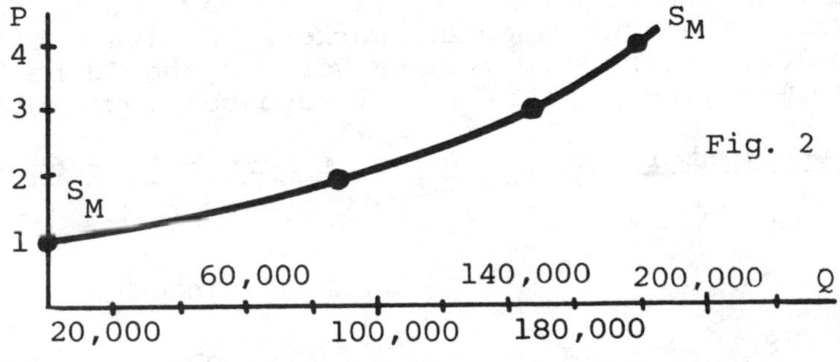

Fig. 2

in this example, there are 30 producers, each with exactly the same supply curve. That is, at P = \$1, the quantity supplied by the market will be 30 x 0 = 0. At P = \$2 the market would supply 30 x 3,000 = 90,000 units. Similarly, at P = 3, Q_M = 150,000 = 30 x 5,000 and at P = 4, Q_M = 180,000 = 30 x 6,000. The market supply curve is shown in figure 2.

• PROBLEM 18-16

If four firms in a competitive industry have supply schedules given by the following equations:

$Q_1^s = 16 + 4P$ $\qquad$ $Q_3^s = 32 + 8P$

$Q_2^s = 5 - 5P$ $\qquad$ $Q_4^s = 60 - 10P$

What is their combined supply?

Solution: The combined supply of these four producers would be a horizontal summation of each of the four individual supply curves. Note that at any given price P_0 (the independent variable) the combined supply would be the quantity supplied by the first producer Q_1^s plus that of the second Q_2^s plus the third Q_3^s and the fourth, Q_4^s , or $Q_1^s + Q_2^s + Q_3^s + Q_4^s = Q_{total}$. Therefore, to get the combined supply of the four producers, simply add the given equations:

$$Q^s_{total} = Q_1^s + Q_2^s + Q_3^s + Q_4^s =$$

$$= (16 + 4P) + (5 - 5P) + (32 + 8P) + (60 - 10P)$$

$$= (16 + 5 + 32 + 60) + (4P - 5P + 8P - 10P)$$

$$Q^s_{total} = 113 - 3P.$$

SHORT RUN PROFIT MAXIMIZATION

• PROBLEM 18-17

Suppose that the wage rate is \$30 per day and a factory owner is considering how many workers to hire. Using the table below, determine how many workers should be hired in order to maximize profits (total revenues less total costs).

Input (Labor)	Value of Marginal Product per day
6	\$50
7	70
8	35

9	20
10	10

Solution: Clearly, the profit-maximizing factory owner will hire workers until the point where the next worker hired costs the owner more in wages than this worker can provide in extra output. Since the wage rate is $30, the factory owner will hire additional workers as long as the value of the daily marginal product of labor is greater than or equal to $30. We see that this occurs when the total number of workers hired is eight (value of MP = $35).

If the factory owner were to hire a ninth worker, total daily revenue would increase by $20 (value of MP) while total costs would increase by $30 (daily wage rate). Since the net effect of this would be a loss of $10, the profit-maximizing owner would not hire additional workers beyond the eighth worker.

• PROBLEM 18-18

In figure 1, MC shows Astro Corporation's (a perfect competitor) Marginal Costs of producing commodity A. P_M represents the market price of A. Why wouldn't Astro produce quantities Q_s or Q_L. How much of A will they choose to produce?

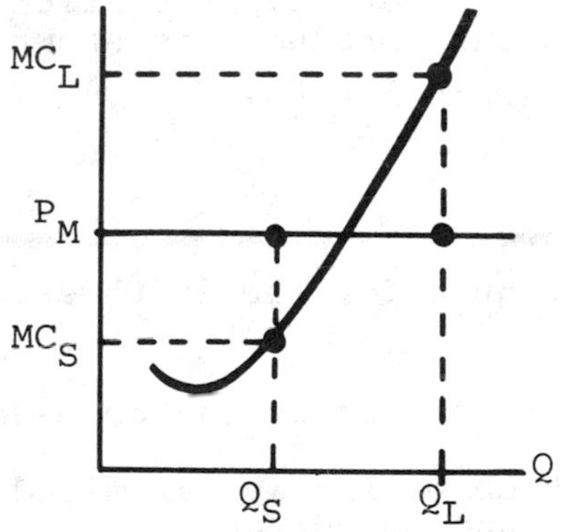

Fig. 1

Solution: This question is asking why a producer in a perfectly competitive market should choose not to produce where the cost of the last unit produced (Marginal Cost) is either greater or less than the market price. Intuitively, if commodity A is selling for $3 per unit, and the last unit of output cost only $2.00 to produce (don't forget that the economist's definition of cost includes a "normal" profit for the producer) then Astro could increase its net revenues by increasing its production level. Here, by increasing output even by 1 unit, Astro would add $3 - $2 = $1.00 on the last unit produced to its net revenue (total revenue - total cost). By increasing its production level to the point where the cost of producing the last unit of output (MC) was just equal to the price of the good, P_m, Astro would be maximizing its profits (net revenue).

Similarly Astro would not produce where the cost of producing the last unit of output was greater than the price received for it. That is, if the market price was $3, it wouldn't make sense for Astro to produce an additional unit if it cost $4 to produce.

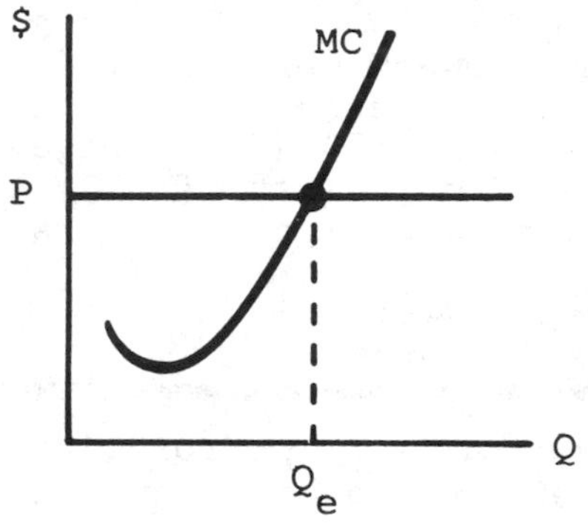

Fig. 2

Since the firm will choose to increase production whenever MC is less than the Price, and it will decrease production whenever MC is bigger than the Price, then the point where the firm should produce, as shown by Q_e in figure 2, will occur where P = MC.

• PROBLEM 18-19

Given the cost schedule for the Northwestern Lumber Company, find

a) the range over which profit can be made

b) the point at which profit is maximized, if price = $52.50 per thousand board feet.

Solution: a) Profits are being made whenever price is greater than the average total costs. Looking at column 7, we see that average total cost is less than $52.50 (the price) over the range of 6,000 board feet per day to 10,000 board feet per day. Therefore any point in this range would be profitable.

b) As long as price is greater than average variable costs, profits will be maximized by producing that quantity for which the marginal cost equals price. With price =

(1) Output per Day (Thousand Board Feet)	(2) Total Cost Fixed	(3) Total Variable Cost	(4) Total of All Costs (Fixed and Variable)	(5) Average Fixed Cost	(6) Average Variable Cost	(7) Average of All Costs (Fixed and Variable)	(8) Marginal Cost
1	$60.00	$ 81.00	$ 141.00	$60.00	$81.00	$141.00	....
2	60.00	131.00	191.00	30.00	65.50	95.50	$50.00
3	60.00	166.00	226.00	20.00	55.33	75.33	35.00
4	60.00	192.00	252.00	15.00	48.00	63.00	26.00
5	60.00	219.00	279.00	12.00	43.80	55.80	27.00
6	60.00	248.00	308.00	10.00	41.33	51.33	29.00
7	60.00	281.50	341.50	8.57	40.21	48.78	33.50
8	60.00	322.50	382.50	7.50	40.31	47.81	41.00
9	60.00	375.00	435.00	6.67	41.66	48.33	52.50
10	60.00	440.00	500.00	6.00	44.00	50.00	65.00

$52.50, we look down column 8 until we reach marginal cost = $52.50. So, profits are maximized at output = 9,000 board feet per day.

• PROBLEM 18-20

Given the following graph, describe the situation created by each of the four different MR curves in terms of profitability at the point where MC = MR.

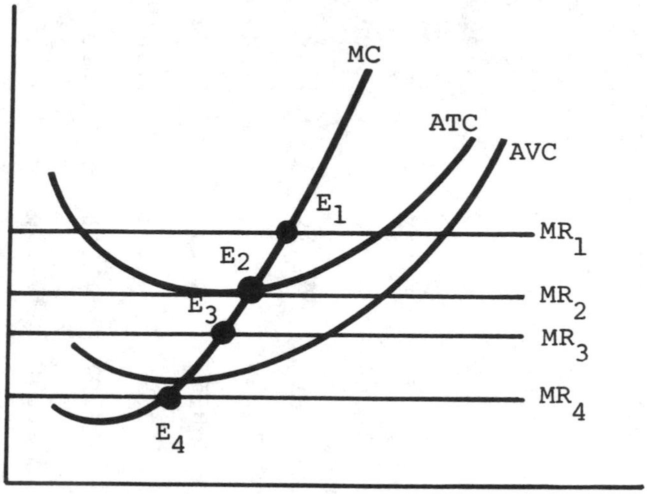

Solution: MR_1 intersects MC at E_1 , a point above the ATC curve. Therefore at this point, the firm involved would be making "economic profits" as well as "normal profits".

MR_2 intersects MC at E_2 , the lowest point of the ATC curve. The output at this point would bring about only normal profits, since at E_2 , price per unit = MR_2 = total cost per unit.

MR_3 intersects MC at E_3 , a point between the AVC and ATC curves. Since a portion of fixed costs is being covered, the firm would continue to operate even though it is incurring a loss. E_3 represents the point of loss minimization.

Finally at E_4 , MR_4 intersects MC. Here price is not only less than ATC but is also less than AVC. Revenues cannot even cover variable costs. Hence, at E_4 the firm shuts down operations.

• PROBLEM 18-21

Figure 3 represents cost curves for Firms A and B, both perfect competitors, where P_A and P_B represent market price to A and B respectively and Q_A and Q_B represent each firm's output. Are either of these firms making an economic profit or loss? If so, show the amount of this profit or loss in total and on a per unit basis.

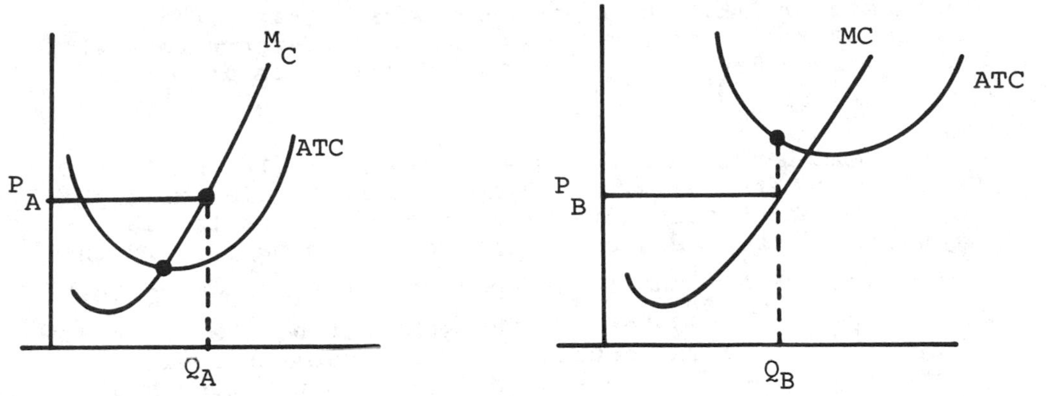

Firm A Fig. 3 Firm B

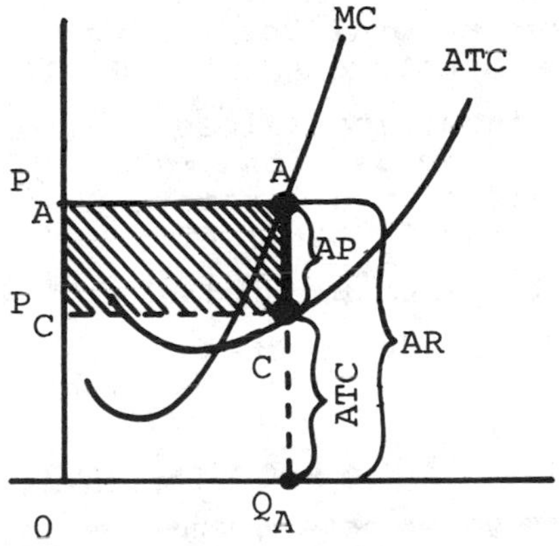

Fig. 1

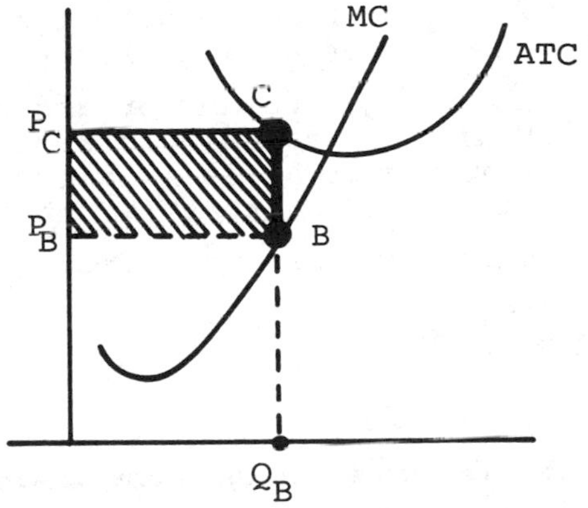

Fig. 2

<u>Solution</u>: Economic profits which are also referred to as pure profits or excess profits, are defined as Total Revenue minus Total Cost, TP = TR - TC. Where TP is a positive number, (TR>TC), the firm is making economic profits. Where TP is negative, (TR<TC), the firm is incurring losses. Note, that profit on a per unit basis, that is Average Profit (AP), can be determined by dividing TP by Q:

$$AP \equiv \frac{TP}{Q} \equiv \frac{TR}{Q} - \frac{TC}{Q}$$

Remember that $\frac{TR}{Q} \equiv$ Average Revenue (AR) and $\frac{TC}{Q} \equiv$ Average Total Cost (ATC) which gives:

$$\frac{TP}{Q} = AP = AR - ATC.$$

When a firm is making profits, AP would be a positive number, which implies that AR would be greater than ATC. If a firm was incurring losses, then AP would be negative. This would imply that AR was less than ATC.

Keeping this in mind, note in Fig. 2 that for Firm A, at its production level of Q_A, ATC lies below Average Revenue $\left(AR = \frac{TR}{Q} = \frac{PQ}{Q} = P\right)$. That is Firm A is making an economic profit. On a per unit basis, this profit, Average Profit, can be shown as the difference between the Average Revenue and Average Total Costs at Q_A, or distance AP in Figure 1.

Remember that ATC x Q = TC, AR x Q = TR and AP x Q = TP. Geometrically, one side of a rectangle, multiplied by an adjacent side gives the area of the rectangle. Thus, TC is represented by the rectangle oP_CCQ_A, TR is rectangle oP_AAQ_A and TP is rectangle P_CP_AAC. Note that TP could also be determined by subtracting the TC rectangle from the TR rectangle. Thus, geometrically, profit on a per unit basis to Firm A is the length of line from A to C, while Firm A's Total Profit can be represented by the area of the shaded rectangle P_CP_AAC.

For Firm B, note that the Average Total Cost curve lies above Average Revenue at Q_B. Therefore AP = AR - ATC is a negative number and Firm B is incurring a loss. Using the same logic as for Firm A, Firm B's loss on a per unit basis is shown in Figure 2 as the distance from C to B, that is, the distance from Q_B to C, ATC, minus the distance from Q_B to B, AR. Firm B's total loss can be shown by the area of the shaded rectangle P_BP_CCB.

• PROBLEM 18-22

Given the following situations defined by the three different marginal revenue curves, show in what situation a profit would be made, in what situation a loss would occur, and in what case a firm would break even.

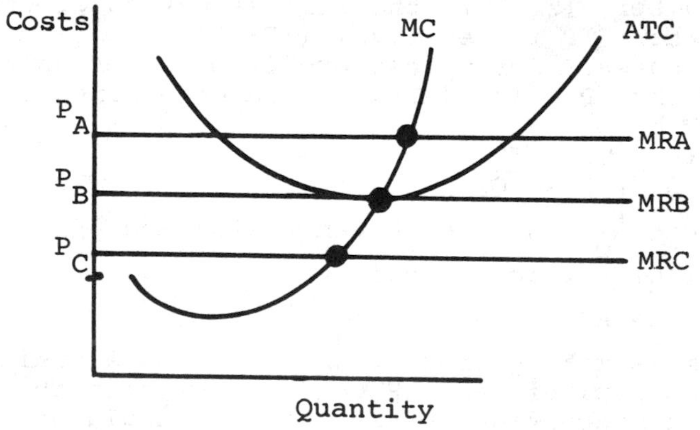

Solution: We assume that this firm is profit-maximizing. Therefore it will produce at the point where MR = MC. Under perfect competition, MR = price = average revenue.

If we look at MR_A, we see that at the point at

which it intersects MC, Price P_A>ATC. That is, since Average Revenue per unit (P_A) is greater than the Average Cost per unit, the firm is making a positive profit on every unit sold. Therefore at this point, profits will be maximized and will be positive.

Looking at MR_B, we see that at the intersection of MC and MR_B, MC = MR_B = Price = ATC. That is, at this point, Average Revenue per unit (P_B) is the same as Average Cost per unit and the firm is making neither a profit nor a loss. Therefore at this point, the firm will break even.

Finally MR_C intersects MC at a quantity where ATC>Price. Therefore a loss occurs here.

• PROBLEM 18-23

Mr. A owns 1,000 shares of General Electric common stock. If he tries to sell some, he finds he can get a price of \$61.50 per share for all 1,000 shares. If he offers only 500 shares, he can get a price of \$61.625 which is \$0.125 more per share. That is, reducing his amount sold by a half, he can get a price that is higher by about 1/500. If he sought a price of \$61.75, he would sell nothing. Mr. A considers this an insignificant rise in price as a result of withholding his supply. Is this an example of a price-takers' market? Compute Mr. A's marginal revenues as best you can with the given data.

Solution: Yes, since Mr. A considers the difference in price insignificant, this is an example of a price-takers' market, although in strict terms, we assume that there is no rise in price as a result of withholding some of the good which one might otherwise supply.

Marginal revenue is computed as follows:

At 1,000 shares for \$61.50 per share TR = \$61,500

At 500 shares for \$61.625 per share TR = \$30,812.50

Total revenue difference is (\$61,500 - \$30,812.50) = \$30,687.50 for 500 shares change in sales. Marginal revenue is therefore about $\frac{\$30,687.50}{500}$ or \$61.375 per share.

• PROBLEM 18-24

On the basis of the following information which shows all available techniques by which 30 units of wheat can be produced, answer questions (a) and (b) below.

Resource	Resource Prices	Units of resource used for each technique #1	#2	#3	#4	#5
Land	\$6	3	6	3	6	6
Labor	5	2	3	6	2	5

Capital	5	4	1	2	1	3
Entrepreneurial ability	4	1	2	3	4	5

a) Given the resource prices above, identify the economically most efficient production technique(s).

b) According to your results in (a), if the 30 units of wheat, which can be produced with each technique, can be sold for $3 per unit, what would be the economic profit of the firm?

Solution: a) To identify the most economically efficient production techniques we multiply the quantities of various resources, required by the resource prices, by each of the 5 techniques as follows:

Resource	Cost for each production technique #1	#2	#3	#4	#5
Land	\$6x3=\$18	\$6x6=\$36	\$6x3=\$18	\$6x6=\$36	\$6x6=\$36
Labor	\$5x2=\$10	\$5x3=\$15	\$5x6=\$30	\$5x2=\$10	\$5x5=\$25
Capital	\$5x4=\$20	\$5x1=\$ 5	\$5x2=\$10	\$5x1=\$ 5	\$5x3=\$15
Entrepreneurial ability	\$4x1=\$ 4	\$4x2=\$ 8	\$4x3=\$12	\$4x4=\$16	\$4x5=\$20
Total cost	\$52	\$64	\$70	\$67	\$96

As the computations above indicate, technique 1 is the most economically efficient of the five, because it gives the least costly method of producing the 30 units of wheat.

b) The difference between how much the wheat industry earns by selling wheat and how much the industry spends on production of wheat equals total economic profit.

Total profit = 30 units x 3 = \$60
Less Total (least) Cost = 52
\$ 8

Hence, the wheat industry realized an economic profit of \$8.

The president of National Widget Corporation has just been given the set of cost curves, shown in figure 1, by his economists. If the economists' estimation of NWC's cost curves is correct, should the president change the quantity of widgets currently being produced, Q_E, or the price at which NWC is currently selling its widgets, P_E? Why or why not?

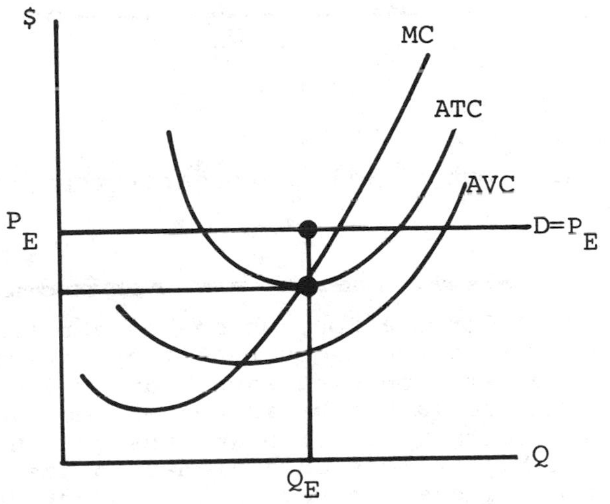

Fig. 1

Solution: This question is asking whether or not NWC is currently maximizing its profits. The profit maximizing rule says to set Marginal Revenue equal to Marginal Cost. Under perfect competition, the demand curve is a horizontal line which implies that D = P = MR = AR.

This means that to maximize his profits, the perfect competitor should set MC = P (=MR). Since NWC's demand curve is a horizontal line, this means that NWC must be a perfect competitor, and therefore, NWC should not change its price from P_E. However, to maximize its profits, NWC should increase its production, until MC = P_E, to Q_M in figure 2. Note that by doing so NWC loses the excess profits represented by the rectangle $P_C P_E EC$ (TR - TC = $(oP_E EQ_E) - (oP_C CQ_E)$). At its profit maximizing equilibrium, P_E and Q_P there are no excess profits (since TR - TC = $(oP_E MQ_M) - (oP_E MQ_M) = 0$). The reason why NWC should be willing to sacrifice its excess profit, is that the increase in normal profit that comes

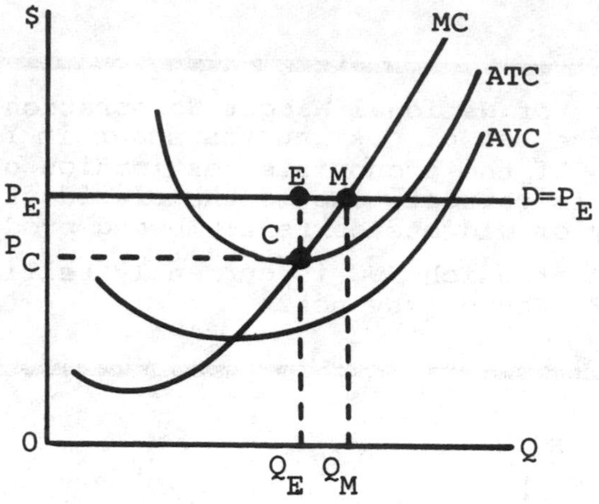

Fig. 2

with increasing output will be greater than the excess profit lost.

• PROBLEM 18-26

American Widget Corporation, which has a rising short run Marginal Cost curve is currently operating at a loss. AWC's chief economist says that if P rises a little, output should not be increased because, if it were, Marginal Costs would rise and the company would end up with a bigger loss on a higher volume. Should AWC's president listen to the chief economist? Why or why not?

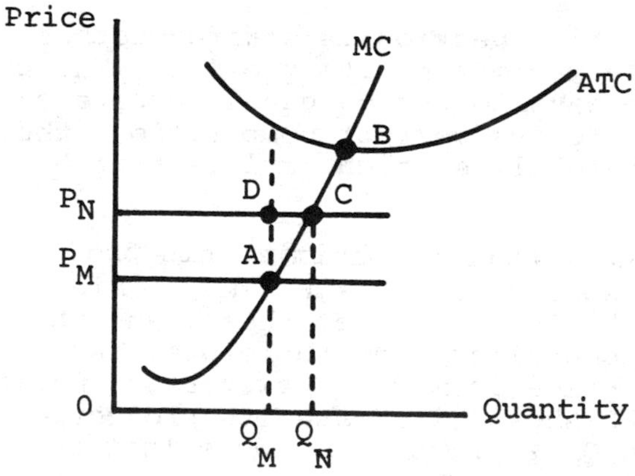

Fig. 1

<u>Solution</u>: This question is asking whether a company, attempting to minimize its losses, should change its quantity of output in response to a price increase. Using the rising Marginal Cost curve in figure 1, B is the break-even point, i.e., where total revenue equals total costs, P_M is the current market price and Q_M is

the quantity currently being produced. Suppose the market price rises to P_N. If AWC continues to produce Q_M then its marginal cost, that is, the cost of producing the last unit, will still be P_M. But the market is now willing to pay P_N for this last unit. Since the new price P_N is greater than marginal cost P_M, AWC would increase its total revenue by more than it increased its total cost. AWC increases production to the level Q_N, at which the cost of producing the last unit of output is exactly equal to what the market was willing to pay for it (point C). That is, the additional revenue from producing the additional output $Q_N - Q_M$ is represented in Figure 1 by the rectangle DCQ_NQ_M; and the additional cost of producing that output is represented by ACQ_NQ_M. Thus there is a gain in net revenue represented by triangle ADC from producing the additional output $Q_N - Q_M$. Thus, it would decrease the loss that it is taking.

In other words, a profit maximizing (or loss-minimizing) perfectly competitive firm should always set P = MC. In AWC's case, with its rising MC curve, this would require an increase in output to quantity Q_N in the figure. Therefore AWC's president should disregard his chief economist's advice on this matter.

• PROBLEM 18-27

Assume that B Corporation has the following total profit function equation:
Total Profit = π = $-\$3,000 - \$2,400\,Q + \$350Q^2 - \$8.333Q^3$
a) Compute the marginal profit
b) Determine its output quantities

Solution: a) Marginal profit is obtained by taking the first derivative of the total profit function

$$\text{Marginal Profit} = \frac{d\pi}{dQ} = -\$2,400 + \$700Q - \$25Q^2$$

b) The marginal profit function is in the form

$Y = ax^2 + bx + c$ which is a quadratic equation. Note that the coefficients in the marginal cost equation correspond to the coefficients in the general form of a quadratic equation as follows:

X = Q
a = -25
b = 700
c = -2,400

The two roots for any quadratic equation may be found

using the following formula:

$$X_1, X_2 = \frac{-b \pm \sqrt{b^2 - 4ac}}{2a}$$

By substituting the values of the marginal profit function into the quadratic equation, we can obtain its output quantities as follows:

$$X_1, X_2 = \frac{-700 \pm \sqrt{700^2 - 4\ (-25)(-2,400)}}{2\ (-25)}$$

$$= \frac{-700 \pm \sqrt{490,000 - 240,000}}{-50}$$

$$= \frac{-700 \pm \sqrt{250,000}}{-50}$$

$$X = \frac{-700 \pm 500}{-50}$$

The first quantity is:

$$X_1 = \frac{-700 - 500}{-50}$$

$$= \frac{-1,200}{-50}$$

$$X_1 = 24 \text{ units.}$$

The second quantity is:

$$X_2 = \frac{-700 + 500}{-50}$$

$$= \frac{-200}{-50}$$

$$X_2 = 4 \text{ units.}$$

The output quantities therefore are 24 and 4 units. By definition, Profit is maximized when Marginal Profit is equal to zero. Therefore, to check that $\frac{d\pi}{dQ} = 0$ for X_1 and X_2 substitute them into $\frac{d\pi}{dQ}$ as follows:

Marginal Profit $= \frac{d\pi}{dQ} = -\$2,400 + \$700Q - \$25Q^2 = 0$

For $X_1 = 24$ units,

$$= -\$2,400 + \$700\ (24) - \$25\ (24)^2 = 0$$
$$= -\$2,400 + 16,800 - \$25\ (576) = 0$$
$$= -\$2,400 + 16,800 - \$14,400 = 0$$
$$= -\$16,800 + 16,800 = 0$$

For $X_2 = 4$ units,

$$= -\$2,400 + \$700\ (4) - \$25\ (4)^2 = 0$$
$$= -\$2,400 + \$2,800 - \$25\ (16) = 0$$
$$= -\$2,400 + \$2,800 - \$400 = 0$$
$$= -\$2,800 + \$2,800 = 0$$

Assume that a firm operates with the total revenue (TR) and total cost (TC) functions:

$$TR = 41.5Q - 1.1Q^2$$

$$TC = 150 + 10Q - 0.5Q^2 + 0.02Q^3$$

where Q represents the quantity of output produced and sold.

a) Determine the profit-maximizing output level for this firm via the TR - TC approach.

b) Solve for the profit-maximizing output level by using the MR = MC approach.

Solution: a) By definition,

$$\begin{aligned} \pi &= TR - TC \\ &= (41.5Q - 1.1Q^2) - (150 + 10Q - 0.5Q^2 + 0.02Q^3) \\ &= 41.5Q - 1.1Q^2 - 150 - 10Q + 0.5Q^2 - 0.02Q^3 \\ &= -150 + (41.5Q - 10Q) + (-1.1Q^2 + 0.5Q^2) - 0.02Q^3 \\ &= -150 + 31.5Q - 0.6Q^2 - 0.02Q^3 \end{aligned}$$

Recall that to find the maximum point on the profit function, the derivative with respect to Q should be set equal to zero, as follows:

$$M\pi = \frac{d\pi}{dQ} = 31.5 - 1.2Q - 0.06Q^2 = 0$$

This is a quadratic equation, and the corresponding output levels are computed as follows:

$$\begin{aligned} X_1, X_2 &= \frac{-b \pm \sqrt{b^2 - 4ac}}{2a} \\ &= \frac{-(-1.2) \pm \sqrt{(-1.2)^2 - 4(-.06)(31.5)}}{2(-.06)} \\ &= \frac{+1.2 \pm \sqrt{1.44 - 4(-1.89)}}{-.12} \\ &= \frac{+1.2 \pm \sqrt{1.44 - (-7.56)}}{-.12} \\ &= \frac{1.2 \pm \sqrt{1.44 + 7.56}}{-.12} \\ &= \frac{1.2 \pm \sqrt{9}}{-.12} \\ &= \frac{1.2 \pm 3}{-.12} \end{aligned}$$

$$X_1 = \frac{1.2 - 3}{-.12} = \frac{-1.8}{-.12} \qquad X_2 = \frac{1.2 + 3}{-.12} = \frac{4.2}{-.12}$$

$X_1 = 15$ units $\qquad X_2 = -35$

Since it is not feasible to have negative quantities, X_2 is a nonfeasible solution and can be discarded.

Therefore, profit-maximizing output level would be 15 units.

b) Recall that $MR = \frac{dTR}{dQ}$ and $MC = \frac{dTC}{dQ}$. Thus, using the MR = MC approach, to find the profit maximizing output level, differentiate the total revenue and total cost functions:

$$MR = \frac{dTR}{dQ} = 41.5 - 2.2Q$$

$$MC = \frac{dTC}{dQ} = 10 - Q + 0.06Q^2$$

At the profit-maximizing output level, MR = MC. Thus

$MR = 41.5 - 2.2Q = 10 - Q + 0.06Q^2 = MC$

Combining terms, we obtain:

$$41.5 - 2.2Q - 10 + Q - 0.06Q^2 = 0$$

$$31.5 - 1.2Q - 0.06Q^2 = 0$$

Note that the resulting equation in the MR = MC approach has different signs than the TR - TC method. However solving for its output quantities (again using the quadratic equation), will result in the same quantities as we obtained before. This can be shown as follows:

$$X = \frac{-b \pm \sqrt{b^2 - 4ac}}{2a}$$

$$= \frac{-(-1.2) \pm \sqrt{(-1.2)^2 - 4(31.5)(-.06)}}{2(-.06)}$$

$$= \frac{1.2 \pm \sqrt{1.44 - 4(-1.89)}}{-.12}$$

$$= \frac{1.2 \pm \sqrt{1.44 - (-7.56)}}{-.12}$$

$$= \frac{1.2 \pm \sqrt{1.44 + 7.56}}{-.12}$$

$$= \frac{1.2 \pm \sqrt{9}}{-.12}$$

$$= \frac{1.2 \pm 3}{-.12}$$

$$X_1 = \frac{1.2 - 3}{-.12} \qquad X_2 = \frac{1.2 + 3}{-.12}$$

$$X_1 = \frac{-1.8}{-.12} \qquad X_2 = \frac{4.2}{-.12}$$

$$X_1 = 15 \text{ units} \qquad X_2 = -35$$

As before, disregard X_2 since it represents a negative output level. Therefore, $X_1 = 15$ is the profit maximizing output.

Note that the profit maximizing output level is the same, regardless of which method is used.

Given that firm A has demand function $P = 15 - .05q$ and total cost function, $TC = q + .02q^2$.

a) find the point of profit maximization

b) find maximum profit if a \$1/unit tax is imposed.

Solution: Since profit maximization occurs where MR = MC, the way to solve this problem is to solve for MR and MC and then equate the two. Demand is given as $P = 15 - .05q$. Since $TR = q \times p$, then $q(15 - .05q) = TR = 15q - .05q^2$. Marginal Revenue is defined as, $MR = \frac{d(TR)}{dQ}$,

therefore, $MR = d\left(15q - .05q^2\right)/dq$

or $MR = 15 - 0.1q$

Similarly, $MC = d(TC)/dQ$. Therefore

$$MC = d\left(q + .02q^2\right)/dq$$

or $$= 1 + 0.04q$$

At profit maximization, MR = MC, or

$$15 - 0.1q = 1 + 0.04q.$$

Solving for q: $0.14q = 14$

yields the profit-maximizing q, q*: $q^* = 100$

To find the profit maximizing price level, p*, substitute q* into the original demand function, $P = 15 - .05q$,

This gives $P = 15 - (0.05)(100)$

or $P = 10$

b) Now we must include a \$1/unit tax in our total cost function. Originally we had $TC = q + 0.02q^2$. Now we have $TC_T = q + 0.02q^2 + \text{tax}$. If tax = \$1/unit and we sell q units then the tax = q. Therefore $TC_T = q + 0.02q^2 + q = 2q + 0.02q^2$

Finding MC, we get $MC = 2 + 0.04q$.

Equating MR and MC to reach profit maximization, we have

$$15 - 0.1q = 2 + 0.04q$$

$$0.14q = 13$$

$$q^* = \frac{1300}{14} \approx 93$$

$$\text{At } q^* = 1300/14, \; P^* = 15 - (0.05)\left(\frac{1300}{14}\right)$$

$$P^* = \$10.36$$

So we see that a \$1/unit tax causes sales to drop from 100 to approximately 93 and price to rise from \$10 to \$10.36.

• PROBLEM 18-30

Y Corporation, a manufacturing entity, has the following profit function:

$$\pi = - \$10{,}000 + \$400Q - \$2Q^2$$

where π = Total profit and Q is output in units

a) What will happen if output is zero?

b) At what output level is profit maximized?

Solution: a) If output is zero, the company will incur a loss of \$10,000 since fixed costs are \$10,000. To show this, solve the profit function for Q = 0 as follows:

$$\pi = -\$10{,}000 + \$400(0) - \$2(0)^2$$

$$= -\$10{,}000 + 0 - 0$$

$$\pi = -\$10{,}000$$

b) The maximum profit level can be found by finding the derivative of the function

$$\frac{d\pi}{dQ},$$

setting this derivative equal to zero and then determining the resulting value of Q, as follows:

$$\frac{d\pi}{dQ} = 400 - 4Q$$

$$400 - 4Q = 0$$

$$-4Q = -400$$

$$Q = 100.$$

Therefore, when Q = 100, profit is maximized.

• PROBLEM 18-31

Given the following graph, explain why a firm in perfect competition would remain in production in the short run even though the prevailing market price is less than average total costs (ATC).

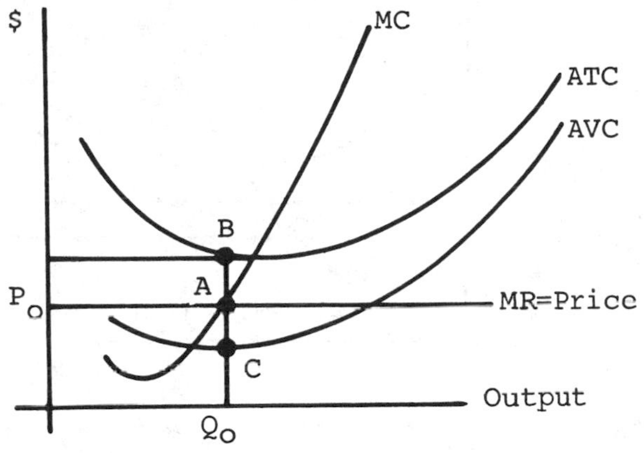

Solution: Theory tells us that in order to maximize profits, a firm should produce the output at which Marginal Cost = Marginal Revenue. On the graph above, Marginal Cost intersects Marginal Revenue at point A. Therefore the firm would produce the output, Q_o, corresponding to point A.

However, at this output Average Total Cost is less than Price. Since Total Revenue ≡ (Price x Quantity), and Total Cost ≡ (ATC x Quantity), Total Cost exceeds Total Revenue. Therefore the firm will incur a loss.

Yet the firm will continue operations. The reason is that price is still greater than AVC (Average variable costs) at output Q_o, So (Price x Quantity) ≡ Total Revenue is greater than (AVC x Quantity) ≡ Total Variable Cost. The difference between AVC and ATC is fixed costs. (As output increases, fixed costs per unit of output, Average Fixed Costs (AFC), become smaller and the ATC and AVC curves come closer to one another). Since fixed costs have, by definition, already been incurred by the firm regardless of the level of output, the fact that only a portion of them are being covered by the firm's revenue is not relevant to the firm's (future) choice of output. At output Q_o, variable costs are completely covered (price lies above AVC) and fixed costs are partially covered. Were the firm to shut down, there would be no variable costs but no revenue either, and fixed costs would not be covered at all. Even though the firm is operating at a loss, it is minimizing its loss by remaining in operation and producing an output, Q_o at which MC = MR, and at which the excess of Total Revenue (Price x Q_o) over Total Variable Cost (AVC x Q_o) is greatest, because the difference between Price and AVC is greatest.

• PROBLEM 18-32

Given the following curves, explain why a firm would remain in operation in the short run if price was at MR_1, but would shut down if price was at MR_2.

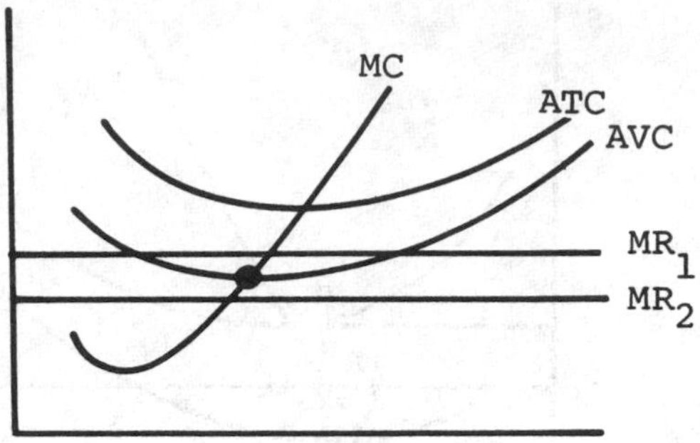

Solution: Notice that both MR_1 and MR_2 hover about the intersection point of MC and AVC. It is this point, the minimum value of AVC, which decides whether a plant will remain open or shut down. The critical thing to remember here is that there are two types of costs: fixed and variable. Whether production is undertaken or not, the fixed costs must be paid. Therefore if we have MR_1, we will produce even though price (MR_1) < ATC. We see from the graphs that in this situation, price > AVC. Therefore all variable costs plus a portion of fixed costs are being paid by revenue. The actual loss is equal to the portion of fixed costs not paid by revenue. Were the firm to shut down, the actual loss would equal all of total fixed costs. Therefore it is more profitable to remain in operation.

In the second situation, MR_2 not only lies below ATC but also lies below AVC. Therefore since price < AVC, not even the variable costs of the firm are being met by staying in operation. Therefore if operation continues, the loss will equal fixed costs plus a portion of variable costs. Under these conditions, a firm would shut down, and face a loss equal only to its fixed costs.

• PROBLEM 18-33

Given the curves in figure 1, explain the effect of a per-unit tax on the graphs of MC, ATC, and AVC.

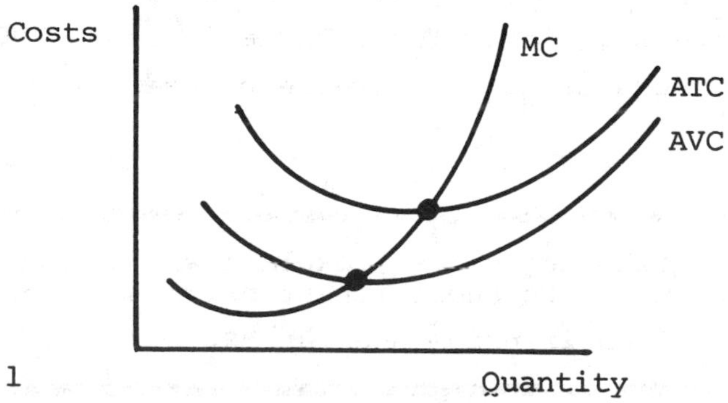

Fig. 1

Solution: To solve this problem, note that the tax is imposed on each unit of production. This means that the graphs shown, MC, AVC and ATC, would change by a constant amount throughout. At each quantity costs would increase by the amount of the per-unit tax, as shown in Figure 2.

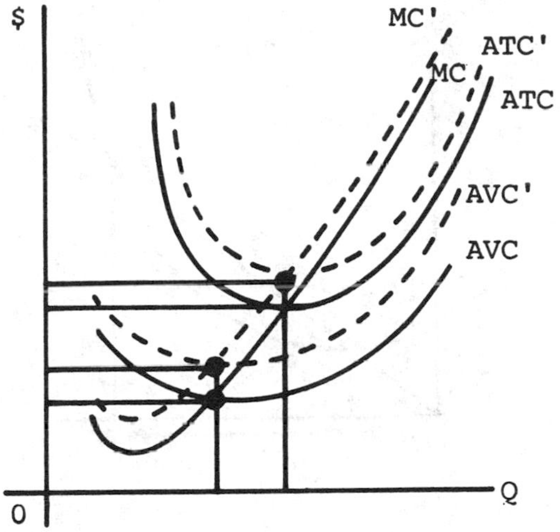

Fig. 2

That is, the distance between MC and MC', ATC and ATC', or AVC and AVC' are all the same, exactly the amount of the per unit tax. Notice that since the curves have been shifted only upward, the minimum Average Cost point will occur at exactly the same quantity produced as before. The only difference is that Average Cost per unit will be higher, by the amount of the per unit tax.

• PROBLEM 18-34

Given, in figure 1, the total cost and total revenue curves for a perfectly competitive firm,

a) Explain why total revenue is a straight line.

b) Show the range where profits can be realized.

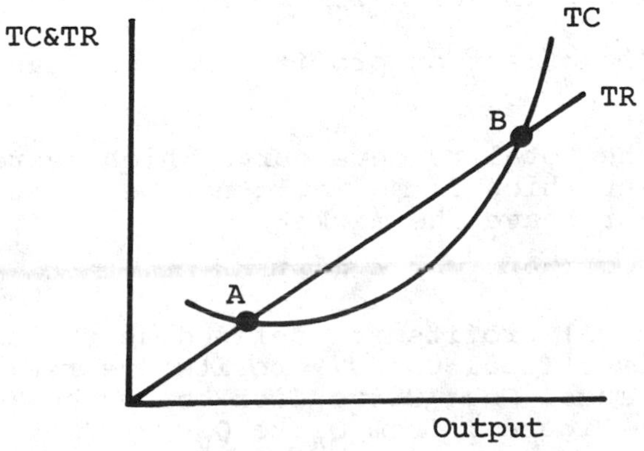

Fig. 1

Solution: a) We know from theory that under perfect competition, the demand curve faced by a firm is horizontal, i.e., the price that the market will pay is constant. Total revenue (TR) is defined as price x quantity, and since price is constant, TR = cQ, where c = P. We can see that this equation is a straight line with slope = c.

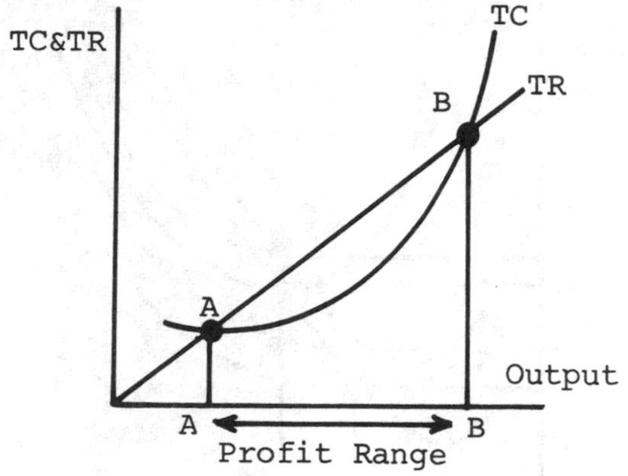

Fig. 2

b) Profits will be realized as long as TR $\geq$ TC. When TR = TC, we say that the firm is realizing a normal profit. We also call this the break-even point. Looking at the graph we see that TC = TR (the two graphs intersect) at points A and B. In the interval between points A and B, TR > TC. Therefore, the firm is realizing excess profits here. At any point to the left of A or to the right of B, TC > TR. So at these points, the company would incur a loss.

Therefore the range of profits is from Output = A to Output = B, as shown in figure 2.

• PROBLEM 18-35

Given the Total Cost and Total Revenue curves in Figure A for a perfectly competitive firm,

a) show the point of maximum profits.

b) show the effect on profits of a decrease in the market price.

c) show the total revenue curve which represents the market price at which firms would not be encouraged to either enter or leave the market.

Solution: a) Profits are defined as the excess of Total Revenue over Total Cost. Profits are realized everywhere that the Total Cost Curve lies below the Total Revenue curve, in Figure 1 from Q_A to Q_B.

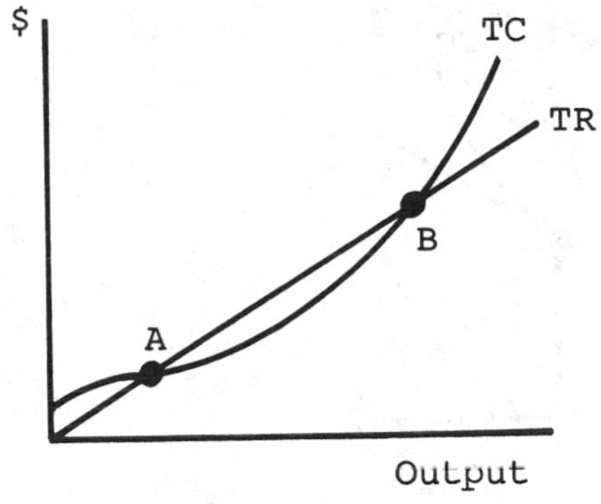

Fig. A

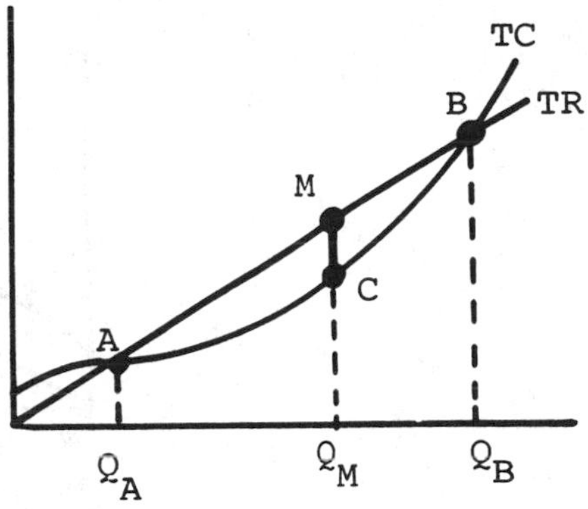

Fig. 1

The maximum profit point would occur at that quantity where the distance between TC and TR is the greatest. In Figure 1 this occurs at Q_M, where the value of the excess profit is represented by the length of the line from M to C. (Note, that a tangent to TC drawn at Q_M is parallel to TR. This represents the MC = MR profit maximizing condition.)

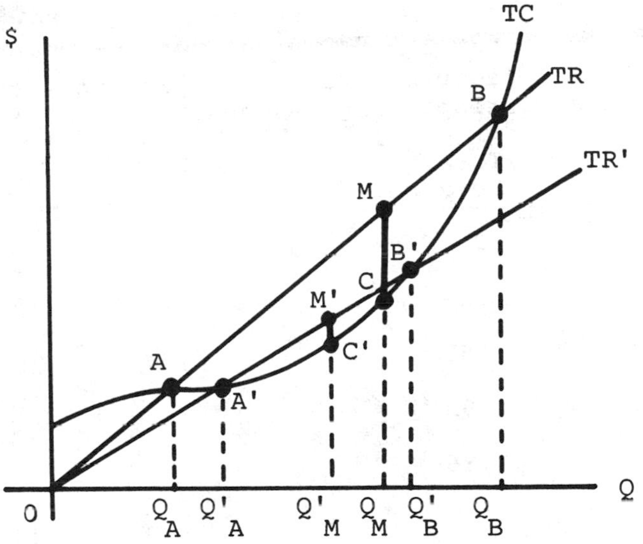

Fig. 2

b) The market price is shown in this diagram as the value of the slope of the TR curve. A decrease in the market price will decrease the value of the slope of TR resulting in TR' in Figure 2. Note that the range over which profits can be made shrinks to Q_A' to Q_B'. Also note the maximum profit point shifts to the left, to Q_M' and that the value of the maximized excess profits, M' to C', is less.

c) A market price where firms would not be encouraged to either enter or leave the market would occur where neither economic profits nor losses were being incurred. This would

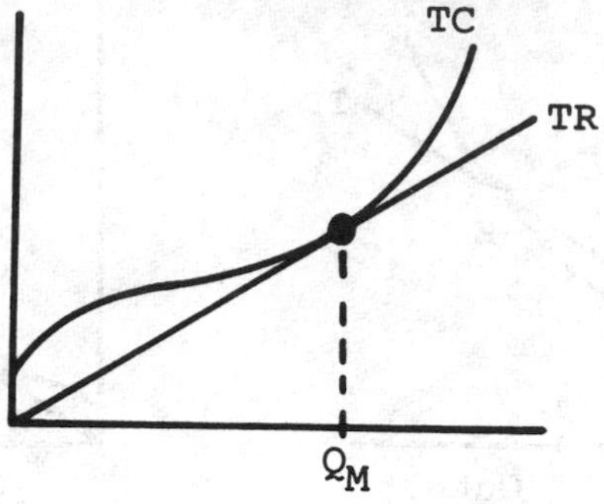

Fig. 3

occur where the TC curve was never below the TR curve and the TR curve was never above the TC curve. That is, where TR and TC just touch at one point, as shown in Figure 3.

The market price in this situation is the value of the slope of the TR curve.

• PROBLEM 18-36

Mr. White, a manufacturer, has the following record of output and its corresponding revenue.

Units of Output	Total Revenue
0	\$ 0
1	19
2	52
3	93
4	136
5	175
6	210
7	217
8	208

Compute the

a) Marginal Revenue

b) Average Revenue

Solution:

Units of Output (1)	Total Revenue (2)	Marginal Revenue (3)	Average Revenue (4)
0	$ 0	$ 0	-
1	19	19	19
2	52	33	26
3	93	41	31
4	136	43	34
5	175	39	35
6	210	35	35
7	217	7	31
8	208	-9	26

Marginal revenues are computed as follows:

Marginal revenues = MR's = change (Δ) in revenue

= $0 - $0 = $0

= 19 - 0 = 19

= 52 - 19 = 33

= 93 - 52 = 41

= 136 - 93 = 43

= 175 - 136 = 39

= 210 - 175 = 35

= 217 - 210 = 7

= 208 - 217 = -9

Average revenues are obtained as follows:

Average revenues = Total revenue ÷ Units of Output

= $0/0 = 0

= $19/1 = $19

= $52/2 = 26

= $93/3 = 31

= $136/4 = 34

= $175/5 = 35

$= \$210/6 = 35$

$= \$217/7 = 31$

$= \$208/8 = 26$

The interpretation of the above computations is that since the marginal revenue of the eighth unit is negative, revenues are reduced if output is raised to that level. Thus, maximization of revenue occurs at the point where the marginal relationship shifts from positive to negative.

LONG RUN INDUSTRY EQUILIBRIUM

• PROBLEM 18-37

The current equilibrium point for Astro Corporation's main product, commodity A, is P_M and Q_M, as shown in the Figure 1. S_1 S_2 and S_3 each represent relevant supply curves for A, where the only difference in calculating the curves is the length of time which Astro has to actually produce and ship more or less A to the market. Which curve, S_1, S_2 or S_3 corresponds to Astro's supply of A to the market for any given a) day b) month or c) year?

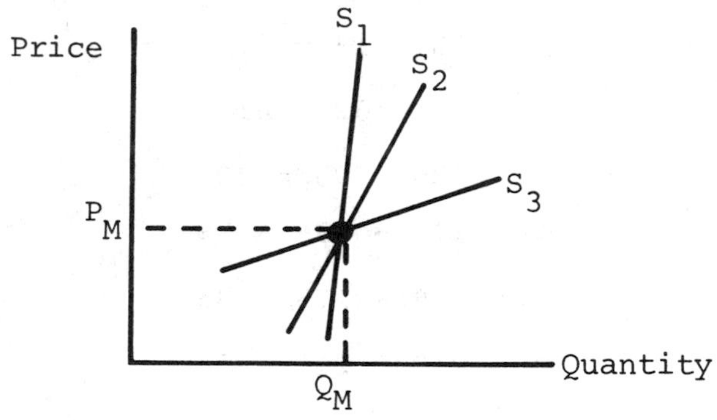

Fig. 1

Solution: This question is asking how the time span considered when calculating a supply curve will affect the slope of that curve. That is, how will the time frame under consideration effect the costs of increasing or decreasing the producer's quantity supplied to the market. The solution to this problem lies in realizing that changing the quantity supplied to the market means changing current production procedures and that the costs involved in changing even the most easily varied costs of production are much higher in the very short run then they are when a longer time frame is considered. Therefore, in response to a change in market price, a firm which is maximizing its profits, setting Price = Marginal Cost, would change its output least in the short run and most in the long run. That is, since Marginal Cost varies with output most (is the steepest) in the short run, as costs vary with output most quickly, the producer's response in terms of output changes to any change in the market price will be much less than it would be in the long run where Marginal Cost changes more slowly; is flatter.

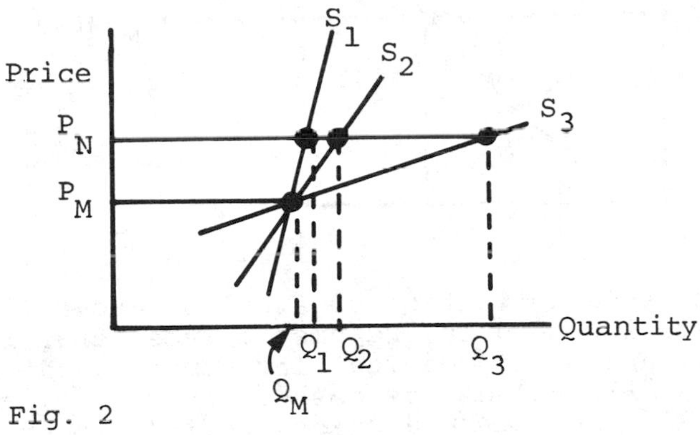

Fig. 2

To decide which of S_1 S_2 or S_3 corresponds to a larger or shorter time span, consider an increase in the market price from P_M to P_N in figure 2. Q_1, Q_2 and Q_3 show the new quantities supplied by Astro as scheduled by S_1, S_2 and S_3 respectively. Note that as P_N rises, S_1 shows the smallest response, indicating that it reflects the highest costs involved with changing the level of production. Therefore S_1 corresponds to the shortest-run considered, Astro's supply to the market for any given day. S_3 shows the greatest response, reflecting the lowest costs incurred by changing the level of output. Therefore, Astro's supply to the market for any given year is S_3. Similarly, S_2 shows Astro's supply to the market for the intermediate case, for one month.

• PROBLEM 18-38

Economists claim that the equilibrium position of each firm in a perfectly competitive industry in industry equilibrium can be pictured as in the diagram.

Notice that at the equilibrium market price Average Revenue per unit is exactly equal to Average Cost per unit. This means that AR x Q_M is exactly equal to AC x Q_M, which means that Total Revenue is the same as Total Cost. Since Costs and Revenues are exactly the same here, this means that there are no profits. Why would any producer stay in business if there are no profits to be gained from doing so?

Solution: The solution to this problem lies in recalling

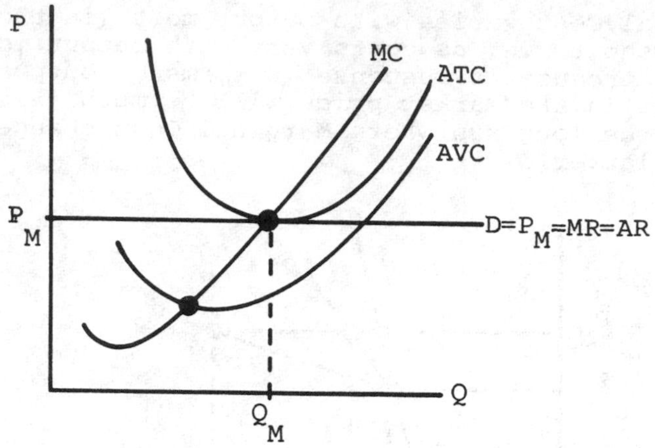

the economist's definition of Profits. So-called normal profits are included in the cost curves, that is, the owner's salary, return on his capital investments and entrepreneurial skills are all included as costs. Therefore, what the layman normally considers a "nice profit", to the economist, is a cost of the firm. The Total Profit obtained by subtracting Total Costs from Total Revenues (TR - TC) is known as "excess-profits". Under perfect competition, these excess profits are competed away, but the normal profits remain, keeping the firm in the market.

• PROBLEM 18-39

Given the set of cost curves in figure 1, for one firm in an industry, what will probably happen to the number of firms in this industry?

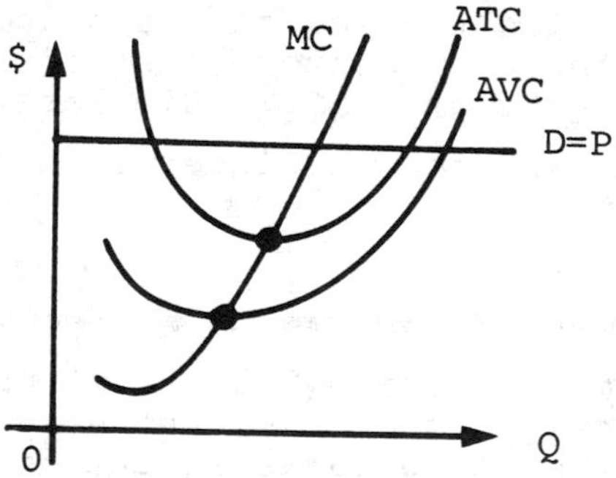

Fig. 1

Solution: Recall that the number of firms entering or leaving a particular market will most likely be affected by the profits or losses incurred by firms already in the market. With this in mind, the way to solve this problem is to decide whether the representative producer, whose cost curves are given in the problem, is incurring a loss or a profit.

Using Figure 2, since this producer is a perfect competitor, he will set P_R = MC at R and produce the quantity Q_A. The area of the rectangle OP_RRQ_A represents the pro-

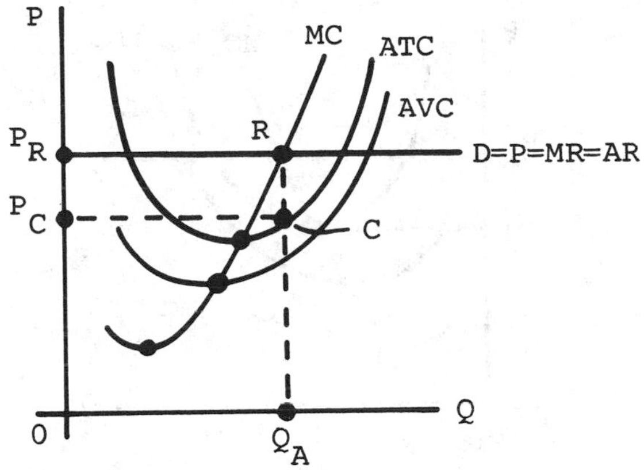

Fig. 2

ducers total revenue. That is, P x Q or here, $P_R \times Q_A$ which is equal to the rectangle OP_RRQ_A, is total revenue. Total Cost can be determined by multiplying Average Cost per unit times the quantity produced, AC x Q. Here, that is $P_C \times Q_A$ or the area of the rectangle OP_CCQ_A. Total revenue minus total cost is total profit, so rectangle OP_RRQ_A minus rectangle OP_CCQ_A leaves rectangle P_RRCP_C. This area shows the value of total profit, which here, since total revenue is greater than total cost, is positive. That is, this producer is incurring a profit rather than a loss. Since excess profits by those already in the market will tend to draw new producers into the market, it can be expected that the number of producers in the market shown in this problem will increase.

• PROBLEM 18-40

Given the set of cost curves in Figure A, which represents costs and demand to one small firm, it can be determined that since the market price P_R is greater than the minimum cost of producing each unit, P_M, the number of firms in the market is likely to increase. If the costs to this producer do not change, how will the number of firms in the market affect this single manufacturer's production decisions?

Solution: This question is asking you to determine what in the diagram given will be changed by an increase in the number of producers in the market. Such an increase in producers might cause the availability of raw materials to decrease. This would be reflected by a rise in the price of these raw materials. This, however, would change the costs to the producer, a situation which the problem states need not be considered for this problem. Given that the cost curves are unchanged, the only element left in the diagram which could change the manufacturer's production decisions would be the demand curve. The solution to this problem

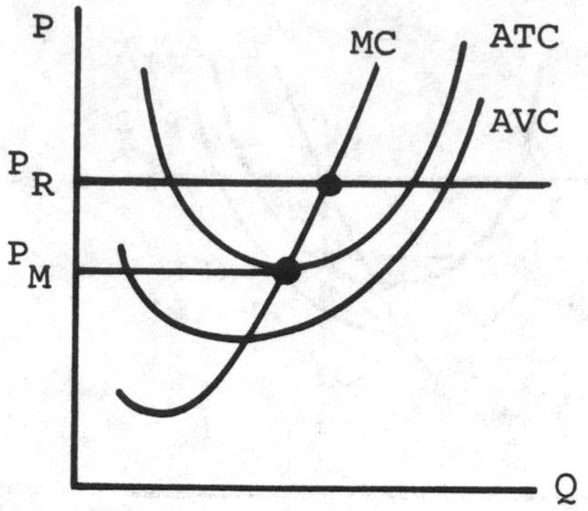

Fig. A

lies in recognizing that while the demand curve to a single producer is horizontal, market demand, for the quantity produced by all producers taken together is a downward sloping curve.

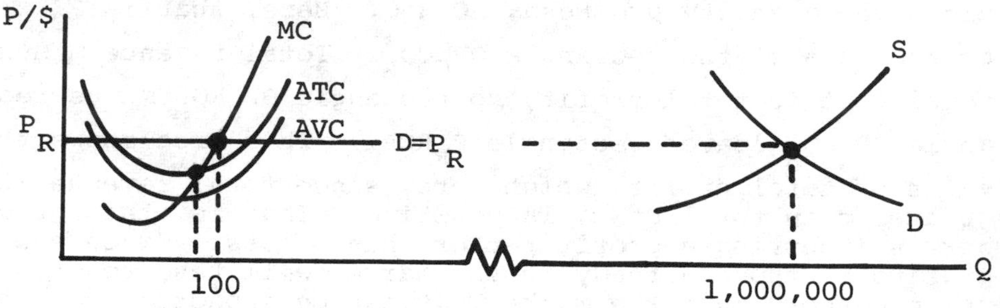

Fig. 1

As shown in Figure 1 each manufacturer is producing 100 units at price P_r. But this price, P_R was set by the interaction of market demand, D_M, and market supply, S_M. That is, in Figure 1, equilibrium for the entire market was reached at price P_R where quantity 1,000,000 units was produced.

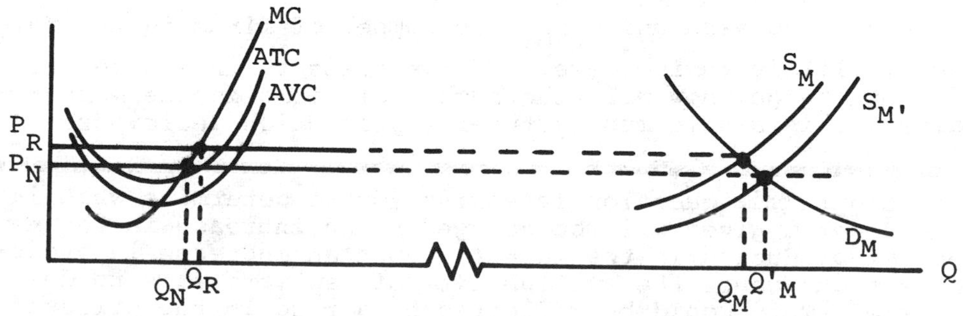

Fig. 2

Now, if excess profits by manufacturers already in the market draws new manufacturers into the market, then market supply, S_M would shift outward to S_M' as shown in Figure 2. This would result in a new equilibrium market price, P_N. Looking at the representative manufacturer, this new price level, P_N will cause the individual manufacturer to supply less, in Figure 2, quantity Q_N, even though the entire market has increased the amount it is supplying from Q_M to Q'_M. Thus, with an influx of new producers, assuming no change in costs, each of the manufacturers will supply less of the product to the market, in response to the new lowered market price. This decrease in Quantity produced will lower TR and, eventually, profits will be competed away for the industry.

• PROBLEM 18-41

Suppose an economy possesses presently 60 million automobiles; and that each automobile must be replaced every 5 years.

Suppose also that the present population of 240 million people grows 2% per year.

Calculate on the basis of these data, all other things remaining equal, the expected demand for automobiles for this year.

Solution: The total demand for automobiles consists of the replacement demand plus the new demand for automobiles. In terms of investment in the capital stock of automobiles, the gross investment consists of the replacement investment plus the net investment: gross investment = replacement + net investment. Of the existing stock of automobiles, $\frac{1}{5}$ = 20% must be replaced each year. (If each automobile had to be replaced every 10 years, only $\frac{1}{10}$ = 10% should be replaced each year.) In this year, therefore, 0.20 x 60 million = 12 million automobiles should be replaced.

The present population numbers 240 million people and grows 2% per year. Thus this year there is a net addition to population of 0.02 x 240 = 4.8 million persons. The present 240 million persons possess 60 million automobiles; that is on average one automobile per every 4 persons.

If all other things remain equal, it may be expected that this ratio of the number of automobiles to the number of persons also holds for the new contingent of 4.8 million persons. Thus, these additional 4.8 million persons will demand $\frac{4.8}{4}$ = 1.2 million new automobiles. (This process of expansion of the capital stock by an increasing population, with a constant capital/labor ratio (=1/4), is called "capital widening".)

On the basis of the calculations it may, therefore, be expected that there will be a total demand for new automobiles of 12 million (to be replaced) + 1.2 million (additional) = 13.2 million automobiles.

• PROBLEM 18-42

Differentiate economies from diseconomies of scale and give its point of reference.

Solution: Economies of scale occur when a firm experiences a more than proportionate increase in its output as a result of increasing all of its factor inputs. For example, if a firm were to double all its inputs-labor, capital (including material inputs), land- with the result that its output more than doubled, this would indicate economies of scale. Likewise, diseconomies of scale exist if a firm experiences a less than proportionate increase in output when it increases all of its factor inputs. In such a case, a firm that doubles all its inputs finds that it produces less than twice as much as its previous output.

Economies and diseconomies of scale relate to single plant firms or to individual plants owned by firms that operate more than a single plant. A plant in this respect, is a factory or other production complex in some particular geographic location. It may be included in a single building or a large number of buildings spread over several acres. A firm may operate only one plant or a number of plants. For example, large U.S. firms in the bread industry typically operate regional plants, while it is unusual for even the largest firms in the tool industry to operate more than a single plant. Economies and diseconomies of scale refer to expansions of a single plant rather than to expansions of a firm into more plants than it operated originally.

• PROBLEM 18-43

State one important reason why Smith's principle of the "invisible hand" does not assure the "perfect functioning," without government intervention, of the U.S. economy today.

Solution: For Smith's principle of the "invisible hand" to be completely effective there must be perfect competition. Perfect competition means that no supplier of any good or service is so large, in comparison to the market for the good or service in question, that the price of the good or service will be affected by the supplier's withholding his share from the market. As thus defined, perfect competition exists in few, if any, sectors of the U.S. economy today.

Where markets are not perfectly competitive, the benefits resulting from Smith's principle may still be realized if government intervenes in the market in order to create conditions or results approximating those of perfect competition. For example, antitrust laws attempt to prevent the acquisition or exercise of monopoly power in most industries. Where monopolies are deemed necessary (for example, public utilities), government attempts to create results approximating those of perfect competition through regulation of price and service.

• PROBLEM 18-44

What is meant by the exclusion principle? How does this relate to the concept of externalities? What effect do externalities have on the operation of the market?

Solution: The exclusion principle refers to a situation in which the owner of a good or service can prevent others from deriving satisfaction from it. For example, the owner at a zoo can erect a fence to prohibit people from enjoying it without paying him.

An example of a non-exclusive good is national defense. If a multi-billion dollar missile system is implemented, it is theoretically and practically not possible to exclude any citizens from the security it provides.

An example of a non-exclusive "bad" imposing costs on others is pollution. When a factory discharges wastes into a river, all users of the river must suffer its ill effects as it is difficult to isolate the polluters among the users from the non-polluters.

Both of these examples involve externalities--benefits or costs imposed on persons who do not share in the cost or benefit of the good itself. In such a case, the market operates inefficiently since the price of the good providing the externality fails to take into account the total cost or benefit of the good. Hence the price of national defense will be overstated (it is more valuable than its cost reflects) while that of the good which caused the pollution will be understated (it is less valuable, taking into account the cost of the pollution, than its price reflects).

• PROBLEM 18-45

Suppose consumers are willing to pay up to $20 for a burglar alarm, and will buy more alarms the lower the price is. If no alarms are supplied at a price of $20, does this mean that the price mechanism and consumer sovereignty must have broken down?

Solution: This situation, where consumers are willing to buy at a price of $20, but nobody is willing to sell at a price of $20, is fully compatible with the workings of the price mechanism and consumer sovereignty. Consumer sovereignty simply means that consumers decide the types and quantities of goods produced, as long as the firms producing these goods can make normal profits. If firms cannot make normal profits in selling a product at a price acceptable to consumers, they will not produce the product. If firms cannot make alarms at a cost less than $25 per alarm, and consumers are only willing to pay $20 per alarm, firms have no incentive to produce burglar alarms. They will lose money if they do so. Consumer sovereignty requires that firms produce only if they can make at least normal profits.

If no alarms are supplied because of cost considerations, then this situation is completely consistent with the operation of the price mechanism. The price system sets guidelines for allocational efficiency, and creates incentives for firms and individuals to follow the guidelines. In this case, the price system shows that the value society places on burlar alarms ($20) is less than the value society places on the resources expended in making alarms (say, $25). So, it would be inefficient from a societal perspective to produce burglar alarms. It would be more efficient to use the resources to produce something that society values more highly (say, fire alarms for which buyers will pay $30 each). The fact that no burglar alarms are supplied at a price of $20 shows that the price system has created incentives for firms not to produce them at a price of $20. The incentive (or disincentive) is simple: any firm that produces this good will lose money in doing so. The fact that a good is not produced, even though there is some demand for it, can be fully consistent with the functioning of the price mechanism.

In both of the explanations offered, it was assumed that the costs of production exceeded the price. Consumer sovereignty and the price system can only explain the result if this is the case. If burglar alarms can be produced at less than $20 per alarm, then these explanations are invalid. This does not mean that the concepts of Consumer sovereignty and the pricing mechanism are invalid; it just means that some distortions (government restraints, immobility of resources, etc.) have disrupted the explanations based on these concepts (concepts which are valid in pure capitalism). The example in the question cannot refute either of the two concepts. If the costs of production are over $20 per alarm, the concepts can explain the result. If the costs of production are under $20 per alarm, then there are distortions which merely limit the applicability of the two concepts.

Answer
To be covered when testing yourself

SHORT ANSWER QUESTIONS FOR REVIEW

Choose the correct answer.

1. The break even point for a perfectly competitive firm that is maximizing profits occurs where the price equals (a) the minimum point on the ATC curve (b) Marginal Cost (c) Marginal Revenue (d) Average Revenue (e) all of the above, simultaneously. — e

2. The supply curve of a firm in perfect competition is the same thing as (a) its entire Average Cost curve (b) the rising segment of its Average Cost curve (c) that part of the Total Cost curve in which Total Cost rises or remains constant as output increases (d) the rising segment of its Marginal Cost Curve, above Average Variable Cost (e) none of the above. — d

3. If a firm must sell its product at the market price, whatever that price may be, and wants to earn as much profit as that price makes possible, it should: (a) try to sell all the output it can produce (b) never let Marginal Cost rise up to the market price, since this is the point where profits reach zero (c) try to produce and sell that quantity of output at which Marginal Cost has risen to equality with price (d) always produce where Average Costs are lowest (e) always produce where Marginal Costs have reached a minimum. — c

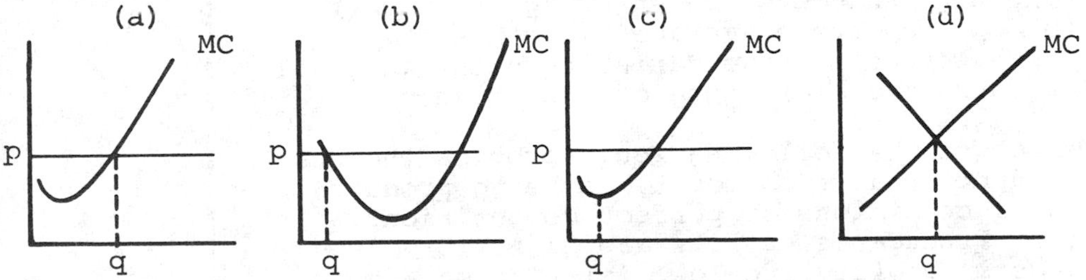

4. Which of the accompanying diagrams accurately indicates the level of output which a profit maximizing supplier in a perfectly competitive industry will produce, given that he produces a positive amount? (a) a (b) b (c) c (d) d (e) none of these represent accurately how a perfect competitor would react. — a

5. If a perfectly competitive firm finds that

at its best possible operating position, Total Revenue is not sufficient to cover Total Variable Costs, it should: (a) increase the price that it's charging (b) decrease the price that it's charging (c) increase the quantity that it's producing (d) decrease the quantity that it's producing (e) go out of business. e

6. Which of the following would occur if a single farm in pure competition lowered its price for wheat below the equilibrium market price for wheat? (a) All other farms would lower their wheat prices. (b) This farm would increase its market share of wheat, which would lead to higher profits. (c) Other farms would be driven out of the industry. (d) This farm would receive lower Total Profits than it would have if it had sold all of its wheat at the market price. (e) Most other farmers would switch over to corn. d

7. The industry's long run supply curve: (a) is the sum of all member firms' Total Cost Curves (b) is the sum of all member firms long-run Marginal Cost Curves (c) is the sum of all member firms long-run Average Cost Curves (d) is found by adding horizontally all the short-run Marginal Cost curves of member firms (e) is not properly described by any of the above. b

8. It will sometimes pay for a firm to operate at a loss under pure competition so long as (a) new producers are entering the market (b) price covers Average Fixed Costs (c) price covers Average Variable Costs (d) all of the above (e) none of the above. e

9. Which of the following would provide the best evidence that a commodity is being produced under conditions of perfect competition? (a) Producer's profits are high. (b) Producers' profits are low. (c) The market is very large. (d) The total supply curve is highly inelastic. (e) The demand curve facing any one producer is infinitely elastic. e

10. If prices fall in a perfectly competitive industry, the firms in the industry in the short run will: (a) not decrease in number (b) keep output at the same level but make losses (c) try to reduce production or

SHORT ANSWER QUESTIONS FOR REVIEW

	Answer To be covered when testing yourself
shut down (d) advertise (e) none of the above.	c
11. In a market economy, the price system reacts to an oversupply of a commodity by: (a) raising the price and the producer's profits (b) lowering the price and the producer's profits (c) lowering the price but raising the producer's profits (d) raising the price but lowering producer's profits (e) keeping output the same but lowering producers' profits.	b
12. Which of the following is compatible with a firm in a purely competitive market? (a) The firm will advertise. (b) Marginal Cost is falling. (c) The firm is very large. (d) Demand to the producer is infinitely elastic at the prevailing price. (e) None of the above.	d
13. Which of the following is correct? (a) A supplier in a perfectly competitive market cannot influence the price of the commodity he sells. (b) A supplier in a perfectly competitive market cannot influence the costs of the commodity he sells. (c) A supplier in a perfectly competitive market will not sell all he can at the prevailing price in an attempt to drive up the market price. (d) A supplier in a perfectly competitive market is able to influence appreciably the market price for his commodity. (e) none of these are correct.	a
14. If a firm must sell its output at the going price and wants to earn as much profit as possible, it should not: (a) produce where Marginal Cost is equal to price (b) try to sell all the output it produces (c) produce where Marginal Cost is at its minimum (d) produce along the rising portion of its marginal cost curve (e) none of the above.	c
15. Under conditions of pure competition, the firm will maximize profits when: (a) price and marginal cost are rising (b) average fixed cost is falling (c) price and marginal cost are equated (d) average fixed cost and marginal cost are falling (e) none of the above	c
16. If all the firms in an industry which is char-	

SHORT ANSWER QUESTIONS FOR REVIEW

acterized by decreasing costs are changing to a price equal to Marginal Cost, an upward shift in demand, in the long run will (a) increase industry output and lower price (b) decrease industry output and raise price (c) alter neither industry output nor price (d) result in a much more complicated industry structure (e) do none of the above. a

17. The nature of the long-run supply curve of a constant-cost industry is: (a) perfectly inelastic (b) inelastic (c) elastic (d) upward sloping (e) perfectly elastic e

18. Price is constant or "given" to the individual firm in a purely competitive market because: (a) the firm's demand curve is down-sloping (b) of product differentiation, reinforced by advertising (c) each seller supplies a negligible fraction of total supply (d) there are no good substitutes for his product (e) it is a profit maximizing price. c

Fill in the blanks.

19. To get the __________ for a good, add horizontally all the supply curves of the independent producers of that good. market supply curve

20. __________ at any output level is the extra cost incurred by producing one additional unit of output. Marginal cost

21. To maximize profits, a perfect competitor should produce where the __________ is equal to __________. market price, marginal cost

22. A perfect competitor's supply curve is simply the rising portion of its __________ above Average Variable Costs. marginal cost curve

23. The break-even point for a perfectly competitive firm occurs where the price equals the minimum point on the __________ curve. Average Total Cost

24. The point where Total Revenue is just equal to Total Cost is called the __________ point. break-even

25. The __________ occurs at some critically low market prices, where the perfectly competi-

Answer
To be covered when testing yourself

tive firm just recovers its variable costs of producing. Below this price it will produce nothing. — shut-down point

26. (Increasing/Decreasing) Long-run Average Cost can lead to the break-down of perfect competition. — Decreasing

Determine whether the following statements are true or false.

27. Efficient allocation of resources calls for a perfectly flexible price pattern. — True

28. Marginal Cost is the cost to the firm which just breaks even at the current price. — False

29. A perfect competitor is one who can sell all he wants to at the prevailing market price. — True

30. A competitive firm should produce where it's Marginal Cost curve is at a minimum. — False

31. A competitive firm should always produce at the minimum point on its Average Total Cost curve. — False

32. We can add horizontally the supply curves of firms to get a market supply curve even for low prices, although in the short-run some firms will close down if they cannot cover their Fixed Costs. — True

33. Price and Marginal Revenue are identical for an individual purely competitive seller. — True

34. Under Pure Competition, nonprice competition is not ruled out. — False

35. Full employment minimum costs are just covered by normal price at equilibrium. — True

36. Abnormal losses would lower the Average Cost curve. — False

37. If, in the short-run, the firm's Average Variable Cost curve is initially downward sloping, then the firm's supply curve is initially downward sloping. — False

38. The long-run U-shaped Average Cost curve

SHORT ANSWER QUESTIONS FOR REVIEW

A

To b
when
yo

is derived by passing a curve through the minimum points of all associated short-run U-shaped Average Cost curves. — Fal

39. In the long-run, the industry's supply curve may reflect constant, increasing or decreasing costs. — True

40. MC equal to AC holds true for a profit maximizing competitive firm in long-run equilibrium. — True

41. The long-run supply curve for a purely competitive increasing cost industry will be upward-sloping. — True

42. If a competitive firm is producing at some level less than the profit maximizing output, we can conclude that Marginal Costs exceed Marginal Revenue. — Fals

SHORT ANSWER QUESTIONS FOR REVIEW

	Answer To be covered when testing yourself
tive firm just recovers its variable costs of producing. Below this price it will produce nothing.	shut-down point
26. (Increasing/Decreasing) Long-run Average Cost can lead to the break-down of perfect competition.	Decreasing
Determine whether the following statements are true or false.	
27. Efficient allocation of resources calls for a perfectly flexible price pattern.	True
28. Marginal Cost is the cost to the firm which just breaks even at the current price.	False
29. A perfect competitor is one who can sell all he wants to at the prevailing market price.	True
30. A competitive firm should produce where it's Marginal Cost curve is at a minimum.	False
31. A competitive firm should always produce at the minimum point on its Average Total Cost curve.	False
32. We can add horizontally the supply curves of firms to get a market supply curve even for low prices, although in the short-run some firms will close down if they cannot cover their Fixed Costs.	True
33. Price and Marginal Revenue are identical for an individual purely competitive seller.	True
34. Under Pure Competition, nonprice competition is not ruled out.	False
35. Full employment minimum costs are just covered by normal price at equilibrium.	True
36. Abnormal losses would lower the Average Cost curve.	False
37. If, in the short-run, the firm's Average Variable Cost curve is initially downward sloping, then the firm's supply curve is initially downward sloping.	False
38. The long-run U-shaped Average Cost curve	

Answer
To be covered when testing yourself

	is derived by passing a curve through the minimum points of all associated short-run U-shaped Average Cost curves.	False
39.	In the long-run, the industry's supply curve may reflect constant, increasing or decreasing costs.	True
40.	MC equal to AC holds true for a profit maximizing competitive firm in long-run equilibrium.	True
41.	The long-run supply curve for a purely competitive increasing cost industry will be upward-sloping.	True
42.	If a competitive firm is producing at some level less than the profit maximizing output, we can conclude that Marginal Costs exceed Marginal Revenue.	False

CHAPTER 19

MONOPOLY

Basic Attacks and Strategies for Solving Problems in this Chapter. See pages 697 to 728 for step-by-step solutions to problems.

A monopoly is defined as an industry composed of a single firm which sells a product with no close substitutes, with high barriers to entry. Because one firm is the industry, the market demand curve for the product is also the demand curve facing the industry.

There are industries called natural monopolies. They are typically characterized by average total cost curves that decline continuously over the full range of likely output for the industry. This means that one firm can produce the output demanded by the market more efficiently than several smaller firms, each producing lesser amounts. In fact, one firm is the only likely stable condition in the industry.

As in perfect competition, the most important issues in monopoly are the determination of the short run and long run equilibrium positions and an evaluation of long run equilibrium. In short run equilibrium, the profit-maximizing monopolist will produce the level of output where marginal revenue (MR) equals marginal cost (MC). At levels of output where $MR > MC$, the firm can add to its profits by producing more since additional units sold will add more to revenue than to costs. If $MR < MC$, the firm will reduce profits by producing more since additional units add more to cost than to revenue.

Since the demand curve facing the firm has a negative slope, the firm's marginal revenue curve lies below it. The profit-maximizing monopolist will charge the highest price possible for the level of output produced, meaning that the price charged will exceed *MR*.

In the short run, monopolists may make economic profits, but these are not guaranteed by any means. Short run losses are also a possibility. As in the case of perfect competition, the monopolist will continue to produce if losses occur but price exceeds average variable cost. The firm will shut down if price is less than average variable cost.

Typically, monopolists do not have to worry about entry in the long run if economic profits are being made. This means that economic profits can exist in long run equilibrium.

Most economists consider monopoly an undesirable market structure for several reasons. For one thing, monopolists are alleged to charge too high a price and produce too small a quantity. Since monopolists set $MR = MC$ and the price they charge exceeds MR, this means that they charge a price that exceeds MC. Since the price of the product is a measure of its value to society, and its MC is a measure of the cost to society of producing additional units, this means that additional units of output would provide a greater benefit to society than they would cost, but will not be produced because additional units would reduce the monopolist's profits. Second, having a protected market position means that monopolists are not under constant pressure to produce as efficiently as possible. Third, monopolists can earn economic profits in the long run.

An interesting problem is the effect of a tax on monopoly price, output, and profit. A "lump-sum" tax would have no effect on price and quantity. The profit maximizing price/quantity combination is unchanged by the presence or absence of this type of tax. The reason is because this tax has no effect on either demand or variable costs. It does affect fixed costs, but fixed costs are irrelevant for short run decision-making. The lump-sum tax would reduce monopoly profits dollar for dollar, however. A per-unit tax does not affect demand, but will raise variable costs. This will lead to a reduction in quantity and a consequent increase in product price. Monopoly profits will also be reduced, but here the consumer bears some of the burden.

When monopoly exists, a possibility is that price discrimination will be practiced. Price discrimination is the practice of selling a product at different prices to different people, when price differences are not justified by cost differences. There are three types of price discrimination. First-degree, or perfect, price discrimination occurs when consumers are charged the highest price they could possibly pay for each unit of the product, leading to the firm appropriating all the consumer's surplus for itself. Second-degree occurs when different prices are charged for blocks of the product. Third-degree occurs when markets are separated and different prices are charged in different markets.

Successful price discrimination will raise the profits of the discriminator, but there is a beneficial side-effect. Price discrimination will lead the monopolist to produce a greater quantity of output, potentially eliminating one of the objections to monopoly stated above. Price discrimination can only take place when the firm can identify separate markets and prevent resale between the different markets.

Step-by-Step Solutions to Problems in this Chapter, "Monopoly"

BASIC CONCEPTS

• **PROBLEM 19-1**

What is a monopoly?

Solution: A monopoly is a firm which is the sole producer of a good. A monopolist's power involves the control of the supply of this good to a degree sufficient to fix its price and prevent competition in its sale.

In a monopoly, since there is only one supplier, the industry's demand curve and the monopolist's demand curve are one and the same. In pure competition, industry demand is ordinarily downward-sloping while individual firm demand is perfectly elastic. Here the monopolist's (industry) demand curve is downward-sloping.

• **PROBLEM 19-2**

What are natural monopolies?

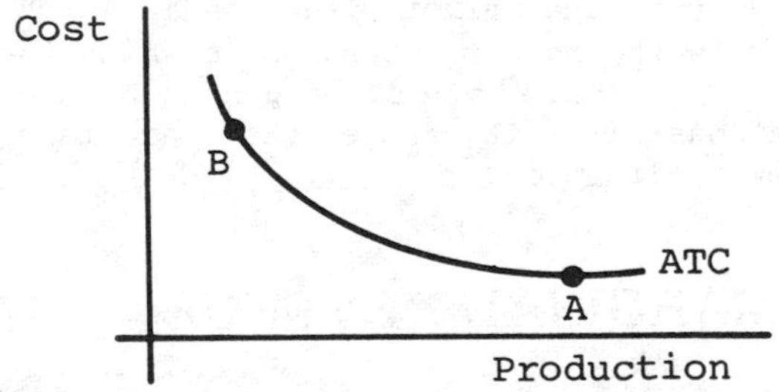

Solution: Natural monopolies are industries in which competition is impractical, inconvenient, or simply unworkable.

The primary reason justifying the existence and promotion of natural monopolies is the existence of economies of scale. In a natural monopoly, the average total cost curve will usually look something like the curve in the figure.

Suppose the curve represents ATC for an electric company in a large city, where by having one firm produce at point A, all demand is satisfied. Now suppose the city government decided to break up this natural monopoly into five smaller companies of equal sizes. This would place each of the five companies at point B on the average cost curve, which represents considerably higher average cost. Thus, by allowing natural monopolies to exist, an economy is able to produce at a lower cost.

Natural monopolies are also justified in some cases where competition would be very inconvenient. Suppose there were five telephone companies instead of just one. The streets would be lined with the various telephone company wires and confusion would ensue as people called outside of their own companies.

As a result of these considerations, the government will usually grant an exclusive franchise to a single firm when a tendency toward natural monopoly exists. Examples of this would be water, electricity, natural gas, and telephone service. However, in return for this gift of non-competition from the government, natural monopolies are subject to price control. This is necessary to prevent the natural monopolist from earning monopoly profits by restricting output and charging a high price.

• **PROBLEM 19-3**

What is bilateral monopoly?

Solution: Bilateral monopoly is a market situation in which a single seller faces a single buyer, i.e., the seller is a monopolist and the buyer is a monopsonist. In such a situation, bargaining takes place between buyer and seller, with each usually trying to maximize his individual wealth.

• **PROBLEM 19-4**

What is the difference between monopoly and monopsony?

Solution: Both words contain the part "mono" coming from the Greek word for "one". Monopoly is the market situation in which there is only one seller. Monopsony is the market situation in which there is only one buyer. The model of perfect competition cannot be used to explain either of these situations since it assumes there are many buyers and many sellers in a market situation.

DEMAND AND MARGINAL REVENUE

• **PROBLEM 19-5**

What is marginal revenue? How does the elasticity of demand affect marginal revenue?

Solution: Marginal revenue is defined as the change in total revenue that results from an increase in quantity demanded by one unit. Suppose we have the following excerpt from a company's demand schedule:

	Quantity demanded	Price
A.	8	$11
B.	9	$10

In case A, Total Revenue = Price x Quantity demanded = $11 x 8 = $88. In case B, Total Revenue = $10 x 9 = $90. Then since marginal revenue is the change in total revenue as quantity demanded increases by one unit, marginal revenue = $90 - $88 = $2.

One way to study elasticity of demand is in relation to total revenue. We saw when first considering demand elasticity, that if demand is elastic, total revenue increases as price falls. Now a falling price is equivalent to a rising quantity demanded (due to the downward-sloping nature of demand curves). Therefore if demand is elastic, total revenue will increase as quantity demanded increases and marginal revenue will be positive if demand is elastic.

Similarly, if demand is inelastic, total revenue decreases as price falls. Therefore total revenue decreases as quantity demanded is increased and marginal revenue is negative.

Finally, if demand is unitarily elastic, total revenue does not change as price is maneuvered. Therefore marginal revenue is zero.

• PROBLEM 19-6

Given the following demand schedule for a monopolistic firm, plot the demand curve and the marginal revenue curve.

Quantity	Price
1	$30.00
2	$26.75
3	$23.50
4	$20.25
5	$17.00
6	$13.75

Solution: To compute the marginal revenue, first find total revenue (price x quantity). Marginal revenue is equal to the change in total revenue as quantity is increased.

Quantity	Price	Total Revenue	Marginal Revenue
1	$30.00	$30.00	$30.00
2	$26.75	$53.50	$23.50
3	$23.50	$70.50	$17.00
4	$20.25	$81.00	$10.50
5	$17.00	$85.00	$ 4.00
6	$13.75	$82.50	$-2.50

To graph the demand and marginal revenue curves, we simply plot points, noticing that as quantity increases by 1, price decreases by $3.25 and marginal revenue decreases by $6.50. Therefore slope of demand = -3.25 and slope of marginal revenue = -6.50, (see Figure.)

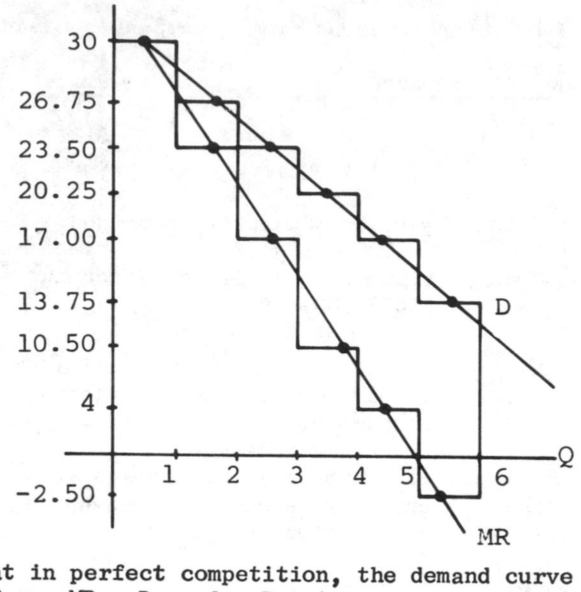

Remember that in perfect competition, the demand curve is a horizontal line; therefore, MR = Demand. But in monopoly, demand is downward-sloping, so MR is also downward-sloping, but with an even steeper slope.

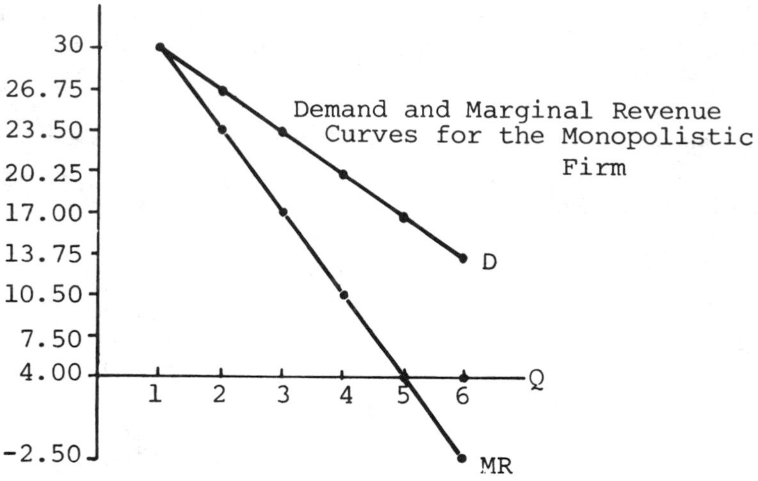

To see why MR is steeper than Demand, examine where they originate and examine the behavior of the two graphs. At Q = 0, TR = 0. Therefore at Q = 1, Price = TR = MR. But when Q > 1, price falls. And if price is falling, the new lower price must apply to all units sold. In our example at Q = 1, P = \$30.00, while at Q = 2, P = \$26.75. Now by selling 2 items, we gain \$26.75 from the sale of the second item, but lose \$3.25 (\$30.00 - \$26.75) on the first item which could have originally been sold for \$30.00. Therefore MR = \$26.75 - \$3.25 = \$23.50. This pattern will continue throughout the curves and MR will always be steeper than Demand.

• PROBLEM 19-7

Answer the following questions concerning the demand schedule below.

a. Complete the total-revenue, marginal-revenue, and average-revenue data:

Price	Quantity	Revenue: Total	Marginal	Average
20	2	40		20
19	3	57	+17	19
18	4	72	+15	18
17	5	-	-	-
16	6	-	-	-
15	7	-	-	-
14	8	-	-	-
13	9	-	-	-
12	10	-	-	-
11	11	-	-	-
10	12	-	-	-
9	13	-	-	-

b. What happens to the difference between selling price and marginal revenue?

Solution: a.

Price	Quantity	Revenue: Total	Marginal	Average
20	2	40		20
19	3	57	17	19
18	4	72	15	18
17	5	85	13	17
16	6	96	11	16
15	7	105	9	15
14	8	112	7	14
13	9	117	5	13
12	10	120	3	12
11	11	121	1	11
10	12	120	-1	10
9	13	117	-3	9

Marginal Revenue as shown above, is the rate of change in total revenue which results from the sale of one more unit of output.

Average Revenue is total revenue divided by its quantity.

b. The difference between selling price and marginal revenue goes to the purchasers as a lower price. For example, between a price of $18 and $19 with sales of four and three units, respectively, the marginal revenue, $15, is less than the average revenue, $18, by $3. This amount is distributed to buyers of the three units at $19 by charging a price $18, that is $1 lower than before (3 purchasers x $1 savings each = $3). We are assuming here that all purchasers pay the same price, i.e., no price discrimination exists.

• PROBLEM 19-8

Situation A represents pure competition. Situation B represents monopoly.

Situation A: Quantity demanded	Price	Situation B: Quantity demanded	Price
1	$2	1	$9

Situation A		Situation B	(contd.)
Quantity demanded	Price	Quantity demanded	Price
2	$2	2	$8
3	$2	3	$7
4	$2	4	$6

Draw the marginal revenue and demand curves for both situations, pointing out the differences shown between pure competition and monopoly.

Solution: To find the marginal revenue (MR), first find total revenue (TR) using the formula: TR = (Quantity Demanded) x (Price). From this, MR can be evaluated with the formula:

$$MR = \Delta TR$$

Reconstructing the table for Situation A,

Quantity		Price	TR	MR(= ΔTR)
1	(x)	$2	$2	
				$2
2	(x)	$2	$4	
				$2
3	(x)	$2	$6	
				$2
4	(x)	$2	$8	

Note that Price = MR = $2. Demand and MR are plotted on the graph in Figure 1, (note that they are the same line.)

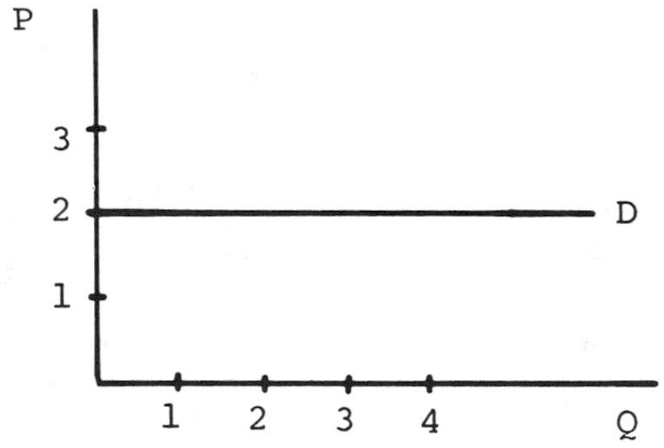

Fig. 1

Reconstructing the table for Situation B,

Quantity	Price	TR	MR
1	$9	$9	
			$7
2	$8	$16	
			$5
3	$7	$21	
			$3
4	$6	$24	

Here, Price ≠ MR and both are decreasing as quantity demanded increases. Plotting demand and MR on a graph, we get Figure 2.

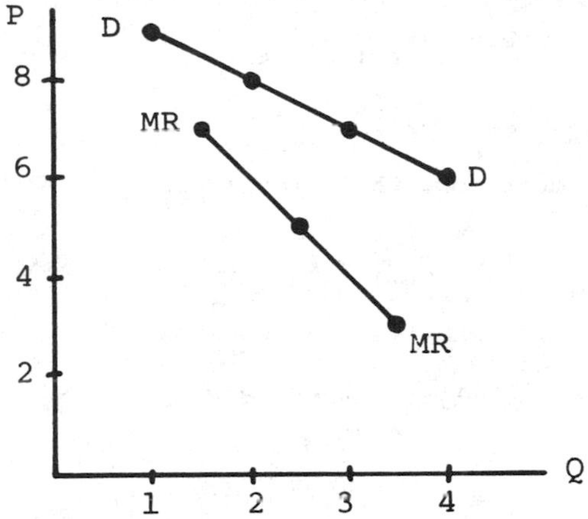

Fig. 2

Thus, under pure competition, Price = MR = Constant, and so, the demand curve is the same as the MR curve. But under monopoly, Price $\neq$ MR and both price and marginal revenue decrease as quantity demanded increases.

• PROBLEM 19-9

If demand is downward sloping, prove that marginal revenue is less than price, (see Figure.)

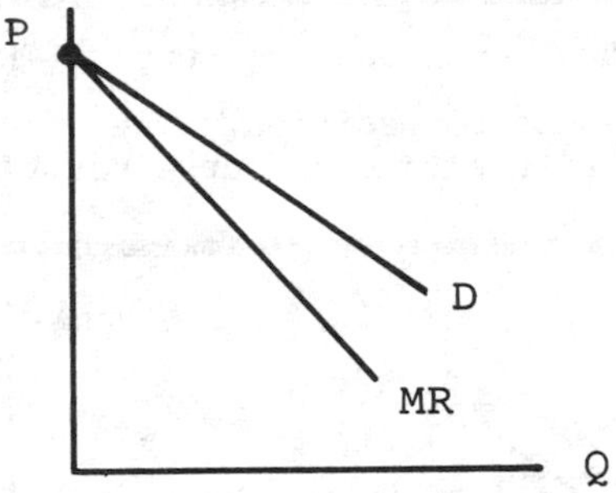

Solution: For the first unit sold, $MR_1 = P_1$ (as the intersection of MR and D shows in the graph.) But for the second unit sold, $q = q_2$, $P_2 < P_1$, due to the downward slope of the demand curve.

Therefore, since $TR_2 = 2P_2$ and $TR_1 = P_1$, $MR_2 = 2P_2 - P_1$.

Now we must show that $MR_2 < P_2$. Since

$$P_2 < P_1$$

$$P_2 + P_2 < P_1 + P_2$$

$$2P_2 < P_1 + P_2$$

$$2P_2 - P_1 < P_2$$

Substituting back, we get $MR_2 < P_2$

In general we wish to show that

$MR_{n+1} < P_{n+1}$, where $MR_{n+1} = TR_{n+1} - TR_n$

and

$TR_n = nP_n$ and $TR_{n+1} = (n+1)P_{n+1}$.

Therefore we must show that $(n+1)P_{n+1} - nP_n < P_{n+1}$

given that

$$P_{n+1} < P_n \text{ .}$$

We start off with what we want to show:

$$(n+1)P_{n+1} - nP_n < P_{n+1}$$

$$nP_{n+1} + P_{n+1} - nP_n < P_{n+1}$$

$$nP_{n+1} - nP_n < 0$$

$$nP_{n+1} < nP_n$$

$$P_{n+1} < P_n$$

Since we know from the downward shape of the demand curve that $P_{n+1} < P_n$, we have proven that $MR < P$.

• PROBLEM 19-10

Given in Figure 1 are two total revenue curves, TR_1 and TR_2. One describes a situation of pure competition. The other describes a monopoly. Determine which market situation each curve describes.

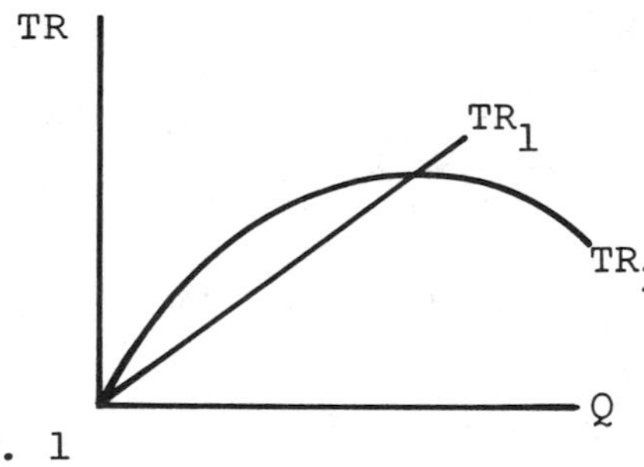

Fig. 1

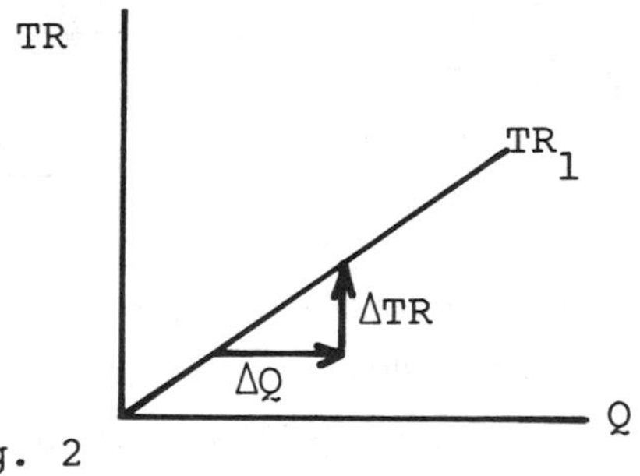

Fig. 2

Solution: Let us examine each of the two curves separately, first looking at TR_1, (see Fig. 2.) By definition the marginal revenue = $\Delta TR/\Delta Q$, which is the same as the slope of the TR-function. For TR_1 above, $MR_1 = \Delta TR_1/\Delta Q$ = constant since TR_1 is a straight line (constant slope). Therefore MR_1 is as plotted in Figure 3.

At this point, MR_1 should look familiar. It is in fact the marginal revenue curve which exists under pure competition where Price = Marginal Revenue = Demand = Constant.

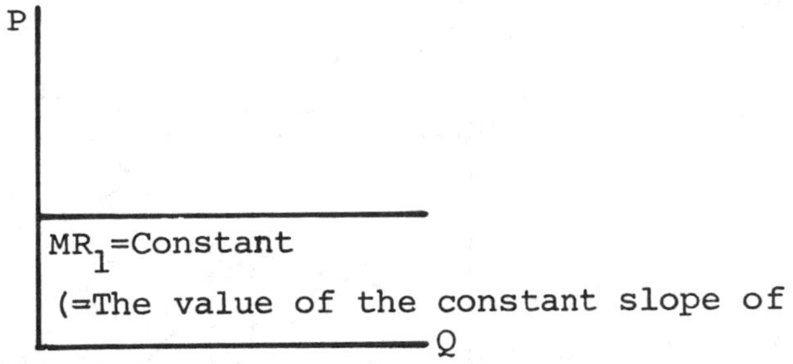

Fig. 3

Let us now examine TR_2 in Figure 4.

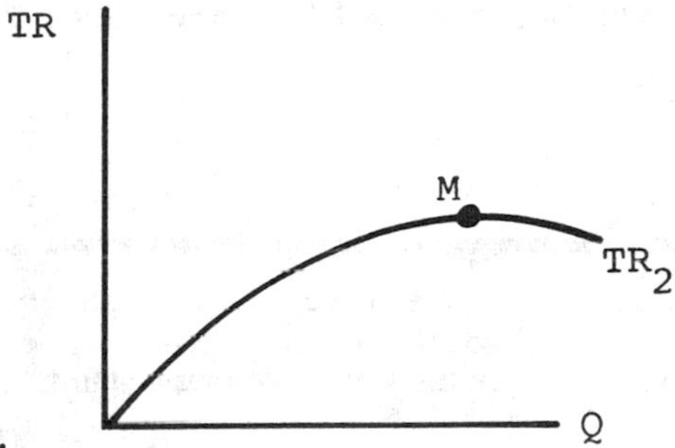

Fig. 4

In this situation total revenue is no longer linear, but rather assumes a parabolic shape. By examining the graph, note that as quantity increases, total revenue increases, but at a slower and slower rate until it reaches a point, M, after which total revenue actually starts to fall. Since TR is at first growing at a decreasing rate, and, beyond point M, it is falling as Q is increasing and since $TR = P \times Q$, then P must be falling as Q is increasing. Now, that is the same as saying that the demand curve is downward-sloping. So TR_2 describes a monopoly situation.

PROFIT MAXIMIZATION

• PROBLEM 19-11

Suppose a monopolist is currently producing at E_1. If he switches to E_2 what will be the effect on a) profit; b) total revenue, (see Figure.)

Solution: a) At E_1, the monopolist is selling Q_1 units which corresponds to the point of profit maximization, the intersection of the MC and MR curves. Therefore if the monopolist lowers price to P_2 or changes the price in either direction, profits will fall since he is already at his profit maximization point.
b) To see whether dropping the price from P_1 to P_2 will increase or decrease total revenue, examine the marginal revenue over this range. Since marginal revenue is a function of quantity demanded, consider its behavior as Q goes from Q_1 to Q_2. Notice that $MR > 0$ over that

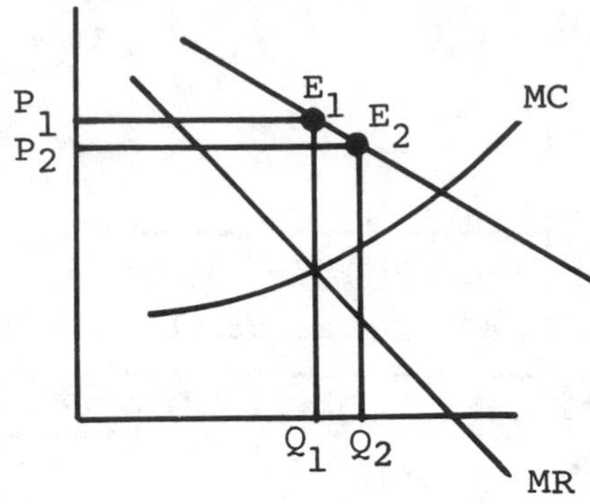

range. Therefore as the quantity sold is increased from Q_1 to Q_2, TR increases since $\Delta TR(MR) > 0$.

• PROBLEM 19-12

Suppose the graph shown in Figure 1 represents an industry with many buyers and many sellers. What would be the effect on equilibrium price and output of monopolizing this industry. (Assume that there are no changes in costs.)

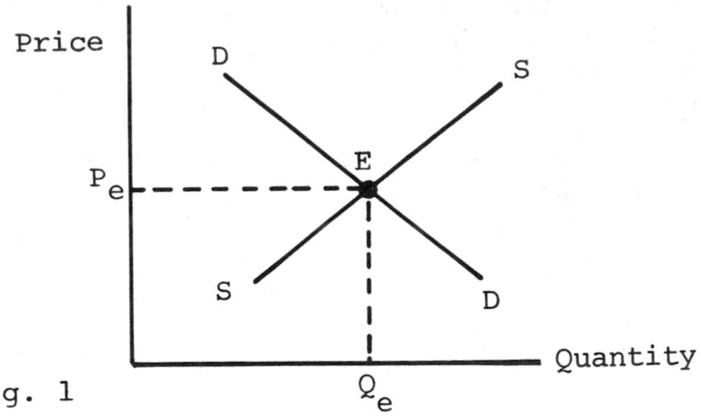

Fig. 1

Solution: Before monopolization, as shown in Figure 1, the market supply curve, SS, is composed of the summation of the individual supply curves of the firms in the industry. The equilibrium point is E, the intersection of SS and the market demand curve, DD. Equilibrium price would be P_e and equilibrium quantity would be Q_e.

As the industry suddenly becomes monopolized, we make the assumption that the only thing changing is that the monopolist now realizes that he faces the entire downward-sloping demand curve.

Before the change, each perfectly competitive supplier faced a horizontal demand curve and therefore a horizontal marginal revenue curve. For each supplier, the selling price was P_e and the sum of all the quantities sold by all of the competitors, was Q_e. Now, with monopolization, the monopolist faces the entire downward sloping demand curve. He also faces a downward sloping marginal revenue curve as shown in Figure 2, rather than the horizontal MR curve faced by each pure competitor. Now, the monopolist will produce, not at the equil-

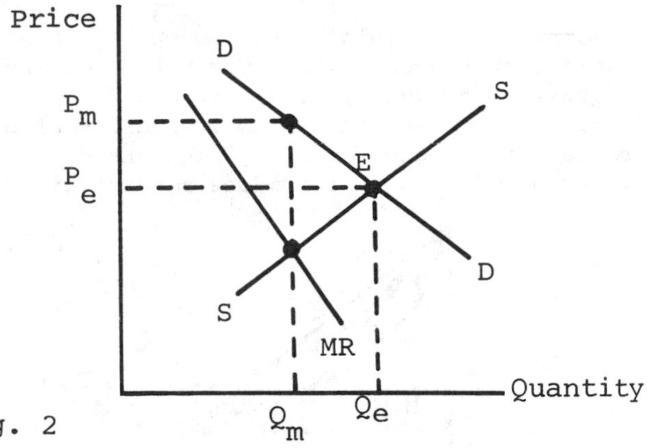

Fig. 2

ibrium point, E, but rather at the output level where MR = MC. Marginal cost for the monopolist is SS since this is the summation of the individual marginal cost curves. Therefore the monopolist produces at Q_m and charges the price P_m. Notice that $P_m > P_e$ and $Q_m < Q_e$, that is, the monopolist charges more and produces less than a comparable competitive situation.

• PROBLEM 19-13

Suppose that the graph drawn in Figure 1 represents a natural monopoly.
a) Where would the profit maximizing monopolist produce? Show his profit graphically.
b) If the government regulated the situation and forced the monopolist to produce as if in a competitive situation, where would the monopolist produce? Show graphically his profit.

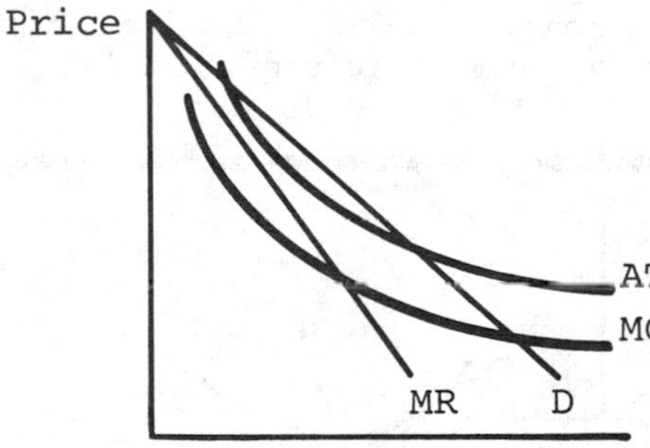

Fig. 1

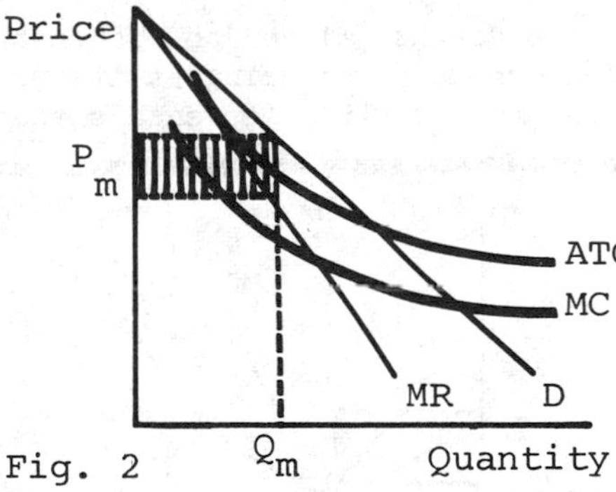

Fig. 2

Solution: a) The profit maximizing monopolist will produce at the output level indicated by MR = MC. On the graph in Figure 2, we see that at the profit maximizing point, quantity demanded is Q_m and the price that corresponds to Q_m is P_m.

The shaded portion of the graph represents the profits of the monopolist. To construct this rectangle, find the profit per unit on the vertical axis (measured as Price-ATC at Q_m) and multiply it by the total Quantity sold, Q_m.

b) Were the government to regulate this monopoly, changes would take place in the monopolist's production. One method of regulation, is to force the monopolist to produce at the intersection of the demand curve and the supply curve (represented by the marginal cost curve), i.e., as if this were competition where P = MC. Using the graph in Figure 3, note that the regulated monopolist will produce a quantity, Q_r, at a price, P_r.

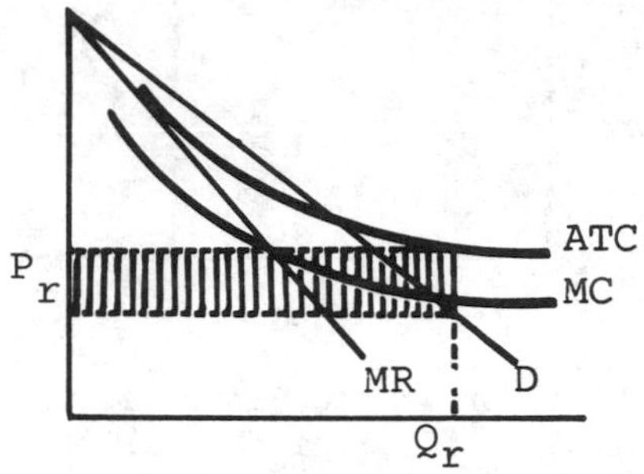

Fig. 3

The shaded portion of the graph represents the difference between Price and ATC, multiplied by Q_r. But since ATC > Price, this is in fact the loss, not the profit, which the monopolist would suffer under such regulation.

The monopolist, of course, could not sustain such a regulated position for long. Eventually the loss involved in producing under this type of government regulation would drive the monopolist out of business. Therefore some assistance, such as subsidization or the right to price discriminate, must be given to this monopolist.

• PROBLEM 19-14

The two graphs (a) and (b) demonstrate a monopoly making normal profits and a monopoly producing at its point of maximum efficiency. Decide which graph applies for each situation.

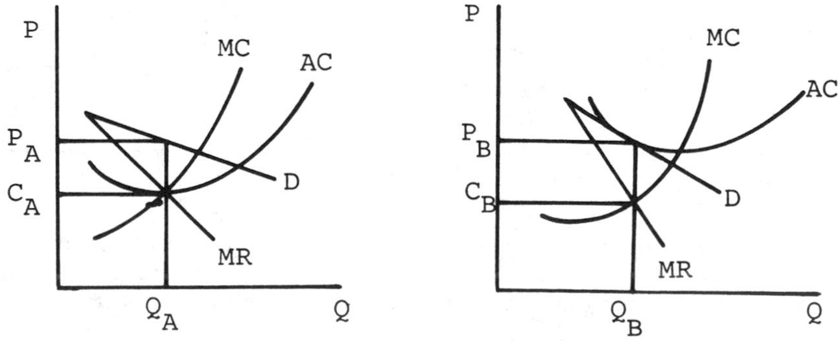

(a) (b)

Solution: This problem is asking for an interpretation of the two graphs. It is given that one represents a monopoly earning normal profits, (no excess profits) and the other shows a monopoly producing at maximum efficiency (where average costs are minimized). Beginning with graph (a) at MC = MR, the profit maximization monopolist will produce Q_A

units of output at a price of P_A. Note that at this intersection of MC and MR, the MC also intersects AC. Recall now that MC intersects AC only at the minimum point on the AC curve. Therefore by producing an output of Q_A at the point of minimum average costs, the monopolist in graph (a) is at maximum efficiency. A profit of C_AP_A per unit is being earned.

In graph (b), MC = MR when output is Q_B. The corresponding price for this output is P_B, which is also the average cost when output is Q_B. Therefore, since price = average cost, the monopolist in graph (b) is earning only normal profits.

The reader should be warned at this point that the two situations shown above are not likely to occur in the real world. They illustrate two special cases, where profit maximization just happens to occur jointly with maximum efficiency or normal profits. Normally a monopolist will incur above-minimum average costs and earn higher-than-normal profits.

• PROBLEM 19-15

Suppose the various curves for a monopolist are as presented in Figure 1.

Using the graph, determine the following:

a) profit maximizing output and price;
b) socially optimal output and price;
c) "fair return" output and price.

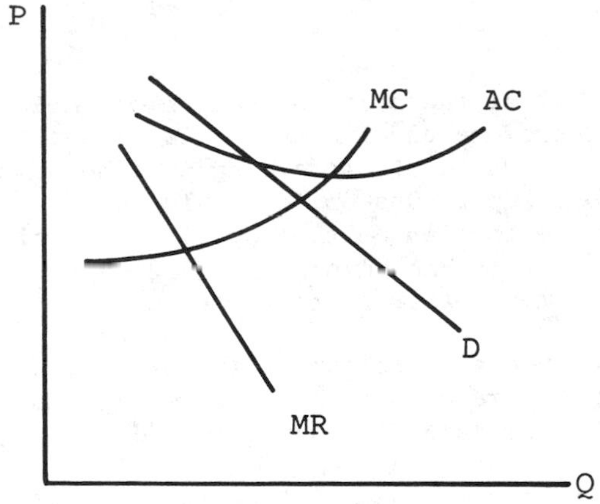

Fig. 1

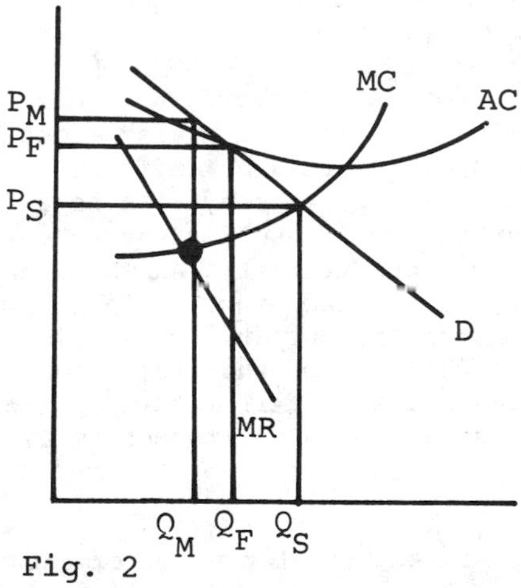

Fig. 2

Solution: To solve this problem, use the curves from Figure 1, with the various price-output combinations drawn in, (Figure 2).

a) To find the profit maximizing output and price, look for the intersection of the MR and MC curves. In Figure 2, MR intersects MC at Q_M. At Q_M, look for the appropriate price paid by the consumer, as shown by the demand curve. This price turns out to be P_M in Figure 2.

b) Under ordinary circumstances, we would expect a monopolist to price his product as shown in part a). If, however a socially optimal situation is desired, some sort of regulation must be implemented to force the monopolist to charge a socially optimal price.

The way to reach this socially optimal price is to set a ceiling price at the point where MC intersects the demand curve. In such a situation the demand curve becomes perfectly elastic over a range as shown in Figure 3.

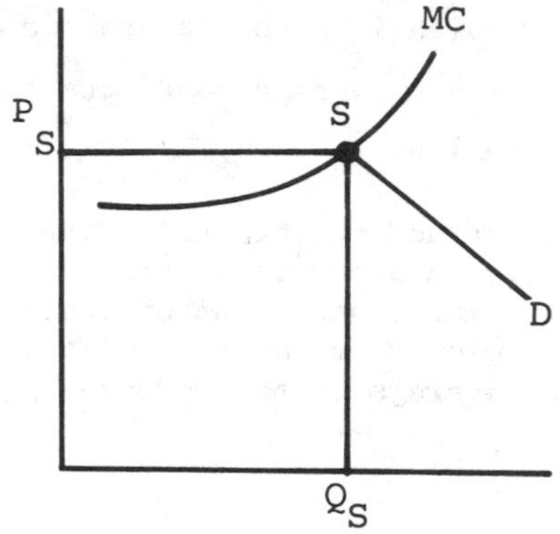

Fig. 3

The effective demand curve has now become P_sSD with the MR curve being equivalent to the demand curve over the range P_sS (as if in a pure competition situation). Under such restrictions, the monopolist will maximize profits when MC = MR = P at point S. In Figures 2 and 3, the socially optimal price is then P_s and the socially optimal output is Q_s.

Notice, however, in Figure 2, that at the point of social optimality, price is less than average cost. Therefore under such a situation the monopolist would be suffering a loss. Obviously something must be done or else this company will soon go bankrupt. One option would be a public subsidy sufficient to cover the loss which the socially optimal price would entail. Another option, which has often been adopted by regulatory agencies, is to allow the monopolist a "fair return" in pricing his output.

c) Remembering that total costs include a normal or "fair" profit, we see that the "fair return" price in Figure 2 would be realized at the point where AC intersects D. The corresponding output would be Q_F and the price, P_F.

To sum up, let us refer back to Figure 2. In terms of social optimality, P_S is the proper regulatory price. But due to the nature of the demand and cost curves, such a price entails losses for the producer. Therefore one solution is to allow a "fair return" to monopolists by setting price = P_F = average cost. However, as Figure 2 indicates, such a solution sets price higher than socially optimal and output lower than socially optimal. Finally, the unregulated monopoly situation represents even further movement away from social optimality and hence is the reason for regulation in the first place.

It is clear from the definition of profit why a monopolist would maximize profit at the point where the difference between Total Revenue and Total Cost is greatest. Yet it is not intuitively clear why this is necessarily the same point where Marginal Revenue = Marginal Cost. Explain why the first rule of profit maximization (Maximize TR - TC) is equivalent to the second rule of profit maximization (MC = MR).

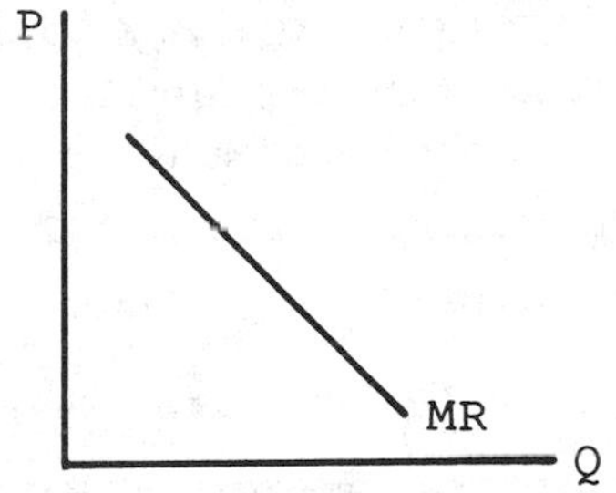

Fig. 1

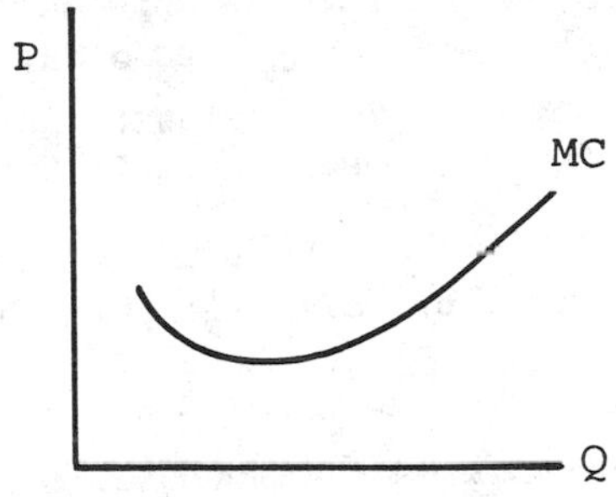

Fig. 2

Solution: When we consider the marginal revenue curve for a monopoly, we imagine a downward-sloping line as shown in Figure 1.

Marginal cost, on the other hand, is thought to have a U-shape such as shown in Figure 2.

In dealing with the MC and MR curves together, we generally ignore the "decreasing marginal cost" portion of the MC curve to ease explanation. Therefore combining the MC and MR curves, we get the situation shown in Figure 3.

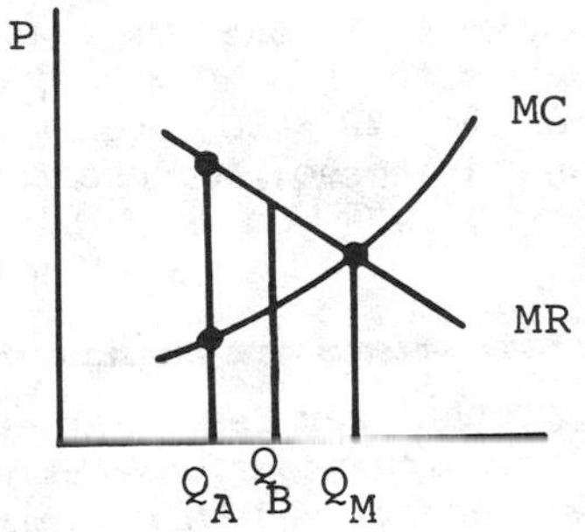

Fig. 3

Suppose we are currently producing at Q_A in Figure 3 and we are considering an increase of output to Q_B. How will this affect profit?

Notice that throughout the range from Q_A to Q_B, MR > MC. This means that if we increase output from Q_A to Q_B, TR will increase by more than TC will increase. Therefore profit will be greater at Q_B than at Q_A. In general, as long as MR > MC, an increase in output will cause TR to increase by more than TC, resulting in an increase in profits.

By looking at the graph in Figure 3 again, we see that MR ≥ MC as long as output $\leq Q_M$. Therefore profit will increase up to the point Q_M. After the point, Q_M, MC > MR. Therefore if we increase output beyond Q_M, TC will increase by more than TR, thereby causing a drop in profit. Thus profit maximization occurs when MC = MR at Q_M.

To show that this is equivalent to maximizing the difference between TR and TC, imagine the behavior of TR and TC as we move along the MR and MC graphs in Figure 3 from Q_A to Q_M. Since MR > MC along this path, the difference between TR and TC is growing as we go from Q_A to Q_M. After Q_M, MC > MR. Therefore after Q_M, the difference between TR and TC begins to shrink. Since this difference between TR and TC increases until it hits Q_M and decreases after passing Q_M, the point Q_M represents the maximum difference between TR and TC. And this, by definition, is the point of profit maximization.

• PROBLEM 19-17

In monopoly, profit maximization occurs when marginal revenue = marginal cost. In pure competition, profit maximization occurs when price = marginal cost. How is pure competition just a special case of imperfect competition?

Solution: While a monopolist faces a downward-sloping demand curve, the pure competitor faces a perfectly elastic demand curve, i.e., price is constant throughout the demand curve. Therefore, since price is constant, total revenue changes by a constant amount, the price of one unit, with the additional selling of one unit, and marginal revenue = constant = price. When we apply the MR = MC rule to a pure competition situation, it reduces to P = MR = MC , or P = MC. That is, the pure competitor follows the MR = MC profit maximizing rule also. The pure competitor is a special case, because for him MR = P.

• PROBLEM 19-18

Suppose the following graph describes a market situation in which a monopsonistic buyer is hiring homogeneous workers where S = Supply Curve, MRP = Marginal Revenue Product, and MSC = Marginal Supply Cost of Labor.

a) Why does MSC always lie above S?

b) What quantity of labor would the profit maximizing monopsonist hire?

c) What wage would he pay? How is this a non-deliberate exploitation?

Solution: a) The MSC, or the Marginal Supply Cost of labor represents the Marginal Cost to the buyer that results from the "purchase" of one extra unit of labor. To show why this curve will always lie above the supply curve, (which represents the average costs to the buyers), notice that the supply curve for labor, S, like any other supply curve is upward sloping. This means that as more people are hired, the wage rate must increase. Since all workers are assumed to be homogeneous, the wage rate must be the same for all workers. Therefore, the cost of hiring one additional laborer is greater than that one worker's wage rate since all previously employed workers must also receive the new higher wage rate. This means that the marginal supply cost of labor, the marginal cost of hiring that one extra laborer, will lie above the supply curve, or the average costs of hiring any given number of laborers, as long as supply is upward sloping.

b) Just as the profit maximizing monopolist produces at the point where MC = MR, the profit maximizing monopsonist will hire up until the point where Marginal Supply Cost of Labor = Marginal Revenue Product. At this point, R in the given diagram, the quantity hired = 0Q.

c) When MSC = MRP at point R, the profit-maximizing monopsonist will pay the wage rate just necessary to call forth an employment level of 0Q. This wage level is determined by the supply curve. To hire just 0Q amount of workers, the monopsonist must pay QT (or OP) level of wages. Note that here, the demand (MRP) price of labor is not equal to, but is greater than the supply price.

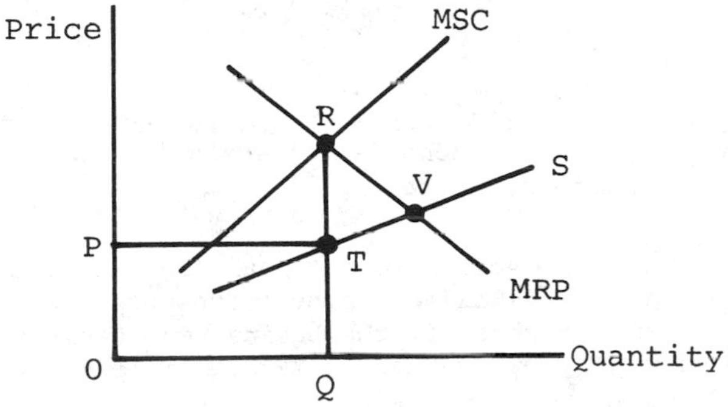

Exploitation would occur in this case if the wage rate were below the marginal revenue product. Since at an employment level of 0Q, wage rate (QT) < marginal revenue product (QR), exploitation has occurred. However economic theory shows no evidence of deliberate exploitation on the part of the monopsonist . This theoretical monopsonist's purpose is not to exploit labor, rather he is just acting as a rational decision maker who seeks to maximize profits. Thus since he faces a less than perfectly elastic supply curve of labor, and hence a marginal supply cost curve for labor above the supply curve, the theory shows a non-deliberate exploitation.

• PROBLEM 19-19

Suppose a monopolist has the following demand and marginal revenue schedules with marginal cost = average cost = $5.

P	Quantity Demanded	Marginal Revenue
40	0	
		30
30	1	
		10
20	2	
		-10
10	3	

Because a monopolist can manipulate output and price, it is often alleged that a monopolist will charge the highest price he can get. Why is this assertion wrong?

Solution: Economic theory tells us that the monopolist (like any other profit maximizing producer) will produce at the point where marginal revenue = marginal cost. On the schedule above, profit would be maximized at a production level of 2, with profit = TR - TC

$$= (2 \times \$20) - (2 \times \$5)$$
$$= \$40 - \$10$$
$$= \$30 .$$

Suppose the monopolist charged the highest price possible. Since the demand curve facing the monopolist is always downward-sloping, the highest possible price must be realized at the point where quantity produced = 1 unit. On the schedules above, at quantity = 1,

$$\text{Profit} = TR - TC$$
$$= (1 \times \$30) - (1 \times \$5)$$
$$= \$30 - \$5$$
$$= \$25$$

Generally, the point of maximum profits and maximum price will not be the same, due to the economies of scale that are associated with most modern production processes.

In the case above, where marginal cost and average cost are constant at $5, the point of maximum price represents the point of maximum per-unit profits. In general, the businessman would not seek to maximize per-unit profits, but rather to maximize total profits.

• PROBLEM 19-20

Even if profit maximization were possible for a monopolist, he might purposely charge a lower price and produce a greater output than expected under profit maximization because of certain long-run considerations. What are some of these considerations?

Solution: Given that the monopolist knows where to locate price and output so as to maximize profit, it is commonly held that full exploitation of monopoly position in the short run can destroy monopoly position in the long run.

The important idea here is that a monopoly does not have anonymity. Specifically a monopoly is constantly under scrutiny from three groups: consumers, government, and business.

Suppose consumers become aware of the fact that a certain monopoly is making extraordinary profits. Consumer groups might soon make this monopoly a target of public criticism which could lead to a loss of goodwill. Thus, various monopolies advertise, not so much to influence sales but rather to help the consumer formulate a nice image of their companies.

Government's response to high profits can be more painful for the monopolist. If the monopolist fully exploits his market position, government might intervene by initiating antitrust action, rate regulation, or, at the extreme, nationalization of the firm.

Finally, the monopolist might limit his profits because of the possible response of the business community, i.e., if potential rivals see those high profit figures, they may double their efforts to overcome the monopoly's barriers. Remember that no barriers to entry can last forever.

EFFECT OF A TAX

• PROBLEM 19-21

One way for government to control monopoly is through taxation. Show the effect of an annual fixed amount monopoly tax on output, price, and profit.

Solution: To determine output and price in a monopoly, we equate MR and MC. Since demand would be unaffected by a monopoly tax, marginal revenue would also be unaffected. Marginal cost would also be unaffected because a fixed "lump-sum" tax would be counted as part of a firms fixed costs. That is this fixed amount will not change as the firm changes its production levels; therefore, the fixed tax does not affect MC. To illustrate this point, suppose we have a schedule of costs as shown below:

Annual Output	Total Cost	Marginal Cost
0	50	
		20
1	70	
		10
2	80	
		20
3	100	

Now suppose an annual monopoly tax of $20 is imposed. As the table below shows, total costs increase by $20 at each output, thus leaving MC the same as before the tax. In mathematical terms, $(TR_{i+1} + 20) - (TR_i + 20) = TR_{i+1} - TR_i$.

Annual Output	Total Cost	Marginal Cost
0	70	
		20
1	90	
		10
2	100	
		20
3	120	

Therefore, since MC and MR are unchanged by a fixed amount tax, output and price will be the same before and after the tax. At this point, you might wonder why such a tax would be employed if output and price remain untouched by it. The answer is apparent when we study the effect of the tax upon the monopolist's profits.

On the accompanying graph, we see the effect of a fixed amount tax upon average costs (AC).

As the tax is imposed, total costs increase at each level of output. Therefore, average costs increase at each level of output. In the graph, AC represents average costs before the tax and AC_2, average costs after

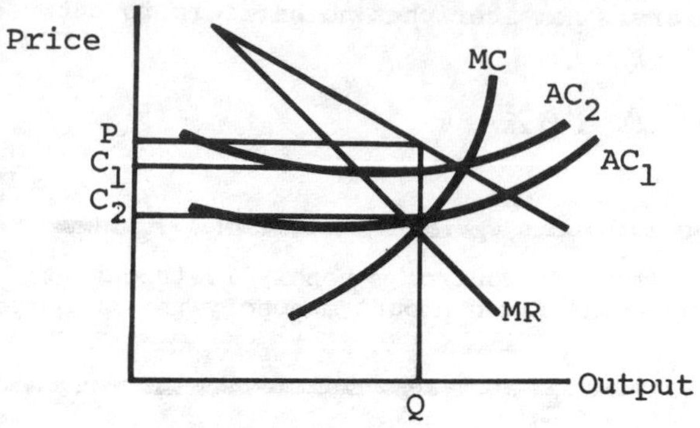

the tax. Using the difference between the price charged and the average costs to represent per-unit profit, we see that per-unit profit before the tax = C_2P. (Profit-maximizing output = Q, price = P). After the tax, per-unit profit has fallen to C_1P. So the pure profits of the monopolist have been cut down and the distribution of income has changed.

Note also that because price and output have remained constant, none of the fixed tax has been borne by the consumer. Instead it has been drawn completely from the monopolist's profits.

• PROBLEM 19-22

Suppose the government decides to regulate a certain monopoly with a fixed per unit tax. How will this affect price, output, and profits?

Solution: A tax on a monopolist is assumed to leave demand and marginal revenue unaffected. That is, a tax on the local (monopoly) power company will not generally change your demand for electric power. However, the monopolist's costs, both marginal cost and average cost, will be affected by a fixed per unit tax. Therefore price, output and profits will also be affected.

Suppose a monopolist has the following cost schedule before the tax is imposed:

Output	Total Cost
0	10
1	20
2	24
3	33

Now suppose the government imposes a tax of $1/unit on the monopolist. The new total cost schedule would be the following:

Output	Total Cost
0	10
1	21
2	26
3	36

Now, compute marginal cost and average cost to see how they are affected by the tax.

	Before Tax			After Tax		
Output	TC	AC	MC	TC	AC	MC
0	10	-		10	-	
			10			11
1	20	20		21	21	
			4			5
2	24	12		26	13	
			9			10
3	33	11		36	12	

Looking at the above table, note that the per unit tax affects marginal cost and average cost in the same way, i.e., at each level of output MC and AC increase by the amount of the per-unit tax.

For the mathematically inclined, this can be shown as follows. For Average costs, let the subscript b stand for "before tax", the subscript t stand for "after tax", c be the amount of the tax per unit, and the subscript i stand for "output i". Then,

$$AC_{bi} = \frac{TC_{bi}}{i}$$

$$AC_{ti} = \frac{TC_{ti}}{i}$$

$$= \frac{TC_{bi} + ci}{i}$$

$$= \frac{TC_{bi}}{i} + \frac{ci}{i}$$

$$= AC_{bi} + c$$

For marginal cost:

$$MC_{bi} = TC_{bi} - TC_{b(i-1)}$$

$$MC_{ti} = TC_{ti} - TC_{t(i-1)}$$

$$= (TC_{bi} + ci) - \left(TC_{b(i-1)} + c(i-1)\right)$$

$$= \left(TC_{bi} - TC_{b(i-1)}\right) + (ci - c(i-1))$$

$$= MC_{bi} + ci - ci + c$$

$$= MC_{bi} + c$$

So with marginal cost and average cost changing by constant amounts at each level of output, let us examine the cost graphs to see how price, output, and profit change. Let AC_1 and MC_1 be "before tax" while AC_2 and MC_2 are "after tax".

On the graph, we see that price rises from P_{A1} to P_{A2} as

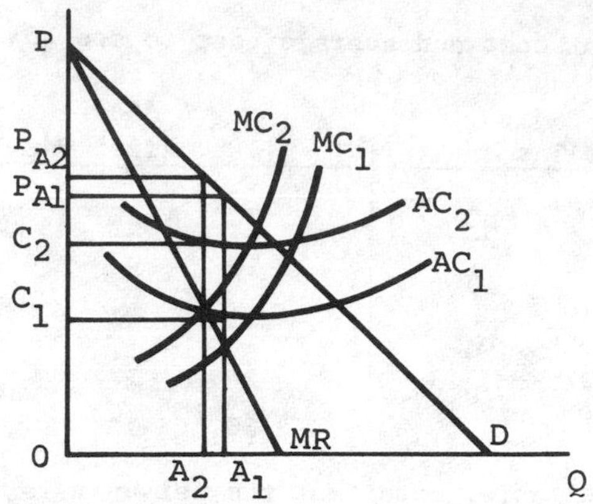

the tax is imposed while output falls from A_1 to A_2. Thus the consumer is paying a higher price and getting less total product as a result of this tax.

Using the difference between price and average cost as per-unit profit, we see that per-unit profit drops from c_1P_{A1} to c_2P_{A2} as the tax is imposed. Thus the pure profits of the monopolist have been cut down somewhat.

Note that in this example price rises while profit falls. Thus the monopolist bears part of the burden of the tax through a drop in profit while the consumer bears the rest of the tax by paying a higher price for the monopolist's product.

• PROBLEM 19-23

Given below are price and cost figures for a monopolist:

Quantity	Price	Total Cost
0	200	145
1	180	175
2	160	200
3	140	220
4	120	250
5	100	300
6	80	370
7	60	460
8	40	570

a) Find the Total Revenue, Marginal Revenue, and Marginal Cost columns. Where is profit maximized?
b) How will a tax of $100 per day affect profit maximization?

Solution: Total Revenue is given by the formula, $TR = P \times Q$. Marginal Revenue = Δ Total Revenue/Δ Quantity. Marginal Cost = Δ Total Cost/Δ Quantity. Therefore TR, MR and MC are:

Q	P	TR	MR	TC	MC
0	200	0		145	
			180		30
1	180	180		175	
			140		25
2	160	320		200	
			100		20
3	140	420		220	
			60		30
4	120	480		250	
			20		50
5	100	500		300	
			-20		70
6	80	480		370	
			-60		90
7	60	420		460	
			-100		110
8	40	320		570	

Looking at the table above, we see that as Q increases from 3 to 4, MR = 60. Also, as Q goes from 4 to 5, MR = 20. Therefore, at the point Q = 4, assuming linearity, MR is halfway between 60 and 20, or MR = (60 + 20)/2 = 40.

Similarly, as Q goes from 3 to 4, MC = 30, and as Q goes from 4 to 5, MC = 50. Therefore at Q = 4, MC = (30 + 50)/2 = 40.

Since MC = MR at Q = 4, this represents the point of profit maximization. The price at Q = 4 is $120. The profit is $480 - $250 = $230.

b) The effect of the flat sum tax will be to shift the total cost curve upward at each Q by a constant amount, c. Marginal revenue will clearly not be affected by this since the tax is imposed upon the producer. Marginal cost will also not be affected by this tax. (Since

$$MC = \frac{d(TC + c)}{dQ} = \frac{d(TC)}{dQ},$$

i.e., shifting the TC curve by a constant does not change the slope, MC, of the curve). Therefore since MC and MR are unchanged, profit maximization will remain at Q = 4, P = $120. Of course, at the point of the profit maximization, total profit will be lower than in the original case.

PRICE DISCRIMINATION

• PROBLEM 19-24

What is price discrimination? How does a monopoly situation often make price discrimination possible?

Solution: Price discrimination is the practice of selling a product at different prices to different people, when price differences are not justified by cost differences.

Since there is only one seller in a monopoly situation, consumers must accept the monopolist's price. The consumer may see that the price paid is not uniform, but he will buy the monopolist's product anyway since there are no other suppliers.

It is important to realize that a monopolist can practice price discrimination only if no customer can resell the monopolist's product. If the product could be resold, those paying less for the product could sell to those paying more, undercutting the monopolist. In general reselling is not possible when the output consists of services, such as legal advice, or medical services.

• PROBLEM 19-25

Suppose a monopolist's demand schedule is as follows:

Quantity	Price
1	109
2	105
3	100
4	96
5	91

If Total costs at the optimal output of 5 units are $405,
a) How much profit will this monopolist earn without price discrimination?
b) How much profit can he potentially earn with price discrimination?

Solution: a) Ordinarily, the monopolist would charge $91 for each of 5 units. Therefore Total Revenue would be $91 x 5 = $455. Then Profit = Total Revenue - Total Cost

= $455 - $405

= $50

b) The monopolist's downward sloping demand curve suggests that price discrimination can be a highly profitable policy. Specifically, we see by looking at the monopolist's demand curve, that he stands to earn even more profits if he can somehow segregate his market. That is, the monopolist has one customer out there willing to pay $109 for his product (more than the going rate of $91) another consumer is willing to pay $105, and so on.

Therefore rather than charging a uniform price of $91, this monopolist can charge different people different prices, even though they are receiving the same product. Total revenue would then be

$109 + $105 + $100 +$96 + $91 = $501

Profit = Total Revenue - Total Cost

= $501 - $405

= $96 .

So by practicing price discrimination, this monopolist can increase profit by $41 from $55 to $96.

• PROBLEM 19-26

When a person invents a new product, he is often granted a patent which is intended to protect his idea from being stolen by others. Explain how the issuance of patents fosters the growth of monopoly.

Solution: Patents, by protecting inventors, encourage innovation and new invention. They assure the inventor that he need have no fear that his ideas will be stolen. However what happens is that one individual (or corporation) is given the right to supply a product, to the exclusion of all other possible suppliers. By limiting the suppliers to one, a monopoly situation has been created. That is, a patent, as a barrier to entry, may cause a monopoly to arise.

• PROBLEM 19-27

What are economies of scale? What is meant by "indivisibilities in the technology?"

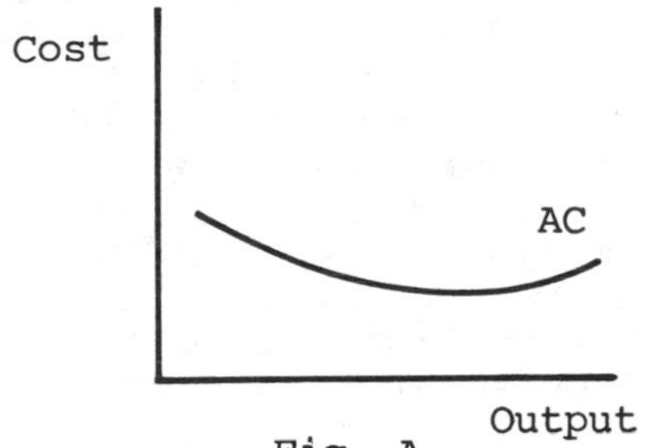

Fig. A

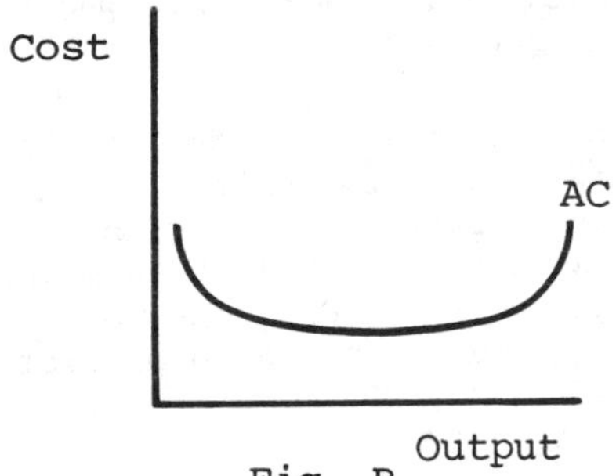

Fig. B

Solution: Economies of scale or increasing returns to scale, refer to the changes in a firm's average costs resulting from scalar changes of the inputs in the production process. That is, suppose every input into the production process is changed by some multiple, say, doubled. If average costs rise by the same factor, i.e., they also double, then the firm is said to show constant returns to scale. If average costs rise by more than this factor, the firm shows decreasing returns to scale and if average costs decline, then the firm shows increasing returns to scale.

In Figure A, there are increasing returns to scale, or economies of scale present. In figure B, no such economies exist.

"Indivisibilities in the technology" is a term used to apply to industries in which economies of scale exist. Take the automobile industry, for example. Suppose we have an assembly line producing 100 cars per day. Indivisibility of technology tells us that it is not possible to create a mini-assembly line, using 1/100 of the equipment and labor, which would produce only 1 car each day.

Such indivisibilities of technology thus help explain the existence of much large-scale production.

Compare and contrast the environment for technological advance in pure competition to the one in monopoly.

Solution: Whether pure competition or monopoly provides a better environment for innovation is a point still being debated by economists, businessmen and government regulators alike.

In pure competition, the nature of the market tends to deprive firms of economic profit. Thus the funds necessary to support the research and development involved in technological advance are missing.

But suppose that the funds are available. We still might find a firm in pure competition reluctant to innovate. This is because an innovating firm in a competitive industry will soon find its many rivals duplicating or imitating any technological advances it has achieved. The result is that our innovating firm pays the costs of technological research while its rivals share in the rewards.

In contrast to pure competition, a monopolist may persistently realize substantial economic profits. Thus the funds are available if a monopolist wishes to innovate. But whether or not the monopolist possesses the incentive to innovate is open to debate.

Those who maintain that the monopolist's incentive to advance technologically is weak argue that the absence of competition removes the stimulus to innovate. Whereas in pure competition, the rule is "be efficient or perish", it is held by many that the monopolist is often inefficient and lethargic, due to his sheltered market position. It is even suggested that the monopolist may withhold technological improvements in order to more fully exploit existing capital equipment.

Those who maintain that monopolists do in fact have incentives to innovate argue that monopolists view technological advance as a means of lowering unit costs and thereby expanding profits. Also, some view research and technological advance as a barrier to entry for the monopolist, essential to the maintenance of monopoly. It is felt that unless the monopolist can continually show advancements, his potential rivals will soon catch up to him. By keeping one step ahead of possible competitors, the monopolistic firm guarantees its existence into the future.

Answer

To be covered when testing yourself

SHORT ANSWER QUESTIONS FOR REVIEW

Choose the correct answer.

1. Which of the following describes any firm at its maximum-profit equilibrium? (a) marginal cost equals average cost (b) demand is unitarily elastic (c) the slopes of the Total Revenue and Total Cost curves are the same (d) demand exceeds supply. c

2. Suppose a firm is producing an output at which marginal revenue equals marginal cost. However selling price is less than average total costs. This firm is: (a) likely to raise price (b) a monopoly (c) minimizing losses (d) making an accounting profit. c

3. A monopolist finds that at his present level of output and sales, Marginal Revenue = $3.10 and Marginal Cost = $2.50. Which of the following will maximize profits? (a) Leave price and output unchanged (b) Decrease price and leave output unchanged (c) Increase price and leave output unchanged (d) Increase price and decrease output (e) Decrease price and increase output. e

4. In a pure monopoly situation, (a) product price and production are the same as they would be in pure competition (b) product price is ordinarily higher and production lower than they would be in pure competition (c) product price and production are ordinarily lower than they would be in pure competition (d) product price and production are higher than they would be in pure competition (e) product price is lower and production higher than they would be in pure competition. b

5. Which of the following helps cause perfect competition to produce a more efficient allocation of resources than monopoly? (a) A firm in perfect competition has no control over market price while monopolies can gain from creating a divergence between price and marginal cost. (b) Firms in perfect competition try to set low prices while monopolists set high prices. (c) Firms in perfect competition try to minimize cost while monopolies try to maximize profits. (d) Firms in perfect competition try to maximize output while monopolies try to maximize profit. a

Answer

To be covered when testing yourself

SHORT ANSWER QUESTIONS FOR REVIEW

6. Of the following statements, which describe a monopoly at maximum-profit equilibrium? 1. Marginal Revenue equals Marginal Cost. 2. The slope of the total profit curve is zero. 3. The slopes of Total Revenue and Total Cost are parallel. (a) 1 only (b) 1 and 2 only (c) 1 and 3 only (d) 2 and 3 only (e) All three. — e

7. If a monopolist could find buyers for 9 units at a price of $5 (no excess quantity demanded), and if Marginal Revenue due to the tenth unit were $2, the highest price at which this monopolist could find buyers for 10 units must be: (a) $2.00 (b) $3.00 (c) $4.70 (d) $4.80 (e) $5.20. — c

8. The fact that a firm in a pure-monopoly situation is able to prevent new firms from entering the market means most certainly that: (a) the firm is able to satisfy its present customers (b) new firms are not attracted by extra profit (c) the firm must be operating at a loss (d) monopoly profit could exist indefinitely (e) the firm is highly efficient. — d

9. How does the presence of a monopoly in an otherwise competitive full-employment economy tend to affect output of monopoly and competitive products? (a) The output of both is too small. (b) The output of both is too large. (c) The output of the monopoly products is too small while the ouput of the competitive products is relatively too large. (d) The output of the monopoly products is relatively too large and the output of the competitive products is too small. — c

10. In a monopsonistic labor buying situation with no market imperfections, once the employer determines the level of employment which will maximize profits (or minimize costs), he sets wages as dictated by examining: (a) demand for labor (b) supply of labor (c) substitutability of capital equipment for labor (d) union requirements and government wage laws. — b

11. All but one of the following are barriers to entry that help explain the existence of monopoly. Which is not such a barrier? (a) economies of scale (b) control of

	Answer — To be covered when testing yourself
essential raw materials (c) patent ownership (d) highly inelastic demand (e) unfair competitive practices.	d
12. In a monopoly with downward-sloping demand, marginal revenue is greater than price (a) if demand is elastic (b) if demand is inelastic (c) if MC = MR lies to the right of minimum ATC (d) if the monopoly is under government regulation (e) at no time for a profit maximizing monopsonist.	e
13. The existence of monopolies can be economically justified when (a) international trade is a part of the monopoly's business (b) an economy is in an early growth stage (c) economies of scale exist (d) cost and demand figures are not obtainable.	c
14. Price discrimination takes place when: (a) a given product is sold at more than one price and these price differences are not justified by cost differences (b) different prices, to compensate for differences in the characteristics of the product, are charged (c) the price is equal to the per unit cost of the product (d) increased price lowers the supply of the product	a
15. Charging a discriminatory fee is economically desirable because: (a) it redistributes income from the rich to the poor (b) the survival of certain vital industries may depend upon the practice of price discrimination (c) $MR > P$ (d) marginal cost exceeds price at all profitable levels of production	a

Fill in the blanks.

16. In a monopoly the supply and demand curves to the monopolist and the industry are ________.	equivalent
17. Profit is maximized when ________ equals ________.	marginal revenue, marginal cost
18. A sells product X to B for \$5 and to C for \$10. This is an example of ________.	price discrimination

SHORT ANSWER QUESTIONS FOR REVIEW

Answer
To be covered when testing yourself

19. The Interstate Commerce Commission, Federal Power Commission, Federal Communications Commission, and Civil Aeronautics Board are all examples of ________. — regulatory commissions

20. If P = ATC, we say a firm is making normal profits. If P > ATC, we say a firm is making ________. — economic or excess profits

21. If a firm like IBM controls 80% of its market, this is an example of a ________ monopoly. — near

22. If the government imposed a fixed amount tax on a monopoly, price and output would ________ while profit would ________. — be unaffected, fall

23. When a market has a single buyer, we call it a ________. — monopsony

24. Monopolies for which it would be impractical for producers to compete are called ________. — natural monopolies

25. Antitrust rulings, in their attempt to break monopolies into pure competition, have instead turned monopolies into ________. — oligopolies

26. When government regulates a monopoly so that price equals average total costs, we say that the monopolist's profit represents a ________. — fair return

27. If Marginal Cost is greater than Marginal Revenue, the profit-maximizing monopolist should ________ output. — decrease

28. When compared with a pure competition situation, a monopoly has ________ prices and ________ output. — higher, lower

29. If elasticity of demand equals one, marginal revenue equals ________. — zero

30. A market situation similar to monopoly in that demand is downward sloping even though many firms exist in the industry is called ________. — monopolistic competition

Determine whether the following statements are true or false.

31. The long-run profit-maximizing monopolist always aims for the largest attainable per-

SHORT ANSWER QUESTIONS FOR REVIEW

	Answer (To be covered when testing yourself)
unit profit.	False
32. In price discrimination, the buyer who pays the higher price has a more inelastic demand.	True
33. If demand is downward-sloping, then marginal cost always lies beneath demand.	False
34. A monopolist will always benefit by increasing his price.	False
35. A pure monopolist is guaranteed to receive at least a normal profit.	False
36. If the ABC Company can sell 9 units per week at $10 per unit and 8 units per week at $11 per unit, the marginal revenue of the ninth unit is $2.	True
37. Because of his control over price, the pure monopolist is able to increase his price and increase his volume of sales simultaneously.	False
38. If a per-unit tax is imposed upon monopolies, consumers will pay more per unit and get less total output.	True
39. The only monopolies unregulated by government are those which prove sufficient economies of scale.	False
40. Since the consumer has nowhere else to go when buying from a monopolist, he must often pay a discriminatory price even though he is aware of the monopolist's practice.	True
41. If price is less than average total cost in a monopoly, there is no need for government to regulate this monopoly since a loss is already being incurred.	False
42. The socially optimal point occurs at the point where Marginal Cost intersects Average Total Cost.	False
43. In the long-run, monopolies always earn only normal profits.	False
44. In pure competition, (in the long-run), equilibrium price = minimum ATC = MC = MR. In monopoly equilibrium price > MC, thereby signalling a misallocation of resources.	True

SHORT ANSWER QUESTIONS FOR REVIEW

Answer
To be covered when testing yourself

45. If a lump sum tax is imposed on a monopolist, consumers will pay more and get less total output.

False

CHAPTER 20

MONOPOLISTIC COMPETITION

Basic Attacks and Strategies for Solving Problems in this Chapter. See pages 729 to 753 for step-by-step solutions to problems.

Monopolistic competition is an industry structure characterized by a large number of firms, ease of entry and exit, and product differentiation. As its name indicates, the industry incorporates elements of both competition and monopoly. The competitive element is that there is a large number of firms and easy entry and exit. The monopoly element results from product differentiation. Since each firm produces a similar but slightly different product, each firm can be considered a single seller of its unique product. Consequently, some brand loyalty can be built up, meaning that some consumers will prefer a particular product even if its price is slightly higher than that of its competitors. The implication of this is that the demand curve facing the monopolistically competitive firm has a negative slope to it, indicating that its elasticity is less than infinity.

Product differentiation in monopolistic competition can be real or perceived. In the case of perceived product differentiation, advertising is often cited as the reason why consumers believe differences exist between products that are actually the same.

The concept of the industry becomes ambiguous in monopolistic competition. Presumably, an industry consists of all firms that sell the same or a similar product, but how similar do products have to be to be considered members of the same industry?

Short run equilibrium in monopolistic competition is similar to the case of monopoly. The negatively-sloped demand curve yields a marginal revenue curve that lies beneath the demand curve with a steeper slope. A profit-maximizing firm will locate where $MR = MC$ and charge the highest price consumers are willing to pay for that quantity. In the short run, monopolistically competitive firms can earn economic or normal profits or losses.

In the long run, firm entry or exit can occur. If short run profits are being earned, entry will take place. New firms will begin doing business selling a slightly differentiated product which is likely to appeal to some segment of the market. This will take away business from existing firms, causing their demand curves to shift inward. Entry will cease when economic profits have been reduced to zero. Losses will lead to the departure of firms and a consequent increase in demand for the product of the remaining firms. Exit will cease when profits have returned to the normal level.

The key element of long run equilibrium can be seen in the diagram. The negatively-sloped demand curve means that long run equilibrium must take place on the negatively-sloped segment of the average cost curve. This has given rise to a debate in the economics profession about the "Excess Capacity Theorem." One view is that long run equilibrium occurs where average cost is higher than the minimum. This results from the fact that there are too many firms producing too little output, in other words, there is excess capacity. Consequently, this market structure is inefficient.

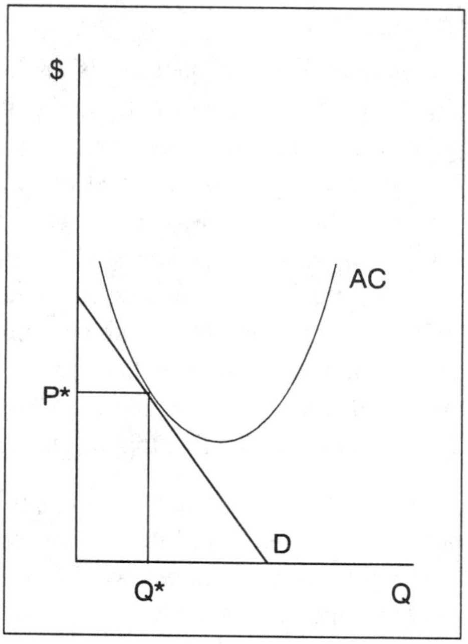

Long Run Equilibrium in Monopolistic Competition

The other view is that the excess capacity results from the fact that demand curves have negative slopes due to product differentiation. Since product differentiation means more choice when it comes to goods and services, the excess capacity is actually desirable because it means we have more variety in our lives.

The role of advertising is a controversial subject in the discipline. Some economists believe that advertising, at least as we are used to it in the United States, exerts a net negative influence on society. They argue that advertising allows some producers to achieve monopoly power, leading to monopoly distortions. They also point out that much advertising lacks any significant informational content. Rather, it appears to be trying to create a demand for a product by creating a pleasing image, irrespective of the facts. In addition, some advertising is false or misleading.

Other economists believe that the bulk of advertising is, in fact, informative. It allows firms to gain a foothold in a market they might otherwise not be able to enter, enhancing competition. They also believe that consumers are not as easy to manipulate and deceive as the critics seem to believe.

Step-by-Step Solutions to Problems in this Chapter, "Monopolistic Competition"

BASIC CONCEPTS

• PROBLEM 20-1

List the three main characteristics of monopolistic competition and discuss briefly the implications of these characteristics.

<u>Solution</u>: The three defining characteristics of monopolistic competition are a) a large number of competitors b) product differentiation and c) relatively free entry into and exit from the market.

The large number of competitors limits the control any individual firm has over market price. It also prevents price-fixing because of the difficulties involved in getting a large number of firms to act together. Monopolistic competition does not require the presence of hundreds of firms but only a fairly large number--say between 25 and 70.

Product differentiation gives each firm some control over the price of its products since consumers no longer perceive rivals' product as identical. That is, product differentiation gives the firm something of a monopoly where there are many close substitutes. Product differentiation also leads to nonprice competition among firms. This competition can focus on advertising or it can focus on the quality and workmanship of the competing products.

Ease of entry simply prevents firms from maintaining excess profits year after year. Suppose a firm is making extraordinary profits. If barriers to entry are low, other firms will soon enter the industry since it appears so lucrative. As new firms enter the market profits will be reduced to "normal" levels.

• PROBLEM 20-2

Discuss the similarities and differences between pure

competition and monopolistic competition.

Solution: Monopolistic competition is similar to pure competition in that there are a large number of sellers, each of whom offers a relatively small amount of the total amount offered for sale.

Monopolistic competition differs in that each firm sells a differentiated product, thereby having some control over its price. Also product differentiation results in some restriction to entry.

• PROBLEM 20-3

What is the importance of product differentiation in monopolistic competition?

Solution: Product differentiation is an essential concept in monopolistic competition; in fact, product differentiation is what defines monopolistic competition. Monopolistic competition is also called the "many differentiated sellers model" by some economists. Because there is product differentiation, each firm faces a slightly different market, and thus a different demand curve. Since each firm has a different demand curve, each firm will have some control over price.

The women's garment industry is an excellent example of an industry where, even though firms might all be selling blouses, there is still product differentiation. Because of this differentiation, different firms can charge different prices for the same good (blouses). Product differentiation, then, is important in monopolistic competition in that it defines monopolistic competition. Because of the different demand curves for each firm resulting from differentiation, the industry is no longer purely competitive.

• PROBLEM 20-4

Is it possible for many firms to sell exactly the same product, and still be in monopolistic competition?

Solution: Yes, it is entirely possible for this to happen. The essence of monopolistic competition is product differentiation, but this differentiation can be in two forms. The first is if there are slight differences in the actual product sold. The second form, the one that concerns us here, occurs when the products are the same, but there are still differences among the products from the consumers point of view. These differences can arise from differences in location (one store or gas station might be closer than the others) or they could arise as the result of an especially effective advertising campaign (one firm may convince consumers that its product is superior to all the others, when it could be identical to the others). The phrase 'product differentiation,' then, covers much more than actual differences between products; it covers any difference between products that the consumer perceives. Because of this broad application of 'product differentiation,' it is possible for firms to sell exactly the same products and still be in monopolistic competition.

• PROBLEM 20-5

Why is it realistic to expect relatively free entry and exit in a monopolistically competitive industry?

Solution: It is realistic to expect free entry and exit in a monopolistically competitive industry because, by definition, there are numerous, small firms. Because firms are small, it takes relatively little capital to start up a new firm. Some monopolistically competitive industries, like beauty salons and retail gas outlets, can be entered into by individuals with relatively little cash. Other industries, with bigger though still differentiated markets, might require larger amounts of capital. Because monopolistic competition, by definition, is limited to industries where there are many firms, it is not unrealistic to expect relatively free entry and exit in monopolistically competitive industries.

• PROBLEM 20-6

Why is it difficult sometimes to define monopolistically competitive industries?

Solution: The problem with defining monopolistically competitive industries is that it can sometimes be hard to tell where one industry ends and another begins. With product differentiation, the product of one firm may not be a perfect substitute for the products of other firms. As the goods produced by different firms become less and less perfect substitutes, it becomes hard to define exactly what product a certain industry produces. Though some monopolistically competitive industries can be rather easily isolated and defined, some industries tend to gradually shade into others. Product differentiation, then, with the consequent loss of perfect substitutability, can lead to problems of industry definition as one industry shades off into another.

• PROBLEM 20-7

What is a product group?

Solution: 'Product group' is the term Edward Chamberlin, one of the most famous theorists on monopolistic competition, used to describe a group of firms producing similar, but not identical, products. In other words, it is his name for a monopolistically competitive industry. He used this term to try to defend his theory against the criticism that monopolistically competitive industries could not be adequately defined, since all of the firms produce different products. Chamberlin asserted that meaningful classifications of industries could be made.

• PROBLEM 20-8

In making his original analysis of monopolistic competition, Edward Chamberlin assumed that all of the firms in an industry face similar cost and demand curves. What is the problem with this assumption?

Solution: The assumption of similar demand and cost curves throughout an industry runs into problems because it is hard to reconcile this assumption with product differentiation. Product differentiation would seem to mean that firms would have different costs, either in the production process or in advertising. Product differentiation almost certainly means that firms face different demand curves. It is hard to imagine a situation where all the different product varieties have similar demand conditions. This is especially true for retail outlets, where location can tremendously affect demand. This assumption by Chamberlin of similar cost and demand curves has been widely criticized, and is one of the reasons why the entire theory of monopolistic competition has been criticized.

• PROBLEM 20-9

What do sales (the lowering of prices to stimulate purchasing) at stores indicate about competition in many retail industries?

Solution: A sale at a store implies that the store is not in a purely competitive industry. In pure competition, firms are price-takers. Any deviation from the market price will result quickly in either excess supply or excess demand. Furthermore, since in an equilibrium position profits are zero in pure competition, deviations from the market price, sales, would result in losses to the store. As is obvious from the widespread use of sales, stores have some control over prices. Since sales do not usually result in sudden gaps in demand and supply, the use of sales seems to indicate at least monopolistic competition, and possibly oligopolistic competition.

DEMAND AND MARGINAL REVENUE

• PROBLEM 20-10

Why will firms in monopolistic competition tend to have highly elastic (not quite horizontal) demand schedules?

Solution: Firms in a monopolistically competitive industry will tend to have highly elastic demand schedules because they produce goods that are fairly close substitutes for each other. The fact that they are fairly close substitutes means that a firm has some control over price, but not much. If the firm raises prices too much, customers will switch to the similar, but not identical, products of other firms in the industry. This implies that moderate changes in price will have large effects on output--that is, the demand schedule will have a slight downward slope. A slight downward slope (large changes in quantity in response to moderate changes in price) means that the demand schedule is highly elastic. Note that the demand schedule cannot be perfectly elastic (horizontal) in monopolistic competition. This would imply that the firms cannot control price at all. In monopolistic competition, because of product differentiation, firms do have some control over price.

• PROBLEM 20-11

Why is marginal revenue below the demand curve for the monopolistically competitive firm?

Solution: The marginal revenue is the change in total revenue caused by selling an extra unit of output. As such, it is different from the average revenue (average revenue = $\frac{\text{total revenue}}{\text{quantity}}$ = price = demand schedule). It might seem at first that marginal revenue should equal the price paid for the last unit sold. But this is not the case. It is true that when an extra unit is sold, total revenue increases by the amount charged for that extra unit. However, at the same time, the price of all units is falling. Therefore the total revenue from all previous units sold is falling as well. And so the combined effect of an addition to total revenue from an extra unit sold and a subtraction from total revenue due to the price drop is that marginal revenue lies below the demand curve.

An example should make this clearer. In the table below, the demand schedule (quantity and price coordinates) is given for a firm. From this schedule we can calculate total and marginal revenue.

Quantity	Price	Total Revenue	Marginal Revenue
1	50	50	50
2	45	90	40 (90-50)
3	40	120	30
4	35	140	20
5	30	150	10
6	25	150	0

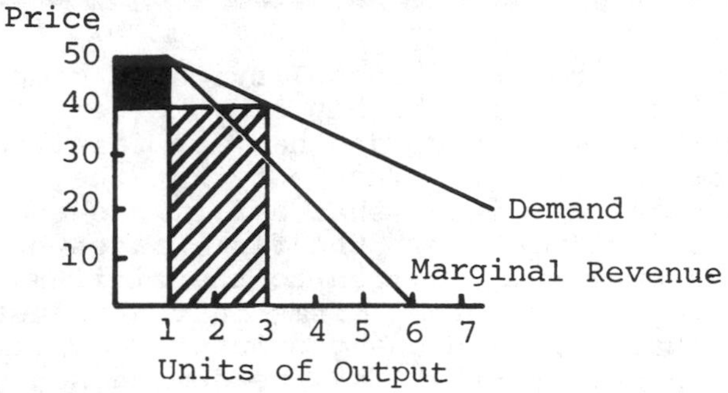

Put on a graph, this table clearly shows that marginal revenue is less than price (the y-coordinate of demand). When the price drops from 50 to 40, and the quantity sold increases from 1 unit to 3, there is a large gain in revenue (shaded area ▨) from the extra two units sold. However, there is also a loss, since the original unit sold at 50 would now be sold at 40. To calculate marginal revenue, we have to subtract this loss (blackened square ■ on graph) from the gain. So, marginal revenue does not equal price, and therefore is below the demand curve, because the price of all units has to be lowered to the price of the last unit sold. Marginal revenue will always be less than price whenever a firm faces a downward-sloping demand schedule, and so has to lower the price of all units of output in order to increase sales.

• PROBLEM 20-12

Does the following diagram correctly show a monopolistic competitor's cost and revenue curves? Why or why not?

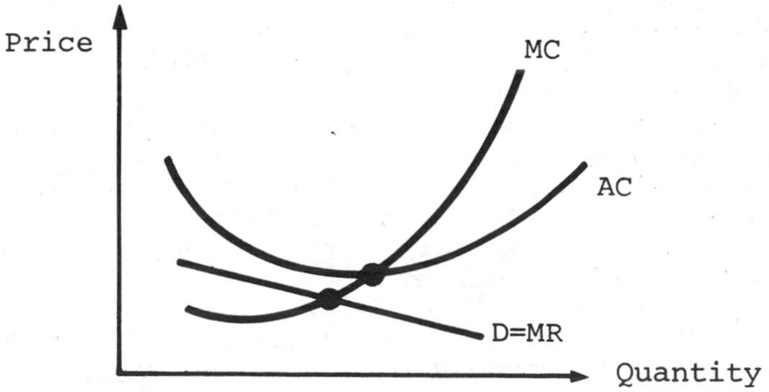

Solution: In the diagram, note that D is represented as being equal to MR, even though the demand curve is shown as downward sloping. However, with a downward sloping demand curve, increases in the quantity purchased result in increases to the total revenue, not by the last unit times the new price, but by the last unit times the new price minus the decrease in price times all previous units. That is, since the demand curve is assumed to slope downward, any increase in the quantity sold must come about because of a decline in price. This price decline must be true not just for the last unit sold, but for all units sold. Therefore, when the quantity sold is increased the marginal revenue will be less than the average revenue (demand) at that point, not equal as shown in the diagram.

PROFIT MAXIMIZATION

• PROBLEM 20-13

Does the graph in Figure 1 show a potential profit-maximizing equilibrium point for a monopolistic competitor? Why or why not?

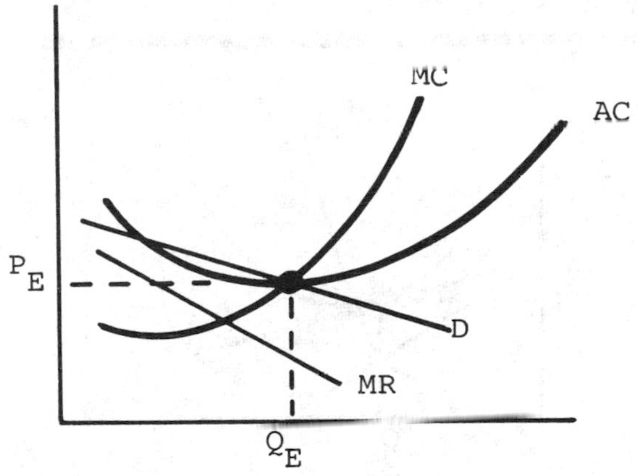

Fig. 1

Solution: The profit maximizing condition for any firm is to produce at the quantity where MR = MC. The firm in the diagram can be identified as a monopolistic competitor by its highly elastic, downward sloping demand curve. Using the diagram in the question, note that this firm has chosen to produce at the minimum average cost level, Q_E, with its associated price, P_E, where no excess profit is earned. (At Q_E, the AC curve is exactly equal to the demand, or AR curve.) Note that if this firm were to decrease its production to Q_M where MR = MC, and increase its price to P_M, as shown in Figure 2,

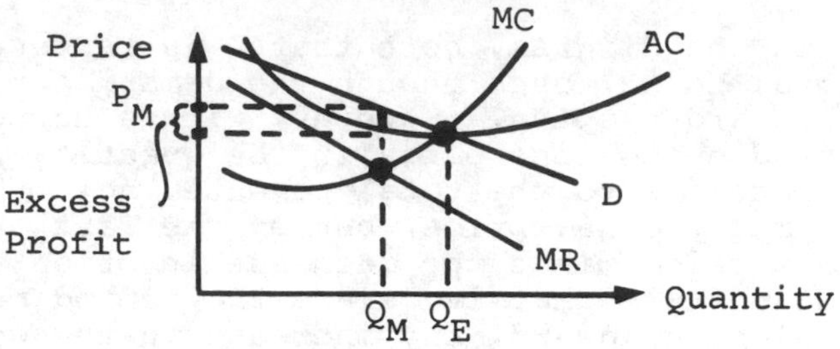

Fig. 2

excess profits could be earned. (At Q_M, the AC curve lies below the AR curve, with the distance between the two representing the excess profit per unit.) Therefore, since Q_M, with its associated price of P_M, not Q_E, with price P_E, is the profit-maximizing point for this monopolistic competitor, the diagram given in the question does not correctly show a profit-maximizing equilibrium.

• PROBLEM 20-14

Draw a diagram for a firm in monopolistic competition, including the marginal cost, average total cost, marginal revenue, and demand schedules. Show what the equilibrium price and output will be.

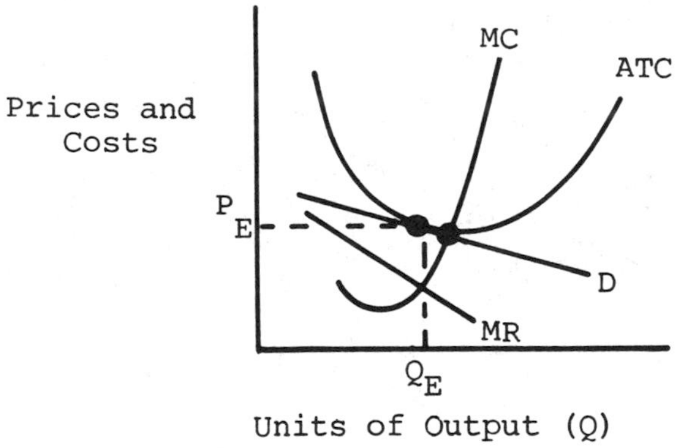

Solution: In this diagram, P_e and Q_e represent the equilibrium levels of price and quantity, respectively. The quantity of output is determined by the intersection of the marginal cost (MC) and marginal revenue (MR) curves, just as in pure competition. This is because if the firm produces any more, marginal cost will be greater than marginal revenue resulting in the firms losing money. If the firm produces less than Q_e, marginal revenue will be greater than marginal cost, resulting in the firms not taking full advantage of its profit-making capability. The price is determined by finding the price associated with the quantity produced (Q_e). This is done by finding the point on the demand curve (D) above Q_e and then finding the price level (P_e) that is associated with this point on the demand curve.

Two aspects of this diagram are notable. First, the cost curves and the efficiency condition (MC = MR) are the same as in the pure competition model. The difference between the two models lies in the downward sloping demand schedule (caused by product differentiation) facing the firm under monopolistic competition. This results in $P \neq MC = MR$. The second notable aspect of this model is that no economic profits are made. At the equilibrium level of output, the price of each unit equals the average total cost (ATC) of each unit. This happens for the same reason as in pure competition--free entry and exit into the market. With free entry, if there are economic profits being made, more firms will enter the market. They will enter until profits are no longer being made, that is until price equals average total cost. (Price equals average total cost when the demand schedule has been adjusted so that it is tangent to the average total cost curve.)

• PROBLEM 20-15

Differentiate between the demand curve faced by the perfect competitor and the demand curve faced by the imperfect competitor.

Solution: A perfect competitor is being defined as a firm that has no control over price but it can sell all it wants without ever depressing market price. In other words, the firm faces an essentially horizontal dd curve along which it can sell as much or as little output as it likes. The reason why the firm has no control over price is that any single competitive firm constitutes just a very small segment in relation to the entire market that any action that he has with regards to price has no bearing with the action of the firm. The firm demand under perfect competition may be shown graphically as in Figure 1.

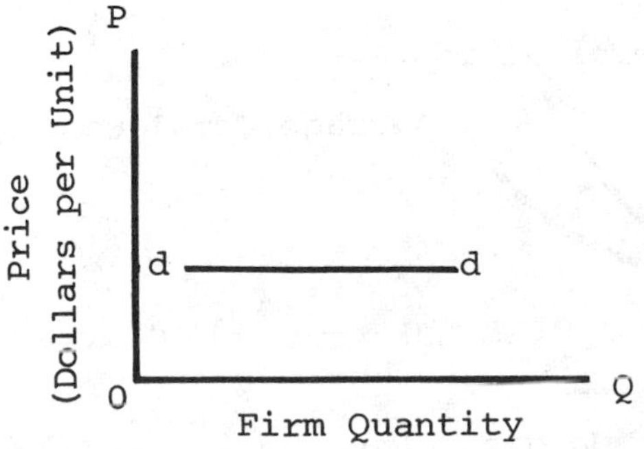

Fig. 1

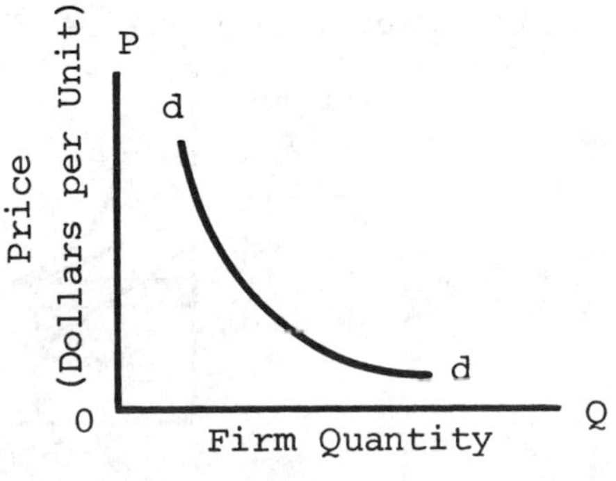

Fig. 2

On the other hand, "imperfect competition" prevails in an industry or group of industries wherever the individual sellers are imperfect competitors, facing their own nonhorizontal dd curves as shown in Figure 2.

In other words, the imperfect competitor finds itself facing a demand curve which slopes appreciably downward--which means that when it insists on throwing more on the market it definitely does depress price along its dd curve.

• PROBLEM 20-16

Using Figure 1, find the price level for this monopolistically competitive firm. Is it higher or lower than the price of a purely competitive firm?

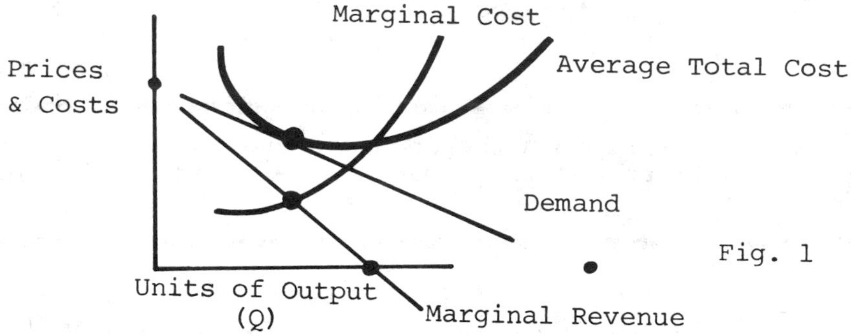

Fig. 1

Solution: For any firm that is not purely competitive, price is determined by the optimal quantity, and the optimal quantity is determined by the intersection of the marginal cost (MC) and marginal revenue (MR) curves. After finding the quantity (Q_e) associated with the intersection of the MC and MR curves, the point on the demand schedule that corresponds to this quantity has to be located. Corresponding to this point, Q_e, on the demand curve is a specific price (P_e). This price is the equilibrium price. (See Figure 2.)

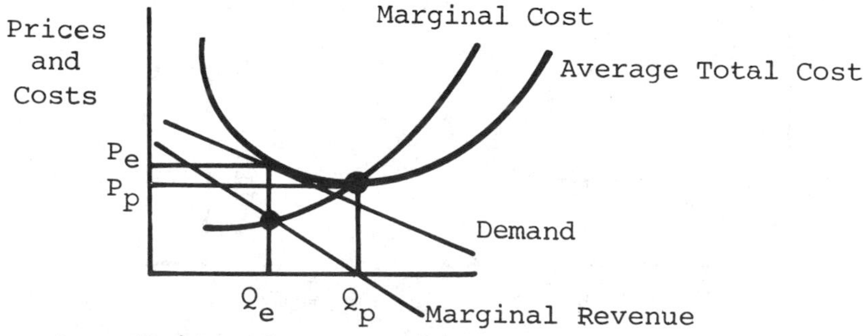

Fig. 2

With pure competition, output in the long run would be Q_p, where marginal cost equals average total cost. The corresponding price level would be P_p. It is obvious that monopolistic competition not only supplies fewer goods, but also charges a higher price to consumers.

INDUSTRY EQUILIBRIUM

• PROBLEM 20-17

Using Figure 1, calculate this firm's (Firm X) profit-maximizing price, output and economic (pure) profit. What will happen if other firms enter this industry (assume constant costs)?

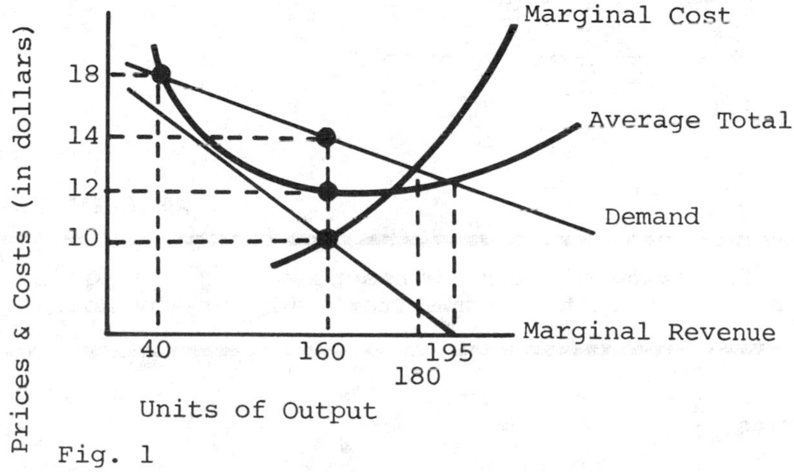

Fig. 1

Solution: The firm's optimal output level will be 160 units. This is the quantity that corresponds to the point where marginal cost equals marginal revenue (MC = MR). The profit-maximizing price at this optimal output is \$14 per unit. To calculate the excess (or economic) profit, subtract the cost per unit (average total cost for each of the 160 units produced = \$12) from the price, \$14, and multiply by the quantity produced, ((14-12) x 160 units = \$320). This firm's excess profits are \$320.

If other firms enter this industry, the demand schedule will shift downwards and become more elastic (more horizontal) since the new firms will introduce more substitutes for this firm's product. So, Firm X will have less control over price (if prices are raised too high, consumers will switch to the now more numerous substitutes). Firms will enter this industry until there are no excess profits left to be had, that is, until Firm X's demand schedule has shifted so it is tangent to the average total cost curve. At this tangency, no economic profits will be made, only 'normal' profits. So the entry of more firms into the industry will eliminate Firm X's excess profits, lower the price it can charge, and reduce its output. These last two results will occur because of the shift of the demand schedule. (As the demand schedule shifts down, the price will have to drop. The marginal revenue curve will also shift down and to the left, thus moving the intersection of marginal cost and marginal revenue to the left and reducing output.) This is shown in Figure 2.

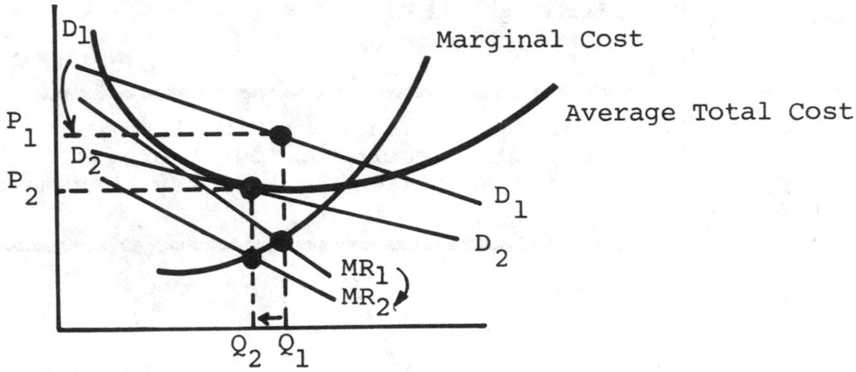

Fig. 2

• PROBLEM 20-18

Could the following diagram represent a long run equilibrium for a monopolistic competitor? Why or why not?

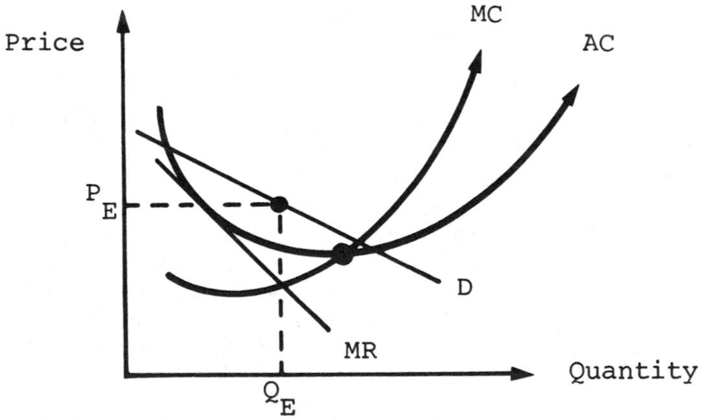

Solution: In the long run, because of the free entry and exit assumption, all of the monopolistic competitor's excess profits are assumed to be competed away. That is, if, in the short run, the monopolistic competitor is earning excess profits, new firms will enter the industry, decreasing the demand for the original firm's product, and raising costs to the original firm. If, in the short run, a monopolistically competitive industry is incurring losses, many of its firms may decide to leave the industry, decreasing costs and increasing demand to the remaining firms. Thus, in the long run, all excess profits are assumed to be competed to zero.

In the diagram, note that at Q_e, the profit-maximizing output level, the AC curve lies below the AR curve. That is, at this point the given firm is earning excess profits. Therefore, the given diagram does not show a long run equilibrium point for a monopolistic competitor.

• PROBLEM 20-19

Monopolistic competitors produce less goods at a higher average cost than pure competitors. Could a purely competitive market degenerate into a monopolistically competitive market? If so, why would the lower prices of the pure competitors fail to drive out the higher-priced monopolistic competitor?

Solution: A market could degenerate easily from pure competition to monopolistic competition. All that is needed is the introduction of product differentiation. This could be done by advertising, or actual changes in the product itself. Once this has happened, even if only one firm does it, then the lower prices of pure competitors become irrelevant. By introducing product differentiation, the firm has isolated its own little market. Even though other firms might offer lower prices, they are serving a different market. Because of this, the monopolistic competitor is to a certain extent isolated from price competition.

• PROBLEM 20-20

Monopolistic competition will usually result in normal profits for the firms in an industry in the long run. Describe three factors which might change this result.

Solution: There are three reasons why either below-normal or above-normal profits could persist in the long run in a monopolistically competitive industry. The first two could lead to excess profit, the third to below-normal profits.

To start off, a firm could have some measure of product differentiation that cannot be duplicated. A patent or prime location (for example, a rathskellar near a college campus) could enable a firm to achieve excess profits.

Another possibility is that product differentiation could cause greater barriers to entry than would otherwise be the case. Though these barriers are usually not enough to deny entry completely, they could keep out some potential competitors and help boost up profits.

The final factor works to reduce profits. Imagine the case of the sole proprietor (tavern owner, bakery owner, etc.). Such a businessman might stay in business even though profits are below normal. To him, his business is a way of life, i.e. profit is measured in more than monetary terms.

So, these factors, as given above, show us that economists cannot state rigidly that firms will always have normal profits in the long run in a monopolistically competitive industry.

• PROBLEM 20-21

If there is a monopolistically competitive industry with firms enjoying above-normal profits, what will probably happen to costs as other firms enter the industry?

Solution: As new firms enter a monopolistically competitive market, costs will tend to rise for two basic reasons. First, increases in the number of firms bidding for scarce input resources will cause the prices of these factors of production to rise, causing an increase in a firm's average costs at all points. Second, as new firms enter the industry, the established firms will try to protect, or even increase, their profits. They could use advertising or technical improvement in an effort to distinguish their product and maintain the market for it. These additional attempts at product differentiation, however, cost money. The established firms will have a rise in costs due to their attempts to preserve their profits. This rise, of course, will immediately diminish their profits unless offset by a rise in output. Since new firms are entering the industry, and all the established firms are taking similar steps to protect their profits, it is doubtful if any of the older firms will be able to expand their markets. The result of new firms entering the market, then, is not only increased costs, but increased average total cost (cost per unit of output).

• PROBLEM 20-22

The market for pizza pie behaves as follows: Government has set the price at $3.00 a pie and the quantity demanded is assumed to be constant at 1,000,000 pies per year. There are five companies in the market, each selling exactly 20% of the total quantity. The five companies' products are identical and cost each company $2.00 each to produce.

Early this year, Company A added a secret ingredient to its product which costs $0.30 for each pie. As a result, Company A's share of total pizza sales increased to 40%, at the expense of the four other companies whose market share dropped to 15% apiece.

With the industry in an uproar over the shift away from equal shares of the market, Company A's president offered to tell what the secret ingredient was if each company would pay him $35,000, reasoning that each other company could double its sales, just as Company A had, and would therefore be more than willing to pay the $35,000.

a) What is the fallacy here?

b) Should the other companies accept A's offer? What should they propose instead if they wish to return to an evenly divided market with a uniform product?

Solution: a) The fallacy here is that of composition. That is, it is assumed by Company A that what is true for it can necessarily be true for the whole pizza industry. To show this we must investigate what would happen if the other companies accepted Company A's proposal. When A introduced the secret ingredient into its pizza, there no longer was a market of uniform products and consumers began to prefer pizza A. But A's doubling of sales came completely at the expense of the four other companies due to the fact that the quantity demanded is constant at 1,000,000 pies per year. Therefore if Company A sold the secret, the market share of the four other companies would rise but only to the point where market share for each firm was once again 20%, since we would have now another undifferentiated product market. Company A's market share would therefore have to drop from 40% to 20%.

The lesson is clear. If demand is constant, gains in total sales can only be had at the expense of competitors. (This is an example of a zero-sum game.) It is possible for an individual firm to double sales, but impossible for the industry as a whole to do so, when demand is constant.

b) If the other companies accept Company A's offer, their sales will rise from 150,000 to 200,000, but profit will drop from $1.00 per unit to $0.70 per unit since it costs $0.30 to add the secret ingredient to the pizza. Therefore, actual profits will fall from (150,000)($1.00 per unit) = $150,000 to ($200,000)(.70 per unit) = $140,000. Note that this does not even account for the $35,000 cost of acquiring the secret information. It would therefore be foolish to buy the information.

By buying the information, the five companies would once again achieve perfect competition. But profit per unit would be $0.70 as opposed to the profit per unit of $1.00 which existed before Company A introduced its secret ingredient. It would be to the advantage of the four firms in the industry to pay Company A the $35,000 each which A requested, but not to buy the rights to the secret information. Rather they should pay A to disregard its secret and return to producing pizza without the secret ingredient. That way equal shares of the market would be restored with profit of $1.00 per unit.

For Company A, if it understood the fallacy which it is invoking, it would realize that its best strategy is not to sell its secret at all (unless a large enough payment can be commanded from each firm to offset the ensuing loss of profits) and should continue to produce its unique pizza, thereby continuing its dominance of the market.

• PROBLEM 20-23

In an oligopolistic market, firms pay close attention to the strategies of their rivals. In monopolistic competition, with a large number of sellers, it is assumed that there is not this kind of rivalry, or interdependence. Why is there probably some rivalry in many monopolistically competitive markets?

Solution: There is probably some rivalry in many monopolistically competitive markets because of the effect location can have on product differentiation. Firms who realize that good location is one of the reasons they are preferred by customers, will watch closely the actions of firms nearby. Thus two restaurants or cigar shops across the street from each other will probably pay close attention to each other. Similarly, two blouse manufacturers will pay attention to the styles introduced by each other. It is obvious that there are many situations where the oligopolistic element of rivalry could be felt in monopolistically competitive markets because of either geographical or stylistic closeness between firms.

EFFICIENCY AND WELFARE

• PROBLEM 20-24

Given the following graph for a firm in monopolistic competition, explain why it is not advisable to produce at the most efficient point if profit maximization is desired.

Solution: If the firm wants to maximize profits, it will produce at the point, Q_p, where marginal cost equals marginal revenue. Note that at this point the monopolistic competitor is not producing as efficiently as he could. For at the most efficient point, Q_E, marginal cost equals average total costs. However since the monopolistic competitor faces a downward sloping demand curve, at this point, MC = ATC, marginal cost is greater than marginal revenue, thereby eliminating profit maximization. Therefore, in general, it can be concluded that firms in imperfect competition (with downsloping demand curves) fail to produce at their most efficient points.

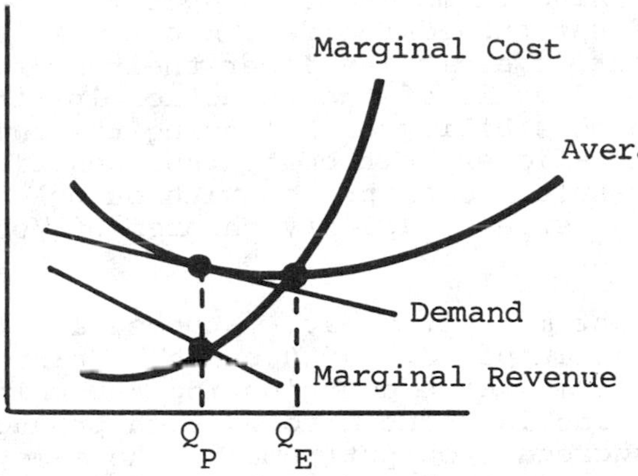

• PROBLEM 20-25

The profit-maximizing equilibrium for a monopolistically competitive firm leaves marginal cost below price. Explain why this is inefficient from a societal perspective.

Solution: A situation leaving marginal cost below price is inefficient from a societal perspective because it does not equate the benefits and losses that accrue to society as a result of a firm's production. The marginal cost is not only the marginal cost to the firm; it is also the marginal cost to society of using the factors of production in that firm, rather than somewhere else. The price of a unit of output also reflects societal preferences; it reflects how much society is willing to pay for an extra unit of output. When price and marginal cost are equated, the price society is willing to pay for the last unit is equal to the cost to society of producing. Society's consumption of the product reflects the real social costs in producing it. When price equals marginal cost, there is a socially efficient allocation of resources. When price is above marginal cost, society does not get enough output. Society would receive marginal benefits from more output. This extra output could be provided without using up factors in greater demand anywhere else. So, when price is greater than marginal cost, there is not a socially efficient allocation of resources.

• PROBLEM 20-26

Explain the excess capacity theorem of monopolistic competition.

Solution: Because monopolistically competitive firms do not operate at the most efficient point (where average cost per unit is lowest), it may be possible to lower costs while maintaining output by reducing the number of firms in the industry. By reducing the number of firms, the remaining firms might be able to expand. This expansion, if not pushed too far, might make the firms more efficient, i.e. it may lower their average cost per unit. As a result of the reduction in firms, there would be the possibility of producing the same aggregate output at a lower unit cost, thus benefitting consumers. This result, lower prices with output constant, is called the excess capacity theorem of monopolistic competition.

An example might make it clear. Suppose a particular industry has a total output of 6,000 units. This output is produced by 12 firms, each contributing 500 units. If the number of firms is reduced to 3, each producing 2,000 units, the aggregate output remains the same. If the expansion in output of these three firms results in lower unit costs (say from \$4 to \$3), there is a net gain to the community of \$6,000 without any reduction in output. In this demonstration of the excess capacity theorem, total costs to the industry were reduced from \$24,000 to \$18,000 because of the elimination of the inefficiencies of monopolistic competition.

• PROBLEM 20-27

Given that an industry with monopolistic competition is not economically efficient (compared to pure competition), what are some possible compensating advantages of monopolistic competition?

Solution: An industry with monopolistic competition may be able to compensate for its inefficiency because of other factors. Monopolistic competition can offer the consumer a wider variety of choice than pure competition can with its homogenous product. In addition to this, there can be tremendous non-price competition. Some of this non-price competition might be wasteful, like advertising, but some can be beneficial to the consumer. A firm could try to improve the quality of its product, or customer service, in an effort to win more business. Traditionally, monopolistically competitive industries have been marked by vigorous competition in areas other than price. So, an industry with monopolistic competition may compensate for economic inefficiency by widening consumer choice and improving quality and service. The consumer, though, has to pay for these compensations through the higher prices and lower quantities supplied because of the inefficiency of monopolistic competition.

• PROBLEM 20-28

Product differentiation and development are two of the compensating advantages of monopolistic competition. Yet some people claim that they can be disadvantages as well. How can they be disadvantageous to the consumer?

Solution: Product differentiation and development can be disadvantageous to consumers if these competitive tools are used to excess. Product differentiation, for example, can give greater choice to consumers, but it can reach the point where there are so many product variations that consumers become confused. In this case, the consumer cannot even take advantage of product differentiation, because there are so many products that a rational choice would simply take too long. In such a situation, price is often taken as the sole indication of quality.

Similarly, though product development can obviously benefit consumers, it can also hurt the consumer. Critics charge that much of product development is merely superficial. They point to the 'planned obsolescence' of some durable consumer goods as a wasteful example of product development. Here critics argue that firms improve their product only by that amount necessary to make the average consumer dissatisfied with last year's model. Some people believe that these inefficient aspects of product differentiation overrule the beneficial aspects. Because of this, they favor public policies designed to correct these abuses.

• PROBLEM 20-29

A monopolistically competitive producer can shift the demand schedule for his product by changing consumers' perceptions of it. He can do this by actually changing the product, or he can do it through advertising. Distinguish the two types of advertising and draw out the implications for economic efficiency of each type.

Solution: The two types of advertising are informative and competitive. Informative advertising accurately describes the qualities and prices of products, as in classified advertisements. Since it informs the consumer of the options available, informative advertising helps the consumer make a rational, efficient choice. Because of this, informative advertising is generally considered to improve economic efficiency.

Competitive advertising is more controversial. It consists of simple exhortations to buy a product because a celebrity endorses it or an announcer says it's great. Some economists feel that this kind of advertising can be beneficial. If the demand for a firm's product rises because of competitive advertising, then the firm can expand its production and realize economies of scale. A monopolistically competitive producer might thus be able to reach a more efficient level of production. Even including the additional advertising costs, the firm still might be able to achieve lower unit costs because of the expanded scale of production. Critics argue that advertising by one firm merely offsets advertising by another. As a result, competitive advertising results in higher unit costs due to advertising expenditures; it does not result in expanded production for any firm. These critics point to the cigarette industry, where millions of dollars are spent each year simply as a defensive measure by firms to protect their market shares. The costs, of course, are paid for by consumers.

The economic aspects of advertising are a matter of fierce debate. Though informative advertising is considered desirable, it is sometimes hard to disentangle from competitive advertising. As for competitive advertising, there are very different opinions as to its desirability.

• PROBLEM 20-30

Economists have taken opposite stands on the effect advertising can have on the level of competition in a monopolistically competitive industry. Describe how advertising could increase, and how it could decrease, competition in a monopolistically competitive industry.

Solution: Some claim that advertising in a monopolistically competitive industry promotes the growth of monopoly power. They argue advertising expenditures create large obstacles to entry in an industry, thus securing the market power of the established firms. In addition to this, the creation of brand loyalty will give firms greater control over price, thereby gaining monopoly power. Another danger is that firms that are not successful advertisers might be forced out of the market. This, plus the financial barrier to free entry caused by extensive advertising, could lead to an oligopolistic situation.

Other economists dispute these points. They believe that advertising, by providing information on a large number of substitutes, prevents, and even diminishes, monopoly power. As for the argument that advertising prevents free entry, they believe that advertising gives new firms and new products a chance to diminish the tremendous advantage that established products have. They point to empirical evidence that new firms have frequently gained entrance to an industry by extensive advertising, thus increasing competition.

So, it seems that economists have taken completely

opposite stands as regards the effects of advertising on the level of competition. Some hold that it can change monopolistic competition to oligopoly or monopoly; others think that it could enable monopolistic competition to approximate pure competition more closely.

Answer

To be covered when testing yourself

SHORT ANSWER QUESTIONS FOR REVIEW

Choose the correct answers.

1. In the short run, monopolistically competitive firms will (a) realize normal profits (b) realize excess profits (c) lose money (d) either lose money, make money or break even, depending on the particular firm and industry. d

2. The tendency of monopolistically competitive firms to make normal profits in the long run arises from (a) the counteracting effects of advertising (b) the perfectly elastic demand curve (c) the relative absence of barriers to entry (d) product differentiation and development. c

3. Monopolistic competition consists of (a) a few firms selling differentiated products (b) a few firms selling a uniform product (c) many firms selling differentiated products (d) many firms selling a uniform product. c

4. Consider a monopolistically competitive firm's demand curve; the degree of elasticity depends on: (a) the number of rivals and non-rivals (b) the number of rivals and the degree of product differentiation (c) product differentiation and development (d) the level of profit in the firm b

5. Monopolistic competition is less efficient than pure competition because (a) of misleading advertizing (b) of price-fixing by sellers (c) there is too high a turnover of firms (d) none of the above. d

6. The profit-maximizing condition of a monopolistically competitive firm is producing at the point where (a) marginal revenue equals marginal cost (b) marginal cost equals price (c) marginal revenue equals average cost (d) total revenue is at a maximum. a

7. Product differentiation refers to (a) entirely different products produced by the same firm (b) entirely different products produced by different firms (c) consumer preferences (d) any differences perceived by consumers between products. d

8. In monopolistic competition, as opposed to perfect competition, (a) prices are higher, but so is output (b) both prices and output

	Answer To be covered when testing yourself
are lower (c) output is higher because prices are lower (d) output is lower and prices are higher.	d
9. Multi-priced industries tend to be characteristic of (a) pure competition (b) monopolistic competition (c) pure monopoly (d) no particular market structure.	b
10. In monopolistic competition, marginal revenue is (a) less than price (b) equal to price (c) equal to demand (d) always greater than zero.	a
Fill in the blanks.	
11. The downward-sloping demand curve facing a monopolistically competitive firm is the result of ____________________.	product differentiation
12. One feature which compensates for the inefficiencies of monopolistic competition is ____________________ which results in greater __________ for the consumer.	product differentiation, choice
13. The ____________________ theorem refers to the underutilization of plants characteristic of monopolistic competition.	excess capacity
14. A large part of the debate on monopolistic competition centers on the usefulness of advertising, specifically on the differences between __________ and __________ advertising.	informative, competitive
15. Chamberlin's term for a monopolistically competitive industry is ____________________.	product group
Determine whether the following statements are true or false.	
16. If free entry into an industry shifts each firm's sloping demand curve far enough to the left to eliminate all profits, then the inefficiencies of monopolistic competition have been eliminated.	False
17. For a monopolistically competitive firm, price is always above marginal cost at the maximum-profit equilibrium.	True
18. If all firms in an industry sell identical	

		Answer To be covered when testing yourself
	products, then it would never pay to advertise.	False
19.	Monopolistic competition resembles pure competition because barriers to entry are weak or virtually nonexistent in both cases.	True
20.	As new firms enter a monopolistically competitive industry, average total costs (costs per unit) tend to rise for the established firms.	True
21.	The larger the number of firms and the less pronounced the degree of product differentiation, the more elastic the demand curve of a monopolistically competitive seller will be.	True
22.	Monopolistic competition is typical of retail industries.	True
23.	Because of the expenses of advertising and product development, monopolistically competitive firms usually prefer price competition over non-price competition.	False
24.	The major difference between pure competition and monopolistic competition is that the purely competitive industries have fewer firms.	False
25.	The marginal revenue schedule of a monopolistically competitive firm slopes downward because of the heavy advertising and development costs incurred in the attempt to increase sales.	False
26.	The less elastic (more inelastic) the demand schedule facing a monopolistically competitive firm, the greater the control the firm has over price.	True
27.	If firms could differentiate their products as much as they desire to, a monopolistically competitive situation would degenerate into a group of small monopolies.	True
28.	In monopolistic competition, marginal revenue equals price.	False
29.	If consumers would sacrifice product variety, they could get more of a product at a lower price.	True
30.	A monopolistically competitive firm has the	

SHORT ANSWER QUESTIONS FOR REVIEW

Answer

To be covered when testing yourself

same profit-maximization condition as a purely competitive firm, marginal revenue equals marginal cost.

True

CHAPTER 21

OLIGOPOLY

Basic Attacks and Strategies for Solving Problems in this Chapter. See pages 754 to 779 for step-by-step solutions to problems.

An oligopoly is an industry dominated by a few very large firms and in which there is "mutual dependence recognized." There are homogenous oligopolies in which firms produce identical products, and differentiated oligopolies in which firms produce similar but slightly differentiated products.

The key element in the oligopoly definition is "mutual dependence recognized." This means that the success of the business strategy each firm follows will depend on the strategies followed by all the other firms, and each firm realizes this. Consequently, each firm takes into account expected reactions by its rivals in formulating its business strategy.

Because firms recognize their mutual dependence and the small number of firms in the industry, there is the potential for collusion between the market participants. Collusion means that firms cooperate with each other to try to extract monopoly profits from the public. Collusion can be explicit or tacit, formal or informal.

Unlike the cases of perfect competition, monopoly, or monopolistic competition, there is no widely-accepted theory of oligopoly. Rather, there are many oligopoly models that attempt to capture aspects of the oligopoly problem.

One insightful model is the duopoly (industry composed of two firms) model of firm location. Assume two firms are trying to locate themselves on a street along which population is evenly distributed. People will buy from the firm closest to them. Firm location will represent a reaction to the expected location of the rival firm. It can be shown that in equilibrium, both firms will locate side-by-side at the center of the street. This model shows that imitative behavior is a likely outcome of duopolistic situations, among other things.

Another well-known model is the kinked demand curve. This model assumes that firms believe that rivals will match any price cuts but will not follow price increases. This assumption results in a demand curve displaying a kink at the current price. The segment above the kink will be highly elastic; the segment below the kink will be highly inelastic. An implication of this model is that prices will tend to be inflexible over the business cycle.

The welfare implications of oligopoly is a source of controversy. Some economists believe that the structure of the industry, in particular the small number of firms, reflects the existence of economies of scale meaning that few firms can produce more efficiently than many firms. Other economists emphasize the likelihood of collusion as the source of suspicions that the industry would display monopoly-like distortions.

Step-by-Step Solutions to Problems in this Chapter, "Oligopoly"

BASIC CONCEPTS

• PROBLEM 21-1

What is economic concentration?

Solution: Economic concentration measures the control of a particular economic activity by a small number of firms in an industry. For example, in the cigarette industry, the top four firms produce 80% of the industry's total output. We would say that this industry is highly concentrated, or has a high concentration ratio. Oligopolies typically possess high concentration ratios.

• PROBLEM 21-2

Suppose we are told that an industry is composed of a small number of firms. Can we immediately call this industry oligopolistic? Explain.

Solution: The term "oligopoly" literally means "few sellers." However, it is not the actual number of sellers that is important in studying oligopoly. Rather it is the existence of interactions between the sellers that concern us in studying oligopoly. A market has an oligopolistic structure if actions by one firm have such important effects upon rivals that these rivals will contemplate appropriate reactions, which may affect the original firm. In other words, an oligopoly exists when each firm in an industry must contemplate the possible reactions of its rivals in deciding its own behavior.

• PROBLEM 21-3

What is the difference between a homogeneous and a differentiated oligopoly?

Solution: In a homogeneous oligopoly, the firms produce standardized products, that is, the consumer perceives the different firms' products as being essentially the same. Examples of homogeneous oligopolies would be the steel and lead industries.

In differentiated oligopolies, products are no longer perceived by the consumer as being the same. Examples of differentiated oligopolies would be the automobile and cigarette industries.

Notice the emphasis of the word "perception" above. In some instances of differentiated oligopoly, the degree of difference perceived by consumers is far greater than the real difference that exists between products.

• PROBLEM 21-4

What is the difference between explicit and tacit collusion?

Solution: Explicit collusion is an open agreement between two or more companies determining the prices for their products. Since the greatest fear of the oligopolist is to get caught in a price war, collusion is a very attractive alternative. Unfortunately for the oligopolists, explicit collusion is illegal in the United States. Years ago, however, it was common practice for various oligopolistic sellers, such as the steel producers, to meet together at dinners and collusively set some kind of monopoly price, restricting it somewhat only for fear of attracting new entries into the industry.

Tacit collusion, on the other hand, implies that oligopolistic sellers begin to sell at similar prices, without ever agreeing upon collusive pricing.

• PROBLEM 21-5

Explain the following as applied to oligopoly: cartel, gentlemen's agreements, price leadership.

Solution: All three of the terms mentioned above describe a collusive situation in an oligopoly.

A cartel is by far the most blatant collusive arrangement of the three. Cartels are formal arrangements among producers to regulate price or output or to divide markets. Cartels are illegal in the United States. OPEC is an example of a cartel.

Gentlemen's agreements are more informal and subtle than cartels, and hence are undoubtedly widespread in our economy. Such agreements arise when competing oligopolists reach a verbal agreement on price or some other aspect of their strategies. Although they too collide with antitrust laws, gentlemen's agreements are difficult to detect and prosecute successfully due to their informal, sub rosa character.

Finally, price leadership is an even less formal means by which oligopolists coordinate their price behavior and avoid the uncertainty inherent in non-collusive action. In this case, one firm--usually the industry leader--initiates price changes, and all other firms more-or-less automatically follow that price change. Because price leadership is an informal, tacit agreement involving no written or spoken commitments, it is generally accepted as a legal technique by the courts in interpreting antitrust laws. The American steel industry is an example of a price leadership arrangement.

• PROBLEM 21-6

What is countervailing power?

Solution: Suppose that a certain industry is oligopolistic. Galbraith tells us that the presence of oligopolistic sellers tends to stimulate the growth of oligopsonistic buyers, and vice versa. More specifically, there is a tendency for "countervailing power" to develop on the opposite sides of markets in which "original power" has already developed.

The motivation of the group which tries to develop countervailing power is as follows: seeing that their partners on the other side of the market have developed an original-power position, this group bands together to protect itself against any abuses of the original-power position (defense) and to try to gain a share of the profits made possible by the original-power position (offense). Such "across-the-market" competition can thus be an important competitive force in those markets in which "same-side-of-the-market" competition is weak. When countervailing power has evolved, buyer and seller power will work against each other so as to cancel the potential market abuses of one another, with the resulting compromise price and output being closer to the competitive level than would have been attained ordinarily under oligopoly.

An example of countervailing power that exists in the American economy is the tire industry where four large producers (oligopoly) sell the majority of their products to three large car producers (oligopoly).

INTERDEPENDENCE

• PROBLEM 21-7

In dealing with price-setting, there is one important difference between the oligopolist's considerations and those of the monopolist. What is it?

Solution: We know that a monopolist has no competitors (by definition) and that when setting his price, his only concern is picking the price which maximizes his total revenue. We also know that the oligopolist must always consider carefully the possible actions of his competitors when setting or changing his price. Therefore the difference between these two forms of imperfect competition is interdependence. For example, suppose there are two firms, A and B, competing oligopolists. If A wants to raise its price, it must analyze what B might do in response to a price raise. Unless B also raises its price, A might lose enough business to result in a decrease in total revenue. However, suppose A was a monopolist. By raising his price A will certainly lose some business (since he faces a downward sloping demand curve), however, depending upon his demand and cost curves this may even result in an increase in total revenue.

Thus while a monopolist's only concern is locating a profit maximizing point, the oligopolist must maximize his profits while considering carefully the actions of his competitors. Problems like this often bring about collusion in oligopolies.

• PROBLEM 21-8

Suppose that Jack and Bill wish to sell lemonade on Elm St. where there are 10 identical houses as shown in Figure 1.

The residents of Elm St. consider Jack's lemonade to be the same as Bill's. Therefore, these people will buy lemonade from whoever is within closer walking distance since both Jack and Bill charge 25¢ a glass.

At the beginning of the day, Jack set up his stand between houses #1 and #2 while Bill set up his stand between houses #9 and #10.

a) If the two boys wish to maximize profit, where will they eventually relocate?

b) If we wished to maximize society's (the block's) welfare, where would we locate Jack and Bill?

Solution: The situation in Figure 1 represents an undifferentiated oligopoly in which our only independent variable is location.

The original positions of the two boys are as shown in Figure 2.

Fig. 1

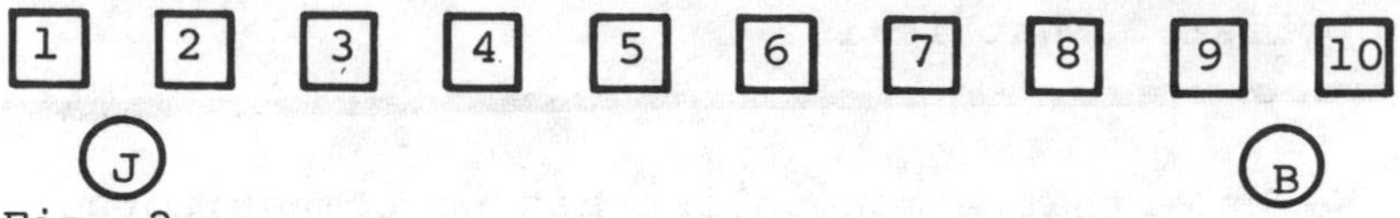

Fig. 2

a) Looking at the above situation, we see that since Jack sits between house #1 and Bill, house #1 would definitely buy from Jack. We call house #1 Jack's sheltered market. Similarly house #10 represents a sheltered market for Bill.

Since by nature your sheltered market will always buy from you, it would be to the boys' advantage to try to increase their sheltered markets, hence relocate.

Suppose Jack moves first. With the objective of maximizing his sheltered market in mind, Jack would relocate his stand directly to the left of Bill as shown in Figure 3.

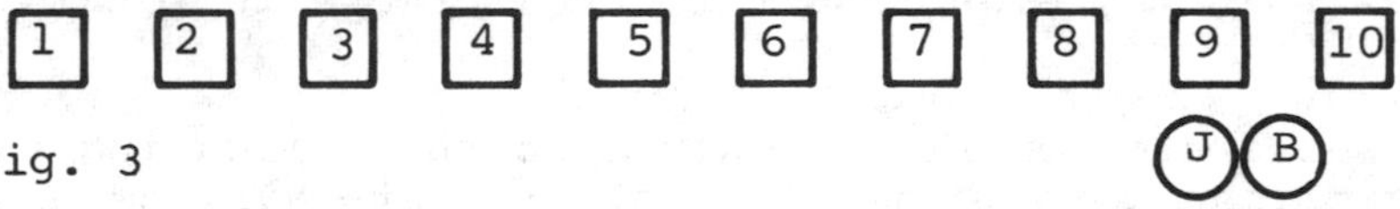

Fig. 3

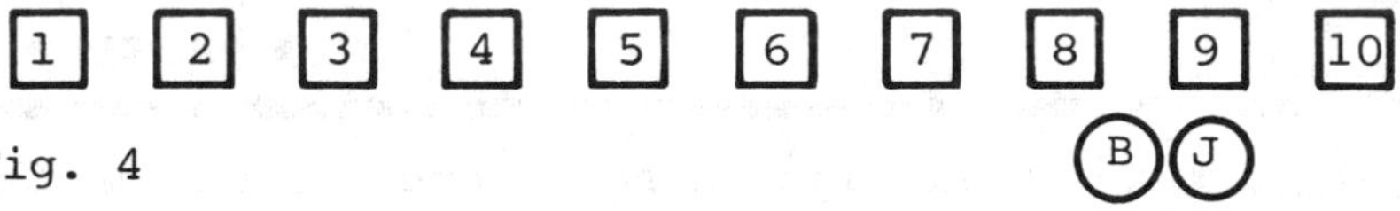

Fig. 4

Now Jack has acquired all the business of houses #1-#9. But this is only a temporary dominance, since Bill can just as easily move his stand to the left of Jack, as shown in Figure 4.

Now Bill has houses #1-#8 as a sheltered market while Jack has only houses #9 and #10.

The leap-frogging will continue until neither of the boys can increase their market share by moving any further. The equilibrium position will have Jack and Bill located between houses #5 and #6 as shown in Figure 5. Whoever is on the left will serve houses #1-#5 while the boy on the right will serve #6-#10.

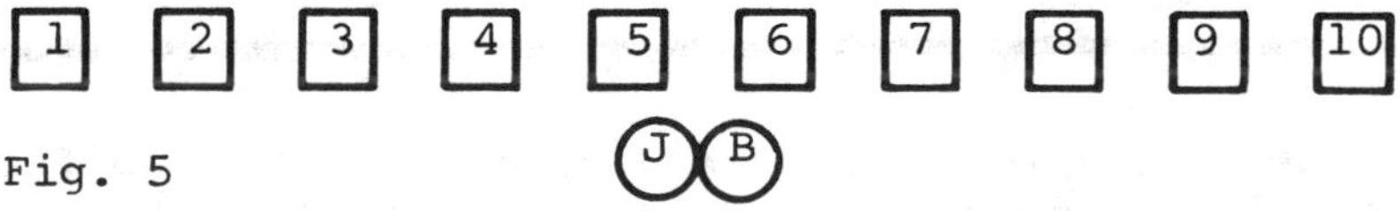

Fig. 5

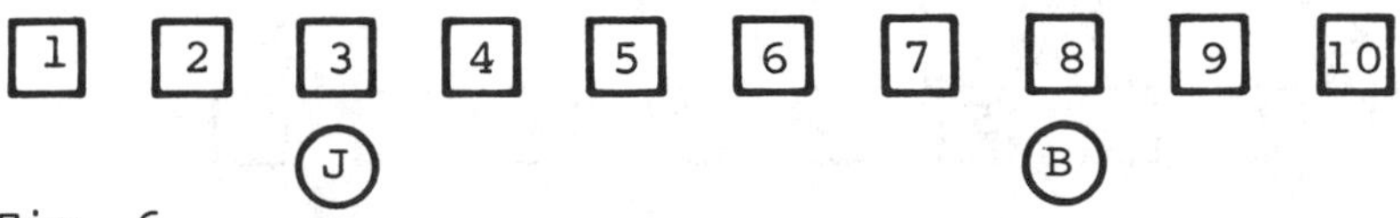

Fig. 6

b) At first glance it seems strange that two sellers should locate directly next to each other. From the point of view of society (the block) this is clearly not optimal since we wish to minimize the total distance traveled to obtain lemonade (remember our only independent variable is location). Rather, if we wished to minimize total distance, we would divide the block into two equal regions, houses #1-#5 and houses #6-#10, and locate Jack in one region and Bill in the other. Specifically we would place the boys directly at the midpoints of their respective regions, as shown in Figure 6.

Notice that under this situation, both boys still have sheltered markets of five houses, as in the equilibrium situation of part a). So Jack and Bill have nothing to lose by adopting these positions. However, unless forced to remain in front of houses #3 and #8, both boys would soon move so as to increase their sheltered markets, eventually relocating once again between houses #5 and #6.

It is not hard to find examples of such behavior in the real world. In New York, for example, three of the city's largest department stores, Gimbel's, Korvettes and Macy's are situated within a block of each other while other areas of the city go without even one department store.

• PROBLEM 21-9

Firms X and Y represent a duopoly in which the two rivals are fighting for the largest share of the market. In order to gain market share, Firm X is considering three methods of advertising, A_1, A_2 and A_3. Firm Y is also trying to gain market share; it is considering four possible packaging schemes, P_1, P_2, P_3, and P_4. Suppose it were possible to assess the share of the market resulting from these alternative strategies, as shown in Table 1 for Firm X.

Table 1: Market share (%) for Firm X,

		Firm Y's choices			
		P_1	P_2	P_3	P_4
Firm X's choices	A_1	48	93	16	22
	A_2	30	3	7	99
	A_3	60	37	6	33

Given the nature of the oligopoly, what are the best choices Firms X and Y can make?

Solution: Let us consider first the situation for Firm X. If Firm X could choose a strategy for itself and for Firm Y, it would select A_2 for itself and P_4 for Y, thereby granting itself a 99% market share. But no such choice is permitted in an oligopoly. Instead Firm X must choose an advertising strategy, aware of the fact that Firm Y will be choosing a packaging strategy that will affect the impact of that advertising strategy. For example suppose Firm X chooses A_1. This part of the market share picture is shown below:

	P_1	P_2	P_3	P_4
A_1	48	93	16	22

Firm Y now has to choose a packaging strategy. Since Y wants to maximize its own market share, it will seek to minimize X's market share on the section of the matrix shown above. Thus Firm Y would select packaging strategy P_3 and Firm X's market share would be 16%.

Similarly if Firm X chose A_2, Firm Y would retaliate with P_2 thus granting X a market share of 3%. If Firm X chose A_3, Firm Y would respond with P_3 giving Firm X a market share of 6%.

Since Firm X knows that Firm Y will respond in the manner described above (this being an oligopoly), we would expect Firm X to select strategy A_1 which would give it maximum market share of 16%.

Now consider the situation for Firm Y. To ease the analysis, it is useful to create a market share matrix for Firm Y, realizing that Market Share (x) + Market Share (Y) = 100%, or Market Share (Y) = 100 - Market Share (X), as in Table 2.

Table 2: Market share (%) for Firm Y,

		Firm X's choices			
		P_1	P_2	P_3	P_4
Firm Y's choices	A_1	52	7	84	78
	A_2	70	97	93	1
	A_3	40	63	94	67

Now we once again consider each strategy alternative, this time for Firm Y. Suppose Firm Y picks P_1. Firm X must respond and has chosen as shown in Table 3 (extracted from the preceding matrix.)

Table 3:

	P_1
A_1	52
A_2	70
A_3	40

Firm X, in its attempt to maximize its own market share, will try to minimize Firm Y's market share. Therefore it would pick A_3 giving Firm Y a market share of 40%.

Similarly, if Y picks P_2, X will respond with A_1, giving Y a market share of 7%. If Y picks P_3, X will pick A_1, giving Y a market share of 84%. Finally, if Y picks P_4, X will respond with A_2, giving Y a market share of A_2.

In its attempt to maximize its own market share, Y will then pick P_3, since it knows X will respond to whatever strategy it picks. At this point Y's market share will be 84%.

So we see that the two firms in analyzing strategy and counter-strategy, have agreed upon a cell in the table. The A_1P_3 cell is Firm X's best choice, given Firm Y's reaction; it is also Firm Y's best choice, given Firm X's reaction. Thus, both rivals have selected a strategy, and it will yield 16% of the market to Firm X and 84% of the market to Firm Y.

• PROBLEM 21-10

Given the profits-payoff table (Fig. 1) for a differentiated duopoly, assume firms C and D are both currently charging a price of $35.

a) Explain price rigidity by using the profit figures.

b) If C and D were both charging $30 and decided to collude why would they both agree to charge $35, but not $40? What if joint profit maximization were the objective?

D's Price \ C's Price	$40	$35	$30
$40	I 50 60	II 59 55	III 57 49
$35	IV 48 69	V 55 58	VI 56 50
$30	VII 40 70	VIII 49 60	IX 51 52

Fig. 1

Solution: a) If both C and D are charging $35, we are located in box V of the profits-payoff table with C's profit = $55 and D's profit = $58.

Looking at the table, we see that if C could lower its price to $30 without D reacting to the price cut (Box VI), its profits would rise to $56. Similarly if D could lower its price to $30 without C reacting to the price cut (Box VIII) its profits would rise to $60. But herein lies the reason for the price rigidity. There is no reason to assume your competition will not react to your price cuts. In fact, it is most likely that an oligopolist competitor will match or even undercut your price cut. This ease of reciprocal action helps explain why price cutting is rarely a part of an oligopolist's strategy.

In our example, suppose firm C cut its price to $30, hoping to attain box VI. Upon finding out about the price cut, firm D would realize that its profits had dropped from $58 (in box V) to $50 (in box VI). In order to retaliate D would lower its price to $30 (thus attaining a profit of $52 in box IX).

Similarly, if D took the initial move and lowered its price to $30 (box VIII), firm C would react by lowering its price to $30 also, thus bringing us once again to box IX.

So both price-cutting strategies eventually lead us to box IX where both C and D charge $30. Notice that once in box IX, neither firm will change its price independently since a raise in price by one firm will cause a drop in profit. Therefore, once at box IX, we would expect both firms to remain at a price of $30.

b) Now collusion enters the picture. Both firms are currently charging $30, and would like to increase their profits. But independent raising of prices by one firm will not be matched by the other firm, and hence profits for the higher priced firm will drop. However, if the two firms act together in raising price, profits can be raised for both firms. Specifically, should both firms agree to charge $35 (box V), C's profit will increase from $51 to $55 while D's profits will increase from $52 to $58. So both firms will gladly welcome a joint increase to $35. However, we would not expect C to agree to an increase in price to $40 (box I). In this case profit for C would be

$50, or $1 less than it currently has at a price of $30. It would make more sense for C to keep its price at $30 or only to raise it to $35.

C's Price / D's Price	$40	$35	$30
$40	I 110	II 114	III 106
$35	IV 117	V 113	VI 106
$30	VII 110	VIII 109	IX 103

Fig. 2

If joint profit maximization is the objective, we will no longer consider individual profit for C and D, but rather combine the profits in each profit-payoff cell, as shown in Figure 2.

According to our revised payoff table, joint profit would be maximized in box IV. Here D would charge $35 and C would charge $40.

Note also that ironically enough, box IX, the cell from which neither C nor D was willing to move independently, represents the lowest joint profit for the two firms.

DEMAND AND MARGINAL REVENUE

• PROBLEM 21-11

Explain the rationale behind the kinked demand curve used by economists to describe oligopoly.

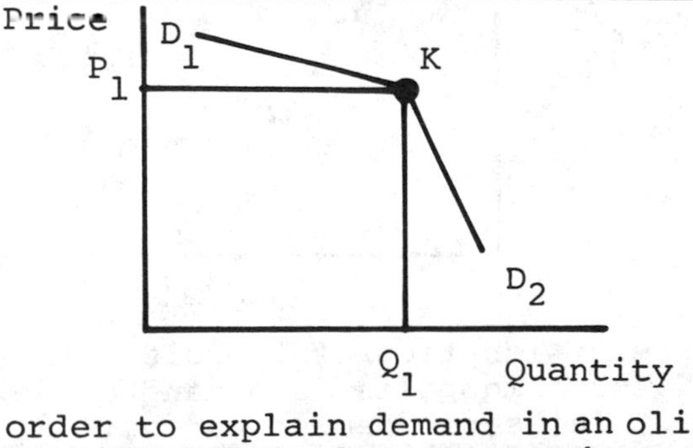

Solution: In order to explain demand in an oligopoly, economists use a kinked demand curve, such as illustrated in the figure.

The kinked demand curve is used to explain the price inflexibility that characterizes oligopoly. Let us consider the price strategy of an oligopolist selling Q_1 units of output at price = P_1. This point (k) is called the kink. If the oligopolist lowers his price, his competitors will follow suit and lower their prices also. Therefore the curve shows that as he lowers price, quantity demanded increases very slowly. As price falls along this inelastic portion of the curve, the oligopolists total revenue (P x Q) will fall. On the other hand, if the oligopolist raises his price, his competitors will most likely not raise their prices. When this happens, the high priced product will no longer be so attractive to the customer and quantity demanded will drop a great deal. Here, the demand curve is highly elastic, that is, by increasing his prices, the oligopolist's total revenue will decline. Therefore according to the kinked demand curve, it does not pay for the oligopolist to raise or lower prices.

• PROBLEM 21-12

Suppose that there are three firms, A, B, and C, in an oligopolistic industry. In analyzing the market, Firm A has come to the conclusion that B and C will follow any price change A initiates. Does the kinked demand curve apply here?

Solution: The kinked demand curve is used to illustrate a market situation where Firms B and C would match the price cuts of Firm A but would ignore any price increases by Firm A. In the situation here B and C match both price cuts and price increases. So the kinked demand curve does not apply to this oligopoly.

• PROBLEM 21-13

Explain why the marginal revenue curve is discontinuous at the kink on an oligopolist's demand curve.

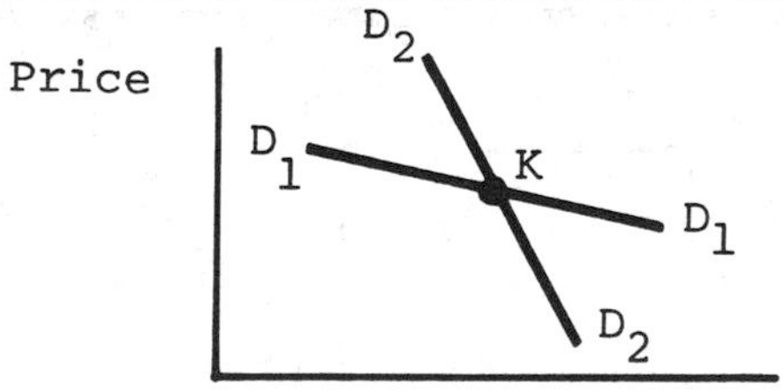

Fig. 1

Solution: The explanation of the discontinuity lies in the derivation of the oligopolist's demand curve. Essentially an oligopolist faces two demand curves. D_1 is consumer demand for his product if the oligopolist's rivals do not follow his price changes. D_2 is consumer's demand for his product if they do follow his price changes. Note that D_1 is more elastic than D_2. Suppose our oligopolist is at point K in figure 1, that is, his prices are currently consistent with those of his rivals. If our oligopolist were to raise his prices, his rivals would have two choices. They could react with similar price changes, moving upwards along D_2, (this is the price leadership model), or they could react by not changing their prices, putting our oligopolist on D_1. Our oligopolist would then lose a considerable percentage of his market to his rivals resulting in decreased total revenue for himself and increased total revenue for his rivals. We will assume that oligopolists take the latter course leaving us with D_1 as our oligopolist's demand curve above point K.

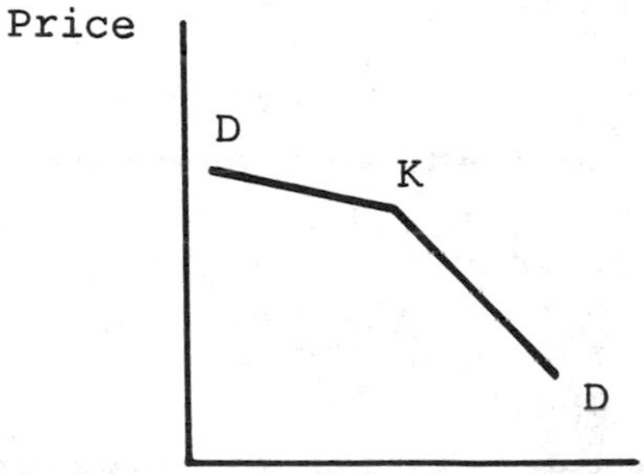

Fig. 2

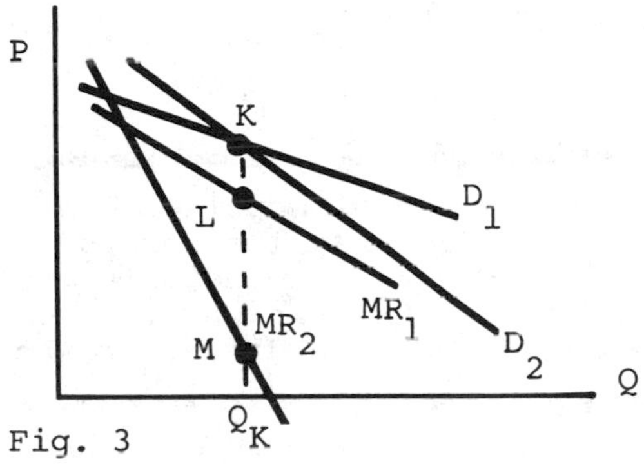

Fig. 3

Similar logic may be applied to a decrease in prices. That is, if our oligopolist were to lower his prices, his rivals would follow his actions, putting him on D_2, rather than ignoring the change and allowing him to capture a larger market share. Thus the final demand curve would be as drawn in Figure 2.

When demand is downward sloping, MR is downward sloping as well, with even greater steepness. Therefore the MR curves for our original demand curves (D_1 and D_2) would be as shown in Figure 3.

Fig. 4

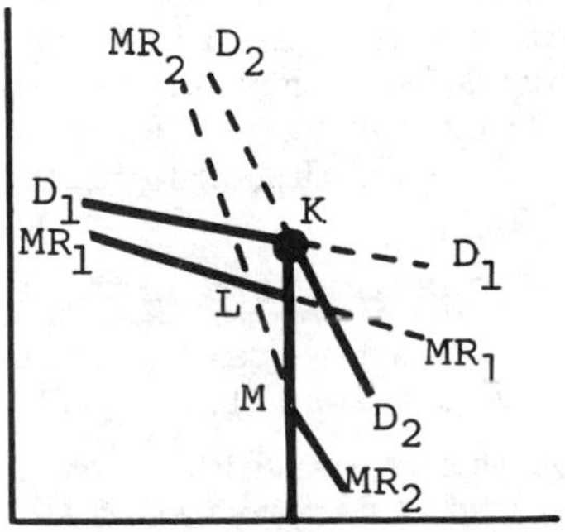

Fig. 5

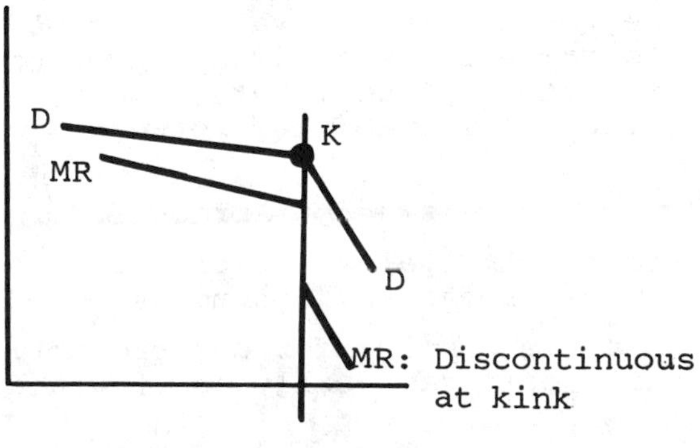

We have decided that D_1 is the relevant demand curve above point K. At point K the oligopolist is producing Quantity Q_K. Any quantity less than Q_K would have its price defined by the D_1 demand curve. Therefore, from the P axis to point L at Q_K level of production, MR, is the relevant MR curve. At levels of production greater than Q_K, D_2 is the relevant demand curve. Therefore, we use MR_2 beyond Q_K, that is the portion beyond point M. The relevant portions of the Demand and Marginal Revenue curves are shown in figure 4. From this we can see that the MR curve for the oligopolist would not be continuous.

The finished demand and MR curves would be as in Figure 5.

• PROBLEM 21-14

In describing oligopolies, we characteristically use graph (a) to describe demand. However we often use graph (b) to describe the demand situation present in a differentiated oligopoly. Explain why the demand curve might possess a different shape in a differentiated oligopoly.

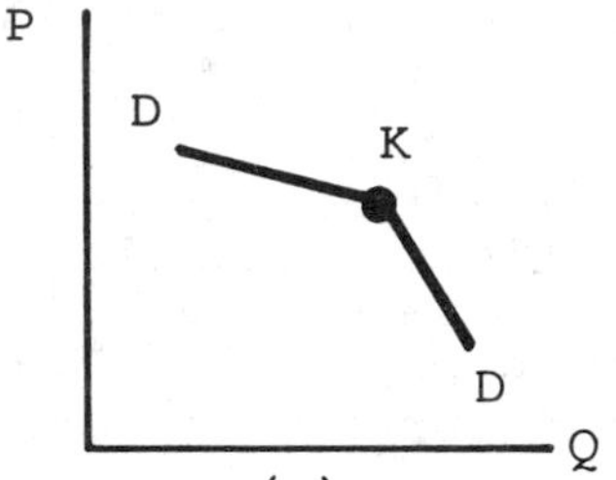

(a)

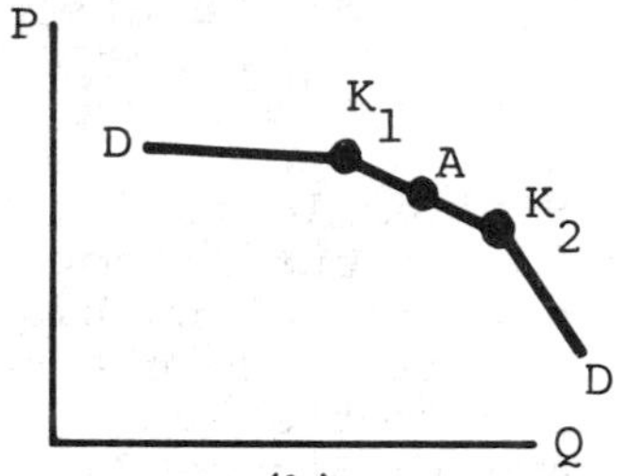

(b)

Solution: In a differentiated oligopoly, industry members produce slightly dissimilar products. Product differences encourage consumer preferences, which in turn induce brand loyalty.

Looking at the graphs, we see that undifferentiated oligopoly (graph (a)), a raise in price will cause a drastic drop in quantity demanded, due to the fact that the other firms in the industry will keep their prices low. But in the differentiated oligopoly (graph (b)), some degree of brand loyalty exists. Therefore if our firm were to raise its price, loyal customers would be somewhat reluctant to switch to other brands. Thus we have an area of price flexibility between K_1 and K_2 on our demand curve.

In raising our price from A to K_1, customers would be somewhat loyal as described above. But if we were to raise prices above K_1, consumers would no longer be willing to pay the premium for our product, and quantity demanded would drop off drastically as it would in an undifferentiated oligopoly.

Similarly in lowering its price, competitive firms in a differentiated oligopoly will not react immediately since some difference in price is tolerated due to differences in product. However, beyond some point, K_2, on graph (b), other firms will have little choice but to reduce their prices to avoid losing a large number of their once-brand-loyal customers to the low-priced brand. The result of lowering price below K_2 would be the same as lowering price in an undifferentiated oligopoly.

Since the feature of differentiation gives the oligopolistic firm some flexibility in the pricing of its product, it is often strived for. As a firm's product grows more differentiated in the minds of potential buyers, price becomes more flexible for the firm, and hence more able to be manipulated as if in a monopoly.

• PROBLEM 21-15

Given a kinked demand curve, such as the one in Figure 1 where demand is elastic to the left of point A and inelastic to the right of Point L, explain why an oligopolist would not want to alter his price from point A (assuming no changes in cost or demand curves.)

Price

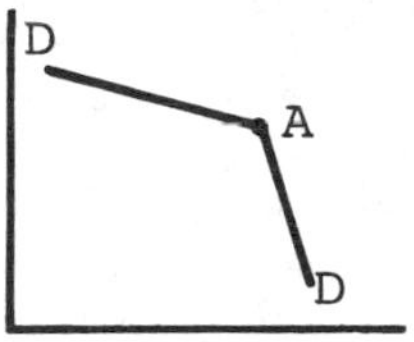

Fig. 1

Quantity

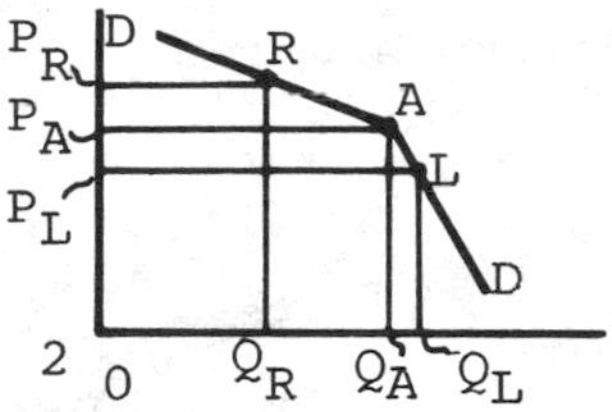

Fig. 2

Solution: Our oligopolist is currently producing at point A on the demand curve. He is faced with three alternatives. He can keep price constant at A, lower price to L or raise price to R.

If he raises his price, the other firms in the industry will leave their prices low. Therefore the quantity of goods demanded from our firm will fall greatly, as illustrated by the elastic end of the kinked demand curve in Figure 2, from Q_A to Q_R and total revenue will fall from OP_AAQ_A to OP_RRQ_R, (see Figure 2.)

If he lowers price, the other firms in the industry will follow suit. Subsequently, the quantity demanded will increase only slightly (as shown by the inelastic side of the demand curve) from Q_A to Q_L. All the firms in the industry will therefore suffer a drop in profits, the drop for each of them represented by the difference between OP_AAQ_A and OP_LLQ_L. Since raising the price and lowering the price would be mistakes, the oligopolist's only remaining choice is to keep price steady at point A.

• PROBLEM 21-16

Explain the rigidity of prices in an oligopoly in terms of the discontinuous MR curve.

Solution: Using the standard kinked demand curve as shown in the figure, our oligopolist is initially facing demand PAD, his marginal revenue curve is PBCMR, and his marginal cost curve is MC_1. To maximize his profits he follows the MC = MR rule and decides to produce at quantity Q. For this quantity consumers are willing to pay price P. Now, suppose our oligopolist's costs rise and the MC curve shifts from MC_1 to MC_2. Ordinarily, we would expect an increase in costs to cause a drop in output and possibly a price increase. But as our curves indicate below, the discontinuity of the MR curve allows the firm to set its price at the kink even when costs are changing. That is, even though his costs have risen, the oligopolist will still produce amount Q for price P.

If the MC curve intersects the MR curve at any point on the line segment where the MR curve is discontinuous, that is anywhere from B to C, price and output will remain the same at P and Q. This lends a great deal of rigidity to an oligopolist's prices.

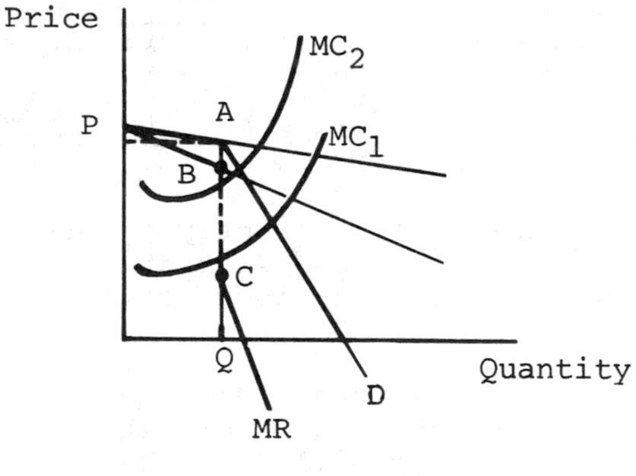

• PROBLEM 21-17

Given in Figure 1 are the kinked demand curve and corresponding marginal revenue curve for an oligopolistic firm. Note that there is a break in the marginal revenue curve due to the kink in the demand curve. The dotted line indicates the discontinuity.

Explain the price inflexibility present in oligopoly in terms of the MC = MR profit maximization concept.

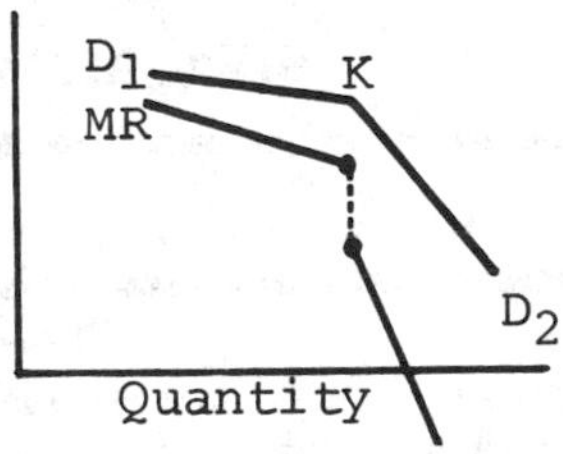

Fig. 1

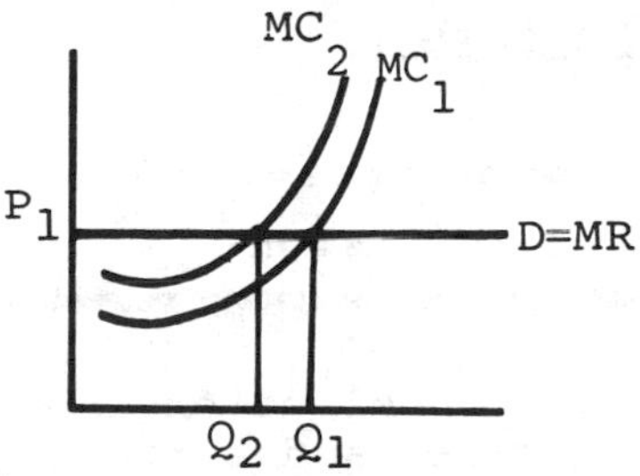

Fig. 2

Pure Competition

Solution: We know that profit will be maximized where marginal cost = marginal revenue. In an ordinary situation, any change in the marginal cost curve will result in a change in output or price or both (as illustrated in Figures 2 and 3).

Under pure competition, a rise in the marginal cost curve from MC_1 to MC_2 will cause a reduction in output from Q_1 to Q_2. Here, since a pure competitor's demand curve is horizontal by definition, no change in price will result from this one competitor's decreased production. Under monopoly, a rise in the marginal cost curve from MC_1 to MC_2 will cause a reduction in output from Q_1 to Q_2. Since the monopolist faces a downward sloping demand curve, this decrease in the quantity supplied results in an increase in the price received from P_1 to P_2.

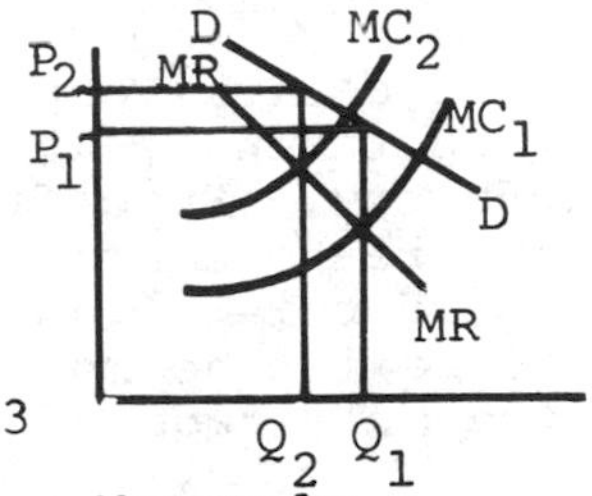

Fig. 3

Monopoly

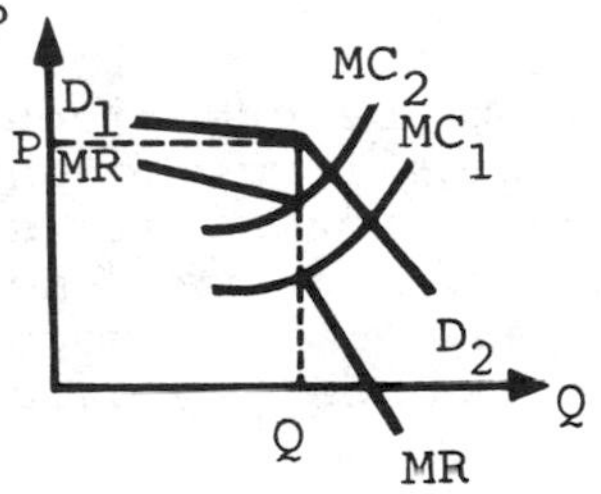

Fig. 4

Under oligopoly, the situation is quite different due to the kinked demand curve. Marginal revenue is discontinuous at the kink, and therefore complications set in when trying to evaluate profit maximization. In Figure 4, we see that both MC_1 and MC_2 intersect the marginal revenue curve at the kink. Both MC curves result in the firm's decision to produce quantity Q and receive price P. We can also see that any MC curve which falls between MC_1 and MC_2, that is, which crosses MR along the discontinuous section, will result in the oligopolist deciding to produce quantity Q for price P. Because of the range of positions that the marginal cost curve can occupy while still intersecting the marginal revenue curve along the vertical line, the price in an oligopoly is very inflexible.

COLLUSION

• PROBLEM 21-18

What is collusion?

Solution: Collusion is the practice whereby several firms get together and secretly agree upon how their market should be divided or what prices should be charged. The practice is often linked to oligopolies.

• PROBLEM 21-19

Suppose that the four firms in an oligopoly are getting together to collude. How might ease of entry into their industry affect how high they set their prices?

Solution: Just because an industry is currently oligopolistic does not mean that it will remain so permanently. Suppose the four oligopolists above set their prices at an extremely high level and consequently earn a very large profit. In this situation, other businessmen will be tempted to enter this industry that shows such high profits. (Whereas before the collusion, profits were relatively low). If there is ease of entry, many businessmen will be attracted by the high-profit industry and hence, as the number of firms increase, our market structure will grow less and less oligopolistic. The ability to collude will also diminish.

The lesson to be learned is that if collusive price setting is to be practiced, care must be taken if it is easy for other firms to enter your industry. Specifically, prices should not be set so high as to create a profit which attracts too many new entrants. If this rule should be disobeyed, your oligopoly might soon exist no more and collusion becomes impossible due to the multitude of producers.

• PROBLEM 21-20

What are the resale price maintenance laws? How do they represent, in effect, cartels with free entry?

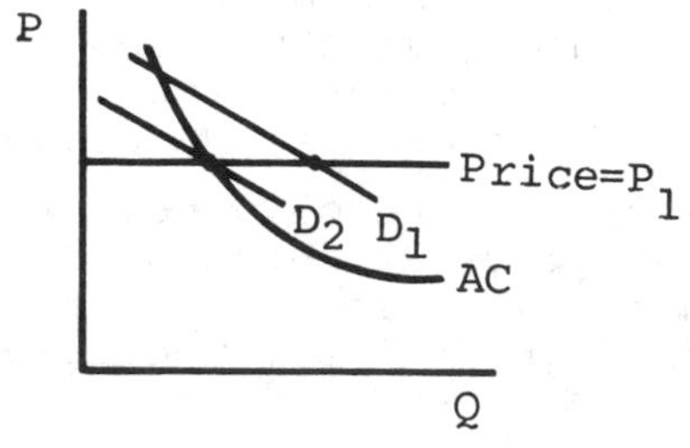

Solution: Resale price maintenance laws are the so-called "fair trade" laws which permit manufacturers to stipulate minimum prices in contracts with their retailers. Then if a contract is violated, the manufacturer can sue the price cutter. In fact under the "non-signer" clause included in most fair trade laws, the manufacturer may sue any retailer selling below the minimum price even if he has not signed an agreement, provided only that some dealer in the state in which this dealer does business has signed such an agreement. Resale price maintenance has been common in the past in the sale of drugs, cosmetics, liquors, and small appliances.

In effect, by enacting fair trade laws, the manufacturer has banded the retailers together into a sort of forced cartel whereby the sellers agree to maintain prices above a certain level.

One might assume that individual stores would enjoy such fair trade laws since higher price will mean higher profits. But this is only in the short-run, since there are no barriers to entry in this cartel, i.e., we are encountering a "cartel with free entry." Using the curves in the figure, we see that for an individual store, with demand D_1, substantial profits will result from setting price at P_1. But these profits will disappear because of the new stores it attracts into the trade. The new crop of stores cannot drive down the price under the fair trade laws, but they can spread the volume of the trade thinner and thinner until the demand at an individual store is down to D_2.

When Price = P_1 on the D_2 curve, P_1 = Average Cost. Therefore excess profits are zero.

In the long run, retail stores in general will not gain much. The net effect will simply be higher costs at each store, but no greater profits than before.

COMPARISON WITH OTHER MARKET FORMS

• PROBLEM 21-21

In oligopoly we have a "few" firms and hence we do not reap all the benefits of perfect competition. The other side of the coin is an industry in which there are an excessive number of sellers. Explain the consequences of this situation.

Solution: Many industries are characterized by an excessive number of firms, most of which do a small volume of business and remain in the industry only until they have lost their capital. As soon as these excessive unprofitable firms leave the industry, it seems that new firms enter the industry.

The results of an over-crowded industry tend to be negative all around. The fact that there are so many firms present prevents the sellers from realizing full production. Hence, there are resources being wasted and losses incurred by the producers. In addition, producers tend to charge a high price, due to their inefficient production, and so consumers suffer through higher prices.

• PROBLEM 21-22

How might the traditional view of economic efficiency in an oligopoly and the historical facts surrounding many oligopolistic manufacturing industries disagree with each other?

Solution: The traditional view holds that because oligopoly is close to pure monopoly in structure, we should expect it to operate in a similar way. Characterized by barriers to entry, oligopoly can be expected to result in a restriction of output so that lowest unit costs are not attained and market price is high enough to yield a substantial profit. Ceteris paribus, the price and output under such an oligopoly would be clearly inferior to that of pure competition.

However, the above traditional view does not necessarily describe what has happened in oligopolistic industries in the past. For instance the farm equipment, steel and electronics industries are oligopolistic and have been characterized by falling product prices, improvements in product quality, and expanding levels of output and employment over a period of years. It would seem that historical data contradicts theory. But caution should be taken here. The real issue to study here is whether this progress would have been even greater if these industries had been organized on a purely competitive basis.

• PROBLEM 21-23

Suppose Industry A is populated by many small firms each producing at or near point P on the Long Run Average-cost curve (Fig. 1). DD^1 repesents total market demand.

Why might such a competitive industry evolve into an oligopoly?

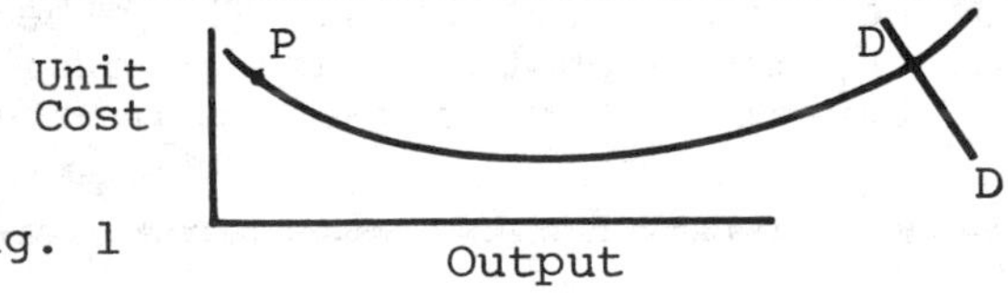

Fig. 1

Solution: The shape of this average cost curve tells us that there are great economies of scale in this industry. That is, increasing the output of each firm will result in lower per unit costs. At point P, each firm is producing quantity Q_P at an average cost of AC_P, (see Fig. 2). Note

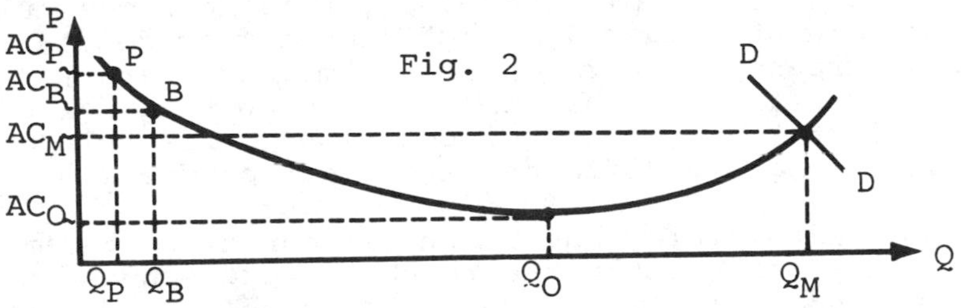

Fig. 2

if any one firm decided to double its output to Q_B (shifting from P to B on the curve) its average costs would drop from AC_P to AC_B. Thus a firm which could produce a greater output than that of point P could experience considerably lower unit costs. Upon realizing this, the firms in industry A would be encouraged to expand their output. Since we assume that demand is constant throughout this situation, one firm can increase its output only at the expense of another firm's output. So we would expect a firm's output to increase either through merger or by replacing the output of firms that go out of existence. In either case there is a shrinking of producers over time, changing industry A from an industry of many small producers to one of a few large producers. Note the location of the market demand curve. Its location to the right of the minimum point on the AC curve, where Average Costs have begun to rise again, tells us that industry A will not tend toward monopoly. If any one firm were to try and capture the entire market, that is, produce at Q_M, its average costs would rise to AC_M. Here smaller firms, with lower average costs could compete successfully for the monopolist's share of the market.

In the long run, we would probably expect this market to be split between two oligopolists, each producing Q_O with average costs of AC_O.

• PROBLEM 21-24

Explain why advertising tends to not exist in pure competition and pure monopoly, while often existing in oligopolies.

Solution: Under pure competition no seller has any motive to advertise. By definition, a purely competitive producer can sell all of his product at the going price without any advertising outlay. The act of advertising would only serve to add to the producer's costs.

A monopolist will find some advertising to be profitable, especially when introducing a new product or trying to reach a new group of consumers. However, once a monopolist has neared saturation of his product's potential market, advertising will often serve little use in increasing profit. And since there is no competition in monopoly, advertising would not be expected.

However, under oligopoly, advertising comes fully into its own. In an oligopoly, each producer is constantly trying to increase his portion of the market share. Due to the ease of retaliation inherent in price-cutting, oligopolists often resort to non-price competition, an example of which is advertising, to differentiate their products.

Once advertising has begun, it can often become a life-and-death matter due to the interdependent nature of firms in an oligopoly. Since a change in advertising by one firm can affect the other firms in an industry, an oligopolist who fails to follow the "advertising norm" set by his competitors may soon find his customers drifting off to rival products.

• PROBLEM 21-25

What is the difference between collusion, cooperation, and competition? How would you define collusion between two people so as to exclude partnerships and corporate joint ownership from the concept of collusion? Why is collusion considered undesirable?

Solution: Collusion connotes elements of deception in seeking to negotiate exchanges in the pretense that the sellers are acting as independent competitors. Buyers are misled into presuming sellers are acting independently. If buyers knew sellers were in agreement, buyers would be alerted to the incentive of each seller not to bid as he otherwise would. Without the element of secrecy, buyers are aware of the lack of inter-seller conflict of interests--as, for example, among the two salesmen of the same firm. The pretense of competing with respect to prices and quality is designed to induce buyer to think he is already obtaining advantages of inter-seller competition.

With open collusion, such as mergers, there is no pretense. Buyers are not deceived and can then obtain offers from other independent sellers. Open agreements not to compete are not deceptive and consequently are much less effective in open markets. Partnerships, being open, are not deceptive, hence do not connote elements of collusion. Elements of deception are undesirable.

Competition connotes elements of method of resolving who will get what of existing resources, while cooperation connotes joint action to increase total stock of wealth to be distributed. Some actions do both at the same time. Thus, exchange with specialization is both competitive and cooperative in increasing wealth as well as in allocating it.

Answer

To be covered when testing yourself

SHORT ANSWER QUESTIONS FOR REVIEW

Choose the correct answer.

1. Which of the following is a characteristic of oligopoly? (a) A market situation with only a few competing buyers (b) A market situation with only a few competing sellers (c) A market situation with only one seller (c) An open market for the best interests of the consumer (e) Government control of prices. b

2. Mr. Bill owns numerous shoestores on the north side of town. Mr. Mike owns numerous shoestores on the south side of town. If the two men combine operation into Bill & Mike Shoes, this type of merger is called: (a) collusion (b) vertical combination (c) horizontal combination (d) holding company. c

3. Galbraith has focused the attention of economists on: (a) the large corporation's staff of technocrats who may often move with ease between corporate decisions and political decisions (b) the kinked demand curve as an explanation for rigid price (c) the need for oligopoly in a Veblenian world (d) the great technological achievements of American industry. a

4. Price discrimination means: (a) selling below cost (b) selling above cost (c) charging different prices to different buyers (d) making all buyers pay the same price. c

5. High concentration in most individual industries is: (a) desirable because it leads to more intense competition (b) desirable because it better enables firms to coordinate policies and activities to best serve the consumer (c) undesirable because it is thought to lead to less effective competition and inefficient resource allocation (d) cannot be deemed desirable or undesirable on the grounds listed above. c

6. Ceteris paribus, high barriers to entry into an industry are likely to be: (a) associated with a high degree of economic competition (b) associated with a low degree of economic competition (c) unrelated to competition (d) impossible to evaluate in relation to competition. b

7. In the accompanying diagram, the oligopolist is (a) making a profit (b) breaking even (c) losing money, and should close (d) losing money, but should stay in business. a

Answer
To be covere[d]
when testin[g]
yourself

SHORT ANSWER QUESTIONS FOR REVIEW

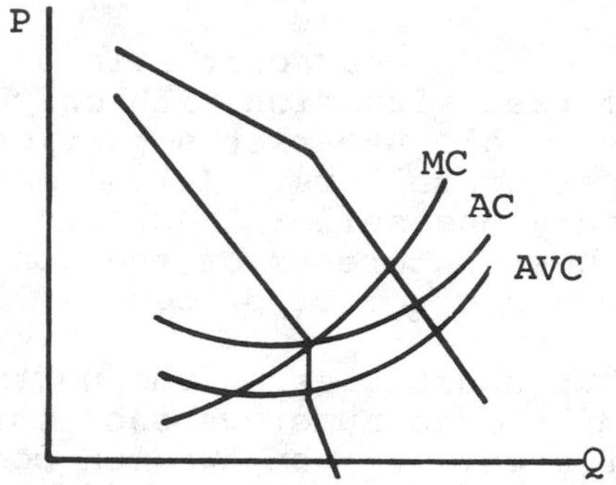

8. In the most standard usage, the term "price leadership" refers to (a) pre-emptive pricing made possible by the learning curve (b) a form, in effect, of price collusion (c) the maintenance of a monopolistic price (d) cutthroat competition. b

9. Markup pricing: (a) refers to the practice of setting a product's price by adding some constant percentage markup to an estimate of marginal cost (b) is equivalent to profit maximization under imperfect competition (c) exists exclusively in the agricultural sector of the economy (d) is adopted, in part, because of the difficulty of estimating marginal revenue and marginal cost. d

10. The kinked demand curve and the preceding broken marginal-revenue curve, under noncollusive oligopoly, explain that within a certain range, high cost changes will have no effect on: (a) price and marginal revenue (b) output and marginal cost (c) marginal revenue and marginal cost (d) price and marginal cost (e) output and price e

11. Of the following which is an outstanding feature of oligopoly? (a) many firms (b) small firms (c) few firms (d) medium firms c

12. Prices are likely to be least flexible under: (a) pure competition (b) oligopoly (c) monopolistic competition (d) monopoly. b

13. Economists are not very interested in noncollusive oligopoly as they are in collusive oligopoly because: (a) gentlemen's agreements

	Answer (To be covered when testing yourself)
are not widespread in the economy (b) there is no intra-industry competition (c) it does not provide a more satisfactory explanation of price and output behavior (d) of the uncertainties about the behavior of other firms in the industry	c
14. Countervailing power is ineffective as a competitive force during periods of inflation because: (a) with excess demand, buyers are no longer able to restrain sellers (b) oligopolies tend to evolve into pure monopolies (c) with excess supply buyers are no longer able to restrain sellers (d) oligopolies tend to evolve into pure competition	a
15. In a situation where the demand and cost are given under oligopoly, it will pay for the oligopolist to be: (a) expansionary (b) sales-conscious (c) restrictive (d) profit-maximizing	c
Fill in the blanks.	
16. Demand in an oligopolistic market is typically explained by the ______________ curve.	kinked demand
17. When producers agree to charge the same price, they are practicing ______________.	collusion
18. Two types of collusion are ______________ and ______________.	tacit, explicit
19. Using the kinked demand analysis, if oligopolist A raises the price of his product, oligopolist B will probably ______________ increase in price.	ignore
20. If several oligopolistic firms collude, the resulting price and output will most likely resemble that of ______________.	pure monopoly
21. The creative function of the large corporation was emphasized in the writings of ______________.	Schumpeter
22. When the farmer buys feed for his pigs, he has to pay the price demanded. This is an example of ______________ prices.	administered
23. When industry members produce slightly dissim-	

SHORT ANSWER QUESTIONS FOR REVIEW

	Answer To be covered when testing yourself
ilar products, we say that this is a __________ oligopoly.	differen ated
24. The practice of firms in an industry following the price changes initiated by one member of the industry is called ______________.	price leadersh
25. Price agreements among sellers is most clearly illegal according to the ______________.	Sherman Act
26. Price discrimination is most clearly illegal according to the ______________.	Clayton Act
27. Competition through advertising is popular in many oligopolies. One type of competition which is often shunned by oligopolists is competition based on ______________.	price
28. A situation of few buyers is called ___________.	oligopso
29. Monopolistic competition and oligopoly are alike in that ______________ competition is common to both.	nonprice
30. Above the kink in an oligopolist's demand curve, demand is ______________ while below the kink, demand is ______________.	elastic, inelasti

<u>Determine whether the following statements are true or false.</u>

31. If a firm sets prices by a cost plus markup rule, we know that it cannot be maximizing profit.	False
32. Countervailing power refers to the competition between such rivals as General Motors and Ford.	False
33. If consumers were willing to sacrifice the differentiation of product, the price of the product could be lower.	True
34. If free entry into an industry shifts each firm's sloping demand curve far enough to the left to eliminate all profits, then most of the so-called "wastes of imperfect competition" have been eliminated.	False
35. Reciprocity means a firm's practice of buying supplies from its subsidiaries and others, who are then expected or pressured to purchase from it.	True

	Answer To be covered when testing yourself
SHORT ANSWER QUESTIONS FOR REVIEW	
36. Firms involved in exporting, thus helping our balance of payments, are exempt from antitrust legislation.	False
37. Countervailing power frequently does not function very effectively during inflation.	True
38. Under oligopolistic industry, the firms may produce standardized or differentiated products.	True
39. Collusive oligopolists might keep price at a less than maximum level in order to not attract new entrants into their industry.	True
40. "Mutual interdependence" means that oligopolists rely upon price competition to determine their market shares.	False
41. In an oligopolistic industry with firms B, C and D, if B cuts price, its sales will increase very modestly, because its two rivals will follow suit.	True
42. Under oligopoly, equilibrium price is equal to marginal cost.	False
43. Since collusion tends to increase profits and attract many new producers to the industry, it inevitably results in pure competition in the long-run.	False
44. In oligopoly it is possible that change in unit costs will have no effect upon equilibrium price and output.	True
45. In strongly decreasing-cost industries, there is no hope for natural perfect competition.	True

CHAPTER 22

THEORY OF PRODUCTION

Basic Attacks and Strategies for Solving Problems in this Chapter. See pages 780 to 813 for step-by-step solutions to problems.

Business firms use factors of production—land, labor, capital, and entrepreneurship—to produce goods and services. The analysis of the relationship between the inputs used and the output produced is known as the theory of production. An important concept is that of the production function. A production function is a schedule or equation which shows how much output of a particular product can be produced for given amounts of the inputs, assuming the most efficient production methods are used. If X is output and I_i stands for the various inputs, a production function in general form can be written as $X = f(I_1, I_2, ..., I_n)$.

Over short periods of time, inputs can be divided into two categories: fixed and variable. Fixed inputs are those whose quantity cannot be increased or decreased. Variable inputs are those whose quantity can be increased or decreased. The short run is defined as a period of time so short that at least one of the inputs must be considered fixed in amount. The long run is a period so long that all inputs can be considered variable.

The analysis of short run production considers the impact on total production of altering the amount of variable inputs used. An important concept here is the law of diminishing returns. As equal amounts of a variable input are added to the fixed input, the additions to total output eventually begin to diminish.

The graphs on the following page illustrate some important relationships in the short run theory of production. The upper graph plots total product (TP) against the amount of variable input (VI) used (for a given amount of the fixed factors). Note the distinctive shape of this curve. At low levels of variable input usage, *TP* increases at an increasing rate. This results from specialization and division of labor. After point *a*, *TP* increases at a decreasing rate. This is the region of diminishing returns which lasts until *b*, after which *TP* actually falls.

The lower graph plots average product (AP) and marginal product (MP). *AP* is defined as *TP/VI*. *MP* is the increase in *TP* from using one more unit of *VI*. It is defined as $\frac{\Delta TP}{\Delta VI}$. The region of diminishing returns runs from the high point of *MP* until the point where *MP* = 0. Note that *MP* intersects *AP* at *AP*'s high point. When *AP* is rising, *MP* lies above it. When *AP* is falling, *MP* lies below it.

The analysis of long run production considers the impact on total production of altering all the inputs. The production function defined earlier, $X = f(I_1, I_2, \ldots, I_n)$, can be used to illustrate some important relationships between input and output. If all the inputs are altered by a certain factor and output increases by more than that factor, then there are economies of scale, such as if each input is doubled and output more than doubles. If output increases by less than the factor, there are diseconomies of scale.

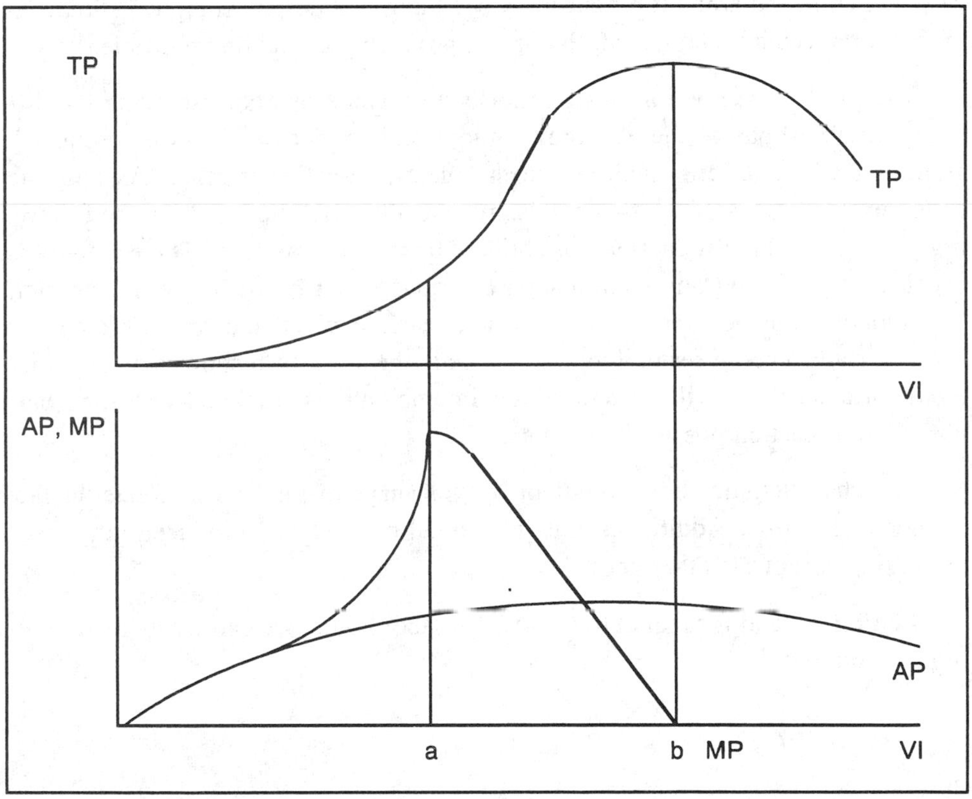

Production in the Short Run

Achieving technological efficiency in production is an important goal of both firms and the economy as a whole. The condition for technological efficiency is the following:

$$\frac{MP_1}{P_1} = \frac{MP_2}{P_2} = \ldots = \frac{MP_n}{P_n},$$

where MP stands for marginal product of factor i and P stands for the market price of factor i. The term MP_i/P_i refers to the marginal product of the last dollar spent on factor i. In equilibrium the marginal product of the last dollar spent on each input should be equal. If they were not, if $MP_1/P_1 > MP_2/P_2$, then output could be increased by spending one dollar less on input 2 and using that dollar to purchase input 1. As this reallocation takes place, MP_1/P_1 decreases (due to the law of diminishing returns) and MP_2/P_2 increases (for the same reason). If $MP_1/P_1 = MP_2/P_2$, then the amount of output lost by spending one dollar less on input 2 would be matched by the amount produced by spending that dollar on input 1. Since no more output could be produced, the firm is producing at maximum efficiency.

The production possibilities frontier is a schedule or graph showing the different combinations of the economy's goods and services that can be produced, assuming all inputs are employed in the most productive manner. Assume the economy can only produce two goods, guns and butter. The graph on the following page shows the production possibilities frontier in this case. The economy is capable of producing any combination of goods either on or inside the frontier. Combinations outside the frontier are not feasible given the existing stock of resources and level of technology. Increases in the stock of resources or improvements in technology will make additional combinations feasible by shifting outward the production possibilities frontier.

The characteristic "bowed-out" or convex shape of the curve reflects the law of increasing costs. Additional units of a good can only be produced at an ever increasing cost of the other good.

Letting Q stand for real output and L for labor hours, we can write the following equation:

$$Q = \frac{Q}{L} * L.$$

The term Q/L is the average product of labor, or, simply, the productivity of labor. What the equation says is that we can increase our output (or our standard of living) in two fundamental ways. We can work more hours or increase the productivity of each hour we work. Clearly, our long run growth in living standards has been more the result of the latter, not the former.

The key factors which have contributed to the increase in labor productivity

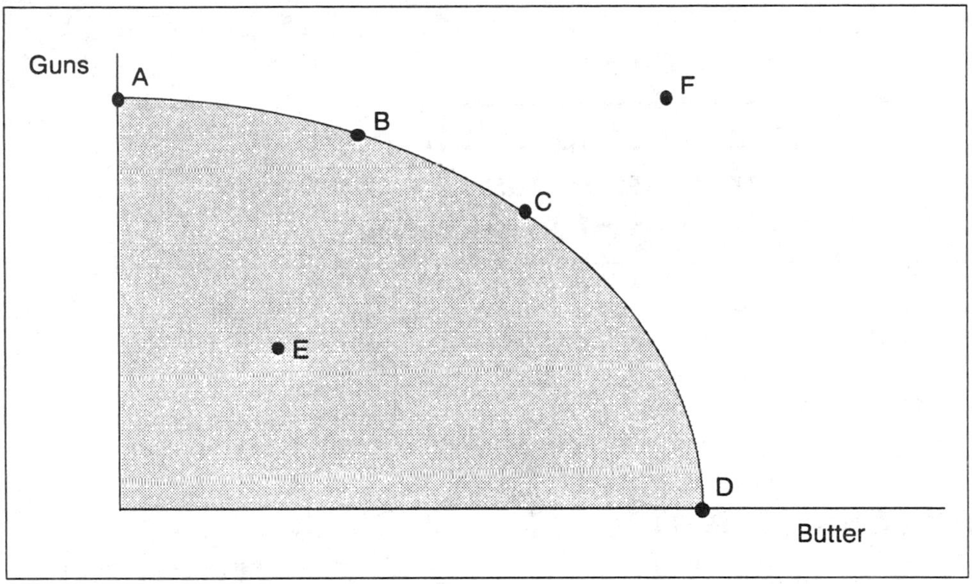

include capital investment, technological change, and improvements in worker education and skills. Intuitively, labor is able to produce more each hour when it has access to sophisticated capital equipment and the skills to operate the equipment. Productivity growth is the result of many other less tangible factors also.

The capital/output ratio (*K/Y*) shows the relationship between capital required and output produced. It can be used to predict the level of investment needed to produce an increased quantity of output. For example, assume the subscripts refer to year, there is no depreciation, and desired investment can be completed within one year. Investment in year 2 (I_2) equals the change in desired capital between years 1 and 2 ($K_2 - K_1$), where $K_i = \left(\frac{K}{Y}\right)_i * Y_i$, or $I_2 = K_2 - K_1 = \left(\frac{K}{Y}\right)_2 * Y_2 - \left(\frac{K}{Y}\right)_1 * Y_1$. This assumes the capital/output ratio is fixed over time, a dubious assumption in most instances.

Step-by-Step Solutions to Problems in this Chapter, "Theory of Production"

FACTORS OF PRODUCTION

• PROBLEM 22-1

What are the major factors of production?

Solution: The categories of the factors of production are common to practically all modern economies. All the goods created by men to assist in the production of other goods and services are generally classified as capital goods. All the people involved in the production of these goods and services are characterized as labor force. Land refers to all the natural resources involved in the production processes, in other words, the resources available through nature, not through men. Finally, economists often include entrepreneurial talents in the category of factors of production alluding to the importance of the concepts of maximization and efficiency for the outcome of production processes.

• PROBLEM 22-2

Does efficient production assume that perfect knowledge exists? Explain.

Solution: No. It merely assumes that existing knowledge can be used and subjected to performance tests. It assumes no restrictions on rights to purchase or exchange knowledge. Knowledge is a valuable (economic) resource. To assume it is free is, for example, to deny that schools exist and that teachers perform a useful desired service. A substantial fraction of our wealth is devoted to gathering information of one kind or another.

CAPITAL GOODS

• PROBLEM 22-3

What are the distinguishing characteristics of a capital good that differentiate it from the other factors of production? As an aid to production, what are its relative risks?

Solution: First of all, capital goods are produced so as to produce other goods and services more efficiently. That is, capital goods, such as factories and machines, are not produced to be directly consumed by consumers, but rather to produce consumer goods or other capital goods at a lower cost. We produce mechanical looms, for example, because much more cloth per unit of resource input can be woven with such machines than by hand weaving. Even when the cost of producing the looms is included, cloth is still produced at a far lower cost with the looms than without them.

Capital is characterized by durability. Factory buildings, blast furnaces, auto body presses, computers, and mechanical looms are produced and bought with the expectation that they will last for a considerable period of time.

Capital goods are artifacts, not a gift of nature, as are labor and land - the other factors of production. While we frequently invest in labor by educating or training workers, and we invest in land by draining or irrigating for farming, much labor and land can be employed in production without extensive investment. Capital, by contrast, can only be created through investment, which is defined as the purchase of capital goods.

As an aid to production, it has the following weaknesses:

The first is a time problem. Capital goods must be bought in advance of the production of consumer goods and services. For example, an investment in a factory building today may not begin to pay off for several years.

Second, there may be substantial risk involved, since the use of capital goods is envisioned for the future. For example, a machine that a businessman planned to use for twenty years may turn out to be obsolete after only two years because a new and more efficient machine has been invented. Also, a sharp decline in demand for a good will decrease the value of the capital equipment designed to produce it.

• PROBLEM 22-4

When the capital/output ratio for the annual output is 2, what is it for quarterly output?

Solution: The capital/output ratio shows the amount of capital required to produce a unit of output per time period, usually a year. The theory of this capital requirements approach assumes that there is a fixed relationship between the level of output for a given period of time and the amount of capital equipment required to produce it. A capital/output ratio for annual output of 2 means that $2 million capital is required to produce $1 million output per year = $250,000 output per quarter. Now if the capital/output ratio per quarter is measured it would have a value of

$\frac{2 \text{ million}}{250{,}000} = 8$. The capital/output ratio is a normal input-output ratio; it measures the input of capital into the production process relative to the output produced. Labor/output ratios, or material/output ratios can also be considered. But the capital/output ratio is thought to be more fixed than these other ratios - plant and equipment cannot be changed overnight, but (at least in theory), the labor input can, for example, by increasing the number of workshifts per day.

The capital/output ratio K/Y, divided by the labor/output ratio L/Y, gives the capital/labor ratio K/L, an important indicator of the relative capital- respectively labor - intensity of the production process. The capital/output ratio is determined partly by technical, partly by cost considerations.

• PROBLEM 22-5

Assume that the capital/output ratio is 2. From a present level of $600 million, GNP increases in the coming 10 years, by 2, 6, 4, 5, 6, 6, 3, 5, 2, and 0 percent, in the respective years. How could the investments be expected to behave in those 10 years?

Solution: Notice that the investments fluctuate by a greater proportion than does the GNP. The acceleration principle states that the level of investment will vary with changes in the level of output, rather than with the level of output itself.

First, calculate the levels of output in the coming 10 years, and the related levels of capital stock required to produce these outputs. Then calculate the differences between the stocks of required capital for each year to determine how much investment is needed. (See Table 1.)

Table 1

Year	GNP (=Y)	Change in GNP amount	Change in GNP in %	Capital Required	Capital Available	Net Investment
0	680	ΔY		1360		
1	694	+14	2	1388	1360	28
2	735	+41	6	1470	1388	82
3	765	+30	4	1530	1470	60
4	803	+38	5	1606	1530	76
5	851	+48	6	1702	1606	96
6	902	+51	6	1804	1702	102
7	929	+27	3	1858	1804	54
8	976	+47	5	1952	1858	94
9	995	+19	2	1990	1952	38
10	995	+ 0	0	1990	1990	0

The capital required is calculated by multiplying the GNP (=Y) by the capital/output ratio(K/Y); so $K_{req\ t} = Y_t \times (K/Y)$, which, by substitution, $= Y_t \times 2$. It is assumed that the net investment needed is actually invested, i.e. added to the available stock of capital. Therefore, the investment is calculated as the difference between the required stock of capital and the available stock of capital. Thus, the capital stock available in year t equals the sum of the capital stock available in the preceding year t-1, plus the net investment in year t. From Table 1, it is seen that, although GNP grows continuously, investment varies, both increasing and decreasing. And the ratio of investment to the change in output equals 2, the capital/output ratio. Thus the 1 level of investment is related to the change in the level of output. The fluctuation in the net investment can also be arrived at, by calculating the differences between the levels of net investment of congruent years, and taking percentages (See Table 2).

Table 2

Year	Change in GNP in %	Net Investment	ΔI Change in Net Investment amount	in %
1	+2	28		
2	+6	82	+54	193
3	+4	60	-22	- 27
4	+5	76	+16	+ 27
5	+6	96	+20	+ 26
6	+6	102	+ 6	+ 6
7	+3	54	-48	- 47
8	+5	94	+40	+ 74
9	+2	38	-56	- 60
10	+0	0	-38	-100

Although the change in GNP is small and positive in each year, the change in investment is forceful, and both positive and negative changes are evident, depending on the year. Because investments form an important component of aggregate demand, and the effects of changes in the level of investments are amplified in the economy by the multiplier effect, there is a need for the government to counteract these changes in the level of investment by decreasing, respectively, increasing the government deficit to give the appropriate stimulus to the economy.

• PROBLEM 22-6

If the capital/output ratio is 2.5, and GNP rises from $985 billion to $1,055 billion, by how much can investment be expected to increase, assuming no depreciation? Also, if the marginal propensity to consume is 0.5, what will be the extra changes in GNP induced by the original rise?

Solution: There are two amplifying, and therefore destabilizing, mechanisms working in the economy, which cause the major swings: the accelerator and the multiplier. The accelerator principle states that the level of investment will vary with changes in the level of output, rather than with the level of output itself. The multiplier principle states that small changes in the autonomous expenditures cause larger changes in total expenditures. In period t, the capital, K_t has a fixed relationship to the output in period t,

$$Y_t: \quad K_t = aY_t \tag{1}$$

where $a = \frac{K_t}{Y_t}$ = the capital/output ratio, which is considered to be a constant input-output ratio. Similarly for the preceding period t-1:

$$K_{t-1} = aY_{t-1} \tag{2}$$

When equation (2) is subtracted from equation (1), the result is:

$$K_t - K_{t-1} = \Delta K = aY_t - aY_{t-1}$$

$$= a(Y_t - Y_{t-1}) = a\Delta Y$$

ΔK is the change in the capital stock, and because there is no depreciation, this equals investment I_t. Thus $\Delta K = I$, so that $I_t = a\Delta Y$, where ΔY is the change in output between two subsequent periods. This is the formal statement of the simple accelerator - the investment in period t is proportional to the change in output in period t.

GNP rises from \$985 billion to \$1055 in the first period, so $\Delta Y = Y_1 - Y_0 = 1055 - 985 = \$70$ billion. The capital/output ratio is given as 2.5, and so the investment in the first year is

$$I_1 = a\Delta Y = 2.5 \times 70 = \$175 \text{ billion.}$$

This investment in period 1 will have repercussions on income and consumption in the following period 2. Assume that the consumption of period t is dependent on the income in the preceding period t-1. Then $C_t = cY_{t-1}$ (no autonomous consumption). In the first period then

$$C_t = 0.5 \times 985 = \$492.5 \text{ billion.}$$

Investments jumped up from zero to \$175 billion, as demonstrated. This means an extra addition to aggregate demand.

The multiplier is $\frac{1}{1 - \text{MPC}} = \frac{1}{1 - 0.5} = 2$, thus the increase in investments boosts the economy further upwards in the next period by another 2 × 175 = $350 billion.

Thus it is seen that a relatively small increase in GNP of $70 billion is amplified 5-fold in the next period, if all other conditions remain unchanged. [How powerful becomes even clearer from a formal analysis]. We know that aggregate demand

$$Y_t = C_t + I_t + G_t + (E_x - I_m)_t$$

where G_t - budget deficit, and $(E_x - I_m)$ - surplus on the trade balance. Substituting the consumption function and the accelerator relationship gives

$$Y_t = cY_{t-1} + a(Y_t - Y_{t-1}) + G_t + (E_x - I_m)_t$$

$$= aY_t + (c-a)Y_{t-1} + G_t + (E_x - I_m)_t$$

or $$(1-a)Y_t = (c-a)Y_{t-1} + G_t + (E_x - I_m)_t.$$

Dividing both sides by 1-a results in

$$Y_t = \frac{c-a}{1-a} Y_{t-1} + G_t + (E_x - I_m)_t.$$

This expression represents the dynamics of the economic system. The first term at the right hand side indicates the autonomous system dynamics, while $[G_t + (E_x - I_m)]$, thus the budget deficit and the trade surplus are seen to be the driving forces of the system.

Substituting the values in

$$Y_t = \frac{0.5 - 2}{1 - 2} Y_{t-1} + G_t(E_x - I_m).$$

The power of the accelerator-multiplier system is represented by the coefficient of 1.5; the current GNP level in 1.5 × the preceding GNP level, plus some additional expenditures. Thus

$$1{,}055 = 1.5 \quad 905 + G_t + (E_x - I_m)_t$$

$$= 1{,}477.5 + [G_t + (E_x - I_m)_t]$$

or $$G_t + (E_x - I_m)_t = -422.t.$$

In other words the government budget must show a surplus, or the trade balance a deficit, or both in the year when GNP is 1,055, in order to have created such a calm increase in GNP. Both have a dampening effect.]

• PROBLEM 22-7

Characterize and differentiate capital widening from capital deepening.

Solution: Capital widening is the term used when more workers are provided with capital goods to increase their productivity. Capital deepening means that each worker is provided with a greater amount of capital goods in order to be more productive.

Capital widening occurs when the labor force increases and the additional workers are provided with as much capital as the original work force had been using before. For example, a construction company digging a foundation may be using four men, each using a hand shovel to do the digging. The Company might want to quadruple output by hiring twelve more men and widening its capital stock by buying twelve more shovels. Alternatively, however, the company might quadruple output by selling its four shovels, buying four steam shovels, and having each of its workers operate one steam shovel. This would be a case of capital deepening.

MARGINAL PRODUCTS AND DIMINISHING RETURNS

• PROBLEM 22-8

What is meant by the marginal product of a productive factor?

Solution: The marginal product of a factor input is the amount by which total output increases due to the addition of one unit of a given factor while the amount used of other factors of production remains unchanged. For example, if the addition of an extra worker to the plant assembling cars does not change the total amount of cars assembled then the marginal product of labor on this plant is zero.

• PROBLEM 22-9

Given the following production schedule, compute the marginal products of Factor B.

Factor A Units of Input	Factor B Units of Input	Total Product
10	0	0
10	1	40
10	2	55
10	3	65
10	4	70

Solution: The amount of additional output that is produced when one unit of a variable input is added to a fixed input is called the marginal product. To evaluate marginal products above, we evaluate the change in total product associated with each one-unit change in input B. The marginal product computations are shown below.

Units of Input B	Total Product	Marginal Product
0	0	
		> 40 - 0 = 40
1	40	
		> 55 - 40 = 15
2	55	
		> 65 - 55 = 10
3	65	
		> 70 - 65 = 5
4	70	

Notice above that marginal product grows smaller as more and more units of the variable input are added. This is due to the law of diminishing marginal returns which states that as units of a variable resource are added to fixed resources, beyond some point, the output generated by each additional unit of the variable resource will decline.

• PROBLEM 22-10

Distinguish between the diminishing returns to a factor input and diminishing returns to scale.

Solution: The fact that a certain production process is characterized by diminishing returns to a given factor input means that beyond some level of output each successive unit of a given factor added, while the amounts of all other factor inputs are being held constant, will result in a smaller and smaller additions to the total output produced.

Diminishing returns to scale describe the tendency of extra output (again, beyond a certain output level) produced as a result of each successive increase of all factor inputs by a certain number, say 2 (all inputs doubled), to become smaller and smaller. The essential difference is that in the case of returns to a factor all the inputs but one are assumed to be fixed while when the returns to scale are considered, all the inputs without exception are allowed to change simultaneously.

• PROBLEM 22-11

What are the major determinants of productivity increases? Briefly describe each.

Solution: The more important determinants or causes of productivity increases can be grouped into four categories as follows:

(1) increasing returns to scale
(2) factor substitution
(3) increasing quality of factors
(4) technological progress.

We have increasing returns to scale if output rises by more than 50 percent when all inputs are increased by 50 percent. The significant point here is that in those industries in which economies of scale or returns to scale exist (where an increase in all the factor inputs causes a more than proportionate increase in output), productivity increases as the economy grows. Here population increase or higher disposable per capita income will increase demand, and this will enable firms to take advantage of the economies of scale possible within their existing technology. Also, increased demand for firms' products may allow them to increase productivity by adopting different and more sophisticated organizing techniques - possibly involving mass production.

A second determinant of productivity growth is the substitution of a more productive factor for one that is less productive. This may involve substitution within a factor category (one machine for another, or one type of skilled worker for another) or between different factors, such as capital for land or for labor. Significant productivity gains have occurred from the substitution of capital for labor, and when labor is provided with more efficient capital, fewer workers are required to produce the same amount of output. The resulting decrease in cost will normally yield a decrease in price and this, in turn, an increase in the quantity demanded - possibly to the degree that more workers will be hired. Of course, the substitution of capital for labor may not always lead to a price decrease. The new capital equipment may cost more, the remaining workers may be successful in bargaining for higher wages, and firms' owners may take higher profits. In that case, the industry would experience a constant level of output, less employment of labor, and higher returns to individual factor units.

A third determinant of productivity increases is improvement in the quality of factors. Companies may discover higher grades of raw materials or better land for special purposes; more sophisticated capital equipment may be developed; and labor's quality may be greatly enhanced through training and education.

Finally, technological progress - the advance in knowledge of the industrial arts that permits new methods of production and new products - is a major determinant of productivity gains. Technological change creates demand for new or improved products and thereby gives rise to economies of scale. The substitution of capital for labor may likely be a result of a technological advance in a capital good. And the quality improvement in either land, capital or labor may be a function of technological progress.

DEMAND FOR FACTORS OF PRODUCTION

• PROBLEM 22-12

Why do economists stress the cross-elasticities between different factors of production?

Solution: The term cross-elasticity is used in economic theory to describe the extent to which the change in the price of one good (factor) influences the demand for another good (factor). As is the case with consumer goods, factors of production often interact, at times by complementing each other's functions, at times serving as each other's substitute. For example, labor requires access to a sufficient amount of capital in order to become more productive. Therefore, the demand for additional labor will depend not only on the cost of hiring but also on the price of capital. It is in this respect that cross-elasticity between the factors of production is important.

• PROBLEM 22-13

Suppose a firm faces a unitarily elastic demand curve throughout its schedule. If it wished to maximize profit, how many units of output would the firm produce? Assume the cost curve looks like the following:

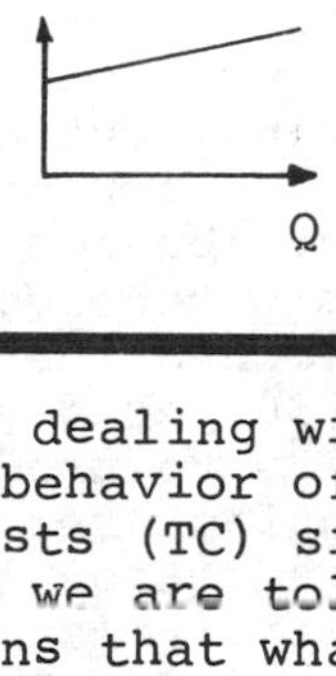

Solution: Ordinarily, in dealing with profit maximization, one must investigate the behavior of two variables, total revenue (TR) and total costs (TC) since profit = TR - TC. However, in this example, we are told that demand is unitarily elastic. This means that whatever the output (for all outputs greater than zero), total revenue is constant. Since TR is constant, it is no longer a factor in trying to find the output at which profit will be maximized. Therefore, if we want to maximize profit, we are left now only with the task of minimizing total costs.

To find the point of minimum total costs, one should examine the behavior of costs. Before any output at all is produced, there are some fixed costs which must be met. Then with the addition of each unit of output, total costs increase by the addition of variable costs to fixed costs. Therefore the cost to produce two units of output is greater than the cost to produce one unit of output and the cost to produce X units of output is greater than the cost to produce X-1 units of output. The output, then, at which TC is maximized would be zero. However, this is not the point of profit maximization since TR = 0 at Q = 0 (remember TR =

$P \times Q$). So we move one unit to the right and get a slightly higher TC than at $Q = 0$, but get the TR figure which is constant throughout the demand curve. Therefore, at an output of one, profit will be maximized.

• PROBLEM 22-14

What, if any, are the differences between the nature of demand for land and, say, the nature of demand for cars?

Solution: The essential point is that a car is an example of a finished product while land is a factor input in the production of wheat, corn, etc. Therefore, the major characteristic of the demand for land is that it is a derived demand, meaning it depends strongly on the demand for final products which use land as a factor input. For example, a significant increase in the demand for grains will be likely to cause the rent on land to go up. At the same time the demand for cars depends mostly on the consumer tastes regarding automobiles.

• PROBLEM 22-15

What is the fundamental difference between consumer demand for goods and services and employer demand for workers?

Solution: The fundamental difference between consumer demand for goods and services and the employer demand for workers is that consumers buy goods and services for the satisfactions that they bring, but employers hire workers in order to make profits. An employer compares the cost of hiring a worker to the contribution that the worker is expected to make to the firm's revenue. For example, if a necktie manufacturer determines that an additional necktie industry worker will add $30 per day to his costs and that this worker enables the firm to produce an additional $40 worth of neckties, the manufacturer will want to hire the worker. If, instead, the additional worker is expected to contribute only $20 to this firm's revenue, he will not be hired. Therefore, the demand for labor depends upon the additional output that another worker can contribute, the price of that additional output, and the cost to the employer of hiring the additional worker.

SUPPLY OF LABOR AND PRODUCTIVITY

• PROBLEM 22-16

Describe the major factors which influence the economy's supply of labor.

Solution: Certainly in the market economy the supply of any good including a factor of production depends primarily on the price that is paid for it. Therefore, in case of labor supply, the wage-rate is of major significance. But wage is not the only factor influencing the supply of labor. Population size, for example, sets a definite natural limit on how much labor can be available at any wage-rate. The legal framework of employment (laws on child labor, retirement age, working hours, etc.) can expand or restrict the size of the available labor force. Also the opportunities for training and education along with numerous non-monetary factors such as working environment, attractiveness of leisure, etc. play a role in the determination of the size and of the nature of the labor force.

• PROBLEM 22-17

What determines the elasticity of resource demand?

<u>Solution:</u> First of all, we will consider a purely technical factor. The rate at which the marginal physical product of the resource, say labor, declines is important. If the marginal physical product of labor declines slowly as additional units are added to a fixed amount of capital, the demand curve for labor will decline slowly and tend to be highly elastic. Conversely, if the marginal productivity of labor declines sharply, the demand curve will decline rapidly and tend to be highly inelastic.

The degree to which resources can be substituted for one another is a second important determinant of elasticity. The larger the number of good substitute resources available, the greater will be the elasticity of demand for a particular resource. If a shoe manufacturer finds that five different types of leather are equally satisfactory for making shoes, a rise in the price of any one type of leather may cause a very sharp drop in the amount demanded, as the producer readily substitutes other leathers.

Thirdly, the elasticity of demand for any resource will depend upon the elasticity of demand for the product which it helps produce. The greater the elasticity of product demand, the greater the elasticity of resource demand. The fact that resource demand is a derived demand would lead us to expect this relationship.

Finally, the ratio of resource cost to total cost plays a part in determining the elasticity of demand. Specifically, the larger the portion of total production costs accounted for by a resource, the greater will be the elasticity of demand for that resource.

• PROBLEM 22-18

Define productivity. Give its importance in union-management collective bargaining negotiations as well as its policy implications in curbing inflation.

Solution: Productivity of a factor input is defined as the amount of output it produces during a certain period of time taken as a unit e.g. man-hours. Labor productivity is the one most widely used in economics and politics. It is often used to substantiate the argument of trade-union leaders that wage increases should match the price increases and productivity increases combined. Employers in turn tend to attribute output increases to the higher productivity of capital not of labor. Of course, technical knowledge and personal perceptions are not less important in these arguments than economic theory. Government also quite often advances the argument that increased returns to factors above what is justified by higher productivity are inflationary, and therefore unacceptable. One can see how important the concept of productivity is in labor economics and in the formulation of national economic policy.

• **PROBLEM 22-19**

Define productivity of labor and give an example of it.

Solution: Productivity of labor is the amount of output produced by each worker on the average. Thus, if a firm uses 20 workers and 8 units of capital to produce 100 units of output, the productivity of its labor is 5 units. If at a later time a firm changes its input combination to 25 workers and 15 units of capital while output rises to 200 units, the new productivity of labor becomes 8 units. One can say that as a result of this change the labor productivity has risen by $(\frac{8-5}{5} \cdot 100 = 60)$ 60%.

• **PROBLEM 22-20**

Why is it that in the United States, labor constitutes the single most important factor of production?

Solution: Labor in the United States is the single most important factor of production because wages and salaries make up about 80 percent of national income in the United States. With very few exceptions, people are either workers, retired workers, or prospective workers. Understandably, people have stronger feelings about the labor factor than about land or capital. The return for his labor constitutes most of an individual's lifetime income, and the working conditions and prestige attached to his work status significantly affect his well-being.

• **PROBLEM 22-21**

Enumerate the important variables which have an influence on the supply of labor and briefly describe each.

Solution: The supply of labor, like the supply of other factors and of commodities, depends to a considerable degree on its price, i.e. the wage rate. Other variables which have an important influence on the supply of labor include:

(1) population - the number of potential workers available;
(2) societal practices - the number of years of schooling, the age of retirement, and the degree of sex discrimination;
(3) legal restrictions - child labor laws, social security programs, and licensing requirements;
(4) availability of education and training - the number of places available in medical schools or the number of apprenticeships permitted by an electricians' union;
(5) the length of the training period,
(6) nonmonetary or psychic income like pleasant working environment and psychologically fulfilling jobs.

• PROBLEM 22-22

Enumerate and briefly explain the factors that give rise to the high productivity of American labor.

Solution: The factors that give rise to the high productivity of the American labor are as follows.

1. Capital - American workers are used in conjunction with large amounts of capital equipment. For example, the average American worker is assisted by some $27,000 worth of machinery and equipment.

2. Natural Resources - The fact that American workers have large amounts of high-quality natural resources to work with is perhaps most evident in agriculture where, historically, the growth of productivity has been dramatic.

3. Technology - The level of technological advance is generally higher in the United States than in foreign nations. American workers in most industries use not only more capital equipment but better (that is, technologically superior) equipment than do foreign workers. Similarly, work methods are steadily being improved through detailed scientific study and research.

4. Labor Quality - The health, vigor, education and training, work attitudes, and adaptability of American workers to the discipline of factory production are generally superior to those of the labor of other nations. This means that, even with the same quantity and quality of natural and capital resources, American workers typically would be somewhat more efficient than their foreign counterparts.

5. Other Factors - Less tangible, yet important, items underlying the high productivity of American labor are

(a) the efficiency and flexibility of American management;
(b) a business, social, and political environment

which puts great emphasis upon production and productivity; and

(c) the vast size of the domestic market, which provides the opportunity for firms to realize mass-production economies.

• PROBLEM 22-23

In the past few years, economists have started to use 'human capital analysis.' Describe this analysis, concentrating on the micro-economic aspect of it.

Solution: Human capital analysis focuses on investments made in people (education, good health care, etc.) rather than in machines or land. This analysis has two aspects. The macroeconomic aspect stresses the contribution human capital investment can make to national growth and output. This perspective emphasizes the benefits to the economy that arise from national expenditures on education and other measures. The micro-economic aspect examines the returns to the individual from human capital investments. This analysis, for example, could examine the returns to a college education. The analysis would determine the cost (including opportunity cost) of college and then determine the benefits. Human capital analysis is closely related to the economic analysis of the opportunity cost of time. It is simply an extension of utility calculations and cost-benefit analysis to decisions people make about how to increase their future earnings.

ECONOMIES VS. DISECONOMIES OF SCALE

• PROBLEM 22-24

Define the terms economies of scale and diseconomies of scale and explain what they refer to.

Solution: Suppose a firm increases all of its inputs involved in the production process by a certain factor and as a consequence experiences a more than proportionate increase in its output. This increase is attributed to the existence of economies of scale. On the other hand, if an increase in all of the factor inputs leads to a less than proportionate increase in the firm's output, then diseconomies of scale are said to occur.

The modern economies are characterized by a variety of firms some of which operate only one plant while others operate many. It is important to realize that economies of scale refer to the expansions of single plants, not to a firm expanding the number of plants it operates. In other words, the term economies of scale always characterizes the production process, and not the manner in which a firm is administrated.

• **PROBLEM 22-25**

What gives rise to the so-called pecuniary economies or diseconomies of scale?

Solution: Pecuniary economies or diseconomies of scale refer to those changes in the long-run cost per unit of output which arise due to the variations in the prices of inputs. Thus, a discount received by a big corporation on a large purchase of steel would be a pecuniary economy, while the necessity to raise wages due to a trade-union pressure would constitute a pecuniary diseconomy.

• **PROBLEM 22-27**

What is meant by the technically efficient method of production?

Solution: Suppose that a certain method of production is technically efficient. This implies that there is no other method of production such that the same level of output is maintained using lower quantity of one of the factor inputs without increasing the quantity of at least one other factor input used. The existence of such a different method of production would mean that the given method is technically inefficient.

• **PROBLEM 22-26**

Over what time period are the economies and diseconomies of scale defined?

Solution: Both economies and diseconomies of scale are long-run concepts. They are defined over a period of time that is long enough to make it possible to change the amount of all the factor inputs involved in the production process. It should be kept in mind that in the short run output can be varied by adding to or subtracting from the active labor force with the major capital stock being fixed. Such variations are discussed in the theory of diminishing marginal returns. Economies of scale can appear only in the long-run where all the factor inputs can be altered in order to reach the desired level of output.

PRODUCTION METHODS AND INPUT COMBINATION DECISIONS

• **PROBLEM 22-28**

In a competitive market economy, the firms which do the producing are those which employ the economically most efficient technique of production. What determines the most efficient technique?

Solution: Economic efficiency entails getting a given output of product with the cheapest combination of scarce resources, money and terms. Economic efficiency depends on available technology and resource prices. The state of technology determines what alternative combinations of resources can produce a given amount of output. Resource prices determine which combination of resources is the least-cost, and hence the most efficient, combination. A technique which can produce a given output with only a few inputs may be less efficient if those inputs are very expensive, than an alternative technique which uses less expensive resources.

• PROBLEM 22-29

What economic factors influence the choice of the best combination of inputs by a firm?

Solution: The best combination of factor inputs is that combination which allows production of a given level of output at the least possible cost. Two things have to be taken into account. The production function of a firm shows the technologically efficient ways to produce different amounts of output using the minimal amount of inputs. The prices of inputs can then be used to determine which factor combination is economically efficient or best from the firm's standpoint.

• PROBLEM 22-30

Sigma Corporation is studying the following production method together with its various input combinations that will produce 10 dozen pairs of shoes per day.

Production Method	Quantity of Shoes Produced per day (in dozens)	Number of Shoe Workers (in 8-hour days)	Number of Shoemaking Machines (in 8-hour days)
alpha	10	30	10
beta	10	25	7
gamma	10	22	5
delta	10	20	6
epsilon	10	20	5

Management has also determined that the precise relationship among shoe workers (W), the shoemaking machinery (M) and the quantity of shoes produced (S) to be:

$$S = \sqrt{W \cdot M}$$

where shoe output will be measured in numbers of pairs of

shoes per day and the inputs on the basis of a standard 8-hour day.

Which of the five different production methods should management choose so that it will be technically efficient and consequently efficient with the production function?

Solution: First of all the equation $S = \sqrt{W \cdot M}$ may be read as follows: The quantity of shoes prcduce per day is equal to the square root of the number of shoe workers working an 8-hour day multiplied by the number of shoemaking machines operating for 8 hours.

Management should use production method epsilon as is shown below

$$S - \sqrt{W \cdot M}$$

$$= \sqrt{20 \cdot 5}$$

$$= \sqrt{100}$$

$$S = 10.$$

Therefore, it is technically efficient and consequently is consistent with the production function. On the other hand, production methods alpha and beta use more workers and more machines than do epsilon and are therefore technically inefficient. Production method gamma uses the same amount of machines as epsilon, but requires two more workers. Production method delta uses the same amount of workers, but one more machine. Hence, both gamma and delta are also technically inefficient.

• PROBLEM 22-31

The engineers of the Long-Last Shoe Company after considerable studies, have come out with the following minimum in input combinations for producing ten dozen pairs of shoes per day.

Minimum Input Combinations and Total Cost for Producing Ten Dozen Pairs of Shoes per Day

Quantity of Shoes Produced per Day (in dozens)	Number of Shoe Workers (in 8-hour days)	Number of Shoe-making Machines (in 8-hour days)
10	100	1
10	50	2
10	25	4
10	20	5
10	10	10
10	5	20
10	4	25
10	2	50
10	1	100

Assume that the firm does not influence input costs so that the cost of shoe workers is $30 per 8-hour day and the cost of shoemaking machines is $100 per 8-hour day, for all quantities as shown in the above table. Determine which of these combinations is considered to be the most economically efficient.

Solution: Economic efficiency is being defined as the most technically efficient combination of resources that represents the lowest cost to the firm. To determine which of these combinations is the economically efficient, it is necessary that we determine the total cost per day. These cost figures are derived merely by adding together the cost of workers and the cost of machines for each combination. For example, the firm can employ 5 workers at a per worker rate of $30 per 8-hour day, or $150, and use 20 machines at a cost of $100 each per 8-hour day, or $2,000, so that the combination of 5 workers and 20 machines costs the firm $2,150. Following the same procedure, we arrive at the following cost figures for each minimum input combination below.

Number of Shoe Workers (in 8-hour days)	Number of Shoe-making Machines (in 8-hour days)	Total Cost per Day (in dollars)
100	1	$ 3,100
50	2	1,700
25	4	1,150
20	5	1,100
10	10	1,300
5	20	2,150
4	25	2,620
2	50	5,060
1	100	10,030

From the above, we can see that the combination of 20 workers and 5 machines is the most economically efficient since it costs less than any other combination.

To summarize, once the technically inefficient production methods have been weeded out, only the alternatives consistent with the production function are left. From these, the most technically efficient alternative can be adopted by the firm.

• PROBLEM 22-32

What is the primary objective of management in managerial economics?

Solution: In managerial economics, the primary objective of management is assumed to be maximization of the firm's value. This objective is expressed in the following equation form.

$$\text{Value} = \sum_{t=1}^{h} \frac{\text{Profit}}{(1+i)^t} = \sum_{t=1}^{h} \frac{\text{Total Revenue}_t - \text{Total Cost}_T}{(1+i)^t}$$

where t represents the time period of the year and i is the appropriate interest rate.

The above expression has given us the value of the firm which actually is the present value of expected future profits. Another way of expressing this PV (present value) is as follows:

$$\text{PV of expected future profits} = \frac{\pi_1}{(1+i)^1} + \frac{\pi_2}{(1+i)^2} + \ldots \frac{\pi_n}{(1+i)^n}$$

$$= \sum_{t=1}^{h} \frac{\pi_t}{(1+i)^t}$$

where π_1, π_2, and so forth represent the expected profits in each year, t; and i is the appropriate interest rate.

• PROBLEM 22-33

Why is the division of labor an effective ingredient of efficient production?

Solution: The division of labor allows a drastic increase in the efficiency of production and consequently the amount of output produced. A. Smith first illustrated this fact with his example of a pin factory and gave the following reasons for it:

a) workers' concentration on a specific narrow task or group of tasks tends to improve their skill in performing it and to increase their productivity.

b) time that is otherwise taken by switching from one process to another is saved

c) time-saving and input-saving innovations are more likely to be introduced by workers who perform the same task many times over. In particular, the inventions of new machines are characteristic of a high degree of specialization

d) finally, the division of labor makes the use of machines in production possible.

• PROBLEM 22-34

What are the human costs and benefits one can derive from the division of labor? Briefly explain each.

Solution: A. Smith in the Wealth of Nations showed that extensive division of labor was essential for the achievement of economic efficiency. A high degree of specialization entails enormous benefits in terms of productivity and consumption. Without the division of labor much longer hours of hard work would be necessary to maintain a much lower standard of living than the one we enjoy today. Nevertheless, along with these benefits the division of labor involves certain costs. It is dull for a worker to perform the same simple processes many times over and it is not very rewarding to perform a minor insignificant part of the production process without the presence of a sense of final result. In the age of mass production repetitiveness and the monotonous character of many production processes are difficult to avoid.

PRODUCTION POSSIBILITIES CURVE

• **PROBLEM 22-35**

Describe a production function statement.

Solution: The production function can be described in many different ways. One of them would be to account for every input which is used in the production process. For example, the function

$$X = f(I_1, I_2, I_3, \ldots, I_n)$$

states that certain quantities of different inputs from I_1 to I_n are required to produce the output X. It is common in economic theory to simplify the production function by making all the factor inputs either a part of capital input or a part of labor input. The type of production function most commonly used in economics is therefore:

$$X = f(L,K).$$

• **PROBLEM 22-36**

What is production possibility?

Solution: Production possibility describes the limited number of goods and services that an economy can produce during any given time period. Production possibility is an expression of the basic economic questions; societies possess limited resources (land, labor and capital) requiring choices to be made concerning the uses to which these resources are put. Resources and therefore goods and services are scarce. The decision to produce certain goods and services involves an opportunity cost in terms of the goods or services that are not being produced instead. The opportunity cost of production is sometimes expressed as a trade-off, with the amount of one good or service that must be traded off or given up to gain a certain quantity of another good or service expressing the price of the latter good or service.

Production Possibilities

Production	A	B	C	D	E
Shoes (thousands of pairs)	0	10	20	30	40
Soybeans (thousand of tons)	100	90	70	40	0

For example, suppose a small country, Ruritania, produces only two goods, shoes and soybeans. Its economic resources are limited, so any factors of production (land, labor or capital) which are added to shoe production must be taken from soybean production, and vice versa, consequently to produce less of another. The table shows various combinations of quantities of shoes and soybeans which Ruritania can produce.

To construct the production-possibility curve we employ a simple two-dimensional graph, putting the output of shoes on the vertical axis and that of soybeans on the horizontal axis.(see figure)

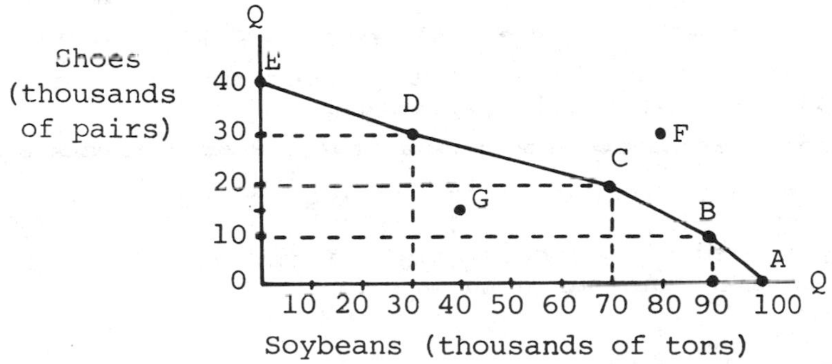

Once the axes are constructed, the various production possibilities (A, B, etc.) are plotted by reading from the table. When all the production possibilities have been plotted, they are joined by a smooth cruve.

It is important to note the underlying assumption of the production possibility curve, that the curve represents a set of possibilities for the economy operating with full employment of its resources. The economy can never move outside the curve (Point F) without a change in its economic resources (the discovery of oil, for example) or in technology (discovery of a way to grow 100 instead of 50 bushels of corn on every acre).

An economy may operate inside the curve (Point G) if it is at less than full employment.

• PROBLEM 22-37

Are the concepts of production possibility frontier and production function different? How?

Solution: The production possibility frontier refers to an outer limit on the finished consumer good that a society can produce given its resources and the state of technical knowledge. For example, if all of the American workers were employed in the automobile industry, they would still produce a finite number of cars. Such a distribution of resources is certainly unlikely but it represents a point on the production possibility frontier where an economy produces only cars. Alternative ways of employing available resources will give additional points on the production possibility frontier.

The production function, on the other hand, describes how various inputs should be employed in order to produce a given amount of output. Thus, to say that the production of 10 units of a certain good requires 7 units of labor and 5 units of capital is to describe the production function. At the same time, to say that the economy can at the most produce 12 units of one good when it produces 6 units of another good is to describe a point on the production possibility frontier.

• PROBLEM 22-38

What is meant when it is said that an economy is producing on its production possibility frontier?

<u>Solution:</u> When an economy is producing on its production possibilities curve, it is fully utilizing its resources and hence, in order to produce more of any one good, it must sacrifice some of another good.

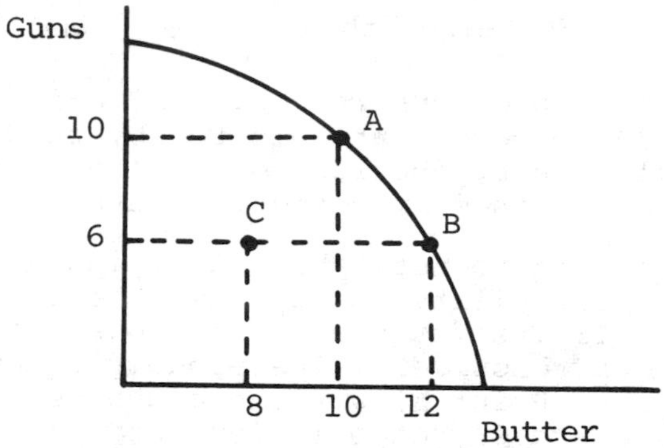

For example, in the accompanying diagram, if the economy is operating at point A (10 guns and 10 pounds of butter being produced), and it wishes to increase butter production to 12 pounds at point B, it must sacrifice 4 guns.

However, if the economy were originally operating inside the production possibility frontier, say at point C, and wished to increase butter production to 12 pounds, it could do so while maintaining its production at 6 guns, by operating more efficiently.

• PROBLEM 22-39

Suppose that on the production-possibilities graphs in the figure, AA represents the present, with BB and CC representing possible p-p frontiers ten years from now. Explain why choosing X_1 now would result in CC later, while choosing X_2 now would result in BB later.

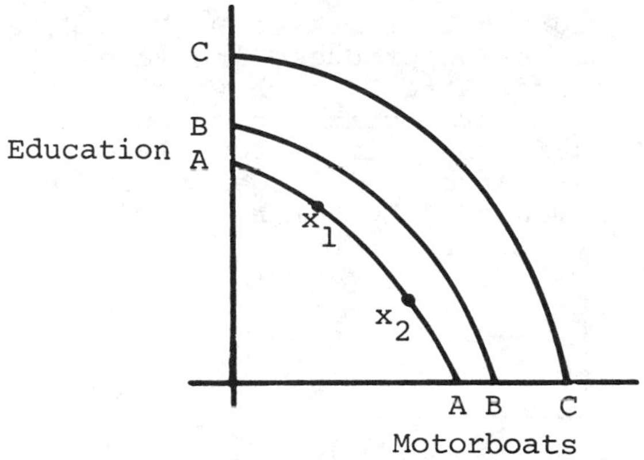

Solution: At point X_1, our society decides to devote more resources to education than to motoboats. This will result in a greater shift outward (to CC) of the production-possibility curve since education represents a preparation for the future. Point X_2, on the other hand, will result in a smaller shift of the production-possibilities curve (to BB) since producing motorboats means placing more emphasis on goods that are consumed now.

In general, when a society places its greatest emphasis on capital goods, its future growth will be greater than a society whose emphasis is on consumer goods.

• PROBLEM 22-40

How does the convex production-possibility curve reflect the law of increasing relative costs? If the production-possibility curve were a straight line, would this reflect the law of increasing cost?

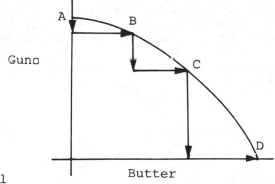

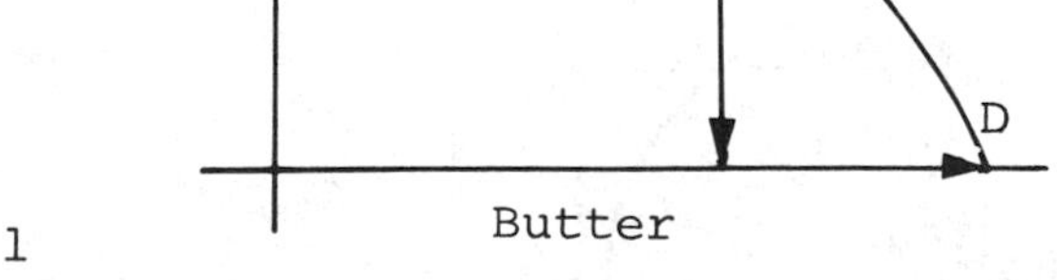

Fig. 1

Solution: The law of increasing costs says that in order to get equal extra amounts of one good, society must sacrifice increasing amounts of the second good.

We can see that the production-possibility curve agrees with the law by examining its concave shape. On the graph in Figure 1, we illustrate this with the use of arrows.

We see on the graph that from A to B, B to C, and C to D, the amount of butter being produced increases by an equal amount. But as we go from A to D, each vertical arrow, which indicates the drop in gun production which must take place in order to increase butter production, grows larger. This indicates that it takes a larger and larger sacrifice of guns to produce equal increments of butter as we move down the production-possibility curve.

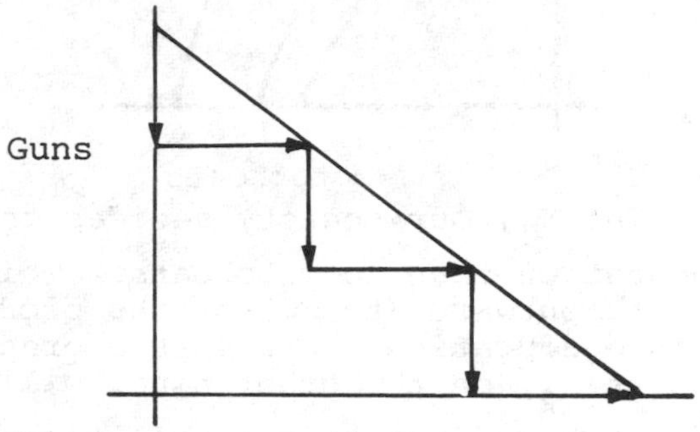

Fig. 2

To investigate the case where the production-possibility curve is a straight line, we will draw such a curve and once again examine with arrows how much of a change is required in one variable to cause a constant change in the other variable.

We see on the graph in Figure 2 that as butter production increases by a constant amount, gun production decreases by a constant amount. This result contradicts the law of increasing costs and so represents an exceptional case. Economists call this a case of "constant (relative) costs."

• PROBLEM 22-41

Figure 1 represents a production possibility frontier of a certain economy.
Points A and B show different combinations of goods and services which a nation may want to produce. Are these combinations attainable? What do they mean in terms of the nation's economy?

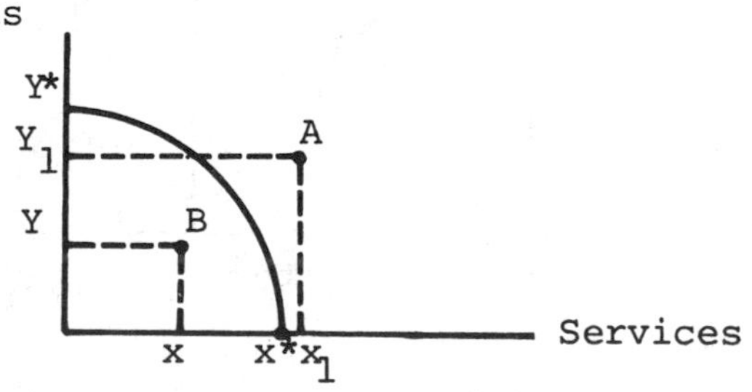

Fig. 1

Solution: Given the production possibility frontier shown in Fig. 1 point A is clearly unattainable. The existing techology and natural resources allow the nation's economy to produce at the most X* units of services and even this is possible only if no goods are produced. The choice of Y_1 units of goods in this simplified economy limits the attainable amount of service-units to the point on the production possibility frontier corresponding to Y_1 units of goods. At the same time, assuming there are no environmental limitations, point B represents an 'underproducing' economy, i.e. an economy not producing at full capacity. This could happen for reasons of unemployment or inefficiency or both. Practically all modern economies have some unemployment and allow some waste and non-optimal production. This means that at any point inside the production possibility frontier the economy can improve and thereby increase its output of both goods and services. Once some point on the production possibility frontier is reached only a trade-off between goods and services becomes possible in the short run. Any increase in the amount of goods produced requires giving up some units of services and vice versa.

• PROBLEM 22-42

Consider a nation that is producing at point A in the accompanying figure.

Suppose now that this nation would like to produce as much as possible - to raise the standard of living of the population - and that there are no environmental reasons for limiting maximum production. What does this tell us about the nation's economy?

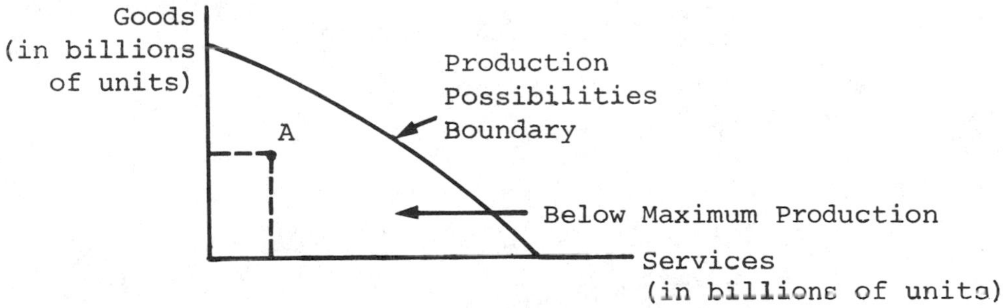

Solution: One or both of the following two possibilities will explain the above nation's position at A.

(1) unemployment of resources
(2) inefficient use of resources

(1) Point A production may be the result of some idle resources. For example, workers may not be able to find jobs; deposits may not be mined; or machines for automobile bodies may not be in operation because not enough cars are being sold.

(2) The other circumstance that gives rise to producing below the production possibilities boundary is inefficient use of resources. This could be due to outright waste - for example, not permitting qualified and healthy people over the age of sixty-five to hold jobs. Alternatively, it

could be due to combining resources in a less than optimal way. If, for instance, each individual Chevrolet fender were cut out by hand instead of stamped out by a press, the cost of production would be substantially increased. Whenever goods or services are produced at higher cost than could be achieved by using an alternative combination of resources, production is not efficient.

Point A production - or some other point below the production possibilities boundary - is a very likely combination for this nation to be producing in a particular year. Few nations do not experience some unemployment of resources and some production inefficiencies. It is important to understand, however, that a nation producing below its production possibilities boundary is able to improve - in this country's case, to produce more goods or more services, or more of both - without an expansion of its resource base or its technological knowledge, both of which take a long time to achieve. By contrast, if this nation were producing on its production possibilities boundary, it could increase its production of goods in the short run only by decreasing its production of services. Alternatively, it could increase its production of services only by decreasing its production of goods.

SHORT ANSWER QUESTIONS FOR REVIEW

Answer
To be covered when testing yourself

Choose the correct answer.

1. The theory of distribution: (a) explains how market relations, not power relations, determine the shares of national income for both labor and property (b) explains little, since the theory is still so unsettled (c) analyzes the determination of rents, wages, and interest (d) explains how power relations, not market relations, determine property's share of national income (e) explains how power relations, not market relations, determine labor's share of national income. — c

2. The marginal-revenue-product is: (a) the selling price of the last unit of output (b) the increment of Total Revenue resulting from the use of an additional unit of input (c) used in determining marginal-physical-product (d) harder to determine in pure competition than in monopoly (e) harder to determine in pure competition than in oligopoly. — b

3. A firm achieves Least-cost in production by substituting factors until: (a) their factor prices are equal (b) their marginal-physical-products are equal (c) their marginal-physical-products are each equal to their factor prices (d) their marginal-physical-products are each zero (e) none of the above are true. — e

4. Diminishing marginal returns occur: (a) after some point, as increasing amounts of a factor are added to fixed amounts of other factors of production (b) when the marginal utility of income just equals the marginal utility of leisure, but not before (c) because, basically, as more workers are employed in a plant they talk more and produce less (d) because of the laws of physics and engineering (e) because of the operation of a general economic principle called economies of scale. — a

5. If input A is used in producing finished commodity X (i.e., A's price is a cost of production for X), the price of X will determine the price of A: (a) if the number of X producers is large and the number of A suppliers is small (b) If A is fixed in supply available and useful only in production of X (c) if the supply curve for A is perfectly elastic (d) only if the demand for A is highly inelastic (e) in none of these circumstances. — b

Answer

SHORT ANSWER QUESTIONS FOR REVIEW

To be covered when testing yourself

6. Which of the following is a strong economic efficiency reason for desiring that each factor be paid the value of its marginal-product? (a) It would eliminate both the social and economic need for labor unions. (b) It would bring about much more antitrust activity by the government. (c) It would eliminate the need for expensive apprenticeship programs in crafts and industry. (d) It would help ensure that no reallocation of factors could increase the production of one good without decreasing that of the other. (e) It would make the distribution of income clearly ethical. d

7. An increase in the price of a particular factor: (a) will cause the marginal-revenue-product curve for this factor to shift downward (b) will usually result in the substitution of other factors for this factor, and hence will cause employment of this factor to fall (c) will result in less employment if firms have monopoly power in product markets (d) will have no effect on the amount of it being used according to the marginal-product principle of Least-cost which requires only that the MPP of each factor be proportional to its price, not equal to it (e) would not result in diminished use of this factor if output were not decreased at the same time. b

8. In the short run, (a) barriers to entry prevent new firms from entering the industry (b) a firm does not have sufficient time to change the amounts of any of the resources it employs (c) the firm does not have sufficient time to cut its rate of output to zero (d) the firm does not have sufficient time to change the size of its plant. c

9. A distinguishing characteristic of the long run period is that (a) all costs are fixed costs (b) all costs are variable costs (c) fixed costs tend to be greater than variable costs (d) fixed costs tend to be lesser than variable costs. b

10. Which of the following represents a long-run adjustment? (a) A farmer uses an extra dose of fertilizer on his corn crop. (b) A supermarket hires four additional checkout girls. (c) A steel manufacturer cuts back on its purchases of coke and iron ore. (d) Unable to

Answer
To be covered when testing yourself

meet foreign competition, an American watch manufacturer sells the real assets of one of its branch plants. — d

11. Average fixed cost is the ratio of total fixed cost to the corresponding output; that is (a) AFC declines initially, reaches a minimum, and then increases again as output increases (b) AFC is independent of output (c) AFC declines as output decreases (d) AFC declines as output increases — d

12. The marginal cost curve cuts the Average Variable Cost and the Average Total Cost curves at what points? (a) minimum and center points, respectively (b) minimum points (c) center points (d) none of the above — b

Answer questions 13 and 14 on the basis of the accompanying diagram.

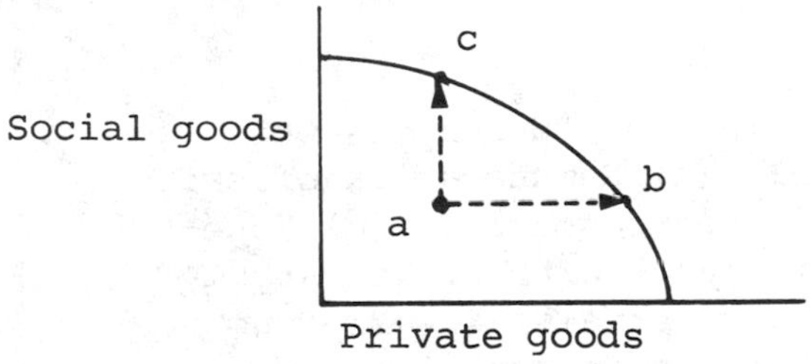

13. The movement from b to c suggests that: (a) more private goods are being produced by employing currently idle resources (b) more social goods are being produced by employing currently idle resources (c) more social goods are being produced at the expense of less private goods (d) more private goods are being produced at the expense of less social goods. — c

14. The movement from point a to c suggests that: (a) more private goods are being produced at the expense of less social goods (b) more social goods are being produced at the expense of less private goods (c) more social goods are being produced by employing currently idle

Answer
To be covered when testing yourself

resources (d) more private goods are being produced by employing currently idle resources (e) none of the above. c

15. When an economy is operating with maximum efficiency, the production of more of commodity A will entail the production of less of commodity B because: (a) of the law of increasing real costs (b) material wants are insatiable (c) the structure of demand is fixed at any point in time (d) resources are limited (e) resources are specialized and only imperfectly shiftable. d

16. The least per unit cost at which any quantity of a product can be produced by a firm, after it has had the time to properly readjust its plant size, can be illustrated by the (a) AVC curve (b) short-run ATC curve (c) long-run ATC curve (d) ATC curve c

17. Which of the following explain the down sloping part of the long-run ATC curve? (a) Diseconomies of large-scale production (b) Economies of mass production (c) Higher average total costs (d) Law of Diminishing Returns b

18. Which of the following best describes what explicit costs are? (a) Remuneration of self-owned and self-employed resources (b) Monetary payments firms make to those who supply labor services, raw materials (c) Minimum payments to keep talents in the firm (d) Maximum payments to keep talents in the firm b

19. Which of the following pertains to the long-run? (a) the firm can revert to a smaller plant but can not alter its plant capacity (b) the average costs of production is always constant (c) sufficient amount of time for new firms to enter or firms to leave an industry (d) the amount of extra output pro-

SHORT ANSWER QUESTIONS FOR REVIEW

	Answer To be covered when testing yourself
duced reduces considerably	c
Fill in the blanks.	
20. A purely competitive firm should hire an additional worker if marginal-revenue-product would be more than the ____________.	wage rate
21. When a competitive firm has reached a level of output at which the marginal-revenue product of each input is equal to the price of that input, it is at ____________ output level and is producing that output at least possible cost.	maximum-profit
22. Since income depends upon the price of the ____________ a person has to sell multiplied by the quantity sold, an increase in the marginal physical productivity of a service can increase income by making the service more desirable.	productive service
23. In the U.S. as a whole, a 1 per cent increase in labor increases output by about ____________ times as much as does a 1 per cent increase in capital.	3
24. In ____________ simplified theory of production, the wage rate is equal to the marginal product of labor, and total payments to labor are given by the product of employment and the wage rate.	Clark's
25. The equality everywhere of factor proportions and marginal-products would be denied if ____________ returns to scale prevailed.	increasing
26. The ____________ of labor is the amount of extra output that is produced when one extra worker is added to a fixed amount of other factors.	marginal-physical-product
27. The ____________ is best described as the marginal-physical-product times the Marginal Revenue received from the sale of an extra unit of output.	marginal-revenue-product
28. A firm achieves ____________ in production by substituting factors until the ratio of their marginal-physical-product equals the ratio of their prices.	least-cost
29. Technological change has been increasing output in the U.S. at an annual rate of about ________ per cent.	2

SHORT ANSWER QUESTIONS FOR REVIEW

	Answer To be covered when testing yourself
30. The equality everywhere of factor proportions and marginal-products will result, as Clark suggested, in ____________ returns to scale if all inputs are increased in balanced proportion.	constant
31. ____________ version of the concept of exploitation of labor does not depend upon monopoly or other imperfections of bargaining power between employer and employees.	Oskar Lange's
32. The production function is stated only in terms of the given state of ____________.	technical knowledge
33. When a firm is at a Maximum-profit position, it is also necessarily at a ____________ position.	Least-cost
34. The increase of ____________ per worker in the U.S. has shifted labor's productivity wages up faster than technological change would alone.	capital

<u>Determine whether the following statements are true or false.</u>

35. Marginal-revenue-product is the extra revenue you get by increasing output by one unit.	False
36. The general Least-cost substitution principle is: Equate the marginal-products of all factors.	False
37. Clark proved that all factors can be thought of as having their distributive shares determined by their respective interdependent marginal-products.	True
38. Despite changing birth rates and technology, labor's relative share of national product has dropped over the decades.	False
39. The amount of labor hired by a producer depends not only on the price of labor but on the price of machinery and other inputs.	True
40. An increase in the price of one factor (without an equivalent increase in its productivity), will cause employment of that factor to fall, both because of substitution of cheaper factors and because the Maximum-profit output may now be smaller.	True
41. The quantity demanded of a factor (say labor) at a specified wage is that quantity of labor whose marginal-revenue-product just equals the specified wage.	True

SHORT ANSWER QUESTIONS FOR REVIEW

	Answer To be covered when testing yourself
42. The marginal-physical-product of a factor is the resulting increase in production when the amounts of all factors being used are increased by one unit.	False
43. When all factors' marginal-physical-products are exactly proportional to those factors' respective market prices, then the firm is necessarily maximizing its profits.	False
44. The rule that the marginal-revenue-product of each factor be equal to the price of the factor ensures that the firm will not only be using a Least-cost combination of factors but will also be at its Maximum-profit position.	True
45. To achieve a Least-cost combination of factors for each possible output, the business firm should equate the marginal-physical-product of each factor to its market price.	False
46. The period of time in which all resources can be varied, is the short-run.	False
47. The main factor causing diseconomies of scale is related to inefficiency in managing and coordinating a large-scale business enterprise.	True
48. When diseconomies of scale outweigh economies of scale, the long-run average cost curve rises.	True
49. The long-run average cost curve is U-shaped because of large scale economies.	False

CHAPTER 23

WAGE DETERMINATION

Basic Attacks and Strategies for Solving Problems in this Chapter. **See pages 814 to 840 for step-by-step solutions to problems.**

While it is recognized that human labor is not the same thing as other commodities, issues such as wage rates, labor force participation, and employment can be analyzed using demand and supply analysis as in the case of other commodities.

The demand for labor is analyzed using the marginal productivity theory. Each worker a firm hires produces output that can be sold in the market place. Consequently, each worker contributes something to the firm's revenue. If the firm sells in a perfectly competitive market, this contribution is known as the worker's value of the marginal product (VMP). In imperfectly competitive markets, the same concept is called marginal revenue product (MRP). Both VMP and MRP decline as more labor is hired. The firm will hire labor as long as the worker's contribution to the firm's revenue exceeds what the worker costs (the wage) because the firm's profits will be increased. The firm will maximize profits when labor is hired up to the point where the wage equals VMP or MRP.

For any wage, we can determine the amount the firm will want to hire by consulting the VMP or MRP schedule. Consequently, these schedules are the firm's demand curve for labor. To go from the firm level to the market level is a somewhat complicated task. We cannot simply add demand curves horizontally as in the case of consumer goods and services. The problem is that as firms hire more labor, more output is produced, which lowers product price and decreases labor's VMP or MRP. The exact details of constructing the market demand curve for labor are best left to more advanced courses. Nonetheless, market demand curves can be constructed that represent the marginal product of labor.

The labor supply problem can be analyzed as a typical problem of consumer choice. The worker must decide how to allocate her scarce time (only 24 hours per day for everyone) between working and not working. The worker will compare the reward from working with the utility of non-work activities and choose an allocation. The labor supply curve represents how many hours the worker would like to work at each wage rate.

The slope of this curve is an important issue in labor economics. The reason is because wage changes affect workers in two ways. There is a substitution effect. The substitution effect is that as wages rise, not working becomes more expensive. In other words, you sacrifice more by not working. This should lead the worker to choose more hours. There is also an income effect. As wages rise, the worker can earn the same income and work fewer hours, which workers may opt to do since work at the margin is presumably a source of disutility. Both effects are present at all times for all workers. Which effect is stronger determines the slope of the labor supply curve. If the substitution effect is stronger, the labor supply curve should have a positive slope. If the income effect is stronger, the labor supply curve should have a negative slope. Many economists believe a "backward-bending" supply curve is possible, one that has a positive slope at low wages but bends back and has a negative slope at higher wages.

Summing the individual labor supply curves horizontally will give the market supply curve.

The intersection of the relevant market demand and supply curves will give equilibrium wages and employment levels in particular occupations and industries. The labor market works as the markets for other commodities do. If the wage rate is below the equilibrium level, a shortage of labor will be created which will force wage rates up. If the wage rate is above the equilibrium level, there will be a surplus, forcing wages down. The standard analysis of the minimum wage postulates that the legislation creates a wage floor above the equilibrium level resulting in a permanent surplus of labor. In short, minimum wage legislation will create unemployment.

What creates wage differentials among workers? It is all a matter of supply and demand. Wage differentials among workers reflect the fact that equilibrium levels differ between markets. Markets with relatively high demand and scarce supply will naturally lead to higher equilibrium wage rates, and the reasons may have little to do with the intrinsic value of the work or the moral character of workers. If rock stars earn more than teachers, it is simply dictated by market conditions.

In the long run, wage differentials can be reduced simply by the mechanism of labor mobility. Labor will exit markets with low wages and enter markets with high wages, causing wage differentials to decrease. In some cases, wage differentials can persist in the long run. This results from barriers to mobility between markets. One barrier results from the cost of acquiring the skills to perform in certain jobs. Another barrier results from worker tastes. Some jobs have features making them unattractive. A wage differential is required to compensate workers for these unattractive characteristics. A third set of barriers results from various market imperfections, such as lack of knowledge of job opportunities, discrimination, and reluctance to leave familiar surroundings.

Labor unions are organizations of workers. Their goals are to improve wages and working conditions, provide political representation, and give social support for their members. The economic goals of unions can be analyzed using demand and supply analysis.

Unions have four methods at their disposal to improve wages. Use the accompanying graph for the following analysis. Let D_0 and S_0 be the market demand and supply curves for labor in the absence of unions.

2) They can restrict the supply of labor to particular occupations. Unions of skilled workers (craft unions) are able to do this through the provision of apprenticeship opportunities. Union lobbying for occupational licensing laws and similar restrictions on entry into occupations can accomplish the same thing. Graphically, union policies can shift in the supply curve (from S_0 to S_1) raising equilibrium wage, but lowering the quantity of employment.

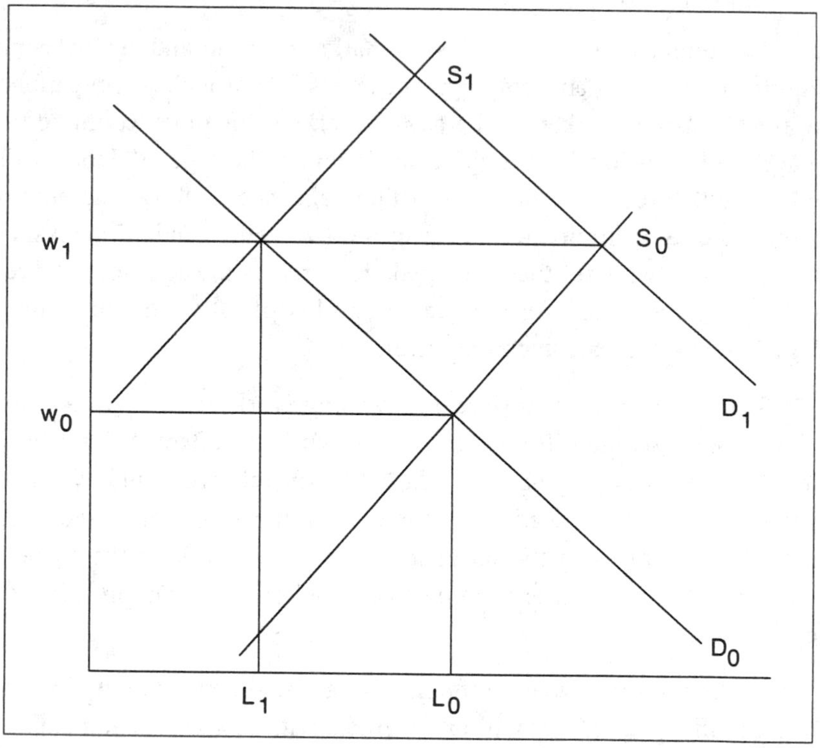

Effect of Unions

2) They can raise the standard wage rate. Unions may bargain with employers to set a wage higher than the equilibrium in particular markets. Unions are likely to be successful at this to the extent they are

able to organize a large segment of the labor force, develop cohesiveness among their members, and skillfully use the tactics of bargaining, including the willingness to call and endure strikes. What is not often appreciated is that union standard rate policies can have adverse effects on the level of employment in an industry. Graphically, assume a union is able to win a wage, w_1, in excess of the equilibrium rate. Employers will respond by reducing employment to L_1.

3) Unions can increase the demand for labor in particular markets. Political lobbying for specific programs, union label campaigns, and image advertising can all play a role here. Graphically, this policy has the effect of raising demand to D_1, also raising equilibrium wage and the quantity of employment.

4) Unions can also resist exploitation of labor by monopsonistic employers. This issue is more a theoretical curiosity because true monopsony is not very common. The graphical analysis cannot be shown here.

Step-by-Step Solutions to Problems in this Chapter, "Wage Determination"

WAGES AND LABOR MARKET EQUILIBRIUM

• **PROBLEM 23-1**

Describe the classical theory of wages.

Solution: The classical or non-marginal theory of wage determination rests on the concepts of subsistence wage and of the wages fund. The first one was often held by people sharing the Malthusian view of population growth. The idea is that in the long run wages can be neither at higher nor at lower than the subsistence level or the level necessary to sustain human life. A higher long run wage is impossible due to constant competition from the reserve army of the unemployed fed by the ever increasing population. Lower wages on the other hand, would be simply insufficient to support the workers' continued existence.

The concept of wage fund means essentially that entrepreneurs provide the resources necessary for the workers' existence for as long as the production process continues and workers' product is sold. The wage rate in these circumstances is obtained by dividing the number of workers employed into the total wage fund.

• **PROBLEM 23-2**

Distinguish between money wages and real wages.

Solution: Money wages are simply the amount of cash workers receive per unit of time on the job. Consequently money wages are representative only of the amount of currency workers hold, not of its value. Real wages, on the other hand, indicate the actual value of the money wages or their purchasing power. Therefore, the higher the price level the lower the real value of a given money wage received by a worker. It is important to point out that the direction of a change in the money wages and in the real wages need not coincide. A higher money wage may mean a lower real wage if the rate of growth of prices exceeds that of the money wages.

• **PROBLEM 23-3**

Suppose that dd' is the demand for labor and ss' the supply of labor in a two-factor production system.

Show what portion of total product goes to wages and what portion goes to rent, (see Figure 1).

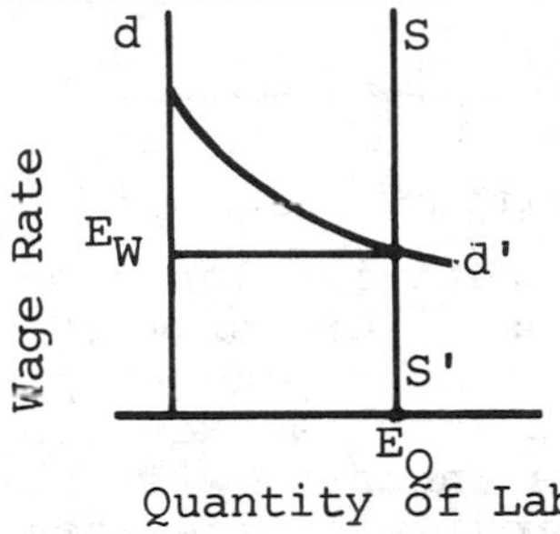

Fig. 1

Solution: Since the demand curve for labor is the same as the marginal-product of labor, the total product can be drawn in as the area under the dd curve from $x = 0$ to $x = E_Q$ (In other words, the sum of the marginal product for each worker = total product) shown in figure 2.

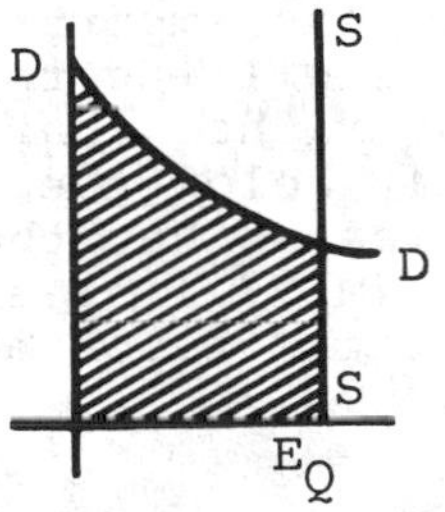

Fig. 2

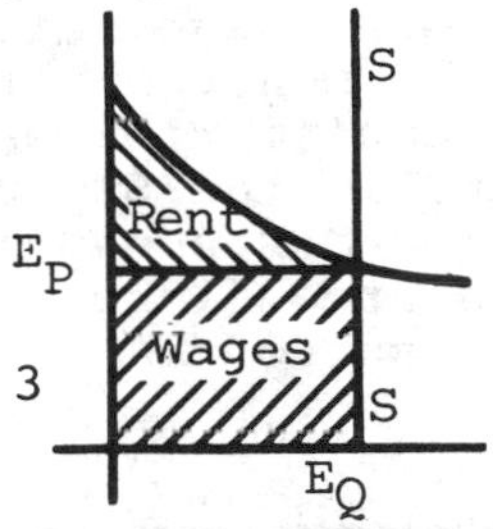

Fig. 3

Now, according to economic theory each laborer will receive as wages the marginal product of the last worker hired. In our case, the last worker is hired when the dd curve intersects the ss-curve. Since wages are constant for all workers and E_Q workers are hired, total wages can be represented by the rectangle portion of the total product shown in figure 3.

Finally, since rent represents the remainder of the total product not given over to wages, the triangular portion of total product above wages will represent rent, or the excess over final marginal product that workers provided but never got paid for.

• **PROBLEM 23-4**

Consider the accompanying figure of the wage rate and the level of employment:

a) Assuming we have a purely (perfect) competitive market, how much labor will the industry hire, and what wage rate will it pay?

b) Will the answer be the same if we have a monopsonistic labor market? Explain.

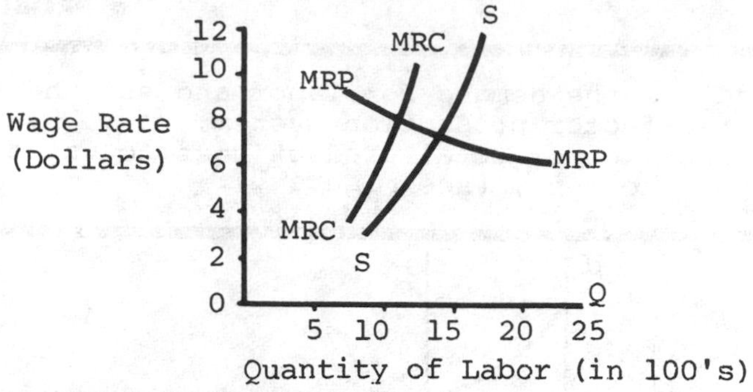

Solution: a) Under a competitive labor market the equilibrium wage rate and the number of workers to be employed are determined by the intersection of the supply SS curve and the demand DD curve or the Marginal Revenue Product (MRP). Therefore, the competitive industry will hire approximately 14 workers and pay an approximate wage rate of $7.20.

b) The answer will not be the same if we have a monopsonistic labor market because the monopsonist will hire workers and pay a wage rate at the point where the marginal resource cost is equal to labor's marginal revenue product. So the monopsonistic firm will hire around 11 workers and pay a much lower wage rate of $4.10. The important point here is that a monopsonist will not be willing to pay the competitive equilibrium wage rate but rather that the wage rate is found in the SS curve directly below the intersection of the MRC and MRP schedules. This means that the employers marginal resource (labor) cost curve (MRC) lies above the labor supply curve (CS) in a monopsonistic labor market.

• PROBLEM 23-5

Describe how the equilibrium wage rate and the equilibrium level of employment are determined in a perfectly competitive market.

Solution: The assumption of a perfectly competitive market means that none of the individual firms is large enough to influence the going wage rate by its hiring decision. Each firm faces a perfectly elastic labor supply curve and can hire as many workers as it wishes at the going wage rate. Therefore the marginal cost of hiring an extra worker is constant and the same for every firm. The equilibrium wage rate and the level of employment in a competive market will be given, of course by the intersection of the labor supply and labor demand curves (see fig. 1).

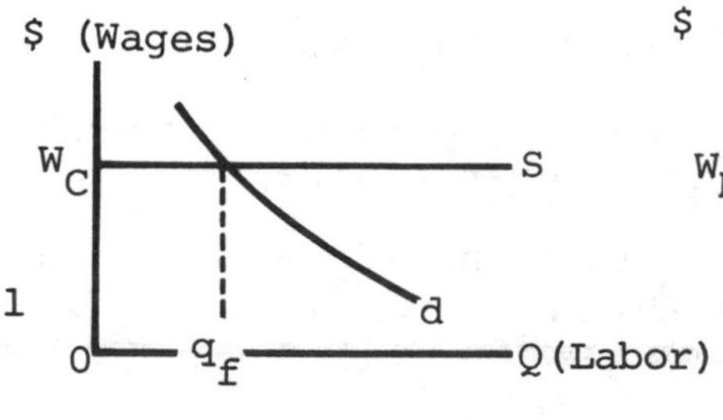

Fig. 1

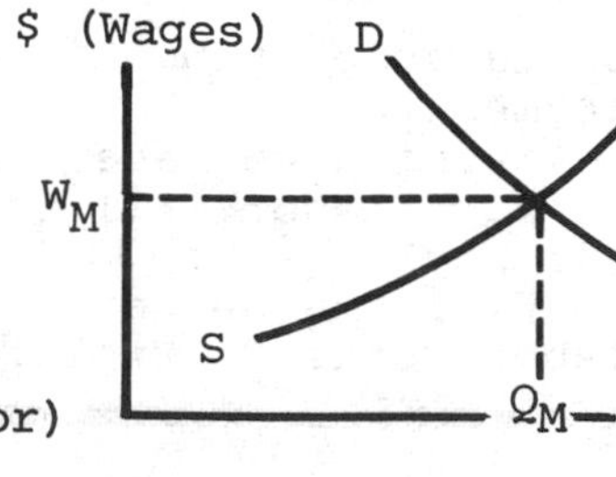

Fig. 2

The interaction of all the typical firms in the market (fig. 1) gives the aggregate result as shown in fig. 2. Q_m is the number of workers employed, W_m is the equilibrium wage rate.

• PROBLEM 23-6

Given the following information explain the profit maximization concept graphically.

Falbo Factory

No. of Men	Total Physical Product	Price	Total Revenue	MRP	MRC
1	15	$10	$150	$150	$50
2	25	10	250	100	50
3	33	10	330	80	50
4	38	10	380	50	50
5	42	10	420	40	50

Also, show what would happen to the number of men employed if minimum wage rates for factory workers were suddenly set at $80 per day.

Solution: The marginal revenue product schedule represents the demand schedule for the factor of production, in this case men. The inverse relationship is due to the law of diminishing returns.

In our example we assume that any number of workers may be hired for $50 each, the Marginal Resource Cost of hiring an additional laborer is constant at $50. Hence the Marginal Resource Cost schedule and the Supply of labor schedule coincide. The $50 wage schedule is actually a supply schedule for labor.

Depicting the situation graphically, we see that the number of workers hired (so as to achieve profit maximization) is determined by the intersection of the demand (MRP) curve and supply curve (wage rate), (see figure).

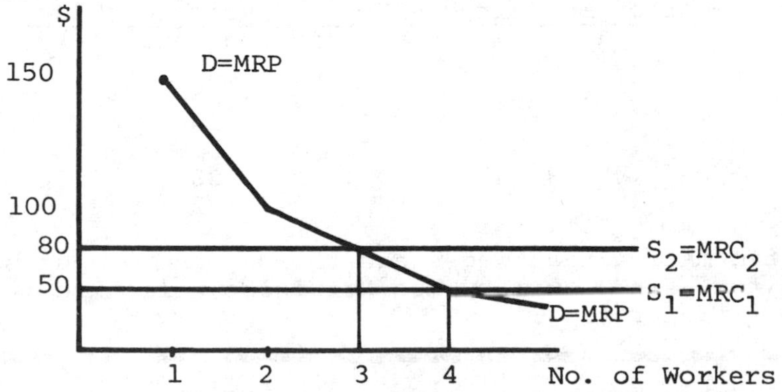

So, at a wage of $50 per day, the employer will hire

four workers.

If minimum wages are fixed at $80 per day, the workers will be receiving higher wages but only 3 workers will be hired, as shown by the intersection of MRC_2 (S_2) and MRP above.

WAGES AND LABOR PRODUCTIVITY

• PROBLEM 23-7

Describe the connection between labor productivity and wage determination. What factors contribute to the high productivity of American labor?

Solution: Labor productivity is directly connected with the demand for labor. Generally, as labor productivity rises the demand for labor also rises. Given the size of the available labor force the increase in the demand for labor results in higher real wages being received by the workers. American labor is highly demanded and receives relatively high real wages in part because it is in most cases more productive and efficient than labor abroad. There are several reasons for this situation. Most American industries use large amounts of capital in conjunction with labor in their production processes and thereby make labor more productive. Also the technological superiority of the American capital equipment contributes to the efficiency of production. The abundance of land and mineral resources per worker is another reason behind the impressive productivity of American labor particularly in agriculture. Finally, the high quality of American labor and management based on education, training and work attitudes, and the vast size of the American market create a favorable environment for the growth of labor productivity.

• PROBLEM 23-8

Given the schedule of productivity below for the Falbo Factory

Number of men hired	Total Physical Product (in tons per day)
1	15
2	25
3	33
4	38
5	42

and the information that wages are $50/day and output sells for $10 a ton, find how many men Mr. Falbo will hire in order to maximize profits.

Solution: To solve this problem, we must think in terms of the familiar MR = MC formula. Only the vocabulary is a bit different here.

Working analogously to the MR = MC problem, our profit-maximizing factory owner will hire workers until the point where the increase in total revenue due to hiring an additional man, called the marginal revenue product (MRP), is equal to cost of hiring an additional worker, called the marginal resource cost (MRC). In this case MRC = wage rate = $50 per day.

To find out MRP, we must first multiply the total physical products given in the table by $10 (the price of one ton) to get the total revenue corresponding to each level of employment. Then we measure MRP's as the changes in total revenue due to each successive additional worker. Constructing a table we get:

No. of Workers	Total Physical Product	Price	Total Revenue	MRP	MRC
1	15	$10	$150	$150	50
				($250-150)	
2	25	10	250	100	50
				(330-250)	
3	33	10	330	80	50
				(380-330)	
4	38	10	380	50	50
				(420-380)	
5	42	10	420	40	50

Looking at the table, we see that profit is maximized when no. of men employed = 4, since that is where MRC (50) = MRP (50).

THE MINIMUM WAGE

• PROBLEM 23-9

What are the pros and cons in the minimum-wage controversy? Which view is correct?

Solution: Since the enactment of the Fair Labor Standards Act in 1938, the United States has had a Federal minimum wage. There are some who insist that ferocity in exploiting labor ensures efficiency. Others argue that a minimum wage prevents Darwin's view of competition in the jungle from becoming a reality among human beings.

A. Case for the Minimum Wage - Advocates of the minimum wage claim that the imposition of a minimum wage in a monopsonistic labor market can raise wages without causing unemployment; indeed, they contend that higher minimum wages may even result in more jobs by eliminating the monopsonistic employer's motive to restrict employment. Furthermore, the imposition of an effective minimum wage may increase labor productivity, shifting the labor demand curve to the right and offsetting any unemployment effects which the minimum wage might otherwise induce. There are several ways in which minimum wage increases productivity. First, a minimum wage may have a shock effect upon employers. That is, firms using low-wage workers may tend to be inefficient in the use of labor; the higher wage rates imposed by the minimum wage will presumably force these firms to use labor more efficiently, and so the productivity of labor rises. Second, it is argued that higher wages will tend to increase the incomes and therefore the health, vigor, and motivation of workers, making them more productive, and better tools for maximizing profits.

B. Case against the Minimum Wage - Critics, reasoning in terms of the inclusive or industrial unionism concept, contend that the imposition of effective (above-equilibrium) minimum wages will simply push employers back up their MRP or labor demand curves because it is now profitable to hire fewer workers. The higher wage costs may even force some firms out of business. The result is that many of the poor, low-wage workers whom the minimum wage was designed to help will find themselves out of work. Therefore, a worker who is unemployed at a minimum wage of $2.30 per hour is clearly worse off than if he were employed at the market wage rate of, say, $1.75 per hour. Some discharged workers may drift off into other labor markets and find employment, but in so doing they increase the supply of labor in these markets and tend to depress wage rates therein.

After considering the pros and cons of the minimum wage controversy, we can conclude that it is hard to say which view is correct because empirical studies of the effects of increases in the minimum wage run into the problems of distinguishing the effects of the minimum wage per se from the effects of other developments - growth, inflation, recession - occuring in the economy. On balance, however, the evidence seems to suggest that periodic increases in the minimum wage are followed by employment declines in affected industries. Empirical studies suggest that those who remain employed receive higher incomes and tend to escape poverty, while those who lose their jobs are plunged deeper into poverty.

• PROBLEM 23-10

Suppose the demand and supply curves for messengers in Omaha are as shown in Figure 1.
What would happen if the federal government set a minimum wage rate of $3.00 per hour?

<u>Solution</u>: Currently the wage rate is $2.00 per hour and there are 400 messengers working in Omaha. If the minimum wage rate is established at $3.00 per hour, the equlibrium point of supply and demand will no longer be realized, as shown in Figure 2.

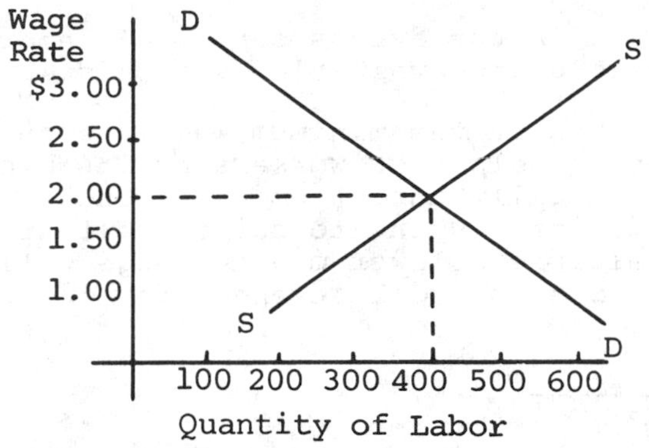

As seen from the graph, at a wage rate of $3.00 per hour, employment will drop from 400 messengers to 200 messengers. A surplus of 400 workers will exist, since 600 workers will be willing to work as messengers, while only 200 will be demanded.

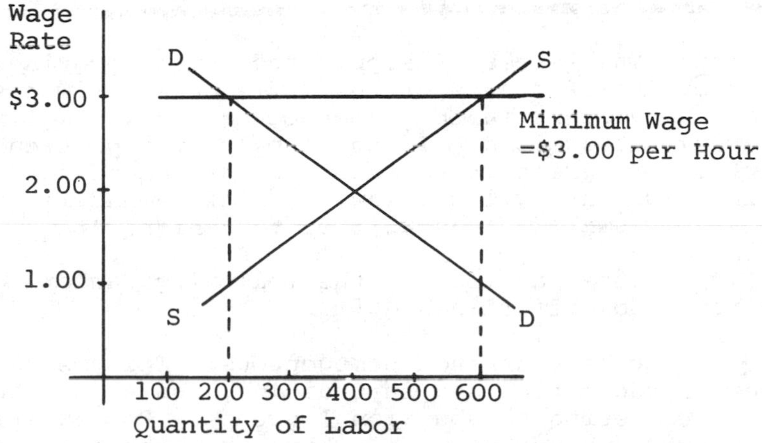

Fig. 2

• PROBLEM 23-11

Suppose at E, (see figure), wage = $2.00, but government sets a minimum wage rate at $2.65. How does this hurt those it is trying to help?

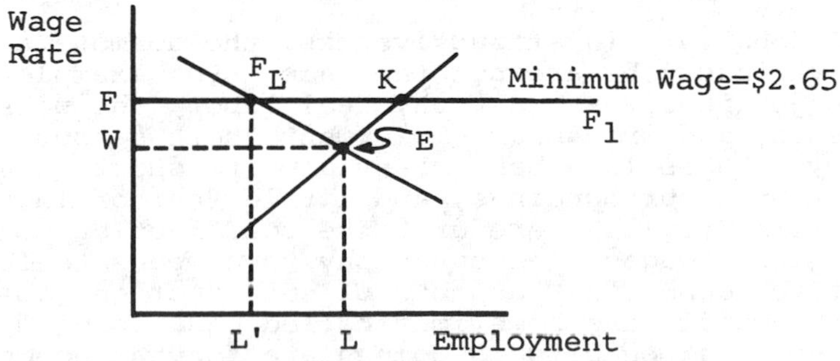

Solution: The competitive equilibrium is reached at E, where L workers are paid wage W. Suppose now the government establishes a minimum wage at F in excess of equilibrium W. This action would result in the excess supply of labor, i.e. in unemployment (K workers are available, yet only F_L of them are demanded by the firms at the minimum wage). Thus a government who intended to help poor workers by its minimum wage measure may have actually hurt them by making these workers unemployed. It is interesting to point out that if the labor demand curve is elastic a lower minimum wage will actually result in higher total payroll revenues for the workers.

WAGE DIFFERENTIALS

• PROBLEM 23-12

Briefly explain the factors that give rise to the existence of wage differentials:

Solution: The forces of supply and demand provide a general answer on the existence of the differences of wages among different individuals in the same occupations as well as those in different occupations. If the supply of a particular type of labor is very great in relation to the demand for it, the resulting wage rate will be low. But if demand is great and the supply very small, wages will be very high.

To be more particular, the following factors explain why wage rates do differ in practice.

(1) Workers are not homogeneous. This means that they differ in capacities and in training, and as a result, fall into noncompeting occuputaional groups. For example, a relatively small number of people have the inherent capacity to be lawyers, dentists, brain surgeons, concert violinists, and even fewer have the financial means of acquiring the necessary training. The result is that the supplies of these particular types of labor are very small in relation to the demand for them and that the consequent wages and salaries are high. These and similar groups do not compete with one another or with other skilled or semiskilled workers. The lawyer does not compete with the dentist, nor does the research chemist compete with the garbage collector.

(2) Jobs vary in attractiveness; the nonmonetary aspects of various jobs are not the same - For example, the construction job involves heavy physical labor, the possibility of accidents, and irregular employment, both seasonally and cyclically. A job in a bank means a white shirt, pleasant air-conditioned surroundings, and little fear of injury (outside New York City). Therefore, the construction contractors must pay higher wages than banks pay to compensate for the unattractive nonmonetary aspects of construction jobs. These wage differentials are sometimes called equalizing differences because they must be paid to compensate for the nonmonetary differences in various jobs.

(3) Labor markets are typically characterized by imperfections. This may be explained under three headings:

a) Geographic Immobilities - workers take root geographically. They are reluctant to leave friends, relatives, and associates, to force their children to change schools, to sell their houses, and to incur the costs and inconveniences of adjusting to a new job and a new community. The reluctance or inability of workers to move causes geographic wage differentials for the same occupation to persist.

b) Institutional Immobilities - Geographic immobilities may be reinforced by artificial restrictions on mobility which are imposed by institutions. As an example, the low paid nonunion peanut picker of Atlanta, Georgia may be willing to move to Washington in pursuit of higher wages, but his chances of successfully doing so are slim. He will probably be unable to get a union card and hence a job, specially if it is a craft union.

c) Sociological Immobilities - Despite recent regulatory legislation to the contrary, women workers frequently receive less pay than men working at the same job. The consequence of racial and ethnic discrimination is that Negroes, Hispanics, and other minority groups are often forced to accept lower wages on given jobs than fellow workers receive.

• PROBLEM 23-13

What is meant by psychic income?

Solution: Psychic income refers to the nonmonetary benefits a person receives from a job. Clearly this income can be negative or positive. Differences in salaries (money income) between two jobs are sometimes explained by taking psychic income into account.

• PROBLEM 23-14

With no institutional factors present in an economy (such as unions and employer power), give two reasons why there still could be large differences in competitive wage rates in various occupations.

Solution: Some jobs are more attractive than others. Some jobs offer comfortable working conditions, or other compensations for wages less than the market rate. Other jobs, like a steelworker or a police officer, have particular disadvantages that have to be compensated for by relatively high wages. These wage differences, called equalizing differences, arise from the different pecuniary conditions of particular jobs.

A second cause of wage differentials is the qualitative differences of ability among people. These differences can be natural, or they can be environmental in origin. Natural differences could explain the high wages of an opera star or basketball player. Environmental differences could explain the disparity in incomes between adults who were educated in the suburbs, and adults who were educated in ghetto schools. These qualitative differences, whether actual or imagined, can lead to large differences in wage rates, even in a competitive situation.

• PROBLEM 23-15

How does discrimination affect the labor market? What are the social costs of this discrimination?

Solution: Discrimination is reflected in the labor market in the demand schedule. In the demand schedule for a particular type of labor (machinist, doctor, etc.), prejudice results in a shift in the demand curve for the members of the group discriminated against from d_1d_1' to d_2d_2'. This shift lowers their wages and lowers the quantity of labor employed. So, members of this group are paid less, and work less in this particular field, than they would if there were no discrimination, (see figure).

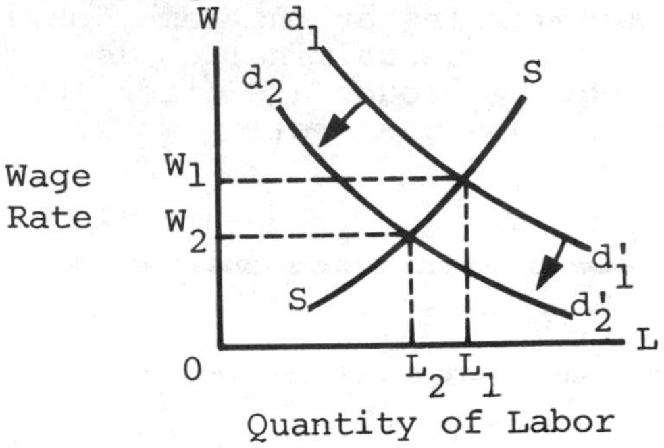

The social costs of discrimination arise because members of the group discriminated against do not contribute as much to total output as they would if there was not any discrimination. So, society as a whole loses some output because of irrational prejudice.

Discrimination results in a deviation from the optimum distribution of resources. The shift in the demand curve misallocates the supply of labor. This shift misallocates labor because some laborers are no longer paid their actual marginal product (recall that the demand schedule for labor is the same as the schedule of the marginal-product of labor). This is an example where irrational, non-economic factors can impair economic efficiency by distorting economic judgements (the value of the labor of the group discriminated against).

• PROBLEM 23-16

Why is it that in a perfectly competitive market, firms hiring labor, as a group will be forced to pay higher wage rates to obtain more workers?

Solution: In the absence of unemployment workers tend to have several alternative employment opportunities. Assuming it is realistic to expect a worker to be able to switch to a different industry or to work in the same industry but in a different area, makes it necessary for a competitive firm, or a group of firms to raise wages in order to obtain more workers. In a perfectly competitive market characterized by full employment, workers, unless offered higher wages by the firm, will be likely to choose alternative employment offers. Firms that want to increase the size of their labor force must be prepared to pay higher wages in order to obtain the needed workers.

SUPPLY CURVE OF LABOR

• PROBLEM 23-17

Because of labor market rigidities (unions, legislation, etc.), Keynes drew a kinked supply curve for labor. In the accompanying diagram of this supply curve, L' stands for the full employment supply of labor. Give a verbal explication of what this graph means.

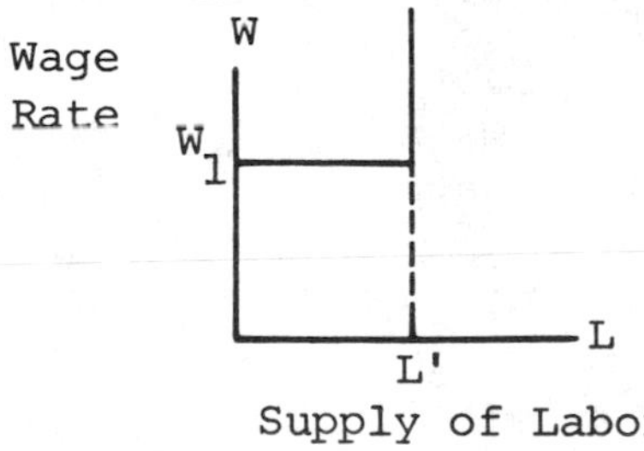

Solution: This graph shows an almost constant wage rate at all levels of employment below full employment, and above full employment there are no increases in the quantity of labor supplied, even at very high wage rates. What Keynes meant by this is that even with large amounts of unemployment, wages will not fall by much, if at all, because unions will resist any attempt to lower wages. So, because of unionization, the wage rate is fixed at all levels of employment below full employment. Above full employment, Keynes said that no increases in wages, no matter how large, can increase the supply of labor because there is no more labor to be had. As a result of this, the supply of labor will be perfectly inelastic (vertical) at full employment and above. In this diagram, Keynes was trying to present a realistic picture of the rigidities in the supply of labor caused by institutional factors.

• PROBLEM 23-18

Explain the backward bending supply curve for labor drawn on the following page.

Solution: In general, as wages rise, everything else being equal, the quantity of labor offered to the market will increase. This explains our supply curve above up to point A. But then supply starts moving backwards. As wages are raised,

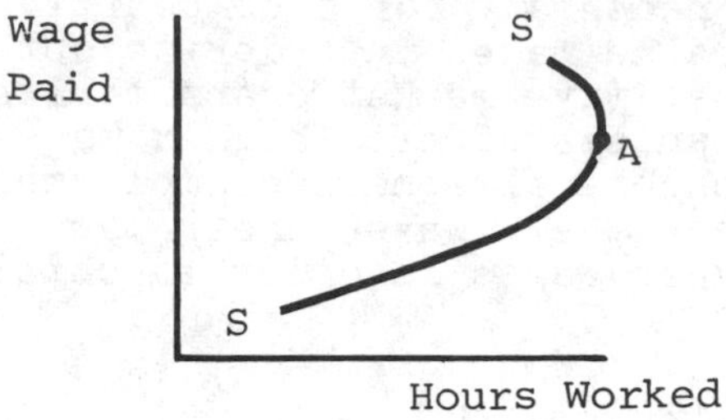

our curve tells us that workers will work less hours. The reason for this is that as wages become extremely high, workers will be making so much money that they will no longer need to work a full week. Also, as salary increases, the attractiveness of leisure time will increase for the workers and labor hours supplied will decline.

• PROBLEM 23-19

Consider the following hypothetical data on the supply of labor in a monopsonistic market

(1) Units of labor	(2) Wage Rate
1	$ 6
2	7
3	8
4	9
5	10
6	11

From the above data, determine

I. a. Total labor cost (wage bill)
b. Marginal resource (labor) cost

II. Analyze the results of your computations.

Solution: I. a) The total labor cost (wage bill) is determined by multiplying the units of labor by the wage rate.

b) The marginal resource (labor) cost is determined by getting the increments of the total labor cost. To complete the table, we have as follows:

(1) Units of labor	(2) Wage rate	(3) Total labor cost (wage bill)	(4) Marginal resource (labor cost)
			$ 6
1	$ 6	$ 6	
			8
2	7	14	
			10
3	8	24	

			12
4	9	36	
			14
5	10	50	
			16
6	11	66	

II. As we can see from the above table, one worker can be hired at a wage rate of $6. But the hire of a second worker forces the firm to pay a higher wage rate of $7. Marginal resource (labor) cost is $8 - the $7 paid the second worker plus a $1 raise for the first worker. Similarly, the marginal labor cost of the third worker is $10 - the $8 which must be paid to attract him from alternative employments plus $1 raises for the first two workers. The important point is that to the monopsonist, marginal resource (labor) cost will exceed the wage rate. This will be the case because the higher wages involved in attracting additional workers will also have to be paid to all workers currently employed at lower wage rates. If not, labor morale will surely deteriorate, and the employer will be plagued with serious problems of labor unrest because of the wage-rate differentials existing for the same job. As for cost, the payment of a uniform wage to all workers will mean that the cost of an extra worker - the marginal resource (labor) cost (MRC) - will exceed the wage rate by the amount necessary to bring the wage rate of all workers currently employed up to the new wage level.

• PROBLEM 23-20

It is said that as wages rise, there are two opposite effects on the supply of labor: the "substitution-effect" versus the "income-effect." Evaluate the meaning of this notion as to what effect wage rates will have on the number of hours worked per year.

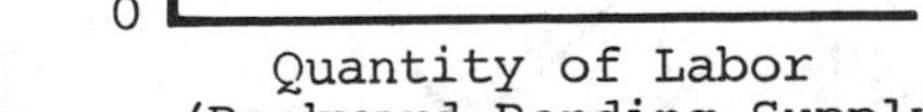

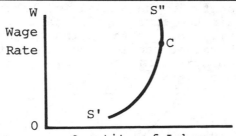

(Backward-Bending Supply Curve)

Solution: To explain this notion, the accompanying diagram makes the issues clear.
The diagram shows the supply curve of total hours that a group of people will want to work at each different wage. As we can notice, the supply curve rises at first in a northeasterly direction; then at the critical point c, it begins to bend back in a northwesterly direction which signifies the fact that higher wages may either increase or decrease the quantity of labor supplied. This phenomena may be explained as follows:

Put yourself in the shoes of a worker who has just been offered higher hourly rates and is free to choose the number of hours worked. You are torn two different ways: On the one hand, you are tempted to work some extra hours because now each hour of work is better paid. Each hour of leisure has become more expensive. But acting against this so-called "substitution-effect" is an opposing income effect. With the higher wage, you are, in effect, a richer man. Being richer, you will want to buy more clothes, more insurance, better food, more of other consumer goods. But most important for the present-problem, you will tend to buy more leisure. Now you can afford to take a Saturday off, have a week's vacation in the winter or an extra week in the summer.

These therefore, are the two opposing effects accompanying an increase in the wage rate. To determine which of the two is more powerful has no definite answer because it will depend upon the individual concerned.

• PROBLEM 23-21

From a societal perspective, what is the error in the lump-of-labor argument especially as it is used to oppose technological progress?

Solution: The lump-of-labor argument suggests that there is only so much remunerative work to be done in any particular economic society. The implication is that restrictive labor regulations (forbidding immigration, overtime, etc.) can protect employed workers without decreasing the potential output available to society. This argument is used to argue for these restrictive policies, and is sometimes used as an argument against introducing more efficient technologies into the workplace.

This argument runs into two problems. First of all, technical progress increases the productivity of labor. This is reflected in a shift in the demand for labor (the demand schedule for labor is the same as the schedule of the marginal-product of labor). So, technical innovation shifts the demand curve, which raises wages and employment. Since both productivity and employment increase, it is obvious that total output also increases, (see figure).

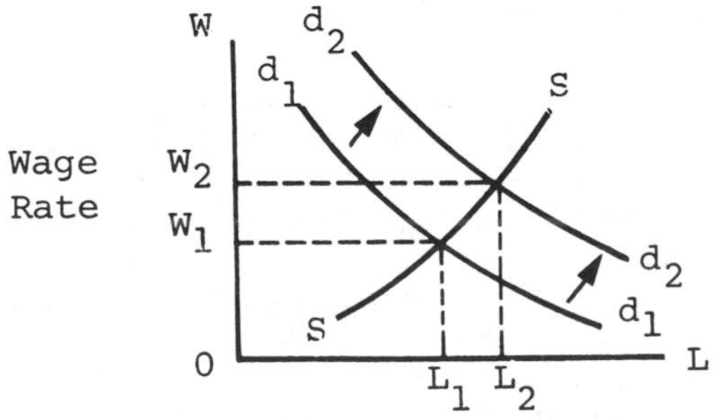

So, with technical innovation, wages and output both increase (as has been the pattern in the United States and Europe).

The lump-of-labor argument fails to take into account that, even with a fixed number of workers, technical progress increases total output in society. So the economic pie to be distributed is constantly growing.

The lump-of-labor argument holds that technical progress can create unemployment as machines replace men. While this is undoubtedly true in particular industries, it is not true for society as a whole. Government policies can stimulate employment to prevent large-scale technological unemployment. In addition to this, retraining programs can minimize the effect of new technology on workers with specific skills that have become obsolete.

THE UNION

• PROBLEM 23-22

Explain why the opportunity for unions to increase the demand for labor is limited.

Solution: The labor unions usually concentrate the efforts to increase the wage rate paid to their members by trying to affect the supply side of the market. This happens because unions generally have very limited means at their disposal to influence the demand for labor. Labor productivity which is the major ingredient in the demand for labor, depends largely on the amount and quality of capital equipment with which labor is provided. Unions generally have no influence over the way firms use the capital equipment and consequently over the number of workers they demand. The campaigns supporting tariff protection which unions often conduct are designed primarily to stop the decline in the demand for labor and not to actually increase the existing demand.

• PROBLEM 23-23

What are the four main methods by which a union can raise wages?

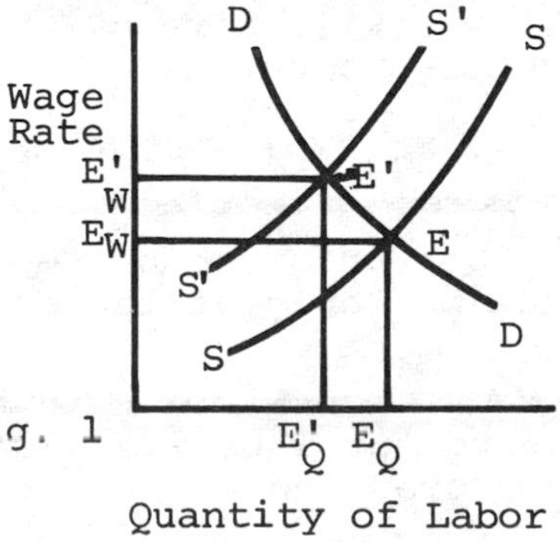

Fig. 1

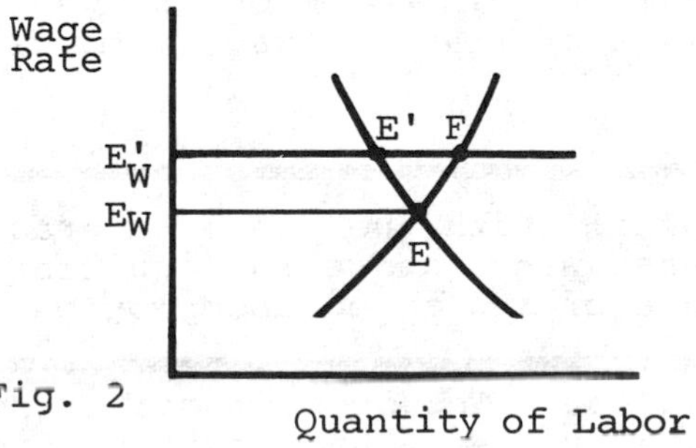

Fig. 2

Solution: 1) Unions can raise wages by restricting the supply of labor. In the supply and demand curves shown in figure

1, a shift fron SS to S'S' would cause equilibrium wage rate to rise from E_W to E_W'. Note that the total number of workers employed in this situation would fall from E_Q to E_Q'.

Some methods of restricting supply are maximum hour legislation and refusal to let nonunion members work.

2) A second method of raising wages is to raise standard wage rates. Whereas a shift in the supply curve represents a direct restriction of labor supply, minimum standard wage rates represents an indirect restriction. Here, unions get employers to agree to a minimum wage above the equilibrium wage determined by competitive forces. As shown in Figure 2, wage rates rise from E_W to E_W' while total employed falls. The difference between E' and F represents the workers who wish to be hired at the high minimum wage, but have been effectively excluded from jobs as if the union had directly limited supply (as in case 1).

3) A union may hope to increase wages by any policy that causes the derived demand curve for labor to shift upward. As in Figure 3, an increase in demand will increase both total men employed and equilibrium wage rate.

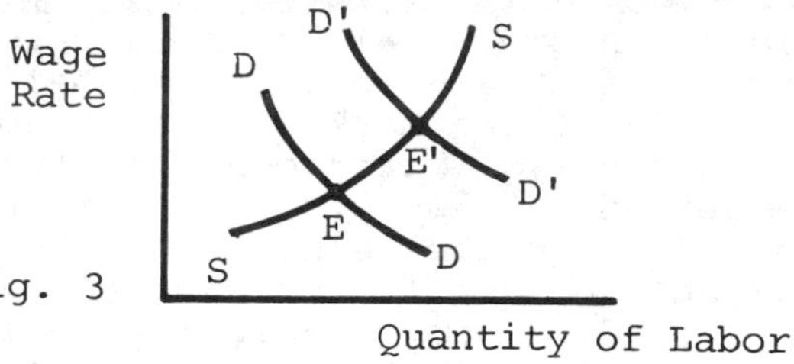

Fig. 3

Some ways to increase demand for labor would be to increase the productivity of labor or to fight for a tariff to protect the laborers' industry.

4) Finally, unions can raise wages by resisting exploitation of laborers by a monopsonist employer. When an employer is the only hirer in town, there is no reason why he should pay wages at the point where they are equal to total revenue product. Instead, he pays a low wage rate. In this case organizing a union can result in higher wages without any decline in employment. For the presence of the union will counteract the monopsonist power of the employer and force him to become a "wage-taker," who will hire by the rule that standard wage = marginal revenue product.

• PROBLEM 23-24

Explain, with the use of a graph, how labor unions can increase wages above the equilibrium level but only at the expense of increased unemployment.

Solution: Suppose the market demand curve for labor is defined by the amount of other factors employed and by the product demand conditions.
The perfectly competitive market equilibrium in the absence of union interference is reached at E (fig. 1) where L_c work-

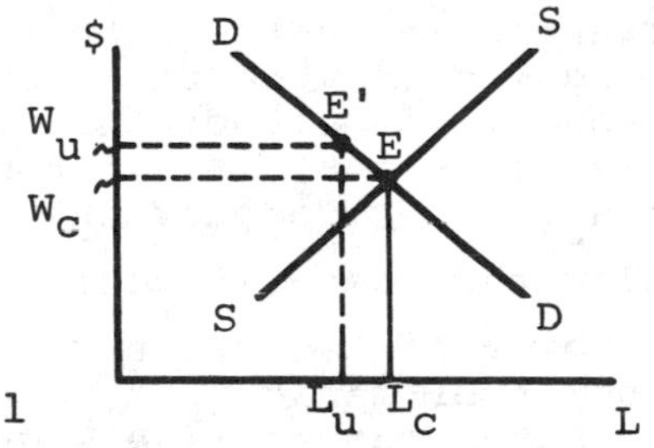

Fig. 1

ers are employed each receiving a wage of W_c. In this situation an attempt on the part of the union to raise the wage up to W_u will result in the reduction of demand for labor, in firms being driven to other industries and eventually in increased unemployment. As it often happens in reality, unions here (fig. 1) are faced with the dilemma of a trade-off between a higher wage rate (W_u) and a lower level of employment (L_u).

• PROBLEM 23-25

Describe what will happen if a strong industrial union is formed in a labor market which is not competitive but monopsonistic.

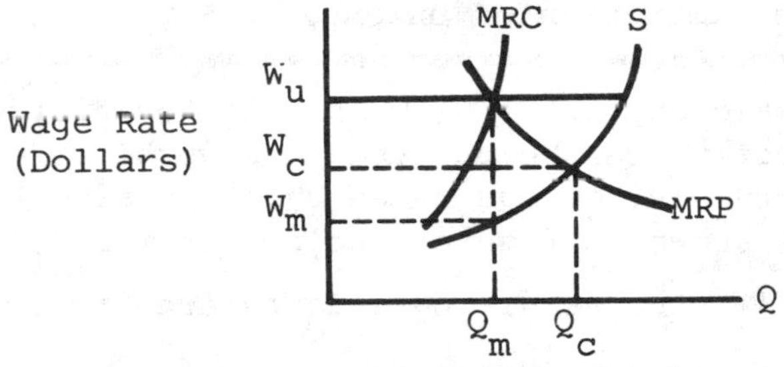

Solution: If a strong industrial union is formed in a labor market which is not competitive but monopsonistic, then we have the situation of a bilateral monopoly wherein the union is a monopolistic "seller" of labor in that it can exert an influence over wage rates. On the other hand, it faces a monopsonistic employer of labor who can also affect wages. This situation can be shown graphically in the accompanying figure.

The monopsonistic employer will seek the wage rate W_m and the union presumably will press for some above-equilibrium wage rate such as W_u. The actual outcome of this is logically indeterminate in the sense that economic theory does not explain what the resulting wage rate will be. We should expect the resulting wage to lie somewhere between W_m and W_u. Beyond that, about all we can say is that the party with the most bargaining power and the most effective bargaining strategy will be able to get his opponent to agree to a wage close to the one he seeks.

Another important point here is that the kind of labor market we are dealing with may be an important manifestation of countervailing power. If either the union or management prevailed in this market - that is, if the actual wage rate were determined at W_u, or W_m, employment would be restricted to Q_m, which is below the competitive level. But supposing the countervailing power of the union roughly offsets the original monopsony power of management, a bargained wage rate at about W_c, which is the competitive wage, is agreed upon. Once management agrees to this wage rate, its incentive to restrict employment disappears; no longer can the employer depress wage rates by restricting employment. Thus management equates the bargained wage rate W_c (=MRC) with MRP and finds it most profitable to hire Q_c workers. In short, with monopoly on both sides of the labor market, it may be possible that the resulting wage rate and level of employment will be closer to competitive levels than if monopoly existed on only one side of the market.

• PROBLEM 23-26

Demonstrate and illustrate graphically why the most desirable technique for raising wage rates is to increase the demand for labor from the union's point of view and, also explain the main limitation of unions.

Solution: The basic objective of unions is to raise wage rates. This objective can be pursued in several different ways. If unions can raise wage rates by increasing the demand for labor as shown in figure 1 below (from D_1D_1 to D_2D_2) (see figure 1), the resulting effects are higher wage

UNIONS AND THE DEMAND FOR LABOR

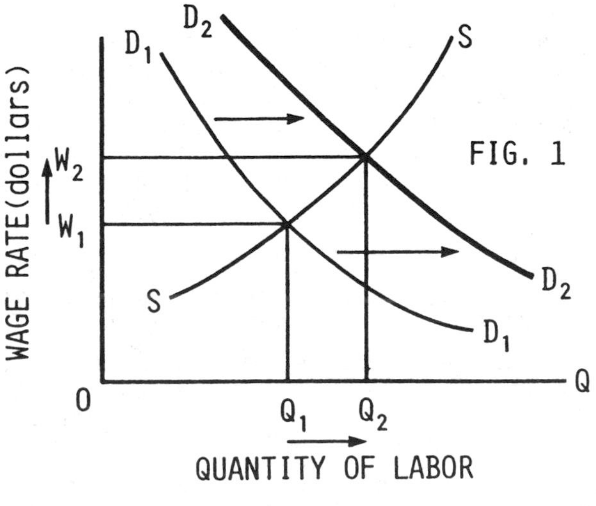

rates (from W_1 to W_2) and a large number of jobs (Q_1 to Q_2).

Comparatively, under Exclusive (Craft) Unionism and Inclusive (Industrial) Unionism, the unions' ability to raise wage rates results in fewer employment opportunities, as is shown respectively in figure 2 and figure 3. The wage rate rises from W_1 to W_2, while the level of employment falls from Q_1 to Q_2 (see figure 2); likewise in figure 3, the

EXCLUSIVE OR CRAFT UNIONISM

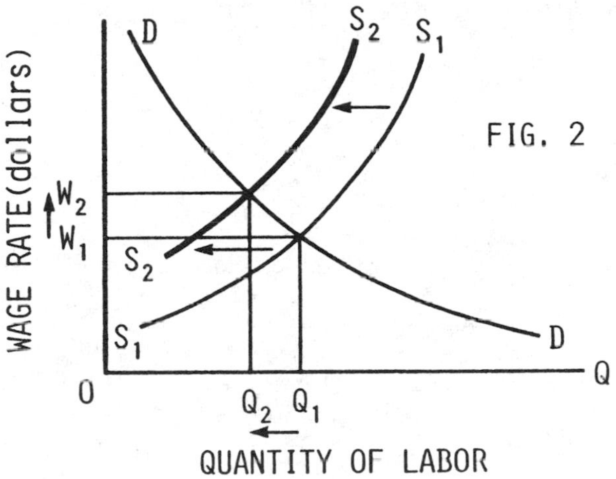

FIG. 2

wage rate rises from W_c to W_u, while the level of employment falls from Q_c to Q_u (see figure 3). Therefore, the

INCLUSIVE OR INDUSTRIAL UNIONISM

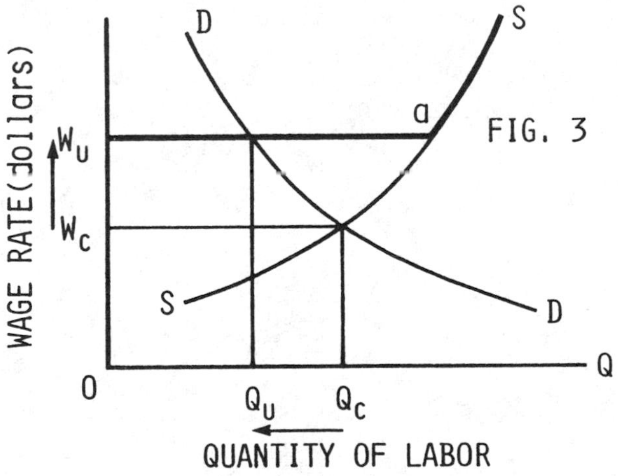

FIG. 3

above analysis indicates the ability of unions to raise wage rates by increasing the demand for labor is the most desirable of the three outcomes. However, in the real world the ability of unions to raise wage rates by increasing demand for labor is limited. The basic forces underlying the productivity of, and therfore the demand for, labor are to a large extent outside the control of labor unions. For example, unions have little or no control over the quantity and quality of the capital equipment with which labor is matched. These are the basic determinants of labor productivity in most firms. Consequently, union efforts to increase wage rates have concentrated upon the supply side of the market.

	Answer
## SHORT ANSWER QUESTIONS FOR REVIEW	To be covered when testing yourself

Choose the correct answer.

1. Of the following which reason is usually cited for the decline in productivity growth in the United States? (a) The general level of wages is low (b) Population increase has exceeded the job market's point of full capacity (c) Intensified efforts of government to prevent greater income equality (d) Values and attitudes have changed in recent years so as to impede productivity growth	d
2. What is the basic factor in wage determination by union and management? (a) the fear that Congress will pass unfavorable legislation (b) the welfare of the nation (c) the bargaining strength and skill of both parties (d) the welfare of the consumer (e) the corpus of labor legislation and judicial decisions.	c
3. The kind of labor market characterized by bilateral monopoly may be an important manifestation of what? (a) Monopolistic power (b) Monopsonistic power (c) Countervailing power (d) Craft Unionist power	c
4. Unions have been known to use all the following to raise wages except: (a) restricting of labor supply (b) raising standard wage rates (c) shifting the derived demand curve upward (d) making the derived demand curve less inelastic (e) removing exploitation by the monopsonist.	d
5. How does the presence of monopoly or oligopoly power affect the analysis of a monopsonistic labor market? (a) Through the supply curve of labor (b) Through the wage rate (c) Through the labor demand curve (d) Through the labor cost	c
6. The economic cost to the nation of a strike that raises wage rates can best be measured by: (a) the income lost by strikers minus the additional income resulting from higher wages (b) the value of the lost output which would have been produced had no strike occurred (c) the induced decrease in profits minus the higher incomes of the union members (d) the induced increase in prices minus the additional	

future income accruing to the union members (e) the induced increase in prices. b

7. Other things being equal, the monopolistically competitive demand curve is much more elastic than that of the pure monopolist because: (a) the pure monopolist has few rivals (b) the monopolistically competitive seller is faced with few number of rivals producing close-substitute goods (c) the monopolistically competitive seller sets a low price (d) the monopolistically competitive seller is faced with a large number of rivals producing close-substitute goods d

8. A logically possible relationship between wages (W) and number of hours worked (L) is: (a) lower W causes L to increase because the "substitution-effect" predominates over the "income-effect" (b) higher W causes L to increase because the "income-effect" is less than the "substitution-effect" (c) higher W causes L to decrease because the "income-effect" is not large enough to predominate over the "substitution-effect" (d) higher W causes L to increase because the "income-effect" predominates over the "substitution-effect" (e) none of the above. b

9. Industrial unions are characterized by workers such as: (a) carpenters (b) professional employees (c) steel workers (d) plumbers c

10. If through collective bargaining a union succeeds in raising its members' wages, then: (a) the supply curve of labor will shift upward as workers substitute leisure for work (b) this will necessarily cause the demand curve for labor to shift downward (c) the union must be simultaneously placing restrictions on union membership (d) the observed wage and employment levels will be indicated by the intersection of the horizontal wage line with the demand curve (e) this would raise total wages earned. d

11. Construction laborers receive better wages than do beginning bank clerks because: (a) the construction job involves the hazard of accidents (b) the construction job entails

SHORT ANSWER QUESTIONS FOR REVIEW

	Answer (To be covered when testing yourself)
little fear of layoff (c) the construction job involves regular employment (d) of labor market imperfections	a
12. Changes in real wages are calculated by comparing changes in money wages with changes in the: (a) tax rate (b) effort of the work (c) cost of living (d) rate of profits.	c
13. Which of the following unions best represents the exclusive unionism model? (a) the mine workers (b) the teamsters (c) the steelworkers (d) the carpenters.	d
14. If a person receives a higher wage than would be necessary to induce him to work, he is said to be receiving: (a) marginal product (b) surtax income (c) interest (d) profit (e) rent.	e
15. The economic term which refers to a firm which is the sole employer in a nonunion community, is: (a) countervailing power (b) monopsonist (c) monopolist (d) bilateral competitor (e) bilateral monopolist.	b
<u>Fill in the blanks.</u>	
16. If wages rise, the number of hours which labor will contribute to production will __________.	increase
17. Suppliers of labor (that is, individual households), are generally motivated by maximizing ______________.	personal satisfaction
18. We can draw a supply curve for a laborer. In general, as wages rise, everything else being equal, the quantity of labor offered to the market will _____________.	increase
19. If wages continue to _____________, there will be a point beyond which labor supplied declines.	rise
20. The individual supply curve for labor starts by rising, but slopes _____________ after a point.	backward
21. The market supply of labor shows a regular supply curve because workers will respond to a wage _____________.	increase
22. Wages vary for different workers. For example: A worker whose skills are the result of long years of training will generally receive higher	

SHORT ANSWER QUESTIONS FOR REVIEW

Answer
To be covered when testing yourself

	Answer
wages than one who is unskilled. This will be true only if his _____________ are needed by his employer.	skills
23. The _____________ argument suggests a belief that the total amount of work to be done is constant in the short run.	lump-of-labor
24. The United Mine Workers are a good illustration of _____________ unionism.	inclusive
25. When wages are increased, reductions in employment may occur when the demand for labor is _____________.	elastic
26. _____________ refers to the amount by which a firm's total resource cost increases as the result of hiring one more unit of the resource.	Marginal resource cost
27. _____________ differentials generally have little to do with imperfections of competition.	Nonequalizing wage
28. The _____________ holds that the imposition of an effective minimum wage will force firms to use labor and other resources more efficiently.	shock effect
29. The notion of _____________ is used to explain wage rate differences based upon differing nonmonetary aspects of jobs.	equalizin differenc
30. A monopsonistic employer in a _____________ labor market will pay a wage rate less than labor's marginal revenue product.	unorganized or nonunion
31. A firm which has monopoly power in the labor market pays a wage rate which is less than the _____________ of labor.	marginal-revenue-product
32. If an industrial union is formed to bargain with a _____________ employer, we can conclude that in this labor market, employment may either increase or decrease.	monopsonistic
33. A _____________ union attempts to increase wage rates by shifting the labor supply curve to the left.	craft
34. From a firm that maximizes profit, labor will certainly receive a wage not equal to its marginal-revenue-profit if the firm has a _____________ position in the labor market.	monopolistic

SHORT ANSWER QUESTIONS FOR REVIEW

Answer
To be covered when testing yourself

35. Minimum-wage legislation is less likely to have adverse effects upon employment when the affected labor market is ____________. — monopsonistic

36. Critics of ____________ legislation argue that it causes unemployment. — minimum-wage

37. As compared to a ____________ labor market, in a nonunionized monopsonistic labor market, wages and employment will both be lower. — purely competitive

Determine whether the following statements are true or false.

38. The average level of real wages received by labor both organized and unorganized has been raised substantially by unions. — False

39. In a monopsony situation, the organization of a union is hardly likely to bring about higher wages with no decline in employment. — False

40. Advocates of the minimum wage argue that its effects should be analyzed within the context of a dynamic and imperfectly competitive labor market. — True

41. The "shock effect" refers to the fact that high wages tend to make it necessary for industry to develop more efficient means of production. — True

42. The monopsonistic power of employers is complete in the sense that there is only one employer in the labor market. — True

43. The law of diminishing returns helps explain why a union may fight for a shorter working week. — True

44. Money wages are the quantity of goods and services which one can obtain with real wages or the "purchasing power" of real wages. — False

45. Since the demand for labor is a derived demand, any change in general wages will not shift the general demand curve for labor. — False

46. The supply curve for labor is always upward sloping, reflecting the fact that in the absence of unemployment hiring firms, as a group, will pay lower wage rates to obtain

	Answer (To be covered when testing yourself)
more workers.	False
47. In a monopsony situation, the wage paid may not equal the marginal-revenue-product of the worker.	True
48. In a Constant-Cost industry, the expansion of the industry through the entry of new firms will have a decreasing effect upon resource prices and, therefore, upon production costs.	False
49. Most wage differentials that are not of the "equalizing" type are probably due to imperfect competition in the labor market.	False
50. If the general level of product prices falls at a more rapid rate than does money wages, real wages will rise.	True

CHAPTER 24

PRICING OF FACTOR INPUTS: LAND AND OTHER RESOURCES

Basic Attacks and Strategies for Solving Problems in this Chapter. See pages 841 to 859 for step-by-step solutions to problems.

The demand for any factor of production is considered a derived demand. This reflects how factors of production are used. Unlike goods and services that are a direct source of utility to consumers, the value of factors derives from the fact that they are used to produce goods and services. It is the demand for goods and services that creates a demand for factors. They would not be demanded otherwise. One important implication of this idea is that in a competitive system, high prices for goods and services lead to high prices for factor inputs, not the other way around.

Rent is the payment for a factor input in excess of its transfer cost. Transfer cost is an opportunity cost. It is the price a factor could command in its next best opportunity. A factor will not be made available for use in any particular activity unless it receives a payment at least equal to what it can get from some other activity (payments must be appropriately adjusted for other compensating factors).

The term "rent" is frequently used in connection with land. This usage follows correctly from the above discussion. Simplifying somewhat, land is fixed in supply (there is a vertical supply curve at the quantity of land available). Consequently, its transfer cost can be considered zero. The same amount of land will be available regardless of its price. The demand for land will establish its market price which is considered rent because it is in excess of its transfer price of zero.

The concept of profit is a source of considerable controversy among economists. Among critics of capitalism, profits are viewed as an "unearned surplus," a payment to owners of capital that can be extracted simply because of the power that goes along with ownership of a vital resource. Even among supporters of capitalism, there is little agreement about where profits come from.

A normal profit is defined as a return equal to what an investment could earn in its next best alternative. In a sense, it can be considered a payment to the entrepreneurial function of managing and directing the other factors of production. That entrepreneurs do perform a valuable activity is not questioned.

An economic profit is a return in excess of a normal profit. The legitimacy and source of economic profits is an issue not yet fully resolved. On one side, economic profits are viewed as the result of temporary disequilibrium situations, as a reward for innovation, or as compensation for risk. In each case, profits are a necessary part of the economic system. In the first instance, they serve to guide resources into their most productive uses. In the second and third instances, they are appropriate compensation for necessary activities.

The other side of the argument sees economic profits as primarily the return extracted by someone with the good fortune of having a monopoly position.

Present value is an important concept in economic decision-making. The basis of the concept is the notion that money received in the future does not have the same value as an equivalent amount of money received today.

To see this, consider the following problem. Assuming away inflation and other risks, what would you pay for the privilege of receiving \$1.00 one year from today? Hopefully you would not pay \$1.00. A dollar invested today would yield more in a year than paying a dollar to get a dollar. The maximum amount you would pay (the worth to you of \$1.00 in one year) is the amount that if invested at the going rate of interest would yield \$1.00 in one year. Letting X stand for the amount and i for the interest rate, if you invested X today, you would receive $X(1 + i)$ in one year. Therefore $X(1 + i) = \$1.00$ in one year, or $X = \$1.00/(1 + i)$. X is known as the present value of \$1.00 in one year.

How much would you pay for \$1.00 in two years? The maximum amount you would pay would be the amount that invested today would yield \$1.00 in two years. Investing X at i would yield $X(1 + i)(1 + i) = X(1 + i)^2$ in two years. Therefore $X(1 + i)^2 = \$1.00$ in two years so $X = \$1.00/(1 + i)^2$.

Generalizing, the present value of \$1.00 received n years in the future is $\$1.00/(1 + i)^n$.

The present value formula is used to convert future streams of income into a current equivalent. The formula is especially useful in investment decisions. The cost of an investment can be compared to the present value of the returns.

Step-by-Step Solutions to Problems in this Chapter, "Pricing of Factor Inputs: Land and Other Resources"

DEMAND FOR FACTORS: A DERIVED DEMAND

• PROBLEM 24-1

How is the demand for a factor of production such as land a derived demand?

Solution: When a consumer demands a finished product such as an ear of corn, he does so because of the satisfaction he hopes to obtain from its use. But when a businessman demands a factor input such as land, he surely is not looking for direct satisfaction. Rather the businessman demands land and other factors of production because these factors permit him to produce a good which consumers are willing to pay for. The demand for land then is ultimately derived from consumers' desires and demands for final goods.

• PROBLEM 24-2

Suppose as a result of certain economic developments the price of cars and the price of steel both increase. What might be the reasons behind this upsurge in prices, assuming the automobile industry is fairly competitive and the supply of steel is constant in the short run?

Solution: The fact that demand for factor inputs is a derived demand determines to a large extent the level of prices for these inputs. Assuming the competitiveness of the automobile industry (only a theoretically valid assumption) and no major change in costs, the price of cars could only rise due to an increased demand for cars. Since steel is a major input in the production of cars, the automobile industry desiring to expand output will increase its demand for steel. Thereby the price of steel will be rising as long as the demand for cars increases. Despite the fact that the automobile industry is in reality oligopolistic and therefore subject to different conditions, the above argument shows a theoretically important fact. In a competitive world, the impression that cars are expensive because of the high price of steel or that wheat is expensive because of the high rent on land would be false. The demand for factor inputs and therefore their prices in the short run are derived from the consumer demand for final goods in the production of which these inputs are utilized.

TRANSFER EARNINGS, RENT AND COSTS

• PROBLEM 24-3

a) What is economic rent?
b) Draw the supply and demand curves for land.
c) Show the effect of an increase in demand on the price of land and the quantity of land demanded at the equilibrium point.

Solution: a) Economic rent is the price paid for the use of land and other natural resources which are completely fixed in total supply. b) Since our definition above tells us that land is fixed in total supply, the supply curve for land is perfectly inelastic (SS) and the price paid for land is an example of economic rent. Graphically, we have figure 1. The equilibrium price will therefore be R. c) To show the effects of an increase in demand on price and quantity, we once again draw a graph where DD is the original demand and D_1D_1 is the increased demand (see Figure 2).

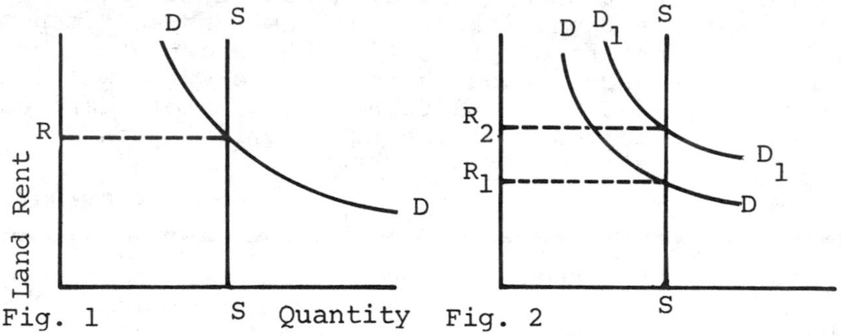

Fig. 1 Fig. 2

We see from figure 2 that land rent increases from R_1 to R_2 as demand increases. But the quantity of land demanded remains constant no matter how much demand changes. This is due to the perfect inelasticity of the supply, land being a fixed resource.

• PROBLEM 24-4

What will happen to transfer earnings and economic rent if land has only a single use?

Solution: If land has only a single use, transfer earnings are zero and the price of the land is entirely made up of economic rent. Alternatively, if the price that a piece of land can command in its present use is no higher than what it can command for its next best use, economic rent is zero and the price is entirely made up of transfer earnings.

• PROBLEM 24-5

Distinguish between the transfer earnings of a piece of land and economic rent on a piece of land.

Solution: The part of the price of a piece of land that will be paid for this land in its best alternative use represents the transfer earnings. Everything that is paid for a piece of land over and above its transfer earnings represents the economic rent on this land. It follows from the given definitions that in the absence of alternative uses all of the price of land is economic rent and transfer earnings are zero. Similarly, as soon as the value of rent falls below zero, a given piece of land will be applied to a different use.

• PROBLEM 24-6

Consider the graphs in figures 1, 2 and 3 on the demand and supply of land.

Which of these three graphs represent the following extreme and normal cases and explain why it is so:

a) the extreme case in which the whole price is transfer earnings;
b) the normal case in which the price consists of some transfer earnings and some economic rent;
c) the extreme case in which the whole price is economic rent.

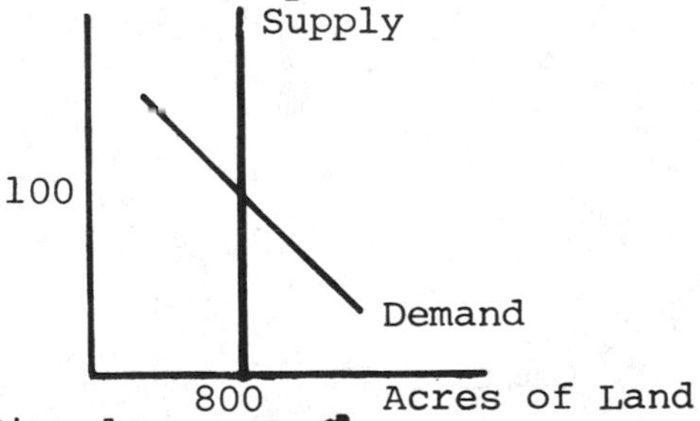

Fig. 1

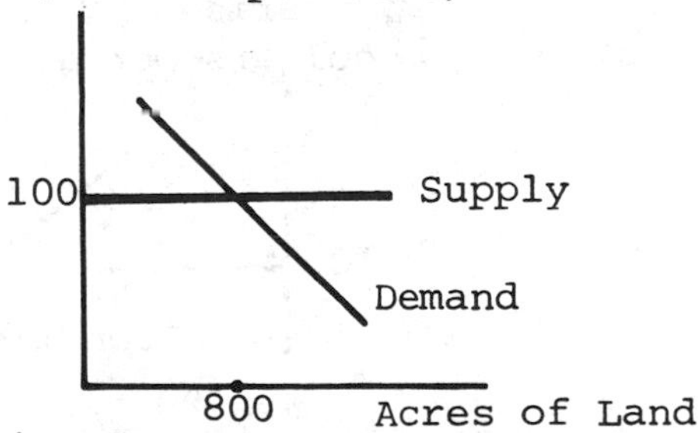

Fig. 2

Solution: (a) Figure 2 illustrates the extreme case where the whole price is transfer earnings. This is the case because the supply curve here is a horizontal straight line, which indicates that virtually unlimited amounts of land are available at that price. If the price were any lower than $100 per acre, these 800 acres would transfer to another use. Thus the entire price for the 800 acres ($80,000) is transfer earnings. Figure 4 is the completed graph for this case.

Fig. 3

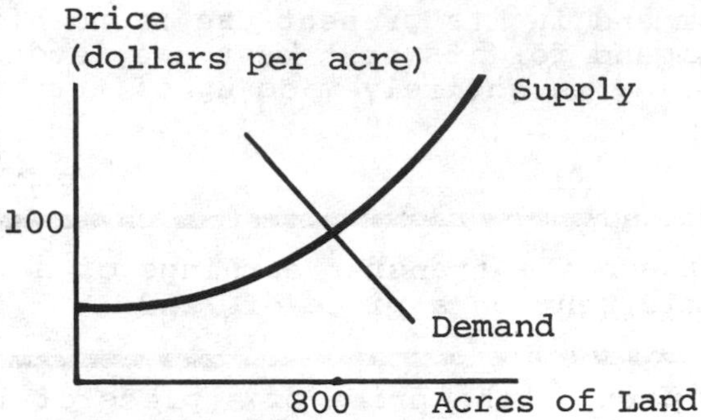

Fig. 4

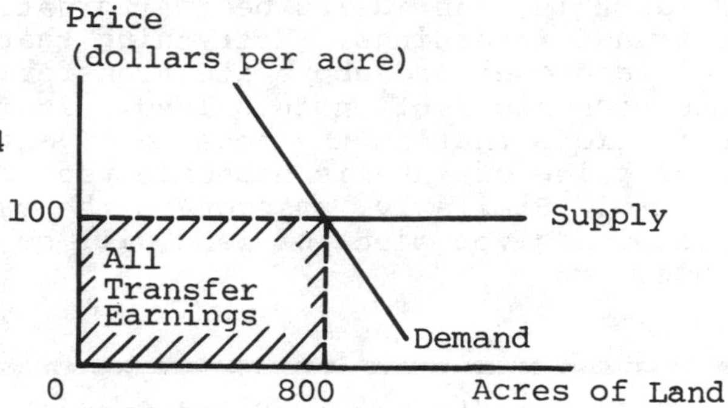

All Transfer Earnings

Fig. 5

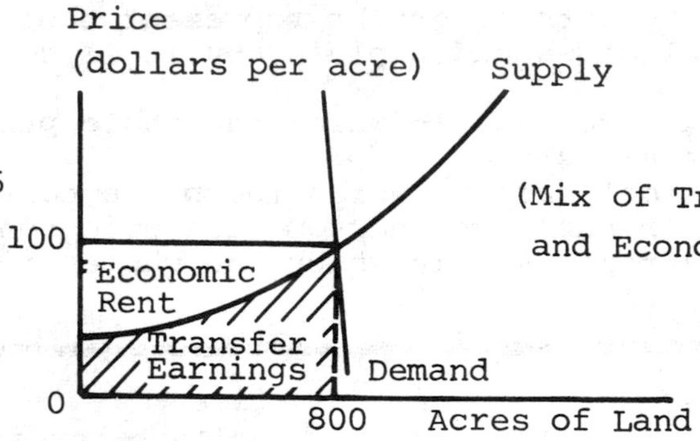

(Mix of Transfer Earnings and Economic Rent)

Fig. 6

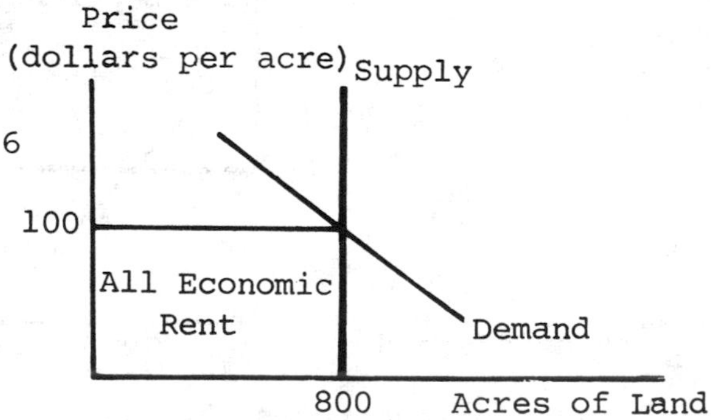

(All Economic Rent)

(b) Figure 3 illustrates a normal situation where the supply of land for a particular use is neither fixed nor extremely responsive to changes in price. The price for the 800 acres is $80,000, but this time, it is partially made up of transfer earnings with the remainder economic rent. (see Figure 5).

(c) Figure 1 illustrates the extreme case in which the whole price is economic rent. Here the supply of land is fixed and has only one use. The demand for that use and thus for the land will determine the price. Transfer earnings are zero, and thus the entire price for the 800 acres ($80,000) is economic rent. (see Figure 6).

• PROBLEM 24-7

How is the use of land a cost, not counting the rent one has to pay to use the land?

Solution: The above question differentiates the concepts of both explicit and implicit costs. The rental one has to pay for the use of the land takes the form of an explicit cost in the sense that it involves cash outlays, that is monetary payments which a firm makes to the "outsiders" who supply the said land resource. On the other hand, the use of the land also constitutes a cost, in this sense an implicit cost, that is the money payments which the land resource could have earned in their best alternative employments. For example, suppose Tim uses the land that he rented for raising wheat. Therefore, Tim sacrifices the income which he could have earned by planting corn on it.

• PROBLEM 24-8

The production of a unit of good Y requires the employment of 3 workers and 7 units of capital. The going wage is $4. The rent on a unit of capital is $1. What should be the marginal physical product of capital in order for the production to be carried out at the least cost and what is this cost if the marginal physical product of labor is $2?

Solution: Using the cost-minimization rule which requires a firm to equalize marginal product per dollar spent on each of the factor inputs we get:

$$\frac{MPPL}{\$4} = \frac{MPPK}{\$1} \quad \text{at the minimum cost.}$$

We are given MPPL = 2. Therefore

$$MPPK = \frac{2 \cdot \$1}{\$4} = \frac{1}{2}$$

To answer the second part of the question we have to define first the production function of Y

$$Y = f(K,L).$$

It is given that the firm employs 3 workers and pays them $4 each, and utilizes 7 units of capital costing $1 each. Therefore, the total cost of production or the total cost of all inputs is:

$$TC = 3 \cdot \$4 + 7 \cdot \$1 = \$19.$$

The production of a unit of Y costs a firm $19.

FACTOR PRICING AND EFFICIENCY

• PROBLEM 24-9

How does the price system regulate the distribution of total output in pure capitalism?

Solution: In pure capitalism, the price system regulates the distribution of output in two ways. First of all, what a consumer can buy is determined by his income. This income, in turn, depends upon the resources which the consumer can supply, and the prices of these resources in the resource market. The endowments of resources (natural abilities, inheritances, etc.) and the prices of these resources, determine the income levels of consumers.

Within the limits of his income, a consumer will buy products on the basis of his tastes and relative product prices. If good X has a high price, and there are low-priced substitutes for good X available, the consumer might decide to purchase one of the substitutes. So, product prices play an important role in determining the expenditure patterns of consumers.

Distribution of output, then, is regulated by the ability and willingness of consumers to pay for specific products. Their ability to pay depends on resource distributions and resource prices. Their willingness to pay depends on tastes and relative prices. In both aspects, the price system plays a role in distribution.

• PROBLEM 24-10

The Council of Economic Advisers (to the President of the United States) has argued that keeping down the price of cattle could keep down the price of meat to the consumer. Explain how the application of demand analysis to market pricing and allocation rejects the argument.

Solution: Holding down the wholesale price of cattle to the meat processors increases the spread between purchase price and selling price for the processors. The price to consumers would rise anyway because of the increased demand for meat. The wealth that would have been available to cattle growers is instead given to the cattle processors.

• PROBLEM 24-11

"New business firms can underprice older firms, because the

newer firms can buy the latest equipment and are not burdened with the older, less economical equipment which older firms must retire before they can economically adopt the new. This is why continued technological progress contributes to maintaining a competitive economic system." Explain the errors in both sentences.

Solution: Old firms are not burdened by old equipment. They too can switch to new goods. That they don't simply means they can compete by using old equipment, whose value is recapitalized to whatever level will enable it to continue to be used - unless its value is zero, in which case it will certainly be retired. The first sentence is typical of a very common error - an error that ignores the market's valuation process of existing goods.

As for the second sentence, continued technological progress can often create barriers to entry, violating one of the axioms for perfect competition to exist. Consider the following contemporary example: Swiss watchmakers are switching over to the production of electronic watches. But since the Japanese are technologically superior in this area, the Swiss effort is being nipped in the bud.

• **PROBLEM 24-12**

How does the price mechanism act to conserve those products and resources which are most scarce?

Solution: If a resource becomes very scarce, the price of that resource will rise. This price rise will induce buyers to switch to other, less expensive, less scarce, resources. The high price transfers consumer purchases to substitute resources. By substituting other goods, society conserves those goods that are most scarce.

The scarcity reflected in the high price of oil has induced industrialized countries to search for alternative energy sources. By substituting other fuels for oil, these countries can cut down on their consumption of oil, and thus make the existing supply of oil last longer. The effect of the price mechanism is to induce consumers to search for substitutes, an act which will tend to conserve the scarce resource.

PROFITS AND THE ROLE OF TAKING RISKS

• **PROBLEM 24-13**

What are the various theories of profits? Describe each.

Solution: The various theories of profit can be described

as follows:

a) Frictional Theory of Profit.

First, there exists a "normal rate of profit," which is simply the return on capital necessary to induce savers to invest some of their funds rather than consume their entire income or "to put their savings in a mattress." In a static economy, all businesses would be equal to the desired level of business investment.

Secondly, shocks occasionally occur in the economy, producing disequilibrium conditions that give rise to abnormal profits for some firms. For example, the emergence of a new product such as the automobile might lead to a marked increase in the demand for steel, and this might cause profits of steel firms to rise above the normal level for a time. Alternatively, a rise in the use of plastics might drive the steel firms' profits down. In the long run, barring impassable barriers to entry and exit, resources would flow into or out of the steel industry, driving rates of return back to normal levels. But during interim periods, profits might be above or below normal because of these frictional factors.

b) Monopoly Theory of Profit.

This is an extension of the frictional theory. It asserts that some firms, because of such factors as economies of scale, possession of unique natural resources, patent protection, or the like, are able to build up monopoly positions and keep their profits above normal for indefinitely long periods.

c) Innovation Theory of Profit.

Under this theory, as a compensation for successful innovation, above normal profits exist.

d) Compensatory Theory of Profit.

This is otherwise known as the functional theory which holds that profits arise as a payment for entrepreneurial services; i.e., profits are the compensation for promoting, managing, and assuming the risks of a business enterprise.

• PROBLEM 24-14

What is the difference between economic profits and normal profits? What effects do these different types of profits have on the number of firms in an industry?

Solution: A normal profit is the return to the entrepreneur for the functions he performs in organizing and combining the other resources in the production of a commodity. The entrepreneurial resource must be paid for like any other resource. A normal profit is the minimum reward required to induce entrepreneurs to utilize their skills.

An economic profit is any revenue over and above costs (including normal profit). This additional profit usually accrues to the entrepreneur. Since this profit exceeds the amount needed to keep the entrepreneur in the firm (normal profit), it is not considered a cost, but a pure or economic profit.

In any industry, firms must be realizing normal profits in the long run to stay in business.

When an industry is realizing normal profits, the number of firms in the industry will remain stable. Since firms are making normal profits, the entrepreneurs will be paid enough for their resource that they will not leave the industry. If more firms enter the industry in which only normal profits are being made resources allocated to it would become abundant, increasing the industry's output, and lowering the market price of that output. Hence the rate of profit would decline. Some entrepreneurs would pull their firms out of the industry to find an industry where profits are higher. Thus the influx of firms into an industry in which only normal profits are being made would be quickly offset by an outflow of firms. So, the overall number of firms remains steady. If firms are not realizing normal profits, the entrepreneurs will switch to industries where a normal profit can be realized. Industries that cannot realize normal profits will be declining or contracting.

If the firms in an industry are making economic profits, new firms will enter the industry. They will enter because entrepreneurs will be attracted by the prospect of earning a higher than normal return on their resources. As more firms enter the industry, the quantity of resources in this industry increases and economic profits go down until the firms in the industry are making only normal profits.

• PROBLEM 24-15

In theoretical terms, what are the three possible attitudes toward risk? Describe each.

Solution: In theory, there are three possible attitudes toward risk:

1) A desire for risk.
2) An aversion to risk.
3) An indifference to risk.

Description:

1) A risk seeker is a person who, when confronted with a choice between two investments with different risks but with the same expected monetary returns, will select the riskier investment.

2) Faced with the same choice, i.e., between more and less risky investments, the risk averter will prefer the less risky investment.

3) The person who is indifferent to risk is also indifferent to which investment he selects.

DECISIONS

• PROBLEM 24-16

A particular firm considers a project to invest \$100,000 in new equipment that will last about 5 years before it has to be replaced. At the time of replacement the scrap value of the equipment is expected to be zero. The demand for goods produced with the new equipment is expected to be about 2000 items per year. The present price of one item is \$30, but is expected to increase by 6% each year, due to inflation. The present cost (or expense to the producer) is \$20, but is expected to rise by 5% each year. When the firm is confronted with a rate of interest of 8%, if it borrows the funds to invest in the project at present, should it invest? Also, evaluate this project when the rate of interest for borrowing is 6% and 10%, respectively. Take year-end prices.

Solution: This firm is considering investing in a new project, but must borrow funds to do so. Therefore it considers the profitability of investment. The sales revenues must recover not only the initial principal investment of \$100,000, but also the interest costs of 8% of \$100,000 = \$8,000 per year. The rate of interest with which the firm is confronted is its cost-of-capital, or its "opportunity-cost," because it could also "invest" the \$100,000 in bonds, an alternative investment project, assuming that this would earn at least 8% per year on the invested capital.

What may the firm expect for the future 5 years? It expects a constant demand per year of 2000 items. The present price is \$30 per item; but the price rises with 6% per year, so the sales revenues also increase at 6% per year. In fact the firm expects the revenue flow shown in Table 1.

Table 1

Year	1	2	3	4	5
Sales Revenue	63,600	67,416	71,461	75,749	80,294

Remember that sales revenue = price × quantity sold = price × 2,000; and the price at year t is 1.06 × price of preceding year t - 1. We take year-end prices, thus, for example, the sales revenues in year 1 are 1.06 × 30 × 2000 = 63,600; in year 2 they are 1.06 × (1.06 × 30 × 2000) = $(1.06)^2 \times 30 \times 2000$ = 67,416; and so on. The expenses to produce the items = cost per item × quantity sold = cost per item × 2,000. The cost per item of year t is 1.05 × cost of preceding year t-1. Thus, for example, the expenses in year 1 are 1.05 × 20 × 2,000 = 42,000; in year two are $(1.05)^2 \times 20 \times 2{,}000 = 44{,}100$, and so on.

The expected expenses are shown in Table 2.

Table 2

Year	1	2	3	4	5
Expenses	42,000	44,100	46,305	48,620	51,051

The firm is interested in the profit in each year: profit = sales revenues - expenses. Thus over the years the current profits are expected to be, 63,600 - 42,000 = 21,600 in year 1; 67,416 - 44,100 = 23,316 in year 2; and so on.

The expected profits are shown in Table 3.

Table 3

Year	1	2	3	4	5
"Profits"	21,600	23,316	25,156	27,129	29,243

But what is the present value of these future profits? The present value of the future profits has to be calculated and compared with the current initial investment to determine whether the project is worthwhile for the firm to undertake. For example, if 100 dollars is invested now, and these 100 dollars are borrowed at a rate of interest of 8%, the project in which they are invested must produce a return on investment of at least 8% in order to make it worthwhile to undertake. In other words, at the end of the first year, in order for the project to be profitable, more than 108 dollars must be accumulated, so that the principal investment sum of 100 dollars, plus the cost-of-capital of 0.08 × 100= 8 dollars can be repayed. Thus 108 dollars a year from now equals 100 dollars at present.

However, the firm in question is confronted with profits spread out over 5 years. Thus it must calculate the present value of each of these annual profits, add the present values together, and compare this total with the initial $100,000 investment. If the sum total of the present values is greater than the initial investment, the project is worthwhile; if it is less, the project should be discarded.

From the above example, it can be seen that

$$\underset{\text{future value}}{\underset{\uparrow}{108}} = \underset{(1 + \text{interest rate})}{\underset{\uparrow}{1.08}} \times \underset{\text{present value}}{\underset{\uparrow}{100}}$$

Thus,
$$\underset{\text{present value}}{\underset{\uparrow}{100}} = \frac{108}{1.08} \begin{array}{l} \leftarrow \text{future value} \\ \leftarrow 1 + \text{interest rate} \end{array}$$

For the second year,

$$116.64 = (1.08) \times (1.08) \times 100, \quad \text{or}$$

$$\underset{\substack{\uparrow \\ \text{present value}}}{100} = \frac{116.64 \leftarrow \text{future value}}{(1.08)^2 \leftarrow \text{number of years}}$$

$$\qquad\qquad \uparrow \; 1 + \text{interest rate.}$$

Now the present value of the future profits can be calculated. The present value of the profit in year 1 is

$$\frac{21{,}600}{1.08} = 20{,}000;$$

and of the profit in year 2:

$$\frac{23{,}316}{(1.08)^2} = 19{,}990; \quad \text{and so on.}$$

The present values of the future profits for all five years are given in Table 4.

Table 4

Year	1	2	3	4	5	sum
Present value of profits	20,000	19,990	19,970	19,941	19,902	99,803

The final sum is $99,803, less than the $100,000 initial investment. Thus, given the condition, and with an 8% interest rate, the project would not be profitable.

Given the formula for calculating the present value of a future sum

$$\text{present value} = \frac{\text{future value}}{(1 + r)^n},$$

where r = interest rate, and n = number of years, it can be seen that if the interest rate is increased, the present value of a given future value must decrease. Thus if the cost of borrowing is increased above the 8%, say, to 10%, the investment project should also be discarded.

However, for a lower cost-of-capital, the opposite is the case. Calculating again the present value of the future profits, but now for a 6% interest rate, and summing them, produces Table 5.

Table 5

Year	1	2	3	4	5	sum
Present value of profits	20,377	20,751	21,121	21,489	21,852	105,590

The sum of these present values is $105,590, more than the $100,000 initial investment. Thus at a 6% rate of interest it is worthwhile to undertake the project.

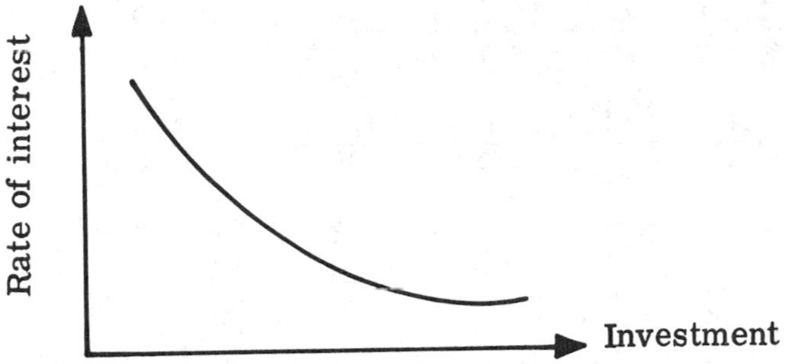

FIG. 1 The Keynesian Investment Schedule

This pattern of behavior is common to all investing firms: the lower the interest rate, the more projects become profitable and worthwhile to undertake. In the aggregate, a downward sloping investment schedule may be expected then, showing that at lower interest rates, more investments take place. See Figure 1.

• PROBLEM 24-17

Suppose that a businessman is contemplating the purchase of a $35,000 machine, and that he estimates that the machine will provide a return (net of operating costs) of $10,000 per year for 4 years. Assume that the going rate of interest is

a) 8 percent,
b) 2 percent.

Should he buy it?

Solution: First of all, it is necessary that we calculate the discounted present value of the $40,000 income stream ($10,000 per year × 4 years) which is given by the formula:

$$PV = \frac{X}{(1 + i)^T}$$

Where: PV is the present value,
X is the future return,
i is the rate of interest.

Therefore, at a) 8 percent, we arrive at the following solution:

$$PV = \frac{\$10,000}{1.08} + \frac{\$10,000}{(1.08)^2} + \frac{\$10,000}{(1.08)^3} + \frac{\$10,000}{(1.08)^4}$$

$$= \frac{\$10,000}{1.08} + \frac{\$10,000}{1.1664} + \frac{\$10,000}{1.2597} + \frac{\$10,000}{1.3605}$$

$$= \$9,259.26 + \$8,573.39 + \$7,938.40 + \$7,350.24$$

$= \$33,121.29.$

for b) 2 percent, the present value would be:

$$PV = \frac{\$10,000}{1.02} + \frac{\$10,000}{(1.02)^2} + \frac{\$10,000}{(1.02)^3} + \frac{\$10,000}{(1.02)^4}$$

$$= \frac{\$10,000}{1.02} + \frac{\$10,000}{1.0404} + \frac{\$10,000}{1.0612} + \frac{\$10,000}{1.0824}$$

$$= \$9,803.92 + \$9,611.69 + \$9,423.29 + \$9,238.73$$

$$= \$38,077.63.$$

When the interest rate was 8 percent, the cost of the machine ($35,000) was greater than the present value of the return from that machine, $33,121.29 and, therefore, we would not expect a businessman to buy it. In the case where the interest rate was only 2 percent, the present value of the return from the machine, $38,077.63, exceeded the cost of the machine, $35,000, and, therefore, we would expect a businessman to buy it.

The general rule to follow is that if the computed present value of the return exceeds the cost of the capital equipment or machinery, then, it is worthwhile to invest in such machinery or equipment; it is not worthwhile to invest if the computed present value of the return is less than the cost of the capital goods.

LIQUIDITY OF AN ASSET

• PROBLEM 24-18

What is "liquidity," and why might one consider the liquidity of an asset?

Solution: "Liquidity" refers to the nearness of an asset to currency or cash with which you can freely purchase another asset. A dollar bill is highly liquid. A house is not a very liquid asset. Obtaining cash for a house may involve much work and a long period of time. In deciding on what assets to hold, a household or business may want to hold some assets according to their expected need for cash, or a liquid asset. This is especially important if large outlays of cash are anticipated, and cash will be necessary on short notice.

• PROBLEM 24-19

Common stock or bonds are considered more liquid assets than an automobile. What would be the reason for this?

Solution: In the case of stocks and bonds, highly efficient and fast markets exist. By simply making a phone call, not only can one trade or sell these assets for cash, but an accurate value or price may be determined. In converting an automobile to cash, not only will much time and effort be necessary, but an accurate value of the automobile may be difficult to determine.

Answer
To be covered when testing yourself

SHORT ANSWER QUESTIONS FOR REVIEW

Choose the correct answer.

1. Suppose $20 left at the market interest rate yielded $1.40 at the end of the year. What was the mentioned rate of interest? (a) 5% (b) 7% (c) 17% (d) .7%. — b

2. A state government is considering investing funds in a certain building project. Which of the following values for the net productivity of the project will make the undertaking worthwhile if the market interest rate is 12%? (a) 9% (b) 11.5% (c) 12.041% (d) all of the above. — c

3. According to the law of diminishing marginal returns, as society applies more and more capital to its natural resources the yield on its investment projects will tend to (a) remain constant (b) increase over time (c) decrease over time (d) decrease unless technological innovations are introduced. — d

4. When faced with risk, bankers will tend to (a) reduce the interest rate on their loans (b) increase the interest rate on their loans (c) alter the market interest rate (d) increase the total money supply. — b

5. An increase in society's propensity to save is likely to result in (a) a higher market interest rate (b) a lower market interest rate (c) no changes in the market interest rate (d) inflation. — b

6. The long run equilibrium of the capital market (assuming no technological improvements) occurs at a point where: (a) interest rate is 0 (b) MC = MR (c) net saving is 0 (d) net investment is equal to 0. — c

7. Zero-interest rate (a) has often been recorded in the American economy (b) is equivalent to the complete lack of savings (c) is advantageous in that it makes economy work more efficiently (d) none of the above. — d

8. The higher the rate of inflation (a) the bigger is the disparity between the money and the real interest rates (b) the higher is the real interest rate (c) the smaller

Answer
To be covered when testing yourself

is the nominal interest rate (d) all of the above. — a

9. The yearly price rise was recorded to be 12%. What was the real return to the owner of a governmental bond with an annual yield of 15%? (a) 15% (b) 3% (c) 12% (d) Impossible to determine. — b

10. A savings bond with yield of 8% was purchased for $1,000. How much money will the customer get in returns in the following year if the inflation rate is expected to be 10%? (a) $1100 (b) $1020 (c) $1080 (d) $1180. — c

11. The money interest rate is equal to the real interest rate when (a) there is no inflation (b) the economy is at full employment (c) investments are free of risk (d) net saving is equal to zero.

12. Which of the following comes closest to the definition of profits? (a) revenue (b) returns to capital (c) yield on investment (d) the difference between total revenues and total costs. — d

13. In the world of perfect competition firms will earn (a) positive profits (b) zero profits (c) negative profits (d) different profits depending on their productivity. — b

Fill in the blanks.

14. Rent, unlike other kinds of economic payments, is made for the use of resources __________ in supply. — fixed

15. A __________ demand for money depends on the expected future changes in the market interest rate. — speculative

16. The higher the market interest rate the __________ is the amount of money people will want to hold for speculative purposes. — lower

17. The desire to hold a certain amount of cash available for transactions on a daily basis describes best the __________ demand for money. — transactions

18. A precautionary demand for money increases with an __________ in the level of national income. — increase

SHORT ANSWER QUESTIONS FOR REVIEW

Answer

To be covered when testing yourself

19. As the risk of default on any given loan increases, the interest rate a lender will charge on it ________.	rises
20. The major difference between what most businessmen perceive as profits and the concept of economic profits is the fact that the latter accounts for both ________ and ________ costs while the former accounts only for ________ costs.	explicit, implicit, explicit
21. When the firm's profits fall short of ________ in the long run its resources will be applied to alternative uses.	normal profits
22. The existence of positive profits under perfectly competitive conditions will cause immediate ________ into the industry.	entry
23. The monopolist is in a better position to earn positive economic profits than a competitor because of his ability to restrict ________ and, to a certain extent, to control ________.	output, prices
24. Rent payments for the use of land may be considered a ________ since their presence has no effect whatsoever on the supply of land.	surplus
27. Government can encourage the ________ in the economy by combining generous increases in the money supply with tight fiscal policies.	formation of capital
28. The demand for ________ depends on the consumer demand for those final goods whose production process utilizes them regularly as ________.	factors of production, factor inputs

<u>Determine whether the following statements are true or false.</u>

29. The demand for factors of production is correlated with the amount of satisfaction that can be obtained from their use.	False
30. An increased demand for housing is likely to result in a higher demand and higher prices for building cement since cement is an input in the construction of houses.	True
31. The supply curve for land as a factor of pro-	

SHORT ANSWER QUESTIONS FOR REVIEW

	Answer To be covered when testing yourself
duction is close to being perfectly inelastic.	True
32. Fluctuations in the price of wheat depend on the fluctuations in the rent on the farmland.	False
33. For farmers who work on their own land rent is not a part of the production costs.	False
34. The supply curve of land for an individual producer, unlike the supply facing the whole community, is infinitely elastic and is considered to be a part of the production costs.	True
35. A single tax on the unearned income acquired from the ownership of land proposed by Henry George would shift both the market demand and the equilibrium rent received by the landowners down.	False
36. The price of a factor of production depends on the existence and the availability of close substitutes that can perform the same function.	True
37. Extensive farming, characteristic of America is an example of how factor pricing contributes to the efficiency of the economy in general.	True
38. The term "pure rent" describes the situation when the earnings of a factor of production remain untaxed.	False
39. Capital goods differ from the primary factors of production in that they are produced by the economy as outputs and are used as inputs for further production.	True
40. The interest rate is the yield per year of the primary factors of production.	False
41. The higher the annual yield on money invested in a production project, the more productive the capital used in this project is considered to be.	True
42. Any investment is foregone present consumption.	True

CHAPTER 25

THEORY OF COMPARATIVE ADVANTAGE

Basic Attacks and Strategies for Solving Problems in this Chapter. See pages 860 to 879 for step-by-step solutions to problems.

An open economy is one that has economic relationships with other nations of the world. An open economy can import and export goods and services as well as make or receive loans or buy and sell financial or real capital across national boundaries.

In the simple multiplier model of the economy, the expression for aggregate demand is expanded to include both exports (X) and imports (M):

$$Y_d = C + In + G + (X - M),$$

where the term in parentheses is net exports ($Xn = X - M$). Note that exports add to Y_d. Exports represent foreign demand for the goods and services of domestic firms. Imports reduce Y_d. The demand for imports represents a diversion of domestic purchasing power to the products of foreign firms.

An important component of international economics is an analysis of the gains from trade. Economists believe that voluntary trade benefits all parties, and use a theory first developed over 150 years ago to establish the case, the theory of comparative advantage.

A country possesses an **absolute advantage** in the production of a good or service if it is the most efficient producer of the item. For example, since herring only swim in cold waters and bananas can only grow in warm, moist climates, Norway has an absolute advantage in fishing for herring and Guatemala has an absolute advantage in growing bananas. Norway is better off by devoting resources to fishing and using the herring caught to trade for Guatemalan bananas than trying to grow bananas itself. Likewise, Guatemala is better off growing bananas to trade for herring rather than devoting resources to fishing in colder waters.

The law of **comparative advantage** explains why trade is beneficial between two nations even if one of the nations holds an absolute advantage in the production of all goods and services. In other words, absolute advantage is irrelevant to explaining the pattern of specialization and trade.

Assume a world of two nations of about equal size, called Japan and the United States. They are each capable of producing only two goods, telephones and VCRs. Resources are fully employed in both nations. The table shows total productivity in the production of both goods.

	Telephones per Unit of Resources	VCRs per Unit of Resources
Japan	2	6
U.S.	1	1

Note that Japan has an absolute advantage in the production of both goods. Note also the opportunity costs of production in both countries.

	Cost of One Telephone	Cost of One VCR
Japan	3 VCRs	⅓ telephone
U.S.	1 VCR	1 telephone

Opportunity costs are computed as follows. In Japan, if one unit of resources is shifted from VCR to telephone production, 6 VCRs must be given up to get 2 telephones. Therefore, 2 T = 6 VCR, or 1 T = 3 VCR. The opportunity cost of good *X* in terms of good *Y* is

$$\frac{Y \text{ per unit of resources}}{X \text{ per unit of resources}}.$$

A country has a comparative advantage in the production of a good if it has the lowest opportunity cost. Here Japan has the comparative advantage in VCRs because they cost only ⅓ telephone as compared to 1 telephone in the United States. The United States, despite being less efficient than Japan in telephone production, has a comparative advantage because telephones cost only 1 VCR, as opposed to 3 in Japan. As a general rule, regardless of how inefficient a producer a country is, it is bound to have a comparative advantage in something.

Why and what will the Japanese trade with the United States? If the Japanese try to produce telephones, it will cost them 3 VCRs for every unit of resources shifted to telephone production. It may be cheaper to buy telephones in the United States where they cost only 1 VCR. Similarly, domestically produced VCRs cost 1 telephone in the United States, but the United States may be able to buy them cheaper in Japan, where they only cost ⅓ VCR. Even though Japan has an absolute advantage in the production of telephones, it makes sense for them to buy from the United States. Even though the United States lacks an absolute advantage in telephone production, it can be a successful competitor in the world market.

The magnitude of the gains from trade will depend on the world prices that arise for VCRs and telephones. The United States may charge Japan more than 1 VCR per telephone. As long as the price is less than 3 VCRs, the Japanese are better off trading for telephones than producing them themselves. The same could be said about the United States and VCRs.

The price of telephones and VCRs in the world market (the exchange ratio between telephones and VCRs) cannot be determined precisely. We know it must be between 1 T = 1 VCR and 1 T = 3 VCR for both countries to be able to benefit from trade.

Regardless of the countless complications that could be added to this model, the lesson of the law of comparative advantage continues to hold.

The key policy implication of the law of comparative advantage is that the gains to a nation from specializing and trading exceed the losses. Anything that artificially interferes with the development of trading relationships (e.g., tariffs, quotas, etc.) is harmful to both nations in the long run.

The implications of this theory can be shown graphically using production possibilities curves. Assume the tables show some of the points on the production possibilities curves for Japan and the United States.

United States

VCRs	30	27	24	21	18	15	12	9	6	3	0
Phones	0	3	6	9	12	15	18	21	24	27	30

Japan

VCRs	100	90	80	70	60	50	40	30	20	10	0
Phones	0	3.3	6.6	10	13.3	16.6	20	23.3	26.6	30	33.3

Graphs of each country's production possibilities curve are shown following:

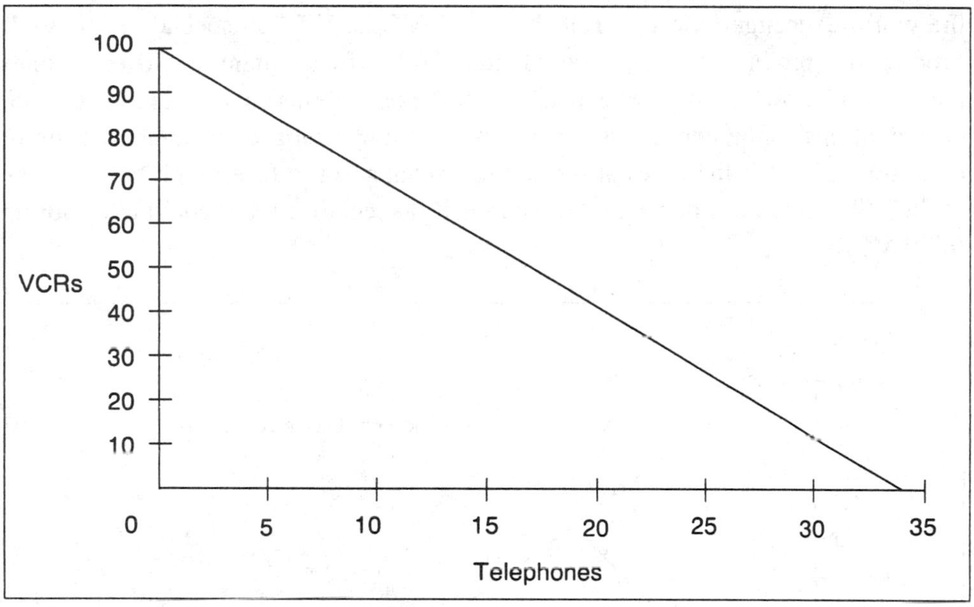

Japan's Production Possibilities Curve

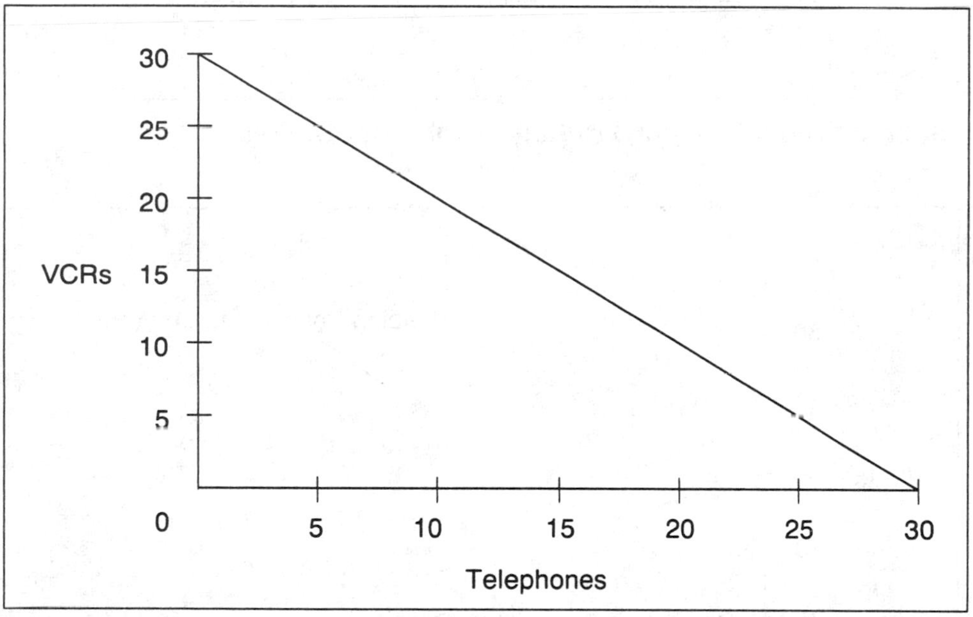

United States' Production Possibilities Curve

If both countries try to be self-sufficient and neither trades, the production possibilities curves are also their consumption possibilities curves, where the consumption possibilities curve shows all combinations of the two goods that can be consumed by the country.

Assume now that trade opens up between Japan and the United States, and the world exchange ratio is 1 Telephone = 2 VCRs. If Japan specialized in VCR production (producing 100), it could trade VCRs for as many as 50 telephones (see graph below). This gives Japan's trading possibilities curve, which shows all combinations of the two goods it could have if it specialized in the production of one and traded for the other at the world exchange ratio (see graph below). The United States could produce 30 telephones if it specialized, but could trade for up to 60 VCRs.

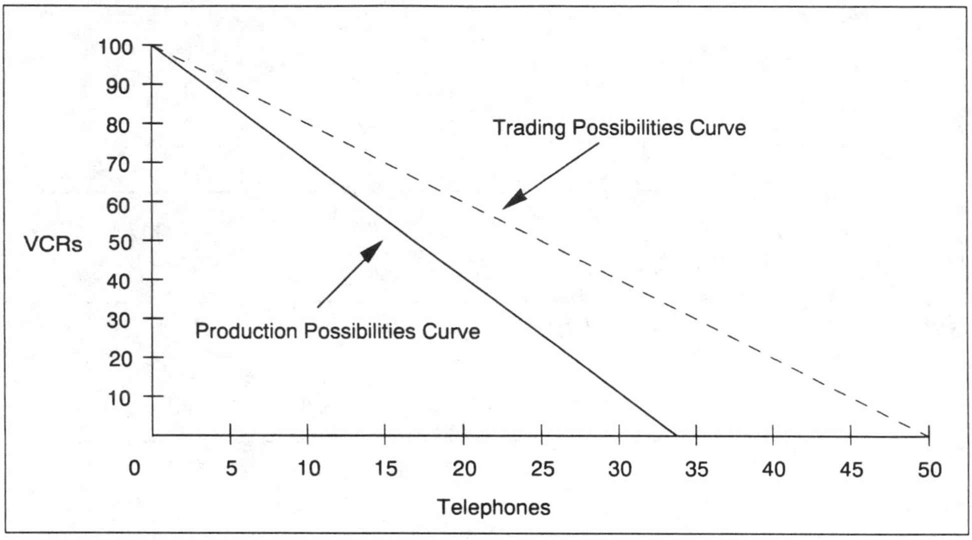

Japan's Production and Trading Possibilities Curves

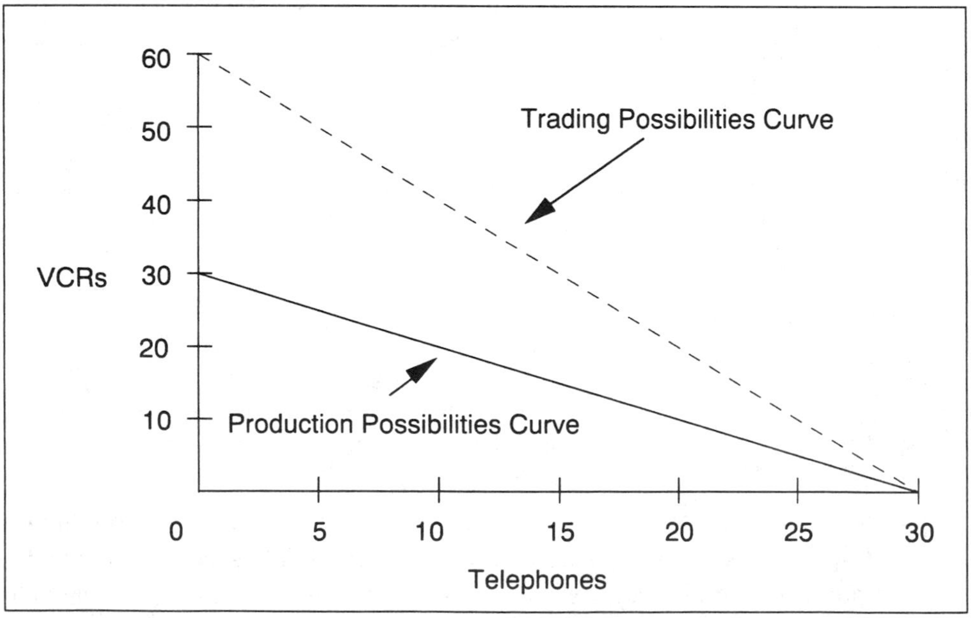

United States' Production and Trading Possibilities Curves

With specialization and trade, the trading possibilities becomes the new consumption possibilities curve.

Note the increased quantities of both goods that can be consumed, implying that each nation's overall standard of living will rise as the result of specialization and trade.

While some individuals may suffer from trade (telephone producers in Japan and VCR producers in the United States, the nation as a whole benefits (and the afflicted producers will be able to find jobs in the expanding sectors of their economies).

Step-by-Step Solutions to Problems in this Chapter, "Theory of Comparative Advantage"

BASIC CONCEPTS OF INTERNATIONAL TRADE

• PROBLEM 25-1

What gives rise to the difference in the aggregate demand for a nontrading or closed economy from a trading or open economy?

Solution: The components of the aggregate demand for a nontrading or closed economy are consumption, investment, and government purchases given by the formula C + In + G. But for a trading or open economy, another item is added which is the net exports (Xn) which is equal to (X - M), where X is total exports and M is total imports so that the aggregate demand is given by the formula C + In + G + (X - M) or C + In + G + Xn.

From the above, we can say that a closed economy is characterized by the absence of the trade components which in turn gives rise to exports and imports as in the case for a trading or open economy.

• PROBLEM 25-2

What determines the volume of a nation's exports and imports?

Solution: The volume of a nation's exports and imports will depend primarily and directly upon the levels of incomes in foreign nations. Take the case of the United States' exports with respect to its major trading partners. That is, if such major trading partners as Japan, West Germany and Britain are prosperous in terms of economic growth, they will purchase more from the United States with the result that the American exports will be relatively large. But if these economies are depressed, their purchases from the United States will be relatively small. However, it is important to note here that the American exports are independent of the level of domestic national income. On the other hand, it is reasonable to assume that any nation's imports will vary directly with domestic income in the same general fashion as domestic consumption. To illustrate, if the domestic net national product (NNP) rises, it would be expected that households will buy not only more Fords and GM's, but also more Toyotas and Volvos.

• PROBLEM 25-3

What is the rationale of subtracting expenditures for imports in measuring aggregate demand as compared to adding exports as a new component of aggregate demand?

Solution: The rationale of subtracting expenditures for imports in measuring aggregate demand for domestic goods is that imports of a country represent spending by its citizens on foreign goods--which will induce production and create jobs and incomes abroad rather than domestically. Differently stated, imports--like the leakages of savings and taxes--represent a use of income other than spending on domestic goods and services.

On the other hand, exports give rise to domestic production, income, and employment despite the fact that goods and services produced in response to such spending flow abroad. This is because such foreign spending on domestic goods increases production and creates jobs and incomes for the home country.

• PROBLEM 25-4

Explain David Ricardo's Theory of Comparative Advantage. Give an example to illustrate the point of the theory.

Solution: David Ricardo's Theory of Comparative Advantage states that the exchange (especially in international trade) is most efficient if each trader offers the particular good of which he has advantage in production relative to the good he receives in exchange. Alternatively stated, foreign trade is mutually beneficial, even when one nation is absolutely more efficient in the production of every good, as long as there are differences in the relative costs of producing the various goods in the two potential trading nations. Thus, the theory of comparative advantage is closely tied to the concept of opportunity costs.

As an example, assume that lawyer Smith can earn $35 an hour as a corporate lawyer. Assume further that he can type twice as fast as his secretary to whom he pays $6 an hour. But Mr. Smith can earn $35 an hour as a lawyer. Therefore, even if he has an absolute advantage in secretarial services, it is not worth his while to save $6 an hour in typing at the expense of $35 an hour as a lawyer. He would be better off using his training as a corporate lawyer, even if he is the most efficient typist in the office.

• PROBLEM 25-5

What relevance do 'terms of trade' have to the principle of comparative advantage? What limits are set to the terms of trade?

Solution: The 'terms of trade' simply express the exchange ratios of trade. So, if ten tons of food exchange for one ton of steel, on the international market, the terms of trade are defined for food-steel exchanges.

The principle of comparative advantage only identifies what goods a country should specialize in producing. It does not specify at what exchange ratio the countries will trade with each other.

The limits to the terms of trade are the internal ratios of substitution in the trading nations. If the international terms of trade are ten tons of steel for one ton of food, while the country can produce one ton of food for every five tons of steel forgone, the country will not specialize in steel and trade for food on the world market. So, the limits to the terms of trade are internal relative costs of the trading nations. A nation will specialize in a good if it can substitute production of it for another at less cost than it can when substituting by trading.

The terms of trade, then, determine which countries benefit most from trade. The limits to the terms of trade are the exchange ratios which are enough so that countries will specialize and trade for the other goods that they need.

• PROBLEM 25-6

What is absolute advantage?

Solution: Absolute advantage exists when one nation can produce a good more cheaply and efficiently than another. Thus Brazil because of its climate, natural resources, and labor force has an absolute advantage over the United States in producing coffee while the United States has an absolute advantage over Brazil in producing computers.

• PROBLEM 25-7

Does the principle of comparative advantage apply only to international trade?

Solution: The principle of comparative advantage applies wherever productive units have different relative efficiencies. These productive units can be countries, states, divisions of a firm, or even people. If an executive is an excellent business manager and an excellent typist, he will concentrate on business management, leaving the typing to a secretary. Even if he is a better typist than the secretary, it pays for him to concentrate in his most valuable area. In this example, the executive has an absolute and comparative advantage in business management, while the secretary has a comparative advantage in typing. This application of the principle of comparative advantage shows how the principle can be useful even in interpersonal 'trade.'

The reason why comparative advantage is usually dealt with in international trade theory is that comparative advantage provides the theoretical basis for the benefits of free trade. While people do not argue about the executive leaving typing to a secretary, some do argue vehemently against free trade. Comparative advantage, while almost absurdly simple in the case of the executive, has to be explained at length in international trade theory to defend free trade against protectionist arguments.

So, although international trade is the principal user of the theory, it does not diminish the relevance of comparative advantage to any area where productive units (whether Japan and the United States, or the executive and the secretary) have different relative efficiencies.

• PROBLEM 25-8

What is the 'trading possibilities frontier'?

Solution: The trading possibilities frontier illustrates the potential output of a nation after the gains from trade are taken into account. Since specialization and trade result in a more efficient allocation of resources, potential combined output of two trading countries is increased. Comparative advantage, and the consequent specialization, is the major reason for the benefits of trade as measured by the trading possibilities frontier.

COMPARATIVE ADVANTAGE

• PROBLEM 25-9

The cost of producing one ton of steel in the United States is one ton less of coffee. The cost of producing one ton of steel in Brazil is foregoing two tons of coffee. Given that Brazil specializes in coffee production and the United State specializes in steel production, how will the price of steel (in terms of coffee) change in the United States? How will the price of steel change in Brazil? Generalize this result for any two nations trading on the basis of comparative advantage.

Solution: As the United States engages in trade and specializes in steel production, the demand for United States steel will rise. This is because in addition to the previous domestic demand for steel, there is now also the Brazilian demand for United States steel. As a result of this rise in demand, the price of steel in the United States will rise. It will now take more than one ton of coffee forgone to produce one ton of steel. The rise in the demand for steel has another implication. As the demand for steel is now international (domestic and Brazilian), the market is now united and so there is a single price for steel. Brazil will pay the same price for steel as the Unites States will. Yet the price of steel in Brazil will fall. This is because while the demand for steel has remained constant (taking Brazil by itself), the supply has increased (the principle of comparative advantage holds that the production possibilities expand with trade; that is, the supplies of goods increase). Because the supply increases, the price falls. The new, international price of steel, then, is higher than the old United States price of one ton of coffee forgone, and lower than the old Brazilian price of steel of two tons of coffee forgone. This implies that the new, international price of coffee (in terms of steel) is lower for the United States, and higher for Brazil.

This result contains two important points. The first is that international trade and specialization bring about changes in supply and demand which tend to equalize product prices in the trading countries. The second point deals with the directions in which price changes will take place. A country which specializes in production of a good for the world market can expect the price of that good to rise, because of an increase in demand. A country which imports a product can expect the price of the import to be lower than the price of the older, comparable, domestic product, because of an increase in supply. Comparative advantage, then, not only tends to equalize worldwide prices, but also tends to push product prices in specific directions.

• PROBLEM 25-10

In a frictionless world economy, resources would be perfectly mobile. As it is now, immigration, emigration and capital outflow restrictions severely limit resource mobility. How do the changes in supply and demand, and the consequent price changes, brought about by application of comparative advantage, tend to compensate for the immobility of resources.

Solution: Comparative advantage brings about price changes in trading nations. In a country with abundant capital, the price of capital will be low. So, this country will have a comparative advantage in capital-intensive industries. The expansion of these industries, because of trade, however, will lead to an increased demand for capital. The result of this process is to increase the formerly low price of capital. Similarly, in a country with an abundance of labor, trade will tend to increase the price of labor. Because of the specialization in labor-intensive industries, there will be a drop in demand for capital, leading to a lower price of capital. The overall trend is for resource prices throughout the world to equalize. The original low price of capital in the capital-abundant country will rise, and the original high price of capital in the capital-scarce (labor-abundant) society will tend to fall as the demand of industries shifts to labor. This result, rough equality of resource prices, is close to the result that would be gained from resource mobility. The implication is that trade roughly matches up the worldwide demand for resources, with the world-wide supply. This rough equality of supply and demand points to the partial success of trade in compensating for immobility of resources. Though there would probably be greater efficiency with resource mobility, trade can approximate the results of this mobility.

• PROBLEM 25-11

In an industrial country, capital is abundant. In a rural country, land is abundant. If these two countries trade, each specializing in the good it has a comparative advantage in, what will happen to the prices of the resources (capital and land) in the two countries?

Solution: Before trade, resource prices in these two countries were very different. With capital abundant, the industrial society had a relatively low price of capital, while land had a relatively high price. In the rural country, land would have had a relatively low price while capital would have had a high price. With trade, the imbalances between the resource prices of the two countries would tend to disappear. This is because the industrial society would specialize in capital-intensive goods (because of abundant, low-priced capital) which, in turn would bid up the price of capital. Since land would not be in much demand in capital-intensive industries, the price of land would decline, even though land is scarce. With trade, the rural country would specialize in land-intensive goods (agricultural goods), thus driving up the price of land. Since capital is not in demand, its price would fall relative to the price of land. The trend in both countries is for the high-priced resource to fall in price while the abundant resource would rise in price because of specialization. International trade thus shifts demand from the scarce to the abundant resource in both economies. Because of this, resource prices tend to equalize in the two countries.

The principle of comparative advantage, which encourages a country to specialize in areas where they have abundant, low-priced resources, tends also to equalize the prices of resources in the trading countries.

• PROBLEM 25-12

Even if the United States is at a comparative disadvantage

in agriculture, why might it still be more efficient for the United States to specialize in agricultural production?

Solution: It might be efficient for the United States to specialize in agricultural production, even when at a comparative disadvantage, if there are decreasing costs (increasing returns to scale). If there are increasing returns, absolute efficiency becomes more important than relative efficiency. The advantages of 'mass' agricultural production would override the comparative disadvantage. Trade, by expanding the markets of agricultural producers, would stimulate greater efficiency, though not by the usual method of comparative advantages.

• PROBLEM 25-13

An argument frequently used against free trade is that it throws Americans (or Germans or Italians) out of work and lowers the wages of those who remain employed. It is argued that American labor cannot compete against cheap, exploited, foreign labor. Evaluate this argument using the principle of comparative advantage.

Solution: The principle of comparative advantage holds that a country will benefit from free trade if it specializes in the industries in which it has the highest relative efficiency. The price of cheap, foreign labor has little to do with it. The American industries which will decline because of foreign trade are those industries which are least efficient, compared to other American industries. Protectionists will still argue that American workers are thrown out of jobs because of foreign trade, because some industries do decline. A free trade advocate will argue that the decline of certain industries will free resources (labor and capital) so that the more efficient industries will be able to expand. The workers laid off because of trade will be able to find jobs in other industries, because of trade. As for the wage level, American workers will have a higher real wage because of trade. This higher real wage occurs because some imported goods (like cars, stereos, etc.) will be cheaper than the old domestically produced goods were. In addition to this, there will also be a larger quantity of goods available to Americans, without any increase in work. Measured in terms of how much a day's labor will buy, it is clear that Americans' standard of living rises because of free trade. (The proof of this is simple. The trade possibilities frontier shows that a country can consume a larger quantity of goods without increasing work simply by producing according to the principle of comparative advantage.)

The principle of comparative advantage, then, demonstrates the fallacies of these arguments. Trade will not cause permanent unemployment (though there may be some temporary unemployment) and trade will increase, and not decrease, a worker's standard of living.

• PROBLEM 25-14

If a rich country and a poor country trade with each other, without any restrictions, and the rich country gains $50 million, while the poor country only gains $5 million, is the rich country exploiting the poor country?

Solution: In a situation like this, the rich country is gaining more from trade, but it cannot be said that it is exploiting the poor country. The distribution of the gains derived from trade is regulated by the terms of trade, the exchange ratio. The terms, in turn, are regulated by the supply and demand conditions of the world market. So, the real determinants of which countries gain most from trade are the supply and demand conditions. As long as there are not any government-imposed restrictions such as tariffs or quotas (there are not any in this case), then it is impossible for any country to be 'exploiting' another. It is market conditions that determine the returns from trade for each country.

An example of this would be the gains from trade received by an oil-exporting nation, and a nation selling trinkets. Though the poor nation might sell a tremendous number of trinkets to the oil-rich nation, it is really not surprising that the richer country, the country exporting oil, gains more from the trade. It is not really a case of the rich country exploiting the poor country; it is simply that there is a huge demand, relative to supply, for the rich country's export.

• PROBLEM 25-15

If the United States could produce five automobiles instead of one ton of food (that is, the opportunity cost of producing one ton of food is five automobiles) and maximum food production is five million tons, then the maximum automobile production is twenty-five million. Given that on the international market ten automobiles can be exchanged for one ton of food, compare the production possibilities frontier with the trading possibilities frontier.

Solution: The accompanying diagram illustrates the gains to the United States from trade. Without trade, the United States could produce, at most, twenty-five million automobiles. By specializing in food production and engaging in trade, the United States can double its potential car consumption. Depending on domestic food requirements, the United States can increase its car consumption without reducing food consumption simply by engaging in trade. The Trading Possibilities Frontier represents the new schedule of combinations of consumption due to trade. As is obvious from the diagram, this new schedule substantially increases the consumption possibilities open to society.

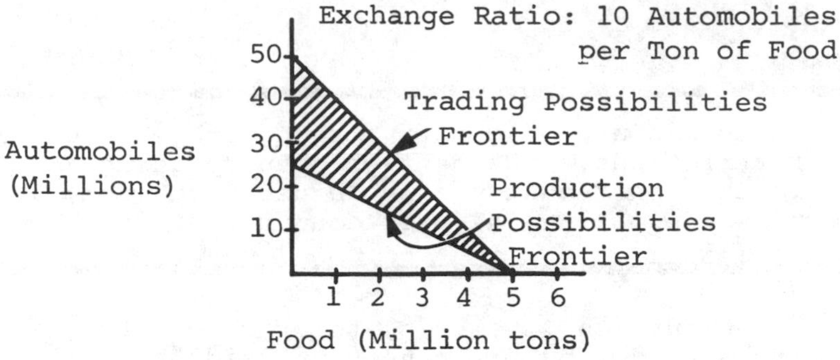

The reason why the trading possibilities frontier is different from the production possibilities frontier is that the international exchange ratio is different from the internal exchange ratio (five automobiles to one ton of food). The international ratio is different because other countries have different comparative efficiencies (internal ratios). Thus, even though the United States might be able to produce automobiles cheaper than any other country, if other countries can produce automobiles more efficiently with respect to food (say if Japan can produce twenty times as many automobiles as tons of food), then it will pay for the United States to specialize in food production. The trading possibilities frontier, then, demonstrates the concrete advantages of specialization according to the principle of comparative advantage.

• PROBLEM 25-16

The theory of comparative advantage explains how nations benefit from trade. Not everyone in these nations benefits equally, however. Explain. Relate this to some of the groups clamoring for protectionist measures.

Solution: The benefits from trade are not shared equally because trade causes some industries to expand and some to decline. Both the employers and employees of the declining industries can suffer losses during the initial period of trade. The owners of the industries lose their investment (unless they can sell their equipment to the competing, foreign firms). The employees either lose their jobs outright, or else do not get the wage increases other workers get.

However, with proper government policies, the shifting of workers and capital from one industry to another can be relatively painless. But these workers and owners still do not share the immediate gains that workers and owners in the expanding industries receive.

The relative loss of workers and owners in the declining industries is probably the major factor in protectionist (anti-trade) sentiment. Unions, such as the maritime workers and steelworkers, that have seen their members laid off because of foreign competition, sometimes bitterly attack free trade measures. Likewise, employers in these industries sometimes try to protect their industries from foreign competition. Once it is realized that some people benefit less from free trade than others, it becomes fairly obvious why some groups oppose free trade. While comparative advantage shows that free trade will result in higher per capita wealth (because the production possibilities frontier expands to the trading possibilities frontier) and lower prices for the imported goods (compared to the domestic competition), these advantages do not outweigh the disadvantages in the minds of many people involved with the declining industries.

• PROBLEM 25-17

If American agriculture is the most efficient in the world, could the United States still import food?

Solution: Even if American agriculture is the most efficient, it still might be more efficient for the economy as a whole to import food. This is because trade is not based on absolute efficiency, but relative efficiency. So, if the United States can produce computers and machinery with even greater efficiency than it can produce food, and other nations can produce food more efficiently than computers and machinery, then the other nations would have a comparative advantage in agriculture. As a result, the United States could import food for the greatest efficiency in using resources. Remember that the principle of comparative advantage stresses relative efficiencies within an economy, and not absolute efficiency.

• PROBLEM 25-18

There is a country, Freedonia, with the production possibilities frontier as shown in Figure 1. Since Freedonia needs two million tons of food to feed its one million people, it produces at point A on the production possibilities frontier (two million tons of food, one million garments.) If the international exchange ratio is 2 garments for every ton of food, draw Freedonia's trading possibilities frontier and determine where on the frontier the economy will produce (given the stated need for food).

Fig. 1

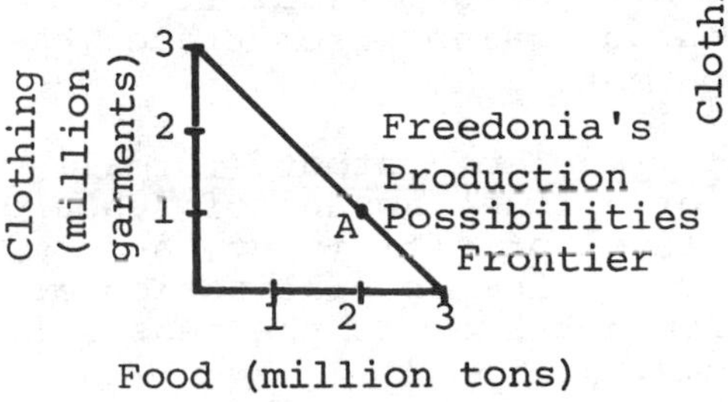

Fig. 2

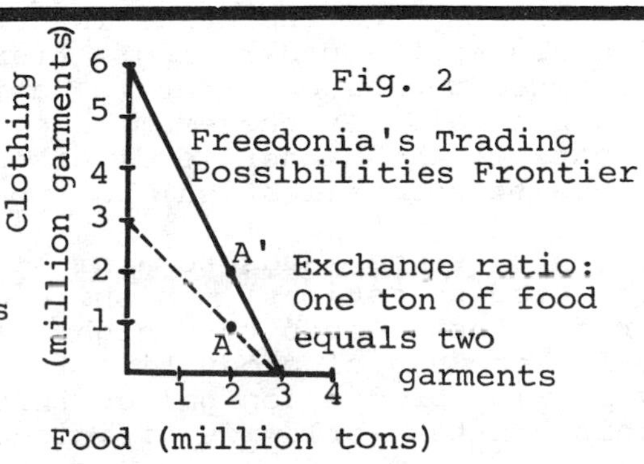

Solution: The trading possibilities frontier for Freedonia is easily determined. Freedonia can produce three million tons of food and have no clothing, or it can produce this three million tons of food and trade it for six million garments. The diagram shows these two extremes, and the range of possibilities lying between them, (see Figure 2.)

The economy will produce at point A[1]. At this point, the economy will produce three million tons of food, but one million tons will be traded in exchange for two million garments. As a result of trade, the inhabitants of Freedonia will have twice as many garments while still consuming as much food as before (two million tons).

Actually, there are also other choices for Freedonia. If the nation decides to consume more food it can do so and also have more garments by a correct choice. For example, the point (2¼, 1½) lies on the new exchange ratio line. Thus the effect of free trade is the same as a technological innovation that shifts the production possibilities frontier outwards.

• PROBLEM 25-19

Show simply how international trade (through comparative advantage) leads to a more efficient use of the productive forces of the world.

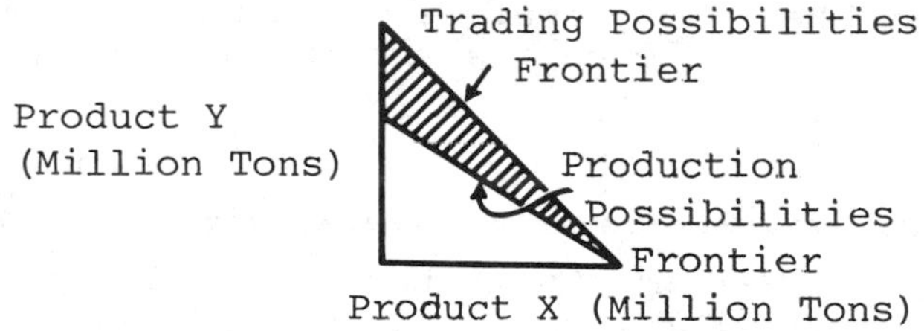

Solution: To show how international trade leads to a more efficient use of productive forces, all that is needed is a definition of efficiency and trading possibilities frontiers. Efficiency is simply the degree of output squeezed out of scarce resources. The higher the level of output produced from fixed resources, the more efficient the productive process is. Trading possibilities frontiers show graphically the increases in output possible from trade. The assumption underlying a trading possibilities frontier is fixed resources, that is, a fixed amount of land, labor and capital. In the example of a trading possibilities frontier, the higher level of output gained from trade (because of specialization) is apparent.

So, trade leads to a higher level of output (for all of the trading nations) in spite of a fixed amount of resources. Trade, then, leads to a higher level of efficiency, a more efficient use of productive forces. The specialization of worldwide production gained through trade, is the reason for this greater worldwide efficiency.

• PROBLEM 25-21

Given that Sri Lanka can produce two tons of tea at a cost of one ton of steel production, while the United States can produce one ton of steel at a cost of one ton of tea production, which country will produce steel? Which will produce tea? Draw the production possibilities frontier for each country (given that the United States can produce at most twenty tons of tea, while Sri Lanka can produce at most only ten).

Solution: According to the principle of comparative advantage, each country will produce the good it can produce at relatively lower cost. Sri Lanka can produce tea at a relatively lower cost than the U.S., so it will produce tea. The United States can produce steel at a relatively lower cost than Sri Lanka (the U.S. has to give up only one ton of tea to produce a ton of steel while Sri Lanka would have to forego two tons). The United States, then, will produce steel. Each country will produce the good it has the comparative advantage at producing (the good that has the smallest opportunity cost) in relation to the other country.

The production possibilities frontier of the United States can be deduced from the fact that twenty tons of tea can be produced, with all resources devoted to tea production. This implies that only twenty tons of steel can be produced at most since the opportunity cost of each ton of steel is one ton of tea production. The production possibilities frontier in Figure 1 shows that the United States can produce any combination of tea and steel along (or below) the line connecting the two extreme positions.

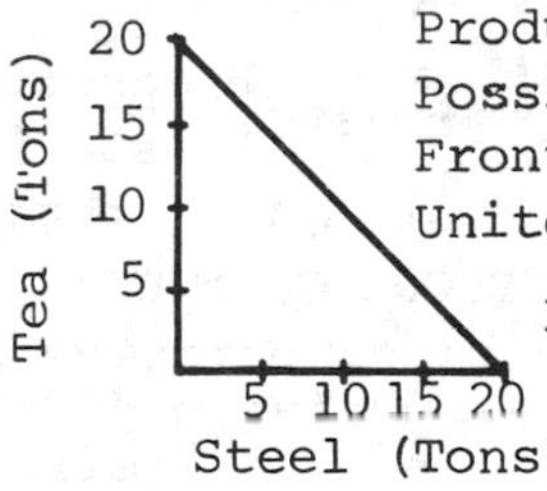

Production Possibilities Frontier of The United States

Fig. 1

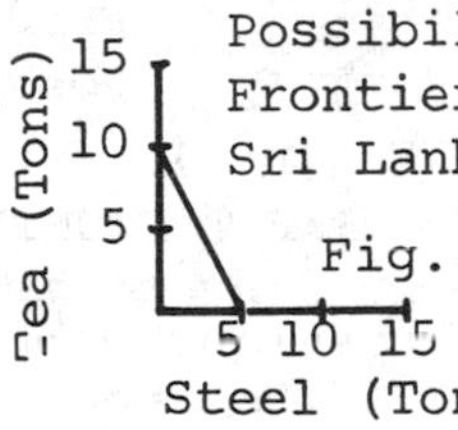

Production Possibilities Frontier of Sri Lanka

Fig. 2

Sri Lanka can produce ten tons of tea at most. Since each 2 tons of tea cost it one ton of steel production, its total potential steel production is 10 tons of tea ÷ (2 tons of tea/ton of steel) = five tons of steel. The production possibilities frontier for Sri Lanka, as shown in Figure 2 is the line connecting these two points.

• PROBLEM 25-20

What is the effect of increasing costs (decreasing returns to scale) on specialization?

Solution: Increasing costs effect specialization because

specialization is based on relative costs between industries (comparative advantages and disadvantages). As the scale of production is increased, these relative costs will change when there are increasing (or decreasing) costs. A country which has a comparative advantage in steel and begins to expand production for export, will find that its comparative advantage decreases as production and average costs increase. The country that can produce two tons of steel, at a cost of one ton of food, while other countries produce one ton of steel at a cost of one ton of food, will find that its comparative advantage shrinks as it expands steel production and incurs increasing average costs of producing steel in terms of foregone food. Any country that specializes because of trade will find that increasing costs puts a limit on the degree of specialization. The more they specialize and the more they expand production, the more the gains from specialization are exhausted. For the world as a whole, increasing costs will not eliminate specialization (with the accompanying allocational efficiency), but they will tend to make specialization less complete than it otherwise would be. For the steel producing country, e.g., this means other countries might continue producing steel.

• PROBLEM 25-22

According to the principle of comparative advantage, what would be the effect on the production possibilities frontier if countries specialized in the production of goods in which they have a comparative advantage?

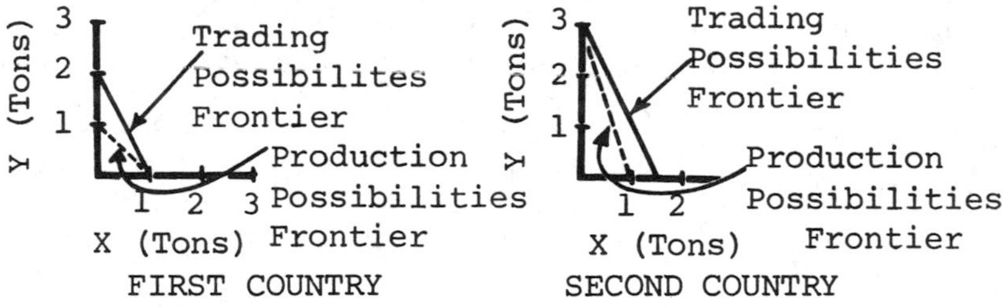

Solution: According to the principle of comparative advantage, specialization by countries in producing what each has a comparative advantage in will result in a more efficient allocation of resources. Since resources will be used more efficiently, the combined potential output will increase. This increase in potential output will be reflected in an expansion of the world's production possibilities frontier.

If, for example, a country has the resources to produce one ton of product X or one ton of product Y, or any combination of the two up to one ton total, it will probably produce some combination. If another country can produce Y at a relatively lower cost in terms of foregone X (it can produce three tons of Y, or one ton of X), then it would benefit both countries to specialize and trade at a world market price of, say, two tons of Y for every ton of X.

In these two diagrams, the gains to each country are made obvious. By specializing in X, and then trading for Y, the first country can increase the maximum amount of Y it can have by one ton. Likewise the second country can increase the maximum amount of X it can have by ½ ton. These gains are the concrete advantages of specializing and then trading.

• PROBLEM 25-23

If every country in the world has the exact same opportunity costs, so that no nation has a comparative advantage in any line of production, could there still be a basis for trade?

Solution: Even if no nation has a comparative advantage, there still could be a basis for trade. Differences in taste of countries could motivate exchange, and these differences could encourage specialization. Trade increases the size of markets, so any trade (whether induced by comparative advantage or by differences in taste) would tend to increase specialization and efficiency. Differences in taste, leading to exchange between nations, would stimulate trade regardless of the absence of comparative advantages.

• PROBLEM 25-24

Consider the following production possibilities for Country A and Country B.

Production Possibilities

Country	Units of wool	Units of steel
A	60	60
B	40	20

Apply the principle of the theory of comparative advantage to the above production possibilities schedule.

Solution: As we can see, Country A can produce either 60 units of wool or 60 units of steel with a given amount of resources and Country B can produce either 40 units of wool or 20 units of steel with the same resource input. It is clear that Country A has an absolute advantage in both wool and steel production, since it can produce both more steel and more wool than Country B with an equal quantity of inputs. However, it will be worthwhile for Country A to specialize in steel production and to use the surplus steel to trade with Country B for wool. This is because Country A can produce 1 unit of steel for each unit of wool it foregoes, whereas Country B can produce only ½ unit of steel for each unit of wool it gives up. Thus, if Country A produces their wool at home by cutting back on steel production, their opportunity cost is 1 unit of steel for each unit of wool. The opportunity cost in Country B on the other hand, is only

½ unit of steel for each unit of wool. Because the cost of wool, in terms of steel, is relatively less in Country B than in Country A, Country B is said to have a comparative advantage in wool production. It will therefore pay Country A to specialize in steel production and procure their wool by trade from Country B, where a unit of wool can be obtained for ½ unit of steel, rather than to make it at home, where the opportunity cost of a unit of wool is 1 unit of steel.

Conversely, Country A has a comparative advantage in steel as far as Country B is concerned. The opportunity cost of 1 unit of steel in Country B is 2 units of wool, that is, Country B must forego 2 units of wool in order to obtain 1 unit of steel. In Country A, nevertheless, the opportunity cost of a unit of steel is only 1 unit of wool. Because of the fact that steel, in terms of wool, is relatively cheaper in Country A, Country B would do well to put their resources into wool production, trading some of the surplus for steel. For Country B, it would not be economically sensible to produce steel instead of wool.

• PROBLEM 25-25

If only the limits to the terms of trade between two countries can be determined by their relative opportunity costs, how are the actual terms of trade determined?

Solution: The final terms of trade, i.e., the actual exchange ratios, are determined by world supply and demand conditions. If world demand for steel is high, and world demand for coffee is low, then the exchange ratio of steel and coffee will be nearer the cost ratio in the country with the comparative advantage in coffee production (the steel importing country). It will be farther from the cost ratio in the country with the comparative advantage in steel production (the steel exporting country). If world demand for steel is low and the world demand for coffee is high, then the exchange ratio of steel and coffee will be nearer the cost ratio in the country with the comparative advantage in steel production (the coffee importing country), and farther from the cost ratio in the country with the comparative advantage in coffee production (the coffee exporting country).

• PROBLEM 25-26

Relate the principle of comparative advantage to the concept of opportunity cost.

Solution: The principle of comparative advantage rests upon the concept of opportunity cost. Comparative advantage means that a country can produce the good in which it has a comparative advantage with a lower opportunity cost than another country; that is, the good costs less in terms of other goods foregone. Trade based on comparative advantage exists because opportunity costs for different countries vary. There might be a high opportunity cost for Japan to produce food instead of radios, while for Australia there might be a high opportunity cost in producing radios instead of food. Because of these different opportunity costs, i.e., the comparative advantage that Japan has in radios and Australia has in food, Japan and Australia can both gain if they specialize in and export radios and food respectively. Comparative advantages thus exist because of the varying opportunity costs of countries.

• PROBLEM 25-27

Give the significance of the "most favored nation clause" in the Gatt agreement.

Solution: The General Agreement on Tariffs and Trade (always called GATT) was set up for the purpose of reducing existing tariff barriers by all countries at the same time, in a mutually cooperative effort as well as to try and dismantle the very high tariff barriers which grew up in the years prior to World War II. One of its most important provisions is the so-called "most favored nation clause." To illustrate this, suppose the United States and France, both members of the Gatt, start negotiating. The United States is perhaps most interested in selling machinery to France; France in selling textiles to the United States. Both countries bargain, reaching an agreement that France will cut its machinery tariff by so much if America cuts its textile tariff by a certain amount.

The tariff cuts then apply to all textiles (not only French) imported into the United States, and all machinery imported into France, because of the most favored nation clause in the GATT agreement.

From the above, we can say that the most "favored nation clause" is the agreement that no member of GATT will be treated worse than the "most favored nation"--in effect, that no member country's imports can be charged a higher tariff than any other member country, unless special exceptions have been made. Although it has been a long process, GATT has resulted in a major reduction in world tariff barriers since the agreement first went into operation.

SHORT ANSWER QUESTIONS FOR REVIEW

Answer
To be covered when testing yourself

Choose the correct answer.

1. A necessary assumption of the theory of comparative advantage if we are to prove gains from trade is (a) one country cannot have an absolute advantage in the production of both goods (b) one country must be relatively more efficient in the production of one of the goods (c) one country must be considerably larger than the other (d) factors of production have to be free to move between countries. b

2. Assume that American agriculture is the most efficient in the world; then (a) America will never import food (b) America cannot gain from trading because it is self-sufficient (c) America will export food (d) it is still impossible to determine whether America will export food or import food only on the basis of the assumption. d

3. The simple theory of two-good, two-country comparative advantage in itself will not enable us to determine (a) the price ratios at which the goods must exchange after trade (b) which country exports which good (c) the pattern of geographical specialization (d) the direction in which relative goods prices will be moved in each country by trade. a

4. A country relatively rich in labor resources and relatively poor in capital resources would be more likely to gain from trade by (a) producing goods having labor-intensive production methods (b) producing goods having capital-intensive production methods (c) imposing very high import and export tariffs (d) using production methods in which the cost of production rises as output rises. a

5. With a given quantity of labor and capital, Country X can produce 20 tons of steel or 20 tons of coal, but Country Y can produce 10 tons of steel or 16 tons of coal. Assuming constant costs, Y should (a) import coal and export steel (b) import both coal and steel (c) export coal and import steel (d) export both coal and steel. c

6. Under increasing costs, two countries producing the same goods (a) find it unprofitable to trade unless their tastes are different (b) may continue to produce something of both goods

SHORT ANSWER QUESTIONS FOR REVIEW

Answer
To be covered when testing yourself

after trade (c) realize that under trade, one country benefits at the expense of another (d) will each specialize in the production of some goods as much as in the constant costs case. — b

7. Beef, shoes, and bread require (10,10,10) hours of labor in the U.S., and (12,11,13) hours in the U.K. This means that (a) the U.S. must never export beef (b) the U.S. must never export bread (c) the U.S. must never export shoes (d) the U.S. will never import anything. — c

8. International goods movements can be a substitute for international factor movements (a) if no factors are scarce (b) only if the principle of comparative advantage is denied (c) only if the goods movements are strictly regulated (d) when trade makes the scarce factor in each country less scarce. — d

9. Trade based on comparative advantage improves allocational efficiency because (a) less productive countries do not produce anything at all (b) absolute efficiency determines which country will produce each product (c) of specialization based on relative efficiency (d) everyone and every country all benefit equally from it. — c

10. Trade (a) tends to make product prices in different countries roughly equal (b) does not affect product prices at all (c) leads to inflation because of increased world demand (d) leads to lower prices because of increased supply of goods. — a

Fill in the blanks.

11. When one nation can produce a good more efficiently than another nation, then the efficient nation has an _____________ over the inefficient nation. — absolute advantage

12. When the production possibilities frontier is altered to include trade, the new frontier is known as the _____________ frontier. — trading possibilities

13. A major reason why specialization is not always complete is _____________. — increasing costs

14. A nation has a _____________ in producing good X when it is relatively more efficient in producing good X, even though other nations might

SHORT ANSWER QUESTIONS FOR REVIEW

Answer
To be covered when testing yourself

Question	Answer
be absolutely more efficient in producing the good.	comparative advantage
15. The easiest way to measure relative efficiencies is to compare _______________.	opportunity costs

Determine whether the following statements are true or false.

Question	Answer
16. International trade between Countries X and Y can be mutually profitable even though X can produce every commodity more cheaply than Y.	True
17. If full employment prevails in both countries before trade, then it is impossible for both countries to be better off after trade.	False
18. According to the theory of comparative advantage, prices of all different goods must be equal after trade.	False
19. Relative to constant costs, decreasing costs increase the likelihood of mutually advantageous trade.	True
20. By the terms of trade, we mean the relative price ratios of the goods exchanged.	True
21. Under increasing costs, two quite different countries might end up each having to produce something of all goods; this would be virtually impossible under constant costs.	True
22. If two nations specialize and trade in accordance with comparative advantage, the prices of the relative resources will tend toward equality.	True
23. If the American ratio of clothing price to food price is 3/1 and in Europe is 2/1 before trade, then if trade is opened up, America would most likely export food.	True
24. It would be possible for a country which had been importing a certain commodity to switch to exporting it, because of a change in demand, even though the underlying comparative-cost conditions are unchanged (provided that there are more than two commodities involved in trade).	True
25. Everyone in a nation will benefit equally from the opening up of international trade.	False

SHORT ANSWER QUESTIONS FOR REVIEW

	Answer To be covered when testing yourself
26. If a country is especially plentifully endowed with land, then free trade may cause rents to rise relative to wages.	True
27. While free trade does maximize world production, nevertheless if we are selfish, we in the well-endowed United States can maximize our own production by self-sufficiency.	False
28. It follows from the theory of comparative advantage that the opening up of trade could not lead to unemployment even in the short run.	False
29. Differences in factor-prices resulting from differing factor endowments can be reduced by free movement of goods, or of factors, or of both.	True
30. Where posttrade price ratios will fall, in the interval between pretrade ratios, depends on the strength of reciprocal demands.	True

CHAPTER 26

PROTECTIVE TARIFFS, QUOTAS, AND FREE TRADE

Basic Attacks and Strategies for Solving Problems in this Chapter. See pages 880 to 909 for step-by-step solutions to problems.

The theory of comparative advantage discussed in Chapter 25 has an unambiguous implication for the appropriate policy a government should follow toward trade with other countries. Namely, free trade is the best policy. Under free trade, nations will specialize in those products in which they possess a comparative advantage. The result is maximum world production of all products, leading to the attainment of the highest possible living standard. Nonetheless, policies that interfere with free trade, namely, tariffs and quotas, remain widespread.

A tariff is a tax applied to an imported good or service. A quota is a limitation on the amount of a good that can be imported. Both tariffs and quotas make foreign goods less competitive with domestic products, with the result that foreign producers and domestic consumers are hurt while domestic producers and foreign consumers are helped.

Common arguments made in favor of trade restrictions include:

Cheap Foreign Wages – It is frequently asserted that low foreign wages enable foreign industries to out-compete domestic industries. The inevitable result is that domestic producers will be forced out of business, American workers will lose jobs, and our standard of living will fall (to the level of the foreigners!). Consequently, we need to provide protection for American industries.

The argument is almost wholly fallacious. The absolute level of wages is not what determines how competitive an industry is. Rather, it is the level of wages relative to the productivity of workers. If an American industry has high wages, but equally high productivity, it may very well be quite competitive with its foreign counterparts. In fact, it is high wage American industries that are some of our best performers in the international marketplace. The grain of truth in the argument is that some low wage foreign industries may, in fact, out-compete

American industries, but this simply means that is where their comparative advantage lies and ours does not.

Infant Industry—The infant industry argument says that some new industries need time to develop the skills, techniques, and efficiency necessary to be "world-class." Failure to protect these industries will lead to their being "snuffed-out" before they had a fair chance. Protection of selected industries is alleged to be behind the rise to prominence of Japan, Taiwan, South Korea, and Singapore, and is a significant part of the case made for industrial policy. The argument is valid as far as it goes, but it does not explain how a country is able to separate the "winners" from the "losers." Some economists feel that what will happen in practice is that politically influential but senile industries will end up being protected.

Terms of Trade—There are certain conditions (whose description must await more advanced courses) where a country may benefit at the expense of others by using tariffs. However, these conditions do not always exist, and countries must be prepared for the imposition of retaliatory tariffs, which end up making everyone worse-off.

Antidumping—There is widespread belief that some foreign governments subsidize their industries to allow them to sell below cost (dump) in the United States. American industries are said to be victims of "unfair competition." What is seldom explained is why Americans should be upset if foreign governments help us buy products at low prices.

National Defense—The necessity of maintaining particular industries for national defense is often used as an argument to support protectionism. Like the infant industry argument, it is not illogical and cannot be completely evaluated in economic terms. Also like the infant industry argument, it suffers from the practical problem of how to identify those industries that are absolutely vital.

Probably the most valid general explanation for the existence of trade restrictions is simply the power of special interest groups in the political process. The potential gainers from trade restrictions, domestic producers, are a relatively small group that individually will benefit significantly from restrictions. The potential losers, domestic consumers, are a relatively large group that individually will lose only a little. The potential gainers have a greater economic incentive and fewer practical impediments to cooperating to apply political pressure than the potential losers have to resist. In many instances, this proves decisive.

Supply and demand can be used to analyze trade restrictions. The figure on the following page shows the market for a tradable good in countries A and B. If there was no trade between the countries, the good would sell for P_1 in A and P_2 in B. If free trade is encouraged, then country B producers would export to country A to take advantage of the higher price. The increased supply in country A would reduce the product's price there, and the decreased supply in country *B* would raise the price there. In equilibrium the price of the product would be equal in both countries (P_0) and the excess supply in *B* at price P_0 ($Q_6 - Q_5$) will be exported to *A* to satisfy *A*'s excess demand ($Q_4 - Q_1$) .

That this is a more efficient outcome is easily shown. Recall that the industry supply curve measures marginal cost of production. Prior to free trade, marginal cost is higher in *A* than *B*. Free trade causes *A*'s higher cost domestic producers to reduce production while *B*'s lower cost producers expand. Consequently, total costs of production will be lower.

Now assume that *A* imposes a tariff on the product that raises its price in *A* to P_3. There are benefits and costs of this policy to the various parties. In *A*, domestic producers benefit because they can sell more (Q_2) at a higher price. Domestic consumers lose for that reason. Also, the government of A receives revenue from the tariff. Country *B* producers will lose because they can no longer sell as much in *A* ($Q_3 - Q_2$ instead of $Q_4 - Q_1$) and must sell at a lower price in *B*. Country *B*'s consumers will gain from lower domestic prices.

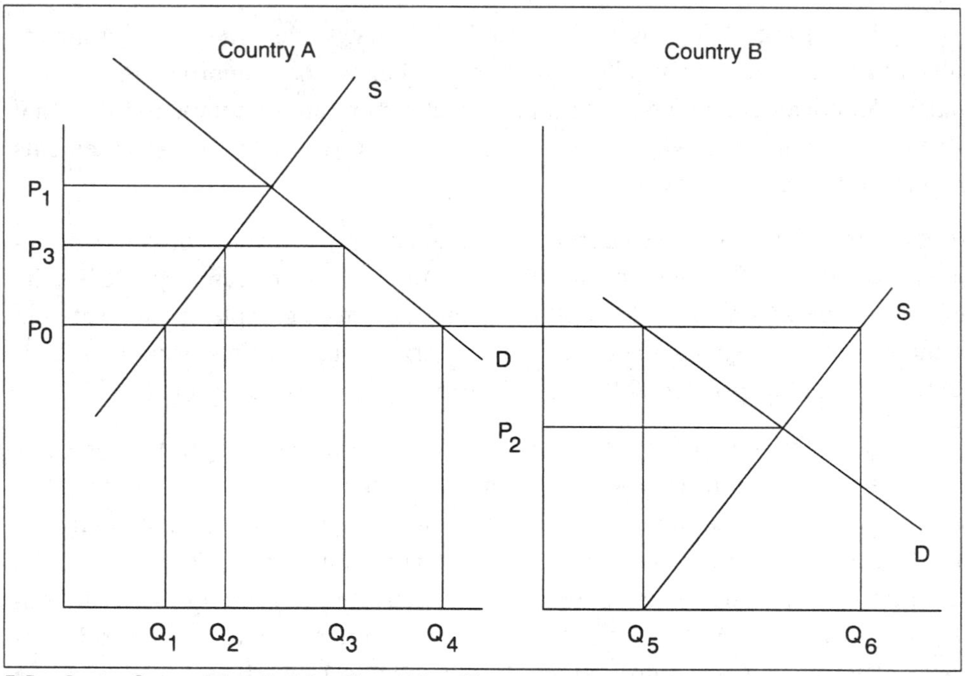

Markets for a Tradable Good in Country A and B

The effects of a quota imposed by country *A* on imports from *B* are similar to those of a tariff. If *A* can only import $Q_3 - Q_2$ instead of $Q_4 - Q_1$, price would rise to P_3, helping domestic producers (who could now sell Q_2 units at P_3 instead of Q_1 at P_0) while hurting domestic consumers. The import restriction would hurt some of *B*'s domestic producers (those who cannot get import licenses) and help domestic consumers. The difference from the tariff case is that country *B* producers who can obtain import licenses into *A* will reap windfall profits, and country *A*'s government will not be receiving tariff revenue. In a sense, compared to tariffs, quotas hurt the imposing country's government and help the other country's producers.

Regional economic integration can be defined as any measures taken by two or more countries within a region to reduce or remove barriers to commerce between the countries. There are several distinct approaches to integration. These include free trade areas, customs unions, and a common market. The best example is the European Economic Community (EEC). By 1992 all significant barriers to trade should be removed between the members of the EEC.

The goal of economic integration is to allow the region to achieve the benefits of specialization and division of labor.

PROBLEM 26-17

What is the so-called European Economic Community?

Solution: The European Economic Community (EEC), better known as the European Common Market, is a group of European nations which have agreed to strive for economic integration. It was established in 1957 by the Treaty of Rome, the original signatories to which were Belgium, France, Italy, Luxembourg, the Netherlands, and West Germany.

The Treaty required all internal tariffs (except on farm products) between member countries to be gradually reduced and eventually eliminated. The various external tariffs of the members were also to be equalized over time until they constituted a common external barrier to goods produced outside the community. Finally, the signatories agreed to eliminate barriers to the free movement of factors of production (labor and capital) among themselves. As of this point in time, the goals regarding internal and external tariffs have been achieved. The next important date for the Common Market is 1992. At that time all restrictions on capital and labor mobility will cease. An EEC passport will come into being, which will permit citizens of any EEC country to travel freely within the EEC. Also, the members will standardize their government regulations regarding product quality. In recent years they have taken preliminary steps to monetary union by establishing fixed exchange rates among all member currencies. Later plans call for full coordination of monetary policies.

Since, 1957, the original signatories have been joined by Great Britain, Spain, Portugal, Denmark, Ireland, and Greece.

Step-by-Step Solutions to Problems in this Chapter, "Protective Tariffs, Quotas, and Free Trade"

RATIONALE FOR PROTECTION

• PROBLEM 26-1

What yardsticks do economists use to evaluate foreign trade policies? Explain each.

Solution: Essentially, the criteria used to evaluate foreign trade policies are much the same as those employed in analyzing domestic economic measures, namely, international trade is judged in terms of its efficiency and equity as well as its effect on economic stability and growth.

Foreign trade is efficient when it results in a greater amount of goods and services available to each of the trading nations. It has been an argument that an expanding trade between the United States and the USSR will lead to efficiency. It is claimed that the net effects will be both more natural gas for American households and more meat for Russian consumers.

Another yardstick for evaluating foreign trade is equity, for international trade policies can affect the distribution of income. As an example, it was argued that the oil import quotas of the 1960s benefitted the high-income stockholders of American oil companies at the expense of the low-income fuel, oil and gasoline consumers who were forced to pay higher prices.

Stability is the third criterion for judging international trade policy, such questions as the effect of foreign trade on the level of domestic employment and prices has to be considered.

Finally, international trade can be evaluated in terms of its impact on economic growth. Government officials must therefore consider trade policy when planning an overall rate of growth.

• PROBLEM 26-2

What are typical motivations for the imposition of protective tariffs and import quotas?

Solution: The imposition of protective tariffs and import quotas may result from any of several motivations or combinations of such motivations. The most important of these motivations are as follows:

1. The desire to protect special interests which are able to exert political influence is a common motivation. While nations as a whole may benefit from free international trade, there are particular industries or resource producers (such as miners or farmers) who may suffer, at least in the short run, as a result of it. The long-run effect of free trade is to cause each country to shift the use of its factors of production (such as land, labor and capital) from uses in which the country does not enjoy a comparative advantage, to other uses in which it does. For example, if Country X has a comparative advantage in shoe manufacturing and a comparative disadvantage in cattle raising, as compared to Country Y, the logical end-result of free trade between X and Y is that Y will specialize in cattle raising and will export hides to X, which will use the hides to make shoes, some of which will be exported back to Y. If, before free trade with X begins, Y has a substantial shoe manufacturing industry, the long-run result of free trade will be that factors of production in Y will be shifted from shoe manufacturing to cattle raising and to other uses in which they can be more profitably employed. The short-run result for Y, however, will be decreased volume and profits for its shoe industry and less employment for shoemakers. If ~~the~~ shoe manufacturers and the shoemakers' union in Y are politically powerful, they may successfully lobby the government to impose or keep protective tariffs or import quotas on shoes. Similarly, those involved in cattle raising in Country X may lobby their government to impose or preserve tariffs or quotas on cattle or cattle hides in order to protect themselves against competition from Y.

2. A second important motivation for imposing protective tariffs or quotas is to provide stimulus for the domestic economy. This motivation is especially important during periods of recession or depression, when many countries have typically attempted to follow what are called "beggar-thy-neighbor" policies. These policies are implemented by imposing tariffs or quotas, or both, which effectively keep out most foreign goods, except those which the country imposing the tariffs or quotas cannot produce itself. The effect of these tariffs or quotas is to artificially stimulate the economy of the country imposing them by enabling industries in which the country does not enjoy a comparative international advantage to increase their level of production. A decline in imports will cause the aggregate demand schedule of the country imposing the tariffs or quotas to shift upward. This, in turn, will stimulate both domestic income and employment.

3. A third major motivation for the imposition of protective tariffs and quotas is defense, or national security. If a country has domestic resource producers or industries whose goods are required for national defense, it may seek to protect these producers or industries from foreign competition if they do not enjoy a comparative advantage under free trade. The rationale for this is that in time of war access to foreign sources of goods may be denied. Therefore, it is argued, it is important to keep domestic producers alive and healthy so they will be readily available to supply needed goods during wartime.

4. A final important motivation for imposing protective tariffs and quotas stems from the so-called "infant industries" argument. This motivation is particularly important in less developed countries. These countries may have embryonic manufacturing industries which do not presently enjoy comparative advantage vis a vis their counterparts in industrialized countries. It is often argued that such "infant industries", if afforded protection by tariffs, quotas, or both, can develop under such protection to a point at which they enjoy comparative advantage in the world market.

• PROBLEM 26-3

What is the "cheap labor" argument in favor of protecting tariffs and quotas? What are its weaknesses?

Solution: The "cheap foreign labor" argument in favor of protective tariffs and quotas is one which is usually used in highly industrialized countries where wage rates are high, such as the United States. The argument asserts that, since foreign wages are lower than American wages, protective trade barriers are necessary in order to prevent foreign goods, produced by "cheap" labor, from underselling American goods and thereby pricing them off the market.

The "cheap foreign labor" argument's primary weakness is that it would be applicable only if labor were the only factor of production, the cost of which must be considered in determining the price of goods. However, it must be remembered that the comparative costs of other factors of production have to be taken into account in determining overall marginal cost and comparative advantage. For capital intensive industries, in which countries like the U.S. enjoy their greatest comparative advantage due, mainly, to their advanced technology, the "cheap foreign labor" argument is largely irrelevant. In the case of labor intensive industries it may hold some truth. However, such industries are ones in which countries like the U.S. do not hold a comparative advantage in international trade. It would be in the long-run best interest of the U.S. economy to allow foreign competitors to force these industries to employ their factors of production in more economically efficient pursuits.

• **PROBLEM 26-4**

Differentiate the national security argument from the cheap foreign labor argument in favor of protection.

Solution: The national security argument in favor of protection holds that certain industries are essential to the nation's defense and must therefore be protected despite the fact that cheaper sources of supply are available in peacetime. On the other hand, the cheap foreign labor argument in favor of protection holds that since wages in the United States are substantially higher than in other nations, tariffs and similar barriers are necessary to keep out goods produced by low-paid foreign workers. Otherwise, low-cost imports will outsell American-made goods, and the result will be widespread domestic unemployment or lower wages and living standards for American workers.

• **PROBLEM 26-5**

What is the so-called foreign trade multiplier argument? What conclusion can we derive from the said argument?

Solution: The foreign trade multiplier argument is a special version of the cheap foreign labor argument and is often heard during periods of economic depression. Based on the formula $Y = C + I + G + X$ (where X represents net exports), this argument holds that because an increase in any one of the components of national income will stimulate the economy and raise the level of employment, an attempt should be made to increase X. In the short run, the simplest way to increase X is by means of reducing imports by imposing tariffs and quotas. However, the weakness of such an approach has been illustrated many times. This is by virtue of the fact that since one nation's imports are another nation's exports, any attempts to increase domestic employment in Country A through reducing imports from Country B will have a negative effect on Country B's net exports and employment. Country B would then reciprocate with its own tariffs and quotas, and A's exports to B would decline.

From this, we can see that tariffs and quotas usually fail as devices for stimulating net exports and domestic employment. Although it is true that initially some domestic industries will expand, very soon employment in the traditional export industries will decline in response to the imposition of retaliatory measures by foreign nations. In other words, the final result is rarely an expansion of overall economic activity. Instead, the previous pattern of exports and imports is replaced by a less efficient use of resources, as workers shift from the former export industries in which the nation had a comparative advantage, into protected high-cost industries.

What was the significance of the Trade Agreements Act of 1934, passed by the U.S. Congress in that year and signed into law by President Franklin D. Roosevelt? What were the effects of the "escape clause" and the "peril point" amendments to that Act?

Solution: The Trade Amendments Act of 1934 represented a significant innovation in the mechanics of setting tariff rates. Before the passage of the 1934 Act, all tariff rates (that is, the amount of duty charged on any given imported commodity, whether on an ad valorem or a specific basis) were fixed by Act of Congress and could be changed only by further legislation. The 1934 Act gave the president authority to negotiate reciprocal trade agreements, which could alter existing tariff rates by as much as fifty percent of existing rates without any requirements for Congressional action. The overall effect of the 1934 Act, therefore, was to make United States tariff and trade policy much more flexible than it previously had been.

After World War II, however, Congress added two amendments to the 1934 Act which significantly limited the Tariff Commission's authority to alter tariff rates. These were the "peril point" and "escape clause" amendments. The escape clause was intended to offer relief to American industries or producers who claimed they had been injured by reductions in tariff rates already negotiated by the Tariff Commission. Such industries or producers were allowed, under the escape clause, to petition the Tariff Commission for relief in the form of a new, higher tariff rate. In deciding whether or not relief should be granted under such petitions, the Commission was directed to "take into consideration a downward trend of production, employment, prices, profits or wages in the domestic industry concerned, or a decline in sales, an increase in imports, either actual or relative to domestic production, a higher or growing inventory, or a decline in the proportion of the domestic market supplied by domestic producers." It is important to note here that an American firm could petition for higher tariffs, although its sales were increasing, so long as imports were increasing faster. The peril point amendment, unlike the escape clause, was designed to prevent, before the fact, tariff reductions which might adversely affect American industries or producers. Under the peril point amendment the president was directed to list the products on which he planned to make tariff concessions at meetings of the General Agreement on Tariffs and Trade. The Tariff Commission was then required to decide what minimum tariff rates were required on each of these products in order to prevent injury to American industry. These minimum rates were referred to as "peril points", since it was believed that any reduction of tariffs below these rates would imperil domestic producers. In the ensuing negotiations, the president could reduce rates below the peril points, but was required to justify his action in a special message to Congress.

• **PROBLEM 26-7**

Explain the "infant industries" argument in favoring protection of domestic industries from foreign competition. Is there a validity with such an argument?

Solution: The "infant industries" argument is one of the oldest arguments in favor of protection which comes from those who feel that new domestic industries must be shielded temporarily from foreign competition. This was first presented in the eighteenth century by Alexander Hamilton, in his report on manufacturers. Hamilton claimed that because a new industry may lack trained workmen, established suppliers of raw materials, and the necessary technological know-how, it should be protected from low-cost imports until it achieves the level of efficiency of its foreign competitors. Recent versions of the infant industry argument stress that unless such an industry is granted protection, its volume of sales may never reach the level where it can enjoy economies of scale. In theory, then, the protection of infant industries is seen as temporary. Once the new industry reaches efficient levels of production, it will be able to compete in terms of price with foreign competitors, and tariffs or quotas can be removed.

As to its validity, it is difficult to make a strong case for the infant industry argument in mature economies like those of the United States, Western Europe, or Japan. In developing nations, it may have more validity, although even there it is difficult often to determine which industries have the potential to compete in world markets and which will never reach the required levels of efficiency. Furthermore, the record shows that protection originally afforded as a temporary measure frequently persists, even after an infant industry has reached maturity and has become an efficient producer. The result is permanently higher prices for the consumer and frequently higher profit margins for the fortunate industry. Finally, many point out that even in those cases where an infant industry legitimately deserves some help, there are cheaper ways than tariffs or quotas to accomplish this end, including direct cash subsidies, government manpower training programs, and tax abatement.

TARIFFS AND QUOTAS

• **PROBLEM 26-8**

Differentiate tariffs from quotas as barriers to free trade.

Solution: Tariffs are generally, a scale of charges, but specifically in international trade, a tax which must be paid on imported goods. They are levied for two basic reasons: to raise revenue and to protect domestic industries.

On the other hand, a quota sets a maximum on the quantity of a good that may be imported during a given period of time.

• PROBLEM 26-9

Describe the effect of an export quota and export tax on such a product as soybeans.

Solution: An export quota and export tax have an effect opposite to that of an import quota or tax. This implies that an export quota or export tax will benefit domestic consumers rather than domestic producers. Assume, for instance, that the world price of soybeans is $200 a ton. In country A, a soybean producer, the prevailing price of soybeans is $100 a ton. If the government of country A decides to impose a quota on the amount of soybeans that domestic producers may export, these producers will be forced to sell the amount they produce in excess of the export quota at the lower prevailing domestic price. If the producers attempt to drive up the domestic price by withholding soybeans from the domestic market, the government may be forced to impose price controls. The result of this policy will be to keep the domestic price of soybeans in country A at $100 a ton below the world price, thus benefitting domestic consumers.

If, instead of a quota, the government decides to impose an export tax on soybeans, the result will be similar. To be effective, the tax should equal the difference between the export price of soybeans and the domestic price. This will eliminate any economic incentive for domestic producers to export soybeans, thus assuring supply and price stability at the $100 per ton level within country A.

• PROBLEM 26-10

Whether imposed for protective purposes or to raise revenue, tariffs can be imposed in two different ways. Define these two methods of imposing tariffs, and give an example of each.

Solution: There are two common methods of imposing tariffs, namely, a) ad valorem and b) specific.

Ad valorem tariffs are import taxes equal to a percentage of the value of an imported good. As an example, if an imported car costs $50,000 and the ad valorem tariff on automobiles is 20 percent, the amount of tariff imposed will be $50,000 x .2 = $10,000. If the cost of the imported car is only $5000, the tariff will be $1000.

A specific tariff, on the other hand, is a fixed tax

levied upon each unit or quantity of an imported good. An example of a specific tariff is a tariff of $5 per bale on imported cotton. In this case, the tariff payable on any specific bale is $5, whether the cost of the bale to the importer is $20, $50 or some other cost.

• PROBLEM 26-11

Define tariffs, and differentiate revenue tariffs from protective tariffs.

Solution: Tariffs are excise taxes on imported goods. They may be imposed for either of two reasons, and sometimes for both reasons combined. These two reasons are: (1) to raise revenue for the government of the country imposing the tariff, and (2) to protect producers of goods in the country imposing the tariff from foreign competition.

Revenue tariffs are those which are imposed primarily for the purpose of raising revenue. They are usually applied to products which are not produced in the country imposing the tariff. The United States, for example, would be most likely to impose revenue tariffs on tropical agricultural products (such as bananas) which it cannot grow domestically in sufficient quantities to meet demand, or on raw materials such as chromium ore which do not exist in sufficient quantities domestically to meet the needs of American industry. Since the United States does not and cannot have a significant domestic banana-growing or chromium ore extraction industry, tariffs on these goods do not serve a protective purpose.

Protective tariffs are distinguishable from revenue tariffs in that their primary function is to protect domestic producers from foreign competition. Although protective tariffs are usually not high enough to completely prohibit the importation of foreign goods, they put foreign producers at a competitive disadvantage in selling their goods in the domestic market of the country imposing the tariff. Protective tariffs do, of course, raise revenue. However, it could be said that the less revenue they raise the more effectively they are performing their primary function. The less revenue they produce, the fewer foreign products which are being imported, and, therefore, the greater the protection which is being afforded to domestic producers.

• PROBLEM 26-12

Evaluate the effect of a tariff on textiles in terms of benefits and losses for the citizens of the importing country, Country A.

Solution: Evaluating the consequences of a tariff on textiles in terms of the benefits and losses for the citizens of Country A, those who are likely to suffer are the consumers of Country A who, as a result of the tariff, have to pay a higher price for textile goods and find fewer such goods available on the market. The beneficiaries will be textile producers in Country A. Two groups of such producers will benefit in different ways. The first group consists of high cost producers, i.e., those whose costs of production exceed the costs of production in Country B, the textile exporting country. These producers would be forced out of the textile market in Country A if a tariff were not imposed. Imposition of the tariff, therefore, allows these relatively inefficient producers in Country A to remain in the textile business, because the tariff ensures that the cost of goods imported from Country B will equal or exceed the cost of goods produced by them.

The expressed purpose of most tariffs is to achieve this result--the protection of high cost, low efficiency domestic producers from low cost, high efficiency foreign competitors. However, there is likely to be a secondary group of beneficiaries, the low cost producers of Country A. Although these producers are not threatened with elimination from the textile market by competition from Country B because they can produce goods at equal or less cost than can Country B's manufacturers, the tariff will, by maintaining an artificially high price for textiles in Country A, allow these low-cost producers to maintain higher profit margins than they could realize under free trade. The benefit, to these producers, measured in dollars, is likely to be much greater than the benefit to high-cost producers because (1) the low-cost producers are likely to be much larger, more efficient firms, and (2) the high-cost producers could, in the absence of a tariff, shift the use of their capital and labor resources to the production of non-textile goods which they could sell at a profit. Thus, the irony of the tariff is that it produces the greatest benefit for those producers whom it is not intended to protect.

• PROBLEM 26-13

The figures on the next page demonstrate the effect of levying tariffs on imported goods such as textiles. Refering to Figures 1,2 and 3, describe the effects of the tariffs on a) Country A, which imports textile goods and b) Country B which is an exporter.

Solution: The line labeled P*, which crosses figures 1, 2 and 3 at the same level, represents the prevailing world price for textiles. In figure 1, the P* line intersects S_A, the supply curve for textiles in Country A, at the point (Q_A^S, P^*), and Q_A^S represents the quantity of textiles which will be produced in Country A at the price P*. The demand curve for textiles in Country A, D_A intersects the P* line at (Q_A^D, P^*), and Q_A^D is the quantity of textiles which consumers in Country A are willing to buy at the world price. The distance between these points, $Q_A^D - Q_A^S$,

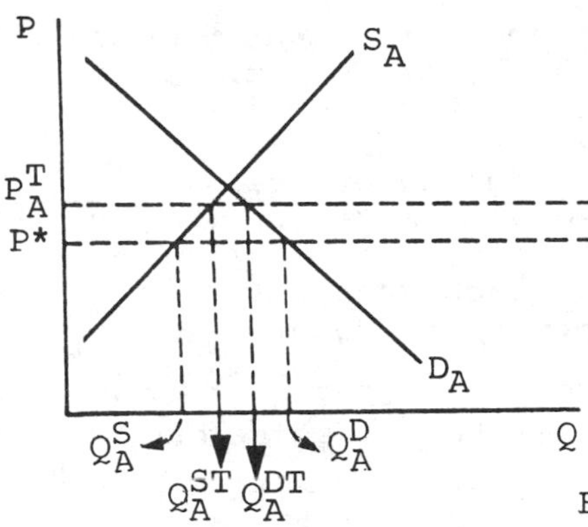

Fig. 1 Country A Demand and Supply

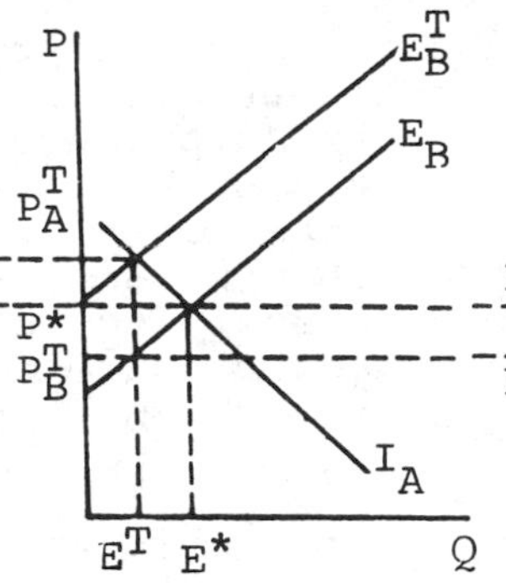

Fig. 2 Import and Export Curves after Tariff

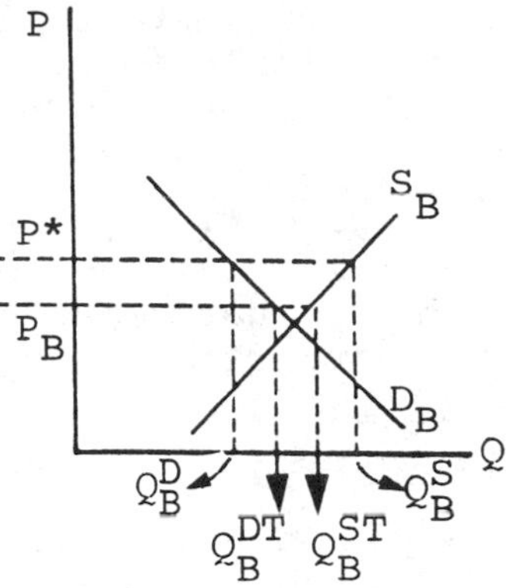

Fig. 3 Country B Demand and Supply

equals the shortfall of supply in Country A at the world price. Note that the world price line intersects the supply and demand curves for Country A beneath the intersection of the supply and demand curves, and the result of this (which is true for all normal cases of increasing supply and decreasing demand with respect to increasing price) is that demand exceeds supply.

Figure 3, however, shows that the intersection of the supply (S_B) and demand (D_B) curves for Country B intersect P* above the point where S_B and D_B intersect. The result is that, at the world price, supply exceeds demand in an amount equal to $Q_B^S - Q_B^D$.

If trade between countries A and B were unrestricted, the result would be that Country A would be willing to import a quantity of textiles equal to $Q_A^D - Q_A^S$ at price P*. Conversely, Country B would be willing to export a quantity of textiles equal to $Q_B^S - Q_A^D$ at the same price. By referring to the export curve for Country B (E_B) and the import curve for Country A (I_A), on Figure 2, it can be seen that they intersect at P* and that the quantity of textiles which Country B will export to Country A is equal to E*. The net result is that producers in Country A can produce and sell Q_A^S of textiles in Country A at price P*, and consumers in Country A can buy Q_A^D of textiles at the same price. Producers in Country B can produce and sell Q_B^S of textiles at price P*, Q_B^D of which will be sold on the home market and the remainder ($Q_B^S - Q_B^D$) of which will be exported (including the quantity E*, which will be exported to Country A). Thus, demand and supply will be in equilibrium in Countries A and B at the world price P*.

The effect of a tariff on textiles imposed by Country

A is to increase the cost to the producers in Country B of textiles exported to Country A. This is, because the tariff is, in effect, a tax on producers of textiles in countries such as Country B which export textiles to Country A. An increase in the cost of producing or selling goods will, all other things being equal, cause the supply curve for such goods to shift to the left, since the producer must receive a higher price for each quantity sold in order to cover costs. The net result for Country B is to cause its export curve (the supply curve for goods exported to Country A) to shift from E_B to E_B^T, as can be seen on Figure 2. Note that the new export curve E_B^T intersects Country A's import curve I_A at a new price, P_A^T, which is in excess of the world price P*. The difference, $P_A^T - P^*$, is equal to the amount of the tariff.

Since textile goods imported from Country B now cost consumers in Country A more ($P_A^T - P^*$) than before the imposition of the tariff, producers in Country A are now able to increase their prices to P_A^T. They are also able to sell more textiles on the home market. Referring again to Figure 2, it can be seen that Country B's new export curve E_B^T intersects Country A's import curve I_A at a quantity, E^T, which is less than the quantity (E*) which Country B exported to Country A under free trade conditions.

The consequences of the tariff for producers and consumers in Country A can be seen by referring to Figure 1. The horizontal line beginning at P_A^T is the new price of textiles in Country A. This line intersects the supply curve S_A at the point (S_A^{ST}, P_A^T), which is above and to the right of the point (Q_A^S, P*) at which the world price line intersects Country A's supply curve. Therefore, producers in Country A can now sell more textiles (the difference being equal to $Q_A^{ST} - Q_A^S$) on the home market, for which they will receive a higher price (the difference being equal to $P_A^T - P^*$ for each unit sold).

The new price P_A^T intersects Country A's demand curve D_A at a point (Q_A^{DT}, P_A^T) which is above and to the left of the point (Q_A^D, P*) at which the world price line intersects D_A. Therefore, consumers in Country A will now purchase fewer textile goods (the difference being equal to $Q_A^D - Q_A^{DT}$) for which they will pay a higher price per unit (the difference being equal to $P_A^T - P^*$).

The effect of Country A's tariff on the domestic textile market of Country B, the exporter, will be just the opposite of its effect on the domestic market of Country A. Since Country B is now exporting less ($E^* - E^T$) textiles to Country A, there will (assuming other export markets are saturated) be more textiles produced in Country B available for sale domestically. The effect of this increase in available textiles on Country B's home market can be seen by referring to Figure 3. The effect of an increase in the available supply (all other things being equal) is to cause the price to fall, which it does, to the level represented by the line beginning at point P_B^T. This line intersects Country B's supply curve S_B at a point (Q_B^{ST}, P_B^T) below and to the left of the point (Q_B^S, P^*) at which the world price line intersects it. Therefore, producers in Country B will be able to sell a smaller quantity of textiles (the difference being equal to $Q_B^S - Q_B^{ST}$) for which they will receive a lower price per unit (the difference being equal to $P^* - P_B^T$). It is important to note that although producers in Country B are able to sell more textiles on the domestic market at the lower price, the difference in the amount they are able to sell in the export market ($E^* - E^T$) is more than enough to offset this gain and cause an overall decrease in the quantity they are able to sell.

The new price line P_B^T intersects Country B's demand curve D_B at a point (Q_B^{DT}, P_B^T) below and to the right of the point (Q_B^D, P^*) at which the world price line intersects it. Consumers in Country B can therefore buy more textile goods (the difference being equal to $Q_B^{DT} - Q_B^D$) at a lower price (the difference being equal to $P^* - P_B^T$).

In summary, the effect of a tariff on textiles imposed by a textile importing country, Country A, is to benefit textile producers in Country A (who can now sell more textile goods at a higher price) and consumers in the textile exporting country, Country B (who can now buy more textile goods at a lower price). The tariff penalizes consumers in Country A (who can now purchase fewer textile goods at a higher price) and textile producers in Country B (who can now sell less at a lower price).

• PROBLEM 26-14

Suppose Country A, which imports textile goods from Country B, decides to impose a quota on textile goods imported from Country B. The two given figures illustrate the effects of the imposition of the quota. Referring to the figures, describe the effects of the quota on producers and consumers in Country A. Distinguish the effect of a quota from that of a tariff.

Fig. 1

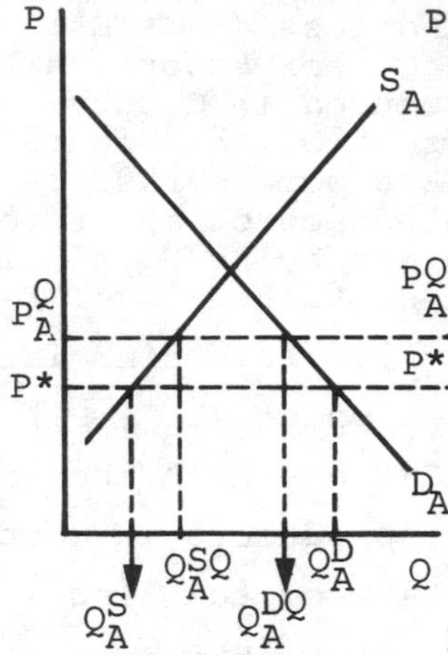

Country A Supply and Demand

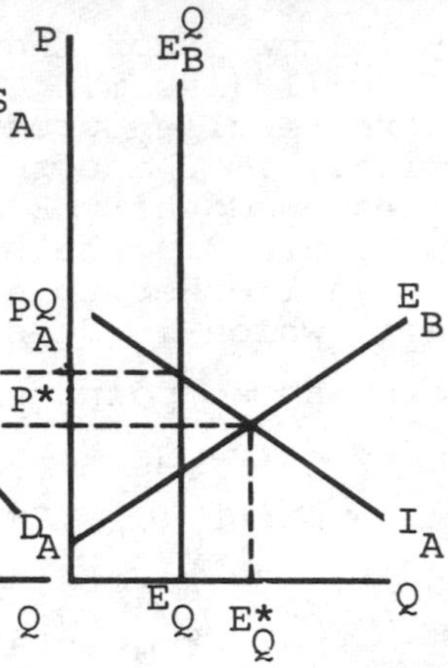

Fig. 2

Export and Import Curves

Solution: A quota is defined as a quantitative limit on imports. Unlike a tariff, it generates no tax revenue for the government of the importing country.

Before the imposition of the quota, the price of textile goods in Country A is P*, which is the prevailing world price under free trade conditions. Referring to Figure 1, it can be seen that the line extending horizontally from P* intersects Country A's supply curve, S_A, at a point (Q_A^S, P*) below and to the left of the intersection of S_A and Country A's demand curve, D_A. It intersects the demand curve at a point (Q_A^D, P*) below and to the right of the intersection of S_A and D_A. Demand and supply in Country A are therefore in disequilibrium at price P*, since Country A's producers are only willing to produce Q_A^S of textile goods at price P*, while consumers will demand Q_A^D at the same price, equilibrium is achieved through imports from Country B. Referring to Figure 2, it can be seen that Country A's import curve I_A intersects Country B's export curve E_B at the point (E_Q^*, P*). This results in the quantity E_Q^* of textile goods being exported from Country B to Country A. For the sake of simplicity, it is assumed that Country B is the only exporter of textiles to Country A, and that E_Q^* equals the excess of demand over supply (Q_A^D - Q_A^S on Figure 1) in Country A, so that Country B's exports allow demand and supply in Country A to reach equilibrium at price P*.

If Country A imposes an import quota prohibiting imports of textile goods in excess of a quantity which is less than E_Q^*, the result will be to transform Country B's export curve to a vertical line originating on the Q-axis a point representing the amount of the quota. This can be seen on Figure 2 as line E_B^Q. It originates at point E_Q, which is equal to the quota amount. Note that the new export curve E_B^Q intersects Country A's import curve I_A at a price, P_A^Q, which is greater than P*. This is the price which textile producers in Country B can now demand for textile goods exported to Country A.

Because imposition of the quota has resulted in an increase in the price of imports, textile producers in Country A are also free to raise their prices to P_A^Q, which becomes the prevailing price of textile goods in Country A. Note from Figure 1 that the line originating at P_A^Q intersects the supply curve S_A at a point (Q_A^{SQ}, P_A^Q) above and to the right of (Q_A^S, P^*), and the demand curve D_A at a point (Q_A^{DQ}, P_A^Q) at a point above and to the left of (Q_A^D, P^*). This means that textile producers in Country A can sell a greater quantity of textile goods (the difference being equal to $Q_A^{SQ} - Q_A^S$) than they could before the quota, and receive a higher price (the difference being equal to $P_A^Q - P^*$) for each unit sold. Consumers in Country A will, as a result of the quota, purchase fewer textile goods (the difference being equal to $Q_A^D - Q_A^{DQ}$) for which they will pay a higher price (P_A^Q). The effect of the quota on producers and consumers in Country A is, therefore, identical to the effect of a tariff on textile goods imposed by Country A in that it benefits producers and penalizes consumers.

In one respect, however, the effect of a quota can be distinguished from the effect of a tariff. This is in respect to its effect on textile producers in the exporting country, Country B. Since a quota, unlike a tariff, does not increase the cost to producers of goods exported, and since it results in an increase in the price received by producers for exported goods, those producers in Country B whose goods are exported to Country A under the quota will receive profits in excess of what they would receive under conditions of free trade and considerably in excess of what they would receive under a tariff.

REGIONAL ECONOMIC INTEGRATION

• PROBLEM 26-15

Define regional economic integration and give an example

of how it may be implemented.

Solution: Regional economic integration may be defined as any measures taken by two or more countries within a region, the result of which is to reduce or eliminate barriers to economic activity among the countries in the region.

Examples of such measures include: (1) the reduction or elimination of tariffs, quotas and other barriers to trade among the countries within the region; (2) equalizing tariffs and other trade restrictions directed at countries outside the region; (3) minimizing or eliminating barriers to the movement of factors of production (labor and capital) among the countries within the region; and (4) coordination of monetary, fiscal and regulatory policies among the countries within the region.

• PROBLEM 26-16

What are the three distinct approaches to the integration of markets among countries? Describe and give an example of each.

Solution: The three distinct approaches to the integration of markets among countries are: (a) free trade areas, (b) customs unions, and (c) common markets.

A description of each type follows:

A free trade area consists of a group of countries that have removed all trade barriers, including tariffs and quotas, on commodities produced within the area. However, each country may still enforce its own separate barriers to trade originating outside the free trade area. An example of this is the European Free Trade Area (EFTA) which was organized in the early 1960's by seven European nations, including the United Kingdom. The U.K. has since withdrawn from EFTA and has become a member of the EEC, described below.

A customs union is a form of economic integration in which the member countries adjust their own tariffs and quotas to establish a common set of barriers against goods produced outside the region, while eliminating barriers to trade among the member nations as in a free trade area. The Zollverein, or customs union, was the first attempt toward the unification of the various states in Germany in the mid-19th century. Another example of a customs union is the Benelux, which was established by Belgium, the Netherlands and Luxembourg in 1948. The Benelux countries are now members of the EEC.

A common market, like a customs union, is characterized by an absence of internal barriers to trade (such as tariffs and quotas) and by a unification of external barriers. The additional characteristic of a common market which distinguishes it from a customs union is the elimination of internal barriers to the free movement of factors of production (capital and labor) among the member nations. Thus, citizens or companies of one member country may build factories in other member countries, or may organize, or acquire control of, companies in other member countries. Similarly, workers who are citizens of one member country are free to seek employment in other member countries. The European Economic Community (EEC), otherwise known as the European Common Market, is the most important example of a common market in modern times.

• PROBLEM 26-17

What is the so-called European Economic Community?

Solution: The European Economic Community (EEC), better known as the European Common Market, is a group of Western European nations which have agreed to strive for economic integration. It was established in 1957 by the Treaty of Rome, the original signatories to which were Belgium, France, Italy, Luxembourg, the Netherlands and West Germany.

The Treaty required all internal tariffs (except farm products) between member countries to be gradually reduced and eventually eliminated. The various external tariffs of the members were also to be equalized over time until they constituted a common external barrier to goods produced outside the community. Finally, the signatories agreed to eliminate barriers to the free movement of factors of production (labor and capital) among themselves. In recent years they have also taken preliminary steps towards monetary union by attempting to stabilize the exchange rates of their various currencies against each other.

Since 1957, the original signatories have been joined by Denmark, the United Kingdom, and the Republic of Ireland. Greece has recently been approved for membership, and Portugal, Spain and Turkey have expressed interest in eventual membership.

• PROBLEM 26-18

What are the immediate factors that led to the formation of the European Common Market?

Solution: The immediate factors that led to the formation of the European Common Market are as follows:

a) the rapid Post-World War II economic recovery of Western Europe, which was spurred by massive United States aid provided through the European Recovery Program (more commonly called the Marshall Plan after the the Secretary of State, George C. Marshall).

b) the decision by many Europeans that Europe should not remain a group of small, politically and economically weak, competing nations.

c) the success of the European Coal and Steel Community, founded in 1952. The success of this led to plans to extend the elimination of internal trade barriers, which originally applied only to coal and steel, to include all other nonfarm products.

d) the formation in 1948 by the Netherlands, Belgium and Luxembourg of a customs union (Benelux), which was also a success.

FREE TRADE

• PROBLEM 26-19

Describe how the principle of economic efficiency may be used to demonstrate the advantages of free trade.

Solution: One demonstration of the advantages of free trade is based upon the principle of economic efficiency. This principle requires that the marginal cost of producing a good be equal for all producers and equal to the price paid by consumers. Consider the two given figures:

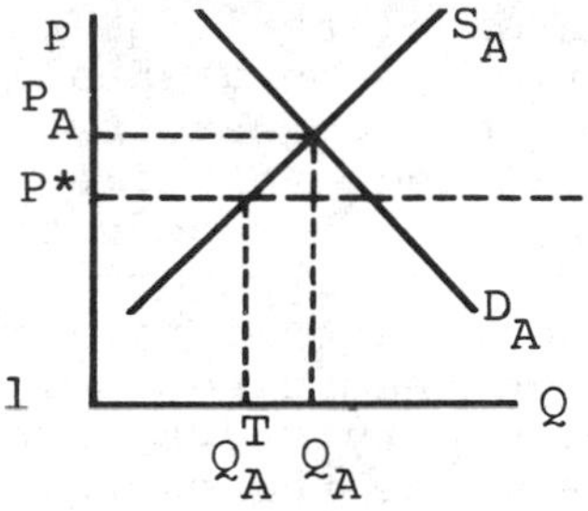

Fig. 1

Country A Supply and Demand for Wheat

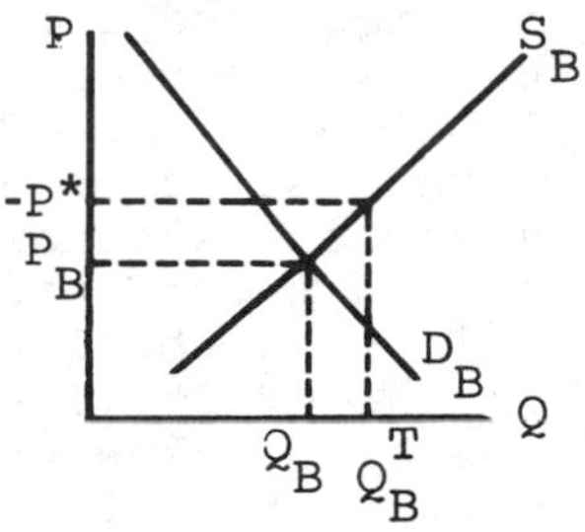

Fig. 2

Country B Supply and Demand for Wheat

Figure 1 shows the supply (S_A) and demand (D_A) curves for wheat in Country A. The curves intersect at a price level P_A which is the prevailing price for wheat in Country A assuming none is imported. At this price level, Q_A of wheat is produced. Figure 2 shows the comparable supply (S_B) and demand (D_B) curves for Country B, which intersect at price level P_B and quantity Q_B. The dashed line which runs across both figures represents the prevailing world price (P*) for wheat, which is lower than P_A but higher than P_B.

If Figure 2 were to be superimposed on Figure 1, it could be seen that S_B, the supply curve for Country B, lies to the right of S_A, the supply curve for Country A, while the two countries' demand curves are equal. This equality of demand in Countries A and B is assumed for purposes of illustration, but is not likely to occur in reality. The superimposition of Figure 2 on Figure 1 is illustrated in Figure 3.

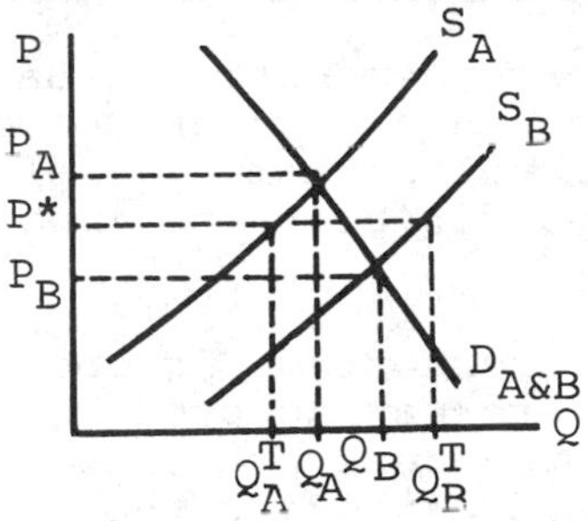

Fig. 3 Supply Curves for Wheat in Country A (S_A) and Country B (S_B), with Common Demand Curve ($D_{A\&B}$).

The fact that Country B's supply curve for wheat lies to the right of Country A's implies that the marginal cost of producing a unit (say a bushel) of wheat in Country B is less than in Country A, since it requires a lower price P in Country B to produce a given quantity Q of wheat.

The principle of economic efficiency states that whenever the marginal cost of one producer (or producing country) exceeds that of another, the total cost of producing any given quantity of the product in question can be reduced by shifting production from the higher marginal cost producer to the lower one. Equilibrium is reached when the marginal costs of all producers are equal, at which point maximum economic efficiency is realized because it is then impossible to shift production from one producer to another without increasing the total cost of producing a given quantity.

Maximum economic efficiency in the wheat market of Countries A and B can be achieved only by allowing free trade in wheat between the two countries, thereby allowing a shift in wheat production from the high cost Country A producers to the low cost Country B producers until the marginal costs of production in both countries are equal. This will occur when the price of wheat in both countries is allowed to stabilize at P*, which is the price level for wheat when all producers are operating at the same marginal cost level. This will result, referring to Figures 1, 2 and 3, in a decrease in wheat production in Country A, the high marginal cost producer, from Q_A to Q_A^T, and an increase in production in Country B, the low marginal cost producer, from Q_B to Q_B^T. The marginal cost of Country A's producers at production level Q_A^T will equal the marginal cost of Country B's producers at production level Q_B^T, and maximum economic efficiency will thereby be realized.

• PROBLEM 26-20

Is it possible in economic terms, for the benefits associated with free trade to be outweighed by the detriments? Explain using the example of two countries, A and B, one of which is a net importer and the other of which is a net exporter of soybeans.

Solution: It is always possible to demonstrate that, in purely economic terms, free trade in any given commodity, such as soybeans, will result in net economic benefits or, at worst, a break-even situation, for both the importing and exporting countries.

For example, suppose that before trade is opened consumers of soybeans in Country A are paying producers in Country A $11 a bushel. These producers are incurring a $10 per bushel cost in growing and marketing their soybeans, and receiving a $1 per bushel economic profit. Suppose now that trade is opened with Country B, and that B's soybean producers can sell their product in Country A for $7 a bushel. The result is a $4 per bushel benefit for soybean consumers in A, who previously were required to pay $11 per bushel.

Soybean producers in Country A would, however, suffer a $3 per bushel loss if they continued to sell soybeans in A, since their cost of production is $10 per bushel and competition from B has reduced the market price in A to $7 per bushel. These producers, however, have the option of using the resources (land, labor and capital) presently employed in soybean production in some alternative use (such as cotton or wheat production) in which they can at least sell what they produce at a price equal to their cost of production (including a normal bookkeeping profit) but at zero economic profit. In doing so, they would forego the $1 per bushel economic profit they received for soybeans. Recall, however, that the economic benefit to consumers in Country A from free trade is $4 per bushel. The result of free trade in soybeans for Country A is, therefore, a net economic benefit.

If the cost of producing the soybeans in Country B were higher, so that soybeans from B could be sold in Country A for $10 a bushel instead of $7, the result of free trade for A would be a break-even situation. Soybean producers in A could compete with those in B by reducing their price to $10 a bushel and foregoing their $1 per bushel economic profit, while consumers in A would enjoy a $1 per bushel benefit.

Note, however, that if the cost of producing soybeans in Country B and selling them in Country A is greater than $10 per bushel, no soybeans from B will be sold in A because A's soybean producers will always be able to undersell B's. In this case, the consumers in Country A receive no benefit, and producers in Country A suffer no detriment. Under no circumstances can the detriment suffered by producers in the importing country (Country A) as a result of free trade, outweigh, in economic terms, the benefits enjoyed by consumers in the importing country.

It can also be demonstrated that the result of free trade for the exporting country (Country B) will always be either a net economic benefit or a break-even situation.

Suppose that, before opening free trade in soybeans with Country A, soybean producers in B were able to sell their product on the domestic market for $5 a bushel, which equalled their economic cost of production. Opening trade with Country A enables these producers to increase their price to the world equilibrium price of $7 per bushel. Therefore, the producers in Country B can now earn a $2 per bushel economic profit on soybeans sold in B's domestic market.

Consumers in Country B, however, now have to pay $2 more per bushel for soybeans. Nevertheless, their total economic detriment will only equal the benefit to producers in B ($2) in the extreme case in which demand for soybeans in B is completely inelastic. In this case, consumers in B would continue to buy the same quantity of soybeans after free trade had opened as before, suffering a $2 per bushel detriment which would exactly balance the $2 per bushel benefit enjoyed by B's producers. If, as is more likely, there is some elasticity of demand for soybeans in Country B, consumers in B will be able to substitute other products for the now more expensive soybeans, and their economic detriment will be less than the economic benefit to B's producers. The overall result, therefore, is a net economic benefit for the exporting country, Country B.

• PROBLEM 26-21

What was the theory of mercantilism? How was it rebutted by the classical economists?

Solution: The mercantilist theory held that a nation must export more than it imports to prosper. It was based upon the assumption that the real wealth of a nation was determined by its reserves of precious metals, such as gold and silver. These reserves could, the mercantilists believed, be expanded if the nation retains a favorable balance of trade, that is, an excess of exports over imports. If foreign purchasers were required to pay for exports in gold or silver, the nation with a favorable trade balance would be able to increase its gold and silver reserves. Mercantilists, therefore, believed that the best interests of a nation were served by pursuing policies which strictly limited imports (such as high tariffs and low import quotas), while undertaking other policies (such as artificially keeping domestic prices low) which encouraged domestic producers to export as much as possible.

The classical economists, beginning with Adam Smith, pointed out several fallacies in the mercantilist theory. The most basic of these fallacies was the belief that money (gold and silver) constituted real wealth. Wealth, the classical economists pointed out, is properly measured as the value (which may conveniently be expressed in monetary terms) of the goods and services available to consumers. If a nation were consistently able to export more than it imported, the result would be that fewer goods would be available on the domestic market. If the excess of exports over imports was paid for in gold or silver, the further result would be that the value of these metals in terms of their ability to command goods and services in the domestic economy would decline, because there would be more gold and silver chasing fewer goods and services. In other words, there would be inflation. This inflation would, in turn, frustrate mercantilist policy by pricing the exporting country's goods out of the world market. Spain, which aggressively pursued a mercantilist policy, did in fact suffer severe inflation.

The classical economists also pointed out further self-defeating aspects of mercantilist policy. Increases in trade barriers (tariffs and quotas) by one country, they observed, would be likely to result in retaliation increases in trade barriers by other countries. The end result of such "beggar-thy-neighbor" policies would be a decrease in the overall amount of international trade. This would not only frustrate the intent of mercantilist nations to expand their precious metal reserves at the expense of other nations, but would also result in less quantity and variety of goods being available on the domestic market of any nation than would be available under conditions of free trade. As the classical economists pointed out, free trade would result in a greater quantity and variety of goods being made available to consumers at a lower price because of the operation of the principles of specialization and comparative advantage.

• PROBLEM 26-22

The supply and demand curves for beef in Country A are illustrated in the accompanying figure.

Supply and demand for beef in Country A are in equilibrium at price P_O and quantity Q_O when there is no external trade in beef. Assume the world price of beef is P*. Under free trade conditions will Country A become an exporter or importer of beef? Referring to the figure, describe the effects on beef producers and consumers in Country A if free trade in beef is allowed.

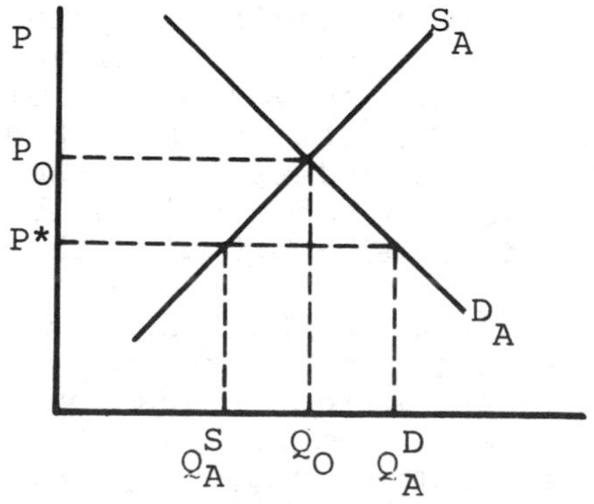

Solution: Under conditions of free trade, Country A will become an importer of beef because its domestic equilibrium price P_O exceeds the prevailing world price P*. Because of this, foreign beef producers will be eager to sell their beef in Country A, where they will receive a higher price than elsewhere. The resulting influx of imported beef into Country A will increase the available supply and cause the price of beef to drop until it stabilizes at the world price P*. It will stabilize at P* because, when it reaches this point, foreign producers will not find it profitable to increase their exports of beef to Country A, and because domestic producers will be forced to reduce their prices to this level in order to meet foreign competition.

Note in the figure that the horizontal dashed line extending from price P* intersects the supply curve S_A at a point (Q_A^S, P*) which is below and to the left of the supply and demand equilibrium point (Q_o, P_o). The quantity Q_A^S is the amount of beef which domestic producers will produce at price P*. It is less than the amount which they would produce at price P_o, the difference being equal to $Q_o - Q_A^S$.

Note also that the P* line intersects the demand curve D_A at a point (Q_A^D, P*) which is below and to the right of the equilibrium point. The quantity Q_A^D is the amount of beef which consumers in Country A will buy at price P*. It is more than they would buy at price P_o, the difference being equal to $Q_A^D - Q_o$.

Under conditions of free trade, therefore, beef producers in Country A will produce less beef than they would if no imports were allowed, and they will receive a lower price for what they produce. The immediate consequence of free trade will be that these producers will suffer. The least efficient of these producers--those operating in the portion of the supply curve between (Q_o, P_o) and (Q_A^S, P*)--will be unable to meet foreign competition and will therefore be forced to withdraw their factors of production (land, labor, etc.) from beef production and put them to other uses which are profitable. The more efficient producers--those operating in the portion of the supply curve below and to the left of (Q_A^S, P*)--will also suffer because the decline in price from P_o to P* will erode their profit margins. These producers will respond by attempting to use their resources more efficiently in order to cut costs and thereby restore profits. The ultimate consequence of free trade for producers in Country A, therefore, will be that they will allocate and use their resources in a more efficient manner.

The consequence of free trade for consumers in Country A will be that they will be able to purchase more beef at a lower price. Poor persons who could not previously afford beef will be able to add it to their diets. More affluent consumers will be able to consume more beef than before.

This increase in beef consumption will have further repercussions on the supply side of the economy because producers of substitute commodities (such as pork, poultry and fish) will experience a decrease in demand and a consequent lowering of prices. These producers will thus be forced to make adjustments in the allocation and use of their resources similar to, but less dramatic than, those made by beef producers.

• PROBLEM 26-23

The supply and demand curves for beef in Country B are illustrated in the accompanying figure.

Supply and demand for beef in Country B are in equilibrium at price P_1 and quantity Q_1 when there is no external trade in beef. Assume the world price of beef is P*. Under free trade conditions, will Country B become an exporter or importer of beef? Referring to the figure, describe the effects on beef producers and consumers in Country B if free trade in beef is allowed.

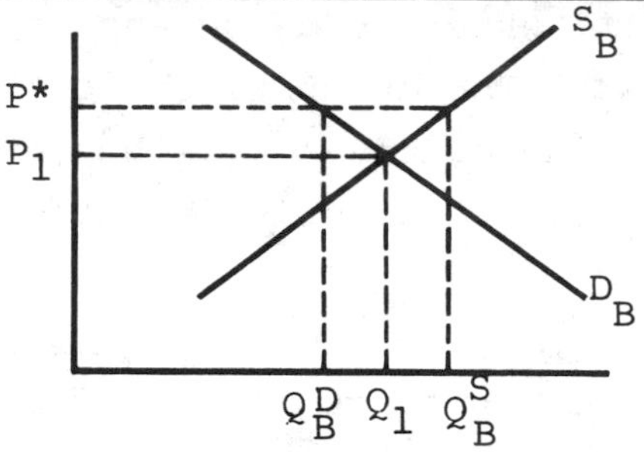

Solution: Under conditions of free trade, Country B will become an exporter of beef because its domestic equilibrium price P_1 is less than the prevailing world price P*. Producers of beef in Country B will, therefore, wish to sell as much of their beef as possible in foreign markets because they can receive a higher price for it abroad than they can in the domestic market. This will result in a decrease in the supply of beef available in Country B, which in turn will cause the price of beef in Country B to rise until it stabilizes at the world price P*. It will stabilize at this level because, if the domestic price rises above P*, domestic producers will not find it profitable to increase their exports and because an increase in the price in Country B above the world price will cause foreign producers to export beef to Country B, thereby increasing the supply and driving down the price.

Note in the figure that the horizontal dashed line extending from price P* intersects the supply curve S_B at a point (Q_B^S, P*) which is above and to the right of the supply and demand equilibrium point (Q_1, P_1). The quantity Q_B^S is the amount of beef which producers in Country B will produce at price P*. It is more than the amount which they would produce at price P_1, the difference being equal to $Q_B^S - Q_1$.

Note also that the P* line intersects the demand curve D_B at a point (Q_B^D, P*) which is above and to the left of the equilibrium point. The quantity Q_B^D is the amount of beef which consumers in Country B will buy at price P*. It is less than they would buy at P_1, the difference being equal to $Q_1 - Q_B^D$.

Under conditions of free trade, therefore, beef producers in Country B will benefit because they will produce more beef for which they will receive a higher price. Thus, in the short run, both their volume of business and their profit margin will increase. In the long run, the increased profitability of the beef business in Country B is likely to result in a diversion of resources such as land and labor from less profitable uses to beef production.

Consumers in Country B will, however, be penalized by free trade because they will be able to purchase less beef, for which they will be forced to pay a higher price. Poorer consumers may be forced to eliminate beef from their diets, and the more affluent will reduce their beef consumption. This will, in turn, affect the supply side of the economy by increasing the demand for (and thereby increasing the price of) substitute commodities such as pork, poultry and fish.

Answer

To be cover
when testi
yourself

SHORT ANSWER QUESTIONS FOR REVIEW

Choose the correct answer.

1. The advocates of tariff say that the imposition of high tariffs, assuming there is no retaliation, will increase money wages. A correct criticism of this argument is: (a) such tariffs would tend to lower money wages, not increase them (b) such tariffs would have no effect upon money wages (c) any rise in money wages would be offset by a drop in employment (d) that any rise in money wages would tend to be offset by a rise in the cost of living (e) none of the above. d

2. The Common Market as an institution has contributed to: (a) the expansion of member nations' economies (b) eliminating all trade barriers between member nations and nonmember nations (c) free movement of capital and labor across international boundaries (d) lower tariffs among member nations and nonmember nations a

3. The infant-economy argument for tariff protection (a) is true if a country specializes in the production of only one good (b) contradicts the theory of comparative advantage (c) says that the long-run terms of trade are always shifting against agricultural products (d) is designed to stabilize a country's production possibilities (e) is valid if the production-possibility curve can be shifted outward in the direction of a new comparative advantage. e

4. The General Agreement on Tariffs and Trade (GATT) was formed to: (a) monitor American tariff system efficiently (b) achieve tariff reduction and eliminate import quotas (c) relax highly restrictive trade policies (d) increase the volume of trade between the international economies b

5. By the "terms of trade," we mean: (a) the difference between exports and imports (b) the ratio of exports to imports (c) the difference between current account and capital account (d) the ratio of short-term capital movements to long-term capital movements (e) the ratio of export prices to import prices. e

6. In addition to raising prices and attracting

Answer
To be covered when testing yourself

gold or international reserves into a country, a highly protectionist tariff may: (a) cause general living standards to rise (b) leave real wages unchanged, although money wages rise (c) increase money wages more than the cost of living so that real wages fall (d) increase money wages less than the cost of living so that real wages fall (e) do none of the above. — d

7. Of the following, which one failed to serve as a stimulant in the American economy and resulted in retaliatory restrictions by affected nations? (a) Sherman Act (b) Smoot-Hawley Act (c) Reciprocal Trade Act (d) Kennedy Act — b

8. Which one of the following arguments for a tariff may be a valid economic argument, in the sense of benefiting all countries in the long run? (a) the peril-point tariff (b) the cheap-foreign-labor (c) the terms of trade (d) the infant industry (e) the scientific tariff. — d

9. Which one of the following best describes the protectionist view? (a) That free trade contributes to structural adjustment and resource employment (b) In the long-run a nation must cut off all imports to survive (c) Introduce intranational trade restrictions to protect small firms (d) Free trade contributes to malstructural adjustment and resource unemployment — d

10. A subsidy, rather than a tariff or a quota, might be the appropriate measure if: (a) we wish to maintain employment in ship-building (b) we wish to maintain the level of employment (c) the oil reserves and capacity are considered necessary for national security (d) demand is growing for precision products, currently being made in Germany and Japan (e) all the above are true. — c

11. Beggar-my-neighbor high-tariff policies: (a) might increase employment at home in the short run (b) are designed to reduce unemployment abroad (c) are based on a foreign nation's absolute advantage in production (d) are designed to raise needed government revenue (e) do none of the above. — a

SHORT ANSWER QUESTIONS FOR REVIEW

Answer
To be covered when testing yourself

12. Which one of the following did the Geneva Round not concentrate on? (a) Nontariff barriers (b) Freedom of access to raw materials (c) Freedom of access to foodstuffs (d) Tariff barriers (e) Import quotas and licensing requirements — d

13. To diversify, lessen risk, and guard against deteriorating export-import terms of trade is an argument popular with: (a) AFL-CIO trade unionists (b) Japan and the common market (c) the military-industrial complex (d) Latin-Americans (e) jingoists and chauvinists. — d

14. Which of the following arguments comes closest to constituting a legitimate economic exception to the case for free trade? (a) the increase in domestic employment argument (b) the protect high domestic wages argument (c) the diversification for stability argument (d) the military self-sufficiency argument (e) the infant industry argument. — e

15. An American tariff on linen will tend to: (a) raise U.S. real wages (b) help domestic linen producers and factors with a domestic comparative advantage in linen production (c) help nonlinen producers here (d) create deadweight loss to the degree that the consumer pays dollars to the tax collector (e) do none of the above. — b

<u>Fill in the blanks.</u>

16. The ______________ argument calls for increasing quotas or duties if domestic production becomes very small — peril-point tariff

17. The ______________ argument for tariff protection presupposes that the comparative advantage which is based upon technological superiority is more transient than the one which is based upon resource endowments. — diffusion-of-technology

18. The ______________ can best be described as an excise tax on an imported good. — tariff

19. An ______________ tariff is a tariff that will somewhat improve a country's terms of trade and keep imports and exports at a level favorable to that country. — optimal

SHORT ANSWER QUESTIONS FOR REVIEW

	Answer (To be covered when testing yourself)
20. By the ____________, we mean the ratio of the export prices to the import prices.	terms of trade
21. A tariff on imports of goods into America that labor can produce more cheaply abroad would tend to ____________ the price of those goods to the U.S. public.	raise
22. ____________ are equivalent to tariffs if the government auctions off the limited supply of quota licenses to the highest bidders.	Quotas
23. The basic effect of a tariff is to divert resources from their most ____________ uses.	efficient
24. The ____________ argument for tariffs will only improve one country's terms of trade if it is assumed that other countries do not retaliate.	terms-of-trade
25. ____________ quotas are designed to persuade foreigners to place limits on their exports to the United States.	Voluntary
26. Leontief claimed that America tends to import ____________-intensive rather than labor-intensive goods.	capital
27. The ____________ clause in reciprocal trade agreements means that any tariff reductions in the United States negotiated with a specific nation will automatically apply to many other nations.	most-favored-nation
28. If oil reserves and capacity are considered necessary for U.S. national defense, economists might recommend that oil imports be encouraged and ____________ be granted for exploration of standby oil reserves.	subsidies
29. If we have a tariff just large enough to equalize foreign costs of production with ours, we shall negate the benefits of ____________.	comparative advantage
30. "____________ tariff reductions benefit the economies of foreign countries at the expense of American workers and their employers" is an incorrect statement for it ignores the fact that "American workers and their employers" in some industries would benefit from increased exports.	multilateral

Determine whether the following statements are true or false.

SHORT ANSWER QUESTIONS FOR REVIEW

Answer

To be covered when testing yourself

31. A tariff can never increase real wages for workers in the protected industry. — False

32. An argument for free trade is that it encourages a more efficient allocation of resources. — True

33. Cutting tariffs might increase government revenues from tariffs. — True

34. GATT as an international organization is responsible for negotiating comprehensive trade agreements among international governments. — False

35. A customs duty aids in the optimal allocation of international resources. — False

36. A tariff which increases the money wages of domestic workers is not necessarily a good thing either for the public or for those workers. — True

37. Many tariffs are the results of political pressures. — True

38. The International Trade Organization is comprised of seven European nations and dedicated to the purpose of abolishing trade barriers and integrating their economies. — False

39. A sales tax is a less distorting way of raising revenue from a tariff. — True

40. In international trade and finance, to correct a payment deficit, one should reduce exports and increase imports. — False

41. Careful analysis shows that no one gains from a tariff for protection against the competition of cheap foreign labor. — False

42. If a foreign country imposes a tariff on our exports, then it would always pay for us to retaliate. — False

43. The optimal tariff is one large enough to improve the terms of trade and low enough to maintain a favorable level of exchange of goods. — True

44. Noneconomic goals may constitute valid arguments for freer trade as well as for tariffs. — True

45. An invisible tariff is one low enough to improve

Answer

To be covered when testing yourself

the terms of trade and high enough to maintain a favorable level of exchange of goods. | False

CHAPTER 27

BALANCE OF PAYMENTS

Basic Attacks and Strategies for Solving Problems in this Chapter. See pages 910 to 922 for step-by-step solutions to problems.

Buying goods, services, or assets from foreign countries is complicated by the fact that countries use different monetary systems. In order for these transactions to take place, there must be some way to change domestic into foreign money and vice-versa. The foreign exchange market is where these transactions take place. Its participants include banks and other financial intermediaries, consumers, business firms, and governments.

The **balance of payments** is a summary statement of the transactions that take place between a country and the rest of the world during a given period of time.

The balance of payments uses a double-entry system of bookkeeping. Transactions are recorded as debits and credits. From the standpoint of the United States, a debit transaction is one that requires us to supply dollars. Examples of debit transactions are:

1) imports of goods and services

2) gifts made to foreigners (also known as remittances)

3) acquisition of a long-term asset or reduction of a long-term liability (i.e., stocks, bonds, real capital)

4) acquisition of a short-term asset or reduction of a short-term liability (i.e., checking account balances or short-term bonds)

From the standpoint of the United States, a credit transaction is one that causes foreigners to demand dollars. Examples of credit transactions are:

1) exports of goods and services

2) gifts received from foreigners

3) sale of a long-term asset or long-term liability increased

4) sale of a short-term asset or short-term liability incurred

All transactions are placed into specific categories. The simplest breakdown is between the current account and the capital account. The current account records all transactions involving goods and services. The capital account records all transactions involving short- and long-term assets. A blank balance of payments ledger might appear as in the table.

	Debit	Credit
Current Account		
Capital Account		

Schematic of the Balance of Payments Account

The beginning of wisdom regarding the balance of payments is to realize that **every transaction gives rise to both debit and credit entries.** Consequently, the balance of payments must always balance in an accounting sense. For example,

1) Americans buy $800,000 in automobiles from Germany, paying for them with dollar checks drawn on American banks. The import of goods leads to a $800,000 debit in the current account. The German acquisition of dollar demand deposits increases our short-term liabilities and results in a credit of $800,000 to the capital account. Enter these transactions in the ledger.

2) The French buy the equivalent of $2,000,000 in private American corporation bonds, paying for them with franc checks. The sale of the bonds (long-term assets) led to a $2,000,000 credit in the capital account. The acquisition of francs (short-term assets) leads to a $2,000,000 debit in the capital account. Enter these transactions in the ledger.

3) American tourists travel in Holland, spending the equivalent of $5,000 on souvenirs. The guilders spent were obtained by exchanging dollars at a Dutch bank. The souvenirs are an import resulting in a $5,000 debit in the current account. The Dutch have acquired dollars, leading to a $5,000 credit in the capital account. Enter these transactions in the ledger.

If we sum all debits and credits, both sides must be equal. See the table below.

	Debit	Credit
Current Account	$ 800,000 5,000	
Capital Account	2,000,000	$ 800,000 2,000,000 5,000
Total	$2,805,000	$2,805,000

Balance of Payments Example

Balance of payments "imbalances" result from looking at just a portion of the ledger. Some important balances are:

1) **Balance of Trade**—The net balance of debits and credits for goods. Now shown in the table above.

2) **Balance on Current Account**—The net balance of debits and credits for goods and services. A $805,000 debit balance in the table above.

3) **Balance on Capital Account**—The net balance of debits and credits for short- and long-term assets. A $805,000 credit balance in the table above.

The **exchange rate** is simply the price of one nation's currency in terms of another's. The table on the following page shows exchange rates existing between the United States dollar and selected other currencies on March 12, 1990. For example, $1 buys 1.917 Dutch guilders, therefore 1 guilder buys $.5216 (If $1.00 buys 1.917 guilders, then 1 guilder buys $1.00/1.917 = $.5216). A product costing $25.00 in the United States would cost 47.93 guilders; a product costing 100 guilders would cost $52.16 (this ignores transportation and transaction costs).

Selected Exchange Rates, March 12, 1990	
\$1.00 = .6202 British pounds	1 pound = \$1.6123
\$1.00 = 5.753 French francs	1 franc = \$.1738
\$1.00 = 1.917 Dutch guilders	1 guilder = \$.5216
\$1.00 = 152.15 Japanese yen	1 yen = \$.006572
\$1.00 = 1.7065 German marks	1 mark = \$.5860
\$1.00 = 2747.93 Mexican pesos	1 peso = \$.000365
\$1.00 = 1.1802 Canadian dollars	1 dollar = \$.8473

If the dollar/guilder rate changes to \$1 = 2.25 guilders, we say the dollar has appreciated. Each dollar will buy more guilders. The dollar has become more valuable. The guilder has depreciated because each guilder will now buy fewer dollars than before.

Exchange rates are set in the foreign exchange market by the forces of demand and supply. For example, if the Dutch want to acquire our goods, services, and assets, they must acquire dollars. This is the basis of the demand curve for dollars. The more valuable the guilder, the greater the quantity demanded of dollars because a valuable guilder makes American goods, services, and assets a better buy to the Dutch. If Americans want to acquire Dutch goods, services, and assets, they must acquire guilders. To do so, they must supply dollars. Here, the more valuable the dollar, the greater the quantity supplied (more advanced treatments allow the supply curve to have a negative slope in some cases).

At the exchange rate \$1 = 2.25 guilders, the strength of the American dollar makes Dutch goods, services, and assets a good buy for Americans. The weakness of the guilder makes American goods, services, and assets less attractive to the Dutch. Consequently, there is an excess supply of dollars and that will drive down the exchange.

At the exchange rate \$1 = 1.75 guilders, the weakness of the dollar makes Dutch goods, services, and assets a bad buy for Americans. The strength of the guilder makes American goods, services, and assets more attractive to the Dutch. Consequently, there is an excess demand for dollars and that will drive up the exchange rate.

At the exchange rate \$1 = 2 guilders, quantity demanded equals quantity supplied and the market is in equilibrium.

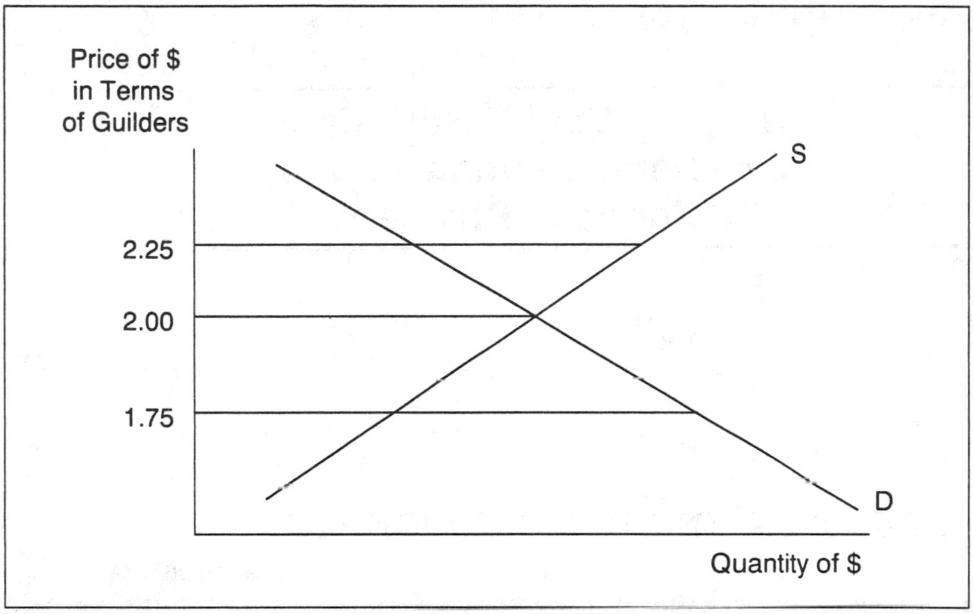

Equilibrium in the Market for Dollars

Other factors influencing the demand and supply of dollars include relative national income, relative national price levels, and relative interest rates. Any factor making American goods, services, and assets more attractive—a rise in foreign income or price levels or a fall in interest rates relative to American levels—will increase the demand for dollars. Any factor making foreign goods, services, and assets more attractive—a rise in American income or price levels or a fall in interest rates relative to foreign levels—will increase the supply of dollars.

The purchasing power parity doctrine (PPP) says exchange rates will adjust to equalize the purchasing power of a unit of currency in all countries. For example, assume perfume sells for \$20 a bottle in the U.S. and 50 guilders a bottle in Holland. PPP says the exchange rate will adjust to \$1 = 2.5 guilders, so that both Americans and the Dutch are indifferent between buying the perfume in America or Holland. If the exchange rate was \$1 = 3 guilders, perfume in Holland would cost Americans \$16.67 and perfume in America would cost the Dutch 60 guilders. This would lead both countries to buy perfume in Holland and the guilder would appreciate in value. If the exchange rate was \$1 = 2 guilders, perfume would be cheaper in America (can you calculate the price in guilders?). The demand for dollars would cause the dollar to appreciate. The only equilibrium is at PPP.

Step-by-Step Solutions to Problems in this Chapter, "Balance of Payments"

DEFINITION AND BASIC CONCEPTS

• PROBLEM 27-1

What is the international balance of payments?

Solution: The international balance of payments is an annual accounting statement, prepared by the various nations of the world. In it all the transactions which take place between a nation's residents (including individuals, businesses, and governmental units) and the residents of all other foreign nations are summarized.

Despite being called a "balance" of payments, this statement is more like a profit and loss statement than a balance sheet. On it a nation records all sales and purchases from foreign nations and accounts for any differences between sales (receipts) and purchases (expenditures).

• PROBLEM 27-2

In speaking about the balance of payments, what are autonomous and accommodating transactions?

Solution: Autonomous transactions are independent of the balance of payments in the sense that they arise from, or are caused by, factors lying outside the balance of payments statement itself. Five autonomous items are: exports, imports, remittances, public transactions, and net capital movements. Imports and exports come about because of differences in comparative costs. Remittances and public transactions are based upon humanitarian, political, or military considerations. Capital movements arise because of expectations about returns on foreign investments.

Accommodating transactions, on the other hand, occur in order to account or compensate for differences between the inpayments and outpayments which arise from a nation's autonomous transactions. Accommodating transactions can be thought of as balancing transactions, which take place, to accommodate or finance payment imbalances associated with autonomous transactions. For example, suppose a nation's autonomous transactions are such that its exports are $20 billion and its imports are $25 billion, it receives remittances of $2 billion, public grants of $1 billion, and net capital inflows of $1 billion. Thus the outpayments are $25 billion, while the inpayments are only $24 (20 + 2 + 1 + 1) billion. This country has a $1 billion disequilibrium, or deficit in its balance of payments. Therefore this nation must undertake $1 billion of financing, or accommodating transactions to account for the difference between autonomous inpayments and outpayments. We can therefore say that the occurrence of accommodating or financing transactions is evidence of a balance of payments disequilibrium.

• PROBLEM 27-3

The following items are components of the United States Balance of Payments: Remittances, Government Transactions, Capital Movements. Explain each.

Solution: Remittances are private gifts or grants given by people in one country to people in another country. Examples of remittances are contributions to overseas missions and pensions for American citizens living abroad. In 1976, net remittances amounted to an outlay of $1.9 billion by the United States.

Government transactions involve the loans and grants made by one nation's government to another nation. In the case of the United States, these loans and grants are for economic and military aid and in part reflect our ideological competition with the Soviet Union. In 1976, net government transactions amounted to an outlay of $3.1 billion.

Capital movements occur when people invest money or real capital in interests outside of their home country. A corporation might decide to construct a plant in Asia. An investor might place money in a Swiss bank. These are both examples of capital movements.

If investors can realize greater profit overseas than in the United States, they will surely go international with their investments. And so in 1976, $40.5 billion were invested abroad by Americans. Also that year $20 billion was invested in the United States by foreigners so that net capital movements amounted to an outflow of $20.5 billion.

• PROBLEM 27-4

What is Gresham's Law?

Solution: Gresham's Law simply stated, is "Bad money drives out good". This means that when two types of money are in circulation and they have equal stated values, but they are not equally demanded (that is one currency has a much stronger backing than the other, causing people to prefer it) the less desirable type will drive the other out of circulation. Why? Because people will substitute the desired type of money for the less desired type in their money balances, i.e., they will hoard the desired type and spend the undesired type as quickly as possible. Because less and less of the desired type of money is left in circulation its desirability will increase even further, accelerating the process. Finally the only type of money left in circulation is the undesired type of money.

DEPRECIATION VS. DEVALUATION

• PROBLEM 27-5

If the price of a pound falls from \$2.10 to \$2.00, is that depreciation or devaluation? Explain the difference.

Solution: By definition, the fall in the price of one currency in terms of one or all others is called "depreciation." The drop in the price of the pound above therefore is an instance of depreciation. Devaluation, on the other hand, is usually defined to mean a rise in the price of gold relative to the currency in question. Therefore if gold prices increase from \$420 to \$450 an ounce, a devaluation of the currency has occurred.

• PROBLEM 27-6

Why did the United States have to devalue its dollar in 1971 and again in 1973?

Solution: Nations cause changes in their exchange rates to avoid disequilibrium in the balance of payments.

The very strong dollar became an obstacle to exports. Domestic inflation within the United States was higher than the inflation rates abroad, in particular in Japan and West Germany. American export prices rose rapidly and the American export products became less competitive in the world markets. As a result the exports decreased. Simultaneously, foreign import products being cheaper, imports increased dramatically. The U.S. balance of payments worsened, and huge amounts of dollars, in payment of the imports, began to inundate the financial markets, in West-Europe in particular, and created the phenomenon of the uncontrollable Euro-dollar. The monetary authorities in West-Europe began to lose control over their domestic money stocks, and alarmed, started to pressure the United States to lower the value of the dollar versus their currencies. For example, the West German Bundesbank had to buy billions of dollars in 1972 to keep the price of a dollar from falling below 3.2 DM. Finally, the United States, struggling with a worsening balance of payments decided to devalue its dollar, rather than attempting to correct the deficit of the balance of payments by pursuing a tight money policy.

EXCHANGE RATES AND THE FLOW OF MONEY

• **PROBLEM 27-7**

Suppose an American firm sells a large piece of machinery to a British firm for $40,000. Describe the flow of money in this situation. Assume the exchange rate is $2 = £1.

Solution: Since the exchange rate is $2 for £1, the British importer must pay $\$40,000 \times \frac{£1}{\$2} = £20,000$ to the American exporter. To pay the £20,000, the British buyer draws a check on his demand deposit in a London bank for £20,000 and sends this to the American seller.

Since the American exporter can not pay his expenses with pounds, he takes the check for £20,000 and sells it to some large American bank, probably located in New York, which is a dealer in foreign exchange. The American firm is then given $40,000 in demand deposits in the New York bank in exchange for the £20,000.

Finally the New York bank deposits the check for £20,000 in a London bank for future sale.

• **PROBLEM 27-8**

Suppose the balance sheet of an American bank looks, in its simplified form as follows (in 1000 dollars):

Assets		Liabilities and Capital	
Cash	$2,000	Demand deposits	$12,000
		Time & savings deposits	1,200
Balances in British bank	1,000	Deposits of states	600
U.S. Securities	1,500	Common stock	200
Obligations	3,000	Surplus	1,000
Loans	9,000	Undivided profits	1,500
	$16,500		$16,500

An American importer who is a depositor at this bank, buys $700 worth of British pounds to pay for his imports from Great Britain. British exporter deposits $2000 worth of British pounds in the bank in exchange for dollars. The State of New York sells an obligation of $1,000 to the bank and withdraws $700 in the form of cash.

How is the balance statement of this bank changed? How much are the excess reserves in the original and in the new situation if the legal reserve requirement is 24%?

Solution: We will solve this problem step by step by tracing the effects on the assets, liabilities, and net worth.

When the American importer buys $700 worth of British pounds, the balances in the British bank and the demand deposits are both decreased by $700.

Assets		Liabilities	
Balances in British bank	-700	Demand deposits	-700

The British exporter sells $2000 worth of British pounds to the bank; assuming that he has a deposit in the bank we see that both the balances in the British bank and the demand deposits are increased by $2,000.

Assets		Liabilities	
Balances in British bank	+2,000	Demand deposits	+2,000

The State of New York sells an obligation of $1,000 to the bank. The obligation is an asset for the bank. The bank in return increases the deposit of the New York State, subsumed under Deposits of States, by $1,000. The Deposits of States is a liability: the deposit is a promise to keep money ready when needed.

Assets		Liabilities	
Obligations	+$1,000	Deposits of States	+$1,000

The next step is that the State of New York takes out the cash needed; so the cash balance decreases by $700 and the New York State deposit decreases by $700.

Assets		Liabilities	
Cash	-$700	Deposits of States	-$700

When we substitute these four changes into the original balance statement the following statement results:

Assets		Liabilities and Capital	
Cash	1,300	Demand deposits	13,300
Balances in British bank	2,300	Time & Savings deposits	1,200
U.S. Securities	1,500	Deposits of States	900
Obligations	4,000	Common Stock	200
Loans	9,000	Surplus	1,000
	18,100	Undivided profits	1,500
			18,100

The actual reserves in the original situation totalled 2,000 cash + 1,000 worth of British pounds = $3,000, and the actual reserve/demand deposit ratio was

$$\frac{3,000}{12,000} = 0.25$$

In the new situation the total of the reserves is

$$1,300 + 2,300 = \$3,600$$

and the actual reserve/demand deposit ratio is

$$\frac{3,600}{13,300} = 0.27$$

The legal reserve requirement is 0.24 so in both situations there are excess reserves; in the new situation more than in the original situation. In the original situation the required reserves are 0.24 x 12,000 = $2,880. So the excess reserves are 3,000 - 2,880 = $120. In the new situation the required reserves are 0.24 x 13,300 = $3,192; in this case the excess reserves are 3,600 - 3,192 = $408.

• PROBLEM 27-9

Suppose Americans experience an increase in demand for British racing cars. How will this affect the exchange rate between the U.S. dollar and the British pound?

Solution: As demand for British sports cars increases, demand for the pound will increase. This is due to the fact that U.S. demand for pounds is a derived demand schedule. On Figure 1, demand increases from DD to D^1D^1. D^1D^1.

Assuming that the supply of pounds is not perfectly elastic and has remained stable, the equilibrium rate will increase from P to P^1. At P^1, a pound is worth more (in dollars) than at P.

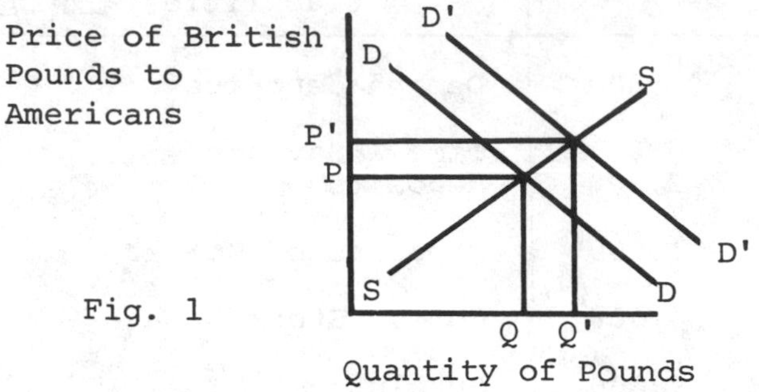

Fig. 1

We can see the same effect from the following sequence:

(1) As Americans buy English sports cars, the amount of dollars in England increases, since the Americans buy in dollars.

(2) This means that, temporarily, the supply of dollars in England is greater than the demand for dollars. Thus, the price of dollars in terms of pounds must fall, or equivalently, the price of pounds (in dollars) must rise.

• PROBLEM 27-10

Suppose the price of a British pound is \$2.00 and the price of a German mark is \$0.40.

a) What should the price of a British pound be in terms of German marks?

b) If the market was paying 6 marks for every British pound, how might an Englishman make an arbitrage profit?

Solution: a) We are given the value of pounds and marks in terms of dollars, but must now compute the value of a pound in terms of marks. We will use the following operations to compute "marks per pound".

marks per pound = marks per dollar x dollar per pound

We are told that dollars per pound = 2. To compute marks per dollar, we notice that dollars per mark = 0.40. Therefore to find marks per dollar, we take the reciprocal. So marks per dollar = $\frac{1}{0.40}$ = 2.5.

Returning to,

marks per pound = marks per dollar x dollars per pound

we get,

marks per pound = 2.5 x 2

= 5.

Therefore each pound has a price of 5 marks.

b) We see above that pounds have an equilibrium price of 5 marks. If the market was paying 6 marks for every pound, an Englishman could sell one pound for six marks. Then he could convert six marks into 0.40 x 6 = $2.40 using the U.S.-German exchange rate of 1 mark = $0.40. Finally realizing that 1 pound = $2.40, our Englishman could get back his original one pound and still have $2.40 - 2.00 = $0.40 left over as profit. When a profit can be made by juggling various currencies as above, we refer to this as arbitrage profit.

• PROBLEM 27-11

Mr. Morris wishes to purchase an MGB convertible. When he called on his local British-Leyland dealer he was quoted a price of £3500. Mr. Morris had planned on spending no more than $7500 for the car.

a) If the exchange rate is £1 = $2.20, can he afford the car?

b) How low must the exchange rate be in order for Mr. Morris to buy the car?

Solution: a) With the MGB costing £3500 and an exchange rate of £1 = $2.20, we find that the price in dollars =

$$3500 \times \frac{\$2.20}{£1} = \$7700 .$$

Therefore since Mr. Morris had only wanted to spend $7500, he can not afford the sports car.

b) In order for him to be able to afford it, the price of the pound must go down (assuming the price of the MGB is constant at £3500). To compute just how far down the price of the pound must go, we return to the equation in part a) substituting "x" for the exchange rate, i.e.,

$$\$3500\ x = \$7500$$

$$x = \$2.14$$

Therefore the price of the pound must be $2.14 in order for the MGB to cost $7500. If £1 > $2.14 Mr. Morris can not afford the MGB (as shown in part a). If £1 < $2.14, Mr. Morris will have money left over after he purchases the car.

Answer
To be covered when testing yourself

SHORT ANSWER QUESTIONS FOR REVIEW

Choose the correct answer.

1. A country experiences net capital outflow. What is the most plausible explanation for it? (a) Appreciation of currency (b) Lowering of tariff's on the country's products (c) Higher rates of return on foreign investments (d) Introduction of the gold standard. — c

2. The balance of payments deficit can be financed by (a) devaluation of currency (b) increasing the foreign holdings of domestic currency (c) spending the reserves of foreign currencies (d) b and c. — d

3. An organization whose major function is to stabilize international monetary relations is (a) EEC (b) IMF (c) OPEC (d) Federal Reserve. — b

4. The purpose of governmental action to control foreign exchange and ration the inflowing foreign funds among producers might be to (a) restrict imports and eliminate the balance of payments deficit (b) increase the value of domestic currency (c) to develop the slow growing industries (d) all of the above. — a

5. A serious problem with the Gold Standard system is that (a) it poses a threat of severe inflation or depression as a result of the process of monetary adjustment (b) there is not enough gold in the world to make it a good medium of exchange (c) disequilibrium often persists (d) prices have a strong tendency to fluctuate. — a

6. The Gold Standard can be effective as an international monetary system only if (a) all nations possess gold (b) gold is allowed to move freely in and out of the countries (c) all the currencies are directly convertible into gold (d) the price of gold is fixed. — b

7. The system of freely fluctuating exchange rates (a) is safer than the Gold Standard for those involved in international trade (b) makes international trade a risky undertaking (c) has a stabilizing effect on the economies (d) improves a non-exporting nation's terms of trade. — b

8. The U.S. had balance of payments problems over recent years, namely, the balance consistently showed deficit. This situation was caused by

(a) excess of American exports over imports (b) excess of American imports over exports (c) large net outflow of capital and substantial aid to foreign countries (d) lack of demand for American goods. c

9. The transactions undertaken for the sole purpose of accommodating the balance of payments surplus/deficit are called (a) autonomous transactions (b) equilibrating transactions (c) accommodating transactions (d) export-import transactions. c

10. The U.S. sells grain to other countries because (a) of its balance of payments deficit (b) it has a comparative advantage in the production of grain (c) its government is more thoughtful of other people's needs than other governments (d) it wants to reduce domestic grain prices. b

11. Which of the following has a positive effect on the balance of payments? (a) tariffs (b) quotas (c) reduction of imports (d) all of the above. d

12. The net result of autonomous and accommodating transactions is (a) always a zero-balance (b) usually deficit (c) usually surplus (d) impossible to predict. a

13. Suppose an American dollar depreciated in value relative to a Swiss franc. This means that for an American firm under contract to buy 10,000 Swiss watches the transaction becomes (a) more profitable (b) more risky (c) economically less attractive since the dollar price of watches increased automatically with the depreciation of the dollar (d) in no way different. c

14. The U.S. government makes a decision to decrease its possessions of foreign currencies and at the same time to increase the amount of dollars held by foreigners. This action is likely to be the result of (a) balance of payments surplus (b) Gold Standard (c) balance of payments deficit (d) inflation. a

15. A country's balance of payments statement for 1975 shows no accommodating transactions. This means that (a) the country lives under the Gold Standard (b) the worth of inflowing and outflowing goods and capital, as a result of foreign trade and international transactions which the country engaged in, is one and the

SHORT ANSWER QUESTIONS FOR REVIEW

	Answer To be covered when testing yourself
same (c) the exchange rates float freely (d) imports are equal to exports.	b
Fill in the blanks.	
16. Pensions paid to American citizens living abroad have a ____________ effect on the American balance of payments.	negative
17. Governments often use ____________ to reduce the incentive for foreign companies to sell goods in their countries.	tariffs
18. ____________ is a policy of setting a specific quantitative limit on the amount of certain foreign products which can be sold in a country.	Quota
19. Under the system of ____________ the depreciation of a currency is caused solely and directly by the reduction in the market demand for it.	freely floating exchange rates
20. When the world currencies are tied to gold the equilibrating mechanism cited by Hume ensures that the price level in the countries having a balance of payments surplus will ____________ and their exports will become ____________.	rise, more expensive
21. An American firm entering an agreement to buy Japanese cars at a given price is mostly worried about the possible ____________.	deprecia- tion of the dollar
22. When, under the Gold Standard, the American dollar is devalued and the German mark is not, devaluation also becomes ____________.	depreciatio
23. When the exchange rate floats freely the expectations abroad of a high future level of inflation in the U.S. are likely to cause the demand for American dollars to ____________ and their value in terms of other currencies to ____________	fall, be reduced
24. Devaluations are characteristic of the ________ system.	Gold Standard
25. A transaction involving a net expenditure of a foreign currency is registered as a ____________ on the balance of payments list.	debit item
26. If the rate of inflation in one country is consistently higher than in another and the exchange rates are flexible, the currency of the first country is likely to ____________ relative to the currency of the second country.	depreciate

SHORT ANSWER QUESTIONS FOR REVIEW

Answer
To be covered when testing yourself

Question	Answer
27. Suppose today's price of a British pound in the exchange market is \$2.50. An American importer will be indifferent between paying £100 or ____________ for a British good.	\$250
28. The balance of payments statement is technically always ____________.	in balance
29. A country's payments deficit or surplus are determined by the net effect of ____________ transactions.	autonomous
30. Quotas and tariffs have a function of protecting local industries from ____________.	foreign competition

Determine whether the following statements are true or false.

Question	Answer
31. Foreign trade is beneficial for any state because it expands the possibilities of consumption for the population.	True
32. The exchange rates between a dollar and a German mark, and between a British pound and a dollar are completely independent.	False
33. Under the Gold Standard the exchange rates are basically stable.	True
34. Under the floating system the exchange rates are fixed by the government.	False
35. The Gold Standard system creates the situation where the wealth of a population is determined strictly by the state reserves of gold.	False
36. Increase in the demand for foreign goods may make the foreign currencies more expensive relative to a dollar and is therefore likely to be inflationary.	True
37. A price and wage rise of 50%, with everything else held constant, will inflate the value of a currency by the same 50%.	True
38. The rise in the price of gold relative to a currency automatically depreciates this currency.	False
39. Depreciation and devaluation are not mutually exclusive.	True
40. The restoration of equilibrium of the international trade markets require the appreciation	

	Answer To be covered when testing yourself
of undervalued currencies.	True
41. One of the disadvantages of the Gold Standard is that the rate of gold mining may have a destabilizing influence on the level of prices in the economy.	True
42. On the balance of international payments sheet any item that adds to the country's supply of foreign currencies is a debit item.	False
43. Both the visible merchandise items and the invisible service items play a role in the national balance of payments.	True
44. The expansion of tourist activity can be part of the program to eliminate the balance of payments deficit in an economy.	False
45. The military aid to allies of the U.S. is a credit item for the U.S. since it is equivalent to investing capital abroad.	False

CHAPTER 28

AGRICULTURAL ECONOMICS

Basic Attacks and Strategies for Solving Problems in this Chapter. See pages 923 to 948 for step-by-step solutions to problems.

Agriculture is an industry that is undeniably important to a nation's well-being, yet in country after country there is discussion of the "farm problem." There are striking similarities in the "farm problem" from one nation to the next, and analysis of the issues involved is an enlightening way to show the usefulness of basic economic theory.

Fundamentally, there are two basic farm problems, a long run and a short run problem. The long run problem is the downward trend in the prices of agricultural commodities. This is easily understandable. For one thing, the income elasticity of farm products is likely to be quite low. People need to satisfy their need for food before most other needs. Consequently, expenditures on food will be a large proportion of a household's budget when income is low. Once minimal standards are attained, people are unlikely to want to increase their food consumption very much, so expenditures are not likely to rise very rapidly as income rises so the proportion of the budget spent on food will be lower at higher incomes. For another thing, the supply curve of food has been shifting outward rapidly. This is because technological progress has been very rapid. A large increase in supply coupled with a moderate increase in demand will lead to declining prices.

The short run problem is instability in agricultural prices, and, consequently, instability in farm incomes. This is the result of the fact that both the short run demand and supply curves for agricultural products tend to be inelastic. The demand curve is inelastic because there are few substitutes for food. The supply curve is inelastic because growing seasons cannot be significantly shortened and farmers are unwilling to destroy crops in the ground. What this means is that moderate shifts in demand and supply will have dramatic effects on prices. A major reason for supply curve shifts is weather problems. Demand curve shifts can result from a variety of causes, including weather problems in another region.

The figure on the following page shows the market for an agricultural com-

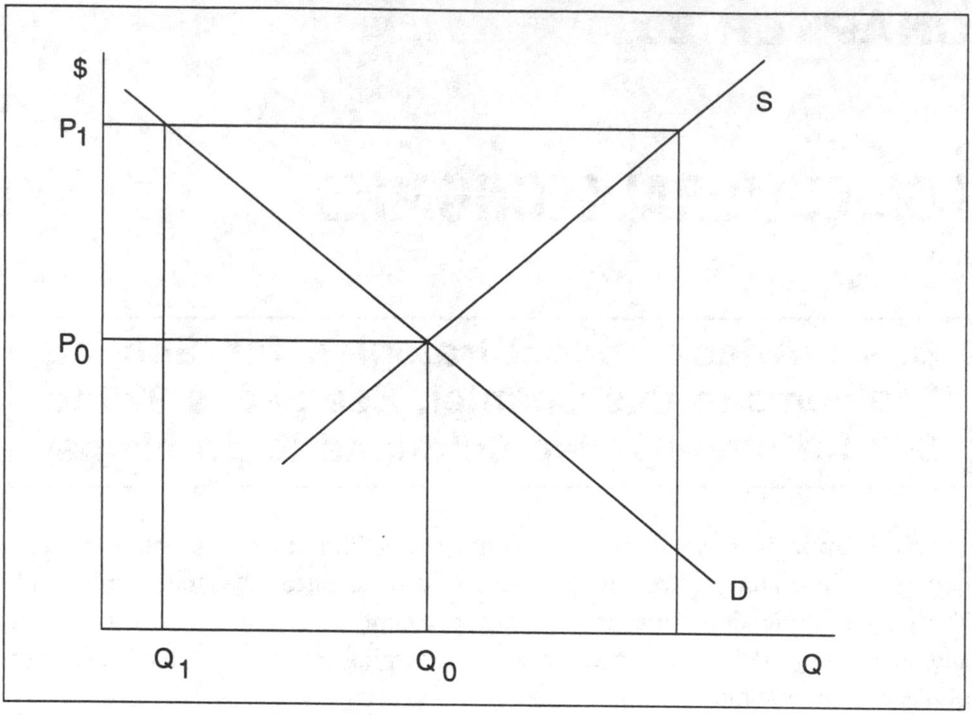

Market for a Farm Product

modity. Assume, as a consequence of the long run problem discussed above, the equilibrium price is too low to provide "decent" incomes to farmers. What types of policies are available to deal with this issue? There are many options government could consider. One is that government could make relief payments available to farmers in need. Second, the government could design programs to increase the demand for farm products. Examples might include information campaigns on proper diets, and aggressively marketing American products in foreign countries (including breaking down trade barriers). Third, government could enlist farmers in crop limitation programs. This would decrease the supply of various crops, and, given the inelastic demand curve for farm products, farmers would enjoy higher incomes as a result.

Fourth, government could guarantee farmers a price higher than would have been provided in the market, for example, P_1 instead of P_0. It would work like this. Farmers would supply Q_1 to the market at P_1, and government would promise to purchase the rest $(Q_2 - Q_1)$ at that price. One major problem with this is that government will be forced to dispose of excess commodities. Storage is expensive; destruction distasteful. Frequently this type of program requires crop limitations as an adjunct policy.

Fifth, government can design purchase-and-resale differential subsidy plans. Essentially, farmers are expected to sell their crop at the equilibrium price (P_0), and government will make up the difference between P_1 and P_0 with a subsidy payment.

Step-by-Step Solutions to Problems in this Chapter, "Agricultural Economics"

CONCEPTS OF AGRICULTURAL ECONOMICS

• PROBLEM 28-1

The following terms are frequently encountered in the subject of agricultural economics. Briefly describe each of these terms: a) Income elasticity, b) Price supports, c) Parity d) Surplus.

Solution: a) Income elasticity is the proportionate change in consumer expenditure on a product occurring due to a 1% increase in consumer income.

b) One of the forms of governmental help to the farmers is the establishment of a price level, above the competitive market price. Farmers are guaranteed that they will be able to dispose of all of their product at this price, which is called a support price. Government does not allow transactions below this price. It then buys up everything that is not purchased by private consumers. Clearly, under this system farmers are guaranteed a fixed revenue in exchange for their output.

c) The concept of parity has to do with the comparison between the real, not nominal, worth of farmer's revenue and its real value in some other period, say in the beginning of the century. The 'fair' price argument says that prices should be high enough to secure farmers reimbursement equal to what they received in some good years.

d) Surplus occurs when there is some sort of intervention with the competitive forces in the market and results in a situation where there is not enough demand for all the products supplied to the market.

• PROBLEM 28-2

What are the five principal forms of government aid to farmers?

Solution: 1) Outright gifts or relief payments given to farmers who have established their need.

2) Demand promotion and research. By demand promotion we mean government's attempts to increase the use of farm products by consumers. An example would be the distribution of circulars explaining how to improve one's diet. Research involves finding ways to increase the productivity of farmers.

3) Crop-limitation programs that aim to cut down on supply. At first, such programs might not seem helpful to the farmer, but when we realize that demand for farm products is generally inelastic, we can see that a drop in production will raise price more than proportionally and cause total revenue to rise. In effect, government is using its power to simulate monopoly.

4) Purchase loan storage programs to support farm prices. Here the government guarantees the farmer a price higher than would have prevailed in the market. This price floor is shown in the figure.

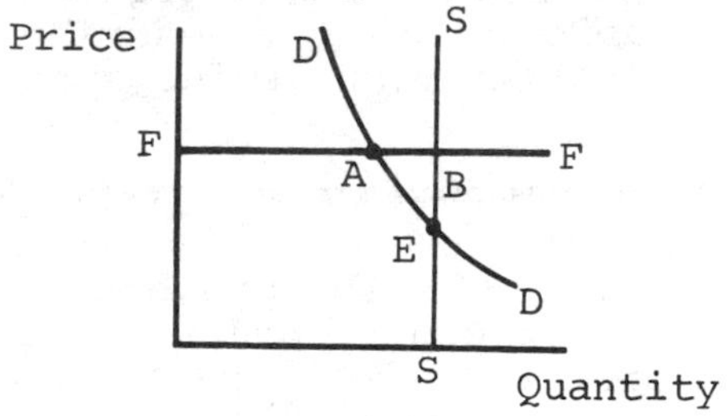

At so high a price, consumers will not buy all the crop supplied at the floor price. Government then must buy the unsold portion between B and A.

5) Purchase-and-resale differential subsidy plans. Here the government purchases the farmer's product at the price floor (as in case 4 above) but now resells it to the public at whatever market price it will bring. The government does not deal in the purchase-and-resale but rather sends a check to the farmers for the difference between the market price and price floor on all units sold.

• PROBLEM 28-3

What is the chief reason why farm policy was not conceived as simply part of an overall income distribution policy?

Solution: The chief reason that farm policy was not conceived as simply part of an overall income distribution policy was its historical context, Farm prices and incomes had been falling and farmers had become worse relative to others in the economy, (even during the boom period of the 1920's), and agricultural policy was regarded as an attempt to restore the original relationship. The policy of price support stressed the fundamental notion of "parity"--the ratio of farm to other prices that happened to rule just prior to World War I--and all supports were fixed relative to the parity price. A policy approach of this kind necessarily implied that the very rich farmer who had become merely rich was to be restored to his original relative position, along with the poor farmer who was now very poor.

THE FARMING PROBLEM

• PROBLEM 28-4

Graphically analyze agriculture's long-run decline particularly concentrating on its farm-price trends.

Solution: The following diagram would explain the sagging trend of farm prices as the years go by.

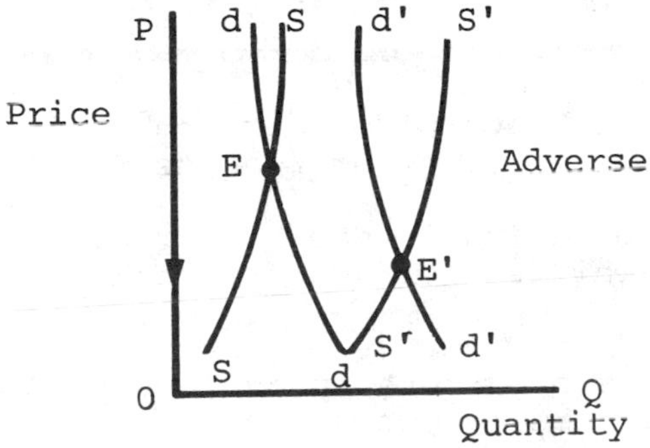

Adverse Farm-Price Trends

At the above figure, the point E represents the initial equilibrium of supply and demand at some earlier period. Let's analyze now the repercussions on the curves with the passing of time. As we can see, the demand curve dd will shift to the right which is the consequence of an increment in population and a much higher real income which will cause the people to consume more food at the prevailing price. However, the increase in consumption would not be applicable to all kinds of food because some foods, specifically basic foods, are the kinds of necessities which do not increase in the family budget at all proportionately to increases in real income. Also, the United States population no longer grows at the prodigious percentage rates of the nineteenth century. So, the rightward demand shift to d'd' is of the modest amount.

On the supply side, though many make the mistake of thinking of farming as a backward business, statistical records show that productivity in American agriculture has increased at a pace even faster than productivity in industry. So each new improvement helps to shift the ss curve a great deal to the right.

With the shift of the dd and the ss curves to the right, a new equilibrium E' has resulted. A question might be posed here to what will happen to the new equilibrium E' that would prevail in the market if the government did not intervene. One possible effect of a shift in supply that outstrips the shift in demand would be a downward trend of market prices (relative, to the general price level, so that the effects of overall inflation are disregarded). This declining price trend would result in financial pressure and hardship on those farmers and rural workers whose efficiency has not undergone tremendous increase and this in turn would mean that there will be considerable pressure for people to leave the countryside for jobs in industry. It also means that consumers are paying lower prices for the raw-material component of their foods and that the economy is reallocating its resources toward the things that are now most demanded in the expanding society. All of this would mean strong political pressures for government aid to agriculture.

• PROBLEM 28-5

Enumerate the main reasons why the exodus of human resources from farming may be coming to an end.

Solution: The flow of labor from farming to industry should start declining for the following reasons.

First, farm population is now historically low, and therefore, the possibility of further outmigration is diminished.

Second, the rate of growth in agricultural productivity seems to be declining in recent years.

Finally, there has been an increase in agricultural demand as a result of which the demand for labor also rises.

• PROBLEM 28-6

What are some reasons why there has been a relative shift from farming?

Solution: There has been a relative shift away from farming. People seek the higher incomes of the city, shorter hours, and what many seem to regard as the better social life in town with the result that they flee from ancient discriminations.

However, it is important to note that this out-migration from the countryside is lucky, because birth rates are higher in rural areas as compared to the cities. If it were not for this migration, cities might grow smaller and smaller; the rural share of total population would grow larger and larger. Such an eventuality would mean, according to the law of diminishing returns, a great reduction in the productivity of each man-hour spent on the farm. The land would become crowded with many people, each producing little and each unable to buy many of the comforts of life with his produce.

• PROBLEM 28-7

Give some economic justifications for the public aid to farmers.

Solution: Aside from such subjective arguments as the importance of farmers to the American way of life or their extraordinary vulnerability to the harmful forces of nature, more objective economic reasons can be stated to explain why it would be fair for the government to support the farmers. It can be mentioned that agriculture as an industry having made incredible progress in the quantity and quality of its output, nevertheless remained one of the most significant labor sources for the city. At the same time, due to the structure of the markets and because of the peculiarities of agricultural production, farmers ended up paying for most of the progress they helped to generate by receiving consistently lower incomes than workers in other industries. It should be also noted that agricultural markets represent the closest approximation available in the U.S. economy to the theory of perfect competition. Agricultural markets include thousands and thousands of farmers producing homogenous products, each farmer having completely no power over price. Such a vulnerable market position, along with the traditional American belief in economic competition, is another good reason for the government to consider support of the farmers in "bad times" as necessary and fair.

• PROBLEM 28-8

What do we mean when we say that the farm problem may be correctly envisioned as a problem of resource misallocation?

Solution: Big differentials between the farmers' income and the income in other industries would not have persisted were it not for a significant degree of resource misallocation. Theoretically, competitive forces should drive the failing farmers off the land into the city in search of alternative uses for their labor. This process indeed has been taking place, but very slowly. Large fixed costs, a long tradition of work on the land, and often strong attachments to the rural life style make a lot of farmers suffer through the bad times and hope for a better future on the land. Land itself is a fixed input. In most cases it cannot be put to alternative uses as a response to a reduced demand. This created in a sense an excess 'supply' of farmers sharing in a diminishing agricultural income. Consequently the farm problem as it is often presented is to a large degree a problem of resource misallocation.

• PROBLEM 28-9

Enumerate the strategies the government has followed to

augment the demand for agricultural products.

Solution: One approach to the problem of reversing the long run tendency of farm incomes to fall is to encourage demand for agricultural products. The U.S. government pursued various policies designed to increase the demand facing the farmers. Numerous federal welfare programs involving subsidized purchases of food (e.g., food stamps) have been put into life. Government itself became a major domestic purchaser of grain with the development of advanced storing facilities. Internationally, the U.S. government negotiated credit agreements with the less developed countries for the purchases of food and reduced tariffs abroad for American agricultural products. Research is being done in the area of alternative uses of food. All these policies have often been helpful but not quite capable of reversing the general trend of decline in agriculture.

• **PROBLEM 28-10**

Enumerate the causes of the long-and short-run farm problems.

Solution: The agricultural sector of the U.S. economy can be generally characterized by a consistent decline in its income since the beginning of the century and by a great price instability of agricultural markets at any particular period. Decline is a long run problem, instability is a short run difficulty. There are objective economic reasons for agriculture's inability to match the income growth of other sectors.

The specificity of the demand for farm products is such that it is quite inelastic and basically unchanging over time. The amount of food people want to consume does not vary a great deal with the change in their real incomes. At the same time agricultural supply grew noticeably over time due to technological progress. This created a long run problem of over-supply and consequently low prices and low incomes for farmers. Large fixed costs of agricultural production as well as virtual immobility of resources make it difficult to eliminate the problem.

In the short run demand and supply are highly inelastic and even small changes in one of them can cause the price to fluctuate significantly. Agricultural markets are characteristically competitive and individual farmers are at the mercy of the market price for their product. Every short-run price change inevitably alters farmers' incomes, thus making them very unstable.

• **PROBLEM 28-11**

Enumerate and briefly explain some of the major differences between the economic properties of the markets for farm products and those for manufacturers.

Solution: Problems of agricultural policy arise in almost every country, but they can often be more acute in industrialized countries because there are major differences--which are universal in character--between the economic properties of the markets for farm products and those for manufacturers. These differences are:

(1) The relatively low elasticity of demand for farm products and the relatively small expansion of this demand, over time, in the richer countries. Both these properties occur because farm production is predominantly food production; in the richer countries, people can be well fed by spending only part of their income on food and do not change the quantity they eat very much in the face of changes in food prices or their own incomes.

(2) The relatively low elasticity of supply of farm products in the short run. Once a farmer has planted his crop, he will harvest it at any price which is not so low that it will not cover the actual harvest and marketing cost. Thus price changes during 1979 will have little effect on the quantity of most farm crops during that year. However, because of weather conditions, there will be considerable season-to-season fluctuation in farm output.

(3) Technological progress in agriculture has been, and is, rapid. This has pronounced effects in richer countries, which can adopt the new technology easily, but the effects remain only potential in many of the poor countries.

(4) Farming represents a form of social specialization. A shift from agriculture to industry requires more social and structural change than a shift from one industry to another.

• **PROBLEM 28-12**

Explain the two arguments that have always been advanced for a special policy towards farmers.

Solution: Two arguments have always been a strong element in the claim for a special policy towards farmers. The first one is national security, the argument that the country should preserve farm capacity against the possibility of imported supplies being cut off. This argument is not special to agriculture and is used by almost every sector of the economy when it seeks special treatment.

The second argument deals with preserving the rural life. This has a considerable sentimental element, but there are probably genuine externalities involved. Urban dwellers do gain something from seeing farms and crops along the highways, and are very likely willing to pay something for this.

This last argument seems to provide a case for treating

agriculture differently from other sectors. It is an inevitable consequence of economic change and development that prices in some sectors will decline relative to those in others and that industries will disappear. Preservation of rural society, especially in the versions that generate most nostaliga, is probably impossible, and, in any case, is not the answer to guaranteeing incomes sufficient to keep people on the land.

• PROBLEM 28-13

Why is it that even though the price the farmer gets for the food he sells will fall, the retail price need not fall so much--or may even rise?

Solution: It is the claim of the agricultural experts that the fall in the retail price is not so much because railroads, packers, and supermarkets extort an undue share of the food dollar, as that consumers today want their food more and more fabricated (e.g., frozen, cut, cleaned, cooked, minutely packaged, premixed for baking, and so forth) and that greater technological progress may be taking place in producing raw food than in processing and marketing it. In the 1970's, the farmer got less than one third of the retail food dollar, as compared with about one-half in earlier years of high farm prices.

ELASTICITY OF FARM PRODUCTS

• PROBLEM 28-14

Briefly describe the effect of demand changes on farm prices and incomes.

Solution: The short-run instability and drastic price fluctuations on the agricultural markets can be graphically illustrated in the following way:

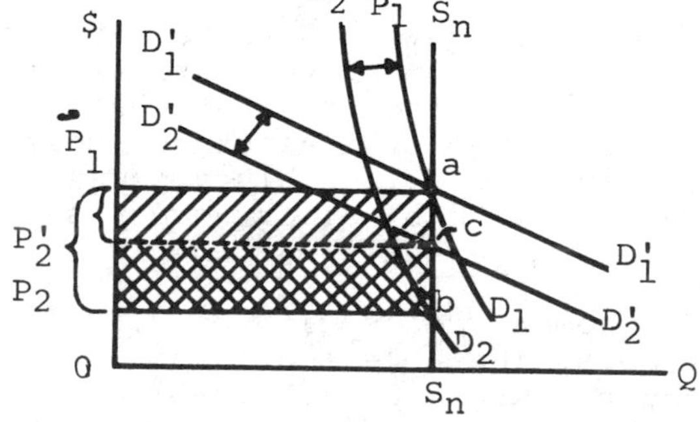

Line S_n on the graph signifies the amount of output farmers produced in the year n. As long as D_1D_1 is the market demand curve farmers sell at a price P_1 and receive a revenue equal to the area of rectangle OP_1aS_n. As shown on the graph a small decrease in the demand, equal precisely to the distance between D_1D_1 and D_2D_2, will cause the price to fall all the way to P_2 reducing the farmers' income by as much as the area $P_1a\ bP_2$. Should the demand curve be more elastic, like $D_1'\ D_1'$ on the graph, an equally small reduction in demand drops the price only to the level of P_2' and the resulting change in income is not as big, just the area $P_1ac\ P_2'$.

This illustration shows that farmers' incomes are very sensitive to market demand because of its inelasticity. Farmers cannot reduce the disastrous impact of a fall in market demand on their income by withdrawing the output from the market because huge fixed costs make such a move completely insensible for every individual producer.

• PROBLEM 28-15

In a study conducted on aggregate farm products, it was estimated that the elasticity coefficient lay between .20 and .25. These figures suggest that the prices of agricultural products would have to fall by 40 to 50 percent in order for consumers to increase their purchases by a mere 10 percent which in turn indicates that consumers apparently put a low value on additional agricultural output as compared with alternative goods. Why is this so?

Solution: In the long run, consumers apparently put a low value on additional agricultural output as compared with alternative goods. The rationale behind this is that since substitutability is the basic determinant of elasticity of demand, when the price of a product falls, the consumer will tend to substitute that product for other products whose prices presumably have not fallen. But in wealthy societies, this "substitution effect" is very modest. Food consumption remains much the same, since people rarely eat more than three meals a day. An individual's capacity to substitute food for other products is subject to very real biological constraints. The inelasticity of agricultural demand can also be explained in terms of diminishing marginal utility. In a wealthy society, the population, by and large, is well fed and well clothed. Therefore, additional agricultural output entails rapidly diminishing marginal utility. Thus it takes very large price cuts to induce small increases in consumption.

• PROBLEM 28-16

Graphically differentiate the effects on farm income of a short crop from a bumper crop. What logical conclusion can be derived from the said analysis?

Solution: The following figure is pertinent to illustrate the effect of output changes on farm prices and incomes.

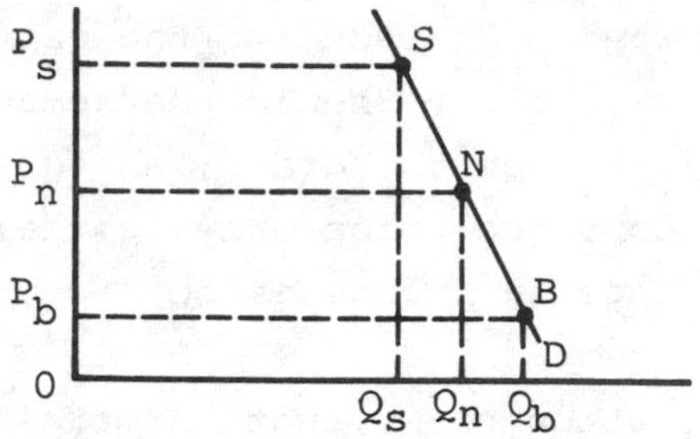

Now, putting the instability of farm production with the inelastic demand for farm products, we can see why farm prices and consequently incomes are unstable from the above figure.

Assuming now that the market demand for agricultural products is stable at D, the inelastic nature of demand will magnify small changes in output into relatively large changes in farm prices and income. As an illustration, assume that a "normal" crop of Q_n results in a "normal" price of P_n and a "normal" farm income of OP_nNQ_n. But a bumper crop or a short crop will cause large deviations from these normal prices and incomes which are both the consequences of the inelasticity of demand for farm products.

Considering each individual case, we can say that an unusually good growing season, resulting in a bumper crop of Q_6 will cause farm incomes to fall from $OP_n\ NQ_n$ to OP_6BQ_6 This stems from the fact that when demand is inelastic, an increase in the quantity sold will be accompanied by a more than proportionate decline in price. The net result is that total receipts, that is, total farm income will decline. Similarly, for farmers as a group, a short crop caused by bad weather conditions, may boost farm incomes. A short crop of Q_s will raise total farm income from OP_nNQ_n to OP_sSQ_s because a diminution in output will cause a more than proportionate increment in price when demand is inelastic. Ironically, for farmers as a group, a short crop may be a blessing and a bumper crop a hardship.

The logical conclusion that we can derive from the above analysis is this: Given a stable market demand for farm products, the inelasticity of that demand will turn relatively small changes in output into relatively larger changes in farm prices and incomes.

• PROBLEM 28-17

Analyze the effects of the low elasticities of both demand

and short-run supply, coupled with output variations due to weather, on farm price and income.

Solution: The causes mentioned above can often result in dramatic price-changes of agricultural products from one year to the next. Another problem related to this would be due to technological progress. New techniques enable farmers to produce more with the same land and the same (or less) labor. Since the demand for farm products remains relatively constant, the expansion in output causes a fall in prices. The low elasticity of demand implies that absorption of a small increase in output will require a relatively large fall in price.

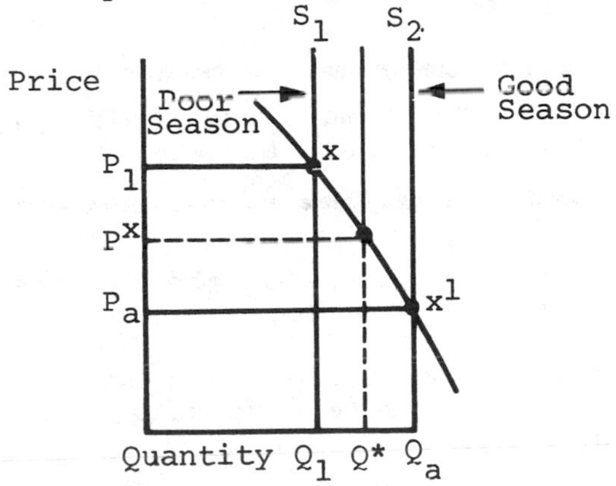

The given figure illustrates the above argument. It is assumed that the market is always cleared, i.e., that whatever is harvested is sold, no matter what the price. This assumption yields an inelastic short-run supply curve. S_1 and S_2 are two such curves. Since the demand curve is steeply sloping due to low elasticity of demand, the fluctuations in harvest between Q_1 of the supply curve S_1 and Q_2 of the supply curve S_2, will result in the relatively large price fluctuations between P_1 and P_2. The relationship between the fluctuations in price and those in quantity is given directly by the elasticity of demand, since the demand curve remains the same.

Not only does a low elasticity of demand result in large price fluctuations, it results in large income fluctuations to farmers. If the elasticity of demand is low (less than unity), total revenue from farm sales, which determines farm income, will move in the same direction as price. This means that incomes will be low when output is high (S_2) and high when output is low (S_1). If the demand for farm products had unit elasticity, price fluctuations would have no effect on incomes--under these conditions, the fall in quantity and rise in price would balance each other.

Since low elasticity of demand is the general rule, incomes will tend to fall in years of good harvest and rise in years of bad harvest. On the other hand, there is no incentive for the individual farmer to hold back production in a good year since he cannot affect the price by his own actions. However low the price, each individual farmer will make more income by selling more, although farmers as a group will make less income if they all behave the same way.

Thus farm incomes, because of the low demand elasticity, are a victim of the fallacy of composition--what is good for each individual is not good for all farmers taken together. It is this special property of farm incomes that gives rise to pressure for some government or other centralized control in an industry which is, in other respects, close to the classic view of perfect competition.

• PROBLEM 28-18

Briefly enumerate two reasons why the supply curves of the farmers are relatively inelastic.

Solution: The supply curves of the farmers are relatively inelastic for at least two reasons:

(a) When the price is low, his own effort to increase output may intensify, as he desperately tries to maintain family income.

(b) Many of his costs go on anyway, whether he produces much or little, and he can save little extra cost by cutting his Q.

GOVERNMENT SUBSIDIES

• PROBLEM 28-19

When does subsidization instead of price stabilization of agriculture occur?

Solution: When the agriculturists have strong political support, they will apply pressure for stabilization of prices. This pressure, however, will not be for a true stabilization scheme but for a price support scheme. Farmers will prefer to obtain the free market price when that is high, but the support price when the market price is low. This leads to a program whereby the government buys when the price is depressed, but cannot sell overtly when the price is high--although governments can often sneak some of their surpluses into the market.

Therefore under these conditions, we do not have price stabilization but subsidization of agriculture.

• PROBLEM 28-20

Give the importance of buffer stocks in the agricultural

market model.

Solution: In the idealized simple model, the government could hold the price at P* by accumulating buffer stocks in good crop years and running them down in bad crop years. On the average, over the years, the stabilized price P* will give rise to purchases of Q* and the buffer stocks will go up and down from season to season but maintain a constant average level. With an ideal buffer stock scheme, the government does not need any direct price controls. By simply offering to buy or sell at a constant price P*, the market price will be stabilized at that level and the buffer stocks will fluctuate with the seasonal events.

With such a scheme, no financial burden is imposed on the government (except the pure costs of administration and interest on the value of the buffer stocks) over the years, since purchases into and sales from the buffer stocks are made at the same price and cancel out over the years.

• PROBLEM 28-21

Describe how price stabilization as a policy operates in times of a good crop year as well as in a bad crop period.

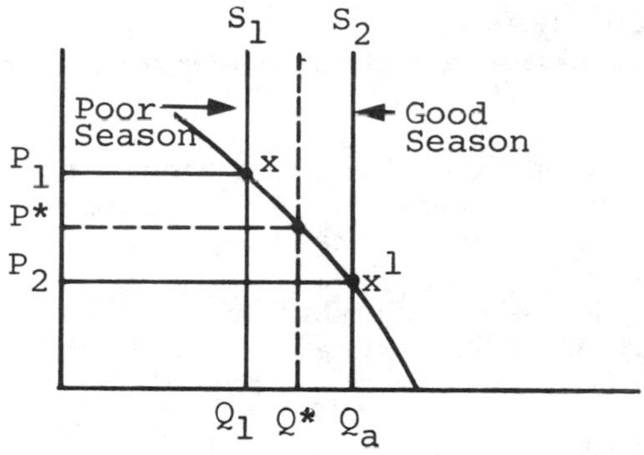

Solution: Consider the given diagram. If government maintains the price at P*, amount Q* will be purchased. In a good crop, with supply at S_2, P* will be above the market price P_2. But buyers will only purchase amount Q* at this price and there will be excess supply equal to Q_2 - Q*. The government will then normally have to do one of two things:

(1) Ration supply, by allowing each farmer to sell only a proportion of his crop and making him destroy the rest--equiproportionate rationing would require each farmer to destroy a fraction of his crop equal to (Q_2 - Q*) / Q_2. Note that each farmer would have increased income, compared with the free market situation, even though he has destroyed part of his crop, because of low demand elasticity.

(2) Add to demand an amount Q_2 - Q^*_1 either by buying

up the surplus, or paying the farmer to store it and not sell.

During a bad crop year, when supply drops to S_1, the free market price would rise to P_1 in the absence of intervention. If the price ceiling was fixed at P*, however, there would be excess demand equal to $Q^* - Q_1$. The government could handle this by certain procedures:

(a) Rationing demand--which in this case is difficult to accomplish because farm policy usually gives the government control over farmers, not their customers.

(b) Adding to this an amount $Q^* - Q_1$, which it can only do if it holds large quantities of farm products, or buffer stocks, just for this purpose.

• PROBLEM 28-22

Consider the following news item: "Seoul, Korea. The city government ordered the capital's 1,500 restaurants not to sell any meal containing rice during lunch hours. The measure is designed to encourage the customers to take other food. South Korea is experiencing a serious food shortage because of a poor rice crop." Would open market prices achieve the same result?

Solution: Two main facts are given in the problem: 1) There is a poor rice crop; 2) The government is eliminating the "demand for rice at lunch in restaurants," leaving only "all other demands for rice" operative.

The question asks whether the price and the quantity exchanged under this government intervention would be the same as they would in the absence of the intervention.

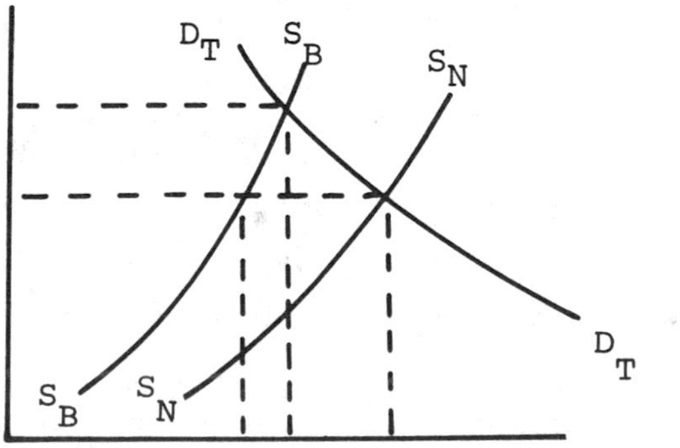

Fig. 1

"A poor rice crop" can be represented by a supply curve $S_B S_B$ for rice that is above and to the left of the "normal" supply curve $S_N S_N$ as shown in Figure 1. Without any government intervention, the new market equilibrium would occur where the demand curve D_T D_T intersects the new "bad crop" supply curve S_B S_B. Thus, the free market equilibrium price would rise from P_N to P_F, and the equilibrium quantity exchanged would fall from Q_N to Q_F.

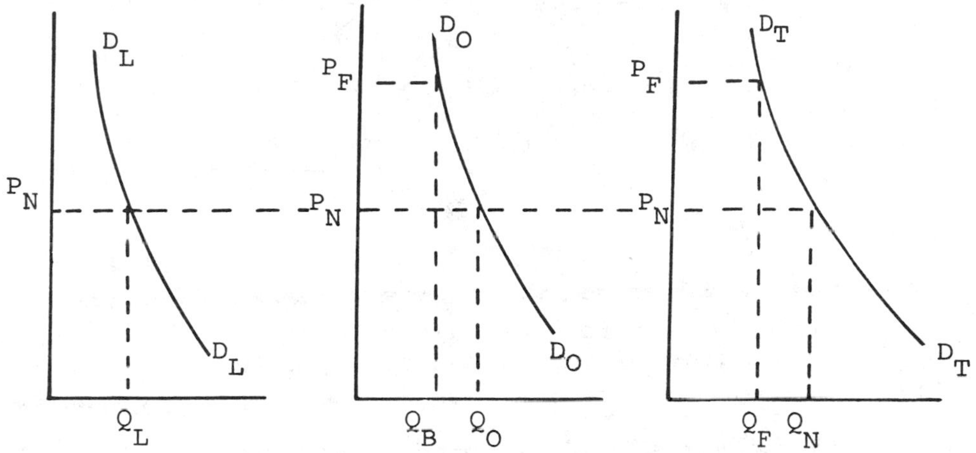

Fig. 2

The government is attempting to alleviate the shortage that would occur at price P_N (measured by Q_N - Q_A, the distance between D_T D_T and S_B S_B at P_N) by reducing demand. Total demand can be represented at the horizontal summation of the demand curve for "rice in restaurants at lunch," D_L D_L in Figure 2, and "all other demand for rice," D_O D_O. This total demand for rice is represented by D_T D_T. At any given price, the total quantity demanded is the sum of the quantity demanded for lunch and that demanded for all other purposes. E.g., at P_N, $Q_L + Q_O = Q_N$. The intervention prohibiting the sale of rice at lunch eliminates that component of demand. If we assume (rather unrealistically) that demand for all other purposes does not increase as a result of the government prohibition, then total demand is shifted down and to the left from D_T D_T to D_O D_O. The intervention, then results in a new equilibrium of P_G and an equilibrium quantity exchanged of Q_G, as shown in Figure 3.

Thus, the free market result in a higher equilibrium price, P_F, and a greater quantity bought and sold, Q_F, than occur with the government restriction, namely P_G and Q_G, respectively. Notice that the government is essentially subsidizing the "all other" category of demand at the expense of the "lunch" demand. Under the government restriction, there is more rice demanded for all other purposes, Q_G, at a lower price, P_G, than would be the case without the intervention, where quantity Q_B would be demanded at price P_F.

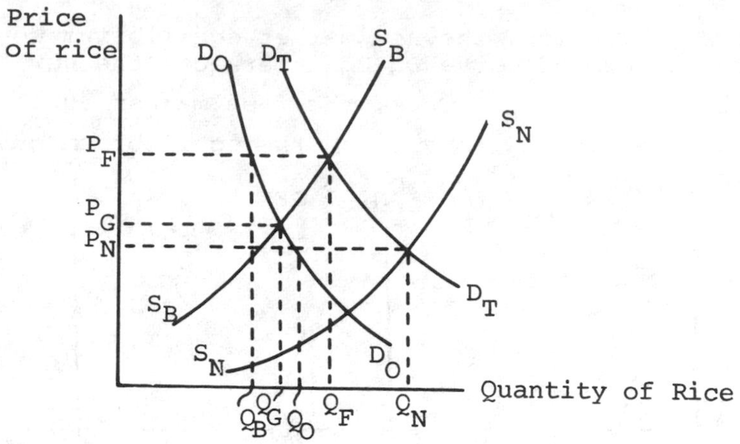

• PROBLEM 28-23

Explain how the purchase-and-resale differential subsidy plans as a form of government aid operates.

Solution: The subsidized producer-consumer price differential involves paying an artificially high price to farmers, but reselling food to consumers at whatever low price the market will set.

Here the farmer would be guaranteed the parity price of BB' as shown in the following figure, which also illustrates the new fact that food, instead of being left to rot in storage, is to be resold to the public for current consumption at whatever market price it will bring.

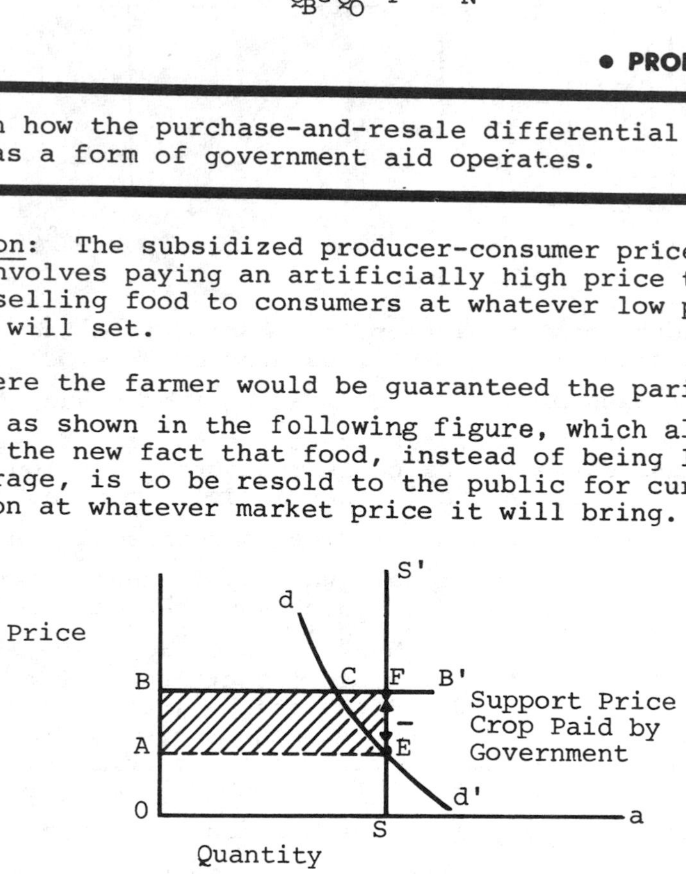

Every bit produced, as shown by the ss' supply curve, will now go to the consumer. Consumption will end up at the original point E because the "law of supply and demand" explains the fact that for consumers to buy the full crop, price must fall to the point where the demand curve intersects the market supply. But producers are promised the parity price for their entire crop. So the price they are to receive is indicated by F. The government pays the difference by sending each primary producer a check, whose amount per bushel is shown by the vertical arrow EF. The cost to the government is indicated by the shaded area AEFB, which shows that the government must pay the difference between the producer's and consumer's price on each and every unit produced.

Therefore, direct payments to farmers, equal to the shortfall of the market price below the support price, results in low prices to the consumer, high consumption and avoids storage of rotting surpluses.

• PROBLEM 28-24

What does the government do when agricultural prices fall below the parity price? Explain the rationale behind such an approach using a graph to illustrate your point more clearly.

Solution: When the prices of the farm products fall below the parity price, the government resorts to outright purchase or some kind of loan red tape to acquire the unsold farm products. The following graph will illustrate this point more clearly.

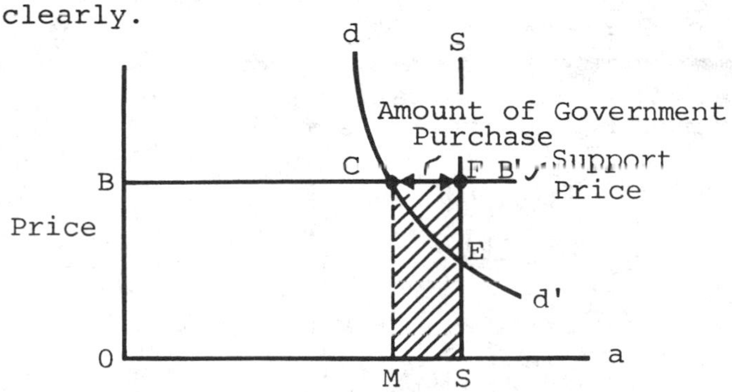

The "price floor" or the parity price, which is determined by a ratio of the prices a farmer receives for his products to the prices he must pay for goods, is shown by the line BB' in the above figure. Line ss' represents the farmer's supply in the market place. It is assumed to be almost perfectly inelastic due to the time lag involved between planting and harvesting. That is, it is impossible to decide in September to have planted more back in April. Line dd' shows the consumer demand curve. At so high a price, consumers will not buy all the crop supplied. Consumers will be on the demand curve at C. But farmers are supplying the full amount as shown by F. If government does nothing, price must fall to E, which is below the parity price. What the government will do now would be to acquire the unsold portion between C and F, marked with an arrow, by outright purchase or through some kind of loan red tape. This will go into storage, or will be sent abroad as part of foreign aid. The consequence of this would be that the government has increased the price received by the farmer from E to F and with the increased price serving as an incentive to them, the farmers can now sell as much as they want, representing a clear increase in their incomes. The consumers are now paying a higher price and buying less.

To them, parity price through loan support or government purchase is just as bad as the crop restriction program. The government, through taxes, is now footing the bill for the extra income now received by the farmers. The Treasury Department is having to spend an amount of dollars equal to the part of the crop it must buy times the full market price as shown by the shaded MCF_s in the graph.

Summarizing the above result, we have the following points:

To guarantee a price higher than the free market would dictate, government must purchase the gap between supply and demand at the support price, storing the difference or dumping it abroad.

• PROBLEM 28-25

Describe how the crop-limitation programs of the government such as acreage allotments or crop quotas to each farm cut down on supply and consequently raise prices.

Solution: The crop-limitation program of the government may be illustrated graphically as follows:

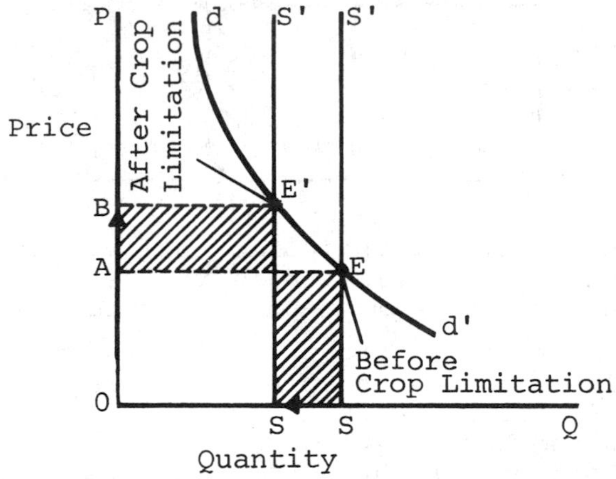

Before the intervention of the government, the ss' supply curve intersects the inelastic dd' curve at the low price shown at point E. Since the agricultural industry closely resembles that of a perfectly competitive industry, each farmer has no motive to do anything to improve the situation. But if all together can get government to put monopolistic limits on their total Q_1, they can benefit.

When production controls cut supply from ss' to SS', P rises to E'. Because demand is inelastic, total gross farm income is thereby increased. Furthermore, PXQ revenues at E and E' are measured, respectively, by the 0_sEA and 0SE'B rectangular areas.

Generalizing the above results, we can say therefore that if the demand for farm products is inelastic rather than elastic, then a program of enforced crop reduction will result in higher total receipts to the farmer. And since he also saves a little on total costs when he produces less, his net revenue goes up by even more than his total receipts do.

However, it is important to note that this form of farm aid is not necessarily bad since noneconomic ethical and political issues are also involved. But it does suggest that each bit of benefit to some farmers is being bought at a greater sacrifice to the rest of the community than is economically and technically necessary. It does suggest that society look around for more efficient methods.

INTERNATIONAL AGRICULTURAL ECONOMICS

• PROBLEM 28-26

Why is it that on the whole, international stabilization schemes have been only moderately successful in their attempts to stabilize prices of various products such as wheat, rice, sugar and coffee?

Solution: On the whole, international stabilization schemes have been only moderately successful in stabilizing the price at some level or between certain limits. Their failures have usually been because the agreed price turned out to be inappropriate to the conditions for which it was developed, or because either buyers or sellers left (or refused to renew) agreements when free market prices were especially favorable to them. Thus, international stabilization schemes suffer from the same problem as internal schemes (primarily one of prediction) with the additional problem that the buyers and sellers are different countries and a solution satisfactory to one side cannot be imposed on the other--something which the government can always do within a country.

• PROBLEM 28-27

What is the so-called International Wheat Agreement?

Solution: The International Wheat Agreement is one of the international programs that attempt to stabilize the price at some level or between certain limits. It set forth the upper and lower limits and attempted to solve the excess demand and excess supply problems by buyer and seller quotas--exporting countries guaranteed to sell importing countries a certain maximum amount if the price reached the upper limit, and importing countries guaranteed to buy a certain minimum quota if the price reached the lower limit.

• PROBLEM 28-28

Give the significance of the Agricultural Adjustment Act of 1933.

Solution: The Agricultural Adjustment Act of 1933 established the concept of parity as a cornerstone of agricultural policy. In both real and money terms, we can envision the simple rationale of the parity concept. In real terms, parity says that year after year for a given output of farm products, a farmer should be able to acquire a given total amount of goods and services. Stated differently, a given real output should always result in the same real income. To illustrate, if Mr. X should take a bushel of peanuts to town in 1978 and sell it and buy himself some shoes, he should be able to take a bushel of peanuts to town today and buy shoes. On the other hand, the parity concept in money terms suggests that the relationship between the prices received by farmers for their output and the prices they must pay for goods and services should remain constant. Therefore, if the prices of the items farmers purchase increase, then the prices which farmers receive for their products should rise accordingly.

• PROBLEM 28-29

What were the factors that contributed to the failure of agriculture to share in the prosperity that other segments of the economy did immediately after the post-war depression in 1920?

Solution: Four main factors that led to the failure of agriculture to regain its "Golden Age" are:

a) European agriculture recovered quickly and expanded rapidly due to new technological advances. This caused foreign demand for U.S. goods to level off and finally decline.

b) During this period, the U.S. was maintaining high tariffs on imports. These tariffs restricted the foreigner's ability to sell to the U.S. and consequently to earn the funds needed to purchase American agricultural products.

c) Domestic demand for farm products did not rise very much in the twenties. Increases in income were devoted to the purchase of automobiles, refrigerators and many other products previously unavailable for mass consumption.

d) Technological advances also effected supply. Farm output increased sharply.

These four factors combined to cause a lagging, inelastic demand and a sharply increasing supply which led to low farm prices and incomes.

• **PROBLEM 28-30**

Why is it that the two decades prior to World War I have been dubbed "the golden age of American agriculture"?

Solution: The two decades prior to World War I have been dubbed as "the golden age of American agriculture" because it has been an exceedingly prosperous one for the agricultural industry. The demand for farm products, farm prices, and farm incomes all rose. World War I generated a greater demand for American agricultural products in Europe. This demand continued to increase after the war since the war-torn nations of Europe had few resources for agriculture.

SHORT ANSWER QUESTIONS FOR REVIEW

Answer
To be covered when testing yourself

Choose the correct answer.

1. The proportion of population employed in agriculture has been (a) increasing since 1910 (b) basically unchanged since the beginning of the century (c) declining due to the improved technology of production (d) always more than 10%. — c

2. The process of migration of farmers to the city occurs (a) because of a particularly unfair income distribution in the rural areas (b) when bad weather harms the crops (c) because life in the city is more interesting (d) incomes in agriculture are consistently lower than wages in industry. — d

3. The prices of agricultural products are: (a) usually very stable (b) changing rapidly in the short run (c) determined by farmers (d) subject to bargaining. — b

4. Lower tariffs on U.S. agricultural products abroad will (a) shift domestic demand to the right (b) create grain shortages in the U.S. (c) increase the farmers' income (d) make domestic grain prices lower. — c

5. Prices on farm products fluctuate in the short run because: (a) both supply and demand are inelastic (b) agricultural production is very unstable (c) perfect competition always results in unstable prices (d) none of the above. — a

6. What is the purpose of government intervention in agricultural markets? (a) to prevent their monopolization (b) to assure that farmers' income does not become intolerably low under adverse market conditions (c) to make farmers produce more grain (d) all of the above. — b

7. The average income of a farmer is (a) lower than per capita income in the U.S. (b) higher than the average nonfarm income (c) rising every year (d) approximately $10,000. — a

8. Technological progress (a) benefitted all the farmers equally (b) had an adverse effect on the farmers' income (c) was not apparent in agriculture as much as it was in the industry (d) drastically increased the demand for agricultural products. — b

Answer

To be covered when testing yourself

SHORT ANSWER QUESTIONS FOR REVIEW

9. Suppose government decides to implement a price-support aid program. In order to do this it will have to (a) purchase the surplus grain from farmers at a support price (b) allow no transactions at a price below the support price (c) purchase the market surplus at a competitive price (d) a and b (e) b and c. — d

10. Which of the following is a cause of resource misallocation in agriculture? (a) income misallocation (b) high birth-rate in rural areas (c) large fixed costs of production and unavailability of land for alternative uses (d) all of the above. — c

11. Grain prices in the U.S. can be increased by (a) farmers (b) the government (c) restrictions on the supply of grain (d) payment of subsidies to the farmers. — c

12. Of all federal aid programs for the farmers the one with the lowest social cost is (a) the crop restriction program (b) the program involving direct money payments to the farmers (c) the program of storing all of the surplus grain to future consumption (d) a and c combined. — b

13. What can be done to make the demand curve for farm products more elastic? (a) people can be forced to eat more (b) alternative uses for farm products can be searched for (c) more grain can be stored (d) nothing. — b

14. In the short-run the supply of the agricultural products can be graphically represented in the form of a (a) horizontal line (b) positively sloped curve (c) vertical line (d) negatively sloped curve. — c

15. Suppose a market for wheat satisfies completely all the theoretical assumptions of perfect competition. Then the demand curve facing an individual farmer is (a) less elastic than the market demand curve (b) graphically a horizontal line (c) not infinitely elastic (d) equivalent to the market demand curve. — b

Fill in the blanks.

16 Rent on the land is part of the farmer's _______ cost. — fixed

SHORT ANSWER QUESTIONS FOR REVIEW

Question	Answer (To be covered when testing yourself)
17. The demand for food has not increased as fast as the _____________ with the improvement of agricultural technology.	supply of food
18. A _____________ is created when a higher than competitive price is supported artificially.	surplus
19. A high birth-rate in rural areas has been a factor in the process of _____________.	migration to the cities
20. In the U.S. approximately _____________ of the working population is employed in agriculture.	4%
21. Price-support programs help the farmers' income but result in a _____________.	consumer loss
22. As society gets more prosperous, the proportion of its productive force which is employed in agriculture gets _____________.	smaller
23. Government invests in the research on possible alternative uses of agricultural products in order to _____________ for these products.	increase demand
24. Lower tariffs on U.S. grain are likely to result in _____________ prices.	higher domestic
25. The U.S. enjoys _____________ in the international grain markets due to the high level of mechanization of its agriculture.	comparative advantage
26. The U.S. often allows the underdeveloped countries to use _____________ to pay for the American grain.	local currencies
27. Farmers cannot withhold their output in response to a low market price because of the considerable size of their _____________.	fixed costs
28. It is the function of _____________ to execute federal farm aid programs.	the Department of Agriculture
29. The shape of the demand curve for an individual farmer suggests that he is a _____________.	price taker
30. The future of agriculture is highly dependent on whether the problem of _____________ can be solved.	resource misallocation

Determine whether the following statements are true or false.

SHORT ANSWER QUESTIONS FOR REVIEW

	Question	Answer To be covered when testing yourself
31.	The farm problem has strong historical roots. Incomes in agriculture were consistently low and declining throughout this century and nothing could be done about this.	False
32.	The depression of the 1930's had a particularly devastating effect on the farmers due to their strong susceptibility to competitive pressures.	True
33.	Large-size farms are generally more prosperous than small ones.	True
34.	The demand for agricultural products is inelastic only in the long run.	False
35.	The feeling of solidarity with others prevents an individual farmer from raising his price and thus compensating for the reduced sales.	False
36.	Rapid economic growth is to a large degree responsible for making the demand for agricultural products as inelastic as it is.	True
37.	Farm income is very unstable and fluctuates a lot in the long run.	False
38.	The more prosperous farmers have more market power than their poorer counterparts.	False
39.	Price support policy always generates a surplus which is later purchased by the government at a set price higher than the market price.	True
40.	Price supports are beneficial to both consumers and farmers since it is the government who pays for them.	False
41.	Given an opportunity farmers would probably vote against food stamp and school lunch programs since they add almost nothing to the farmers' income.	False
42.	Price support and crop restriction programs are similar in that they result in a higher price but different in that the first one acts on the demand side and the second one on the supply side of the market.	True
43.	A direct payments aid program is the most beneficial way of supporting farmers from the consumer point of view.	True

SHORT ANSWER QUESTIONS FOR REVIEW

Answer
To be covered when testing yourself

44. Prospects of a better future for the American farmers depend mostly on their realization of an increase in the domestic demand for agricultural products. — True

45. Agricultural markets in their structure probably come closer to theoretically defined perfect competition than any other markets in the U.S. economy. — True

CHAPTER 29

GROWTH AND DEVELOPMENT

Basic Attacks and Strategies for Solving Problems in this Chapter. See pages 949 to 979 for step-by-step solutions to problems.

Economic growth refers to an increase in a nation's output per capita, or, in other words, the nation's standard of living. Growth is depicted graphically by an outward shift in the production possibilities frontier. This shift provides some insight into the necessary preconditions for growth. A production possibilities frontier is drawn showing the maximum feasible output combinations from a given stock of factors of production. Growth, then, can only result from a nation increasing its stock of factors of production.

On a less abstract level, examples of events that could lead to growth would include but not be limited to increases in population, increases in labor force participation rates, development of greater skills or more education by the work force, investment leading to capital accumulation, research and development fostering technological improvements, development of better managerial techniques, discovery and recovery of valuable natural resources, lowering of governmentally-imposed barriers to production and trade, and development of a stronger entrepreneurial spirit. Note, that each example mentioned represents an increase in either land, labor, capital, entrepreneurship, or technology. Of course, these increases are not free. All require some short-term sacrifice on the part of society. As an example of the type of sacrifice required to achieve growth objectives, capital accumulation requires that society forego current consumption in favor of savings.

The term growth must be distinguished from the terms development and expansion. Not every economic system provides a nurturing environment for growth. Development refers to the structural, institutional, and value changes a society must undergo before it can grow. Expansion involves an increase in output per capita, but it is qualitatively different from growth. Expansion means putting all available resources to work and getting the greatest possible output from existing resources. Graphically, it is represented by moving from a point inside the production possibilities frontier to a point on it.

The arithmetic of growth is fascinating. From the end of World War II to the mid-1960s, the United States economy grew approximately 3% a year, a rate that economists in hindsight agree was satisfactory. Since that time the rate of growth has been approximately 1% a year, a rate that is deeply troubling. A two percentage point difference may not seem that significant, but it actually is quite significant once the rule of 72 is considered. The rule of 72 says that if you divide the growth rate of something into the number 72, you will get the approximate amount of time it will take that thing to double in size. An economy growing at 3% per year will double in size (or double its standard of living) every 24 years (72/3 = 24), or about once a generation. An economy growing 1% per year will double every 72 years, or about once a lifetime. Looked at from this perspective, the difference in growth rates is quite significant.

How does a nation grow? Let Q be the quantity of output, L be the amount of hours worked, and Q/L be the productivity of labor (how much output labor produces each hour). Then

$$Q = \frac{Q}{L} * L.$$

Q will grow if either L or Q/L increases. L increases if the labor force grows either through higher population or a higher labor force participation rate, or if workers work more hours. Q/L grows if labor works harder or "smarter." Working smarter includes such things as using more and better (technologically more sophisticated) capital equipment, bringing more skills (human capital) to the job, and better management techniques. Of course, the increase in output achieved must exceed the growth in population for living standards to rise.

Growth is easier said than done. The problem is that the key elements in growth—capital investment, technological change, and human capital development—all require that society sacrifice some current consumption in favor of saving and investment.

There is a continuing debate over whether growth is unmitigatedly a good thing. Some commentators point to undesirable side effects, such as pollution, dehumanization of work, and the obsolescence of skills. Many believe that the problem of poverty will only be solved by growth. "A rising tide lifts all boats." Others are not so sure. These critics believe that poverty is essentially a problem of the distribution of income. People are poor if their standard of living is far below the societal norm, regardless of what society's absolute standard of living is. Unless growth is accompanied by a compression in the distribution of income, the poverty problem will not be solved.

Step-by-Step Solutions to Problems in this Chapter, "Growth and Development"

DEFINITION AND SIGNIFICANCE

• **PROBLEM 29-1**

Illustrate the concept of economic growth with the use of a production frontier.

The Production Frontier and Economic Growth

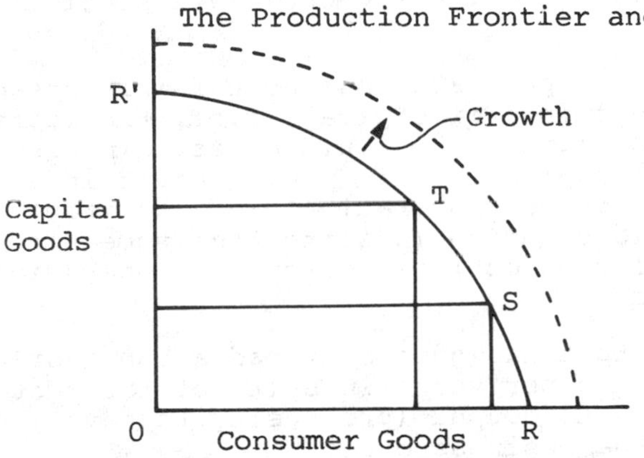

Solution: In a simplified model we assume that there are two "commodities": consumer goods and capital goods. Along the production frontier RR' in the figure we have the choice of producing quantity OR of consumer goods, quantity OR' of capital goods, or some combination of consumer and capital goods on RR', such as at Point S or Point T. Note that at any particular moment of time, our productive factors, and hence the amount of production possible, are strictly limited. Therefore, on the production frontier, we cannot produce more of one kind of good except by producing less of the other.

Economic growth is shown by the pushing out of the production frontier, RR' to a higher position, shown by the dashed curve in the diagram. On the new frontier, we can produce more of either good, the quantity of the other remaining the same, or more of both, than we could when confined to the old frontier (RR'). This growth must take place over a period of time, augmenting the limited factors of production. With increases in resource supplies and/or technological progress, economic growth is made possible.

• PROBLEM 29-2

Identify briefly six major trends in the growth of the advanced nations.

Solution: The six major trends of the advanced nations have been as follows:

1) Capital accumulation has proceeded faster than population growth, resulting in a higher capital-labor ratio or a 'deepening' of capital.

2) Real wage rates have consequently risen sharply.

3) Labor's share of output and capital's share have remained fairly steady. Wages and salaries are perhaps a slightly larger percentage of national income than they were before.

4) The rate of return to capital has not shown any particular pattern at all. The oscillations of these rates have generally reflected the oscillations of the business cycle.

5) The capital-output ratio has been fairly steady. Because of the 'deepening' of capital, i.e., the increase in the capital-labor ratio, one would expect diminishing marginal returns to capital. This would result in an increase in the capital-output ratio. So, the stable capital-output ratio seems to indicate that something (probably technical progress) has offset the operation of diminishing returns.

6) National output has generally had a constant percentage rate of growth per year, in spite of the fact that the ratio of savings to output (propensity to save) seems to oscillate with the business cycle.

• PROBLEM 29-3

Is there any difference between growth and development?

Solution: 'Growth' and 'development' are closely related concepts, but they do have different implications. Growth is generally used to describe expansion of output, without any major changes in composition of output or in the structure of the economy. Development is used to describe situations where major changes are needed to bring about expansion of output. A peasant society, for example, can only achieve limited 'growth' (expansion in output). However, by industrializing, shifting population away from the land, and creating new economic institutions, considerable 'development' is possible. Over a long period of time, continuous growth will involve structural change, but this change can be considered a byproduct of growth, rather than a prerequisite to growth. The emphasis on structural change to promote an expansion in output is the major difference between an economist's use of the concept of development, and his use of the concept of growth.

• PROBLEM 29-4

Why are slight differences in growth rate percentages so important?

Solution: Slight differences in growth rate percentages are important because they can reflect large differences in potential output. The difference to the United States in 1977 (with a GNP of $1265 billion in 1972 dollars) between a 3 and 4 percent growth rate comes to over $12 billion worth of output per year. Over a ten year period, the difference would amount to some $170 billion. For poor countries, these differences in growth rate percentages can be the difference between survival and disaster.

• PROBLEM 29-5

Why do economists use per capita figures so often when discussing growth?

Solution: Economists use concepts like per capita output (total output divided by population, or average output per person) to explain growth because they feel that per capita figures measure growth more accurately than aggregate figures. They are considered a better index of changes in individual welfare. If output in an economy grew by 3% in a year, but population grew by 5%, then economists would not say that the economy showed real growth. Although that society's aggregate wealth grew slightly, the individual people in the society became poorer on average. Per capita income (income per head) went down because the economy did not grow as fast as the population. By using per capita figures, economists attempt to discover if the individual people in an economy are growing richer or poorer, and not just whether an economy as a whole is growing or not.

• PROBLEM 29-6

Drawn below are the production-possibility frontiers for a small country, before and after development. Describe what happens as the country develops.

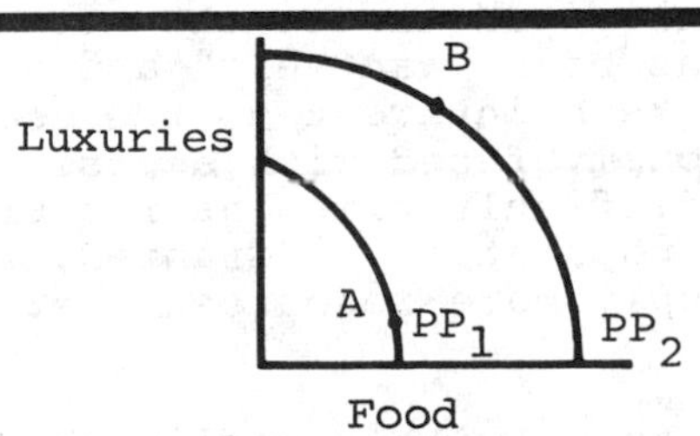

Solution: Prior to development this country is situated on PP_1 at point A. At this point the country is devoting almost all its resources to food production, thereby enjoying few of the luxuries of life.

Following development, the country has moved its production-possibility curve outward to PP_2 and now lies on PP_2 at point B. Notice that as it moved from A to B food consumption increased very little, whereas consumption of luxuries increased a good deal.

• PROBLEM 29-7

What is the rule of 72?

Solution: In dealing with populations, we often use the so-called "rule of 72." It is used to approximate the doubling time of the population, or of interest. Suppose you estimate that the population of a country will grow at an annual rate of 6% for the next 25 years. To find out when the population will be double its present size, you could use a logarithm table or a calculator. But if neither are handy, you can simply divide the annual growth rate into 72 to approximate the doubling time. Therefore doubling time $\sim$ 72/6 = 12 years. If we use a calculator, we find that the true answer is 11.8956 years. So we see that the error by using this rule of thumb is slight.

Keep in mind that the rule of 72 can also be used in determining doubling time for interest accounts at banks or in any compound interest situation.

• PROBLEM 29-8

Define net reproduction rate (NRR). What does it mean if NRR is (1) greater than one, and (2) less than one? Why is the net reproduction rate of interest to the economist?

Solution: The net reproduction rate for any group is defined as the average number of female babies that will be born to a newly born female, representative of the group, during her lifetime.

If the NRR for a group is greater than one (and stays there), the group's population will ultimately grow. If NRR is less than one, the population of the group will ultimately decline.

Since economics deals with the allocation of scarce resources in the face of unlimited wants, the actual number of persons in an economy (as both "want-ers" and contributors of resources) is of keen interest to the economist. A stagnant or declining economy faced with a positive or increasing NRR can expect difficult times as resources grow more scarce in relation to population. (Granted, the increased population will supply more resources, yet natural resources are fixed.)

Similarly, an economy faced with a declining NRR can

expect an easing as resources become less scarce in relation to population. (Such an economy must be aware of the fact that a declining NRR also means a lower future level of resource supplies, though.)

POPULATION

• PROBLEM 29-9

How can rapid population growth contribute to economic progress? How can this growth detract from progress?

Solution: Rapid population growth is desirable when non-labor resources are tremendously underutilized. During a large part of the history of the United States, there were large tracts of land that were unused. As people moved into this land, output grew tremendously. As more people moved in, farms became technically efficient units of production, instead of sprawling, wasteful domains that could not possibly be farmed by one family. So, rapid population growth in these empty lands was accompanied by a more than proportionate increase in production, resulting from the extension of the division of labor and increasing marginal returns to labor applied to land, and contributed strongly to economic progress.

There is usually a point, however, beyond which future population growth can detract from progress. With given supplies of capital and natural resources, and a given state of technology, diminishing returns to labor will set in as population increases. Once the optimum level of population has been passed, diminishing returns will pull down the average labor income. Rapid population growth, then, can also wipe out progress. Even where there is technological progress, population growth without a proportionate rate of capital accumulation can outstrip the increase in output, as in India, for example. The possible contributions or detractions that population growth can make to economic progress depend on the initial relative abundances of population, natural resources, and capital.

• PROBLEM 29-10

Using the data provided in the accompanying table, compute the marginal and average physical productivities. What is the "optimum" population (level of population with highest per capita income) for this economy?

Population (Thousands)	Total Physical Product (Thousand Tons)	Marginal Physical Product (Thousand Tons)	Average Physical Product (Tons)
1	10	-	-
2	22	-	-

3	36	-	-
4	52	-	-
5	70	-	-
6	90	-	-
7	108	-	-
8	124	-	-
9	135	-	-

Solution: The marginal physical product per thousand people is computed by determining how much the total physical product is increased by the addition of an extra thousand people to the economy. So, when the first thousand people arrive they have a marginal physical product of 10 thousand tons. When the second thousand people arrive, 12 thousand tons (22 - 10) are added to the total physical product. The marginal physical productivity of this group, then, is 12 thousand tons. This process is repeated to compute the other marginal productivities.

The average physical product is computed by dividing the total physical production by the corresponding total population. So, for the first one thousand people, the average physical product is ten tons. For two thousand people, the average physical product is 11 tons per thousand. By repeating this process for the other levels of population, the following table is obtained:

Population (Thousands)	Total Physical Product (Thousand Tons)	Marginal Physical Product (Thousand Tons)		Average Physical Product (Tons)	
1	10	10		10	$(\frac{10}{1})$
2	22	12	(22 - 10)	11	$(\frac{22}{2})$
3	36	14	(36 - 22)	12	$(\frac{36}{3})$
4	52	16	(52 - 36)	13	$(\frac{52}{4})$
5	70	18	(70 - 52)	14	$(\frac{70}{5})$
6	90	20	(90 - 70)	15	$(\frac{90}{6})$
7	108	18	(108 - 90)	15.4	$(\frac{108}{7})$
8	124	16	(124 - 108)	15.5	$(\frac{124}{8})$
9	135	11	(135 - 124)	15	$(\frac{135}{9})$

To determine the optimum population, find the level of population that has the highest average physical product. The average physical product is simply another way of saying per capita output, or per capita income. So per capita income (average physical product) is highest when the population is 8 thousand people, with a per capita income of 15.5 tons of product. Note that the average physical product is not highest where marginal physical product is highest. Average physical product continues to rise after marginal physical product has started to fall, because marginal product (18 with 7 thousand people) is still higher than average product (15.4 with 7 thousand people). Average product will rise whenever it is less than marginal product, even if marginal product is decreasing.

CAPITAL ACCUMULATION

• PROBLEM 29-11

What is the cost of capital accumulation to society?

Solution: The cost of capital accumulation is the consumption society sacrifices today for the prospect of higher potential consumption tomorrow. Capital accumulation results from increased levels of productive investment, which will increase potential output. But to accumulate capital, to save, a society has to forgo some consumption. It follows that the faster the rate of capital accumulation, the greater the consumption loss in the present and the greater the potetial gain in the future. The cost incurred, then, is simply a reflection of how much society values present consumption, compared to future consumption.

• PROBLEM 29-12

What is the difference between gross capital accumulation and net capital accumulation? Which is the better indicator of growth?

Solution: Gross capital accumulation (or formation) is the total amount of investment in capital goods in a given period, usually a year. Some of this investment, however, is merely replacing worn-out or obsolete, i.e., depreciated, equipment. Gross capital accumulation, then, includes capital invested to offset depreciation. Net capital accumulation is the addition to the stock of capital goods; that is, it does not include depreciation costs. So the difference between net capital accumulation and gross capital accumulation is that gross accumulation includes depreciation costs, i.e., the depreciation allowance.

Because net capital accumulation does not include the depreciation allowance, it is the better indicator of growth. It indicates by how much the stock of capital goods has been increased. This additional investment expands output capacity. Investment to replace worn-out equipment does not add to output capacity, it merely maintains output capacity at the same level. So, net capital accumulation provides some indication of how much productive capacity is being expanded by investment. Gross capital accumulation does not tell us how much investment is being used to expand capacity, and how much is simply replacing old equipment.

• **PROBLEM 29-13**

What is the capital-output ratio?

Solution: The capital-output ratio (or incremental capital -output ratio) describes the relationship between increases in net investment and the resulting increases in the productive capacity of society. If, for example, 4 dollars of net investment makes the economy capable of producing one additional dollar's worth of output, then the capital-output ratio is 4 to 1. This ratio is used to translate changes in the average propensity to save (and hence changes in capital accumulation) to changes in the growth rate.

• **PROBLEM 29-14**

What is meant by the "deepening" of capital? How would this affect growth (assume a fixed technology)?

Solution: The deepening of capital simply describes the rise of the capital to labor ratio; that is, more and more capital is being added to a fixed supply of labor. Applying the law of diminishing returns to this situation, it is clear that the marginal return to capital will go down, i.e., successive increments of capital will induce smaller and smaller increases in output. Eventually, capital accumulation and investment would have no effect at all on output. There would be no growth. As the marginal returns to capital decline, interest rates and profits would also decline since capital is in relatively more abundant supply. The increase in the quantity of capital per worker, on the other hand, causes the marginal product of labor (now the relatively more scarce factor) to rise, and likewise the wage rate that employers are willing to pay. Because the increases in the stock of capital have less and less effect on output, the capital-output ratio would also rise. The deepening of capital, then, could result in a no-growth, stationary state if there is no technological progress.

• **PROBLEM 29-15**

What is 'human capital' and what are the implications of this for growth?

Solution: Human capital is investment made in people, as opposed to physical capital, which is investment in factories and machinery. Investments in human capital can be made by refining the talents and abilities of a person. The most basic investments would be in health and education. A healthy, educated person is capable of producing more than an ill-fed, illiterate one.

The relationship of human capital to growth is fairly straightforward. Nations can make investments in human capital just as they can make investments in physical capital. By feeding and educating workers, nations can increase productivity. Firms can also increase productivity, and output, by having training and remedial education programs. Social investments in human capital, in training engineers and college professors, can increase growth rates and per capita income just as investments in traditional capital can. Economists have only recently realized that advanced equipment does not increase growth at all unless there are properly trained workers available to operate the equipment.

• PROBLEM 29-16

What is social overhead capital?

Solution: Social overhead capital refers to those public investments that are necessary for growth and development. Roads, dams, irrigation projects, and public health measures are usually prerequisites for any substantial private investment. Public facilities benefit society and build up an "infrastructure" for private investments. A country's "infrastructure" is the communications, transportation, educational, and public health networks needed for economic growth.

It is often noted that social overhead capital often involves projects where there are increasing returns to scale. The larger a hydroelectric plant is, for example, the more technically efficient it usually is. Because of the large scale of these projects, and the wide diffusion of benefits from which it is difficult or impossible to exclude beneficiaries, it is often argued that social overhead projects should be undertaken by the public authorities. Since many of these projects would show profits only after a considerable period of time, many economists argue that private investors will not undertake such investments. These social overhead capital projects are often cited as examples of beneficial public investment. Sometimes these projects will be undertaken in order to induce greater private investment. Only rarely will they actually replace private investment. The concept of social overhead capital has become vitally important in theories of underdevelopment, and in theories of growth of the more advanced nations.

• PROBLEM 29-17

In highly centralized, socialist countries, the government can decide directly how much capital accumulation there will be. In capitalist countries, the government can only influence the rate of capital accumulation indirectly. Describe some measures the government of a capitalist country can take if it wants to increase the rate of capital accumulation.

Solution: The government can try to increase the rate of capital accumulation by taking measures that would increase the cost of consumption and decrease the cost of investment. This can be done by increasing taxes on consumer goods, while giving investment tax credits to businesses, and permitting firms to deduct greater depreciation allowances from their taxable revenues. These measures will make it more expensive to consume goods, while inducing businesses to make more investments. In addition to these measures, which change the prices of consumption and investment, the government can increase taxes on personal incomes. This tax increase simply enlarges the amount of forced public savings. The government can use this money, most of which would have gone to consumption, for public, social investment (such as roads, schools, etc.) or it can use the money to finance private investment. Either way, the government has increased capital accumulation by forcibly reducing personal accumulation. Though a government in a capitalistic country cannot directly set the rate of capital accumulation, it is obvious that it still can influence this rate by a variety of means.

• PROBLEM 29-18

If a mature economy could grow only by capital accumulation or population growth, which would be preferred? Why?

Solution: With a choice of either capital accumulation or population growth, capital accumulation would usually be preferred as the means to growth. With more capital per worker, the marginal productivity of labor can increase. This increase in per capita output would increase per capita income. So, capital accumulation would lead to a higher standard of living for the people. Population growth alone does not necessarily achieve this. While an increased population will bring about an increase in output, it will also mean that there are more people to share the increase. This increase in output would, due to the diminishing marginal product of labor as there is less capital per worker, be proportionally smaller than the increase in population. In this case, per capita income, the measure of the material standard of living, would go down. Individuals would be materially worse off than they were before the population increase. It is obvious that if a certain amount of capital accumulation, and a certain increase in population, could both bring about the same increase in output, the capital accumulation would always result in a higher level of per capita income. Because of increases in per capita income caused by capital accumulation it is normally preferred as the engine of economic growth. The only time it would not be preferred is if a country was seriously underpopulated. This case does not seem to have widespread relevance.

• PROBLEM 29-19

Given that the aim of growth is to increase per capita consumption, is it possible for there to be too much investment?

Solution: It is possible for there to be so much investment

in an economy that investment cuts into future consumption. The reason this is possible is that capital investment requires more future investment to offset depreciation if the capital stock is to be maintained at the new higher level. If there is too much investment, future depreciation replacement costs will offset future consumption gains. In this case, there is too much capital accumulation to achieve maximum per capita consumption.

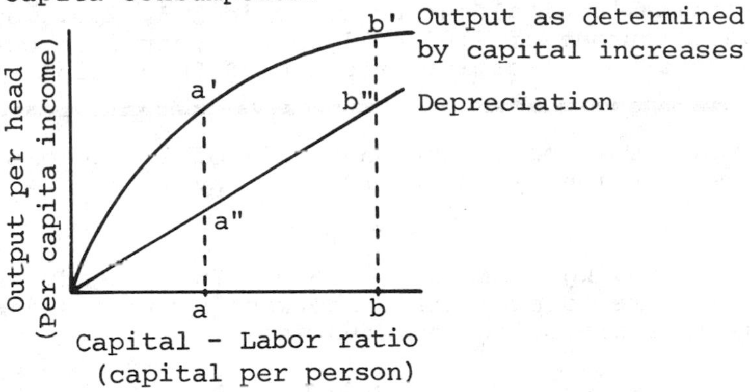

This can be illustrated graphically by using the per capita income and the capital-labor ratio (average amount of capital per worker) in an economy with no technological progress and a steady or growing population. Because technology is fixed by assumption, as each worker gets more capital to work with (as the capital-labor ratio rises), each successive increase in capital will result in a smaller and smaller increase in output. In other words, as the amount of capital increases with respect to labor, capital will be subject to diminishing returns. On the graph, this is illustrated by the decreasing slope of the output curve. The slope is decreasing because each increase in the capital-labor ratio brings about a smaller increase in output and so, a smaller increase in per capita income. In this graph, depreciation is shown as a positively-sloped straight line. The positive slope reflects the fact that each increase in investment (each increase in the capital-labor ratio) will be accompanied by an increase in depreciation costs if the capital stock is to be maintained at the new higher level. If, for example, a company has ten machines, each of which has to be replaced every ten years, then the company has to replace an average of one machine a year; if the company has one hundred machines, it has to replace an average of ten machines per year. As the company's investment in machines rises, so do its future depreciation costs if it plans to maintain its larger capital stock. The straight line is used only for simplicity; as long as the slope is positive, the line may be curved or straight.

Now from the graph we can see that the amount of output per person after deducting depreciation costs is higher at point a than at point b. The distance a'a" is greater than the distance b'b". The greater depreciation costs at point b offset the greater output. This is a clear illustration of how too high a level of investment can reduce per capita consumption. The individuals in this economy would be better off with the lower per capita investment level of a, than the investment level of b. Because of depreciation costs, not even future consumption would be increased at point b.

• PROBLEM 29-20

What do you expect the rate of growth to be of an economy where, on average, the population saves 15% of its income and marginal capital/output ratio is 2.5, i.e., an increase in output of $100 billion per year is produced by an increse in the capital stock of $250 billion.

Solution: The population saves 15% of its income, so the savings function can be represented by

$$S = 0.15Y \qquad (1)$$

where S ≡ Savings, and Y ≡ income. In a steady growth economy there is equilibrium between savings and investment: all savings are being invested, so

$$I = S \qquad (2)$$

where I ≡ investment. Combining (1) and (2) yields $I = 0.15Y$. Investment is equal to the net addition to capital (depreciation is ignored in this example, so that gross investment = net investment), ΔK in a steady state, so $I = \Delta K$, and

$$\Delta K = 0.15Y \qquad (3)$$

The marginal capital/output ratio is 2.5, thus $\frac{\Delta K}{\Delta Y} = 2.5$; its reciprocal, the output/capital ratio is

$$\frac{\Delta Y}{\Delta K} = \frac{1}{2.5} = 0.40 \qquad (4)$$

Substituting equation (3), into equation (4) for ΔK, results in

$$\frac{\Delta Y}{0.15Y} = 0.40 \quad .$$

Multiplying both sides by 0.15 gives the rate of growth in national income $\frac{\Delta Y}{Y} = 0.15 \times 0.40 = 0.06$, or 6% per year. In effect we have multiplied the average propensity to save, $s = 0.15$, with the marginal output/capital ratio $\frac{\Delta Y}{\Delta K} = 0.40$ or, what is the same, we have divided the average propensity to save, $s = 0.15$, by the marginal capital/output ratio $\frac{\Delta K}{\Delta Y} = 2.5$ in order to find the expected growth rate of the economy $\frac{\Delta Y}{Y}$.

• PROBLEM 29-21

When the population of a country consumes 90% of its income, and its technology is such that, at the margin, a $100 billion increase in its capital stock increases its output by $25 billion, what would you expect the growth rate of this society to be?

Solution: Income, Y, is composed of consumption, C, and savings, S:

$$Y = C + S \quad . \tag{1}$$

The population consumes 90% of its income; therefore

$$C = 0.90Y \tag{2}$$

(this is the average consumption function). Substituting equation (2) into equation (1) yields

$$Y = 0.90Y + S \quad .$$

Thus savings are

$$S = Y - 0.90Y = 0.10Y \quad , \tag{3}$$

i.e., 10% of income. All savings are assumed to be invested. Therefore,

$$S = I \tag{4}$$

where I = investment. Substituting equation (4) into equation (3) yields

$$I = 0.10Y \quad . \tag{5}$$

Investment is defined as the increase in the capital stock, K, i.e., $I = \Delta K$. Therefore equation (5) may be written as:

$$\Delta K = 0.10Y \tag{6}$$

The marginal capital/output ratio, determined by the country's technology is

$$\frac{\Delta K}{\Delta Y} = \frac{\$100 \text{ billion}}{\$25 \text{ billion}} = 4$$

or

$$\Delta K = 4 \times \Delta Y \tag{7}$$

That is, each addition to future annual output requires a current addition to the capital stock equal to $4. When we substitute equation (7) into equation (6) the result is $4\Delta Y = 0.10Y$. Dividing both sides by 4Y gives the growth rate of national income

$$\frac{\Delta Y}{Y} = \frac{0.10}{4} = 0.025 \quad , \text{ or } \quad 2.5\%$$

per year. In effect, we have divided the average propensity to save s = 0.10, by the marginal capital/output ratio $\frac{\Delta K}{\Delta Y} = 4$, to determine the expected rate of growth in national income.

TECHNOLOGICAL INNOVATION

• PROBLEM 29-22

Describe research, innovation, and the diffusion of technology.

Solution: A technology is a way of combining resources so as to accomplish an objective.

During the research stage we witness investment of resources in the development of new knowledge. For example Henry Ford tried repeatedly to develop a new method of automobile production before hitting upon the assembly line method.

The innovation stage involves the initial application of the new knowledge to the production of goods and services. After Henry Ford developed the assembly line, he put all his efforts into the commercial production of automobiles using his new technology.

Finally, diffusion involves the widespread use of the new technology in production. In Ford's case, other producers were forced to imitate his new tachnology since the assembly line was a more efficient means of production.

• PROBLEM 29-23

How can economies of scale contribute to growth?

Solution: Economies of scale, because of the advantages of mass production, contribute to growth by enabling firms, and countries, to produce goods at lower average cost. Economies of scale characterize production processes which use less inputs per unit of output as the scale of production increases. Because these processes use less input per unit output than smaller scale production of the same goods would use, output can be expanded without a proportionate increase in inputs. An increment of resources which, in the absence of economies of scale, would be required in order to expand the scale of production of a given commodity, is instead available for production of other commodities. Because of economies of scale, these resources can be used to increase production in another sector, without decreasinq production in the sector they were originally allotted to. Economies of scale, then, can lead to increased production, or growth, in many sectors of the economy.

• PROBLEM 29-24

Why is the principle of diminishing returns so important to growth theory?

Solution: With fixed natural resources and a fixed technology, diminishing marginal returns would indicate that capital accumulation and population growth alone cannot indefinitely increase output. In agriculture, for example, after a certain stage of mechanization has been achieved, neither more capital nor more laborers will be able to increase food production from a given land area. In a factory that uses raw materials, more workers using more machines will be able to produce only so much from a fixed amount of raw materials. Diminishing returns, in regards to natural resources (specifically land) was the basis of Thomas Malthus's dire prediction about the limits of growth. Once those limits were achieved, he said, population growth would force a decline in per capita income, possibly down to the starvation level. So, the principle of diminishing marginal returns, and any factors which might overcome the operation of the principle, has tremendous importance to growth theory, especially as regards the limits of growth.

• PROBLEM 29-25

Malthus used diminishing returns to predict an end to growth and possible disaster. The Club of Rome has also predicted an end to growth and almost certain disaster. What basis does this group have for its predictions?

Solution: The Club of Rome uses a more sophisticated version of diminishing returns, but basically it uses the same analytical concept of diminishing returns that Malthus used. For the theorists of the Club of Rome, there are two crucial fixed quantities. The first, as in Malthus' model, is the supply of natural resources. Modern technology and industry are heavily dependent on the use of non-renewable resources. When these resources run out, an event the Club of Rome regards as fairly imminent, they think that modern industry will decline rapidly. The other fixed-quantity is the capacity of the earth to absorb industrial waste and pollution. The Club of Rome theorists believe that the increased waste which will be the result of growth will eventually choke off the possibility of any more growth. When diminishing returns are applied to these fixed quantities, they think that an end to growth is inevitable.

Using elaborate computer models, they predict that a sudden and uncontrollable collapse will take place well before the year 2100. Even when they assume twice the amount of known resources, quadruple the productivity of land and raw materials, cut pollution by three-fourths, and half the population growth, their models still predict collapse before 2100. So, using the limits to resources and diminishing returns, the Club of Rome theorists have predicted a Doomsday scenario not unlike the one predicted by Malthus.

• PROBLEM 29-26

Given a fixed amount of natural resources, the Law of Diminishing Returns would indicate that capital accumulation and population growth could not by themselves prevent the eventual emergence of a no-growth state. Cite several factors which could offset the Law of Diminishing Returns.

Solution: The factors are: a) more efficient use of inputs,
b) increasing returns to scale,
c) technological innovation.

a) If inputs in the production process are used more efficiently, then this would at least partially offset the limited amount of natural resources. This efficiency could be attained, through streamlined production and more stringent cost controls.

b) Increasing returns to scale is the economic term used to denote the technical efficiency gains of mass production. Cars, for example, are produced more cheaply when manufactured by the thousands in huge factories, than when they are built by the hundreds in smaller factories. The tendency of increasing returns to scale in some areas of production is one way of using capital accumulation to offset the diminishing returns on natural resources. Capital accumulation is necessary in order to take advantage of increasing returns; without large amounts of capital, mass production is not possible.

c) Technological innovation has been historically the greatest source of economic growth. Breakthroughs in science and engineering have increased the productivity of both labor and capital. With these constantly increasing productivities, it seems that the fixed amount of natural resources can be completely offset. Technological advances, moreover, imbue with the quality of resource materials that had previously been completely useless, as, for example, nuclear technology did with uranium, and as new technology transformed oil from a waste product of kerosene into a major energy source. Technological innovation and resource availability are not independent factors, but are intimately related. Further, such innovation is likely to accelerate as exhaustable resources become depleted and their prices rise. Technological innovation is also important in that it seems the only permanent way to keep increasing productivity. There are definite limits to the productivity of better management of factor inputs and increasing returns to scale. There does not seem to be any corresponding limitation to innovation.

• PROBLEM 29-27

Use the concept of capital deepening to explain why economists think that technological progress has been the most important factor for growth for advanced countries.

Solution: Capital deepening would imply that the capital-output ratio would rise because of diminishing returns to the increases in capital. In fact, there has been capital deepening; the capital-labor ratio has increased tremendously over the past century. The capital-output ratio has not risen, though. It has remained fairly stable. This would imply that some factor has offset diminishing returns. The massive increases in the capital-labor ratio would seem to indicate that output would rise more slowly than the capital stock. Economists think that technological progress is the factor that has been most instrumental in offsetting diminishing returns. Capital accumulation, by introducing embodied technological progress to production processes, has managed to avoid diminishing returns. Instead of merely adding to the previous stock of capital, new investments have also introduced new, more productive technologies. So, technological progress has proceeded simultaneously with capital deepening. Economists feel that the offsetting, by more productive technologies, of diminishing returns as a result of capital deepening demonstrates the importance of technological progress.

• PROBLEM 29-28

Technological innovation has been one of the most important causes of economic growth. Explain what embodied technological progress is and discuss its relationship to capital accumulation.

Solution: Embodied technological progress is progress that requires new forms of either human or physical capital in order to put the technology into practice. In contrast to this, disembodied progress does not require new capital; it uses the present factors of production in a more efficient way. The term "embodied" refers to the fact that the new technology is "in" the new machine, or "in" new skills; it cannot be utilized without an investment in these machines or skills.

Since the use of embodied technological progress depends on capital investment, the use of this progress necessarily depends on capital accumulation as well. Even if there is not any net accumulation of capital (if only enough is accumulated to replace worn-out equipment), the new technology can still be introduced. The old, worn-out equipment (or the retiring workers) can be replaced with the new equipment (or with young workers with new skills). It is obvious, though, that the new technology can be introduced faster if there is net capital accumulation as well. The more capital that is accumulated, the faster technological progress can be put to use. The higher the rate of embodied technological progress (that is, the rate at which new technology can be utilized in production processes), the higher the growth rate of per capita income. Since most technological progress is embodied, this implies that capital accumulation has a large effect on the introduction of new technology. Capital accumulation and embodied technological progress, then, are very closely related.

• PROBLEM 29-29

How did Joseph Schumpeter build his theory of the business cycle, and of growth, from the idea of embodied technological progress?

Solution: Schumpeter considered the activity of those entrepreneurs who embodied the new technologies to be the key to the capitalist system. These innovators would take the financial risks of introducing new technologies to the market place. If they were successful, other, less imaginative, entrepreneurs would then copy the new technology. The effect of the embodiment of the new technology would be a spurt in growth. The new technology would provide the incentive for new investment, thus increasing the potential output of society. Schumpeter thought that as each cycle of innovation played itself out, the economy would slump until the next new technology was embodied. For Schumpeter, technological progress and imaginative, risk-taking innovators were the keys to the business cycle, and to growth.

EFFICIENCY AND RESOURCE UTILIZATION

• PROBLEM 29-30

A factor contributing to growth in the past has been allocational efficiency. Describe the micro and macro aspects of this efficiency.

Solution: Allocational efficiency is getting the most highly valued combination of goods and services out of a given supply of land, labor and capital, with a fixed state of technology. The micro aspects of the increases in allocational efficiency deal with the efforts of firms to cut costs and to direct resources to the production of goods and services for which the demand has increased, and out of lines of production where demand has fallen. Firms streamline company organization, improve factory lay-outs, and search for the lowest-priced raw materials and machinery. In these ways, firms lower their own costs and lower the costs to society. In addition, firms try to exercise constant alertness to changes in consumer tastes and are prepared to adjust their product mix accordingly. The macro aspects deal with the changing structure of the economy. Labor and other resources are transferred from one sector of the economy to another as conditions change. There has been a marked decrease, for example, in agricultural workers, a decrease matched by an increase in service industry workers. This is a transfer of resources from an area where they would have been less productive, to an area where they are more productive. Similarly, as some industries, like coal, decline, workers transfer to other industries where they are needed. Sometimes these transfers are hindered by union or company pressure on behalf of the contracting industries, but in order to achieve allocational efficiency and maximum growth they must eventually take place. In this way, the productive capacity of society is increased. Both the micro and macro aspects of allocational efficiency help stimulate growth, without an increase in the supply of factor resources.

• PROBLEM 29-31

How does the price system help allocative efficiency? Explain how prices can act as 'feedback mechanisms' to offset the depletion of resources?

Solution: The price system helps allocative efficiency by identifying the cheapest production processes and by reallocating resources. A firm, for example, can choose the most efficient combination of capital and labor by comparing the prices (and productivities) of capital and labor. These factor (capital and labor) prices are determined by the supplies of the factors, relative to the demand for the factors. Thus in a country with an abundant population, but little capital, profit-maximizing firms will probably use relatively labor-intensive methods of production because the price of labor will be relatively low due to its abundance. The scarcer factor of production, capital, will have a relatively higher price and will therefore be conserved and applied only in its most highly valued uses. This analysis of factor prices also applies to non-renewable, natural resources. As, for example, oil becomes more scarce, its price rises. As its price climbs, there are two reactions. First of all, people tend to cut down on oil consumption; they try to curtail their use of oil so they do not have to spend so much of their incomes on it. In addition to conservation, they look for alternative energy sources. Thus, as the price of oil has climbed in the past few years, the search for other energy sources (coal, solar energy, etc.) has intensified. The second reaction to the higher price is that firms now have incentives to expand output by drilling deeper costlier wells, or, as is the case with other natural resources, by recycling them. So, the price mechanism automatically induces responses to alleviate shortages of resources. This tends to offset, and overrule, the rapid depletion of resources. Prices, then, help determine the rate of growth by contributing to allocative efficiency, and by inducing consumers to economize on scarce resources. This tends to undermine predictions of economic collapse based on shortages of resources. Shortages will be reflected in higher prices, which will spur consumers and producers to use alternative resources.

• PROBLEM 29-32

Is the achievement of full employment sufficient for the maintenance of growth?

Solution: While full employment is necessary for maximum growth, it will not by itself insure growth, i.e., an increase in per capita output. In fact, full employment could even be associated with a decrease in per capita output. If, for example, full employment is maintained in the face of population growth by decreasing wages (as wages go down, employers hire more workers and absorb the increased labor force) then there will be a lower per capita income (though total output might increase some). If, with either a stable or growing population, there is no net investment, then there will be little, if any, per capita growth.

A society could maintain full employment simply by replacing worn-out equipment, without making any provisions whatsoever for new investments. Without new investments the society will not grow, or it can only grow very little. Without new investments, diminishing returns will apply to increases in the number of workers employed to work with a fixed amount of equipment.

Economic growth depends on capital accumulation, increasing returns to scale, technological progress, and other factors. Full employment, by itself, does not guarantee that any of these factors will come into play. It is entirely possible to maintain full employment equilibrium, and yet have a no-growth economy.

• PROBLEM 29-33

Most discussions of growth focus on the supply aspect of growth. Explain how unemployment due to lack of demand for goods can affect growth.

Solution: Unemployment can depress growth even in subsequent years when there is full employment. When there is unemployment, investment and capital accumulation generally decline. Firms are reluctant to invest in a situation where there is a lack of effective demand for goods and services. In fact, firms usually 'disinvest,' i.e., reduce their stock of capital goods, during recessionary times by getting rid of excess inventories. This lack of investment will not only depress or nullify the growth rate during the recession, but will also have repercussions on the growth rate after the economy has recovered. The lack of capital accumulation during the recession will depress the long-term rate of growth by lowering the amount of capital available for new (net) investment. Merely replacing worn-out equipment could use up all the available capital. Because of the decline in net investment, the introduction of new technology could also be slowed. Since technological progress is a very important source of growth, this slowing down could also depress the growth rate. These effects on physical capital apply to human capital as well. For example, people will not make the sacrifices to become engineers if the job market for engineers is tight. When the economy recovers, there may be a lack of engineers and other skilled personnel, thus putting a drag on potential growth.

So, unemployment and unemployment cycles in economic activity can seriously impair growth. The obstacles to growth caused by these cycles can persist, and depress growth, long after the economy has recovered. Thus unemployment has a more than transitory effect. Because of this, adequate fiscal and monetary policies which insure that bouts of unemployment become less severe and less frequent are imperative.

• PROBLEM 29-34

If an economy recovers from a recession (like the American recession of 1974-75), is the recovery considered growth?

Solution: Growth does not refer to short-term cyclical variations in economic activity, such as a recovery or a recession. In the example of a recovery, the recovery would be considered a movement back to potential output, and not economic growth. To abstract from the fluctuations of the economy, economists use either measures of potential output or long-term averages of output. In this way, they hope to concentrate on long-term trends without being distracted by short-term variations.

OTHER FACTORS

• PROBLEM 29-35

What do property rights have to do with growth?

Solution: Investment, either expanding existing facilities or introducing new technologies, is one of the major factors of the rate of growth. In capitalist countries, a large share of investment is investment by the private sector. Firms and individuals, however, will be reluctant to invest if their ownership of their investments is in question. Companies, for example, will not invest in countries where they think their factories will be nationalized. So some countries experience a lack of private investment because property rights are not secure, and these countries suffer lower rates of growth. Some economists have asserted that the economic development of Western Europe was based on the development of secure property rights. Secure property rights will induce people to invest, which will contribute to growth. Property rights, then, are important as influences on economic growth.

• PROBLEM 29-36

Most discussions of growth economics concentrate on a single economy which is isolated from all others. Discuss two ways in which international factors can affect growth.

Solution: International considerations can affect growth in two different ways. The first is through trade, and the consequent specialization in production. Specialization by a nation according to its comparative advantage will lead to growth (expansion of potential output) and to a structural change in the economy. This structural change will come about because those industries which enjoy a comparative cost advantage will expand to increase exports, while other industries which suffer a comparative cost disadvantage will decline because of competition from imports. So, international trade will contribute to growth, but it will also change the direction of growth. This change of direction is not detrimental to the economy; in fact, it is helpful. Trade will weed out the relatively inefficient industries while encouraging the expansion of the relatively more efficient industries. Because it stimulates the expansion of the most efficient industries, trade will lead to a more efficient allocation of resources in the world economy, which will in turn add to domestic growth. So trade will increase the growth of the economy both directly, through comparative advantage, and indirectly, through improved allocational efficiency.

The other way in which international considerations can effect growth is through resource mobility. The resources needed for more rapid growth, capital, natural resources, and labor, can be obtained from abroad. Immigration can increase the labor force, natural resources can be purchased, and capital can be borrowed from other countries. In addition to this, 'brain draining' and purchasing advanced technology can also stimulate growth.

Trade and resource mobility, then, are international aspects of growth theory. Both can increase an economy's potential beyond that of a closed, isolated economy.

HARROD-DOMAR GROWTH MODEL

• PROBLEM 29-37

Give a simple explanation of the mechanism of the Harrod-Domar growth model.

Solution: The Harrod-Domar growth model uses the average propensity to save and the capital-output ratio to determine the rate of growth. The average propensity to save is used because this gives the rate of capital accumulation. The average propensity to save yields the percentage of total income that is invested. (In this simple model, savings are equal to investment.) After the rate of capital accumulation (rate of investment) has been determined, it is necessary to find how much an increase in capital investment will add to output capacity. This is given by the capital-output ratio. With an average propensity to save of 10%, and a capital-output ratio of 4 to 1, the growth rate will be 2.5%. The 10% average propensity to save tells us that the economy will have an additional 10 dollars capital next year for every 100 dollars of output this year, and the capital-output ratio tells us that this additional 10 dollars will increase output capacity by 2.5 dollars (10 ÷ 4). So, the rate of growth is 2.5% ($2.5/$100). The Harrod-Domar model, then, divides the average propensity to save by the capital-output ratio $\left(\frac{\text{average propensity to save}}{\text{capital-output ratio}}\right)$ to determine the growth rate.

• PROBLEM 29-38

What assumption in the Harrod-Domar model is particularly troublesome? If the assumption is dropped, how could the model lead to chronic instability?

Solution: The troublesome assumption in the Harrod-Domar model is that planned savings equal planned investment. It could be argued that when investment increases, firms bid up the interest rate in a competition to get financing, and this higher interest rate will induce higher savings. The problem with this argument is that savings are mainly a function of income, not of the interest rate. So, this assumption of the equality of planned savings and investment seems to make the model unrealistic.

If this assumption is dropped, however, the model has further problems. If more money is saved than is invested, there is the possibility of depression and collapse. This is because more money has been taken out (saved) of the flow of expenditure than has been put back in (invested). The result is that the level of demand (both consumption and investment) will not be high enough to absorb the total supply of output at prevailing prices. As a result, output will decline, possibly to depression levels. Similarly, if planned investment exceeds savings, demand will exceed the total supply of output at prevailing prices. This could very well stimulate price inflation. So, if the assumption that planned savings equals planned investment is dropped, the economy could easily be lead into inflation or depression rather than growth. Instead of a continuous growth rate, there could be chronic instability.

• PROBLEM 29-39

How could government policy eliminate the instability of the Harrod-Domar model?

Solution: Government policy can both directly and indirectly eliminate the cause of instability (namely, the lack of a mechanism to insure that planned savings equal planned investment) in the Harrod-Domar growth model. If planned savings is greater than planned investment, the government can absorb the excess savings and undertake growth-generating investment itself. So, if, in the United States, planned private investment is not large enough to absorb savings, the government can invest the excess savings in capital goods such as highways, public housing, and dams. If investment exceeds savings, the government can increase taxes to force a reduction in consumption. Forced public savings would make up the difference between savings and investment. It is clear that a government could manipulate both savings and investment either to increase or decrease the rate of growth. Government policy can determine the growth rate of a country directly.

A government can increase the rate of growth in another way. By redistributing income from rich to poor, the government can lower the average propensity to save because the propensity to save depends on the level of income. If most people have low incomes, the country as a whole will have a low propensity to save. By taking income from those who have higher propensities to save, the average propensity will be lowered even further. In the Harrod-Domar model, a lower propensity to save means a lower growth rate. Similarly, a government could redistribute income from the poor to the rich to increase the propensity to save and so, to increase the growth rate. In poorer countries, there is a dilemma in that reducing income equality (redistributing income from the rich to the poor) could result in a lower growth rate, and so, perpetual poverty.

Governmental policy, then, can affect the growth rate either directly, or indirectly, and so eliminate the instability of the Harrod-Domar growth model.

• PROBLEM 29-40

What does the Harrod-Domar model, taken with the Keynesian theory of savings, imply for the growth rates of poor countries?

Solution: The Keynesian theory of savings holds that the level of income is the main determinant of savings. In the Harrod-Domar model, savings is very important in determining growth rates. The higher the level of savings, the higher the growth rate. Taken together, these theories imply that poor, low-income countries will have low levels of savings (a low average propensity to save) which will mean that these countries will have low growth rates. So, the poor countries will stay poor, while the rich countries, with high levels of savings, will get richer. This is a simplified version of the "vicious cycle of poverty." In this cycle, poor countries cannot save income and invest (accumulate capital) because they are poor, which means they will have low growth rates that will keep them poor. The Harrod-Domar model with the Keynesian theory of savings gives one explanation of why poor countries tend to remain poor.

CONTROVERSY OVER GROWTH

• PROBLEM 29-41

It is often claimed that one of the beneficial results of growth has been the abatement of poverty. Why do some anti-growth economists challenge this claim? How do mainstream economists reply?

Solution: Anti-growth economists believe that the elimination of poverty is essentially a problem of distribution, and not a problem of production. That is, total production is sufficient to provide an "adequate" standard of living for everyone, but the inequality of individual incomes means that some people are poor. Since the problem is one of distribution, further growth will not eliminate poverty. Rather, they recommend the redistribution of existing incomes more equally. They argue that the United States has had the productive capacity to insure a decent standard of living for every one of its citizens, but has simply not done so.

Mainstream economists believe that growth is the only practical way of achieving a more nearly equal distribution of income. They believe that the middle- and upper-income groups will be more likely to vote for some redistribution if they are satisfied with their own prosperity. The basic point is that prosperous people are more generous. Since World War II, the distribution of income has remained relatively stable. Mainstream economists argue that the easiest way to better the position of the poor is to raise the entire range of incomes by increasing output. So, growth would be the primary force eliminating poverty. Further, they point out that continuous redistribution of incomes is likely to have adverse effects on work incentives, and hence on productivity and output, thereby lowering the income of almost everyone in the long run. These economists also point out that growth is almost certainly the only way for poor countries to achieve a higher standard of living. These economists generally regard growth as essential to achieve the goal of eliminating poverty.

• PROBLEM 29-42

Much of the controversy surrounding growth is based on the alleged side-effects of growth, such as pollution, the rapid obsolescence of skills, and the dehumanization of work. Relate these complaints against growth to the concept of externalities.

Solution: Externalities are the beneficial or harmful effects of a given action on people other than those taking that action. A firm that dumps raw sewage into a public stream, for example, does not pay the full cost for damages that the sewage inflicts. Likewise, the customers of the firm do not pay for the damages. The cost is borne by the people who live along the stream. Any cost or benefit of an economic act that does not accrue to the buyer or seller is called an externality (external cost or benefit).

The harmful side-effects of growth listed are all externalities. The costs of pollution, the dehumanization of work, and the rapid obsolescence of skills are not borne exclusively by either the manufacturing firms or their customers. They are borne by society as a whole. There is a difference, then, between the (private) costs of production to a firm, and the costs of production to society. This difference is the external cost. Anti-growth activists argue that these social costs of growth are greater than its benefits to society.

Economists argue that these extra social costs can be removed by eliminating externalities. If a firm is forced to take account of the costs of pollution (because of possible fines, or anti-pollution regulation), then the firm's decisions and costs will more accurately reflect social costs. Given the allocative efficiency of the pricing mechanism, the elimination of externalities (forcing firms to pay the social costs of growth) will result in growth that has to take account of the full costs of growth. If the costs are greater than the benefits, a particular investment will not be made. If the benefits exceed the costs, then the investment will be made, and there will be growth. In this way (the elimination of externalities), any growth that is undertaken will be beneficial, even when the side-effects are taken into account. Using this argument, economists can defend growth while still conceding that not all actual growth is beneficial.

Answer

To be covered when testing yourself

SHORT ANSWER QUESTIONS FOR REVIEW

Choose the correct answer.

1. The production possibility frontier indicates: (a) various maximum combinations of products producible, given your resource and technology restrictions (b) various maximum combinations of products producible, given your largest real total income (c) various minimum combinations of products producible, given technology restrictions (d) the absolute expansion of consumption which growth entails — a

2. According to Malthus's doctrine, workers' productivity will decline if: (a) more and more workers work on a variable amount of land (b) per capita incomes are low (c) the population is too large relative to domestic economy (d) more and more workers work on a fixed amount of land — d

3. The rightward shift of the production possibilities curve indicates that: (a) output has increased as a result of declining inputs (b) a movement from a point inside to a point on the production possibilities curve (c) labor is now being utilized efficiently (d) output has increased as a result of increase in input(s) — d

4. Assume an economy with a growth rate of 12 percent and capital-output ratio of 2. Using the Harrod-Domar model determine the Average Propensity to save. (a) 0.25 (b) 0.06 (c) 0.24 (d) 0.12 — c

5. The term "capital-labor" ratio means: (a) the worth of capital to a given number of workers (b) the amount of capital per worker (c) the amount of capital needed by labor to produce a given output (d) the quantity of capital goods per consumer good — b

6. In a full-employment economy, capital accumulation requires (a) that saving be reduced (b) low interest rates (c) that the economy restrain its consumption (d) foreign loans. — c

7. Of the following, which one is not conducive to economic growth? (a) material progress (b) positive job attitudes (c) moral taboos (d) capital formation — c

Answer

To be covered when testing yourself

8. Antigrowth economists argue that: (a) domestic poverty is a problem of distribution, not production (b) domestic poverty is a problem of production, not distribution (c) growth is a necessary factor for a decent standard of living (d) zero population growth policy should be pursued during inflation — a

9. Because of the allocative efficiency of the price mechanism, labor in the United States has shifted from (a) agriculture to services and the public sector (b) government to services (c) manufacturing to agriculture (d) services to manufacturing. — a

10. Per capita income is highest when (a) the marginal productivity of labor is highest (b) the average product of labor is highest (c) total output is highest (d) there is no saving. — b

11. For a given economy, with no depreciation and all resources fully employed, the levels of consumption and investment were \$480 billion and \$60 billion respectively, for the first year. If the capital-output ratio is 3/1, what will be the full employment NNP? (a) \$540 billion (b) \$560 billion (c) \$500 billion (d) \$220 billion — b

12. The embodiment of new technology will proceed faster (a) the larger the economy is (b) the higher wages are (c) the larger net investment is (d) in an economy with unemployment where wages are low. — c

13. Given the capital-output ratio, a decrease in the average propensity to save will: (a) reduce the full-employment growth rate (b) reduce employment below the national average (c) increase the full-employment growth rate (d) increase the production per industry in the domestic economy — a

14. Increased allocative efficiency, increasing returns to scale, and technological progress have all served to offset (a) the lack of social overhead capital in some countries (b) the lack of capital accumulation in advanced countries (c) the decline in the labor force of the advanced countries (d)

SHORT ANSWER QUESTIONS FOR REVIEW

Answer

To be covered when testing yourself

diminishing returns as a result of capital deepening. — d

15. The most important single source of growth for the United States has been (a) capital accumulation (b) population growth (c) technological progress (d) the increase in education. — c

16. The means by which market economies signal and respond to changes in relative scarcity is: (a) the market system (b) the price system (c) income distribution (d) the wage rates and profit rates of giant corporations — b

17. Government policy aimed at keeping savings and investment equal will (a) lead to less private investment (b) depress the growth rate (c) stabilize the economy and the growth rate (d) lead to an overabundance of social capital and a shortage of private, productive capital — c

18. One of the most important methods of increasing the growth rate is to (a) increase the percentage of output used for investment (b) institute a highly progressive tax structure (c) increase unemployment in order to free labor and capital resources (d) increase the population. — a

19. Savings is mainly a function of income levels, but it can also be directly affected by (a) the capital-output ratio (b) population growth (c) educational background (d) government tax policies. — d

20. Mainstream economists do not think growth is more harmful than beneficial. They feel, however, that the harm that does result from growth arises from (a) the fact that resources are limited while human wants are infinite (b) externalities in the production of some goods, leading to social costs greater than private costs (c) unintentional miscalculations by firms (d) the interference of governments in the economy. — b

Fill in the blanks.

21. There is an ____________ when private costs do not equal social costs, in a certain situa-

	Answer To be cover when testi yourself
tion.	externali
22. A continuous increase in the capital-labor ratio is the same as the ___________ of capital.	deepening
23. Increases in education and health care will probably increase a nation's stock of ___________ capital.	human
24. The ___________ model of growth identifies the average propensity to save and the capital-output ratio as the main determinants of growth.	Harrod-Domar
25. ___________ is gross investment minus depreciation costs.	Net investmen
26. Because of ___________, population growth with fixed resources and technology will eventually result in decreasing per capita income.	diminishi returns
27. To implement ___________ technological progress, some new investment capital is needed, either to buy new machines or retrain workers or both.	embodied
28. The ___________ tends "automatically" to react to shortages of resources and compensate for these shortages by inducing people to cut down on consumption of the scarce resource.	price mechanism
29. The increase in potential output created by an increase in net investment is given by the ___________.	capital-output ratio
30. The long-term trend in advanced nations has been for wage rates to ___________.	rise

Determine whether the following statements are true or false.

31. Because the level of savings increases in a growing full-employment economy, the level of investment must also increase if full employment is to be sustained.	True

SHORT ANSWER QUESTIONS FOR REVIEW

	Answer To be covered when testing yourself
32. Other things being equal, a higher average propensity to save causes a higher growth rate.	True
33. If the labor force is doubled and non-labor resources remain constant, total output will double.	False
34. Disembodied technological progress will not increase labor productivity.	False
35. A declining capital-output ratio implies that capital goods are becoming more productive.	True
36. Taxation will always hinder capital accumulation.	False
37. When capital is deepened, and there is no technical change, the profit rate will rise.	False
38. As the capital-labor ratio in the advanced countries has increased over the years, diminishing returns have set in, causing the capital-output ratio to rise sharply.	False
39. A higher rate of growth is likely to imply greater total consumption, but a lower proportion of income consumed.	True
40. Per capita output cannot equal per capital income because of savings.	False
41. The cost of capital accumulation is the consumption that society sacrifices today for the prospect of higher potential consumption in the future.	True
42. If the stock of capital increases by 5 percent, and the labor force increases by 1 percent, per capita output will always increase by 3 percent.	False
43. Capital accumulation, education, and technological progress have all contributed to increasing labor productivity.	True
44. Capital accumulation, other things being equal, will lead to higher wage rates and lower profit rates.	True
45. A high growth rate in total output is generally preferable to a high growth rate in per capita output.	False

CHAPTER 30

ECONOMICS OF INCOME DISTRIBUTION

Basic Attacks and Strategies for Solving Problems in this Chapter. See pages 980 to 989 for step-by-step solutions to problems.

The related issues of poverty and inequality continue to be among the most crucial facing the United States.

In 1987, 13.5% of the American population was considered to be living in poverty. The level of poverty was determined by an "absolute" standard known as the "poverty line." The poverty line is an income threshold. In 1987 the threshold was $11,611 for a family of four. The threshold was adjusted up or down for larger or smaller families. The poverty line is supposed to represent an "acceptable" standard of living. Any family with an income below the poverty line is considered poor, regardless of whether its income was $1 or $10,000 below the line. Any family with an income above the line was considered not poor, again regardless of how far above the line its income was.

The poverty line is not a scientifically valid measure of what constitutes an "acceptable" standard of living because no such measure exists or could exist. It is primarily an arbitrary measure of living standards whose chief virtue is that it has been consistently applied for many years so that we can follow the trend in poverty. Consequently, the measure is always open to the criticism that it is either too high or too low.

A fundamental criticism of our use of an absolute standard to measure poverty is that it does not really reflect the way society views the problem. Consider the following points. A family with a real income of $11,610 would be counted as poor in the United States, but would not be considered poor if it lived in Ethiopia (one of the poorest nations on earth). The same family would also not have been considered poor if it had lived in the United States two centuries ago. This suggests that what constitutes poverty depends on the general standard of living of society. Families are poor if their income does not keep up with the rest of society, almost regardless of how high their income is in absolute terms.

The implication of this is that what is important is the level of income inequality. A society with a more equal distribution of income will have less poverty than one with a less equal distribution, everything else held equal.

The Lorenz curve is a commonly-used graphical device to represent the degree of income inequality. The diagram is constructed as follows. Rank the units under consideration (families, households, etc.) from poorest to richest and divide into equal proportional groups, such as quintiles (poorest 20%, next poorest 20%, etc.) or deciles (poorest 10%, next poorest 10%, etc.). Referring to the figure, the bottom horizontal axis is used to plot the population of units from poorest (on the left) to richest (on the right). The left vertical axis is used to plot the cumulative distribution of income, the proportion of total income received by each group and all poorer groups. For example, curve *A* shows that the poorest 20% of the units received 5% of all the income, the poorest 40% received 15% of the income (the 5% of the poorest quintile plus the 10% of the next quintile), the poorest 60% received 30%, the poorest 80% received 60%, and the poorest 100% received 100% of the income.

The degree of inequality is represented by how "bowed-out" the curve is from the diagonal. Curve *B* represents greater inequality than curve *A*. A curve lying along the diagonal represents "perfect equality;" each quintile receives the same proportion of the income. A curve lying along the bottom horizontal and right vertical represents "perfect inequality;" one person receives all the income.

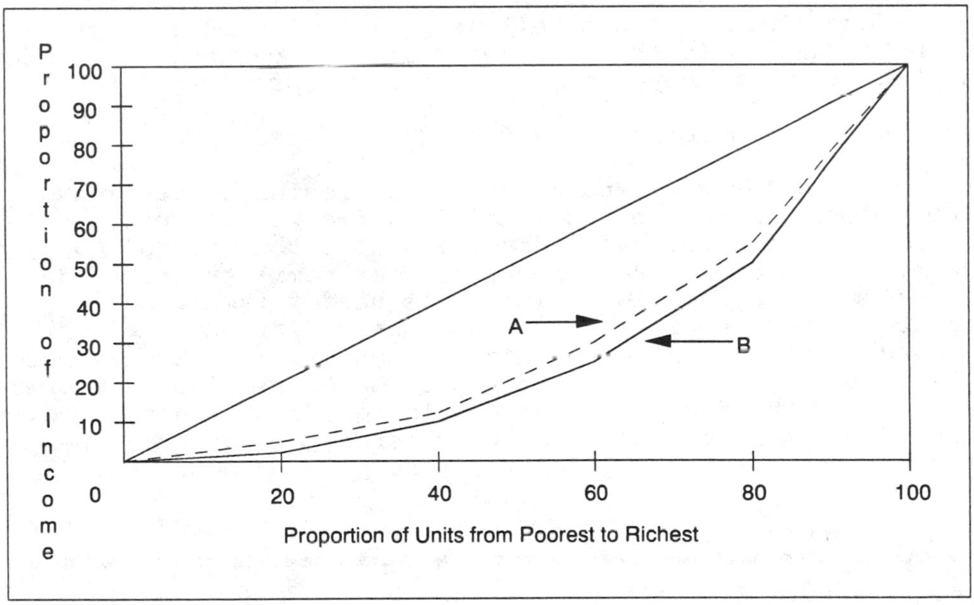

The Lorenz Curve

Step-by-Step Solutions to Problems in this Chapter, "Economics of Income Distribution"

POVERTY AND INCOME INEQUALITY

• **PROBLEM 30-1**

Define poverty.

Solution: Poverty is the condition of having too little money to fulfill basic needs as society currently defines those needs. As a broad generalization we might say a family lives in poverty when its basic needs exceed its available means of satisfying them. A family's needs have many determinants, its size, its health, the ages of its members, and so forth. Its means include currently earned income, transfer payments, past savings, property owned, and so on. The definitions of poverty accepted by concerned government agencies are based on family size.

The poverty population has a greater proportion of the elderly, female-headed families, blacks, the poorly educated, and unrelated individuals than the general population. For example, 46 percent of poor families are headed by a female, and children in female-headed families are about 6 times as likely to be poor as children in male-headed families (52 percent vs 9 percent). Blacks are more than 3 times as likely as whites to be poor; blacks comprise almost one-third of the poor population, compared to a poverty rate of 12 percent for the general population. The elderly constitute 14 percent of the poverty population.

• **PROBLEM 30-2**

Define income inequality.

Solution: The sources of income are wages, salaries, rents, profits and interest. Among various segments of the economy "Income Inequality" exists in distribution of income and wealth ownership.

Some of the more specific factors contributing to income inequality include: 1) native abilities. Nature has been very arbitrary in apportioning mental, and physical talents. In brief, native talents put some individuals in a position to make contributions to total output which command very high incomes. Others are in much less fortunate circumstances. Second, training education, opportunities to advance, to develop talents and to acquire new abilities are not equally available to all. Discrimination on basis of race, religion, ethnic background, and sex blocks many paths.

THE LORENZ CURVE

• PROBLEM 30-3

Given in the figure are Lorenz curves of income distribution for the United States and Sweden. To which country is income more equally distributed? In which country would one be more likely to find a more progressive income tax structure?

Solution: In order to understand income distribution under the Lorenz curve, we must draw a 45° line from the origin which represents perfect equality.

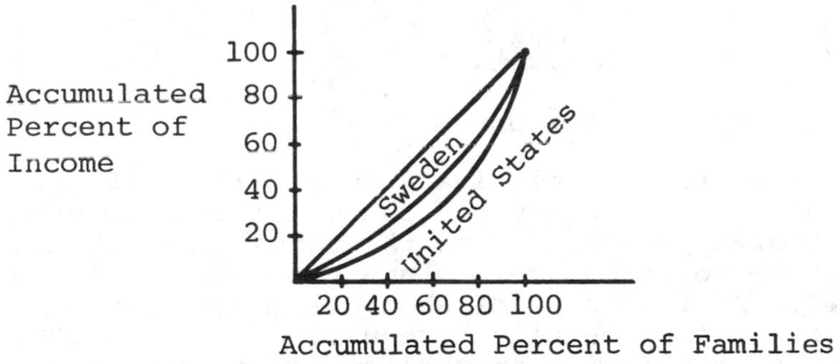

To understand why the 45° line represents perfect equality, we need simply examine any of the points on it. By definition, all points on the 45° line are such that x = y, or accumulated percent of families = accumulated percent of income. Since this is true, all families are making the same income, i.e., there is perfect equality.

To decide which country has income more equally distributed, we simply examine the graphs given and decide which one better approaches the perfect equality line. In this case Sweden has income more equally distributed.

In a progressive tax structure, the percentage of income paid as taxes increases as income increases. Under such a system, income can become somewhat more evenly distributed. Therefore we would expect to find a more progressive tax structure in Sweden.

Suppose that on a small Pacific island 50% of the population has no wealth while the other 50% has equal wealth.

a) Using the Lorenz curve, graph the distribution of wealth on this island.

b) How might you measure the relative inequality of wealth on this island?

Solution: To show the actual distribution of wealth, we plot percent of people on the x-axis and percent of wealth on the y-axis. We see above that the first 50% of the population has no wealth, so the first part of the curve from x = 0% to x = 50% will be the x-axis. The rest of the population shares their wealth equally. Therefore from x = 50% to x = 100%, percent of income will increase in straight line form terminating at x = 100%, y = 100%. The graph is given along with the curve of absolute equality.

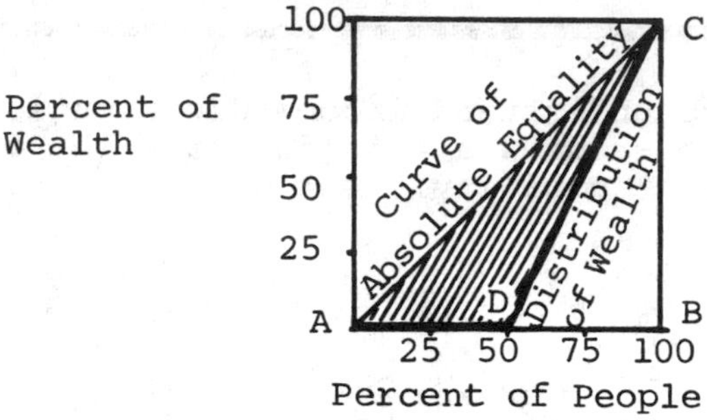

b) To measure the relative inequality of this income distribution, we must study the shaded region above. If the curve of absolute equality were the actual distribution, there would be no shaded region and the relative inequality would be 0%. If the curve of absolute inequality were the actual distribution, relative inequality would be 100%. We can see now that relative inequality can be measured as the ratio of the area of the shaded region (the region bounded by the curve of absolute equality and the actual distribution) to the area of the triangle ABC with sides determined by the curve of absolute equality and the curve of absolute inequality.

On the graph above, it is easy to determine the relative inequality of the wealth distribution since the distribution is plotted with a straight line. Using basic geometry we see Area $\Delta ABC = AB \cdot BC/2$ and Area $\Delta DBC = DB \cdot BC/2$. Since $DB = \frac{1}{2} AB$, Area $\Delta DBC = AB \cdot BC/4 = \frac{1}{2}$ Area ΔABC. Therefore Area ΔADC (shaded region) = $\frac{1}{2}$ Area ΔABC. The relative inequality then

$$= \frac{\text{Area } \Delta ADC}{\text{Area } \Delta ABC}$$

$$= \frac{\frac{1}{2} \text{ Area } \Delta ABC}{\text{Area } \Delta ABC}$$

$$= \frac{1}{2} = 50\%$$

• PROBLEM 30-5

On the Lorenz curve shown,

a) Where is the curve of absolute equality?

b) What does the shaded region region represent?

c) What would be the curve of absolute inequality?

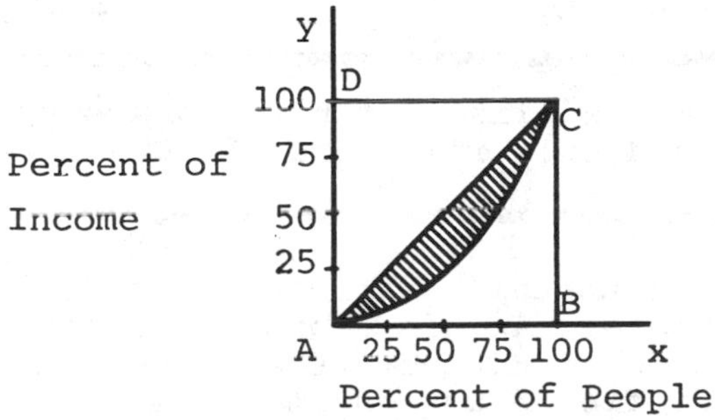

Solution: a) Under absolute equality, each person would receive the same income. Algebraically this would be the line $y = x$. Looking at the graph, we see that the curve of absolute equality is the 45° line which passes through the origin and the point (100,100).

b) Assuming that the curved line below the curve of absolute equality represents the actual distribution of income, the shaded region represents deviation from absolute equality, or relative inequality of income. The greater the shaded region, the greater is the inequality of income distribution.

c) Under absolute inequality, all people in a country but one would be making no income. That one person of course would be earning all of the country's income. Looking at the graphy, we can see this case exists if we examine the kinked curve, defined by the x-axis $(0 \leq x < 100)$ and the line $x = 100$. We see on this curve that as we move along the x-axis there is no income being earned until we reach the last person (at $x = 100\%$). Then we see that all income is earned by this one person as the curve of income distribution becomes a vertical line terminating at the point (100,100).

INCOME DISTRIBUTION IN THE U. S.

• PROBLEM 30-6

How might the nature of ownership of American monopolies contribute to income inequality?

Solution: By virtue of their market power, monopolists charge a higher price than would a purely competitive firm with the same costs. Therefore most monopolists are able to realize substantial economic profits.

In the modern corporation, ownership lies in the hands of the stockholders, with most stockholders coming from the upper income groups. Therefore as monopolies earn profits, upper income owners of monopolistic enterprises tend to be enriched at the expense of the rest of the society.

• PROBLEM 30-7

"In capitalism, commercialism dominates and suppresses social, artistic, and cultural values." Evaluate.

Solution: According to this criticism, a person is so influenced by his interest in his economic wealth that other criteria are dominated. However, the exchanging of goods does not make it difficult for anyone to be influenced by the artistic, social, humanitarian, or cultural uses to which he can put his goods and services.

Playwrights complain that the financial "backer" invokes his crass monetary standards. Artists complain that businessmen want mere display copy, not true art. The architect complains because builders do not want the artistic designs he proposes. What they really are objecting to are other people's tastes and preferences. But the issue is rarely put in so embarrassing a way.

Saying that only lowbrow products sell well seems to suggest that this is a result of the money-value system. But that system effectively reveals and enforces the "lowbrow" tastes and desires of the public. The actors and writers wish the public valued such quality more than it does. Hence, actors and artists are frustrated because other people don't want as much "quality" as the artists would like to provide at the prices they would like to get. Or putting it differently, the artists must admit that the income they can get from "low-quality" work is so high that they prefer to produce low-quality plays and get a big income rather than produce high-quality plays and live with a lower income. In this case, it is also the artists' and actors' own tastes for more wealth, not merely that of the public's, that precludes quality.

SHORT ANSWER QUESTIONS FOR REVIEW

Answer
To be covered when testing yourself

Choose the correct answer.

1. Unequal income distribution can be defended on the grounds that it (a) improves the functioning of the political system (b) increases the productivity of the economy (c) makes poor people work harder (d) creates economic incentives. — d

2. Poor people in the U.S. (a) are in the majority (b) are economically weak but politically very active (c) have a hard time making themselves visible to the law-makers and to the public (d) all live in rural areas. — c

3. Paying off different amounts to two workers of white and non-white race for the work of the same quality and intensity is an example of (a) wage discrimination (b) price discrimination (c) occupational discrimination (d) superiority of white workers. — a

4. Poverty is partially the result of (a) individual laziness and irresponsibility (b) social deficiencies (c) discrimination in employment (d) all of the above. — d

5. Which of the following is a program designed to alleviate poverty in a society (a) SSI (b) tax increase (c) ITT (d) none of the above. — a

6. Welfare programs turned out to be inflationary because of the (a) reduced incentives to work that resulted (b) deficits that the government had to maintain (c) abundance of 'loopholes' in these programs (d) administrative difficulties of maintaining them. — b

7. Which of the following will the negative income tax not do? (a) equalize the personal incomes in a society (b) secure a certain minimum income for the poor (c) preserve incentives to get a higher paying job (d) reduce the administrative cost of welfare assistance. — a

8. The families living below the poverty level (as defined at a given point in space-time) (a) have more than 50% likelihood of being dissolved (b) are going to become rich if they work harder (c) are likely to stay poor

Answer
To be covered when testing yourself

in the following year (d) are a rarely seen exception in the American economic system. c

9. The law of diminishing marginal utility when applied to the concept of consumer satisfaction is an argument (a) in favor of the unequal income distribution (b) for the more equal distribution of income (c) which has nothing to do with the problems of income distribution (d) none of the above. b

10. Poverty often stems from various forms of discrimination. The fact that the rate of unemployment among blacks is statistically higher than it is among whites is a sign of (a) lack of participation in the economy on the part of blacks (b) racial discrimination in the South (c) difficulties of achieving full employment (d) employment discrimination. d

11. A much smaller percentage of blacks than whites gets an opportunity to engage in various high quality educational and training programs. This is an example of (a) difference between the utility functions for blacks and for whites (b) racial discrimination in the admissions policies of the American educational institutions (c) poverty resulting in the inability to invest in personal improvements (d) high rate of investment in human capital on the part of the blacks. c

12. The existence of wage discrimination and occupational discrimination tend to (a) create numerous incentives for blacks to invest in job-related self-improvement (b) reduce the motivation of those discriminated against to invest in training and education (c) improve the productivity of the economy as a whole (d) be important only in theory. b

13. Which of the following cannot be part of the program to reduce poverty and income inequality? (a) private charity (b) food stamps (c) progressive income tax (d) negative income tax. c

14. If income distribution in the U.S. were absolutely equal the present richest 5% of American population would receive (a) one

Answer
To be covered when testing yourself

fifth of total national income (b) one twentieth of total national income (c) half of the national income (d) approximately 20% of the total income — b

15. Doctors are capable of maintaining high incomes because (a) the medical profession requires a lot of personal investments in money and time (b) the demand for medical services is permanently large (c) of the high quality standards imposed by the medical societies and organizations (d) all of the above. — d

Fill in the blanks.

16. The distribution of ____________ is generally more unequal than the distribution of income. — wealth

17. As the economy gets wealthier its estimate of the subsistence income ____________. — rises

18. The families with most of their income provided by a woman are more likely ____________ than are the families supported by men. — to be poor

19. Half of the American families receive the income which is above the ____________ for the U.S. — median income

20. If the society's mean income falls below the subsistence level of income it must be regarded as ____________. — poor

21. The closer to unity the negative income tax rate comes the lesser the economic ____________ become. — incentives to work

22. Colleges, medical schools, job related training programs all take part in the formation of __________, and therefore in increasing the productivity of the economy. — human capital

23. The statistical finding that the relative shares of national income in the U.S. do not change significantly over time __________ the prediction of Marx about the route of development of any capitalist system. — contradicts

24. Poor countries show ____________ of poverty and wealth than do the developed countries. — greater extremes

25. Along with other efforts to decrease the im-

Answer
To be covered when testing yourself

pact of poverty the government introduced __________ which involved federal subsidies to help the aged bear the high costs of medical treatment. — Medicare

26. Accumulations of savings and capital caused by income inequality play a positive role in promoting __________ without which, as Keynes stated, no capitalist economy can survive. — economic growth

27. The existence of a significant amount of rich people among the consumers is essential for the development of __________ which typically face high costs and therefore have to require high prices for their products. — new industries

28. To bar the members of minority ethnic groups from occupying executive positions in the Defense industry would constitute an example of __________. — occupational discrimination

29. Ideally, any welfare program should assure that individual incomes do not fall below an accepted minimum and that at the same time __________ are maintained. — work incentives

30. Differences in natural abilities, education, training, wealth endowments can all be cited as the __________ of unequal income distribution. — causes

<u>Determine whether the following statements are true or false.</u>

31. Marx's statement "The rich get richer and the poor poorer" accurately describes the main economic trend in American society over the last 100 years. — False

32. It is generally the case that the distribution of income is more equal in the poor countries than in the developed industrialized states. — False

33. The equality in the distribution of income does not necessarily imply equality in the distribution of wealth. — True

34. Lawyers have the largest average professional earnings in America. — False

35. A minimum subsistence level of income differs

	Answer To be covered when testing yourself
among the nations because at different stages of development and industrialization of a society the term subsistence assumes different meanings.	True
36. An artificial attempt by the government to interfere with the natural distributive processes is likely to create disefficiencies and to reduce the GNP.	True
37. Any permanent job offered to a person on welfare represents an opportunity to increase his/her net income and therefore is likely to be accepted.	False
38. A negative income tax is proposed by both liberal and conservative economists as a possible alternative to the complex welfare assistance system.	True
39. It is a fact of life that a small part of American families receive a disproportionately high share of total personal income.	True
40. The ability to control supply and the possession of a certain degree of market power have a strong impact on the income distribution within a society.	True
41. Both absolute and relative incomes fluctuate up and down from year to year.	False
42. The fact that both high and low incomes grew at approximately the same rate shows that the dollar differentials between the incomes of the rich and the poor remained basically stable over a given period of time.	False
43. Taxes prove to be the most effective governmental tool of equalizing the distribution of income.	False
44. Income inequality, though aesthetically unpleasant, is economically desirable since being a result of an undisturbed free competitive system it assures efficient allocation of resources.	False
45. The existence of large privately owned accumulations of money resulting from income inequality promotes economic growth.	True

CHAPTER 31

LABOR AND INDUSTRIAL RELATIONS

Basic Attacks and Strategies for Solving Problems in this Chapter. See pages 990 to 1005 for step-by-step solutions to problems.

Labor unions are an important institution in modern industrial society. Unions perform a number of services for their members. First, they represent workers in their dealings with employers. Many people feel there is unequal bargaining power between worker and employer, individual workers cannot possibly bargain on even terms with their employers. By combining workers together in one organization, bargaining power can be equalized. A consequence will be better wages and working conditions. Unions will be able to achieve these goals through collective bargaining over a contract that will cover employment conditions at the firm. The union also acts as the voice of workers between contract negotiations, frequently by processing grievances for workers.

Second, unions act as the political representatives of the workers' interests. Unions engage in election campaign activities and lobbying. Third, unions provide social support for workers. They support such social activities as Christmas parties and scholarship funds for workers' children, and provide a sense of "solidarity" with other individuals in similar circumstances.

There are two main types of unions. Craft unions join together workers who possess the same industrial skill. Unions of plumbers or electricians would be examples. The power of these unions comes from the fact that they control the supply of a vital resource. Industrial unions join together all workers in the same industry. The auto workers or steel workers would be examples. Often a large proportion of the membership of an industrial union consists of unskilled and semi-skilled workers. The power of an industrial union comes from its ability to control the entire labor supply to an industry.

Except in certain pockets of industry where economic conditions were favorable, the development of a strong labor movement in the United States required the passage of protective legislation. The most important piece of legislation was the Wagner Act. This act made it public policy to support the development of unions, protected the organizing activities of workers and unions, and required employers to bargain in "good faith" with the representatives of their employees.

After growing rapidly in the three decades following the enactment of the Wagner Act, the union movement in America has undergone a period of contraction since the 1970s. While changes in the geographic, industrial, and occupational structure of industry, and the demographic characteristics of the labor force may have played a role in this, some commentators believe an employer counter-offensive coupled with lax enforcement of the protective laws may be more important explanatory factors.

Economists are divided on the impact of unions on the economy. While the evidence is clear that unions tend to improve wages and working conditions for their members, side-effects of union activities are more controversial. Economists using the conventional analysis conclude that union gains come at the expense of other workers. In addition, union activities hurt national productivity and may impart an inflationary bias to the economy. Other economists point to evidence that union gains come at the expense of profits, not other workers, unions have a net positive impact on productivity and unions are not the cause of inflationary pressures.

Step-by-Step Solutions to Problems in this Chapter, "Labor and Industrial Relations"

BASIC DEFINITIONS

• PROBLEM 31-1

What is the economic definition of labor?

Solution: "Labor," in the economic sense, consists of all human abilities or talents which may be used in the production of goods and services. By the type and quality of service it renders, labor is classified as unskilled, semi-skilled and skilled. The economic definition of "labor" therefore includes the work of ditchdigger, factory worker and neurosurgeon.

It should be noted that some economists (for example, McConnell) exclude from the economic definition of "labor" one type of mental ability, entrepreneural ability, and classify it as a separate economic resource or factor of production.

The proficiency of labor depends in large part on the amount of investment that has been made in human resources. Education and training are considered as investment in human capital.

Labor in the United States is the single most important factor of production. Wages and salaries make up about 80 percent of national income.

• PROBLEM 31-2

How are craft unions different from industrial unions?

Solution: Craft unions join together workers with one particular skill, for instance, masons. Industrial unions, on the other hand, are not based upon skill but rather include workers in a particular plant or industry. An example of this would be a union of automobile assembly line workers.

• PROBLEM 31-3

Explain how the MC = MR rule can be applied to the hiring of labor in a perfectly competitive market.

Solution: To deal with factors of production such as labor, we change the terms in the MC = MR rule, but the concepts are the same. Instead of MC, we use Marginal Resource Cost (MRC) and instead of MR, we use Marginal Revenue Product (MRP). In a perfectly competitive market, MRC = MRP for labor and a firm will pay each worker a wage equal to the MRP of the last worker hired.

• PROBLEM 31-4

The following are the terms commonly encountered as a result of a breakdown in negotiations between labor and management.

a) lockout
b) strike
c) picketing
d) boycott
e) secondary boycott
f) jurisdictional strike
g) featherbedding

Briefly describe each of the above concepts.

Solution: a) A lockout is a work stoppage in which the employer closes his plant to his workers.

b) A strike is a stoppage in which the workers refuse to work. The strike is the ultimate weapon of the union. It is frequently supported by other weapons, such as picketing and boycotts.

c) Picketing refers to the parading of striking workers before the entrance of their plant with the hope of convincing others not to enter the plant.

d) A boycott is an attempt to block the distribution of the products sold by the employer. It may involve only a refusal to purchase on the part of the striking employees themselves, but more likely, it will include a request that others also refuse to patronize the firm.

e) A secondary boycott is a boycott against an employer other than the one with which the union has a dispute.

f) A jurisdictional strike is a strike called by a union against an employer who is already legitimately bargaining with another union.

g) Featherbedding is the practice of forcing an employer to pay "for services which are not performed."

• PROBLEM 31-5

Why is the Wagner Act (officially the National Labor Relations Act), considered to be "labor's Magna Charta"?

Solution: The Wagner Act, otherwise known as the National Labor Relations Act, is considered to be "labor's Magna Charta" because it gave labor two basic rights: the right of self-organization and the right to bargain collectively with employers. The Act also listed a number of "unfair labor practices" on the part of management. Specifically, it

1. Forbade employers from interfering with the right of workers to form unions.

2. Outlawed company unions.

3. Prohibited antiunion discrimination by employers in hiring, firing, and promoting.

4. Outlawed discrimination against any worker who files charges or gives testimony under the Act.

5. Obligated employers to bargain in good faith with a union duly established by their employees.

The Wagner Act was tailored to accelerate union growth, and it was extremely successful in achieving this goal.

• PROBLEM 31-6

Define collective bargaining and give its importance to labor.

Solution: Collective bargaining is the approach used by labor organizations--usually unions representing employees--to negotiate with employers or their representatives. Workers have come to demand collective bargaining because of their feeling of relative powerlessness as compared with their employers. An individual worker with no unique skill may find that he is at a decided disadvantage when attempting to bargain with his employer. He may be confronted with a "take it or leave it" situation--the employer being able to get along quite well without the individual worker's services, but the worker requiring the job for his livelihood. A large factory will not stop producing just because it loses a single machine operator, clerk, or janitor. It will continue to function while a suitable replacement is found. But an unemployed worker may find it difficult to get along. Collective bargaining can therefore be used by labor as a forum where their grievances may be expressed and where security and tenure of jobs can be attained.

• PROBLEM 31-7

Discuss the common issues in collective bargaining, including among other things the terms commonly contained in the contract as well as the contractual relationship that must exist between labor and management over the life of the contract.

Solution: Collective bargaining attempts to find terms satisfactory to both employees and management regarding many important issues. Once agreed upon, these terms are carefully set down in the form of a labor contract. The issues fall very broadly into two categories: (1) the conditions of employment, and (2) the relationship between the union and management.

The conditions of employment include wages, fringe benefits, work standards, and job security. Wage issues include the basic rate for each job category as well as the pay steps for advancement within each category. Fringe benefits include items such as pensions, life insurance, health plans, severance pay, as well as paid vacations, holidays and even coffee breaks and cleanup time. Work standards specify the amount of work to be performed--for example, the crew size to accomplish a standard job or the number of units to be handled on an assembly line. Finally, job security entails job continuance and the handling of grievances. Job continuance is usually determined by seniority rules--for example, the worker who has been on the job the longest is the last to be laid off and the first to be recalled when the firm hires again.

Union and management must also agree on their own relationship over the life of the contract. They have to decide upon the definition of the bargaining unit which identifies the workers for whom the union is bargaining and, therefore, to whom the labor contract applies. They must agree upon the privileges given to shop stewards, who are workers elected to represent the union on the job. As an example, stewards may be allowed to confer with workers and supervisors during working hours. Union and management may also agree upon provisions for the "checkoff" of union dues. The checkoff is a form of union security in which the employer deducts union dues from workers' paychecks and pays those dues directly to the union. Labor contracts frequently include provisions for arbitration, a procedure to settle union-management disputes by an outside neutral party. Finally, the union and management must agree on when the contract begins and ends and how it might be renewed.

• PROBLEM 31-8

Give the classifications of bargaining arrangements and briefly discuss each.

Solution: Basically, there are three kinds of bargaining

arrangements: (1) the closed shop, (2) the open shop, and (3) the union shop.

The closed shop is the strongest form of union security, requiring employers to hire only union members. This allows unions virtually to control the supply and, therefore, the wages of the workers. In 1947, the Taft-Hartley Act made it illegal for unions to maintain a closed shop.

In sharp contrast, the open shop allows employers to hire union and nonunion workers alike. The union represents its members but has no jurisdiction over the rest of the workers. This provides the least security for the union, since employers can always hire nonunion employees if unions attempt to raise wages more than the employer feels is necessary to attract the number of workers he needs.

The union shop is a compromise between the first two. Under this arrangement employers can hire union or nonunion workers, but every nonunion worker must join the union within a specified period of time after he is employed. The union shop provides a fair amount of union security. The wage negotiated by the union will not be undercut by new workers, since they are required to join the union within a matter of days.

• PROBLEM 31-9

Describe the methods of solving the problem of impasse in the labor and management contract.

Solution: The methods of reaching an agreement in case of impasse in the labor and management contract are:

1. Conciliation - which refers to the attempts at peaceful settlement by direct negotiations between employer and employees (or their representatives) without the intervention of the outside parties. Others however use the term to mean the intervention by a third party who attempts rather informally to bring the two sides together. Such a third party may suggest the terms of a settlement, but without the power to compel. He may guide discussions, but cannot make decisions.

2. Mediation - which is considered to be more formal than conciliation, involves the use of a commission before which the two parties will appear with their attorneys. The mediator may investigate the situation and suggest solutions, but he cannot compel the parties to accept.

3. Voluntary Arbitration - is resorted to when mediation fails. They will agree to have a third party enter the case and, furthermore, they will agree to accept his decision. In some union contracts, the conditions under which the parties will resort to arbitration are spelled out. For example, it may be decided that the arbitrator's authority will be limited to interpretation of the terms of the contract.

4. Compulsory arbitration exists when government directly or indirectly compels the parties to submit their differences to an impartial outsider for adjudication.

• PROBLEM 31-10

Briefly describe the weapons used by unions to get their demands.

Solution: The following are the weapons used by labor to win their demands:

1. Agency shop - which make it a requirement to all workers to pay their dues to the union because the union acts as their agent in bargaining, but workers are not required to join the union. This would reduce the tension among those who feel that a worker should have a right to join or not to join a union without being discriminated against in employment.

2. Checkoff agreement - which might be asked by the union from the employer, whereby the latter would deduct from the employee's paycheck his union dues. This guarantees continuity of membership and protects union authority.

3. Maintenance-of-membership shop which requires all workers to continue their membership in the union for the duration of the contract under which they are working. If they are not members of the union, they do not have to join.

4. Preferential shop exists when management agrees to hire union members as long as they are available, in preference to nonunion workers.

5. Union label signifies that the product was made by union workers and according to union standards. This is an attempt of the organized labor to make consumers conscious of buying only goods with such labels.

6. Slowdown - this happens when workers purposely reduce the speed at which they work. The consequence of this would be an increase in the cost of production to the employer and will reduce his profits.

7. Political action such as helping candidates to important government offices by giving financial contributions, meeting halls, posters and sound trucks with the expectation that the said political candidates would further the cause of labor if elected.

• PROBLEM 31-11

Describe the weapons used by management to combat unions.

Solution: The weapons used by management to counteract labor which have frequently been very effective but have been considered extremely harsh by labor are as follows:

1. Company unions were set up by management to discourage or prevent workers from joining an existing union or starting a union of their own. These unions were largely dominated by management.

2. Yellow-dog contracts which make it compulsory for workers to sign a contract not to join a union as a condition of employment. If they did join a union, they violated the contract and were subject not only to being discharged but to being sued as well.

3. Blacklists containing the names of union organizers were circulated among employers to prevent these men from getting jobs and to warn employers of what these men might try to do if hired to work for a company.

4. Injunction, a court order restraining some person or group from particular actions. Employers would request judges to issue injunctions to prevent unions from striking or picketing, claiming such action threatened their property.

• PROBLEM 31-12

Describe the economic and non-economic grievances that have motivated labor to organization into unions.

Solution: The grievances that have motivated labor to organization are varied, some economic and some non-economic. The ones typically used are as follows:

1. Wage reductions. It has always been a principle of the labor movement to resist any wage reduction. With the wage reductions may come an equal reduction in working time or without a reduction in working time. Both industrial and craft unions have begun organizing campaigns over this issue.

2. Fixed wages. When Samuel Gompers was president of the American Federation of Labor, the basic philosophy was "more." It is for the purpose of increasing the wages paid to its members that a union is organized and often resistance to wage increases by management has resulted in the organization and strike of the union.

3. Working conditions. Poor working conditions have been the major thorn in the side of labor in many industrial situations. It is in response to unsafe or unsanitary conditions that the union will be organized.

4. Reduction in hours with no reduction in pay. This has been one of labor's earliest objectives, the purpose of which is both economic in that a shorter day with the same pay is higher wages, and non-economic in that the shorter day is of social benefit to the workers.

5. Unfair treatment of union members. There had been a number of organizing drives which started with employer discharges or discrimination against men who were union members,

or who were attempting to organize one. The result of this will be that men who otherwise would not be in sympathy with the union would be motivated by the unfair treatment to join with the union.

6. Conditions not related to employment. There are many cases where the major grievance is not against the company in its wage policy, but its treatment of members outside the job. Labors' drive to organization and recognition has been caused by the exorbitant prices imposed by the company towns and company stores. In many cases, management would compound the grievance by expelling union families from company housing and cutting off credit at the company store.

7. Radicalization. In some cases, the union grievance was not directed at the particular employer, but the whole employer-employee relationship. Reaction to capitalism, the system of private property, was sometimes the motivation of union movement.

• PROBLEM 31-13

Enumerate the major influences that acted to bring the merging of the American Federation of Labor and the Congress of Industrial Organizations.

Solution: The major influences that acted to bring the two giant unions together were:

1. The feeling that unity might provide organized labor with greater political power to stem legislative attacks.

2. The change in leadership within the unions, eliminating some of the personal animosities that had been an obstacle to a merger.

3. The minimal growth in membership that set in after the close of World War II.

4. The interest on the part of the AFL in using industrial organization.

• PROBLEM 31-14

What are the major factors that are largely responsible for the slow growth of the early unionism?

Solution: The major factors that are largely responsible for the slow growth of early unionism are as follows:

1. The lack of any federal policy recognizing unions as collective bargaining agents for workers.

2. The hostility of the courts, which prosecuted unions under conspiracy laws.

3. The strong resistance on the part of American business-

men to accepting unions.

4. The individualism of the American worker.

5. The lack of effective communications necessary to the success of mass movements.

• PROBLEM 31-15

Suppose that a strong union is able to bargain for an increase in wages of 5 percent when productivity has gone up only 3 percent. Assume further that as a result of such an increase in wages, management increases the price of its products by 2 percent to pay for the additional cost. Analyze the effects of such increases in wages and price on the part of labor, management and consumers.

Solution: If a strong union is able to bargain for an increase in wages of 5 percent when productivity has gone up only 3 percent, then there will be an increase in the production cost per unit and the employer will be forced to pay for it by cutting into his profits or by raising prices to the consumer. The latter will be the result in industries where there is little competition. On the other hand, prices will rise immediately in competitive industries because of the additional purchasing power in the hands of the workers, who are at the same time, also the consumers. In the interim however, some of the weakest firms will be forced out of business. Given these conditions, unemployment will probably rise and thereby cause wages to fall.

If prices rise 2 percent to pay for the additional cost, the 5 percent increase in wages will have a purchasing power of only 3 percent, which we can note as the same as the increase in productivity. This has been the argument used by the critics of labor to the effect that labor is responsible for what is called a cost-push inflation. They argued that wage increases that are above the increased productivity per man-hour have raised costs and forced prices up. This has been rebutted by the defenders of labor by saying that the cost for additional wages should come from excessively high profits. They further argued that business welcomes the opportunity to give a wage increase because such action permits raising prices not only high enough to pay for the additional labor cost but even higher, so that profits will be larger than ever.

• PROBLEM 31-16

Describe the preconditions that must be met in order for the organizing strike to be successful.

Solution: The preconditions that must be met in order for the organizing strike to be successful are the economic conditions, since they relate to the union's role in the production process as a factor of production, and they relate to the structure of the particular market. These economic preconditions are that the factor be a limitational factor and be a limitative factor. If either of these two conditions is not met, the probability of success in the union's attempt at organization and recognition may be quite small. We define these two factors in turn and the reason for their necessity:

1. The Limitational Factor. A factor is considered to be a limitational factor if an increase in its use, all other factors constant, does not increase total output, and an increase in any or all other factors, the factor under consideration remaining constant, does not increase total output. In qualitative terms, a factor is a limitational factor when its particular role in the production process is such that substitution is not technically or legally possible.

The reason that limitationality is a necessary precondition to successful organization of labor into a recognized union is the fact that limitationality precludes substitution from other classes of labor. Because of the fact that the union in most cases faces strong opposition from the employers, it is important that the union be able to bring effective economic pressure against the employer to force him to recognize and bargain with the union. To achieve this, the union is typically forced to strike the plant. If the union does not represent a limitational factor (or very close to a limitational factor), then the organization strike will be largely ineffective. The employer will merely substitute other classes of labor for the labor unit that is on strike; production, though possibly hampered, will continue. A labor union that cannot inflict severe economic losses on the employer will not be able to force that employer to recognize the union. Therefore, a union may be able to exert sufficient pressure if it is not a limitational factor, but the lack of that essential characteristic makes its job extremely difficult and lowers the likelihood of success.

2. The Limitative Factor. A factor was characterized as a limitative factor if an increase in its use produced an increase in total product, while an increase in any or all other variable factors did not produce an increase in total product.

The reason that it is necessary for a factor of production to be a limitative factor before a successful organizational strike can be accomplished is basically the same as the limitational factor.

SHORT ANSWER QUESTIONS FOR REVIEW

Answer

To be cove
when test
yourself

Choose the correct answer.

1. In a labor-management struggle, a weapon employed by management to counteract workers' strike is: (a) closed shop (b) union shop (c) lockout (d) company unions — c

2. One reason for the creation of the CIO was the reluctance of the AFL to: (a) engage in political lobbying (b) give up its great authority over local unions (c) admit the railroad brotherhoods to membership (d) organize mass-production workers (e) sanction the establishment of closed shops. — d

3. "Right-to-work" laws: (a) make compulsory union membership (e.g., the union shop) illegal (b) prohibit unions from discriminating against minority groups in recruiting members (c) prohibit employers from discriminating against minority groups in hiring workers (d) permit employers to hire nonunion workers only if union labor is unavailable. — a

4. Business unionism: (a) means the attempt to raise wages through political action (b) is synonymous with company unions (c) refers to employer organizations to raise incomes (d) refers to unions organized along industrial rather than craft lines (e) is not properly described by any of the above. — e

5. In the late 1800s and early 1900s, American businessmen applied lots of antiunion techniques to disrupt the growth of unions. One of the major antiunion techniques fostered was: (a) American Federation of Labor (b) Taft-Hartley Act (c) Green-dog Contract (d) Yellow-dog Contract — d

6. Over the past 60 years, hours worked have been steadily reduced, while both money wages and real wages have continued generally to rise. What factor is primarily responsible for this trend? (a) Minimum-wage laws (b) Right-to-work legislation (c) Reduction in profit margins (d) Increased output per man-hour (e) None of the above. — d

7. Trade autonomy under unionism allows: (a) unions to organize on the basis of bar-

Answer
To be covered when testing yourself

gaining power (b) the establishment of producer cooperatives (c) unions to organize on the basis of specific crafts (d) unions to trade with a considerable degree of freedom — c

8. Previous to the merger with the CIO, an AFL union was: (a) primarily an industrial union (b) primarily a revolutionary union (c) primarily a craft union (d) entirely a craft union. — c

9. The Landrum-Griffin Act states that: (a) an individual worker has the right to take part in union meetings and vote, but the act does not allow any worker to pursue legal action if any of his rights are denied (b) there should be government regulation on union elections and that certain rights of union members must be observed (c) there should be no government intervention on union elections and that certain rights of union members must be observed — b

10. Which of the following would be generally accepted by the representatives of both labor and management? (a) Industrial disputes should be settled without the coercive intervention of government (b) Price controls should be substituted for further increases in both wages and prices (c) Wage rates should be determined by arbitration rather than collective bargaining (d) Wage rates should be directly tied to profit rates (e) None of the above. — a

11. Many economists feel that growth of the labor movement has slowed substantially in the postwar period. Which of the following is not usually cited as a causal factor? (a) changes in the occupational structure of the labor force (b) internal disputes between CIO and AFL leaders (c) a change in public policy in the direction of a more neutral or even antilabor position (d) most currently unorganized workers are in the mass-production industries and therefore difficult to unionize. — d

12. Which of the following union practices would decrease the supply of a particular kind of labor? (a) Higher minimum wages (b) Lengthening the apprenticeship period, while keeping the number of apprentices fixed (c) Intro-

ducing incentive-rate provisions into union-management contracts (d) Raising tariff rates (e) Using union labels on consumer goods. b

13. "Specific crafts, safe and sane business unionism, rejection of government intervention in labor-management relations and collective bargaining, are the guidelines American labor should pursue" is the basic philosophy of: (a) Wagner and the management unions (b) Sherman and Wagner (c) American Federation of Labor and Wagner (d) Gompers and the American Federation of Labor d

14. The outlook for general union growth looks bleak, but one of the following is not a valid reason for this (a) Increasing use is being made of the lockout to prevent strikes (b) Women are not easy to organize (c) Automation means a trend toward white-collar workers who are difficult to organize (d) One of the faster growing parts of the country, the South, is a region difficult to organize (e) Some legislatures and much of the public are hostile to unions. a

15. Which two labor-management relations acts were successful in curtailing "unfair labor practices" and enhancing union growth? (a) Sherman Act and Miller-Tydings Act (b) Taft-Hartley Act and Landrum-Griffin Act (c) Landrum-Griffin Act and Sherman Act (d) Norris-La Guardia Act and Wagner Act d

Fill in the blanks.

16. The ____________ modified the Wagner Act chiefly by citing unfair labor union practices. Taft-Hartley Act

17. ____________ clauses gear wages to changes in the cost of living. Escalator

18. Prior membership in a union as a condition for employment is prohibited by the ________. Taft-Hartley Act

SHORT ANSWER QUESTIONS FOR REVIEW

Answer
To be covered when testing yourself

Question	Answer
19. ____________ outlawed the injunction as an employer weapon against unions.	Norris-LaGuardia Act
20. The Taft-Hartley Act allows states to pass ____________ laws.	right-to work
21. ____________ outlawed the "yellow dog" contract.	Norris-LaGuardia Act
22. Under a ____________ agreement, one must belong to the union before being hired.	closed-shop
23. The ____________ established the National Labor Relations Board.	Wagner Act
24. During the 1920s, ____________ were not used by companies to fight unions.	picket lines
25. The ____________ held union officials strictly accountable for the use of union funds.	Landrum-Griffin Act
26. The single union with the largest membership is the ____________.	Teamsters
27. ____________ outlawed secondary boycotts.	Taft-Hartley Act
28. ____________ refers to rules imposed on an employer for the purpose of keeping up the demand for workers.	Feather-bedding
29. The labor provisions of the ____________ were designed to remove labor from prosecution under the Sherman Antitrust Act.	Clayton Act
30. ____________ is the Magna Carta of organized labor.	Wagner Act

<u>Determine whether the following statements are true or false.</u>

Question	Answer
31. Company unions are unions that are composed of specific types of skilled workers.	False

SHORT ANSWER QUESTIONS FOR REVIEW

Answer
To be covered when testing yourself

32. The term "industrial union" is synonymous with "national union". — False

33. The Landrum-Griffin Act has made it possible for union officials to be closely checked and held accountable for union funds and property. — True

34. Less than one-third of the nonagricultural working force is made up of union workers. — True

35. The open shop retains that a firm hires those workers who have union membership already. — False

36. Widespread annual percentage wage increases which exceed the percentage increase in net productivity would tend to result in increases in the price level. — True

37. "Featherbedding" is when labor and management come to terms on modifying existing work conditions. — False

38. Lenin argued that large parts of the working classes in affluent colonizing nations would be impoverished according to the Marxian laws of motion. — False

39. The "yellow-dog" contract was one of the driving forces in fostering the growth of unions. — False

40. The AFL's concept of "exclusive jurisdiction" thwarted its efforts to organize the mass-production industries. — True

41. The Taft-Hartley Act reinforced the Wagner Act in the sense that both acts outlined "unfair labor practices" on the part of management. — False

42. "Checkoff" is a term relating to a forbidden employer practice of blacklisting employees thought to be active in union organization. — False

43. Compulsory union membership under the closed shop was outlawed by the Norris-La Guardia Act. — False

44. Some of the new labor elite have recently

Answer
To be covered when testing yourself

changed their political affiliations as they have become more capitalistic than socialistic in nature. — True

45. The Knights of Labor began the philosophy of business unionism. — False

CHAPTER 32

COMPARATIVE ECONOMIC SYSTEMS

Basic Attacks and Strategies for Solving Problems in this Chapter. See pages 1006 to 1032 for step-by-step solutions to problems.

All societies face the same three basic economic problems. They are

1) What goods and services to produce

2) How to produce goods and services

3) For whom shall the goods and services be produced

These problems are frequently referred to as simply the "What," "How," and "For Whom" problems.

A nation's economic system refers to the institutions, rules and values that govern its economic life. There are as many economic systems as there are nations, and economic systems are constantly changing. Nonetheless, there are three models that represent the primary pure forms that economic systems can take. They are:

1) Traditional Economy

2) Market Economy

3) Command Economy

In a traditional economy, the answers to the three basic economic problems are found by reference to tradition. The goods and services produced, the production methods used, and the distribution of the product follow rules laid down in the past and passed down through the ages. Traditional economies tend to be static, primitive societies, although there are some traditional elements in even the most modern society. For example, in many households in our own society today the division of labor between husband and wife represents simply traditional ways of doing things.

In a market economy, the decisions about What and How are made individually by the members of society. Individuals decide for themselves how much to spend and save, and how much to spend on specific goods and services. They decide for themselves what business they will enter (as worker or entrepreneur) and what production methods they will use. They make these decisions by reference to their own self-interest. Government, which can be thought of as a method of collective decision-making, plays a minimal role in this type of economy. Limited government is called laissez-faire.

On its face, the market economy seems like a recipe for chaos, with everyone "doing their own thing," but, in fact, if certain conditions are met, it is capable of working quite nicely. The key to a market economy is the market. The market acts to restrain and coordinate the actions of individuals so that what is demanded gets produced, and efficient methods are used in production. Market prices become both a source of information and incentives. Prices indicate what products are in high demand and what resources are scarce. They also provide the reward for those who supply the products most desired or scarce. The distribution of income is also a result of the market. Individuals offering services in high demand and who are most productive will end up with the highest incomes.

The main criticisms of the market economy are that it is prone to instability and likely to exhibit a high degree of inequality.

The term capitalism is frequently used in conjunction with the market economy, although they are not synonymous. The vital characteristic of a capitalistic economy is that productive resources (the means of production) are owned privately. In fact, virtually every capitalistic economy is organized along market lines because the systems are highly congruent.

A command economy is one where the decisions about What, How, and For Whom are made by a central authority. The central authority can either be a dictator or a democratically-elected central administration. The key is that individual choices do not matter. Everyone is required to follow a plan determined "at the top."

At first glance, this would seem to be a reasonable method that would allow society to use its resources to meet society's goals. The chief problems with this system have to do with information and incentives. A pure command economy does not rely on markets so there are no market prices. It is very difficult for a central authority to keep track of what is in high demand and what is scarce. In addition, since prices are not used, there is little in the way of tangible rewards for the most productive individuals. In short, command economies are criticized for being inefficient.

A command economy is not necessarily the same thing as socialism, but the systems are highly congruent. Socialism is defined as a system where productive resources (the means of production) are owned collectively by all of society. The congruence with a command economy stems from the fact that if society owns the resources, society can legitimately make decisions about how to use them.

A mixed economy is one that contains elements of each of the economic systems just described. In fact, all real-world economies are mixed economies, but each differ greatly in terms of the mix. For example, the United States economy is primarily market-oriented, but government does play a major role setting rules and regulations, buying output, taxing, and borrowing. The Soviet economy, by way of contrast, is primarily command-oriented, but there are limited market elements, most notably in agriculture. The system is currently undergoing important restructuring called "perestroika."

Step-by-Step Solutions to Problems in this Chapter, "Comparative Economic Systems"

FUNCTION OF AN ECONOMIC SYSTEM

• PROBLEM 32-1

What are the basic problems with which all economic systems must deal?

Solution: If all goods were super-abundant, i.e., if they existed in sufficient quantities that all human desires could be satisfied by these quantities, then "the economic problem" would not exist. The economic problem arises from the scarcity of goods in relation to human wants. The economic problem then is how to allocate scarce goods (means) which have more than one possible use among competing ends in such a way as to yield the greatest possible satisfaction (utility).

This fundamental economic problem can be analyzed into three basic subproblems. The first problem with which all economic systems are concerned is, what shall be produced. At which point on the production possibilities curve will the society be? Which among the many possible combinations of goods will it produce?

The second problem is how to produce the particular combination of goods and services decided upon. Which of the possible combinations of scarce resources are to be devoted to the production of each good and service? By what technology is each to be produced? And who shall perform the various types of labor involved (e.g., manual, technical, managerial)?

Third, what share of the output that is produced jointly through the cooperation of many individuals is to go to each of them. That is, how is the "distribution" of the output determined?

These three basic problems, though they can be isolated conceptually, are in reality mutually interdependent. The choice of what to produce is constrained by the resources available, and depends upon who will be getting the output.

The distribution of output will likewise be dependent upon what is being produced. And similarly, the resources available at a given moment for future production depend on prior output and distribution.

TYPES OF SYSTEMS

• PROBLEM 32-2

What are the essential features of pure capitalism?

Solution: Capitalism is the system of organization of a monetary economy with division of labor characterized by private ownership of the means of production. A primitive economy composed of relatively small self-sufficient units (e.g., family, tribe) which engage in no trade cannot be a capitalist economy. Nor can it qualify as a capitalist economy after it has begun to discover the productive advantages of the division of labor and progressed to the stage of barter trade. Only when the extent of its specialization and the complexity of its trade has reached the point where the use of a medium of exchange (money) is required to carry on this trade does capitalism potentially emerge. If not only consumption goods but also the means of production in such an advanced economy (i.e., the capital goods) are owned and operated privately, rather than collectively through the state, then it is a capitalist economy.

Capitalism entails private ownership of, and free trade in, not only consumption goods, but also producers' goods (capital goods) and ownership titles (stocks). Hence one of its chief distinguishing characteristics is the existence of markets for the various individual factors of production and a stock market on which ownership shares in firms are bought and sold. The existence of such markets provides a means by which "objective" monetary comparisons can be made of the values of various resources and resource combinations in producing goods which satisfy consumers' demands (a means unavailable to a socialist economy).

The private ownership of the means of production under capitalism has several corollaries. First, it implies "freedom of enterprise," i.e., the freedom to acquire productive resources and to use them as one sees fit. Private ownership of productive assets would be virtually meaningless without the power to allocate them according to one's own judgment as to their most profitable uses.

Second, private ownership of the means of production, in conjunction with freedom of consumers to spend their incomes in accordance with their own preferences, ensures that, with certain exceptions (e.g., monopoly), "consumer sovereignty" prevails. That is, owners of productive assets must utilize them in accordance with consumers' demands or face bankruptcy and the loss of these assets. Under "consumer sovereignty," only capitalists who use their capital to produce what consumers want retain it.

A third corollary is competition among production enterprises. Firms' efforts to satisfy consumers' desires, in order to avoid losses and make profits, imposes on them the necessity of offering to consumers goods or services at least as attractive as other firms are offering. Competition in product markets stimulates competition also in factor markets, and thus provides labor with choice in employment.

In no contemporary nation does capitalism in its pure form exist. In all countries there is some public ownership, direction and regulation of productive enterprises.

• PROBLEM 32-3

"Economic theory is applicable only to a capitalist society." Evaluate.

Solution: The market-exchange system characteristic of private property (capitalism) has been the dominant institutional context of many discussions. The economic theory used in the analysis is applicable to any system of competition (capitalist, communist) for resolving conflicts of interest among people arising from the fact of scarcity. In fact, the analysis of allocation with prices at less than the free-market price is an application of economics to a socialist society in which free-market prices are not used.

Many communist systems rely on money prices and private property to ration existing stocks of some consumers' goods. In Russia, many goods are sold for money,and individuals get money income from wages and salaries--but not from ownership of productive physical capital goods and instruments and land. Given a person's money income, he is allowed to choose among a variety of consumption patterns by voluntary exchanges with other people via controlled (as distinct from open) market prices.

The postulates are not idiosyncratic to capitalist systems. They hold for all known societies. The laws of demand and production hold also, whether or not exchange of resources via a private-property exchange system is used.

• PROBLEM 32-4

What are the essential features of a socialist economy?

Solution: A socialist economy is a specialized economy (i.e., one employing the principle of the division of labor) in which the means of production are controlled by the state and production operations are centrally planned by an agency of the state (the central planning board or commission). The central planning board sets priorities and physical production targets for all commodities, and determines the physical quantities of all resources, including labor, to be used as inputs in the production of each commodity.

Consumers have no direct voice in production decisions. They may have a choice in what they consume, however, subject to the limits imposed by the central planners' decisions regarding the production of consumers' goods. If consumption goods are not distributed by command, then consumers are free to buy consumption goods in markets at government-set prices. Laborers may be assigned to their jobs or the central planners may set wage rates in such a way as to try to achieve the allocation of labor among industries called for by their plan.

• PROBLEM 32-5

What is a Command Economy?

Solution: A Command Economy is one in which resources are allocated according to the commands of a central planning authority. All means of production are owned and operated by the state and directed by the central planners. They determine how much final output of each good is to be produced, how much of each input, including labor, is to be allocated to the production of each commodity, and the quantity and composition of output to be received by all workers, including managers.

No use is made of markets in allocating productive resources or consumption goods. Consumers thus have no means of expressing or enforcing observation of their preferences. Only the preferences of the central planning agency or the government determine production and distribution.

The command economy does not exist in pure form in any contemporary nation, even in the Soviet Union or China. All essentially command systems are supplemented to some degree by market-like institutions.

• PROBLEM 32-6

What is a "mixed economy"?

Solution: A "mixed economy" is one in which some of the means of production are privately owned and some are owned and operated by government. It is also characterized by government policies which attempt the following: i) avoid general business fluctuations, ii) alter the distribution of wealth from the free market pattern in such a way as to provide every individual with at least a certain minimum income, iii) regulate working conditions in private industry, iv) regulate business behavior (mergers, product safety, etc.) in the market, v) etc. It is thus a system resulting from the modification of the pure type of free market capitalism by interventions characteristic of socialist economies.

Virtually all countries today have some variety of a mixed economy. There is none in which either the pure capitalist type or the pure socialist, centrally-planned type exists unmodified.

• PROBLEM 32-7

What are the economic functions of government in mixed capitalism?

Solution: Economies are "mixed" when government and private business share the functions of the economy. American capitalism is predominantly a market economy. At the same time, the economic functions of Federal, State and local government are of considerable significance. In American capitalism a number of strategic economic decisions are rendered not by individuals as such, but collectively through government. In short, the economy of the United States can be accurately described as mixed capitalism.

The economic functions of government are many, and they are varied. In fact, the economic role of government is so broad in scope that it is virtually impossible to establish an all-inclusive list of its functions.

First, some of the economic functions of government are designed to strengthen and facilitate the operation of the price system. The two major activities of government in this area are first, providing the legal foundation and social environment conducive to the effective operation of the price system; second, maintaining competition; third, redistributing wealth and resources.

• PROBLEM 32-8

Explain the concept of Laissez-faire. Is governmental activity of the past in support of a Laissez Faire system?

Solution: Laissez-faire, otherwise known as pure capitalism, may be described under the following three main headings:

I. Underlying assumption

Each economic unit decides what choices and policies are best for it; such choices will prove to be in the social interest.

II. Institutional characteristics

Private ownership of resources and business institutions; freedom of choice for consumers, resource suppliers, and enterprisers.

III. Method of solving the economizing problem

Emphasis upon a system of free, competitive markets--virtually no governmental planning or control.

Actually the economic role of government has been a generally expanding one. More and more activities in our complex, interdependent society have been coming under direct regulation and control such as tariff legislation, pure-food laws, utility and railroad regulation, minimum-wage laws, fair-labor-practice acts, social security price ceilings and floors, public works, national defense, national and local taxation, police protection and judicial redress, zoning ordinances, municipal water or gas works, and so forth.

• PROBLEM 32-9

What are the chief characteristics of the British brand of socialism?

Solution: British socialism, first of all, has been evolutionary rather than revolutionary. That is, the nationalization of industries which has taken place in Britain has been carried out gradually by democratically elected governments, rather than, as in Russia and China, at one fell swoop by governments which came to power through violent revolutions. This process is in accordance with the theories of the English Fabian socialists who overshadow the orthodox Marxian socialists in their influence on English thought.

The principal features of the British system are government ownership and direction of the "commanding heights" of industry, such as the coal, power, railroad, shipping and other critical industries; extensive government planning of land use and provision of housing; a nationalized health service; heavy redistributive income and estate taxes; and a great proliferation of social welfare agencies. Over half of the total British labor force, as opposed to less than one-fourth of the American labor force, is unionized. The percentage is higher in the nationalized industries.

The remainder of British industry and agriculture is, though highly regulated, owned and operated privately.

• PROBLEM 32-10

What is Market Socialism?

Solution: Market Socialism is an economic system designed to try to incorporate the "best" features of capitalistic markets and of socialist planning into one system. It is characterized, on the one hand, by state ownership of land and capital. The state determines the aggregate amount of capital that will be invested in productive capacity. But it does not dictate in what specific lines it shall be utilized. Rather, it sets "prices" for the various factors of production. The state-owned "firms" are instructed to "bid" for factors on the basis of these prices, although they do not necessarily actually pay these prices to the state. On the basis of these revealed "demands," the state adjusts factor prices to balance the "demands" with the respective factor supplies.

State-owned "firms" are to produce and sell goods in the market, with the proviso that their prices be set equal to marginal cost. These "firms" purchase labor in the market, with wages being determined by market forces. Wages earned by workers are subject to some redistribution by the state; however, consumers are free to allocate their incomes as they wish among consumer goods.

Critics of market socialism point to several flaws in the system. First, the managers of state-owned "firms" cannot be expected to have as much incentive to improve efficiency and make profits if it is not they alone who reap the profits or bear the losses from the firms' operations. Second, income redistribution is likely to have an adverse effect on workers' incentives to work. Third, if the bids by firms for productive factors do not entail corresponding payments to the state (the owner of the factors), there is no assurance that equilibrium factor "prices" set by the state secure efficient resource allocation.

• PROBLEM 32-11

What is "indicative planning"? How does it differ from socialist central planning?

Solution: Indicative planning is a system, practiced in France, in which representatives of government and private industries draw up what they consider to be a realistic and realizable national economic plan. The quantitative goals of the plan are submitted to business leaders at large for their response as to how the plan will affect their respective industries. These goals are then recalculated in light of this new information, and a final plan evolved. Unlike socialist enterprises, private firms are not absolutely compelled to cooperate with the indicated plan. However, indirect government pressures, exerted primarily through its control of access to the liquid capital markets, are used to encourage participation in the plan.

The purpose of the plan is to provide a degree of inter-industry coordination of future plans above and beyond that provided by market price signals.

• PROBLEM 32-12

What is Fascism as an economic system?

Solution: A Fascist system retains the institutional forms of a capitalist economy, i.e., private property in the means of production, markets, prices, etc., while subjecting these institutions to such extensive control and regulation by the government that commerce and industry are virtually nationalized. Prices and wages are controlled; industry is cartelized; tariffs and import quotas are imposed to reduce imports and encourage economic "self-sufficiency," while certain export industries are subsidized; foreign exchange control is imposed to limit investment abroad; some key industries, such as the railroads, may be nationalized outright. Although the allocation of resources is not directly controlled by a central planning board, as in a socialist economy, a fascist government exercises effective control over resource allocation through its extensive powers of intervention in the economy.

PURE CAPITALISM VS. PURE SOCIALISM

• PROBLEM 32-13

Contrast the ways in which the amounts and types of goods and services to be produced are determined under the capitalist and socialist systems, respectively.

Solution: Capitalism is characterized by private ownership of the means of production. A privately-owned firm has no source of revenue other than the sale of its output. In order for a producer to recover his costs of production and perhaps make a profit as well, consumers must find his products sufficiently attractive, compared to all the available alternative uses of their incomes, to buy them. Each producer in a capitalist, market economy is continually under the necessity of adjusting the types and quantities of his products to suit the (ever-changing) desires of consumers, in order to avoid making losses and eventually dissipating his capital. Thus, it is ultimately the consumers in a capitalist system who, by their buying patterns, determine which lines of production are profitable and which not, and hence into which lines of production profit-seeking entrepreneurs will direct resources.

The socialist system, on the other hand, is characterized by control of the means of production by the central government. In determining what is to be produced and in what quantity, the central planning board is not primarily influenced by considerations of consumer demand (and profitability). In contrast to the market economy, where resources are attracted through profits and losses into those lines of production most urgently demanded by consumers, central planners can redirect resources from "profitable" industries (i.e., where total revenues exceed total costs) into "unprofitable" industries (i.e., where total revenues fall short of total costs), in accordance with state-determined priorities, regardless of the revealed preferences of consumers. Since no independent producers compete with the state-run industries, consumers in a socialist economy have little choice but to accept the types and quantities of goods decided upon by the central planners and produced by the state industires. Nevertheless, shortages and excesses of various goods are the chronic outcome of the inability (and/or unwillingness) of central planners to accurately gauge and plan for consumers' demands for different products, without the guidance of competitively determined market prices.

• PROBLEM 32-14

Contrast the capitalist and socialist methods of organizing production.

Solution: In a capitalist economy production is directed by privately owned firms or entrepreneurs, who attempt to select the products which are in greatest demand and to produce them with the lowest-price combination of resources in order to make profits which they are entitled to keep. Firms or entrepreneurs that fail to make profits (or at least to avoid losses) are forced to contract their operations, and, unless they avoid continued losses, to stop them altogether. In this way, command over resources (in the form of capital) is continually transferred from those less skilled in directing production to meet consumers' demands to those who have shown more skill.

Capitalist firms and entrepreneurs must bid against one another to attract the amounts and kinds of capital and labor resources they require in order to carry out their production plans. It is this competitive bidding process that determines wage rates and resource prices.

In a socialist economy, where at least most of the means of production are controlled by the government, production is directed by a central planning board, whose members have no financial interests in the industries they direct. The planners' function is to see that the production priorities determined by the government are fulfilled. The standard of profitability as a measure of success in directing production is inapplicable to centrally directed production where the government rather than consumers at large decides what is to be produced. Planners' performance is instead judged by how well they meet their assigned production quotas.

Since there do not exist independent firms in a socialist economy, and hence there is no competitive bidding for factor inputs (capital and labor), the central planning authority must try to achieve the allocation of resources appropriate to its plan either by coercion or by trying to choose a set of prices which will induce just the right amounts of resources into the various desired uses.

• PROBLEM 32-15

Contrast the process of income distribution in capitalist

vs. centrally planned economies.

Solution: In a capitalist economy, where the means of production are privately owned, the functional distribution of income among the various factors of production is determined by demand and supply in the factor markets. The wage rates, salaries, rents, and interest rates which firms are willing to pay for the services of each unit of labor, management, land, and capital, respectively, depend on its marginal revenue product, i.e., the value at the margin of its contribution to firms' sales revenues. In the market economy, firms' sales revenues depend on consumers' valuations of their products. Thus, the demand for factors tends to mirror consumers' implicit valuations of the contribution to output made by each factor. The quantity of each factor that will be supplied at any given price, on the other hand, depends on the valuations placed by owners of the factor on alternative uses of their resource (opportunity cost) relative to that price. The aggregate share of income (output) received by each factor of production in a capitalist market economy, then, is determined by the interplay of Consumers' and factor owners' valuations of each factor, i.e., demand and supply, respectively.

In a centrally planned economy, on the other hand, there are no freely operating factor markets. All factors, except perhaps labor, are owned by the government. Nonhuman factors are allocated by command in accordance with the priorities of the government. Wages are set and paid by the government in such a way as to try to elicit the amounts of labor required for each industry to meet the production quota assigned to it by the central planners. Thus, in a centrally planned economy, both the pattern of production and the distribution of income among factors is determined by the government.

• PROBLEM 32-16

What is the difference in the way prices are determined in centrally planned vs. capitalist economies? What consequences does this difference have in terms of the function prices perform in the two systems?

Solution: In the market economy of a capitalist system, prices are the outcome of the interplay of demand and supply. Demand conditions reflect the relative intensity of consumers' preferences for a certain good, and supply conditions reflect the value in alternative uses of the resources required to produce it. The equilibrium market price equates the quantity demanded to the quantity supplied.

In a system of central planning, on the other hand, the quantity of each of the various commodities to be produced is predetermined by the state. Likewise, the planners try to estimate the quantities of the various inputs which, on average, are technically necessary to produce each of the final products. They then try to set all input and output prices in such a way that the price of each unit of output covers the average money cost of all the inputs used in its production, plus a "planned profit" of, say, 5 to 10 percent. Using these prices as accounting tools, the planners are able to monitor the technical efficiency of the various production units. Plants using relatively fewer units of inputs will show higher "profits" than those which are less technically efficient.

Thus, market-determined prices reflect relative consumer demands for and relative scarcities of goods, and direct resources to those uses on which consumers place the highest relative values. Prices set by central planning agencies, on the other hand, are for the purpose only of judging the comparative technical efficiency of various production units in fulfilling their pre-assigned output quotas, and thus do not reflect, as market prices tend to do, the relative scarcities of resources.

• PROBLEM 32-17

Contrast the way in which economic information is utilized and disseminated in capitalist and socialist economies, respectively.

Solution: In an advanced economy, individuals are specialized in their experience, training, skills, and knowledge. There are a vast multitude of labor skills and machines with various technical capabilities available for utilization in productive processes. Any single individual can have direct knowledge of only a tiny fraction of the possibilities for combining inputs to produce commodities.

In a capitalist economy, it is the function of the entrepreneur to choose from among this vast array of diverse types of skills and technologies available, that combination which will produce the most highly valued output at the lowest possible resource cost. In performing this function, indispensable aid is rendered to entrepreneurs by the system of market prices. This system of prices conveys to them in highly compact form and at minimal cost essential information about the available supply of various types of labor skills and machines to reach rational decisions as to the optimal combinations to use in their respective production processes. This dissemination of information via market prices obviates the need for massive detailed data collection by each entrepreneur or by government.

In a centrally planned socialist economy, however, where market prices are absent, the planners do not have access to price-conveyed information. They are thus forced to resort to massive data collection efforts in attempting to formulate a feasible economic plan.

In short, we can picture information in the market economy (capitalism) as flowing from each particular market outwards to all other markets in a decentralized pattern. In a centrally planned economy, information flows not from sector to sector, but rather it is channelled to a central point where all the major allocation and production decisions are made.

• PROBLEM 32-18

What role can Input-Output analysis play in a centrally-planned socialist economy? What are the limits of that role?

Solution: Input-Output analysis shows the technological relationships that exist among all categories of commodities and labor in an economy. An Input-Output table summarizes these relationships, showing how much of each of the commodities (including labor) in the economy is used, directly and indirectly, in the production of a given amount of each commodity. It illustrates the interdependence of all production processes in an advanced, highly specialized economy.

In attempting to construct a consistent national economic plan, the central planners of a socialist economy must not only set targets for net output of each commodity, but must also determine how much of each commodity must be produced for use as an input, directly or indirectly, in the production of all other commodities. Using Input-Output analysis, central planners can determine the total production of each commodity that is required to yield the respective targeted levels of net output of each commodity.

What Input-Output analysis cannot tell an economy's central planners is what their net production targets "ought" to be. That is, once the planners have already decided their net production targets to aim at, they can apply Input-Output analysis to determine the total production of each commodity necessary to meet these targets. But it cannot determine what net production levels would be "desirable" or "optimal." A more technical limitation of Input-Output analysis is that it is based on the assumption of constant-returns-to-scale production. To the extent that a nation's industries do not conform to this restriction, input-output calculations by central planners will be subject to error.

• PROBLEM 32-19

Can personal liberties co-exist with socialist economic organization?

Solution: Many people contend that centralized control of the means of production (socialism) is compatible with personal liberty. They argue that democratic election of government officials will restrain central planners in charge of resource allocation and production from employing coercion to execute their plan, and from infringing on traditional Western Civil liberties. Advocates of this position also point to the cases of Great Britain and the Scandinavian countries as actual historical examples supporting their contention.

Those who dispute the compatibility of freedom and central planning maintain that the state's role as sole owner of the means of production and sole employer necessarily gives it irresistible powers over the individual's livelihood and thereby over his actions. The right to vote is no defense of freedom, they say, as long as votes must be cast under the duress of massive state powers of retaliation. Moreover, state control of the means of mass communication enables the ruling group to insure that the public hears and sees primarily what it permits the public to hear and see, thus helping the group in power to perpetuate its power. Disputants of the compatibility of freedom and socialism reject those historical interpretations of British and Scandinavian socialism claiming full preservation of freedoms. They perceive a definite, if limited, erosion of freedom in Britain and Scandinavia commensurate with the extent of their socialization, which is far from complete.

• PROBLEM 32-20

Compare the situation of the worker in a centrally planned socialist economy to that of his counterpart in a capitalist economy.

Solution: Consider an economy in which productive resources are controlled by a central planning authority. The authority can allocate resources either by coercion or by trying to find a set of wages that will induce laborers into the desired lines of production. In practice, some combination of both methods is usually used by socialist governments. Monetary incentives such as piecework rates, and bonuses and premiums are used to spur worker productivity, just as, to some extent, such monetary incentives are used in capitalist economies. Socialist economies, to a much greater extent than capitalist economies, use non-wage rewards and punishments to encourage skill and productivity. These range on the one hand from recognition by the state entailing preferential treatment regarding taxes, state-owned housing, state transportation facilities, etc., to fines, eviction from state housing, denial of freedom to change jobs, and ultimately imprisonment or exile in "correctional labor camps," on the other. Whereas in a capitalist economy the right of workers collectively to negotiate wage bargains with employers, and even to engage in peaceful strikes, is recognized and protected, in a socialist economy the central planning board alone has authority to set wages.

In their role as the major group of consumers, workers in a capitalist economy exercise the primary, if indirect, influence over what is produced and offered for sale to consumers and at what prices. Consumers are "sovereign." In a centrally planned socialist economy, however, workers' choices in consumption are restricted to those products which the central planners decide to make available. In practice, the plans of most socialist countries have provided a relatively lower proportion of output for consumer goods than have the decentralized economies of capitalist countries.

• PROBLEM 32-21

Compare and contrast the alleged virtues and shortcomings of capitalism and socialism.

Solution: It should be recognized that this topic involves not only economic analysis but ethical judgments which are strictly beyond the scope of economics. At the same time, comparative economic analysis is essential to making informed ethical judgments of the two systems.

One possible criterion for judging the two systems is efficiency in satisfying the desires of consumers. Under socialism, the absence of free markets for consumer goods renders it virtually impossible for consumers to express their demands effectively and for the central planners to adjust production to them if that were their primary aim. Generally, however, the governments priorities take precedence over those of the consumers, which are secondary. Under capitalism, on the other hand, consumers are able to register the relative intensities of their demands for various goods through the prices they are willing to pay in the market. The multitude of firms competing in the economy must adjust their outputs, quantitatively and qualitatively, to these demands in order to make profits or avoid losses. Thus capitalistic markets provide a mechanism through which the pattern of consumer demand can be translated into the pattern of production. Imperfections in this translation may stem from such sources as monopoly, externalities, and advertising. Nevertheless, the market achieves a high degree of efficiency in discovering and providing for consumers' desires.

A second criterion by which the two systems might be judged is the distribution of income which they generate. Although a hallmark of socialist rhetoric has been equality of income distribution, such equality is not inherent in a system of central planning, and, indeed, the actual experience of centrally planned economies has forced them to sacrifice the goal of equality of income in order more nearly to achieve their production goals. They have been forced to introduce differential wage rates to reward special skills, and to pay bonuses to elicit greater productivity from workers. While the fact of inequality of income under capitalism is not disputed, it may be questioned whether the degree of this inequality is significantly greater than exists in socialist economies. And, indeed, it is a moot question for economics whether greater or lesser inequality in income distribution is desirable or not.

A third criterion of comparison is the achievement of the goals of economic stability and full employment. Marxian theory ascribes to the workings of a capitalist economy an inherent tendency towards increasing unemployment. Keynesian theory predicts cyclical unemployment under capitalism. Monetarists and others, on the other hand, contend that it is government interventions in the market that have been the primary source of aggregate instability and cyclical unemployment. In a socialist economy, there is less of an unemployment problem, due to the fact that central planners have the power, unlike capitalist firms, to allocate labor to production processes with little regard for the saleability of the product or the cost of the labor.

Fourthly, the two systems may be compared on the basis of personal freedoms. Government ownership and control of the means of production under socialism gives it virtually irresistible powers over the individual. The decentralized ownership characteristic of capitalism, and the competition that ensues from this decentralization, provides the individual with a considerable range of choice of employment and hence a degree of economic independence that insulates him to a greater extent from government coercion, and permits him to exercise a greater range of freedoms.

• PROBLEM 32-22

Radical economists insist that there are basic differences of interest among social groups. Mainstream economists can agree with this, but still point to the mediating roles of the free market and government. Why do radicals disagree that government can help resolve conflicts?

Solution: The radicals argue that the government is one of the participants in social conflicts, rather than a neutral "umpire," as supposed by non-radicals. In their view, the state is dominated by the giant corporations. They point to the failure of the regulatory agencies, and the consideration given by political leaders to business 'confidence' as evidence for this view. Radical economists do not think that the government will help try to resolve conflicts impartially because the government is essentially a tool by which corporations preserve their power and promote their own interests.

In order to free government of this influence, they believe, the source of the domination must be eliminated. Private ownership of the means of production must be ended if the government is to really serve all groups.

In this radical analysis of the role of government, it is clearly seen how political and social considerations interact with economic theory in radical economics. Their analysis of the domination of government strongly influences their evaluation and choice of economic systems.

• PROBLEM 32-23

Marx prided himself on his 'scientific' analysis of capitalism. Through this analysis, he felt he had proved how the problems facing the nineteenth century were intimately related to the capitalist mode of production. Modern radical economists hold the similar view that the problems of modern Western society are inherent in capitalist production. Give the orthodox rebuttal to this viewpoint.

Solution: Orthodox economists are highly skeptical of this assertion because many other societies, with very different economic and ideological bases, seem to be suffering from the same problems as Western, capitalist countries. Evidence of exploitation, pollution, economic and social inequality, alienation, imperialism, discrimination, and wasteful production can be found in many (if not most) non-capitalist societies.

To take two specific examples, it is obvious that imperialism and alienation are not limited to capitalist societies. The Soviet Union, for example, had a remarkable record as to its relations with neighboring countries. Almost every one of its neighbors was dominated, or faced the threat of domination, by the Soviet Union. Imperialism not only exists now in non-capitalist societies, but it existed well before capitalism ever developed in various types of societies.

As for alienation, there is no evidence that a worker on a capitalist production line is more alienated than a worker in socialist production. Sweden, the Soviet Union and other socialist countries have had major problems with worker boredom and dissatisfaction. Indeed, these are factors that contributed to the weakening and, ultimately, the break-up of the Soviet Union in 1991. To say that these problems can be eliminated by the elimination of capitalism fails to explain why other societies have not eradicated these problems.

THE AMERICAN VS. THE SOVIET ECONOMY

• PROBLEM 32-24

In what major ways did the institutions of the Soviet economy differ from the American and other Western economies?

Solution: There are three primary institutional differences between the Soviet and Western economies. First, the government owned virtually all the material means of production in the former Soviet Union, whereas in the Western nations, ownership of much or most productive capacity is by private individuals and corporations. The principal exception to the rule of government ownership in the Soviet Union was that agricultural families were permitted to own small farms.

Second, the Soviet economy's allocation of resources was decided at the top by a single body of central planners, who drew up a comprehensive production plan. In the private sectors that constitute the greater part of the Western economies, market prices that reflect consumers' demands and producers' supplies direct the flow of resources to their various uses. Allocation decisions are "decentralized" and reflect the priorities of market participants as a whole, rather than those of the ruling body alone.

Finally, economic freedoms fairly widespread in Western societies were little known in the Soviet Union. The "consumer sovereignty" enjoyed by Western consumers in determining what shall be produced and what they shall consume was absent in the Soviet economy, where consumers had only the freedom to choose the consumption goods provided by the central planners.

• PROBLEM 32-25

What major microeconomic problems plagued the Soviet planned economy?

Solution: First, there was the problem of efficient satisfaction of consumers' desires. Because prices in the Soviet economy were set by the State Planning Commission rather than determined by the interplay of supply and demand, they did not reflect the desires of consumers. Without market-determined prices as signals, planners had no way of learning what array of products consumers wanted most. Consequently, the mix of consumer goods chosen by the Gosplan to be produced may have borne little resemblance to the mix desired by consumers, and large inventories of unsaleable goods accumulated, while long waiting lists or lines formed for other goods that were in short supply.

Second, the narrow emphasis of Soviet planning on output measured in physical terms obscured the economically relevant considerations of quality and cost. Managers were judged primarily on the basis of whether or not they achieved their numerical production quotas, and only secondarily on the quality and cost of the products. Thus, the product mix resulting from the physical units in which the production quotas were specified was frequently not at all that desired by the planners. Moreover, since Gosplan-determined resource prices were mere accounting devices and did not reflect real resource costs, there was no way of determining, and therefore of minimizing, real production costs.

Third, the introduction of superior technologies was resisted by managers because of the higher production quotas that were assigned to them as a result. Managers seemed to have a greater interest in keeping these quotas as low as possible, in order to more easily fulfill them, than in maximizing their output.

Note that all three of the above problems are also present in the American economy. Advertising and monopoly power restrict consumer sovereignty. The emphasis on minimizing costs and deliberate production of shoddy goods (so that consumers will buy the new, "improved" product) and, finally, the phenomenon of planned obsolescence all result in a lower quality of American products. Lastly, since ownership of economically important corporations is diversified, managers are no longer owners and are content to maintain their share of the market.

• PROBLEM 32-26

How and with what degree of success did Soviet planning attempt to solve the problem of coordinating production that is solved in a capitalist economy by the price system?

Solution: There were three basic methods by which the Soviet State Planning Commission (Gosplan) attempted to coordinate production. First, it gathered masses of statistical data from the subordinate ministries that oversaw the operations of individual industries. On the basis of these data, it constructed a tentative overall plan. It then submitted the component parts of the plan to the respective supervisory ministries concerned with evaluation and criticism. With the comments of the supervisors of individual industries and plants, the Gosplan constructed a revised plan which was ready for implementation.

The second method of coordination, called by Lenin the principle of "decisive links," was the establishment by the Gosplan of priorities among the output goals of various sectors. In case some planned output goals were not being achieved, resources were redirected from industries which had been assigned lower priority by Gosplan (e.g., automobiles, agriculture) to those which had received higher priority (e.g., machinery, chemicals, steel).

Third, in order to avoid input shortages, stocks of inputs were held in reserve.

Despite these measures, however, production bottlenecks and stoppages, and hence failure to meet assigned production quotas, were regular occurrences in the Soviet economy, just as gluts and shortages and widespread unemployment are cyclic occurrences in the American economy.

• PROBLEM 32-27

How were productive resources allocated in the Soviet economy? How did this differ from market allocation?

Solution: The Gosbank was the Soviet State banking system. Its function was to allocate bank credit among all the production units in the Soviet economy in accordance with the directives of the Soviet planning authority (Gosplan). It kept accounts of these units' expenditures and receipts, and thereby monitored their success or failure in achieving the production targets set for them with their assigned quotas of resources. The Gosbank's monopoly of loanable funds ensured that each productive unit would have command over just that quantity of resources assigned to it in the national economic plan. The Gosbank could redistribute funds from "profitable" to "unprofitable" industries as the Gosplan's priorities dictated.

In a market economy, capital owners invest their capital in those lines of production in which they expect it to yield the highest return. They invest funds in the production of those commodities which entrepreneurs believe will yield the greatest profit and for which there is consequently the greatest unexploited demand. Thus, in a decentralized market economy the allocation of capital resources is not dictated by a single body through its control of credit. Rather, numerous firms and entrepreneurs must compete for money capital and for real resources in order to implement their production plans, which are subjected in the market to the test of consumers' approval or disapproval. Firms and entrepreneurs who fail this test lose their wealth and their control over productive resources.

• PROBLEM 32-28

What role did the "turnover tax" play in the Soviet economy?

Solution: The prices of consumer goods set by the central planning board were not, in general, market-clearing prices (i.e., those which just balance the quantities demanded by consumers with those supplied by producers). The problem then arose of how to manipulate the relative demands for the various consumer goods in such a way that the quantities demanded corresponded, at least roughly, with the respective quantities that the planners had chosen to produce, in order to avoid excesses of demand or supply and the necessity of some form of direct government rationing.

The function of allocating consumer goods was assigned to the "turnover tax." The turnover tax was an increment to the price set by the central planners. The greater the amount of the tax, the greater was the excess demand for the good at the planners' artificially set price, and the less it was, the less was the excess demand, or the greater the excess supply. The turnover tax was thus a device for adjusting the total money costs to consumers of each consumer good to a level at which the quantity demanded corresponded at least roughly to the quantity available.

Thus, the turnover tax was the means by which Soviet planners attempted to manipulate the pattern and level of demand into conformity with the pattern and level of consumer goods produced.

• PROBLEM 32-29

How did the Soviet economy provide incentives for workers to be productive and managers to be efficient? How effective were they?

Solution: The Soviet system employed a variety of rewards and punishments, monetary and non-monetary, to workers and managers to try to elicit the greatest possible effort in fulfilling the goals of the national economic plan. Monetary rewards included piece rates for workers and differential wages for various grades of skill and productivity. Managers who succeeded in fulfilling or surpassing assigned production quotas earned higher salaries and bonuses.

Non-monetary rewards for workers took the form of public awards and the more tangible benefits of better housing, free transportation, more and better vacations, and tax breaks. Superior managerial performances could lead to promotion.

The threat of punishment hung over any worker or manager whose performance was judged not up to standards. Punishments ranged from fines, pay reductions, loss of job, eviction from state housing, and reduction of social insurance benefits to harassment by the secret police, imprisonment, or assignment to "correctional labor camps."

In spite of these numerous positive and negative incentives, there were considerable difficulties for the Soviet authorities in securing desired behavior. Worker absenteeism and tardiness were significant problems. Cutthroat competition among managers for the best workers was a prevalent practice which the authorities tried, with far from complete success, to eliminate, as workers were eager to transfer to better jobs.

• PROBLEM 32-30

What were the Liberman Reforms? What problems did they attempt to solve? What were their limitations?

Solution: There were three essential features of the Liberman Reforms. First, Soviet enterprises were not required simply to fulfill a physical production quota set by Gosplan, but were permitted to produce to fill orders from other enterprises or consumer goods retailers. Moreover, the managers of enterprises had some latitude in setting the prices of their products. This reform allowed greater responsiveness of production to the desires for the various types of consumers' goods, and to the requirements of other productive units for the appropriate inputs.

Second, enterprises were allowed some latitude in the wage rates they paid their workers. This gave managers greater control over the quantity and quality of workers they employed, and thus greater control over their money costs.

In addition to greater discretion as to the prices and quantities of their output and the wages paid their laborers, enterprises were charged with the responsibility of seeing that their output was actually bought. Thus, the new criterion of the success of an enterprise under the Liberman Reforms was "profitability," calculated in relation to the total capital of the enterprise. Management and labor were rewarded with bonuses according to the "profitability" of their enterprise.

The influence of these reforms, however, was limited. The operations of Soviet enterprises were subject to review by the State Planning Commission for consistency with the economic goals and priorities the commission adopted. It was still able to enforce its priorities through control over the allocation of bank credit to enterprises. Furthermore, the limitation on the authority of enterprises to set prices prevented these prices from reflecting with greater accuracy real scarcities and real resource costs. Thus, this limitation constituted a barrier to the achievement of greater allocative efficiency in the Soviet economy.

• PROBLEM 32-31

Compare the demand management policies of the American mixed economy and the Soviet socialist economy.

Solution: Both governments have used taxes as an instrument of demand management. In the American case it is taxes in conjunction with government expenditure, i.e., the government budget deficit or surplus, that is the critical magnitude; whereas, government expenditure played no such role in Soviet demand management.

Moreover, the type of tax is entirely different in the two cases. The Soviets used a form of excise tax (called the "turnover tax") to choke off excess consumer demand. Only income taxes and tariffs play a role in the U.S. government demand management policies.

A further difference lies in the fact that the "turnover tax" was applied at different rates to different goods, so that Soviet policy undertook to perform the function not only of macroeconomic aggregate demand management, as U.S. government policy does, but of microeconomic manipulation of demands for individual products as well. The problem of microeconomic equilibrium which is left in the American economy largely to market price adjustment to solve must be dealt with by deliberate policy decision in the Soviet economy. Another means by which Soviet policy curtailed demand for certain particularly scarce luxury goods was direct rationing, a method not usually employed by U.S. policy in peacetime.

• PROBLEM 32-32

Compare the patterns of consumption and investment in the Soviet and American economies.

Solution: The considerable differences in the form of economic organization in the United States and the former Soviet

Union are reflected in significant divergences in the patterns of consumption and investment. The Soviet government, which exerted far greater control over the Russian economy than the U.S. government exerts over the American economy, pursued a policy of forced rapid industrialization. Thus, it had been allocating a relatively large share of the nation's total output to investment in industrial development. (This share has been estimated at 30 percent of Soviet GNP). In the United States, on the other hand, where investment decisions are made independently by numerous individuals in accordance with their own preferences, a smaller share of total output has been devoted to investment (estimated at 15 percent of U.S. GNP.) Given that U.S. GNP is estimated to be roughly twice that of what the Soviet Union's was, aggregate gross investment was roughly the same in the two economies. With a smaller population base, per capita investment is somewhat greater in the U.S.

Conversely, American consumers are able to consume a much larger portion of their output than Soviet consumers were permitted to consume. Estimates place American consumption at 5/8 of U.S. GNP compared to one-half of Soviet GNP consumed by Russians. This would mean that total American consumption is roughly two and one-half times that of what the Soviet Union's was, despite a smaller population.

Caution is required in making such quantitative comparisons because the structure of relative prices differed greatly in the two countries. In the U.S. they are market-determined, and in the former U.S.S.R. they were arbitrarily set by the State Planning Commission. Consequently, dollar price comparison of the two GNP's yields a significantly different result from comparisons in which both GNP's are calculated in rubles according to ruble prices as they were set by the State Planning Commission.

SHORT ANSWER QUESTIONS FOR REVIEW

Answer
To be covered when testing yourself

Choose the correct answer.

1. A feature not common to the American and Soviet economies is: (a) the division of labor (b) intervention to control fluctuations in national income (c) consumer sovereignty (d) abundance of natural resources. **c**

2. A socialist system does not allow (a) use of money (b) private ownership of capital goods (c) inequality of incomes (d) private ownership of consumer goods. **b**

3. Which of the following is not a distinguishing feature of capitalism? (a) freedom of enterprise (b) government control of industry (c) freedom of consumer choice (d) competition. **b**

4. Indicative planning is carried out through (a) government control of labor unions (b) tax incentives (c) government ownership of industry (d) government control over the capital markets. **d**

5. The principal problem of the Soviet economy was (a) allocative efficiency (b) lack of natural resources (c) poor monetary policy (d) a low growth rate. **a**

6. The American economy is not a pure capitalistic economy because (a) the government uses fiscal and monetary policies to try to control business fluctuations (b) the government uses its power of taxation to redistribute income (c) the government owns and operates a number of productive enterprises, such as the TVA, the Postal Service, etc. (d) all of the above. **d**

7. The Yugoslavian economic system could most accurately be described as (a) a command economy (b) fascism (c) market socialism (d) indicative planning. **c**

8. In the Soviet economy, the decision as to what to produce was made by: (a) production managers (b) consumers (c) central planners (d) engineers. **c**

9. Before the Liberman reforms, Soviet production directives were couched in terms of: (a) equalizing Marginal Revenue and Marginal Cost

Answer
To be covered when testing yourself

(b) physical output targets (c) maximizing net revenues (d) equalizing Total Revenue and Total Cost. b

10. Critics of socialism contend that freedom cannot co-exist with state ownership and control of the means of production because: (a) the state, as the sole employer, has overwhelming power over the livelihood of each individual (b) there are no elections in socialist states (c) there is only one political party in socialist states (d) entrepreneurs are prohibited from keeping their profits. a

11. In a planned economy, economic information must flow from: (a) consumers to producers (b) labor to management (c) production managers to central planners (d) politicians to voters. c

12. The Liberman Reforms were designed to: (a) give central planners more authority to plan Soviet production (b) redistribute income more equally (c) democratize the Soviet election process (d) give Soviet plant managers greater flexibility in hiring labor, setting prices, and planning production. d

13. The main purpose of the Soviet Gosbank was: (a) to assure the stability of the price level (b) to regulate interest rates (c) to finance government operations (d) to allocate capital. d

14. Introduction of new technology to Soviet industry: (a) had been more rapid than in the American economy (b) had been resisted by production managers who feared it would mean higher production targets assigned to them (c) was responsible for the high rate of growth of the Soviet economy (d) had caused a serious unemployment problem. b

15. Worker incentives in the Soviet economy consisted of: (a) piece-rates for laborers (b) longer and better vacations for superior productivity (c) threat of eviction from state housing (d) all of the above. d

SHORT ANSWER QUESTIONS FOR REVIEW

Answer
To be covered when testing yourself

<u>Fill in the blanks.</u>

16. The economic system in which the means of production are privately owned and operated is called ____________.

capitalism

17. The economic system in which the government owns and operates the basic industries is called ____________.

socialism

18. The economic system in which the outward form of private ownership of the means of production remains, but which is in reality a command economy with no freedom of enterprise is ____________.

fascism

19. The economy system of the United States is sometimes referred to as a ____________.

mixed economy

20. An economy in which all decisions concerning resource allocation are made by a central authority is a ____________ economy.

command

21. The ____________ hypothesis predicts that the Eastern socialist economies and the Western "mixed capitalist" economies are both tending toward some hybrid system incorporating some elements of each system.

convergence

22. The attempt to introduce market-like incentives into Soviet industry was the____________Reforms.

Liberman

23. The adjustment of the prices of consumer goods set by the Soviet central planners to market clearing levels was the purpose of the ________.

turnover tax

24. The ____________ was the agency through which Soviet planners ensured that each industry had command over just that amount of resources which they were assigned to.

Gosbank

25. ____________ was the Soviet State Planning Commission.

Gosplan

26. In formulating their plan for the allocation of resources among different industries, the Soviet planners looked to ____________ Analysis for guidance.

Input-Output

27. Both the American and Soviet governments used ____________ policy to attempt to control fluctuations in GNP.

demand management

28. ____________ planning is a type of planning in which government does not own and direct the operation of industry, but uses indirect pres-

Answer
To be covered when testing yourself

sures to produce conformity to its plan by private industry. — **Indicative**

29. ______________ is an attempt to combine the allocative efficiency of the market with state control of aggregate investment. — **Market socialism**

30. ______________ socialism holds that socialism can and should be achieved peacefully and democratically. — **Fabian**

Determine whether the following statements are true or false.

31. The questions of what to produce, how to produce it, and for whom it is produced can be solved only by a system of central planning. — **False**

32. Inequality of income is no less the case in contemporary socialist economies than in contemporary "mixed" economies. — **True**

33. The socialist system does away with the institution of money. — **False**

34. Prices play a much different role in a socialist economy from the role they play in a capitalist economy. — **True**

35. The term "command economy" refers to one in which the consumers are sovereign. — **False**

36. The term "mixed economy" applies to one in which there is a healthy balance of consumption and investment. — **False**

37. In a socialist economy, no goods are privately owned. — **False**

38. The Fascist economic system maintains the appearance of private ownership of the means of production, but in fact production is directed by the government. — **True**

39. Indicative planning is similar to Soviet central planning in that government control of liquid capital is the key to implementing them both. — **True**

40. The "turnover tax" was the device by which the prices of consumer goods set by the Soviet planners were corrected so as to clear the markets for consumer goods. — **True**

SHORT ANSWER QUESTIONS FOR REVIEW

	Answer To be covered when testing yourself
41. It is universally agreed that democratic election of socialist governments could prevent them from behaving despotically.	**False**
42. The Liberman Reforms introduced full consumer sovereignty into the Soviet economy.	**False**
43. Physical output targets set by Soviet planners invited production managers to sacrifice quality in order to meet them.	**True**
44. Input-Output analysis enables socialist planners to calculate the economic costs of various production plans.	**False**
45. Workers in the Soviet economy had ultimate authority over production decisions.	**False**

CHAPTER 33

HISTORY OF ECONOMIC THOUGHT

Basic Attacks and Strategies for Solving Problems in this Chapter. See pages 1033 to 1061 for step-by-step solutions to problems.

Economics has been and remains a controversial discipline. This is understandable. First, the issues under debate are fundamental. They are all directly or indirectly related to our material well-being. Second, clear analysis is complicated by the fact that human behavior is inherently ambiguous and the total effect of human actions is often unclear. Third, interpretations of events can be influenced by subjective desires, in addition to objective reality.

Consequently, the history of economics as a discipline is one of the rise and fall of different schools of thought. Schools of thought in economics can be thought of as groups of economists who analyze economic issues in a similar way and emphasize similar economic problems.

The leading schools of thought that have made appearances in the discipline include the Mercantilists, Physiocrats, Classicals, Neoclassicals (or Marginalists), Marxists, Institutionalists, Keynesians, Post-Keynesians, and Monetarists. Many other schools would argue for inclusion on this list.

There are certain issues that continue to reappear in economic debates. How we approach these issues may help define the fundamental nature of the discipline. They include growth (factors causing and long run prospects for), distribution (determinants of and issues of equity), value (fundamental determinants of prices), competition and efficiency (conditions required for an efficient allocation of resources), international trade (benefits of), business cycles (is the economy fundamentally stable or not), and economic policy (what is the proper role of government). Comparing and contrasting the views of the different schools in each of these areas is a useful exercise. By studying the various views, students of economics can develop an appreciation for how economic thought develops and the complexity of the discipline. Frequently, other schools provide insightful perspectives on particular issues, even if you are unlikely to subscribe to that school's views as a whole.

Step-by-Step Solutions to Problems in this Chapter, "History of Economic Thought"

INTRODUCTION

• PROBLEM 33-1

Generally speaking, economic theory has gone through three stages: classical, neoclassical (marginalist), and post-Keynesian. Evaluate the statement: 'Economic theory has progressed smoothly and uneventfully through the last two centuries.'

Solution: The three stages of theory do not mark a smooth progression, but rather, abrupt changes in direction and emphasis. In every case, the early writers of each stage saw themselves as starting a revolution in theory. Adam Smith, W. S. Jevons, and Keynes all attacked strongly the prevailing doctrine of their times. All of them felt that their theories would signal the demise of the preceeding doctrines. It is true that as each stage matured, later writers would incorporate earlier work into the general body of theory. Thus Samuelson, the post-Keynesian, includes many elements of neo-classical theory into his economic theorizing. Marshall, the marginalist, also incorporated doctrines of the classical school in his work. This still does not obscure the sharp breaks that occur during the transitions between stages.

Even within each school of thought there have been sharp disputes. Thus the followers of Ricardo often attacked Adam Smith's ideas, and hardly considered themselves as members of the same school as Smith. To depict economic theory as a smooth progression is to ignore all of the disputes and dissensions which have brought economics to its present position.

WEALTH AND GROWTH THEORY

• PROBLEM 33-2

Francois Quesnay and the Physiocrats argued twenty years before Adam Smith that the source of all wealth is agriculture. Why?

Solution: Economic theorists have posited three sources of wealth--commerce, industry, and agriculture. The Physiocrats considered commerce and trade as a mere transfer of wealth from one area (or person) to another. They did not think that trade added anything to wealth.

The Physiocrats regarded industry as merely a transformation of wealth into a different form. Thus a weaver would change a certain amount of yarn into cloth, but this change would be merely a change in form, not a change in value.

This leaves agriculture as the only possible source of new wealth. Here, a farmer gets something of value from land that previously was bare. The farmer physically creates value by working the land.

The Physiocrats, then, ruled out two of the three possible sources of wealth, and then tried to show how the third is the source of wealth.

• PROBLEM 33-3

Discuss how Adam Smith developed the concept of the division of labor.

Solution: The division of labor is a plan of production that separates work into many different tasks in order to take advantage of the specialization of labor. The concept, introduced by Adam Smith in his famous book, The Wealth of Nations (1776), has had a profound effect on the development of modern industry. Smith argued that the division of labor was a necessary ingredient of efficient production.

As an example Smith described a pin factory he had visited. "One man draws out the wire, another straights it, a third cuts it, a fourth points it, a fifth grinds it"--eighteen distinct operations in all. In that particular factory only ten men were employed, and consequently some performed more than a single task. He observed that although they had poor machinery to work with, "they could, when they exerted themselves, make among them . . . upwards of forty-eight thousand pins in a day . . . But if they had all [worked] separately and independently . . . they certainly could not each of them have made twenty, perhaps not one pin in a day . . ." Thus has evolved the term "Division of Labor".

• PROBLEM 33-4

Adam Smith described in great detail the superior productivity of the division of labor. What did he think division of labor was limited by?

Solution: Smith thought (as do modern economists) that division of labor was limited by the size of the prospective markets. Even if a capitalist had the capital and technology to produce 10,000 cars a day, it would not be worthwhile to undertake mass production making use of extensive division of labor if he could only sell 500 cars a day. In Smith's day, the extent of division of labor was severely limited because firms often could only sell products in local markets. So, Smith saw the extent of potential markets as the crucial factor in limiting the extent of the division of labor, and hence, productive efficiency.

• PROBLEM 33-5

Describe the processes of classical growth theory.

Solution: The driving force of growth in classical theory is capital accumulation. Capital accumulation, in turn, is determined by savings. These early theorists thought that the amount of savings is determined by the interest rate. The higher the interest rate, the larger the amount people would be willing to save. Interest rates are determined by the returns to capital. Because of diminishing marginal productivity, the returns to capital would be greatest when the amount of capital is low. So, in a poor country with little capital there would be high returns to capital, and so the interest rate would be high. This high interest rate would, in turn, induce high savings, which will lead to rapid capital accumulation. As the country becomes richer, the returns to capital would drop (because of diminishing marginal productivity), lowering the interest rate and thus slowing down the rate of capital accumulation.

As a result of this chain of events, poor countries would grow rapidly while rich countries would have a slow rate of growth. Eventually rich countries will reach a stage where they have no growth at all, because the returns to additional amounts of capital will be negligible. Classical growth theory, then, predicted rapid growth for poor countries and eventual stagnation for rich countries.

• PROBLEM 33-6

What change did Keynes make in classical growth theory? How would this change affect the predictions of growth theory?

Solution: Keynes objected to the assertion in classical growth theory that the amount of savings is determined by the interest rate. Keynes held that the amount of savings is determined by the level of income, not by the interest rate. So, a rich person will save more than a poor person, and a rich country will save more than a poor country. A poor country, with a small national income, will save little, if at all. So, there will be little capital accumulation and little growth. In contrast to this, a rich country will save more and grow faster.

By postulating a different determinant of saving (income instead of interest rates), Keynes completely altered the predictions of the classical model. Instead of poor countries growing more rapidly than rich countries, rich countries, according to Keynes, gain an even bigger advantage over poorer countries. Poor countries remain in the poverty cycle of low income, low savings, and hence low growth.

The change made by Keynes generated drastically different predictions about the relative growth rates of rich and poor countries.

• PROBLEM 33-7

Why, according to Marx, are capitalists forced to accumulate?

Solution: Capitalists are forced to accumulate because of the fierce competition of the free market. In order to survive, a capitalist must continually become more efficient and cost conscious. To increase efficiency, he must expand his production to take advantages of economies of scale. To expand, he must accumulate. As all capitalists expand, the competition grows even fiercer. After a while, the amounts of capital needed to compete grow so large that only monopolies or cartels can survive. This is the end result of Marx's Law of Accumulation.

• PROBLEM 33-8

What is the Malthusian Theory of Population? What factors have prevented Malthus' prediction from coming true?

Solution: The Malthusian Theory of Population was propounded by Thomas Malthus, an English clergyman of the early nineteenth century. Malthus believed that the natural tendency of human population, if unchecked by war, famine or diseases, was to grow at a geometric progression, that is, a progression in which each succeeding number is an equal multiple of the preceding number, such as 1, 2, 4, 8, etc. Since, however, there is only a fixed amount of arable land available for food production, the law of diminishing returns would prevent agricultural output from growing at a rate greater than a simple arithmetic progression, that is, one in which the difference between each succeeding number is equal, such as 1, 2, 3, 4, etc. Therefore, the growth in the food supply could never keep pace with the growth in population. Although wars, famines and epidemics could be relied upon to keep population growth in check, the general lot of humanity could never improve.

Malthus' prediction failed to prove true, at least in the industrialized countries, for two reasons. First, the birth rate in these countries has declined rather than continuing at its unchecked potential. Second, technological progress has allowed production of the necessities of life, including food, to expand at a rate much greater than that of population growth. Meanwhile, Malthus' theory remains true in many less developed countries as disease, poverty and war continue.

• **PROBLEM 33-9**

What is the Malthusian Doctrine and how does the theory of diminishing marginal returns agree with this doctrine?

Solution: According to Malthus, there is a tendency for population to outrun its means of subsistence. To be specific, Malthus believed that population increases in a geometric ratio, whereas food supply increases in an arithmetic ratio. If population doubles every 25 years, the Malthusian predictions would go as follows:

	0 yr.	25 yr.	50 yr.	75 yr.	100 yr.
Population	1	2	4	8	16
Food Supply	1	2	3	4	5

We can see that whereas there is enough food for the population at the beginning (0 years), food supply per capita shrinks considerably as time goes on. After 100 years, the per capita food supply is 5/16 of what it was.

This theory coincides with the theory of diminishing marginal returns which tells us that as the quantity of land is held constant, an increase in labor (population) and even capital fails to produce a proportionate increase in food supply.

DISTRIBUTION THEORY

• **PROBLEM 33-10**

Ricardo's theory of distribution assumed that the supply of land was fixed, while the country's population and capital stock were constantly increasing. On the basis of these assumptions, he predicted eventual stagnation of the economy. How would this happen according to Ricardo?

Solution: With the population constantly increasing, the demand for food, and hence the demand for land, would increase. Since the supply of land is fixed, the increased demand for land would result in a higher price for land. The price of the services of land is its rent. So the result of the increasing number of mouths to feed, with a fixed supply of land, is that rents increase.

The landlords are made richer without lifting a finger. Unlike capitalists, landlords cannot increase their future incomes by investing a part of their present incomes to increase the supply of their resource, since it is fixed. Hence, landlords tend to consume their incomes, contributing nothing to the accumulation of wealth.

The crucial question for Ricardo is where this extra income of the landlords comes from. It cannot come out of the wages of workers which Ricardo assumed to be determined by the needs of subsistence. Rising food prices would force the workers to demand raises in the wage rate and since capitalists were not prepared to see their workforce die off, they would have to grant the pay raises. These pay raises would have to be taken out of profits, for if producers raised the prices of products the workers' real incomes would again be reduced below subsistence levels. This is the crucial point for Ricardo. The increasing population leads to an increased demand for land. This, in turn, eventually leads to a decline in profits. Moreover, since the population is constantly increasing, the rate of profit would be steadily declining. Eventually profits would be zero and hence there would exist no incentive for further investment. Capital accumulation would cease. The (marginal) productivity of workers and output per capita would fall. There would then be economic stagnation, and decline.

In summary, the eventual consequences of the population increase is a redistribution of income from capitalists to landlords. Since the landlords consume their incomes, this would mean that eventually there would be no investment; and hence no growth, and even a decline in per capita income. Classical economics was thus labelled the "dismal science" for its pessimistic predictions.

• PROBLEM 33-11

How did Ricardo's observation of fixed land with an increasing population lead to the economic concept of rent?

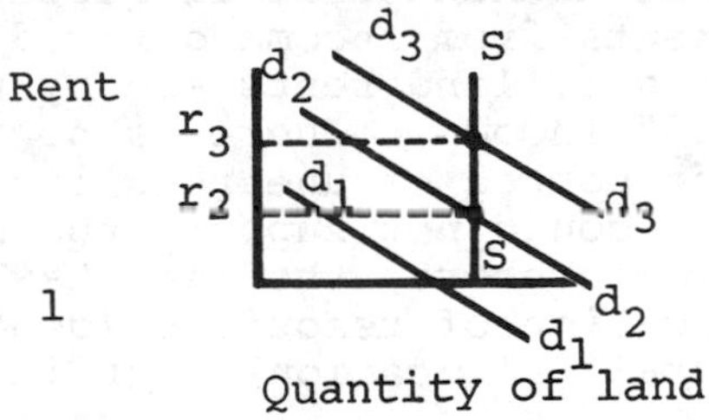

Fig. 1

Solution: The demand curve d_1d_1 in Figure 1 represents a situation in which the population (density) of a country is so low that land rent would be zero. This is because land would not be scarce in relation to demand. If a landowner tried to charge rent, people would simply move to an area that was not occupied. In England of Ricardo's time however, land was a scarce resource, and a rapidly expanding population meant that it was becoming more and more scarce relative to the demand for it. This process is depicted in Figure 1 as a shift of the demand curve for land from d_2d_2 to d_3d_3, with the consequent rise in rent from r_2 to r_3.

Generalizing from the case of land, economists have defined economic rent as the payment for any resource whose supply is perfectly inelastic. Rent does not affect the quantity of the good supplied, but it does affect the allocation. Whoever is willing to pay the highest price will have control over the good. As a result, the price (rent) is completely determined by demand.

• PROBLEM 33-12

The Ricardian theory of land rents led to a movement in the late nineteenth century called the single-tax movement. What was the goal of this movement and what was its economic rationale?

Solution: The goal of this movement was to eliminate all taxes but a tax on land. This tax would equal the 'pure' rent from the land. ('Pure' rent is the difference between gross rent and the rent that a piece of land could obtain in its next most valuable use, if any).

The rationale behind this tax was simple. As the population grew, rents rose, thus giving tremendous windfall gains to landlords. By taxing the pure rent, the land-tax supporters wanted the gains caused by society's growth to be distributed "fairly". They did not feel they were burdening landlords unfairly, since the tax was on "unearned" income. Since the tax would not be applied to income derived from capital improvements of land, they did not feel the tax would dampen investment. The rationale, then, was primarily on ethical judgment about "unearned" income, which could not be attacked on economic grounds. For in economics, redistribution of "unearned" income has no costs except the actual transfer costs.

The single-tax movement did ignore some complications. First of all, it would be tremendously difficult in practice to separate pure rents from income derived from capital improvement. Second of all, land rents are by no means the only source of "unearned" income. There is no particular logic in taxing just one source of unearned income. Last of all, a land tax alone could not support the current level of government spending. In short, the land tax has a neutral effect on the allocation of resources (other kinds of taxes distort the 'natural' allocation), but it still has some problems.

• PROBLEM 33-13

Identify briefly the following elements of Marxian economics: Alienation, Variable Capital, Reserve Army of the Unemployed, and Reproduction.

Solution: Alienation is the term used to describe a worker's increasing repression under capitalism. A worker is brainwashed by advertising and the media, exploited by government and big business and made to work like a robot at his job.

Variable Capital consists of the outlay of employers for wages. So variable capital purchases labor ('live labor') while any other capital purchases machines and raw materials ('dead labor'). In the Marxian scheme, capitalists can only make profits by squeezing unpaid labor out of workers. Profits, then, are related only to the amount of wages (variable capital) paid. Variable capital, and not capital in general, is the source of capitalistic profits.

The Reserve Army of the Unemployed is created under capitalism because of the introduction of labor-saving machinery. This machinery is introduced because each capitalist wants to gain a competitive edge over other capitalists. As the reserve army grows in size over time, a fierce competition for jobs will develop among laborers. This competition will depress wages to the subsistence level (wages cannot stay below this level for long). The size of the reserve army, then, regulates the level of wages, and indirectly affects the size of profits (the lower wages fall, the higher profits rise).

Reproduction is a crucial element in Marxian theory. Marx insisted that an economy must not only function in the present, but must continually reproduce itself, at either a constant level of production, or an expanding level. So, Marx set up series of equations to show that an economy can maintain an equilibrium over time. In doing this, he anticipated general equilibrium theory, growth theory, and input-output analysis.

• PROBLEM 33-14

Briefly describe Marx's theory of surplus value.

Solution: Surplus value is the concept developed by Marx to describe the result of the exploitation of workers by capitalists. Surplus value is the difference between the value that a worker produces, and the value that he is paid. Using prices instead of values, this surplus (which the capitalist receives) is the difference between a worker's wage and the price of the goods he produces. This surplus value is the source of profit and wealth for the capitalist class. Marx believed that, under capitalism, workers would inevitably be paid less than the value of what they produced.

• PROBLEM 33-15

Neoclassical economists explained interest rates by the concept of time preference. How?

Solution: Time preference simply means that people would rather consume today than consume at some later date. People value consumption (and money) now more than they value consumption (and money) in the future.

Neoclassical economists used this concept to say that interest is the reward to people for postponing consumption. The higher the rate of interest, the more consumption they will be induced to postpone. It follows that the higher the rate of interest, the more money people will lend out. For these economists, the time preferences of individuals (how much they value consumption today over consumption later) are reflected in their willingness to lend at different interest rates. The equilibrium rate of interest would be the rate at which the demand for loans would equal the amount people would be willing to lend (given their schedule of time preferences).

There are two complications to this analysis. First of all, people do not lend money for capital investment, financial institutions do. Neoclassical economists simply said that these institutions get their money from people's savings and the amount of their savings is determined by the interest rates and time preferences. The other complication is that the economists used marginal analysis in their use of time preferences. They said that consumers will lend (or save) money as long as the marginal disutility of postponing more consumption is less than the rate of interest. This refinement simply adds analytical rigor while not changing the basic uses of time preferences as determining the supply of capital resources (the supply of savings people will be willing to lend).

• PROBLEM 33-16

One aspect of Marxian economics is that some of the predictions of Marx were proven wrong. As a result of this, some radical economists have only adopted the tools of Marxian analysis, without necessarily accepting Marx's conclusions. In the nineteenth century, other Marxists became 'revisionists'. Explain briefly what distinguishes a revisionist from a Marxist.

Solution: The failure of some of Marx's predictions (declining rate of profit, growing misery of workers, increasing unemployment, subsistence level of wages, among others) led to a critical re-examination of Marxist theories by some radicals. The revisionists no longer believed that capitalism must end in a violent revolution, as orthodox Marxists did. They believed that there can be a gradual evolution towards socialism by means of political action and trade unionism. So, they rejected the idea of violent class struggle while still holding to the ideal of a classless society.

Some of these socialists rejected Marxism because of theoretical differences. Eduard Bernstein, for example, could not accept the labor theory of value. He argued for a socialism based on mainstream economic methodology. There is some evidence that Marx himself, late in his life, conceded the possibility of evolutionary change, though Marxists adhere to his earlier revolutionary doctrine.

• PROBLEM 33-17

What contribution did Lenin make to Marxist economic theory?

Solution: Lenin contributed to Marxist economic theory an explanation of imperialism. His theory of imperialism was based on Marx's predictions that there would be an overexpansion of investment in capitalist countries which would lead to declining profits. One of the reasons for this excess of investment would be that workers could not buy the entire supply of goods on the market due to their low wages. To make profits, then, capitalists would have to find new markets for their goods, and new markets for investments. Lenin's theory holds that capitalists would come to rely on imperialism as the way to accomplish these goals. Colonies would provide new markets for goods and opportunities for investment. Lenin thought that 'capitalistic imperialism' only delayed revolution. Eventually colonies would also be saturated with capital, and so the original crisis conditions that prevailed in the capitalist countries would also prevail in the colonies. Capitalists postponed the inevitable by exploiting backward countries but they did not eliminate the basic tendency inherent in capitalist production--the tendency toward economic crisis.

VALUE THEORY

• PROBLEM 33-18

Marx (and the classical school) held that a commodity's value is determined by the amount of homogenous labor enbodied in the commodity. How does he reconcile this with the varied skills and natural abilities of people?

Solution: There are two different questions being asked here, and, so, Marx has two different answers. With respect to differences in skill, Marx answers that skills are acquired, and thus have a labor cost themselves. The value of skilled labor, then, can be computed from training costs and measured in terms of units of unskilled labor. Marx uses units of unskilled labor for simplicity of analysis.

In reference to differences in natural abilities, Marx simply averages these differences into the term 'socially necessary labor'. Thus if it takes, on the average, 100 hours of 'socially necessary labor' to produce an aluminum table, all aluminum tables have a value of 100 labor units. Even if it takes an uncoordinated person 150 hours of his own labor to make this table, its value will still be only 100 labor units. By attempting to measure the values of different qualities of labor by including the training costs of producing skilled labor, and by taking average or "socially necessary" labor as his standard of measurement, Marx tried to overcome the problem in labor value theory of differences in talents and skills.

• PROBLEM 33-19

Define 'marginalism' (as used in economics).

Solution: Marginalism is the method of analysis that concentrates attention on the last unit (whether in production or consumption). Economic agents make their decisions based on the costs or benefits of one extra unit. The prices of goods are determined by the respective utilities and costs of the last units. Thus, firms do not decide merely whether to produce some or none; they decide whether to produce one unit more or one unit less. To make the decision, a firm has to calculate the marginal cost of producing the last unit, and the marginal revenue derived from producing it. Marginalist analysis is the basis of modern microeconomic theory.

• PROBLEM 33-20

What is 'cardinal utility'? What school used this concept?

Solution: Cardinal utility refers to measurable utility. As such, is not only a preference ordering, it also indicates the strength or intensity of preferences. Since it is an absolute quantity (not merely a relative ranking), marginal utilities are also quantities of utility.

The problem with cardinal utility is that there is no convenient way to measure these quantities. Money cannot be used, since money is also a good and so its utility depends on its scarcity or abundance. Neoclassical (marginalist) economists believed that these quantities of marginal and total utility could be measured subjectively, through introspective experiments. These measurements would be measured in utils rather than objective units (like money). The neoclassical economists used this concept to illustrate the principle of diminishing marginal utility. With cardinal utility, an increase in the quantity of a good consumed would lead to a measurable decrease in the utility received from the last, or marginal, unit.

Most economists today find simple preferences (ordinal utility), a more satisfactory tool of analysis than cardinal utility.

• PROBLEM 33-21

Contrast the pure labor theory of value with the utility theory.

Solution: The labor theory of value states that all exchange values of commodities are determined by the amount of labor used in producing the commodities. That is, relative prices are determined by the relative amounts of labor needed to produce the goods. If it takes, on the average, two hours to make a hammer, and one hour to make a screwdriver, then the hammer will be worth twice as much as the screwdriver. In this view, machines do not add any new value to products; they just transfer the value of the labor incorporated in each machine to the product.

The marginal utility theory holds that the value of a commodity depends on the utility or satisfaction that people derive from it. So, relative prices are determined by their demands for the object.

The labor theory holds that, to have value, an object must have some utility, but its relative value is not determined by this utility. Utility theory holds that a good, such as land, would have value, even if no labor at all was expended on it, if it has the capacity to satisfy a human want.

• PROBLEM 33-22

Classical economists could not understand how utility could be the basis of prices when water, which is so necessary for life, is cheap, while diamonds, which are not at all necessary for life, are expensive. Explain how the neoclassical (marginalist) school solved the diamond-water paradox.

Solution: The neoclassical school said it is not total utility, but marginal utility that determines price. Marginal utility, in turn, to a large extent depends on scarcity or abundance. Since water is very abundant, its marginal utility is usually very low (while it can get expensive during a drought). In the same manner, since diamonds are very scarce, their marginal utility is very high.

In the accompanying graph, the marginal utility schedules for water and diamonds are shown (diminishing marginal utility is assumed).

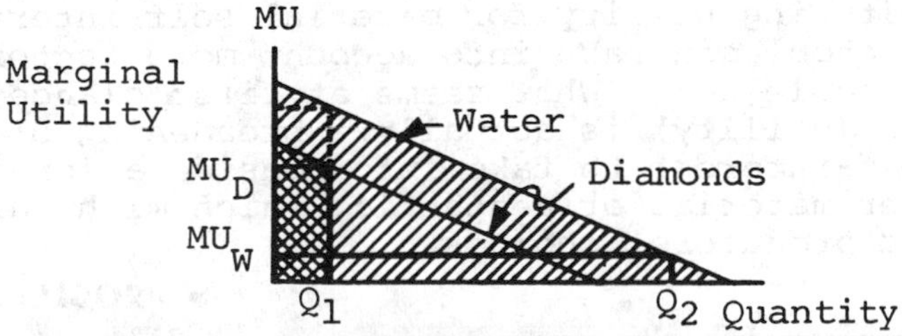

At quantity Q_1 of diamonds, the marginal utility of diamonds is MU_D. At quantity Q_2 of water, the marginal utility is MU_W. The marginal utility (and hence the price people are willing to pay) is higher for diamonds than water because diamonds are much more scarce than water, that is, Q_2 is much greater than Q_1.

Total utility is measured by the area under the marginal utility curve to the level of consumption (either D_1 or W_1). The total utility received from quantity Q_2 of water is marked by the area shaded . The total utility derived from quantity Q_1 of diamonds is shaded . It is clear that even though water provides a much greater total utility than diamonds, diamonds have a higher marginal utility.

Using marginal utility analysis, the neoclassical economists were able to resolve the diamond-water paradox. They showed how diamonds could have a higher price, even though they furnish less total utility, because of their relative scarcity.

• PROBLEM 33-23

Classical economists assumed self-interest, specifically financial self-interest. The incentive of material self-interest would put the free market economy in motion. How did this concept of self-interest change when utility (marginal utility) became the basis for neoclassical economic theory?

Solution: Material self-interest takes into account only material rewards. Utility also takes into account non-material rewards ('psychic income'). What utility theory does is broaden the sphere of self-interest. Now instead of money being the sole goal of economic activity, happiness (utility) is the goal. A worker, for example, might take a lower-paying job if the working conditions are more pleasant than the working conditions of a higher-paying job. In this case, the marginal utility derived from the greater pleasantness of the working conditions is greater than the marginal utility derived from the extra amount of pay at the other job. The worker is still following the dictates of his self-interest; it is just that his self-interest also includes non-financial considerations when utility is the basis of judgment.

By substituting utility for material self-interest the neoclassical school can take into account more factors in describing how people act. What seems at first glance a restrictive term (utility) is actually a broadening of the concept of self-interest to take into consideration any factor, whether material or aesthetic, which might affect consumers' and producers' choices.

• PROBLEM 33-24

The classical economists emphasized cost of production as the determinant of price. The early marginalists thought that demand determined price. What was Alfred Marshall's contribution to this debate?

Solution: Marshall brought together both of these views in his theory of price. In the immediate period, demand would determine price, because supply is fixed. In the short-run, a firm can hardly change the supply at all by changes in the use of its existing facilities. In the long run, the firm can change the facilities of production; so supply is very flexible over the long run. This analysis of supply and demand, with the emphasis on time determining the flexibility of supply, synthesized the views of earlier writers into a new theory of price. This was Marshall's contribution.

COMPETITION AND EFFICIENCY

• PROBLEM 33-25

Adam Smith relied on the workings of the profit motive in his theory of the 'invisible hand'. Yet, at the same time, he attacked businessmen for their attempts at 'conspiracy against the public'. How did Smith reconcile his economic system with the greed of some businessmen? Would he call for government intervention in order to break up these conspiracies?

Solution: Smith not only relied on the profit motive, he also placed tremendous emphasis on the value of competition. He believed, in the absence of legal monopolies, that free competition could regulate and control the profit motive and channel it into socially beneficial activities. In the instance of a business conspiracy to fix a high price for their product, Smith believed that other businessmen (or even some of those involved in the conspiracy) would undercut the fixed price in order to "steal" sales from the conspirators. So, competition would prevent price-fixing conspiracies. The first firm that undersold the cartel would do tremendous business, while the cartel members would lose business.

Smith would definitely not call for government intervention in this situation. Since he believed that competition could, and would, bring about the most efficient allocation of resources, any actions by the government could only interfere with this allocation. Even a well-intentioned government policy could do damage to the economy. So, Adam Smith believed that the profit motive, when harnessed to a competitive market system, could lead to increased national wealth.

• PROBLEM 33-26

Adam Smith could count on self-interest to spur businessmen to greater efficiency. Now, with the rise of large corporations, can modern economists also count on self-interest to produce efficiency?

Solution: Modern economists have had problems in dealing

with the role of self-interest. For two reasons, they cannot make the same automatic assumption that Adam Smith made. The first reason is that Adam Smith dealt in a world where by and large the manager of a firm also owned the firm. What was good for one was good for the other. With a large corporation where ownership and management are separated, what is good for executives (higher salaries, padded expense accounts, luxurious offices, etc.), might not be in the best interests of stockholders. To a certain extent, the self-interest of executives runs counter to the efficiency and profit interests of stockholders. The second reason for not making Smith's assumption is that the owners of corporations (the stockholders) may not really have the capacity to effectively discipline the management. If stockholders could oversee the executives, they could prevent the abuses just described. The problem is that with thousands of small stockholders and the management use of absentee ballots, it is difficult to kick out incompetent or greedy managers. Not only can management spend the stockholders' money on themselves, but there is also a good chance that they will get away with it. For these reasons, simple assumptions about self-interest leading to efficiency have become much more problematic in the last fifty years. Economists have had trouble reconciling self-interest with efficiency.

• PROBLEM 33-27

Neoclassical economists developed a production function in which all the factors of production (land, capital, labor) received the value of their marginal product; that is, the interest paid to capital equals the contribution capital makes to the product, wages paid to labor equals the value of the marginal product of labor, etc. Some economists suggested that this result showed that the distribution of free, competitive capitalism is morally right and just. What is wrong with this suggestion?

Solution: The problem with this suggestion is that it assumes that ownership of resources (land, capital) means that the owner is entitled to all the benefits of the resource. The landlord's collection of rent is morally just because he happens to own land that is needed for food. To make this assertion, the economists would have had to make the additional assertion that mere ownership of resources, under any circumstances, is right and just. Without this assertion, these economists could not answer the socialist charge that resources belong to a nation, and so the profits from such resources should be distributed among all the people. These economists did not realize that, in addition to the marginal-productivity basis of distribution, they also needed to make explicit value judgments about the original distribution of resources, about the original ownership of resources.

• PROBLEM 33-28

The neoclassical approach to macroeconomics relies on pure competition, and price and wage flexibility to maintain full employment and a stable economy. How would the presence of huge corporations with large shares of their markets affect the first two assumptions (pure competition and price flexibility)?

Solution: The presence of large corporations with large shares of their markets would tend to diminish the plausibility and validity of the neoclassical assumptions. Because of the large market shares, there could not be pure competition. Pure competition describes a market where there are numerous sellers, none of which have any significant share of the market.

Related to the concept of pure competition is the idea of price flexibility. Since in a purely competitive market none of the sellers individually can set his own prices (if he tried to, he would be undercut by other competitors), price is set by the interaction of supply and demand. As supply and demand change, prices adjust--there is price flexibility. When there is not pure competition, there is no assurance that there is price flexibility. While there could be price competition between large corporations, there could also be oligopolistic price-setting. The firms could engage in tacit agreements to keep prices high. So, the presence of large corporations with significant market shares would eliminate the possibility of pure competition and give rise to the possibility of price-fixing.

Since the plausibility of these two assumptions would become questionable, the validity of using them as the basis of policy recommendations also becomes questionable. The presence of large corporations, and the consequent dubious validity of neoclassical assumptions, is one of the reasons for the decline in the belief in the self-regulating purely competitive economy of neoclassical theory.

• PROBLEM 33-29

With the emergence of corporate giants, John Kenneth Galbraith theorized a new version of price regulation. Describe his concept of 'countervailing power'.

Solution: Galbraith's concept of 'countervailing power' describes the situation where neoclassical competition is not effective in regulating prices. Instead, giant corporations have their power checked by other giant concerns. Thus, e.g., Lockheed cannot set high prices for its products and pay low wages to its workers, for the workers are represented by another large entity--a union, while buyers consist either of other powerful corporations or the government. Lockheed cannot simply dictate prices and wages, but has to negotiate them with other large, powerful organizations. Countervailing power, then, describes the restraints that are placed on giant corporations in the absence of competition.

• PROBLEM 33-30

In socialist (or communist) economic theory, the system of E. Liberman has been introduced for efficiency purposes. What is Libermanism?

Solution: Libermanism is the evaluation of enterprise efficiency using the "profit" criterion. Accounting principles are used to record the costs of factor inputs (labor, capital) and the output of each particular enterprise. If "profits" are made, managers and workers will receive bonuses, the size of which depends on the size of the profits. Enterprises may take orders from their customers and negotiate with other enterprises for inputs. Even limited advertising and salespeople were used in the Soviet Union after the implementation of Libermanism. There was even a small amount of wage and price flexibility for individual units permitted.

The intention of this whole system is to take supply (factor inputs) and demand considerations into account within a centralized framework.

The increase in allocative efficiency induced by Libermanism led to the adoption of it by over 80 percent of Soviet industry. Libermanism, then, is the attempt at utilization, within strict limits, of supply and demand to allocate resources in a basically centralized command economy.

INTERNATIONAL TRADE THEORY

• PROBLEM 33-31

Since the time of Adam Smith, economists have usually advocated free trade measures. The Mercantilists, however, supported a strong protectionist policy during the 17th and 18th centuries. Briefly explain their position.

Solution: The Mercantilists believed that a nation's strength could be measured by its gold reserves. So, they advocated policies which would bring gold into the country, and which would keep the gold in the country. Specifically, they wanted tariffs and quotas to restrict imports (which would have to be paid for in gold). They also wanted subsidies to encourage exports which would bring in gold. Mercantilists also supported strict limitations on the emigration of skilled labor and on the use of foreign ships for trading purposes. As is obvious from these policies, these economists were quite willing to sacrifice allocative efficiency in favor of building up gold reserves. They simply were guided by the belief that a plentiful gold supply would make a nation prosperous and powerful, and that the prosperity and power of one nation could come only at the expense of the prosperity and power of other nations.

• PROBLEM 33-32

Adam Smith argued for free trade for reasons of economic efficiency. He thought goods should be produced wherever they could be produced with the fewest resources. How did Ricardo modify this theory?

Solution: Ricardo formulated the Law of Comparative Advantage. This states that trade can be beneficial to two countries, even if one of the countries can produce every good with fewer resources than the other country. An example illustrating this is the case of an important executive who is also an excellent typist. The executive can do both jobs better; the executive is more proficient at both jobs. Yet the secretary has a comparative advantage in typing because, while her typing ability may be slightly less than that of the executive, her managerial abilities are vastly inferior to those of the executive. So, having the secretary do all the typing, leaving the executive to do all managerial work is the most productive arrangement.

The principle illustrated by this example can be applied to trade between nations. Even if one nation is more technically efficient in producing every type of product than another nation, it still would be most productive overall for that nation to concentrate its efforts on producing those products in which its advantage over the other nation is greatest, leaving production of products in which its advantage is least to the other nation.

So, Ricardo did not argue for free trade on the same grounds as Adam Smith. Ricardo argues that specialization and free trade can be mutually beneficial, even for a nation which cannot produce anything at the lowest cost.

BUSINESS CYCLE THEORY

• PROBLEM 33-33

Explain Say's Law and discuss its weakness.

Solution: Say's Law, in short, holds that the economy will always be close to full employment; that is, the economy will regulate itself and return to equilibrium without any intervention from the government. It says that prolonged unemployment is impossible because 'supply creates its own demand.' This last phrase means that as firms produce goods, they also create income. This income (to workers, to other firms) will then be spent in the economy. So all payments to factors of production will go to consumption or investment - thus equating aggregate supply and aggregate demand at a full-employment level of aggregate output, and a stable price level.

The problem with this theory is that it assumes any

income saved is automatically invested. If some income is saved but not invested, then supply will be greater than the demand for current output at the existing price level. Desired consumption and investment would be less than production. Individuals (or firms) may save without investing in capital goods either out of caution or uncertainty about the future of the economy, or other factors. Say's Law, then, is only valid in situations where all savings are invested.

• PROBLEM 33-34

What school of economists defended Say's Law? Which prominent economist disputed this theory?

Solution: Since Say's Law states that the economy will always be close to full employment, it implies there is no need for intervention in the economy by the government. It is clear, then, that any school adopting Say's Law would tend to downgrade the role of government in stabilizing the economy. The classical school did show this tendency, as it did generally accept Say's Law (Say himself was a contemporary of Smith and Ricardo). Laissez-faire is a position characteristic of the adherents of Say's Law of the classical school.

Keynes disputed Say's Law. One of his most important points against it was that the decision to invest savings in capital equipment is far from automatic. Because savings may not be fully invested in productive equipment, consumption and investment may fall short of production, and the economy could not maintain stability of aggregate income. So Keynes rejected Say's Law because of the assumption that any income saved is invested. Keynes' arguments on this point were instrumental in discrediting Say's Law among contemporary economists.

• PROBLEM 33-35

How did Jevons use sunspots to explain business cycles? Why would his theory be less important in industrialized nations?

Solutions: Jevons used sunspots to explain business cycles caused by fluctuations in agricultural production. Sunspots influence the weather, and the weather obviously influences agricultural production. A good year in agriculture could stimulate business activity by increasing the demand for farm equipment, transportation and credit. Similarly, a terrible year in agriculture could lead to a drop in business activity. So, Jevons used sunspots to explain the business cycle by using them to explain fluctuations in farm production.

In an industrialized nation, agriculture plays a less significant role in the economy. Because of this, fluctuations in agricultural production have less effect on the overall level of business activity. So, any theory that explains business cycles by using fluctuations in agricultural production is less important in an industrialized nation than in a primarily agricultural nation.

• PROBLEM 33-36

How did Joseph Schumpeter distinguish the innovator from the inventor? On which did he base his theory of the business cycle?

Solution: For Schumpeter, inventors make discoveries, whether of new machines, new methods or new products. Innovators interested in income invest in inventions, incidentally introducing inventions into industry. The innovators are the ones who take the financial risk in investing in these inventions.

Schumpeter based his theory of business cycles on innovation, and hence, innovators. He believed that the tremendous investments made in basic inventions, such as the railroad and automobiles, stimulated the economy and led to an expansion of output. Innovation, the introduction of inventions into the market place, was the primary force behind economic booms.

Eventually, the wave of investments in innovative products would run its course, and the economy would slip into a recession. Even though inventions are made during periods of economic contraction, they would not affect the economy until innovators invested in them. The investments of the innovators in these inventions would start a new phase of business activity.

ECONOMIC POLICY

• PROBLEM 33-37

During the Great Depression, Keynes advocated deficit spending to increase employment. What would a neoclassical economist have recommended?

Solution: A neoclassical economist would consider this situation a situation of excess supply of labor. The answer to any situation of excess supply is to lower the price (the price of labor is the real wage).

In the accompanying Figure 1, the neoclassical view is clear. Employment can be increased from L_D to the equilibrium position L^* by lowering the real wage from W_o to W^*. At a wage of W_o, the high price of labor has attracted L_s jobseekers into the labor market. So, unemployment is not the difference between L_D and L^*, but the difference between L_D and L_S.

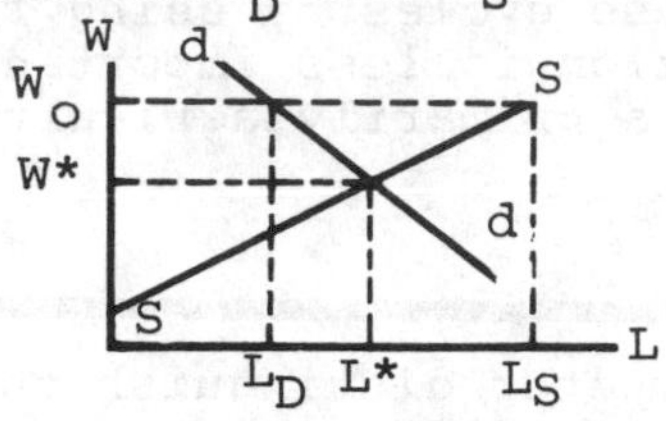

Real Wage

Fig. 1

Quantity of Labor

Many economists during the thirties did recommend lowering the wage rate as a solution to the massive amount of unemployment. It was not until after Keynes made his recommendations (and his criticisms of this proposed solution) that the neoclassical position was modified.

• PROBLEM 33-38

Classical and neoclassical (marginalist) theorists have usually supported the market system of allocation. Because of this, they usually opposed government intervention in the economy. Keynes advocated government intervention. Does this mean he was against the market economy?

Solution: If Keynes had been against the free market system, he would have advocated replacing the system. But his theory aimed to stabilize the market economy. Because of the variability of business investment, he believed that a completely free private enterprise economy was inherently unstable. So, he wanted government intervention to smooth out the fluctuations of the free enterprise economy. In his General Theory, he remarked that he did not care whether governments expanded their responsibilities or not; all he wanted was some government action (fiscal and monetary policy) to control inflation and unemployment.

• PROBLEM 33-39

Government intervention in the economy not only effects the level of economic activity, but it can also result in the redistribution of resources (from rich to poor people, for example). What school of economists has traditionally supported government intervention for both of these reasons?

Solution: The Keynesians have supported government intervention as a means of affecting the level of economic activity. They have also, however, been strongly in favor of using this intervention to achieve other goals. The manipulation of taxes, in their view, can be used to stimulate (or to depress) the economy and to redistribute income from the rich to the poor. Likewise government spending can be used to finance transfer payments, or public housing for the poor. Keynesians have generally preferred fiscal policy over monetary policy because fiscal policy does have the capability directly to redistribute resources.

Institutionalists also favored government intervention to redistribute income, but they did not have the analytical structure to make any general predictions about the effects of fiscal policy on the aggregate level of economic activity. They were interested in social reform, but they did not realize the 'multiplier' effects that these reforms could have.

• PROBLEM 33-40

John Maynard Keynes actively supported direct government intervention in the economy. In particular, he advocated deficit spending as a means to end the Great Depression because he thought business was not investing enough, even with low interest rates to maintain national income and employment at their pre-Depression levels. Why did business, in the view of Keynes, fail to invest in response to the low interest rates?

Solution: Business decisions are determined by the profit motive. Firms invest because they anticipate that they will make a profit from the investment. It is clear that interest rates are a factor in business costs and hence in determining profits. But interest rates are not the sole factor determining the profitability of investments. During the Depression, most business firms faced extraordinarily low demand. Because of this, many firms did not expect that investments would be profitable, whether interest rates were low or not. So, low interest rates could not stimulate a recovery during the Depression. Because of this, Keynes considered the idea of self-regulating economy of the classical school a delusion. In its place, he proposed government intervention to mitigate the business cycle.

• PROBLEM 33-41

Government intervention in the economy has now been accepted as desirable and necessary by many economists. Monetarists do not agree with this position. Briefly state the monetarist viewpoint.

Solution: Monetarists, most notably Milton Friedman, believe in the importance of a stable monetary framework for the economy. They believe that changes in the money supply have significant effects on the economy. So, it is important to keep the money supply from rapidly fluctuating. Generally, then, monetarists believe that the Fed should aim for a stable and moderate growth rate in the money supply. They do not believe that the Fed should actively use monetary policy to 'fine tune' the economy.

In their view, though monetary policy has significant effects, it is also somewhat unpredictable in the timing of its effects. It therefore should only be used passively - by aiming for moderate increases in the money supply.

Monetarists further believe that fiscal policy should not be used. Some, like Friedman, argue that deficit spending does not increase total income, it just 'crowds out' private investment. The argument is that an increase in government spending will only raise income temporarily. This temporary rise in income, with a fixed money supply, will cause interest rates to rise (a rise in income increases the demand for money, which will raise interest rates). This rise in interest rates will lead to a decline in business investment. This decline in investment will offset the original rise in income generated by the additional government spending. Even if the effects of the additional government spending are not completely negated by the decrease in investment, private investment has still been hurt by the use of fiscal policy. Because of this, monetarists strongly oppose the use of active fiscal policy.

Taken with their cautious appraisal of monetary policy, it is clear that monetarists believe government intervention in the economy should be kept to a minimum. Overall, monetarists are much more confident of the efficiency and usefulness of free markets than other economists.

• PROBLEM 33-42

Mainstream economic theory holds that monetary policy effects the economy by influencing interest rates and hence investment. What did A.C. Pigou contribute to the analysis of the effects of monetary policy?

Solution: Pigou contributed an additional explanation as to how monetary policy works. He believed that an increase (or decrease) in the money supply could affect the economy independently of the effect of changes in the interest rate on investment. He held that an increase in the money supply with prices held constant, or a decrease in prices with the money supply held constant, would increase the real value of people's cash balances, and thus their wealth. This effect of changes in the money supply, the Pigou effect, works by increasing consumption. Because they are wealthier, people tend to spend more. This would stimulate an increase in investment.

The Pigou effect would predict that a drop in prices during a recession would increase the real wealth of people, which would stimulate spending and economic recovery. So, if there is price flexibility, the economy will be self-regulating. The changes in price levels will cause changes in real wealth, and so, countercyclical changes in spending patterns.

While this analysis of Pigou does not contradict mainstream theory, it does considerably change its emphasis. By describing an alternate monetary policy mechanism, Pigou supplemented mainstream theory. By then drawing out the implications (the self-regulating nature of the economy) of this mechanism, Pigou reached conclusions differing from most post-Keynesian economists.

• PROBLEM 33-43

Keynes' analysis of the economy aimed to show how aggregate demand and the money market interact to determine the equilibrium level of income for the economy. Soon after his analysis was published, Keynesian economists emphasized the aggregate demand for goods to the exclusion of the role of money in the economy. Why?

Solution: The Keynesian economists believed the Depression showed the relative unimportance of monetary factors in determining the level of national income and employment. During the years 1929 to 1933, a large increase in the supply of money failed to stop the tremendous fall in output and employment that occurred during this period. After this, the situation gradually improved until 1937, when the government tightened up fiscal policy. In 1937, the tighter fiscal policy led to another drop in output and employment. The Depression was not finally ended until expansionary fiscal policy was used at the start of massive government purchases of World War Two.

The failure of monetary policy to control the Depression, and the two instances of the effectiveness of fiscal policy led Keynesians to believe that monetary policy was not as important as fiscal aggregate demand policies.

• PROBLEM 33-44

After the initial rejection of monetary policy by Keynesians, why did they change their minds and include both monetary and fiscal policy as policy options?

Solution: There were two related reasons accounting for this change to a balanced mix of both monetary and fiscal policy. The first was the failure of predictions based on fiscal policy alone to accurately account for the behavior of the economy. It was predicted that after World War Two ended, the large cutbacks in government spending would induce another depression. There were large cutbacks in spending but there was no depression. In fact, there was rapid postwar growth. There were problems with inflation, and these were kept under control by monetary, not fiscal, policies. The success of monetary policy to stimulate growth and then to control inflation led to a re-evaluation of the fiscal policy emphasis.

The other reason for the adoption of monetary policy

was the wealth of empirical research done by monetarists. Milton Friedman published a series of studies giving evidence of the past effectiveness of monetary policy. Though his claim that only monetary policy is effective is a matter of dispute, Friedman's studies did convince most economists that monetary policy is important.

The combination of the failure of predictions based only on fiscal considerations, and empirical research on the effects of changes in the money supply, led to the balanced position of present-day mainstream economics: monetary and fiscal policy both have an important effect on income and employment.

• PROBLEM 33-45

What is meant by the 'new economics'?

Solution: The 'new economics' is used to describe the synthesis of Keynesian and monetarist position. This school of economists holds that both monetary and fiscal policy have an important role in macroeconomic policy. This school uses basically the Keynesian structure in analyzing policy options.

The new economics rose to prominence during the sixties. During this period, Keynesian economic theory was used for the first time as the basis for economic policy. The 'new economics' has lost some of its lustre because of its seeming inability to solve the problems that have plagued the seventies.

• PROBLEM 33-46

Why did the institutionalists of the early twentieth century reject laissez-faire?

Solution: The institutionalists were not satisfied with the state of the economy. They were disturbed by the widespread poverty and the fluctuations of the business cycle. Because of the persistence of these problems, they were unwilling to simply wait for the laws of supply and demand to solve these problems as laissez-faire economists would. They rejected the abstract, theoretical approach of the neoclassical school in favor of empirical study of the economy and institutions. From this research, they advocated selective government intervention (social security, for example) as a means to social and economic reform. Though they did favor government intervention, they retreated from the militancy and drastic change of socialism.

SHORT ANSWER QUESTIONS FOR REVIEW

Answer

To be covered when testing yourself

Choose the correct answer.

1. The marginal utility theory of value was developed among others (a) by Karl Marx (b) in the eighteenth century (c) by Alfred Marshall (d) by David Ricardo. — c

2. The value of a commodity for a consumer is determined by (a) its marginal utility (b) its total utility (c) its importance for survival (d) all of the above. — a

3. Alfred Marshall suggested that (a) marginal utility for every commodity was diminishing (b) consumers tried to maximize their utilities (c) consumers equalized marginal utilities of every product in their consumption market (d) all of the above. — d

4. In Malthus' view the growth of population will (a) benefit capitalists in the long run (b) benefit workers (c) drive the workers' wages down to the subsistence level (d) promote the class struggle. — c

5. The theories of neoclassical economists were primarily concerned with (a) macroeconomics (b) microeconomics (c) econometrics (d) prospects for revolution. — b

6. Marx claimed that human history was shaped primarily by (a) economic factors (b) political factors (c) divine scheme (d) class consciousness. — a

7. For Keynes, the prosperity of a state was determined (a) by the amount of bullion a state owned (b) by the national income (c) by the level of investment (d) by the same factors mercantilists thought it was. — b

8. Keynes believed (a) the invisible hand was sufficient to stabilize the national economy (b) investment opportunities in capitalist countries were increasing (c) the American economy to be uncontrollable (d) government should intervene and there should be deficit spending in the event of depression. — d

9. Keynes suggested that for the capitalist economy to survive, it has to (a) include elements of socialism (b) grow (c) periodic-

SHORT ANSWER QUESTIONS FOR REVIEW

	Answer To be covered when testing yourself
ally contract (d) keep the government's budget balanced	b
10. The use of mathematical tools for the purposes of checking the validity of economic models in the real world is characteristic of (a) game theory (b) classical economics (c) econometrics (d) John K. Galbraith.	c
11. Marshall's partial equilibrium analysis is based on the fact that (a) market price is determined by interaction of supply and demand (b) marginal utility is diminishing (c) marginal productivity is diminishing (d) empirically the economy is never fully at equilibrium.	a
12. The "Paradox of Value" reflected in the low price of certain necessities can be explained by (a) their low total utility (b) their low productivity (c) their low marginal utility (d) the fact that they are "inferior goods".	c
13. Marx believed that the destruction of capitalism and the seizure of power by the proletariat (a) were economically inevitable (b) were to come through a class struggle (c) were to lead to socialism (d) all of the above.	d
14. Keynes' writings (a) support Say's law (b) dispute Say's law (c) are not related to the subject of Say's law (d) are practically in agreement with Say's law.	b
15. Adam Smith saw (a) no role for government in the functioning of the economy (b) the establishment of protective tariffs as the major governmental function (c) the main duties of the government within the economic system in providing national defense and social services (d) the ideal economic system as one strictly regulated and controlled by the government.	c
<u>Fill in the blanks.</u>	
16. The ______________ states that the price of a good is determined by the amount of labor which goes into its production.	labor theory of value
17. Both Malthus and Ricardo shared a ______________ view of the economic future.	pessimistic

SHORT ANSWER QUESTIONS FOR REVIEW

Answer
To be covered when testing yourself

18. ______________ are the modern school of thought closest in their views to the laissez-faire approach taken by Adam Smith. — Monetarists

19. "______________ creates its own ______________" is the statement of Say's law of market. — supply, demand

20. The ______________ economists assume that a consumer maximizes total utility and equalizes the marginal utilities of the products he consumes. — neo-classical

21. In the works of the ______________, agriculture is considered to be the sector of major importance in the economy. — Physiocrats

22. ______________ claimed that restraint, misery and vice were the only possible checks on the otherwise geometrically growing population. — Malthus

23. Mercantilists believed that ______________ was basically the determinate of the wealth of a society, Keynes thought ______________ was such a determinant. — gold, national income

24. The concept of self-regulating economy as developed by Adam Smith assumes ______________ among the producers and lack of ______________ influences on the market. — competition, monopolistic

25. The ________________ refused to accept the ideas of classical economists and sought an alternative to the capitalist system of production. — Utopian socialists

26. One of the most important achievements of Alfred Marshall was ______________ analysis. — partial equilibrium

Determine whether the following statements are true or false.

27. Mercantilists were a group of 17th century economists, pragmatic in their views, who encouraged frequent government intervention in order to establish law and order in the economy. — False

28. Mercantilists emphasized the importance of a favorable balance of trade largely because of the confusion between money and wealth. — True

29. Mercantilists considered trade in terms of competition and warfare, not in terms of mutual benefit. This is contrary to the view of inter-

SHORT ANSWER QUESTIONS FOR REVIEW

Answer
To be covered when testing yourself

national trade accepted today. — True

30. The major precepts of the economic philosophy of the Physiocrats are economic flows subject to natural rules and interdependence of the elements of the economy. — True

31. Physiocrats, as a school of thought, were prophets of Industrial Revolution in that they recognized the potential of industrial growth and emphasized the economic importance of industry as compared to agriculture. — False

32. Adam Smith did not favor massive government intervention in the economy but supported the mercantilists' view that international trade should be regulated, because he, too, realized the importance of precious metals for national prosperity. — False

33. Adam Smith was an earnest defender of laissez-faire policy because he believed the capitalist economy to be self-regulatory. — True

34. For Adam Smith, the natural price of a commodity on the free competitive market is equivalent to the cost of the production of the commodity. — True

35. <u>Wealth of Nations</u> shows the division of labor and capital accumulation to be the major means of economic expansion and growth. — True

36. Say's Law of Markets, if accepted, makes excess supply an impossibility even in the short run. — False

37. Utopian socialists were the first group to look for alternatives to the free market and to classical economic theory. — True

38. For Marx, dialectical materialism was the theory of economic justice. — False

39. Adam Smith saw capitalism as self-regulatory, while Karl Marx saw capitalism as self-destructive. — True

40. Marx based his critique of capitalism as a system and his predictions of its future failure on the fact that all capitalists were highly amoral. — False

INDEX

Numbers on this page refer to PROBLEM NUMBERS, not page numbers

Numbers on this page refer to PROBLEM NUMBERS, not page numbers

Numbers on this page refer to **PROBLEM NUMBERS,** not page numbers

Numbers on this page refer to PROBLEM NUMBERS, not page numbers

Numbers on this page refer to PROBLEM NUMBERS, not page numbers

Numbers on this page refer to PROBLEM NUMBERS, not page numbers

Numbers on this page refer to PROBLEM NUMBERS, not page numbers

Numbers on this page refer to **PROBLEM NUMBERS,** not page numbers

Numbers on this page refer to **PROBLEM NUMBERS,** not page numbers

Numbers on this page refer to PROBLEM NUMBERS, not page numbers